The Ships of Trafalgar

ACKNOWLEDGEMENTS

This work, like previous publications, could not have been produced without the generous assistance of museum colleagues, friends and institutions. First I must thank all the staff at the National Archives, Kew, where the core research was undertaken. Second I wish to thank the staff at the Royal Naval Museum, Portsmouth, namely Matthew Sheldon, Head of Research Collections and Curator of Manuscripts, Allison Wareham, Librarian and Head of Information Services and Stephen Courtney, Curator of Photograph Collections, for extensive use of their resources. Equally I thank Jeremy Michell, Curator of Historic Photographs and Ships at the National Maritime Museum for providing copies of the plans from the Admiralty Sailing Navy Collection (Ship Draughts), an invaluable source for detailed information and generating illustrations. I thank Frank Nowosielski for his support. A special thanks is extended to my friend and university colleague José Manuel Matés Luque who provided information about Spanish ship designers and a wealth of material (unfortunately more than I could handle within a tight schedule) from the Spanish archives in Santander, and to fellow researcher Frederic Nabbe Degenkolbe for statistics about Spanish naval ships. My gratitude also extends to Jenny Wraight, Head Librarian, and Iain MacKenzie, Curatorial Officer, of the Naval Historical Branch at the Admiralty Library, Portsmouth, for use of their extensive records, Norman Swales for supplying useful illustrative material related to ship draughts, and marine artist William Bishop for providing other supportive information and material. My thanks extend also to marine artists Geoff Hunt RSMA, Derek Gardner RSMA, Robin Brooks and Gordon Frickers who have enhanced this book with their stimulating contemporary paintings.

Regarding my publishers, Conway Maritime Press, yet again I express a special thanks to John Lee for undertaking the publication of this work in the first place. I am indebted to his direction and remarkable patience, especially as he fully understood the ramifications of the mammoth task ahead. This thanks is also bestowed upon project editor Stuart Robertson for patiently dealing with the complexities arising from the work, especially during its final stages. I likewise acknowledge Steve Dent for his exceptional skill planning the final layouts. I very much thank my colleague historian Dr Ann Coats, University of Portsmouth, who undertook the painstaking task of editing this work, throughout which her guidance and knowledge proved invaluable.

I cannot conclude without acknowledging my wife Katy, Curator and Local History Officer of the Portsmouth Museums and Records Service. Besides providing images from the Portsmouth Museums collection and assisting with research, as my wife, companion and friend I am indebted to Katy for her infinite patience during the past thirty months spent working on this project. While the later stages of collating a book are the most challenging for the publisher, the person closest to the author endures the trials of creativity from their onset to the final moments.

Peter Goodwin MPhil. IEng. MIMarEST. 25 April 2005

Text and drawings © Peter Goodwin 2005
Volume © Conway Maritime Press 2005

First published in Great Britain in 2005 by
Conway Maritime Press

An imprint of Chrysalis Books Group plc

The Chrysalis Building
Bramley Road
London W10 6SP
www.conwaymaritime.com

All rights reserved. No part of this publication may be reproduced, stored in a retrieval system, or transmitted in any form or by any means, electronic, mechanical, photocopying, recording or otherwise, without the prior permission of the publisher.

Peter Goodwin has asserted his moral right to be identified as the author of this work.

British Library Cataloguing in Publication Data
A record of this title is available on request from the British Library.

ISBN 1 84486 015 9

Printed and bound in China

The Ships of Trafalgar

The British, French and Spanish Fleets
October 1805

Peter Goodwin

Conway Maritime Press

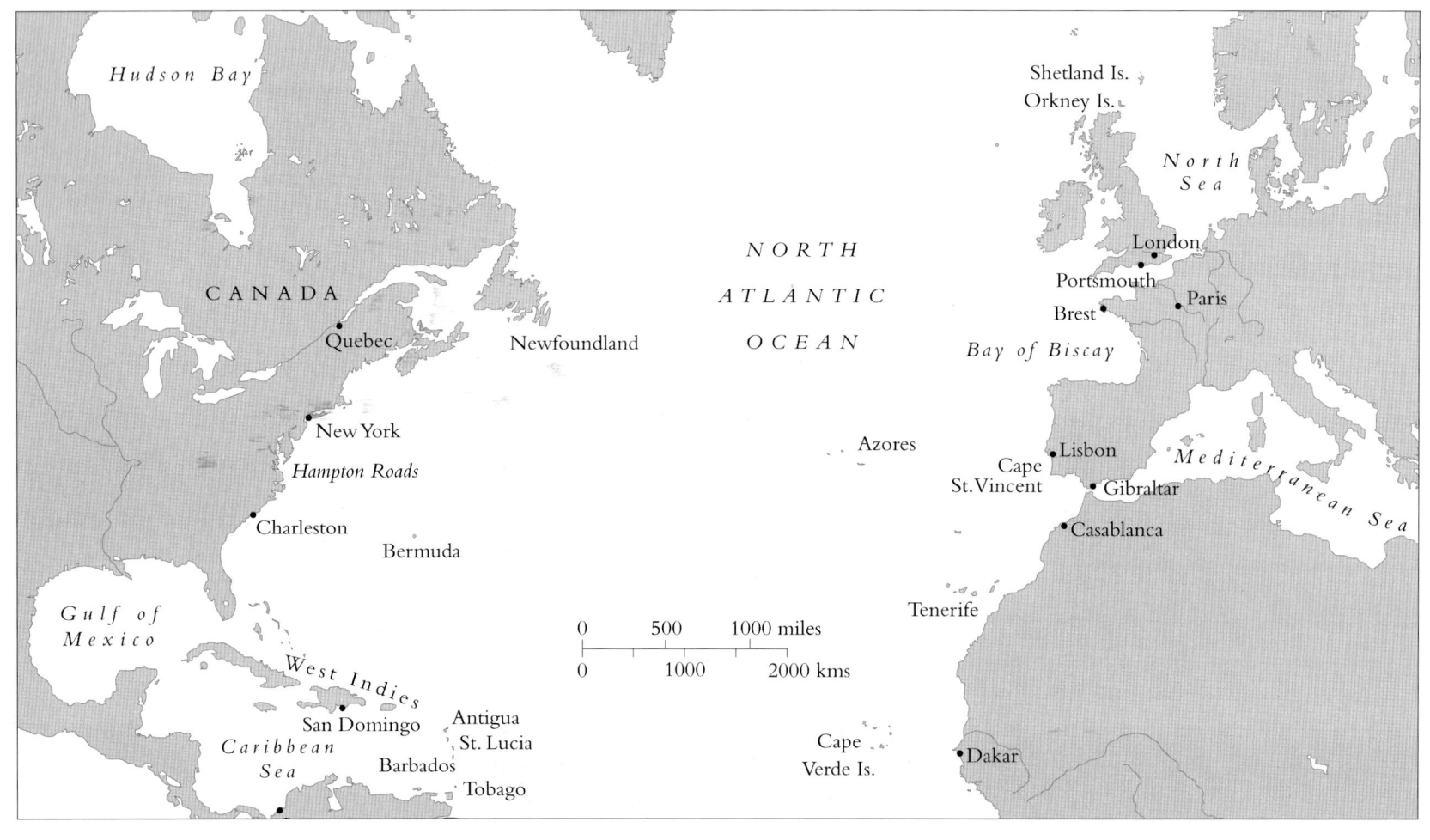

MAPS
Showing the main theatres of operations mentioned in this book.

CONTENTS

Introduction 6

Part 1: THE BRITISH FLEET

Introduction 10

Part 1 Chapter 1: **The British First Rate Ships** 12
The 100 gun ship *Britannia* • The 100 gun ship *Royal Sovereign* • The 100 gun ship *Victory*

Part 1 Chapter 2: **The British Second Rate Ships** 34
The 98 gun ship *Dreadnought* • The 98 gun ship *Neptune* • The 98 gun ship *Téméraire* • The 98 gun ship *Prince* • The 80 gun ship *Tonnant*

Part 1 Chapter 3: **The British Third Rate 74 gun Ships** 55
The 74 gun ship *Achille* • The 74 gun ship *Ajax* • The 74 gun ship *Belleisle* • The 74 gun ship *Bellerophon* • The 74 gun ship *Colossus* • The 74 gun ship *Conqueror* • The 74 gun ship *Defence* • The 74 gun ship *Defiance* • The 74 gun ship *Leviathan* • The 74 gun ship *Mars* • The 74 gun ship *Minotaur* The 74 gun ship *Orion* • The 74 gun ship *Revenge* • The 74 gun ship *Spartiate* • The 74 gun ship *Swiftsure* • The 74 gun ship *Thunderer*

Part 1 Chapter 4: **The British Third Rate 64 gun Ships** 118
The 64 gun ship *Africa* • The 64 gun ship *Agamemnon* • The 64 gun ship *Polyphemus*

Part 1 Chapter 5: **The British Fifth Rate Ships** 135
The 38 gun ship *Naiad* • The 36 gun ship *Euryalus* • The 36 gun ship *Phœbe* • The 36 gun ship *Sirius*

Part 1 Chapter 6: **The Other British Ships** 154
The Armed Schooner *Pickle* • The Armed Cutter *Entreprenante*

Part 2: THE FRENCH FLEET

Introduction 163

Part 2 Chapter 1: **The French Second Rate Ships** 164
The 80 gun ship *Bucentaure* • The 80 gun ship *Formidable* • The 80 gun ship *Indomptable* • The 80 gun ship *Neptune*

Part 2 Chapter 2: **The French Third Rate Ships** 172
The 74 gun ship *Achille* • The 74 gun ship *Aigle* • The 74 gun ship *Algésiras* • The 74 gun ship *Argonaute* • The 74 gun ship *Berwick* The 74 gun ship *Duguay Trouin* • The 74 gun ship *Fougueux* • The 74 gun ship *Héros* • The 74 gun ship *Intrépide* • The 74 gun ship *Mont Blanc* The 74 gun ship *Pluton* • The 74 gun ship *Redoutable* • The 74 gun ship *Scipion* • The 74 gun ship *Swiftsure*

Part 2 Chapter 3: **The Five French Frigates** 201
The 40 gun ship *Cornélie* • The 40 gun ship *Hermione* • The 40 gun ship *Hortense* • The 40 gun ship *Rhin* • The 40 gun ship *Thémis*

Part 2 Chapter 4: **The Two French Brigs** 206
The Brig *Furet* • The Brig *Argus*

Part 3: THE SPANISH FLEET

Introduction 208

Part 3 Chapter 1: **The Spanish First Rate Ships** 209
The 136 gun ship *Nuestra Señora de Santísima Trinidad* • The 112 gun ship *Principe de Asturias* • The 112 gun ship *Santa Ana* • The 100 gun ship *Rayo*

Part 3 Chapter 2: **The Spanish Third Rate Ships** 219
The 80 gun ship *Argonauta* • The 80 gun ship *Montañez* • The 80 gun ship *Neptuno* • The 74 gun ship *Bahama* The 74 gun ship *Monarca* • The 74 gun ship *San Agustin* • The 74 gun ship *San Francisco de Asis* • The 74 gun ship *San Ildefonso* The 74 gun ship *San Juan Nepomuceno* • The 74 gun ship *San Justo* • The 74 gun ship *San Leandro*

Conclusion 235
Appendices 243
Bibliography 253
Index 255

INTRODUCTION

For two hundred years, many of the published works about the battle of Trafalgar 21 October 1805 have covered the battle, the strategic and political issues surrounding the Trafalgar campaign and the threat of invasion, Nelson's battle tactics and biographies of admirals and captains. Inevitably, much has been written about Vice-Admiral Horatio Lord Nelson. Histories of this momentous battle have been influenced by the victors and the patriotic perspectives of Victorian and Edwardian naval historians and Nelson enthusiasts. With few exceptions little has been published about individual British, French or Spanish Trafalgar ships. These are Nelson's *Victory*, because she still exists and through personal association with Nelson symbolises the long reach of British naval heritage. Other ship histories relate to *Agamemnon*, 'Nelson's favourite', again through personal association, and *Bellerophon*, well covered in David Cordingly's recent publication *Billy Ruffian*. Paradoxically, *Bellerophon* has as great an association with Napoleon as she does with Nelson. There are also works on *Implacable*, formerly the French *Duguay Trouin*, because she became a training ship and because she was scuttled so controversially in 1949. But little has been written from the perspective of the French and Spanish ships present. Apart from articles on *Santísima Trinidad*, *Rayo* and *San Juan Nepomuceno*, little has been published on the Iberian aspect outside Spain. Consequently the French and Spanish sections are shorter, but it is hoped that current French and Spanish research into their ships will soon become available and that points raised in this book will stimulate further dialogue. Differences between British, French and Spanish naval administration may be deduced from the juxtaposed accounts. The latter two were more centralised, standardised, hierarchical and autocratic. Despite the revolution the French navy was in 1805 officered by many obvious aristocrats. British naval administration, despite accountability and interlocking branches, seems less centralised and standardised, and more flexible, eccentric and resourceful. Differences in shipkeeping, tactics and gunnery methods are very apparent.

For the context of battle, ships and personalities this book owes a debt to past and contemporary historians Edward Brenton, David Cordingly, Anthony Deane, Robert Gardiner, William James, Brian Lavery, David Lyon, William Laird Clowes, Dudley Pope and Alan Schom. They have allowed this volume to focus on new primary sources and construct statistical tables to cast fresh light on a familiar subject, taking an old story in new directions and furnishing original material for social and economic historians.

The value of working as HMS *Victory*'s Keeper and Curator for 14 years has lain in excavating the ship as an archaeological site. Returning the ship to its 1805 configuration has revealed successive layers of structures, timbers and metals. Restoring the magazine has led to breakthroughs in understanding the function of contemporary ships' magazines. Personal experience obtained during an earlier naval career has been invaluable in deconstructing 200-year-old dockyard practices, protocols and parallels.

Transcribed primary sources are invaluable building blocks of new research. Juxtaposing the ships' captains' and masters' logs highlights new details and discrepancies, leading to further research. Printing observations of sailing qualities allows further discussion of significant divergences from standard designs and their effect on sailing qualities. Progress reports, minutely detailing dockyard maintenance and repairs carried out on each ship, balanced major repairs or wholesale modifications with the seasonal repairs which kept blockading ships at their station off Brest for weeks on end. 'Captains and Ships' reveals fresh information about short commissions which add to the overall picture of ship command and officer turnover. Prominent commanders are familiar, but the successive listing of every commander, some acting, gives a more realistic picture of frequent short term commands, often during refit or before commissioning. Were they older experienced officers who did not want long postings but could be trusted to oversee all the detail of refitting or pre-commission, a stopgap to give an officer favoured by the Admiralty more time in town 'on his private affairs', or practice for young inexperienced officers who could be overseen within a dockyard? These and other questions arise from detailed examination of primary sources.

The objectives of *The Ships of Trafalgar* are thus twofold. The first is to present a history of every ship that took part in the battle on Monday 21 October; not only the British fleet commanded by Vice-Admiral Horatio Lord Nelson but also the combined Franco-Spanish fleet under the overall command of Vice-Admiral Pierre Villeneuve. It has long been accepted that the British Trafalgar fleet comprised 27 British sail of the line opposing 33 Franco-Spanish sail of the line, totalling 60 vessels. But if we include the supporting frigates, brigs, cutters and schooners, 73 ships were collectively involved in the battle. These 13 supporting vessels (six British and seven French) did not stand in the line of fire, but each played a specific rôle in the engagement, whether relaying signals, towing out damaged ships or picking up survivors. In total the British, French and Spanish fleets comprised the following number and type of ships:

Ships Rate or Type	Guns	British Fleet No.	French Fleet No.	Spanish Fleet No.
1st Rate	136	0	0	1
1st Rate	112	0	0	2
1st Rate	100	3	0	1
2nd Rate	98	4	0	0
3rd Rate	80/84	1	4	1
3rd Rate	74	16	14	9
3rd Rate	64	1	0	1
5th Rate	40	0	5	0
5th Rate	38	1	0	0
5th Rate	36	3	0	0
Brig	18	0	1	0
Brig	16	0	1	0
Armed Schooner	12	1	0	0
Armed Cutter	10	1	0	0
TOTAL		33	25	15

Each individual ship, like the men who manned or commanded it, has its own story. Like the men, each ship had its own characteristics, abilities and failings, its fortune or misfortune reliant on its preparation and the chance of war.

War, the inevitable consequence when all other means of political diplomacy fails,[1] is the last resort to which the consolidated will of a group, country or state engages itself financially, materially and morally in order to defeat opposition to its will. To achieve this in 18th-19th century terms, national resources and labour are directed towards supporting the army and navy which, as the martial bodies under government authority, implement state policy by force. The second objective of this work is to analyse collectively the 73 ships forming the Trafalgar fleet in relation to contemporary industrial output achieved by ship designers, technology and science, matériel and procurement policy. The new iron industries were located on the coalfields around the Firth of Forth, South Wales and Staffordshire/Shropshire; copper production on the coalfields of South Wales and Lancashire. What, in terms of timber, iron and copper, rope, canvas and blocks, iron guns, powder and shot, did the ships of the Trafalgar fleets represent as the product of national policy, industrial capacity, limitations, experience, innovation and enterprise?

Timber for British hull construction, mainly oak, came from forests near dockyards or private building centres. In England this was Kent, Sussex, and Suffolk, the Forest of Bere and New Forest in Hampshire, the Forests of Dean and Holt and private estates. Shipbuilding centred on the royal dockyards at Chatham, Deptford, Portsmouth, Plymouth, Sheerness and Woolwich. In addition there were private sites from Harwich in Suffolk to Buckler's Hard on the River Beaulieu, Hampshire, and shipyards along the River Thames. Timber was hauled out of the woods on wagons, then transported along rivers or canals. The main building centres in France were Brest, Lorient, Rochefort, and Toulon where rivers could be utilised as supply routes. Spanish shipbuilding was centred at Cadiz, Cartagena and Guarnizo, Santander, although some ships were 'foreign built' in the royal arsenal at Havana. The Havana-built ships used cedar and mahogany. By this period oak was also being imported from Canada and Prussia via the port of Danzig (modern Gdansk). Timber for masts, yards and booms – fir, pine, or spruce – was, for all countries, imported from the Baltic. Equally important materials such as hemp for making ropes and canvas, and preservatives in the form of tar, turpentine and rosin were also supplied from Scandinavia, the Baltic states and Russia. Other important materials were iron and copper, the former for manufacturing guns, shot, iron knees, bolts and nails, the latter for producing copper plating to sheath the underwater hulls of the ships and other fastenings. While Britain had become virtually self-sufficient for these two materials, France was still importing iron ore from Sweden and, ironically, copper sheathing from Britain.

Documents also reveal the proportion of ships built in merchant yards rather than dockyards - the dockyards' main function was to repair and keep ships at sea. Portsmouth and Plymouth were the prominent repairing dockyards because their location was most suitable for maintaining blockades off Brest and fitting out expeditions for the Mediterranean, West and East Indies. The Thames yards and Chatham, because of their distance from the south-west, were used for research, development, shipbuilding and long term repairs. Service histories and progress books pinpoint strengths and weaknesses of ships designed by particular surveyors and master shipwrights such as Sir Thomas Slade and Sir John Henslow. Why did some ships (*Dreadnought*, *Neptune*) deteriorate more quickly than the norm; what was the norm; why did some ships need modifications (*Prince*); how did differences between specifications and completed ships arise; how much standardisation and non- standardisation existed? Generalisations cannot be made without reference to particulars.

Master Shipwright Joseph Tucker's unique list of shipwrights' hull repairs at Plymouth in 1803 tells us much more than its title suggests: it is a concrete manifestation of Earl St Vincent's dockyard reforms. It appears to be a unique report written specially for St Vincent who was closely linked to the Tucker family. Joseph, who would became joint Surveyor of the Navy with Sir Robert Seppings, was the brother of Benjamin who had been St Vincent's purser in 1798, a Navy Commissioner 1801-1803 and second Secretary to the Admiralty in 1804 and 1806-1807.[2] St Vincent had become First Lord of the Admiralty in 1801 suspecting that dockyard workers were thieves and that the Navy Board condoned abuses. He initiated a Commission of Naval Enquiry to investigate them and sought to justify his innovations as First Lord of the Admiralty 1801-1804.[3] Such detail was proof of new efficiency and accountability, but its itemised technical information gives us new information about working practices, quantities and prices.

Furthermore, ships' progress reports give a realistic picture of more regular dockyard procedures, in particular the frequency of docking and recoppering hulls to maintain efficient shiphandling in difficult conditions. Most of this work was done with man- or horse-powered winches and tackle, although dockyards were spearheading steam-driven pumps, winches and dredgers. The dockyards were the point at which government, parliament, Admiralty and Navy Board hierarchies and distribution networks meshed. By looking just at battles, officers and ships, we see only the tip of the iceberg of naval history. By leaving out the dockyards most of the iceberg is missed. Further study of dockyard procedures will yield many more answers to the actions of officers, men, ships and the operations in which they engaged.[4]

This book embodies the concept of historic ships as heritage. Although only *Victory* and the frigates *Trincomalee* (*Foudroyant*) and *Unicorn* remain as the most famous examples of British ship conservation, the spirit of *Téméraire*, *Duguay Trouin*, *Bucentaure* and the rest live through these pages. Their subsequent fates show the wide uses of a naval ship: prison (*Neptune*, *Téméraire*, *Defiance*, *Leviathan*, *Bellerophon*, *Euryalus*); hospital (*Britannia*, *Dreadnought*); receiving ships (*Prince*, *Téméraire*, *Mars*, *Swiftsure*, *Phœbe*); officer training (*Britannia*); target (*Leviathan*); slop-clothing (*Phœbe*); accommodation (*Polyphemus*); powder magazine (*Polyphemus*); sheer hulk (*Spartiate*); coal depôt (*Naiad*); and icon (*Victory*, *Téméraire*). Poignantly, *Revenge* was laid up for 30 years before being broken up.

These documents make an original contribution to social and economic history. Diet is particularised by accounts of fresh meat, vegetables, fruit, cocoa (*Neptune*) and lemon juice (*Dreadnought*) taken on board from victuallers. Composition of ships' companies is detailed. For instance, *Dreadnought* was a heavily Portsmouth-manned ship. The international composition of *Téméraire*'s crew and Captain Rotheram's dossier of descriptions and statistics of *Bellerophon*'s crew are invaluable, as are comments on volunteers, quotamen (*Revenge*) and pressed men. The discipline of the navy is highlighted by comparative punishment regimes across the fleet in time and location. Documents from *Agamemnon* and *Neptune* provide new primary sources for the Nore mutiny and accounts of mutinies in the preceding period. They also provide evidence of discipline of warrant officers. On *Orion* in 1810, 'A second court martial was held the following day to try William Fogwell, the ship's boatswain, for drunkenness and beating a man unmercifully', evidence that the Admiralty was overtly curbing cruelty to seamen. Across the fleets, the distinctive activities of different types of ships, and their tempo of operations, are seen: frigates clearly had the most frequently exciting and daring actions.

Cultural history is illuminated. Logs reveal contemporary language that has passed into common use: 'steer clear', masts and rigging 'going by the board'. Our emotions are stretched by the first hand accounts. To twenty-first century eyes the battle scenes are brutal, horrific, vindictive. They are also compassionate, brave, humorous, honourable. Snapshots from 21 October 1805 allow us to empathise with seaman: *Ajax*'s men were polishing the guns, 'as though an inspection were about to take place instead of martial combat, while three or four, as if in mere bravado, were dancing a hornpipe'; *Victory*'s crew were taking their meal of 'pork and wine' at their guns at 11 a.m., an hour before facing death. Participants of all three navies, with few exceptions, must have been traumatised by the slaughter, death of close friends and loved officers, guilt at their own survival, terror of dying by weapon, cannon or explosion, exhausted by physical effort; but the following day most crews had to fight desperately to save their own or other ships from a foe common to all of them, the weather.

This book's unique contribution to the scholarship of Trafalgar is its evaluation of the material needed to produce in a physical sense, over very many years of hard-won experience and effort, the ships of Trafalgar, and the environmental and human resources which placed the ships off Trafalgar on the morning of 21 October 1805. Naturally this great battle and its ships cannot be fully understood without reviewing the events leading up to it.

On 27 March 1802 the Treaty of Amiens was signed, formally concluding the war between Britain and revolutionary France. After 14 months this fragile peace ended when war was declared between Britain and France on 16 May 1803. Almost immediately Vice-Admiral Nelson took up his appointment as Commander-in-Chief of the Mediterranean Fleet stationed off Toulon, blockading the French Fleet. France was now led by the ambitious Napoleon Bonaparte who planned to invade Britain. Such an invasion plan could not be undertaken without a large fleet drawn from the entire French navy, much of which was under close blockade. When British frigates attacked the Spanish frigate *Mercedes* and her consort in late 1804, Spain allied herself immediately with France and entered the war against Britain on 12 December 1804. Napoleon, who had been proclaimed Emperor of France on 18 May 1804, welcomed this new ally to reinforce his ambitions. With the Spanish navy at his disposal, new orders were issued. These extra ships would support his invasion flotilla gathering at the ports of Texel, Ostend, Dunkirk, Calais, Boulogne and Le Havre. French naval expeditions were also prepared at Brest, Rochefort, and Toulon, while Spanish ships and troops were made ready at Ferrol, Cadiz, and Cartagena. Newly appointed to command the fleet at Toulon was Vice-Admiral Pierre Villeneuve, an experienced seaman who had fought against Nelson at the Battle of the Nile in August 1798. With orders from Vice-Admiral Decrès, French naval minister, Villeneuve was to sail and rendezvous with other French forces sent to the West Indies. Their objective was to attack British colonies in the Caribbean, but more importantly, to lure British blockading forces away from the Channel to allow an attempt at invasion to take place. But bad weather detained the Toulon fleet from sailing, and Villeneuve was reluctant, remembering his defeat by his adversary at the Nile.

Although the battle of Trafalgar in 1805 did not decisively change the course of the war in Europe, it was the 'grande finale' of two years' dogged pursuit and harassment by British naval forces against the French in the English Channel and the Mediterranean. As a result, each of Napoleon's grandiose plans to invade Britain were dissolved piecemeal by the Royal Navy. His ambitions of French expansion were confined to mainland Europe. The two naval commanders upsetting Napoleon's intentions were Vice-Admiral Lord Nelson, Commander in Chief of the Mediterranean fleet, and Vice-Admiral Sir William Cornwallis commanding the Channel fleet. Both men were appointed when hostilities with France reopened in May 1803. Historians have ignored or underestimated the part that Cornwallis played within the overall campaign, his tenacious efforts overshadowed by Nelson's venerated genius. Under Cornwallis the Channel Fleet diligently blockaded the entire shoreline of France and Spain, preventing any attempt by Napoleon to coalesce and invade. Irrespective of weather or season, and stretched to the limits of their resources, Cornwallis's ships were unrelentingly in their vigilance.

Nelson, zealously blockading Toulon with eleven ships and two frigates, prevented Villeneuve from sailing as ordered in December 1804. After prolonged excuses, Villeneuve informed Decrès that the 'enemy have not appeared' and left the harbour on 18 January 1805. Struck immediately by north-westerly gales, his ships battered, he returned to port. Napoleon's fourth invasion plan was thereby aborted. In March Napoleon again revised his plans and further pressure was placed on Villeneuve to sail from Toulon. This time he was successful, for adverse weather conditions had forced Nelson to drop his vigil and withdraw his ships to Sardinia for maintenance, leaving two frigates, his 'eyes of the fleet', to watch over Toulon. Villeneuve broke out of harbour on 30 March, and, after refusing to supplement his squadron with Spanish warships from Cartagena, made for the Straits of Gibraltar.[5]

At 8 a.m. 4 April, while making his way to Pulla Bay off the SW coast of Sardinia, Nelson received news from the frigate *Phœbe* of Villeneuve's escape. Wasting no time he weighed anchor and sailed east for Sicily, believing that French intentions lay with Egypt. When Villeneuve reached Cadiz on 9 April to combine forces with the Spanish, he surprised the blockading fleet under Vice Admiral Sir John Orde. Orde, outnumbered, went north to support the British squadron laying off Brest, confident that Villeneuve's combined squadron would now rendezvous with Admiral Ganteaume's ships within that port. Tactically this proved a grave error. Now united with the Spanish squadron under Admiral Gravina, the combined force totalling 17 ships and 5,262 troops set course for the West Indies following Napoleon's seventh plan. Hearing no news of Villeneuve to the east, Nelson sailed west. Trusting his intuition he realised the French had left the Mediterranean, and conjectured they were bound for Ireland in readiness for invasion. Hampered by westerly winds, Nelson's squadron finally reached Gibraltar on the 7 May and proceeded north but found no trace of the enemy. On 12 May he wrote, 'My lot is cast, and I am going to the West Indies where, although I am late, yet chance may have given them a bad passage and me a good one'. Leaving word for the Admiralty, Nelson sailed in hot pursuit.

Villeneuve arrived at Fort de France, Martinique, on 16 May after a passage of 35 days. After receiving new orders he captured Diamond Rock on 2 June. The following day, as Nelson arrived off Barbados, reports suggested that Villeneuve's fleet had sailed south to Tobago. With no alternative, Nelson reluctantly followed, expecting to catch the enemy in the Bay of Paria. Meanwhile, Admiral Magon arrived with two ships from Rochefort. Adhering to orders, Villeneuve attacked British interests. When he captured 15 merchantmen on the 7th, he learned of Nelson's presence. To avoid confrontation Villeneuve ordered his fleet, now comprising 20 vessels, to return to Ferrol, and sailed eastward for Europe. He totally ignored Napoleon's orders to land troops, attack British possessions and wait, as instructed, 35 days for Ganteaume to arrive with further reinforcements. Two days later Nelson learnt of the hasty French departure and followed, sending the 18 gun brig *Curieux* ahead with his dispatches. Taking a northerly course Curieux sighted the combined fleet en route. When *Curieux* arrived in Plymouth on 7 July news of the enemy was conveyed to Lord Barham at the Admiralty. Instantly orders were sent to alert Vice Admiral Sir Robert Calder whose squadron lay off Finisterre. Nelson had by this time arrived and anchored at Gibraltar on 19 June and 'went on shore for the first time since the 16th June, 1803, and for wanting my foot out of the *Victory*, two years and ten days.'[6]

Villeneuve fell in with Calder's squadron off Finisterre on 22 July. After many hours' manœuvring, Calder, flying his flag in the 98 gun *Prince of Wales*, finally got to grips with his opponent around 5.45. p.m. A chaotic battle, hampered by poor visibility caused by smoke and fog, continued until about 8.30 p.m. when Calder called off the action. Two Spanish 74 gun ships *Firma* and *San Rafael* were captured and five other ships badly mauled. Calder's squadron had also suffered considerable damage. Next day, due to the persistent fog, neither side was willing to renew engagement. Although weather conditions improved on 24 July, Calder 'would neither attack nor retreat', allowing Villeneuve to escape. Had he re-engaged the enemy more persistently, a second fleet engagement off Cape Trafalgar might not have taken place. As a result of his actions and the British humiliation it caused, Calder was relieved of command and recalled to face an Admiralty court of inquiry. Because of weather and damage, Gravina and Villeneuve agreed to proceed to Cadiz, but dwindling supplies forced them to make for Vigo Bay. After a brief respite they sailed for the safety of Ferrol, reaching harbour on 2 August. Utterly worn out and overdue a rest, Nelson sailed for home in *Victory* with *Superb* (74), landing at Portsmouth on 18 August.[7]

Napoleon had reviewed his Grande Armée at Boulogne while waiting for Villeneuve's fleet to arrive with its additional squadrons from other French ports to fulfil what was now his eighth plan. But on 11 August Villeneuve decided otherwise and instead of sailing north from Ferrol, turned south for Cadiz, a decision that infuriated the Emperor and had historic implications. Villeneuve's combined fleet reached Cadiz on 21 August, while news of Villeneuve's blatant disobedience devastated the Emperor's invasion plans. Napoleon also found himself facing a new enemy as Austria had entered the war against France. Totally thwarted, Napoleon ordered his Grande Armée to break camp at Boulogne on 26 August and march south-east to oppose the Austrian threat. As all opportunity of invading Britain dissipated, Napoleon discarded his invasion plan and devised a ninth plan, intending to send the combined fleet back into the Mediterranean to Naples to support his new campaign against Austria. Deeply unimpressed with Villeneuve, Napoleon appointed Admiral Rosily to take command of the fleet at Cadiz. In France Decrès issued new orders that clearly directed the combined fleet to sail for Naples and support the new theatre of war on the Austrian front. Despite this, it is still commonly believed that Villeneuve's fleet sailed from Cadiz to support an invasion of Britain and that Nelson's action off Trafalgar prevented this French invasion. These misconceptions have distorted the story of Trafalgar and Nelson, and have contributed to the mythological notion that Trafalgar was a decisive blow against Napoleon or indeed that it put an end to war at sea in the period to 1815. Although it removed a possible future threat, its most important and often ignored effect was that Napoleon could not utilise any troops or support that Villeneuve was carrying, to bolster the proposed Italian campaign against the Austrians.

Villeneuve was now confronted by innumerable problems. Much needed provisions proved difficult to procure due to shortages of money and credit, many of the ships were 'in want of repair' and ordnance supplies were exhausted. The fleet was also undermanned by 2,000, numbers reduced by illness and desertion. Villeneuve therefore called a 'conseil de guerre' on 8 October, where the officers voted unanimously not to sail immediately. In effect the entire fleet mutinied against Napoleon. But when Villeneuve received news that Rosily was to relieve him of command he rescinded these actions and ordered the fleet to sail on 18 October. At 6 a.m. next day Villeneuve's combined fleet comprising 40 ships carrying 30,000 men began to weigh anchor and put to sea. With the weather deteriorating the combined fleet struggled to get into formation as they encountered rain, squalls and strong south-westerly winds. Further hampered by shifting winds, Villeneuve's fleet fell into further disarray.

Victory's log for Sunday 20 October says little more than 'Performed Divine Service', while *Victory* received further news of the enemy's strength and position from Nelson's old ship *Agamemnon*.[8] By nightfall all Nelson's ships had cleared for battle and were steering a course WNW south-west of Cadiz, with Villeneuve 25 miles further north. Expecting to prevent the enemy making for the Straits of Gibraltar, Nelson soon realised he had over-anticipated the situation and had placed his ships too far to the south. Finally, at 5 p.m., much to Nelson's relief, *Naiad* reported that the enemy was now sailing due south. An hour later Nelson's own fleet was sighted by the French *Achille*. Villeneuve marshalled his ships into line of battle and stood towards the Straits of Gibraltar. As night closed Blackwood's frigates silently stalked the combined fleet. Their signal instructions were: 'If the enemy are standing to the southward, or towards the Strait, burn two blue lights together, every hour, in order to make a greater blaze. If the enemy are standing to the westward three guns quick, every hour.' The blue lights burned on through the night.

As night mists dissipated in the morning light of Monday 21 October 1805, the fleets of three nations prepared for an historic battle. To the east stood the combined fleet, a myriad of masts silhouetted against a pale autumn sun, sailing south towards the Straits of Gibraltar. After many frustrating months Nelson, now commanding the British fleet carrying 17,000 men, was at last confronting the enemy. Following his battle plan Nelson displayed signal number 72, ordering his fleet to get into formation behind its respective lead ships, *Victory* (100) and *Royal Sovereign* (100). This signal was followed by number 76, 'Bear up and sail large ENE'. At about 8 a.m. Villeneuve ordered his fleet to wear and reversing his sailing order, proceeded northward towards Cadiz and Nelson's ships. Just before noon French and Spanish ships opened fire on the British fleet, bringing into action 73 floating embodiments of industrial output, technology, natural resources and human will. Each of these ships has a history from which there is much to discover about the qualitative and quantitative demands of fighting at sea.

Notes
1. 'War is a mere continuation of policy by other means.' Von Clausewitz, Karl, trans. Howard, M / Paret, P, *Vom Kriege* (Princeton University Press, 1976/1984, 1st pub. Dummlers Verlag, Berlin, 1832), Book I On the Nature of War, Chapter I What is War? Introduction.
2. My thanks to Matthew Sheldon of the Royal Naval Museum which holds papers (MSS 259) of Admiral John Jervis collected by Jedediah Stephen Tucker, Benjamin's son and St Vincent's biographer.
3. RNM, Admiralty Library Portfolio I (3). His secretary was Benjamin Tucker whose eldest son, Jedediah Stevens Tucker, published *Memoirs of the Earl of St Vincent* (1844) compiled from his father's notes.
4. See Naval Dockyards Society *Transactions*, 'Portsmouth Dockyard in the Age of Nelson', Conference 30 April-1 May 2005, forthcoming summer 2005.
5. P Goodwin, 'The Battle of Trafalgar: A short account in two parts: The Prelude and The Battle.' (Unpublished, 1995).
6. TNA: PRO, ADM 51/1482 part 6; ADM 51/4514 part 3.
7. Goodwin, 'The Battle of Trafalgar' (1995).
8. TNA: PRO, ADM 51/4514/3.

∞ A Note on Sources ∞

In a book of this size it has been necessary to keep referencing to a minimum. Therefore primary sources have been listed in the footnotes in an abbreviated form while commonly used secondary sources have been referred to by author name, volume, page number (and year of publication where necessary). The reader is directed to the following list of abbreviations and the bibliography where the full source references will be found.

List of Abbreviations

ADM	Admiralty	NRS	Navy Records Society
Br	Brig	pdr	pounder
Bs	bomb ship	PRO	Public Record Office
Bv	bomb vessel	qtr	quarter weight
cwt	hundredweight	Rep[d]	repaired
Do	ditto	Ss	Stores ship
Fs	fireship	TNA	The National Archives
ft	foot / feet	WO	War Office
fm	fathom	Wr	weather
Gb	Gun-brigs of between 12 & 14 guns:	yd	yard
Hs	Hospital ship		
ins	inch / inches		
kts	knots		
lbs	pounds weight		
NMM	National Maritime Museum		

Because all recorded dimensions, weights, and quantities are pertinent to a period when the imperial system was in use, the reader can determine their metric or alternative equivalents from the following conversion tables.

1 in = 2.54 cm
12 ins = 1 ft = 30.48 cm = 0.3048 metres
3 feet (ft) = 1 yd = 0.9144 metres
6 ft = 1 fathom = 1.8288 metres
101 fathoms = 1 anchor cable = 606 feet = 184.7 metres.
1 nautical cable = 608 feet = 185.3 metres.
10 cables = 1 nautical mile = 6080 feet = 1 minute of latitude = 1853.18 metres
1 league = 3 nautical miles = 5.5695 kilometres

1 oz = 0.0284 kg
16 ozs = 1lb = 0.454 kg
28 lbs = 1 qtr = 12.71 kg
4 qtrs = 112 lbs = 1cwt = 50.848 kg
20 cwt = 2240 lbs = 1 ton = 1016.96 kilograms = 1 tonne

1 pint = 0.568 litres
2 pints = 1 quart = 1.136 litres
8 pints = 4 quarts = 1 gallon = 4.544 litres
225 gallons = 1 ton of water = 1022.4 litres

All monetary values are given in pounds (£), shillings (s) and pence (d).

PART 1
THE BRITISH FLEET

The British fleet present at the Battle of Trafalgar, under the overall command of Lord Nelson, Vice-Admiral of the White, comprised thirty-three ships consisting of 27 line of battle ships, four 5th rate frigates, an armed schooner and an armed cutter. This fleet was assembled from Lord Nelson's Mediterranean squadron which had pursued Vice-Admiral Villeneuve's ships across the Atlantic and back, and Vice-Admiral Cuthbert Collingwood's squadron blockading Cadiz. Before joining Nelson, Collingwood and his squadron had been wearing the blue ensign of the Channel squadron. During the weeks preceding the battle, while the British fleet watched over Villeneuve's combined Franco-Spanish fleet blockaded within Cadiz, commanders exchanged ships to meet Nelson's requirements ready for the potential battle. Ships were still preparing to sail from England to join the Trafalgar fleet. *Superb* (74), for example, was completing her refit at Plymouth and failed to arrive on time, meeting the schooner *Pickle* in the Channel approaches returning in early November with news of the battle. Other ships, especially those of Admiral Louis' squadron, were deployed elsewhere or in Gibraltar when the battle took place, for example *Donegal* (74). Nelson's fleet that fought off Trafalgar on Monday 21 October 1805 therefore comprised the following ships, flag officers and commanders:

THE BRITISH FLEET AT TRAFALGAR

Ship's Name	Rate or Type	Guns	Class Group Name Class	Date	Designer
Britannia	1st	100	Royal George	1745	Est. Establishment
Royal Sovereign	1st	100	Royal Sovereign	1772	John Williams
Victory	1st	100	Victory	1759	Thomas Slade
Dreadnought	2nd	98	Neptune/Dreadnought	1788	John Henslow
Neptune	2nd	98	Neptune/Dreadnought	1788	John Henslow
Téméraire	2nd	98	Neptune/Dreadnought	1788	John Henslow
Prince	2nd	98	London	1759	Thomas Slade
Tonnant	2nd	80	Ex-French *Tonnant*	1789	Noel Sane
Achille	3rd	74	*Achille* (French lines of *Pompée*)	1795	Copy of French lines
Ajax	3rd	74	Kent	1795	Thomas Slade
Belleisle	3rd	74	Ex-French *Formidable*, ex-*Marat*, Ex-*Lion*	1790	Jacques Noel Sane
Bellerophon	3rd	74	Arrogant	1758	Thomas Slade
Colossus	3rd	74	Colossus	1798	John Henslow
Conqueror	3rd	74	Conqueror (mod. *Mars* design)	1795	John Henslow
Defence	3rd	74	Arrogant	1758	John Henslow
Defiance	3rd	74	Elizabeth	1766	Thomas Slade
Leviathan	3rd	74	Leviathan	1779	Copy of French lines
Mars	3rd	74	Mars	1788	John Henslow
Minotaur	3rd	74	Leviathan	1779	Copy of French lines
Orion	3rd	74	Canada	1759	William Bately
Revenge	3rd	74	Revenge	1796	John Henslow
Spartiate	3rd	74	Ex-French *Spartiate*	1797	Jacques Noel Sane
Swiftsure	3rd	74	Swiftsure	1800	John Henslow
Thunderer	3rd	74	Culloden/Thunderer	1769	Thomas Slade
Africa	3rd	64	Inflexible	1777	John Williams
Agamemnon	3rd	64	Ardent	1761	Thomas Slade
Polyphemus	3rd	64	Intrepid/Magnanime	1765	John Williams
Naiad	5th	38	Naiad	1795	William Rule
Euryalus	5th	36	Apollo/Euryalus	1798	William Rule
Phœbe	5th	36	Phœbe	1794	Edward Hunt
Sirius	5th	36	Sirius (Lines of French *San Fiorenzo* class)	1795	Copy of French lines
Pickle	Schooner	12	Purchased	1802	Unknown
Entreprenante	Cutter	10	Ex-French *Entreprenante*	1798	Unknown

Ship's Name	Rate or Type	Guns	Flag Officer and/or Commander
Britannia	1st	100	Rear-Admiral William Earl of Northesk (White) Captain Charles Bullen
Royal Sovereign	1st	100	Vice-Admiral Cuthbert Collingwood (Blue) Captain Edward Rotheram
Victory	1st	100	Vice-Admiral Horatio Lord Nelson (White) Captain Thomas Masterman Hardy
Dreadnought	2nd	98	Captain John Conn
Neptune	2nd	98	Captain Thomas Francis Freemantle
Téméraire	2nd	98	Captain Eliab Harvey
Prince	2nd	98	Captain Richard Grindall
Tonnant	2nd	80	Captain Charles Tyler
Achille	3rd	74	Captain Richard King
Ajax	3rd	74	Lieutenant John Pilford: acting
Belleisle	3rd	74	Captain William Hargood
Bellerophon	3rd	74	Captain John Cooke
Colossus	3rd	74	Captain James Nicoll Morris
Conqueror	3rd	74	Captain Israel Pellew
Defence	3rd	74	Captain George Hope
Defiance	3rd	74	Captain Phillip Charles Durham
Leviathan	3rd	74	Captain Henry William Bayntun
Mars	3rd	74	Captain George Duff
Minotaur	3rd	74	Captain Charles John Moore Mansfield
Orion	3rd	74	Captain Edward Codrington
Revenge	3rd	74	Captain Robert Moorsom
Spartiate	3rd	74	Captain Sir Francis Laforey Bt
Swiftsure	3rd	74	Captain William Gordon Rutherford
Thunderer	3rd	74	Lieutenant John Stockham: acting.
Africa	3rd	64	Captain Henry Digby
Agamemnon	3rd	64	Captain Sir Edward Berry
Polyphemus	3rd	64	Captain Robert Redmill
Naiad	5th	38	Captain Thomas Dundas
Euryalus	5th	36	Captain Henry Blackwood
Phœbe	5th	36	Captain Hon. Thomas Bladen Capell
Sirius	5th	36	Captain William Prowse
Pickle	Schooner	12	Lieutenant John Richards Lapenotière
Entreprenante	Cutter	10	Lieutenant Robert Benjamin Young

The ships assembled off Trafalgar were typical of the British fleet, embracing a wide variety of ships, rates and classes, conceived from differing designers and introduced at varying periods. These ships varied considerably in age; all except a few had been in action prior to Trafalgar. *Revenge* (74), launched on 13 April 1805, had barely five months to shape her ship's company into a cohesive fighting unit. That she would sustain just 28 killed and 51 wounded under prolonged action pays tribute to the crew's training under Captain Moorsom.

Apart from the three 1st rate 100 gun ships *Britannia*, *Royal Sovereign* and *Victory*, which were built as individual designs, the vessels comprised four 98 gun ships of which three were the same class, one ex-French 80 gun ship captured at the battle of the Nile in 1798 and designed by the celebrated Frenchman Jacques Noel Sane, and sixteen 74 gun ships of varying class types, two of which were ex-French prizes also designed by Sane. Irrespective of class group, most of the British-built Trafalgar ships were designed by Thomas Slade and John Henslow. Slade, who designed the *Victory*, was perhaps the most innovative of the eighteenth century naval warship designers. Until the 1750s ship specifications had been constrained

SUMMARY OF BRITISH FLEET SERVICE LENGTH

Ship's Name	Dockyard Built	Date Launched	Ship's Age in 1805	Date when Ship Disposed or Lost	Age when Disposed or Lost
Britannia	Portsmouth	1762	43	1825	63
Royal Sovereign	Plymouth	1786	19	1841	55
Victory	Chatham	1765	40	Still in service	240+
Dreadnought	Portsmouth	1801	4	1857	56
Neptune	Deptford	1797	8	1818	21
Téméraire	Chatham	1798	7	1838	40
Prince	Woolwich	1788	17	1837	50
Tonnant	Toulon – Captured 1798	1789	16	1821	32
Achille	Gravesend	1798	7	1865	67
Ajax	Rotherhithe	1798	7	1807	9 ★
Belleisle	Rochefort – Captured 1795	1790 ?	15	1841	51
Bellerophon	Frindsbury	1786	19	1836	50
Colossus	Deptford	1803	2	1826	23
Conqueror	Harwich	1801	4	1822	21
Defence	Plymouth	1763	42	1811	48 ★
Defiance	Rotherhithe	1783	22	1817	32
Leviathan	Chatham	1790	15	1848	58
Mars	Deptford	1794	11	1823	29
Minotaur	Chatham	1793	12	1810	17 ★
Orion	Deptford	1787	18	1814	27
Revenge	Chatham	1805	6 months	1849	44
Spartiate	Captured	1798 ?	7	1857	59
Swiftsure	Buckler's Hard	1804	1	1841	37
Thunderer	Deptford	1783	22	1814	31
Africa	Deptford	1781	24	1814	33
Agamemnon	Buckler's Hard	1781	24	1807	26 ★
Polyphemus	Sheerness	1782	23	1827	45
Naiad	Limehouse	1797	8	1866	69
Euryalus	Buckler's Hard	1803	2	1860	57
Phœbe	Deptford	1795	10	1841	26
Sirius	Deptford	1797	8	1810	13 ★
Pickle	Purchased at Plymouth	1801	4	1808	7 ★
Entreprenante	Captured 1798	1798	7	1812	14

Note: Ships marked with ★ were lost through foundering or fire.

by a series of particulars proposed by the somewhat conservative Navy Board and ratified by the Board of Admiralty. These authorised specifications, or establishments, first introduced in 1706, were reviewed and upgraded periodically. However, being restrictive, they left little room for inventiveness in improving ship design and speed. In France where initiative and understanding of hydrodynamics was encouraged as a science, ship designers produced far better hull forms giving their ships far greater speed and manoeuvrability. Realising that reform was necessary, Slade, with the aid of his kinsman Benjamin Slade, analysed the lines of captured French ships. This investigation was supported by Lord Anson and the Board of Admiralty who readily appointed Slade as Surveyor of the Navy. Slade then persuaded the Admiralty to make variations to the 1745 Establishments and revolutionised British naval ship design based on French lines. Although hull form altered, specific timber dimensions and scantling lists forming the ship remained. Henslow carried Slade's concepts through into the nineteenth century.

Nineteen of the British ships were built in royal dockyards: eight at Deptford, five at Chatham, two at Portsmouth, two at Plymouth and one at each of Woolwich and Sheerness. Excluding the four captured French ships, the ten remaining vessels were built at private shipyards on the River Thames or in the south of England, three being constructed at Buckler's Hard on the River Beaulieu in the New Forest, Hampshire.

While most vessels had been in service for a considerable time before Trafalgar and would continue to do so afterwards, some (with an asterisk) were later lost through foundering or fire; the frigate *Sirius* was burnt deliberately to avoid capture after grounding in an action against the French. *Victory*, now preserved in dry dock at Portsmouth, is 240 years old at the time of writing. As the oldest ship commissioned ship in the world she continues to serve in the Royal Navy as the flagship of the Second Sea Lord/Commander-in-Chief Naval Home Command. The only other ship that remains commissioned in service from this period is the American 44 gun frigate USS *Constitution* which, launched precisely eight years before Trafalgar on 21 October 1797, is conserved afloat today at Boston, Massachusetts. Nelson's *Victory*, as she is colloquially termed, was not however the oldest British ship at Trafalgar, the 1st rate *Britannia* being 43 and *Defence* 42 years old when they went into battle that day. Only 14 of the 33 ships present (42 per cent) were aged 10 years or less, the youngest vessels to fight in the British fleet that day being the 74 gun ships *Revenge* and *Swiftsure*.

Manned with 17,000 men, the entire fleet of 33 ships carried a total armament of 2,370 guns, comprising 2,186 standard carriage guns and 184 carronades. The number and type of each calibre are given in the table. By calculation this weight of armament amounted to 4,945.2 tons (4,683.9 tonnes) of iron. The total number of guns carried by the 27 line of battle ships that actually fought in the battle was 2,166 guns comprising 2,038 carriage guns and 128 carronades. The number and type of each calibre are given in the table. This quantity of ordnance weighed 4,610 tons (4,683.9 tonnes) in total. If each gun of the 33 ships fired a single round the cumulative firepower amounts to 23.20 tons (23.6 tonnes) of iron and that for the 27 line of battle ships 21.43 tons (21.8 tonnes).

As no British ship was captured or destroyed during the battle, or lost in the horrific storm afterwards, their individual service stories continue until the end of the Napoleonic War and often beyond.

FIREPOWER OF THE BRITISH FLEET OF 33 SHIPS

Gun Type and Calibre	Total No. of Guns	Total Broadside Weight if all guns fired one round of Iron Round Shot (lbs)	(tons)	(kgs)	Total Gunpowder Expended if all guns fired one round (lbs)	(tons)	(kgs)
32 pounder carriage gun	624	19,968	8.91	8,986	6,656	2.96	2,995
24 pounder carriage gun	374	8,976	4.01	4,039	2,992	1.27	1,346
18 pounder carriage gun	756	13,608	6.08	6,124	4,536	2.03	2,756
12 pounder carriage gun	162	1,944	0.86	874.8	648	0.29	292
9 pounder carriage gun	238	2,124	0.96	956	708	0.32	319
6 pounder carriage gun	32	192	0.09	86.4	64	0.03	29
68 pounder carronnade	2	136	0.06	61	12	0.005	6
32 pounder carronnade	128	4,096	1.83	1,843	341	0.15	154
24 pounder carronnade	6	144	0.06	65	12	0.005	6
18 pounder carronnade	30	540	0.24	243	45	0.02	20
12 pounder carronnade	18	216	0.10	97.2	18	0.008	8
TOTAL	2,370	51,962	23.20	23,383	16,032	7.16	7,214

FIREPOWER OF THE 27 BRITISH LINE OF BATTLE SHIPS (100 TO 64 GUN SHIPS)

Gun Type and Calibre	Total No. of Guns	Total Broadside Weight if all guns fired one round of Iron Round Shot (lbs)	(tons)	(kgs)	Total Gunpowder Expended if all guns fired one round (lbs)	(tons)	(kgs)
32 pounder carriage gun	624	19,968	8.91	8,986	6,656	2.96	2,995
24 pounder carriage gun	374	8,976	4.01	4,039	2,992	1.27	1,346
18 pounder carriage gun	624	11,232	5.01	5,054	3,744	1,67	1685
12 pounder carriage gun	162	1,944	0.86	875	648	0.29	292
9 pounder carriage gun	222	1,998	0.89	899	666	0.30	300
6 pounder carriage gun	32	192	0.09	86.4	64	0.03	29
68 pounder carronnade	2	136	0.06	61	12	0.005	6
32 pounder carronnade	90	2,880	1.29	1.296	240	0.11	108
24 pounder carronnade	6	144	0.06	65	12	0.005	6
18 pounder carronnade	30	540	0.24	243	45	0.02	20
TOTAL	2166	48,010	21.43	21,605	15,079	6.73	6,786

PART 1: CHAPTER 1
THE BRITISH FIRST RATE SHIPS

The 100 gun ship *BRITANNIA*

Named after Britannia, the female figure who represents Britain, the *Britannia* that fought at Trafalgar was the third Royal Naval ship to bear this name. The first *Britannia* was a 1st rate ship of 100 guns built at Chatham in 1682. Taken to pieces in 1715, her frames were transferred to Woolwich and used to construct the second *Britannia*, also a 100 gun ship, launched there in 3 October 1719. This ship remained in service until broken up at Chatham in September 1749.[1] The Trafalgar *Britannia*, again a 1st rate of 100 guns, was ordered on two consecutive occasions, the first date being 28 March 1751, the second date 21 May 1757. Built at Portsmouth, she was finally launched on 19 October 1762. Using the first order date, Colledge suggests that she was eleven years on the stocks, construction work commencing under Master Shipwright Peirson Lock. When work resumed after she was reordered in 1757, the work was supervised by Master Shipwright Edward Allin, Lock transferring to Chatham where he would soon commence constructing the 100 gun *Victory*. After a further six years' building, *Britannia* was finally launched on 19 October 1762.[2] Built to similar lines as the ill-fated 100 gun *Royal George*, launched at Woolwich in 1756, some 288,000 cubic feet of timber was used to construct *Britannia*, which equates to about 5,760 loads, or an equivalent number of trees taken from about 96 acres of woodland. The initial building cost for her hull was £39,644 10s 10d with a further £79 10s 4d spent the year after her launch, while her overall expenditure for rigging and stores amounted to £6,120 1s 6d.[3]

SERVICE HISTORY

1772: Although launched at the end of the Seven Years' War, *Britannia* was not put into commission until France intervened with the American War of Independence. Placed into dock at Portsmouth for a small repair and graving on 3 April, *Britannia* was re-launched on 28 August, the cost of her refit amounting to £6,371 11s 11d; £5,746 0s 8d of which was expended on her hull and £625 11s 3d for rigging and stores.[4]

1778: With France joining the American War of Independence in support of the rebel colonists, and Spain entering the war shortly after, *Britannia*, like *Victory* (100), which had also not been operational since her launch at the end of the Seven Years' War, was finally put into commission on 30 August under Captain John Moutray and deployed in home waters.[5]

1779: On 2 March 1779 Moutray transferred into *Ramillies* (74) and his successor, Captain Charles Morice Pole, entered *Britannia* on 1 April.[6]

1780: On 9 June command of *Britannia* was superseded by Captain Thomas Allen. However, Allen remained in the ship for only a few months until succeeded by Captain James Bradley on 26 August. *Britannia* then joined the Channel squadron commanded by Rear-Admiral Richard Kempenfelt.[7]

1781: In November the Admiralty received intelligence that Admiral de Guichen was preparing to sail from Brest with a large convoy of transports carrying much needed naval supplies, part for the West Indies, the rest for Admiral de Grasse's fleet stationed in the East Indies. Ordered to intercept them, Kempenfelt put to sea on 2 December. With twelve line of battle ships escorting his convoy De Guichen eventually sailed on 10 December. Flying his flag in *Victory* (100), Kempenfelt's squadron comprised the following ships:

Rate	No.	Guns	Ships' names
1st	2	100	*Britannia, Victory*
2nd	2	98	*Duke, Queen*
2nd	2	90	*Ocean, Union*
3rd	4	74	*Alexander, Courageux, Edgar, Valiant*
3rd	1	64	*Agamemnon*
3rd	1	60	*Medway*
4th	1	50	*Renown*
5th	1	38	*Arethusa*
5th	2	36	*Monsieur, Prudente*
5th	1	28	*Tartar*
Fire ship	1	8	*Tisiphone*
TOTAL	18	1192	

Having deployed his fleet 150 miles SW of Ushant, Kempenfelt sighted the French on the afternoon of 12 December and, taking advantage of the fact that de Guichen had stationed his squadron to leeward of the transports, swiftly made his attack. While the convoy scattered, the French warships remained powerless as ship after ship struck their flags to Kempenfelt's squadron. In all 15 transports and their valuable stores were captured before nightfall. In the ensuing days violent weather dispersed the remains of the French fleet, most returning to Brest while only *Triomphant* (84), *Brave* (74) and five transports completed their voyage to the West Indies.[8]

1782: On 7 April Captain Benjamin Hill succeeded command of *Britannia*.[9]

SPECIFICATIONS: *BRITANNIA*

Rate	1st	Length on the range of the gun deck	178 ft	Ordnance - lower gun deck	28 x 42 pounders (later 32 pounders)
Guns	100	Length of keel for tonnage	144 ft 6½ ins	Ordnance - middle gun deck	28 x 24 pounders
Class	*Royal George*	Extreme breadth	51 ft 10 ins	Ordnance - upper gun deck	28 x long 12 pounders
Designer	1745 Establishment	Depth in hold	21 ft 6 ins	Ordnance - quarter deck	12 x 6 pounders
Builder	Peirson Lock/Edward Allin	Tons burthen	2065. 58/94	Ordnance - forecastle	4 x 6 pounders
Dockyard	Portsmouth	Draught afore	23 ft	Single broadside weight	1140 pounds (1000 pounds)
Date ordered	28 March 1751/ re-ordered 21 May 1757	Draught abaft	24 ft	Fate	Hulked at Plymouth as prison ship
Date keel laid	1751 (11 years building)	Complement	850		1815 renamed *Saint George* as flag and receiving ship
Date launched	19 October 1762				1825 renamed *Barfleur* and later broken up

Note: Ordnance listed as for 1803/1805 Trafalgar campaign.

Source: Lyon, *Sailing Navy List*, p. 63.

THE 100 GUN SHIP *BRITANNIA*

CAPTAINS OF *BRITANNIA* (MSS 248/4 and 248/6)

Name	Time of Entry	Time of Discharge	On What Occasion
John Moutray	30 August 1778	2 March 1779	To the *Ramillies*
Charles Morice Pole	1 Aril 1779	8 June 1780	Superseded
Thomas Allen	9 June 1780	25 August 1780	Superseded
James Bradley	26 August 1780	6 April 1782	Superseded
Benjamin Hill	7 April 1782	13 March 1783	Paid Off at Portsmouth
John Doling	3 October 1790	26 November 1790	Paid Off at Portsmouth – Acting
John Holloway	8 January 1793	30 June 1795	Appointed First Captain of the Fleet
Shuldham Peard	1 July 1795	17 January 1796	To the *St George*
Thomas Foley	18 January 1796	23 March 1797	To the *Goliath*
Edward Marsh	24 March 1797	14 February 1798	Paid Off at Portsmouth
Edward Kittroe	12 April 1803	4 June 1803	Superseded
Rt. Hon. Earl of Northesk	5 June 1803	31 December 1803	New Book
Rt. Hon. Earl of Northesk	1 January 1804	5 May 1805	Superseded
Thomas George Shorthand	4 May 1804	26 June 1804	Superseded
Charles Bullen	3 June 1804	20 June 1806	Paid Off
Henry Sheen	18 February 1823	14 September 1823	Dead
W H Bruce	4 October 1823	3 April 1824	Paid Off

1783: As the war against the American colonists and their allies France, Spain and Holland had finished, Captain Hill paid off *Britannia* on 13 March at Portsmouth where she remained for the next seven years.

1790: When Spain re-armed and the British fleet was mobilised *Britannia* was brought out of the ordinary and recommissioned under Captain John Doling in an acting capacity on 3 October, but with the threat of war disappearing the ship was decommissioned again on 26 November.[10]

1793: When war with revolutionary France became imminent *Britannia* was recommissioned under Captain John Holloway on 8 January, then sent to the Mediterranean with Vice-Admiral Lord Hood's fleet to watch over the French port of Toulon. *Britannia* served as the flagship of Vice-Admiral William Hotham, Hood's second in command.[11]

1794: In November Vice-Admiral Hotham, flying his flag in *Britannia*, assumed command of the Mediterranean fleet when Hood sailed home in *Victory*.[12]

1795: When Hotham received news that the French had been seen off the Isle Ste Marguerite, *Britannia*, with the rest of the British fleet comprising three 98 gun ships, eight 74s, two 64s three 5th rate frigates and several smaller vessels including two Neapolitan frigates, sailed from Leghorn on 9 March. Two days later the French fleet containing some 15 line of battle ships, six frigates and two brigs was sighted, Hotham shadowing their movements. Closing with the French off Genoa on 13 March, Hotham ordered a general chase which evolved into a spasmodic action continuing into the next day with the result that only two ships, *Ça Ira* (80) and *Censeur* (74) were captured. During this engagement *Britannia* suffered one killed and eighteen wounded. On 13 July *Britannia* was involved with Hotham's indecisive action off Hyères just south of Toulon.[13] On 30 June Captain Holloway was appointed First Captain of the Fleet and command of *Britannia* was superseded the following day by Captain Shuldham Peard.[14]

1796: Continuing her deployment in the Mediterranean, command of the ship was succeeded by Captain Thomas Foley on 18 January, Captain Peard turning over into *St George* (98), Foley's previous command.[15]

1797: Under Captain Foley *Britannia* served as the flagship of Vice-Admiral Charles Thompson, operating with Admiral Sir John Jervis's squadron operating off Cadiz at the beginning of this year. On 14 February *Britannia* took part in the action off Cape St Vincent against the Spanish fleet of 27 line of battle ships commanded by Admiral Don José de Córdoba. Probably because of her poor sailing qualities, *Britannia* played little part in the close action, suffering only one seaman wounded.[16] Shortly after this battle Captain Foley transferred into *Goliath* (74), his successor, Captain Edward Marsh, assuming command on 24 March.[17]

1798: Recalled home, Marsh paid off *Britannia* at Portsmouth on 14 February, a full year after the battle of Cape St Vincent.[18]

1804: *Britannia* was recommissioned under Captain the Rt Hon Earl of Northesk on 1 January. While Northesk would remain in the ship for the next two years, on his promotion to admiral command was provisionally succeeded by Captain Thomas George Shorthand on 4 May. Just four weeks later Shorthand was superseded by Captain Charles Bullen on 3 June. Bullen,

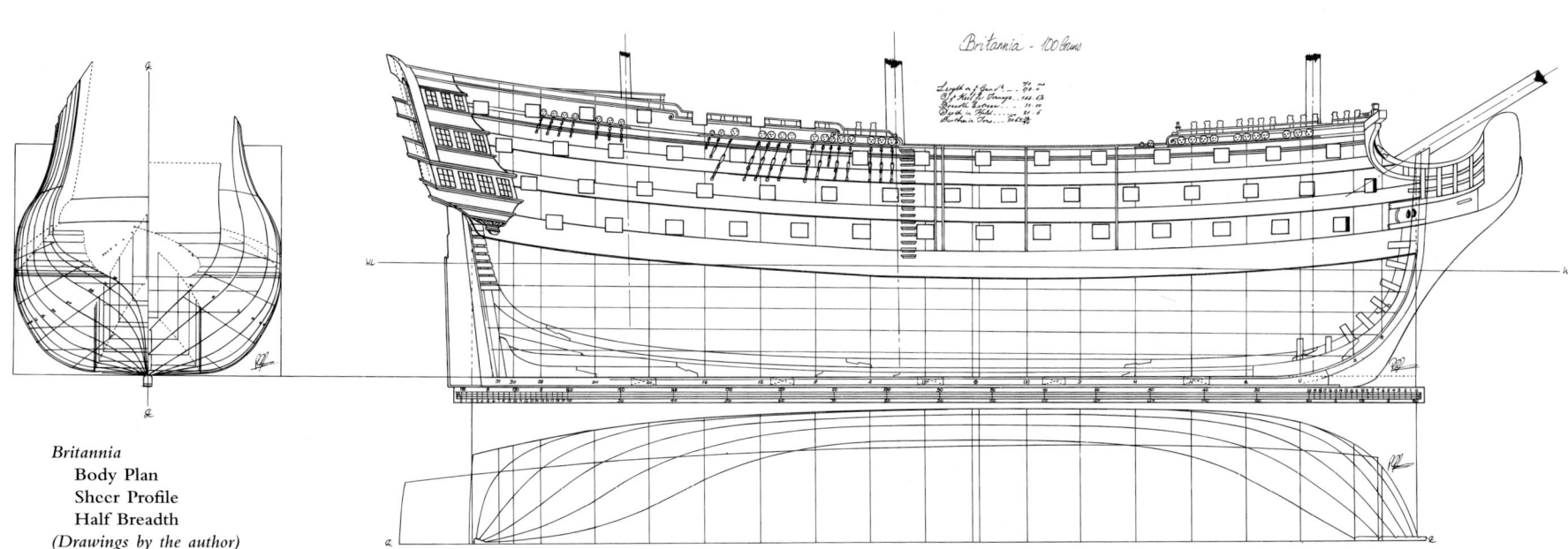

Britannia
Body Plan
Sheer Profile
Half Breadth
(Drawings by the author)

Britannia
Full Upper deck plan
(Drawing by the author)

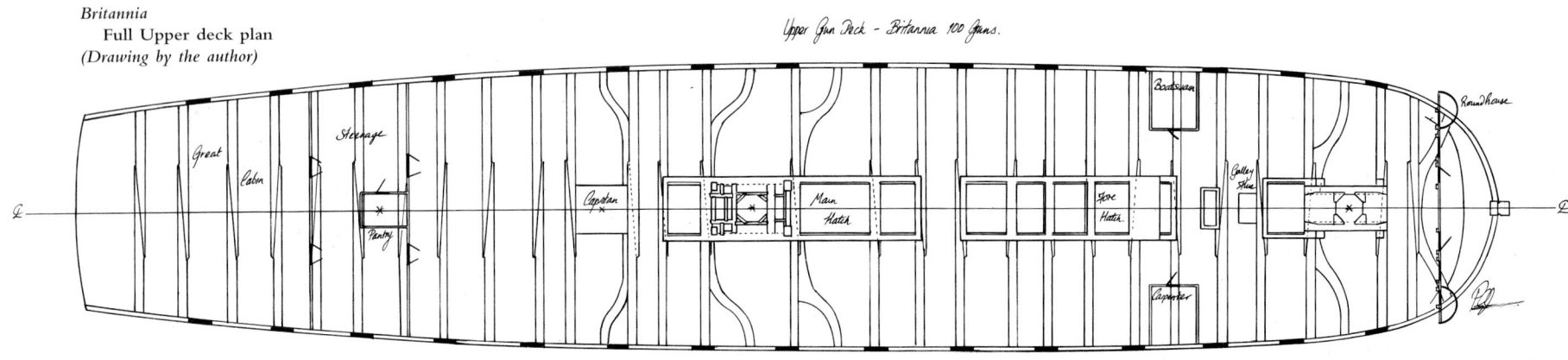

like *Victory*'s commander Thomas Hardy at Trafalgar, was a Dorset man.[19]

1805: Going into Plymouth on 19 February, *Britannia* was docked for one day on 3 March to repair defects and sailed again for duty two weeks later.[20] In late September Rear-Admiral William Earl of Northesk, later appointed by Nelson to be third in command at the battle of Trafalgar, re-hoisted his flag in *Britannia* and sailed from England to join Nelson's fleet blockading Cadiz. Serving with Captain Bullen as *Britannia*'s First Lieutenant was Arthur Atchison. Arriving off Cadiz in early October, *Britannia*'s ship's company settled down to blockade duty. For amusement and to alleviate boredom, some members of *Britannia*'s crew, directed by Second Lieutenant of Marines Halloran, involved themselves with amateur dramatics. Initially staged in the fore cabins of Northesk's quarters, these productions proved so popular that the admiral gave permission to have the fore cabin bulkhead taken down, opening up the whole upper deck to a greater audience. The layout of the cabin doors leading to the admiral's day cabin beyond the after bulkhead proved useful entry and exit points for the actors. Performances included the *Siege of Colchester*, *Miss in her Teens*, *Lord Hastings* and *The Mock Doctor*. Using deals and canvas, scenery was ably constructed by the ship's carpenter and painted by Mr Adams, a master's mate who had exceptional artistic talents. On 9 October the play *Columbus, or a World Discovered* proved a particularly popular performance. Published bills were prepared:

> 'In the course of the performance will be two splendid processions, a view of the interior of the Temple of the sun with a Grand Altar burning incense, etc. Grand Hymn of the Priestesses etc. Towards the close of the play the Destruction of the Temple by an Earthquake accompanied by Thunder, Lightning and Hail Storms with the rescue of Cora from the ruins by Alonzo - Doors to open at 6.30 To begin at 7.0.'

All officers and crew were seated in time, some seamen squatting by guns. The cast wore wigs skilfully made from teased out rope, their faces rouged with red lead; Lieutenant Wilson playing the part of the High Priestess of the Sun.[21] That day the ship's log records that *Britannia* lay in latitude 36° 3' M and longitude 7° 3' W. Cape Trafalgar N84E 20 leagues, occurrences being 'PM light airs & clear made & shortend sail Occasionally Joind C°. HM Ship *Royal Sovereign* rec[d] from the Malabar Victualler 7 Bags Cocoa 9 barrels Sugar 8 Boxes lemons'.[22] Apart from stating ships lying nearby – *Africa*, *Agamemnon*, *Belleisle* and the frigate *Nimble* – and that she received 97 yards of bunting and four barrels of tar from the *Royal Sovereign*, log entries over the next few days record little. Captain Bullen, it appears, punished quite severely, for on Thursday 17 October one seaman got 36 lashes for drunkenness, a second twelve lashes for neglect of duty while another two received 46 and 24 lashes respectively for theft. On 19 October Nelson received news that the combined fleet were getting out of Cadiz so he ordered *Britannia*, a poor sailer, to take her station as convenient. *Britannia* 'repeated the Admirals signal with 3 guns and wore'.[23] On the night before battle Northesk wrote to his wife:

> *Britannia*, off Cadiz at 10 o'clock p.m. Oct 20 1805
>
> My Dearest Wife
> We have every hope of bring the enemy to action; if I should not survive the glorious day; take care of yourself and my dear children and I beg you may have one [the one was deleted and two written above] thousand pounds after my death for your own use and at your disposal beside that I left you by will - made in Scotland and at Battle - Believe me ever to have been your affectionate husband, Northesk.

Folding the paper, he pressed his seal into the warm black wax and simply addressed the paper 'Countess of Northesk'.[24]

TRAFALGAR

Deployed with Nelson's windward division at the beginning of the battle, *Britannia* was placed sixth in the line with the ships *Conqueror* (74) and *Agamemnon* (64) ahead and abaft her respectively. Apart from general sail evolutions, Bullen's entry in *Britannia*'s log for Monday 21 October is characteristically brief: 'at 4.30 wore at day light Enemies Fleet ESE 4 leagues consisting of 33 sail of the line 4 Frigates & 2 Brigs bore up and made all sail to close with them Cleared for Action'.[25] Having gone to quarters at 8.0 a.m., Marine Lieutenant Halloran took his station at the after end of the lower gun deck. To his delight he listened to seamen quoting lines from his theatrical productions to alleviate the emotional intensity of approaching battle, a popular verse being 'We have great guns of tragedy loaded so well, If they do but go off they will certainly tell'.[26] Like many of the British ships that saw Nelson's signal 'England Expects…' at 11.25 a.m., *Britannia*'s crew cheered in response.

Britannia's log 22 October commences:

> PM light airs and cloudy 12.20 Vice Admiral Collingwood commenced the Action by a Vigorous attack on the Enemies rear 12.40 Lord nelson in the *Victory* attacked their centre 12.50 we began to engage three of the Enemys ships having opened their fire on us while edging down.[27]

Britannia was firing her larboard guns at long range into *Bucentaure*. Bullen's log continued:

> 1.10 observed the Ship we were engaging on our larboard quarter totally dismasted continued our course in order to break through the Centre of the Enemys line Engaging on both sides in passing between their Ships.[28]

Britannia then turned to larboard and ran down firing some broadsides into *Santisima Trinidad*, which, as Lieutenant Halloran wrote, 'shattered the rich display of sculpture, figures, ornaments and inscriptions with which she was adorned. I never saw so beautiful a ship'.[29] After this *Britannia* engaged the Spanish vessels *Rayo* (100) and *San Francisco de Asis* (74). At about 3 p.m., following Hardy's signal from *Victory*, *Britannia* manœuvred to bring Dumanoir's four ships into action as they bore down back into the mêlée, the log stating:

> ... at 3 passed through the line 4.30 hauled to the Wind on a Starboard tack pr Signal 5.30 ceased firing at 6 observed *Achille* a French line of Battle Ship on fire which soon after blew up 7.30 observed 12 Ships of the Enemys line making off for Cadiz in great confusion and three others standing to the Southward all the rest (of which seven was dismasted) appearing in our possession 10.30 sent an officer with sixty men including a party of marines to assist securing the French Ship *Aigle*.[30]

When the French *Achille* caught fire many casualties were blown from her and recovered, including a women whom Lieutenant Halloran records: 'This poor creature was brought on board with scarcely any covering and our senior subaltern Lt. Jackson, gave her a dressing-gown for clothing'; Halloran also stated that a Turk and his son were among those embarked into *Britannia*, both of whom died later that night.[31] From the outset of battle *Britannia*, because of her slowness, was obliged to move obliquely from Nelson's intended line to draw more wind to maintain better speed. Despite this complication, Northesk's inability to get into the thick of the affray remains questionable, especially when *Victory* and *Royal Sovereign* were nearly overwhelmed at the climax of the fighting: a crucial moment when *Britannia*'s firepower would have been invaluable. Odder still, Northesk was never challenged about his apparently reluctant behaviour. Because *Britannia* saw little action she sustained minimal damage: only 52 casualties comprising ten killed and 42 wounded. Among the dead was Lieutenant Francis Roskruge; officers wounded were Stephen Trounce, the ship's Master and Midshipman William Grint.[32] After the action two of *Britannia*'s midshipmen were promoted to lieutenant.[33] Completing the log for 22 October next morning, the entry states 'AM Fresh Breezes with Constant rain at 11 took the *Berwick* in tow (French Prize) Sent new sails in lieu of those shot away received a number of French Prisoners'.[34] Next day, 23 October, *Britannia* struck her topgallant mast and yards to ease her movement in the rising storm and 'bent a new Fore topsail'. Shortly after wearing at 12.30 Bullen assembled the ship's company and 'committed the Body of Lieut. Frances Roskruge to the deep'. On Thursday Bullen found that towing the battered prize *Aigle* in the current sea conditions proved difficult, and in preparation for casting off the tow, *Britannia*'s crew were 'employed getting Prisoners out of the Prize', and 'at 3.30 Cast off the tow'. Shortly afterwards *Britannia* observed, '11 of the Enemies Ships under weigh 3 leagues from Cadiz', and, like the other British ships, cleared for action in anticipation of a second battle. Seeing the enemy ships returning to port, the transfer of prisoners out of *Aigle* recommenced. *Britannia*'s log on Friday 25 October then records: 'PM Fresh Breezes and Cloudy boats employed getting prisoners onboard at 3 wore at 6 backed the main T.sail cleared the Prize of men & set her on fire filled & made sail sounded in 48 fms AM D° W[r] [ditto weather] at 4 fired 3 Guns & wore at 7 wore & set the reefd Courses carried away the gaff employed filling salt water', into the empty fresh water casks to maintain the trim of the ship. The last significant log entry made on Thursday 31 October records that Bullen mustered *Britannia*'s crew and 'read Adm[l] Collingwood's thanks to the Ship's C°'.[35]

1806: Returning to Plymouth on 1 June 1806, Captain Bullen paid off *Britannia* on 20 June, after which the ship was laid up in the Hamoaze for seven years.[36]

1813: Taken into dock on 16 July, *Britannia* had her 'Copper taken off & Re-coppered to light Draft of water' and underwent remedial repairs to stop her leaks. She was undocked the following day and returned to her moorings to await her fate. On 27 October the ship was 'taken in hand' and 'Fitted for a Prison Ship', the work being completed in December. *Britannia* was employed in this rôle for two years.[37]

PROGRESS BOOK – *BRITANNIA* 1st RATE OF 100 GUNS: Source: ADM 180/2 Entry 14 & ADM 180/10 Entry 6

At what Port	Arrived	Docked	Coppered	Launched or Undocked	Sailed	Built or Nature of Repair	Cost of Hull, Masts & Yards Materials £ s d	Cost of Rigging & Stores Materials £ s d	Grand Total
Portsmouth	Began	1 July 1751*	(Admiralty Order 21 May 1757 to Build this ship by the Draught of the *Royal George*)						
Portsmouth			Graved October 1762			Built	39,644. 10s. 10d.	2,084. 16s. 3d.	41,729. 7s. 1d.
				1763			79. 10s 4d.	27. 11s. 0d.	107. 1s. 4d.
				1764				4,007. 14s. 3d.	4,007. 14s. 3d.
							39,724. 1s. 2d.	6,120. 1s. 6d.	45,844. 2s. 8d.
Portsmouth		13 Nov 1765	Graved Nov 1765	14 Nov 1765		Trunnelled transom		342. 19s. 2d.	342. 19s. 2d.
Portsmouth		11 Oct 1768	Graved Oct 1768	25 Oct 1768		Ditto		81. 4s. 8d.	81. 4s. 8d.
					Expense 1769		625. 11s. 3d.	6,371. 11s. 11d.	
					Expense 1770		921. 2s. 7d.	921. 2s. 7d.	
					Expense 1771			3,269. 1s. 9d.	3,269. 1s. 9d.
Portsmouth		3 April 1772	Graved Aug 1772	28 August 1772		Small Repair	5,746. 0s. 8d.	625. 11s. 3d.	6,371. 11s. 11d.
Plymouth	19 Feb 1805	3 March 1805	3 March 1805	18 March 1805	Defects				
Plymouth	1 June 1806	16 July 1813	Copper taken off & Re-coppered to light Draft of water	27 July 1813		To Stops leaks			
Plymouth		Taken in hand 27 October 1813 and completed Dec 1813				Fitted for a Prison Ship			
			March	1813					
Plymouth		Taken in hand 27 March Repaired, Coppered and completed June 1815				Fitted for a Flag & Receiving Ship			
Plymouth		4 Feb 1825							
		Taken to Pieces 25 Feb[y] 1825							

Notes:
1. The date denoted by * should perhaps read 1 July 1757 not 1751. However the Observations do record 'Keel Laid April 1758'. Likewise the statement preceding this entry reads: 'Ad. Order 28th March 1757 to Build a new 1st rate of 100 Guns in the room of one of the old 1st Rates taken to pieces. Ad. Order 25th Apr. 1757 to Build her by the Establish'd Draught with some variation thereon, but strictly to observe the Principall [sic] Dim[s]. Established the 27th March 1746 - And to register her on the list by the name of the *Britannia*'.
2. No costs are recorded after 1804.

1815: As *Britannia* was serving as a prison ship the Admiralty decided to build a new ship of the same name in her room. Consequently the Trafalgar *Britannia* was renamed *Saint George* and under this name she was taken in hand at Plymouth and 'Fitted for a Flag & Receiving Ship'. Repaired and re-coppered to fulfil her receiving rôle, *Britannia*'s refit was completed in June, the cost of which is unrecorded.[38]

1819: According to the progress book *Britannia* was renamed *Barfleur* on 2 June.

1823: Commissioned under Captain Henry Sheen on 18 February, he unexpectedly died on 14 September, so command of *Britannia* was not fulfilled by Captain W H Bruce until 4 October.[39]

FATE

No longer required for service, *Britannia* was paid off again at Plymouth on 3 April 1824, taken into dock on 4 February 1825 and 'Taken to Pieces'.[40] The succeeding *Britannia*, a 1st rate ship of 120 guns of the *Caledonia* class designed by William Rule, which had been ordered on 6 November 1812, was laid down at Plymouth in December 1813 and finally launched on 20 October 1820. Hulked as a hospital ship in 1855, she was moved to Dartmouth as an officer cadet training ship in 1859. In 1869 it was decided to move the officer cadets ashore into a new purpose-built training establishment at Dartmouth, so the ship *Britannia* was broken up at Devonport the same year.[41] Much expanded, the Royal Naval College *Britannia* continues today as the primary establishment for training new entry officer cadets.

The 100 gun ship ROYAL SOVEREIGN

Designed by John Williams, with Edward Hunt joint Surveyor of the Navy, the 100 gun 1st rate *Royal Sovereign* which served as Vice-Admiral Cuthbert Collingwood's flagship leading the leeward division of the British fleet at the battle of Trafalgar, was the third ship to bear this name. The first *Royal Sovereign* was in fact the *Sovereign of the Seas*, the navy's first three decked 100 gun ship, launched at Woolwich on 14 October 1637. Renamed *Sovereign* during the English Civil War and rebuilt at Chatham in 1659, she was renamed *Royal Sovereign* in 1660. Having fought in the three Dutch Wars the ship was rebuilt for a second time in 1685 and accidentally destroyed by fire in 1696 while awaiting her third rebuild. The second *Royal Sovereign*, also a 100 gun ship, was launched at Woolwich in July 1701. Rebuilt at Chatham in 1728, she remained in service until broken up at Chatham in April 1768. Ordered on 3 February 1772, the keel of Williams' Trafalgar *Royal Sovereign* was laid down at Plymouth dockyard in January 1774. This ship spent over twelve years and nine months on the stocks, this time possibly related to budget constraints imposed by the costs of the American War of Independence, 1776-1782. Initially launched on 11 September 1786, she went into dock the next day to be coppered before her launch on 25 September. Building costs amounted to £67,458 9s 4d of which £61,254 14s 7d was expended on hulls, masts and coppering and £6,203 14s 10d for rigging and stores.[42]

SERVICE CAREER

1787: In September *Royal Sovereign* was taken in hand, 'partly fitted for Sea', and on 1 October first commissioned under Captain James Lambert. However, after undergoing several weeks of sea trials she was paid off on 10 December and laid up for three years.

1790: When the navy was mobilised to meet the threat of the Spanish armament, *Royal Sovereign* was taken in hand on 6 May and fitted for sea service, the work being completed in August. While refitting, the ship was recommissioned on 19 May under Captain Richard Fisher. *Royal Sovereign* was then captained successively by commanders John Hamilton, John Dilkes and William Domett, the latter assuming command on 10 October. Going into Plymouth on 16 November, Domett paid off the ship on 4 December.[43]

1793: When war was declared between revolutionary France and Britain *Royal Sovereign* was taken out of ordinary and recommissioned under Captain Henry Nicholls on 27 February. Docked on 12 March to have her copper repaired and launched two days later, she was then fitted for sea and sailed on deployment on 17 June, flying the flag of Vice-Admiral Thomas Graves, returning to Plymouth on 28 December.

1794: Docked again on 3 January, *Royal Sovereign* was entirely re-coppered and launched two weeks later. Still flying the flag of Vice-Admiral Graves, the ship sailed on 13 February with the Channel fleet commanded by Admiral Richard Howe. When news was received that a grain convoy escorted by Rear-Admiral Louis Villaret-Joyeuse was due from America, Howe, flying his flag in *Queen Charlotte* (100), took the Channel fleet immediately to sea in pursuit. The first engagement between the two fleets commenced on 28 May, during which *Royal Sovereign* took little part and it was not until 1 June that the ship played a significant rôle in the ensuing battle. Later named The Glorious First of June, action began at 9.24 with the French opening distant fire upon Howe's ships as they bore down towards Villaret's van. Seeing that *Queen* (98) had become isolated and under fire from several ships, Howe signalled his squadron to form line ahead astern of him and bore up on a starboard tack towards Villaret. Following him in *Queen Charlotte* were *Barfleur* (98), *Thunderer* (74), *Royal Sovereign* (100), *Valiant* (74) and *Leviathan* (74). Entering the mêlée, Captain Nicholl ordered

---

SPECIFICATIONS: *ROYAL SOVEREIGN*

Rate	1st	Length on the range of the gun deck	186 ft	Ordnance - lower gun deck	28 x 42 pounders (later 32 pounders)
Guns	100	Length of keel for tonnage	152 ft 6 ins	Ordnance - middle gun deck	28 x 24 pounders
Class	Royal Sovereign 1772	Extreme breadth	52 ft	Ordnance - upper gun deck	30 x long 12 pounders
Designer	John Williams	Depth in hold	22 ft 3 ins	Ordnance - quarter deck	10 x 6 pounders (later 12 pounders)
Builder	Dockyard	Tons burthen	2193. 38/94	Ordnance - forecastle	4 x 6 pounders (later 12 pounders)
Dockyard	Plymouth	Draught afore	24 ft 6 ins	Single broadside weight	1146 pounds (1048 pounds)
Date ordered	3 February 1772	Draught abaft	25 ft 1ins	Fate	Hulked at Plymouth and renamed *Captain*. 1841 broken up.
Date keel laid	January 1774	Complement	850		
Date launched	11 September 1786				

Note: Ordnance listed as for 1803/1805 Trafalgar campaign.

Source: Lyon, *Sailing Navy List*, p. 63.

Royal Sovereign's gunners to fire into *Terrible* (110) but was engaging at too great a distance so Howe ordered *Royal Sovereign* to engage more closely. Closing with *Terrible*, *Royal Sovereign* forced the French ship to bear up and in doing so Nicholl's gunners repeatedly raked the great three decker as she yawed in the swell. *Royal Sovereign*, now supported by *Valiant*, then gave chase until *Montagne* (120) and *Jacobin* (80) came to *Terrible*'s aid. *Royal Sovereign* suffered 14 killed and 44 wounded.[44] Returning to Plymouth on 12 June, the ship was overhauled to repair her battle damage and sailed twelve days later.[45]

1795: On 10 March Captain John Whitby superseded command of the ship, Captain Nicholls transferring into *Marlborough* (74).[46] At the time *Royal Sovereign* was still deployed with the Channel fleet and shortly after Whitby took command Vice-Admiral the Hon. William Cornwallis hoisted his flag in the ship. On 30 May Cornwallis sailed from Spithead with a small squadron to cruise off Ushant. Cornwallis's squadron comprised the following ships:

Rate	No. Guns.		Ships	Commanders
1st	1	100	*Royal Sovereign*	Vice Admiral Hon William Cornwallis
				Captain John Whitby
3rd	1	74	*Bellerophon*	Captain James Lord Cranston
3rd	1	74	*Brunswick*	Captain Lord Charles Fitzgerald
3rd	1	74	*Mars*	Captain Sir Charles Cotton
3rd	1	74	*Triumph*	Captain Sir Erasmus Gower Kt.
5th	1	38	*Phæton*	Captain Hon. Robert Stopford
5th	1	32	*Pallas*	Captain Hon. Henry Curzon
6th	1	18	*Kingfisher*	Commander Thomas Le Marchant Gosselin
TOTAL	8	484		

On 8 June they sighted a French squadron off Ushant commanded by Rear-Admiral Vence, escorting a large convoy of merchantmen bound from Bordeaux to Brest. Seeing the British ships Vence immediately stood in for Belle Isle, pursued by Cornwallis's squadron. *Triumph* (74), *Phæton* (38) and the 18 gun sloop *Kingfisher* closed and fired into the rearmost French ships. Meanwhile the rest of Cornwallis's ships chased two frigates and engaged the shore batteries on the island. When news reached Brest that Vence had been attacked by British ships, Vice-Admiral Villaret-Joyeuse, flying his flag in *Peuple* (120) sailed on 12 June with a squadron comprising nine sail of the line, two fifty gun ships rasés, seven frigates and four corvettes. Three days later Villaret met Vence off the Isle de Groix and proceeded with him

CAPTAINS OF *ROYAL SOVEREIGN* (MSS 248/4 and 248/6)

Name	Time of Entry	Time of Discharge	On What Occasion
James Lambert	1 October 1787	10 December 1787	Paid Off
Richard Fisher	19 May 1790	8 September 1790	Superseded
John Hamilton	9 September 1790	26 September 1790	Superseded
John Dilkes	27 September 1790	9 October 1790	Superseded
William Domett	10 October 1790	4 December 1790	Paid Off
Henry Nicholls	27 February 1793	9 March 1795	To the *Malborough*
John Whitby	10 March 1795	16 June 1796	Superseded
William Bedford	17 June 1796	4 September 1800	Superseded
John Miller	2 March 1797	29 March 1797	Superseded Acting
Richard Browne	5 September 1800	22 January 1801	Superseded
Richard Haggett	23 January 1801	26 April 1802	Paid Off at Portsmouth
Richard Curry	12 April 1803	31 December 1803	New Book
Richard Curry	1 January 1804	16 January 1804	Superseded
Pulteney Malcolm	17 January 1804	26 March 1804	To the *Kent*
John Stuart	27 March 1804	10 May 1805	To the *Swiftsure*
Mark Robinson	11 May 1805	13 September 1805	Superseded
John Conn	14 September 1805	14 October 1805	To the *Dreadnought*
Edward Rotheram	11 October 1805	1 November 1805	To the *Bellerophon*
Henry Garrett	25 November 1805	1 August 1808	Superseded
David Colby	2 August 1808	25 November 1809	To the *Apollo*
A Ferris	26 November 1809	19 February 1810	Superseded
H W Pearce	20 February 1810	30 June 1810	Superseded
Josiah Spear	1 July 1810	10 March 1811	To the *Téméraire*
John Harvey	11 March 1811	25 December 1811	Superseded
William Bedford	26 December 1811	19 October 1812	Superseded
James Bissett	20 October 1812	22 December 1813	Superseded
T G Caulfield	23 December 1813	28 March 1814	Superseded
C T Smith	29 March 1814	27 May 1814	To the *Duncan*
Robert Lambert	28 May 1814	10 August 1814	Paid Off at Portsmouth
Edward P Brenton	11 April 1815	6 June 1815	Superseded
Edward R Broughton	7 June 1815	28 August 1815	Paid Off at Plymouth

to Brest. When they sighted the British squadron off Penmarck on 16 June, Cornwallis formed his ships into line ahead, *Brunswick* taking the lead, followed by *Royal Sovereign*, *Bellerophon*, *Triumph* and *Mars*. At 2 p.m. Villaret divided his squadron in two and pursued Cornwallis on the same tack. At daylight on the 17th the French formed three divisions: the weather column comprising three sail of the line and five frigates; the centre line five sail of the line; and the leeward column four sail of the line, five frigates, two brigs and two cutters. By 9 a.m. the weather column brought up on the

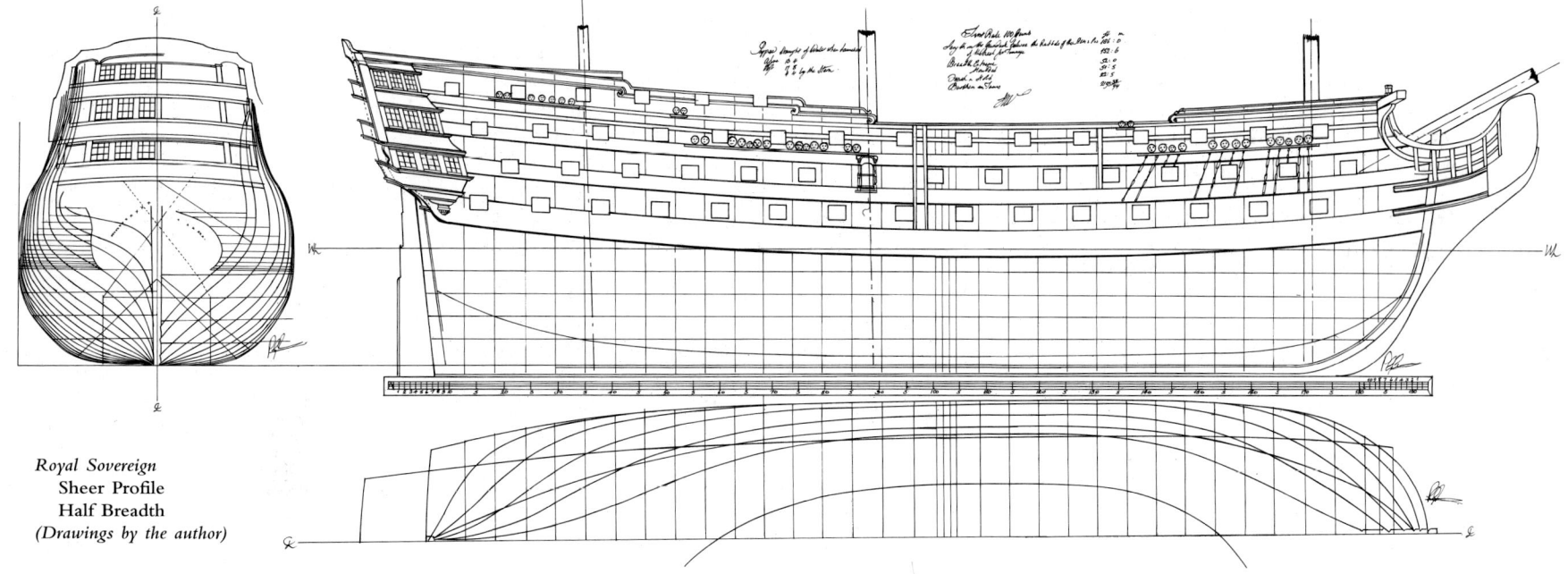

Royal Sovereign
Sheer Profile
Half Breadth
(Drawings by the author)

British rear and fired upon *Mars*. Totally outnumbered, Cornwallis decided to fight a rearguard action as he retreated and sent the slow sailing *Bellerophon* ahead. Detached from the squadron, *Phæton* proceeded to make signals to an illusory fleet beyond the horizon, a ruse that certainly demoralised the French commanders. At noon *Royal Sovereign* and the remaining ships commenced firing stern chase and quarter guns as they bore. This action continued for some three hours until *Mars*, damaged aloft, fell off to leeward. To support her Cornwallis stood *Royal Sovereign* towards her followed by *Triumph*, and poured well-aimed broadsides into the foremost French ships closing upon *Mars*. The chase continued until about 6 p.m., after which the French ships shortened sail and abandoned pursuit. During the chase the British ships, *Royal Sovereign* included, sustained considerable damage to their stern framing and galleries, not only from French gunfire, but also from the necessity to cut extra ports to mount heavier long range guns astern.[47]

1796: In his history of the Royal Navy, Clowes states that Cornwallis sailed in *Royal Sovereign* on 29 February with reinforcements for the West Indies, but suffering considerable damage aloft in an ensuing gale, was obliged to return to Spithead on 14 March. While this fact is undeniable, the ship's progress book clearly records that the ship went into Portsmouth on 29 February and was docked 9 April to have her copper repaired, 'made good her damages' and re-launched on 9 May.[48] In the meantime, and Clowes is lucid on this point, Cornwallis was tried by a court martial on 17 April for failing to transfer his flag from *Royal Sovereign* into *Astræa* and defying orders by returning home. Although acquitted on the grounds that he was in poor health, Cornwallis struck his flag on his own accord and never hoisted it in any ship until February 1801.[49] On 17 June command of the ship was superseded by Captain William Bedford who remained in the ship for four years.[50]

1797: When Captain Bedford temporarily moved out of the ship on 2 March command of the *Royal Sovereign* was given over to John Miller who held acting command until Bedford returned at the end of the month. Stationed with the Channel Fleet at the Nore, *Royal Sovereign* became involved in the infamous mutiny led by Richard Parker. Although the mutiny was finally quashed and Parker was hanged on board *Sandwich* (74) on 29 June, further outbreaks of insurrection broke out in several ships throughout the summer. One such vessel was *Royal Sovereign*, others being *Pompée* (80), the 74 gun ships *Bedford*, *Saturn*, *Mars* and *Marlborough*, *Ardent* (64), *Beaulieu* (40), *Phœnix* (38) *Calypso* (16) and the storeship *Grampus*. The perpetrators were either flogged round the fleet or hanged.[51]

1799: Returning to Portsmouth on 6 February, *Royal Sovereign* was docked, re-coppered and refitted at a total cost of £11,556, of which £6,817 was expended on her hull, masts and yards. Flying the flag of Vice-Admiral Sir Alan Gardner, *Royal Sovereign* sailed on 16 June with *Cæsar* (80), *Magnificent* (74) and *Russell* (74) to join Lord Keith laying off the Tagus. The objective of this detached squadron was to escort back to England a convoy of prize ships captured by Nelson at the battle of the Nile.[52]

1800-1802: Throughout this period *Royal Sovereign* remained in home waters attached to the Channel fleet. On 5 September command of the ship was given over to Captain Richard Browne who was superseded on 23 January 1801 by Captain Richard Haggett. On 27 March 1802 the Treaty of Amiens was signed, bringing temporary peace between France and Britain. Consequently *Royal Sovereign* went into Portsmouth 19 April where one week later Haggett paid off the ship, then she was 'fitted'.[53]

1803: When it was realised that war between Britain and France would re-open, *Royal Sovereign* was recommissioned on 12 April under Captain Richard Curry and made ready for sea. War against Napoleonic France was formally declared on 16 May.[54]

1804: On 17 January command of the *Royal Sovereign* was succeeded by Captain Pulteney Malcolm. Then she sailed for the Mediterranean, joining Vice-Admiral Lord Nelson's fleet cruising off the French coast on 15 February. In the following month Nelson's squadron, including *Royal Sovereign*, resumed its station off Capes Sicié and Cepet, blockading the French arsenal of Toulon.[55] Superseded by Captain John Stuart 27 March, Captain Malcolm transferred into *Kent* (74).[56]

1805: Still cruising with Nelson's ships blockading Toulon, *Royal Sovereign* was now serving as the flagship of Rear-Admiral of the Red, Sir Richard Bickerton Bt. On 17 January the French fleet comprising four 80s, seven 74s, seven frigates and two brigs evaded the British fleet and sailed from Toulon. In command was Vice Admiral Pierre Villeneuve flying his flag in *Bucentaure* (80). *Royal Sovereign* was, at this time, repairing in Agincourt Sound with most of Nelson's ships. Receiving news at 4.30 p.m. on 19 January from frigates *Active* and *Seahorse* that the French had made their escape, Nelson immediately ordered his squadron to weigh. Besides *Royal Sovereign* and the two frigates aforementioned, the British squadron comprised ten vessels, five of which would fight at Trafalgar: *Victory* (100), *Belleisle* (74), *Conqueror* (74), *Leviathan* (74), and *Swiftsure* (74). From this point began the long chase which would culminate off Cape Trafalgar.[57]

Royal Sovereign
  Inboard profile
  (Drawing by the author)

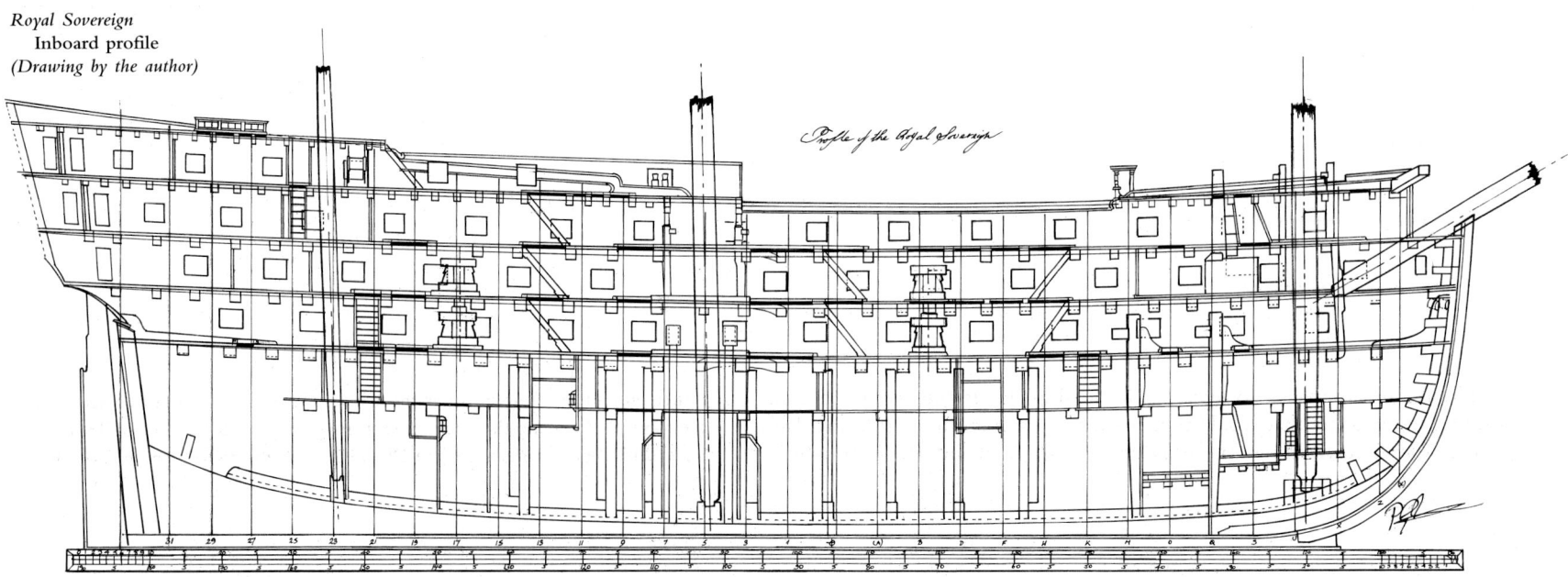

Anchored in Rosia Bay, Gibraltar, on 7 May, Rear-Admiral Bickerton shifted his flag out of *Royal Sovereign* and transferred into *Amphitrite* (40) to command the Mediterranean fleet, while Nelson prepared his ships to sail westward to chase Villeneuve. Three days later Captain Stuart transferred into *Swiftsure* (74), newly arrived from England. Consequently command of *Royal Sovereign* was superseded by Captain Mark Robinson on 11 May. Lying off Cape St Vincent on 12 May, Nelson weakened his own force by detaching *Royal Sovereign* to escort an important convoy of transports carrying 5,000 troops bound from England to the Mediterranean.[58]

Arriving in England *Royal Sovereign* entered Plymouth to refit on 19 July. Taken into dock on 11 August, her copper was removed, her hull re-bored in several places to drive new or replace bolts, and she was entirely re-coppered. Undocked on 28 August, she left Plymouth dockyard on 10 September and anchored in Cawsand Bay to prepare for sea. Four days later Captain John Conn superseded command of the ship and sailed to rejoin Nelson's squadron off Cadiz.[59] Arriving on Thursday 10 October, Captain Conn received orders from Nelson that the ship was to carry the flag of his appointed second in command, Vice-Admiral Cuthbert Collingwood. Consequently the ship's log of 11 October states: 'at 5.30 Capt[n] Conn left the ship at 6.00 Admiral Collingwood and Capt[n] Rotheram joined the ship'. Exchanging with Captain Conn, Collingwood transferred his flag out of *Dreadnought* (98) and entered *Royal Sovereign*, taking his captain with him.[59]

As *Royal Sovereign* was carrying fresh stores from Plymouth, the next day Rotheram:

Supplied the *Prince* with 3 Barrels of Tar *Mars* D[o] 3 *Colossus* Ness D[o] 3 *Polyphemus* D[o] 2 at Noon D[o] Weather sent two Cables on Board of the *Malabar* Transport'. On the Sunday he 'Supplied *Britannia* and *Revenge* with Sundry Boatswain's Stores.

The log then states:

Parted Company his Majesty[s] ship *Prince of Wales* [taking Admiral Calder back to face court martial in England] ...Joined Company his Majesty[s] ship *Africa* delivered a cable to the *Malabar* Transport Punished 3 Seamen with 12 Lashes each for Drunkenness.[61]

It may be noted that a high proportion of the *Royal Sovereign*'s complement comprised Irish and Italians, a combination which obviously proved interesting if not difficult.[62] Over the next few days the crew were exercised at the great guns and many references are made to ships joining or leaving the fleet and convoys of transports and victuallers to and from Gibraltar, comprising *Agamemnon* (64), the frigates *Amphion*, *Amiable* and *Renommée*, and the brig *Weazle*.

TRAFALGAR

On Sunday 20 October, Rotheram wrote in his log:

PM Moderate breezes set steering sails Joined Company his Majesty[s] ship *Mars Colossus Defence Phœbe* and *Pickle* schooner at 8 AM Cape Trafalgar bore ES 7 or 8 Leagues at 9 Admiral Collingwood went on board the *Victory* at 10 Returned at Noon fresh breezes and squally Reefed topsails made the Signal for the Larb[d] Division of the fleet to Keep Close Order Adm[l] and fleet in C[o].

Oddly, Rotheram makes no reference in the ship's log to the combined fleet putting to sea, a fact that would perhaps appear paramount considering that *Royal Sovereign* carried the flag of the second-in-command. *Royal Sovereign*'s log for Monday 21 October commences: 'PM Moderate Breezes and fine wea[r] - at Day Light Discovered the Enemys Fleet to Leeward bearing from ESE to EBN the Signal was made to Chase and form the Line of battle in two Columns Each Ship to Engage her 1 opponent Set studding sails at 11.00 Brought the Ship under her courses'. Leading the British leeward division of 14 ships, *Royal Sovereign* stood towards the combined fleet. Standing on the quarter deck of the ship that morning with Vice-Admiral Cuthbert Collingwood and Captain Rotheram were *Royal Sovereign*'s two First Lieutenants, John Ellis and William Stephens. Although *Royal Sovereign* was to be the first into battle, Nelson had earlier signalled *Mars* to take the lead. The probable reason for this was that *Mars*, noted for her highly trained Scots gunners, would rapidly inflict considerable damage to enemy ships at the opening of the action. This was not to be, however, for *Royal Sovereign*, with her freshly coppered bottom, surged well ahead and became isolated from the rest of the British line. Concluding the ship's log that day Rotheram wrote: 'at 11.50 began to Engage a Spanish 3 Deck Ship at Noon DW no other ship in Action'.[63]

Collingwood had directed *Royal Sovereign* towards the centre of the combined fleet, intending to break the enemy line between Admiral Alava's flagship *Santa Ana* (112) and *Fougueux* (74), directly astern. The first broadside of the battle, fired from the French *Fougueux*, was directed at *Royal Sovereign* as she bore down. Carrying the ship through the line ten minutes later, *Royal Sovereign*'s larboard battery, double shotted, opened fire, raking the stern of *Santa Ana* (112) with devastating effect, her starboard broadside simultaneously, though less potently, raking the head of *Fougueux*. Reeling from *Royal Sovereign*'s timely executed gunnery the Spanish officers momentarily took stock: there were 400 casualties and 14 guns were out of action. Rotheram ordered the helm to starboard and brought *Royal Sovereign* alongside *Santa-Ana*'s starboard bow, pouring more broadsides into her while the starboard battery continued firing into *Fougueux*; *Indomptable* now ranged in close proximity. On the first ship to be fully engaged, Collingwood remarked, 'Rotheram, what would Nelson give to be here'. Brave words maybe, but *Royal Sovereign* soon found herself in great danger as nearby ships manœuvred to bring their broadsides to bear upon her. Raked by *Fougueux* from astern and *San Leandro* (64) ahead, her starboard side was also receiving broadsides from the two 74s *Indomptable* and *San Justo*. It was 15 minutes before *Belleisle* (74) hauled up to draw off surrounding fire.[64] At the point of capitulation, *Royal Sovereign*'s mizzen mast went overboard and her main mast collapsed shortly after. The heated duel between *Royal Sovereign* and *Santa Ana* continued for 45 minutes; much beaten and having lost all three masts, the Spanish ship was compelled to strike her colours. *Royal Sovereign*'s log of Tuesday 22 October recalls; 'PM Moderate Breezes still in Action at 12.40 the Spanish 3 Decker [the *Santa Ana*] struck her Colours, at this Time the *Bellisle* [sic] came up and began to Engage a Spanish 84 when then we Lost our Mizen Mast, the whole Fleet came up in turn and the Action begun General, at 3.30 the main Mast went by the Board'.[65] At about 4.40 *Victory*'s remaining boat came alongside *Royal Sovereign* carrying Captain Blackwood and Lieutenant Hills. The two officers clambered up the ship's entry steps to give Collingwood the news that Nelson had died. Collingwood therefore assumed overall command of the British fleet. By this point *Royal Sovereign* was in a terrible condition, her fore topsail yard had gone, and having lost her main and mizzen masts there was so little supportive rigging left that her fore mast was left tottering precariously.[66] Realising the situation, Collingwood made preparations to transfer his flag into Blackwood's frigate *Euryalus* (36) to command the fleet.[67] The ship's log entry continues:

... at 5.00 the firing Cease'd [sic] When *Eurilius* [sic] Frigate came and towed us out of the line Admiral Collingwood then went on board the *Eurilius* and hoisted his Flag there the French and Spanish ships which struck was Nineteen and one Blown up at the Close of the action Employed securing the foremast Clearing the decks & securing the Guns &[c] at 8 Cape Trafalgar bore SEbE 7 or 8 leagues Cut the Clynch [sic] off the cable being Nearly shot away and bent them again at 12 wore ship Rigged a jury Main mast AM fresh breezes unbent the foresail and cast off from the *Eurylius* When the *Neptune* took us in Tow at Noon strong breezes with four of the Fleet in sight *Neptune* Towing us.[68]

Surpassed only marginally by *Victory*, *Royal Sovereign* sustained 141 casualties. The 47 killed comprised William Chalmers, the Master; Lieutenant Brice Gilliland, Lieutenant of Marines Robert Green, Midshipmen John Aikenhead and Thomas Braund, 29 seamen and 13 marines. Among the 94 wounded were Lieutenants James Bashford and John Clavell, Lieutenant of Marines James le Vesconte, Master's Mate William Watson, Midshipmen John Campbell, John Farrant, Gilbert Kennicot and Grenville Thompson, Boatswain Isaac Wilkinson, 69 seamen and 16 marines.[69]

By Wednesday 23 October the predicted storm reached the ships, *Royal Sovereign*'s log stating:

> Strong Gales with rain Thunder and Lightning, most part of the Fleet in Sight at 5.00 Committed the Body of John Coomb seaman to the deep at 11.30 wore ship Departed this life Ant[y] Parral M [marine] Committed the Body of the Deceased to the deep at 5 AM bent a Spritsail for a Foresail at 9.30 Departed this life James Allen Marine Committed the Body to the deep at Noon D[o] W[r] still in Tow.

At 2.30 p.m. Thursday the tow line from *Neptune* was cast off and at 6 that evening *Royal Sovereign* was 'taken in Tow by the *Mars*'. After running in and securing the middle deck guns the following morning at noon Rotheram 'Read the articles of war and Punished two Seamen for drunkenness and disobedience of orders'. Although the weather had moderated by Friday a second force hit the fleet on Saturday 26 October, the log recording 'Strong Gales with rain at 5.30 our Fore Mast went by the Board and with it all the sails standing and running Rigging Cleared the Wreck'. As if this was not enough the ship's predicament got worse for 'at 5.45 Carried away the Tow Rope Rigged a jury Fore Mast and fired several Guns to Windward and Leeward and sounded Evry [sic] half hour lost overboard one of the Poop Carronades by the Violent Rowling of the ship AM Obs[d] 17 sail in Sight most Part at Anchor hove overboard our Boats'. The latter action was undertaken to reduce top weight and ease the roll of the ship. Next day *Royal Sovereign* anchored off Cape Chipiona, spending the next three days rigging jury masts, clearing the decks and making good her repairs. During this period she 'Received from his Majesty[s] Frigate *Eurilius* [sic] a Main Top Sail Yard', and on the 29 October the crew were busy; 'swaying up the Main and Main Top Sail Yards Employ'd Stowing the Booms and Bending Sails'. The log also states that she 'Received on Board 300 French and Spanish Prisoners from his Majesty[s] ships *Donegal* and *Swiftsure*'. There were now some 1,150 people within the ship, so the coopers were 'Employ'd shaking Butts to make room for the Prisoners in the Hold Obs[d] one of the Prizes Blow up'. The term 'shaking' or more correctly 'shaking down' describes removing the hoops from barrels which allowed the barrel staves to collapse, after which they were tied together complete with hoops and headers and stored ready for return to the victualling yards; in effect all barrels could be 'flat-packed'. Weighing anchor on Wednesday 30 October *Royal Sovereign* put to sea under her jury rig; later that day Rotheram 'punished 8 seamen for drunkenness'.[70]

Laying some 3 leagues ENE of Cape Spartel on the morning of Saturday 2 November, *Royal Sovereign* made sail eastward with 'several of the fleet in Company' and at PM Sunday 3 November was 'standing in for Gibraltar'; 'at 4.40 shortened Sail and came too with the best bower in 29 fathoms water in Rosio Bay'. Having veered and moored the log states: 'found lying here Two Prizes and some of the Fleet'. Next day the log records 'PM Light Breezes Sailed his Majesty[s] ship[s] *Victory Prince Agamemnon* and *Niger* Carpenter Employ'd stoping shot holes out side arrived here his Majesty[s] Ship *Etnea* [sic] at 6:25 sailed HM Ship *Etnea* [sic] sent away the Spanish Prisoners in transports Boats emp[d] Removing Cap[t] Rotheram[s] things to the *Bellerophon*'. On Tuesday 5 November: 'left the ship Cap[t] Edward Rotheram Joined Lieutenant Roberts arrived his Majesty[s] Brig *Weazle* sailed his Majesty[s] ship *Bellerophon*'.[71] According to the list of commanders and their ships at the Royal Naval Museum, MS 248/6, Rotheram turned over into *Bellerophon* on 1 November, but the log confirms that command

actually changed four days later. Rotheram's successor, Captain Henry Garrett, would remain in *Royal Sovereign* until August 1808. Having changed command, *Royal Sovereign* returned to Plymouth on 6 December.[72]

1806: Finally going into dock on 2 May, *Royal Sovereign* commenced a 'Between Middling & Large Repair' when her copper was replaced. Coming out of the dock on 10 November, she was moored in the Hamoaze being 'fitted'.[73]

1807: Sailing on 23 January, the ship returned to the Mediterranean with Garrett still holding command.

1808-1810: Throughout these years the ship continued her deployment in the Mediterranean. While serving as flagship to Vice-Admiral Edward Thornborough in 1808, Captain Garrett was succeeded on 2 August by Captain David Colby. When Colby was appointed commander of *Apollo* in 1809 his successor, Captain A Ferris, took command of *Royal Sovereign* on 26 November 1809. Ferris remained in the ship until superseded by Captain Henry Pearce on 20 February 1810. Five months later on 1 July Pearce was succeeded by Captain Josiah Spear.[74]

1811: When Captain John Harvey assumed command of the ship on 11 March his predecessor Josiah Spear transferred into *Téméraire* (98). Towards the end of the year *Royal Sovereign* was recalled home, reaching Plymouth on 11 December. Two weeks later Captain William Bedford assumed command of the ship.[75]

1812: After spending the first two weeks of this year in dock having defects repaired and being re-coppered, on 1 April *Royal Sovereign* sailed from Plymouth for duty.[76] Bedford remained in the ship until superseded by Captain James Bissett on 20 October.[77]

1813: Returning to Plymouth 19 July the ship was docked 12 August for two days to have her copper 'repaired & dressed down' and afterwards remained in port where, on 23 December, command of the ship was given to Captain T G Caulfield.

1814: *Royal Sovereign* eventually left Plymouth on 22 January. Appointed as flagship conveying Vice-Admiral Sir Sidney Smith to the Mediterranean, command of the ship was, under the admiral's instruction, given to Captain Charles Thurlow Smith on 28 March. On arrival at Palermo Sir Sidney Smith transferred his flag into *Hibernia* (110), taking Captain Smith with him. However, according to the list of commanders and their ships, Charles Smith moved into *Duncan* (74) on 27 May, but was certainly in *Hibernia* in August that year. Smith's successor, Captain Robert Lambert, assumed command of the ship on 8 May. By this time the war against France had finished and Napoleon had been exiled on the island of Elba. Consequently *Royal Sovereign* was recalled home. Although Lambert officially paid off the ship on 10 August, sources are contradictory about which port the ship was decommissioned, one source states Portsmouth, the other Plymouth. The ship's progress book clearly states that *Royal Sovereign* returned to Plymouth on 4 August.[78] No longer required for service the *Royal Sovereign* was docked six days after being decommissioned to have her 'Copper taken off to Ordinary height', after which she was 'Fitted for Ordinary'.

1815: After escaping from Elba, Napoleon landed in France on 1 March and marched from Cannes, gathering an army to restart the war. *Royal Sovereign* was placed back in commission under Captain Edward P Brenton on 11 April. 'Fitted for Sea', her bottom was re-coppered to her 'Load Draft of Water'. Once stored she sailed for duty on 18 May. Brenton remained in the ship until superseded by Captain Edward R Broughton on 7 June. With Napoleon's final defeat at the battle of Waterloo on 18 June, *Royal Sovereign*

PROGRESS BOOK - ROYAL SOVEREIGN 1st RATE OF 100 GUNS: Source: ADM 180/6 Entry 3 & ADM 180/10 Entry 9

At what Port	Arrived	Docked	Coppered	Launched or Undocked	Sailed	Built or Nature of Repair	Cost of Hull, Masts & Yards Materials £ s d	Cost of Rigging & Stores Materials £ s d	Grand Total
Plymouth	Began	Jan 1774		11 Sep 1786	Built		61,254. 14s. 7	6,203. 14s. 10d.	67,458. 9s. 4d.
Plymouth		12 Sep 1786	Coppered Sep 1786	25 Sep 1786		Coppered	Included in above	Included in above	Included in above
Plymouth		Taken in hand September 1787 & partly fitted for Sea					3,737. 0s. 4d	3,023. 6s. 10d	6,760. 7s. 2d.
Plymouth		Taken in hand 6 May 1790 completed August 1790				Fitted	3,092. 14s. 10d	4,219. 3s. 4d.	7,311. 18s. 2d.
Plymouth	16 Nov 1790	12 Mar 1793	Copper repaired March 1793	14 Mar 1793	17 June 1793	Fitted	8,482	13,699	22,181
Plymouth	28 Dec 1793	3 Jan 1794	Copper taken off Re-coppered Jan 1794	18 Jan 1794	13 Feb 1794	Refitted	Included in above	Included in above	Included in above
Plymouth	12 June 1794				24 July 1794	Refitted	5,905	5,536	11,441
Portsmouth	29 Feb 1796	9 April 1796	Copper repaired	9 May 1796	23 May 1796	Made good her damages	3,965	5,707	9,672
Portsmouth	6 Feb 1799	20 Feb 1799	Copper taken off and Re-coppered Feb 1799	6 April 1799	13 April 1799	Refitted	6,817	4,739	11,556
Portsmouth	19 Apr 1802		Copper repaired	16 June 1803	Fitted				
Plymouth	19 July 1805	11 Aug 1805	Copper taken off bored Re-coppered Aug 1805	28 Aug 1805	10 Sep 1805	Refitted			
Plymouth	6 Dec 1805	2 May 1806	Copper taken off May Re-coppered Nov 1806	10 Nov 1806	23 Jan 1807	Between Middling & Large Repair; Fitted			
Plymouth	11 Dec 1811	2 Jan 1812	Copper taken off and Re-coppered	13 Jan 1812	1 April 1812	Defects			
Plymouth	29 July 1813	12 Aug 1813	Copper repaired & dressed down	14 Aug 1813	22 Jan 1814	Defects			
Plymouth	4 Aug 1814	16 Aug 1814	Copper taken off to Ordinary height	17 Aug 1814		Fitted for Ordinary			
Plymouth			Coppered Bottom to Load Draft of Water April 1815		18 May 1815	Fitted for Sea			
Plymouth	21 July 1815		Copper taken off to Ordinary Draft of Water Nov 1815						
Plymouth	17 June 1825		Copper taken off and re-coppered & fixed protectors	15 August 1825		Fitted for a Receiving Ship			
Plymouth		August 1841	defects from April 1833 to August 1841						
		Taken to Pieces August 1841							
		Value of Stores returned from Hull - £5,996							

returned to Plymouth on 21 July and again had her copper removed to her light draft waterline. Captain Broughton finally paid the ship off at Plymouth on 28 August and for the next ten years the ship remained laid up in ordinary.[79]

FATE

With orders to be fitted out as a receiving ship, *Royal Sovereign* was docked at Plymouth on 17 June 1825 when she had her copper removed, after which she is described as 're-coppered & fixed protectors'. What is meant by 'protectors' at the time of writing is unclear; however it does suggest that some form of anode being fitted to her hull to prevent galvanic action between dissimilar metals. This implies that an understanding of metallurgy had advanced considerably by the 1820s. Renamed *Captain*, the ship was undocked on 15 August and remained in her new rôle accommodating men entering the navy until 1841. No longer required for service, *Captain* (*Royal Sovereign*) was docked at Plymouth in August 1841 and taken to pieces, the value of her returned stores removed beforehand amounting to £5,996.[80]

The 100 gun ship VICTORY

Victory is famous for being the only surviving battleship from the French Revolutionary and Napoleonic Wars and for serving as Nelson's flagship at the Battle of Trafalgar on 21 October 1805. Restored to her Trafalgar configuration, the ship remains commissioned in the Royal Navy as the flagship of the Second Sea Lord and Commander-in-Chief Naval Home Command. Nelson's *Victory* is the sixth ship to bear the name *Victory* in the Royal Navy, the previous ships being:

Victory I. The *Great Christopher*, a merchant vessel purchased in 1560 and renamed *Victory*. Rebuilt in 1586, she was listed as a ship of 800 tons with an armament of twelve 18 pounders, nine 6 pounders and 20 smaller guns. Fighting against the Spanish Armada in 1588, her complement comprised 300 mariners, 34 gunners and 400 soldiers. She was broken up in 1608.

Victory II. A 42 gun ship of 870 tons designed by Phineas Pett and built at Deptford in 1620. She was rebuilt at Chatham in 1666 as a 2nd rate of 82 guns and 1,020 tons. She fought against the Dutch off Dover in 1652, Portland, Gabbard, and Scheveningen 1653, Orfordness 1666, Solebay 1672 and Texel in 1673. She also fought against the French at Barfleur before being broken up at Woolwich in 1691.

Victory III. Referred to as *Little Victory* and not often accounted for, this ship was a 5th rate of 28 guns of 175 tons built at Chatham in 1665 and expended as a fireship in 1671.

Victory IV. Originally called *Victoire*, this *Victory* was a 5th rate of 38 guns

Part 1: The British Fleet

The Ships of Trafalgar

SPECIFICATIONS: *VICTORY*

Rate	1st	*Length on the range of the gun deck*	184 ft	*Ordnance - lower gun deck*	30 x 42 pounders (later 32 pounders)
Guns	100	*Length of keel for tonnage*	152 ft 6⅝ ins	*Ordnance - middle gun deck*	28 x 24 pounders
Class	Victory 1759	*Extreme breadth*	51 ft 10 ins	*Ordnance - upper gun deck*	30 x long 12 pounders
Designer	Thomas Slade	*Depth in hold*	21 ft 6 ins	*Ordnance - quarter deck*	12 x 6 pounders (later short 12 pounders)
Builder	John Lock, Edward Allin	*Tons burthen*	2162. 53/94	*Ordnance - forecastle*	4 x 6 pounders
Dockyard	Chatham	*Draught afore*	23 ft		(later 2 x medium 12 pounders & 2 x 68 pounder carronades)
Date ordered	13 December 1758/14 June 1759	*Draught abaft*	24 ft	*Single broadside weight*	1194 pounds (1148 pounds)
Date keel laid	23 July 1759	*Complement*	850	*Fate*	Dry docked for preservation in 1922 and remains in commission today
Date launched	7 May 1765				

Note: Ordnance listed as built and as fitted for 1803/1805 Trafalgar campaign.

Source: Lyon, *Sailing Navy List*, pp. 62-63.

captured from the French on 5 April 1666 and later captured by the Dutch in 1672.

Victory V. A 1st rate ship of 100 guns laid down at Portsmouth on 23 February 1726 and launched on 23 February 1737. This ship was in fact a rebuild of the *Royal James* built in 1675. *Royal James*, renamed *Victory* in 1691, was rebuilt at Chatham in 1695, renamed *Royal George* on the 27 October 1714 and again renamed *Victory* in September 1715. This ship was accidentally burnt in 1721 and taken to pieces in April that same year, her timber frames were laid aside and re-used for the construction of the *Victory* launched in 1737. Serving under the flag of Admiral Balchen, this fifth *Victory* was wrecked on the notorious Casquets that lay off the Channel Islands, 5 October 1744, with a loss of 1,000 lives.

SERVICE HISTORY

The career of the Trafalgar *Victory* commenced 40 years before the momentous battle. One of twelve ships ordered by the Navy Board on 6 June 1759 to supplement the fleet during the Seven Years' War, this 1st rate 100 gun ship was designed by the Surveyor of the Navy, Sir Thomas Slade, the most innovative and successful eighteenth century naval architect who adopted many of his designs from captured French ships during Lord Anson's administration. After Slade's designs were approved by the Board of the Admiralty on 14 June, authorisation to build was given on 7 July 1759. As yet unnamed, the ship's keel was laid in the old single dock at Chatham dockyard 23 July 1759, the construction work overseen by Master Shipwright John Lock. This was the *Annus Mirabilis* or 'marvellous year', the turning point of the war for Britain. Victories had been won at Lagos, Minden, Quebec, and Quiberon Bay, the latter where Admiral Hawke, in a rising gale, fought and smashed the French fleet on shore. These facts may well have been instrumental in the naming of this ship, confirmed as *Victory* by Admiralty Order 30 October 1760. 1759 was also the year that William Pitt the Younger, later to lead the war against France, was born and William Boyce wrote the song 'Heart of Oak'. Ironically 1759 was the year that James Watt invented his steam engine with a separate condenser: within 70 years this innovation would begin to oust sailing ships.

John Lock died in 1762; thus completion of the ship was left to his capable successor Edward Allin. In 1763 the war ended, some of the dockyard workforce was paid off and the work rate on *Victory* was reduced. Her cost, when 'floated out of the dock' on 7 May 1765, amounted to £63,176 3s 0d: £57,748 1s 7d for hull, masts and yards and £5,426 1s 5d for stores and rigging.[81] Her initial armament comprised thirty short 42 pounders, twenty-eight medium 24 pounders, thirty long 12 pounders and twelve long 6 pounders. Not required for service immediately after sea trials, *Victory* was laid up in ordinary for thirteen years 'at Gillingham Water' until France joined the American War of Independence in 1778.[82]

1768: Having sprung some leaks, *Victory* was docked at Chatham on 7 March to repair defective planking and undocked two weeks later.[83]

1771: *Victory* went into dock again at Chatham on 18 May for a 'Small

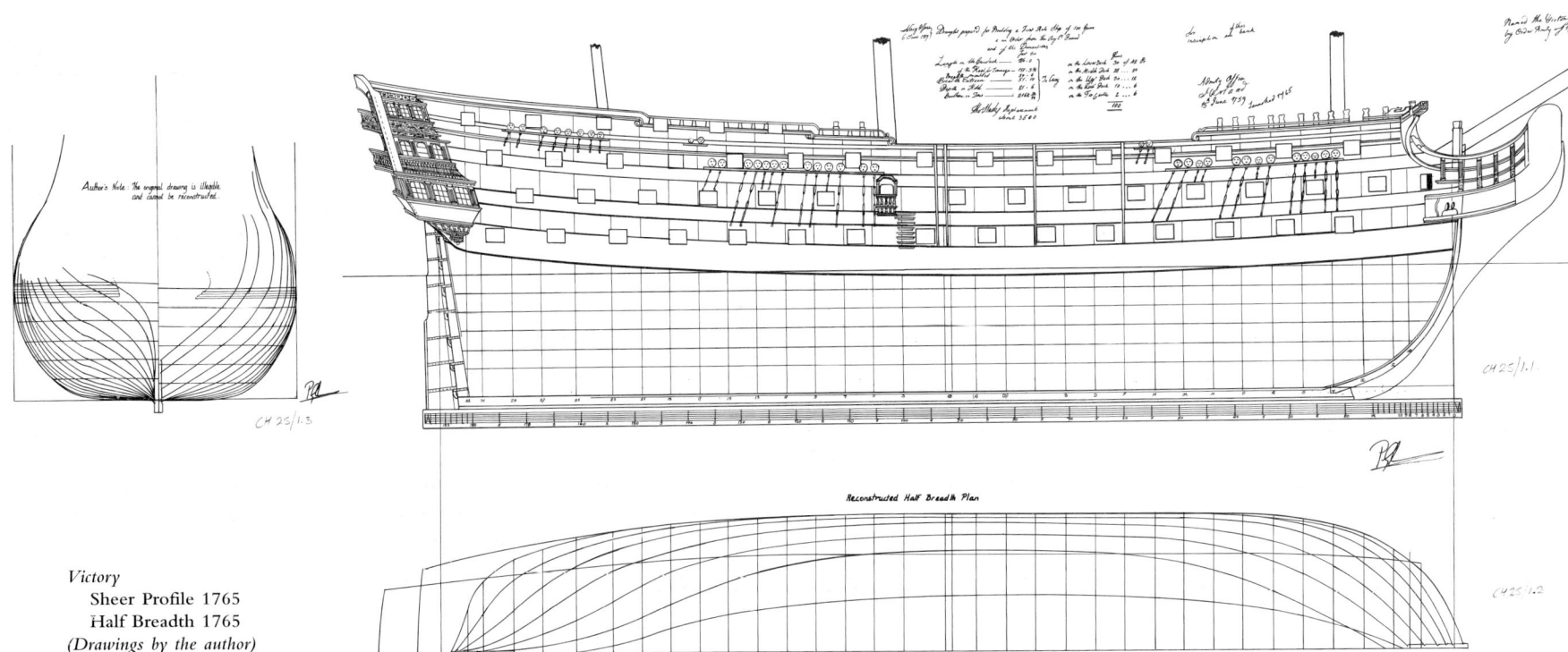

Victory
Sheer Profile 1765
Half Breadth 1765
(Drawings by the author)

Repair' at a cost of £4,276 9s 9d and re-launched on 10 October.[84]

1778: When France and Spain entered the War of American Independence with the Americans, *Victory* was commissioned on Thursday 12 March under her first commander, Captain John Lindsay, who recorded: 'At 1 PM Came down here, hoisted the Pendant on Board His Majestys Ship Victory & put her in Commission'.[85] Between Tuesday 17 March and 13 April the ship was prepared for war, taking on ballast, guns, stores and cables, while 40 riggers rigged her masts and yards. After *Victory* sailed and 'Moor'd at Black Stakes' at the mouth of the River Medway, on Monday 13 April she continued storing and taking on crew.[86] When King George III visited Chatham dockyard in his yacht *Royal Charlotte* on Monday 27 April he went on board *Victory*. Lindsay 'Hoisted the [Royal] Standard' at the truck of *Victory*'s masthead. Accompanying the King were Lord Sandwich, First Lord of the Admiralty, the Marquis of Lothian, Admiral Campbell, and Commissioner Charles Proby. Besides Captain Lindsay and his officers, also present were 'all the Navy Officers from the Nore'. The King went back 'on Board the *Royal Charlotte*, where he was Saluted with 21 Guns'.[87]

Ready for sea on Friday 8 May, '*Victory* weighed & made Sail' for Spithead. Two days later the ship suffered her first fatality: at '½ past 3 John Smith fell over Board & was drowned'. Arriving at Spithead on 13 May, *Victory* joined the Channel Fleet assembling for deployment off the NW coast of France under Admiral Keppel. Next day 'Came on Board Adm.^l Keppel, Rear Adm.^l Campbell, & Captn Faulknor to view the Ship'. Succeeded by Captain Jonathan Faulknor that same day, John Lindsay transferred into *Prince George* (90).[88] Having embarked the admiral's retinue on Saturday 16 May, Faulknor wrote in *Victory*'s log: 'at sun set Adm.^l Keppel Shifted His Flag from y.^e *Pri*. [*Prince*] *George* to the *Victory*'.[89] This statement, together with the previous note concerning Lindsay's transfer into the *Prince George*, is quite typical inasmuch that admirals often transferred their own captains from one ship to another with them.

Before sailing Keppel ordered *Victory*'s thirty 42 pounder guns to be replaced by lighter and more manageable 32 pounders. This reduced her broadside weight to 1,032 pounds. Leading Keppel's Grand Fleet, *Victory* sailed on Saturday 30 May for Ushant to blockade Brest. On Wednesday 17 June the armed cutter *Alert*, later captured, joined the fleet.[90] When most of Keppel's ships took shelter in Torbay at the end of June the French fleet commanded by Admiral Compte d'Orvilliers broke out of Brest on 8 July. Receiving news of their escape next day, Keppel ordered his fleet to weigh and returned off Ushant on 15 July. Although D'Orvilliers' squadron was sighted on Friday 24 July, hard squalls prevented the two fleets closing, the British fleet all the while pursuing the French further into the Atlantic. Before the two fleets engaged on Monday 27 July Faulknor 'Served an Allowance of Grog to the Ships Company'. Faulknor states that when the British van began to engage at 11.30 a.m. the French fleet was reaching to windward on an opposite tack and 'Firing as they Pass our Ships, Several of them Fired at the *Victory* but seeing we could fetch the *Bretagne* we Passed 2 of their Ships Reserving our Fire for the Adm.^ls Ship at ¾ past 11 got along side the *Bretagne* and at Noon Engaging the *Ville de Paris*'.[91] At 1 p.m. (on Tuesday 28 July) while *Victory* was engaging the six ships astern of d'Orvilliers' flagship *Bretagne*, Faulknor records that Keppel signalled the fleet to wear because, as Faulknor notes: 'Our Ships Greatly Damaged: Rigg.^g & Sails', from enemy fire. As a manœuvre wearing put more strain on the rigging than tacking. At 2 o'clock Keppel signalled the fleet to form line ahead one cable length (600 feet) distance between each ship, when *Victory* was brought to, 'to repair the Sails & Rigg.^g'. At 2.45 p.m. the French fleet 'Wore & formed the Line with their Heads Towards us'. Keppel then made several signals to get his ships steering SSE, 'to Join the main Body of our fleet to Leeward & form the Line'. Although this signal was repeated at 4.30 and at 5 p.m. the British line had fallen into disorder. Keppel then signalled Sir Robert Harland's division to make more sail and form the line in the van. Still hove to, *Victory*'s seamen had 'Unbent ye Maintopsail & bent a new one', and were 'Emp.^d Splicing the Rigg.^g' which is very much damaged'. With Sir Hugh Palliser's division failing to get back into action the two fleets did not close again. Thus ended the first battle of Ushant. Although indecisive, *Victory* had received her baptism of fire.[92]

Much damaged, *Victory*, with Keppel's fleet, made for Cawsand Bay to make repairs. On Sunday 23 August *Victory* weighed and sailed again to blockade off Ushant. Accompanying her were *Sandwich* (98), the 74 gun ships *Berwick*, *Cumberland*, *Defiance*, *Thunderer* and *Valiant*, the 64 gun *Stirling Castle* (64), the 28 gun frigates *Andromeda*, *Fox*, *Milford* and *Proserpine*, the 24 gun *Porcupine* (24) and 14 gun sloop *Rattlesnake*.[93]

When *Victory* returned to Spithead on Tuesday 27 October for minor repairs shipwrights re-caulked the decks, her rudder was unshipped and sent into the dockyard with her sails; *Victory* also 'Rec'd on board a new Capstern'. By the number of punishments given during this period, some for mutinous behaviour, Faulknor still had problems with his crew.[94]

1779: *Victory* remained at Spithead until Wednesday 10 March when she moved into Portsmouth harbour. On Saturday 27 March 'Captain Collins Came on Board Superseded Captain Faulknor and Read His Commission to the Ships Company'.[95] Having refitted, *Victory* returned to Spithead where, on Monday 17 May, Collins wrote: 'AM Admiral Sr Chas Hardy hoisted his Flag, which the Ships of the Fleet Salut.^d by Cheers'. One month later *Victory* sailed for deployment in the Channel approaches and Ushant, returning to Spithead Thursday 25 November.

1780: On 8 February *Victory* went into Portsmouth harbour to comply with a new Admiralty regulation. She was docked in March to have her bottom sheathed with 3,923 sheets of copper plating which would protect her hull from the boring ship-worm *teredo navalis* and deter marine growth, to improve her speed. Coming out of dock at the end of the month the ship commenced embarking ballast, stores and provisions.[96]

On 13 April the log recalls that 'Admiral Evans hoist.^d his Flag on Board the *Victory* & at 11 he shift.^d it to *Formidable*'. While *Victory*'s crew 'got on Board 15 of the lower Deck Guns' on Wednesday 19 April, Captain John Clayton entered the ship, 'Read his Commission & Superseded Captain Collins'. *Victory*'s armament was increased: the thirty lower deck 32 pounders were replaced with thirty 42 pounders as originally armed and she was equipped with carronades; two 24 pounder carronades on her forecastle and six 18 pounder carronades on her poop deck. In all she now had a broadside weight of 1,260 lbs (567 kgs).

On 13 May command of *Victory* was temporarily superseded by Captain Parker, flag captain to Admiral Sir Francis Geary. Geary hoisted his flag in *Victory* on 24 May and although *Victory* was appointed to the Channel fleet, she spent most of this period at Spithead.[97] Captain Clayton returned to the ship 16 August, twelve days before Geary lowered his flag and left *Victory*.[98]

1781: When Captain Clayton transferred out of *Victory* on 16 April her new commander, John Howarth, remained in the ship until superseded on 22 November by Captain Henry Cromwell who, at 2 p.m. on Saturday 23 November, 'read my Commission to the Ships Company'. Shortly after Admiral Richard Kempenfelt hoisted his flag in the ship and on Monday 2 December *Victory* sailed with Kempenfelt's squadron for Ushant to intercept an expected French convoy. On Wednesday 12 December Cromwell wrote: 'we discovered the whole of the Enemy Fleet to leeward forming the line of Battle ahead the Convoy', comprising 19 sail of the line escorting a convoy of troopships from Brest to the West Indies. Kempenfelt engaged the French fleet on the 13 December. Although his squadron was numerically inferior, he captured the entire convoy from under the escort's noses. After *Victory* triumphantly returned to Spithead on Friday 21 December Kempenfelt transferred his flag into the ill-fated *Royal George* (100).[99]

1782: On Tuesday 9 April Cromwell was superseded by Captain John Bowmaster who, just ten days later, was succeeded by Captain Henry

Duncan.[100] Still attached to the Channel squadron, *Victory* spent most of this year escorting convoys between the Channel approaches and the North Sea, returning to Spithead on Tuesday 13 August. Under the flag of Admiral Richard Howe *Victory* and her squadron sailed again on 11 September 1782, escorting a convoy to Portugal. After taking part in an action off Cape Spartel and supporting the relief of Gibraltar in October she returned to Spithead on Friday 15 November. Ready for refitting, *Victory* moved into Portsmouth harbour 27 November and on Thursday 5 December was moored alongside a sheer hulk to have her masts removed. Two days later Captain Duncan moved *Victory* into dock where the crew 'got out 304 tons shingle ballast'.

1783: Decommissioned, *Victory* commenced a 'middling repair', during which it was found that she was suffering serious structural defects caused by her coppering three years earlier. This is highlighted in Captain Ferguson's letter to his brother dated 1 March 1783.

> Some time ago I stepped into a dry dock, Where a Ship was under repair, which had been Copper'd, and observed the whole Bolts and Iron Work in the Bottom, between 4 and 5 Inches from the outside corroded and nothing but rusty dust, and having mentioned this in different Companies, I found myself laughed at. But on the *Victory* being lately carried into Dock, it is found, That all the Bolts for 4 to 5 Inches inwards from the Copper, is sound and all the rest inwards to the Hold, nothing but rust and it is the general opinion of the Officers and Carpenters, who have inspected her, that had she touched the Ground ever so slightly she must have gone to pieces. And on further Inquiry, I find the whole Ships which have been Copper'd to two years are in the same condition, and even my old ship *Venus*, which I Copper'd in Antigua...[101]

The same problem affected most ships in the fleet; therefore all vessels had to have their underwater iron fastenings replaced with those made of copper or other non-ferrous alloys (at great expense). For *Victory* this was over £2,000.[102] The total cost of her refit of March 1783 amounted to £15,372 19s 9d. Her quarter deck and forecastle 6 pounder guns were replaced with 12 pounders which effectively increased her broadside weight to 1,290 pounds. Her sides, previously paid 'bright' with rosin above the lower deck ports, were now painted dull yellow ochre; the area below remaining painted black. *Victory* was then laid up in ordinary 'At Moorings in Portsmouth Harbour' until 1787.

1787: *Victory* was initially recommissioned again Saturday 6 October 1787 by Lieutenant John Doling. Her true commander, Captain Charles Hope, who entered the ship shortly after, was only in command until 5 December. After *Victory*'s crew removed all ballast the ship was docked for refitting on Saturday 27 October. At 11 a.m. on Saturday 10 November Hope recorded that *Victory* was 'haul'd out of the Dock, alongside the Jetty Came on Board the Clerk of the Cheque and Muster'd the Ships Company'.[103] *Victory*'s 'large repair' had cost £37,523 17s 1d Besides lengthening her quarter deck and forecastle and having the main and fore masts re-positioned, her hull was strengthened by fitting thirty-three breadth, middle and top riders along each side. These extended from the flat of the orlop to the deckhead of the upper gun deck.[104] Although recommissioned under the flags of Howe and then Lord Hood, on Tuesday 27 November *Victory* 'Received Orders to Put Ourselves under the Command of Rear Admiral Sir Francis Drake, at Sun set Vice Admiral Lord Hood struck His Flag. AM Rear Admiral Drake was Saluted by H M Ships at Spithead and in the Harbour'.[105] *Victory* only remained in commission until Saturday 1 December, Hope recording: 'Came on Board the Clerk of the Cheque and paid Bounty Money to y^e. Volunteers'. Having made this payment *Victory* decommissioned, her log entry on Wednesday 5 December 1787 stating, 'Carried the ships Company on Shore to the Pay Office to be paid off at PM Haul'd down the Pendant of His Majestys Ship *Victory* and Put her out of Commission'.

1790: *Victory* remained out of service until Sunday 16 May 1790 when 'Lieut. Hallowell, came on Board and put the Ship in Commission' on behalf of her new commander, Captain John Knight. In 1798 Benjamin Hallowell would command *Swiftsure* (74) at the battle of the Nile. In the succeeding weeks while *Victory* was re-rigged, she received her officers and crew.[106]

Victory sailed on Tuesday 28 June accompanied by Admiral Barrington in *Barfleur* (98), with *Impregnable* (98), *Princess Royal* (90), *Alcide* (74), *Arrogant* (74), *Bellona* (74), *Bombay Castle* (74), *Carnatic* (74), *Colossus* (74), *Culloden* (74), *Cumberland* (74), *Edgar* (74), *Magnificent* (74), *Valiant* (74), and *Director* (64). They proceeded down the Channel passing Portland Bill and Berry Head for Torbay. Although Knight meted out punishment justly, discipline within *Victory* was frequently violated with cases of drunkenness, insolence, theft, neglect of duty and uncleanness, probably because the ship was laying idle in Torbay. After an uneventful deployment, on Friday 24 September 1790 *Victory* returned to Spithead, where she remained at anchor.[107]

1791: On Wednesday 12 January *Victory* went into Portsmouth harbour for bricklayers to lay new bricks under the iron fire-hearth in the galley, carpenters to repair boats and the gunner to receive 'on Board part of our Gun carriages'. Throughout March and April Knight constantly exercised his men at the great guns to alleviate the monotony of being anchored at Spithead.[108]

As flagship, *Victory* often received prestigious visitors. On Tuesday 31 May 'His Serene Highness the Duke of Wertenburgh came on board', and on Sunday 19 June, 'His Grace the Duke of Hamilton… and His Excellency the Ambassador to the Landgrave of Hesse'. Other distinguished visitors: 'His Royal Highness the Duke of Gloucester Prince W^m. Henry and Princess Sophia of Gloucester' embarked into *Victory* Friday 1 July, when Knight reported: 'Hoisted the Standard and the Fleet Saluted' with 21 Guns. Tuesday 26 July saw yet another visit, this time Knight wrote: 'Saluted the R^t. Honble Messrs. Pitt, Dundas &c. with 15 Guns on their coming on Board and 15 on their quitting the Ship'. When no longer required for service 'The Commissioner Came on board to Pay the Ship off' on Friday 2 September. Knight concluded *Victory*'s log next day, recording 'PM fresh breezes and cloudy. At 3 the Commissioner left the Ship having paid the Ship off'.[109]

1793: Before war was declared against revolutionary France on 1 February *Victory* was quickly prepared for sea service and recommissioned under Captain John Knight. Anchored at Spithead on Tuesday 13 January, Knight records that following a court martial, 'at ¼ before Noon 5 of the Mutineers were executed on Board the *Culloden*'. On 24 January, while still taking on crew, *Victory* was hauled 'into Dock again the lead being torn from her Fore Foot in heaving out of the Dock'.[110]

Appointed flagship to Admiral Hood, *Victory* sailed for the Mediterranean with a large force to blockade the French Fleet at Toulon. Hood's main objective was to assist French Royalists in Toulon against 30,000 revolutionary forces laying siege to the city under the command of General Dugommier. Hood therefore stood off the port on 4 August with his entire fleet of 51 ships of the following types.[111]

Guns	100	98	74	64	50	36	32	28	24	20	14	12	FS	SS	HS
No.	2	3	12	5	1	4	8	3	1	1	4	2	2	2	1

Note: FS = Fire ship: SS = Store ships: HS = Hospital ship.

Supported by a squadron of allied Spanish ships, by 29 August Hood had captured nineteen ships of the Toulon fleet to prevent then falling into the hands of the revolutionaries. After discussions with the royalists on 26 August, Hood prepared to take possession of the city. He landed 1,500 troops and 200 seamen and marines next day. Although aided by Spanish forces, he was hard pushed to maintain control. In December, when Toulon fell to the revolutionary forces led by General Bonaparte, Hood withdrew his fleet to Corsica.

1794: During the earlier part of the year *Victory* supported the campaign of the Corsican General Pasquale de Paoli against French forces, assisting Nelson's attacks where required, first on Bastia and then Calvi in April. At the end of the year Hood, his health deteriorating, transferred command of the Mediterranean fleet to Admiral William Hotham in *Britannia* (100) and returned home in *Victory*.

1795: Flying the blue flag of Rear-Admiral Robert Man at her mizzen topgallant mast, *Victory* rejoined the Mediterranean fleet off Toulon under Admiral William Hotham on 8 May. Sixteen days later Hotham withdrew his ships to San Fiorenzo to water. Receiving news from Nelson that the French fleet under Vice-Admiral Martin had used this opportunity to break out of Toulon, *Victory* with the rest of Hotham's fleet weighed and put to sea. Hotham's fleet which encountered Martin's ships off the island of Hyéres on Monday 12 July was composed of the following 31 vessels:[112]

Rate	1st	2nd	2nd	3rd	3rd	3rd	5th	5th	5th	6th	6th	Brigs	Cutters
Guns	100	98	90	80	74	64	32	28	24	20	18	14	12
No.	2	3	1	1	14	2	1	1	1	2	1	1	1

Heavy gales hampered the British ships that night and when *Victory*'s 'Main Topsail split' next morning her seamen bent on a spare topsail while clearing for battle. *Victory*'s log states: 'hoisted our Colours employed getting up with the enemy, 11 returned the Cheer of the *Agamemnon*, *Cumberland*, *Culloden* and *Defence*'. By noon the wind eased and the French fleet, formed in line ahead on a larboard tack, were only three quarters of a mile from Hotham's van. Then, '½ past 12 the wind shifted from SWW to North which brought the enemys sides to bear on us when the three Ships of the [French] Rear began to fire'. *Victory* then returned her 'fire on the Sternmost Ships at 1 ceased firing until we got our guns to bear as did the Enemy'. *Victory*, *Culloden* and *Cumberland* took the heaviest fire of the French broadsides and at 1.10 p.m. *Victory* recommenced, 'firing on the Sternmost Ships'. Action continued until 2.23 p.m. when Knight entered in *Victory*'s log, 'ordered the retreat to be beat to repair our rigging not being able to make Sail having lost the Fore Topsail Yard Main Top Gall[t]. Mast all the Masts wounded with the Main Stay cut away sever[l]. of the Shrouds all the Braces and running rigging'.[113] Why Hotham made this extraordinary decision, signalling the fleet to withdraw just when *Agamemnon*, *Blenheim*, *Captain* and *Defence* were getting into action, is incomprehensible. After listing the damage sustained in battle Knight wrote in *Victory*'s log, 'Killed 2 Midshipmen 3 Marines Wounded officers 4 Seamen 9'.[114] Clowes erroneously states 15 wounded. James quite rightly refers to the battle as 'this miserable action'. One of *Victory*'s officers commented critically: 'Had the British fleet only put their heads the same way as the Enemy's and stood inshore at four o'clock, the whole French line might have been cut from the land, taken, or destroyed: and even afterwards, they might have been followed into Fréjus bay and wholly destroyed'. Hotham's indecisiveness cost him his post. His successor, the firm disciplinarian Admiral Sir John Jervis, would soon hoist his flag in *Victory*. Needing repairs, *Victory* sailed with Hotham's fleet for San Fiorenzo, where she remained for the rest of the year.[115] After five years in command Knight's last log entry, dated Thursday 3 December 1795, states: 'Came onboard Capt. Grey, & Superseded Capt. Knight, read Captain Grey's Commission and mustered the ships company'.[116] George Grey was to remain in the ship until 31 December 1796.[117]

Captain Grey's first log entry Friday 4 December 1795 states, 'Light wind & Clear. Employed in the Holds. 8 PM Hoisted Sir John Jarvis [sic] Commander in Chief & fired the Evening Gun'.[118]

1796: Unmooring at 6.0 a.m. Sunday 13 December, *Victory* finally sailed to take up station off Cape Sicié, her log stating: 'Employed running out of the Bay fleet in Compy. Consisting of the following Ships Viz.'[119]

St George	*Pss. Royal* [*Princess Royal*]
Blenheim	*Britannia*
Gibraltar	*Zealous*
Excellent	*Captain*
	Guiscardo Sannite Neapolitans
Minerva	*frigate*
Comet fireship & *Fox Cutter*	

1796: *Victory* returned to San Fiorenzo on Friday 15 January. Two days later *Victory*'s log states that with Hotham returning to England, Vice-Admiral Sir Hyde Parker shifted his flag onto *Britannia*. Over the next three weeks *Victory* embarked large quantities of fresh provisions and livestock, undertook minor repairs and dealt with the sick, sending some 'to the Hospital Ship' accompanying the fleet. Ready for sea, *Victory* sailed on Tuesday 9 February for Leghorn and returned to San Fiorenzo on Thursday 24 March.[120]

While anchored at San Fiorenzo Tuesday 13 April Grey records the event that *Ça Ira*, captured at Hotham's action off Genoa 14 March 1795, 'made the Signal of distress & soon afterwards perceiv'd her on Fire which burnt Rapidly' to the waterline. *Victory* lost, 'in towing her Clear a Cablet of 5? Inches, two Fire Grapnels Eight Buckets and one Broad Axe'.[121] *Victory* sailed later that day and spent the next few months cruising with the fleet between Genoa, the island of Levant, and Cape Sicié while sickness prevailed. When *Dolphin* (44), serving as a hospital ship, joined Jervis's fleet on Friday 20 May, Grey 'Hoisted the Boats out and sent 15 Seamen and two Marines (Sick) on board her'. Seven days later the squadron was reinforced by *Barfleur* (Vice Admiral Waldegrave), *Britannia*, *St. George*, *Bombay Castle*, *Excellent*, *Boston*, *Comet* and transports *Liberty* and *Pitt* which transferred

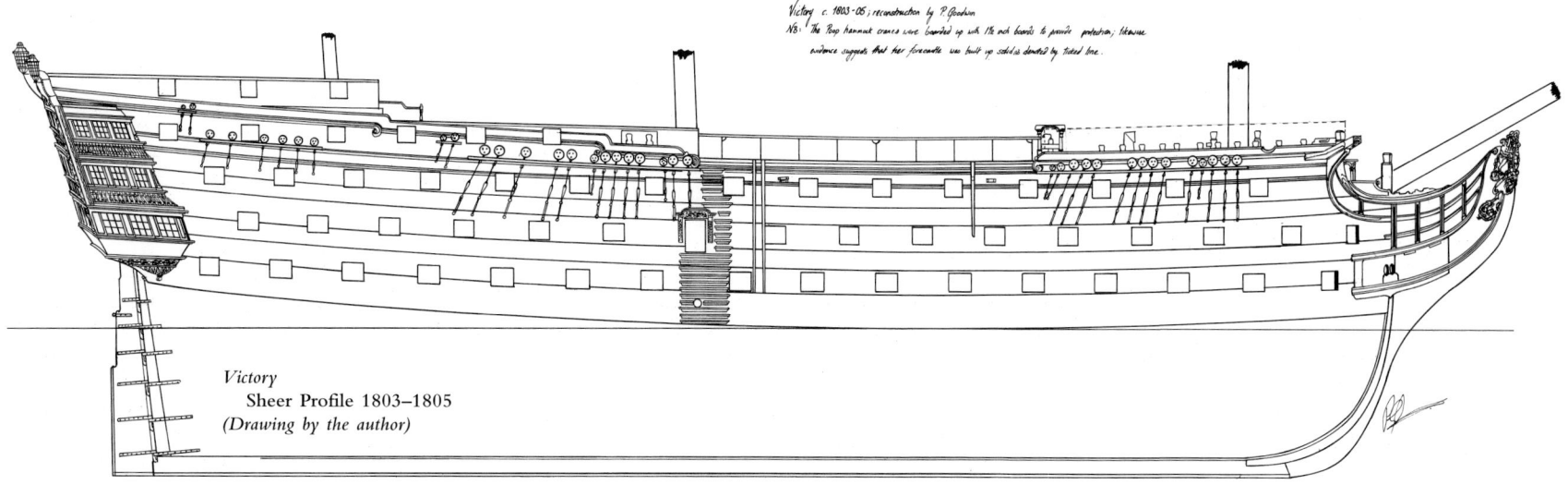

Victory
Sheer Profile 1803–1805
(Drawing by the author)

provisions into *Victory* while at sea. *Victory* returned to San Fiorenzo on Monday 10 October. By November the pendulum of power had swung in favour of France, forcing Jervis to withdraw from the Mediterranean, now effectively a French lake. Corsica was no different, hostilities rendering it inhospitable as a base. On Wednesday 2 November *Victory*'s log states that after *Minerva* (38) and *Surprise* (24) had sailed, 'the Ships and launches (armed) firing on the Enemy who had Attacked our Guard at the Watering place. At 11 Unmoor'd, the convoy under sailed turning out of the bay Noon Calm Launches still firing at the Enemy'.[122]

When Jervis's fleet arrived at Gibraltar on Thursday 1 December the frigate *Blanche* (32) collided with *Victory* 'and carried away our Fore Yard in the Slings'. Grey then 'Got Main Topsail yard across for a Fore one & bent the Main topsail for a Fore Sail & a Mizen topsail for a Fore topsail'. Sailing again on Friday 16 December for Lisbon, *Victory* arrived in the River Tagus on 22 December.[123]

1797: In January Sir Robert Calder joined the *Victory* as First Captain to the Fleet, Grey remaining in command. On 13 February Jervis received news that a Spanish fleet of 27 ships, commanded by Admiral Don José de Córdoba flying his flag in *Santisima Trinidad* (136), had been sighted escorting a convoy carrying mercury from the Americas. Jervis immediately gave orders to clear for action and intercept and by 10 a.m. 14 February he had already despatched *Blenheim* (98), *Prince George* (98), *Culloden* (74), *Orion* (74), *Irresistible* (74) and *Colossus* (74) to give chase to the SW. At 10.57 Jervis ordered his fleet to form line of battle 'as convenient' ahead and astern of *Victory* and steer SSW. When Jervis gave the decisive signal, 'The Admiral means to pass through the enemy line' at 11.26, this confounded the Spanish who, with little room to manœuvre, inadvertently fell into two divisions, leaving Admiral Moreno in *Principe de Asturias* (112) and six ships to leeward, the weathermost ships continuing north. Action began at 12.10, with *Culloden* (74) and then *Irresistible* (74) firing their broadsides into the *Principe de Asturias* which veered away from their onslaught. *Victory* then opened her fire into Moreno's flagship, inflicting more damage to this severely mauled vessel. Around 12.30 the British line turned to starboard, pursuing the enemy van to windward. Seeing the Spanish could escape, Nelson in *Captain* (74), followed by Collingwood in *Excellent* (74), turned out of the line to cut off their retreat, resulting in several Spanish ships including the *San Josef* (112) and *San Nicholas* (74), being taken. Throughout the battle *Victory* added her weight of broadsides as opportunity arose, her main opponent being *Salvador del Mundo*. In *Victory* only one man was killed and five wounded. At around 11.00 a.m. next day *Victory* with the fleet and their prizes sailed for Lagos Bay to make repairs.[124]

When Captain Thomas Sotheby assumed command of *Victory* Friday 31 March, Captain Grey transferred with his admiral into *Ville de Paris* (110). Recording the event, *Victory*'s log states; 'Fresh Gales & Cloudy W[r]. with Light Rain PM Employed Shifting Men between the *Ville de Paris* and *Victory* removing stores &c. AM Sir John Jervis's Flag was Shifted to the *Ville de Paris* Unmoored Ship P[r]. signal and got all ready for sea'. Next day *Victory* stood out to sea and on Monday 3 April got involved in another collision when at; '1/2 past 8 Ran foul of H.M.S. *Goliath* & Carried away Our Q[tr]. Gallery, Poop Lanthorns and Stove the Cutter'. *Victory* had a third collision Sunday 16 April; mustering the ship's company by divisions Southeby then 'Performed Divine Service During which Time the *Theseus* came on Board us & carried away part of the Larboard Quarter Gallery', causing further damage to *Victory*'s elaborate stern.[125] *Victory* remained off Cadiz for the next two months. On Tuesday 20 June, when 'Cap[n]. Sotheby left the Ship & took Command of the *Namur*', command was succeeded by Captain William Cummings.[126] On 6 July when *Victory*'s barge and launch were employed attacking 'the Enemys Gun Boats and town of Cadiz', the launch 'received a Shell through her', and although 'Entirely destroyed', the crew were 'taken up by the Boats around her'.[127]

Recalled, *Victory* sailed for England on 22 August with the Spanish prize *Salvador del Mundo*. After encountering heavy weather she arrived at Spithead on Friday 6 October. Nine days later she sailed for the Nore, mooring at Blackstakes on Tuesday 17 October where she discharged stores and shot until 12.30 p.m. On 8 November she sailed up the River Medway. Anchoring three hours later 'a little below the Dockyard at Chatham', the crew commenced de-rigging and sending anchors and cables into the dockyard. Ten days later the sheer hulk was warped alongside to remove *Victory*'s masts and bowsprit. With all stores and ballast removed by Friday 24 November, Cummings landed the marines, discharged the crew to other ships, and paid off *Victory* that afternoon.[128] Thirty-two years old and unfit for further service, the Admiralty issued orders on 8 December for *Victory* to be converted into a hospital ship for prisoners of war. Consequently the ship was taken in hand and fitted out and used accordingly.

1799: The loss of the 1st rate *Impregnable* (98) near Chichester Harbour on 8 October was fortuitous for *Victory*. Needing to replace this loss while still at war *Victory* was surveyed at Chatham and found 'in want of a middling repair', estimated at £23,500.

1800: Once refitting commenced, a second survey revealed considerable defects: many parts of the hull required rebuilding, over 50 per cent of her knees needed refastening or replacing and many port lids needed refitting. When Grey had been in command he had reported that her stern structure worked open at sea. Because this defect was common in around 160 vessels

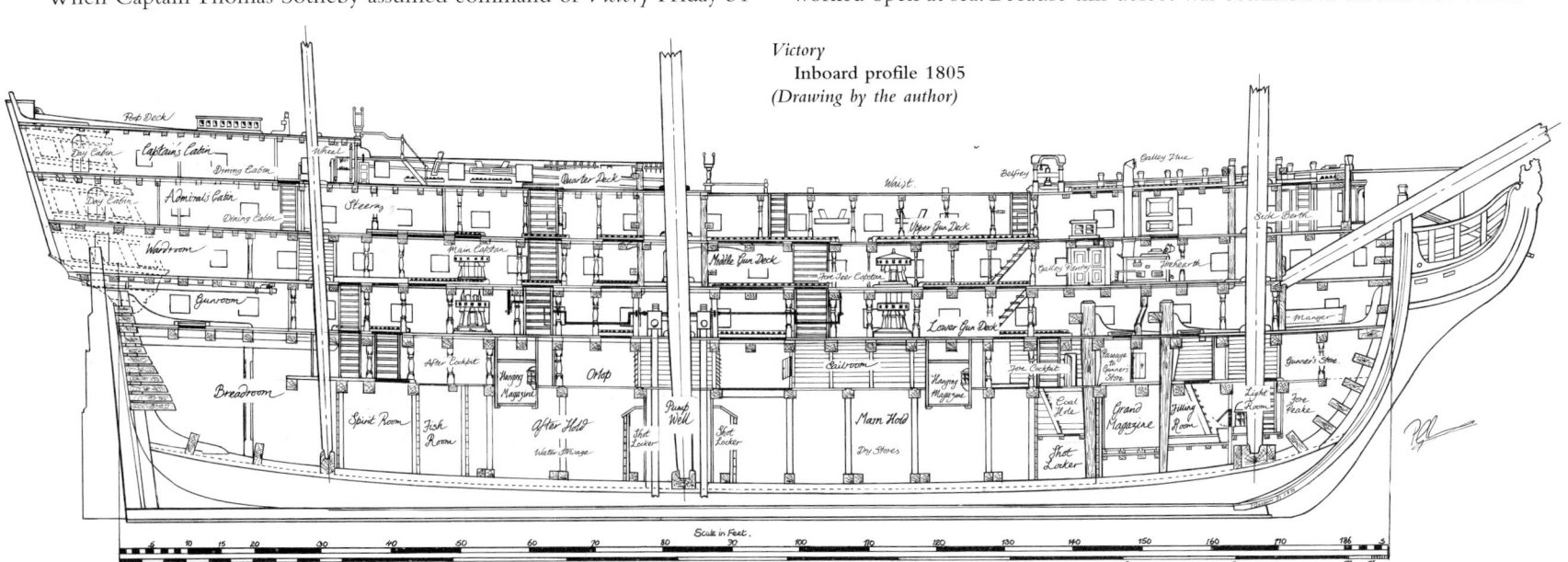

Victory
Inboard profile 1805
(Drawing by the author)

built with open galleries, the Admiralty abolished the open stern in 1798. Therefore *Victory*'s open galleries were removed and her entire stern was closed in.[129] Two extra ports were cut at the fore end of her lower gun deck and the magazines were lined in copper, lead and plaster, conforming to recent authorised practice. Passageways leading to the grand magazine and light room were lined with lathe and plaster as an anti-flash precaution and their decks covered in lead, 'well turned in the corners so as to hold water', to de-activate loose powder spilt when transferring cartridges.[130] The heavy ornate figurehead, now rotten, was replaced with a simpler, lighter design as presently fitted. This, together with reduced ornate work on the stern, corresponded with contemporary restrictions on carving expenses. While it is believed that her lower masts were replaced at this time with composite masts banded with iron hoops, it is more probable that her original pole masts had been replaced in 1787 after mast contracts with New England had been terminated. The ship was also repainted with the black and yellow ochre livery seen today, although the port lids remained yellow. It was later under Nelson's command that the port lids were painted black producing the much imitated 'Nelson chequer' pattern.

1801: By April war had exhausted Britain and France; William Pitt, the Prime Minister, resigned in February, leaving Henry Addington and his government to negotiate peace terms. Moreover Napoleon's ambitions were destroyed when the Danes were defeated at Copenhagen on 2 April.

1803-1804: While *Victory* was still completing her 'great repair', it was predictable that hostilities with France would re-open, thus on 14 March 1803 orders were issued to Chatham to have her fitted for sea. *Victory* was recommissioned under Captain Samuel Sutton on 9 April and undocked two days later. Her refit had cost £70,933, 66 per cent higher than estimated. After storing and embarking, her ordnance was inspected and officially accounted for on 28 April 1803.[131] Her armament now comprised thirty 32 pounders, twenty-eight 24 pounders, thirty long 12 pounders on her upper gun deck, twelve short 12 pounders on her quarter deck and two medium 12 pounder carriage guns and two 24 pounder carronades on her forecastle. The six 18 pounder carronades mounted on her poop had been removed. Reduced by 15 per cent, *Victory*'s broadside weight was now 1,092 pounds (491.4 kgs). Sutton sailed for Portsmouth on 14 May. That same day Nelson was appointed Commander-in-Chief Mediterranean Fleet. Two days later war with France was declared and when *Victory* arrived at Portsmouth on 18 May, Nelson, now a Vice-Admiral of the White, hoisted his flag at her foremast.[132] *Victory*, however, had been provisionally appointed for Admiral William Cornwallis, commanding the Channel Fleet already stationed off Ushant blockading Brest. As *Victory* was not yet ready and because Nelson needed to get into the Mediterranean quickly, he lowered his flag two days later and took passage in *Amphion* commanded by Captain Thomas Masterman Hardy. Before leaving, Nelson told Sutton that should Cornwallis not wish to transfer into *Victory* Sutton should join him off Toulon. Hoisting Cornwallis's blue flag, Sutton sailed. On reaching Ushant Cornwallis ordered Sutton to give *Victory* to Nelson, taking with her six of Cornwallis's hall chairs, which, not being returned to their owner, have remained in *Victory* to this day. Sutton reached Nelson's fleet cruising off Cape Sicié at the end of July. Nelson, taking Hardy with him as his flag captain, immediately transferred into *Victory* on 31 July. It is at this point that Nelson and *Victory* became synonymous. Hardy's log, commencing Sunday 31 July states: 'Joined this Ship and superseded Capt[n]. Sutton hoisted L[d]. Nelson's Flag employed getting on Board Lord Nelson's Baggage frm [sic] y[e] *Amphion*'. Sutton shifted into *Amphion*. For the next 18 months *Victory*, with ten other 'liners' and two frigates, cruised off Cape St Sebastian and Cape Sicié, methodically blockading the French fleet in Toulon. When needing to effect repairs or replenish, Nelson's ships periodically retreated to the Gulf of Palma, Sardinia, or the safe Corsican anchorages of Pulla Roads, Cagliari or Agincourt Sound off the island of Magdelena.[133]

1805: When Nelson received news on 4 April that Villeneuve had finally escaped from Toulon, he wasted no time, ordering his ships to weigh. Believing that the French were proceeding to Egypt, *Victory* and her consorts sailed for Sicily. Hearing nothing there of Villeneuve's whereabouts, Nelson sailed west, reaching Gibraltar on 7 May and then north, but to no avail. Five days later Nelson and his squadron commenced the long chase to the West Indies and back. *Victory* reached Barbados on 3 June and finding that Villeneuve had headed back to Europe, Nelson sailed in pursuit. Anchoring briefly at Gibraltar on 19 July, Nelson 'went on shore for the first time since the 16th June, 1803, and for wanting my foot out of the *Victory*, two years and ten days'. Reaching Ushant on Friday 16 August (ship's time) Nelson handed his fleet over to Cornwallis and, utterly worn out and overdue a rest, sailed for home. When *Victory* finally anchored at Spithead Tuesday 20 August and Nelson went ashore, Hardy wrote in the log, 'At 9 hauled Down Lord Nelson's Flag'. *Victory*'s crew commenced refitting her masts, rigging and sails, undertaking minor hull and internal repairs and landing her guns at the Gun Wharf for inspection.[134]

Friday 13 September *Victory* unmoored, made sail and anchored in St. Helens. Next day, when Nelson returned to the ship at 11.30. a.m, Hardy wrote, 'Hoisted the Flag of the Right Hon[ble]. Lord Nelson KB &c.', then on Sunday 15 September he wrote; 'At 6 Weighed & made sail... Light Breezes from the SSE... *Euryalus* in Company'. *Victory*, bearing her great commander, slipped down the Solent into the English Channel and on Sunday 29 September, 'At 10 joined the Fleet off Cadiz under the Command of Vice Admiral Collingwood'.[135]

Very little happened in *Victory* for the next three weeks until signals from the inshore squadron revealed on Saturday 18 October that Villeneuve's combined fleet was hoisting and crossing their yards ready to sail. Next day Hardy states little in the log except that after they had 'Shifted the Main Top Sail', he punished ten seamen with 36 lashes each, all for drunkenness. Within 48 hours these men would be in battle.

TRAFALGAR

Victory's terse log, commencing at noon on Monday 21 October 1805, states:

> Light Breezes and Squally with rain. At 2 Taken aback came to the wind on the Starboard Tack. At 4 Wore ship and up Top Gall[t.] Yards – Look out Ships making signals of the Enemy's Position – At 8.40 Wore Ship at 12 D[o] Weather At 4 wore ship – At 6 Observed the Enemy bearing EbS Dist. 10 or 11 Miles bore up to the East[wd] out all reef Topsails, set steering Sails and Royals – cleared for Quarters.[136]

As the 'Trafalgar dawn' emerged, Villeneuve's combined Franco-Spanish fleet, a myriad of masts silhouetted against a reluctant autumn sun, lay to the east. Numbering 33 ships of the line carrying some 30,000 men and 2,632 guns, Villeneuve stood his fleet towards the Straits of Gibraltar. At last able to do battle after many frustrating months, the British fleet was going into action. Nelson telegraphed signal number 72, ordering his fleet to get into formation behind its respective lead ships, *Victory* (100) and *Royal Sovereign* (100), followed by 76, 'Bear up and sail large ENE'. At 6.22 a.m. *Victory* hoisted signal number 13, 'Prepare for Action'. Nelson signalled further instructions at 6.45 a.m. directing his fleet to 'Come round two points to starboard and steer East'. *Victory*'s log continues:

> At 8 Light Breezes and Cloudy Body of the Enemys Fleet EbS Dist. 9 or 10 Miles – Mile [word in singular repeated erroneously in the log] Still Standing for the Enemys van The *Royal Sovereign* and her Line of Battle steering for the Centre of the Enemys Line – The Enemys Line extending about NNE and SSW At 11.40 *Royal Sovereign* commenced firing in the Enemy they having began on her At 11.30 –.

Whether this means the *Royal Sovereign* was under fire as early as 11.30 a.m.

or that another event happening at 11.30 was not recorded remains a mystery. However a separate note made on the left hand page of *Victory*'s log states: 'At Noon Commenced Action with Combined Fleets cape Trafalgar bore EbS Dist. 5 Leagues'.[137]

Victory's crew had gone to quarters at 11 a.m. and piped to dinner shortly after, taking their meal of 'pork and wine' at their guns. At 11.25 a.m. *Victory* hoisted Nelson's famous signal, 'England Expects that Every Man will do his Duty' in eleven separate hoists to the head of the mizzen mast, immediately followed by Nelson's last signal, number 16: 'Engage the enemy more closely', which remained flying until shot away during the mêlée. At 11.40 the opening broadside was fired from *Fougueux* (74) and ten minutes later *Victory*, still unable to bring her guns to bear, came under heavy fire from the augmented guns of *Fougueux* (74), *Héros* (74), *Santisima Trinidad* (130), *Bucentaure* (80) and *Redoutable* (74). Double headed shot carried away *Victory*'s mizzen topmast, round shot peppered *Victory*'s fore topsail and smashed the yard, carried away her studding sails and brought down her fore topgallant mast. One ball also smashed the steering wheel, fortunately without loss of life. *Victory* was temporarily out of control but this was allayed as the Master, Mr Atkinson, went to the gun room to organise secondary steering, using 20 men a side to haul on tackle rigged to the tiller. It is believed that helm orders were shouted down to Atkinson but this might not have been the case; it is possible that *Victory* was fitted with copper speaking tubes from the quarter deck to the tiller position. Recent research has revealed that ships refitting in 1803 were furnished with such devices and there is no reason why *Victory* could not have been so fitted. Speaking tubes would explain how *Victory* effortlessly negotiated her counter-turn to pass through the enemy line.

Victory's log Tuesday 22 October commences:

> Light Airs and Cloudy Standing towards the Enemy Van, with all Sails set, At 4 Minutes past 12 opened our Fire on the Enemys Van in passing down their Line At 12.20 In attempting to pass through their Line fell on board the 10th & 11th Ships when the action became General.[138]

As *Victory* crossed *Bucentaure*'s stern she fired her larboard 68 pounder carronade loaded with one round shot and a canister of 500 musket balls, followed by every broadside gun as it bore. The blast from *Victory*'s double shotted volley mercilessly cut a swathe through the crowded decks of the French flagship, carrying death and destruction. Twenty guns were dismounted and 325 Frenchmen fell dead or disabled. While *Victory* poured shot into Villeneuve's flagship, she unavoidably ran aboard *Redoutable*'s larboard side and getting entangled, the two ships, locked in deadly combat, drifted to leeward. Embraced muzzle to muzzle, both ships fought ferociously, the British seamen manning *Victory*'s starboard battery dashing buckets of water out through the ports as they fired their guns to prevent the burning wads catching *Redoutable* ablaze. Well trained by *Redoutable*'s commander Captain Jean-Jacques Lucas, the French crew maintained a fierce fusillade of musketry fire from their main, fore, and mizzen tops onto the decks of *Victory*, most directed towards the quarter deck, the nerve centre of the ship. Lucas' men also lobbed over 200 grenades, their sharp explosions scattering *Victory*'s defenders for cover and causing more casualties. Small fires broke out on *Victory*'s forecastle but were soon extinguished. Amid the affray Nelson and Hardy unpretentiously paced the quarter deck. Then, as they turned by the hatchway, tragedy stuck. *Victory*'s log states: 'About 1.15 the Right Hon[ble]. Lord Visc[t]. Nelson KB and Commander in Chief was wounded in the shoulder'.[139] Hit by a musket ball fired from *Redoutable*'s mizzen top, Nelson fell to his knees on the spot where his secretary had fallen earlier. Instantly Marine Sergeant Secker, Able Seaman James Sharman, and one other rushed to support the admiral. Nelson told Hardy, 'They have done for me at last, Hardy', adding, 'my backbone is shot through'. As the admiral was carried below to the after cockpit, Midshipmen Pollard and Collingwood turned their muskets towards *Redoutable*'s mizzen top, their volley despatching all the Frenchmen manning it.[140]

Although most of *Victory*'s upper deck 12 pounders were now out of action, her larboard battery continued firing into *Santisima Trinidad* and *Bucentaure*. Still tangled with *Victory*, *Redoutable* drifted south east, colliding with *Téméraire*. Believing *Victory* to be in difficulty, Captain Harvey fired his larboard guns and 32 pounder carronades into Lucas's ship. Thinking that *Redoutable* was ready to surrender, *Victory* momentarily ceased firing. *Téméraire*'s guns created more carnage within his ship, but Lucas refused to surrender and prepared to board *Victory*. Ordering the slings of his main yard to be cut, the yard crashed down upon the *Victory*'s waist, forming a bridge over which hordes of French seamen clambered while others succeeded in getting onto *Victory*'s starboard anchors. Instantaneously Captain Charles Adair called up his marines from *Victory*'s lower decks to repulse the attack. The ensuing skirmish was bloody: 19 officers and men were killed and 22 wounded, Adair included, fatally shot by a musket ball through his neck. For a brief moment it appeared that *Victory* would be overwhelmed but carronades swiftly obliterated the enemy boarders with grape shot. Reopening fire, Lieutenants Williams, King Yule and Brown ordered *Victory*'s guns to be depressed and loaded with reduced charges to prevent shot passing through *Redoutable* into *Téméraire*. *Victory*'s treble shotted guns ripped into *Redoutable*, penetrating her orlop and starting fires. Totally crippled and with rising casualties, *Redoutable* finally capitulated.[141]

The capture of *Redoutable* had been hard earned. *Victory*'s log states,

> At 1.30 the *Redoutable* having Struck her Colours we ceased firing our Starboard Guns but continued engaged with the *Santissima Trinidad* and some of the Enemy's Ships on the Larboard Side Observed the *Téméraire* between the *Redoutable* and another French Ship of the Line both of which had Struck - the Action continued General until 3 o'clock when several of the Enemy's Ships around had Struck- Observed the *Royal Sovereign* with the Loss of her Main and Mizen Masts and several of the Enemy Ships around her dismasted At 3.30 Observed 4 Sail of the Enemy's Van, Tack and stand along our Weather Line to Windward fired our Larboard Guns at those that would would reach At 3.40 made the Signal for out Ships to keep their Wind and engage the Enemys Van coming along our Weather Line - At 4.15 - The Spanish Rear Admiral to Windward Struck to some of our ships, which had Tacked after them.[142]

The Spanish ship referred to was *Santa Ana* (112).

On *Victory*'s orlop Chevalier, Nelson's servant, fearing that his Lordship was near to death, summoned Surgeon Beatty. While Beatty took Nelson's hand and felt his pulse and cold forehead the admiral opened his eyes briefly, then peacefully closed them. The surgeon left to help the wounded but after five minutes when Beatty was recalled, Chevalier announced that 'he believed his Lordship had expired" It was 4.30 p.m. when, according to Beatty, Nelson died.

Victory's log continues:

> Observed one of the Enemy's Ships blow up and 14 sail of the Enemys' Ships standing to the Southward - Partial Firing continued untill 3.40 when a Victory having been reported to the Right Hon[ble]. Viscount Lord Nelson KB and Commander in Chief he died of his Wound.

There is a time difference of about one hour between *Victory*'s log and Beatty's account of Nelson's death; this is clearly shown by the time given for *Achille* blowing up which differs considerably with other ships' logs. *Victory*'s log then reports:

> At 5 the Mizen Mast fell about 10 feet above the Poop The Lower Masts, Yards, and Bowsprit all crippled - Rigging and Sails very much cut - The Ships around us much crippled Several of our Ships pursuing the Enemy to Leeward Saw Vice Admiral Collingwoods flag flying on board H.M. Ship *Euryalus* and some of our ships taking Possession of the Prizes - Struck Top Gall[t]. Mats, Got up runners and tackles to secure the Lower Masts Employed clearing the Wrecks of the Yards and rigging - Wore Ship and Sounded in 32 fm Sandy

Bottom - Stood to the Southward under the Remnants of the Fore sails and Mizen Top Sail, Sounded from 13 to 19 fm. At 2 Wore Ship At Day Light Saw our Fleet and Prizes 43 sail in Sight still closing with our Fleet - At 6 cape Trafalgar bore SEbE Dist. 4 or 5 Leagues - At 6.30 Saw 3 of the Enemy's Ships to Leeward standing towards Cadiz Fresh Breezes and Cloudy - Employed Knotting the fore and main Rigging and Fishing and securing the Lower Masts Struck the Fore Top Mast for a Fish for the Fore mast which was very badly wounded - at Noon Fresh Breezes and Hazy -.[143]

Casualties in *Victory* were high: 54 dead rising to 57, three men dying later of their wounds. As for the wounded, the final number was 102, as 27 more men were reported to Beatty after he made his official return of 75.

Necessitated by the rising storm, work proceeded to get *Victory* into a seaworthy state. On Wednesday 23 October the seamen 'bent a Fore Sail for a Main Sail, the old Main Sail Shot all to Pieces…Watch employed, Woolding the Lower Masts &c.…bent a Main Top Sail old one Shot to Pieces - Got a Jib Boom up and rigged for a Jury Mizen - Employed securing the Masts, Yards and Rigging - Carpenters Employed stopping the Shot Holes &c as necessary'. Meanwhile *Victory* was making 12 inches (30 cm) of water in the hold hourly, her chain pumps continuously manned. Afterwards, 'clearing the wreck of the Mizen Mast', on Thursday 24 October, *Victory* encountered 'Strong Gales and Heavy Squalls with rain and a Heavy Sea from the West…At 11 HM Ship *Polyphemus* took us in tow'. Still; Setting up the fore Rigging', on Friday they 'Got up a Jurry Fore Top Mast and a Main Top Gall.t Yard for a Fore Top Sail Yard and bent the Mizen Top Sail for a Fore Top Sail…At 9.20 Wore, Observed a Ship on Fire astern, At 9.45 she blew up'.[144] This could have been one of two prizes; *Intrépide* or *San Agustin*, which unable to endure the storm had to be burnt. Alternatively it was either *Indomptable* or *Rayo* which went ashore and burnt.

On Saturday 26 October *Victory* fared poorly in the storm: 'At 4.15 Heavy Squalls, At 5.10 Carried away the Main Yard - Split the Main Top Sail and Main Sail all to Pieces…*Polyphemus* increased her Distance from us Supposing the Hawser had Parted - Hard Gales and a Heavy Swell from the WSW Bent a Fore sail and Set the main Stay Sail'. With her tow rope parted, *Victory* was now left to her own devices. Next morning Hardy recorded that seaman Henry Cramwell (Seaman) died of his battle wound and *Africa* was seen with all her masts gone sending distress signals. After setting up a jury main yard and fitting the main topsail yard, *Neptune* (98) took *Victory* in tow; also on Sunday James Gordon, one of *Victory*'s 31 boys, died of his wounds. Still off Trafalgar Monday 28 October, *Victory*'s ordeal was not over: again the tow rope parted and *Neptune* 'Carried away her Fore Top Mast'. Finally reaching Gibraltar on Tuesday 29 October (Log time), *Victory* anchored in Rosia Bay at 7 a.m. Next morning Midshipman Palmer died from his wounds.[145]

Refitted with jury masts, *Victory* sailed on Monday 4 November for Portsmouth, later accompanied by *Belleisle* and *Bellerophon*. After entering the English Channel on Sunday 1 December, *Victory* was taken in tow the next day by *Warrior* (74). Finally, at 10 o'clock on Thursday 5 December (log time), she anchored at Spithead.[146] Over the next few days the ship was pressed with visitors, amongst whom was the artist Arthur Devis, commissioned by Nelson's prize agent Alexander Davidson to paint the renowned work, 'The Death of Nelson'. The original worked up canvas is on public display within *Victory* today. The painting has since raised a debate about the place where Nelson died.[147] After provisioning, *Victory*, still with Nelson's body on board, sailed for Chatham on Wednesday 11 December. Mooring in the Swin on Monday 23 December, *Victory*'s log states memorably: 'Came alongside Commissioner Grays Yacht from Sheerness & rec.d the Remains of the late Lord Viscount Nelson KB and Vice Admiral of the White'. Nelson's body, now contained in a casket, was conveyed up the Thames in the yacht *Chatham* to Greenwich. Later proceeding up the Medway, *Victory* moored at the 'Lower Part of Long Reach' on Christmas Day and commenced disembarking her guns, powder and shot.[148]

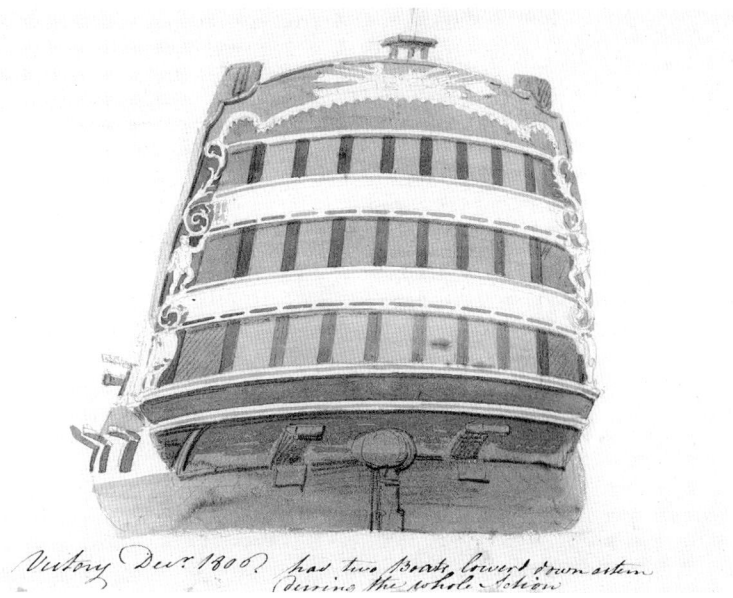

Victory. Sketch by John Livesay, Drawing Master at the Royal Naval Academy in Portsmouth, dated December 1806. Original caption says 'had two Boats lowered down astern during the whole action'. *(Courtesy of the Royal Naval Museum)*

1806: Wednesday 1 January started badly when 'Will.m Patterson was killed by a Fall out of the fore Top on the Forecastle'. Over the next two weeks most of *Victory*'s crew were transferred into the ships *Ocean, Gleyheid Bloodhound, Mariner*. After disembarking 'the Marines to head Quarters' at Chatham on Wednesday 15 January 1806, Hardy 'hauled the Pendant Down', and paid off the ship.[149]

Docked at Chatham on 6 March, *Victory* commenced refitting, overseen by Master Shipwright Robert Seppings. While inspecting the battle damage to her flat vulnerable beakhead bulkhead, Seppings, an ingenious innovative man later to be Surveyor of the Navy, conceived the design of building ships with what was later termed the 'round bow'.[150] With her copper replaced and completed at a cost of £9,936, *Victory* was undocked on 3 May.[151] Afterwards her ordnance was altered; 8 of the quarter deck short 12 pounders being substituted with 32 pounder carronades and all her forecastle guns replaced with just two 32 pounder carronades, giving her a broadside weight of 1,180 lbs.

1807: During this year the ship was docked twice; once on 23 April to have her copper dressed and re-nailed at a cost of £3,488 with £317 covering labour costs, and again on 18 November. During this second docking, lasting nearly six weeks, *Victory* was refitted and reduced to a 2nd rate ship of 98 guns at a total cost of £12,148.[152]

1808: *Victory* was recommissioned at Chatham Sunday 31 January under Captain John Serrell (often written Searle) who wrote in his log, 'Joined the Ship and took Command received the Crew of the *Pompée* leave of absence P.r Admiralty Order for 14 Days PM D.o W.r the remaining part of the Crew employed in the Hulk'.[153] Serrell was superseded within two months. On Saturday 5 March 1808 *Victory* completed her 'Account of Iron Ordnance' ,after embarking her guns. Not only was her ordnance reduced, all 24 pounders were replaced with lighter 18 pounders to lessen the weight borne by her aged hull and, to allow smaller gun crews leaving more space for carrying troops when required.[154]

Lower gun deck	= Thirty 32 pounder carriage guns
Middle gun deck	= Twenty-eight 18 pounder carriage guns
Upper gun deck	= Thirty long 12 pounder carriage guns
Quarter deck	= Eight 32 pounder carronades
Forecastle	= Two medium 12 pounder carriage guns

Broadside weight = 1052 lbs

Captain Philip Dumaresq entered the ship on 22 March and superseded John Serrell.[155] Dumaresq would remain in *Victory* while she served as flagship for Vice-Admiral Sir James Saumarez Bt KB during the Baltic campaigns. Embarking provisions at Spithead on Thursday 17 November, *Victory* received orders to sail for Spain to assist evacuating General Sir John Moore's army from Corunna. She sailed on Saturday 10 December with *Barfleur* (98) in company.[156]

Retreating from the French army, Moore reached Corunna on 11 December and prepared to withdraw his army by sea at Vigo. Although Moore and Sir David Baird, his second in command, were overwhelmed, they defeated Marshall Soult's advancing forces during their final rearguard action, on 16 December. Moore was mortally wounded. *Victory* and her consorts arrived off Vigo just two days later.[157]

1809: On 12 January *Victory* sailed from Vigo Bay with a convoy of transports. Anchoring off Corunna at 11.30 a.m. on Sunday 15 January, Dumaresq wrote, 'found lying here HMS *Tonnant* bearing the Flag of Rear Adm^l. De Courcey out all boats'. Like the evacuation of the British Expeditionary Forces from Dunkirk in 1940, *Victory* rescued Moore's army, her log states: 'Boats emp^d. embarking Troops Observed a firing on Shore between the British and French armies'. Next day Dumaresq wrote: 'Observed a heavy fire of Artillery & Musquetry between the 2 Armies, which lasted till Dark. Rece'd wounded Troops and a party of the 81st Regm^t. & their Baggage Found that Genl. Sir Jno. Moore had been kill'd & Sir Dav^d. Baird severely wounded'. While *Victory*'s carpenters were 'fitting up a Berth on the Main Deck for the Sick & Wounded Soldiers' on Tuesday 17 January, her crew, still embarking soldiers, saw the French army advance towards the remaining troops on shore and open fire on the British ships.[158] *Victory* sailed shortly after, returning to England on 23 January. After disembarking the troops she sailed for the Nore to make minor repairs and prepare for another deployment in the Baltic.[159] On Thursday 27 April, after Vice-Admiral Sir James Saumarez, with his Captain of the Fleet, Captain (later Admiral Sir) George Hope, entered the ship, *Victory* made sail with '*Minotaur & Owen Glendower* in C^o.', for Sweden and arrived at Winga Sound near Karlskrona on Monday 8 May. Besides *Minotaur*, the other Trafalgar ship present was *Téméraire*.[160] Two log books were maintained in *Victory*, Dumaresq's and Hope's. To thwart Napoleon's Treaty of Tilsit, Saumarez's objectives were to maintain diplomatic relations with Sweden, keep the Baltic trade lines open, blockade the Russian fleet at Kronstadt and watch over the Danes; *Victory* became virtually a floating embassy. In May the ship was indirectly involved in the capture of the Danish island of Anholt before returning to Karlskrona on Sunday 4 June, anchoring near *Bellerophon* (74) and *Implacable* (74), formerly the French *Duguay Trouin*.[161] Remaining in the Baltic, *Victory* sailed home late September.[162]

1810: *Victory* was docked at Portsmouth on Wednesday 24 January and re-launched 12 February. During this refit *Victory* had her copper replaced which, with all other work, amounted to £11,043.[163] Evidence suggests that during this refit *Victory* was first fitted with beam end chocks and Robert's iron plate knees to replace defective wooden hanging knees.[164] Sailing on 28 April, *Victory* returned to the Baltic under Saumarez's flag, arriving at Hawke Roads, Anholt, on Saturday 22 May; then to Wingo Sound. She remained operating between these two places until the end of November 1810, when she returned to home waters. Arriving at Spithead on Tuesday 11 December, Saumarez struck his flag and temporarily quitted the ship. With a number of guns removed, *Victory* was temporarily converted into a troopship.[165]

1811: Having embarked troops of the 42 Regiment of Foot to reinforce Wellington's army in the Peninsula Campaign and hoisting the flag of Rear Admiral Yorke, *Victory* sailed for Lisbon on Wednesday 30 January. In company were *Formidable* (90), the 74 gun ships *Ganges*, *Orion*, *Pompée*, and *Revenge*, the 44 gun ships *Argo* and *Vengeur* (44), the 36 gun frigates *Fisgard* and *Ethalion*, the 10 gun brig-sloop *Primrose* and transports. When *Victory* returned to Spithead on Tuesday 26 March 1811, Admiral Yorke lowered his flag and quitted the ship, after which she was reconverted and re-armed.[166] Saumarez re-hoisted his flag on 2 April and sailed for the Baltic in late April, reaching Wingo Sound on 2 May. Here *Victory* remained until September, supporting amphibious assaults.[167]

PROGRESS BOOK – VICTORY 1st RATE OF 100 GUNS:

At what Port	Arrived	Docked	Coppered
Chatham	Began	23 July 1759	
Chatham		7 Mar 1768	Graved March 1768
Chatham		18 May 1771	Graved October 1771
Chatham	1775		
Chatham	Feb 1778		
Plymouth	Aug 1778		
Portsmouth	April 1779		
Portsmouth	March 1780		
Portsmouth	Nov 1782		
Portsmouth	Dec 1787		
Portsmouth	1789		
Portsmouth	Feb 1791		
Portsmouth	Dec 1792		
Portsmouth	Dec 1794		
Chatham	Dec 1797		
Chatham	Feb 1800		
Chatham	24 Dec 1805	6 March 1806	Copper taken off March; Re-coppered April 1806
Chatham		23 April 1807	Dressed & Re-nailed Copper
Chatham		18 Nov 1807	Copper Repaired
Portsmouth	22 Dec 1809	24 Jan 1810	Copper taken off Jan Re-coppered Feb 1810
Portsmouth	4 Dec 1812	26 Mar 1814	Copper taken off Mar 1810; Re-coppered Jan 1816
Portsmouth			Completed Housing over 1820
Portsmouth		26 June 1823	Copper taken off and. Re-coppered
Portsmouth		Taken in Hand Dec 1823 & Completed Aug 1824	
Portsmouth		27 May 1827	Shifted 6 Upper Strakes of Copper each side
Portsmouth			Copper Repaired January 1832
Portsmouth		16 Sep 1836	Copper Repaired
Portsmouth			Shifted defective Copper on Bottom
Portsmouth			Copper repaired July 1757 Defects to 31 March
Portsmouth		18 Sep 1757	Repaired 3 Strakes of copper; Re-coppered the bottom
Portsmouth			Removed Pillars from Hold to make a Table for Model of Battle of Trafalgar
Portsmouth			
Portsmouth			

ADDITIONAL ENTRIES NOT GIVEN IN THE ORIGINAL PROGRESS BOOKS

Portsmouth		1888	Copper Repaired & Replaced
Portsmouth			Copper Repaired
Portsmouth			*Placed in No 2 Dock 12 January 1922*
Portsmouth	*Taken in Hand and commenced Large Repair 1960 and completed December 2004*		

1812: On 6 January 1812 Captain Lewis Shepheard took command of the ship while she remained in home waters, with Dumaresq resuming command when she sailed under Saumarez's flag for the Baltic. By September the Baltic campaign was over. Recalled home, *Victory* arrived at Spithead on Saturday 1 November where she remained for a month removing guns and stores ready to pay off. Sailing for her last time on Friday 4 December, *Victory* entered Portsmouth harbour where she continued de-storing, removing ballast, and taking down her topmasts. After cleaning ship and drafting the ship's company into *Royal William* on Thursday 17 December, Dumaresq's last log entry on Friday 18 December reads: 'Moderate breezes and Snowy weather Emp^d. returning the remaining stores to the Victualling Office & Dock Yard etc'.[168] *Victory* was now 47 years old.

Source: ADM 180/2 Folio 11 and 180/10

Launched or Undocked	Sailed	Built or Nature of Repair	Cost of Hull, Masts & Yards Materials £	Workmen £	Cost of Masts & Yards Materials £	Workmen £	Cost of Rigging & Stores Materials £	Workmen £	Grand Total £
7 May 1765		Built	57,748. 1s. 7d				5,426. 1s. 5d.		63,174. 3s. 0d
21 March 1768	–	Trien. Trimming ?							
10 Oct 1771		Small Repair	4,276. 9s. 9d.						4,276. 9s. 9d.
		Repair Defects							3,075
April 1778		Fitted							13,296
		Repaired							
		Refitted							8,301
		Refitted							8,941
March 1783		Repaired & Refitted						15,372	
April 1788		Large Repair							37,523
		Fitted							6,451
		Repair defects							3,376
Feb 1793		Refitted							8,177
Feb 1795		Repair							13,154
		Fitted for a Hospital Ship							
April 1803		Large Repair							70,933
3 May 1806		Refitted	4,005	1,977	3,504	241		209	9,936
24 April 1807		Fitted	3,488	317	206	31	–	–	4,042
30 Dec 1807	1 April 1808	Reduced to a 98 Gun Ship and Fitted	253	287	714	62	10,822	10	12,148
12 Feb 1810	17 March 1810	Refitted	2,041	1,183	443	13	7,289	74	1,043
Housed Jan 1816		Between Middling and Large Repair	61,615	14,512	3,223	44	204	174	79,772
25 Aug 1823		Defects made good	1,381	1,193	–	28	–	–	2,602
		Fitted for a Guardship	3,817	1,917	3,025	34	8,103	24	17,010
			635	451	83	4	1,409	39	2,621
		Total for Guardship	4,452	2,368	3,108	38	9,512	63	19,631
9 June 1827		Defects made good	2,046	964	12	35	1,150	82	4,289
		Defects	1,564	1,059	8	24	3,054	209	5,918
7 Nov 1836		Fitted for the Captain of the Ordinary	328	254	–	–	392	70	1,044
			548	878	160	33	1,628	58	3,305
			590	549	28	–	2,860	35	3,882
		Total for Do. Ordinary	1,466	1,681	188	33	4,700	163	8,231
8 April 1854		Defects to 31 March 1856	2,067	2,327	118	–	7,182	–	11,694
9 160 - 1 636 - 916									
13 April 1858		Defects							
		Refitted	3,200	3,244	924	–	2,074	–	9,442
		Defects Aug 1859 in Commission	253	176	3	–	1,125		1,557
	Expenses to 31 March 1860		As above				As above		
	First Cost, Built & Fitted for Sea; from 1759 to 1778		See abstract of Progresses No.3						
	Subsequent Repairs from 1778 to 1803		See abstract of Progresses No.3						
	Subsequent Repairs from 1805 to 1860		87,950	31,448	13,001		48,822		181,221
		Defects							
		Docked to repair collision damage							

to Restore the ship to her 1805 Condition and completed 1928.

Author's Note: This table has been extended beyond Progress Book date of 1860 to reflect recent works undertaken.

COMMANDING OFFICERS OF *VICTORY*: 1778-1827

Commander	Time of Entry	Time of Discharge	On what Occasion
Sir John Lindsay	9 Apr 1778	15 May 1778	*Prince George*
Jonathan Faulknor	14 May 1778	27 Mar 1779	Superseded
Henry Collins	28 Mar 1779	12 May 1780	Ditto
John Clayton	13 May 1780	16 Apr 1781	*Centurion*
John Howarth	17 Apr 1781	22 Nov 1781	Superseded
Henry Cromwell	23 Nov 1781	8 Apr 1782	Ditto
John Bourmaster	9 Apr 1782	18 Apr 1782	Ditto
Henry Duncan	19 Apr 1781	5 Dec 1782	Ditto
Roger Curtis	6 Dec 1782	8 Dec 1782	Ditto
Thomas Byard	9 Dec 1782	17 Feb 1783	Paid off at Portsmouth
Charles Hope	1 Oct 1787	5 Dec 1787	Ditto
John Knight	13 May 1790	15 Jan 1791	Ditto
John Knight	16 Jan 1791	2 Sep 1791	Ditto
John Knight	29 Dec 1792	3 Dec 1795	Superseded
George Grey	4 Dec 1795	30 Mar 1797	*Ville De Paris*
Thomas Sotheby	1 Apr 1797	20 June 1797	*Namur*
William Cumming	21 June 1797	26 Nov 1797	Paid off at Chatham
Samuel Sutton	9 Apr 1803	30 July 1803	*Amphion*
Thomas M Hardy	31 July 1803	31 Dec 1803	Next Book
Thomas M Hardy	1 Jan 1804	15 Jan 1806	Paid off at Chatham
John Searle (Serrell)	27 Jan 1808	22 Mar 1808	Superseded
Philip Dumaresq	23 Mar 1808	18 Dec 1812	Paid off at Portsmouth
John Searle (Serrell)	20 Nov 1808	18 Dec 1812	Ditto
Lewis Shepheard	6 Jan 1812	8 Mar 1813	Superseded Recommissioned
Charles Inglis	31 Jan 1824	30 Apr 1827	Paid off

Source: Royal Naval Museum and Admiralty Library.
MSS 248/4 (Vol.4); Ships and their Commanding Officers 1764-1803.
MSS 248/6 (Vol.6); Ships and their Commanding Officers 1804-1823.

1813-1922 On 8 March 1813 Captain Lewis Shepheard officially left *Victory*, even though she was virtually laid up in ordinary.[169] Docked at Portsmouth on 26 March 1814, *Victory* commenced her 'Between middling and large Repair', when she was altered to comply with Seppings' new designs. Completed at a total cost of £79,772, *Victory* came out of dock on 15 January 1816 and was 'housed' before being laid up in ordinary, as war with France had ended. According to the progress book they 'Completed housing over July 1820' which implies that *Victory* had a roof built over to protect her hull. She was again docked in June for two months to have her copper replaced at a cost of £1,381 plus £1,193 for labour. In December 1823 *Victory* was 'Taken in hand' and 'Fitted for a Guardship' at a cost of £17,010.[170] Although not completed until August 1824, records show that she was commissioned again on 31 January under Captain Charles Inglis who remained in the ship until 30 April 1827.[171] Throughout this time *Victory* was employed as flagship for the Port Admiral until paid off again 24 April 1830. For the next year *Victory* served as a residence for the Captain of the Ordinary until October 1831 when she was listed for disposal. However luck again intervened. Hardy, *Victory*'s former commander at Trafalgar, was now First Sea Lord, and, at his wife's request, refused to sign the disposal order, thus giving *Victory* her second reprieve. Recommissioned in October 1831 as flagship for the Port Admiral, *Victory* retained this rôle until paid off August 1836. Commissioned again in 1837, *Victory* then became flagship of the Admiral Superintendent for Portsmouth. During this year *Victory*'s stern acquired the ornate Prince of Wales plume of feathers which were removed from *Prince* (98). Docked again on 18 September 1857, *Victory* had her bottom coppered and re-launched on 13 April 1858. The following year *Victory* was commissioned as flagship of the Commander in Chief, Portsmouth and in 1869 became tender to the *Duke of Wellington* (131) which underwrote the duty of Commander-in-Chief's flagship. During these years *Victory* started to receive public visitors by boat; naval veterans provided unofficial tours, and a small museum developed within the ship. Refitted in 1888, she was re-coppered for the fifteenth and last time and in 1889 she became flagship for the Commander in Chief Naval Home Command.

FLAG OFFICERS (ADMIRALS) OF *VICTORY*: 1778-1812

Flag Rank	Name	From	To
Admiral	The Hon. Augustus Keppel	16 May 1778	28 October 1778
Admiral	Sir Charles Hardy	19 March 1779	14 May 1779
Admiral	Sir Francis Geary	24 May 1780	28 August 1780
Admiral	Sir Francis W Drake	26 September 1780	29 December 1780
Vice Admiral	Hyde Parker	20 March 1781	31 May 1781
Commodore	John Elliot	June 1781	August 1781
Rear Admiral	Richard Kempenfelt	10 September 1781	11 March 1782
Admiral	Lord Richard Howe	20 April 1782	14 November 1782
Admiral	Lord Richard Howe	July 1790	August 1790
Admiral	Lord Alexander Hood	August 1790	August 1791
Rear Admiral	Sir Hyde Parker	6 February 1793	May 1793
Admiral	Lord Alexander Hood	6 May 1793	15 December 1794
Rear Admiral	John Mann	8 July 1795	27 September 1795
Vice Admiral	Robert Linzee	October 1795	November 1795
Admiral	Sir John Jervis	3 December 1795	30 March 1797
Vice Admiral	Lord Horatio Nelson	18 May 1803	20 May 1803
Vice Admiral	Lord Horatio Nelson	July 1803	21 October 1805
Admiral	Sir James Saumarez	18 March 1808	9 December 1808
Admiral	Sir James Saumarez	8 April 1809	December 1809
Admiral	Sir James Saumarez	11 March 1810	3 December 1810
Rear Admiral	Sir Joseph Yorke	December 1810	March 1811
Admiral	Sir James Saumarez	2 April 1811	December 1811
Admiral	Sir James Saumarez	14 April 1812	15 October 1812

Source: HMS *Victory* Curatorial Archives.

Disaster struck in 1903 when *Victory* had to be docked for emergency repairs after being accidentally rammed by *Neptune* which was under tow to the breakers. This event, together with the forthcoming Trafalgar centenary, raised questions about her future, but the First World War intervened. Finally, through a national appeal raised by the Society for Nautical Research, *Victory* was put into her current dock on 12 January 1922 and restored under the authority of the Victory Technical Committee to her 1805 appearance and opened to the public in 1928. In 1955 *Victory* was found to have inherent timber problems and under a re-appointed Victory Advisory Technical Committee (VATC), large sections of her hull were rebuilt, the work completed in 1996. In September 1991 *Victory* appointed her first Keeper and Curator, working as the technical and historical adviser to the ship's Commanding Officer. From this date *Victory* commenced a final restoration programme. Besides internal structural improvements, the ship has been equipped throughout with a vast range of artefacts, weapons, tools and domestic necessities that provide an accurate interpretation of life at sea within Nelson's ships.

Sick berth aboard *Victory*. All British ships of the line had by this period been fitted with sick berths on the starboard side under the forecastle. (*Author's collection*)

Notes to Part 1: Chapter 1

1. Colledge, 1, p. 90
2. Lyon, *Sailing Navy List*, p. 63.
3. TNA: PRO, ADM 180/2 Entry 14.
4. TNA: PRO, ADM 180/2.
5. RNM, MS 248/4.
6. *Ibid.*
7. *Ibid.*
8. Clowes, 3, pp. 509–510.
9. RNM, MS 248/4.
10. *Ibid.*
11. Clowes, 4, p. 203.
12. Clowes, 4, p. 246.
13. Clowes, 4, pp. 272–274.
14. RNM, MS 248/4.
15. RNM, MS 248/4
16. Clowes 4, pp. 309, 316.
17. RNM, MS 248/4.
18. *Ibid.*
19. RNM, MS 248/6.
20. Rnm, ADM 180/10 Entry 6.
21. Pope, *England Expects*, pp. 175–176.
22. TNA: PRO, ADM 51/1552 part 1.
23. *Ibid.*
24. Pope, *England Expects*, p. 196.
25. TNA: PRO, ADM 51/1552 part 1.
26. Pope, *England Expects*, p. 217.
27. TNA: PRO, ADM 51/1552 part 1.
28. *Ibid.*
29. Pope, *England Expects*, p. 265.
30. TNA: PRO, ADM 51/1552 part 1.
31. Pope, *England Expects*, pp. 318–319.
32. James, 4, p. 79; Clowes, 5, p. 158.
33. Clowes, 5, p. 168.
34. TNA: PRO, ADM 51/1552 part 1.
35. *Ibid.*
36. RNM, MS 248/6.
37. TNA: PRO ADM 180/10.
38. TNA: PRO, ADM 180/10.
39. RNM, MS 248/6.
40. TNA: PRO, ADM 180/10 Entry 6.
41. Lyon, p. 104; Colledge, p. 91.
42. TNA: PRO, ADM 180/6 Entry 3; Lyon, p. 10; Colledge, 1, pp. 475, 516.
43. TNA: PRO, ADM 180/6; RNM, MS 248/4.
44. Clowes, 4, pp. 226–230.
45. TNA: PRO, ADM 180/6.
46. RNM, MS 248/4.
47. Clowes, 4, pp. 257–259.
48. TNA: PRO, ADM 180/6.
49. Clowes, 4, pp. 291–292.
50. RNM, MS 248/6.
51. Clowes, 4, p. 176.
52. Clowes, 4, p. 387.
53. TNA: PRO, ADM 180/6 & MS 248/4.
54. RNM, MS 248/6.
55. Clowes, 5, pp. 72–73.
56. RNM, MS 248/6.
57. Clowes, 5, pp. 88–90.
58. Clowes, 5, p. 102.
59. TNA: PRO, ADM 180/10.
60. TNA: PRO, ADM 51/494 part 1; RNM, MS 248/6.
61. TNA: PRO, ADM 51/494 part 1.
62. TNA: PRO, ADM 35.
63. TNA: PRO, ADM 51/4494 part 1.
64. James, 4, pp. 35–36; Clowes, 5, pp. 136–137.
65. TNA: PRO, ADM 51/4494 part 1.
66. James, 4, p. 79.
67. James, 4, p. 87.
68. TNA: PRO, ADM 51/4494 part 1.
69. James, 4, pp. 45–46.
70. TNA: PRO, ADM 51/4494 part 1.
71. *Ibid.*
72. TNA: PRO, ADM 180/10 Entry 9.
73. *Ibid.*
74. RNM, MS 248/6.
75. *Ibid.*
76. TNA: PRO, ADM 180/10 Entry 9.
77. RNM, MS 248/6.
78. RNM, MS 248/6; TNA: PRO, ADM 180/10 Entry 9.
79. *Ibid.*
80. TNA: PRO, ADM 180/10 Entry 9.
81. TNA: PRO, ADM 180/2 folio 11.
82. Goodwin, *Nelson's Ships*, p. 234.
83. TNA: PRO, ADM 180/2 folio 11.
84. *Ibid.*
85. TNA: PRO, ADM 51/1036 part 1.
86. *Ibid.*
87. TNA: PRO, ADM 51/1036 part 1; Goodwin, *Nelson's Ships*, p. 235.
88. TNA: PRO, ADM 51/1036 part 1; RNM MS 248/4.
89. TNA: PRO, ADM 51/1036 part 1.
90. Goodwin, *The Naval Cutter Alert 1777*, p. 12.
91. TNA: PRO, ADM 51/1036 part 1.
92. *Ibid.*
93. *Berwick*, *Defiance* and *Thunderer* would later fight at Trafalgar, although *Berwick* would be under a French flag.
94. TNA: PRO, ADM 51/1036 part 1.
95. *Ibid.*
96. Throughout this period the ship took on considerable stores, the details of which are fully expanded in Goodwin, *Nelson's Ships*, p. 239.
97. TNA: PRO, ADM 51/1036 part 3.
98. TNA: PRO, ADM 51/1036 part 4.
99. TNA: PRO, ADM 51/1036 part 6.
100. TNA: PRO, ADM 51/1036 part 6.
101. Cited in P Goodwin, 'The Influence of Industrial Technology and Material Procurement on the Design, Construction and Development of HMS *Victory*' (M Phil, University of St Andrews, 1998), p. 149.
102. *Ibid.*
103. TNA: PRO, ADM 51/1023 part 4.
104. TNA: PRO, ADM 180 Progress Book.
105. TNA: PRO, ADM 51/1023 part 4.
106. Details are fully expanded in Goodwin, *Nelson's Ships*, p. 241
107. TNA: PRO, ADM 51/1023 part 4.
108. TNA: PRO, ADM 51/1023 part 5.
109. *Ibid.*
110. TNA: PRO, ADM 51/1105/6. Details concerning crew joining the ship and provisioning are well covered in Goodwin, *Nelson's Ships*, p. 243
111. Goodwin, *Nelson's Ships*, p. 120; Clowes, 4, p. 203.
112. Clowes, 4, p. 274; G. Callender, *The Story of HMS Victory*, passim.
113. TNA: PRO, ADM 51/1105 part 6.
114. TNA: PRO, ADM 51/1105 part 6.
115. Clowes, 4, p. 276.
116. TNA: PRO, ADM 51/1105 part 6.
117. All above – Goodwin, *Op Cit*, p. 243.
118. TNA: PRO, ADM 51/1181 part 8. While Grey appears to have misspelt the admiral's surname, it is phonetically correct as the 'e' is in fact pronounced as an 'a'. This fact was clarified by Jervis's descendant who attended the Battle of Cape St Vincent Conference held at Portsmouth in 1997.
119. TNA: PRO, ADM 51/1181 part 8.
120. P Goodwin, *Op Cit*, p. 244; TNA: PRO, ADM 51/1181 part 8.
121. TNA: PRO, ADM 51/1181 part 8.
122. TNA: PRO, ADM 51/1181 part 8; Goodwin *Op Cit* p. 245. The former ship is not to be confused with Nelson's *Minerve*; the latter, formerly the French *Unité*, likewise should not be confused with Nelson's ship of identical name.
123. TNA: PRO, ADM 51/1181 part 8.
124. Clowes, 4, pp. 307–317; Goodwin, *Op Cit*, pp. 138, 245; White, *1797: Nelson's Year of Destiny*, pp. 47–71.
125. TNA: PRO, ADM 51/1186.
126. *Ibid.*
127. TNA: PRO, ADM 51/1207 part 3. For provisioning details, the influence of insurrection, and other daily occurrences for July and August see Goodwin, *Op Cit*, p. 246.
128. *Ibid.*
129. Goodwin, 'The Influence of Industrial Technology'.
130. Steel, *Naval Architecture*; unpublished notes of Goodwin, Keeper & Curator of HMS *Victory*; Minutes of the Victory Advisory Technical Committee 1999 & 2000.
131. TNA: PRO, ADM 160/154, Accounts of Ordnance carried on Ships.
132. Goodwin, *Op Cit*, p. 249.
133. TNA: PRO, ADM 51/4514 part 1. For details see Goodwin, *Nelson's Ships*, pp. 250–254.
134. TNA: PRO, ADM 51/1482 part 6; ADM 51/4514 part 3; Goodwin, *Nelson's Ships*, pp. 254–255, for detailed account of refitting.
135. TNA: PRO, ADM 51/4514 part 3.
136. *Ibid.*
137. TNA: PRO, ADM 51/4514 part 3; Goodwin, *Nelson's Ships*, pp. 257–258; Goodwin, 'The Battle of Trafalgar: A short account in two parts; The Prelude, and The Battle', Unpublished article, 1995.
138. TNA: PRO, ADM 51/4514/ part 3.
139. *Ibid.*
140. Goodwin, *Nelson's Ships* p. 259; Goodwin, 'The Battle of Trafalgar'.
141. Goodwin, *Nelson's Ships* pp. 259–260; Goodwin, 'The Battle of Trafalgar'.
142. TNA: PRO, ADM 51/4514 part 3; Beatty, *The Death of Lord Nelson: The Authentic Narrative*, pp. 47–52.
143. TNA: PRO, ADM 51/4514 part 3.
144. TNA: PRO, ADM 51/4514 part 3.
145. *Ibid.*
146. *Ibid.*
147. Goodwin, 'Where Nelson Died: An Historical Riddle resolved by Archaeology', *Mariner's Mirror*, 1998.
148. TNA: PRO, ADM 51/4514 part 3.
149. ADM 51/4514 part 3.
150. Goodwin, 'The Influence of Industrial Technology'.
151. TNA: PRO, ADM 180/10.
152. TNA: PRO, ADM 180/10.
153. TNA: PRO, ADM 51/1776 part 5.
154. TNA: PRO, ADM 160/154 Accounts of Ordnance carried on Ships. See also the William Rivers Papers, Royal Naval Museum MSS 1998/41/1. (See Goodwin, *Nelson's Ships*, p. 263.)
155. TNA: PRO, ADM 51/1776/5.
156. TNA: PRO, ADM 51/4514 part 7
157. Hume & Smollett, *The History of England*, Vol. 3, London 1857; Chandler, *Dictionary of the Napoleonic Wars*, pp. 107, 287; Haythornthwaite, *Who was Who in the Napoleonic Wars*, p. 222; Goodwin, *Op Cit*, p. 263.
158. TNA: PRO, ADM 51/4514 part 7.
159. TNA: PRO, ADM 51/2934 part 3.
160. TNA: PRO, ADM 51/2934 part 3 & ADM 51/1971 part 6.
161. Goodwin, *Op Cit*, p. 264; TNA: PRO, ADM 51/2934 part 3 and ADM 51/1971 part 6.
162. TNA: PRO, ADM 51/2934 part 4.
163. TNA: PRO, ADM 180/10 folio 10.
164. Goodwin, 'The Influence of Industrial Technology'.
165. TNA: PRO, ADM 51/2934 part 5.
166. TNA: PRO, ADM 51/2934 part 6.
167. TNA: PRO, ADM 51/2934 part 7 & ADM 51/2934 part 8.
168. TNA: PRO, ADM 51/2934 part 10.
169. TNA: PRO, MS 248/6.
170. TNA: PRO, ADM 180/10.
171. RNM, MS 248/6.

PART 1: CHAPTER 2
THE BRITISH SECOND RATE SHIPS

The 98 gun ship *DREADNOUGHT*

The *Dreadnought*, a 2nd rate ship of 98 guns, was the seventh Royal Naval ship to bear this name. The first *Dreadnought* listed was a 40 gun ship which served in 1553. The second *Dreadnought*, a vessel of 450 tons, launched at Deptford on 10 November 1573, was rebuilt in 1592 and again in 1614 when her size was increased to 552 tons. Carrying 41 guns, her initial ordnance comprised two 60 pounders, four 18 pounders, eleven 9 pounders, ten 6 pounders and 12 smaller guns. After a long career, during which she fought against the Spanish Armada in 1588, she was finally broken up in 1648. The third *Dreadnought* was in fact the 52 gun ship *Torrington* of 732 tons built by Johnson at Blackwall in 1654. Renamed *Dreadnought* in 1660 when the monarchy was restored under Charles II, this vessel foundered off the North Foreland on 16 November 1690. The fourth *Dreadnought*, also built by Johnson at Blackwall, was a 4th rate ship of 60 guns launched in 1691 to replace her predecessor. Originally measuring 142 feet in length and 36 feet 6 inches in breadth, she was rebuilt at Blackwall in 1706, her tonnage being increased from 852 to 910 tons. Having been in action and hulked in 1740, she was broken up at Portsmouth on September 1748. The fifth *Dreadnought*, also a 4th rate of 60 guns, was built by Wells and launched at Deptford on 23 June 1742. Much larger than her predecessor, she measured 144 feet on her gun deck, 42 feet in breadth and had a tonnage of 1,093 tons. Seeing service in the War of the Austrian Succession, the Seven Years' War and War of American Independence, this vessel was sold in 1784. The sixth vessel to bear the name of *Dreadnought* was in fact called *Dreadnought Prize*, a sloop 62 feet in length, 21 feet in breadth and 109 tons which was captured from the French by the fifth *Dreadnought* in 1748. This sloop was sold in the same year. After the Trafalgar *Dreadnought* were three further vessels, two of which have had historic importance, *Dreadnought* being the first of the great 17,000 ton battleships introduced in 1906; and *Dreadnought* was the name given to Britain's first nuclear submarine in 1960.[1]

The Trafalgar *Dreadnought*, the seventh of her name, was designed by the Surveyor of the Navy, Sir John Henslow. Ordered on 17 January and again on 22 March 1788, her keel was laid down at Portsmouth dockyard on July 1788 and launched thirteen years later on 13 June 1801. Why building took so long must relate to the priority of refitting of ships already in service. The construction of a 98 gun ship would consume some 5,760 loads (288,000 cubic feet of timber) before conversion into specific components. This figure equates to approximately 5,700 trees, of which 90 per cent was oak, felled from 95 acres of woodland. *Dreadnought* was docked on the same day as her launch to be coppered and re-launched on 15 June. The fact that her bottom was sheathed with some 3,500 plates, each held with 140 copper nails, within two days, is a remarkable achievement. This suggests that the teams of men employed doing this work were large; moreover, scaffolding also had to be erected to permit this work to be undertaken and removed again afterwards. The entire cost for building and fitting out the ship totalled £60,484 of which £53,609 was spent on her hull, masts and yards and £6,875 for rigging and stores.[2]

CAPTAINS OF *DREADNOUGHT* (MSS 248/4 and 248/6)

Name	Time of Entry	Time of Discharge	On What Occasion
James Vashon	23 June 1801	15 July 1802	Paid Off
James Bowen	15 March 1803	7 September 1803	Superseded
Edward Bruce	3 April 1803	7 September 1803	Superseded
John C Purvis	8 September 1801	31 December 1803	New Book
John C Purvis	1 January 1804	12 May 1804	Promoted to Rear Admiral of the Blue
R C Reynolds	13 May 1804	21 August 1804	Superseded
George Reynolds	22 August 1804	14 December 1804	Superseded
Edward Rotheram	15 December 1804	10 October 1804	To the *Royal Sovereign*
John Conn	11 October 1804	12 June 1806	Paid Off
William Lechmere	27 December 1806	8 April 1808	Superseded
George B Salt	9 April 1808	8 January 1810	Superseded
Valentine Collard	9 January 1810	13 September 1810	Superseded
S Hood Singer	14 September 1810	8 December 1812	Paid Off

SERVICE HISTORY

1801: Fitted out, *Dreadnought* was first commissioned under Captain James Vashon on 23 June and deployed with the Channel squadron, but with the war with France drawing to a stalemate, she saw little service.[3]

1802: Not required for service, *Dreadnought* was paid off at Portsmouth by Captain Vashon on 15 July.[4]

1803: With a declaration of war with France imminent, *Dreadnought* was recommissioned under Captain James Bowen on 15 March and made ready for sea. When hostilities with France formally reopened on 16 May, *Dreadnought* was already deployed with the Channel fleet anchored in Cawsand Bay outside Plymouth, awaiting orders to sail. Having already

SPECIFICATIONS: *DREADNOUGHT*

Rate	2nd	Length on the range of the gun deck	185 ft	Ordnance - lower gun deck	28 x 32 pounders
Guns	98	Length of keel for tonnage	152 ft 6⅜ ins	Ordnance - middle gun deck	28/30 x 18 pounders
Class	Dreadnought/Neptune 1788	Extreme breadth	51 ft	Ordnance - upper gun deck	30 x 18 pounders
Designer	John Henslow	Depth in hold	21 ft 6 ins	Ordnance - quarter deck	8 x 12 pounders
Builder	George White	Tons burthen	2110. 53/94	Ordnance - forecastle	2 x 12 pounders
Dockyard	Portsmouth	Draught afore	22 ft 6 ins	Single broadside weight	1030/1048 pounds
Date ordered	17 January and 22 March 1788	Draught abaft	23 ft 6 ins	Fate	1825 Hulked, then became a lazaretto at Pembroke. 1831 sent to Greenwich as a seaman's hospital. 1857 broken up
Date keel laid	July 1788	Complement	750		
Date launched	13 June 1801				

Source: Lyon, *Sailing Navy List*, pp. 106–107.

34

Dreadnought
Sheer Profile 1765   Half Breadth 1765   Stern 1765

(Drawings by the author)

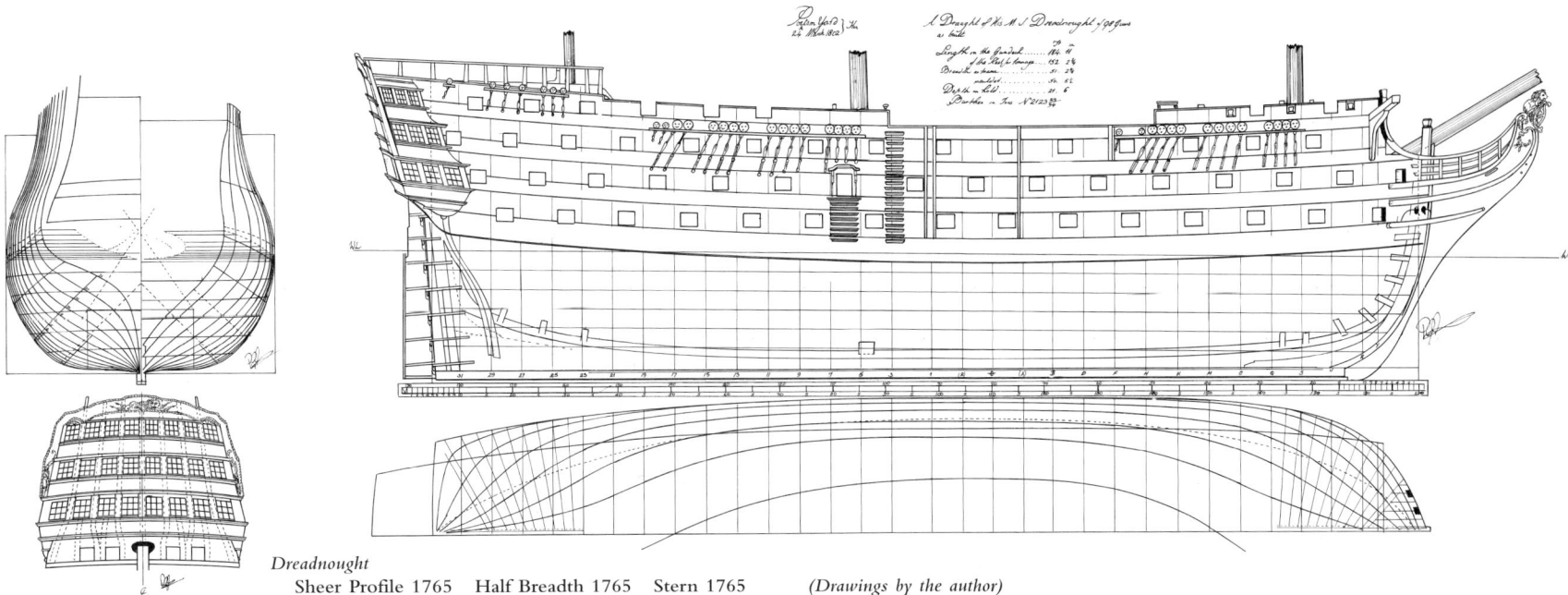

embarked additional stores and provisions, Admiral the Hon. William Cornwallis came on board, hoisted his flag and issued orders for his squadron to sail. Cornwallis's squadron, comprising ten sail of the line and a number of frigates, sailed at 7 p.m. on 17 May to take up station off Ushant to watch over the French fleet within the naval port of Brest. The French ships within Brest comprised six sail of the line ready to sail, eighteen undergoing repairs and three on the stocks still fitting out. Knowing that this blockade would be a lengthy deployment, Cornwallis decided to transfer his flag into the more commodious 112 gun *Ville de Paris* on 9 July.[5] On 8 September Captain Bowen was superseded by Captain John C Purvis, although the ship had been under the temporary command of Edward Bruce since 3 April.[6]

1804: When Captain Purvis was promoted Rear Admiral of the Blue and transferred out of the ship on 12 May, he was superseded by Captain R Reynolds who remained in *Dreadnought* only until 21 August. Taking command the next day, his successor Captain George Reynolds was himself superseded by Captain Edward Rotheram on 15 December.[7] Throughout the year the ship had been stationed on continuous blockade duty off Rochefort on the Atlantic coast of France. The months of working ship within the Bay of Biscay took its toll on the British fleet and its men and *Dreadnought*, now the flagship of Vice-Admiral Cuthbert Collingwood, suffered considerably during the winter gales of mid-November 1804. Constantly leaking, with water entering her magazine, Collingwood remarked 'that I fear there is little serviceable powder' remaining.[8]

1805: Things did not improve; in a letter, received by Admiralty Secretary William Marsden on 6 January 1805, Cornwallis complained bitterly about the condition of his ships: 'It has blown exceedingly hard since that time (3rd December)... both the *Ville de Paris*' tillers have given way, and Captain Guion of the *Prince*, has reported the same.' In a second letter, written two days later, Cornwallis confirmed that further storm damage had affected his ships, stating that Collingwood's *Dreadnought* was the 'only ship of the line I have seen since the 15th of last month, when I put to sea from Torbay with eleven sail of the line', and that his ship 'labours most exceedingly', in a 'great deal of sea or swell'.[9] In March 1805 Cornwallis, under Admiralty orders, made preparations to form a detached squadron under Collingwood to act independently of the Channel fleet. Collingwood, still flying his flag in *Dreadnought*, was given *Tonnant* (80) and three 74s, *Illustrious*, *Mars* and *Minotaur*.[10]

Still flying Collingwood's flag with Captain Rotheram in command, *Dreadnought* received orders to sail south. Parting from Cornwallis's main squadron, *Dreadnought*, together with the two 74s *Achille* and *Colossus*, took up station off Cadiz on 17 July. The object was to prevent any French or Spanish vessels getting into that port.[11] Cruising off Cape St Vincent on 20 August, Collingwood was chased by a number of ships from Villeneuve's fleet which were sailing south after engaging with Admiral Calder's squadron a few weeks earlier. Collingwood, having insufficient ships, was drawn from his station, allowing Villeneuve to get into the safety of Cadiz. All too late, *Mars* (74) joined Collingwood from Tangier at midnight.[12]

Nelson joined Collingwood's squadron off Cadiz on 29 September and assumed overall command, sending orders for Collingwood to turn over into *Royal Sovereign* (100), newly arrived from Plymouth. Consequently on 10 October (ship's log date Friday 11 October) Collingwood, taking Captain Rotheram with him, transferred into the 100 gun ship. *Dreadnought*'s log book notes, 'Moderate W^r Employed shifting Baggage and Occasionally joined Company His Majestys Ship *Belleisle* and *Ætna* Bomb Adm Collingwood left the ship and went into the *Roy^l Sovereign* Captain Conn superseded Captain Rotheram hoisted in the launch and made sail'.[13] *Dreadnought* was very much a Portsmouth ship, for not only did her entire company of marines came from the Portsmouth Division, but her percentage of seamen from Portsmouth was far higher than any other Trafalgar ship.[14] As the combined fleet began to leave Cadiz *Dreadnought*'s log, Saturday 19 October, states, 'saw from the Masthead 15 sail of the Enemys ship[s] in the North q^r made signal to the Admiral for them'.[15]

TRAFALGAR

On Monday 21 October 1805 *Dreadnought*'s log states:

PM Fresh breezes and squally with rain at times at 10.30 sent down TopGallantyards shifted the Foretopsail hived [*sic*] up the Maintopsail to repace [*sic* - replace] at 4 mod^t made and shortened sail occasionally at 7.30 observed sev^l blue lights and Rockets in the ENE q^r. at 10 set the mainsail at 12 D^o W^r. fleet in Company AM at 4 D^o W^r answered the *Victorys* Signal to Wear General Bore up Cleared for Action made all sail to the Enemys Fleet which Consisted of 33 sail of the Line 4 frigates and 2 Brigs at 12 *Victory* made N°. 63 with Preparative N°. 8 27 sail of the Line 4 frigates 1 Schooner and Cutter in Company...

Dreadnought was stationed eleventh in line of Collingwood's leeward division bearing down on the centre and rear of their opponents' line, the *Swiftsure* (74) being more or less abreast to starboard. In command was Captain John Conn, his First Lieutenant John Clavell. A poor sailer, *Dreadnought* lay slightly to windward of the formal line whereby, taking this station, she could draw more wind to sail as fast as her counterparts to get into battle. The ship's log entry for Tuesday 22 October states:

> PM Light airs made all possible sail towards the Enemys Rear at 12.10 Observed the Enemy open a fire on the Roy*l* Sovereign which the Roy Sovereign returned at 12.20 the Roy Sovereign broke their Line near the centre at 12.45 the Victory commenced Action with the Enemys van at 12. 55 Observed the Victorys Mizen T.mast shot away…

Although Collingwood's division were the first ships to engage it was not until after one o'clock that she finally got into action, discharging her broadsides into *San Juan Nepomuceno* and *Principe de Austurias*. The ship's log proceeds:

> At 1.25 the *Dreadnought* Commenced Action with a Spanish three Deck Ship and a 74 at 2 the S*r*. Juan a Spanish 2 Deck Ship Struck to the *Dreadnought*, sent an Officer and Boats Crew to take Possession of her at 12.15 [this time appears to be an error and should perhaps read 2.15] Opened a Fire on a Spanish three Decker, Observed several of the Enemys ships Dismasted and Strike their Colours at 4.5 Repeated 101 General [signal] made and shortened sail Occasionally to get our Guns to bear on the Enemy at 5.15 answered N°. 99 General from *Victory*: at 5.45 observed a French 2 Deck ship Blow up.[16]

With battle over Captain Conn then recorded the aftermath, writing;

> At 6 Saw 4 French Ships of the Line make sail to Windward, at 12 ships of the Line 4 Frigates and 2 Brigs make sail towards Cadiz, Employed sending Men into and taking Prisoners out of the Prize at 7 made sail to the Southward Fleet and several Prizes in Company the Enemy not in sight Employed Knotting and splicing Rigging and shifting the Maintopsail yard which had been shot away at 11 set the Maintopsail at 12 Wore as p*r* Signal Fished the Foreyard at 4 Moderate W*r* Fleet and some Prizes in company at 5.35 Wore as p*r* Signal to take Possession of a Prize at 8 Moderate W*r* Fleet and Prizes in sight at 9 took the French *Swiftsure* in tow Employed occasionally Non Fresh gales Prize in tow the Fleet and ships of the Line Prizes in Company Coniel EBS 5 or 6 Leagues (7 killed and 30 Wounded in Action).[17]

Compared with other British ships *Dreadnought* played a marginal rôle in the battle. Conn's casualty figures were higher than those stated in James and Clowes, both of whom state seven killed but only 26 wounded. Among the wounded were Lieutenant James Lloyd, Midshipmen Andrew McCulloch and James Sabban.[18] As for material damage, besides losing her main topsail yard, her fore yard, as stated in the log, had to be fished. However the storms after the battle further took their toll, *Dreadnought*'s log entry on Wednesday 23 October recording 'Fresh gales and cloudy'. Then Captain Conn 'shortened sail [and] sent down TopGallantyards and struck the TopGallantmasts'. The log then says,

> At 3.30 in Fore and Mizentopsails at 4 D° W*r* the *Swiftsure* in tow shifted the Foretopsail a great part of the Body of it being blown away at 8 Strong breezes and squally, at 8.30 taken aback broke the hawser which broke the White Cutter a Drift and was Lost AM fresh Gales with Lightning at 4 D° W*r* Prizes in sight part of the Fleet in Company 19 sail of the Enemys ships at Anchor and under Weigh, at 10 observed the Enemys Ships under weigh Admiral SBW…[19]

With gales continuing on Thursday 23 October, the ship was under reefed topsails and a main staysail. After the crew 'handed the Topsails' at 9.30 p.m. they 'housed the Middle Deck Guns', the weather all the while being 'strong Gales and Squally with Lightning'. At 8.30 next morning *Dreadnought* hove to, boats were lowered and sent 'to the *Augustine* Spanish Prize for Prisoners at 11.30 in Boats and made sail'. That afternoon they 'shook [down] water casks to make room for the Prisoners'. The prize *San*

PROGRESS BOOK – *DREADNOUGHT* 2nd RATE OF 98 GUNS:

At what Port	Arrived	Docked	Coppered
Portsmouth	Began	July 1788	
Portsmouth		13 June 1801	Coppered June 1801
Portsmouth	5 July 1802		Copper repaired March 1803
Portsmouth	2 June 1806	1 Sep 1806	Copper taken off Sept. Re-coppered Nov 1806
Plymouth	5 May 1810	19 May 1810	Copper Repaired
Plymouth	12 Jan 1812		
Portsmouth	20 June 1812	13 Aug 1812	Copper taken off Aug 1812; Re-coppered Mar 1814
Portsmouth		5 Sep 1815	Copper taken off and Re-coppered
Pembroke	29 Sep 1825		to be a Lazaretto
Woolwich	Sep 1830		
Sheerness	Dec 1830	30 Mar 1831	Copper taken off
Woolwich	May 1831		
Deptford			
Sheerness	28 July 1840	28 July 1840	
Deptford			
Deptford	1 Aug 1840	21 July 1849	
Woolwich	21 July 1849	21 July 1849	Payed the Bottom
Deptford	16 Oct 1849		
Woolwich	24 Feb 1857	24 Feb 1857	
Completed taking to pieces 31 March 1857			

Agustin was then left to her fate. On the Friday Conn records that the mainsail had to be changed and they observed one of the prize ships which had been set on fire blow up at 9.30 p.m. The log also clarifies that the *Dreadnought* mizzen mast had to be fished and after 'making a fish for the Mainmast', they then got the 'Preventer shouds over the Main and Mizenmasthead' to give support where the other lower shrouds had been shot away. To do this, *Dreadnought*'s crew, under the expert leadership of the boatswain, had to send the main and mizzen topgallant masts down on deck, no easy task in squally weather with the sea in a heavy swell. However, such tasks clearly indicate the professional ability of British seamen crews. After noting that *Britannia*, *Neptune* and *Defiance* were in company, *Dreadnought*'s log for Saturday 26 October then records 'AM Moderate and clear set the Fore and Mizentopsails pointed the TopGallantmasts through the Caps Sailmakers repairing shotholes Employ[ed] washing decks'. While shot holes at and below the waterline were plugged by the carpenter's crew using lead sheeting, oakum and conical wooden bungs, holes in the ship's upperworks were generally sealed with patches of tar-covered canvas nailed in place. Carpenters and sailmakers continued their repairs over the next few days and on Tuesday 29 October the seamen 'Bent the sheet cable and new Best Bower' anchor, after which they 'fitted and put over the Head [of the mast] a Spring Stay the other being shot through the Collar'. Further work involved shifting the fore topsail and main spring stay and taking in '5 inches of the Mainstay'. Events recorded on Wednesday: at 6.20 Conn 'observed a Ship on Fire in the EBS Q*r* [quarter]' which 'at 7.40 Blew up'. Conn then recorded at 8.45 a.m. that there was a 'French Frigate and a Brig withe [sic] the Fleet with a Flag of Truce', which parted company at noon under an English frigate.escort. Throughout this week *Dreadnought* plied between Cape Trafalgar and Cape Spartel with *Britannia*. On Monday 4 November *Queen* (100) and sloop *Bittern* (18), which had been built at Buckler's Hard, joined *Dreadnought* after which Conn 'sent a Spanish Commodore and Captain onboard the *Melpomene*'. Being officers they could be exchanged for English prisoners. *Melpomene*, a 38 gun frigate, had been captured from the French at Calvi in 1794. Not forgetting

36

Source: ADM 180/6 Entry 27 & ADM 180/10 Entry 19

Launched or Undocked	Sailed	Built or Nature of Repair	Cost of Hull, Masts & Yards Materials £	Workmen £	Cost of Masts & Yards Materials £	Workmen £	Cost of Rigging & Stores Materials £	Workmen £	Grand Total £
13 June 1801		Built	53,609				6,875		60,484
15 June 1801	9 August 1801	Fitted	as above				as above		as above
7 Nov 1806	13 Jan 1807	Fitted							
21 May 1810	25 June 1810	Defects							
	17 June 1812	Defects							
25 Mar 1814		Large Repair	49,491	13,963	2,749	47	6,110	151	72,511
13 Sep 1825	26 Sep 1825	Fitted for a Lazaretto to Be at Milford							
	Aug 1830	Navigated to Woolwich							
	28 Dec 1830	to Sheerness							
6 April 1831 to Woolwich	7 May 1831	Fitted for an Hospital Ship for seamen							
	20 June 1831	Ditto							
	28 July 1840	to Sheerness	1,311	936	1	9	1,167		3,424
31 July 1840	1 Aug 1840	To Deptford; Defects	51	263					314
		Defects 31 March 1844	613	597			455	3	1,668
		Defects	432	484	30	21	901	11	1,879
16 Oct 1849	16 Oct 1849	Defects	1,565	1,890			62	9	3,526
24 Feb 1857		From Greenwich	227	208				357	792
		Broken Up	45	1,015				42	* 1,002
Stores returned on taking to pieces} Hull - £3,389									

Note: The total expense given for her being taken to pieces; i.e. £1002 [denoted above by ★] within the original document is erroneous and should, by calculation, read £1,102.

Dreadnought's other duties of stopping and searching any merchantmen, at 4 p.m. Conn sent boarders into 'an English Ship from Newfoundland bound to Naples' which proves that vessels of all nationalities, British included, were subject to Royal Naval policy.

On Tuesday 5 November *Dreadnought* received '16 boxes of Lemon Juice from His Majestys Ship *Bittern*', sailmakers were still repairing sails and the carpenters putting up bulkheads two weeks after the battle. With most of the crew actively busy these past two weeks, discipline had been not been compromised, but with the ship's company falling back into a standard routine the usual problems began to reappear. Captain Conn punished seamen James Cummins and John Smith with 24 lashes for drunkenness and fighting; Thomas Powell and David Arthur, 'the 1st with 12 lashes, the 2nd with 6 lashes for neglect of Duty', and 'Wm Armstrong (Marine) with 24 lashes for Drunkenness and Fighting'. The following day the log records that topgallant yards and mast had to be sent down due to squally weather and that they 'Committed the body of Samuel Harris (S) Deceased to the deep'. Sailing with the *Dreadnought* on Friday 8 November were ten sail of the line, one frigate and one brig and that night *Donegal* (74) and sloop *Martin* (18), part of Admiral Louis' squadron, joined company. The weather did not abate and still just four leagues from Cape Spartel on Saturday, at 11 p.m. the *Dreadnought* was obliged to take 'in Top Gallantsails down Jib and Staysails'. Further punishment was meted out that day: 'Geo Bloom & Andw Hogue with 12 lashes for drunkenness Jno Fitzgerald and Thoms Rice (Seamen) the 1st with 24 lashes the 2nd 18 lashes for Negligence of Duty, and fighting and Jno Smith (Marine) with 24 lashes for Drunkenness and leaving his Post'. Finally, reaching Gibraltar on Monday 11 November at 1 p.m. the *Dreadnought* 'came to with the small Bower in 34 fms Water, Veered away and Moored Europa Point SE½E Caberitta NBS½S hoisted out all Boats and sent the Spanish Prisoners ashore on the Neutral Ground'. After this the crew were turned to 'Rounding the Bower cables and occasionally Coopers up water casks'. Next morning, while landsmen were cleaning ship, the more skilled 'cast off and knotted the mainstay, it being shot through'. They were also 'Pointing the Best Bower cables'. After sending the ship's launch inshore for water, *Dreadnought* received four bullocks from *Niger* (32). At 4.20 that afternoon the ship received '70 Casks of Bread from the *Johanna Friderica*' and '10 Pipes of Wine and Bread from the Transports'. Rigging repairs continued and having got the Spritsail yard in, the seamen 'Fluted the deadeye of the Main Rigging', while the carpenters were sent 'to Work on board the *Neptune*'. The ship also received a Maintopsail yard which they 'got it a Cross for a Foreyard'. All the while the ship's boats plied to and fro bringing on provisions and otherwise employed 'with the Warrant Officers at the Dock yard'.[20] After refitting, the *Dreadnought* resumed her duties until sailing for England the following year.

1806: *Dreadnought* returned to Portsmouth on 2 June 1806 where, eight days later, Captain Conn paid the ship off.[21] On 1 September the ship went into dock and after scaffolders had erected staging around the parts of the hull where the dockside steps did not provide easy access, teams of men replaced *Dreadnought*'s old copper, the ship being undocked on 7 November.[22] The old copper was reworked into serviceable sheets within Portsmouth dockyard itself, special facilities for smelting and rolling being set up in a building adjacent to the Block Mills where wooden pulley blocks for rigging were manufactured. The Block Mills, operational by 1803, contained the world's first ever mass production machinery designed by the ingenious French emigré Marc Brunel. Fitted for sea service *Dreadnought* was then recommissioned under Captain William Lechmere on 27 December.[23]

1807: *Dreadnought* had previously mounted long 18 pounders on her middle and upper guns decks, but she was now ten years old and weaker, so her upper gun deck armament was reduced to lighter 12 pounder guns.[24] With her ordnance embarked, the ship finally quit Portsmouth harbour on 13 January 1807 to undertake her new duties.

1808: On 9 April command of the ship was succeeded by Captain George B Salt who remained in *Dreadnought* until 1810.[25] During these years the ship remained deployed near home and played little part in operations.

1810: On 9 January Captain Valentine Collard superseded Salt in command of the ship and taking her into Plymouth on 5 May, *Dreadnought* was docked on 19 May for two days to have her copper repaired.[26] Flying the flag of Rear-Admiral Thomas Sotheby, *Dreadnought* sailed from Plymouth on 25 June, for deployment off Ushant. On 7 September Sotheby received news from the armed schooner *Snapper* (4), Lieutenant Williams Jenkins in command, that a vessel had been seen close by the rocks west of Ushant. *Dreadnought* immediately stood to the east, rounded the island and discovered the vessel laying to in a small bay at 6 a.m. next day. Given orders from Sotheby to cut out the stranded vessel, Collard stood *Dreadnought* back out to sea to avoid detection. When darkness fell he bore up towards the location. During the night boats were swung out and lowered in preparation and at 5 a.m. on the 9th seven boats, manned and armed, commanded by Lieutenant Thomas Pettman, set out for the bay. On their approach they were instantly fired upon by troops and a 4 pounder field gun hidden in the rocks. Despite this Pettman pressed his men on and boarded the vessel which proved to be the Spanish *Maria Antonia*, a prize taken by the French vessel moored in a nearby creek. This triumph was short-lived; suddenly 600 French troops appeared on the cliff and commenced firing upon the boats. With just one 18 pounder carronade to supplement any return fire against the tremendous volleys, Pettman was obliged to withdraw. Six men were killed in the action, Master's Mate Henry Middleton, Midshipman William Robinson, two seamen and two marines. Among the wounded were Lieutenants Henry Elton and Stewart Blacker, Midshipmen George Burt and Henry Dennis, 18 seamen and nine marines. In addition six men were missing, presumed captured with the two boats that went on shore.[27] On 14 September Captain Collard was superseded by Captain S Hood Singer.

1812: Captain Singer eventually brought *Dreadnought* into Plymouth on 12 January to make good defects. While undergoing repairs it was discovered that she was much in need of a large repair. With all docks occupied with other ships in repair, Singer received orders to sail for Portsmouth where docks were available. Putting to sea on 17 June, *Dreadnought* arrived at Portsmouth dockyard three days later and after discharging her guns stores, provisions, and ballast, went into dock on 13 August to commence her 'Large Repair'. Once docked her copper was removed to effect structural repairs to her hull. The Admiralty deemed it too expensive to keep the ship in commission, consequently on 8 December Singer paid off the ship.[28]

1813-1814: With no urgency to complete the ship, *Dreadnought* remained under refit for these years. Finally re-coppered in March 1814, she was undocked 25th of that month. The cost of *Dreadnought*'s large repair amounted to £72,511, of which hull costs comprised £49,491 plus £13,963 for labour, £2,749 and £47 labour for masts and yards, with the remainder expended on rigging and stores.[29] The war with France was now over, consequently *Dreadnought* was moored in Portsmouth harbour to await her fate.

FATE

Found unsuitable for further service, *Dreadnought* was docked at Portsmouth on 15 September 1815 and after having her copper removed was 'Fitted for a Lazaretto to Be at Milford'. This work, which really only involved taking her down to a flush-decked two-decker, was not completed for ten years. After being re-coppered, she was finally undocked on 13 September 1825. Sailing on 26 September, she arrived at Pembroke dockyard three days later. Here she remained until August 1830 when she was 'navigated to Woolwich', arriving there in September. Sailing again 28 December she was taken down to Sheerness and docked on 30 March 1831 to have her copper removed. Coming out on 6 April *Dreadnought* was then returned to Woolwich on 7 May to be 'Fitted for an Hospital Ship for Seamen'. This work was completed in June 1831 after which she was taken to Greenwich where she remained until disposed of in 1857. She went into dock at Sheerness in July 1840 to make good defects then returned to Deptford. The overall cost of this refit amounted to £3,738, the greater amount being spent on the hull. On 21 July 1849 the ship was docked at Woolwich to fix more defects and have her bottom paid. Undocked on 16 October, she returned to her berth near Deptford. Surveyed and found unserviceable, *Dreadnought* went into dock at Woolwich on 25 February and was taken to pieces at a total cost of £1,102 while the value of stores returned amounted to £3,389.[30] Retaining the name of *Dreadnought*, the hospital itself was re-established within a new building erected to the west of Sir Christopher Wren's original hospital opposite the National Maritime Museum. Today *Dreadnought*'s building is used partly by the *Cutty Sark* restoration team.

The 98 gun ship NEPTUNE

The *Neptune*, a 2nd rate ship of 98 guns, was the third Royal Naval ship to bear the name of the Roman god of the sea, adopted from the Greek god Poseidon who ruled the sea. The first *Neptune*, a 2nd rate carrying 90 guns, had a lengthy career. Launched at Deptford on 17 April 1683, this vessel was rebuilt at Blackwall in 1710 and again at Woolwich in 1730. Renamed *Torbay* in 1750, this ship remained in service until sold on 17 August 1784. The second *Neptune*, also a 2nd rate of 90 guns, was built at Portsmouth and launched on 17 July 1757. Converted to a sheer hulk in 1784, this *Neptune* was broken up at Portsmouth in October 1816. The *Neptune* which fought at Trafalgar was one of three *Dreadnought/Neptune* class 98 gun three-decked ships designed by John Henslow. Ordered on 15 February 1790, her keel was laid down at Deptford dockyard on April 1791

SPECIFICATIONS: *NEPTUNE*

Class	Dreadnought/Neptune 1788	Length on the range of the gun deck	185 ft	Ordnance - lower gun deck	28 x 32 pounders
Designer	John Henslow	Length of keel for tonnage	152 ft 6⅜ ins	Ordnance - middle gun deck	28/30 x 18 pounders
Builder	Thomas Pollard	Extreme breadth	51 ft	Ordnance - upper gun deck	30 x 18 pounders
Dockyard	Deptford	Depth in hold	21 ft 6 ins	Ordnance - quarter deck	8 x 12 pounders
Date ordered	15 February 1790	Tons burthen	2110. 53/94	Ordnance - forecastle	2 x 12 pounders
Date keel laid	April 1791	Draught afore	22 ft 6 ins	Single broadside weight	of fire 1030/1048 pounds
Date launched	28 January 1797	Draught abaft	23 ft 6 ins	Fate	1813 Hulked at Plymouth and converted to temporary prison ship
		Complement	750		1818 Broken up

Source: Lyon, *Sailing Navy List*, pp. 106-107.

and launched six years later on 28 January 1797. Building a vessel of this size consumed some 5,760 loads (288,000 cubic feet of timber) before conversion into specific components. This figure equates to some 5,700 trees felled from about 95 acres of Kentish woodland, of which 90 per cent was oak. Once launched, the ship was moved to Woolwich on 12 February and went into dock that same day to have her bottom coppered. Launched again on 1 March, the ship completed fitting out and receiving her masts and yards, etc. Her final building costs, totalling £77,053, comprised £61,172 for her hull, masts and yards and £15,881 for rigging and stores.[31]

CAPTAINS OF *NEPTUNE* (MSS 248/4 and 248/6)

Name	Time of Entry	Time of Discharge	On What Occasion
Henry Edward Stanhope	25 March 1797	27 September 1797	Superseded
Sir Erasmus Gower	28 September 1797	28 February 1799	Promoted to Rear Admiral of the White
Herbert Sawyer	25 October 1798	22 January 1799	Superseded Acting
James Vashon	5 March 1799	26 March 1801	Superseded
Edward Brace	27 March 1801	11 September 1801	Superseded
Francis William Austen	12 September 1801	29 April 1802	Paid Off at Portsmouth
Francis William Austen	30 April 1802	30 September 1802	Superseded
William O'Brian Drury	1 October 1802	31 December 1803	New Book
William O'Brian Drury	1 January 1804	13 May 1804	Promoted to Rear Admiral of the White
Sir Thomas Williams Kt	14 May 1804	7 May 1805	Invalided
Thomas Francis Freemantle	8 May 1805	6 December 1805	Paid Off at Portsmout
Sir Thomas Williams Kt	18 August 1807	8 November 1808	Superseded
Thomas Pinto	9 November 1808	20 December 1808	Superseded
Charles Dilkes	21 December 1808	31 July 1809	To the *Pompée*
J A Wood	2 August 1809	18 March 1810	To the *Pompée*
Charles Dilkes	20 March 1810	1 September 1810	Allowed six weeks
N V Ballard (Acting)	22 July 1810	20 December 1810	Paid Off at Portsmouth

SERVICE HISTORY

1797: Commissioned 25 March 1797 under the command of Captain Henry Edward Stanhope, the ship left Woolwich on 11 June 1797 flying the broad pendant of Commodore Sir Erasmus Gower and sailed for the Nore. Directly on arrival *Neptune* became involved with the Nore Mutiny led by Richard Parker in early June. Laying near Gravesend, *Neptune*, together with *Lancaster* (64), *Agincourt* (64) and diverse gunboats, was ordered to intercept and attack the seditious ships anchored at Nore. Realising that further remonstration would not break the will of the Admiralty, most mutineers resolved to negotiate through the Earl of Northesk, Captain of *Monmouth* (64). By the 9 June the entire mutiny was on the verge of collapse with the result that *Neptune* was fortunately relieved of the task of attacking.[32] On 21 September Captain Sir Erasmus Gower superseded Stanhope in command of *Neptune*.[33] After this the ship remained deployed with the Channel fleet.

1799: When Sir Erasmus Gower received his promotion to Rear Admiral of the White and left *Neptune* on 28 February, command of the ship was formally given over to Captain James Vashon on 5 March. Prior to this Herbert Sawyer had temporarily held command in an acting capacity until 22 January.[34] While the *Neptune* remained deployed with the Channel fleet for the first half of the year, in June Vashon received orders to join Vice-Admiral Lord Keith's Mediterranean command together with 15 other sail of the line. This detached squadron, commanded by Rear-Admiral Sir Charles Cotton flying his flag in *Prince* (98), joined Keith at Minorca on 7 July. Having 31 vessels at his disposal, Keith intended to intercept a combined Franco-Spanish squadron of 42 ships commanded by Admirals Bruix and Massaredo. *Neptune*, with Keith's squadron, weighed and proceeded to sea on 10 July but unfortunately for the British, the allied fleet gave Keith the slip and by 9 August was safely moored in Brest Roads.[35]

Neptune remained with the Mediterranean fleet for the next two years.

1801: On 27 March command of the ship was succeeded by Captain Edward Brace who remained in the *Neptune* until superseded by Captain Francis William Austen on 12 September.[36]

1802: As the war with France had finished, *Neptune*, along with many of the ships stationed in the Mediterranean, returned home, *Neptune* going into Portsmouth on 24 February. On 29 April Captain Austen paid off the ship, but surprisingly he recommissioned the ship next day. Although *Neptune*'s progress books do not record when she went in and out of dock at Portsmouth during this year, they do state that she had her copper repaired which would be necessary considering how long the ship had been on active service. No docking dates are given, implying that if the repairs to her copper were minimal, it did not warrant taking the ship into dock. Having fitted out at a total cost of £5,728, of which £2,895 was expended on hull, masts and yards, command of the ship was superseded by Captain William O'Brian Drury on 1 October. Provisioned and stored, *Neptune* sailed from the dockyard to join the Channel fleet laying at Spithead on 29 October.[37]

1804: Promoted to Rear Admiral of the White, Captain Drury left *Neptune* on 13 May, his successor, Captain Thomas Williams Kt assuming command the next day. For most of this year *Neptune* remained deployed with part of the Channel squadron blockading the French ports on her Atlantic coast.[38]

1805: Suffering from ill health, Captain Williams was invalided out on the 7 May. His successor, Captain Thomas Francis Freemantle, took command of *Neptune* the following day and appointed George Acklom the ship's First Lieutenant.[39] Writing home on 23 June, Freemantle refered to the ship's livestock stating that 'Malhuer, the only poor goat that was in the ship, fell down the hatchway yesterday and I am obliged to drink my breakfast without a drop of milk'. It appears that the goat recovered for on 15 July he wrote, 'Make yourself happy on the score that the goat that fell down the hatchway, it is living and very nearly recovered and gives us a small quantity of milk twice a day'.[40] Shortly after Freemantle received orders to join Collingwood's newly formed squadron watching over Cadiz and would consequently form part of Nelson's fleet at the battle of Trafalgar on 21 October 1805.

TRAFALGAR

At the opening of the action *Neptune* was stationed third in line of Nelson's windward squadron. William Stanhope Lovell, who served as an officer in *Neptune* at the time, later described the allied ships at the battle:

> Some of them were painted like ourselves - with double yellow sides; some with a single red or yellow streak; others all black; the noble *Santisima Trinidad* with four distinct lines of red, with a white ribbon between them... the *Santa Anna*... was painted all black... It was remarked (by Nelson) that the enemy had the iron hoops round their masts painted black. Orders were issued by signal to whitewash those of his fleet, that, in the event of all ensigns being shot away, his ships might be distinguished by their white masts and hoops.[41]

While it is commonly believed that all the British ships at this period had their lower masts painted yellow/buff as seen on the *Victory* at Portsmouth today, this statement by Lieutenant Lovell suggests that this may not be the case and that the later practice of painting lower masts white may have began earlier. Furthermore, the practice of using white for masts had occasionally been employed on ships in tropical waters before 1805; white paint being more reflective, it delayed mast deterioration from strong sunlight and for this reason it is quite possible that *Bounty* had white lower masts when she sailed on her disastrous voyage to the Pacific in 1788.

It was about 1.45 p.m. when *Neptune* finally got into action. Bringing her close under *Bucentaure*'s stern, Freemantle ordered his larboard guns to fire and delivered a double shotted broadside into Villeneuve's already crippled ship with devastating effect. Freemantle then steered *Neptune* around the stern of *Santisima Trinidad* and brought her up and engaged the starboard side of the great Spanish flagship, while *Neptune* was being mauled in turn by several ships of the combined fleet as they passed. Total casualties sustained by *Neptune* were 34 wounded, one of whom was Richard Hurrell, the Captain's Clerk, and ten dead.[42] After Collingwood transferred into *Euryalus* at the close of battle, *Neptune* took the much battered *Royal Sovereign* in tow. On Wednesday 23 October Freemantle recorded that with the wind freshening to strong breezes he had the topgallant yards and the fore topgallant mast sent down. *Neptune*'s log then states:

> At 2 the *Mars* SSW *Phœbe* S½W with a Prize in Tow *Revenge* SSE with a Prize in Tow, a Frigate with the *Téméraire* in tow EbS a Ship of the Line with a Prize in Tow 2 Ships of the Line EbN ¼ past 2 Obs^d one of the Prizes Foremast fall - at 4 heavy Wea^r & Blowing Strong *Royal Sovereign* in Tow at 6 very squally Wea^r at 8 Strong gales at 10 heavy Squalls the Maintopsail blew to pieces ? past 11 wore & set the fore Sail at 12 hard rain Burnt a Blue Light to ships to leeward at 1 set Mainsail & single topsail more moderate Wea^r at 4 moderate & Cloudy Weath^r Saw Lights on the Lee Bow at daylight counted 10 Sail in different Directions Bent a new MaintopSail Lowerd the boats & Pick'd up 3 men floating on a Wreck...[43]

At noon on 24 October *Neptune*'s log records that there were 19 sail of the Line, three frigates, one Brig, one Cutter, a schooner and seven Prizes in sight. After hauling the wind onto a larboard tack at 2 p.m., Freemantle, obeying Collingwood's signal wrote: 'ans^d our Sig^l to cast off the *Royal Sovereign* 10 M^s [minutes] past 2 slip'd the stream cable', then at '? past 2 the French Commander in Chief & Suite came on board from the *Mars*'. This was Vice-Admiral Villeneuve and his entourage of flag captains who had been taken into *Mars* when his flagship *Bucentaure* (80) surrendered. Clarifying the deteriorating weather conditions and the difficulties of maintaining the damaged prize ships at sea, *Neptune*'s log then states:

> 9 sail of the Enemy NE at ½ past 5 wore 21 Sail of the Line & 9 Prizes in C^o close reef^d Blowing fresh with rain at ½ past 7 got down Main & Mizentopgallt Y^ds & furl^d the MizenTopsail at 11 Clewed up the foretopsail Blowing hard with rain at 12 D^o Wea^r the Commander in Chief SSW 3 - 4 miles at 2 furl^d the Foretopsail & Mainsail - at 8 out 4th & 3rd reefs & up Main & Mizen Topgallant Y^ds CinC NbE Hove to at 9 Bore up ans^d Gen Sig^l to shift Prisoners & Destroy the Prizes ans^d Sig^l to assist the Prince on that Duty at ? past 11 Hove to, out all Boats & sent them to the *Santisima Trinidad*...

Neptune's boats, with others, battled in the rising sea amid squally winds and lightning, transferring prisoners out of the crippled Spanish ship and sending them down into *Neptune*'s hold. With weather easing and land in sight on Saturday 26 October, *Neptune*'s log then states: 'at Noon moderate & cloudy with flying showers [of rain] Bore up towards the *Victory* to take her in tow'. The log entry next day (afternoon) continues '2 M^s past 1 Shortend Sail & Hove to by the *Victory* Sent the Boats with hawsers to bend to her stream cable at 4 D^o Wea^r took her in tow, up Boats & made sail at 5 got up the Maintopgall^t Yard & Set the sail - bent a foretopsle for a Maintopsail'. Finally on reaching Gibraltar on Monday 28 October, Freemantle wrote in *Neptune*'s log: 'at 6 Squally with flying showers ? past 8 Wore Ship the *Victory* in tow at 10 the *Victory* cast off the Tow rope, hove it in spoke one of our Ships with a Hulk in Tow'. Nelson's flagship now brought safely to Gibraltar, he recorded later that day: 'at daylight saw the *Conqueror* with the *Africa* Dismasted in Tow & one Ship at Anchor'. According to *Victory*'s log, *Neptune* on the same day 'Carried away her Fore Top Mast'.[44] Why Freemantle did not record this is incomprehensible.

PROGRESS BOOK – *NEPTUNE* 2nd RATE OF 98 GUNS:

At what Port	Arrived	Docked	Coppered
Deptford	Began	April 1791	
Woolwich	12 Feb 1797	12 Feb 1797	Coppered February 1797
Portsmouth	24 Feb 1802		Copper Repaired
Plymouth	17 July 1803	2 August 1803	Copper taken off &. Re-coppered Aug 1803
Portsmouth	23 Nov 1806	24 Mar 1807	Copper taken off Mar Re-coppered Aug 1807
Plymouth	26 Oct 1810	9 Nov 1810	
		Taken in hand 22 Nov and Completed Dec 1813	
		Taken to Pieces October 1818	

Finally, sailing for England, *Neptune* reached Portsmouth where Freemantle paid the ship off on 6 December.[45]

1806: *Neptune* returned to Spithead and went into Portsmouth on 23 November where she remained at moorings until commencing a refit the following spring.

1807: When docked on the 24 March *Neptune*'s copper sheathing was removed and her hull refitted. Coppered before being re-launched 20 August, the overall cost of *Neptune*'s refit totalled £29,053, of which £12,466 was spent on her hull, £2,128 for masts and yards and £8,597 for rigging and stores, with labour costs £5,862.[46] Following her refit, *Neptune*, like her sister ship *Dreadnought*, had her ordnance reduced, her upper gun deck long 18 pounders being substituted with 12 pounders of lesser weight.[47] This suggests that surveys taken during her refit revealed either that Henslow's design had proved poor or that the hulls of this class of ship had become weakened prematurely. The ship had recommissioned three days before her launch by Captain Thomas Williams Kt who had previously commanded the ship before being taken ill.[48]

1808: During this year *Neptune* was sent to the West Indies where, on 9 November, command of ship was superseded by Captain Thomas Pinto. Pinto remained in the ship only six weeks before being succeeded by Captain Charles Dilkes on 20 December.[49]

1809: In early January a large fleet was assembled at Carlisle Bay, Barbados, preparing to make an attack on French Martinique governed by Vice-Admiral Villaret-Joyeuse. Command of the expedition was given to Rear-Admiral Sir Alexander Cochrane who hoisted his red flag in *Neptune*. The entire naval force which sailed on 28 January, comprised 44 vessels, together with a fleet of transports to convey 10,000 troops commanded by Lieutenant-General Beckwith.

Vice-Admiral Cochrane's Fleet January 1809.

Guns	98	74	64	44	40	38	36	32	24	20	18	16	14	12	10	6	Sch.
No.	1	4	1	1	1	2	2	2	1	1	15	3	5	1	2	1	1

Cochrane's squadron arrived off Martinique on 30 January where 3,000 troops, led by Major-General Maitland, were put onshore at Pointe Sainte Luce without meeting resistance. A further 600 men under Major Henderson were landed at Cape Salomon. Both landings were directed by Captain William Fahie, commanded of the other Trafalgar veteran ship present, the 74 gun *Belleisle*. Meanwhile a major force of 6,500 troops, commanded by Lieutenant-General Sir George Provost, landed on the north side of the island. By 2 February the majority of the French forces had retreated to Fort Desaix. After capturing the fort on Pointe Salomon Major Henderson, considerably supported by the brigades of British seamen led by

Source: ADM 180/6 Entry 28 & ADM 180/10 Entry 24

Launched or Undocked	Sailed	Built or Nature of Repair	Cost of Hull, Masts & Yards Materials £	Workmen £	Cost of Masts & Yards Materials £	Workmen £	Cost of Rigging & Stores Materials £	Workmen £	Grand Total £
28 Jan 1797		Built	61,172				15,881		77,053
1 March 1797	11 June 1797	Fitted	as above				as above		as above
	29 October 1802	Fitted	2,895				2,833		5,728
18 August 1803	12 Dec 1803	Defects							
20 Aug 1807	15 Nov 1807	Fitted	12,466	5,162	2,128	490	8,597	210	29,053
8 Dec 1810	25 June 1810	Fitted for Ordinary	693	20					713
		Fitted for a temporary Prison Ship							

Captain George Cockburn, set up gun batteries and commenced his attack on Pigeon Island on St Lucia. Two days later, after twelve hours continuous bombardment, the island capitulated. Cochrane now stood his fleet inshore to support the troops and by 10 February both St Pierre and Fort Royal had been taken on Martinique. Cochrane's ships began bombarding Fort Desaix on 19 February, continuing for almost five days. The fort finally capitulated at 9 a.m. on 24 February. Naval casualties accrued during the attacks on Pigeon Island and Fort Desaix amounted to eight killed and 19 wounded.[50]

Neptune's squadron, comprising *York* (74), *Pompée* (74), *Polyphemus* (64), *Acasta* (40), *Recruit* (18) and *Hazard* (18), remained on station blockading Martinique. In March Commodore Troude, flying his pendant in *d'Hautpoult* (74), arrived off Martinique escorted by *Courageux* and *Polonais*, both 74s, and two transports. Finding the British had taken Martinique, he anchored off the two small islands known as the Saintes. With the French posing a potential threat, Cochrane, still in command, decided to capture the Saintes. An assault using 2,500 troops, was made on 14 April, when two 8 inch howitzers were landed and hoisted 800 feet up a promontory called Mourne-Russel to fire upon the French ships. Threatened, Commodore Troude put to sea with his three warships, whose movements were tracked by *Hazard* (18). Receiving signals from *Hazard*, Cochrane set sail with his squadron in pursuit. At 10 p.m. *Pompée* closed with the rearmost French ship and fired two broadsides to bring her to, but having the wind gauge the vessel continued undeterred. Fifteen minutes later the brig-sloop *Recruit* caught up with *Pompée* and also fired her guns at the Frenchman. Setting more sail *Neptune* joined the chase at 11 p.m. The pursuit continued through the night and by 4 a.m. *Recruit*, being the handier vessel, finally closed with *d'Hautpoult* and fired at her, when the three French ships formed line abreast and commenced firing their stern chase guns into the sloop, wounding Captain Napier's sergeant of marines. The chase continued for two days and on 17 April *Pompée* eventually captured *d'Hautpoult* after a hot engagement.[51] On 31 July Captain Dilkes transferred into *Pompée* and although not evident from the wording of the documents, this move suggests that Dilkes had been taken ill. His successor, Captain J A Wood, assumed command of *Neptune* on 2 August.[52]

1810: On 20 March Captain Dilkes resumed command of *Neptune*, while Wood exchanged into *Pompée*. Captain N Ballard took command of *Neptune* in an acting capacity on 22 July and when Dilkes finally left the ship on 1 September he was 'Allowed six weeks', further suggesting that he was ill. Recalled home *Neptune* reached Plymouth on 26 October and was taken into dock on 9 November to be fitted out for the ordinary.[53] Here sources conflict; while the progress book clearly states that the ship was at Plymouth, the list of ship's commanders states that acting Captain Ballard paid off the ship at Portsmouth on 20 December.[54]

FATE

Fitting *Neptune* for the ordinary involved stripping out bulkheads and other less structural fitting, removing strakes of 'quick work' (non-structural inner lining planking) and taking up part of the deck planking throughout in order to ensure that the vessel's hull, especially her frames, was continuously ventilated to prevent timber decay. The entire cost of fitting the ship for ordinary amounted to £713. When undocked on 8 December the ship was laid up at moorings in the Hamoaze where she remained until late autumn 1813. Like her sister ship *Dreadnought*, the hull of *Neptune* appears to have deteriorated more quickly than expected and she was deemed unfit for sea service after just 13 years. The Admiralty, at the Navy Board's proposal, ordered her to be converted into a prison ship. The ship was therefore 'Taken in hand 22 November' and 'Fitted for a temp[y] Prison Ship', the work being completed in December 1813. Serving this role for three years, *Neptune* was then taken to pieces in October 1818.[55]

The 98 gun ship *TÉMÉRAIRE*

The *Téméraire* which fought at Trafalgar was the second ship to bear this name in the Royal Navy. Her predecessor was a 3rd rate ship of 74 guns captured from the French at Lagos on 18 August 1759 during the Seven Years' War (1756-1763). Proving a successful ship, this *Téméraire* remained in service until sold in June 1784 after seeing active service during the American War of Independence. The Trafalgar *Téméraire* was one of three 98 gun ships of the *Dreadnought/Neptune* class designed by Sir John Henslow, Surveyor of the Navy, in 1788. Ordered on 9 December 1790, her keel was laid down at Chatham dockyard in July 1793 and launched five years later on 11 June 1798. Building was first overseen by Master Shipwright Thomas Pollard and from 25 June 1795 by Edward Sison. Like her sister ships *Dreadnought* and *Neptune*, the construction of *Téméraire* required some 5,760 loads (288,000 cubic feet of timber) before conversion into specific components. Most of the 5,700 trees used, of which 90 per cent was oak, was taken from the nearby Wealden forests of Kent and woods further afield in Sussex, Surrey and Essex. The day after her launch the ship was hauled into the graving dock to be coppered, this work taking just two weeks. *Téméraire*'s overall building costs amounted to £73,241 of which £59,428 was expended on her hull, masts and yards and £13,813 for rigging and stores.[56]

Téméraire. Going out in a boat, John Livesay (1750–1826), made these sketches to gather first-hand evidence of the battle-damaged Trafalgar ships returning to Portsmouth. His sketches were then sent to the artist Nicholas Pocock in London, who produced more formal drawings from them. Livesay acted as Pocock's agent and man on the scene, speaking to naval officers in the aftermath of the battle. (*Courtesy of the Royal Naval Museum*)

killed were two Royal Marine officers, Captain Simeon Busigny and Lieutenant John Kingston, Midshipman William Pitts and the Carpenter Lewis Oades. Officers wounded comprised Lieutenants James Mould, and Samuel Payne; Master's Mate Francis Swaine, Midshipman John Eastman and Boatswain John Brooks.[66] In the days that followed 47 more of the *Téméraire*'s crew who had been sent into her two prizes were lost with these ships in the gale that followed. As for battle damage, besides having lost masts, yards and rigging, eight feet of ship's side planking on the starboard of her lower deck had been stove in.

Wednesday 23 October Harvey wrote, 'PM Fresh Breezes No Logg [sic] kept being taken in Tow by the *Sirius* Noon Cape Trafalgar SEBE 7 or 8 Leagues *Sirius* cast off the Hawser and let us go, by Signal'. All this while the crew were busy 'Clearing the Wreck Knotting and Splicing the Rigging &c'. Shortly after she was joined by *Donegal* (74) the weather turned to heavy squalls with rain.[67] On Friday 25 October *Téméraire*'s log states that the ship was positioned 36.36N by 16.00W running on a northerly course some 20 miles south of Cadiz. Having been with *Africa* (64) that afternoon, at 9 p.m. the log records, 'Saw a Ship on Fire bearing North [which] at ? past Blew Up'. Next morning as the weather turned to squalls with lightning and rain, *Téméraire* found herself with the '*Defiance* in Company'. Unable to endure the onslaught of the storm any longer, Harvey gave the order to anchor, at 7.30 p.m. Saturday 26 October *Téméraire* 'came too with the Best Bower in 18 fm [and] Veered to a whole Cable' in Cadiz Bay, after which they 'found the rudder Head quite broke off, Wedged the Head up in clear of the other part'. The crew were then 'Employed Refitting the Jury Yards Sails &c & fitting a Piece of Yard for a Starboard Cat Head it being shot away'. With the heavy winds abating by noon on Tuesday 29 October, they 'opened Hammocks and Aired Bedding. Early next morning Harvey recorded the weather as moderate and cloudy with rain and that they received 39 prisoners. Then, at 8 a.m. the log records; 'the *Euryalus* bearing Adm[l] Collingwood 's Flag coming towards us with the *Defyance* [sic] & *Polyphemus* Rec[d]. 15 men from y[e] *Euryalus* who had been left on Board one of the Ships who Struck to us Capt[n] Harvey went on Board the *Euryalus* Rec[d] from the *Defiance* a main TSail Yard' After receiving 95 prisoners out of *Defiance* on Wednesday afternoon and 'getting up TG Mast for Jury Mast & out riggers for the Rudder —— to steer by', the lower yards were swayed up and at 8 the ship weighed 'and came to Sail under Stay Sails'. Half an hour later, '*Defiance* took us in Tow'. Harvey then 'Sent Returns of Killed and Wounded and Drowned'.

On Friday 1 November the tow hawser had to be cut because, '*Defiance* dropping Onb[d] us', the tow being taken up again later. Finally on Sunday 3 November, after supplying *Orion* (74) with twenty empty water butts and casting off the tow from *Defiance*, *Téméraire* finally 'came too in Gibraltar Bay in 26 fm Water and after mooring ship a cable each way they sent they unshipped the rudder and sent it together with the main top into the dockyard for repairs and sent the sick and wounded onshore to the hospital.'[68] For their part in the battle, every one of *Téméraire*'s lieutenants was promoted to commander and consequent to Captain Harvey being promoted to Rear-Admiral, command of the ship was superseded by Captain John Lorimer on 6 December. Having made all necessary repairs, *Téméraire*, with *Royal Sovereign*, *Tonnant*, *Colossus* and *Leviathan*, returned to England, reaching Portsmouth on 19 December.

1806: While waiting to go into dock to refit, Captain Lorimer paid off the ship and on 8 January transferred into *Audacious* (74). *Téméraire* was finally docked on 18 June, her copper being taken off during November.[69]

1807: Re-coppered, the ship was undocked on 23 March and recommissioned under Captain Sir Charles Hamilton on 1 April.[70] The cost of *Téméraire*'s refit totalled £23,352, of which £6,039 covered hull costs, £421 for masts and yards and £11,362 for rigging and stores. Labour amounted to £3,740.[71] *Téméraire* eventually sailed from the dockyard on 17 September to join the Mediterranean fleet watching Toulon.

1808: Returning to Plymouth on 26 April the ship, was docked on 9 May to have her 'Copper Repaired & Redressed' and undocked 17 days later. The entire cost of fitting her defects totalled £8,700. With Spain changing sides and declaring war on France, the ship sailed on 15 June to join the naval forces deployed off the Spanish coast supporting the Peninsular War.

1809: On 9 February Captain Edward Clay took command of the ship in an acting capacity until Hamilton formally left the ship 1 May. All the while *Téméraire* was with the squadron laying off the coast of Spain, mainly operating out of Lisbon.

1810: *Téméraire* returned again to Plymouth 2 January to be docked six days later for one day to have her copper repaired and make good other defects. Command of the ship was then superseded by Captain Edwin H Chamberlayne on 25 January.

1811: With Captain Joseph Spear assuming command on 11 March, *Téméraire* was deployed to the Mediterranean as flagship to Rear-Admiral

PROGRESS BOOK – *TÉMÉRAIRE* 2nd RATE OF 98 GUNS:

At what Port	Arrived	Docked	Coppered
Chatham	Began	July 1793	
Chatham		12 Sep 1798	Coppered Sep 1798
Plymouth	28 Sep 1802	22 May 1803	Copper Repaired
Plymouth	19 Feb 1805	4 March 1805	Copper taken off and Re-coppered Mar 1805
Portsmouth	19 Dec 1805	18 June 1806	Copper taken off Nov 1806 Re-coppered Mar 1807
Plymouth	26 April 1808	9 May 1808	Copper Repaired & Redressed
Plymouth	2 Jan 1810	8 Jan 1810	Copper Repaired
Plymouth	9 Feb 1812	27 Feb 1812	Copper Repaired
		Taken in hand 22 Nov[r] & Completed December 1813	
		6 Sep 1819	Copper taken off and Re-coppered
Sheerness	28 June 1820	Defects from 1 April 1833 to 16 August 1838	

Sold 16 August to Mr J Beatson for £5,530

Pickmore, third in command of Admiral Sir Edward Pellew's Mediterranean fleet cruising off Toulon. Getting under way out of Hyéres Bay on 13 August the wind fell off, causing her to drift too close to a battery of 36 pounders mounted upon Cap des Medes at the N.E. end of the island of Porquerolles. The French gunners opened fire and one of the shots struck *Téméraire*'s Master, Mr Robert Duncan, as he stood conversing with Captain Spear. It carried away one leg and badly wounded the other. The same shot dismounted one of the quarter deck guns and wounded five seamen with splinters. *Téméraire* instantly returned a heavy fire against the French battery, preventing them from continuing firing while the ship was towed out of range. Taken below, Mr Duncan refused to allow the surgeon to operate until a miniature of his wife had been hung around his neck and eventually made a good recovery. Spear then took *Téméraire* to Port Mahon to make good her damage and refit her main mast which had been sprung for some considerable time. While in harbour, refitting fever broke out in the ship resulting in nearly half *Téméraire*'s officers and crew, including Captain Spear, being confined to the naval hospital. Rear-Admiral Pickmore shifted into *Royal George* (100) sent out to relieve her but due to Captain Spear's poor health, Pellew decided to send him home commanding *Téméraire*. Once near Cape St Vincent, health within the ship, including Captain Spear's, improved.

1812: Recalled to England she entered Plymouth on 9 February and docked to have her copper repaired and defects fixed on 27 February. Although it had been earlier recorded in her 'Sailing Qualities' that she showed 'no particular signs of weakness', recent surveys had revealed that she was 'A well built and strong Ship but apparently much decay'd'.[72] While in dock command of the ship was succeeded by Captain I H Linzee, however his tenure was short for once she came out of dock on 13 March, Linzee paid off the ship seven days later.[73]

FATE

Taken in hand in Plymouth dockyard on 22 November 1813, *Téméraire* was fitted out for a temporary prison ship, the work completed that December. The costs for this work are not recorded. Performing this rôle for six years in the River Tamar, the ship went back into dock on 6 September 1819 to be re-coppered, fitted out as a receiving ship and re-launched on 21 September. Finally completed at a cost of £27,733, *Téméraire* sailed from Plymouth for Sheerness on 21 June 1820, arriving there one week later. For the next 18 years she successfully fulfilled her rôle. commanded indirectly by the Superintendent of Sheerness dockyard who, in 1834, was Captain Thomas Fortescue Kennedy. Serving as *Téméraire*'s First Lieutenant at Trafalgar, Kennedy had led the boarding party into *Fougueux*.[74] Throughout this period *Téméraire* accumulated £4,244 in costs for defects. In June 1838 the Superintendent of Sheerness dockyard received orders that *Téméraire* was to be 'prepared for Sale'. This task was given to Captain Sir John Hill, commander of nearby *Ocean*. Within *Ocean*'s log Hill provides a detailed account of stripping *Téméraire* down to her bare hull beforehand. His entry, dated 4 July, states 'commenced dismantling the *Téméraire* - sent Top masts & Yards on deck & unrigged the Fore and Mizen Masts', leaving her lower masts to be removed using the sheerlegs at Sheerness. Next day Hill records, 'return Stores from the *Téméraire* & prepare her for sale'. With the stores sent into the dockyard on 6 July the ship's bower anchors were removed four days later and on 13 July the log entry records: 'get the Guns & Ordnance Store out'.[75] With all guns masts rigging and stores removed, the small contingent that made up *Téméraire*'s crew went on board *Ocean* and was paid by the Navy Board representative. Auctioned on 16 August 1838 with twelve other vessels including the gun ship *Venerable* (74), Admiral Duncan's former flagship which fought victoriously against the Dutch at the battle of Camperdown on 11 October 1797, *Téméraire* was sold on to Mr John Beatson, a Rotherhithe shipbreaker, for £5,530. Beatson paid a deposit of £1,500 at the auction and the balance eleven days later, after which he had to face the difficult task of towing her up river, 55 miles from Sheerness to Rotherhithe.[76]

Because of *Téméraire*'s great weight, Beatson hired two tugs, *London* and *Samson*, from the Thames Steam Towing Company. With Beatson employed William Scott, a Rotherhithe pilot and his crew of 25 men at an overall cost of £58, to navigate the tugs with their charge up river. Of this sum Scott received £25, ten men £1 5s each, 15 men £1 1s each, 5 shillings for beer and the remainder covered costs for a Mr Burleigh (£4) and another man at Sheerness hired for 10 shillings.[77] The tow from Sheerness began at about 7.30 a.m. just before slack water on 5 September. Arriving at Long Hope Reach they anchored off Greenhithe at about 1.30 p.m. as the tide began to ebb. Continuing at about 8.30 next morning, *Téméraire* and her consorts passed Woolwich, then Greenwich Hospital shortly after noon. Finally entering Limehouse Reach, they arrived off Beatson's Wharf around 2 p.m. where preparations were made to haul her up onto the mud. Though little was recorded in the newspapers about this last journey, it is from this event that the *Téméraire*, one of the last surviving veterans of Trafalgar, became immortalised in the painting 'The Fighting Téméraire' by the renowned painter J M W Turner. In his painting the noble *Téméraire*, glowing ghost-like and majestic, resigns herself to being towed to her death by a paddle tug. Belching acrid smoke from its tall metallic stack, this tug provides an ugly symbol of the industrial age against the grace of the once-powerful

Source: ADM 180/6 Entry 78 & ADM 180/10 Entry 32

Launched or Undocked	Sailed	Built or Nature of Repair	Cost of Hull, Masts & Yards Materials £	Workmen £	Cost of Masts & Yards Materials £	Workmen £	Cost of Rigging & Stores Materials £	Workmen £	Grand Total £
11 Sep 1798		Built	59,428				13,813		73,241
26 Sep 1798	18 May 1799	Fitted	as above				as above		as above
23 May 1803	23 Feb 1804	Fitted	608	813	196	44	15,169	68	16,898
16 March 1805	4 April 1805	Defects	4,006	917	105	46	3,994	75	9,143
23 March 1807	17 Sep 1807	Fitted	6,039	3,072	4,211	563	11,362	105	25,352
26 May 1808	15 June 1808	Defects	2,215	1,156	1,877	-	3,440	12	8,700
9 Jan 1810	12 Feb 1810	Defects	855						
13 March 1812		Defects	314					314	
		Fitted for a temporary Prison Ship Ordinary	Expense not shown						
21 Sep 1819	21 June 1820	Fitted for a Receiving ship	451	6,279	1,936	37	6,892	138	27,733
			2,067	1,200	146	182	262	-	3,857
			Expenses for 1831 to 1832 Not in Office						
			107	280					387

sailing man-of-war. Poignantly, the event is further enhanced by the stillness of the water and the fiery sky, both reflecting the bold light of the evening sun which, full of sadness, is setting over an era that has now passed. Besides this famous painting, her demise gave rise to a series of literary works including Richard Monckton Milnes' lines, 'On Turner's picture of the *Téméraire* man-of-war towed into port by a steamer for the purpose of being broken up', published in 1840; J Duff's song 'The brave old *Téméraire*' in 1857; *The Téméraire* by Herman Melville, published in New York in 1866; and perhaps the most famous poem, *The Fighting Téméraire* by Sir Henry Newbolt, published in London in 1898.

Once berthed, the slow process of dismantling *Téméraire* began and, by agreement with the Admiralty, all copper sheathing plates, rudder pintles and gudgeons, copper bolts, nails, and other fastenings were sold back to them in 1839, Beatson making a profit of £3,000. He then sold off the timber, the buyers varying from house builders to shipyard owners where it was re-used for wharf buildings and small ship parts. Some timber, however, was sold for a more lucrative market and turned into pieces of commemorative furniture, altar chairs and barometers, the most celebrated piece being the gong stand presented to the Duke of York on his marriage to Princess May of Teck on 6 July 1893 (later King George V and Queen Mary).[78] The fighting *Téméraire*, like the *Victory* she had defended at Trafalgar, had thus became embodied within the culture of England.

The 98 gun ship PRINCE

The *Prince* that fought at Trafalgar was the fourth vessel to bear this name in the Royal Navy. The first *Prince* was a 1st rate of 100 guns launched at Chatham in 1670 which when rebuilt in 1692, was renamed *Royal William*. Undergoing a second rebuild at Portsmouth in 1719, this ship remained in active service until *circa* 1790, when she became a guardship. Finally broken up in 1813 after 143 years, her longevity of service is surpassed only by Nelson's *Victory*. The second was in fact the 2nd rate 90 gun ship *Ossory* launched at Portsmouth 1682. Renamed *Prince* in 1705, her name was again altered to *Princess* on 2 January 1716 and to *Princess Royal* in 1728 and she served under this name until broken up in 1771. Like her predecessor, the third *Prince* started her career under a different name. Launched as the 90 gun ship *Triumph* at Chatham in 1698, she was renamed *Prince* on 27 August 1714. Rebuilt and enlarged at Chatham in 1750, this *Prince* remained in service until broken up at Plymouth in 1775.

The Trafalgar *Prince* was a 2nd rate of 98 guns built to the lines of Slade's *London* class of 1759, which also comprised *Impregnable* and *Windsor Castle*. Under the wording 'to cause to be set up & built a Ship of 90 Guns at Woolwich', *Prince* was formally ordered by the Admiralty on 9 December 1779. As stated in the order *Prince* was initially meant to be a 90 gun ship. The keel of *Prince* was laid down at Woolwich dockyard on the River Thames on 1 January 1782 under the supervision of Master Shipwright John Jenner. During the next six years while *Prince* was under construction, work was supervised by four consecutive master shipwrights. When Jenner died 18 December 1782 he was succeeded by Henry Peake. Peake would later become eminent in his profession and share similar status to William Seppings. When Peake transferred to Deptford dockyard in December 1785, work on the *Prince* continued under Martin Ware until he too was superseded in March 1787 by John Nelson. When *Prince* was finally launched on 4 July 1788, her overall construction costs amounted to £55,041 9s 11d of which £8,388 0s 0d was spent on rigging and stores.[79] Three weeks later the ship left Woolwich and arriving at Plymouth on 6 August, went into dock on 17 October to be coppered at a cost of £1,568.

CAPTAINS OF PRINCE (MSS 248/4 and 248/6)

Name	Time of Entry	Time of Discharge	On What Occasion
Jonas Rogers	30 July 1790	8 December 1790	Paid Off – Sir J Jervis's Flag flying
Cuthbert Collingwood	22 February 1793	14 January 1794	Paid Off at Portsmouth – Rear Admiral Bowyer's Flag flying
James Parry	2 October 1794	9 June 1795	Superseded Promoted Rear Admiral of the White
Charles P Hamilton	10 June 1795	23 June 1796	Paid Off at Portsmouth
Thomas Larcom	20 October 1796	23 March 1799	To the *Lancaster*
Samuel Sutton	24 March 1799	5 August 1800	To the *Prince George*
James Walker	6 August 1800	3 October 1800	To the *Isis*
Earl of Northesk	4 October 1800	22 April 1802	Paid Off at Plymouth
John Loring	19 October 1801	19 November 1801	Superseded
Richard Grindall	4 April 1803	31 December 1803	New Book
Richard Grindall	1 January 1804	4 March 1806	Superseded – Promoted to Rear Admiral
Daniel Oliver Guion	14 December 1804	10 February 1805	Superseded Acting
William Godfrey	5 March 1806	12 April 1806	Superseded Acting
William Lechmere	13 April 1806	26 December 1806	Superseded – to the *Dreadnought*
Alexander Fraser	29 December 1806	23 March 1807	Paid Off at Plymouth
RECOMMISSIONED			
George Fawke	12 October 1813	15 May 1815	Superseded
Edmund Boyer	16 May 1815	2 September 1815	Paid Off at Portsmouth

6s. 6d. *Prince* would have been sheathed with 3,500 plates of copper (the slightly larger *Victory* had 3,923), the material cost for each sheet and labour is estimated as about 9 shillings. Mounting twenty-eight 32 pounders on the lower gun deck, thirty 18 pounders on her middle gun deck, thirty 12 pounders on her upper gun deck and two 6 pounders upon the forecastle, *Prince* delivered a single broadside weight of 904 pounds. This class of ship carried no ordnance on the quarter deck. Not required for service, the ship remained laid up in the Hamoaze until 1790.[80]

SPECIFICATIONS: PRINCE

Rate	2nd	Length on the range of the gun deck	177 ft 6 ins (1796 lengthened by 17 ft)	Ordnance – lower gun deck	28 x 32 pounders
Guns	98			Ordnance – middle gun deck	30 x 18 pounders
Class	London 1759	Length of keel for tonnage	146 ft 6 ins	Ordnance – upper gun deck	30 x 12 pounders
Designer	Thomas Slade	Extreme breadth	49 ft	Ordnance – quarter deck	0
Builder	John Jenner, Henry Peake, Martin Ware, John Nelson	Depth in hold	21 ft	Ordnance – forecastle	2 x 6 pounders
		Tons burthen	1870 93/94 (2088 when lengthened)	Single broadside weight	904 pounds
Dockyard	Woolwich			Fate	1816 Hulked as a victualling vessel and for accommodating dockyard officers.
Date ordered	9 December 1779	Draught afore	22 ft 6 ins		
Date keel laid	1 January 1782	Draught abaft	23 ft 6 ins		1837 Broken up
Date launched	4 July 1788	Complement	750		

Note: Ordnance listed as for 1803/1805 Trafalgar campaign.

Source: Lyon, *Sailing Navy List*, p. 64.

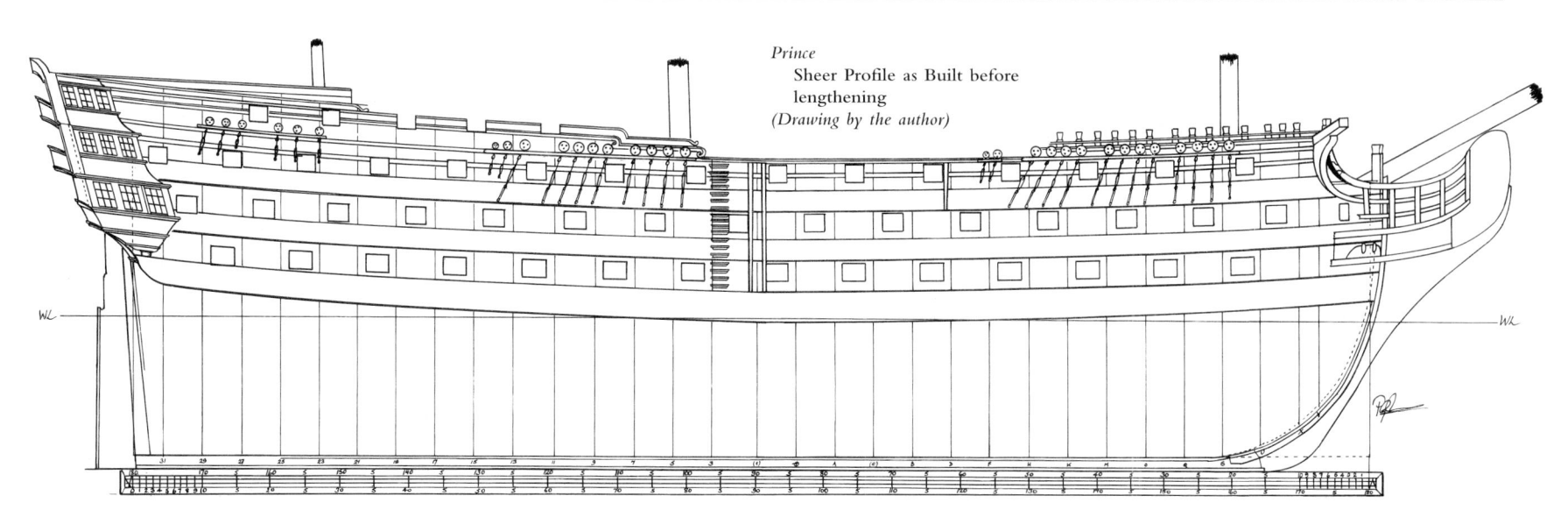

Prince
Sheer Profile as Built before
lengthening
(Drawing by the author)

SERVICE CAREER

1790: With the threat of Spain rearming her navy *Prince* was taken in hand and fitted at an overall cost of £6,227 17s 8d and put into commission for the first time under the command of Captain Jonas Rogers on 30 July.[81] Rogers remained in the ship for five months, during which period she flew the flag of Admiral Sir John Jervis. The threat of war abated, *Prince* returned to Plymouth on 16 November and after de-storing Rogers paid off the ship on 8 December.[82]

1793: When the war with revolutionary France became a certainty, *Prince* was docked on 11 February for two days to have her copper repaired; she was then recommissioned under Captain Cuthbert Collingwood on 22 February. Twelve years later Collingwood would be Nelson's second in command at the battle of Trafalgar. Once fitted for war at an expense of £6,674, *Prince* sailed on 21 June to join the Channel fleet, flying the flag of Rear-Admiral Bowyer.

1794: Having returned into Portsmouth on 31 December, *Prince* was paid off on 14 January and laid up in ordinary for nine months. After being docked on 9 September for three days to have her copper repaired, the ship was recommissioned under Captain James Parry on 2 October but does not appear to have put to sea.[83]

1795: *Prince* finally sailed to rejoin the Channel squadron on 12 April. When Captain Parry was promoted Rear-Admiral of the White, Captain Charles Hamilton succeeded him on 10 June. *Prince* was deployed with Lord Bridport's squadron off Belle Isle watching Villaret's French fleet. Cruising off Isle de Groix on 23 June the two fleets met and engaged. Although *Prince* played little part in the fight and suffered no damage or casualties, she did take one prize in tow afterwards.[84]

1796: Recalled, *Prince* re-entered Portsmouth on 28 May. On 23 June Hamilton paid off the ship. A decision had been made by the Navy Board to lengthen her. It is not known why. *Prince* was docked at Portsmouth on 21 June and had her copper removed in July before the hull was lengthened by 17 feet. The 'cut' was made at a position referred to as the 'dead flat', where the hull frames remain parallel for a short distance before curving towards the ship's bow and stern. This cut was also made on a double frame that formed the fore or after side of the gun ports at each deck level which, in *Prince*'s case, would have been a middle gun deck port. All fore and aft structural members were stripped back to their next line of butts or joint lines. This included the keel, the hog (rising wood), keelson, beam clamps, spirketting, the external wales and all runs of internal lining and thick stuff, and external planking. Deck planking at each level was also removed. The two sections of the hull were separated to construct the new middle section. Moving the two hull sections apart was a considerable engineering feat involving rollers, capstans and many teams of horses but a not uncommon one. The distance between the two sections was critical and had to comply with specifications governing the spacing and thickness of the ship's timbers. Adding 17 feet to *Prince*'s hull extended her length to 194 feet 6 inches, giving her six additional gun ports, two per gun deck, on each broadside. Her burthen was increased by 11.6 per cent to 2,088 tons.[85] Re-coppered, *Prince* was undocked on 2 October. The entire cost of *Prince*'s rebuild was £31,267 of which £19,905 covered her extension, the remaining £11,362 expended on rigging and stores.[86] Completed, *Prince* was recommissioned by Captain Thomas Larcom on 20 October and, flying the flag of Rear-Admiral Sir Roger Curtis, sailed to join Lord Bridport's squadron on 28 November.[87] For the next month *Prince* remained with the squadron at Spithead. On 25 December Bridport received news that the French had escaped out of Brest and immediately ordered his squadron to sail. Unfortunately while leaving Spithead *Prince* missed stays and while paying off to make a second attempt to tack she ran aboard the starboard gangway

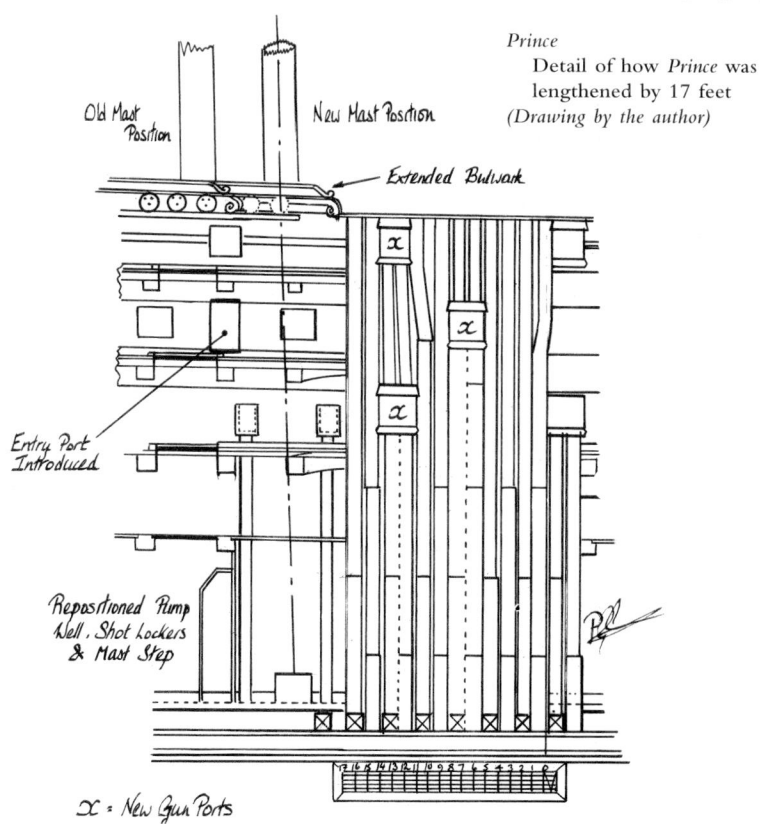

Prince
Detail of how *Prince* was
lengthened by 17 feet
(Drawing by the author)

of *Sans Pareil*, the damage forcing both ships to go into Portsmouth to repair. Sailing was delayed as *Formidable* (90) collided with *Ville de Paris* (110) and *Atlas* (90) ran aground.[88]

1797: While Bridport's fleet finally sailed on 3 January,[89] *Prince* went into Portsmouth on 11 January and was docked on the 29th for a month to have her copper repaired and 'make good damages'. Completed at a total cost of £7,603, she returned to her moorings at Spithead on 6 March.[90]

1798: In May Rear-Admiral Sir Roger Curtis hoisted his flag in *Prince* and sailed under new orders with seven other sail of the line to reinforce Admiral the Earl of St Vincent's squadron operating off Cadiz, arriving there on 24 May.[91] It was shortly after this squadron arrived that *Prince* was involved with subduing the dissension on board *Marlborough*, a ship much troubled with grievances since the Spithead mutiny. Under St Vincent's orders, boats from the fleet, under the overall command of Captain Campbell of *Blenheim*, each manned and armed with carronades carrying twelve rounds, were to rendezvous with *Prince* at 7 a.m. and go alongside and fire into the *Marlborough* if needed to subdue further mutiny.[92]

1799: According to lists of commanders and ships, Captain Samuel Sutton, who would later command *Victory*, was appointed to *Prince* on 24 March. His predecessor, Captain Larcom, turned over into *Lancaster* (64),[93] built as the East Indiaman *Pigot*, and purchased on the stocks in 1797.[94] According to James, Captain Larcom was still in command of Prince. *Prince* was now flying the flag of Rear-Admiral Sir Charles Cotton Bt attached to Lord Bridport's squadron watching over Brest. Inside the port a French fleet commanded by Vice-Admiral Eustache Bruix was preparing to sail. Giving Bridport the slip on the 25 April, Bruix sailed from Brest with twenty-five ships of the line, three frigates, two corvettes and several smaller vessels, to land a force in Ireland. Missing them, Bridport's ships sailed for Cape Clear to search.[95] With Captain Sutton in command and still carrying the flag of Rear-Admiral Sir Charles Cotton, *Prince*, along with twelve other warships, was re-deployed in early July to serve with Lord Keith's Mediterranean fleet operating out of Minorca.[96]

1800: Recalled, *Prince* was laid up alongside a hulk at Portsmouth between 16 February and 25 April rectifying her defects at a cost of £2,034 for hull masts and yards and £2,050 for rigging and stores.[97] Two courts-martial were convened to try marines; the first, held on 7 April, sentenced marine Corporal William Howell to receive 100 lashes for quitting his station in the dockyard and taking Private Barnard Ward from the dockyard gate with him. Ward was also charged for leaving his post. The second court martial convened on 28 April sentenced another marine to be flogged 200 lashes around the fleet for assaulting his marine sergeant. On 5 August Captain Sutton transferred into *Prince George* (90), Captain James Walker commanding *Prince*. Two months later Walker transferred into *Isis* and he was succeeded by the Earl of Northesk who would later command *Britannia* (100) at Trafalgar.

1801: *Prince* remained with the Channel squadron. The Earl of Northesk left the ship for a month on 19 October and John Loring held temporarily command.[98]

1802: Recalled, *Prince* went to Plymouth on 15 April where, one week later, the Earl of Northesk paid off the ship. She docked on 19 May for a 'very small repair', had her copper replaced, was re-launched on 18 June and remained at Plymouth.[99]

1803: When war resumed *Prince* was recommissioned under Captain Richard Grindall and fitted out. The work preparing her for war during this refit is covered in the appendices. Once completed, the *Prince* sailed to join the Channel squadron deployed off the French Atlantic coast.

1804: Captain Grindall handed over his command on an acting basis 14 December to Daniel Oliver Guion. It is probable that *Prince* was refitting when Guion took temporary command.

1805: On 10 February Captain Grindall resumed command of the ship. That summer *Prince* was part of the fleet watching Villeneuve's combined fleet in Cadiz. Laying off Cape St Mary on Wednesday 16 October while the crew were painting the ship, frigates *Renommée* (38) and *Amiable* (32), both originally French, parted company with a convoy. A seaman William Barrett was flogged 'with 24 Lashes for Drunkenness & Insolence'. *Prince* received '15 Ton of water from the *Britannia*' on the 19th. For Sunday 20 October, when the combined fleet were leaving Cadiz, Grindall recorded in *Prince*'s log 'Fresh Breezes & fine W^r. all sail set in Chace at 4 Exercis^d Great Guns at 6 N°. 252 Adm^l Genl. All Sail sett in Chace [N^o.] 265 Adm^l to *Prince* 5.30 Carried away the main Top Mt Studd^g S^l [studding sail] Boom at 6.30 Short^d S^l wore Ship'.[100]

TRAFALGAR

Monday 21 October the log states: 'Fresh Breezes & Squally down Top G^t Yd^s at 2 Wore Ship out 4th Reeffs TopS^{ls} at 4 Wore Ship 4.20 Cross^d Top G^t Yd^s out 3rd & 4th Reeffs TopS^{ls} at 8 Wore ship Pr Sign^l saw the flash of several Guns NE'.[101] On the morning of the battle *Prince* lay 15th in the line of Collingwood's leeward division and consequently, like the *Defence* almost abreast of her, would be late getting into action, primarily because her fore topsail split during the approach. Her log continues, 'AM at 4 Wore ship at daylight saw about 30 Or 40 Sail of the enemy on the Lee Beam & Observ^d. The F. TopS^l T Spilt Unbent D^o. &Bent Another at 5.30 bore up Pr Sign^l with all Sail Sett employed Making all the necessary preparations for Battle at Noon the Enemy on the LB^d tack with all set Steering Down'.

On Tuesday 22 October Grindall's log continues, 'Light Breezes with a swell from the NW. at 12.10 the Action Commenc^d in the Rear of the Enemy at 12.30 the *Victory* Commencing an Action in the Van all sail sett standing down between the 2 Line'. *Prince* was a poor sailer and she had already set a new topsail, then fell off to windward closer to Nelson's division. Her log states, 'at 3 Observ^d several Ships Dismasted in the Centre & Rear —— [abbreviated word illegible] at 4 Discharged 2 broadsides at a Spanish 3 Decker put our Helm aport & Stood for the Rear of the Enemy & after exchanging a few Broad Sides with a French 2 Decker Obsrv^d her on fire'. The French ship was *Achille* (74). One broadside from *Prince* brought down *Achille*'s foremast, the fore top of which was already on fire, and this caused a conflagration which swiftly enveloped the French ship. It was now about 4.30 p.m. Seeing the situation, Grindall ceased firing into *Achille* and 'Wore Ship Hove to out Boats to save the People' escaping from a raging inferno. With the battle virtually over, *Prince* went alongside *Santisima Trinidad* (136), the log recording:

Employ^d Repairing the Rigging Shot away in the Action at 5 saw the *Archillies* [sic] Blow up Sent an Officer & Men to Take Charge of the S^t. *Trinidad* at 12 Took her in Tow at Daylight Observ^d the Fleet 3 or 4 leagues to Windward with the Dismasted Ships in C^o. employ^d Clearing the Wreck on Board the S^t. *Trinidad* at Noon Strong Breezes with Rain Rec^d prisoners on Board from the Diff^t Ships taken in the Action.

Prince, like *Defence*, suffered no casualties and only minimal damage to her mizzen mast.[102]

During the great storm after the battle, on Wednesday 23 October, *Prince*'s mizzen topsail split. As the wind increased Grindall lowered all the topsail yards to avoid further damage. The cable towing the *Santisima Trinidad* parted. Wallowing in the swell next afternoon, Thursday 25 October, *Prince* 'observ^d the Enemy take Possession of Another Dismasted Ship', implying that some vessels had been recaptured earlier. It then says:

... at 8 Tack^d all Square sails the Spanker was Split to Pieces *Santisima Trinidad*

PROGRESS BOOK – PRINCE 2nd RATE OF 98 GUNS: Source: ADM 180/6 folio 23

At what Port	Arrived	Docked	Coppered	Launched or Undocked	Sailed	Built or Nature of Repair	Cost of Hull, Masts & Yards Materials £ s d	Cost of Rigging & Stores Materials £ s d	Grand Total
Woolwich	Began	1 Jan 1782		4 July 1788	25 July 1788 to Plymouth	Built	46,653. 9s. 11d	8,388. 0s. 0d	55,041. 9s. 11d
Plymouth	6 Aug 1788	17 Oct 1788	Coppered Nov 1788	30 Oct 1788		Coppered	1,568. 6s. 6d	1. 15s. 7d	1,570. 2s. 1d
Plymouth		Taken in hand and completed 1790			5 Sep 1790	Fitted	2,131. 2s. 8d	4,096. 15s. 0d	6,227. 17s. 8d.
Plymouth	16 Nov 1790	11 Feb 1793	Coppered Repaired February 1793	13 Feb 1793	21 June 1793	Fitted	2,421	4,253	6,674
Portsmouth	31 Dec 1793	9 Sep 1794	Copper Repaired September 1794	12 Sep 1794	12 April 1795	Fitted	3,192	6,134	9,326
Portsmouth	28 May 1796	21 June 1796	Copper taken off July 1796 Re-coppered Oct 1796	2 Oct 1796	28 Nov 1796	Lengthened the Ship	19,905	11,362	31,267
Portsmouth	11 Jan 1797	29 Jan 1797	Copper Repaired	28 Feb 1797	6 March 1797	Made good damages	3,811	3,792	7,603
Portsmouth	16 Feb 1800				25 April 1800	Made good defects	2,034	2,050	4,084
Plymouth	15 April 1802	19 May 1802	Copper taken off May Re-coppered June 1802	18 June 1802		Very Small Repair			
Portsmouth			Copper Repaired 1803			Defects			
			Broken up 1836						

Note: At the time of writing the remainder of the *Prince*'s Progress Book does not appear to be available.

in Tow with Two Cablets sev[l] Ships in Sight of the Fleet but very much Stragled [sic] at 4 Wore Ship the Tow Broke a Drift in Wearing Lay too by her, at Day light More Mod[e] out Boats and took the Prize in Tow again answer[d] Sign[l] at 9 to Destroy Prizes Cast off the Tow, Hove to out Launch & Pinnace & Bro[t] [brought] Prisoners on Board at Noon *Neptune* & *Ajax* came to assist with Boats.

Efforts were made to remove people from *Santisima Trinidad*. Grindall's log for noon Friday continues:

12.30 Wore Ship at 2 fill[d] & Made Sail Wore Ship & Clear[d] for Action Observ[d] the Enemys fleet take possession of 2 Prizes at 4 Prize in Towe [sic] Enemys Fleet Forth 6 Hailed by *Pickle* had to Cast of the Towe without Receiving orders from the Adm[l]. 12 Struck Top Gall[t] S[ls] 4 Wore Ship 4.30 Clear[d] away the Stream Cable Hawser 5.40 Wore Ship at Day Light saw 44 Sail 7.20 Wore Ship at 8 Took Prize in Towe with a Nine Inch Hawser Much Sea Answ[d] Sign[l] to Destroy Prizes Cast off the Towe Cast off the Towe Out launch & Pinnace & Bro[t]. The Prisoners on Board Strong Breezes 7 a heavy swell Empl[d] Getting Prisoners from the Prize H M Ship *Neptune* came to assist.[103]

Describing this later, Lieutenant John Edwards of *Prince* wrote:

We had the *Santisima Trinidad*, the largest ship in the world, in tow. 'Tis impossible to describe the horrors the morning presented, nothing but distress signals flying in every direction. The signal was made to destroy the prizes. We had no time before to remove the prisoners; but what a sight when we came to remove the wounded, of which there were between three and four hundred. We had to tie the poor mangled wretches round their waists, and lower them down into a tumbling boat, some without arms, others no legs, and lacerated all over in the most dreadful manner...[104]

Such a task must have proved a mammoth undertaking: 'Mod[e] with Much Sea Emply[d] all the afternoon geting [sic] in Prisoners from the Prize we Suppose we have 500 On Board & a great many Wounded'. With her own crew of 750, together with 500 men from the Spanish ship, conditions within *Prince* carrying 1,250 souls in such heavy seas were horrific. It was fortunate that *Prince* had few casualties, otherwise the number needing medical attention would have been dreadful. Working parties were sent into *Santisima Trinidad* to scuttle the ship: 'Cut away the Prizes Anchors & began to Scuttle the Decks Strong Breezes & Squally at 9 came to the Wind on the L[d]. Tk [larboard tack] 9.15 parted C[o]. from the *Trinidad* up Top Gall[t] Y[ds] & Made sail 9.30 saw a Ship Blow up'. Aided by gunfire from *Prince* and *Neptune* (98), *Santisima Trinidad* foundered. For the rest of Saturday *Prince* remained under closed reefed topsails labouring twenty-eight miles off Cadiz, enduring 'Hard Gales & Hard Rain with Much Swell Carrying Sail off a Lee Shore No Vessel in Sight'. Poignantly, Grindall recorded on Sunday 27 October; 'Eleven Sail in Sight expended a Spanish Ensign for the use of the Wounded'. Twelve miles off Cadiz the next day and having to send down her topgallant masts, *Prince* made for Gibraltar and on Tuesday 29 October:

... at Day Light Short[d] Sail *Victory* & *Tonnant* had in Sight from the Mast Head at 8 *Revenge* in C[o]. 11 Short[d] Sail Steering into Gibraltar at ? past Anchored with the Small Bower in 22 Fath[s] Water Moored Ship Best Bower North & Small Bowere South the New Mole Head EbN 2 cables Length found Laying here HMS *Colossus*, *Belleisle*, *Bellerophon*, *Thunderer* & *Agamemenon*, & a Spanish Line of Battle Ship & 2 French Prizes...[105]

Prince spent only four days in Gibraltar. After the Spanish prisoners and officers had been counted and sent away, the ship was cleaned throughout while other crew members fished her mizzen mast and bowsprit, made repairs to rigging, and set up her bobstays and topmast rigging. She took in water, 2,711 pounds of fresh beef, 16 bags of onions, 10 casks of pork, 8 casks of peas, 4 casks of oatmeal, 4 casks of cocoa, 3 casks of flour, 2 casks of sugar, 7 quarter casks of wine, and 12 chaldrons of coal. Before sailing, Grindall 'Sent an Officer & 40 Men On Board the S[r]. *John* [San Juan] Spanish Prize', to assist sailing her to England. In the morning of Sunday 3 November Captain Grindall 'Unmoored Ship hove Short the Best Bow[r] [anchor] out Hawsers & Warp[d] the Ship further Out at 11 a Breeze from the Westward Weighed & Made Sail'. Next day Grindall called all hands on deck and 'Read Vice Adm[l]. Collingwoods Letter of Thanks to the Officers & Ship's Compy, at 12 Turning through the Gut of Gibraltar'.[106]

1806: When *Prince* returned to Plymouth, Captain Grindall was promoted to Rear-Admiral on 4 March. William Godfrey took over command of the ship in an acting capacity until formally relieved by Captain William Lechmere on 13 April. When Lechmere transferred into *Dreadnought* on 26 December his successor Captain Alexander Fraser took command of *Prince* three days later.[107]

1807: After refitting at Plymouth Captain Fraser paid off *Prince* on 23 March. While ships designed by Thomas Slade were renowned for their sailing qualities, it appears from the number of refits and her lengthened hull, that *Prince* was either poorly designed or badly built. She was then laid up in ordinary and moored in the Hamoaze until 1813.[108]

1813: *Prince* was fitted out and recommissioned for harbour service under Captain George Fawke on 12 October.

1815: In spring *Prince* sailed as ordered for Portsmouth where, on 16 May, Captain Fawke was superseded by Captain Edmund Bowyer. Bowyer paid off *Prince* on 2 September.[109]

FATE

From 1818 to 1832 *Prince* remained at Portsmouth on harbour service, then spent four years as a receiving ship. Finally, after 48 years' service, much of it inactive, in 1836 *Prince* was towed away to be broken up. When quitting her moorings, which were to be taken by *Victory*, the carved plume of Prince of Wales feathers on her stern were removed and fitted under the taffrail of the *Victory*, implying that the *Victory* had these fitted upon her at Trafalgar. Once it is discovered what adorned *Victory*'s taffrail at Trafalgar, this 'plume of feathers' will be removed and displayed within the *Victory* Gallery of the Royal Naval Museum, Portsmouth.

The 80 gun ship *TONNANT*

Launched in the French dockyard at Toulon in 1791-1792, the 80 gun *Tonnant* that fought with the British fleet at Trafalgar had been captured from the French at the battle of the Nile on 1 August 1798. Her predecessor, also of 80 guns, fought as the flagship of Commodore M des Herbiers de l'Etenduère against Rear-Admiral Edward Hawke at the battle of Finisterre on 14 October 1747. Hawke, with 14 sail of the line, engaged the French squadron of ten line of battleships convoying 252 merchantmen. In this affray *Tonnant* escaped with *Intrépide* into Brest.[110] In 1758 *Tonnant*, now flying the flag of Admiral du Chaffault, fought against Boscawen's fleet at the capture of Louisbourg.[111] Later, when flagship of M. St Andre du Venger, *Tonnant* fought against Hawke again, this second time at Quiberon Bay on 20 November 1759.

The Trafalgar *Tonnant*, which also carried 80 guns on two decks, would have required 3,500 to 4,000 loads of timber for her construction. This relates to between 175,00 and 200,000 cubic feet of wood before conversion. The actual amount of timber employed for this particular ship cannot be fully ascertained, for following French building practices, her hull was probably constructed less heavily than her British counterparts. *Tonnant*'s armament (based on the 80 gun *Franklin*) at the time of capture was as follows:[112]

Deck	Type	Weight cwt	qtrs	lbs
Lower gun deck	30 iron long 36 pounders			
	2 brass long 36 pounders	73	2	18
Upper gun deck	32 iron long 24 pounders			
	2 brass long 24 pounders	51	0	14
Quarter deck	12 iron long 12 pounders			
	2 brass long 12 pounders	33	1	16
Forecastle	6 brass long 12 pounders			
Poop	6 brass 36 pounder carronades			
Total	92			
Broadside	46			
Broadside weight	1212 pounds*			

* James erroneously states this figure as 1,287 pounds.

SERVICE HISTORY

1793: Based at Toulon, *Tonnant* was one of 18 ships of the line left in French hands after Vice-Admiral Samuel Lord Hood's occupation of Toulon in August. Twenty-five other ships were burnt, destroyed or captured.[113]

1795: On 3 March *Tonnant*, under the command of Commodore du Petit-Thouars put to sea from Toulon with Rear-Admiral Martin's fleet of 15 sail of the line and six frigates. Embarked were 5,000 troops to be landed on Corsica. Falling in with Vice-Admiral William Hotham's squadron off Genoa on 13 March, a spasmodic chase action ensued. Although action resumed next day, it was dogged by contrary winds. At around 8.30 am. *Tonnant* came under fire from the British *Illustrious* (74), which having already suffered considerable damage aloft resulting from her preceding engagement with the *Duquesne* and *Victoire*, was obliged to disengage at 9.15 a.m. leaving *Tonnant* virtually unscathed.[114]

1798: Following Napoleon's plan to invade Egypt, a large fleet comprising 15 sail of the line, 14 frigates, 43 supporting warships and some 400 transports was assembled at Toulon. In command was Vice-Admiral de Brueys, supported by Rear-Admirals Villeneuve, Blanquet du Chayla and Decrès. On board the transports was Napoleon's Grand Army numbering 36,000 troops. Sailing on 19 May, *Tonnant* included, de Brueys' fleet sailed south for Malta where, on 9 June, he combined forces with seventy transports from Civita Vecchia. Landing troops on 10 June, Malta, Gozo and Comino capitulated two days later. Meanwhile Nelson's squadron was in pursuit. De Brueys put to sea again on 19 June and anchored off Alexandria on 1 July. Nelson had left this port only two days before. Napoleon and his troops were landed and Alexandria surrendered the next day. Seeking a more suitable anchorage, de Brueys sailed again on 8 July, taking his main fleet into Abu-Kir Bay twelve miles east. Anchored in a line running NNE, *Tonnant* lay eighth in line directly astern of de Brueys' flagship, the 120 gun *Orient* (formerly the *Dauphin Royal* then *Sans Culotte*). According to Colonel Fawkes, who provided descriptions of most of the British and French ships at the battle of the Nile, *Tonnant* had broad light yellow sides with small black strakes running in line with the muzzles of her guns, and two black

SPECIFICATIONS: *TONNANT*

Rate	2nd	Date launched	1791-2	Complement	700
Guns	80	Length on the range of the gun deck	194 ft 2 ins	Ordnance - lower gun deck	32 x 32 pounders
Class	French *Tonnant* Sane-Border 1787	Length of keel for tonnage	160 ft	Ordnance - middle gun deck	32 x 18 pounders
Designer	Jacques Noel Sane	Extreme breadth	51 ft 9¼ ins	Ordnance - quarter deck	2 x 18 pounders
Builder	French Dockyard	Depth in hold	23 ft 3 ins		14 x 32 pounder carronades
Dockyard	Toulon	Tons burthen	2281 3/94	Ordnance - forecastle	4 x 32 pounder carronades
Date ordered	Captured 1 August 1798	Draught afore	20 ft 9 ins	Single broadside weight	1106 pounds
Date keel laid	No record	Draught abaft	22 ft 10 ins.	Fate	1821 Broken up

Source: Lyon, *Sailing Navy List*, p. 237.

CAPTAINS OF TONNANT (MSS 248/4 and 248/6)

Name	Time of Entry	Time of Discharge	On What Occasion
Commodore du Petit-Thouars (French)	-	1 August 1798	Killed at the battle of the Nile
Loftus Otway Bland	7 November 1798	4 December 1798	Superseded
Robert Louis Fitzgerald	5 December 1798	21 October 1798	Superseded
Richard Hawkins	22 October 1798	9 November 1798	Superseded Acting
Sir Edward Pellew Bt	11 March 1803	31 December 1803	New Book
Sir Edward Pellew Bt	1 January 1804	9 May 1804	Promoted to Rear Admiral of the White
William Henry Jervis	10 May 1804	26 January 1805	Drowned
Justice Finlay	27 January 1805	15 February 1805	Superseded Acting
Charles Tyler	16 February 1805	15 March 1806	Superseded
Alexander Burrowes	24 February 1806	15 March 1806	Superseded Acting
Thomas Brown	16 March 1806	16 July 1806	Superseded
Richard Turner Hancock	17 July 1806	3 March 1809	Superseded
James Bowen	4 March 1809	25 April 1809	Superseded
Thomas G Shortland	21 October 1809	3 December 1809	Superseded
Sir Charles Hamilton Bt	4 December 1809	27 August 1810	Superseded
Hasard Stackpoole	25 January 1810	27 August 1810	Superseded Acting
Sir Thomas Gore	28 August 1810	7 July 1811	Paid Off at Portsmouth
Richard Raggett	15 January 1814	8 February 1814	Superseded
Alexander Skene	6 April 1814	8 June 1814	Superseded
John Wainwright	9 June 1814	3 September 1814	Superseded
Charles Kerr	6 September 1814	5 June 1815	Superseded
Edward P Brenton	6 June 1815	24 August 1815	Paid Off at Plymouth
Edward P Brenton	25 August 1815	10 November 1815	Superseded
John Tailour [*Sic* - Taylor]	11 November 1815	19 November 1818	Paid Off at Plymouth
Thomas G Caulfield	17 November 1818	19 December 1818	Paid Off at Plymouth

lines on her channel wale between her two tiers of gunports.[115] Unlike most of the French ships, *Tonnant* had not laid a mooring line between her and *Heureux* abaft her. When Nelson arrived again with his fleet off Alexandria on 1 August and saw the French fleet to the eastward, he quickly made his plan to attack de Brueys' ships while at anchor. *Tonnant*, like many of the French fleet, had many crew ashore gathering water when Nelson's ships entered the bay to attack in the late afternoon. Battle commenced around 6.20 p.m. and just short of an hour later *Majestic* (74) brought up alongside *Tonnant* and engaged her starboard side. Over the next few hours the crew of *Tonnant* gave a gallant account of themselves, their return fire into *Majestic* bringing down the English main and mizzen masts. *Tonnant*'s commander, Commodore du Petit-Thouars, had both arms and one leg shot away and despite his wounds, before he died he urged his crew not to capitulate. Napoleon, impressed with this courage, named a street in Cairo after him. Like many ships seeing *Orient* on fire, *Tonnant* cut her cables to get clear of the inevitable explosion. Dismasted, and with many casualties, she later struck her colours.[116]

On 7 November command of *Tonnant* was briefly given to Captain Loftus Otway Bland, Richard Hawkins' acting captain. Captain Bland was followed on 5 December by Captain Robert Louis Fitzgerald who remained until she returned to England.

1799: *Tonnant*, like *Spartiate*, which had also been captured at the battle of the Nile, entered Plymouth on 17 July 1799, was paid off by Captain Fitzgerald and laid up in ordinary until she could be refitted.[117]

1801: As war with France had finished for a short time, *Tonnant* was docked at Plymouth on 9 December for a 'Middling Repair' and her copper was removed. Work progressed slowly and she was re-launched on Christmas Day 1802. The cost of this refit has not been recorded in the ship's Progress Book.[118]

1803: With war likely, *Tonnant* was recommissioned under Captain the Hon. Sir Edward Pellew Bt on 11 March and assigned to the Channel fleet. Provisioned and stored, the ship sailed from Plymouth 10 April with a squadron of three other vessels for the Iberian coast. On 26 August *Tonnant* was involved in recapturing the East Indiaman *Lord Nelson* (26).[119] On 2 September Admiral Calder's squadron fell in with and chased the two French 74 gun ships *Duguay Trouin* and *Guerrière* off Cape Ortegal. At the time *Tonnant* and *Culloden* (74) were lying off Ferrol. To prevent the French ships running into Corunna, Sir Edward Pellew immediately made sail to cut off the French escape. Although *Culloden* managed to get within firing range and engage both ships, *Tonnant*, whose main topgallant tye was carried away and jib was split in the high winds, had to leave the chase. She unwittingly entered Spanish waters where she was fired upon from a nearby fort.[120] *Tonnant* remained off Ferrol and Corunna for the rest of the winter and Pellew gathered valuable intelligence.

1804: Noticing a marked increase of French activity within Ferrol and Corunna, Pellew sent dispatches home informing the Admiralty that Spain, although neutral, appeared ready to ally herself with Napoleon. In May Pellew received his promotion to Rear-Admiral of the White so Captain William Henry Jervis was appointed to *Tonnant*.[121]

1805: In early January the *Tonnant* was deployed cruising off Rochefort gathering intelligence. Having gathered considerable information, Captain

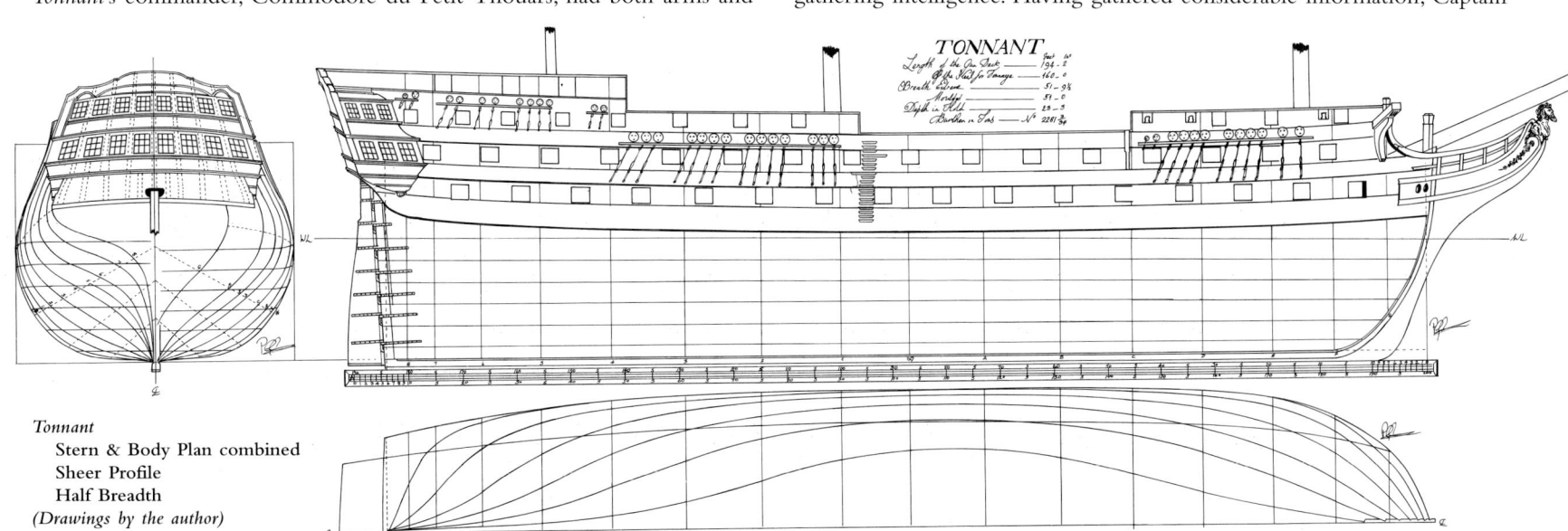

Tonnant
Stern & Body Plan combined
Sheer Profile
Half Breadth
(Drawings by the author)

Jervis made sail to inform his commander-in-chief with the main body of the Channel fleet stationed off Brest. Arriving on 26 January, Jervis immediately set off in his gig for the flagship *San Josef* (112) but was tragically drowned when the boat conveying him from *Tonnant* capsized, spilling the entire boat's crew into the sea. For a while Jervis was supported by his coxswain but when he became exhausted they both went under. Fortunately a good swimmer, the coxswain remained afloat until rescued. The only other survivor of this accident was Captain Patrick Campbell who had recently been wrecked in *Doris* (36) in Quiberon Bay and saved himself by holding onto an oar. Justice Finley briefly took command in an acting capacity until superseded by Captain Charles on 16 February. Britain declared war on Spain on 24 January; in March *Tonnant* with the 74 gun ships *Illustrious*, *Mars* and *Minotaur*, were detached from blockade duty off Brittany to form a new squadron commanded by Vice-Admiral Cuthbert Collingwood flying his flag in *Dreadnought* (98) blockading Cadiz.

TRAFALGAR

Tonnant's log for Monday 21 October concisely states:

> Fresh breezes with rain wore ship down topgall^t yards 4 wore ship out 3rd reef up topgall^t yards Midnight fair weather at 6 am saw the Combined Fleet ESE bore up toward them out 2nd reefs of the topsails & made sail Enemy forming the line 33 sail of the line 3 Frigates & 2 Brigs our force being 26 sail of the line 2 Frigates a Schooner & Cutter at 11 Cape Trafalgar E 5 leagues...[122]

Captain Tyler states that the British fleet had 26 rather than 27 ships of the line because *Africa* (64) had got detached and was entering the battle from the north and was not visible from his perspective. At the opening *Tonnant* was standing fourth in the line of Collingwood's leeward division. Cleared for action with unwanted gear taken into the hold or jettisoned overboard, *Tonnant* bore down upon the combined fleet with her wardroom Windsor chairs strung up on a line raised between her main and mizzen mast. What the French on *Pluton* (74) thought of such a sight remains unrecorded. *Tonnant*'s band was also playing the tunes 'Britons Strike Home' and 'The Downfall of Paris'. Tyler hailed Captain Hargood of *Belleisle* (74), remarking, 'A glorious day for England! We shall have one apiece before night!'[123] Tyler concluded Monday's log entry thus: '11.50 commenced firing on the Enemy', and steered towards *Pluton* which quickly luffed to rake the *Tonnant* but her attempt failed when her mizzen mast was shot away by another French ship, *Fougueux* (74). Making her approach to pass between *Algéciras* and *Monarca*, *Tonnant* fired both broadsides, double-shotted, into the French and Spanish ships, their return fire wounding two bandsmen and nine more of *Tonnant*'s crew.[124]

Tonnant's log dated Tuesday 22 October (actually begun noon Monday) then states:

> At 0.30 PM the French Admirals Ship *Algeciras* came up under our quarter At 1.20 AM I was wounded 1.50 a Spanish Ship struck to us at 2.5 the French Admirals Ship struck to us 5.40 the action ceased 16 or 17 of the Enemy making off with all sail employed clearing the wreck at 11 fresh breeze[s] the *Spartiate* took us in tow.

Tyler's concise journal says little of the part *Tonnant* played in the battle. Captain Tyler directed his ship straight for *Algéciras* but as the French ship backed her sails Tyler was obliged to go across the stern of *Monarca* instead. Raking the Spanish vessel as he passed Tyler then hauled *Tonnant* alongside *Monarca* and commenced firing his broadsides into her. At this point *Algéciras* came up under the stern of the *Tonnant* and raked the ship, wounding Tyler. Despite his wound, Tyler immediately ordered his helmsman to turn to starboard and run his ship on board the larboard bow of *Algéciras*. After this Tyler went below to have his wound attended, leaving Lieutenant John Bedford to command. A duel between the two ships, where the French attempted to board *Tonnant* several times, continued for an hour, but failing and with casualties rising they capitulated. Lieutenant Charles Bennett, accompanied by Lieutenant Arthur Ball and 50 men boarded the French ship and took their surrender. *Tonnant* was also maintaining a steady cannonade with her starboard foremost guns into *San Juan Nepomuceno* which struck her colours just 50 minutes after the French ship had fallen. Tyler sent Lt Benjamin Clements in the one remaining boat to take her surrender but during the crossing the boat was swamped and Clements, who could not swim, was only saved from drowning by a negro

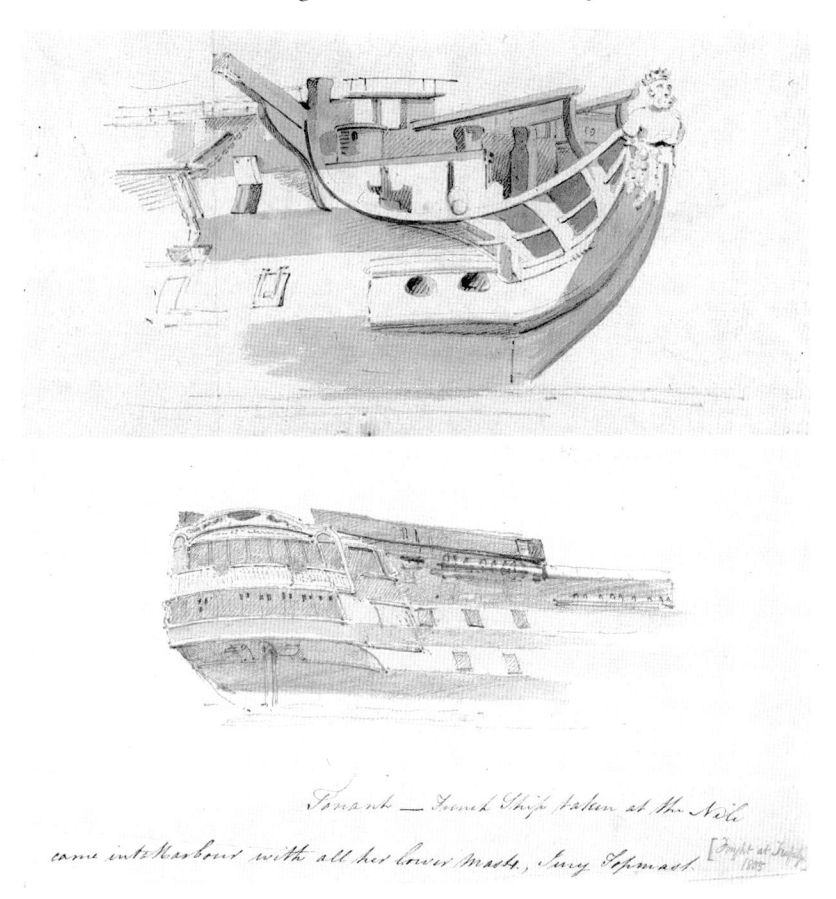

Tonnant. Sketches by Livesay, undated. Original caption to lower sketch says 'French ship taken at the Nile, came into harbour with all her lower masts, jury topmast'. *(Courtesy of the Royal Naval Museum)*

PROGRESS BOOK – TONNANT 2nd RATE OF 80 GUNS:

At what Port	Arrived	Docked	Coppered
Toulon	Began		
Plymouth	17 July 1799	9 Dec 1801	Copper Taken off December 1801 Recoppered Dec 1802
Plymouth	19 Dec 1805	6 Jan 1806	Copper taken off Re-coppered Jan 1806
Plymouth	31 Dec 1806	10 Jan 1807	Coppered Repaired and renailed
Plymouth	1 Oct 1809	22 Nov 1809	Copper taken off and Re-coppered Nov 1809
Plymouth	22 Nov 1811	Coppered upwards above waterline	
Plymouth	28 Feb 1812		
Portsmouth	25 June 1812		
Chatham	14 June 1813	16 Aug 1813	Copper taken off Aug Recoppered in Nov
Chatham	Taken in hand 3 Jan & completed Feb 1814		
Plymouth	27 May 1815	7 June 1815	Copper Repaired
Plymouth	21 Aug 1815		
Plymouth	30 Oct 1818	5 Mar 1821	
Taken To Pieces March 1821			

seaman named McNamara who swam back to *Tonnant* for a lifeline.

Tonnant did little after this except fire her guns intermittently at Admiral Dumanoir's squadron returning to the fight. *Tonnant* lost 26 killed in action, comprising Midshipman William Brown, 16 seamen and nine marines. Among her 50 wounded were Captain Tyler, Henry Ready, Master's Mate, Richard Little, the ship's Boatswain, the Captain's Clerk William Allen, 36 seamen and 16 marines. All three topgallant and topmasts were lost, rigging and the hull was damaged. Ironically, *Spartiate* (74), also captured at the battle of the Nile, took *Tonnant* in tow. Lying 8 leagues WSW½S of Cape Trafalgar next day the crew of *Tonnant* made good repairs, secured her masts, knotted and spliced the rigging and fished the fore yard. The log for Thursday 24 October notes: 'Enemy in Sight NE rigged Jury topmasts Main Yard bent a new fore Staysail & Prepared for Action AM saw the Enemy at Anchor off Cadiz.'[125] *Tonnant*, with the other British ships, cleared for action as a precaution against the remaining ships of the combined fleet resuming battle. After enduring gales over the next few days, on Tuesday 29 October *Tonnant*, with all sail set stood in towards Gibraltar and at '4 shortened Sail & came to Anchor with the best bower in 35 fms. moored Ship HM Ship *Victory* arrived'. The ship remained at Gibraltar until 17 November when considerable repairs were undertaken. Sails were dried, unbent from the yards and sent into the sail loft for repair, her damaged rudder was unhung and sent into the dockyard, the gammoning rope that held the bowsprit down was renewed; a host of carpenters from the dockyard were embarked to fish the fore mast, main mast and fore yard, make new topsail and topgallant yards and undertake repairs. On late Sunday afternoon 3 November the log records that '3 Prizes came in with our Disabled Ships'; on Tuesday following, 'sailed HM Ships *Victory* & *Bellerophon*'. Besides taking on water, receiving fresh beef and vegetables together with boxes of lemons from victualling ships, *Tonnant* returned empty casks to *Peggy's Success* and *Heron* transports, and sent 'into the Store lime juice & Sugar'. On 9 November the log reports the arrival of Admiral Collingwood and the Earl of Northesk with their squadrons. Notable is *Tonnant*'s entry for Monday 13 November:

> Light airs and fair employed watering Rec^d French prisoners from HMS *Britannia* AM D^o weather Rec^d French Prisoners from HMS *Polyphemus* Read a Public letter from Admiral Collingwood and The Officers and Ships Company have agreed that the sum of Two thousand Pounds shall be Paid by the Prize Agents out of Emoluments arising from the Action of the 21st Ult^o [Ultimo] for the Purpose of Erecting a Monument to the memory of the late Lord Viscount Nelson.

Next day *Eurydice* (24) arrived with the recaptured transport *Lady Elgin* and, the day after, 'HM Ships *Prince Thunderer* and *Ajax* sailed'. On the 16 November *Tonnant* had a 'near miss' accident when 'HM Brig *Scout* drifted across our Bow'. Unscathed, however, the ship made preparations to sail. On Sunday 17 November, after making an entry that '*Eurydice* came in with 2 Spanish gun Boats', and receiving five Spanish prisoners, *Tonnant* weighed and made sail for England with '*Téméraire*, *Royal Sovereign* & *Colossus* in Company', *Royal Sovereign* being towed by *Leviathan* (74).[126] *Tonnant* finally arrived at Plymouth on 19 December.[127]

1806: Docked at Plymouth on 6 January, *Tonnant* had her copper replaced and was undocked on 6 February. After being recommissioned under Alexander Burrowes on 24 February the ship completed her refit at a total cost of £17,890. Burrowes, however, had only held acting command and was superseded on 16 March by Captain Thomas Brown. Appointed as flagship of the Channel fleet flying the flag of Rear-Admiral Eliab Harvey, *Tonnant* sailed on 20 March. Admiral Harvey had gallantly commanded *Téméraire* (98) at Trafalgar. Exactly four months later Brown was succeeded by Captain Richard Turner Hancock.[128]

1807: *Tonnant* returned to Plymouth on 31 December 1806 and went into dock on 10 January for two days to have her copper repaired and re-nailed at a cost of £529. With her defects made good and embarking new stores valued at £7,869, she sailed on 1 February flying the flag of Admiral Michael De Courcy who commanded the blockading squadron off Rochefort.

1808: *Tonnant* spent most of the year cruising off the Spanish coast at the beginning of the Peninsular War.

1809: Command of *Tonnant* changed three times: Captain James Bowen entered the ship on 4 March and remained until the ship returned to Plymouth on 1 October; he was superseded by Captain Thomas Shortland three weeks later; and on 22 November the ship went into Plymouth dock for three days to have her copper replaced, when Captain Sir Charles Hamilton Bt took command and sailed for deployment on 19 December.[129]

1810: At the end of January Captain Hasard Stackpoole assumed acting command of the ship until Captain Sir Thomas Gore relieved him on 28 August while deployed on blockade duty off Ushant. On 24 September Gore sighted a French vessel making for Brest. Despite heavy seas and a ris-

Source: ADM 180/9 folio 688 and ADM 180/10 folio 51

Launched or Undocked	Sailed	Built or Nature of Repair	Cost of Hull, Masts & Yards Materials £	Workmen £	Cost of Masts & Yards Materials £	Workmen £	Cost of Rigging & Stores Materials £	Workmen £	Grand Total £
5 Dec 1802	10 April 1803	Middling Repair	NOTE: No Costs Given						
6 Feb 1806	20 March 1806	Refitted	2,773	1,332	2,655	233	10,796	101	17,890
12 Jan 1807	1 Feb 1807	Defects	529	226	256	26	7,869	58	8,964
25 Nov 1809	19 Dec 1809	Defects	4,246	1,227	3,103	108	9,415	98	18,197
	7 Jan 1812	Defects	1,780	772	3,428	53	4,111	122	10,269
8 March 1812		Fitted	included in above	included in above	included in above		included in above		
	10 June 1813	Defects	21	229	5	7	2,776	21	3,059
9 Dec 1813		Small Repair	10,939	5,090	1,642	169	-	38	17,978
	12 March 1814	Fitted for Sea	608	279	326	70	18,427	33	19,743
20 June 1815	24 July 1815	Defects	2,417	1,300	856	15	4,744	186	9,518
14 Nov 1815		Defects	included in above	included in above	included in above		included in above		

ing gale from the NW, Gore immediately gave chase and pursued the Frenchman into Passage du Raz. At about 2 p.m. *Tonnant* lost her main topmast and her fore and mizzen topgallant masts, and abandoned the chase. Then *Tonnant* convoyed troops for General Sir Arthur Wellesley (later the Duke of Wellington)'s army to Lisbon. Under orders of Admiral Sir Thomas Williams, *Tonnant* rejoined his squadron blockading Brest and *Orient*. While cruising in Basque Roads Captain Gore was badly injured when a block falling from the main top struck him on the head.

1811: According to primary sources Captain Gore paid off *Tonnant* at Portsmouth on 7 July.[130] The Progress Book states that she went into Plymouth on 22 November, but this is either a clerk's error in writing 'ditto', implying Plymouth rather than Portsmouth, or some men could have been retained to sail her down the Channel. The probability from later entries is that she remained at Portsmouth. Without going into dock, *Tonnant* was then 'coppered upwards above waterline' to make good her defects.[131]

1812: After refitting, *Tonnant* left the dockyard on 7 January, returning on 28 February for refitting. Completed and laid up on 8 March, the total cost was £10,269 of which £1,780 was spent on her hull, £3,428 for masts and yards and £4,111 on rigging and stores, the remaining £947 covering labour.[132] *Tonnant* then remained out of commission for two years, having further defects made good in Portsmouth dockyard on 25 June and sailing for Chatham on 10 June 1813.

1813: Arriving at Chatham on 14 June *Tonnant* went into dock on 14 August to have her copper replaced and undergo a 'small repair' and was undocked on 9 December.

1814: More ships being needed in the war against America, *Tonnant* was taken in hand on the 3 January, fitted for sea service and completed one month later at a cost of £19,743 of which £18,427 was spent on rigging and stores. While refitting the ship was recommissioned under Captain Richard Raggett from 15 January until 6 April when he was superseded by Captain Alexander Skene. The ship sailed to Bermuda where, on 9 June, Skene was superseded by Captain John Wainwright. *Tonnant* became the flagship of Vice-Admiral Sir Alexander Cochrane, sent to relieve Admiral Sir John Warren. Also entering the ship was the Captain of the Fleet, Rear-Admiral Edward Codrington. Having received Major-General Ross on board, the British squadron sailed on 2 August to assault Washington. This was successfully undertaken by the smaller vessels and boats on 24 August under Cockburn's command and supported by troops under Major-General Ross. Then *Tonnant* sailed to attack Baltimore on 13 September. *Tonnant*'s wounded in assisting troops on shore were Midshipman Charles Ogle, and seamen Matthew Hamstead, Daniel Ross, James Macquire, William Johnson, John Wilson and John Redmonds.[133] Meanwhile Captain Charles Kerr took command on 6 September. Preparations were then made to attack New Orleans. *Tonnant* arrived at Negril Bay, Jamaica, on 22 November and assembled a large force. Her squadron anchored off Lake Borgne at the mouth of the Mississippi on 13 December. The assault, directed at capturing American gunboats defending the approaches to the city, was made next day using 42 boats from the squadron carrying 1,000 seamen and marines led by Commander Nicholas Lockyer of *Sophie* (18). The gunboats were successfully taken but British losses were severe, with 61 killed and 94 wounded. Major-General Sir Edward Pakenham landed troops but the major attack on 8 January 1814 failed miserably because Major-General Andrew Jackson held a good defensive position. British losses amounted to 2,000 killed, wounded, or taken prisoner. *Tonnant* then returned to Bermuda where she remained until recalled to England the following year.[134]

1815: Returning to England, Captain Edward Brenton commanded *Tonnant* from 6 June and paid off the ship at Plymouth on 24 August. Today Brenton is noted for his published accounts of the naval war between 1793 and 1815. *Tonnant* was then ordered to serve as the flagship of Rear-Admiral Sir Benjamin Hallowell on the Cork station. Brenton recommissioned her the following day and sailed for Ireland. On 11 November Brenton was superseded by Captain John Tailour.[135] For the next three years *Tonnant* remained off Cork, serving as Admiral Hallowell's flagship.

1818: Recalled home, Tailour carried *Tonnant* to Plymouth for the last time on 30 October and transferred command of the ship to Captain Thomas Caulfield on 17 November. Two days later Caulfield finally paid off *Tonnant* after 20 years service in the British navy and a previous career serving the French navy.[136]

FATE

After being laid up in ordinary for three years *Tonnant* was taken into dock on 5 March 1821 and taken to pieces.[137]

NOTES TO PART 1: CHAPTER 2

[1] Colledge, 1, p. 172.
[2] TNA: PRO, ADM 180/6 Entry 27.
[3] RNM, MS 248/4.
[4] RNM, MS 248/4.
[5] James, 3, p. 177; Clowes, 5, p. 49.
[6] RNM, MS 248/4.
[7] RNM, MS 248/6.
[8] Schom, p. 180.
[9] *Ibid.*
[10] Schom, p. 201.
[11] Clowes, 5, p. 109.
[12] Clowes, 5, p. 121.
[13] TNA:PRO, ADM 51/1549 part 7.
[14] TNA:PRO, ADM 35/15955.
[15] TNA:PRO, ADM 51/1549 part 7.
[16] *Ibid.*
[17] *Ibid.*
[18] James, 3, pp. 26, 75, 79, 104; Clowes, 5, pp. 152–153.
[19] TNA:PRO, ADM 51/1549 part 7.
[20] *Ibid.*
[21] RNM, MS 249/6.
[22] TNA: PRO, ADM 180/10.
[23] RNM, MS 248/6.
[24] James, 4, p. 279.
[25] RNM, MS 248/6.
[26] RNM, MS 248/6; TNA: PRO, ADM 180/10.
[27] James, 5, p. 236; Clowes, 4, p. 470.
[28] RNM, MS 248/6.
[29] TNA: PRO, ADM 180/10.
[30] *Ibid.*
[31] TNA: PRO, ADM 180/6 Entry 28.
[32] Clowes, 4, p. 175.
[33] RNM, MS 248/4.
[34] *Ibid.*
[35] Clowes, 4, p. 386–387.
[36] RNM, MS 248/4.
[37] TNA: PRO, ADM 180/6 Entry 28; RNM, MS 248/6.
[38] RNM, MS 248/6.
[39] *Ibid.*
[40] *The Wynne Diaries*, 3, pp. 176, 184
[41] Clowes, 5, p. 26; *Personal Narrative of Events from 1799 to 1815*, p. 46.
[42] Clowes, 5, pp. 131, 159.
[43] TNA: PRO, ADM 51/15441 part 1.
[44] TNA: PRO, ADM 51/4514 part 3.
[45] RNM, MS 248/6.
[46] TNA: PRO, ADM 180/10 Entry 24.
[47] James, 4, p. 279.
[48] RNM, MS 248/6.
[49] *Ibid.*
[50] James, 5, p. 206; Clowes, 5, pp. 283–284.
[51] James, 5, pp. 161–164.
[52] RNM, MS 248/6.
[53] TNA: PRO, ADM 180/10 Entry 24.
[54] RNM, MS 248/6.
[55] TNA: PRO, ADM 180/10 Entry 24.
[56] TNA: PRO, ADM 180/6 Entry 78.
[57] RNM, MS 248/4.
[58] TNA: PRO, ADM 51/1418 part 8.
[59] Egerton, *Turner; The Fighting Téméraire*, p. 24.
[60] *Ibid.*
[61] TNA: PRO, ADM 180/6 Entry 78; RNM, MS 248/4.
[62] TNA: PRO, ADM 51/1530 part 5.
[63] James, 4, p. 35; Clowes, 5, p. 134.
[64] TNA: PRO, ADM 51/1530 part 5.
[65] *Ibid.*
[66] Clowes, 5, pp. 131, 157.
[67] TNA: PRO, ADM 51/1530 part 5.
[68] *Ibid.*

ns.

[69] TNA: PRO, ADM 180/10 Entry 32.
[70] RNM, MS 248/6.
[71] TNA: PRO, ADM 180/10 Entry 32.
[72] TNA: PRO, ADM 95/46 folio 156.
[73] RNM, MS 248/6.
[74] Egerton, *Turner; The Fighting Téméraire*, p. 37.
[75] TNA: PRO, ADM 51/3328.
[76] Beatson, MS 4639 folio 456.
[77] Beatson, MS 4639 folio 409.
[78] Egerton, *Turner; The Fighting Téméraire*, passim.
[79] TNA: PRO, ADM 180/6 folio 23
[80] Ibid.
[81] Ibid.
[82] RNM, MS 248/4.
[83] TNA: PRO, ADM 180/6 folio 23.
[84] Clowes, 4, p. 260; Clowes, 4, pp. 263, 1795.
[85] Goodwin, *The Construction and Fitting of the Sailing Man Of War 1750–1850*, passim; Lyon, p. 64.
[86] TNA: PRO, ADM 180/6 folio 23.
[87] RNM, MS 248/4.
[88] James, 2, p. 21.
[89] James, 3, p. 21.
[90] TNA: PRO, ADM 180/6 folio 23, James, 2, pp. 120, 195, 254, 264, 7–91.
[91] James, 2, pp. 195, 254
[92] Clowes, 4, p. 178.
[93] RNM, MS 248/4.
[94] Colledge, 1, p. 309.
[95] James, 2, p. 254.
[96] James, 2, p. 164.
[97] TNA: PRO, ADM 180/66 folio 23.
[98] RNM, MS 248/4.
[99] TNA: PRO, ADM 180/6 folio 23.
[100] TNA: PRO, ADM 51/1543 part 2.
[101] Ibid.
[102] James, 4, pp. 77–91; Clowes, 5, pp. 149, 156, 160
[103] TNA: PRO, ADM 51/1543 part 2.
[104] Legg/Hart-Davis, *Trafalgar: An Eyewitness Account*, p. 118.
[105] TNA: PRO, ADM 51/1543 part 2.
[106] TNA: PRO, ADM 51/1543 part 2; ADM 180/6 folio 2; ADM 180/6 folio 23; ADM 51/1543 part 2; ADM 51/1543 part 2; ADM 51/1543 part 2.
[107] RNM, MS 248/6.
[108] Ibid.
[109] RNM, MS 248/6.
[110] Clowes, 3, p. 127.
[111] Clowes, 3, p. 185.
[112] James, 2, p. 185.
[113] Clowes, 4, p. 204.
[114] Clowes, 4, p. 268–271.
[115] Paul, 'British Ships Painting at Aboukir', *Mariner's Mirror*, 1914, 4, pp. 266–274.
[116] James, 2, passim; Lavery, *Nelson and the Nile*, passim.
[117] TNA: PRO, ADM 180/11.
[118] Ibid.
[119] James, 3, p. 196.
[120] Clowes, 5, p. 323.
[121] RNM, MS 248/6.
[122] TNA: PRO, ADM 51/1547 part 2.
[123] Pope, *England Expects*, pp. 222–223.
[124] Pope, *England Expects*, pp. 284–285.
[125] TNA: PRO, ADM 51/1547 part 2.
[126] Ibid.
[127] TNA: PRO, ADM 180/10 folio 51.
[128] RNM, MS 248/6; ADM 180/10 folio 51.
[129] TNA: PRO, ADM 180/10 folio 51.
[130] RNM, MS 248/6.
[131] TNA: PRO, ADM 150/10 folio 51.
[132] Ibid.
[133] James, 6, pp. 305–321.
[134] TNA: PRO, James, 6, pp. 357–359.
[135] RNM, MS 248/6
[136] RNM, MS 248/6.
[137] TNA: PRO, ADM 180/10 folio 51.

PART 1: CHAPTER 3
THE BRITISH THIRD RATE 74 GUN SHIPS

The 74 gun ship *ACHILLE*

Named after the Greek hero Achilles who was fatally wounded in the heel by an arrow fired by Paris at the siege of Troy, *Achille* was, taking into account those ships named *Achilles*, the sixth vessel to bear this name in the Royal Navy. The first *Achille* was an 8 gun sloop captured from the French in 1744; this vessel was herself captured by the Spanish off Jamaica on 14 November 1745. The second vessel named *Achilles* was an 8 gun schooner purchased into the navy in 1747. Like her predecessor, she was captured by the Spanish in 1748. The third ship, also named *Achilles*, was a 4th rate of 60 guns built by John Barnard at Harwich. Launched 16 May 1757, she saw active service during the Seven Years' War and the American War of Independence until hulked in 1780 and sold in June 1784. The fourth *Achille* was a 14 gun storeship purchased in 1780 and sold 8 January 1784. The fifth *Achille* was a 78 gun ship captured from the French by Howe's squadron at the battle of the Glorious First of June 1794 and broken up at Plymouth in February 1796.[1] The Trafalgar *Achille* is listed in a class on her own because her design was based on the lines of the French 80 gun ship *Pompée* captured at Toulon by Hood's squadron on 29 August 1793. Ordered on 10 June 1795, the contract for building the new *Achille* was given to Cleverley. Laid down at Gravesend in October 1795, the ship was finally launched on 16 April 1798. Her building cost of £50,524 comprised £38,291 for her hull, £2,542 for masts and yards and the remaining £7,711 for rigging and stores; all including labour costs. Mounting thirty 32 pounders on her lower gun deck, thirty 18 pounders on the upper gun deck, four 18 pounders and ten 32 pounder carronades on the quarter deck, two 18 pounders and two 32 pounder carronades on her forecastle, and a further six 18 pounder carronades upon her poop, *Achille* could deliver a single broadside weight of 1,049 pounds. Remarkably her broadside weight equalled that of the 100 gun *Victory*.

SPECIFICATIONS: *ACHILLE*

Rate	3rd	Length on the range of the gun deck	182 ft 2 ins	Ordnance - upper gun deck	30 x 18 pounders
Guns	74	Length of keel for tonnage	149 ft 9¾ ins	Ordnance - quarter deck	4 x 18 pounders
Class	Achille 1795	Extreme breadth	49 ft		10 x 32 pounder carronades
Designer	From French lines of *Pompée*	Depth in hold	21 ft 10 ins	Ordnance - forecastle	2 x 18 pounders
Builder	Cleverley	Tons burthen	1916		2 x 32 pounder carronades
Dockyard	Gravesend	Draught afore	19 ft 3 ins	Ordnance - roundhouse/poop	6 x 18 pounder carronades
Date ordered	10 June 1795	Draught abaft	20 ft 9 ins	Single broadside weight	1049 pounds
Date keel laid	October 1795	Complement	640	Fate	1865 Sold to Castle and Beech and broken up
Date launched	16 April 1798	Ordnance - lower gun deck	30 x 32 pounders		

Source: Lyon, *Sailing Navy List*, p. 110.

CAPTAINS OF ACHILLE (MSS 248/4 and 248/6)

Name	Time of Entry	Time of Discharge	On What Occasion
Henry E Stanhope	23 June 1798	26 February 1799	Superseded
George Murray	27 February 1799	28 February 1801	To the *Edgar*
Edward Buller	1 March 1801	28 April 1802	Paid Off
James Wallis	13 November 1801	14 January 1802	Superseded Acting
Edward Buller	20 April 1802	1 January 1802	Superseded
John Oakes Hardy	2 June 1802	29 June 1802	To the *Courageux*
Richard King	27 May 1805	10 July 1809	Superseded
John Hayes	11 July 1809	5 September 1809	Superseded Acting
Sir Richard King	6 September 1809	2 March 1811	To the *San Josef*
Hon. The G H L Dundas	5 March 1811	15 April 1811	To the *Euryalus*
A P Hollis	16 April 1811	9 August 1815	Paid Off

SERVICE HISTORY

1798: Launched on 16 April and taken to Chatham for fitting out, *Achille* was commissioned on 23 June by Captain Henry Stanhope.

1799: Assigned to the Channel fleet, she was mainly deployed on station blockading Brest. One incident concerned seaman James Hailey striking a midshipman in the execution of his duty and other mutinous conduct. The court martial on 15 February on board *Gladiator* (44) found Hailey guilty and sentenced him to be hanged. On 27 February Captain George Murray took command. Arriving off Plymouth from Ushant on the evening of 13 June *Achille* accidentally ran aboard *Cæsar* (80), losing her bowsprit and fore topmast and one of her crew was killed. Repaired, the ship received orders to embark 50 bullocks and several tons of hay at £5 per ton for their consumption and convey the livestock to Vice-Admiral Pole's squadron at sea.

1800: On 28 August *Achille*, in company with other ships of the Channel fleet, arrived in Plymouth Sound. Receiving new orders from Earl St Vincent on 5 September, all ships made ready and sailed at once from Cawsand Bay to join him, as directed, without delay. With *Achille* were *Royal Sovereign* (100), *Prince George* (90), *Princess Royal* (90), and *Bellona* (74), each of which cleared Penlee Point by nightfall.

1801: Returning to Plymouth on 8 January after cruising off Ushant, *Achille* embarked fresh provisions and stores and rejoined the Channel fleet on 29 January. She remained on station blockading Brest and Rochefort until hostilities with France ceased. On 21 February *Achille* captured a French brig that had become detached from a large convoy dispersed in a gale while making for Brest. Laden with wheat, she was sent immediately to Plymouth. On 28 February Captain Murray exchanged into *Edgar* (74) which, drawing less water, was being sent to the North Sea, an area familiar to Murray. Edward Buller, *Edgar*'s captain, took command of *Achille* on

PROGRESS BOOK - ACHILLE 3rd RATE OF 74 GUNS:

At what Port	Arrived	Docked	Coppered
Plymouth	23 Apr 1803	15 Nov 1803	Copper taken off Nov 1803; Re-coppered Mar 1805
Plymouth	6 Dec 1805	–	Copper repaired
Plymouth	18 June 1807	6 July 1807	Copper repaired
Plymouth	15 Apr 1809	28 Apr 1809	Copper repaired
Portsmouth	8 Oct 1813	23 Oct 1813	Copper taken off Oct; Re-coppered Dec 1813
Chatham	20 July 1815	11 Oct 1817	Copper taken off Oct 1817; Re-coppered Dec 1822 3
Sheerness	21 Apr 1823	9 Oct 1828	Shifted 2 strakes of copper at waters edge
Sheerness		8 Nov 1833	Replaced the Copper removed for Caulking
Sheerness		13 Aug 1839	Copper taken off & re-coppered
Sheerness	13 May 1845		Took off & replaced six upper strakes of Copper & Garboard Supplied copper to Light Line April 1851
		17 May 1852	Repaired Copper

1 March.[2] After going into Plymouth to refit on 15 July, *Achille* returned to her station off Rochefort. Enduring dreadful weather, *Achille* had to return home at the end of October to overhaul her rigging. On 13 November Captain James Wallis took temporary command of the ship until 14 January 1802. Lying in Cawsand Bay on 26 November preparing to join Admiral Mitchell's squadron in Bantry Bay, an unfortunate accident concerned *Achille*. The crew was being paid wages before sailing, attracting bum boats alongside. Anxious that some seamen might desert, Mr Mudge, *Achille*'s First Lieutenant, ordered the traders to stand off from the ship. One boat, quite full of women, did not heed the order, so Lieutenant Mudge took a musket from the gangway sentry. Having confirmed with the sentry that the weapon was not loaded, Mudge took a cartridge, discarded the ball, emptied the powder and wadding down the muzzle, cocked the lock, presented the musket and fired it towards the boat. To his dismay the weapon was loaded and shot the boatman in the face. The luckless victim was immediately taken ashore to the hospital where he died of his wound. Mudge was arrested on the 28th, charged with manslaughter, court-martialled on the

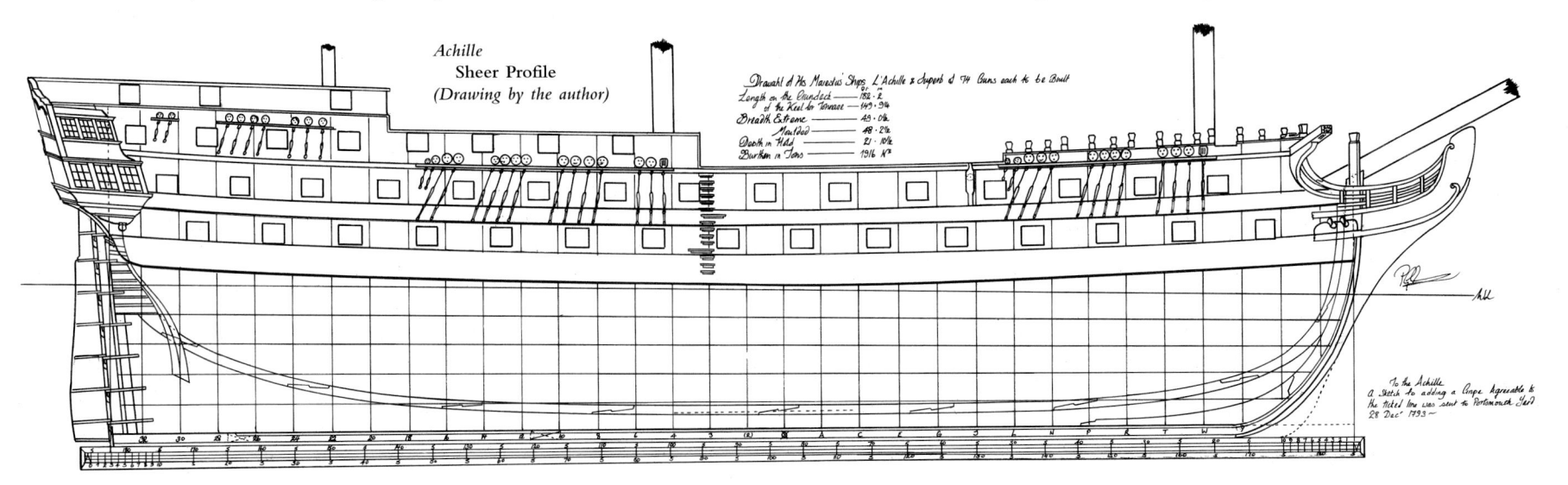

Achille
Sheer Profile
(Drawing by the author)

THE 74 GUN SHIP *ACHILLE*

Source: ADM 180/10/62

Launched or Undocked	Sailed	Built or Nature of Repair	Cost of Hull, Materials £	Workmen £	Cost of Masts & Yards Materials £	Workmen £	Cost of Rigging & Stores Materials £	Workmen £	Grand Total £
30 Mar 1803	8 May 1805	Large Repair	25,603	12.688	2,417	125	7,547	164	50,524
-	29 Jan 1806	Defects	978	483	4,777	107	13,063	89	19.947
7 July 1807	24 July 1807	Defects	482	350	1,337	25	5,048	47	7,269
2 May 1809	29 May 1809	Defect	946	780	692	23	4,801	67	7,389
24 Dec 1813	1 Mar 1814	Defects	10,582	3,555	3,298	41	10.935	120	28.531
0 Dec 1822	April 1823 to Sheerness	Very Large Repair	40,683	13,246	126	197	-	-	54.252
			392	419	3	15	2	-	831
			468	386	7	-	10	19	890
7 Nov 1828	-	-	Expenses from 1831 to 1832						
3 Mar 1836		Defects	180	224	-	-	6	-	410
25 May 1841		Between a Small & Middling Repair – Demonstrated	8,377	6,307	-	11	367	38	15,100
13 June 1845		Advanced Ship	241	2,204	6	6	76	30	2,563
16 June 1852		Co. Defects	As above	Ditto	Ditto	Ditto	Ditto	Ditto	
		Expenses in Ordinary to 31 Mar 1860	114	213	327	-	-	11	338
		Do. To 31 Mar 1861	121	365	-	-	-	2	488
		Surveyed alongside	26	1	-	-	-	-	27

flagship in the Hamoaze and found guilty. Next day *Achille*, amid a snowstorm, sailed for Ireland, leaving Mudge behind to serve his sentence.

1802: When *Achille* went into Portsmouth in January Captain Buller resumed command. Three mutineers from *Téméraire* (74) were hanged aboard *Achille* on 19 January, a further two executed on *Centaur* (74) the same day. When peace was declared between Britain and France *Achille* lay anchored in Torbay. She returned to Plymouth and decommissioned on 27 March, the crew paid off and discharged. Shortly after Captain Buller was ordered to recommission the ship under the previous officers and on 17 May a Royal Marines captain, two lieutenants and sixty privates entered the ship. Unfortunately *Achille* was in need of considerable repairs to her hull so after sailing into the Hamoaze on 23 April and removing all stores an d equipment the ship's crew were paid off 29 June.[3] The French *Achille* at Trafalgar was at this time under construction at Rochefort.[4]

1803: Hostilities with France reopened on 16 May and *Achille* went into dock on 15 November for her much needed 'large repair'. Her copper was removed, the ship remaining in dock throughout 1804.[5]

1805: Re-coppered during March, *Achille* was launched on 30 March, completing her large repair at a total cost of £50,524 of which labour costs amounted to £12,957.[6] Moving out to Cawsand Bay on 8 May, the ship was recommissioned on 27 May under Captain Richard King and deployed immediately with the Channel Fleet, blockading the French Atlantic coast.

1805: In August she was with *Dreadnought* (98), Vice-Admiral Collingwood, and *Colossus* (74), watching Cadiz.[7] In the weeks preceding the Battle of Trafalgar the ship remained operating between latitude 36° 23' and 36° 42'; besides caulking the deck and painting, the ship's company were mustered by divisions; also John Welsh, a boatswain's mate, was punished with 24 lashes for negligence. *Achille*'s log entry for Monday 21 October (starting 12 noon Sunday 20th land time) reads: 'PM. fresh breezes and squally, down topGall[t.] Yards, at 2 Wore, at 4 up topGall[t.] Yards out 2 reefs the topsails - at 8 the admiral NbW 2 or 3 Miles'.[8]

TRAFALGAR

That morning *Achille* lay seventh in the order of sailing within Collingwood's leeward division, her log stating: 'AM. light airs & fine W[r.] At day light saw the combined fleet bearing East; made the all sail towards them, at noon the *Royal Sovereign* Vice Admiral began to engage the Enemy, the rest of the fleet with all sail set going into Action'.[9]

Following astern of *Colossus*, King brought *Achille* quickly across the stern of *Montañez* (74), luffed and engaged her starboard side. After twelve minutes *Montañez*, unable to endure the onslaught from *Achille*'s larboard guns, fell away. King now directed his ship to support the dismasted *Belleisle*, but in so doing fell in with *Argonauta* (74). Running *Achille* alongside her larboard side, King began a close engagement for an hour, then *Argonauta* attempted to make sail. Unable to escape, the Spanish ceased firing, shut their lower deck ports and would have surrendered to *Achille* if the French *Achille* (74) and *Berwick* (74) had not intervened. First fired upon by the opposing *Achille* as she passed, King soon found himself confronted by *Berwick*. For over an hour a hot gunnery duel was fought before *Berwick* hauled down her flag in surrender and *Achille*'s boarding party took possession. Total casualties in *Achille* were 72, of whom 13 were killed and 59 wounded. Among the dead was Midshipman Francis Mug; wounded were Lieutenants Parkins Prynn and Josias Bray; Captain of Marines Palmes Westropp; Lieutenant of Marines William Leddon; George Pegge, Master Mate; Midshipmen William Snow and William Staines; and first class volunteer William Warren.[10] *Achille*'s log dated Tuesday 22 October provides a much briefer account of these events, simply stating:

PM Light breezes & fine W[r.] At ½ past 12 came to Action, and continued until 4 with One french, and One spanish Ship, two decks each, they Struck their Colours, sent a Lieut. men on b[d.] the french Ship took possession of her, which proved to be the *Berwick* of 74 Guns Rec[d.] on b[d.] french prisoners, at ? past 4 made sail Admiral &Prizes in Co[py.] Empl[d..] repairing damages and Reeving Running Rigging afresh, knotting & etc. the *Euryalus* having the *Royal Sovereign* in tow she being dismasted, strong gales and hazy with rain; – counted the Enemy's fleet before the Action, which amounted to 33 sail of the line, 5 Frigates and 2 Brigs saw 21 sail making their escape the rest having surrendered to us...[11]

Next day there were strong gales and in the morning *Achille* 'took the *Monarch* a spanish Prize in tow'. The *Monarch* referred to in the log was in fact the 74 gun *Monarca*. Although the combined fleet had effectively been annihilated, *Achille*'s log entry for Thursday 24 October intimates that a potential threat still remained: 'PM Strong gales and hazy with rain, cleared for Action on seeing 2 sail of the enemy's Ships standing from Cadiz towards the disabled Ships & Prizes.' For the next few days *Achille*, with her prize in tow, endured heavy gales and passing St Lucars light on the Monday 28th, reports: 'Admiral in company. Wore p^r. Signal Cadiz East 3 or 4 leagues, the *Neptune* with *Victory* in Tow parted Company for Gibraltar. Next day the ship had '28 sail in sight, departed this life Joseph Humphries (S) [seaman] in consequence of his wounds received in Action'. Three days later another seaman, William Murphy, died of his wounds and was also committed to the deep; the same day two seamen were given '2 doz^n. lashes each for drunkenness'. On 2 November *Achille* 'rec^d. 100 french prisoners from the HMS *Britannia*' and after parting company, made sail for Gibraltar and finally at 4 p.m. Sunday 3 November *Achille* 'came to Anchor in Gibraltar Bay moored ship, employed getting down the Y^ds. And topmast, knotting and splicing the rigging AM sent the wounded men to Hospital'. *Achille* eventually sailed, arriving at Plymouth on 6 December to make good her defects, the entire work covering hull, masts, rigging, stores and labour costing £19,497.[12]

1806: Still commanded by Richard King, *Achille* sailed from Plymouth dockyard on 29 January and joined Commodore Sir Samuel Hood's squadron blockading Rochefort. Besides *Achille*, this flotilla comprised *Windsor Castle* (98), *Centaur* (74) Hood's flagship *Mars* (74), *Monarch* (74), *Revenge* (74), and *Atalante* (16). On 24 September a French squadron of five frigates and two corvettes commanded by Commodore Soleil escaped from Rochefort with troops bound for the West Indies. Sighted next day by *Monarch*, Hood pursued and although most of the French were taken, *Achille* took no part in this action.[13]

1807: Temporarily commanded by Captain John Hayes, *Achille* continued her deployment off Rochefort during the spring and then after minor refitting at Plymouth between 18 June and 24 July, took up station off Ferrol in December. Within six months Spain re-entered the war on Britain's side against France. Captain John Hayes was employed in the ill-fated expedition to Walcheren. He brought home 700 French soldiers who had been taken prisoner at Flushing and for his skill in personally navigating *Achille* to and from the Roompot (pilots being unavailable) he was appointed to *Freija*.

1808: Now her previous commander, Commodore Richard King's, flagship, *Achille* continued watching Ferrol with *Audacious* (74) and *Theseus* (74).[14]

1809: Returning to Plymouth on 15 April she was docked five days later to have her copper repaired. Coming out of dock 2 May, this refit had cost £7,389 in total. *Achille* sailed on 29 May. On 10 July Captain Richard King was temporarily superseded by Captain John Hayes. Having been knighted King resumed command of the ship on 6 September.[15]

1810: After reaching Cadiz on 28 February, *Achille* sadly witnessed the destruction of one Portuguese and seven Spanish ships of line and 24 merchant vessels after being driven on shore during a heavy gale. To avoid their possible capture all had to be burnt. During the summer a party of men, commanded by Lieutenant Joseph Harrison, were transferred temporarily out of the *Achille* to man a Spanish gunboat employed for the inshore defence of Cadiz.

1811: Captain the Hon. George Dundas took command on 5 March. Sir Richard King transferred into *San Josef* (112). Dundas remained in the ship only until 15 April, so command of the *Achille* was superseded by Captain A P Hollis.[16] Sent to the Mediterranean fleet, *Achille* was initially deployed with the fleet blockading Toulon and later sent to Malta, then Sicily. After this the ship was re-deployed to the Adriatic for eighteen months blockading four enemy ships within the arsenal at Venice.

1813: Operating off Corselazzo on the Adriatic coast on 27 March, boats from *Achille* and *Milford* (74) went inshore and captured and destroyed four enemy coastal vessels. Needing a refit, *Achille* was sent home and went into Portsmouth dock 8 October to have her copper replaced. Completed, she was re-launched on Christmas Eve.

1814: Refitted at a total cost of £28,531, *Achille* sailed on 1 March and briefly joined the Channel fleet blockading Cherbourg before escorting a convoy to South America and joining Vice-Admiral Dixon's squadron based at Rio de Janeiro.

1815: When Dixon's South American squadron was recalled, *Achille* reached Chatham on 20 July, Captain Hollis paid off the ship on 9 August.[17] As usual, *Achille* was stripped of masts, guns, and stores and placed in ordinary until 1817.

FATE

Surveyed afloat, it was revealed that *Achille* much needed a refit and was consequently docked at Chatham on 11 October 1817. Launched five years later on 30 December 1822 having undergone a 'Very Large Repair' at a cost of £54,252 plus additional work amounting to £1,721, she remained at Chatham until docked at Sheerness on 21 April 1823. Re-launched 7 November 1828, the ship was hulked at Sheerness. Docked periodically every six years – 1833, 1839, 1845, and 1852 – to repair her copper, *Achille* remained at Sheerness until 1865 when she was sold to Messrs Castle and Beech and broken up.[18]

The 74 gun ship AJAX

Named after the Greek hero of the Trojan wars, the *Ajax* that fought at Trafalgar was the second ship to bear this name in the Royal Navy.[19] The previous *Ajax* was a *Suffolk* class 3rd rate 74 gun ship designed by Bately and launched at Portsmouth on 23 December 1767. After seeing service during the American War of Independence she was sold on 10 February 1785.[20]

The Trafalgar *Ajax* was one of two 3rd rate 74 gun ships of the *Kent* class based on a modified version of the *Valiant* class of 1757, her sister ship obviously *Kent*. Ordered on 10 June 1795, the building contract was given to Randall who laid down the keel at Rotherhithe during September 1795 and was launched 3 March 1798. Armed with twenty-eight 24 pounders on the lower gun deck, twenty-eight 24 pounder on the upper gun deck, Fourteen 9 pounders on the quarter deck and four 9 pounders on her forecastle, *Ajax* initially fired a single broadside weight of 753 pounds. Before Trafalgar her quarter deck ordnance was amended to carry four 9 pounder carriage guns and eight 32 pounder carronades; this effec-

CAPTAINS OF AJAX (MSS 248/4 and 248/6).

Name	Time of Entry	Time of Discharge	On What Occasion.
John Pakenham	4 June 1798	2 March 1799	Promoted to Rear Admiral
Hon. the Alexander F Cochrane	3 March 1799		Leave 28 February
William Bradley	28 February 1802	19 April 1802	Paid Off at Chatham
Rt. Hon. George Lord Garlies	27 June 1804	21 May 1805	Superseded
Christpher Laroache	17 March 1805	31 May 1805	Superseded Acting
William Brown	1 June 1805	17 December 1805	Superseded
John Pilford	14 October 1805	21 October 1805	Superseded Acting
Hon. Henry Blackwood	22 October 1805	9 April 1807	Paid Off Ship, burnt on 14 February 1807 at the entrance of the Dardanelles

tively increased her broadside weight to 866 pounds.

SERVICE HISTORY

1798: Work completing *Ajax* for service was overseen first by Captain John Whitshed, then Captain J Holloway. *Ajax* was first commissioned in June 1798 by Captain John Pakenham.

1799: Most of this year *Ajax* was deployed with the Channel fleet in Lord Bridport's squadron watching Rochefort. In April Packenham was succeeded by Captain J Osborne, then in May by Captain the Hon. Alexander Cochrane. On 8 June Lord Bridport, flying his flag in the *Royal George* (100), sailed for England with *Atlas* (98), *Achilles* (74), and *Agincourt* (64), leaving Rear Admiral the Hon. George Berkeley, flying his flag in *Mars* (74), in command. *Ajax*, in company with *Ramillies* (74), *Robust* (74), *Renown* (74) and *Venerable* (74), remained on station until returning to Plymouth to refit in October.[21]

1800: Refitted, *Ajax* returned to the Channel fleet deployed with Earl St Vincent's squadron off Brest. On 1 June St Vincent detached a squadron of eighteen ships, including *Ajax*, to support Royalists in Morbihan, Brittany. Under the command of Captain Sir Edward Pellew in *Impétueux* (74), this flotilla carried soldiers of the 2nd, 20th, 36th, 82nd, and 92nd regiments of foot and 200 artillerymen led by Major-General Maitland. *Ajax*, with the other vessels, anchored in Quiberon Bay on 2 June. Over successive days several attacks were made on coastal installations and vessels in which *Ajax* played little or no part.[22]

1801: *Ajax* joined Lord Keith's expedition into the Mediterranean to invade Egypt to oust the French forces. The fleet comprised the following number and type of vessels:

Guns	80	74	64	50	44	38	36	32	28	20	18	16	14	12	Cut	Sch	Bv	Gv	Total
No.	2	5	3	2	6	2	3	7	6	1	3	4	1	1	1	1	2	3	53

Cut = Cutter; Sch = Schooner; Bv = Bomb Vessel; Gv = Gun vessel

With additional transports, Keith's force exceeded 70 vessels. On board were 16,150 troops commanded by General Sir Ralph Abercromby KB, and Major-Generals Sir John Hutchison and Eyre Coote. Anchoring in Abu-Kir Bay on 2 March, bad weather delayed landings until the 8th so all surprise was lost. Disembarkation commenced about 2 a.m. under the direction of Alexander Cochrane, *Ajax*'s captain. By 9 a.m. 320 boats were filled with 7,000 men and proceeded to shore in two lines abreast, gunboats protecting their flanks. Waiting in the dunes were 2,500 French troops commanded by General Louis Friant. As the British forces approached they came under exceedingly heavy fire from the French artillery and guns firing from Fort Bey; grape shot scythed into the boats. By the 9th all the troops had been landed, sustaining heavy casualties. During the assault two of *Ajax*'s men were killed. The troops were later supported by a 1,000 strong division of seamen led by Captain Sir Sidney Smith, Some of these men were from *Ajax*; during actions on 13 and 21 March *Ajax* lost three killed and four wounded.[23]

1802: *Ajax* remained stationed off Egypt until recalled home. Going into Portsmouth on 8 April, she was docked on 27 December to have a 'Middling Repair' and be fitted.[24] Some secondary sources suggest that *Ajax* was refitted at Chatham where *Victory* (100) was nearing completion of her two-year reconstruction. However the Progress Book lists Portsmouth as the refitting yard.

1803: During January *Ajax* had her copper sheathing removed to enable shipwrights to replace underwater planking where necessary while other works were carried out.[25]

1804: Re-coppered, *Ajax* was undocked on 25 July and completed at a total cost of £38,853. These expenses, including labour, comprised £27,422 for the hull, £2,994 for masts and yards, and £8,437 for rigging and stores.[26] *Ajax* had her quarter deck armament altered to include eight 32 pounder carronades bringing her broadside weight of fire up to 866 pounds. When war resumed with France in May *Ajax* was recommissioned under Captain William Brown and soon deployed with the Channel fleet on blockade duty.

1805: Still under the command of William Brown, *Ajax* was deployed with Vice-Admiral Sir Robert Calder's squadron of 15 sail of the line, two frigates, a cutter and a lugger. Cruising off Cape Finisterre on 22 July they sighted Villeneuve's combined Franco-Spanish fleet comprising 20 sail of the line, three large ships armed *en flute*, five frigates and two brigs returning from the West Indies. Sir Robert, flying his flag in *Prince of Wales* (98), made signals to attack at their centre and stood his squadron towards the enemy. *Hero* (74) led the British line followed by *Ajax*. Battle commenced in late afternoon but fog and changeable wind conditions made tactics difficult. Suddenly realising that the enemy, unseen in the mist, had come round on a starboard tack, Brown played a vital part in the action: at 5.45 p.m. he tacked *Ajax* out of line to inform Calder. Because of Brown's initiative Calder was able to bring about a general action, but having fallen back to twelfth position in the line, Brown and *Ajax* had sacrificed their own opportunity. Although the action continued for over four hours Calder was disadvantaged. Villeneuve had the weather gauge but both adversaries

SPECIFICATIONS: AJAX

Rate	3rd	Length on the range of the gun deck	182 ft 3 ins	Ordnance - lower gun deck	28 x 24 pounders
Guns	74	Length of keel for tonnage	141 ft 8¾ ins	Ordnance - upper gun deck	28 x 24 pounders
Class	Kent 1795	Extreme breadth	49 ft 3 ins	Ordnance - quarter deck	14 x 9 pounders (later 4 x 9 pounders and 8 x 32 pounder carronades)
Designer	Modified *Valiant* class	Depth in hold	21 ft 3 ins		
Builder	Randall	Tons burthen	1931 62/94		
Dockyard	Rotherhithe	Draught afore	21 ft 6 ins	Ordnance - forecastle	4 x 9 pounders
Date ordered	10 June 1795	Draught abaft	22 ft 7 ins	Single broadside weight	753 pounds (later 866 pounds)
Date keel laid	September 1795	Complement	690	Fate	11 February 1807 Accidentally burnt off Tenedos
Date launched	3 March 1798				

Source: Lyon, *Sailing Navy List*, p. 110.

Ajax
Sheer Profile
(Drawing by the author)

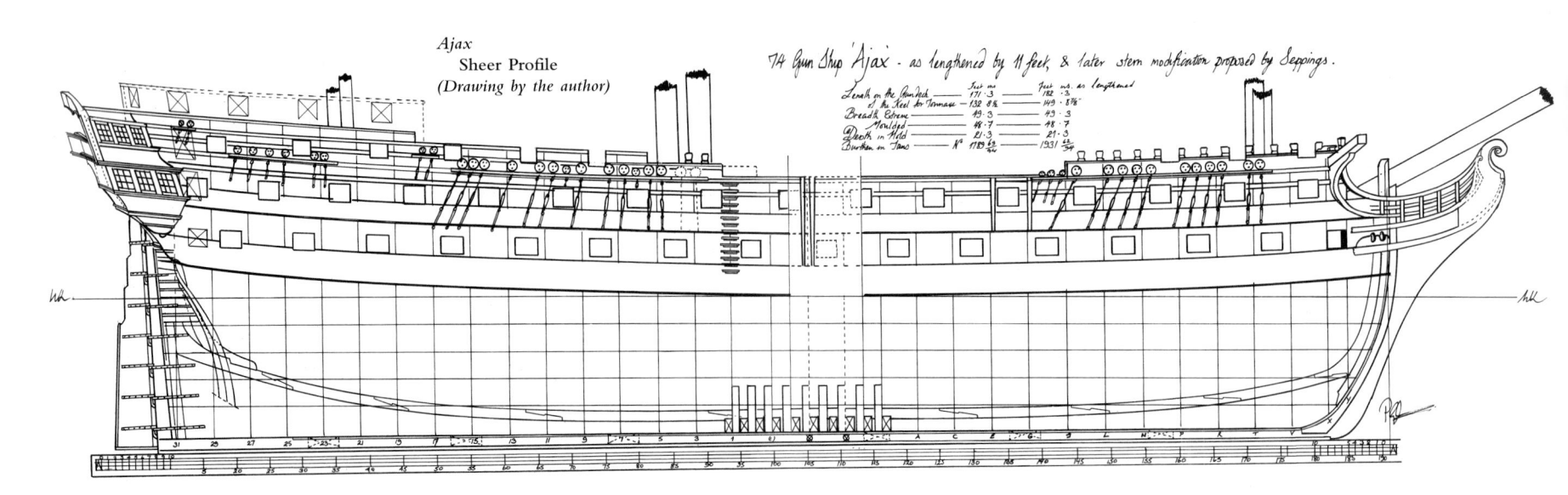

were enveloped in thick fog. Many ships, including *Ajax*, became isolated in the confusion, fighting became sporadic and signalling impossible. Calder could not, therefore, gain a decisive victory. Only two Spanish ships were captured, *San Raphael* (80) and *Firme* (74); the main body of Villeneuve's fleet escaped. In the action *Ajax* lost her main yard and driver boom and suffered 18 casualties, two dead and 16 wounded. *Ajax*'s log that day records:

> D⁰. W^r. *Defiance* made various Signals at ½ past 4 Adm^l. made N⁰. 4 to us & *Defiance* Body of the Enemies fleet bore SEBE 6 Miles at ¼ past 3 Ans^d. Genl. Signal N⁰. 96 at 4 took our station in the line of battle at ¼ past 5 Ans^d. Genl Signal 98, at ¾ past d⁰. Ans^d. Genl Signal to Engage the Enemy at 35 past 5 began to Engage at 50past 5 Tacked ship hove to aBreast of a two Deck one on the weather Bow and one on the Quarter, Thick & foggy W^r. Engaging the Enemy as they came up Spanker Boom and Larb^d. Main yard Arm shot away at 8 Observed that 3 of the Enemies Ships had Struck two Dismasted at 9 the firing ceased and the squadron began to Collect Cut away the flying Jib Boom Jib and all the Rigging. Ans^d. Several Night Signals at 6 AM the Enemy Hove in Sight Body of the fleet bearing WBS 5 or 6 Leags at 20 past 6 Observed the ——— [name illegible] *Sirius* & *Egyptienne* with two of the Enemies Line of Battle in Tow...[27]

Had conditions been better and Calder achieved a conclusive victory, the battle of Trafalgar may not have occurred.[28] Shortly afterwards *Ajax* went into Plymouth for provisions and repairs, when Captain Brown, and the commander of the *Thunderer* (74) received the following orders:[29]

> You are hereby required and directed to put yourself under the command of the R^t. Honble Lort V^t. Nelson, KB Vice Admiral of the White and follow his lordship's orders for your proceedings
> Given &c 5th September 1805
> J Gambier
> P Patton
> Garlies

On 18 September the *Ajax*, in company with *Thunderer*, left Plymouth and joined *Victory* (100) and *Euryalus* (36) which had proceeded from Portsmouth three days earlier. With Nelson in *Victory*, the four ships proceeded south and joined Collingwood off Cadiz on Saturday 28 September.[30] Shortly after Nelson's arrival, Sir Robert Calder was ordered home to face a court martial for his failure off Finisterre in July. Because Captain Brown had been called as a witness, command of *Ajax* was temporarily given to the ship's First Lieutenant, John Pilford.[31] Brown, with Durham of *Defiance*, embarked into Calder's *Prince of Wales* (98).[32]

TRAFALGAR

Captain Pilford's log for Monday 21 October describes proceedings:

> Fresh breezes and hazy W^r. ¼ past set the Jb forsail and topsails – AM at 4 the admiral NE 3 Miles Wore Ship p^r. Signal at daylight saw the Enemy's fleet bearing Eeast [*sic*] bore up for them and made sail p^r. Sig^l. at 6 Ans^d. General Sig^l. 72 at 6.10 Ans^d. Genl Sig^l. 76 with Comp. Sig^l. at 8 light Winds and variable extremes of the Enemies fleet from EbS to SE Ship going large. At 8.30 beat to quarters and prepared for Action. At 9 the enemies fleet separated into two divisions at 10.15 the enemys fleet closed in one line to the number of 33 sail of the Line, all sail set standing down towards them dist. About 4 miles at noon Light airs all sail set Observed five frigates & 2 brigs to leeward of the enemy's line...[33]

Standing eighth in line of Nelson's windward division at the opening of the battle, ahead of *Ajax* lay *Agamemnon* (64) and astern *Orion* (74). Cleared for action, Ellis, *Ajax*'s Lieutenant of Marines, recalled that men below decks were stripped to the waist polishing the guns,

> ... as though an inspection were about to take place instead of martial combat, while three or four, as if in mere bravado, were dancing a hornpipe; but all seemed deeply anxious to come to close quarters with the enemy. Occasionally they would look out of the port and speculate as to the various ships of the enemy, many of whom had been on former occasions engaged by our vessels...[34]

According to *Ajax*'s log of Tuesday 22 October Pilford got into action just after 1 p.m., his journal giving a graphic account of unfolding events:

> At 5' past 12 ans^d. Genl. Sig^l. 63 with a preparative and a white flag the enemys fleet formed on a Larboard Tack, the Lee Division of our fleet bearing down upon the rear of the enemy at 13' past 12 the Enemy commenced firing upon the lee Division, – returned by the R^l. *Sovereign* at ½ past 12 Ans^d. Genl. Signal N⁰. 16 the *Royal Sovereign* broke through the Enemy's line between the Centre and rear at 32 past 12 repeated Genl. Sig^l. N⁰. 16 at 10' past 1 our Fore Topmast

PROGRESS BOOK – *AJAX* 3rd RATE OF 74 GUNS:

At what Port	Arrived	Docked	Coppered
Portsmouth	8 April 1802	27 Dec 1802	Copper taken off January 1803 Re--coppered July 1804
Burnt in Mediterranean 14 Feby 1807			

was shot through at 12' past 1 opened our fire upon the enemy on both sides breaking through the line, at 30' past 1 cut away the all the steering sails and came up to wind on their Starboard side at 55' past one on the smoke clearing away observed several of the Enemy Ships had struck – one Spanish 3 deck'er totally dismasted – at 13' past 3 repeated General Signal N°. 101 at 20' past 3 bore away a little to engage part of the Enemy's Van which was attempting to escape, at 4 a Spanish 2 decker which had rec[d]. our Fire for upwards of half an hour struck her colours with a Rear Admirals flag...

Following Hardy's signal directing ships to bear up, Pilford put *Ajax* on a larboard tack, turning northward to meet the new threat. Firing her larboard broadside into *Intrépide* (74) as she passed, *Ajax* continued her pursuit of *Héros*, *Rayo*, and *San Francisco de Asis* which were hauling round to the NE to make their escape. *Ajax*'s log continues;

– filled and made sail keeping up a heavy raking fore upon the enemys Ships running to leeward, at 45' past 4 one of the french 2 decker Ships struck with the loss of her Main & Mizen Masts – came to the Wind on a Larboard Tack and began to repair damages the Action having ceased from van to Rear found that 22 Sail of the line had struck their colours – one of which was on fire the Signal N°. 101 still flying – in this Action we had 2 men killed and 10 wounded – the rigging and sails much cut and Bumkin shot away – the Jolly Boat was sunk astern and cut adrift – at 10 took possession of the *Intrepide* French 74 and at 10.30 took her in tow – at midnight light airs. AM Fresh Breezes and hazy W[r]. The lights of the Enemys fleet NE and our SSW. Employed repairing damages; – at 2 in the Act of Wearing carried away the tow rope by which two 8 inch Hawsers were lost Hove to by the Prize and sent an officer and party of men on board emp[d]. Getting down the fore TopG[t]. mast to ease the Topmast which was much splintered by shot – at 8 strong Breezes and squally with rain the *Britannia* with a prize in tow near us – the Ship making much Water from shot holes pumps constantly going...[35]

Although *Ajax* did not play an heroic part in the battle her contribution was supportive. Consequently she suffered considerable damage aloft and was much shot below the waterline. The log also corrects the accounts of James and Clowes who state that *Ajax* had nine wounded instead of ten. Hit by the gales on the 23rd Pilford 'sent down top G[t]. Yards and struck topmasts'. With *Intrépide* still in tow *Ajax* endeavoured to ride out the storm just 10 Leagues WSW of Cadiz. Next day they 'bent the sheet cable to the spare anchor leading through the Gun Room port - emp[d]. Clearing ship, and making ready for Action and repairing damages', and in the morning of Friday 25th 'hoisted out our Boats and sent then to the S. Tissimo Trinidada for prisoners', and amid the 'Constant rain' embarked the prisoners from the Spanish ship. That afternoon *Ajax* cast off her tow with *Intrépide* and came to 'Single Anchor Cadiz Light House SSE?E Rota SE' Distance from the nearest shore 3 or 4 Lgs'. With a 'great sea' running the next day, the main and topmasts had to be sent down to ease the strain on the ship and the 'Cutter with an Officer' was sent over to her prize; 'the *Orion* Anchored - Two of the Prizes (hulks) drove on shore - a great sea running'. The storm continued to take its toll. While *Ajax*'s carpenters were busy repairing the damaged barge on Sunday 27 October, the 'launch and Pinnace [were] lost on board the Prize'. Over the next few days *Royal Sovereign*, *Mars*, *Swiftsure* and the prize *Argonauta* anchored nearby, prisoners from the latter being transferred into *Ajax*. On Wednesday 30 October the log states:

... at 4 a French Frigate and Brig joined the Fleet as Flags of Truce from Cadiz. at 6.30 the *Argonaute* Prize went down and the S[r]. *Agustine* blew up - rec[d]. our men (p[r]. *Orion*) which had been to the the S[r]. *Agustine* AM. between 11 & 12 many Guns were fired - some of our Ships standing into Cadiz Bay...[36]

In December, when Pilford was promoted post captain for his part in the battle, command of *Ajax* went to Nelson's distinctive frigate captain Henry Blackwood.

1806: Under Blackwood *Ajax* continued to operate in the Mediterranean.

1807: At the end of January *Ajax* joined Vice-Admiral Duckworth's squadron lying in Valetta, Malta. On 4 February Duckworth, flying his flag in *Royal George* (100), accompanied by *Windsor Castle* (98), *Canopus* (80), *Pompée* (80), *Ajax*, *Thunderer* (74) and *Standard* (64), frigates *Endymion* (40) and *Active* (38), and bomb vessels *Lucifer* and *Mortar*, sailed for the Dardanelles. Arriving off Cape Janissary on the 11th, bad weather compelled the fleet to anchor. A few days later disaster struck the *Ajax*.[37]

FATE

While the *Ajax* lay anchored off the Island of Tenedos near Cape Janissary on 14 February 1807, at about 9 p.m. Blackwood was awoken from his bed by the officer of the watch informing that there 'was a great alarm of fire in the after part of the ship'. Blackwood immediately ordered the drummer to beat to quarters, ordered signal No. 12 to be made, guns to be fired to alarm the fleet, and sent Lieutenant Wood with a midshipman in the boat to warn nearby ships. Gathering other officers, Blackwood went below to the after cockpit to investigate the root of the fire, which had apparently started in the breadroom. The First Lieutenant and other officers were already on the scene. Smashing open the surgeon's cabin door the bulkhead behind suddenly burst into flames, compelling the men to rapidly retreat up the ladder, some being overcome by smoke. Although courageous attempts were made to fight the fire with water buckets, the men were driven back by the intense heat and smoke. Blackwood next ordered the 'lower-deck ports to be hauled up to give air; but very soon finding the harm it produced, I directed them to be lowered down, and the after-hatchway to be covered up, in order to gain time, by stopping the vent of the smoke, for the boats to be hoisted; which measure I was induced to adopt, finding that the fire was of that nature that the ship must soon be in flames'. Most alarmingly, *Ajax* like many other ships, had not yet been fitted with cocks to flood the after magazine, therefore Blackwood ordered 'the carpenter with his screw to scuttle the after part of the ship'. He notes that the smoke was so thick that 'though it was bright moonlight we could not distinguish each other, even on deck'. Once the flames flared through the main hatch Blackwood 'called to everybody to go to the foremost part ship; I desired every one to save himself as fast as he could. I had scarcely reached the forecastle when I saw all parts from the centre of the booms aft in a raging flame. The fire reached the forecastle where 400 of the crew were clambering out on the bowsprit to get to the boats. Blackwood 'jumped overboard from the spritsail yard, and being about half an hour in the water, I was picked up by one of the boats from the *Canopus*, and taken on board that ship much exhausted'. Unable to swim proficiently, Midshipman Duff, a 14 year old from Norwich, clung desperately to the spritsail yard until the

Source: ADM 180/10

Launched or Undocked	Sailed	Built or Nature of Repair	Cost of Hull, Masts & Yards Materials £	Workmen £	Cost of Masts & Yards Materials £	Workmen £	Cost of Rigging & Stores Materials £	Workmen £	Grand Total £
25 July 1804	5 August 1804	Middling Repair & Fitted	17,836	9,586	2,389	605	8,273	164	38,853

The 74 gun ship *BELLEISLE*

Named after the island off Morbihan in Brittany, the *Belleisle* that fought at Trafalgar was the second ship in the Royal Navy to bear this name, the first being the 3rd rate 64 gun ship named *Belle Isle* which, before her capture in 1761, was the French East Indiaman *Bertin*. Used only for harbour service since 1784, this ship was sold 3 February 1819. The Trafalgar *Belleisle*, like her predecessor, was a French prize. Originally launched at Rochefort as *Lion*, her name was later changed to *Marat* and then to *Formidable*, captured in Lord Bridport's action off Isle de Groix against Villaret-Joyeuse on 23 June 1795. Repaired and fitted with English ordnance, *Belleisle* carried thirty 32 pounders on her lower gun deck, thirty 24 pounders on the upper gun deck, two 9 pounders and fourteen 32 pounder carronades on the quarter deck, and two 9 pounder and two 24 pounder carronades on her forecastle. With additional armament on the poop of six 24 pounder carronades, for her size *Belleisle* could pack a powerful broadside weight of 1,178 pounds, in all 30 pounds more than *Victory*.[40]

SERVICE CAREER

1795: Placed under the command of Captain C A L Durand, Compte de Linois's *Formidable* was deployed with the Toulon fleet commanded by Admiral Villaret-Joyeuse. When this fleet combined with Rear-Admiral Vence's squadron on 15 June, the French attained a superior advantage over the British in the Mediterranean.[41]

Within a week *Formidable* saw her first action when Villaret's ships fell in with Admiral Lord Bridport's squadron off Isle de Groix on 23 June. Battle opened at 6.15 a.m. with *Queen Charlotte* (100), Captain Sir Andrew Snape Douglas Kt, bearing down and pummelling *Formidable* with her starboard batteries. *Formidable* returned her broadsides vehemently into her adversary for ten minutes until she also found herself under fire from the formerly French *Sans Pareil* (80). *Formidable* was severely mauled by the two British ships, fires broke out on her poop and her mizzen mast was shot away. Having sustained 320 casualties, killed and wounded, Durand was obliged to strike *Formidable*'s colours. *Formidable* was sent to England with two other prizes, the 74 guns ships *Tigre* and *Alexandre*. As the navy already had a 98 gun ship named *Formidable*, the prize *Formidable* was renamed *Belleisle* under the misconception that Bridport's action was fought off Belle Isle rather than Isle de Groix.[42]

CAPTAINS OF *BELLEISLE* (MSS 248/4 and 248/6)

Name	Time of Entry	Time of Discharge	On What Occasion
Captain C A L Durand	1795	23 June 1795	Ship captured
William Domett	1 November 1800	1 February 1801	Superseded
Charles Boyles	2 February 1801	27 July 1801	Superseded
William Donnell	28 July 1801	6 October 1801	Superseded - Appointed Captain of the Fleet to Admiral Cornwallis
John Whitby	7 October 1801	26 May 1802	Superseded
John Whitby	27 April 1802	31 December 1803	New Book
John Whitby	1 January 1804	17 April 1804	Superseded
William Hargood	18 April 1804	14 January 1806	Paid Off
William Hargood	30 January 1806	14 July 1807	To the *Northumberland*
Nathaniel D Cochrane	15 July 1807	31 October 1807	Superseded
William Maude	1 November 1807	31 July 1808	To the *Wysses*
Edward Woolcoombe	1 August 1808	24 November 1808	To the *Ethalion*
W C Fakie	25 November 1808	28 July 1809	To the *Pompée*
Edward P Brenton	1 April 1809	2 July 1809	Superseded
George Cockburn	3 July 1809	7 October 1809	Paid Off

1800: On her first commission *Belleisle* was commanded by Captain Domett, succeeded by Captain Charles Boyle in February 1801. Throughout this period the ship was deployed in the Channel fleet.

1803: When war with France reopened *Belleisle* was recommissioned immediately under Captain John Whitby and sailed for the Mediterranean. First stationed at Malta, she was soon deployed with the British squadron watching over Toulon. On 30 July Nelson, newly arrived from England in *Amphion* (32) transferred his flag into *Victory* (100) as Commander-in-Chief of the Mediterranean fleet. Besides *Victory* and *Amphion*, accompanying *Belleisle* were *Gibraltar* (80), *Donegal* (74), *Renown* (74), *Monmouth* (64), *Active* (38) and *Phœbe* (36). In early August Nelson's fleet was joined by *Canopus* (80), *Kent* (74) and *Superb* (74). For the rest of the year *Belleisle* endured NW and NE gales while maintaining the blockade off the coast off Cape Sicié, taking occasional respite in Agincourt Sound, Corsica, refitting her rigging.[43]

1805: On 19 January *Belleisle*, now commanded by Captain William

SPECIFICATIONS: *BELLEISLE*

Rate	3rd	Length on the range of the gun deck	184 ft 5 ins	Ordnance - lower gun deck	30 x 32 pounders
Guns	74	Length of keel for tonnage	149 ft 5¼ ins	Ordnance - upper gun deck	30 x 24 pounders
Class	French *Formidable*, ex *Marat*, ex *Lion*	Extreme breadth	48 ft 9 ins	Ordnance - quarter deck	2 x 9 pounders
Designer	Jacques Noel Sane	Depth in hold	21 ft 7½ ins		14 x 32 pounder carronades
Builder	Not Recorded	Tons burthen	1889	Ordnance - forecastle	2 x 9 pounders
Dockyard	Rochefort	Draught afore	22 ft 7 ins		2 x 24 pounder carronades
Date ordered	Captured from French 23 June 1795	Draught abaft	24 ft 7 ins	Ordnance - roundhouse/poop	6 x 24 pounder carronades
Date keel laid		Complement	700	Single broadside weight	1178 pounds
Date launched	1793			Fate	1814 Broken up

Source: Lyon, *Sailing Navy List*, p. 238.

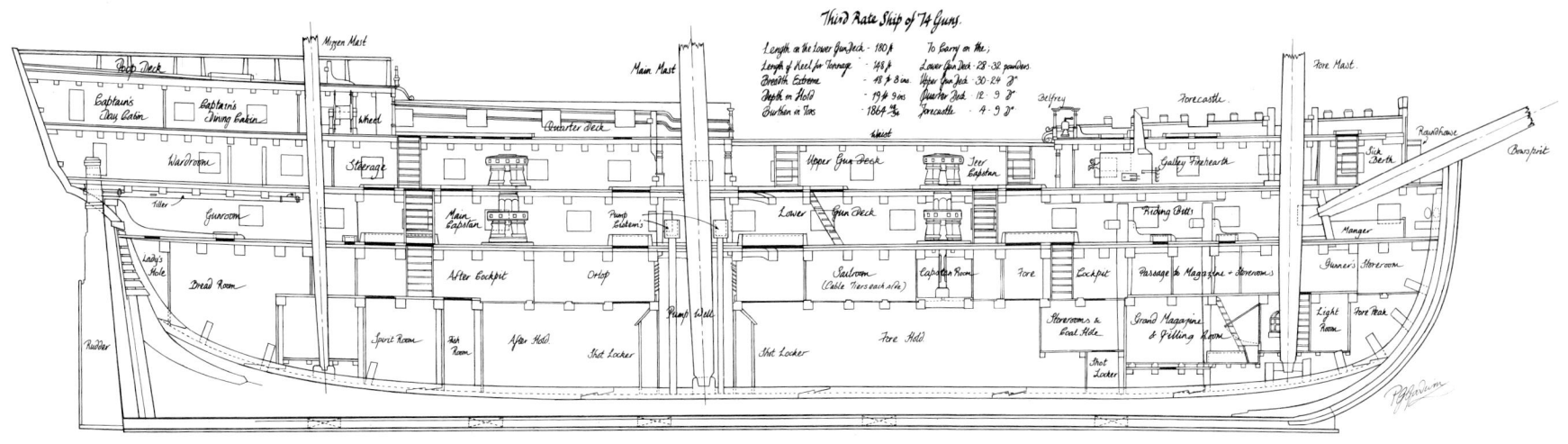

THE 74 GUN SHIP BELLEISLE

Belleisle
Annotated Longitudinal Cross Section
of generic 74 gun ship
(Drawing by the author)

Hargood, lay in Agincourt Sound with the main body of Nelson's fleet when *Active* (38) and *Seahorse* (38) appeared, signalling urgently that Vice-Admiral Villeneuve had escaped from Toulon with eleven line-of-battle ships, seven frigates and two brigs. At 4.30 p.m. Nelson ordered his fleet, including *Belleisle*, to weigh and, to save time, sailed through the narrow channel between Biche and Sardinia.[44] From this point the *Belleisle* would follow Nelson, doggedly pursuing Villeneuve's elusive ships. In short the game was afoot: Napoleon's invasion plan was beginning to take shape. After much searching for Villeneuve, Nelson's fleet reached Gibraltar in early May. Leaving command of the Mediterranean to Rear-Admiral Sir Richard Hussey Bickerton, Nelson weighed anchor on 7 May and, following his hunch, took his ships through the Straits across the Atlantic to the West Indies. Besides *Victory* and *Belleisle* his squadron comprised *Canopus* (80), *Conqueror* (74), *Leviathan* (74), *Spencer* (74), *Superb* (74), *Swiftsure* (74), *Tigre* (74), *Amazon* (38), *Amphion* (32) and *Décade* (36).[45] Returning to Gibraltar from the transatlantic chase in late July, *Belleisle* proceeded to Plymouth to refit.[46] *Belleisle* rejoined Nelson's fleet off Cadiz during the second week of October. On Monday 14 October Hargood recorded, '6.40 parted C^o. *Prince of Wales*', which was returning to England with Admiral Calder. Over the next few days the log states that the *Donegal* (74) and *Weazle* parted company to go into Gibraltar and that *Belleisle* supplied *Achille* with two barrels of pitch.[47]

TRAFALGAR

Belleisle's log entry for Monday 21 October records:

Fresh gales & Squally, down T.G. Yards & Wore at 2 wore & up T.G. Yards, made & short^d. Sail occasionally AM at daylight saw the Enemys Fleet bearing East dist 9 miles consisting of 33 sail of the line, 5 frigates & a Brig. 5.40 answ^d. the gen^l. Sig^l. to form the order of sailing, at 6 answ^d. Genl. Sig^l. to bear up & sail large & to prepare for battle, made all sail bearing down on Enemy, threw overboard unavoidably in clearing for Action Butts in pack 7 D^o. cat for Grog & Tops^l. Hally^d. Tubs 2 D^o. cut for books, Tubs 3 Punchions as harness Casks, 2 Some Beef & Pork in Harness Tubs, Iron hoops & parcels 10 in each, & Bisc^t. bags from the diff^t. births, 9 in N^o. at 8 Light airs, body of the Enemys Fleet SE 6 miles formed in a line of Battle, ¾ p^t. 8 *R. Sovereign* made Sig^l. for Larb^d. Division to make more sail, at 9 Adm^l. Made Genl. Sig^l. to alter course 1 p^t. To Port, 9.20 *R. Sovereign* made *Belleisle* & *Tonnants* Sig^l. to exchange places in the line of Battle & *Belleisle*'s Sig^l. to make more sail, made more sail, 9.30 *R. Sovereign* made *Belleisles* Sig^l. to bear SW of her, 9.40 *R.S* made *Belleisles* Sig^l. to alter Course 1 p^t. to Starboard, 11.50 *R. Sovereign* made *Belleisles* Signal to keep closer order, 11.53 Adm^l. Made Genl. Sig^l to prepare to anchor after close of day, 11.55 Enemy from Centre to Rear opened their fire on *R. Sovereign* & *Belleisle*, which was returned by the *R. Sovereign* & the Adm^l. Made the Sig^l. for closer action, at Noon distance from the Enemy line ? of a Mile, reserving our fire with all sail set to cut their line distance from the *Royal Sovereign* 2 Cables lengths Light airs with a heavy Swell...[48]

Now standing second in line of Collingwood's leeward division, *Belleisle* followed *Royal Sovereign* through the enemy line shortly after noon. First engaging fire with *Monarca* (74) and then pouring a weighty broadside into the lee quarter of *Santa Ana* (74), Hargood ordered the helm over to larboard and fired his starboard guns into *Indomptable* (80). This manoeuvre brought *Belleisle* under direct fire from the larboard batteries of *Fougueux* (74) and *San Juan Nepomuceno* (84), resulting in her main topmast being shot away. Less able to manoeuvre, her position became critical. At about 1 p.m. the French captain of *Fougueux* ran his ship aboard the starboard side of the *Belleisle* and opened a tremendous fire into her, bringing down the mizzen mast. A fierce duel between the two ships ensued during which *Belleisle*'s remaining rigging and masts were totally shot to pieces. Twenty minutes later *Mars* (74) came to Hargood's aid, forcing *Fougueux* to bear off. Although *Belleisle* had been severely mauled, respite was short; within ten minutes the French *Achille* (74) ran alongside and maintained a steady fire into *Belleisle*'s larboard quarter while *Aigle* (74) bombarded her from the other side, aided by the passing *San Justo* (74) and *San Leandro* (64). Virtually surrounded, *Belleisle* took such a severe pounding that, with her mainmast

'*Belleisle*, 15 mins. past Noon, Oct. 21st 1805.' Engraving by E. Duncan, from a painting by W. J. Huggins. Ships left to right are *Fougueux*, *Indomptable*, *Belleisle*, *Santa Ana* and *Royal Sovereign*. (*Courtesy of Stuart Robertson*)

gone, she was rapidly being reduced to a wreck. At about 2.30 p.m. the French *Neptune* (84) drew up and poured raking broadsides into *Belleisle*'s starboard bow, bringing down her fore mast and bowsprit. Completely dismasted, tangled rigging like entrails covering her sides, *Belleisle* was hard put to return fire effectively with her larboard guns. Despite her deplorable condition her ensign bravely flew from the stump of her truncated main mast. *Belleisle*'s precarious situation was further compounded by the battering she was still receiving from the *Achille* and *Aigle*. It was another thirty-five minutes before British ships came to her aid. First *Polyphemus* (64), then *Defiance* (74) and *Swiftsure* (74) drove off the two French 74s. *Naiad* drew alongside, passed a tow and pulled *Belleisle* clear of the battle.[49]

Belleisle's log entry for Tuesday 22 October (PM Monday) reads as follows:

> Light airs & hazy with a heavy swell. 0.5 *R. Sovereign* cut the Enemys line, astern of a Spanish 3 Deck'd Ship bearing a Vice Adm[ls]. Flag, 0.8 open'd our fire on the Enemy, 0.13 cut thru' the line astern of a French 80 Gun Ship 2[d]. to the Spanish Vice Adm[l]. at the same time keeping up a heavy fire on both sides , 0.40 out main Top[mt]. Was shot away, 1.0 French ship bore up to rake us & a ship on each side engaging us, 1.10 the Mizen Mast went 6 feet above the Deck, 1.20 the Enemy Ship on our Starb[d]. Side Sheer'd off 1.30 the enemy ship which had laid herself athwart our Stern plac'd herself on our Larb[d]. Quarter, at the same time a French ship ranged up on our Starb[d]. Side, kept up a heavy fire on them as we could get our Guns to bear, the ship being totally unmanageable, Most of her Rigg[g]. & sails being shot, 2.10 Main M[t]. Went by the Board. 2.30 an Enemy ship placed herself across our Starb[d]. Bow - 2.45 the Foremast & Bowsprit went by the Board still engaging 3 of the Enemy Ships, 3.15 one of our Ships pass'd our Bow and took the fire of the Enemy's ships laying there 3.20 the Enemys Ships on our Starb[d]. Side was engaged by one of our Ships, 3.25 *Swiftsure* pass'd our Stern, cheer'd us & commenced firing into the Enemys Ships on our Larb[d]. Quarter, ceased firing & turn'd the hands up to clear the wreck, sent a boat & took possession of the Spanish 80 Gun Ship *Argonauta*, the action still continuing Genr[y]. Cut away the wreck fore & aft, 4.15 the *Naiad* came down & took us in tow sent a Lieut[t]. the master & a division of men to the Prize...

Manning Hargood's one undamaged boat these personnel comprised William Hudson, *Belleisle*'s Master, and John Owen, Lieutenant of Marines. The log book continues:

> ... saw a French Ship of the line take fire, 5.10 She Blew up, observ'd several of the Enemy Ships had struck several making off to Leeward & 4 French ships of the line going off on the Starb[d]. Tack, 5.30 the Action ceased, People employed securing the Guns, clearing and cleaning the ship. Am variously employed, at 8

'*Belleisle*, 4h.15m.PM, Oct.21st 1805.' Ships are, left to right, *Formidable*, *Naiad*, *Belleisle*, *Santa Ana*, *Royal Sovereign*, *Victory*, and *Achille*. (Courtesy of Stuart Robertson)

PROGRESS BOOK - *BELLEISLE* 3rd RATE OF 74 GUNS:

At what Port	Arrived	Docked	Coppered
Plymouth	24 Aug 1805	27 Aug 1805	Copper taken off; Re-coppered August 1805
Plymouth	5 Dec 1805	–	Copper repaired
Portsmouth	9 Nov 1806	28 Nov 1806	Coppr dress'd & renail'd Dec 1806
Portsmouth	22 Sep 1809	19 July 1814	Copper taken off July 1814
			Taken to Pieces August 1814

> Must[d]. The Ships Company by the Ships Books found killed in battle 2 Lieut[ts]. 1 midshipman & 31 Seamen & Marines & 94 Seamen & Marines wounded at Noon in tow by the *Naiad*, part of the fleet on sight...[50]

Hargood's magnificent and courageous defence of the *Belleisle* remains one of the most memorable actions of the battle. Secondary sources such as Clowes state that *Belleisle* suffered 33 killed and 93 wounded (correctly 94). Officers killed: Lieutenants Ebenezer Geall and John Wood and Midshipman George Nind; officers wounded Lieutenant William Ferrie, Lieutenant of Marines John Owen, Master's Mates William Cutfield and William Pearson, Midshipman Samuel Jago, Boatswain Andrew Gibson and 1st Class Volunteer J Hodge. As her log shows, *Naiad* in fact towed *Belleisle* out of the battle, and not *Polyphemus* as some secondary sources conclude.

In the aftermath Hargood, and his First Lieutenant, Thomas Fife, endeavoured to get *Belleisle* into some semblance of order and during the ensuing gale the ship narrowly escaped being wrecked off Tarifa and reached Gibraltar with great difficulty. Because the ship was 'making much water' chain pumps were continuously operated throughout 23 October. Also that day, 'departed this life Edw[d]. Ford (Seaman)'. Arriving at Gibraltar on Saturday 26 October, Hargood recorded:

> Boats came to assist us, cheer'd occasionally 1.20 let go the Best Bower Anchor, came on board the Master attendant, 1.30 let go the Small Bower, hauled into the mole, employed cleaning Ship, out Boats & sent the wounded men to hospital, got the stumps of the Main & Mizen Masts out...received —— lbs of fresh meat.

Preliminary repairs made, *Belleisle* sailed home to Plymouth to refit, arriving on Thursday 5 December with

> Light airs with thick Fog. PM weighed and warped the Ship towards the harbour At 5 anchored between Drakes Island & the Main AM at 6 weighed & commenced warping the ship up the Harbour, sent all the Powder on shore to the Magazine. At Noon light airs and foggy; Employed warping the ship up the Harbour assisted by Mechanics from the Dock Yard...

and moored in the Hamoaze. At 11.30 Saturday 21 December, 'fell overboard and was drown'd John Avery Seaman'. The next day Hargood mustered the ship's company and 'Discharged into HMS *Formidable* 45 Seamen and 17 Seamen into HMS *Caesar*', many more following over the next few days. Finally on Tuesday 14 January the ship was paid off and 'sent the Cook on shore to the Dock Yard to be paid off, at Sun Set hauld down the pendant'.[51]

1806: Still commanded by Hargood, *Belleisle* was appointed to Rear-Admiral Sir Richard Strachan's squadron being deployed to the West Indies. Strachan, flying his flag in *Caesar* (80), sailed from Plymouth on 19 May with *Belleisle*, *Bellona* (74), *Montagu* (74), *Terrible* (74), *Triumph* (74), *Audacious* (64), *Décade* (36) and *Melampus* (36). After cruising off Madeira the fleet reached Barbados on 8 August. Sailing again five days later in search of the French squadron commanded by Vice-Admiral Jean Baptiste

Source: ADM 180/10/69

Launched or Undocked	Sailed	Built or Nature of Repair	Cost of Hull, Masts & Yards Materials £	Workmen £	Cost of Masts & Yards Materials £	Workmen £	Cost of Rigging & Stores Materials £	Workmen £	Grand Total £
29 Aug 1803	22 Sep 1805	Defects	3,996	1,101	235	75	–	123	5,494
–	14 Apr 1806	Fitted	1,364	495	3,725	20	18,768	12	16,384
15 Dec 1806	13 Jan 1807	Refitted Large Repair	689	555	1,683	151	2,657	63	5,798

Willaumez, Strachan's fleet, like the French, was dispersed in a storm. Following orders, *Belleisle*, *Bellona*, and *Melampus* reached the appointed rendezvous off Cape Henry on 14 September and sighted a French ship under jury masts making for Chesapeake Bay. Making sail the three ships went in pursuit but were unable to actually capture her as they were in neutral waters. But between them they forced the Frenchman to run his ship on onshore and strike his colours. The vessel proved to be *Impétueux* (74), one of Willaumez's ships that had been damaged in the storm. Having taken possession, prisoners were transferred into *Melampus* and *Impétueux* was burnt.[52]

1807: Following Denmark's alliance with France, an expedition was mounted to take possession of their island of St Thomas in the West Indies. Appointed as flagship to Rear-Admiral the Hon. Alexeander Cochrane, *Belleisle*, in company with a squadron carrying troops from Antigua, Grenada and St John commanded by General Bowyer, sailed from Barbados. Reaching St Thomas 21 December, Captain Fahie of *Ethalion* (36) summoned the governor Van Scholton to surrender. Having agreed to avoid bloodshed, 300 troops of the 70th regiment were landed to garrison the island. Cochrane then sailed for St Croix which also capitulated without resistance on Christmas Day.[53]

1808: In the spring Lieutenant Purvis, one of *Belleisle*'s officers, went before a court martial for wounding three French officers while they were being returned in a cartel bound for Martinique. Found guilty of the charge, Purvis was dismissed the service, bringing disrepute to his uncle Admiral John Purvis. On 29 September *Belleisle*'s command was superseded by Captain Edward Woolcombe who had transferred out of *Ulysses* (44). Shortly afterwards Woolcombe was succeeded by Captain William Fahie, late of *Ethalion*.

1809: Deployed with Cochrane's expedition to attack the French island of Martinique, *Belleisle* sailed from Carlisle Bay, Barbados 28 January. Cochrane, flying his flag in *Neptune* (98), was accompanied by *Pompée* (80), *Captain* (74), *York* (74), *Intrepid* (64), *Ulysses* (44), the frigates *Acasta* (40), *Ethalion* (36), *Penelope* (36), *Æolus* (32), *Circe* (32), and *Eurydice* (24) and the sloops and smaller vessels *Amaranthe* (18), *Cherub* (18), *Eclair* (18), *Forester* (18), *Frolic* (18), *Recruit* (18), *Star* (18), *Stork* (18), *Wolverine* (18), *Gorée* (16), *Haughty* (12), *Swinger* (12) and *Express* (6). On board these ships were 3,000 troops commanded by Major-General Frederick Maitland. Arriving off Martinique 30 January, Maitland's troops were landed at Pointe Sainte Luce under the direction of *Belleisle*'s Captain Fahie; meeting no opposition the troops proceeded inland. Before the island capitulated on 25 February, four men from *Belleisle* were wounded while serving on shore. Placed under the command of Captain Edward Brenton, *Belleisle* was directed to return to England. After embarking the French garrison into *Belleisle*, *Ulysses* and seven transports, the convoy sailed for France to exchange the prisoners with an equivalent number of British captives.

Arriving off Quiberon Bay 23 April, the French authorities refused to honour the exchange agreed upon by the terms of war, consequently the ships weighed and sailed for England, taking the grieving Frenchmen with them for internment within the notorious prison hulks.[54]

In Holland, the French, using the Dutch dockyard resources of Antwerp and Flushing, were gathering a considerable force commanded by Rear-Admiral Messiessy. Besides the ten 74 gun ships ready for sea, a further ten 3rd rate ships were on the stocks nearing completion. Fearing this threat, the British Admiralty assembled a large force to attack and destroy the ships and arsenals in the Schelde, Antwerp, Flushing and Ter Neuze and land the army on the islands of Cadzand, Walcheren and Zuid Beveland. This expeditionary fleet, placed under the command of Rear-Admiral Sir Richard Strachan, comprised 645 vessels as follows:

74 and 64 guns	50 guns	44 guns	5th rate frigates	20 guns	Sloops	Brigs	Bomb vessels	Cutters, gunboats & tenders	Transports	TOTAL
37	2	3	23	1	31	23	5	120	400	645

Embarked into the ships were 36,219 troops and 3,000 cavalry commanded by the late Prime Minister William Pitt's elder brother, Lieutenant-General the 2nd Earl of Chatham. To accommodate these forces many of the two decked men of war were armed en flute; their lower deck guns were removed to accommodate troops and their holds converted to carry horses. *Belleisle*, commanded by Captain George Cockburn, joined Strachan's fleet and sailed from the Downs 28 July. On that day Dr William Cullen-Brown, who sailed in the bomb vessel *Ætna*, wrote to his friend:

> July 28th Downs. This morning, at six o'clock, the whole of the Grand Expedition got under way, with a fair wind for Flushing. We are now going along at the rate of eight knots and a half an hour before the wind: and it is not improbable that we may commence operations in the course of tomorrow…10 o'clock P.M. We are now at anchor on what they call Thornton's Ridge, about 18 Miles from Walcheren…[55]

On 30 July *Belleisle* and *Royal Oak* (74) supported the landing of Sir Eyre Coote's division of 17,000 troops on the north end of Walcheren. On 13 August Cockburn transferred out of *Belleisle* into *Plover* (18) to command the bomb ships and gunboats assembled to bombard Flushing. During their attack, which began at 1.30 p.m., Cockburn lost seven men killed and 22 wounded.[56]

FATE

Returning to Portsmouth on 22 September 1809, *Belleisle* was paid off and laid up. Going into dock 19 July 1814, her copper was removed and, according to the Progress Book, it was proposed that she would undergo a 'Large Repair'. However, war with France had ended so this costly work was not undertaken and *Belleisle* was 'Taken to Pieces August 1814'.[57]

The 74 gun ship BELLEROPHON

The *Bellerophon* that fought at Trafalgar was the first vessel to bear this name in the Royal Navy. She was named after the Greek mythological hero who, using the winged horse Pegasus, successfully shot the Chimæra without being burned by its flames.[58]

Designed by Thomas Slade, *Bellerophon* was built to the lines of his *Arrogant* class of 1758. Ordered 11 January 1782, the keel of the *Bellerophon* was laid down in May 1782 at Frindsbury, situated on the northern bank of the River Medway opposite Chatham. Construction was undertaken under contract to the private shipbuilder Edward Greaves. Like other ships of 74 guns, about 3,250 loads of timber, the equivalent of 160,000 cubic feet of timber before conversion, was used in her construction. Much of this timber, the equivalent of 3,250 trees, was taken from the Weald of Kent. Launched 7 October 1786, her hull-only building costs amounted to £30,232 14s 3d. On launch day she was towed across the River Medway to Chatham dockyard where, on 7 March 1787, she was docked for thirteen days to have her bottom coppered and fitted out for the ordinary at a total cost £8,376 15s 2d, of which £3,389 8s 7d was spent on her hull, masts and rigging; the remaining money covering rigging and stores. Although well designed, *Bellerophon* was somewhat ponderous and proved to be a heavy sailer. Carrying 74 guns comprising twenty-eight 32 pounders on her lower gun deck, twenty-eight 18 pounders on the upper gun deck, fourteen 9 pounders on her quarter deck and four 9 pounders upon the forecastle, *Bellerophon* could deliver a single broadside weight of 781 pounds. Embodying her name, she was adorned handsomely with a bold figurehead of the Greek hero of whom only the head now remains. This relic can be seen among the other figureheads displayed within the Royal Naval Museum collection at Portsmouth Historic Dockyard.

SERVICE CAREER

1790: When the navy was mobilised to counter the threat of war with Spain, *Bellerophon* was taken out of ordinary, fitted for sea, and put in commission 19 July under her first commander Captain Thomas Pasley. Pasley, a Scot and veteran seaman, remained in the ship until she was paid off at Chatham 9 September 1791.

1793: When war with revolutionary France began, *Bellerophon* was recommissioned on 12 March under her previous commander Thomas Pasley and deployed with the Channel fleet under Admiral Richard Howe. The entire squadron, including *Bellerophon*, sailed from Spithead 14 July. Encountering squally winds off the Scilly Isles four days later, *Majestic* (74) and *Bellerophon* ran foul of each other. Describing the event Pasley recorded:

> At half-past three I was called in a great hurry and told that the *Majestic* would be aboard us. I ran out and found it was only too true, and past remedy. She came down upon us in the act of wearing and ran over our bowsprit, which she carried away, with the head and stem. There being a good deal of sea, the foremast soon followed, carrying away with it the main topmast and main yard, with a dreadful crash. Not one life was lost nor man hurt, thanks to God.

Having lost her bowsprit, fore mast and main topmast and associated rigging, and with superficial damage to her figurehead and cutwater, *Bellerophon* was compelled to return to port to repair.[59]

1794: On 14 January Pasley was appointed to the rank of Commodore thus command of the ship was superseded the following day by Captain William Johnstone Hope.[60] These dates however conflict with the ship's log, which implies that Pasley first hoisted his pendant on 11 September 1793. However, he probably remained in the captain's post, for Hope did not receive his post rank until 9 January 1794. Over the next five months the ship, flying the broad pendant of Commodore Pasley, cruised off Ushant. With Howe's fleet 400 miles west of Brest on 28 May at 6 a.m., *Bellerophon* received a signal from *Phæton* (38) that she had sighted strange sails to the SSW. The unidentified ships proved to be the fleet of Admiral Villaret-Joyeuse who had sailed west to meet a grain convoy from America. Actions against the French fleet over the next few days culminated in victory on the Glorious First of June. During the initial action, which began on the evening of 28 May, *Bellerophon* closed with and boldly engaged

CAPTAINS OF *BELLEROPHON* (MSS 248/4 and 248/6)

Name	Time of Entry	Time of Discharge	On What Occasion
Thomas Pasley	19 July 1790	9 September 1791	Paid off at Chatham
Thomas Pasley	12 March 1793	14 January 1794	Superseded - Appointed Commodore
William Hope	15 January 1794	30 November 1794	Superseded - Admiral Pasley's Flag flying
Lord Cranstoun	1 December 1794	9 September 1796	Superseded
John Loring	12 April 1796	9 September 1796	Superseded Acting
Henry D Darby	11 September 1796	3 May 1800	Paid Off at Portsmouth
Lord Viscount Garlies	25 June 1801	25 November 1801	Superseded
John Loring	26 November 1801	31 December 1803	New Book
John Loring	1 January 1804	24 April 1805	Superseded
John Cooke	25 April 1805	21 October 1805	Killed in Action off Cape Trafalgar
Richard Thomas	3 November 1805	3 November 1805	Superseded
Edward Rotheram	4 November 1805	7 June 1808	Superseded
Samuel Warren	8 June 1808	22 August 1810	Superseded
John Halsted	23 August 1810	4 November 1810	Superseded
Augustus Brine	5 November 1810	10 February 1813	Superseded
Edward Hawker	17 March 1813	8 April 1815	Superseded
F L Maitland	9 April 1815	13 September 1815	Paid Off

SPECIFICATIONS: *BELLEROPHON*

Rate	3rd	*Length on the range of the gun deck*	68 ft	*Ordnance - lower gun deck*	28 x 32 pounders
Guns	74	*Length of keel for tonnage*	138 ft 1⅜ ins	*Ordnance - upper gun deck*	28 x 18 pounders
Class	Arrogant 1758	*Extreme breadth*	46 ft 9 ins	*Ordnance - quarter deck*	14 x 9 pounders
Designer	Thomas Slade	*Depth in hold*	19 ft 9 ins	*Ordnance - forecastle*	4 x 9 pounders
Builder	Edward Greaves	*Tons burthen*	1604 27/94	*Single broadside weight*	781 pounds
Dockyard	Frindsbury	*Draught afore*	20 ft 9 ins	*Fate*	1816 Hulked as a convict ship at Sheerness
Date ordered	11 January 1782	*Draught abaft*	23 ft 3 ins		1824 Renamed *Captivity*
Date keel laid	May 1782	*Complement*	550		1836 Sold
Date launched	7 October 1786				

Source: Lyon, *Sailing Navy List*, p. 68.

THE 74 GUN SHIP BELLEROPHON

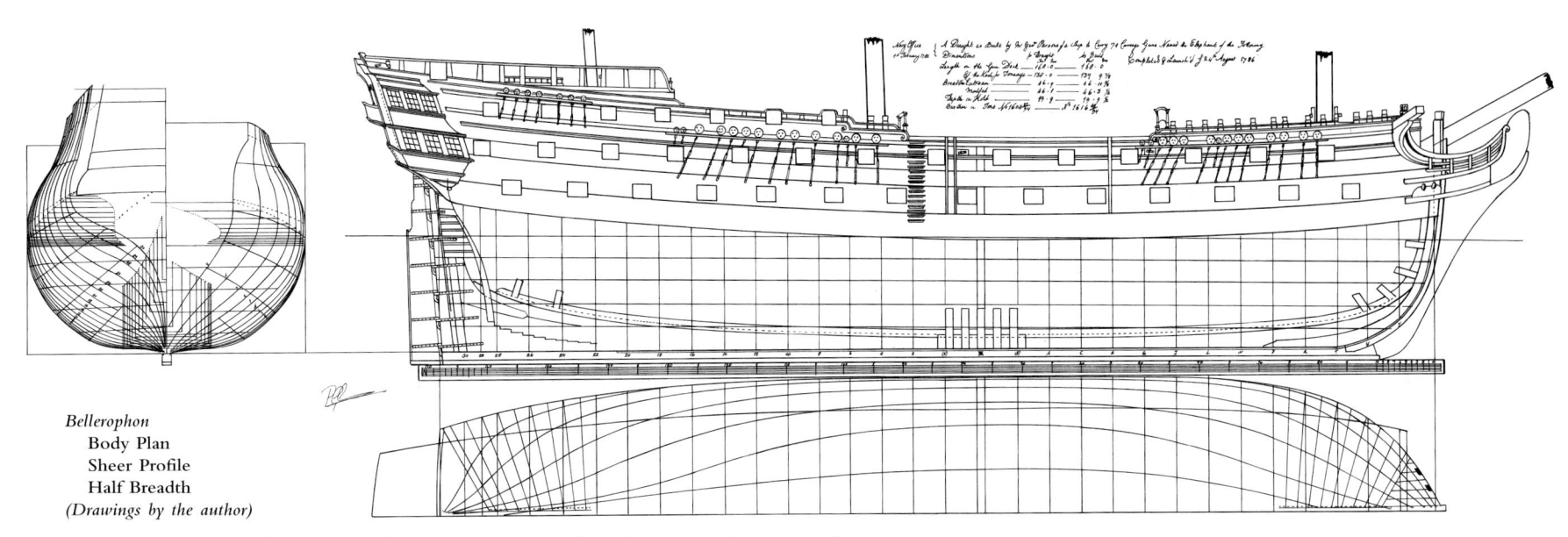

Bellerophon
  Body Plan
  Sheer Profile
  Half Breadth
(Drawings by the author)

Revolutionnaire (110) before any other British vessels of the flying squadron could support her. Sustaining considerable damage to her topmast she was compelled to haul off when other Trafalgar ships *Leviathan* and *Thunderer* arrived. Poor weather prevented the two fleets undertaking a sustained engagement until Saturday 1 June when Howe won Britain's first naval victory of the war. At about 10.40 a.m. the British ships sailed in line abreast towards the French. *Bellerophon*, according to Hope, 'received a very heavy fire from 3 to 4 of the enemies van'. Just before 11 o'clock the ship was hit with a heavy volley of musket and round shot which carried away Admiral Pasley's leg. Midshipman Matthew Flinders, later renowned as an explorer, reported: 'our brave admiral lost a leg by an 18 pound ball which came through the barricade of the quarter-deck' in the heat of the action. When carried below to Alexander White, *Bellerophon*'s surgeon, Pasley appeared more concerned that his flag remain flying than having his leg amputated. Firing rapid broadsides, *Bellerophon* compelled the French *Eole* (74) nearby to withdraw, but by this time *Bellerophon* had taken such a pounding that she had lost all three topmasts and her lower rigging and sails were cut to pieces. Completely disabled and unable to manoeuvre, Hope signalled the frigate *Latona* (38) for assistance. This was a bloody, hard-fought action, and many British ships suffered considerable damage and casualties. Considering the pounding *Bellerophon* had received, remarkably she only lost four killed and 27 wounded. When the ship returned to Portsmouth 10 June to refit, Rear-Admiral Pasley was sent to Haslar hospital near Gosport. On Friday 27 June King George III visited Portsmouth to pay his respects to Howe and his fleet. For their part in the battle Pasley was made a baronet on 26 July with a pension of £1,000 per annum and Captain Hope received a gold medal. Pasley died in 1808 aged 75. On 1 December command of the ship was superseded by Captain Lord Cranstoun.[61]

1795: *Bellerophon* sailed from Spithead 26 May to join Vice-Admiral William Cornwallis's squadron comprising *Royal Sovereign* (100), *Brunswick* (74), *Mars* (74), *Triumph* (74) and two frigates *Phæton* (38) and *Pallas* (32). Arriving off Penmarck on 7 June, the squadron chased and intercepted eight small vessels in Palais Roads off Belle Isle the next day. On 12 June ships commanded by Admiral Villaret sailed from Brest; joining Rear-Admiral Vence off Isle de Groix, the combined force now comprised 13 line of battle ships, two frigates, two brigs and a cutter. Sighting this French fleet at 9 a.m. 16 June, Cornwallis was heavily outnumbered. He made signals as if the remainder of his fleet lay over the horizon and made a tactical withdrawal fighting a rearguard action as he did so. *Bellerophon* took up station with *Brunswick*, firing her stern and quarter guns into the leading French ships.[62] In late June the squadron returned to Cawsand Bay outside Plymouth to re-provision before returning to station off Ushant and Belle Isle. Anchoring at Spithead in mid-September, Cranstoun court-martialled nine *Bellerophon* marines for inciting mutinous behaviour by writing letters of complaint to external parties. As they all had impeccable characters and had shown honour under fire from the French at 'Cornwallis's Retreat' they were acquitted.[63]

1796: In January *Bellerophon* took up station off Ushant watching over Brest, occasionally returning home to re-provision. On 11 September Lord Cranstoun was superseded by the Irish Captain Henry D'Esterre Darby. However, for the previous six months the ship had effectively been commanded by Lieutenant John Loring, appointed acting captain 12 April while Lord Cranstoun took up his new post as Governor of Grenada in the West Indies.[65]

1797: Returning to Plymouth 2 January, *Bellerophon* then joined ships patrolling off Bantry Bay searching for the French invasion fleet heading for Ireland. After weeks of heavy weather she put into Cork where *Polyphemus* (64) lay flying the flag of Admiral Kingsmill. Returning to Spithead in March, *Bellerophon* received new orders to join Sir John Jervis's Mediterranean fleet deployed off Cadiz. Arriving 30 March *Bellerophon* was immediately deployed with the inshore squadron commanded by Rear-Admiral Nelson. At home the great mutiny was enveloping the Channel fleet at Spithead. While several ships were affected by mutiny in Jervis's fleet in June, *Bellerophon* was not one of them.

1798: Under orders from Jervis to observe the French ships at Toulon, Nelson re-entered the Mediterranean in early May. Shortly after Jervis sent a second squadron, led by Captain Thomas Troubridge in *Culloden* to support him. Besides *Bellerophon* and *Culloden* the squadron comprised the 74 gun ships *Defence*, *Goliath*, *Majestic*, *Minotaur*, *Swiftsure*, *Theseus*, and *Zealous*. Consequently *Bellerophon* became involved with Nelson's search of Admiral de Brueys' fleet which finally culminated with his distinguished victory at the battle of the Nile fought in Abu-Kir Bay on 1 August. In the attack *Bellerophon* lay eighth in the British line; directly ahead *Minotaur*; while directly astern followed *Defence*, both of which would later fight at Trafalgar. While it was Darby's intention was to bring *Bellerophon* up alongside *Franklin* (74), by misfortune she inadvertently anchored directly broadside to de Brueys' flagship *Orient* (120), a ship some 38 per cent more powerful. Casablanca, *Orient*'s captain, immediately fired two broadsides into *Bellerophon* with devastating effect, scything down men, dismounting most of her quarter deck guns and shredding rigging; all the boats stowed on the skid beams were smashed to pieces. Besides cannon fire, French musketeers standing in the tops picked their targets. In the hail of shot, ball and flying splinters, Captain Darby was hit in the head rendering him unconscious and was carried below to Bellamy the surgeon. Lieutenants Daniel and Lander,

Bellerophon
Stern View
(Drawing by the author)

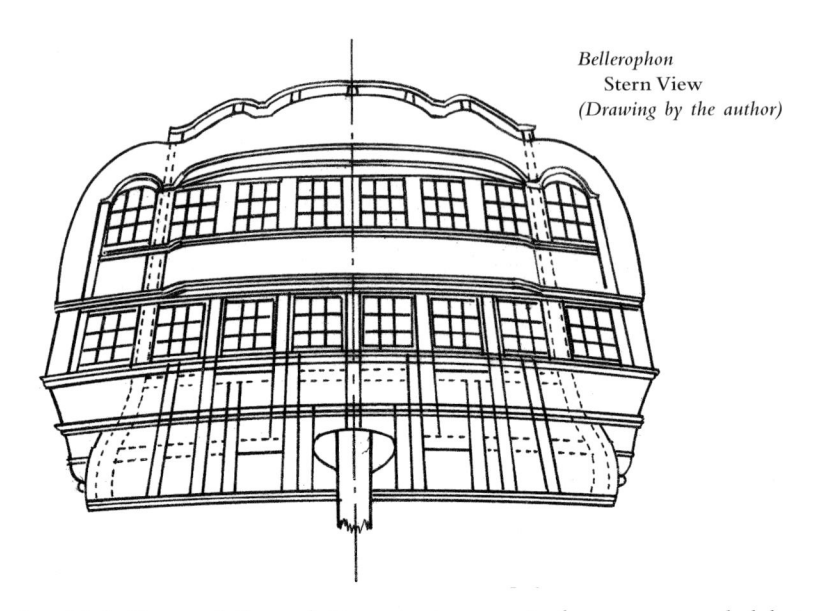

the ship's First and Second Lieutenants respectively, were wounded but remained at their posts. John Hadaway, the Fourth Lieutenant, was also wounded and carried below and George Joliffe, the Fifth Lieutenant was killed instantly. Shortly afterwards Lieutenant Daniel had his right leg carried away by a round shot; while being carried below he was killed outright with a hail of grapeshot which also killed the seamen carrying him. For over an hour *Bellerophon* endured the onslaught meted out by the great French ship until at 8 p.m. her mizzen mast, shot through, collapsed over the stern, the main mast following shortly fell across the waist and forecastle killing Lieutenant Lander and several seamen. With Captain Darby below and other lieutenants killed, command of the ship fell temporarily to the 24 year-old Third Lieutenant Robert Cathcart who now faced the problem that *Orient* was ablaze. He gave orders to cut *Bellerophon*'s cable and, totally dismasted, she drifted some distance before being brought up with the kedge, her only remaining anchor. Although out of the mêlée, she received a broadside from *Tonnant* and more distantly from *Heureux*. Casualties sustained in *Bellerophon* comprised 49 killed and 148 wounded. After making jury masts from wreckage in Abu-Kir Bay *Bellerophon* finally reached Gibraltar to refit.

1800: *Bellerophon* returned to Spithead 2 April 1800 and remained under quarantine for three days. De-stored she went into Portsmouth dockyard on 16 April and was paid off 3 May. It was not until 5 September that she went into dock to refit.

1801: Having undergone a 'middling repair' at a cost of £32,608, *Bellerophon* was recommissioned under Captain Lord Viscount Garlies on 25 June and undocked two days later. Stored for sea, the ship left the dockyard 9 August and sailed 21 August to join the Channel fleet blockading Brest until the end of hostilities. Lord Garlies remained in the ship until succeeded by Captain John Loring on 25 November.

1802: Receiving new orders while laying in Torbay *Bellerophon* was stored and victualled for six months and sailed on 2 March with five other ships of the line to join Admiral Duckworth's squadron in the West Indies. Taking just 25 days to cover the passage between Plymouth and Barbados via the Azores, a distance of 4,700 miles, *Bellerophon* was making 188 miles daily at an average speed of 7.8 knots. *Bellerophon* reached her final destination, Port Royal, Jamaica on 12 April, from where she was deployed for the next 18 months escorting convoys between the Caribbean islands and Halifax, Nova Scotia.[65] When war restarted in May Captain Loring was promoted to Commodore commanding the British squadron. Resuming their offensive they captured French corvette *Mignonne* and a brig in late June. Deployed off Cape François, San Domingo, on 24 July, *Bellerophon*, with *Elephant*, *Theseus* and *Vanguard*, three of Nelson's previous ships, fell in with French ships *Duguay Trouin* (74), *Duquesne* (74) and frigate *Guerrière*. Although *Duquesne* was captured next day, *Duguay Trouin* and the frigate escaped.[66] Within two years *Duguay Trouin* would fight at Trafalgar. Still blockading Cape François in November, Commodore Loring received a communication from General Rochambeau who was commanding the reduced French garrison besieged by black Haitian rebels led by General Dessalines. After negotiations the French were allowed to embark in their ships and leave under British protection only to be escorted by *Bellerophon* and her consorts to Jamaica.[67]

1804: In early February, 212 of *Bellerophon*'s crew contracted malaria and yellow fever; 17 died and of the 100 men ashore into the hospital a further 40 died, among whom were Midshipmen Hewitt and Maxwell. Recalled home, *Bellerophon* sailed from Jamaica on Sunday 17 June escorting a convoy of some 178 merchantmen bound for England. In company were *Duquesne* (74), *Desirée* (40), *Echo* (18), *Snake* (18), *Hunter* (16), *Renard* (16) and the armed schooner *Pickle* (8). After five weeks' passage *Bellerophon* and her convoy anchored in the Downs on 11 August after which Captain Loring took the ship into Portsmouth on 24 August to refit.[68] Docked 5 September, the ship was completely re-coppered and refitted at a total cost of £11,914; £349 for her hull, £2,352 for masts and yards and £5,015 for rigging and stores, the remaining sum accounting for labour costs. Coming out of the dock 8 October the ship sailed on 1 November to join the Channel squadron commanded by Admiral Cornwallis stationed off Brest.[69] Entering Plymouth to re-provision, Loring's long command was superseded by Captain John Cooke on 24 April. For his First Lieutenant Cooke brought William Pryce Cumby.[70]

1805: In May *Bellerophon* joined Vice-Admiral Collingwood's newly formed squadron operating out of Gibraltar watching Cadiz, remaining on this station until returning after the battle.

TRAFALGAR

Because two journals survive from the *Bellerophon*, Captain Cooke's and a lieutenant's, we have good accounts of the events surrounding the battle of Trafalgar and the ensuing storm. Laying off Cape St Mary some 10 leagues SE Friday 10 October, one of the logs states: 'exercised the Landsmen at Great Guns'. In the following morning they 'struck the fore and main Top Gall^t Mast & shifted the Jacks – Parted C^o H.M. Brig *Weazle* Received from the *Malabar* Transport 3 cask of Oatmeal – 13 casks of Beef – 24 of Pork & 5 of Sugar'. Next day the same log states that the ship's company were 'Employed painting the ship's side', and that they 'observed the *Royal Sovereign* hoist Vice Admiral Collingwood's flag', signifying Collingwood transferring out of the *Dreadnought* (98). Also that day seaman John Cook was punished 'with 24 lashes for Drunkenness'. Other events recorded over the next week are the arrival of *Agamemnon* (64) and frigate *Aimable* on Sunday 13 October and the departure of the *Prince of Wales* (98), *Donegal* (74) and the brig *Weazle*. On Tuesday 15 October *Bellerophon* 'received from the *Lord Duncan* Victualler 22 Tierces of Beef & D^o of Pork – 4 HHds [hogsheads] of Flour – 10 Barrels of Rice – 10 D^o of Sugar'.[71]

For Monday 21 October *Bellerophon*'s log states:

Fresh Breezes & Squally W^r with rain ans^d No 53 from *Royal Sovereign* to Larboard Division – 1.45 ans^d N° 106 Genl -made & short^d sail occas^y down TopG^t yards – 2 Wore Ship – 5.20 ans^d Signal from *Victory* 101 & 8 -Saw the Flashes of several Guns & false Fires ans^d Signal to wear – wore Ship AM D^o W^r 4 light airs inclinable to Calm – with a heavy swell from the Westw^d ans^d Signal to wear – 4.15 wore Ship – at daylight Saw the Enemys Fleet ENE ans^d 72 & 76 General Compass ENE out all reefs & made sail towards them – 6.20 ans^d No 13 General – 6.42 ans^d 76 Compass East General – Beat to Quarters & cleared for Action – at Noon light Breezes – ans^d 88 Genl from the *Royal Sovereign* & set steering sails Fleet consisting of 27 Sail of the Line'.[72]

Much briefer, the other log records for Monday:

> ... at daylight Obs^d the Enemy's Fleet to leeward bearing ENE Ans^rd 72 & 76 Genl out reefs and Made sail Beat to Quarters and Clear^d Ship to Action at Noon Lights airs Standing towards the Enemys Fleet Consisting of 33 Sail of the Line, 5 Frigates, and 2 Brigs our Fleet 27 of the Line 4 Frigates 1 Cutter & 1 Schooner...[73]

On the approach towards the combined fleet *Bellerophon* lay fifth in Collingwood's leeward division, ahead lay *Tonnant* (80), astern *Achille* (74) and parallel to larboard the *Colossus* (74). *Bellerophon*'s log Tuesday 22 October continues:

> Light Breezes with a swell from the Westw^d at 10 Minutes past noon the *Royal Sovereign* opened fire on the Enemy's Centre at 13' [minutes past] ans^d 16 Genl at 20' the *Royal Sovereign* broke through the Enemy's Line astern of a Spanish three Decker & engaged to leeward, being followed by HM Ships *Mars*, *Belleisle* and *Tonnant*, which engaged their respective opponents - - 12.15 D^o W^r 12.20 opened our Fire on the Enemy at 30' engaging on both sides in passing through the Enemy's Line; astern of a Spanish two Decker...

which was *Monarca* (74). The log then states:

> ... at 35' while hauling to the Wind [to engage *Monarca*] fell onboard the French two Decked Ship *Aigle*, with our Starb^d Bow on her Larb^d Quarter - our Fore Yard locking with his main One, kept up a brisk fire both on her and the Spanish Ship on the Larb^d Bow, at the same time receiving the Fire of two Ships one astern the other on the Larbd Quarter - at 1 the Main & Mizen Topmasts fell over the side - at 1.15 the Master fell - at 1.11 Captain John Cooke (1st) fell - still foul of the *Aigle*.

At this point the log book terminates with the signature of William Pryce Cumby, *Bellerophon*'s First Lieutenant who took command, with his words 'Captain killed in Action'.[74] During her engagement with *Aigle*, *Bellerophon*'s gunners depressed their guns to shatter the decks of the French ship but at the same time received a continuous hail of musket shot raining down from the poop and tops of her opponent. A witness who saw Captain John Cooke killed recorded the event:

> He had discharged his pistols very frequently at the enemy, who often attempted to board, and he killed a French officer on his own Quarterdeck. He was in the act of reloading his pistols (and upon the same plank where Captain Pasley lost a leg on the 1st June) when he received two musket-balls in the breast, He immediately fell, and upon the quartermaster going up and asking him if he should take him down below, his answer was 'No let me lie quietly one minute Tell Lieutenant Cumby never to strike'.[75]

The second log, again briefer, records Tuesday 22 October as follows:

> Light Breezes with a Swell from the Westw^d Bearing down on the Enemy under all sail at 12.10 *Royal Sovereign* opened fire on the Enemy's Centre being followed by *Mars*, *Belleisle* and *Tonnant* at 12.30 Engaging on both Sides. At 12.36 Fell on Board the French Ship *Aigle* at 1.5 the Master fell, at 1.11 Captain Cooke fell, still foul of the *Aigle* and keeping up a Brisk fire from the Main and Lower Deck Guns, the Quarter Deck, Poop and forecastle being nearly cleard by Troops on board *Aigle* 1.40 *Aigle* dropt to leeward under a Raking fire from us as she fell off on the Smoke clearing away Obs^d several of the Enemy's Ships had Struck at 3 took possession of the Spanish Ship *Monarca* AM D^o W^r Empl^d clearing away the wreck.[76]

When the smoke cleared Cumby saw that the Spanish *Monarca* had struck, and sent an officer and men across in a boat to take possession. At about this point *Bellerophon*'s surgeon came on deck and declaring that there were too many wounded filling the after cockpit, he requested that some be taken to the remains of the captain's cabin; Cumby agreed. At about 5.30 *Bellerophon* took possession of *Bahama* which had earlier fired upon *Bellerophon* as she cut through the line. Including Captain John Cooke, *Bellerophon* lost 28 killed in the action, among whom, as noted in the log, was her Master Edward Overton who died after being carried below with his leg smashed by a round shot, and Midshipman John Simmons. Among the 123 wounded were James Wemyss, Captain Royal Marines; Edward Hartley, Master's mate; midshipmen Thomas Bant, William Jewell, George Pearson and James Stone, and the Boatswain Thomas Robinson. Captain Wemyss, it must be noted, later died after having his arm amputated.[77]

Bellerophon, like *Belleisle*, was in a precarious situation: her main and mizzen topmasts were hanging over the side, her jib boom, mizen boom and gaff had gone, the fore mast was tottering, the rigging was unserviceable, her hull was riddled with shot holes and her uppermost decks had been wrecked by grenades hurled from *Aigle*. With little rigging to balance the ship during the gales following the battle *Bellerophon* rolled so much that it caused considerable discomfort to the wounded as they were thrown around. To prevent further misery Midshipman Daniel Woodriff had capstan bars nailed to the deck of the captain's cabin to hold the cots of the wounded to ease them before they could be discharged into hospital at Gibraltar. Throughout Wednesday 23 October the crew busied themselves re-setting the mizen rigging and 'Got up a Jury Main Topmast and Topsail Yard and set the Sail'. On Thursday at 3 p.m. they 'Obs^d the Enemy's Squad^n to leeward consisting of 8 Sail of the Line', and at around 4.30 that afternoon they 'took in Tow the S^t. Augustine Spanish 74'. The weather the following morning is recorded as 'Strong Gales & Squally with Lightning and Rain'. On Friday 25 October Cumby, with his appointed First Lieutenant Edward Thomas 'Must^d Ships Comp^y found 28 had been killed and 127 wounded in the action'.[78] The scene that day can be imagined, the crew mustered at their divisions standing on a heaving deck with heavy skies and wind-driven rain, each man tentatively listening or answering their names as the roll call was made and their expressions as names were not answered. Stood down they turned to and 'Got up a Jury Mizen Topmast'. Next morning *Bellerophon* lost a twenty-ninth man, the log stating 'AM D^o W^r fell overboard and was drowned Thos^s Bramley (S)'. On Sunday 27 October *Bellerophon* was 'Running in for Gibraltar', with '*Agamemnon* and *Colossus* in Company'. At 7 p.m. next day, 'Came too with the B^t B^r [best bower anchor] in 15 fm^s furled Sails and Moor'd Ship AM D^o W^r Emp^d clearing the ship and taking the wounded People on shore'.[79]

Bellerophon remained at Gibraltar for eight days making repairs with the 'Carpenters Stopping shot holes', restocking the ground and middle tiers of water casks end embarking fresh provisions. Her shattered main topsail yard and topmast were sent down and the fore topmast was lowered and set up as a main topmast. After receiving '72 French Prisoners from the *Phœbe*' on Sunday 3 November, Lieutenant Cumby was, according to the records, succeeded by Captain Richard Thomas.[80] However just before *Bellerophon* weighed next day and sailed for England, command of the ship was superseded by Captain Edward Rotheram who having commanded *Royal Sovereign* was returning home. Repairs had been carried out in harbour but the log records that at sea further work continued, the 'Carpenters making a Jib Boom' and the 'Armourers Emp^d at the Forge', making repairs to iron fittings. Below in the grand magazine filling room men 'Emp^d filling Powder' cartridges, and on 8 November, having survived the battle, 'Departed this Life Joseph Antonio (S) Committed the Body of the Deceased to the Deep'.[81] Accompanying *Bellerophon* home were *Victory* carrying Nelson's body and the equally battered *Belleisle*. Off Start Point *Bellerophon* and *Belleisle* parted company with *Victory* and anchored in Cawsand Bay. Finally going into Plymouth on 14 December, *Bellerophon* went into dock ten days later to have her copper repaired and dressed and undergo general repairs.[82]

1806: Launched again on 20 January, *Bellerophon* was fully refitted at a total cost of £18,082, half of which covered rigging and stores, and sailed for active duty on 26 February. The ship remained under Rotheram's command for the next two years, operating off Ushant blockading Brest and returning to Cawsand Bay or Torbay as necessary to re-provision or avoid Atlantic gales. During his captaincy Rotheram compiled a dossier giving detailed descriptions and statistics of his ship's crew: their height, build, skin variation, facial shapes, even descriptions of tattoos.[84]

1808: When Captain Samuel Warren succeeded command of *Bellerophon* on 8 June the ship was re-deployed to the North Sea blockading the ports of Belgium and Holland. With Napoleon's brother Louis installed as King of Holland and with France dominating most of Northern Europe, this new theatre of war had evolved to prevent Napoleon using the Dutch fleet to support his now much reduced navy. For similar reasons the Royal Navy had attacked and destroyed the Danish fleet in Copenhagen the previous year. *Bellerophon's* squadron, commanded by Rear-Admiral Gardner, was stationed mainly off Flushing where it could easily run for Yarmouth Roads to re-provision.

1809: With Russia supporting France and invading Finland the previous year, *Bellerophon* was sent to join the Baltic fleet commanded by Admiral Sir James Saumarez flying his flag in *Victory* (98). Leaving Gothenburg 24 May, the Baltic fleet reached Karlskrona on 4 June after which *Bellerophon* with *Minotaur* sailed for the Gulf of Finland where they would be joined by the rest of the squadron at the end of the month. Cruising off Hango 19 June, *Bellerophon* and *Minotaur* sent in boats under the command of Robert Pilch, *Bellerophon's* First Lieutenant, to attack a number of suspicious luggers sheltering amid offshore islets. Having taken possession of three of the vessels the British seamen found themselves in a trap, as overlooking the anchorage were four Russian gun batteries. The nearest battery immediately opened fire with round and grape shot, forcing the British seamen to abandon the luggers and set fire to them. Undeterred, Pilch attacked the nearest battery manned by some 100 Russian seamen. Having overwhelmed the defendants, Pilch and his men spiked the 24 pounder guns and blew up the magazine before returning to their ship.[84] On their return *Bellerophon's* log states: 'at 5 the Boats returned on Board with 5 wounded men, Griffith Griffith, Peter Just John Butterfield Thomas MaCarthy & Simon McLean'.[85] With *Implacable* (74), commanded by Captain Thomas Byam Martin, *Melpomene* (38) and *Prometheus* (18), *Bellerophon* was also involved with a second cutting out expedition carried out in Barö Sound, Finland, on 7 July, against eight gunboats each mounting a 32 and a 24 pounder with 46 men. When Lieutenant Hawkey from *Implacable* leading the assault was killed, Lieutenant Charles Allen of *Bellerophon* took command. Although one gunboat managed to get away, one was sunk and the other six were captured, together with ten vessels containing powder and provisions. For his conduct *Bellerophon's* Lieutenant Allen was promoted Commander. After further deployment within the Baltic *Bellerophon* returned home escorting a convoy of merchantmen, arriving off Yarmouth Roads on 21 November.[86]

1810: Entering Sheerness 6 January, *Bellerophon* had her copper repaired while afloat and minor repairs, costing £3,313 of which only £1,098 was spent on her hull, excluding labour costs.[87] Leaving the dockyard on 18 February the ship remained at the Nore until spring when she returned to her station off Holland. On 23 August command of the ship was superseded by Captain John Halsted who was succeeded by Captain Augustus Brine when the ship went into Portsmouth on 5 November.[88] Needing a refit, *Bellerophon* was docked 15 November and had her copper replaced. Re-launched 30 November the ship sailed 13 December and cruised monotonously between the Texel and the Hook of Holland for the next few years.

1813: Back at Portsmouth in December 1812, the ship entered the dock 22 January to repair her copper and doubling, the latter being series of elm planking strakes wrought along the waterline above the copper. One month

PROGRESS BOOK - *BELLEROPHON* 3rd RATE OF 74 GUNS:

At what Port	Arrived	Docked	Coppered
Frindsbury; Edward Breaves	Began	May 1783	
Chatham	7 Oct 1786	7 March 1787	Coppered
Chatham			Coppered Repaired Aug 1790
Sheerness	21 Nov 1790	Taken in hand Mar & completed April 1791	
Chatham	31 Aug 1791	28 Mar 1793	Copper Repaired
Plymouth	21 July 1793		
Poersmouth	12 Oct 1795	27 Oct 1795	Copper Repaired
Portsmouth	16 April 1800	5 Sep 1800	Copper taken off; Re-coppered June 1801
Portsmouth	24 Aug 1804	5 Sep 1804	Copper taken off Sep Re-coppered Oct 1804
Plymouth	14 Dec 1805	24 Dec 1805	Copper Repaired & Dressed
Plymouth	19 Oct 1807	2 Nov 1807	Copper taken off & Re-coppered Nov 1807
Sheerness	3 Jan 1810		Copper Repaired
Portsmouth	6 Nov 1810	15 Nov 1810	Copper taken off & Re-coppered Nov 1810
Portsmouth	19 Dec 1812	22 Jan 1813	Repaired Copper & Doubling
Portsmouth	26 Jan 1814	7 Feb 1814	Copper taken off & Re-coppered
Sheerness	2 Sep 1815	Taken in Hand Dec 1815 & Completed Sep 1816	
		27 April 1826	Copper taken off; Felted & Re-coppered & fixed Protectors
Plymouth	8 June 1826		

Sold 21 January 1836 for £4,030

after the ship was undocked command was superseded by Captain Edward Hawker, who made preparations to receive Vice-Admiral Sir Richard Goodwin Keats and convey him from Spithead to St Johns, where he was to take up the appointment of Governor of Newfoundland. With the admiral entering the ship *Bellerophon* sailed at 4 p.m. on 22 April, escorting a convoy of 72 merchantmen and three other warships. After enduring heavy weather *Bellerophon* arrived at St Johns on 31 May and sailed one week later with a convoy for Bermuda. On her return voyage to St Johns, Hawker captured an American privateer. Sailing with a convoy on 22 November, *Bellerophon* arrived at Torbay on month later and sailed for Portsmouth to refit.

1814: After spending most of February in dock being re-coppered, *Bellerophon* sailed for Newfoundland with a convoy on 26 April and remained cruising North American waters before returning to Spithead in December.

1815: In March *Bellerophon* sailed for the Nore where, on 9 April, Captain Frederick Maitland superseded Hawker in command of the ship. In May Maitland received orders to proceed to Plymouth and join Rear-Admiral Sir Henry Hotham's squadron sailing to blockade the French coast between the Rivers Loire and Gironde. Anchoring off the Basque Roads on 31 May, Maitland noticed two French frigates, *Méduse* and *Saale*, the corvette *Balladiére* and brig *Épervier*, anchored off Île d'Aix. Suspicious of their intentions, *Bellerophon* remained watching for a month when, on 30 June, Maitland received an anonymous note stating that Napoleon was making for Bordeaux after escaping Wellington's triumphant rout of the French army on the field of Waterloo twelve days earlier. On 8 July Napoleon embarked on board *Saale* by which time *Bellerophon* had been joined by the 20 gun frigates *Myrmidon* and *Slaney*. Two days later delegates Count Las Cases and General Savary boarded *Bellerophon* and presented a letter to Maitland concerning the issue of passports permitting Napoleon and his family passage to the United States. Maitland however was under strict

Source: ADM 180/6 Entry 108 & ADM 180/10 folio 67

Launched or Undocked	Sailed	Built or Nature of Repair	Cost of Hull, Masts & Yards Materials £	Workmen £	Cost of Masts & Yards Materials £	Workmen £	Cost of Rigging & Stores Materials £	Workmen £	Grand Total £
7 October 1786	7 October 1786	Built	30,232. 14s. 3d. Hull only						
20 March 1787		Coppered & fitted for Ordinary	3,389. 8s.7d.		4,987.				8,376.15s. 2d.
15 August 1790		Fitted	735. 3s.7d.				3,804. 14s.9d.	4,620. 8s.4d.	
	20 April 1791	Fitted	95				1.733		1,828
29 March 1793	26 April 1793	Fitted	2,128				2,036		4,164
	8 August 1793	Made Good Defects	1,725				2,289		4,014
13 Nov 1795	16 Nov 1795	Made Good Defects	3,266				4,837		8,103
27 June 1801	9 Aug 1801	Middling Repair & Fitted	21,699				10,909		32,608
8 Oct 1804	1 Nov 1804	Fitted	3,349	992	2,352	108	5,015	98	11,914
20 Jan 1806	26 Feb 1806	Defects	3,646	2,049	2,856	41	9,460	30	18,082
5 Nov 1807	23 Jan 1808	Defects	1,589	1,293	1,693	36	3,254	161	8,026
	18 Feb 1810	Defects	1,098	395	188	22	1,603	7	3,313
30 Nov 1810	13 Dec 1810	Refitted	1,525	775	938	11	2,966	45	6,260
17 Feb 1813	26 March 1813	Defects	5,303	1,807	2,034	32	5,528	137	14,856
24 Feb 1814	30 March 1814	Defects	2,836	1,002	888	32	8,121	163	13,042
		Fitted for a Convict Hulk	-	114	-	1	674	1	790
24 May 1826	4 June 1826	Fitted to be navigated to Plymouth	838	395	-	-	-	-	1,233

orders to prevent the defeated French Emperor from leaving France. While in conference the sloop *Falmouth* (20) arrived with orders from Admiral Hotham that no passports were to be issued. Further reinforced by the arrival of *Daphne* (22) and *Cyrus* (20) on 12 July, Maitland deployed all four frigates to prevent the French ships making their escape. By this date France had formally capitulated to the Allied forces; thus Napoleon, now a fugitive and likely to be executed, decided to surrender himself and trust British justice to determine his fate. Leaving his lodgings on the Île d'Aix in the early morning of 15 July, Napoleon boarded *Épervier* which, making sail, proceeded towards *Bellerophon*. Shortly afterwards *Bellerophon*'s barge, commanded by Lieutenant Mott, ran alongside *Épervier* and on boarding the brig Mott informed her commander Captain Jourdon de la Passadiére that he was under strict orders to convey Napoleon back to *Bellerophon*. When the barge got alongside *Bellerophon* at about 7 a.m., Napoleon stepped on board a British man-o-war for the first time. Shortly afterwards *Superb* (74), carrying Admiral Sir Henry Hotham, entered the bay. Making sail at 2 p.m. next day, *Bellerophon*, with *Myrmidon* and *Slaney* escorting her, proceeded to Torbay, arriving on 24 July. Receiving new orders from Lord Keith, *Bellerophon* anchored in Plymouth Sound two days later with the frigates *Eurotus* and *Liffey* acting as guard ships to prevent Napoleon escaping. Meanwhile preparations were being made to transport Napoleon and his entourage into exile. As *Bellerophon* was unfit to make the 10,000 mile return journey to St Helena, Maitland received orders on 3 August to put to sea and stand off to await the arrival of *Northumberland* (74) from Spithead. Joined by *Tonnant* (80) *Bellerophon*, *Eurotus* and *Myrmidon* weighed at 9.30 and made for Start Point on 4 August, later joined by the fireship *Prometheus* (18) carrying Lord Keith and the cutter *Nimble* (12). Finally at 9 a.m. on 6 August *Northumberland* (74), accompanied by troopships *Bucephalus* and *Ceylon*, appeared from the east and anchored off Berry Head, *Bellerophon* and her escorts anchoring likewise. When Napoleon emerged after breakfast to transfer into *Northumberland* on 7 August the entire crew of *Bellerophon*'s were assembled to see his departure. As the Emperor crossed the quarter deck, *Northumberland*'s marines presented their arms to the accompanying drum roll. Acknowledging their salute Napoleon raised his hat, thanked Captain Maitland for his kindness and speaking to *Bellerophon*'s officers, said: 'Gentlemen I have requested your captain to express my gratitude to you for your attention to me and to those who have followed my fortunes'. He then walked to the gangway, faced the *Bellerophon*'s sailors, raised his hat and bowed three times before going down the side into *Northumberland*'s awaiting barge. As the Emperor was rowed over to the *Northumberland*, *Bellerophon*'s seamen lined the side watching their captive of 24 days depart.[89] Like the Greek legend, *Bellerophon* had metaphorically slain the beast Chimæra. Having done so she weighed anchor that evening and with *Tonnant* in company made sail and steered for Plymouth. Soon after Maitland received orders to go to the Medway and be decommissioned. Arriving at Sheerness dockyard 2 September, Maitland paid off *Bellerophon* on 13 September.

FATE

Also like the myth *Bellerophon* was shortly to spend the rest of her days alone within her own Aleian plains as the Navy Board had agreed to have her 'Fitted for a Convict Hulk'. In December 1815 the dockyard took *Bellerophon* in hand and commenced the conversion, removing all unnecessary cabins and storerooms and fitting caged cells throughout her decks. If fitted out like the *Defence* she had twelve cells on each gun deck and 18 cells on the orlop, with warders and other staff being accommodated in the officer's cabins astern. Also part of the upper gun deck was removed to facilitate a chapel between decks that also served as a schoolroom. Completed in September 1816 at a cost of £790, *Bellerophon* was laid up in the Thames estuary near the hulk *Retribution* appearing now, as described in Charles Dickens' novel *Great Expectations*, 'like a wicked Noah's ark. Cribbed and barred and moored by massive rusty chains'. *Bellerophon*'s consort *Retribution* had once been the proud 74 gun ship *Edgar*.[90] Her first batch of prisoners were transferred from the hulk *Portland*, once a 50 gun ship, lying in Langstone harbour. In all 435 prisoners were held within *Bellerophon*. However, following improvements in

71

prison legislation, the ship was used for a boy's prison in 1823. When the 1st rate *Waterloo* (120), the ex-*Talavera*, was renamed *Bellerophon* on 5 October 1824, the Trafalgar *Bellerophon* was renamed, more appropriately, *Captivity*, by Admiralty Order of the same date. Remaining in the Thames for two further years *Captivity* was docked at Sheerness on 26 April 1826 to be 'Fitted to be navigated to Plymouth'. While in dock her old copper was removed; after being felted, she was re-coppered and fixed with protectors at a cost of £1,233, of which £395 covered labour expenses. Re-launched 24 May, *Captivity* left Sheerness on 4 June and was taken to Plymouth, arriving there four days later. Here she remained, fulfilling her role as a convict ship moored off Devonport until she was 'Sold 21st Jany 1836 for £4030'.[91]

The 74 gun ship COLOSSUS

The *Colossus* at Trafalgar was the second Royal Naval ship to bear this name. The previous *Colossus*, a *Leviathan* class 3rd rate of 74 guns based on the line of the French *Courageux*, was built by Cleverley at Gravesend. Launched October 1782 this vessel fought at the Battle of St Vincent on 14 February 1797. In December 1798 this *Colossus*, commanded by Captain George Murray, was escorting a homebound convoy from Lisbon. On the 5th the convoy divided off Ireland and *Colossus*, with eight merchant vessels, proceeded up Channel. Meeting strong winds from the NE Murray decided to stand *Colossus* towards the Scilly Isles for shelter and anchored in St Mary's Roads. On the evening of Friday 7 December the winds increased to gale force, putting the ship in a perilous situation. On Monday 10 December it was found that she was dragging her anchors and when her cables parted the ship commenced to drift and run aground on a shelf of rocks known as Southern Wells. Almost immediately *Colossus* began to fill. Despite pumping, water levels within the ship continued to rise, moreover the rudder was unshipped by the constant pounding against the rocks. By morning the water level had risen to the sills of the upper deck ports and the ship began to break up. By noon next day the entire crew but one man, Richard King the ship's Quartermaster who drowned while sounding, had been removed to safety by local fishing craft. Shortly after the ship fell over on one side and began to break up. Passengers on board comprised Captain Peyton from *Defence* (74) and Mr Harcourt, escorting the body of the late Admiral Shuldham who had recently died of old age in Lisbon. Beside the loss of the ship itself, *Colossus* was carrying a vast fortune of unique Greek and Roman antiquities and Oriental porcelain belonging to Sir William Hamilton which he had collected while serving as Ambassador at the Court of Naples. Having embarked his treasures aboard *Colossus*, Hamilton with his wife Emma Lady Hamilton, and Lord Nelson had returned to England, travelling overland across Europe. In the List of Ships and their Commanding Officers she is written off as 'Paid off Ship lost at Scilley 10 December 1798'.[92] Recent dives on the wreck by marine archaeologists have discovered much of this singular collection with most of the recovered artefacts sold at auction. These dives are now focused on the hull itself and many parts of her ornate stern carving have been recovered.[93]

The Trafalgar *Colossus* was one of two vessels of the *Colossus* class 3rd rate 74 gun ships designed by John Henslow in 1798, her sister ship being *Warspite*. Ordered 23 November 1797, the keel was laid down at Deptford May 1799, building commencing under Master Shipwright Edward Tippett and completed by Henry Peake who succeeded Tippett in March 1803. After the ship was launched on 23 April 1803 she was moved down river to Woolwich on 3 May where she went into dock to be coppered. Launched again 21 May *Colossus* remained at Woolwich fitting and sailed for service 20 June. Unfortunately the Progress Book does not record any costs of her building and fitting out.[94] Armed with twenty-eight 32 pounders on the lower gun deck, thirty 24 pounders on the upper gun deck, four 24 pounders and ten 32 pounder carronades on the quarter deck, two 24 pounders and two 32 pounder carronades upon the forecastle, together with a further six 18 pounder carronades mounted on the poop, *Colossus* delivered a single broadside of 1,126 pounds.

CAPTAINS OF *COLOSSUS* (MSS 248/4 and 248/6)

Name	Time of Entry	Time of Discharge	On What Occasion
George Martin	22 May 1803	31 December 1803	New Book
George Martin	1 January 1804	23 April 1804	To the *Glory*
Michael Seymour	24 February 1804	22 June 1804	Superseded Acting
James N Morris	23 June 1804	29 December 1805	Paid Off
James N Morris	5 July 1806	8 August 1808	Invalided
Thomas Alexander	9 August 1808	17 May 1814	Paid Off

SERVICE HISTORY

1803: Within three weeks of her launch, war between Britain and France had reopened, consequently once launched *Colossus* was taken down to Woolwich 3 May to be fitted out and prepared for sea service. The ship was put in commission on 22 May by Captain George Martin at Woolwich the day after she came out of the dock, and sailed for her deployment in the Mediterranean 20 June.[95]

1804: On 24 February Captain Martin was superseded by Captain Michael Seymour who maintained command in an acting position only until he was succeeded by Captain James Morris on 23 June.[96] Then *Colossus* joined Collingwood's squadron operating off the Iberian coast. On 20 August *Colossus*, with the rest of Collingwood's small squadron, were chased off by French ships as the main body of Villeneuve's fleet made their way into Cadiz.[97] In the days preceding the battle *Colossus*, together with

SPECIFICATIONS: *COLOSSUS*

Rate	3rd	Length on the range of the gun deck	180 ft	Ordnance - lower gun deck	28 x 32 pounders
Guns	74	Length of keel for tonnage	148 ft 3½ ins	Ordnance - upper gun deck	30 x 24 pounders
Class	*Colossus* 1798	Extreme breadth	48 ft 10 ins	Ordnance - quarter deck	4 x 24 pounders
Designer	John Henslow	Depth in hold	21 ft		10 x 32 pounder carronades
Builder	Edward Tippett	Tons burthen	1880 88/94	Ordnance – forecastle	2 x 24 pounders
Dockyard	Deptford	Draught afore	21 ft 2 ins		2 x 32 pounder carronades
Date ordered	23 November 1797	Draught abaft	23 ft 9 ins	Ordnance – roundhouse/poop	6 x 18 pounder carronades
Date keel laid	May 1799	Complement	590	Single broadside weight	1126 pounds
Date launched	23 April 1803			Fate	1826 Broken up

Source: Lyon, *Sailing Navy List*, p. 112.

Colossus
Sheer Profile
(Drawing by the author)

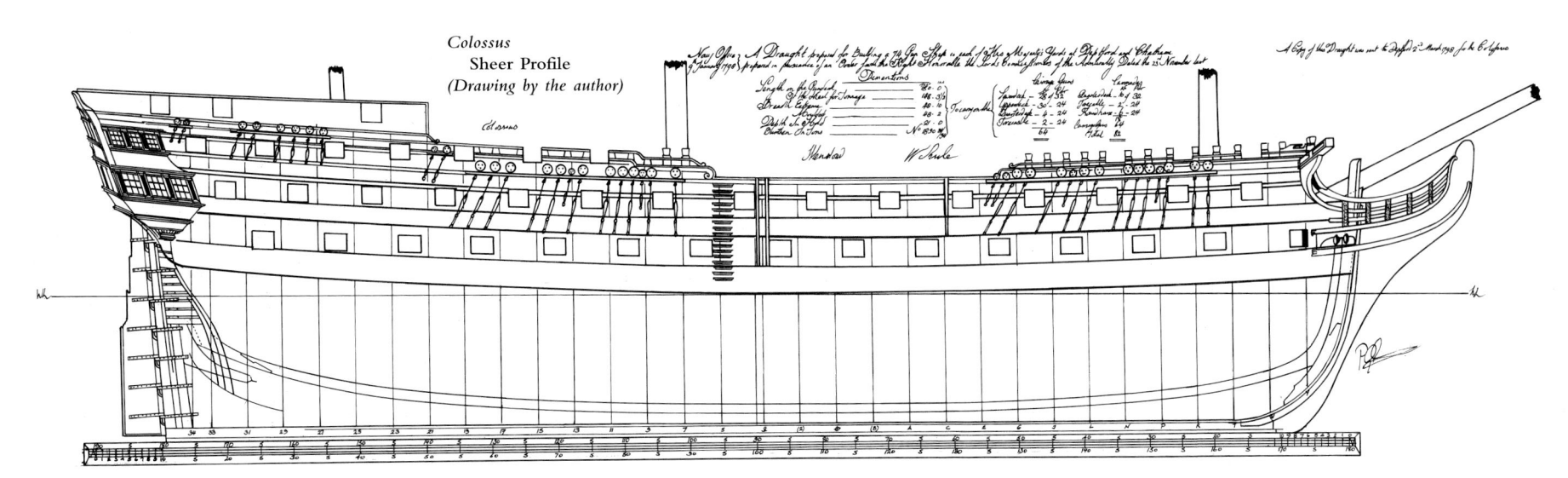

Agamemnon, *Defence* and *Mars*, were deployed to form a chain of communication between *Euryalus* and the other frigates watching Cadiz and the main body of Nelson's fleet 50 miles to seaward. When it was observed that the combined fleet was preparing to leave Cadiz on 19 October, *Colossus* standing in this line relayed signals 249, 354, 864, 875, 756, 986 and 1374 - 'Enemy have their top sails yards hoisted', to *Mars*. At 3 p.m. *Colossus* fired guns for attention and hoisted the signal stating that the combined fleet was now at sea.[98]

TRAFALGAR

Monday 21 October, the log entry for the *Colossus* reads as follows:

> Squally & Rain, obs^d. *Agamemnon* with ~~the~~ [struck thorough in log] her Topmast gone, Wore occasionally; Fleet in C^o. Out 4th and 3rd reefs, shifted Main topsail Yard, & burnt blue lights at intervals, made & short^d. Sail occas^y. recconnoiting [sic] the Enemy. AM. Mod^{te}. & clear - 2 spoke the *Naiad* - at 4 the Enemys light in sight to the Eastw^d. At day light the Enemys Fleet consisting of 33 Sail of the Line 4 frigates & 2 Brigs on the Starb^d. Tk. ESE 6 miles, our Fleet on the weather bow all sail set to close them, cleared Ship for Action.[99]

As the British ships approached the combined fleet that morning, at 12.10 the *Colossus* 'took our Station between the *Bellerophon* and *Achille* the Enemys fleet ahead laying to 33 Sail in Line of Battle opening their fire on the *Royal Sovereign*'.[100] *Colossus* lay sixth in line of Collingwood's leeward division, slightly to starboard lay *Bellerophon* and on her starboard quarter, *Achille*. Morris then recorded, 'at 12.30 Admiral Collingwood commenced the Action, - at 12.50 receiving a galling fire from the Enemys Rear, began firing our Starboard Guns, at 1 passed our opponent in the Enemys Line who bore up as we passed to prevent being raked'. This was in fact the French *Swiftsure*.[101] At this point *Colossus* closed in to support *Bellerophon* which was hard pressed from the French 74 gun ships *Aigle* and *Swiftsure* and the Spanish 74s *Bahama* and *Monarca*. Firing her larboard guns, *Colossus* maintained a steady fire into the stern of *Bahama* as she stood on towards the French *Swiftsure*. As stated in the ship's log at 1 p.m, *Swiftsure* bore up to avoid being raked from astern, whereby *Colossus* was obliged to pass down her starboard side. Amid the volume of smoke, Morris recorded: 'Engaged on both sides all view of the Enemy on the starboard side obscured by smoke until we found ourselves alongside one of the French Ships'. *Colossus* had in fact crashed into the French *Argonaute* (74) and with their yards locked together the two ships exchanged heavy broadsides. Referring to *Argonaute*, *Colossus*'s log then states, 'on whose upper decks after the Ship's touched there was not a man visible, but a fire from the guns which in ten minutes was silenced except a gun in the after part of her cabin'. In ten minutes *Colossus* had silenced all of *Argonaute*'s larboard guns and 'at 1.25 she drop'd clear of us'. As the two vessels drifted apart *Colossus* raked her as she paid off. However at this point one shot from the Frenchman wounded Captain Morris above the knee, obliging him to seek medical attention. All the while *Colossus* was still under fire on her larboard side from *Bahama* and *Swiftsure*, the log stating, 'at the time closely engaged with a French Ship on the Larboard side, and a Spanish Ship a little further distant. At 3 the French Ships fire almost silenced, drop't astern when we were wholly engaged with the Spaniard'. Thomas Toker, *Colossus*'s First Lieutenant, was concentrating her fire into *Bahama*, the rapid fire very effectively penetrating the Spanish ship from waterline to truck. In *Colossus*'s deadly barrage Commodore Galiano was badly bruised by a splinter striking his foot and moments later his telescope was carried out of his hand. His coxswain, retrieving the spyglass, was instantly cut down. The broadsides from *Colossus* cut through *Bahama*'s rigging, bringing down her mizzen mast and yards. With her sailcloth and rigging shielding her guns, the Spanish ship indicated her submission by draping a British Union flag over the hen coops upon her poop. *Colossus*'s log simply records that *Bahama* 'shewed English Colours to us to denote having struck'. Officers from *Colossus* were despatched immediately to take possession. The French *Swiftsure* then bore up under *Colossus*'s stern to rake her but when *Colossus* suddenly wore, the French ship was outmanœuvred. In the log Morris states:

> ... the French ship [*Swiftsure*] at this time endeavoured to bear up under our stern, but we wearing quicker, only received a few shot from her larboard Guns before giving her our Starbd. broadside which brought her Mizen Mast down, and the *Orion* at this moment giving them her first broadside, her mainmast also fell, and they made signs to us of submission.

Colossus had also sustained damage for when she hauled up 'our Mizen Mast fell over the Starb^d. Quarter. sent Lieutenant Huists to bring the two Captains onboard, he returned with the Captain of the French Ship *Swiftsure* and second Captain of the Spanish Ship *Bahama* (her first being slain)'. The log that day concluded, 'observed many of the enemy had surrendered, our Sails & Rigging very much cut and quite unmanageable, four of the Starb^d. Lower Deck Ports knocked off while alongside the Enemy - Received a fire from the Enemys van passing to windward, the *Agamemnon* took us in tow'.[102] Virtually under constant fire throughout the battle, *Colossus* fought with great distinction, suffering high casualties comprising 40 dead and 160 wounded. Those killed included Thomas Scriven, the ship's Master, 31 seamen and eight marines. Among the wounded were Captain Morris, Lieutenants George Bully and William Forster; Lieutenant of Marines John Benson; Master's Mate Henry Milbanke; Midshipmen George Denton, William Herringham, Rawdon Maclean, Thomas Reeve, Timothy Renou, Henry Snellgrove, Frederick Thistlewaite and George Wharrie; and Boatswain William Adamson, together with 115 seamen and

Colossus. Sketch by Livesay, undated. Original caption says 'Only main mast stands, all ye rest [?] jury'. *(Courtesy of the Royal Naval Museum)*

31 marines. Morris, who had refused to quit the deck throughout the battle – even being given first aid to his leg while at his post – finally fainted from loss of blood and was carried below to the surgeon. *Colossus* had suffered considerable damage; in all her hull was very much shattered and, as recorded, four of her starboard side lower deck port lids had been carried away when she engaged *Argonaute*. Three of her boats and two anchors had been completely destroyed and a number of guns had been disabled. Aloft, the ship was in sorry state, her mizzen had been carried away and any remaining masts and rigging were in such a precarious state that during the ensuing storm the seamen had to cut it away and cast it overboard, leaving the ship with only her fore mast to endure the rising storm.[103] Enduring the storm on the 23rd, *Colossus*'s crew were compelled to

> ... cut away the Main mast which in the fall stove the Starb[d]. side of the Q[r]. Deck - [at] 3 parted the Tow Rope, Employed taking it in again - [at] 7 *Agamemnon* took us in tow again…Employed at pumps - carpenters stopping Leaks &c…rigging sheers to get up the a jury Main mast, spliced the messenger to the Stream Achor and gave the ship more Tow Rope.[104]

Next day the men were busy 'overhauling the Breeching & Gun Tackles'. Amid gales and lightning they continued to work, 'double breeching the Guns', the ship still under tow.[105] As they approached Gibraltar in the heavy swell on 28 October, *Colossus*'s crew busied themselves bending the sheet cable and clearing the ship ready and 'at 7 Anchored with the best bower in 10 Fm. abrest [sic] the mole by HM Ship *Belleisle* - hauled into the mole & moored'.[106] On the 29th the wounded were landed and Captain Morris was carried ashore in his cot. Making a full recovery, he later resumed command of the ship. Work repairing *Colossus* between 29 October and 7 November, according to the log, comprised sending the launch into the dock yard for repair, scraping and seaming the decks, stopping shot holes, knotting and splicing the rigging, and coiling down cables, rigging and woolding a jury main mast, gammoning the bowsprit, getting in a new jibboom, fitting a new cap to the foremast and raising jury topmasts, rigging and raising new course and topsail yards, repairing sails and careening the ship. On Sunday 3 November they 'rec[d.] 1821 lbs Fresh beef Lost one quarter overboard weighing 114 lbs', and Tuesday 5th, 'received 1004 lbs Fresh Beef'. Returning to Plymouth 7 December, *Colossus* was paid off on 29 December to await repairs.

1806: On 7 April *Colossus* was taken into dock to effect repairs and have her copper replaced. Undocked 13 June, the total cost of her refit, including 27 small repairs, amounted to £18,105.[107] On 5 July *Colossus* was recommissioned under her previous commander, Captain Morris.[108]

PROGRESS BOOK - *COLOSSUS* 3rd RATE OF 74 GUNS:

At what Port	Arrived	Docked	Coppered
Deptford	Began	May 1799	
Woolwich	3 May 1803	8 May 1803	Coppered May 1803
Portsmouth	7 Dec 1805	7 Apr 1806	Copper taken off April; Re-coppered June 1806
Chatham	25 Jan 1811	9 Feb 1811	Copper taken off Feb; Re-coppered March 1811
Chatham	2 May 1814		Took off Copper to light water mark
		11 Nov 1825	Copper taken off
			Taken to Pieces 8th Feby 1826

1807: Deployed with the Channel fleet, *Colossus* spent much of this year off Ushant blockading Brest.

1808: Still under the command of Morris, *Colossus* was attached to Rear-Admiral Sir Richard Strachan's squadron which would be deployed in the Mediterranean. Flying his flag in *Cæsar* (80), Strachan had with him the 74 gun ships *Colossus*, *Cumberland*, *Renown*, and *Superb*. En route to Gibraltar in late January, the ships endured heavy weather and sustained considerable damage, *Colossus* included. Having made necessary repairs the fleet then proceeded to Palermo where they combined forces with Vice-Admiral Edward Thornborough's squadron.[109] In July *Colossus* suffered the stigma of a court martial, convened on board *Royal Sovereign* on 13 July. On trial was a lieutenant of marines out of *Colossus* who had been charged by the ship's captain for riotous conduct not befitting to gentlemanly behaviour. Found guilty, the marine officer was cashiered. On 9 August Captain Morris, being in ill health, was superseded by Captain Thomas Alexander.[110]

1811: Now under the command of Captain Thomas Alexander, *Colossus* was deployed with part of the Channel squadron operating out of Plymouth. Following a court martial held on board *Salvador del Mundo* lying in the Hamoaze, seaman John Lake out of *Colossus* was hanged on 26 September for mutiny. Shortly after this affair *Colossus* put to sea rejoining the ships operating off the French Atlantic coast. On 1 December boats from *Colossus*, *Conquestador* (74) and *Arrow* (14), commanded by Lieutenants Soady and Stackpoole, staged an attack on a French flotilla comprising three gun brigs, one armed lugger and several pinnaces cruising close inshore near Basque Roads. As the boats were making their approach south of the Chatelaillon shoal the wind shifted from the NW to WSW, allowing the flotilla to press a counter-attack. Although the boats' crews put up a hearty defence and endeavoured to board the lugger, overwhelmed by superior numbers, compounded by covering fire shore batteries, the boats were compelled to row for the shore. On landing some 113 men were taken prisoner and retained in captivity until the war terminated in 1814. Only Lieutenant Soady and his boat's crew managed to escape. Seamen from *Colossus*, *Conquestador* and *Arrow* later subscribed money and clothes which were taken to the British prisoners of war into La Rochelle under a flag of truce. French casualties relating to this incident were, according to Commodore Jacobs, no more than five killed.

1812: With Thomas Alexander still in command, *Colossus* was deployed with one squadron forming part of the Channel fleet commanded by Captain Sir John Gore in *Tonnant* (80). Throughout January and February this squadron was stationed off *Orient* blockading Vice-Admiral Allemend's ships. In company with *Tonnant* and *Colossus* were *Bulwark* (74), *Poictiers* (74), *Pompée* (74), *Tremendous* (74) and the frigate *Diana* (38). On 8 March Allemand's squadron, comprising *Ejlau* (80), *Guillemard* (74), *Marengo* (74), *Vétéren* (74), and two corvettes evaded the British ship and put to sea under cover of fog. Over the next two days *Colossus* with the other ships gave chase, but lost sight of the French in thick weather.[111]

Source: ADM 180/10/73 & ADM 180/11 Entry 592

Launched or Undocked	Sailed	Built or Nature of Repair	Cost of Hull, Masts & Yards Materials £	Workmen £	Cost of Masts & Yards Materials £	Workmen £	Cost of Rigging & Stores Materials £	Workmen £	Grand Total £
23 April 1799	3 May 1803	Built							
21 May 1803	20 June 1803	Fitted							
13 June 1806	3 Aug 1806	Fitted; 27 small repairs	4,914	2,336	1,150	237	9,468	19	18,105
25 Mar 1811	28 Apr 1811	Defects	4,573	1,497	508	117	7,703	127	14,5525
			568	255	–	1	86	21	931

1813: Cruising in the mid-Atlantic on 5 January, *Colossus* fell in with and captured *Dolphin* (12) which proved to be an American letter of marque from Philadelphia for Bordeaux carrying 56 officers and men and four passengers. On the 19 January *Colossus* was equally fortunate to capture the American vessel *Print* of 215 tons bound for Bayonne from Boston.

1814: Arriving at Chatham 2 May, Captain Alexander paid off *Colossus* as ordered on 17 May. After having her copper 'taken off the light water mark', she was laid up in ordinary at Chatham.[112]

FATE

No longer required for service, *Colossus* was docked at Chatham 1 November 1825 to have her copper removed and remained in dock until 'Taken to Pieces 8th Feby. 1826'.[113]

The 74 gun ship CONQUEROR

The *Conqueror* that fought at Trafalgar was the fourth Royal Naval ship to bear this name, the first being a fireship of 8 guns captured from the French in the Mediterranean by *Lowestoffe* (28) in 1745 during the War of Austrian Succession. This ship was sold on 2 March 1748 at the close of the war. The second *Conqueror* was a 3rd rate of 70 guns built by John Barnard, launched at Harwich 24 May 1758 during the Seven Years' War. Commanded by Captain William Lloyd, this ship went aground on rocks near St Nicholas Island while entering the Hamoaze at Plymouth on 26 October 1760. Although she was badly holed and quickly filled up, all her crew and stores were removed. At the enquiry it was concluded that the blame lay with the 'misconduct of the pilot'.[114] The third *Conqueror*, a 74 gun ship of the *Royal Oak* class designed by John Williams, was launched at Plymouth on 10 October 1773. This *Conqueror* actively served in the West Indies during the War of American Independence. Her battle honours relate to Vice-Admiral the Hon. John Byron's action against Compte D'Estaing off Grenada 6 July 1779; Admiral George Rodney's two actions against De Guichen off Martinique on 17 April and 15 May 1780; and being with Rodney at the battle of the Saintes against De Grasse on 12 April 1782.[115] After giving honourable service this vessel was broken up in 1794.[116]

The Trafalgar *Conqueror* designed by John Henslow was a one-off type modified from his *Mars* class of 1788. Ordered 30 April 1795, the keel was laid down at Harwich in October 1795. Overseen by William Graham, the Master Shipwright at that yard, the ship was finally launched 23 November 1801. No expenses for the hull, masts, yards, rigging and stores are recorded in the Progress Book.[117] Armed with twenty-eight 32 pounders on her lower gun deck, thirty 18 pounders on her upper gun deck, fourteen 9 pounders on the quarter deck, two 9 pounders and two 32 pounder carronades on the forecastle together with an additional six 18 pounder carronades on her poop deck, *Conqueror* delivered a single broadside weight of 876 pounds.

CAPTAINS OF CONQUEROR (MSS 248/4 and 248/6)

Name	Time of Entry	Time of Discharge	On What Occasion
Thomas Louis	18 March 1803	31 December 1803	New Book
Thomas Louis	1 January 1804	3 April 1804	Superseded
Israel Pellew	1 May 1804	18 July 1808	Superseded
Edward Fellows	19 July 1808	27 February 1812	Paid Off
John Davie	6 November 1816	25 January 1818	Levant Invalided
James Wallis	26 January 1818	16 September 1818	Superseded
Francis Stanfell	17 September 1818	30 October 1820	Paid Off

SERVICE HISTORY

1802: Built and launched the previous year, *Conqueror* sailed from Harwich on 10 January for Sheerness, arriving there two days later. After spending a

SPECIFICATIONS: CONQUEROR

Rate	3rd	Length on the range of the gun deck	176 ft	Ordnance - lower gun deck	28 x 32 pounders
Guns	74	Length of keel for tonnage	144 ft 3 ins	Ordnance - upper gun deck	30 x 18 pounders
Class	Conqueror 1795 (modified *Mars* design)	Extreme breadth	49 ft	Ordnance - quarter deck	14 x 9 pounders
Designer	John Henslow	Depth in hold	20 ft 9 ins	Ordnance - forecastle	2 x 9 pounders
Builder	William Graham	Tons burthen	1842 24/94		2 x 32 pounder carronades
Dockyard	Harwich	Draught afore	23 ft 10 ins	Ordnance – roundhouse/poop	6 x 18 pounder carronades
Date ordered	30 April 1795	Draught abaft	24 ft 6 ins	Single broadside weight	876 pounds
Date keel laid	October 1795	Complement	590	Fate	1822 Broken up at Chatham
Date launched	23 November 1801				

Source: Lyon, *Sailing Navy List*, p. 110.

month having her masts stepped and rigging set up, she then sailed for Plymouth on 16 February, arriving there twelve days later. Going into dock on 20 March to be coppered, she was re-launched in April. From this it can be surmised that her hull was not sheathed before her initial launching at Harwich. Why this was the case is uncertain; either William Graham did not have the facilities within his yard, or political distribution of work between yards had yet to be established.[118] *Conqueror* had been put in commission but her commander is not listed in the official sources.[119] As the current war with France had ended there was no reason to retain the ship in commission, so *Conqueror* was paid off in February, her ship's company being transferred into *Cambridge* (74) which was serving as flagship at Plymouth. *Conqueror*, meanwhile, was laid up in ordinary alongside *Plantagenet* (74) lying in the stream of the River Tamar. However on 5 March new orders dictated that both ships were needed for service. Consequently on 13 March *Conqueror* was hauled into dock, taken in hand by the dockyard work force and fitted for sea.[120]

1803: On 16 May France declared war on Britain and hostilities recommenced. *Conqueror* was hurried out of the dock and placed in commission under Captain Thomas Louis. Over the next few weeks *Conqueror* was rigged, stored and provisioned after which she sailed from the Hamoaze and anchored in Cawsand Bay. Although commissioned, *Conqueror* still required more people to fulfil her sea-going complement. On 13 June a tender arrived carrying 100 seamen who were sent immediately on board and entered into the ship's books. *Conqueror*, in company with *Malta* (74), *Canopus* (74) and *Sceptre* (74), sailed down the Channel to their respective stations.

1804: Command of the ship was superseded by Captain Israel Pellew, a Cornishman with a high reputation for expertise in gunnery.[121] Ordered to join the Mediterranean fleet, *Conqueror* made sail and joined Nelson off Toulon in July. Shortly after the fleet encountered adverse weather and *Conqueror*, with the rest of Nelson's squadron, retreated to Porto Torres on the island of Pulla in August to take on water.[122]

1805: In January *Conqueror* lay at Agincourt Sound at the south of Corsica refitting with many of Nelson's ships when, on 19 January, Nelson received news that Villeneuve with twenty ships had put to sea. *Conqueror* weighed with Nelson's squadron and began the long chase through the Mediterranean, across the Atlantic and back that consumed the best part of six months. In July *Conqueror* joined the British fleet now assembling off Cadiz.[123]

TRAFALGAR

On Sunday 20 October Pellew records in *Conqueror*'s log:

Light airs & Vble. e. at 2.40 ansd. 81 SebS Genl. Sigl. at 3.50 *Mars* made 403 to Adml. Answd. 252 & 72 Genl. Sigl. & Shortened sail Occasy. 7 AM Do. Wr. Joined Co. HM Ships *Phœbe* and *Pickle* Schooner at 6.30 wore ship 1st reef of topsails at 7.30 filled at 8 Mode. & Cloudy Cape Trafalgar EbS 7 or 8 Leagues, at 8.20 hove to at 9.30 2nd reef of topsails at 11 30 in 3rd Reef of Topsails at Noon Fresh breezes & Squally with rain, *Victory* WbS 2 miles.[124]

On the day of the battle the *Conqueror* took up station fourth in line in Nelson's windward division; ahead of her lay *Neptune* (98) while astern lay *Leviathan* (74), Captain William Bayntun. As the ships descended upon the combined fleet Bayntun crammed on sail in order to get into battle ahead of *Conqueror* and as the first shots were fired a little before midday *Conqueror* and *Leviathan* lay abreast of each other. Shortly afterwards *Leviathan* hauled ahead, leaving *Conqueror* fifth in line of Nelson's column. *Conqueror* got into battle about 1.30 and passing the stern of Villeneuve's battered flagship *Bucentaure*, which had already been successively raked by *Victory*, *Téméraire*, *Neptune* and *Leviathan*, fired another devastating broadside through her

PROGRESS BOOK – CONQUEROR 3rd RATE OF 74 GUNS:

At what Port	Arrived	Docked	Coppered
Harwich; William Graham	Began	Oct 1795	
Sheerness	12 Jan 1802		
Plymouth	28 Feb 1802	20 Mar 1802	Coppered April 1802
Plymouth			Coppered April 1803
Plymouth	11 Dec 1805		Copper repaired December 1805
Plymouth	13 Apr 1807	23 Apr 1807	Copper taken off Apr Re-coppered May 1807
Portsmouth	23 Oct 1808	9 Nov 1808	Copper repaired
Chatham	31 Jan 1812	7 Oct 1812	Copper taken off Oct 1812; Re-coppered Sep 1813
Sheerness	8 Feb 1814		Put on Copper to load Draft of Water[line] Nov 1816
Chatham	8 Oct 1820	23 Apr 1822	Copper taken off
			Taken to Pieces 2nd Augt 1822

stern. *Conqueror* then put her helm to starboard, bringing herself upon *Bucentaure*'s starboard quarter. Firing a series of heavy cannonades from her larboard batteries, she reduced Villeneuve's ship to a floating wreck. Commenting on the gunnery Humphrey Senhouse, a lieutenant in *Conqueror* later wrote, 'Previously to this all the firing had been mere child's play to us, but now a cannonading commenced at so short a distance that every shot flew winged with death and destruction'. Completely dismasted, with some 50 per cent of her ordnance out of action and suffering upwards of 400 casualties, *Bucentaure* was compelled to haul down her colours. To take possession Pellew sent his senior marine officer Captain James Atcherley across in a boat. Gaining the deck Atcherley walked aft to the quarter deck and was immediately confronted with Villeneuve who said: 'To whom have I the honour of surrendering'? Atcherley replied, 'To Captain Pellew of the *Conqueror*'. That the French vice-admiral had surrendered to a ship named *Conqueror* was an historical twist of fate. Atcherley, with Villeneuve and his two captains embarked into the boat and proceeded to return to *Conqueror* for them to surrender their swords to Pellew. Unfortunately Atcherley mistook *Mars* (74) for *Conqueror* and boarded the *Mars* with his captives. His mistake is perfectly understandable for besides confusion through the smoke of battle, *Conqueror* was virtually an improved design of *Mars* (74). Atcherley handed Villeneuve and his captains over to Lieutenant William Hennah, *Mars*' senior officer as Captain Duff had already been killed.

Looking for another opponent, Pellew stood *Conqueror* towards *Santisima Trinidad* (136), which was already hotly engaged on her starboard side by *Neptune* (98). Coming up on her larboard quarter, *Conqueror* began firing her larboard batteries into the great Spanish ship. The combined broadsides of *Conqueror* and *Neptune* hammered through the Spanish ship's decks, bringing down her main and mizzen masts.[125] Describing the event, one of *Conqueror*'s officers later wrote, 'Her immense topsails had every reef out, her royals were sheeted home, but lowered; and the falling of this majestic mass of spars, sails and rigging plunging into the water at the muzzles of our guns, was one of the most magnificent sights I ever beheld'. Shortly afterwards a British Union flag was seen being waved aboard the *Santisima Trinidad*, signifying surrender. Consequently *Conqueror* and *Neptune* ceased their fire.[126] After this *Conqueror*, obeying Captain Hardy's signal concerning Dumanoir's squadron re-entering the battle, made sail northward in pursuit. In company was *Leviathan*.[127] In this final stage of the battle *Conqueror* was briefly engaged with the French *Intrépide* which put up considerable resistance to the British ships surrounding her. Recording events, Lieutenant Senhouse of the *Conqueror* wrote that *Intrépide* finally 'surrendered after one of the most gallant defences I ever witnessed. The Frenchman's name was Infernet, a member of the Legion of honour, and it

THE 74 GUN SHIP *CONQUEROR*

Source: ADM 180/10/78

Launched or Undocked	Sailed	Built or Nature of Repair	Cost of Hull, Masts & Yards Materials £	Workmen £	Cost of Masts & Yards Materials £	Workmen £	Cost of Rigging & Stores Materials £	Workmen £	Grand Total £
23 Nov 1801	10 Jan 1802	Built							
16 Feb 1802									
April 1802	2 April 1802	Fitted							
	8 May 1803								
	13 Feb 1806	Defects	781	512	2,507	81	6,330	126	10,337
8 May 1807	3 June 1807	Defects	3,526	1,415	1,797	9	6,300	44	13,091
19 Nov 1808	16 Dec 1808	Refitted	1,002	667	130	30	4,668	77	6,574
10 Sep 1813	8 Feb 1811 to Sheerness to season	Between Small & Middling Repair	16,466	6,256	664	129	31	162	23,708
	11 Jan 1817	Fitted for Sea	2,626	960	400	19	16,096	19	20,120
		To be Surveyed	-	63	1	4	-	-	68

deserves to be recorded in the memory of those who admire true courage'.[128] An extract from *Conqueror*'s log regarding destroying her prize states: 'AM Fresh Gales Rec.d 99 Prisoners from the *Intrepide* at 5 wore ship at 6.30 wore & Set the Fore & Mizen Topsles at 7.30 hove to at 8 *Britannia* set the *Intrepide* on Fire at 9.10 she Clew up wore ship at 12 fresh breezes with lightning'.[129]

Casualties within *Conqueror* amounted to three killed and nine wounded. Officers killed were Robert Lloyd, *Conqueror*'s First Lieutenant and Lieutenant William St George; those wounded being Lieutenant of Marines Thomas Wearing and Lieutenant Philip Mendal of the Imperial Russian Navy and seven seamen. On Lloyd's death in battle Lieutenant James Couch was instantly promoted to First Lieutenant. In the battle *Conqueror* lost her mizzen topmast and main topgallant, the remaining masts being considerably damaged, likewise her rigging.[130] When *Conqueror* returned to England after the battle she is reputed to have carried a present of roses from Captain William Hoste of *Amphion* (32) for his sister Kate living in Burnham Market, Norfolk.

1806: Returning to home waters *Conqueror*, as part of the Channel fleet, was deployed with the squadron cruising off the French Atlantic coast with the *Prince of Wales* (98), *Centaur* (74), *Monarch* (74), *Revenge* (74), *Polyphemus* (64), *Indefatigable* (44) and *Iris* (32). On the night of 12 July twelve boats assembled from the squadron rowed up the River Gironde to cut out two French corvettes and a convoy lying at anchor. Although the attack on the corvette *César* (16) was successful, her commander Lieutenant Fourré and his crew put a strong defence, inflicting more British casualties than expect-

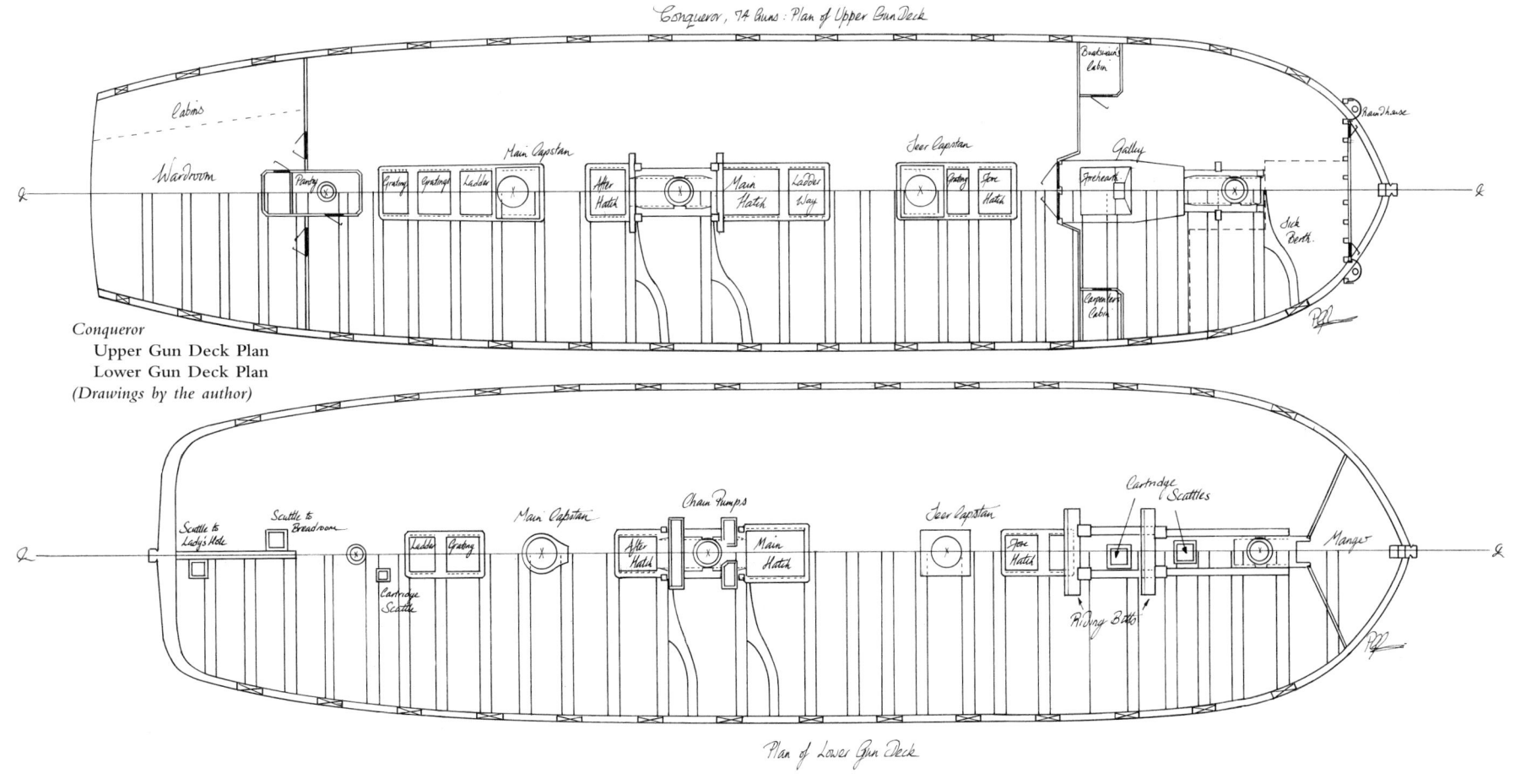

Conqueror
Upper Gun Deck Plan
Lower Gun Deck Plan
(Drawings by the author)

ed. British casualties were nine killed and 39 wounded while 20 men from the *Revenge* were taken prisoner when their boat sank. Among the dead was Lieutenant Charles Manners who led the expedition, and Lieutenant Edward Sibley was also wounded. *Conqueror*'s own casualties comprised Mr Helpman, Master's Mate, who was killed, and two wounded.[131]

1807: When France began to intimidate Portugal and bring her into the war, Dom João commenced threatening British subjects and their property in Lisbon. To counter this the British government authorised the navy to assemble a fleet from the ships at Portsmouth and Plymouth to blockade the port. This main body of the squadron, commanded by Rear-Admiral Sir Sidney Smith flying his blue ensign in *Hibernia* (120), comprised *Conqueror*, together with *London* (98), *Foudroyant* (80), and 74 gun ships *Bedford*, *Elizabeth Marlborough*, *Monarch* and *Plantagenet*. Consequently Dom João relented rather than join with France and her allies. Taking the Portuguese royal family with him, he sailed to Brazil and exile. In the meantime a force of nine Russian ships under Vice-Admiral Seniavine had sailed south to attempt to raise the British blockade. When the Russian ships put into the Tagus, Seniavine found himself counter-blockaded by *Hibernia*, *Conqueror*, *Elizabeth*, *Foudroyant* and *Plantagenet*, Sir Sidney Smith having received intelligence beforehand.[132]

1810: Now under the command of Captain Edward Fellowes, *Conqueror* was deployed in the Mediterranean blockading Vice-Admiral Ganteaume's ships within Toulon. In July Sir Charles Cotton succeeded command of the British squadron of thirteen ships cruising off the French port. The weather being poor, most blockading ships were compelled to run east to Ville Franche, leaving Captain the Hon. Henry Blackwood in *Warspite* (74) together with *Conqueror*, *Ajax* (74), *Euryalus* (36) and *Shearwater* (10) watching the French. Left to his own devices Blackwood stood his squadron, *Conqueror* included, to chase a convoy of twelve French vessels into the port of Bandol just west of Toulon. Although a small squadron of French ships came out of Toulon on 17 July to ensure the convoy reached port, apart from exchange of fire with *Euryalus*, *Conqueror* was not involved.[133]

1811: The Mediterranean squadron watching over Toulon was now under the command of Vice-Admiral Sir Edward Pellew, Cotton having taken command in the Channel. In July when Pellew was with the main body of the fleet cruising off Cape Sicié, *Conqueror*, in company with *Sultan* (74) and several frigates forming the inshore squadron, continued their vigil off Toulon. On 19 July two French 40 gun frigates, *Amélie* and *Adrienne*, carrying naval conscripts from Genoa, made their approach towards Toulon. Hearing of their impending arrival Vice-Admiral Maurice Emeriau put to sea with thirteen ships and *Incorruptible* (40) with intent to draw off the British ships. At 11 a.m. *Conqueror*, ignoring Emeriau's ships, bore down upon *Amélie* and *Adrienne* and run her guns out ready to fire into them, *Sultan* close behind. Before long the two ships were also exchanging fire with the lead vessels of Emeriau's squadron. Being outnumbered, *Conqueror* and *Sultan* were obliged to haul off and make good their escape.[135]

1812: Returning to England, *Conqueror* went into Chatham, decommissioned, and went into dock where she spent the best part of two years under repair.

1814: In May the first Peace of Paris treaty was signed, closing the war with France, consequently *Conqueror*, like many naval vessels no longer required for service, was laid up in ordinary.

1815: *Conqueror*, still in ordinary, was removed to Sheerness.

1816: While many of the Trafalgar ships were being condemned to the breakers *Conqueror* was taken out of ordinary in November and recommissioned under Captain John Davie. Flying the flag of Rear-Admiral Robert Plampin at her mizzen, *Conqueror* sailed for the South Atlantic to the island of St Helena where Napoleon had been exiled in captivity the previous year. Under a special assignment *Conqueror* was deployed as a guard-ship to ensure that Napoleon did not escape. Napoleon remained on St Helena until his death on 5 May 1821.

1818: In April Captain Davie was relieved of his command by Captain Francis Stanfell for having contracted an illness while on this station and had to be sent home. The effects of his illness eventually led to his death at the age of 55 in 1825.

1820: Recalled home, *Conqueror* finally reached Portsmouth on 9 September. Receiving new orders the ship then sailed for Chatham where Captain Stanfell finally paid off *Conqueror* on 30 October.

FATE
No longer fit for service the ship was broken up at Chatham in 1822.

The 74 gun ship DEFENCE

The *Defence* that fought at Trafalgar was the second ship in the Royal Navy to bear this name, the previous vessel being a 10 gun ship of 160 tons builder's measurement purchased in 1588, which remained in service until 1599.[135] Ordered on 5 December 1758 and again 26 January 1759, *Defence* was built to the lines of the *Arrogant* class of 74 gun 3rd rate ships designed by Thomas Slade in 1758. Sister ships in this class were *Audacious*, *Arrogant*, *Bellerophon*, *Cornwall*, *Edgar*, *Elephant*, *Excellent*, *Goliath*, *Illustrious*, *Kent*, *Saturn*, *Vanguard*, and *Zealous*. Laid down at Plymouth on 14 May

SPECIFICATIONS: *DEFENCE*

Rate	3rd	*Date launched*	31 March 1763	*Complement*	550
Guns	74	*Length on the range of the gun deck*	168 ft	*Ordnance - lower gun deck*	28 x 32 pounders
Class	Arrogant 1758	*Length of keel for tonnage*	138 ft 1⅜ ins	*Ordnance - upper gun deck*	28 x 18 pounders
Designer	Thomas Slade	*Extreme breadth*	46 ft 9 ins	*Ordnance - quarter deck*	14 x 9 pounders
Builder	Benjamin Slade ?	*Depth in hold*	19 ft 9 ins	*Ordnance - forecastle*	4 x 9 pounders
Dockyard	Plymouth	*Tons burthen*	1604 27/94	*Single broadside weight*	781 pounds
Date ordered	15 December 1758/26 January 1759	*Draught afore*	21 ft 5 ins	*Fate*	1811. Wrecked
Date keel laid	14 May 1759	*Draught abaft*	23 ft 7 ins		

Source: Lyon, *Sailing Navy List*, p. 68.

1759, *Defence* was launched four years later on 31 March 1763, the costs of her hull, masts and yards amounting to £27,690 3s 4d and £367 10s 0d for rigging and stores.

SERVICE HISTORY

1770: Completed too late to serve in the Seven Years' War, the ship was laid up in ordinary at Plymouth until 1770 when she docked 12 February to be fitted out as a guard ship and consequently commissioned under Captain John Reynolds on 1 March. Fitted at a cost of £2,734 10s 2d, she was undocked, rigged and stored at a cost of £367 10s 0d. *Defence* sailed to Cawsand Bay 19 October to undertake her duties.[136]

1771: On 29 May *Defence* was paid off at Plymouth by Reynolds and laid up in ordinary until 1783. Why the ship was not put into service earlier during the American War of Independence is not known.

1782: Recommissioned by Captain Thomas Newenham on 13 January 1782, *Defence* was deployed with Vice Admiral Sir Edward Hughes' fleet stationed in the East Indies.

1783: While on this station *Defence* saw action in the engagement against Admiral Suffren's French fleet off Cuddalore 20 July. This indecisive battle, fought five months after initial peace treaties had been signed, was the last naval action of the American War of Independence.[137] On 24 December command of the ship was superseded by Captain Thomas Troubridge, Newenham transferring into *Isis* (74).[138]

1784: When Troubridge transferred into *Sultan* (74) on 17 November he was succeeded by Captain Andrew Mitchell.

1785: Remaining on station in the East Indies as the flagship of Commodore Andrew Mitchell, *Defence* eventually returned to England at the end of 1785.

1786: No longer required for service and needing to refit, Mitchell paid off *Defence* at Chatham on 31 January.

1790: Recommissioned under Captain the Rt Hon George Murray on 28 August, *Defence* was briefly deployed with the Channel fleet until paid off again 18 December.

1793: When France declared war against England *Defence* was fitted for sea service immediately and recommissioned under Captain James Gambier on 6 May, after which she was deployed with Admiral Howe's Channel fleet operating out of Torbay. Detached to watch the French port of Brest, on 18 November *Defence*, together with *Audacious* (74), *Bellerophon* (74), *Ganges* (74) and *Russell* (74), chased off a French squadron of ten ships commanded by Commodore Vanstabel in Cancale Bay.[139]

CAPTAINS OF *DEFENCE* (MSS 248/4 and 248/6)

Name	Time of Entry	Time of Discharge	On What Occasion
John Reynolds	1 March 1770	29 May 1771	Paid Off at Plymouth
James Cranstoun	12 June 1778	12 January 1782	Superseded
Thomas Newenham	13 January 1782	23 December 1783	To the *Isis*
Thomas Troubridge	24 December 1783	17 November 1784	To the *Sultan*
Andrew Mitchell	18 November 1784	31 January 1786	Paid Off at Chatham
Rt. Hon. George Murray	28 August 1790	18 December 1790	Superseded
James Gambier	6 May 1793	30 September 1794	To the *Prince George*
Thomas Wells	1 October 1794	1 March 1798	Superseded
William Brown	2 March 1798	30 April 1798	Superseded
John Peyton	1 May 1798	11 November 1798	Superseded
Thomas Stevenson	12 November 1798	9 February 1799	To the *Souverain*
Lord Henry Paulet	10 February 1799	*No entry given*	Superseded ?
George Hope	25 May 1803	31 December 1803	New Book
George Hope	1 January 1804	26 December 1805	Paid Off
Charles Ekins	10 November 1806	23 February 1811	Superseded
David Aitkins	24 February 1811	24 December 1811	Ship lost and only 12 men saved

1794: On 28 May *Defence*, deployed with Howe's squadron of 25 ships of the line, seven frigates and six subsidiary vessels, fell in with the French force commanded by Rear-Admiral Villaret-Joyeuse accompanying a large grain convoy from America. Shadowing the fleet for the next few days, the main attack was made on 1 June, resulting in the first British naval victory of the war. Immediately Howe signalled the fleet to attack, *Defence* bore up for the French line. The battle opened at 9.24 a.m. with the French firing at the British van. Because *Defence* had drawn far ahead of the other British ships and was exposed to enemy fire one officer on board suggested they should bring to until the others caught up, to which Captain Gambier replied that he would remain obedient to the signal which had been made. First to pass through the French line between *Mucius* (74) and *Tourville* (74s), *Defence* was quickly encircled and came under heavy fire, bringing down her main and mizzen masts. Falling away from the two opponents, *Defence* received a heavy broadside from *Républicain* (110) which brought down her foremast, forcing Gambier to signal *Phæton* (38) to tow her clear. During this battle, later dubbed the Glorious First of June, *Defence* suffered considerable casualties; of the 17 killed were William Webster, Master; John Fitzpatrick, Boatswain; eleven seamen and four marines. The 39 wounded were John Elliot, Master's Mate; William Dillon, Midshipman; 26 seamen and eleven marines.[140] On 1 October *Defence*'s command was succeeded by Captain Thomas Wells, Gambier transferring into *Prince George* (98). Sent to the Mediterranean, *Defence* was now deployed with Admiral William Hotham's squadron of 31 ships blockading Toulon. Cruising off the island of Hyères 13 July the British ships fell in with a French force, Hotham giving the order for general chase. Dogged by changeable winds the two fleets failed

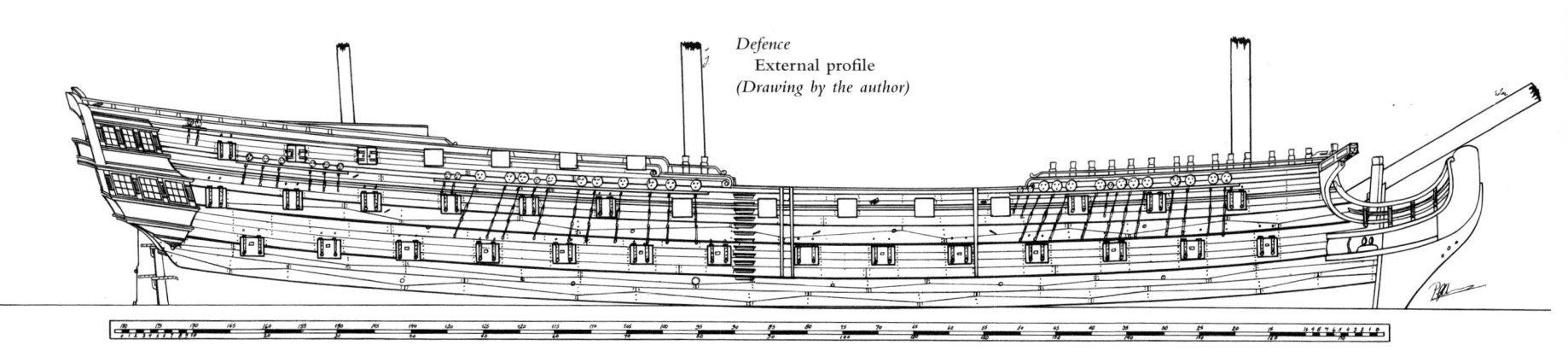

Defence
External profile
(Drawing by the author)

Defence
Inboard profile
(Drawing by the author)

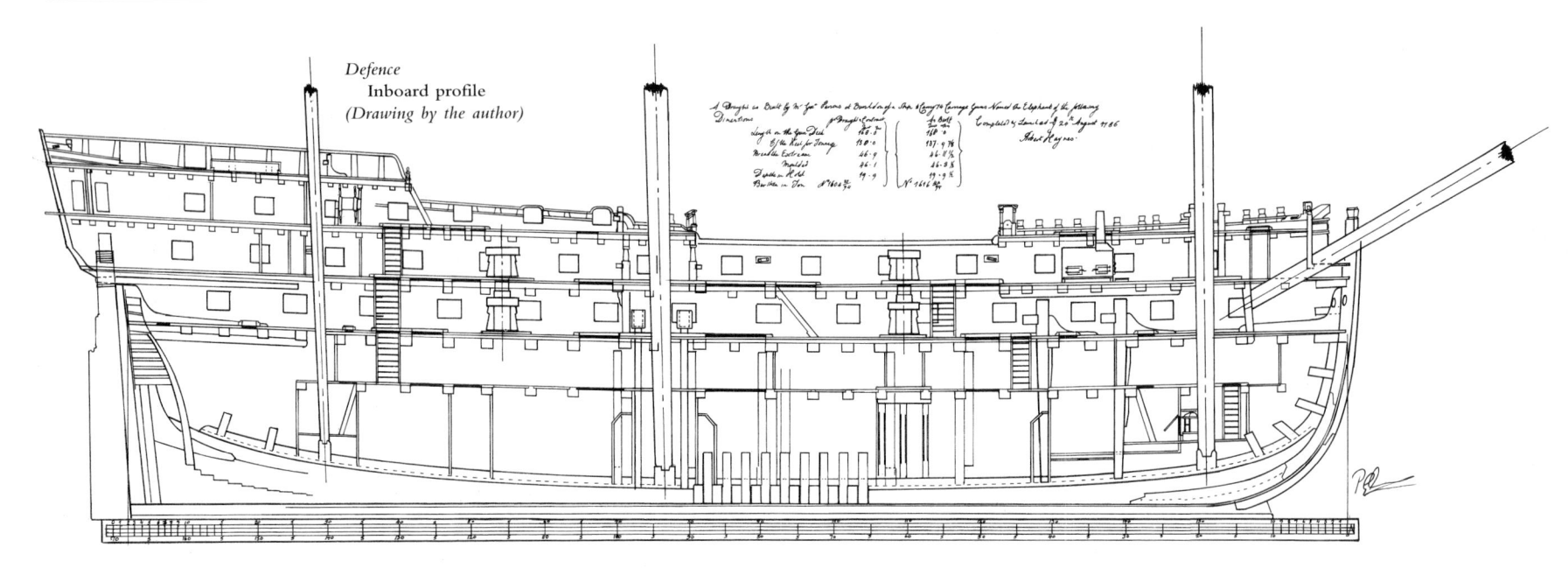

to engage fully, fighting being sporadic. Late into action, *Defence* suffered one killed and six wounded. Stationed with Hotham's fleet at San Fiorenzo, on 5 October *Defence*, in company with seven other ships, was detached under Rear-Admiral Robert Man in the failed pursuit of Rear-Admiral De Richery who had evaded the Toulon blockade.[141]

1797: *Defence* was one of the ships involved in the Spithead Mutiny during April this year.[142] The Admiralty fulfilled most of the demands pressed by the British seamen, but the crew of *Defence* remained dissatisfied. Following further disturbance 19 of *Defence*'s seamen were sentenced to death on 18 September, and six other seamen were flogged and imprisoned.[143]

1798: On 2 March Captain Wells was superseded by Captain William Brown who remained in the ship only until 30 April, superseded the next day by Captain John Peyton. *Defence* joined Rear-Admiral Horatio Nelson's Mediterranean squadron off Corsica in June. Arriving at Naples five days later, Nelson received news that Admiral de Brueys had put to sea from Toulon with a large fleet. Nelson's squadron, including *Defence*, sailed immediately in pursuit of the elusive French fleet. Finding the French anchored in the Bay of Abu-Kir at the mouth of the Nile on 1 August, Nelson, flying his flag in the *Vanguard* (74), ordered his ships to attack. The British fleet comprised thirteen 74 gun ships, the 4th rate 50 gun ship *Leander*, and the 16 gun brig *Mutine*. Five of the thirteen 74 gun ships present that day were later to fight under Nelson at Trafalgar. Including *Defence*, these were *Bellerophon*, *Minotaur*, *Orion* and *Swiftsure*. Entering the bay at 6 p.m. *Defence* lay eighth in order of line and at about 7 p.m. brought herself alongside and engaged *Peuple Souverain* (74). Later, engaging *Franklin* (80), *Defence*'s broadsides brought down her main and mizzen masts forcing her to capitulate. Although a decisive victory *Defence*, like many of Nelson's ships, sustained considerable rigging damage and her fore-topmast was shot away; however her casualties were low, only four killed and eleven wounded.[144] After making repairs *Defence*, in company with *Audacious* (74), *Bellerophon* (74), *Majestic* (74), *Minotaur* (74), *Orion* (74) and *Theseus* (74), together with six French prizes, sailed on 14 August under the command of Captain Sir James Saumarez, reaching Gibraltar 14 September. Peyton was succeeded by Captain Thomas Stevenson on 12 November.[145]

1799: On 10 February Captain Lord Henry Paulet took command of *Defence*, now deployed with Lord Keith's squadron stationed off Lisbon. Ordered to join Earl St Vincent's fleet in the Mediterranean, *Defence* sailed with Rear-Admiral Whitshed's small squadron, joining the Commander-in-Chief on 30 May. With 22 sail of the line the entire fleet then sailed down the Spanish coastline to Barcelona before turning to Port Mahon.[146]

1800: Now deployed with Rear-Admiral Sir John Borlase Warren's squadron off Brest, *Defence* was involved with several boats' actions. On 10 June boats from *Defence* commanded by Lieutenant Stamp, together with boats from *Renown* (74), *Fisgard* (44) and *Unicorn* (36), attacked a convoy lying off Fort St Croix, Penmarck Point. Under heavy fire they collectively captured three armed vessels and eight transports loaded with supplies for Brest; the remaining 20 transports being run onto the rocks. Eleven prizes were taken to Plymouth by *Unicorn* while further boats' actions involving *Defence*, *Renown* and *Fisgard* occurred on 22 June when they attacked a convoy laying in the Quimper River. Forcing the French to retreat upstream, the boats' crews landed and blew up a battery and other works. A third boat action undertaken by boats from *Defence* and *Renown* captured and burnt the French 20 gun corvette *Thérèse* laying in Bourgneuf Bay.[147] In July the coxswain of *Defence* was captured when boats from the ship were attacking a convoy sailing from the Isle de Noirmoutier 20 miles south of St Nazaire. The 74 gun ships *Cæsar*, *Excellent*, *Marlborough* and *Elephant*, now commanded by Rear-Admiral Sir Robert Calder, remained with the squadron off Brest while *Defence* returned to Plymouth 11 November, having sprung her bowsprit in a gale.

1801: To suppress the Northern League comprising Denmark, Russia and

PROGRESS BOOK – DEFENCE 3rd RATE OF 74 GUNS:

At what Port	Arrived	Docked	Coppered
Plymouth	Begun	14 May 1759	Graved March 1763
Plymouth		4 May 1765	Graved May 1765
Plymouth		16 July 1768	Graved Aug 1768
Plymouth		12 Feb 1770	Graved Feb 1770
Plymouth			
Plymouth	7 May 1771	11 June 1771	Graved June 1771
Chatham	3 Oct 1804		
Portsmouth	19 May 1805	25 May 1805	
Portsmouth		2 July 1805	Copper repaired
Chatham	11 Dec 1805	21 Apr 1806	Copper taken off Apr Re-coppered Oct 1806
Chatham	27 June 1808	9 July 1808	Copper repaired
Plymouth	27 Jan 1810	7 Feb 1810	Copper repaired
Plymoth		9 Mar 1810	Copper taken off & Re-coppered Mar 1810
			Lost in 1811

Sweden, a large fleet, including *Defence*, commanded by Lord Henry Paulet, was assembled at Yarmouth Roads to sail for the Baltic under Admiral Sir Hyde Parker. Second in command was Vice-Admiral Lord Nelson, flying his flag in *St George* (98). Parker's first objective was sail to Copenhagen to force the Danes to break their alliance with their two confederates. With all preparations made the main part of Parker's fleet sailed from Yarmouth Roads on 12 March. Arriving off Copenhagen 1 April, *Defence* was ordered to stay with Parker's division to the north while Nelson undertook the main attack the following morning. Being detached throughout the proceedings of the battle, *Defence* suffered no casualties.[148] With imminent threat of invasion from France, *Defence* was shortly recalled and joined the Channel fleet deployed off Brest where she remained until peace was declared in 1802, going into Chatham to refit the following year.

1803: When war reopened *Defence* was commissioned on 25 May under Captain George Hope, operating with the Channel squadron.

1804: For most of this year *Defence* was acting as flagship of Rear-Admiral Edward Thornborough's cruiser squadron deployed off the Texel, comprising the brig-sloop *Scorpion* (18) and sloop *Beaver* (14). Recalled to Chatham in October the ship was refitted to make good various defects at a total cost of £4,131.[149]

1805: Still under the command of Captain George Hope with James Green as First Lieutenant, *Defence* went into Portsmouth 19 May and docked six days later to refit. Undocked on 1 June the ship had to return into dock on 2 July to 'stop leaks' and have copper repaired. The total cost of these two refits amounted to £5,681.[150] Undocked the same day the ship sailed 9 July to join the British squadron blockading the Combined Franco-Spanish fleet in Cadiz. On 14 October the log states that *Defence* 'fired 2 Guns & brought to a Danish Brig from Copenhagen to Leghorn', under the stop and search policy, and that Hope had three marines by the names of Groombridge, Newberry and Turner flogged with '12 lashes each for Drunkenness'.[151]

TRAFALGAR

For Monday 21 October Hope records:

> PM Squally with heavy rain, close reef'd The Topsails, at 1:50 Wore Ship, at 2.15 Wore, At 3 Mod[e]. & Cloudy, at 4:30 out 1st reefs, at 5:00 Tacked Ship saw 24 sail of the Enemys fleet NbW at 6 Tacked Ship at 7:30 Wore Ship at 8 Mod[e].

& Clear, at 9:30 repeated our Sig[l]. with 3 Guns, at 10:30 repeated 3 Guns AM D[o]. W[r]. Wore Ship.[152]

On the eve of battle an officer in *Defence* recorded that 'The absence of moon, and the cloudy state of the weather, rendered it exceedingly dark, so that we came very near to the Combined Fleet without their being able to discern us. While we concealed every light, they continued to exhibit such profusions of theirs and make night signals in such abundance, that we seemed at times in the jaws of a mighty host ready to swallow us'.[153] In the morning *Defence*'s log continues:

> at day light made all sail, saw the Enemys fleet in all 39 sail, bearing S[t]. [south] from fleet — at 7 ans[d]. Gen[l]. Sig[l]. 76, at 8:45 Ans[d]. Sig[l]. Divis[l]. from R[l]. *Sovereign*, at 8:46 Ans[d]. 42 & 88 Divis[l]. from her, at 10:40 made 102 to *Phœbe* & at 10:41 - 88 to *Orion*, Enemys fleet to leeward forming the line, fleet running down with all sail at 11:48 Ans[d]. Gen[l]. —— —— Sig[l]. N[os]. 253, 269, 863, 261, 471, 958, 220, 370, 4, 21, 19, 24 at Noon Light Airs & Clear Running down on the Enemy with all sail.[154]

These numbers represent the individual words of Nelson's 'England Expects…' signal. Laying fourteenth in line of Collingwood's leeward column, it was relatively late when *Defence* got into battle.

Hope's log commencing at Noon ship's time, Tuesday 22 October, states: 'PM Light airs and Clear, at 12:10 Enemy began firing at the R[l]. *Sovereign*, which she returned directly. At 12:40 bisting [?] began, at 2:20 we engaged a French two Deck Ship'. *Defence* was in fact firing into the French *Berwick* at some distance. Then, 'at 3:15 our opponent hauled off to return the *Achilles* fire at which time we engaged a Spanish two Deck Ship'.[155] Having laid *Defence* alongside the *San Ildefonso*, Hope commenced to bombard her. After an hour the Spanish ship was obliged to surrender, the log recording,

> … at 4:15 *San Il Defonso* struck her Colours, sent a Boat onboard, observed several of the Enemy had struck, remainder made sail away, lowered the Boat to take the Prize in tow, at 10 took her in tow AM D[o]. W[r]. wore ship, at 2:30 spoke the *Tonnant*, at 4 Mod[e]. & Cloudy at 5.20 up mainsail at daylight our fleet dispersed, severel dismasted, several Prizes in possession, at 7.30 Hove to employed floatting [sic] the stream Cable into the Prize at 10 filled, at Noon Strong Gales & Squally several sailing…[156]

When the French *Achille* blew up shortly afterwards, one officer in *Defence* recorded:

Source: ADM 180/2/Entry 177 and ADM 180/10/Entry 82

Launched or Undocked	Sailed	Built or Nature of Repair	Cost of Hull, Masts & Yards Materials £	Workmen £	Cost of Masts & Yards Materials £	Workmen £	Cost of Rigging & Stores Materials £	Workmen £	Grand Total £
31 Mar 1763	13 Feb 1806	Built	27,690. 3.4		-				27,690.3.4
8 May 1765		Defects							
1 August 1768		Ditto					367.10.0		367.10.0
24 Feb 1770	19 Oct 1770	Fitted for a Guard Ship	2,734. 10.2				8,474.7. 9		11,208.17.11
	Ditto	Fitted	2,626						
27 June 1771		Refitted	540. 8. 11				58.8.8		606.17.7
	26 Oct 1804	Defects	173	234	81	-	3,515	28	4,131
	1 June 1805	Refitted	858	627	1,245	53	2,808	90	5,681
2 July 1805	9 July 1805	To Stop Leaks							
38 Oct 1806	8 Jan 1807	Between Middling & Large repair	7,809	4,271	1,854	364	9,062	75	23,435
6 Aug 1808	18 Oct 1808	Defects	1,583	742	209	85	3,473	134	6,226
8 Feb 1810		Defects	1,280	1,104	1,560	69	3,223	77	7,313
10 Mar 1810	28 Mar 1810	Defects							

It was a sight the most awful and grand that can be conceived. In a moment the hull burst into a cloud of smoke and fire. A column of vivid flame shot up an enormous height into the atmosphere and terminated by expanding into an immense globe, representing, for a few seconds, a prodigious tree in flames, speckled with many dark spot, which the pieces of timber and bodies of men occasioned while they were suspended in the clouds.[157]

Defence suffered few casualties, only seven killed and 29 wounded.[158]

During the ensuing storm *Defence*, together with *Bahama*, *San Ildefonso*, and *Swiftsure*, relentlessly buffeted by the heavy seas, plied off Cadiz under reefed sails for two days until Friday 25 October when, 'at 5 shortened sail & came to with the Best Bower in 27 f[ms.] veered 2 cables Cadiz SE½E 7 or 8 Miles Rota E½S', with her prize in company. Further attempts were made over the next few days to make sail but *Defence* with *San Ildefonso* were both forced to anchor. At anchor Monday 28 October, Hope had a boat lowered and 'sent one watch onboard the Prize and brought some Prisoners onboard'. On the Wednesday Hope records that 'two French Frigates and a Brig came out [from Cadiz] for the wounded men'. The same day he had the launch sent 'onboard the *Juno* for water', adding, 'saw Adm[l.] Louis' Squadron to windward'. *Defence* and her prize were not yet out of danger, for on Saturday 2 November the log states 'carried away the Hawser, sent the stream cable onboard the Prize', but by morning he had taken her in tow again. Reaching Gibraltar on 3 November, *Defence* and her prize *San Ildefonso* anchored and boats were sent onshore with the prisoners.[159] When the *Defence* eventually reached England the following month Hope paid the ship off 26 December.[160]

1806: Going into dock 21 April, *Defence* was given a 'Middling to Large Repair' and re-coppered in October at a total cost £23,435, of which £4,710 covered labour costs.[161] Launched 28 October, *Defence* was recommissioned under Captain Charles Ekins 10 November.[162]

1807: Sailing from Chatham for Sheerness on 8 January, *Defence* was deployed with the Channel squadron. In July she sailed to join Admiral James Gambier's fleet already assembled off Copenhagen. Arriving on 8 August, Ekins found that Gambier was fully prepared to support the military forces being landed to destroy the dockyard and Danish ships. When the Danish ship *Frederickscoarn* (32) attempted to escape on the night of the 12 August, Gambier ordered *Defence* and *Comus* (22) to sail in pursuit. Brought into engagement on the 14th by *Comus*, after 45 minutes the Danish ship was captured and *Defence* took on board 100 prisoners.[163] After this campaign *Defence* returned to England where she received orders to join Rear-Admiral Sir William Sidney Smith's squadron deployed off Lisbon. In company with *Ganges* (74), *Ruby* (64) and *Agamemnon* (64) *Defence* sailed from Portsmouth on 6 December. Now reinforced, Smith could now maintain an effective blockade of the Portuguese city.[164]

1808: Returning to Chatham 27 June, the ship was docked on 29 July to have her copper repaired. Coming out of the dock again on 6 August *Defence* sailed for active service on 18 October.[165]

1810: Docked at Plymouth 7 February and 9 March, *Defence* was re-coppered and undocked on 10 March. Sailing again on the 28 March the ship returned to duty.[166]

1811: On 24 February command of the *Defence* was superseded by Captain David Atkins, the ship being deployed with part of the Baltic fleet commanded by Admiral Sir James Saumarez. Escorting a convoy pass Heilm Island on 5 July, *Defence*, in company with *Cressy* (74), *Dictator* (64), the brig-sloop *Sheldrake* (16), the gun-brig *Bruiser* (12) were attacked by a Danish flotilla of 17 gunboats and ten heavy row boats, of which four gunboats were captured without loss to the convoy.

FATE

On 16 December 1811 *Defence* sailed from Wingo Sound escorting a large convoy of 150 merchant ships. In company were Admiral Saumarez' flagship *Victory* (100), the *St George* (98) flagship of Admiral Reynolds, *Dreadnought* (98), and 74 gun ships *Cressy*, *Hero*, *Orion* and *Vigo*. When *St George* lost her masts in a gale off Lolland in the Belt, Saumarez ordered *Defence* and *Cressy* to keep close to her. For five days the three ships battled against heavy gales under storm staysails until, at 4.30 a.m. on the morning of 24 December, the wind veered round to the NNW with increased force. *St George*, already disadvantaged with jury rigged masts and a damaged rudder, ran on shore near Ringkobing on the coast of Jutland. Shortly afterwards *Defence*, her storm sails blown out, also struck the ground. According to the narrative of survivor Joseph Page, 'she struck very easy' then 'falling into a trough of the sea, she struck heavy fore and aft… just as the 1st Lt. ordered the masts to be cut away, the main mast, mizzen mast, and fore topsail yard went over the side; about five minutes after, the fore mast went', with the result that the ship broached broadside onto the rocks. Page's narrative continues:

The sea breaking her, the dismal shrieks of the people, the guns breaking adrift, and crushing the men to death, rendered the whole a dreadful scene. I saw the carpenter's wife, with a little girl in her hand, endeavouring to get on the quarterdeck, when a tremendous sea broke in, which washed her, with many of the people, down the hatchway…boats laying on the lee gangway, all dashed to pieces except the pinnace, with about twenty men in her, and she was immediately washed overboard and lay bottom up. I now jumped overboard, and got on the mizzen-top, and the ship parted by the chesstree and gangway…the sheet anchor was driven athwart the forecastle, and killed several men. The sea was now making a fair breach between the forecastle and quarterdeck; the boom were washed away, with nearly a hundred men holding on by them.

With the hull violently pounded against the ground the ship rapidly went to pieces. Page eventually got onto a raft containing 20 men and the Danes waiting on the beach came to his assistance. Of the ship's complement of 530 upwards, only five seamen and one marine survived. Besides Joseph Page these were John Brown, Ralph Teazie, John Platt, Thomas Mullins and David McCormic, the latter dying shortly afterwards when the Danes brought carts to take them to lodgings at Sheltoz. Page further recalls that: 'We soon arrived at a house in the village, where we stript [sic] had dry cloths given us, and were put to bed… When I came to myself, I found Thomas Mullins in bed with me; he came on shore sometime after me on a piece of wreck'.

Over the next few days the Danes buried the bodies washed up on shore from the two ships and later erected a monument to honour those lost in *Defence* and *St George*. Besides Captain Atkins, other *Defence* officers who perished were Lieutenants Baker, De Lisle, Nelson, Peevor and Philpot, the Master Mr Mabson and Purser Mr Nicholson.[167]

The 74 gun ship DEFIANCE

The *Defiance* was the tenth ship in the Royal Navy to bear this name, the first vessel being an 8 gun pinnace hired into the navy to fight against the Spanish Armada in 1588 which remained in service until 1599. The second *Defiance* was a 46 gun ship of 500 tons built in 1590. Rebuilt at Woolwich in 1614 at 700 tons to carry only 34 guns, this ship was sold in 1650. The next *Defiance* was a 10 gun ship captured from the Royalist forces by Parliamentarians in February 1652, which foundered off Anegada, West Indies, in September that same year. The fourth *Defiance* was a 66 gun 3rd rate ship of 890 tons launched at Deptford in 1666. Built by Johnstone and Castle, this ship was accidentally burnt at Chatham dockyard 6 December 1668. The fifth *Defiance*, a 3rd rate of 64 guns, was launched at Chatham in 1675. Rebuilt at Woolwich in 1695, she was reduced to a 4th rate in 1716, hulked in 1743 and broken up at Chatham in June 1749. The sixth ship, purchased into the navy in 1671, is listed as a sloop which remained in service until 1678. The next *Defiance* was a 60 gun ship built by West at Deptford. Launched 12 October 1744, she was sold 10 April 1766. That same year a 20 gun sloop bearing the same name was launched at Bombay dockyard which later captured a brig in August 1782.[168] The ninth *Defiance*, a 3rd rate of 64 guns, was launched at Woolwich 31 August 1772.[169] While on active service during the American War of Independence, commanded by Captain Maximilian Jacobs, she was wrecked off Savannah Bar 18 February 1780.[170] In the list of captains and their ships the entry for this *Defiance* states 'Ship Lost paid Off in Broad Street'.[171] Quite remarkably, it appears that this *Defiance* of 64 guns was fitted with a triple purchase capstan which, comprising a mechanism of epicyclic gearing, provided a three fold advantage. Using a system of planetary gearing set in the trundlehead of the lower part of the capstan, it embodied a central gear integral with the spindle surrounded by three 'star' gears which in turn rotated the outer wheel which was toothed on its inner surface. Dated 1772 on the drawing held in the National Maritime Museum, this type of capstan appears to be fifty years ahead of a similar design generally adapted into naval vessels such as the 1824 frigate *Unicorn* now berthed at Dundee.[172]

Designed by Thomas Slade, the Trafalgar *Defiance* was built to the lines of the *Elizabeth* class which included *Berwick*, *Cumberland*, *Elizabeth*, *Powerful*, *Resolution*, and *Swiftsure*. Ordered on 11 July 1780, the contract was eventually given to John Randall & Co. based at Rotherhithe on the south side of Lower Pool of London. Interestingly the progress books refer to the ship being built on the River Thames, suggesting that this includes any building site along its banks towards its estuary. It was not until April 1782 that the keel was laid down, however construction progressed well, for the ship was launched 10 December 1783. Her building costs for her hull only amounted to £30,757. Removed to Woolwich 4 March 1784 she was completed and furnished with masts, yards, rigging and stores, these additional costs amounting to £8,878.

CAPTAINS OF *DEFIANCE* (MSS 248/4 and 248/6)

Name	Time of Entry	Time of Discharge	On What Occasion
George Keppel	1 August 1794	16 June 1795	Promoted Rear Admiral of the White
Sir George Home	17 June 1795	16 March 1796	To the *Glory*
Theophilus Jones	17 March 1796	26 February 1799	To the *Atlas*
Shuldham Peard	27 February 1799	2 March 1799	Superseded Acting
Thomas R Shivers	27 February 1799	23 December 1800	Superseded
Richard Retalick	24 December 1800	28 October 1801	Paid Off at Portsmouth
Philip Charles Durham	2 June 1803	31 December 1803	New Book
Philip Charles Durham	1 January 1804	1 July 1806	To the *Renown*
Henry Hotham	16 March 1806	16 August 1810	Superseded
Richard Raggett	18 August 1810	10 September 1813	Paid Off

SERVICE CAREER

1784: Docked in mid-March, *Defiance* was coppered and fitted for ordinary, and coming out of the dock at Woolwich 20 April, sailed for Chatham 9 June. Arriving twenty days later, the ship remained laid up in the Medway for nine years.

1793: Although war with France opened on 1 February it was not until 18 November that *Defiance* was docked at Chatham for a 'Middl[g.] Rep[r.] & fitted' to prepare her for war service.

1794: Coming out of the dock 16 May and completing her refit at a total cost of £14,925 of which £3,770 was spent on rigging and stores, *Defiance* was eventually commissioned under Captain George Keppel on 1 August.

1795: Keppel, promoted Rear Admiral of the White, left the ship on 16 June, his successor, Captain Sir George Horne assuming command the next day.

1796: When Horne transferred into *Glory* on 16 March, command of *Defiance* was superseded by Captain Theophilus Jones, who would remain in the *Defiance* until 1799 when the ship was deployed with the Channel fleet.

1797: In April *Defiance* was one of the ships involved in the Great Mutiny at Spithead.[173]

1799: On 27 February command of the ship passed over to Shuldham Peard who took temporary command when Captain Jones transferred into *Atlas*, he was soon superseded by Captain Thomas R Shivers. During this

SPECIFICATIONS: *DEFIANCE*

Rate	3rd	Date launched	10 December 1783	Ordnance - lower gun deck	28 x 32 pounders
Guns	74	Length on the range of the gun deck	168 ft 6 ins	Ordnance - upper gun deck	28 x 18 pounders
Class	Elizabeth 1766	Length of keel for tonnage	138 ft 3¼ ins	Ordnance - quarter deck	14 x 9 pounders
Designer	Thomas Slade	Extreme breadth	46 ft 10 ins	Ordnance - forecastle	4 x 9 pounders
Builder	John Randall & Co.	Depth in hold	19 ft 9 ins	Single broadside weight	781 pounds
Dockyard	Rotherhithe	Tons burthen	1612 88/94	Fate	1813 Hulked as a temporary prison ship at Chatham
Date ordered	11 July 1780	Complement	550/600		1817 Broken up
Date keel laid	April 1782				

Source: Lyon, *Sailing Navy List*, p. 70.

period the ship was deployed with Earl St Vincent's fleet in the Mediterranean. Cruising off Cape de Crues on 30 May, St Vincent received news that Admiral Bruix had sailed with his squadron from Toulon. Realising that Nelson at Palermo was unaware that the French were out, St Vincent detached Rear-Admiral Duckworth with four ships to intercept. Later that day the Commander-in-Chief was reinforced by Rear-Admiral Whitshed in *Queen Charlotte* (100), together with three 74s, including *Defiance*, and the 64 gun *Repulse*. *Defiance*, with the rest of the fleet, sailed down the southern Spanish coast, passing Barcelona.[174]

1800: Lying at Plymouth, *Defiance*, together with *Pompée* (80), *Resolution* (74) and the frigate *Bourdelois* (24), received orders on 3 August to sail for the Downs and were later deployed as part of the Channel squadron operating off the Black Rocks. On 24 December Shivers was superseded by Captain Richard Retalick who, six days later, carried *Defiance* to the aid of a dismasted transport and towed her into Falmouth on 30 December.

1801: The battle of Copenhagen: Flying the flag of Rear-Admiral Thomas Graves, *Defiance* was deployed with Admiral Sir Hyde Parker's fleet that sailed for the Baltic to subdue the Danes at Copenhagen. As Nelson's squadron commenced their attack on the Danish line and defences, *Agamemnon* (64) was forced to anchor; *Bellona* (74) and *Russell* (74) ran aground. Consequently much needed firepower to reduce the Trekoner Forts from these three ships had been lost leaving the *Defiance* and *Monarch* (74) open to considerable fire during the action so that that they both suffered heavy damage and losses. Casualties in *Defiance* amounted to 75, of whom 24 were killed and 51 wounded. Among the dead were Lieutenant George Gray; Mr Matthews, the pilot; 17 seamen, three marines and two soldiers. The wounded comprised the Boatswain Mr Patterson; Midshipman Gallaway; Mr Niblet, captain's clerk; Mr Stevenson, pilot; 35 seamen, five marines and seven soldiers. With an increasing threat of invasion from France *Defiance*, with five other 74s, was recalled in June to reinforce the Channel fleet stationed off Brest.[175] Returning to Portsmouth 8 August the ship was placed in dock for two weeks to have her copper repaired. Remaining at Portsmouth, she was paid off 28 October.[176]

1803: When the war with France was resumed in April *Defiance* was recommissioned under Captain Philip Charles Durham 2 June and deployed with the Channel fleet watching over Brest.

1804: Returning to Portsmouth 5 July, the ship was docked six days later to refit and have her bottom re-coppered. Undocked 7 August, *Defiance* sailed 22 August to resume her station off Brest. In total her refit had cost £5,076.

1805: Still commanded by Captain Durham with William Hellard as First Lieutenant, *Defiance* continued to operate with the Channel fleet, now commanded by Vice-Admiral Sir Robert Calder who was flying his flag in *Prince of Wales* (98). Laying off Finisterre 22 July, Calder's squadron fell in with the combined Franco-Spanish fleet commanded by Vice-Admiral Pierre Villeneuve returning from the West Indies. Villeneuve's fleet comprised 20 ships of the line, six frigates and three corvettes compared with Calder's squadron of 15 line of battle, two frigates, a lugger and a cutter. Severely hampered by thick fog, the action, which lasted four hours, was sporadic and confused. Only two Spanish ships, *San Rafael* (84) and *Firme* (74), were taken; consequently the chance to destroy the combined force designed to support Napoleon's invasion of England was missed. As a result Villeneuve was able to escape south and take his remaining ships into the safe haven of Cadiz. Although *Defiance* suffered some damage to rigging and yards in the action, her casualties were low, comprising one killed and seven wounded.[177] After briefly returning to England for minor refitting *Defiance* sailed and joined Vice-Admiral Nelson's squadron blockading Cadiz on 7 October.

PROGRESS BOOK – *DEFIANCE* 3rd RATE OF 74 GUNS:

At what Port	Arrived	Docked	Coppered
River Thames; Randall & Co.	Began	April 1782	
Deptford	10 Dec 1783		
Woolwich	4 March 1784	15 Mar 1784	Coppered April 1784
Chatham	29 June 1784	18 Nov 1793	Copper taken off Nov 1793 Re-coppered May 1794
Sheerness	8 Jan 1796		
Chatham	16 Mar 1796	8 April 1796	
Portsmouth	31 Aug 1798	12 Sept 1798	Copper taken off Sept 1798 Re-coppered Nov 1798
Plymouth	23 June 1800	7 July 1800	Copper repaired
Portsmouth	8 Aug 1801	29 Aug 1801	Copper repaired
Portsmouth			Coppered May 1803
Portsmouth	5 July 1804	11 July 1804	Copper taken off July Re-coppered Aug 1804
Portsmouth	7 Dec 1805	25 Dec 1805	Copper taken off Dec Re-coppered Mar 1806 & doubled
Plymouth	21 Mar 1808	28 Mar 1808	Copper repaired & re-nailed
Plymouth	17 Mar 1809		Copper repaired
Plymouth	23 June 1810		
Plymouth	9 July 1810	16 July 1810	Copper taken off & Re-coppered July 1810
Chatham	13 Sept 1813	Taken in hand 26 November & completed Dec 1813	
	2 March 1817	***Taken to Pieces May 1817***	

TRAFALGAR

On Monday 21 October the log of the *Defiance* states:

> Fresh Breezes & Hazy *Euryalus* made the Sig[l.] for the Enemys Fleet coming out of Port at 8 light Breezes saw the lights of the Enemy's Fleet AM light airs at day light discovered the Enemy's Fleet EBW Consisting of 33 sail of the Line 7 Frigates & 1 Brig formed in a Line of Battle on the Larb[d.] Tack 6.30 answer[d.] Gen[l.] Sig[l.] N[o.] 13 at 12 Answ[d.] Gen[l.] Signal England expects that every man will do his Duty all sail set Standing for the Enemy's Rear Ships Noon light Airs Inclinable [sic] to Calm Admiral & Fleet in Company.[178]

At noon *Defiance* was standing twelfth in line of Collingwood's leeward division. Describing the opening events in the ship's log for Tuesday 22 October, Durham records:

> Light Breezes & Hazy 12.25 *Royal Sovereign* Commenced action in the centre of the Enemy's Fleet & passed through their Line & the *Victory* Commenced another Action 1.40 we began to Fire and not before a great number of Shot went over us and much of our running rigging shot away to a Spanish 3 Deck Ship the 3rd from the Enemy's Rear at 2.10 she bore up close along side of us keeping a Constant Fire we doing the same at his Hull at 2.40 she hauled off...

The Spanish vessel in which the *Defiance* was partially engaging was the *Principe de Asturias* (112), flagship of Admiral Don Federico Gravina. *Defiance* then 'stood on for French 2 Deck Ship *Aigle* at 3.10 seen alongside of her and made her fast took Possession of her Q[tr.] Deck & Poop struck the French Colours and hoisted English her people still firing from her Tops, Forecastle and Lower Deck'. This initial boarding party, led by Lieutenant Thomas Simens, met considerable resistance, as the French had rallied and were directing a fusillade of musket fire from the forecastle, waist and tops, compelling the British seamen to retire. While retreating back on board *Defiance*, Lieutenant Simens was mortally wounded. When, at '3.35 the Boarders were called from *Aigle*', Durham 'cast off lashings & hauled off

Source: ADM 180/7/Entry 139 and ADM 180/10/Entry 83

Launched or Undocked	Sailed	Built or Nature of Repair	Cost of Hull, Masts & Yards Materials £	Workmen £	Cost of Masts & Yards Materials £	Workmen £	Cost of Rigging & Stores Materials £	Workmen £	Grand Total £
10 Dec 1783		Built	30,757.15s 10d. Hull only		–				30,757.15s 10d Hull Only
	4 March 1784	To Woolwich		4,249				4,629	8,878
20 April 1784	9 June 1784 to Chatham	Coppered & Fitted for Ordinary	Included above				Included above		Included above
16 May 1794	23 Sept 1795	Middling Repair & Fitted	11,155				3,770		14,925
	16 Mar 1796	Making good defects	425				67		492
9 May 1796	1 June 1796	Refitted	1,161				1,335		2,496
23 Nov 1798	28 Dec 1798	Refitted	6,749				3,521		10,270
8 July 1800	1 Aug 1800	Made good defects							
10 Sept 1801		Refitted							
		Fitted							
7 Aug 1804	22 Aug 1804	Refitted	1,838	1,042	146	33	1,934	83	5,076
7 Mar 1806	1 Apr 1806	Refitted	10,784	3,296	2,367	127	7,616	121	24,311
30 Mar 1808	25 April 1808	Defects	1,524	959	1,549	17	5,454	73	9,576
	11 Apr 1809	Defects	664	343	2,440	34	6,877	82	10,440
25 June 1810		Defects	2,817	600	365	22	3,787	53	7,644
18 July 1810	8 Aug 1810	Defects	Included above	ditto	Included above	ditto	Included above	ditto	Included above
		Fitted for a temporary Prison Ship	138 162	183 701	4 –		61 8		386 871

about Pistol shot [about 30 feet] distance & engaged her again about 4 they called for Quarters ceased Firing sent a Boat w[th.] a Lieut. & 20 men to take Possession of her & sail the French Ship to windward standing to Southward with all sail set'. Durham then manœuvred *Defiance* alongside the Spanish *San Juan Nepomuceno* (74), which had succumbed to the tremendous broadsides fired from *Dreadnought* (98,) and took possession of her. Taking this opportunity to inspect the damage in *Defiance*, Durham 'Found Our Bowsprit, Fore Mast, and Main Mast with all the Top Masts Shot thro & Standing & Running Rigging shot to Pieces employed knotting and splicing the rigging'. In the action *Defiance* sustained 70 casualties. Of the 17 killed were Lieutenant Thomas Simens; Midshipman James Williamson; and Boatswain William Forster. The 53 wounded included Captain Durham, together with Master's Mates Robert Browne and James Spratt; and Midshipmen John Hodge and Edmund Chapman.[179] Concluding, the log states:

> ... at 9 let go the B. Bower Anchor Veerd to a Whole C[able] found the ship did not bring up & being near the Shoals of Trafalgar cut the Cable and made sail Rec[d.] 14 French Officers & 70 men At day light Adm[l.] & Fleet in Company. w[th.] a number of Dismasted Ships Prizes none of the y[e.] Enemy's Fleet in sight got out Boats and got Hawsers into them to take the *Aigle* in Tow standing off and on endeavouring to take her in Tow at Noon Strong Breezes and Squally w[th.] heavy Rain empl[d.] as before.[180]

With the rising storm this proved difficult, Durham recording:

> Strong gales and Squally w[th.] Heavy Rain boats endeavouring to get a Hawser on B[d.] the *Aigle* found every attempt ineffective sent Boats for our Men got all on B[d.] except Lieut. Purchas & 12 men which Could not be got without Risking the Loss of H M Ship *Defiance* being so close in w[th.] alee of her up Boats and made sail AM D[o.] W[r.] wth Rain 6 30 Wore Ship at 10 Cadiz EBN ? N 4 or 5 Leagues the Enemy getting under Weigh coming out of Cadiz Noon light Breezes & Hazy Employed Knotting & Splicing.[181]

For the next few days *Defiance* with her prize struggled off Cadiz. On 29 October *Defiance* answered Collingwood's signal to close with the admiral and sent over topsail yards to *Téméraire*. Next day at 9.30 Durham 'Took *Téméraire* in Tow'. With weather moderate and hazy the log then records '*Téméraire* in Tow sent the Boats a head to tow the *Téméraire* nearing us', then suddenly at 10 o'clock irrespective that it was relatively calm the two ships collided, 'the *Téméraire* fell on b[d.] of us cast off ye tow Hawser'. Shortly after the *Defiance* 'got Clear from the & made sail and recovered the tow'. Finally arriving off Gibralter Sunday 3 November *Defiance* was able to 'Cast off the *Téméraire* having towed her to the Anchoring at Gibralter Came to w[th.] ye Best Bower in 40 f[ms]'.[182] *Defiance* eventually returned to Portsmouth 7 December and went into dock on Christmas Day.

1806: Besides having her copper replaced, before being re-launched 7 March, the ship's hull was 'doubled' to improve her strength. Her overall refit costs to repair battle damage, including refitting masts, yards, and rigging and taking on new stores totalled £24,311. *Defiance* sailed on 1 April to resume her mundane duties deployed with the Channel fleet.[183] On 16 March Captain Henry Hotham assumed command of *Defiance*, Durham transferring into *Renown* (74) on 1 July.[184]

1808: Recalled to England, *Defiance* went into Plymouth 21 March to refit and sailed again 25 April.[185]

1809: Still under the command of Captain Hotham, *Defiance* joined Rear-Admiral Stopford's squadron. While pursuing a French squadron commanded by Rear-Admiral Willaumez off Ushant on 23 February, *Naiad* (38) reported seeing three suspicious vessels which later proved to be the French 40 gun frigates *Italienne*, *Calypso*, and *Cybèle*. At 10 a.m. Stopford, flying his flag in *Cæsar* (80), ordered *Defiance*, *Donegal* (74) and *Amelia* (38) to give chase. Gaining shallow waters the frigates took refuge under the Sables d'Olonne batteries to elude the deeper drafted ships. At 10.30 a.m. the British ships stood in, *Defiance* taking the lead. The engagement commenced at 11 a.m., the French returning fire vigorously from the ships and powerful shore batteries to good effect. *Defiance*, having less draft than *Cæsar* and *Donegal*, closed within half a mile, anchored, and opened her fire upon the ensnared ships. By 11.50 a.m. *Italienne* and *Cybèle* had caught fire and were forced to cut their cables and run ashore. *Calypso* also drove on shore stern first and became marooned as the tide fell. Receiving the brunt of the French attack, *Defiance* suffered much damage to her mast before the tide started to ebb. Hotham weighed, made sail and rejoined the squadron. In all *Defiance* sustained two men killed and 25 wounded.[186] During the summer *Defiance* operated off the north coast of Spain with *Amazon* (38). Entering Ferrol on 26 June, the two ships landed seamen and marines and captured the French-occupied fort without meeting resistance. Two days later *Defiance* went into Corunna and on 30 June the Spanish army, comprising 11,00 troops, entered the town.

1810: Back at Plymouth 23 June *Defiance* had another small refit to make good defects and have her copper replaced. She sailed for Cawsand Bay 8 August and ten days later Hotham was succeeded by Captain Richard Raggett.[187]

1811/2: For the most of this year *Defiance* was deployed off Flushing watching over shipping in the River Scheldt and in the following year, operating off the Texel.

1813: Returning to the Medway, her place of origin, *Defiance* was paid off by Captain Raggett on 10 September. Three days later the ship moved into Chatham where she was 'Taken in hand 26 November & completed Dec 1813' and 'Fitted for a temp[y.] Pris[n.] Ship', at a cost of £1,257.

FATE

Defiance remained hulked as a prison ship until 1817 when on 2 March she was finally docked at Chatham and 'Taken to Pieces May 1817'.[188]

The 74 gun ship LEVIATHAN

The Trafalgar *Leviathan* was the second ship in the Royal Navy to bear this name, the previous vessel first called *Northumberland*, a 3rd rate of 70 guns designed to the 1745 Establishment laid down at Plymouth 14 August 1744 and launched 1 December 1750. Converted to a storeship carrying 30 guns, she was renamed *Leviathan* then converted to a 4th rate of 50 guns in 1779. In 1780, while under the command of Captain Robert Lambert, the ship took passage from Jamaica to England. When halfway across the Atlantic the ship began to leak badly and despite constant pumping, jettisoning guns, anchors and stores overboard, and frapping the ship's hull with ropes to prevent the frame timbers working, by 25 February Lambert concluded that the ship could not be saved. Over the next two days the crew were transferred safely into accompanying ships, leaving the stricken vessel, now with eleven feet of water in the hold, to founder.[189]

The Trafalgar *Leviathan* derived from the *Leviathan* class of 1779, the design of which originated from the lines of the French *Courageux* which had been captured by the *Bellona* on 13 August 1761. The other vessels making up the *Leviathan* class comprised the *Carnatic*, *Colossus*, *Minotaur*, *Aboukir* and *Bombay*. Ordered 9 December 1779, *Leviathan*'s keel was laid down at Chatham dockyard in May 1782, building work initially being undertaken by Master Shipwright John Nelson. While under construction Nelson was superseded by Edward Sison and by the time of her launch 9 October 1790 work was completed by Sison's successor Thomas Mitchell. Mounting twenty-eight 32 pounders on lower gun deck, twenty-eight 18 pounders on her upper gun deck, fourteen 9 pounders on the quarter deck and four 9 pounders on her forecastle, *Leviathan* could deliver a single broadside weight of 718 pounds.[190]

CAPTAINS OF *LEVIATHAN* (MSS 248/4 and 248/6)

Name	Time of Entry	Time of Discharge	On What Occasion.
Nathanial Brunton	23 October 1790	23 November 1790	Paid Off Acting
Lord Hugh Coursey	21 January 1793	15 March 1795	To the *Sans Pareil*
William Browell	130 August 1793	26 September 1793	Superseded Acting
George Hope	27 September 1793	11 November 1793	Superseded Acting
John Thomas Duckworth	19 March 1795	22 July 1796	Appointed Commodore
Joseph Bingham	23 July 1796	24 December 1796	Invalided
William Ogilvy	25 December 1796	31 January 1797	Superseded
James Bowen	1 February 1797	21 April 1797	Superseded
John Thomas Duckworth	22 April 1797	14 October 1798	Promoted to Commodore
Henry Digby	15 October 1798	18 November 1798	Supesed
William Buchanan	19 November 1798	30 September 1799	Superseded
James Carpenter	1 October 1799	27 September 1800	Invalided
Edward D King	28 September 1800	4 June 1801	To the *Andromeda*
Christopher Cole	5 June 1801	14 January 1802	To the *Southampton*
Richard D Dunn	15 January 1802	21 July 1803	To the *Hercule*
Henry William Bayntun	22 July 1803	31 December 1803	New Book
Henry William Bayntun	I January 1804	31 December 1805	Paid Off at Portsmouth
Hon. Charles Paget	14 June 1808	10 July 1808	Superseded
John Harvey	11 July 1808	10 March 1811	Superseded
Patrick Campbell	11 March 1811	10 October 1813	Superseded
Adam Drummond	11 October 1813	15 October 1814	Superseded
Thomas Brigg	16 October 1814	19 July 1816	Paid Off at Portsmouth

SPECIFICATIONS: *BRITANNIA*

Rate	3rd	Length on the range of the gun deck	172 ft 3 ins	Ordnance - lower gun deck	28 x 32 pounders
Guns	74	Length of keel for tonnage	140 ft 5¼ ins	Ordnance - upper gun deck	28 x 18 pounders
Class	Leviathan 1779	Extreme breadth	47 ft 9 ins	Ordnance - quarter deck	14 x 9 pounders
Designer	Built to lines of French *Courageux*	Depth in hold	20 ft 9 ins	Ordnance - forecastle	4 x 9 pounders
Builder	John Nelson	Tons burthen	1703 21/94	Single broadside weight	781 pounds
Dockyard	Chatham	Draught afore	22 ft 1 ins	Fate	1816 Hulked as a prison ship at Portsmouth
Date ordered	9 December 1779	Draught abaft	23 ft 5 ins		1846 Became a target ship
Date keel laid	May 1782	Complement	600/640		1848 Sold to be broken up
Date launched	9 October 1790				

Source: Lyon, *Sailing Navy List*, p. 72.

THE 74 GUN SHIP *LEVIATHAN*

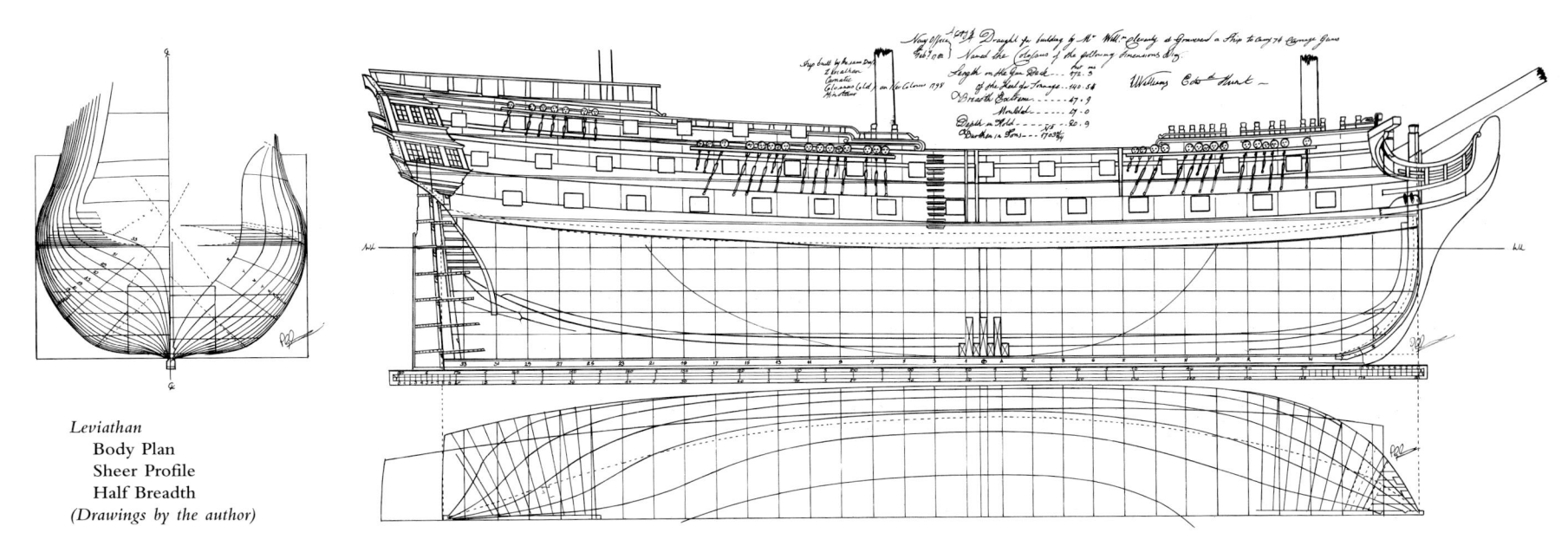

Leviathan
Body Plan
Sheer Profile
Half Breadth
(Drawings by the author)

SERVICE HISTORY

1793: Commissioned at the outbreak of war with revolutionary France in 1793, *Leviathan* was placed under the command of Captain Lord Hugh Seymour and sent to the Mediterranean to join Admiral Hood's squadron deployed with the Spanish fleet off Toulon between August and December that year.[191] The main contribution made by *Leviathan* during this campaign was to assist with the evacuation of French royalists from the city of Toulon while major assaults were being made on French ships within the harbour and dockyard arsenal.[192]

1794: Now deployed with the Channel Fleet, *Leviathan* fought with Admiral Lord Howe's fleet against Admiral Villaret's squadron protecting a grain convoy returning from America. Commencing 28 May, at about 7 p.m. that day *Leviathan* went to the aid of *Bellerophon* (74), *Marlborough* (74), *Russell* (74), and *Thunderer* (74), who were already in chase firing at *Révolutionnaire* (110). Engaging the French three-decker for some thirty minutes before being supported by *Audacious* (74), *Leviathan* engaged the next French ship before reuniting with the main body of Howe's ships. Although she had suffered 400 casualties and her masts and rigging were much damaged, *Révolutionnaire* managed to elude capture from the superior number of British ships involved.[193] That evening Howe signalled his fleet to reform line ahead and astern of his flagship *Queen Charlotte* (100), *Leviathan* laying ninth in the line. On 29 May Howe, needing to close with the rear of Villaret's squadron, made a signal at 7 a.m. for his ships to lay onto a larboard tack to cut through the enemy line and attain the weather gauge. After successive counter manœuvres on both sides the two fleets finally closed and a general action ensued around 1.15 p.m. Fifteen minutes later *Queen Charlotte*, followed by *Bellerophon*, passed through the French line, Seymour driving *Leviathan* closely behind crossing the stern of *Terrible* (110), which lay third from the French rear. Fighting continued between the two fleets until late afternoon during which *Leviathan* was disabled. For two days the British fleet doggedly pursued the French and by the morning of the 1 June they lay some 47∞ 48'N and 18∞ 30'W. At 7.16 a.m. Howe gave the signal that he intended to drive through the French line and engage their ships from leeward and at 8.15 a.m. ordered each ship to attack independently. By 9.45 a.m. action became general, when *Leviathan* engaged, boarded, and took possession of *America* (74).[194]

1795: When Captain John Duckworth assumed command of *Leviathan* in April, the ship was sent to join the West Indies fleet commanded by Rear-Admiral William Parker stationed at Jamaica.

1796: In the spring plans were made to attack French possessions in the West Indies the first being Santo Domingo. While troops, commanded by Major-General Forbes, were landed at Léogane on the 31 March under cover of fire from *Ceres* (32), *Iphigenia* (32), *Cormorant* (18), *Lark* (16), and *Sirène* (16), *Leviathan*, *Swiftsure* (74), and *Africa* (64) bombarded the town and defensive works. French resistance proved more determined than anticipated however, with the result that *Leviathan* and *Africa* suffered considerable damage aloft, so much so that the assault was abandoned. Further attacks made against the French forces on other islands, including St Vincent and Grenada between April and June, were successful.[195]

1797: Returning to England, *Leviathan* was decommissioned and went into refit.

1798: Recommissioned under Captain Henry Digby, *Leviathan* was deployed to the Mediterranean and in the autumn became the flagship to Commodore John Duckworth, her previous commander; consequently Digby became Duckworth's flag captain. At the end of October St Vincent, Commander-in-Chief of the Mediterranean fleet, detached a small squadron commanded by Commodore Duckworth to attack the Spanish island of Minorca. Besides *Leviathan*, this squadron comprised *Centaur* (74), *Argo* (44), *Dolphin* (44), *Aurora* (28), *Cormorant* (20), *Petrel* (16), the storeship *Ulysses* (44), *Calcutta* (74), armed transport *Coromandel* (24), the hired cutter *Constitution* and several merchant transports. Reaching Minorca on 7 November, the troops together with 250 seamen and 100 marines from *Leviathan* and *Centaur* commanded by General the Hon. Charles Stuart, were landed off Fornello on the north side of the island. Meeting no resistance the island was taken without loss of life.[196]

1799: Now commanded by Captain John Buchanan, *Leviathan*, sailing off Majorca on 6 February in company with *Argo* (44), fell in with two Spanish 34 gun frigates *Santa Teresa* and *Proserpina*. On seeing the British ships the two Spaniards split company and while *Argo* gave chase to *Santa Teresa*, *Leviathan*, unable to maintain speed, continued her course, leaving *Proserpina* to get away. After a running fight *Santa Teresa* was captured by *Argo*.[197] Lying at Port Mahon, *Leviathan* weighed and sailed with St Vincent's fleet on 22 May to cruise off Cape de Creus to prevent Masserodo's Spanish ships at Cartagena joining Bruix's fleet based at Toulon. Receiving news on the 30th that the French had sailed from Toulon, thus putting Nelson at Palermo in jeopardy, St Vincent detached Duckworth with *Leviathan*, *Foudroyant* (80), *Majestic* (74) and *Northumberland* (74) to reinforce him.[198] These ships arrived at Palermo on 7 June.[199]

1800: Still the flagship of Commodore Duckworth, command of *Leviathan* had now been given to Captain the Hon. Charles Carpenter. Cruising off Lisbon on the afternoon of 5 April *Leviathan*, together with *Swiftsure* (74) and *Emerald* (36), sighted twelve sail and gave chase. Capturing one of the vessels they discovered that a Spanish convoy of 13 vessels escorted by three frigates had sailed from Cadiz. Next morning boats from *Leviathan* and *Emerald*, commanded by Lieutenant Gregory, took possession of a Spanish 14 gun brig bound for Lima. Continuing the search for the convoy, *Leviathan* sailed to the north while *Swiftsure* and *Emerald* sailed to the south and east respectively. After *Emerald* signalled that she had sighted six sail *Leviathan* joined her at 2 a.m. on 7 April to discover two frigates. At dawn the two ships were hailed to surrender. When they refused, *Leviathan* and *Emerald* fired into the Spanish vessels, disabled their rigging and compelled them to strike their colours. The prizes were *Carmen* (34), Captain Dom Fraquin Porcel, and *Florentina* (34), Captain Dom Manuel Norates. In the action the Spaniards lost two officers and 20 men killed and 26 men wounded. Although the third escort frigate managed to escape, the convoy, which was carrying mercury to Lima, was also taken. The two captured Spanish frigates were later entered into the British navy as 36 gun frigates retaining their original names.[200] In the autumn Duckworth was promoted to Rear-Admiral and appointed Commander-in-Chief of the Leeward Islands. Retaining *Leviathan* as his flagship, he sailed for the West Indies and took up station at Barbados. While the ship lay off Guadaloupe, Carpenter, *Leviathan*'s captain, became ill and had to be shipped home in the merchant vessel *Charlotte*; also on board was Captain Taylor of *Dromedary* which had been wrecked off Trinidad. Consequently Captain Edward King succeeded command of *Leviathan*.

1801: While on station Duckworth decided to attack the islands of St Bartholomew, St Martin and St Thomas. After embarking 1,500 troops commanded by Lieutenant-General Trigge, Duckworth sailed from Barbados on 16 March, the main body of his squadron comprising *Leviathan*, *Andromeda* (32), the brig-sloop *Drake* (14), and armed schooner *Éclair* (12). Later reinforced by the frigate *Proselyte* (32), the sloop *Hornet* (16), and storeship *Coromandel*, each island was taken with little resistance. *Proselyte* was later wrecked off St Martin on 4 August 1801. Shortly after Captain King transferred out of *Leviathan* into *Andromeda* and the ship was recalled to England to refit.

1803: When war with France resumed in April *Leviathan* was recommissioned under Captain Henry Bayntun.

1804: Sent on deployment to the Mediterranean *Leviathan*, together with three bomb vessels, joined Nelson's squadron watching over Toulon on 10 May and on 19 May *Leviathan* with part of Nelson's fleet retired to Agincourt Sound, Corsica.[201] For the next seven months *Leviathan* was either employed keeping station off Toulon as directed or refitting at this safe anchorage.

1805: On 17 January Vice-Admiral Villeneuve, taking advantage of the prevailing NNW wind, evaded the British patrols and escaped from Toulon with his fleet. Villeneuve's force comprised eleven ships of the line, seven frigates and two sloops. At this time *Leviathan* was laying at Agincourt Sound refitting. At 2 a.m. on 19 January Nelson received news from the 38 gun frigates *Active* and *Seahorse* which had been watching the port that the French fleet were at sea. Nelson, flying his flag in *Victory*, immediately ordered his squadron to weigh. Besides *Victory*, *Leviathan* and the two frigates, his Mediterranean squadron comprised *Royal Sovereign* (100), *Canopus* (80), *Belleisle* (74), *Conqueror* (74), *Donegal* (74), *Spencer* (74), *Superb*, (74), *Swiftsure* (74), and *Tigre* (74). By 5 p.m. *Leviathan*, with the other ships, was at sea passing through the narrow channel between Biche and Sardinia. Next morning Nelson ordered *Leviathan* and *Spencer*, his fastest ships, to take up a detached station to windward of his main force.[202] Though unable to find Villeneuve, on 12 March Nelson despatched *Leviathan* to look into

PROGRESS BOOK - *LEVIATHAN* RATE OF 74 GUNS:

At what Port	Arrived	Docked	Coppered
Portsmouth	24 Oct 1803	5 Nov 1803	Copper taken off Nov Re-coppered Dec 1803
Plymouth	11 Dec 1805	20 June 1806	Copper repaired
Plymouth		30 Nov 1807	Copper taken off Nov 1807 Re-coppered May 1808
Portsmouth	4 August 1813	26 Aug 1813	Copper taken off & re-coppered
Portsmouth	2 July 1816	8 Oct 1816	Copper taken off and re-coppered
			Scuttled – removed part of copper Oct 1846

Sold 9th August 1848 to Mr Burns for £805

Barcelona on the pretence that the British were still off the Spanish coast.[203] This proved advantageous for on 16 April *Leviathan* returned to Nelson, who was off Sardinia, with news that the French had been seen off Cape de Gata on 7 April.[204] Finally realising that Villeneuve had sailed for the West Indies, Nelson sailed in pursuit, *Leviathan* in company.[205]

Returning from the great chase across to the West Indies, *Leviathan* put into Gibraltar to refit rigging and take on fresh provisions. Sailing in early October, she took up station off Cadiz on 7 October, where she remained with the rest of Nelson's command blockading Villeneuve's fleet.[206]

TRAFALGAR

At noon the day before the battle Captain Bayntun's 'Remarks &c on board H M Ship *Leviathan*' state:

> Fresh breezes & Squally sent down Top Gall[t.] Yards At ½ past 2 Moderate – ½ P[st.] 3 wore again sent up top Gall[t.] Y[ds.] Fresh breezes & Hazy Observ[d] several Light to luward, Signals at 8 wore ship to the SSW Moderate and Cloudy Fleet in C[o.] Saw several guns blue lights And Rockets fired to the North[d.] Supposed to be our look out ships AM light airs and Cloudy at day light Observed the Enemys fleet to leeward 35 Sail, bore up made P[r.] Signal out 1st reef of Tps Clear[d.] for Action Light airs & Cloudy weather all sail set, down for the Enemys fleet Consisting of 35 Sail of the Line 5 Frigates, and 2 Brigs Employed Clearing ship for action in C[o.] with 27 sail of the line 4 frigates a schooner & Cutter at 5 Minutes before noon the Royal Sovereign Heading the Larb[d.] Division, began to engage the Enemys Rear.[207]

Leviathan, placed fourth in the line of Nelson's windward division, was followed into battle by *Neptune* (98). Prior to the action Nelson had agreed with Captain Bayntun that *Leviathan* could precede *Victory* into action 'if he could'. The order was conveyed by Captain Blackwood after quitting Nelson's flagship and returning to his own command. Although Bayntun crammed on more sail to attain the lead, *Defiance* had only got abreast of *Conqueror* (74) when opening shots began hammering *Victory*. *Leviathan*'s log, dated Tuesday 22 October, records: 'At 20 p[st.] 12 Commenced action engaged the Enemy as oppos[d.] us About 1 the Action became general'.[208] Firing long shots into *Santisima Trinidad* (136), *Leviathan* stood to attack the French *Neptune* (84) but as she had fallen off to windward Bayntun hauled *Leviathan* onto larboard tack and stood towards *San Agustin* (74), and 'at ½ p[st.] 3 laid the *S[t.] Augustine* Aboard carried her'.[209] Although *San Agustin* attempted to rake *Defiance*, Bayntun deftly manœuvred his ship, poured a treble shotted broadside into the quarter of the Spanish two decker, bringing down her mizzen mast. But finding his own rigging already much cut about, Bayntun put *Leviathan*'s helm to starboard, thereby running the larboard side of *Defiance* aboard the Spaniard. Within minutes a party of boarders, led by Lieutenant John Balwin, swarmed onto the Spanish ship, forcing her commander Captain Don Cagilal to surrender. Unwittingly Bayntun

Source: ADM 180/10/Entry 102

Launched or Undocked	Sailed	Built or Nature of Repair	Cost of Hull, Masts & Yards Materials £	Workmen £	Cost of Masts & Yards Materials £	Workmen £	Cost of Rigging & Stores Materials £	Workmen £	Grand Total £
31 Dec 1803	29 Jan 1804	Refitted	8,533	4,441	1,299	221	7,673	94	22,261
20 June 1806			204	–	2	–	112	–	318
8 June 1808	9 Aug 1808	Between Small and Middling Repair	14,048	9,293	3,537	53	12,080	15	39,026
28 Sep 1813	1 Nov 1813	Defects	2,825	1,579	782	2	8,119	89	13,396
Oct 1816		Fitted for a Convict Hulk							
		Target Ship							
		Expense 1847	110	22					132 Refer to Author's Note

Note: In the original document this figure is given as £88 which shows that the clerk subtracted rather than added the two expenses incurred for materials and labour.

then put *Leviathan* in a precarious position, for having lashed his prize alongside the larboard side, all ability to manœuvre was jeopardised. Seeing this, *Intrépide* ranged across *Leviathan*'s head and raked her, then drew herself abreast and commenced firing into *Leviathan*'s starboard side. By good fortune *Orion* (74) and *Africa* (64) came up and, opening fire into the Frenchman, drove her off.[210] Referring to what next happened to *San Agustin*, *Leviathan*'s log continues,

> ... and towed her off. At 20 p[st.] 5 Ceased firing after which only a few shot had struck we fired from either side it appears that 20 sail of the line had Struck One b— and One sunk We had 4 men killed and 25 wounded - Masts and yards &c very much damaged at 4,20t [struck through in log] Employed knotting and Splicing the Rigging Shifting the sails &c took the Prize in tow Commenced with a Fresh on the Starb[d]. bow.

which was in fact *Intrépide*. The log then states 'Light breezes &c Cast off the Prize fitted another tiller the other shot away, one thrown overboard, employed knoting [sic] & spl[g.] The Riging [sic] As daylight emerged next day *Leviathan* 'took the Prize in tow p[st.] *Swiftsure* a Prize and several Hulks hauled on the Main sail & Reefd main Tp[s'.][211] Regarding casualties James states *Leviathan* had only 22 wounded, three less than Bayntun records. Among the wounded was Midshipman James Watson.[212] Also wounded was Seaman Thomas Main who, having had his arm taken clean off by a round shot, rejected help from his shipmates and made his own way to the cockpit where the surgeon successfully operated on his stump. Besides hull damage *Leviathan* was considerably injured aloft with several yards and mast lost or broke.[213]

After the action the ship confronted the storm, her log book entry Wednesday 23 October (Noon Tuesday to Noon Wednesday) stating that the seamen were 'bending Main Tp[s.] and fore staysail Miz[n.] staysail &c Splicing the Rigging & setting up', and when they; 'Handed the Tp[s.] [topsails]', to save the ship from disaster they were 'Oblig[d.] To Cut away the fore and main Course to save the masts'. For the next twelve hours they endured strong gales, squalls and heavy rain, during which they bent new sails, took in 3rd and 4th reefs on the topsails, continued repairs and sent 'Out Stream cable took Prize in tow'. After passing the *Prince of Wales* on the Thursday, at 4 a.m. they joined *Victory* and *Africa*, the 'Artificers [employed] as before caulking the sides where necessary', and blacking the rigging. It appears that Captain Bayntun was determined to restore *Leviathan* to some sense of order after battle, for the log records that seamen were over the ship's side 'painting the Stern & Quarters', and over the next few days they 'white and yellow washed the Inside of the ship'. Likewise the crew 'painted the guns & carriages on the Main deck', and 'White Washed the storerooms'. Although these men had been in battle, discipline still had to be maintained during this week. Bayntun 'Punished John Nelger with 24 lashes and John Green with 36 lashes for Insolence & Disobedience of Orders'.[214] Getting into Gibraltar the wounded were landed, including Thomas Main who unfortunately died of fever in hospital. Arriving at Plymouth 11 December Bayntun paid off *Leviathan* on 31 December.[215]

1806: *Leviathan* eventually went into dock on 20 June to have her copper repaired, and re-launched the same day, the overall cost being £318, after which she was laid up in the Hamoaze.

1807: Docked again at Plymouth 30 November, *Leviathan* underwent a 'small & middling' repair.[216]

1808: Launched 8 June, *Leviathan* completed her refit at a cost of £39,026 and was recommissioned under Captain Hon. Charles Paget on 14 June. After getting the ship in order, he was superseded by Captain John Harvey 11 July.[217] *Leviathan* then spent a short spell operating in the North Sea.

1809: Remaining under Harvey's command, *Leviathan* joined Vice-Admiral Collingwood's Mediterranean Fleet. Operating off the Catalonian coast in October, Collingwood received news that Rear-Admiral Baudin, flying his flag in *Robuste* (80), had sailed westwards from Toulon with two 74s, two 40 gun frigates and number of transports. Without compromising his own forces Collingwood despatched Rear - Admiral George Martin to intercept Baudin. Martin, flying his flag in *Canopus* (80), sailed ENE, with four 74 gun ships, *Leviathan* in company. In the early morning of 24 October the French squadron was sighted but due to shallow waters and an impeding lee shore, the British ships were unable to close for action. Despite this hazard the chase continued with the result that on 26 October Baudin's *Robuste* and her consort *Lion* (74) ran onshore near Frontignan and later blew up. The other French ships were compelled to get into Cette. *Leviathan* with the other ships, then rejoined Collingwood off Cape Sicié.[218] For the next few years *Leviathan* remained in the Mediterranean undertaking monotonous blockade duties.

1811: On 11 March of *Leviathan*'s command was succeeded by Captain Patrick Campbell, from *Unité* (40).

1812: During this year *Leviathan* was deployed in operations in the Gulf of Venice. Cruising off Fréjus on 12 April with *Undaunted* (38), Campbell made preparations to attack a privateer and several merchantmen lying in Agay Roads. Boats from *Leviathan* and *Undaunted*, commanded by Lieutenant Alexander Dobbs, made their way inshore and successfully captured four of the merchant vessels. Bringing out the privateer, however, proved difficult and two men were killed and four were wounded in trying to get her afloat.[219] *Leviathan* was involved in further action on 9 May. In company with *America* (74) and *Eclair* (18), the three ships drove a French convoy of 18 vessels inshore under the gun batteries of Laigueglia.

Determined to destroy the convoy and the batteries, a party of 250 marines from *Leviathan* and *America* were landed under two Royal Marine Captains John Owen and Henry Rea. In the attack one shot from shore sank one of *America*'s boats, drowning eleven men. Despite this setback the assault went well, Captain Owen taking out two gun batteries containing nine guns and a mortar. These guns were turned upon the defendants when *Eclair* moved close inshore and fired upon the town. While this action ensued, boats containing a large force of seamen commanded by Lieutenants Alexander Dobbs, Richard Hambly, Bourchier Molesworth, Robert Moodie, and William Richardson, moved inshore and brought out 16 craft, leaving just two behind, one of which was burnt. Excluding the eleven marines lost in the boat, casualties on this offensive comprised five killed and 20 wounded.[220] Operating off Laigueglia and Alassio again in June, *Leviathan*, in company with *Impérieuse* (38), *Curaçao* (36) and *Eclair* (18), fell in with a French convoy of 18 vessels. Boats from the British squadron made their attack during which nine men were killed and 31 wounded. Although they failed to capture the vessels, they destroyed them by gunfire.[221]

With the Adriatic campaign at an end *Leviathan* was recalled for refit, getting into Portsmouth 4 August. Docked on the 26th to have her copper replaced she was re-launched a month later.[222] On 11 October *Leviathan* was recommissioned under Captain Adam Drummond and on 1 November left Plymouth to lay up in Torbay.

1814: Ordered to join the West Indies squadron, *Leviathan* sailed for her new deployment on 6 January. While on this station command of the ship was superseded by Captain Thomas Briggs on 16 October.

1815: Returning to home waters, *Leviathan* was periodically deployed with the Channel fleet cruising with convoys off Lisbon.

FATE

No longer required for service, *Leviathan* went into Portsmouth 2 July 1816. Paid off by Captain Briggs on 19 July she was laid up in ordinary, joining the many other vessels lying at their moorings within the inner harbour.[223] Although Colledge wrongly states that *Leviathan* was hulked at Chatham, she was in fact, as Lyon agrees, docked at Portsmouth on 16 October 1816 and 'Fitted for a Convict Hulk'. In 1846, after having part of her copper removed she was temporarily scuttled and used as a target ship. Having fulfilled this final service *Leviathan* was 'Sold 7th August 1848 to Mr Burns for £805' and broken up for her timber.[224]

The 74 gun ship MARS

Named after the red planet and the Roman god of war, the *Mars* that fought at Trafalgar was the fifth ship in the Royal Navy to bear this name. The first *Mars*, a 50 gun ship captured from the Dutch in 1665, was sold in 1667. The second *Mars*, a French vessel of 64 guns captured off Cape Clear by *Nottingham* October 1746, grounded and went to pieces when going into Halifax in June 1755.[225] The third *Mars*, launched 15 March 1759, was a 74 gun ship of the Culloden class designed by Joseph Ackworth in 1744. During the Seven Years' War this vessel fought with Hawke at Quiberon Bay 20 November 1759 and also formed part of the expedition led by Keppel to capture Belle Isle in 1761.[226] This vessel remained in service during the American War of Independence until hulked in 1778. Like the first listed, the fourth *Mars* was captured from the Dutch. Taken at the fall of the island of St Eustatius in the West Indies, this 74 gun ship was originally launched at Amsterdam in 1769. No longer required for service this ship was sold in 1784. There was also a Dutch prize called *Mars* taken in the Texel in 1799, a two decked ship 4th rate of 44 guns built at Haarlem. Renamed *Vlieter*, this vessel was cut down and converted to a floating battery. The other vessel was the French privateer *Mars* of 24 guns captured in 1799 and renamed *Garland*.[227]

Designed by John Henslow, the Trafalgar *Mars* appears to be the only ship built to these lines, the only vessel having similar lines being *Conqueror*. Ordered 17 January 1788, the keel of *Mars* was laid down at Deptford 10 October 1789 under the supervision of Master Shipwright Martin Ware. Launched 25 October 1794, her initial building costs totalled £50,270, of which £43,540 was expended for her for hull and masts and £6,730 was spent on rigging and stores. Like other ships building at this time, her long period under construction reflects a low level of manpower while Britain was not at war. In all about 3,250 loads of timber from Kent, the equivalent of 160,000 cubic feet of timber, was used in her construction. Carrying 74 guns comprising twenty-eight 32 pounders, thirty 24 pounders and sixteen 9 pounders, *Mars* could deliver a single broadside weight of 904 pounds.

SERVICE HISTORY

1794: Once launched *Mars* was transported to Woolwich dockyard on 8 November where two days later she was docked to be fitted with copper sheathing. Completed and launched 15 days later this work was done at a cost of £2,843 with a further £356 spent on rigging and stores.[228] Fitted out *Mars* was first commissioned 28 November under the command of Captain Sir Charles Cotton.[229]

1795: Fitted out and provisioned, *Mars* sailed from Woolwich on 13 April for Portsmouth to commence her deployment with the Channel Fleet. Leaving Spithead 30 May with Vice-Admiral Cornwallis' squadron, *Mars* took up station off Ushant. While cruising off Penmarck on 8 June, the British ships were chased by a French squadron under the flag of Rear-Admiral Jean Gasper Vence, who was returning to Brest from the West Indies. During this pursuit *Mars* and the other ships had to fight a rearguard action. News that Vence was unable to get into Brest prompted Vice-

SPECIFICATIONS: *MARS*

Rate	3rd	Date launched	25 October 1794	Complement	640
Guns	74	Length on the range of the gun deck	176 ft	Ordnance - lower gun deck	28 x 32 pounders
Class	Mars 1788	Length of keel for tonnage	144 ft 3 ins	Ordnance - upper gun deck	30 x 24 pounders
Designer	John Henslow	Extreme breadth	49 ft	Ordnance - quarter deck	12 x 9 pounders
Builder	Martin Ware	Depth in hold	20 ft	Ordnance - forecastle	4 x 9 pounders
Dockyard	Deptford	Tons burthen	1842 24/94	Single broadside weight	904 pounds
Date ordered	17 January 1788	Draught afore	23 ft 10 ins	Fate	1814 Hulked as a receiving ship at Portsmouth
Date keel laid	10 October 1789	Draught abaft	24 ft 6 ins		

Source: Lyon, *Sailing Navy List*, p. 109.

CAPTAINS OF *MARS* (MSS 248/4 and 248/6)

Name	Time of Entry	Time of Discharge	On What Occasion
Sir Charles Cotton	28 November 1794	21 February 1797	Promoted Rear Admiral of the Blue
Alexander Hood	22 February 1797	21 April 1798	Killed in Action with *Hercule*
George James Shirley	22 April 1798	7 June 1798	Superseded Acting
John Manley	8 June 1798	13 July 1799	Superseded
James Bowen	14 July 1799	24 January 1801	Superseded
Robert Lloyd	25 January 1801	17 April 1802	Paid Off at Plymouth
John Sutton	14 February 1803	31 December 1803	New Book
John Sutton	1 January 1804	8 May 1804	Promoted to Rear Admiral of the Blue
James Pym	9 May 1804	6 June 1804	Superseded
George Duff	6 June 1804	21 October 1805	Killed in Action off Trafalgar
Robert Dundas Oliver	5 November 1805	18 September 1806	Superseded
William Lukin	19 September 1806	3 September 1810	Superseded - lent 11 July 1810
James Katan	5 February 1809	4 February 1810	Superseded Acting
John S Carden	11 July 1810	17 January 1811	Superseded
Henry Raper	18 January 1811	25 February 1813	Paid Off at Portsmouth

Admiral Villaret-Joyeuse to put to sea on 12 June, sighting Cornwallis near Penmarck 16 June. Outnumbered, Cornwallis ordered his squadron comprising his flagship *Royal Sovereign* (100), and 74s *Brunswick*, *Bellerophon*, *Triumph* and *Mars* to form line ahead. The chase continued into the next day when the leading French 74 gun ship and the 40 gun frigate *Virginie* closed with *Mars* and opened fire, *Mars* retaliating the best she could. At noon all the British ships were engaged. Firing their stern and quarter guns, their fire brought down the fore topgallant mast of the lead Frenchman, compelling her to fall off. The chase continued for a further three hours when *Mars* fell off to leeward, having suffered much damage aloft. Realising that *Mars* might fall prey to the French, Cornwallis bore up and drove *Royal Sovereign* down upon the French ships, *Triumph* following in her wake. This unexpected action forced Villaret to withdraw.[230]

1797: On 22 February *Mars*'s command was superseded by Captain Alexander Hood, her previous commander Sir Charles Cotton Bt being promoted Rear Admiral of the Blue.[231] During this year the *Mars* was involved in the great mutiny that broke out 15 April at Spithead. She was one of the few ships which continued to have grievances after settlements had been made by the Admiralty.[232]

1798: Now under the command of Captain Alexander Hood, *Mars* sailed from St Helens for Ushant on 12 April with Lord Bridport's Channel squadron. Sighting two French sail off Iroise 21 April, Bridport ordered *Mars* and *Ramillies* (74) in pursuit. Losing her fore topmast at 6.20 p.m. *Ramillies* was obliged to fall off, leaving *Mars* to continue alone. In their attempt to escape, the two French ships entered the Pas du Raz but finding the current against them were compelled to anchor. The larger vessel, *Hercule* (74), Captain Louis L'Heretier, laid out springs to manœuvre his ship before *Mars* approached. At 9.15 p.m. the two ships engaged but Hood, finding the tide making it difficult to effect manœuvres, anchored further upstream and paying out the cable, dropped astern to bring his ship alongside *Hercule*. Twenty minutes after the two ships engaged broadsides Captain Hood was hit by a ball in the femoral artery and carried below. Fierce fighting continued until the Frenchman struck his colours at about 10.40 p.m. Hood died of his wound shortly afterwards. Both vessels suffered much damage to their hulls, French losses were 290 killed and wounded. Casualties on *Mars* were 30 killed and 60 wounded. Besides Hood, those killed included Joseph White, Captain of Marines, and Midshipman James Blythe. Amoung the wounded were Lieutenants George Aigles and George Ford and Midshipman Thomas Southey. Command of the ship temporarily passed to William Butterfield, First Lieutenant.[233] *Mars* went into Plymouth on 29 April where formal command was succeeded by Captain George James Shirley, formally appointed on 22 April. Shirley's post was short, however, for after the ship left Plymouth on 2 June he was superseded acting on 8 June by Captain John Manley. On 11 December, when *Mars* had returned and was lying in Cawsand Bay, the ships of the squadron were ordered to man the ship's side to witness a man being flogged around the fleet. As the launch with its prisoner passed by *Mars* the press of men at the ship's side caused her waist rail to give way resulting in 200 seamen being pitched overboard. Although none were drowned many suffered broken limbs.[234]

1799: Carrying the flag of Rear-Admiral the Hon. George Berkeley, *Mars* with the 74 gun ships *Ajax*, *Ramillies*, *Renown*, *Robust* and *Venerable* was deployed blockading Rochefort. Berkeley was joined by ships *Royal George* (100) and *Sans Pareil* (80); in June *Mars* and *Ramillies* parted company for Basque Roads.[235] On 14 July 1799 Captain James Bowen assumed command and remained in the ship until 1802.[236] *Mars* returned to Plymouth on 17 July and went into dock on 2 August to have her copper repaired. Launched five days later *Mars* sailed for duty again on 9 September.[237]

1801: *Mars* returned to Plymouth again on 21 April and went into dock one week later. While in dock her copper sheathing was completely taken off and replaced with new at a cost of £2,784. Launched again on 12 May, the ship sailed on 26 May for a short deployment.[238]

1802: On 25 January command of *Mars* was succeeded by Captain Robert Lloyd Bowen but as the war had virtually ended *Mars* went back into Plymouth on 10 April where, exactly one week later, Bowen paid off the ship.[239] Needing some minor repair work to her copper *Mars* was taken into dock on 17 July and re-launched on 13 August. Taken into dock again at Plymouth on 2 September *Mars* commenced undergoing a 'Middling Repair' of which no costs are recorded in the Progress Book. Completed, the ship was undocked on 10 December.[240]

1803: With resumption of war with France imminent *Mars* was recommissioned under Captain John Sutton 14 February and having taken on stores

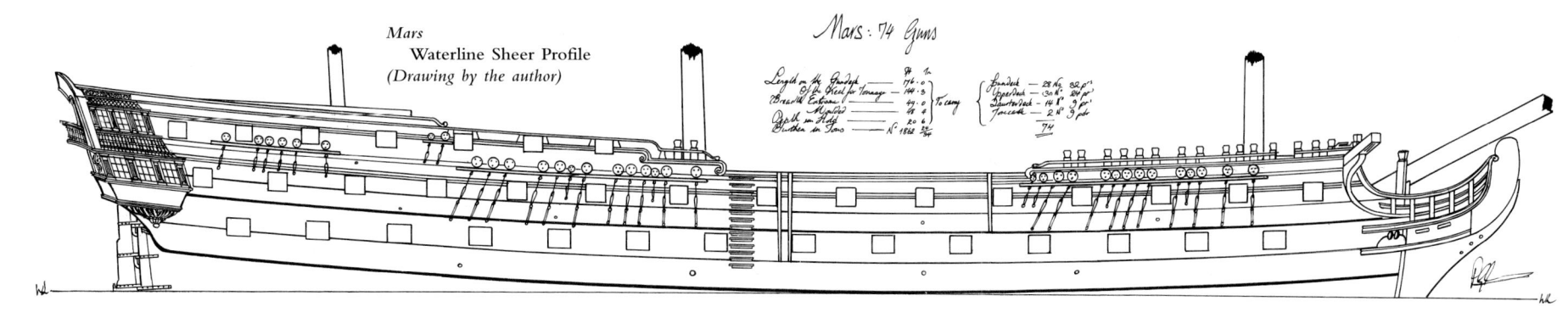

Mars
Waterline Sheer Profile
(Drawing by the author)

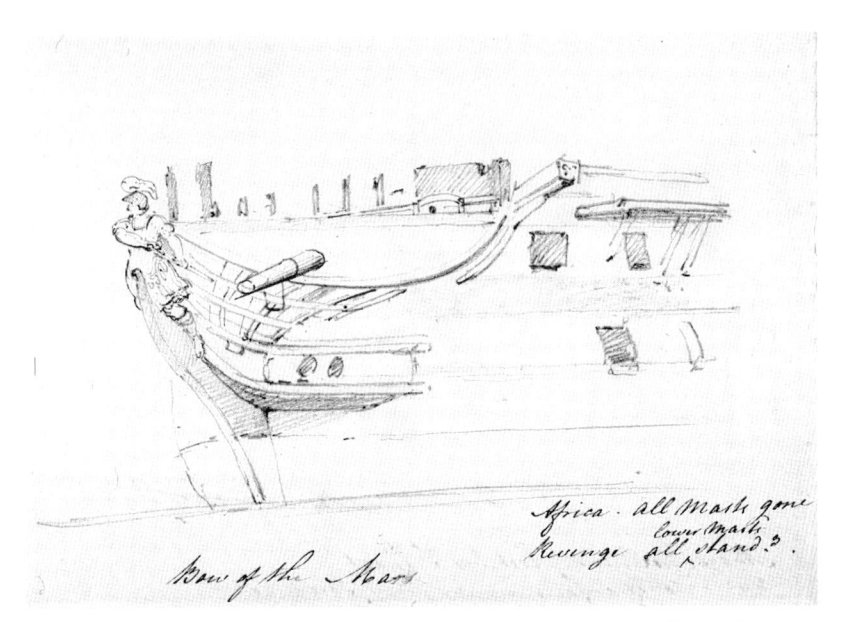

Mars. Sketch by Livesay of the bow, undated. Original caption says '*Africa* - all masts gone, *Revenge* - all lower masts standg.' (*Courtesy of the Royal Naval Museum*)

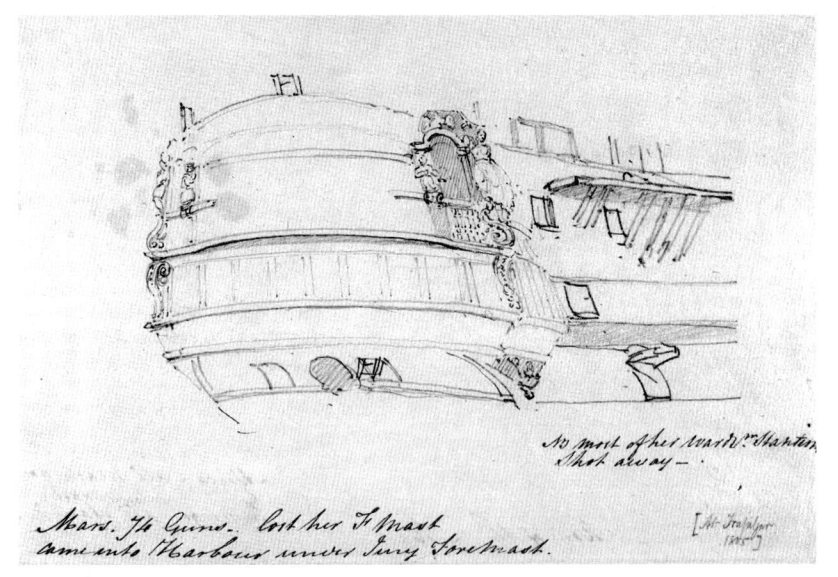

Mars. Sketch by Livesay of the stern, undated. Original caption says '*Mars*, 74 guns, lost her F. Mast, came into harbour under jury foremast. [?] most of her wardroom stantion [?] shot away.' (*Courtesy of the Royal Naval Museum*)

and provisions, sailed from the Hamoaze 23 April.

1804: When John Sutton was promoted to Rear-Admiral of the Blue on 8 May command of the ship was succeeded by Captain James Pym on 9 May. However one month later Pym was superseded by Captain George Duff on 6 June.[241] Going into Plymouth 22 August and docked 4 September, *Mars* was refitted to make good defects and be re-coppered. Launched again four days later *Mars* sailed on 5 October to join the British squadron operating off the Iberian coast.[242]

1805: On the night of 20 August *Mars* sailed from Tangier to join Vice-Admiral Collingwood.[243]

TRAFALGAR

Preceding the battle *Mars* was stationed a little distant from the main body of Nelson's fleet forming a communication link with Blackwood's inshore squadron of frigates. Writing in his journal Saturday 19 October Duff recorded that winds were SEbS, the ship bearing SSE later changing North. He then wrote the following remarks:

PM Light breezes and Clear W[r]. At 4.11 Made *Colossus* Signal N[o]. 6, At 5.30 took in 2nd reef of the topsails, at 6 Calm and Clear W[r]. At 6.20 made *Colossus* Signal N[o]. 154 Compass Signal At 9:35 *Colossus* made Signal to *Mars* N[o]. 370 Repeated D[o]. to the *Victory* out reefs and set the Royals found 2 of the main T.G. Shrouds carried away got the Preventer ones up At noon Calm and Clear Fleet West *Colossus* SbE.[244]

With the combined fleet now at sea, *Mars*'s log on Sunday records that Cadiz bore N36E 20 miles and that her crew were: 'Employed making the Ship perfectly Clear for Action…Fleet with all sail set in Chase at 4.30 *Victory* Signal N[o]. 252'. Later the log states; 'At 8.50 *Victory* made *Mars Colossus* and *Defence* Signals for a Cap[tn]. At 10.30 *Victorys* Signal Gen[l]. N[o]. 72, At noon D[o]. W[r]. *Victory* WbS 6 Miles'. Commencing at noon Sunday the log records the following:

Cape Trafalgar ESE 4 or 5 Miles: PM Strong breezes and Squally with rain, At 4.10 out 3 & 4 reefs of the Topsails Enemies Fleet North Frigates & Ships on the lookout in Shore making Signal of the Enemys fleet being in Sight, At day light saw the Enemys Fleet on our lee beam the Wind being light the Com[der]. in Chief At 6.9 made Gen[l]. Signal N[o]. 72 At 6.14 D[o]. N[o]. 76 with Compass Signal ENE Fleet Formed the order of Sailing in 2 Coloms [*sic*] the Van led by the *Victory* Vice Adm[l]. Lord Nelson and the Rear led by the *Royal Sovereign* under Command of Vice Adm[l]. C. Collingwood and bore up in order to Attack the Enemy At 9.05 Ans[d]. Sig[l]. from the *Victory* for the *Mars* to lead the lee line.

This statement appears to imply that *Mars* was in fact meant to lead Collingwood's leeward division into battle. However, from all accounts *Mars* took up her station astern of the *Belleisle* (74) as the third ship in Collingwood's line of battle. The log of *Mars* continues, 'At 11.45 the Enemy opened a very heavy fire on the *Royal Sovereign*, *Belleisle Mars* and *Tonnant* which was not Returned by us untill [*sic*] we arrived close alongside their Ships At moderate & hazy the *Royal Sovereign Belleisle Mars* & *Tonnant* Warmly Engaged with Enemys lee Division'.[245]

Entering the action at about 12.20 p.m., *Mars* immediately engaged with *Fougueux* (74) which had already run aboard *Belleisle*. Pouring her broadsides into the Frenchman, Duff forced *Fougueux* to disengage and fall off astern.[246] Ten minutes later *Mars* came under fire from *Pluton* (74), which directed her broadsides into the starboard bow, at the same time *Monarco* (74) fired her larboard battery into the starboard broadside of Duff's ship. Countering this attack, Duff immediately ordered his helmsman to turn the ship into the wind to concentrate his starboard guns to bear on *Pluton*. Unfortunately this manœuvre exposed the stern of *Mars* to greater fire from *Algéciras* (74) and *Monarco* (74), their broadsides taking down her rigging. Badly mauled, Duff was obliged to pay off, again bringing *Mars* under heavy fire from *Fougueux* and *Pluton*. The effect, according to Midshipman Robinson, was that 'in a few minutes our poop was totally cleared, the quarter-deck and foc's'le nearly the same, and only the Boatswain and myself and three men left alive'.[247] Unable to manœuvre while intense broadsides pounded into the ship, their deadly fusillade of round shot decapitated Captain Duff while he stood giving orders at the break of the quarter deck, the same ball cutting down two nearby seamen. Written in the hand of William Hennah who, as the First Lieutenant of the *Mars*, assumed command on Captain Duff's death, the log states 'At 1.15 Captain Duff was killed & the poop & Quarterdeck was nearly cleard of officers & Men & all were running rigging shot away, in that the Ship was entirely unserviceable & was frequently raked by the Enemys Ships'.[248] Midshipman Robinson wrote later that when the ship's company heard of their Captain's death, 'they held his body up and gave three cheers to show that they were not discouraged by it, and then returned to their guns'.[249]

With William Hennah now in command of *Mars*, Lieutenant Benjamin

Patey succeeded to the position of First Lieutenant.[250] Further broadsides poured into the ship's quarter beating in her stern and rudder head, overturning guns, bringing down the main topmast an the mizzen boom, and the fore mast was so severely riddled it was ready to go over the side. It was only at about 1 p.m. when *Tonnant* bore down on *Pluton*, that *Mars* was reprieved from further carnage. Shortly after 2 p.m. Villeneuve capitulated his flagship *Bucentaure* to *Conqueror*. The officer sent to receive her surrender, James Atcherley, Captain of Marines, took the French admiral and his two captains to his ship but in the confusion of battle he inadvertently lay his boat alongside *Mars*.[251] Bringing Villeneuve on board, the log of *Mars* simply records: 'At 4 the French Commander in Chief came on Board from the *Bucentaure* with his retinue'.[252] Described by Midshipman Robinson, Villeneuve was a 'thinnish, tall man, a very tranquil, placid English-looking Frenchman; he wore a long-tailed uniform coat, high and flat collar, corduroy pantalons of a greenish colour, with stripes two inches wide, half boots with sharp toes, and a watch-chain with long links'.[253] Villeneuve remained on Duff's ship for the duration of the battle. The final part of the log entry that day reads,

> At 5.30 the firing ceased Emp[d.] splicing & knotting The Rigging All our masts badly wounded & no sails fit to sett so much disabled employed getting Prizes & our own dismasted ships in tow At 8 Cape Trafalgar ESE 4 Leagues at 12 L[t.] Breezes & cloudy W[r.] at 2 worw at 9 mustered Ship's Company & found we had 27 killed & 71 wounded at 10 Strong Gales & heavy Rain Employed about the rigging – At Noon Ditto Weather.

The log is then signed; 'George Duff Captain, Killed as above, W[m.] Hennah Commanding Officer.[254]

Casualties were high; Captain Duff's son Alexander, who was serving as a Master's Mate, died in his younger brother's arms. Thomas Norman, Captain of Marines, also fell, together with Midshipmen Edward Corbyn and Henry Morgan, 17 seamen, and eight marines. These figures, taken from Clowes, differ from those of the ship's log. Clowes also states that there were 69 wounded including Lieutenants Edward Garret and James Black, Mr Thomas Cook the ship's Master, midshipmen William Cook, George Guerin, John Jenkins, Alfred Luckcroft and John Young, 44 seamen and 16 marines; the log however records 71 wounded.[255] Having assumed command Lieutenant Hennah was quick to ensure that the general orders of the ship remained as authorised by Duff, his memorandum as follows:[256]

October 21st 1805
General Order   at 5 o'clock of the afternoon
The Officers, Non-Commissioned Officers and Ship's Company of His Majestys Ship *Mars* will consider the Orders of their late Captain Duff in full force in particular, relative to their particular Duties as they were previous to his Death.

W[m.] Hennah, 1st Lieut.
To the Officers &c. &c. of
His Majestys Ship *Mars*

Reaching Gibraltar, command of *Mars* was succeeded by Captain Robert Dundas Oliver who brought her back into Portsmouth 8 December. According to the log of *Revenge*, *Mars* eventually reached home and anchored at Spithead Tuesday 3 December, *Africa* arriving just a few hours later.[257] Having discharged her gunpowder and other stores, *Mars* entered Portsmouth Harbour on 8 December to effect minor repairs.[258] On 18 December Captain Robert Dudley Oliver, her temporary commander, was superseded by Captain William Lukin.[259]

1806: Her copper needing repair, *Mars* went into dock for four days on 6 February and had her defects made good at a cost of £318. After re-provisioning she sailed from the dockyard 2 March to join Captain John Goodwin Keat's squadron blockading Rochefort.[260] While deployed inshore observing this port on 27 July, *Mars* sighted four French frigates, *Hortense*, *Hermione* and *Rhin*, each of 40 guns, and *Thémis* (36) making for Rochefort from the West Indies. Immediately giving chase, *Mars* closed in upon *Rhin*. The other three frigates tacked and formed line ahead to come down to defend their counterpart but heedful of *Mars*'s firepower made extra sail and hauled off. Abandoned, *Rhin* was soon overhauled and struck her colours 'pour l'honeur du pavillon' after the first broadside.[261] [The log transcript of *Mars* describing this action and the capture of *Rhin* is given in Part 2 Chapter 3.]

Still blockading Rochefort in September, the blockading squadron was now commanded by Commodore Sir Samuel Hood. The ships in company were *Windsor Castle* (98), the 74s *Achille*, *Centaur*, *Monarch*, *Revenge*, and the 16 gun brig *Atalante*. On 24 September a French squadron commanded by Commodore E Soleil, was sighted making for open sea from Rochefort. The French flotilla comprised four 40 gun frigates, *Armide*, *Gloire*, *Indefatigable* and *Minerve*, the 36 gun *Thétis*, and two corvettes, *Lynx* and *Sylph*. Hood gave the signal to chase; *Mars*, with *Centaur* and *Monarch*, took the lead, finally closing with the French at about 5 a.m. the next morning. All four French ships were captured, *Mars* forcing *Indefatigable* to strike her colours at 3 p.m. British casualties comprised nine killed and 29 wounded, Hood himself losing his arm.[262] Afterwards *Mars* returned to Plymouth 6 October to have her copper sheathing repaired and sailed back on duty 6 November.[263]

1807: On 27 July *Mars* sailed from Yarmouth Roads to rendezvous with Admiral James Gambier's fleet that had sailed for Copenhagen. Captain William Lukin commanded the ship. The objective of this expedition was to break the Northern Coalition and destroy the Danish fleet and its arsenal to deprive Napoleon of their use for possible invasion. Gambier, flying his flag in *Prince of Wales* (98), was accompanied by eighteen 74 gun ships including the Trafalgar veterans *Defiance*, *Minotaur*, and *Orion*, together with *Agamemnon* (64). *Mars* joined Gambier on 8 August.[264] Going into Portsmouth 23 December, the ship docked on 4 January to have her copper replaced.

1808: Undocked 28 January and sailing 16 February, still under the command of William Lukin, *Mars* was deployed with the large fleet being assembled for an expedition into the Baltic. Commanded by Vice-Admiral Sir James Saumarez flying his flag in *Victory* (98), the fleet comprised nine 74s, including *Mars* and *Orion*, two 64s, one being *Africa*. five frigates, many bomb vessels, brigs, and fireships, and 200 transports. The object of this force was to protect Sweden from the Northern Coalition of Denmark, Russia and France. Although Gambier had destroyed the Danish fleet the previous year, a threat still came from the Russian fleet that was numerically greater than that of Gustavus VI. During this deployment *Mars* briefly served as flagship to Rear-Admiral John Goodwin Keats. On 30 August *Mars*, with *Victory*, *Goliath* and *Africa*, joined the detached squadron blockading Rogervik. It was planned to send in fireships to destroy the Russian ships lying within the port. However, the defences proved quite impregnable. As the harbour was protected by a heavy boom, the attack was reluctantly aborted.[265]

1809/10: On 5 February 1809 command of the ship was temporarily given to Captain James Katan in an acting capacity until February 1810. The ship now went into Portsmouth and docked 27 February to have her copper repaired. When Captain Lukin was formally lent out of the ship on 11 July 1810 command of *Mars* passed to Captain John Carden.

1811-1814: On 18 January 1811 Captain Henry Raper took command and the ship did little service other than mundane convoy duties while deployed with the Channel fleet. Entering Portsmouth for the last time 31 December 1812, Captain Raper paid off *Mars* on 25 February 1813.

now formed part of Vice-Admiral Lord Keith's squadron blockading Genoa, Keith initially flying his flag in *Audacious* (74). When the 1st rate *Queen Charlotte* (100) accidentally caught fire and blew up off Leghorn on 16 March 1800,[277] Lord Keith shifted his flag into *Minotaur*. During the first three weeks of May Keith's squadron, augmented by frigates, sloops, and a number of Neapolitan gun brigs and mortar boats, lay off Genoa bombarding the city, while Austrian troops attacked the town from landward. In the early hours of 21 May boats from *Minotaur*, commanded by Captain Beaver of *Aurora* (28), went in and stormed *Prima* galley which lay off the mole defending the harbour. Once captured *Prima* was taken in tow. Although the boat's crew came under fire from enemy troops and five seamen were wounded, just after daylight *Prima* was brought to under the stern of the *Minotaur*.[278]

In September *Minotaur* was deployed off Barcelona. On the 3rd, boats from *Minotaur* and the armed flute *Niger*, previously a 12 pounder 32 gun frigate, were sent in to capture two Spanish armed vessels anchored in Barcelona Roads. The expedition, comprising eight boats manned and armed, was commanded by Captain James Hillyer. Also included were Lieutenants Charles Schomberg, Thomas Warrand, Midshipmen James Lowry and Richard Haly, and Lieutenant of Marines, John Jewell. The Spanish ships to be attacked were *Concepción* (formerly the British *Esmerelda*) and *Paz*, each of which carried 22 long 12 pounders, 8 pounders and a quantity of stores. Moving SW, the boats cunningly made for a galliot entering the harbour and having got alongside the entry port and secured a line to the unsuspecting vessel, the boats were towed three-quarters of a mile into the harbour at which point the tow was released. At about 9 p.m. *Concepción* opened fire on the British boats, the shot falling short, but before they could reload the boats lay alongside and carried the prize. Cheers of elation unfortunately provoked *Paz* which cut her cable to run into harbour while the alerted batteries on the mole opened fire. By 11 p.m. *Concepción* and the boats were well clear of the port, but casualties had been sustained. Losses amounted to two seamen and one marine, the wounded comprised Mr Read, the Master of *Minotaur* and 4 seamen. On inspection the prize was found to be carrying some 400 stores bound for Batavia.[279]

1801: Still with Lord Keith's Mediterranean fleet, *Minotaur* sailed from Gibraltar with the intention of invading Egypt. Keith was now flying his flag in *Foudroyant* (80), Captain Philip Beaver. In company with these two ships were *Kent*, Captain William Hope, flying the flag of Rear-Admiral Sir Robert Bickerton Bt, *Ajax*, Captain the Hon. Alexander Cochrane, *Northumberland*, Captain George Martin, *Tigre*, Captain Sir William Sydney Smith, and *Swiftsure*, another Trafalgar ship commanded by Captain Benjamin Hallowell. Also many transports carried a large military force commanded by General Sir Ralph Abercromby. En route the fleet called in at Minorca and Malta before rendezvousing with the Turkish fleet on 31 January 1801 at Marmorice off the coast of Karamania, Asia Minor. The combined Anglo-Turkish fleet, now numbering 70 ships with 16,000 troops, weighed and sailed for Alexandria on 1 February, arriving at Abu-Kir Bay the following day. As soon as the ships anchored boats were lowered and the troops disembarked and landed on shore.[280]

1802: When *Minotaur* arrived back at Chatham 6 February, Captain Louis paid the off the ship on 3 March and two days later she was docked for a 'Small Repair' and to have her bottom recoppered. Undocked 2 July she was laid up in the Medway.[281]

1803: On 11 March *Minotaur* was recommissioned under Captain Charles Mansfield and prepared for sea service. She then proceeded to the Nore to await further orders regarding her deployment with the Channel fleet.[282]

1805: Still under the command of Captain Mansfield *Minotaur* went into Plymouth 21 January and was docked 2 February to have her copper repaired. Coming out of dock the following day the ship sailed for duty 25 February.[283] In March *Minotaur*, under authority from the Admiralty, was detached from Cornwallis's Channel fleet to form a new squadron commanded by Vice-Admiral Collingwood. This independent flotilla, including *Dreadnought* (98), *Tonnant* (80), *Illustrious* (74), and *Mars* (74), was deployed south to watch over the Spanish ports of Ferrol and Cadiz.[284] Before the fleet was assembled off Cadiz *Minotaur* and *Bellerophon* were recalled from their station off Cartagena.[285] Off Cadiz on Friday 11 October *Minotaur*'s log records that *Belleisle* joined them and that she 'Recovered Provisions' from a transport; also noted is that '*Amphion* detained a neutral Ship'. Over the next few days references are made to the sailmakers repairing the mizzen staysail, on the Sunday the ship's company were mustered by divisions and on Wednesday 16 October they 'Exercised the Great Guns & small arms'.[286]

TRAFALGAR

Captain Mansfield kept his ship's journal entries very brief, so his remarks for the morning of Monday 21 October simply state: 'D°· weather, saw the Combined fleets East, at noon light breezes Enemy in a Line of battle from NE to SE 33 sail of the Line'.[287] By 8 a.m. the morning of the 21st Captain Mansfield had cleared *Minotaur* for action. Though brief in his records, Mansfield appears an orator; assembling his ship's company on the quarter deck he gave them a rousing speech:

> Men we are now in the sight of the enemy whom there is every probability of engaging and I trust this day, or tomorrow, will prove the most glorious our country ever saw.

Raising his hand to stifle his seamen's cheers, he continued:

> I shall say nothing to you of courage: our country never produced a coward. For my own part I pledge myself to the officers and ship's company not to quit the ship I may get alongside of till either she strikes or sinks, or I sink. I have only to recommend silence and strict attention to the order of your officers. Be careful to take good aim, for it is to no purpose to throw shot away. You will now, every man, repair to your respective stations, and depend, I will bring the ship into action as soon as possible. God save the King.

After the 'Minotaurs' gave tumultuous cheers, the ship's company disbanded as they were beat to quarters.[288] Mansfield's description of the battle for Tuesday 22 October is as follows:

> Light breezes & Airs at 18 min. past 12 the action began on the Enemys centre the *Royal Sovereign* in close Battle at 1 — of the Enemys Ship on fire Ships on Both sides engaging as they came near Several of the Enemys Ships dismasted 15 min past 1 the Spanish Admirals Ship a Compleat [sic] Wreck ? past 2 Action became general a number of Ships dismasted passed four French and 1 Spanish Ship and brought the Spaniard to action she struck at, at 55 min. past 5 one of the Enemys Ships blew up the Remainder that were not dismasted making for Port AM fresh breezes, bore down to take the Prize in tow, 3 dismasted Ships in Sight - Enemys Ships not in Sight.[289]

Placed eleventh in line of Nelson's windward division, it was about 3.10 p.m. before *Minotaur* hauled herself onto a larboard tack and got into battle and, with support from the *Spartiate* (74), engaged the French ships *Formidable*, *Duguay Trouin*, *Mont Blanc* and *Scipion*, all 74s. These ships, which formed part of Admiral Dumanoir's isolated division, were now attempting to turn and give support to the main body of the combined fleet. Passing to windward they tried to cut off the rear ships of Nelson's division. As *Formidable* bore down *Minotaur* poured her larboard broadside into her bow, reloaded and fired a second volley into the head of *Duguay Trouin*. At 4 p.m. *Minotaur* and *Spartiate* wore and came alongside to engage the Spanish *Neptuno* (80). Using her starboard batteries *Minotaur* vigorously exchanged broadsides with the Spaniard for the next hour. At 5.10 p.m. *Neptuno*, having lost her mizzen mast, main and fore topmasts, together with high casualties, struck her colours. Simultaneously *Minotaur* and *Spartiate* fired their larboard guns into the French *Intrépide*, which being severely mauled by *Orion*, now lay dismasted. In the engagement *Minotaur* suffered much damage to her rigging and had lost her fore topsail yard. Her casualties amounted to three seamen killed and 22 wounded; of the latter were her Boatswain James Robinson, Midshipman John Smith, 17 seamen and three marines.[290]

In the aftermath *Minotaur*'s log says little; references are made on 23 October about Spanish ships coming out of Cadiz to assist the disabled ships to get into port and general work repairing rigging and other damage. The log does, however, indicate how the other British ships were dealing with the foul weather. Sunday 27 October it records that they 'saw the *Royal Sovereign* at anchor', and next day, 'saw the *Téméraire* at Anchor off the mouth of the Seville River lower masts standing'. As for *Minotaur*'s own damage the log entry Tuesday 29 October states: 'drying sails, disabled Ships at Anchor, found the Knee of the Head opening from the Stem'. An entire section of the ship beyond the stem post, that is, the figure, beak deck, head rails, crew's seats of ease and boomkins were in such a precarious condition that they could fall away leaving her beakhead bulkhead, generally of weak structure, entirely exposed to head seas. Next day the log records one French prize ship blowing up and on Friday 1 November *Minotaur* joined *Britannia*, *Dreadnought*, *Neptune*, *Queen* and *Euryalus* to get into Gibraltar.[291] Less damaged than most ships, *Minotaur* did not return immediately to England.

1806: Recalled home *Minotaur* arrived at Chatham 27 November and went into dock 28 December to be re-coppered and her defects made good.

1807: Coming out of the dock 22 February *Minotaur*, still commanded by Captain Mansfield but now flying the flag of Rear-Admiral William Essington, sailed on the 20 March to join the large fleet being assembled at Yarmouth under Admiral James Gambier. The invasion of Denmark by Napoleon's forces immediately posed a threat to Britain inasmuch that the Danish fleet and its arsenal based at Copenhagen could be used by the French to support an invasion of Britain. Drastic measures were immediately put in motion to remove this potential hazard, the purpose of which was to capture or destroy all the Danish warships at Copenhagen. Gambier, flying his flag in the *Prince of Wales* (98), had with him thirteen 74s, which included *Orion*, three 64s, twenty-one frigates, sloops, bomb ships and gun vessels, sailed for the Baltic on 25 July. Arriving in the Sound on 7 August *Minotaur* was soon joined by *Mars* (74) (see chapter 3), *Valiant* (74), *Agamemnon* (64) (see chapter 4), *Leyden* (64), and *Inflexible* (64). In all the British fleet now comprised 25 sail of the line, 40 frigates, sloops, bombs and gun vessels, and 377 transports amounting to 78,420 tons of shipping. On board the transports were 27,000 troops, over half of whom were German. The supreme military commander was Lieutenant-General Lord Cathcart.

The Danish sea-borne defences comprised the 64 gun blockship *Mars*, the 22 gun pram *St Thomas*, 3 prams of 20 guns, 2 floating batteries and 30 gunboats mounting two guns each. Within the Danish arsenal lay 16 sail of the line, 21 frigates and sloops and three 74 guns ships on the stocks in various stages of construction. At 5 p.m. on 15 August the entire British fleet, *Minotaur* included, weighed and sailed for Wedbeck village which lay midway between Elsinore and Copenhagen. While most of the fleet anchored in the bay to land Cathcart and his troops during the morning of 16 August, *Minotaur* with the rest of Essington's flotilla proceeded to another anchorage farther up the Sound. As soon as the landings were executed, the fleet weighed and sailed for Copenhagen. On their arrival, a despatch calling for the Crown Prince to surrender was sent on shore under a flag of truce. This offer being rejected various skirmishes were carried out over the next two weeks against Danish land and sea defences in which *Minotaur* did not participate. By the 2 September all gun and mortar batteries installed by Cathcart's forces were in place. Then Admiral Gambier sent a proclamation to Major-General Peimann, the Danish commander, to surrender the Danish ships over to the British for the duration of the war. Following a second refusal the British fleet opened up a bombardment resulting in setting the city aflame. This bombardment, much augmented by the bomb vessels with their 13 inch shells, continued until 8 a.m. on the 3rd. Partial shelling recommenced that evening and at 7 a.m. on 4 September the barrage was reopened with full fury. Throughout this attack *Minotaur* maintained a steady fire, the great wood yard 440 yards long was ablaze, and churches and buildings on fire could not be extinguished as fire engines had been destroyed during the earlier bombardment. By the night of the 5th the conflagration threatened to destroy the entire city, at which point Peimann sent a flag of truce asking for a 24 hour armistice but because his request omitted the relinquishment of the Danish ships, Gambier refused. Peimann reluctantly relented and negotiations were set in train under Major-General Sir Arthur Wellesley, Lieutenant Colonel George Murray, the Deputy Quartermaster of the British forces and Sir Home Popham, Captain of the Fleet. By the evening of the 6th the surrender terms were drawn up and signed the next morning. Seventeen line-of-battle ships, frigates and sloops were removed ready for passage to England. They comprised three 80 gun ships, fourteen 74s, one 64, six 46s, two 40s, and two 32 gun frigates. Smaller ships consisted of two 20 gun ships two 16 gun sloops, seven 16 gun brig-sloops, two 14 gun brigs, a 12 gun schooner and 25 gunboats. The two 64s *Mars* and *Dittsmarschen*, the 28 gun *Triton* and the 22 gun pram *St Thomas* were found to be rotten and were destroyed. As for the three 74s upon the stocks, two were taken to pieces, their timbers being confiscated, the third vessel, virtually fully planked up, was sawed through, in places over-set. All naval stores, including masts, were removed onto the British ships and carried home. Although the entire expedition was successful in depriving Napoleon of ships and an effective base, it was calamitous for the Danes. Besides the destruction of their fine city, 250 troops were killed, and upwards of 2,000 civilian men, women and children lost their lives in the conflagration.[292]

1808-1810: Apart from a routine refit at Sheerness in December 1808 and being docked at Portsmouth February 1810, *Minotaur* appears to have carried out routine duties.[293]

FATE

Under the command of Captain John Barrett *Minotaur* sailed from Gothenburg for the Downs on the evening of 15 December 1810. In company were *Plantagenet* (74), *Loire* (40) and a convoy of 60 merchant ships. The weather, which that night was tempestuous, did not abate for the next week. Having cleared the most northern point of Denmark the convoy turned south west and meeting heavy seas with poor visibility, *Minotaur* was wrecked on Haak Sands at the mouth of the Texel during the night of 22 December. As soon as the ship struck, her sails were set back to drive her off, simultaneously distress guns were fired to broadcast their plight to the rest of the fleet. Pumps were manned but the ship having bilged they could not cope with incoming water. By 2.30 a.m. the water level had reached the lower gun deck and orders were given to cut away all the masts to ease the ship. With signs that the ship would start breaking up boats were lowered. The first boat, manned by the Gunner Joseph Jones and thirty men set off for the shore. Nearing the beach the yawl capsized with the loss of one man, the others however successfully landed. Encouraged by this Lieutenant Snell filled a second boat to make the hazardous journey. The second yawl, carrying the captain and 60 men however was less fortunate and was swamped with a loss of all life just a short way from the ship. At about 2 p.m. *Minotaur* broke in two and 400 men were drowned as her hull turned over. Langereld, Dutch Chief of Staff of the Third Maritime District of the North Coast, sent a letter to the Admiralty stating that Captain Musquetie, commander in Texel Roads, sent out a pilot on the morning of the 23rd. He had discovered that *Minotaur*, completely dismasted, was lying with her fore part submerged and heavy seas breaking over her after hull. Heavy seas

PROGRESS BOOK – *MINOTAUR* RATE OF 74 GUNS: Source: ADM 180/9 Entry 618 & 180/10 Entry 105

At what Port	Arrived	Docked	Coppered	Launched or Undocked	Sailed	Built or Nature of Repair	Cost of Hull, Masts & Yards Materials £ s d	Cost of Rigging & Stores Materials £ s d	Grand Total
Woolwich	Began	Jan 1788		6 Nov 1793		Built	10,314	10,528	50,842 See Note 1 below
Woolwich		7 Nov 1793	Coppered	Nov 1793	19 Nov 1793	Fitted	As above	As Above	As Above
Plymouth	3 Sep 1796	16 Sep 1796	Copper repaired	19 Sep 1796	2 Nov 1796	Refitted	3,050	4,597	7,647
Plymouth	5 Jan 1797				21 Jan 1797				
Chatham	6 Feb 1802	5 Mar 1802	Copper taken off Mar 1802; Re-coppered June 1802	2 July 1802	24 Nov 1802	Small Repair			See Note 2 below
Sheerness	25 Nov 1802		Coppered to Light Draft of Water Nov 1802	26 April 1803					
Plymouth	21 Jan 1805	2 Feb 1805	Copper Repaired	2 Feb 1805	25 Feb 1805	Defects			
Chatham	27 Nov 1806	28 Dec 1806	Copper taken off Jan Re-coppered Feb 1807	22 Feb 1807	2220 Mar 1807	Defects			
Sheerness	4 Dec 1808		Copper Repaired Mar 1809		26 Mar 1809	Defects			
Portsmouth	5 Feb 1810	21 Feb 1810	Copper taken off Feb Re-coppered Mar 1810	8 March 1810	2 April 1810	Refitted			

Lost 1810, 22nd Dec[r]., on the Haaks Sand

NOTE 1: Written under 'Observations' related to her initial building is the following statement;
Expenses of erecting a Housing over the *Minotaur* while on the Slip, viz:- Materials............£377 19s 3d
Workmanship............£246 6s 10d
£624: 6: 1 See Wool: Officers Letter to the Board, dated 12th Dec[r]. 1792
NOTE 2: No expenses recorded in original document

prevented the pilot providing assistance. Despite the sea conditions 110 survivors of *Minotaur*'s 550 crew managed to save themselves in the boats, landing near the village of Koog, while another four men who had clung to wreckage finally made the shore on the 25th. All survivors were immediately interred for the duration of the war and released in 1814. On their return to England Mr Snell, *Minotaur*'s 2nd Lieutenant and the Master, Mr Thompson, were tried for the loss of the ship. The proceedings of the court martial, held on board the *Gladiator* (44) at Portsmouth, found that the pilot on board assumed the ship to be near Smith's Knowl, when she was in fact some 20 leagues from this shoal; Snell and Thompson were duly acquitted. It was also declared that had the Dutch acted more quickly, more lives would have been saved.[294]

The 74 gun ship **ORION**

Named after the giant and hunter of Greek mythology, and the constellation, the *Orion* which fought at Trafalgar was the first ship to bear this name in the Royal Navy. One of four ships built to the lines of the *Canada* class designed by William Bateley in 1759, her sister ships comprised *Canada*, *Majestic*, and *Captain*, the latter being Nelson's command at the battle of Cape St Vincent, 14 February 1797. Ordered on 2 October 1782, the keel of *Orion* was laid down at Deptford in February 1783. Construction was jointly shared by Henry Adams and John Barnard, both of whom had high reputations as contractors to the Navy Board. *Orion* was finally launched on 1 June 1787, the delay due to a lack of urgency to complete as Britain was not at war, or difficulties with timber procurement, or a combination of both. Overall building costs amounted to £30,144 11s 1d for her hull only and £3,449 for masts and yards. The ship was then rigged and stored at Woolwich at a cost of £7,052.[295] Armed with twenty-eight 32 pounders on lower gun deck, twenty-eight 18 pounders on her upper gun deck, fourteen 9 pounders on the quarter deck and four 9 pounders on her forecastle, *Leviathan* could deliver a single broadside weight of 718 pounds.[296]

SERVICE CAREER

1787: *Orion* was first put into commission at Woolwich on 24 September under the command of Captain Sir Hyde Parker Kt. Sailing 1 November, she went into Plymouth 27 December.[297]

1788: Not required for sea service, the ship was paid off 16 February. Going into dock at Plymouth 7 July, *Orion* was 'Fitted for a Guard Ship' at a total

SPECIFICATIONS: *ORION*

Rate	3rd	Date launched	1 June 1787	Complement	550
Guns	74	Length on the range of the gun deck	170 ft	Ordnance - lower gun deck	28 x 32 pounders
Class	Canada 1759	Length of keel for tonnage	140 ft 5 ins	Ordnance - upper gun deck	28 x 18 pounders
Designer	William Bateley	Extreme breadth	46 ft 7 ins	Ordnance - quarter deck	14 x 9 pounders
Builder	Henry Adams & John Barnard	Depth in hold	20 ft 6 ins	Ordnance - forecastle	4 x 9 pounders
Dockyard	Deptford	Tons burthen	1632 35/94	Single broadside weight	781 pounds
Date ordered	2 October 1782	Draught afore	(light water) 16 ft	Fate	1814 Broken up
Date keel laid	February 1783	Draught abaft	(light water) 19 ft		

Source: Lyon, *Sailing Navy List*, p. 69.

THE 74 GUN SHIP *ORION*

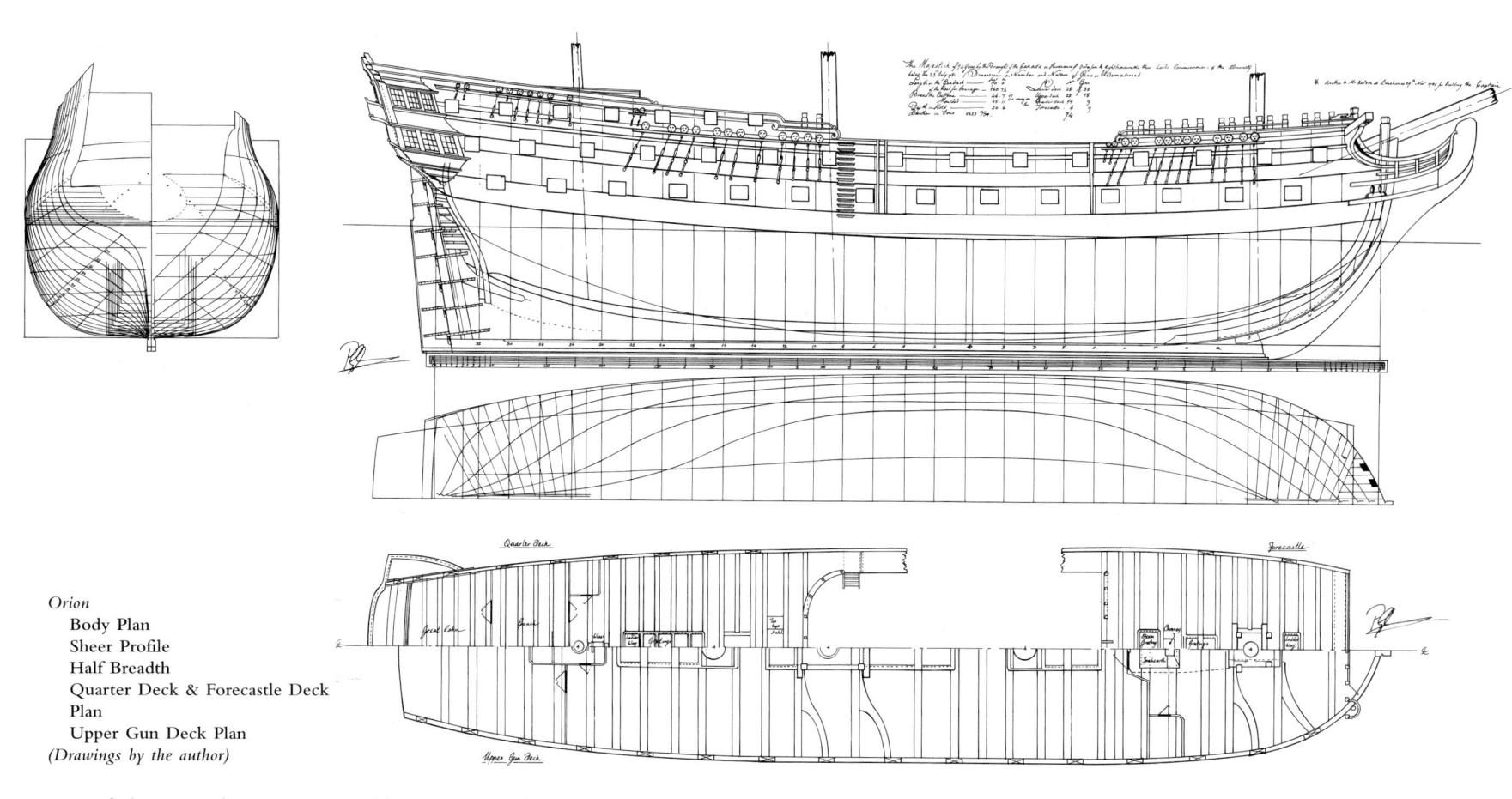

Orion
  Body Plan
  Sheer Profile
  Half Breadth
  Quarter Deck & Forecastle Deck Plan
  Upper Gun Deck Plan
(Drawings by the author)

cost of £4,114 and recommissioned by Captain Andrew Sutherland.[298]

1789: On 1 July command of *Orion* was superseded by Captain Charles Chamberlayne who remained in the ship until paying her off at Plymouth 5 September 1791.

1791: During this year *Orion* was taken in hand by Plymouth dockyard and refitted for normal sea service at a cost of £4,086 and recommissioned under Captain John Thomas Duckworth 16 September.[299]

1794: Under the command of Captain John Thomas Duckworth, *Orion* was detached with Lord Howe's Channel squadron, which fought in the series of engagements against Rear-Admiral Louis Villaret-Joyeuse which, commencing on 28 May, culminated with the distinctive victory on the Glorious First of June. While not wholly involved on the first day, *Orion* did get into action on 29 May. Howe, flying his flag in *Queen Charlotte* (100) formed a column comprising the *Royal George* (100), *Queen* (98), *Cæsar* (80), *Bellerophon* (74), *Invincible* (74), *Russell* (74), *Majestic* (74), *Valiant* (74), and *Orion*. Having turned in succession onto a larboard tack by 7.30 a.m. the entire British squadron, now ranged in line ahead, bore down to pass through the French line. Firing commenced, although at quite a long range, around 10 a.m. After changing tack several times the British ships finally broke the French line at about 1.30 p.m., *Orion* passing between *Vengeur de Peuple* and *Patriote*, and in doing so raked the former. Then, with *Barfleur*, *Orion* hotly engaged *Indomptable* (74), which boldly defended herself until rescued by other French ships. For the next two days the British fleet doggedly pursued Villaret's squadron and at 7.16 on the morning of 1 June Howe signalled for his ships to attack the French centre. Firing commenced two hours later and during the ensuing battle *Orion* engaged *Northumberland* (78) and *Patriote* (74). Though bearing a British name, *Northumberland*, which was captured that day, had in fact been designed by Sané and launched at Brest. Casualties borne by *Orion* that day comprised five killed and 24 wounded. After remedial repairs *Orion*, with the rest of Howe's fleet and six prizes, set a north-easterly course for England. While most of the fleet arrived at Portsmouth on 13 June, *Orion* went into Plymouth the day before.[300] *Orion* was 'Taken in hand', and completed in June, costing £6,232 and docked again in December to replace her copper.[301]

1795: Now commanded by Captain Sir James Saumarez, *Orion* re-joined the Channel fleet which, due to Howe's illness, had been placed under the command of Admiral Lord Bridport. Sailing from Spithead on 12 June, Bridport's squadron sailed to join Commodore Warren who was watching over Admiral Villaret-Joyeuse's fleet anchored near Belle Isle. Bridport, flying his white ensign in *Royal George* (100), was accompanied by the following ships:

Rate	Guns	Ships' names	Total
1st	100	*Royal George, Queen Charlotte*	2
2nd	98	*Barfleur, London, Prince, Prince George, Prince of Wales, Queen*	6
3rd	80	*Sans Pareil*	1
3rd	74	*Colossus, Irresistible, Orion, Russell, Valiant*	5
4th	44	*Révolutionnaire*	1
5th	36	*Nymph, Thalia*	2
5th	32	*Aquilon, Astræa*	2
6th	20	*Babet*	1
Fireship	14	*Megæra, Incendiary*	2
Lugger	14 & 8	*Argus, Dolly*	2
Hospital ship	44	*Charon*	1
TOTAL			25

Arriving off Isle de Groix on 20 June, Bridport was joined by *Robust* (74), *Thunderer* (74), and *Standard* (64). Sighting the French ships at 3.30 a.m. on 22 June, the British ships closed to give battle and at 6.30 a.m. Bridport signalled his faster ships, *Orion* with *Sans Pareil, Colossus, Irresistible, Russell*, and *Valiant*, to give chase. Repeating the signal to the rest of his fleet a quarter of an hour later, the ship crammed on more sail in the falling wind. The chase continued all day until 10.30 p.m. when Bridport's ships were all taken aback and the wind fell away completely. At around 3 a.m. on 23 June

99

CAPTAINS OF ORION (MSS 248/4 and 248/6)

Name	Time of Entry	Time of Discharge	On What Occasion
Sir Hyde Parker	24 September 1787	16 February 1788	Paid Off
Andrew Sutherland	10 July 1788	30 April 1789	Superseded
Charles Chamberlayne	1 July 1789	5 September 1791	Paid Off
John Thomas Duckworth	16 September 1791	18 March 1795	To the *Leviathan*
Sir James Saumarez	19 March 1795	6 January 1799	Paid Off at Plymouth
Ross Donnelly	3 June 1795	10 June 1795	To the *Leviathan* Acting
Robert C Reynolds	28 February 1801	29 November 1801	Superseded
Robert Cuthbert	3 November 1801	10 July 1802	Paid Off
Edward Codrington	24 May 1805	17 December 1806	Superseded
Sir A C Dickson	18 December 1806	8 January 1814	Paid Off at Plymouth

the wind improved and although the British ships had become scattered, *Irresistible* followed by *Queen Charlotte*, *Orion*, *Sans Pareil*, *Colossus*, and *Russell*, continued in pursuit, bearing down on Isle de Groix from the west some eight miles away. By 6 a.m. the gap had closed sufficiently for the rearmost French ships to fire into *Orion* and *Irresistible* who returned their fire. Within thirty minutes *Queen Charlotte*, *London*, *Queen*, *Sans Pareil*, *Colossus*, *Irresistible* and *Russell*, together with *Orion*, were engaged in close combat with *Alexandre*, *Formidable*, *Mucius*, *Nestor*, *Peuple*, *Redoubtable*, (see section 2, chapter 2) *Tigre* and *Wattignies*. The leading French ships, *Droits de Homme*, *Fougueux*, (see section 2, chapter 2) *Jean Bart* and *Zélé*, were too far ahead, and the aftermost British ships too far astern, to participate. In the ensuing action, which continued until about 8.30 a.m., *Orion* sustained 24 casualties; six dead and 18 wounded. French ships captured were *Tigre* (80), *Alexandre* (74), and *Formidable* (74); the former two, previously captured from the British, re-entered the Royal Navy under their original names. *Formidable*, already listed in the navy, was renamed *Belleisle* (see chapter 3 above).[302]

1795: On 18 March Duckworth transferred into *Leviathan*, his successor, Captain Sir James Saumarez Kt, assuming command of *Orion* next day. Apart from 3-10 June 1795 when *Orion* was placed under the acting captaincy of Ross Donnelly, Saumarez remained in command until 1799.[303]

1796: Arriving at Portsmouth 8 February and docking 10 March for one day, *Orion* had her copper repaired, the ship sailing for duty again 24 April.[304]

1797: Still under the command of Captain Saumarez, *Orion* now formed part of Admiral Sir John Jervis's fleet operating off Lisbon after quitting the Mediterranean. With the rest of the squadron *Orion* remained anchored in the Tagus until 18 January when Jervis, flying his flag in *Victory* (100), put to sea with eleven line of battle ships to escort a convoy bound for Brazil. With Spain entering the war on the side of France, Admiral Don José de Córdoba had sailed from Cartagena with 27 sail of the line, twelve frigates, a corvette and other vessels on 1 February, intent on joining the French and Dutch fleets commanded by Admiral Morard de Galles laying at Brest. Receiving news from Nelson in *Minerve* (38) on 13 February that Córdoba was at sea, Jervis immediately prepared his fleet for action and on the morning of 14th his ships lay 8 leagues south west of Cape St Vincent. Sailing in close order, at 9.30 a.m. Jervis detached *Orion* with *Blenheim* (98), *Prince George* (98), *Colossus* (74), *Culloden* (74), and *Irresistible* (74), to chase to the south-west. Action commenced at 11.31 a.m. when *Culloden* opened fire on the leading Spanish ships. Ordered to tack in succession, *Orion* managed to get round and eventually closed with *San Ysidro* and *San Salvador del Mundo* and at about 3 p.m. engaged the mighty *Santísima Trinidad*. While most of the action had ceased by 5 p.m., *Orion* and *Britannia* (100) were still firing at vessels supporting *Santísima Trinidad*. In the battle *Orion* suffered only nine wounded, one of whom was Midshipman Thomas Mansel.[305]

1798: After remaining on station off Cadiz, *Orion* went into Gibraltar, where on 4 May she was, with *Alexander* (74), *Emerald* (36) *Terpsichore* (32), and *Bonne Cityonne* (20) placed under the command of Nelson who had recently arrived from England in *Vanguard* (74). Sailing on 9 May Nelson's small squadron was to re-enter the Mediterranean to watch the large French fleet commanded by Admiral de Brueys being mobilised at Toulon. While off Hyères in the Gulf of Genoa the squadron was beset by extremely heavy gales, the ships were scattered, and *Orion* had to escort *Vanguard* being towed by *Alexander* to Sardinia, anchoring at San Pietro on 22 May.[306] Rejoined by more ships, Nelson finally ran the French fleet to ground in Abu-Kir Bay east of Alexandria on 1 August. Preparing to attack immediately, Nelson's squadron, including *Orion*, comprised the following ships.

Rate	Guns	Ships' names	Total
3rd	74	*Alexander*, *Audacious*, **Bellerophon**. *Culloden*, **Defence**, *Goliath*, *Majestic*, *Minotaur*, *Orion*, *Swiftsure*, *Theseus*, *Vanguard*, *Zealous*.	13
4th	50	*Leander*	1
6th	16	*Mutine*	1
TOTAL			15

NOTE: Those ships denoted in bold type also fought at Trafalgar.

In the battle, which commenced just before 6 p.m., *Orion* entered the bay third in line following *Zealous* which was preparing to anchor and engage *Guerrière*, putting her helm starboard. As *Orion* turned to larboard she poured a raking broadside into *Guerrière*, then running past the outboard side of *Zealous*, Saumarez gave orders to James Barker, his First Lieutenant, to draw *Orion* up alongside *Sérieuse* and fire a broadside into the French ship. So effective were *Orion*'s gunners that *Sérieuse* was left dismasted and taking in water. Having dealt this crippling blow, Saumarez gave the order to let go the anchor and after veering away brought the *Orion* broadside onto the larboard quarter of *Peuple Souverain* and commenced firing into her, at the same time firing her starboard quarter guns into the *Franklin*. By this time her fight against *Peuple Souverain* was supported by *Defence* and by 9.30 p.m. the two ships had brought down her main and fore masts and shot away her cable. The battle continued until about 4 a.m. the next day by which time *Orion* had lost 13 killed and 29 wounded. Among the dead was Mr Baird, the Captain's Clerk.[307] *Orion* remained on station in the Mediterranean until recalled at the end of the year when she returned to Portsmouth 20 December.

1799: On 3 January Captain Saumarez received orders to pay off *Orion* after five years in commission, lowering his pendant three days later. The ship was taken in hand, docked and refitted at Plymouth.

1801: Docked 3 February, *Orion* was refitted at a cost of £2,258 for her hull masts and yards, and a further £7,616 for stores and rigging. On 28 February, *Orion* came out of the dock and was recommissioned under Captain (later Admiral) Robert Carthew Reynolds. *Majestic* (74) was recommissioned the same day. Although preparations were made to move out of the Hamoaze on 9 April, the wind was blowing too hard for *Orion* to sail for Cawsand Bay. Two days later the wind moderated and she sailed for Spithead to join the fleet. After blockading Rochefort *Orion* returned to Cawsand Bay on 12 September, then sailed with a convoy for Ireland with the *Resolution* (74) and *Vengeance* (74). Before returning command was superseded by Captain Robert Cuthbert, 3 November. After enduring considerable gales *Orion* returned to Portsmouth from Bantry Bay on 29 December.

1802: On 7 February *Orion* sailed with a squadron commanded by Rear-Admiral Campbell for Jamaica escorting a convoy, Campbell flying his flag in *Téméraire* (98). Returning to Portsmouth on 24 June, Cuthbert paid off the *Orion* on 10 July, when she was laid up in ordinary and went into refit the following year.

1805: Finally going into dock at Portsmouth 6 April *Orion* was refitted and re-coppered. She was recommissioned by Captain Edward Codrington 24 May and re-launched three days later. Unfortunately the cost of this refit has not been recorded. Sailing out to Spithead 24 July she sailed to join Collingwood's squadron deployed off Cadiz.

TRAFALGAR

On the morning of the battle *Orion* was stationed ninth in line of Nelson's windward division, astern of *Agamemnon* (64). Far away, oblivious of the events about to happen that day, Codrington's wife Jane was in Brighton, but Lady Arden was fretting about her son serving in Codrington's ship.[308] Late getting into battle, Codrington carried *Orion* towards the French *Swiftsure* (74) which had already suffered heavily from broadsides fired from *Colossus* (74). Codrington's extensive account of the battle, given in *Orion*'s log commencing noon Tuesday 22 October, is as follows:

> The Sig.l was made to prepare to Anchor if necessary the Enemys Fleet consisting of 15 sail of Spanish Ships of the line under the command of three Admirals, and 18 Sail of French Ships besides Frigates and a Brig, the French forming their Line to leeward after wearing from Starboard to the Larb.d R, the British Fleet consisting of 27 Sail of the Line besides Frigates, a Brig, a Schooner & a Cutter bearing down to attack then under Steering Sails in Order of Sailing - At 12.15 the gen.l Sigl to engage more closely, the *Victory* made the *Leviathan*'s Sig.l to lead the Van & the *Mars* to lead the lee Line at 35 past the *Royal Sovereign* broke the Enemy's Rear and ranged up under the Lee of the *St. Anna* three decker Spanish Ship, the Larb.d Divisions attacking the remainder of their Rear as they arrived up in succession, the *Victory* after making a faint [sic] of attacking their Van hauled to Starb.d so as to reach their Center [sic] and then wore round to pass under the lee of the *Bucentaure*'s back Ships of our Fleet passed through the Enemys Line with studding sail set, as she arrived up in succession, passed the *St. Anna* dismasted at 2.30 and had struck, the *Royal Sovereign* under her lee with her foremast only standing, passed the *Mars*, *Colossus* & *Tonnant*, aboard and surrounded by several of the Enemy Ships all dismasted or nearly so, passed the *Victory* and *Téméraire* with one French two Decked Ship between and on board of each of them one French two Decker aboard the *Téméraire* on the Starb.d Side also & one other two Decked Ship about a Ships length to windwd. of the *Victory* all in hot action at 2 opened our Fire upon the Stern of one of the Enemy Ships endeav.d. to make off from the ships opposed to her carryed [sic] away her Main Mast and made her strike her Colours - bore up to close up with a Spanish Adm.l to Leeward in the three Decked Ship, but was obliged to haul on a wind by the *Dreadnought* who passed between us, Continued in Action about three cables length with the Enemy's Reserve Line - at 2.25 made a second attempt to Close with the above Spanish Ship passing us on the other B[roadside] - but was again prevented by the *Britannia* ranged in her Line & continued in Action At 3.30 Repeated and obeyed the signal to haul to the Wind on the Larb.d T[ack] - Observed the *Leviathan* closely engaged with a Spanish ship and the whole of the Enemys Van wearing to attack her, made Sail to assist her Observed a French 74 being on the Starboard B and engage warmly between the *Leviathan* who was boarding a Spanish 74 and the *Africa* who appeared to ~~appeared to~~ [struck though in log] have almost Ceased firing made all possible sail passed close astern the *Leviathan*'s stern so as he close with the French 74 - at 4 opened our Fire close on her Larb.d Quarter wore around her Stern and brought to on Lee Bow between the *Africa* and the —— [illegible] Ship Opening up such a well directed fire as carried away her 3 masts & Tiller and preventing her returning us more than one or two Broadsides.[309]

The French ship was *Intrépide* (74) into which *Orion* repeatedly delivered broadsides, obliging her to strike her colours within quarter of an hour. Codrington's log continues,

> ... at 4.45 she struck her Colours, sent the first Lieutenant M.r Croft and a party of men to take possession of her at 6 stood under her Stern with a Rope to take her in tow but Slipt - at 8 PM the *Ajax* took her in tow - at 12 made sail under 3 topsails, the *Ajax* and Prize in sight - at 3 left sight the Prize at Day Light Cape Trafalgar bore SbE 10 or 12 M[iles] - At 8 bore down to the Spanish Ship dismasted (the *Bahama*) at 10 got her in Tow with big 11 Inch Hawser an End at 11 Made Sail very Squally at ½ past 11 Close reefed the Topsails Cape Trafalgar bore SEbS Dis. 4 or 5 Leagues at 12 Very Squally with strong Gales furled the Topsails.[310]

During the entire action *Orion* sustained only one death and 23 wounded, the latter including Midshipmen Charles Cable and Charles Tause. Besides injury aloft, overall damage to the ship was minimal.[311] Writing home to his wife that evening Codrington wrote, 'I feel a little tired; and as I have now nothing to do but keep the ship's head the right way, and take care that the sails are well trimmed, in readiness for the morning.'[312]

Meeting heavy weather next day (ship's log date 23 October), *Orion*'s mainsail was furled and under a storm main staysail, trysail and the fore topmast staysail, she endeavoured to ride out the storm with her prize in tow. At noon beef, pork, and wine were opened and served to the crew. Later that day, 'At 9.30 found the ship settle with the land very fast, let go the small Bower Anchor in 34 fath.m Wore away to a whole Cable prize in tow - at 11 perceived the ships in Cadiz getting under way - at 12 Cut the cable & made sail Cadiz Light House at EbyS ½ S Dis. 9 miles - Prize in Tow - No Obs.ns'. This entry suggests that the *Orion* was box hauled to prevent her closing with the lee shore. Commenting on the ships sailing from Cadiz, at 1 p.m. next day the log states: '7 sail of the Line 3 frigates & a brig of the Enemy's Ships standing for us perceived the *Thunderer* to have cast off her Prize, at 3 the enemy R.d [retired]'. The weather deteriorated, heavy gales obliging *Orion* to reduce sail so much that she began losing leeway. Codrington 'tryed for soundings', which proving to be 60 fathoms he 'Got a range of the Best Bower Cable up', and 'at ½ past 1 judging it not safe to keep the Prize longer in Tow having two bight hawsers fast to the end Cut them and Set the main sail', leaving the prize to her own resources. The log then states that they had to get down the main topsail yard, the starboard yardarm which had been shot away and later, 'hoisted the Boats out & sent them for Prisoners on board the French ship, At 12 stand.g Off & on to keep to windward Lat. By Ob.n 36:36 N'.[313] Getting into Gibraltar *Orion* made good her repairs then continued her deployment.

1806: On 18 December Captain Codrington was superseded by Captain Sir Archibald C Dickson, who remained in command until 1814.

1807: Now deployed with the Home fleet, *Orion* sailed from Yarmouth Roads on 26 July for Copenhagen with Admiral Gambier's forces. This invasion fleet, fully assembled off Elsinore, comprised 25 ships of the line, several frigates, ten gun brigs, four bomb vessels, 377 transports and 27,000 troops. The main attack was made on Copenhagen on the night of 16 August. Finally overwhelmed, the Danes capitulated on 7 September.[314] *Orion* returned to Chatham 9 November and docked 2 December to make good her defects.[315]

1808: Still under Dickson's command, *Orion* joined the Baltic fleet commanded by Vice-Admiral Saumarez, flying his flag in *Victory* (100). Her duties were to support Sweden against the Northern coalition forces of Russia and Denmark.

1809: Returning to Portsmouth 6 October the ship was docked 4 November and refitted.[316]

1810: On 17 November a court martial was convened on board *Orion* to try Mr Henson Barker, *Orion*'s assistant surgeon. Barker was accused of taking ashore medical supplies needed for the ship's company. Found guilty, Barker was dismissed from *Orion* and transferred into a lower rated ship. This would reduce his pay. A second court martial tried William Fogwell,

PROGRESS BOOK - ORION RATE OF 74 GUNS: Source: ADM 180/9/ Entry 615 & ADM 180/10 Entry 110

At what Port	Arrived	Docked	Coppered	Launched or Undocked	Sailed	Built or Nature of Repair	Cost of Hull, Masts & Yards Materials £ s d	Cost of Masts & Yards Materials £ s d	Grand Total
River Thames; Adams & Barnard	Began	February 1783 -		1 June 1787		Built Hull only	30,144s. 1d	-	30,144. 11s 1d
Deptford	1 June 1787			16 June 1787			3,449		3,449
Woolwich	16 June 1787	18 June 1787		16 July 1787	1 Nov 1787	To Plymouth		7,052	7,502
Plymouth	27 Dec 1787	7 July 1788	Taken in hand & docked & shored 1 Aug Coppered Aug 1788	16 Aug 1788	13 July 1789	Fitted for a Guard ship	1,201	2,913	4,114
Plymouth	16 Sep 1789			17 May 1790			375	3,909	4,284
Plymouth	20 Feb 1789		Taken in Hand March & Completed April 1791		19 April 1791	Refitted	1,299	2,787	4,086
Plymouth	21 Aug 1791	7 May 1792	Copper repaired May 1792	8 May 1792	21 June 1792	Refitted			
Plymouth	29 Sep 1792			11 Dec 1792			1,863	3,085	4,948
Plymouth	12 June 1792	Taken in hand & completed June 1794		3 July 1794		Refitted			
Plymouth	16 Dec 1794	24 Dec 1794	Copper taken off and Re-coppered Jan 1795	6 Jan 1795	20 Jan 1795	Refitted	2,005	4,227	6,232
Portsmouth	8 Feb 1796	10 Mar 1796	Copper Repaired	11 March 1796	24 April 1796	Refitted	1,910	1,847	3,757
Plymouth	20 Dec 1798	3 Feb 1801	Copper Repaired	28 Feb 1801	10 April 1801	Fitted	2,258	7,6116	9,874
Portsmouth	28 June 1802	6 April 1805	Copper taken off April Re-coppered May 1805	27 May 1805	24 July 1805	Fitted			
Chatham	9 Nov 1807	2 Dec 1807	Copper Repaired 17 Dec 1807	27 Jan 1808	Defects				
Portsmouth	6 Oct 1809	4 Nov 1809	Copper taken off Nov Re-coppered Dec 1809	19 Dec 1809	23 Jan 1810	Refitted			
Portsmouth	1 Apr 1811		Copper Repaired		7 May 1811	Defects			
Portsmouth	4 Jan 1813		Copper repaired above the Water		8 Mar 1813	Defects			
Plymouth	11 Dec 1813	26 Dec 1813	Copper Repaired	5 Jan 1814		Defects			
		20 June 1814							
				Taken to Pieces July 1814					

NOTE: Regarding the latter expenses, these are not recorded in original document 180/10

the ship's boatswain, for drunkenness and beating a man unmercifully. Like the assistant surgeon, Fogwell was dismissed out of the ship to serve in a lower rated man-of-war, with the same consequences. Pay, for particular officers, varied according to the rating classification of their ship.

1811: Between 1 April and 7 May *Orion* lay within Portsmouth dockyard repairing defects; afterwards she was based at Spithead.[317]

1813: Returning from the Baltic, *Orion* went into Plymouth 11 December and docked on 26 December to refit and have her copper repaired.

1814: Undocked on 5 January, *Orion* was paid off by Captain Dickson three days later and laid up to await her fate.

FATE

After laying at moorings in the Hamoaze for six months the ship was taken into dock on 20 June 1814 and 'Taken to Pieces July 1814'.

The 74 gun ship REVENGE

This was the tenth vessel of the Royal Navy to bear the name *Revenge*; the first was a galleon of 46 guns launched in October 1577. John Hawkins' flagship in the fight against the Spanish Armada in 1588, she was later captured by the Spanish off the Azores 31 August 1591 and foundered five days later. The second *Revenge*, a 42 gun ship purchased by royalists in 1650, was taken by the Parliamentarians in 1652 and renamed *Marmaduke*. During the second Dutch War this vessel was sunk as a blockship in the River Medway. The third vessel, built by Graves, was launched as the 52 gun

SPECIFICATIONS: *REVENGE*

Rate	3rd	Length on the range of the gun deck	182 ft	Ordnance - lower gun deck	28 x 32 pounders
Guns	74	Length of keel for tonnage	150 ft 3 ins	Ordnance - upper gun deck	30 x 24 pounders
Class	Revenge 1796	Extreme breadth	49 ft	Ordnance - quarter deck	14 x 9 pounders
Designer	John Henslow	Depth in hold	20 ft 9 ins	Ordnance - forecastle	2 x 9 pounders
Builder	Edward Sison	Tons burthen	1981 83/94		2 x 32 pounder carronades
Dockyard	Chatham	Draught afore	22 ft 0 ins	Ordnance - roundhouse/poop	6 x 18 pounder carronades
Date ordered	29 September 1796	Draught abaft	24 ft 2 ins	Single broadside weight	966 pounds
Date keel laid	August 1800	Complement	590	Fate	1849 Broken up
Date launched	13 April 1805				

Source: Lyon, *Sailing Navy List*, p. 110.

ship *Newbury* at Limehouse in 1654. Renamed *Revenge* in 1660 on the restoration of the monarchy, she was condemned in 1679. The next *Revenge* was a 3rd rate of 70 guns built by Miller at Deptford. Launched in 1699 and renamed *Buckingham* 16 June 1711 she was hulked in February 1727 and sunk as a foundation in May 1745. The fifth *Revenge* was originally the 70 gun ship *Swiftsure* built by Sir Anthony Deane. Launched at Harwich 8 April 1673 and rebuilt at Deptford in 1796, *Swiftsure* was reduced to 64 guns and renamed *Revenge* 2 January 1716. Rebuilt again in 1742 she was sold 25 May 1787 after 114 years' service. The next *Revenge*, according to Colledge, was a 6th rate frigate of 28 guns launched at Bombay dockyard 22 September 1755 which foundered in the Indian Ocean in April 1782.[318] Where Colledge obtained this information is obscure, for no such ship is listed by Lyon. The seventh *Revenge* was a brig-sloop of 14 guns purchased into service in 1778 and captured the following year by American revolutionaries. According to Lyon, what is effectively the eighth *Revenge* is listed from 1780 to 1782.[319] The ninth *Revenge* was a cutter of 8 guns purchased in 1796 which remained in service until 1798.[320]

Designed by John Henslow, the Trafalgar *Revenge* was a one-off vessel ordered 29 September 1796. Laid down at Chatham in August 1800,[321] construction began under Master Shipwright Edward Sisons, followed by David Polhill 28 July 1801. Polhill was himself succeeded in 18 March 1803 by Robert Seppings who saw *Revenge* through to her launch on 13 April 1805. An innovative builder, within eight years Seppings would become Surveyor of the Navy and introduce many new methods of ship construction. Although the building costs for her hull, masts, yards rigging and stores initially amounted to £44,881, her final cost was £52,653. Armed with twenty-eight 32 pounders on the lower gun deck, thirty 24 pounders on the upper gun deck, fourteen 9 pounders on the quarter deck, two 9 pounders and two 32 pounder carronades on the forecastle, and an additional armament of six 18 pounder carronades on her poop deck, *Revenge* delivered a single broadside weight of 966 pounds.

CAPTAINS OF *REVENGE* (R.N.M, MS 248/6)

Name	Date of entry	Date left	Occasion
Robert Moorsom	9 April 1805	6 January 1806	Superseded
Hon. C E Fleming	7 January 1806	23 February 1806	Superseded
Sir John Gore Kt	24 February 1806	5 August 1808	Superseded
Hon. Charles Paget	6 August 1808	18 October 1810	Superseded
John Nash	19 October 1810	15 June 1812	Superseded
Charles P Bateman	16 June 1812	30 September 1812	Superseded
William Stewart	1 October 1812	26 November 1812	Superseded
Sir John Gore Kt	27 November 1812	23 January 1814	Promoted
F W Carroll	24 January 1814	4 June 1814	To the *Cyrus*
Henry Hart	5 June 1814	10 September 1814	Paid Off at Chatham
Sir Charles Burrard Bt	20 March 1832		

SERVICE HISTORY

1805: *Revenge* was the newest ship to serve with the Trafalgar fleet. Immediately after her launch *Revenge* was put in commission by Captain Robert Moorsom, fitted, rigged and stored for sea. Throughout May while this was happening the ship was crewed with volunteers, pressed men and quota men. One such quota man left an account of his experiences within a man-o-war; although he avoids mentioning *Revenge* by name, it is evident from the content that his story relates to his service within this ship. This work, published in 1836 as *Nautical Economy: or Forecastle Recollections of Events during the last War*, is generally known as *Jack Nastyface*. The author states that on 9 May that he was, as a 'Lord Mayor's Man', confined within the hold of the *Revenge* for two days before being signed on the ship's books. Shortly afterwards *Revenge* was sent to join Vice-Admiral Collingwood's squadron blockading Villeneuve's combined fleet within Cadiz. Following Nelson's orders the ship, like any joining the fleet off Cadiz, was ordered to paint her gun ports black to effect the 'Nelson chequer' and her black mast hoops were painted out with yellow ochre to provide easy identification of friends in the forthcoming battle. When Villeneuve's fleet left Cadiz the British commenced clearing for battle. Preparations in *Revenge* are described in *Jack Nastyface*, the author stating:

> During this time each ship was making the usual preparations, such as breaking away the captain's and officer's cabins, and sending the lumber below, the doctors, parson, purser, and loblolly men were also busy, getting the medicine chests and bandages out, and sails prepared for the wounded to be placed on, that they might be dressed in rotation, as they were taken to the after cockpit.[322]

TRAFALGAR

For Monday 21 October *Revenge*'s log records: 'Fresh Breezes & Hazy with Light Rain made & short[d] sail occas[y] at 1 sent down TG[t]. Y[ds] at 3.30 Wore ship at 4.40 up TG[t]. Y[ds] and made sail'.[323] On the morning of the battle *Revenge* lay eighth in line of Collingwood's leeward division. The log entry continues, 'AM D[o].W[r]. made & short[d] sail occas[y] at 9 Light Airs inclinable to Calm Observed 39 Sail of the Enemy on the Larb[d] Tack - Ans[d]. the *Royal Sovereign*'s Signal No. 88 to make more Sail - Noon Mod[e]. Breezes & Clear - All sail set Prepared for Battle. The log entry commencing Noon 22 October then states; 'at 12.10 took in the studdingsails Enemys Ships in Sight 39 Sail and a Brig - *Victory*'s Signal by Telegraph - England expects every Man will do his duty - at 12.25 *Royal Sovereign* Commenced Action at 12.35 *Revenge* d[o]. at 12.40 *Victory*'s Mizen Topmast shot away'.[324] Running down upon the enemy line, *Revenge* came under fire. One of her seamen later wrote: 'we were favoured with several shots, and some of our men were wounded. Many of the men thought it hard the firing should be all from one side, and became impatient to return the compliment; but our

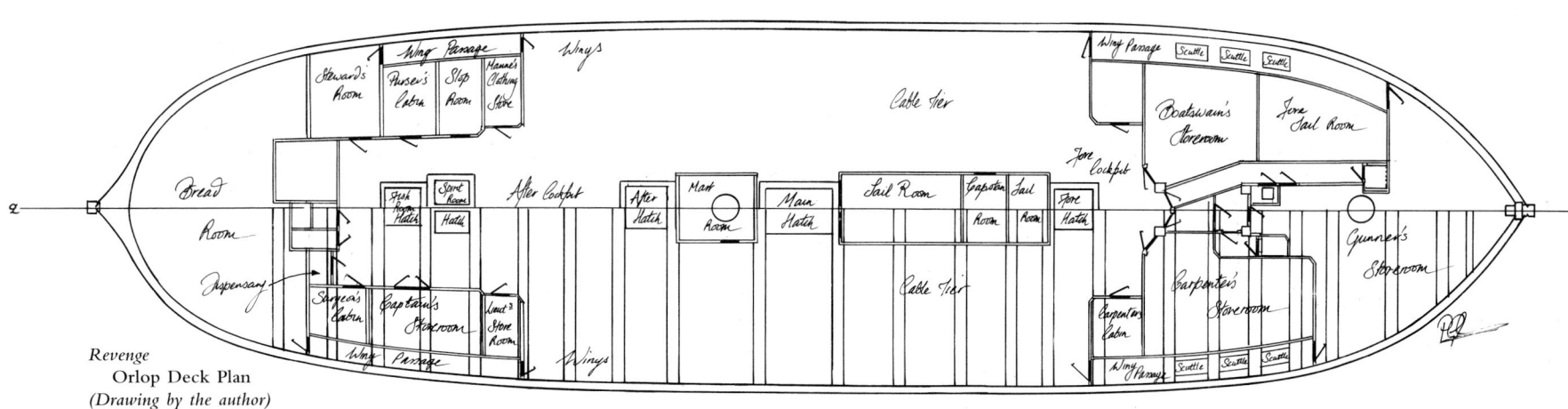

Revenge
Orlop Deck Plan
(Drawing by the author)

Captain had given orders not to fire until we had got close with them'. Getting into action around 12.35 p.m., *Revenge* approached the enemy line obliquely, falling parallel with *San Ildefonso* (74) and the French *Achille* (74), at which point Moorsom ordered his gunners to fire. The deadly timed broadside slammed into *Achille*, shattering her mizzen mast which, beginning to fall, sent her officers scurrying to safety. This was not surprising as Moorsom, considered by his peers a gunnery expert, had the best gunners in the British fleet that day.[325] Moorsom then attempted to drive *Revenge* through the enemy line to rake *Aigle* (74) from ahead. Although he fouled with the French ship's jibboom, his gunners poured several broadsides into *Aigle*'s bow. Getting *Revenge* onto a larboard tack to haul clear, she came under fire from the tremendous broadsides fired from *Principe de Austurias* (112), together with heavy fire from *Neptune* (84), *Indomptable* (80) and *San Justo* (74).[326] In his log Moorsom recorded these events simply:

> ... at 4.40 Men firing with all expectation and Spirit having upon us four French Ships and A Spanish three Decker at 5.50 the Action ceased answered the Genl. Signal to take ships in tow 6.15 the *Achille* french ship Blew up- 14 Ships run dismasted empd. clearing away the Wreck having our Yards Rigging and Sails Cut to pieces and lower Masts very much wounded sounded from 17 to 14 fm. got the Anchors clear - *Victory* N by E 2 or 3 Miles Wore per Signal AM fresh Breezes and cloudy empld. repairing the Rigging sent down T.Masts got the Spritsail Yard up for a foretopsailyard - recd 8 prisoners cape Trafalgar SE about 6 Leagues.[327]

At the close of battle boats from *Pickle* brought on board *Revenge* a woman named Jeanette who had been saved from the blazing inferno of the French *Achille* just before she blew up. Once on board she was, according to Jack Nastyface:

> ... in a state of complete nakedness. Although it was the heat of the battle, yet she received every assistance which at that time was in our power; and her distress of mind was soothed as well as we could, until the officers got to their chests, from whence they supplied her with needles and thread, to convert sheets into chemises, and curtains from their cots to make somewhat of a gown, and other garments, so that by degrees she was made as comfortable as circumstances would admit; for we all tried who would be most kind to her.[328]

Moorsom, recalling the event, stated that he 'Ordered her two purser's shirts to make a petticoat'. Once action had ceased Jeanette was given a cabin by one of *Revenge*'s officers and the chaplain gave her shoes while another found some white stockings. Her distress that she had lost her husband was relieved four days later when he too was found among other survivors in *Revenge*.[329] *Revenge* had suffered considerable damage to hull and rigging; her casualties, amounting to 79 in all, comprised 28 killed including Midshipmen Edward Brooks and Thomas Grier. Among the 51 wounded were Captain Moorsom, Lieutenant John Berry, Luke Brokenshaw, the ship's Master, and Captain of Marines, Peter Lely.[330] During the rising storm on 23 October the winds 'carried away the Crossjack Y^d.', soundings taken revealed 'no ground and the crew 'unbent the Mizen T.S. for a fore TG^t. Sent up spare fore T.Sail Y^d. for a main Yard bent new Sails sunk whole in Action our 25 foot Cutter masts sails Oars breakers &c'.[331] The following day:

> *Euryalus* desired Captain Moorsom to take his Station next the *Euryalus* which Frigate Admiral Collingwod was on board, bore up and made sail at 6 the Enemys Ships bore N by W at 9 carried away the Mizen Topmsail Sheet AM d^o. W^r. at 4 made and shortened sail a necessary at 8.30 took a Prize in tow at 9 wore Ship at 10 the Ships Signal in Distress apparently sinking fast.[332]

On the 26th, *Revenge* received French prisoners from *Pickle* and on the 27th Moorsom 'read a Letter of thanks to the Ships C^oy. From Vice Admiral Collingwood', and 'at three departed this Life And^w Libran (S) at 9.30 comitted his Body to the Deep...'. *Revenge* reached Gibraltar Monday 28

PROGRESS BOOK - *REVENGE* 3rd RATE OF 74 GUNS:

At what Port	Arrived	Docked	Coppered
Chatham	Began	Aug 1800	-
Chatham		14 April 1805	Coppered April 1805
Portsmouth	6 Dec 1805	14 Dec 1805	Copper Repaired
Portsmouth	8 Jan 1807		
Portsmouth	19 July 1808	29 July 1808	Copper taken off & Re-coppered Aug 1808
Portsmouth	30 Mar 1811	6 Apr 1811	Copper taken off & Re-coppered Apr 1811
Chatham	30 Aug 1814		Copper taken off to light water mark
Chatham		24 Feb 1818	Copper taken off Feb 1818 Re-coppered Jan 1823
Chatham		Taken in hand March & Completed Aug 1823	
Portsmouth	26 Apr 1827	13 June 1827	Repaired & dressed down copper
Plymouth	8 Oct 1830	1 Nov 1830	Copper taken off and re-coppered
Plymouth	20 May 1833	3 June 1833	
Portsmouth	27 Feb 1834	12 Mar 1834	Removed the two lower strakes and dressed the copper
Foreign returns			
Portsmouth	20 May 1837	1 Jan 1838	Copper taken off & Re-coppered - raised Copper
Devonport	11 Oct 1839		
Foreign Yards			
Sheerness	15 Feb 1842	26 Apr 1849	Copper taken off
	Taken to Pieces Oct 1849		

	Hull	Masts	Stores	Total
Value of Stores returned......	5,604	1,540	8,028	15,172

October and after carrying out essential repairs sailed on Saturday 9 November for England. She arrived at Spithead Sunday 1 December and waited to go into Portsmouth to refit.[333] Shortly afterwards Captain Charles Fleeming took command of the ship. Unlike Moorsom, who took pains to get the best out of his ship's company, Fleeming had a bad reputation throughout the fleet. Adding insult to injury Fleeming brought further dissatisfaction when he ordered that the 'Nelson chequer', which the crew took as symbolic of the victorious efforts, be painted out, reverting back to single strakes of yellow ochre in the old fashion.[334]

1806: In July *Revenge* with *Prince of Wales* (98), *Centaur* (74), *Conqueror* (74), *Monarch* (74), *Polyphemus* (64), *Indefatigable* (44) and *Iris* (32) was deployed off the Gironde. On the night of 12 July twelve boats, including some from *Revenge*, proceeded up the Gironde to cut out two French corvettes and a convoy anchored in the river. In the assault 20 men from the *Revenge* were taken prisoner after their boat sunk in the action.[335] Continuing her deployment off Rochefort, command was taken by Captain Sir John Gore, while Commodore Sir Samuel Hood took command of the squadron. Although the squadron got into action with the French in September, *Revenge* was not fully involved.[336]

1807: During the early part of this year *Revenge* was deployed blockading Cadiz where she remained until Spain turned against France and entered the war on Britain's side.

1808: By this period command of *Revenge* had been succeeded by Captain the Hon. Charles Paget. Now deployed on convoy duties *Revenge* sailed for the East Indies on 18 September.

1809: Returning to home waters *Revenge* was deployed with the Channel fleet commanded by Admiral Lord Gambier off Ushant watching over Brest. On 21 February a French squadron commanded by Admiral Willaumez attempted to evade the British patrols and put to sea. Flying his

Source: ADM 180/10 Entry 122

Launched or Undocked	Sailed	Built or Nature of Repair	Cost of Hull, Masts & Yards Materials £	Workmen £	Cost of Masts & Yards Materials £	Workmen £	Cost of Rigging & Stores Materials £	Workmen £	Grand Total £
13 April 1805		Built	22,976	11,402	764	401	9,085	253	44,881
16 April 1805	3 June 1805	Fitted							3,449
3 Jan 1806	13 Feb 1806	Refitted			7,052				7,502
14 Jan 1807	10 Feb 1807	Refitted			2,913				4,114
11 Aug 1808	3 Sep 1808	Refitted			3,909				4,284
26 Apr 1811	3 June 1811	Refitted			2,787				4,086
29 Jan 1823		Large Repair			3,085				4,948
	7 Aug 1823	Fitted for a ------ for foreign service							
27 June 1827	29 Jan 1828	Fitted as Guardship; defects made good			4,227				6,232
29 Mar 1831	May 1831	Fitted as a Guardship			1,847				3,757
17 June 1833	9 Aug 1833	Defects							
26 Mar 1834	9 June 1834	Refitted							
14 Dec 1838	1 Aug 1839	Demonstration fitted for Sea							
	5 Nov 1839								
		Surveyed							

flag in *Ocean* (120), Willaumez was accompanied by the 74 guns ships *Aquilon*, *Jean Bart*, *Regulus*, *Tonnerre*, and *Tourville*, together with the 40 gun frigates *Elbe* and *Indienne*, the brig *Nisis* and schooner *Magpie*, the latter vessel formerly British. As the lead ships cleared Passage du Raz they were sighted by *Revenge*. Paget immediately set course for the Glénan Islands to inform Commodore John Poo Beresford flying his pendant in *Theseus* (74). Beresford was at the time stationed off Lorient blockading three French line of battle ships and five frigates with *Triumph*, (74), Captain Thomas Masterman Hardy, and *Valiant* (74). Although the British gave chase, Willaumez eluded Bereford's manœuvres and reached Basque Roads. With the news that a large French force was now trapped in Basque Roads, Gambier, flying his flag in *Caledonia* (120), sailed with more ships including bomb vessels and fireships to support *Revenge* and Beresford's blockading ships. Arriving on 10 April, Gambier planned his attack, his entire now fleet comprised as follows:

Rate or type	Guns	Ships' names	Total
1st	120	*Caledonia*	1
3rd	80	*Cæsar, Gibraltar*	2
3rd	74	*Bellona, Donegal, Hero, Illustrious, Resolution, Revenge, Theseus, Valiant,*	8
4th	44	*Indefatigable*	1
5th	38	*Amelia, Imperieuse*	2
5th	36	*Aigle, Emerald*	2
5th	32	*Mediato, Pallas, Unicorn*	3
6th	18	*Beagle, Doteral, Foxhound*	3
Brigs/sloops	14	*Insolent, Encounter, Growler, Martial*	4
Brigs	12	*Conflict, Fervent*	2
Bomb vessels	8	*Ætna, Thunder*	2
Cutters	-	*King George, Nimrod*	2
Schooner	4	*Whiting*	1
Transport	-	*Cleveland*	1
Fireships	-	20 in number unnamed	20
Explosion vessels	-	3 in number unnamed	3
Storeships	-	Number not recorded	?
TOTAL			57

Although the attack with the fireships led by Lord Cochrane panicked the French commanders to cut their cables, leaving them open to all other forms of attack, many British casualties were caused by the explosions, one of whom was Lieutenant Henry Montgresor of *Revenge*. Meanwhile *Revenge*, *Bellona* and *Valiant* provided fire support to the bomb vessels.[337]

1810: Still under Captain Paget's command, the ship was now attached to the squadron blockading Cherbourg. On the night of 15 November *Revenge*, with *Donegal* (74) and *Niobe* (38), closed inshore to support *Diana* (38) which had chased two French 40 gun frigates *Amazone* and *Eliza* under the safety of shore batteries at Hougue. The four ships made three attempts to get close enough to fire on the frigates, but return fire from the shore batteries which had greater range damaged rigging and masts, forcing the British ships to withdraw.[338]

1811: For a brief period *Revenge* was commanded by Captain Alexander Kerr whose previous command had been *Donegal*. When *Revenge* was redeployed to the squadron stationed off Cadiz as flagship to Rear-Admiral the Hon. Sir Arthur Legge, Kerr was superseded by Captain James Nash.

1812: Still stationed off Cadiz, command of the ship was succeeded by Captain Sir John Gore.

1813: This year saw the last action in which *Revenge* was involved. Operating off the coast of Catalonia on the night of 8 November, her boats, commanded by Lieutenants Thomas Blakiston and William Richards, went into Palamos harbour to cut out a French privateer. The vessel, which proved to be an armed felucca, was successfully captured without suffering a single casualty.[339]

1814: Finally recalled to England *Revenge* was, like many other naval ships, decommissioned and laid up in ordinary.

FATE

Laid up at Portsmouth, *Revenge* was finally broken up in October 1849.

The 74 gun ship SPARTIATE

Built at Toulon as a 2nd rate ship of 80 guns and launched in 1797, *Spartiate*'s service within the French navy was very short as she was captured from the French at Nelson's victorious Battle of the Nile, 1 August 1798. *Spartiate*'s original ordnance comprised twenty-eight 32 pounders on the lower gun deck, thirty 18 pounders on the middle gun deck, two 18 pounders and fourteen 32 pounder carronades on the quarter deck, and two 18 pounders and six 32 pounder carronades on her forecastle. This initially gave *Spartiate* a single broadside weight of 1074 pounds which was somewhat reduced when downrated to a 3rd rate of 74 guns on entering service into the Royal Navy.

CAPTAINS OF SPARTIATE (MSS 248/4, 248/6 and 248/7)

Name	Time of Entry	Time of Discharge	On What Occasion
Charles Pierrepont (French)	1798	1 August 1798	
George Murray	11 April 1803	9 May 1803	
John Manley	10 May 1803	31 December 1803	New Book
John Manley	1 January 1804	3 May 1804	Superseded - Promoted to Rear Admiral
Sir Francis Laforey Bt	4 May 1804	2 December 1809	Paid Off at Portsmouth
Thomas J Maling	1 June 1823	26 June 1823	To the *Cambridge*
Gordon F Falcon	27 June 1823	23 August 1825	Superseded
Graham E Hammond	24 August 1825	22 December 1825	Paid Off
Frederick Warren	23 December 1825		Note: New Book has nothing recorded

SERVICE CAREER

1798: In early April *Spartiate* lay in the arsenal at Toulon being coppered and fitted for sea service along with many other ships ready for Napoleon's expedition to invade Egypt, the fleet being placed under the command of Vice-Admiral de Brueys.[340] De Brueys' fleet, including *Spartiate*, sailed from Toulon 19 May, *Spartiate* commanded by Captain M J Emeriau. En route the ship became involved with the French capture of Malta, which capitulated 12 June. Arriving first at Alexandria, the French fleet moved east to anchor in Abu-Kir Bay. *Spartiate* was initially moored at the head of the line in seven fathoms but as this was too far from shore to effect a good defence de Bruey ordered *Guerrière* and *Conquerant* to anchor ahead of her. So when caught at anchor by Nelson's fleet on 1 August *Spartiate* was stationed third from the head of Admiral de Brueys' line.[341] In the opening stages of the battle *Theseus* (74) brought herself to anchor just astern of *Spartiate* and began firing at her from a range of 300 yards. At about 6.40 p.m, some thirty minutes after the battle had startted, *Vanguard* (74), Nelson's flagship, came up broadside to *Spartiate* and fired into her from about eighty yards. *Vanguard* maintained this fire for a considerable time and about 8.30 p.m. a piece of langridge shot fired from *Spartiate* struck Nelson on the forehead compelling him to go to the cockpit to have his wound dressed. *Spartiate* was soon totally dismasted and at 9 p.m. was obliged to strike her colours.[342]

Repaired after the battle, *Spartiate* was initially placed under the command of Captain Thomas Stephenson, retaining her French name.[343] Items found within her ordnance inventory were fireballs and explosive shells, incendiaries not yet adopted by the British navy.[344] Under Nelson's orders, *Spartiate* joined Saumarez' squadron under the command of Captain the Hon. Charles Pierrepoint (later Viscount Newark), returning to England.[345]

1799: Brought into Plymouth on 17 July, *Spartiate* was decommissioned and laid up in ordinary in the Hamoaze.

1801: Taken into dock at Plymouth on 28 July to be refitted and have her copper replaced, *Spartiate* was undocked on 20 November and placed back in ordinary until fitted for war in 1803.[346]

1803: When it was realised that war with France would reopen an Admiralty messenger arrived at Plymouth on 10 March after a 32 hour journey with dispatches for Rear-Admiral Dacres, the Port Admiral. Acting immediately, Dacres made out orders for all ships in Plymouth to be prepared for sea service and press gangs sent out to recruit. *Spartiate* was taken out of ordinary, fitted for sea service and put in commission. On 16 March a Captain of Marines together with 100 rank and file were embarked into the ship at the north stair. Moving alongside the sheer hulk to receive her masts, by 23 March *Spartiate* had all her lower and topmasts rigged and by 2 April her entire standing rigging had been set down and running rigging complete. At the same time stores for the gunner, boatswain and carpenter had been embarked, together with provisions, while the crew was assembled. Other 74 gun ships following the same procedure in Plymouth were *Mars*, *Malta*, *Plantagenet* and *Tonnant*. At 6 a.m. on 10 April, *Spartiate* made the signal to Admiral Lord Keith that she was ready for sea. Boats were assembled containing the Master Attendant and King's pilots and at 7 a.m. *Spartiate*, in company with *Malta* and *Tonnant*, slipped her moorings and got under weigh under a light NNW wind. As they worked out of the Hamoaze, spectators lined the river on both sides. According to the list of Commanders and their Ships, *Spartiate* was formally commissioned by Captain George Murray on 11 April. Five days later France declared war on Britain. Remaining in Cawsand Bay awaiting orders, Captain Murray was superseded by Captain John Manley on 10 May.[347] *Spartiate* immediately made sail and proceeded to sea in company with *Mars* (74), *Tonnant* (74), *Boadicea* (38), *Hazard* (18), *Seagull* (18), and *Rambler* (14) to cruise the western approaches. Returning to Plymouth on 13 September for a minor refit, *Spartiate* sailed to join the inshore squadron off Black Rock.

1804: When promoted to Rear-Admiral, John Manley was superseded by Captain Sir Francis Laforey Bt on 4 May.[348] Receiving orders to join the blockading squadron lying off the Spanish port of Ferrol, *Spartiate* sailed

SPECIFICATIONS: SPARTIATE

Rate	3rd	Length on the range of the gun deck	182 ft 7 ins	Ordnance - upper gun deck	30 x 18 pounders
Guns	74	Length of keel for tonnage	150 ft 4 ins	Ordnance - quarter deck	2 x 18 pounders
Class	French *Spartiate*	Extreme breadth	49 ft 4½ ins		14 x 32 pounder carronades
Designer	Standard French 80 gun design by Sane	Depth in hold	21 ft 7 ins	Ordnance - forecastle	2 x 18 pounders
Builder	Sane	Tons burthen	1949 41/94		6 x 32 pounder carronades
Dockyard	Toulon	Draught afore	22 ft 1 ins	Single broadside weight	1074 pounds
Date ordered	Captured 1 August 1798	Draught abaft	23 ft 3 ins	Fate	1842 Hulked at Plymouth as a temporarily sheer hulk.
Date keel laid	?	Complement	640		1857 Broken up.
Date launched	1797	Ordnance - lower gun deck	28 x 32 pounders		

Source: Lyon, *Sailing Navy List*, p. 237.

THE 74 GUN SHIP *SPARTIATE*

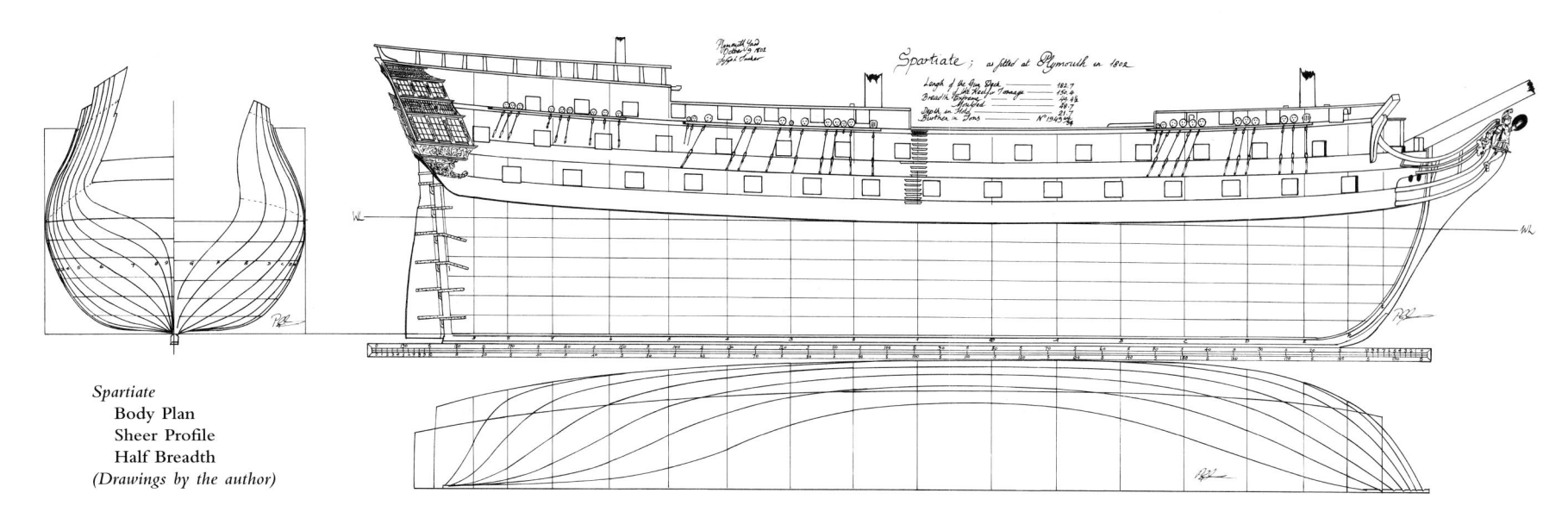

Spartiate
  Body Plan
  Sheer Profile
  Half Breadth
(Drawings by the author)

from Plymouth in early April. At the rendezvous nine ships of the line, some frigates and a cutter were deployed off Corunna. Returning to the Hamoaze in December to refit, command of the ship was superseded by Laforey. After taking on provisions and stores, she sailed to rejoin Sir Edward Pellew's squadron off Ferrol. On 23 December the squadron was hit a by a hurricane and *Spartiate*, driven to leeward, went missing and was feared lost. For nearly three weeks *Spartiate* battled alone against severe gales in the Western Atlantic, when one seaman fell to his death from the main yard, presumably numbed by the excessive cold and losing his grip. *Spartiate* eventually got into Berehaven Bay on 16 January 1805.

1805: Going into to the Hamoaze on 10 March to refit, *Spartiate* then sailed for the West Indies to join Rear-Admiral Cochrane's squadron based at Barbados. When Nelson's squadron, pursuing Villeneuve's combined fleet across the Atlantic, arrived at Barbados on 4 June he found only Cochrane, flying his flag in *Northumberland* (74), and *Spartiate* lying in Carlisle Bay. Needing reinforcements, *Northumberland* and *Spartiate* joined Nelson's fleet and sailed on 5 June for Grenada to seek out the French. Learning four days later that Villeneuve had gone north, Nelson's ships followed, arriving at Antigua 13 June where after landing troops and leaving *Northumberland* in support, set sail for Europe with *Spartiate* now in company. Making good progress, the entire squadron reached Gibraltar, anchoring in Rosia Bay, on 20 July.[349] For the next three months *Spartiate* was deployed with Collingwood's squadron off the Iberian coast.

TRAFALGAR

Spartiate's log for Monday 21 October states:

> Gales & Squally with rain 1-30 wore 2-10 wind shifted to NW under sail ans^d 10b & 8b AN. Mod breezes & hazy with a swell 8-20 wore, heard the report & saw flashes of Guns NNE….[at] 6 crossed Royal Yards at day light 6.10 Saw the Enemys Fleet to leeward NNE laying on a Starb^d. tack & forming a Line of Battle 6-40 bore up and made sail laying in two divisions & cleared for Action 8-55 the enemy wore & brought to the wind on the Larb^d. Tack in One line consisting of 33 Sail of the Line 5 Frigates & 2 Brigs.[350]

On the approach towards the combined fleet *Spartiate* lay eleventh and last in Nelson's windward column and consequently got into battle quite late. Kept in a state of non-activity for considerable time Captain Laforey provides within *Spartiate*'s log perhaps the most informative and detailed step by step account of the battle observed from his perspective. Commencing at noon 22 October Laforey wrote:

> … at 12-9 the action Commenced with the *R.Sovereign* (Vice Adm^l Collingwood) and the Enemy's Centre the *R.S* have gone thru' Line 12-32 the *Royal S.* was engaging (a Spanish 3 decked Ship) mizen topmast was shot away 12-59 HMS *Victory* (Vice Admiral Lord Visc^t Nelson) commenced firing at a Ship ahead of her obscured her bearing down between a Spanish four Decker and a French two Decker (with Admiral's Flag at the Main) 1-4 the *Tonnant* lost her Fore topmast and Yard 1-5 the *Victory* lost her Mizen topmast 1-7 a Spanish two Decker struck to the *Tonnant* 1-19 A Spanish two Deckers Mizen Mast went over the side 1-24 observed one of our 3 Deckers (supposed to be the *Téméraire*) maintopsail Yard shot away 1-25 the Spanish ship engaged by the $R^l.S$ ceased firing and had Struck the ——— [illegible] sail ahead to the next ship 1-36 the *Téméraire*'s maintopmast was shot away 1-39 observed the Spanish 3 Decker (which had struck to the $R^l.S$) masts go by the board 1-42 The French Admiral struck to the *Victory* (1-45 came on board a Lieu^t From HMS *Euryalus* with Orders from Lord Nelson to pass thru' the Enemy's Line wherever we could engage with most effect) 1-49 observed *Tonnant* had wore and had lost her maintopmast, an Enemy Ship appearing to be on board her 1-59 observed a Spanish 2 Decker (engaged by the *Neptune*) Main and Mizen masts go over the Side, 2-25 observed the Spanish 4 Deckers Main & Mizen masts go over the side then engaged by the *Neptune* and *Conqueror* on her starb^d. Quarter the *Africa* in passing Raking a French two Decker and her 2-30 the Spanish two Decker which had struck to the *Neptune* lost her foremast and bowsprit 2-37 the Spanish ——— Deckers foremast was shot away 2-40 observed the $R^l.S$ Main & Mizen masts go over the side 2-57 cut away our studding Sails observing the van of Enemy's Ships had wore to form a junction with their Centre At 3 hailed *Minotaur* to allow us to pass ahead of her hauled our wind to prevent their forming a junction 5 of them bore up 5 kept their wind to engage us and the *Minotaur*, Two French Ships and three Spanish at 3-7 the *Minotaur Spartiate* commenced firing with the headmost ships received and returned the fire of the five in passing with our topsails ——— the mast ——— filled to pass Enemys which had struck 3-40 observed the Spanish aftermost Ships rigging and Sails cut up very much lay to with fore & main topsails aback all the after sails sit on her quarter firing in an oblique direction at times returning the fire from other ports & quarters.

Captain Laforey had brought *Spartiate* abreast of the Spanish *Neptuno* (80) which was attempting to escape. Although the Spanish ship was already engaged on her opposite side by *Minotaur* (74), Laforey ordered his gunners to open fire, then at 4.10 p.m. Laforey 'wore ship to engage on the other Tack, the other four Ships having left her [*Neptuno*] 4-27 observed a French two Decked Ship on Fire in the SE quarter [*Achille*]'. After hammering *Neptuno* continuously for an hour with her broadsides *Spartiate* beat the Spanish ship into submission. *Spartiate*'s log continues, '4-42 the Spanish two Decked Ship Engaged by the *Minotaur* and *Spartiate* had her Mizen mast shot away 5-10 she struck being much disabled'. *Neptuno*, now out of control, drifted off and ran aboard *Téméraire*, lying nearby with two prizes lashed alongside. Laforey then wrote:

> ... 5-20 the firing ceased observed 12 of the Enemy's Ships had struck 5-54 the French ship that caught fire in the SE blew up observed that the *Belle Isle* [*Belleisle*] was totally dismasted The *Téméraire* between two Ships which had struck to her with one of their Mainmasts laying on board her observed the *Victory* & *Colossus* had lost their Mizen masts eight of the Enemy's Ships totally dismasted, the remaining Ships of the five we engaged kept their wind to the South with all Sail set observed also 11 of the Ships of the Enemy under a press of sail Steering to the North East[d]. At 7 sent Twenty of marines with a Cutter with a Mid [midshipman] on board the *Intrepide* (being part of an Officer Guard sent there) 8-20 out Pinnace to take the *Tonnant* in tow AM D[o]. W[r]. Could not get the hawser to the *Tonnant* empl[d]. knotting shrouds, running Rigging &c. at 8 Fresh breezes Fleet and Prizes much scattered at 10 took the *Tonnant* in tow 11-40 wore pr. Signal.

Laforey wrote:

> The damages we received are as follows The Foremast and Bowsprit badly wounded in two places, 1 Shot well thro' the heel of Maintopmast, which splintered it much Fore & Main Shrouds shot away and several of the Topmast D[o]. Backstays running rigging all cut very much and several shots in our hull & several small grape shot in the Fore & Main masts Emp[d]. Rep[g]. the damages & getting the Ship ready to renew Action.

James states that *Spartiate* lost three killed and 20 wounded, whereas Laforey clearly states in his log, '3 killed the Boatswain two Midshipmen 17 men 1 RM & 1 boy W[d].', giving totals of 3 and 22 respectively.[351] Among the wounded were Midshipmen Henry Bellairs and Edward Knapman and the Boatswain John Clark.[352]

During the day following the battle *Spartiate* towed *Tonnant*. To prepare for the approaching stormy weather and relieve strain upon *Spartiate*'s rigging, topgallant yards and masts were sent on deck. Later that day: '10 the *Tonnant*'s two ropes parted'. On Thursday 24th they 'ranged both cables & got springs on both Anchors from our after Gun Deck ports' and on Friday the log states that they closed with 'the *Swiftsure* 1-30 hove to Emp[d] receiving Prisoners from *Swiftsure* and *Intrepide* [at] 9 a Ship on fire NW [at] 10 she blew up'.[353] On the 28th the frigate *Juno*, which had not fought in the battle, joined company and with weather improving *Spartiate*'s topgallant masts and yards could again be sent up and set. The log also gives reference to '2 French frigates & 1 Brig with Cartel Colours flying', seen approaching from Cadiz. At 8.30 a.m. on Thursday 31 October, 'Came on Board the Capt[n]. Of the *Weazle*'. Over the next few days we see from the log that the scattered British fleet began to reassemble with their prizes and make for Gibraltar. Laforey notes the loss of a prize, recording 'drifted in a Prize into Cadiz Bay the *Algeciras*'. Further accounts relate to giving chase and stopping a vessel from Falmouth for Venice, and the loss of *Spartiate*'s cutter. Finally getting into Gibraltar on Sunday 10 November, Laforey wrote:

> Anch[d]. in the bay & moored Ship a cable each way.....[in] 27 f[ms]. water *Queen* & Squadron in the offing', and then list the ship seen at anchor; '*R.Sovereign Téméraire Tonnant Colossus Orion Polyphemus Leviathan Swiftsure Thunderer Niger, Thunder* (bonb) & 4 Prizes Hulk in the bay sent boats for water *R Sovereign* with (Rear Adm[l]. [K]Night's Flag) & the garrison saluted Adm[l]. Collingwood & Fleet 10-30 Anch[d]. HM Ships *Queen Prince Ajax Britannia Sirius* (with the Fellucca —) *Amphion* & *Scout* bent the Sheet Cable & rounded the bower Cables.[354]

Returning to England *Spartiate* went into Plymouth 14 December.

1806. On 9 January Captain Laforey attended Lord Nelson's funeral, travelling in the mourning coach bearing Nelson's standard. *Spartiate*, docked

PROGRESS BOOK - *SPARTIATE* 3rd RATE OF 74 GUNS:

At what Port	Arrived	Docked	Coppered
Plymouth	17 July 1799	28 July 1799	Copper taken off August 1801 Re-coppered November 1801
Plymouth	10 Dec 1804	18 Dec 1804	Copper Repaired
Plymouth	14 Dec 1805	21 Jan 1806	Coppered Repaired
Portsmouth	7 July 1807	13 July 1807	Copper taken off and Re-coppered July 1807
Portsmouth	10 Nov 1809	-	-
Woolwich	15 Sep 1813	6 Apr 1814	Copper taken off Apr 1814 & Re-coppered March 1815
Sheerness	18 May 1815		
Chatham	15 July 1822	1 Dec 1822	Copper taken off Jan 1823 & Re-coppered June 1823
Portsmouth	3 Dec 1825	28 Dec 1825	Copper taken off and Re-coppered
Portsmouth	24 May 1828	27 June 1828	Copper repaired & dressed down
Portsmouth	26 Mar 1830	31 Jan 1831	Copper taken off and Re-coppered
Portsmouth		8 Oct 1832	Copper taken off and Re-coppered
Portsmouth	Jan 1833	-	-
Plymouth	16 Feb 1833	-	-
Plymouth	23 Aug 1835	7 Mar 1837	Shifted four strakes of Copper
Plymouth		6 Aug 1842	Repaired Copper

27 Mar 1857

Completed Taking To Pieces 30 May 1857

on 21 January for three weeks refitting, sailed on 14 March for the Mediterranean, deployed off the coast of Sicily.

1807: Going into Portsmouth 7 July, *Spartiate* went into dock one week later to refit at an overall cost of £9,571, then returned to the Mediterranean, mainly serving with Admiral Sir Richard Strachan's squadron operating out of Palermo.

1809: Deployed with Admiral George Martin's squadron, *Spartiate* sailed from Malazzo on 11 June with *Canopus* (80), Martin's flagship, *Warrior* (74), *Cyane* (22), the brig-sloop *Espoir* (18) and 130 British and Sicilian transports to attack enemy installations upon the Calabrian coast. Joined by *Alceste* (38), two Sicilian frigates and a further 100 transports from Palermo on 15 June, preparations were made for the assault. Sicilian troops, commanded by General Boucard, were landed at Calabria, while diversions of British and Sicilian forces from Melazzo attacked the islands of Procala and Ischia, the former surrendering on 25 June, the latter on 1 July.[355] Recalled, *Spartiate* arrived at Portsmouth 10 November, Laforey paying off the ship 2 December and she was laid up in ordinary until September 1813 when she was transferred to Woolwich.[356]

1814: Going into dock 6 April, *Spartiate* was given a 'middling to large repair'. When undocked 17 May 1815 she had been completed at a cost of £59,787. Next day the ship was sent down river to Sheerness where she remained until sent up the Medway to Chatham 15 July 1822.

1822: In late December *Spartiate* was docked for a 'small to middling repair' costing £36,753.

1823: Still in dock, *Spartiate* was 'fitted for a Flag for Foreign Service' and recommissioned by Captain Thomas J Maling on 1 June. Transferring into

THE 74 GUN SHIP *SPARTIATE*

Source: ADM 180/10 Entry 50

Launched or Undocked	Sailed	Built or Nature of Repair	Cost of Hull, Masts & Yards Materials £	Workmen £	Cost of Masts & Yards Materials £	Workmen £	Cost of Rigging & Stores Materials £	Workmen £	Grand Total £
20 Nov 1801	23 April 1803	Fitted							
19 Dec 1804	18 Jan 1805	Defects	929	555	2,963	49	6,584	158	11,238
13 Feb 1806	14 Mar 1806	Defects	3,239	1,893	2,278	27	9,690	74	17,201
31 July 1807	30 Aug 1807	Refitted	1,884	825	1,2387	19	5,473	83	9,571
-	30 Aug 1813	Defects	214	159	-	7	5,922	1	6,306
24 Apr 1815 Housed Oct 1814	17 May 1815 to Sheerness	Between Middling & Large Repair	36,287	12,941	2,036	355	8,012	156	59,787
15 July 1822 to Chatham			2,444	1,319	7	15	-	1	3,786
8 July 1823	28 Aug 1823	Between Small & Middling Repair & fitted for a Flag for Foreign Service	9,538	4,113	3,644	175	19,152	131	36,753
7 Feb 1826	19 Dec 1826	Defects made good	5,370	2,333	1,695	38	7,583	119	17,138
27 Aug 1828	6 Oct 1828	Defects made good	6,689	2,564	472	78	4,050	131	14,684
28 July 1831		Defects							
10 Oct 1832	7 Nov 1832	Fitted for Sea Service							
-	Feb 1833	Defects	417	391	10	1	2,175	7	3,001
-	Feb 1833	Defects	21	30	-	-	565	-	616
10 Marc 1837		Defects	13	342	-	-	-	-	355
22 Aug 1842		Fitted for a temporary Sheer Hulk	814	1,182	656	168	-	-	2,820
		Defects to March 1856	430	889	-	572	-	476	2,367
		Defects &c.							
		Taken to Pieces	74	774	-	4	-	109	961

Stores returned on taking to pieces Hull £4,448
Rigging &c £3,561
£8,009

Cambridge just 26 days later, Maling was succeeded by Gordon Falcon.

1825 to 1842: On 24 August command of the ship was superseded by Captain Graham E Hammond who remained in the ship until succeeded by Captain Frederick Warren on 23 December. After this *Spartiate* was again docked to make good her defects and was successively maintained in and out of commission at Portsmouth until 1842.

FATE

Docked on 6 August 1842 to be 'Fitted for a temporary Sheer Hulk', *Spartiate* fulfilled this rôle for fifteen years until finally taken into dock on 27 March 1757 and taken to pieces, this work being completed 30 May that same year.[357]

The 74 gun ship *SWIFTSURE*

The *Swiftsure* that fought at Trafalgar was the sixth ship to bear this name in the Royal Navy, the first such ship being a galleon of 41 guns built at Deptford in 1573. Armed with two 60 pounders, five 18 pounders, twelve 9 pounders, eight 6 pounders and fourteen smaller guns, *Swiftsure* fought against the Spanish Armada in 1588. Rebuilt at Woolwich in 1592 to carry 40 guns of more uniform calibre, she was renamed *Speedwell* and was lost near Flushing in November 1624. The second *Swiftsure*, a 46 gun ship of 746 tons, was built at Deptford in 1621. Rebuilt at Woolwich with an increase of 152 tons in 1653, she was captured in 1 June 1666 during the Second Dutch War. The third ship comprised a 3rd rate of 70 guns built by

SPECIFICATIONS: *SWIFTSURE*

Rate	3rd	*Length on the range of the gun deck*	173 ft	*Ordnance - upper gun deck*	28 x 18 pounders
Guns	74	*Length of keel for tonnage*	142 ft	*Ordnance - quarter deck*	4 x 18 pounders
Class	Swiftsure 1800	*Extreme breadth*	47 ft 6 ins		10 x 32 pounder carronades
Designer	John Henslow	*Depth in hold*	20 ft 9 ins	*Ordnance - forecastle*	2 x 18 pounders
Builder	Henry Adams	*Tons burthen*	1704 17/94		2 x 32 pounder carronades
Dockyard	Buckler's Hard	*Draught afore*	21 ft 1 in	*Ordnance - roundhose/poop*	6 x 18 pounder carronades
Date ordered	? 1800/1801	*Draught abaft*	23 ft 6 ins	*Single broadside weight*	1000 pounds
Date keel laid	August 1802	*Complement*	590	*Fate*	1819 Hulked at Portsmouth as a receiving ship
Date launched	23 July 1804	*Ordnance - lower gun deck*	28 x 32 pounders		1845 Broken up

Source: Lyon, *Sailing Navy List*, p. 113.

CAPTAINS OF *SWIFTSURE* (MSS 248/4 and 248/6)

Name	Time of Entry	Time of Discharge	On What Occasion
Mark Robinson	23 August 1804	10 May 1805	To the *Royal Sovereign*
William G Rutherford	11 May 1805	18 November 1807	Superseded
John Conn	9 November 1807	4 May 1810	Drowned
Charles J Austen	13 May 1810	25 September 1810	To the *Cleopatra*
Robert Lloyd Recommissioned	26 September 1810	11 April 1811	Paid Off at Chatham
Temple Hardy	20 August 1811	17 June 1812	Discharged to [Port] Mahon Hospital
Andrew King - Acting	7 May 1812	16 June 1812	Superseded Acting
Jermiah Coghlan - Acting	17 June 1812	9 July 1812	Superseded Acting
William Stuart - Acting	11 July 1812	26 August 1812	Superseded Acting
C J Dickson	27 August 1812	27 June 1814	To the *Rivoli*
Arden Adderley	28 June 1814	8 October 1814	Superseded
William H Webley	9 October 1814	30 August 1815	Paid Off at Portsmouth

Sir Anthony Deane and launched at Harwich 8 April 1673. Rebuilt at Deptford in 1696 she was reduced to 64 guns and renamed *Revenge* on 2 January 1716. Rebuilt for a second time in 1742, this ship was finally sold in 1787.[358] The next *Swiftsure*, constructed to the specifications of the 1745 Establishment, was a 3rd rate of 70 guns launched at Deptford 25 May 1750. After actively serving throughout the Seven Years' War she was sold on 2 June 1773.[359] The fifth *Swiftsure*, designed to the lines of Slade's *Elizabeth* class of 1766, was built by John Wells at Rotherhithe, launched 4 April 1787. Under the command of Captain Benjamin Hallowell, this *Swiftsure* played a significant rôle at the battle of the Nile fought in Abu-Kir Bay 1 August 1798. During this action *Swiftsure* engaged and captured the French *Tonnant* (80) which, taken into the Royal Navy, fought with distinction under Captain Charles Tyler at Trafalgar. Following the battle on 8 August, Hallowell took possession of the batteries set up on the island of Abu-Kir and throwing all the iron guns into the sea and bringing off two mortars and two 12-pounders, all made of brass. Unfortunately, while sailing from Abu-Kir to Malta with a convoy of cartels and light transports on 24 June 1801, Hallowell fell in with four French line of battle ships and a frigate belonging to Admiral Ganteaume's squadron. Hallowell fought gallantly, but this *Swiftsure*, being rather leaky and much in need of refit, was in no fit state to withstand her attackers and was consequently captured. The first news to reach Britain of *Swiftsure's* capture came from the French newspaper *Moniteur*, dated 23 July. The court martial held at Port Mahon 18 August 1801 honourably acquitted Captain Hallowell of all blame, having defended the ship to the utmost. Taken into the French navy under her own name, this *Swiftsure* later served with Vice Admiral Villeneuve's combined fleet at Trafalgar. Re-captured during the battle, she had to be renamed *Irresistible* as a new *Swiftsure* now existed in the fleet. *Irresistible/Swiftsure* was broken up in 1816.[360]

The Trafalgar *Swiftsure* was one of two 3rd rate 74 gun ships built to the lines of the *Swiftsure* class designed by John Henslow in 1800, the other being *Victorious*. Ordered 1800/1801, the keel of the *Swiftsure* was laid down at Buckler's Hard on the River Beaulieu in August 1802 and constructed by Henry Adams.[361] Built using some 3,250 trees taken from the New Forest in Hampshire, the building cost for her hull amounted to £35,787 17s 9d.[362] Unfortunately the expenditure of her masts, yards, rigging and stores has not been recorded within the Progress Book.[363] Completed ten months later than contract, Adams suffered a £500 penalty fine and consequently made little profit from building her. Adams, it must be remarked, had also been late in completing the frigate *Euryalus*. Attending *Swiftsure's* launch on 23 July 1804 were 3,500 people who made their way from the surrounding area by foot or carriage to enjoy the festivities. Although Adams had lost money, 110 guests were entertained at his own expense within the banqueting hall adjoining the Master Builder's house while Charles Hemans, landlord of the Ship Inn, sold five hogsheads of ale (1 hogshead = 448 pints) to the crowd.[364] *Swiftsure* was taken round to Portsmouth dockyard, arriving there 31 July. Docked on 7 August 1804, she was coppered and fitted out for sea service. Armed with twenty-eight 32 pounders on the lower gun deck, twenty-eight 18 pounders on her upper gun deck, four 18 pounders and ten 32 pounder carronades on the quarter deck, two 18 pounders and two 32 pounder carronades on the forecastle and a further six 18 pounder carronades on her poop, *Swiftsure* could deliver a total single broadside weight of 1,000 pounds. Compared with *Victory* (100), which had a single broadside weight of 1,148 pounds, *Swiftsure's* weight of fire was as a 74 considerable.

SERVICE CAREER

1804: Docked, coppered and fitted for sea service between July and August, *Swiftsure* was commissioned 23 August by Captain Mark Robinson and immediately sent to the Mediterranean, joining Nelson's fleet at Agincourt Sound on Christmas Day 25 December.[365]

1805: When Nelson received news on 19 January that Villeneuve had put to sea from Toulon, he immediately ordered his ships to sail. *Swiftsure*, with the rest of Nelson's squadron, weighed at 4.30 and sailed in chase of the French, negotiating the narrow channel between Biche and Sardinia. Besides *Swiftsure* and Nelson's *Victory* the squadron in pursuit comprised *Royal Sovereign* (100), the 74 gun ships *Belleisle, Canopus, Conqueror, Donegal, Leviathan, Superb, Spencer,* and *Tigre*, together with the 38 gun frigates *Active* and *Seahorse*.[366] With the rest of Nelson's ships she sailed first east, across the Mediterranean and to Gibraltar, and then west across the Atlantic to the West Indies in search of Villeneuve, reaching Barbados on 4 June. They re-crossed the Atlantic, arriving off Gibraltar 20 July. Command of the *Swiftsure* was succeeded by Captain William Rutherford and after re-provisioning the ship took up station with the fleet blockading Villeneuve's fleet, now in Cadiz.[367] Preparing two days beforehand for the inevitable battle, *Swiftsure's* log Saturday 19 October records: 'standing off & on Cape S^t. Mary's 11.00 beat to Q^{trs}. & cleared for Action 11.30 beat the retreat'.[368]

TRAFALGAR

Commencing at noon Sunday, *Swiftsure's* log account dated Monday 21 October begins:

PM Fresh Breezes & Cloudy, made & shorten'd sail occas^y. to Keep our Station at 2 observed some Gun fire from the ENE & Sigl^s. flying 6 Adml. & Fleet in Co. at 9 out 2^d reef topsails at 10 Obs^d. our look out Ships firing Guns Rockets & bearing blue lights in the West^d. Quarter AM Light Airs & pleasant W^r. at 5 Discovered the Enemy's Fleet East^d. made all sail to form the Order of Battle beat to Quarters & cleared for Action at 8 all sail set Noon *Victory* & Fleet in Comp^y. Enemy's Fleet from ENE to N consisting of 33 Sail of the line 5 Frigates & 2 corvets [sic] Distance about 1½ or 3 Miles.

Unlike the account given in *Spartiate's* log, Rutherford's log record of the battle, beginning noon Tuesday 22 October is very matter of fact: 'Light Airs & clear 12.15 HMS R. Sovereign broke through the Enemy's line & brought them to Action which was warmly supported by all the rest of the British Fleet 12.30 the Action became general at 4 Cape Trafalgar ESE 3 or 4 leagues'.[369]

Swiftsure was placed tenth in line of Collingwood's leeward division. Ahead of her lay *Polyphemus* (64), astern *Defiance* (74). Being well behind in the line it was a considerable time before *Swiftsure* got into battle. At about 3.15 p.m. *Swiftsure* went to the aid of *Belleisle* which was under considerable fire from various quarters, the French *Achille* raking her stern. Seeing this Rutherford carried *Swiftsure* across *Belleisle's* stern and fired *Swiftsure's* larboard batteries into *Achille* with good effect. This action on Rutherford's

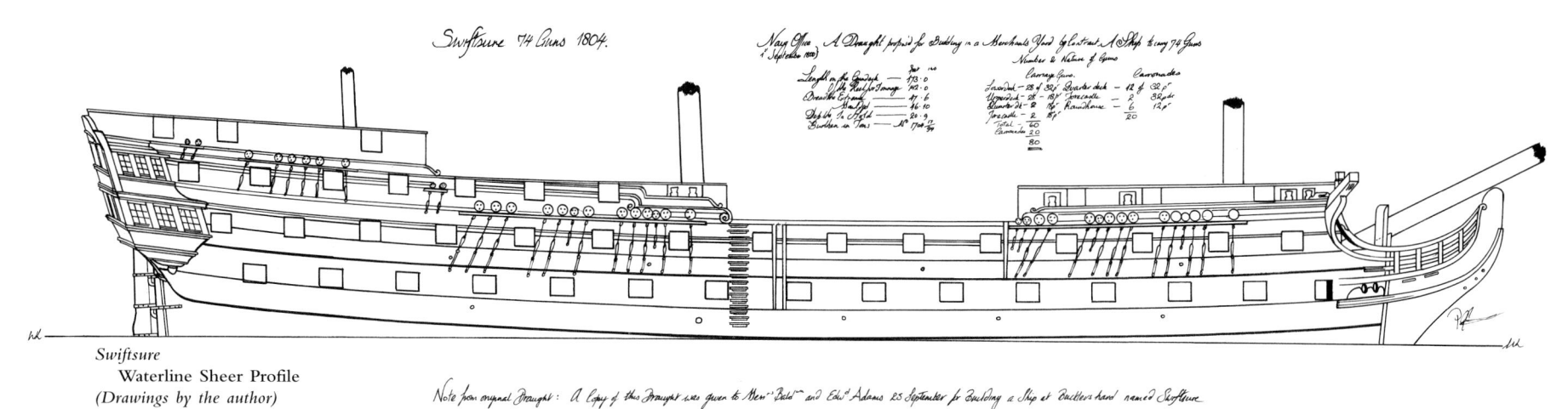

Swiftsure
Waterline Sheer Profile
(Drawings by the author)

part alleviated the consolidated fire directed at *Belleisle*. Rutherford then brought *Swiftsure* to close with *Achille* and drawing up on her stern, fired several raking broadsides before laying his ship alongside the Frenchman's larboard side and persistently mauling *Achille* with broadsides. By 3.35 p.m. *Swiftsure* was joined by *Polyphemus* and others, all firing into *Achille*. Through incessant bombardment, fires started onboard the French ship. As the flames began to engulf *Achille*, *Swiftsure*, being nearby, lowered her boats to rescue survivors, *Pickle* and *Entreprenante* doing the same. Around 200 were rescued before *Achille* blew up with devastating effect. Concluding the day's events in the log Rutherford wrote:

> …4.30 the action ceased when those of the Enemy that were capable bore up for Cadiz while those of our own took in Tow our own crippled Ships & Prizes to clear them of the Shoals of Trafalgar Ans[d.] Sig[l.] to prepare to Anchor People Emp[d.] Repairing the damaged rigging as well as possible took the French Prize *Redoutable* in Tow sounded in 12 fathoms at 6 AM sounded in 25 fathoms & wore p[r.] Sig[l.] at 6 AM Trafalgar EbS 5 or 6 leagues.[370]

Swiftsure suffered few casualties, nine killed and eight wounded, among the latter was Midshipman Alexander Handcock. *Swiftsure* lost her mizzen topmast and sustained some damage to spars and rigging.[371] While his battle account was very concise, Rutherford provides a vivid picture of circumstances surrounding *Redoutable*. Wednesday 23 October:

> Strong Gales & Cloudy at 2 close reef'd the Topsails at 3 *Redoutable* in Tow made the signal of distress out Boats & brought the Prize & People & as many of the Prisoners as possible 8.15 In Boats 10.13 *Redoutable* Prize in Tow went down cut the Tow & lost two cables of 8 Inch & one of 15 to her at 12 wore to the South[d.] 3.30 heard the cries of some people a short distance from us picked up part of the Remaining Crew of Prize who to save their lives had made a raft succeeded in taking them all on board served some Slops [clothes] to those who were destitute of Cloaths more mod[te.] & Clear 8.15 discovered 2 rafts full of men who saved themselves from the wreck of *Redoutable* when sinking sent Boats & brought them on board Noon run alongside the *Victory* to take her in tow Fleet Prizes & crippled Ships much scattered Mount Medina EbS 9 or 10 leagues opened 3 Barrels of American Beef N[o.] 44 Co[ts.] 50 [contents 50 pieces] N[o.] 45 Co[ts.] 50, N[o.] 27 Co[ts.] 50, 200lb each one pipe of wine N[o.] 1107 Co[ts.] 126 Galls Inches Dry 3.[372]

Now burdened with many French prisoners, *Swiftsure*'s log for Thursday 24 October records the measures taken to account for them, 'hove over board p[r.] Captain's Order to make room for Prisoners Water Casks 60 Butts 30 Punch[ns.] 31 Hh[ns.] 20 Barrels, Iron Hoops 1316 in N[o.] '. After bending 'a new Fore Topsail the Old much damaged by shot in the action', on Friday *Swiftsure* came to anchor 'in 2 fathoms Muddy bottom & veered to ? a Cable', Cadiz light still in sight.[373] Rutherford also records that one of the prize ships was on fire. *Swiftsure* remained anchored off Cadiz until Friday 1 November and making sail with the 74 guns ships *Ajax*, *Leviathan* and *Orion*, made for Gibraltar. Arriving there and anchoring in Rosia Bay Sunday 3 November, the crew set about making good repairs to the ship and taking in provisions from *Royal Sovereign* (100).[374] Unlike many of the Trafalgar ships *Swiftsure* did not return home for major refitting.

1807: Finally returning to Portsmouth 29 September, *Swiftsure* went into dock 8 October to refit. Captain John Conn, who had commanded *Dreadnought* (98) at Trafalgar, took command on 9 November and at the beginning of December the ship was sent to Halifax to serve as the flagship for Admiral Sir Charles Borlase Warren, Commander-in-Chief of the North American station.

1810: On 4 May Captain John Conn drowned; consequently, command of the *Swiftsure* ship passed to Captain John Austen from the sloop *Indian* (18) on the 13 May. Austen's stay in *Swiftsure* was brief, for once the ship had been recalled to England he transferred into *Cleopatra* (32) on 25 September. His successor, Captain Robert Lloyd, assumed command the next day. Deployed with part of the Channel fleet, *Swiftsure* spent the rest of the year cruising out of Portsmouth.[375]

1811: Needing to refit, Lloyd sailed for Chatham, arriving there 12 March. Docked ten days later Lloyd paid *Swiftsure* off on 11 April. Refitted at a cost of £14,076 *Swiftsure* was re-launched 23 July and recommissioned under Captain Temple Hardy on 20 August, after which she was sent to the Mediterranean.[376]

1812: Cruising in the Eastern Mediterranean in early May, Captain Hardy was taken ill and acting command was given to Andrew King on 7 May until *Swiftsure* got into Port Mahon on 16 June. Next day, when Captain Hardy was discharged into Port Mahon naval hospital, acting command was superseded by Jeremiah Coghlan and then, on 11 July, by William Stuart. *Swiftsure* finally received a permanent commander in the person of Captain Edward Dickson on 27 August, Dickson having previously commanded *Stately* (64).

1813: Operating off Corsica on 26 November, boats from *Swiftsure* commanded by First Lieutenant William Smith captured the French privateer schooner *Charlemagne* (8) ten miles WNW of Cape Rouse (Rosso). During the engagement *Charlemagne* attempted to get away using her sweeps but when *Swiftsure*'s boats closed with the schooner, *Charlemagne* opened up a devastating fire, causing considerable casualties. Despite this onslaught the schooner was boarded and carried. Casualties comprised Midshipman Joseph Douglas and four seamen killed; 15 wounded among whom were Lieutenants Rose Henry Fuller and John Harvey; Mr Thompson, Lieutenant of Marines; Midshipman Field, and eleven seamen. Lieutenant Henry died later of his wounds. Once taken it was found that the schooner,

PROGRESS BOOK - *SWIFTSURE* 3rd RATE OF 74 GUNS: Source: ADM 180/10 Entry 130

At what Port	Arrived	Docked	Coppered	Launched or Undocked	Sailed	Built or Nature of Repair	Cost of Hull, Masts & Yards Materials £ s d	Cost of Rigging & Stores Materials £ s d	Grand Total
Buckler's Hard; Adams	Began	August 1802		23 July 1804		Built	35,787 Refer Author's Note		35,787 Refer Author's Note 1
Portsmouth	31 July 1804	7 Aug 1804	Coppered Aug 1804	21 Aug 1804	24 Sep 1804	Fitted			
Portsmouth	29 Sep 1807	8 Oct 1807	Copper taken off and re-coppered Oct 1807	30 Oct 1807	21 Nov 1807	Repaired			
Chatham	12 Mar 1811	20 Mar 1811	Copper taken off Apr and Re-coppered July 1811	23 July 1811	22 Sep 1811	Small Repair	10,200 3,876		14,076
Portsmouth	18 Aug 1815		Copper taken off to Light draft of water Sept 1815						
Portsmouth		22 Apr 1819	Copper taken off and re-coppered	7 May 1819		Fitted for a Receiving Ship	863 1,162	453 38	2,516
			Shifted part of the Copper 1844			Expense till Sold	117 83	576	610 Refer Author's Note 2
Sold 18 October 1845 to Mr Barnard for £1,055									

Author's Notes: 1. As the original document has no expenses recorded for the building of the *Swiftsure* the initial building cost, taken from an alternative source, has been added by the author.
2. The last set of figures should read a total of £776; however it appears that the charge for workmen, i.e. £83, has been deducted from the charge of materials for the hull rather than added; hence the difference, £34, when added to the expense for rigging and stores (£576) amounts to £610; consequently it is unsure whether this calculation is deliberate or simply an error on the part of the clerk.

provisioned for six months cruising, had sailed from Genoa twenty-four days earlier.[377]

1814: On 22 February Captain Dickson transferred into *Rivoli*, a 74 gun ship captured from the French in 1812. His successor, Captain Arden Adderley, assumed command of *Swiftsure* six days later and was superseded on 9 October by Captain William H Webley.

1815: Under Webley's command *Swiftsure* was sent to the West Indies where she remained until recalled. Arriving home Webley paid her off at Portsmouth on 30 August, she was then laid up in ordinary.

FATE

No longer fit for service, *Swiftsure* was docked at Portsmouth 22 April 1819 to have her copper sheathing replaced. Re-launched 7 May *Swiftsure* was brought alongside the wall and converted into a receiving ship at a total cost of £2,516. After part of her copper was removed in 1844 for re-use, *Swiftsure* was finally 'Sold 18 Oct 1845 to Mr Barnard for £1,055'.[378]

The 74 gun ship THUNDERER

Thunderer was the third ship of this name in the Royal Navy. The first *Thunderer* was a 3rd rate 74 gun ship of the *Hercules* class designed by Thomas Slade in 1756 which had been launched at Woolwich 19 March 1760. During the American War of Independence this vessel was deployed with a British squadron commanded by Captain Charles Fielding which, at the end of 1779, searched a Dutch convoy suspected of carrying naval stores for the French.[379] While operating off Santo Domingo on 5 October 1780 with a squadron commanded by Rear-Admiral Rowley, she was caught in a violent hurricane with waterspouts. *Thunderer* disappeared and was never seen again.[380] In the List of Ships and their Commanding Officers she is written off as 'Paid off at Broad St. Ship lost & all Crew perished'.[381] A second vessel named *Thunderer*, in service at the same time, was a 14 gun ketch built at St John's in 1776. This was a flat bottomed craft with a swim bow and stern carrying twelve guns and two howitzers employed on the Great Lakes during the American War of Independence until 1779, her fate unknown.[382]

The Trafalgar *Thunderer* was a 3rd rate of 74 guns built to the lines of Slade's *Culloden/Thunderer* class of 1769. Her sister ships comprised *Culloden*, *Hannibal*, *Ramillies*, *Terrible*, *Theseus*, *Venerable*, and *Victorious*; *Theseus* and *Venerable* serving as flagships of Admirals Nelson and Duncan respectively. Ordered 23 August 1781, *Thunderer*'s keel was laid down at Deptford in March 1783 and built by John Wells. Launched 17 November 1783 and carrying twenty-eight 32 pounders on the lower gun deck, twenty-eight 18 pounders on her upper gun deck, fourteen 9 pounders upon the quarter deck and four 9 pounders on the forecastle, *Thunderer* delivered a single broadside weight of 781 pounds.

SERVICE HISTORY

1794: First commissioned under the command of Captain Albemarle Bertie 26 February,[383] *Thunderer* first saw action when deployed with Admiral Howe's grand fleet against the French fleet commanded by Rear-Admiral Louis Villaret-Joyeuse. Cruising with the weathermost division of Howe's

SPECIFICATIONS: *THUNDERER*

Rate	3rd	Date keel laid	March 1783	Complement	550/600
Guns	74	Date launched	17 November 1783	Ordnance - lower gun deck	28 x 32 pounders
Class	Culloden/Thunderer 1769	Length on the range of the gun deck	170 ft	Ordnance - upper gun deck	28 x 18 pounders
Designer	Thomas Slade	Length of keel for tonnage	140 ft 1⅜ ins	Ordnance - quarter deck	14 x 9 pounders
Builder	John Wells	Extreme breadth	47 ft	Ordnance - forecastle	4 x 9 pounders
Dockyard	Deptford	Depth in hold	19 ft 11 ins	Single broadside weight	781 pounds
Date ordered	23 August 1781	Tons burthen	1658 52/94	Fate	1814 Broken up

Source: Lyon, *Sailing Navy List*, p. 71.

CAPTAINS OF THUNDERER (MSS 248/4 and 248/6)

Name	Time of Entry	Time of Discharge	On What Occasion
Albemarle Bertie	26 February 1794	10 March 1796	Superseded
James Ballard	31 January 1796	10 March 1797	To the *Pearl* Acting
James Bowen	11 March 1797	31 January 1797	Superseded
William Ogilvy	1 February 1797	14 May 1798	Superseded
John Loring	15 May 1798	16 June 1798	To the *Carnatic*
John Cochet	17 June 1798	10 January 1799	To the *Valiant*
John Crawley	11 January 1799	11 May 1799	To the *Greyhound*
Temple Hardy	12 May 1799	27 July 1800	Superseded
Robert Mends	28 July 1800	2 April 1801	Superseded
Henry William Bayntun	3 April 1801	16 April 1801	Superseded
Henry Vansittart	17 April 1801	29 June 1801	Paid Off at Chatham
John Delafons	11 August 1801	7 September 1801	Superseded
Soloman Ferris	8 September 1801	4 November 1801	Paid Off at Chatham
William Bedford	12 March 1803	31 December 1803	New Book
William Bedford	1 January 1804	17 February 1805	Paid Off at Plymouth
William Lechmere	2 April 1805	13 October 1805	Superseded
John Stockham	14 October 1805	9 April 1806	Superseded
John Talbot	10 April 1806	26 November 1808	Paid Off at Chatham

fleet under Rear-Admiral Pasley on 28 May, *Thunderer*, with the 74s *Bellerophon*, *Marlborough* and *Russell*, observed Villaret's ships at 8.15 a.m. Howe immediately signalled his fleet to clear for action, the French still being some 3 leagues distant. Howe then ordered Pasley to attack the French rear, but it was not until 6.30 p.m. that *Thunderer*, with *Bellerophon*, *Marlborough* and *Russell*, closed sufficiently to effect this. Backing her main topsails *Thunderer* drew up and began to fire at long range into *Révolutionnaire* (110) and the ships nearby. With some of Howe's ships suffering much damage this initial action was discontinued after a few hours.[384] *Thunderer* played little part in the actions over the next few days. The final encounter between Howe and Villaret commenced at 9.25 a.m. on 1 June, the French opening their fire into *Defence* (74); by 10 a.m. fighting had become general. Hotly contended, the battle continued for two and half hours during which *Thunderer* mainly played mainly a supportive rôle and consequently suffered no casualties and little damage. Of the French fleet of 26 line of battle ships and seven frigates the British captured seven prizes one of which, *Jemmapes* (74), was a recapture. The eighth vessel lost by the French was *Vengeur de Peuple* (74), which foundered shortly after surrendering.[385]

1795: With Bertie still in command *Thunderer* was now operating with Commodore Sir Borlase Warren's inshore squadron standing off Belle Isle watching for Villaret's ships. On 20 June Warren received orders to detach *Thunderer*, *Robust* (74) and *Standard* (64) to reinforce Lord Bridport's cruising fleet further seaward. Because of a shift of wind *Thunderer* and her consorts were unable to join Bridport as ordered and consequently did not take part in Bridport's action against Villaret off Ile de Groix on 23 June.[386]

1796: When command of *Thunderer* was succeeded by Captain James Ballard on 31 January, with Bertie officially leaving the ship on 10 March, *Thunderer* was sent to the West Indies station commanded by Vice-Admiral Sir Hyde Parker.[387] While operating near Jean Rabel on 17 April *Thunderer*, with *Valiant* (74), pursued and drove on shore the French frigate *Harmonie* (44).[388] Serving as flagship for Rear-Admiral Sir Hugh Cloberry Christian a week later, *Thunderer* arrived off St Lucia with a squadron on 27 April. Troops, commanded by Lieutenant-General Sir Ralph Abercromby, were landed next morning in Longueville Bay. More troops were landed in next day in Choc Bay and a third group was landed in Anse La Raye on 29 April. In support a naval brigade of 800 seamen was also landed. After meeting resistance during the assault on Vigie 17 May, the French were eventually forced to withdraw to Morne Fortunée where they finally capitulated on 24 May. After this the squadron, including *Thunderer*, sailed to capture St Vincent and Grenada. The former surrendered on 11 June, the latter a few days later.

1797 to 1800: *Thunderer* operated out of Jamaica for the duration of the war, commanded first by Captain William Ogilvy, with James Bowen holding an acting position during his tenure. In May 1798 John Loring briefly assumed command until transferring into *Carnatic* (74) barely a month later, his successor John Cochet staying in the ship until 16 January 1798. John Crawley then took command until moving into *Valiant* (74) with Captain Temple Hardy taking command on 12 May 1799. *Thunderer*'s final commander here was Robert Mends who replaced Hardy on 28 July 1800.[389]

1801: In April command of the ship passed to Henry William Bayntun for just twelve days and then to Captain Henry Vansittart on 17 April who, recalled to England, paid off *Thunderer* at Chatham on 29 June. *Thunderer* sent into dock for a much needed refit, Mends lowered his pendant 28 April 1801. After refitting, *Thunderer* was recommissioned under John Delafons 11 August. Succeeded by Captain Solomon Ferris on 8 September, *Thunderer* was again paid off at Chatham 4 November.

1803: When the war with France resumed *Thunderer* was instantly recom-

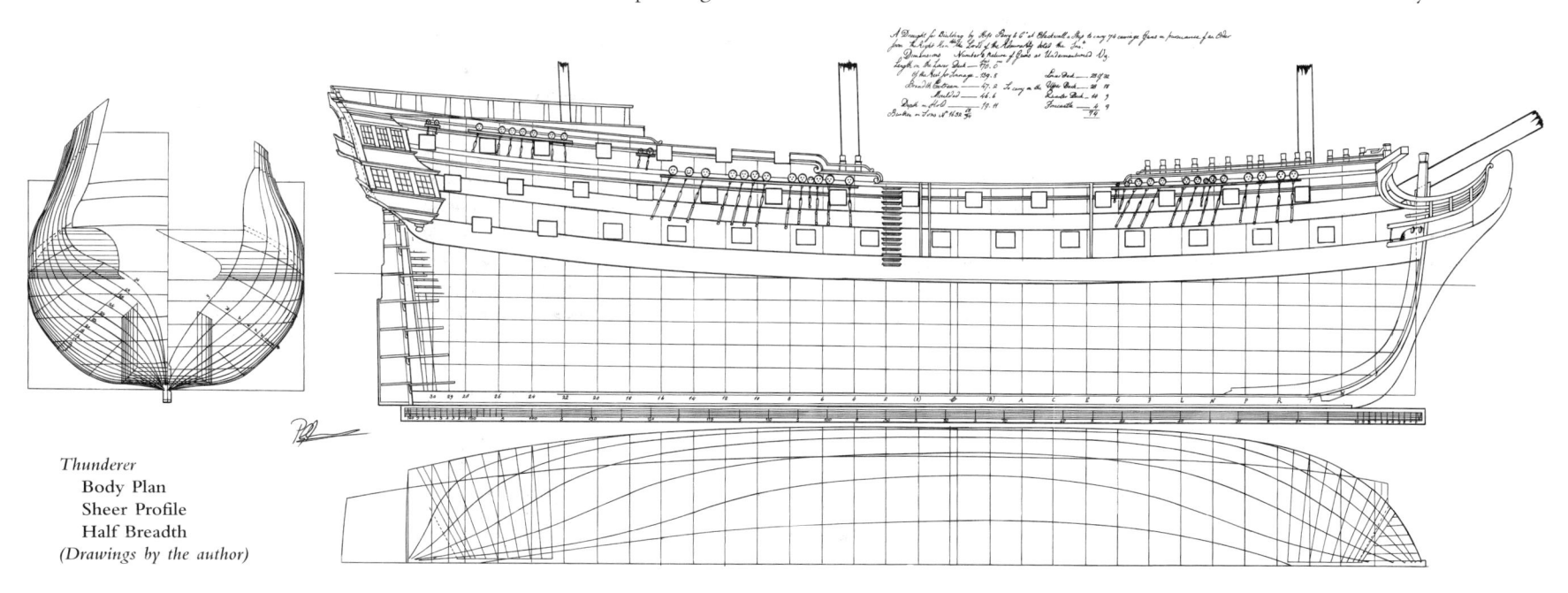

Thunderer
Body Plan
Sheer Profile
Half Breadth
(Drawings by the author)

missioned on 12 March by Captain William Bedford and sailed from Torbay for deployment off Ireland watching the western approaches to the Channel.

1804: Going into Plymouth 16 September the ship was docked five days later to have her copper repaired. Undocked 5 October and prepared for sea *Thunderer* sailed 1 November, returning to her station off Ireland.[390] In late December *Thunderer* accidentally ran aground near Bere Island in Bantry Bay. On the 23rd *Princess Royal* (98) arrived and began taking out *Thunderer*'s stores, guns and shot to lighten the ship. Next morning, 24 December, *Goliath* (74) with a frigate and a transport arrived to help. After disembarking the remaining stores *Thunderer* was successfully refloated without sustaining serious damage.

1805: Getting back into Plymouth 6 February *Thunderer* was taken into dock 17 February to inspect her hull for damage and repair her copper. The same day command was superseded by Captain William Lechmere. Although she was undocked on 27 February it was then decided to replace her copper so she was docked down again on 16 March, re-coppered and fitted and launched again on 3 April.[391] *Thunderer* sailed from Plymouth dockyard 3 June to join Vice-Admiral Sir Robert Calder's squadron deployed off Finisterre. Cruising some 100 miles west of Finisterre on 22 July, Calder, flying his flag in the *Prince of Wales* (100), sighted Villeneuve's combined fleet returning from the West Indies. The two opposing squadrons comprised the following ships:

Calder's British fleet				*Villeneuve's combined Franco-Spanish fleet*			
Rate	Guns	Ship's name	No.	Rate	Guns	Ship's name	No.
2nd	98	*Barfleur, Glory, Prince of Wales* [flagship], and *Windsor Castle*	4	2nd	90	*Argonauta* (S)	1
3rd	80	*Malta*	1	3rd	80	*Bucentaure* (F) [flagship], *Formidable* (F), *Indomptable* (F), *Neptune* (F), and *San Rafael* (S)	5
3rd	74	*Ajax, Defiance, Dragon, Hero, Repulse, Thunderer, Triumph,* and *Warrior*	8	3rd	74	*Achille* (F), *Aigle* (F) *Algésiras* (F), *Atlas* (F), *Berwick* (F), *Firme* (F), *Intrépide* (F), *Mont Blanc* (F), *Pluton* (F), *Scipion* (F), *Swiftsure* (F), and *Terrible* (F)	12
3rd	64	*Agamemnon* and *Raisonnable*	2	3rd	64	*America* (F), *Espana* (S)	2
5th	40	*Egyptienne*	1	5th	40	*Cornelie* (F), *Didon* (F), *Hortense* (F), *Rhin* (F), and *Thémis* (F)	5
5th	36	*Sirius*	1	5th	36	*Sirène* (F)	1
Cutter	12	*Nile*	1	6th	18	*Furet* (F)	1
Lugger	?	*Frisk*	1	Corvette	16	*Naiade* (F), *Santa Magdalene* (S)	1 1
TOTAL			19	TOTAL			29

Source: Clowes, 5 p. 112.

The battle between the two fleets which began on the afternoon of the 22nd was indecisive. Both sides were hampered by poor weather, fog making it difficult to communicate signals and execute the necessary manœuvres to engage fully. During this part of the battle *Thunderer* suffered seven killed and eleven wounded. Next morning the two fleets lay 17 miles apart, *Thunderer* with *Malta* and several frigates lay six miles distant from the admiral and consequently did not close for the second action.[392] *Thunderer* then sailed south with Calder's squadron to join Collingwood's squadron off Cadiz. Shortly afterwards Calder was recalled to England to face a court martial for failing to bring about a decisive action to stop *Villeneuve* getting into the safety of port. Captain Lechmere was also summoned to act a witness. Consequently *Thunderer* sailed for home accompanying Calder in the *Prince of Wales*. Reaching Plymouth, *Thunderer* underwent a short refit where, John Stockham, *Thunderer*'s First Lieutenant, assumed command of the ship during Lechmere's absence. Anchored in Cawsand Bay, Stockham received orders to rejoin Collingwood off Cadiz. Thus on 18 September *Thunderer* with *Ajax* (74) made sail and once out of Plymouth Sound joined company with Nelson's *Victory* (100) and Blackwood's *Euryalus* (36) which had sailed from Spithead three days before.[393]

TRAFALGAR

On the day of the impending great battle *Thunderer* lay thirteenth in line of Collingwood's leeward division and being near the rear, did not get into action until relatively late. After supporting *Revenge* (74), Stockham wore *Thunderer* across the bows of the great *Principe de Asturias* (112) and poured a raking broadside into her before manœuvring onto a starboard tack. While doing so the French *Neptune* (84) came up to assist the Spanish ship, dividing the attention of *Thunderer*'s firepower. Playing little part in the battle after this point *Thunderer* suffered four seamen killed and twelve wounded. Among the latter were Master Mate John Snell and Midshipman Alexander Galloway. For his part in commanding *Thunderer* during the action Lieutenant Stockham was later promoted post-captain.[394]

1806: Still deployed with Collingwood's squadron off Cadiz, in the early morning of 12 March Captain Stockham sighted three suspicious vessels. After making chase for five hours, *Thunderer* brought up and captured the Spanish schooner which proved to be privateer *Santo Christo del Paldo* mounting 14 guns commanded by Jean Gonzales with a crew of 67 men and victualled for four months. Fifteen days out of Bayonne, she had captured the Danish brig *Grunstadt*, the Swedish brig *Pomone*, and a galliot named *Louisa et Emilla*. That evening *Thunderer* recaptured the Danish vessel, carrying linseed and fruit; she was sent back to England with a petty officer. On 10 April Captain John Talbot assumed command of *Thunderer* and joined a small squadron commanded by Rear-Admiral Sir Thomas Louis to reconnoitre the Dardanelles. Flying his flag in *Canopus* (80), Louis' ships comprised *Standard* (64), *Active* (38) and *Nautilus* (18). The intention of this expedition was to determine whether British ships could forcibly pass through to Constantinople (Istanbul) to show a strength of force to deter the Sultan of Turkey from closing the Dardanelles against the Russian fleet. This action had been provoked by a threat from the French ambassador. *Thunderer* with the other ships reached Malta on 8 November and sailed again one week later. The squadron anchored off Tenedos on 21 November for a week while waiting to bring on pilots. Sailing again on 27 November the ships entered the straits and anchored in Azure Bay. *Canopus* with Louis proceeded alone, *Thunderer* and her consorts waited for the remainder of the year.

1807: By January the diplomatic situation with Turkey had become deadlocked so Collingwood received orders to send reinforcements to the Dardanelles. He despatched Vice-Admiral Sir John Duckworth in *Royal George* (100) with eight sail of the line and two mortar vessels to take command of Rear-Admiral Louis' squadron. Duckworth was under strict orders to bombard Constantinople and force the Sultan to hand over the Turkish fleet. Joining Louis' ships off Tenedos on 4 February, Duckworth's squadron now comprised the following ships:

Rate	Guns	Ships' Names	No.
1st	100	*Royal George*	1
2nd	98	*Windsor Castle*	1
3rd	80	*Canopus*	1
3rd	74	*Ajax, Pompée, Repulse,* and *Thunderer,*	4
3rd	64	*Standard*	1
5th	40	*Endymion*	1
5th	38	*Active*	1
Bomb ships	8	*Lucifer* and *Meteor*	2
TOTAL			12

114

THE 74 GUN SHIP *THUNDERER*

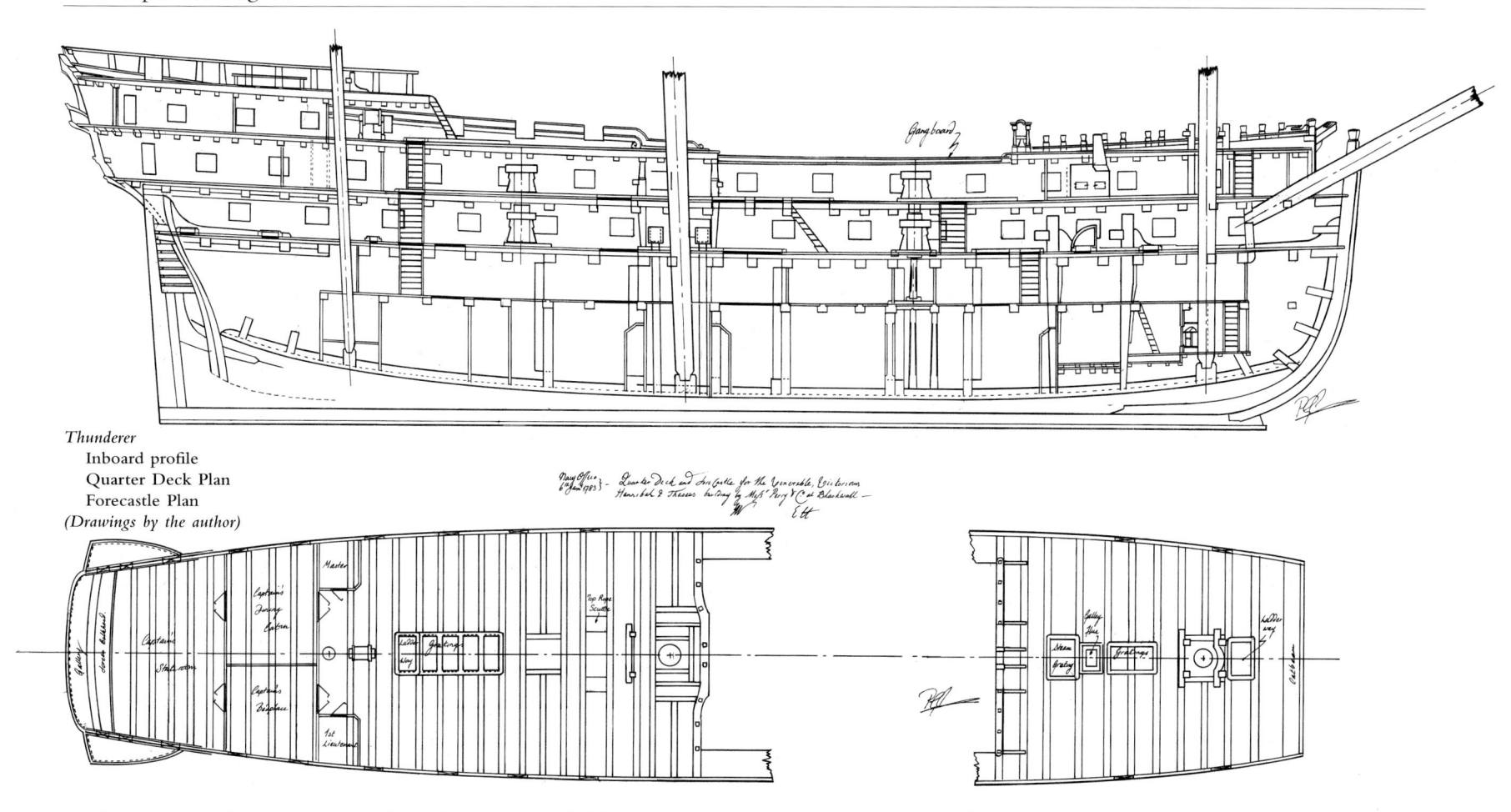

Thunderer
Inboard profile
Quarter Deck Plan
Forecastle Plan
(Drawings by the author)

Duckworth lost *Ajax*, destroyed accidentally by fire on 14 February, but he weighed at 7 a.m. on 19 February and proceeded through the Dardanelles with *Thunderer* initially towing the bomb vessel *Meteor*. At about 9.30 a.m. the ships come under heavy fire from forts on either side but suffering little damage pressed on, reaching a Turkish squadron of one 64 gun ship, four 5th rate frigates, four corvettes, two brigs and three gunboats anchored under the guns of the fort on Point Pesquies. At this point Rear-Admiral Sir Sidney Smith in *Pompée*, together with *Thunderer*, *Standard*, *Endymion* and *Active*, pressed home their attack. Anchoring close by, the British ships opened fire into the Turkish vessels; all but one corvette and a gunboat were taken or driven on shore. During the engagement boats from *Thunderer* and *Standard* were lowered and sent on shore with marines to silence the fort on Point Pesquies whose 31 guns were firing on the British ships. In the attack *Thunderer* suffered the only British fatalities, three seamen and one marine killed. Wounded were one officer, nine seamen and four marines. After this Duckworth and his ships sailed to within eight miles of Constantinople where they remained until 1 March when adverse winds compelled Duckworth to move his ships to open sea, *Thunderer* now towing *Lucifer*. On 3 March, passing the forts previously attacked, Duckworth decided to give them a salute of 13 guns but the Turks mistook this as an aggressive action. Opening fire on Duckworth's squadron from both sides, with heavy guns firing stone shot as well as iron, the Turks inflicted more casualties on the British ships than in the previous engagement. Total casualties were 28 killed and 130 wounded, of which *Thunderer* had two men dead and 14 wounded. Among her wounded were Lieutenants Thomas Colby and John Waller and Midshipman Moore.[395]

1808: Recalled home *Thunderer* joined the squadron operating out of the Downs until 26 November when Talbot paid off the ship at Chatham.

FATE

Having gone into Chatham on 4 November 1808 and been decommissioned, the ship remained moored in the Medway until docked on 8 October 1812 to have her copper removed, and undocked on 4 January. The following year *Thunderer* was again moored in the river. Finally docked at Chatham 7 January 1814, she was taken to pieces two months later.[396]

PROGRESS BOOK – *THUNDERER* RATE OF 74 GUNS: Source: ADM 180/10 Entry 132

At what Port	Arrived	Docked	Coppered	Launched or Undocked	Sailed	Built or Nature of Repair	Cost of Hull, Masts & Yards Materials £ s d	Cost of Rigging & Stores Materials £ s d	Grand Total
Plymouth	16 Sep 1804	21 Sep 1804	Copper Repaired October 1804	5 Oct 1804	1 Nov 1804	Defects			
Plymouth	6 Feb 1805	17 Feb 1805	Copper Repaired	27 Feb 1805		Defects			
Plymouth		16 Mar 1805	Copper taken off Mar Re-coppered April 1805	3 April 1805	3 June 1805	Fitted			
Chatham	4 Nov 1808	8 Oct 1812	Copper taken off	4 Jan 1813					
Chatham	7 Jan 1814								
			Taken to Pieces March 1814						

Author's Note: No expenses were entered on original document

Notes to Part 1: Chapter 3

1. Clowes, 4, p. 226; Colledge, 1, p. 22.
2. RNM, MS 248/4.
3. TNA: PRO, ADM 180/10 Entry 62.
4. Clowes, 5, p. 85.
5. TNA: PRO, ADM 180/10 Entry 62.
6. *Ibid.*
7. Clowes, 5, p. 121.
8. TNA: PRO, ADM 51/1535.
9. *Ibid.*
10. Clowes, 5, pp. 150–160.
11. TNA: PRO, ADM 51/1535.
12. TNA: PRO, ADM 180/10 Entry 62.
13. Clowes, 5, p. 390.
14. Clowes, 5, p. 242.
15. RNM, MS 248/6.
16. *Ibid.*
17. *Ibid.*
18. TNA: PRO, ADM 180/10/62.
19. MacPherson, *Four Ages of Man: The Classical Myths*, p. 117.
20. Lyon, p. 70; Colledge, 1, p. 29.
21. Clowes, 4, pp. 388–389.
22. Clowes, 4, pp. 414–415.
23. Clowes 4, pp. 454–457.
24. TNA: PRO, ADM 180/10.
25. *Ibid.*
26. *Ibid.*
27. TNA: PRO, ADM 51/1562.
28. Clowes, 5, pp. 112–116.
29. Pope, *England Expects*, p. 128.
30. Pope, *England Expects*, p. 151; Clowes, 5, p. 125.
31. Pope, *England Expects*, p. 157.
32. Pope, *England Expects*, p. 168.
33. TNA: PRO, ADM 51/1573.
34. Pope, *England Expects*, p. 218.
35. TNA: PRO, ADM 51/1573; Clowes, 5, pp. 131, 149, 158, 168; Pope, *England Expects*, pp. 322–328.
36. TNA: PRO, ADM 51/1573.
37. Clowes, 5, pp. 219–220.
38. Grocott, *Shipwrecks of the Revolutionary & Napoleonic Wars*, pp. 229–230; Clowes, 5, pp. 221–222.
39. TNA: PRO, ADM 180/10 Entry 63; Banbury, *Shipbuilders of the Thames and Medway*, p. 135.
40. Lyon, p. 238.
41. Clowes, 4, p. 225.
42. Clowes, 4, pp. 262–264.
43. Clowes, 5, p. 54.
44. Clowes, 5, p. 89.
45. Clowes, 5, p. 102.
46. Clowes, 5, p. 110.
47. TNA: PRO, ADM 51/1515.
48. *Ibid.*
49. Clowes, 5, pp. 128–160.
50. TNA: PRO, ADM 51/1515.
51. *Ibid.*
52. Clowes, 5, p. 196.
53. Clowes, 5, p. 239.
54. Clowes, 5, 283.
55. Tracy, *The Naval Chronicle*, 4, p. 273.
56. Clowes, 5, pp. 272–275.
57. TNA: PRO, ADM 180/10.
58. MacPherson, *The Four Ages of Man*, pp. 83–85.
59. Cordingly, *Billy Ruffian*, p. 59.
60. RNM, MS 248/4.
61. James, 1, pp. 128–181; Cordingly, pp. 68–91.
62. Cordingly, p. 97–101; James, 1, pp. 239–243.
63. Cordingly, pp. 101–102.
64. RNM, MS 248/4.
65. Cordingly, pp. 159–166.
66. James, 3, pp. 191–192.
67. James, 3, pp. 207–209.
68. Cordingly, pp. 166–169.
69. TNA: PRO, ADM 180/10 folio 67.
70. RNM, MS 248/6.
71. TNA: PRO, ADM 51/1522 part 2.
72. *Ibid.*
73. TNA: PRO, ADM 51/4417 part 7.
74. TNA: PRO, ADM 51/1522 part 2.
75. Cordingly, *Billy Ruffian*, p. 195.
76. TNA: PRO, ADM 51/4417 part 7.
77. Cordingly, pp. 195–199; James, 4, pp. 29–79; Clowes, 5, pp. 136–163; Pope, p. 358; TNA: PRO, ADM 51/4417 part 7.
78. TNA: PRO, ADM 51/4417 part 7.
79. *Ibid.*
80. RNM, MS 248/6.
81. TNA: PRO, ADM 51/4417 part 7.
82. TNA: PRO, ADM 180/10 folio 67.
83. Cordingly, p. 211.
84. James, 5, p. 180; Clowes, 5, p. 440; *Naval Chronicle*, 22, p. 84.
85. TNA: PRO, ADM 51/1925 part 5.
86. Clowes, 5, p. 441; Cordingly, pp. 220–223. *Victory* had been reduced to a 2nd rate of 98 guns in 1808.
87. TNA: PRO, ADM 180/10 folio 67.
88. RNM, MS 248/6.
89. Cordingly, pp. 228–278.
90. Colledge, 1, p. 183.
91. TNA: PRO, ADM 180/10 folio 67.
92. RNM, MS 248/4.
93. Lyon, p. 72.
94. TNA: PRO, ADM 180/111 Entry 592.
95. TNA: PRO, ADM 180/11 Entry 592; RNM, MSS 248/4 & 248/6.
96. MSS 248/4 & 248/6.
97. Clowes, 5, p. 121.
98. Pope, *England Expects*, pp. 162, 177, 187–188.
99. TNA: PRO, ADM 51/1516 part 1.
100. TNA: PRO, ADM 51/1516 part 1.
101. TNA: PRO, ADM 51/1516 part 1.
102. *Ibid.*
103. James, 4, pp. 52–54; Clowes, 5, pp. 144–160; Pope pp. 300–302.
104. TNA: PRO, ADM 51/1516 part 1.
105. *Ibid.*
106. *Ibid.*
107. TNA: PRO, ADM 180/10 73.
108. RNM, MS 248/6.
109. James, 5, p. 4; Clowes, 5, p. 242.
110. RNM, MS 248/6.
111. James, 6, p. 41; Clowes, 5, p. 303.
112. RNM, MS 248/6; TNA: PRO, ADM 180/10/73.
113. TNA: PRO, ADM 180/10/73.
114. Hepper, p. 44.
115. Clowes, 4, *passim*.
116. Colledge, p. 133; Lyon, p. 70.
117. TNA: PRO, ADM 180/9.
118. *Ibid.*
119. RNM, MS 248/4.
120. See Appendices; Account of Shipwrights' works undertaken at Plymouth, 1803 – Joseph Tucker.
121. Pope, *England Expects*, p. 217.
122. Clowes, 5, p. 76.
123. Clowes, 5, pp. 89–102.
124. TNA: PRO, ADM 51/1529 part 4.
125. James, 4, pp. 64–65; Clowes, 5, pp. 147–148; Pope, *England Expects*, pp. 260–263.
126. Pope, *England Expects*, pp, 265–267.
127. Pope, *England Expects*, p. 322.
128. Pope, *England Expects*, p. 329.
129. TNA: PRO, ADM 51/1529 part 4.
130. James, 4, p. 66; Clowes, 5, p. 158.
131. James, 4, p. 245; Clowes, 5, p. 385; *Naval Chronicle*, 14, p. 506.
132. Clowes, 5, p. 232–233.
133. Clowes, 5, p. 289.
134. Clowes, 5, p. 296.
135. Colledge, 1, p. 156.
136. TNA: PRO, ADM 180/2/177; RNM MS 248/4.
137. Clowes, 3, p. 563.
138. RNM, MS 248/4.
139. Clowes, 4, p. 202.
140. Clowes, 4, pp. 226–231.
141. Clowes, 4, pp. 274–277.
142. Clowes, 4, p. 168.
143. Clowes, 4, p. 180.
144. Clowes, 4, p. 357–369.
145. RNM, MS 248/4.
146. Clowes, 4, p. 384.
147. Clowes, 4, p. 557.
148. Clowes, 4, p. 431.
149. TNA: PRO, ADM 180/10/82.
150. *Ibid.*
151. TNA: PRO, ADM 51/1525.
152. *Ibid.*
153. Legg, *An Eyewitness Account of a Great Battle*, p. 55.
154. TNA: PRO, ADM 51/1525.
155. *Ibid.*
156. *Ibid.*
157. Legg, *An Eyewitness Account of a Great Battle*, pp. 112–113.
158. Clowes, 5, p. 131.
159. TNA: PRO, ADM 51/1525.
160. RNM, MS 248/6.
161. TNA: PRO, ADM 180/10.
162. RNM, MS 248/6.
163. Clowes, 5, p. 210.
164. Clowes, 5, pp. 233–234.
165. TNA: PRO, ADM 180/10.
166. *Ibid.*
167. Grocott, pp. 329–334; Hepper, pp. 138; Clowes, 5, pp. 498, 553.
168. Clowes, 4, p. 116
169. Colledge, 1, pp. 156–157.
170. Clowes, 4, p. 110.
171. RNM, MS 248/4.
172. NMM CHN 002 172/75.
173. Clowes, 4, p. 168.
174. Clowes, 4, p. 384.
175. Clowes, 4, pp. 428–440.
176. TNA: PRO, ADM 1807 & MS 248/4.
177. Clowes, 5, pp. 112–116.
178. TNA: PRO, ADM 51/1640 part 3.
179. Clowes, 5, pp. 127–160.
180. TNA: PRO, ADM 51/1640 part 3.
181. *Ibid.*
182. *Ibid.*
183. TNA: PRO, ADM 180/10.
184. RNM, MS 248/6.
185. TNA: PRO, ADM 180/10.
186. Clowes, 5, pp. 253–255.
187. RNM, MS 248/6.
188. TNA: PRO, ADM 180/10.
189. Lyon, p. 72; Hepper, p. 58; Clowes, 4, p. 110.
190. Lyon, p. 72.
191. Clowes, 4, p. 203.
192. Clowes, 4, p. 210.
193. Clowes, 4, p. 220.
194. Clowes, 4, p. 222–230.
195. Clowes, 4, p. 293.
196. Clowes, 4, p. 377.
197. Clowes, 4, p. 519.
198. Clowes, 4, p. 384.
199. Clowes, 4, p. 391.
200. Clowes, 4, pp. 530–531.
201. Clowes, 5, p. 73.

202 Clowes, 5, pp. 89–90.
203 Clowes, 5, p. 93.
204 Clowes, 5, p. 98.
205 Clowes, 5, p. 102.
206 Clowes, 5, p. 127.
207 TNA: PRO, ADM 51/1526 part 2.
208 Ibid.
209 Ibid.
210 Clowes, 5, p. 147–148.
211 TNA: PRO, ADM 51/1526 part 2.
212 Clowes, 5, p. 158.
213 Clowes, 5, p. 160.
214 TNA: PRO, ADM 51/1526.
215 RNM, MS 248/6.
216 TNA: PRO, ADM 180/10.
217 RNM, MS 248/6.
218 Clowes, 5, pp. 279–280.
219 Clowes, 5, p. 503.
220 James, 6, p. 68; Clowes, 5, p. 505; *Naval Chronicle*, 28, p. 160.
221 Clowes, 5, p. 509.
222 TNA: PRO, ADM 180/10.
223 RNM, MS 248/6.
224 TNA: PRO, ADM 180/10 Entry 102.
225 Clowes, 3, p. 289.
226 Clowes, 3, p. 235.
227 Colledge, 1, p. 348; Lyon, pp. 67, 197, 218, 242, 248.
228 TNA: PRO, ADM 180/7.
229 RNM, MS 248/4.
230 Clowes, 4, pp. 255–259.
231 RNM, MS 248/6.
232 Clowes, 4, pp. 168, 176.
233 Clowes, 4, pp. 336–337.
234 *The Times*, 24 December 1798; Grocott, *Shipwrecks of the Revolutionary & Napoleonic Wars*, p. 65.
235 Clowes, 4, p. 338.
236 RNM, MS 248/4.
237 TNA: PRO, ADM 180/6.
238 Ibid.
239 TNA: PRO, ADM 180/6 & MS 248/6.
240 TNA: PRO, ADM 180/7.
241 RNM, MS 248/6.
242 TNA: PRO, ADM 180/10/Entry 104.
243 Clowes, 5, p. 121.
244 TNA: PRO, ADM 51/1493 part 8.
245 Ibid.
246 Clowes, 5, p. 146.
247 Pope, *England Expects*, p. 282.
248 TNA: PRO, ADM 51/1493 part 8.
249 Pope, *England Expects*, p. 284.
250 Clowes, 5, pp. 151–152.
251 Clowes, 5, p. 148.
252 TNA: PRO, ADM 51/1493 part 8.
253 Ibid; Fraser, *The Enemy at Trafalgar*; Legg, *An Eyewitness Account of a Great Battle*, p. 96.
254 TNA: PRO, ADM 51/1493 part 8.
255 Clowes, 5, p. 159; ADM 51/14913 part 8.
256 'The Trafalgar General Order Book of HMS *Mars*', *Mariner's Mirror*, 22, p. 99.
257 TNA: PRO, ADM 51/1535 part 6.
258 TNA: PRO, ADM 180/10.
259 RNM, MS 248/6.
260 TNA: PRO, ADM 180/10.
261 Clowes, 5, p. 387.
262 Clowes, 5, p. 390.
263 TNA: PRO, ADM 180/10.
264 Clowes, 5, p. 210.
265 Clowes, 5, p. 247.
266 *Oxford Companion to English Literature*, 1953; *The Four Ages of Man: The Classical Myths*.
267 TNA: PRO, ADM 1801/9/Entry 618.
268 James, 2, p. 106.
269 RNM, MS 248/4.
270 Ibid.
271 TNA: PRO, ADM 180/9 Entry 618.
272 James, 2, pp. 20–21.
273 James, 2, pp. 26–27.
274 James, 2, pp. 167–168.
275 James, 2, pp. 174–175.
276 James, 2, p. 183.
277 Lyon, p. 63.
278 James, 3, pp. 9–12.
279 James, 3, pp. 50–51.
280 James, 3, p. 99.
281 TNA: PRO, ADM 180/10 Entry 105.
282 RNM, MS 248/4.
283 TNA: PRO, ADM 180/10/Entry 105.
284 Schom, p. 201.
285 Howarth, p. 31.
286 TNA: PRO, ADM 51/1533 part 4.
287 Ibid.
288 Quoted in Pope, pp. 218–219.
289 TNA: PRO, ADM 51 1533 part 4.
290 James, 4, pp. 26, 73, 100–101; Schom, pp. 35–351; Pope, pp. 321–322; Howarth, p. 122.
291 TNA: PRO, ADM 51 1533 part 4.
292 James, 4, pp. 284–295.
293 TNA: PRO, ADM 180/10 Entry 105.
294 *Naval Chronicle*, 25, p. 56; Hepper, pp. 134–135; Grocott, pp. 302–303.
295 TNA: PRO, ADM 180/9 Entry 615.
296 Lyon, p. 69.
297 RNM, MS 248/4; TNA: PRO, ADM 180/9 Entry 615.
298 Ibid.
299 TNA: PRO, ADM 180/9 & MS 248/4.
300 Clowes, 4, pp. 222–234.
301 TNA: PRO, ADM 180/9 Entry 615.
302 Clowes, 4, pp. 260–264.
303 RNM, MS 248/4.
304 TNA: PRO, ADM 180/9 Entry 615.
305 Clowes, 4, pp. 304–317.
306 Clowes, 4, pp. 351–352; Goodwin, *Nelson's Ships*, p. 170.
307 Clowes, 4, pp. 357–369.
308 Pope, *England Expects*, p. 41.
309 TNA: PRO, ADM 51/1635.
310 Ibid.
311 Clowes, 5, pp. 131–160; Pope, *England Expects*, pp. 327–329.
312 Pope, *England Expects*, p. 190.
313 TNA: PRO, ADM 51/1635.
314 Clowes, 5, pp. 209–215.
315 TNA: PRO, ADM 180/10.
316 TNA: PRO, ADM 180/10.
317 TNA: PRO, ADM 180/10.
318 Colledge, p. 462.
319 Lyon, p. 363.
320 Lyon, p. 263; Colledge, p. 462.
321 Some references state that the ship was laid down August 1796, however the Progress Book clearly states 1800.
322 Clowes, 5, pp. 20–24.
323 TNA: PRO, ADM 51/1535 part 6.
324 Ibid
325 Pope, *England Expects*, pp. 226, 307.
326 James, 4, p. 75
327 TNA: PRO, ADM 51/1535 part 6.
328 Clowes, 5, p. 24.
329 Pope, *England Expects*, pp. 317–318.
330 Clowes, 5, pp. 153–160.
331 TNA: PRO, ADM 51/1535 part 6.
332 Ibid.
333 TNA: PRO, ADM 51/1535 part 6.
334 Clowes, 5, p. 25.
335 Clowes, 5, p. 385.
336 Clowes, 5, p. 390.
337 Clowes, 5, pp. 252–255.
338 Clowes, 5, p. 474.
339 Clowes, 5, p. 539.
340 Lavery, *Nelson and the Nile*, p. 35.
341 Lavery, *Nelson and the Nile*, p. 150.
342 Clowes, 4, pp. 357–364.
343 Clowes, 4, p. 373.
344 Clowes, 4, p. 377.
345 Lavery, pp. 224; RNM, MS 248/6.
346 See Appendices: Account of Shipwrights' works undertaken at Plymouth, 1803.
347 RNM, MS 248/6.
348 Ibid.
349 Clowes, 5, p105–109.
350 TNA: PRO, ADM 51/1543 part 1.
351 Ibid.
352 Clowes, 5, pp. 158.
353 TNA: PRO, ADM 51/1543 part 1.
354 Ibid.
355 Clowes, 5, pp. 242, 440.
356 RNM, MS 248/6.
357 TNA: PRO, ADM 180/10 Entry 50.
358 Colledge, p. 540.
359 Lyon, p. 72.
360 Lyon, p. 70–71.
361 TNA: PRO, ADM 180/10 Entry 130.
362 Holland, *Buckler's Hard: A Rural Shipbuilding Centre*, p. 94.
363 TNA: PRO, ADM 180/10 Entry 130.
364 Holland, *Buckler's Hard: A Rural Shipbuilding Centre*, p. 94.
365 Clowes, 5, p. 79.
366 Clowes, 5, p. 89.
367 James, 3, pp. 241–242, 323, 333; Clowes, 5, p. 102.
368 TNA: PRO, ADM 51 1533 part 1.
369 Ibid.
370 Ibid.
371 James, 4, pp. 77–79; Clowes, 5, pp. 131, 157–161; Schom, pp. 341, 353–354.
372 TNA: PRO, ADM 51 1533 part 1.
373 Ibid.
374 Ibid.
375 RNM, MS 248/6.
376 TNA: PRO, ADM 180/10 & MS 248/6.
377 James, 6, p. 183; Clowes, 5, p. 539; *Naval Chronicle*, 31, p. 75.
378 TNA: PRO, ADM 180/10 Entry 130.
379 Clowes, 4, p. 47.
380 Clowes, 4, pp. 57, 111; Lyon, p. 67.
381 RNM, MS 248/4.
382 Lyon, p. 298.
383 RNM, MS 248/4.
384 Clowes, 4, pp. 218–220.
385 Clowes, 4, pp. 226–235, 555.
386 Clowes, 4, pp. 260, 266.
387 RNM, MS 248/4.
388 Clowes, 4, pp. 334, 555.
389 RNM, MS 248/4.
390 TNA: PRO, ADM 180/10.
391 Ibid.
392 Clowes, 5, p. 116.
393 Clowes, 5, p. 125.
394 Clowes, 5, pp. 156–168.
395 Clowes, 5, pp. 218–229.
396 TNA: PRO, ADM 180/10.

PART 1: CHAPTER 4
THE BRITISH THIRD RATE 64 GUN SHIPS

The 64 gun ship AFRICA

The third ship to bear the name *Africa* in the Royal Navy, the first *Africa* was a 4th rate 46 gun ship hired into service from 1692 to 1695.[1] The second *Africa*, a 3rd rate ship of 64 guns built to the lines of the *Africa/Asia* class designed by Slade in 1758, was in fact one of the first true 64 gun ships designed for the navy that would supersede the earlier 60 gun ships. Built by Perry at Blackwall and launched 1 August 1761, this ship saw little service and was sold in 1777.[2]

The Trafalgar *Africa*, a 3rd rate of 64 guns built to the lines of John William's *Inflexible* class of 1777, was effectively a smaller version of Slade's design of *Albion* class 74 gun ships. *Africa*'s sister ships were *Inflexible*, *Dictator* and *Sceptre*. Ordered 11 February 1778, *Africa*'s keel was laid down in the 'River Thames' on 2 March 1778 and built under contract by Messrs Henry Adams and William Barnard. More precisely, she was built in the Grove Street yard at Deptford owned by William Barnard, son of the renowned shipbuilder John Barnard.[3] According to the contract signed 16 February 1778, *Africa* was to be built in 36 months, but the launch on 11 April 1781 was 23 days later than the contract date. *Africa* was immediately taken into Deptford dockyard for additional work. Moving down to Woolwich on 19 April, *Africa* went into dock five days later to be coppered and fitted out. Re-launched 24 April, the entire cost of her hull, masts and yards amounted to £39,003 14s 7d.[4] Armed with twenty-six 24 pounders on the lower gun deck, twenty-six 18 pounders on the upper gun deck, ten 9 pounders on the quarter deck, and two 9 pounders on the forecastle, *Africa* could fire a single broadside weight of 600 pounds.

SERVICE HISTORY

1781: *Africa* was first put into commission by Captain Thomas Newnham on 25 April, the day after being undocked at Woolwich. Going to sea in July, she was deployed in home waters until 10 December when she went alongside the wall in Plymouth to be refitted.[5]

1782: Refitted at a total cost of £2,564 10s 2d, *Africa* left the dockyard 3 January and ten days later Captain Robert W Donall took command of the ship.[6] Shortly afterwards Donall received orders to escort a convoy of ships to Bombay to reinforce the East Indies fleet commanded by Admiral Sir Edward Hughes KB.

1783: The main duty for Admiral Sir Edward Hughes in this theatre of war was to protect English trade and escort convoys against the French forces under Admiral Suffren based at Cuddalore. Intending to capture this port, the British fleet, including *Africa*, sailed in late March for Madras to launch the assault on Cuddalore. Troops marched south overland and the naval squadron supported the attack from the sea. Suffren sailed from Trincomalee and sighted the British blockading fleet on 13 June. Planning for another encounter with Hughes, Suffren embarked over a thousand troops to strengthen the manpower in his ships and left the harbour on the 18th. On the morning of 20 June the final battle between two adversaries, Hughes and Suffren began. The opposing fleets comprised the following ships.

CAPTAINS OF AFRICA (MSS 248/4 and 248/6)

Name	Time of Entry	Time of Discharge	On What Occasion
Thomas Newnham	25 April 1781	12 January 1782	Superseded
Robert W Donall	13 January 1782	24 May 1784	Paid Off at Plymouth
James Kempthorne	3 November 1790	14 December 1790	Paid Off at Chatham
Roddam Home	9 November 1793	11 October 1796	Paid Off
Henry Digby	31 July 1805	19 February 1806	Superseded
Isaac Wolley	20 February 1806	4 November 1806	Superseded
Henry W Bayntun	5 November 1806	20 January 1808	Superseded
John Barrett	21 January 1808	15 March 1809	Superseded
Loftus Bland	16 March 1809	31 October 1809	To the *Gorgon* HS (hospital ship)
George F Ryves	22 April 1810	23 November 1810	Superseded
John Bastard	24 November 1810	20 March 1813	Paid Off

British Fleet

Rate	Guns	Ships' names	No.
3rd	80	*Gibraltar*	1
3rd	74	*Cumberland, Defence, Hero, Sultan, Superb*	5
3rd	68	*Monarco*	1
3rd	64	*Africa, Burford, Eagle, Exeter, Inflexible, Monmouth, Magnanime, Sceptre, Worcester*	9
4th	50	*Bristol, Isis*	2
5th	32	*Juno*	1
5th	28	*Medea*	1
6th	20	*Seahorse*	1
Total			21

French Fleet

Rate	Guns	Ships' names	No.
3rd	74	*Annibal, Argonaute, Héros, Fendant, Illustre*	5
3rd	64	*Artésien, Ajax, Brilliant, Hardi, Sévère, Sphinx, Vengeur*	7
3rd	60	*St Michel*	1
4th	50	*Flamand, Hannibal*	2
5th	40	*Apollon*	1
5th	38	*Cléopâtre*	1
5th	28	*Coventry*	1
Total			18

The two fleets met off Cuddalore on 20 July, Suffren attempting to lure Hughes into battle. In all the broadside power of the British line of battle ships was 18 per cent greater than that of the French. Hughes formed his ships into line ahead on a larboard tack heading northerly, with the wind coming up from the west; the French kept to the weather side on a parallel course. Closing within 400 yards, action commenced just after 4 p.m. and continued for some three hours. Like previous encounters fought between Hughes and Suffren during this war, the rearmost ships did not get into close action, little damaged was sustained by either squadron and no ships were taken. The contest was close: casualties on the British side were 99 killed and 434 wounded, the French, 102 killed and 386 wounded. Next morning the British ships lay-to and being quite incapacitated, short of

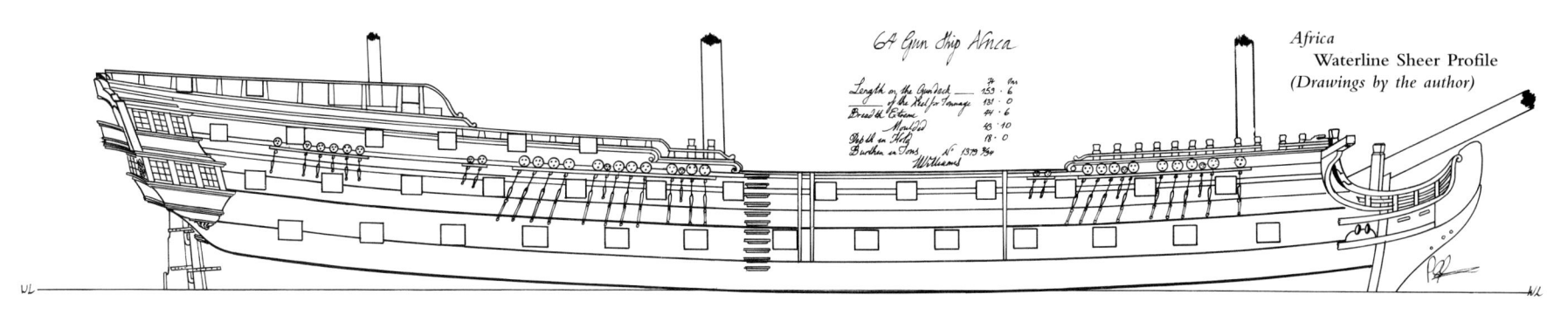

Africa
Waterline Sheer Profile
(Drawings by the author)

water, and with over 1,100 men suffering with scurvy, Hughes sailed for Madras, *Africa* in company, arriving on 25 July. Although this action off Cuddalore was fought five months after initial peace treaties had been signed, it was to be the last naval engagement of the American War of Independence; moreover, it was the last time that British ships would face a royal French fleet.[7]

1784: Recalled to England *Africa* went into Plymouth 4 May, Donall paying off the ship three weeks later. On 2 July the ship went into dock for four days to have her copper repaired and be fitted for the ordinary.[8]

1785: Docked 31 December 1784, *Africa* was given a 'Small Repair' costing £10,727 3s 4d, of which £8,127 11s 4d was spent on her hull, masts and yards. In July her copper, which had been removed in January, was replaced. Re-launched 22 July, *Africa* was again laid up in ordinary.[9]

1790: According to the records *Africa* was briefly recommissioned by Captain James Kempthorne 3 November, paying off the ship at Chatham on 14 December, but the Progress Book does not allude to *Africa* being at Chatham during this period.[10]

1793: Although war with France had opened it was not until 4 September that *Africa* was docked at Plymouth to have her copper replaced and be fitted for sea service. Coming out of the dock 20 September she was put in commission under Captain Roddam Home on 9 November.

1794: Finally completed for sea at a cost of £8,460, *Africa* sailed from Plymouth on 26 February for the West Indies to join Rear-Admiral William Parker stationed at Jamaica.

1796: Still under the command of Captain Home, *Africa* took part in the attack against the French forces in Léogane on the island of Santo Domingo. Troops commanded by Major-General Forbes, had already been assembled at Port au Prince on the same island for embarking into the naval ships. The force, including *Africa*, comprised *Leviathan* (74), *Swiftsure* (74), *Ceres* (32), *Iphigenia* (32), *Cormorant* (18), *Lark* (16) and *Sirène* (16). The attack was made on 21 March with troop landings covered by fire from *Ceres*, *Iphigenia*, *Cormorant*, *Lark* and *Sirène*, *Cormorant* commanded by Captain Cuthbert Collingwood. Meanwhile *Leviathan*, *Swiftsure* and *Africa* shelled the town. However, the French put up a greater defence from the fortifications than anticipated, so *Africa* and *Leviathan* suffered considerable damage aloft and were obliged to draw off, leaving *Swiftsure* to maintain the barrage alone. Unable to destroy the shore batteries and thereby secure a bridgehead for the troops, the attack was aborted, compelling the British forces to withdraw.[11] Recalled to England, *Africa* arrived at Sheerness 6 September and commenced disembarking her powder and other gunner's stores. Sailing up river to Chatham on the 19 September, Captain Home paid off the ship on 11 October. As soon as the *Africa* had arrived in the dockyard she was 'taken in hand' and 'Fitted for a Hospital Ship'.[12]

1798: During wartime, converting *Africa* into a hospital ship was not a priority so she was not completed until 29 September 1798, at a total cost of £3,966. She was then moved to her berth at Sheerness to fulfil her new duties under Lieutenant John Bryant until 1804.[13]

1804: Sailing from Sheerness on 11 September and arriving at Northfleet, *Africa* was given over to Mr Pilcher, a contract shipbuilder, to re-convert her for sea service. Docked 20 October, her old copper was removed the same month.[14]

1805: During this refit a survey found that the ship was weak and actually needed a great repair at considerable expense. To keep costs low it was decided to have her 'doubled' with a second skin of planking: '3 inch deal from ports to first-futtock heads and thence [down] to [the] keel with [one] inch stuff'. Beside improving her strength, this modification, which marginally increased her breadth, also, as recorded in her sailing reports, improved her sailing qualities (see appendices). The fact that she needed doubling, given how little sea service seen, implies that *Africa* was a poorly built ship; however this is unlikely as both Adams and Barnard who built her were well respected shipbuilders. *Africa* was not alone for another 22 line of battleships and five 18 pounder frigates were so fitted, some furnished with diagonal bracing, recommended to the Admiralty by Gabriel Snodgrass, Surveyor of the East India Company.[15] This salient point proves that the introduction of the diagonal bracing system, generally referred to as the Seppings System, cannot be accredited wholly to Robert Seppings. Highly innovative, Snodgrass has been historically overshadowed because of his connection with the East India Company but before entering the HEIC he trained under the renowned eighteenth century naval shipbuilder Sir Thomas Slade.

SPECIFICATIONS: *AFRICA*

Rate	3rd	Length on the range of the gun deck	159 ft 6 ins	Ordnance - lower gun deck	6 x 24 pounders
Guns	64	Length of keel for tonnage	131 ft	Ordnance - upper gun deck	26 x 18 pounders
Class	*Inflexible* 1777	Extreme breadth	44 ft 6 ins	Ordnance - quarter deck	10 x 9 pounders
Designer	John Williams	Depth in hold	18 ft	Ordnance - forecastle	2 x 9 pounders
Builder	Henry Adams & William Barnard	Tons burthen	1379 8/94	Single broadside weight	600 pounds
Dockyard	Deptford	Draught afore	17 ft 6 ins	Fate	1795 -1805 Hospital ship
Date ordered	11 February 1778	Draught abaft	20 ft 11 ins		1805 Re-established as a warship
Date keel laid	2 March 1788	Complement	500		1814 Broken up
Date launched	11 April 1781				

Note: Ordnance listed as for 1803/1805 Trafalgar campaign.

Source: Lyon, *Sailing Navy List*, p. 75.

Africa
Frame Plan
(Drawing by the author)

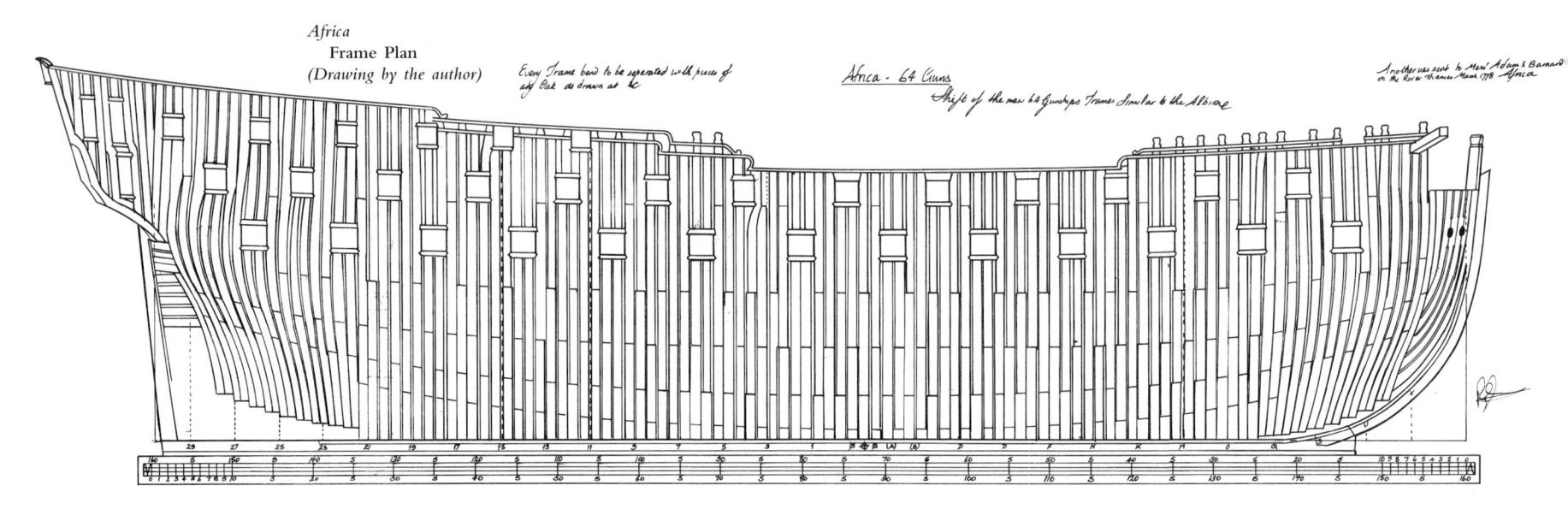

Recoppered in July and undocked on the 13th, the entire cost of *Africa*'s refit, complete with her additional strengthening, was £32,208.[16] *Africa* was then recommissioned under Captain Henry Digby on 31 July.[17] The log of the *Africa* differs, for the entry dated Thursday 3 August states 'Captain Henry Digby took Command of the Ship Lieutenant John Jack joined'. The ship remained off Northfleet until Wednesday 4 September when she moved down the Thames and moored at the Nore next day.[18] Shortly afterwards Digby received orders to join Nelson's squadron lying off Cadiz, thus on Friday 27 September *Africa* made sail. According to Clowes *Africa* reached her station about 9 October; the log however states that she arrived Sunday 15 October.[19] It appears that Digby had problems with his crew, for on Tuesday 15 October he 'Punished G. Ward and Jno Miller (S) with 12 lashes each for gambling J Brown (S) 8 lashes for sleeping on his Watch, G Watson 12 lashes for drunkenness Jno Henry and J^{as} O'Gall— [surname illegible] 12 lashes each for Neglect of duty'. And on the next day: 'James Brand (S) 19 lashes for having liquor on a false acc$^{ct.}$ J$^{as.}$ Neal 20 lashes for drunkenness and P Thompson (S) with 12 lashes for Neglect of duty'. On Friday 18 October further punishment was meted out to 'J^{as} Obray (M) J^{as} Brooks (M) each with 12 lashes each for Quarrelling and neglect of duty'. On Saturday 19 October *Africa*'s seamen painted the ship and on Sunday they were exercised at the 'great Guns and small arms'. Later Thomas Baily was punished with eight lashes for sleeping on watch.[20]

TRAFALGAR

On Monday 21 October, Captain Digby records:

First part fresh Breezes and Squally with rain set the Mainsail and down T Gall^t. Yards Made and shortened sail occasionally during the Night Observed the flashes of Guns and several Rockets in the NE Quarter Wore Ship as necessary at 12 Moderate breezes Wore Ship At 2 set the Mainsail Ships WbS 2 Miles several lights D^o at 3 Obs^d a Ship in the SW Quarter at 4 saw the flashes of several Guns WSW Wore Ship at 6 Wore Ship Trafalgar SE 8 or 9 leagues At 8 light Airs and Clear the Body of the Enemies Fleet S^d. English Fleet SWbW at 10 light airs and clear Enemies Fleet S½W 6 or 7 Miles At 10.53 the admiral made the signal (No 307) with the *Africas* pendants...[21]

From other ships' logs, *Africa* had for some reason became detached from the rest of the fleet during the night. Therefore Nelson had to signal her to make more sail and take her place at the rear of his division. Whether it was because of her isolated position, or whether Digby failed to understand the signal, *Africa* did not enter the action in either Nelson's or Collingwood's divisions. Instead she made her approach separately from the north abeam of *Victory*.[22] *Africa*'s log continues, 'and at 11.20 made N°. 8 with *Britannia*'s pendants at 11.32 N°. 63 with N°. 8 and preparation (general) same time Admiral Collingwood in the *Royal Sovereign* commenced the Action in the Rear of the Enemies Quarter'.[23]

Entering the battle virtually parallel to Villeneuve's line, *Africa* began firing early with her larboard guns into the windward side of the van of the combined fleet:

At 11.40 the *Africa* engaged the headmost Ships of the Enemies van (the *Africa* then on a Starb^d Tack) viz a Spanish two Decker bearing the flag of an Admiral and engaged the whole of the Enemies van Line as we passed them At 12 the Admiral made the Signal N°. 16 with the *Africa*'s pendants Light Airs and clear W^r. Hove overboard to clear for action one hundred and three Bags Bread two casks Beef 13 casks of Pork one cask of Oatmeal One cask Suet one cask Sugar — butts seven puncheons twelve hogsheads ten Lemon Juice cases.

At 12.15 p.m. Tuesday 22 October Digby records: 'the Admiral made the Signal N°. 16. (general) At 1 bore down and with Assistance of the *Neptune* engaging the *Santissima Trinidada* at 1.30 commenced our fire upon her at 1.58 the whole of her Masts went by the board when she struck', then Digby, believing her to have surrendered, 'sent Lieu^t. Smith with a partie to take charge of her'. On reaching the deck John Smith discovered to his embarrassment that the Spanish ship had not surrendered. More surprisingly, he was not challenged by any Spaniard, and therefore made a discreet withdrawal to his boat and returned to *Africa*. The ship's log continues, 'at the same time observed the Enemies Van hauling on a Starb^d Tack at 2.30 obs^d a French two Decker making off made all sail after her At 3.15 bro^t. Her to action at 4.30 her Mizen Mast and Main Topmast went overboard'. *Africa* was engaging the French *Intrépide* (74) which had previously been in contest with *Leviathan* (74) and for the next 40 minutes *Africa*'s gunners maintained a constant fire into her, when,

... at 4.58 the *Orion* came up to our assistance at 5.8 She struck the *Orion* took charge of her she proved to be *Intrepide* Obs^d 19 Sail of the Enemies Ships standing away found our masts very much wounded and the Main Topsail Yard shot away and great part of our Standing and Running Rigging cut up so much disabled that we could not follow them At 12 Moderate breezes Several of the squadron in Company...[24]

In the battle *Africa* suffered eight killed and 44 wounded, her wounded officers comprising Matthew Hay, Acting Lieutenant; James Tynmore, Captain Royal Marines; Master's Mates Abraham Turner and Henry West, and Midshipmen John Bailey, Philip Elmhurst and Frederick White.[25] For the next few days the log records re-rigging and repairs, the lower masts being fished. On Wednesday a marine, his surname illegible, died of his wounds and was buried overboard. By Saturday 26 October *Africa* was in trouble, her log recording:

> Strong gales and Squally Ship labouring very much At 9 the Main Mast went away about 12 feet from the Deck which carried away the Fore and fore topsail yards at 9.15 the Mizen Mast went Employ^d clearing the Wreck, lost a boat from each Quarter with the Wreck of the Mizen Mast at 2.30 the Fore Mast went in three pieces Employ^d clearing the Wreck and Rigging jury Masts latter part D^o. W^r. Made the Signal of being in distress.

More weight had to be removed. Therefore Digby 'hove overboard to ease the Ship 4 - 18 pounder Guns 4 - 32 [pounder] Carronades'. *Africa* still flying her distress signal at noon *Conqueror* came alongside and 'At 4.30 the *Conqueror* took us in Tow'. Although the weather was easing the heavy swell still laboured the ship and at 2 a.m. she was cut off from the *Conqueror* and her jib boom was carried away. On Friday 1 November discipline problems re-emerged: seaman James Dealer received 48 lashes for striking the quartermaster's mate, Matthew Harper twelve lashes for false evidence, one man twelve lashes for uncleanness, another nine for insolence and one eleven lashes for theft. *Africa* finally got into Gibraltar on Sunday (Monday) 3 November and moored with her 'Best Bower'.[26] She arrived at Portsmouth on 8 December and was refitted but not docked.

1806: Moving to Spithead at the beginning of February, Captain Isaac Wolley superseded Digby on the 20th. Wolley was himself succeeded on 5 November by Captain Henry Bayntun who had commanded *Leviathan* at Trafalgar.[27]

1808: Captain John Barrett assumed command of the *Africa* on 21 January.[28] In February Denmark, France's ally, declared war on Sweden. Consequently in April Britain, allied to Sweden, sent a fleet of warships to prevent French troops crossing to Norway. Under Barrett, *Africa* sailed for Gothenburg with a large squadron under the command of Admiral Sir James Saumarez who was flying his flag in *Victory*. Including *Africa* and *Victory* the fleet comprised nine 74s, *Brunswick*, *Centaur*, *Edgar*, *Goliath*, *Implacable*, *Mars*, *Orion*, *Superb* and *Vanguard*, the 64 gun *Dictator*, frigates *Africaine* (38), *Euryalus*, (36), *Salsette* (36), *Tribune* (36) and *Tartar* (32), together with a number of sloops, bomb vessels and fireships. In addition there were 200 transports and 14,000 troops commanded by General Sir John Moore. Arriving 17 May, it was soon realised that a misunderstanding had occurred between the King of Sweden and Moore concerning the requirement of troops. The troops were therefore confined within their transports until returning home in July. The naval force under Saumarez, however, remained, deployed between the Sound, the Great Belt and the Baltic.[29]

While operating off Copenhagen on 18 August, *Africa* was attacked by a large force of Danish gunboats and had to retreat into Malmo. On 30 August *Africa* with *Victory*, *Goliath* and *Mars* joined the Swedish fleet to support the blockade of the Russian port of Roggersvik. It was planned to attack upon the Russian vessels within the port with fireships, but the reconnaissance report from the frigate *Salsette* (36) indicated that a heavy boom and other defences would make this difficult.[30] Two months later on 15 October, *Africa* with *Thunder* bomb vessel and two brigs sailed from Karlskrona escorting a convoy of 137 merchantmen carrying vital supplies and materials. Losing only four vessels en route, the convoy, escorted by the three smaller vessels, reached Malmo on 20 October, while *Africa* anchored eight miles south of Drago on the Danish island of Amag as a lookout. Just after 12.30 p.m. *Africa* sighted a flotilla of 32 Danish gunboats and mortar boats approaching to the convoy. This force comprised 80 guns and 1,600 men. Captain Barrett immediately weighed and stood *Africa* towards the Danish vessels and at 1.15 p.m. shortened sail and cleared the ship for action. Just before 3 p.m. the Danish gunboats came within range and placed their vessels ahead and astern where *Africa* could not bring her main armament to bear, and commenced firing. The engagement lasted for three hours and 45 minutes and *Africa*'s colours were thrice shot away and re-hoisted, but with darkness approaching the Danes retired. For *Africa*'s gunners it was not an easy battle for the gunboats were small targets easily stationed off the ship's blind quarters. In the fight *Africa* suffered nine seamen and marines killed, her 53 wounded comprising Captain Barrett whose wound was slight; Lieutenants of Marines Thomas Brattle and John Richardson; both Captain's Clerks, one Midshipman and 47 seamen and marines. Danish casualties were estimated at 28 killed and 36 wounded. *Africa* also sustained considerable damage to her lower masts and yards, sails and lower rigging, much of which was caused by grapeshot. Afterwards Barrett gave up both his cabins for the wounded and his officers their cots. It had been a close run contest; had light lasted longer, it is possible that *Africa* would have been overwhelmed or sunk. Much in need of repairs, *Africa* returned to Karlskrona.[31] Ten days later *Africa*, with the main body of the British fleet, sailed home for the winter, arriving at the Downs on 8 December. Two days later she went into Chatham to refit.

1809: Going into dock on 7 January, Africa had her copper and doubling repaired. On 16 March *Africa* was commanded by Captain Loftus Bland, previously commander of *Flora* (36), wrecked off the Dutch coast on 19 January.[32] For most of this year *Africa* protected convoys carrying necessary supplies of timber, tar, pitch, turpentine and hemp for British dockyards and consequently support of the fleet. When Bland transferred into the hospital ship *Gorgon* on 31 October, Captain Thomas Dundas took command.

1810: In February *Africa* was docked at Plymouth to have her copper repaired and other defects made good. On 22 April Captain George Frederick Ryves succeeded Dundas. Sailing on 28 March, *Africa* spent most of this year in the North Sea and Baltic maintaining the blockade of Copenhagen. Ryves creditably escorted a convoy of 200 merchantmen through the Great Belt during a gale without losing a single vessel. After delivering this convoy to Yarmouth *Africa* sailed for Portsmouth and entering the Channel experienced more severe weather. Under the advice of the pilot she came to anchor for four days to ride out the gale in safety. Returning to the Baltic in October, a boat from the *Africa* commanded by Lieutenant Finnisnere went inshore under cover of darkness and destroyed a Danish privateer near the Falstubo Reef. When *Africa* was recalled home Captain Ryves transferred into the *Mars* (74) and his successor, Captain John Bastard, took command on 24 November.[33] John Marshall, *Africa*'s First Lieutenant, was promoted commander on 21 October in commemoration of Trafalgar; 19 other lieutenants throughout the fleet were similarly promoted.

1811: With the possibility of imminent war with the United States, *Africa* was deployed to Halifax, Newfoundland, under the overall command of Rear-Admiral Herbert Sawyer, then Commander-in-Chief of the North American station.

1812: Rear-Admiral Sawyer received news on 26 June from the frigate *Belvidera* (36) that she had been in action three days earlier with an American squadron off New York. Consequently Sawyer despatched a squadron comprising *Africa*, *Shannon* (38) and *Æolus* (32) on 5 July, which, sailing east of Nantucket four days later, was joined by *Guerrière* (38). During the morning of 16 July the squadron captured the American brig USS *Nautilus* even though her lee guns were heaved overboard in her endeavours to escape. That afternoon the British squadron sighted a strange sail and gave chase, the vessel later proving to be the heavy American frigate USS *Constitution* of 44 guns commanded by Captain Isaac Hull which had sailed from Chesapeake four days before. Bearing up, the British ships stood towards *Constitution* and gave chase and as dawn broke on the 17th *Guerrière* was only two miles away. At 5.30 a.m. the wind fell off, compelling *Constitution* to lower her boats and take her under tow; at the same time

Part 1: **The British Fleet**   The Ships of Trafalgar

PROGRESS BOOK – *AFRICA* 3rd RATE OF 64 GUNS. Source: ADM 180/7 Entry 137 & ADM 180/10 Entry 168

At what Port	Arrived	Docked	Coppered	Launched or Undocked	Sailed	Built or Nature of Repair	Cost of Hull, Materials £ s d	Cost of Masts & Yards Materials £ s d	Grand Total
River Thames; Adams & Barnard	Began	2 March 1778	11 April 1781	11 April 1781		Built	25,047 3s 1d	207. 14s. 1d. Masts yards etc & Extra works	25,254. 17s. 8d.
Deptford	11 April 1781				19 April 1781 to Woolwich	–	3,237 19s. 7d	8,618 14s. 5d.	11,856 14s. 0d.
Woolwich	19 April 1781	24 April 1781	Coppered May 1781	5 May 1781	July 1781	Fitted	1,859 14s. 2d.	32 8s. 9d.	1,892 2s. 11d.
						Overall Building & Fitting See note.			**39,003 14s. 7d**
Plymouth	10 Dec 1781				3 Jan 1782	Refitted	274 0s. 1d. 2,290 10s. 1d.	2,564 10s. 2d.	
Plymouth	4 May 1784	2 July 1784	Copper Repaired July 1784	6 July 1784		Fitted for Ordinary			
Plymouth		31 Dec 1784	Copper taken off Jan 1785, Re-coppered July 1785	22 July 1785		Small Repair	8,127 11d. 4d.	2,599 12s. 0d.	10,727 3s. 4d.
Plymouth		4 Sep 1793	Copper taken off Sep 1793, Re-coppered Sep 1793	20 Sep 1793	26 Feb 1794	Fitted	4,896	3564	8,446
Sheerness	6 Sep 1796				19 Sep 1796		5		5
Chatham	19 Sep 1796		Taken in Hand & Completed Sep 1798		29 Sep 1798	Fitted for a Hospital Ship	1,206	2,760	3,966
Sheerness	29 Sep 1798			11 Sep 1804					
Northfleet; Mr Pilcher ?	12 Sep 1804	20 Oct 1804	Copper taken off Oct 1804. Re-coppered & Doubled July 1805	13 July 1805 See Note		Repaired & Fitted	32,208 to the Merchant		32,208
Portsmouth	8 Dec 1805		Copper Repaired Dec 1805		2 Feb 1806	Refitted			
Chatham	10 Dec 1808	7 Jan 1809	Copper & Doubling Repaired Feb 1809	14 Feb 1809	6 April 1809	Defects			
Plymouth	17 Feb 1810	26 Feb 1810	Copper Repaired	27 Feb 1810	28 March 1810	Defects			
Portsmouth	5 March 1813	1 April 1813	Copper taken off	9 April 1813					
			9 May 1814 *Taken To Pieces May 1814*						

NOTE: She was doubled during this repair. See also Appendices – Quality of Sailing, which likewise refers to the ship being doubled.

Captain Hull ordered three of her 24 pounders to be hoisted from the main deck, and cutting away part of the taffrail, pointed them astern. Within 15 minutes every British ship, including *Africa*, was also under tow. At 6 a.m. *Constitution* turned south and Hull, at the recommendation of his First Lieutenant Charles Morris, laid out the kedge anchor to warp the ship ahead. At 7.30 a.m. Hull hoisted the American colours and commenced firing at *Belvidera* which had come within range. Following Hull's example Byron, *Belvidera*'s captain, also employed kedges and warps but he cunningly employed two kedges working together, paying the warp out through one hawse-hole and in through the opposite. By 2 p.m. *Belvidera* had closed with *Constitution* sufficiently for both to exchange fire with bow and stern chase guns respectively but without much effect. With wind freshening early next morning *Shannon* joined *Belvidera* in the chase but by 8.30 a.m. *Constitution* had hauled well ahead and eventually got into Boston. During this attack *Africa*, being the larger and heavier ship, was left behind.

1813: Ordered home, *Africa* entered Portsmouth on 5 March and was paid off on 20 March and decommissioned. *Africa* was docked on 1 April, had her copper removed, was stripped of her essential and reusable equipment and laid up in ordinary to await her fate.[34]

FATE

Taken into dock at Portsmouth on 9 May 1814, *Africa* was 'Taken to Pieces'.[35]

The 64 gun ship AGAMEMNON

Named after the Greek king *Agamemnon* who, according to Homer, ruled the ancient city of Mycenæ and Argos in the sixteenth century BC, this was the first ship to bear this name in the Royal Navy.[36]

Considered 'Nelson's favourite', *Agamemnon* was a 3rd rate of 64 guns built to the lines of the *Ardent* class designed by Thomas Slade and built at the private yard of Henry Adams at Buckler's Hard on the River Beaulieu, Hampshire. Ordered on 5 February 1777, her keel was laid down in May, the timber for her construction being supplied from the surrounding New Forest. When launched 10 April 1781, the *Hampshire Chronicle* recorded the day as, 'a blustery day when the rain fell in torrents so that only a few people were present'. *Agamemnon* was then towed to Portsmouth, arriving on 15 April and on 23 April she was docked to have her bottom coppered. Undocked on 7 May the ship completed fitting out and having her masts installed. Overall building costs amounted to £38,303 15s 4d of which £28,579 1s. 7d. was expended on her hull, the remaining £9,724 13s 9d covered rigging and stores.[37]

SERVICE HISTORY

1781: *Agamemnon* was first commissioned under Captain Benjamin Caldwell on 28 March, 13 days before her launch.[38] Also entering the ship at this period was Lieutenant Thomas Masterman Hardy who later served as Nelson's flag captain in *Victory*. Although Agamemnon left the dockyard and moored at Spithead on 9 July, her first true deployment began when she sailed 2 December 1781 with Rear Admiral Kempenfelt's fleet to cruise off Ushant. Kempenfelt's objective was to intercept an expected French force of 20 merchantmen and 19 men of war commanded by Rear-Admiral

CAPTAINS OF *AGAMEMNON* (MSS 248/4 and 248/6)

Name	Time of Entry	Time of Discharge	On What Occasion
Benjamin Caldwell	28 March 1781	10 June 1783	Paid Off at Chatham
Horatio Nelson	31 January 1793	10 June 1796	To the *Captain*
John Samuel Smith	11 June 1796	19 September 1796	Paid Off at Chatham
Robert Devereux Fancourt	23 November 1796	12 April 1802	Paid Off at Chatham
John Harvey	31 July 1804	16 September 1805	Superseded
Sir Edward Berry	17 September 1805	29 June 1806	Superseded
Joseph Spear	30 June 1806	8 July 1806	Superseded
Jonas Rose	9 July 1806	7 August 1809	Dawn transports for passage to England - Ship Lost

de Guichen bound for the West Indies. Besides *Agamemnon*, the British fleet comprised Kempenfelt's flagship *Victory*, one 50 gun ship, four frigates, and the fireship *Tisiphone*. Kempenfelt's squadron fell in with de Guichen's ships on 12 December and taking advantage of the fact that the French escorting squadron was leeward of the convoy, the British ships bore down on the undefended merchantmen and captured 15. *Agamemnon* returned to Spithead on 30 December.[39]

1782: Posted to the West Indies, *Agamemnon* sailed from Spithead on 6 February with Admiral Sir George Rodney's squadron of twelve ships escorting a convoy to Antigua. Rodney flew his flag in *Formidable* (98) and his second in command Rear-Admiral Sir Samuel Hood in *Barfleur* (98). *Agamemnon* was involved in two actions against the fleet of French Admiral Compte de Grasse. When Rodney received news that de Grasse had sailed from Martinique on 8 April with 33 ships to capture Jamaica, he immediately ordered his ships at St Lucia to sail in pursuit. In all the British squadron comprised 56 vessels of the following number and types.[40]

Guns	98	90	74	70	64	44	40	36	32	28	24	16	14	BV	FS
No.	4	1	20	1	11	1	1	3	3	4	2	2	1	1	1

Note: BV = Bomb vessel. FS = Fireship

The first action took part on 9 April. It resulted in Hood withdrawing his badly mauled ships to repair. The second and more decisive action commenced off the Île de Saintes on 12 April during which *Agamemnon* lay sixteenth in the line of battle. Firing broadside to broadside, action begun at around 8.30 a.m. At 9.15 the Rodney suddenly turned *Formidable* to starboard and breaking out of the battle line, cut straight through the French line, firing her broadsides through the stern of *Glorieux* (74) as she passed. By dividing the French fleet in two, Rodney's manœuvre had effectively confused his opponent. When Rodney ordered the fleet to tack at 11.33 a.m. the French line was further divided into three, bringing *Agamemnon* and other British ships into closer action. Nelson would use a similar tactic of subdividing the French fleet into three at Trafalgar. Battle continued until 6.30 p.m. when five French ships including de Grasse's flagship *Ville de Paris* had been captured, one had blown up, while de Vandreuil had escaped with 26 vessels. A prisoner of war, de Grasse was taken to England.[41] In the thick of the fight *Agamemnon* suffered much damage, her fore topmast had been shot away and her sails and rigging cut to shreds. As for her hull, the outer planking in the wake of number eight gun port on the lower deck was severely damaged. *Agamemnon*'s casualties were relatively high, as her master's log dated Sunday 14 April records: 'Departed this Life Lieutenant William Brice At 2 also departed this Life James Hawkins Mariner.... Mustered the Ship's Company and found 14 Men killed and 22 wounded.' *Agamemnon* then sailed to Jamaica for repairs.[42]

1783: When the Treaty of Versailles was signed on 3 September ending the American War of Independence, *Agamemnon* returned from the West Indies and entered Chatham dockyard on 3 June, Caldwell paying off the ship one week later.[43] She then went into dock on 29 October for a 'Small Repair' and to have her copper replaced.[44]

1784: Coming out of the dock on 4 June 1784 her refit costs amounted to £10,593 0s 9d with a further sum of £2,000 spent on rigging and stores. Completed, *Agamemnon* was then laid up in ordinary.[45]

1787: Docked again at Chatham on 1 November for ten days, *Agamemnon* was 'Partly fitted' at a cost of £504 9s 7d.[46]

1790: With the potential threat of war with Spain and Russian hostility in the Black Sea, *Agamemnon* was 'Taken in hand' in October and 'Fitt'd for Sea'. From the survey it was soon evident that she needed far more extensive work than anticipated, so went into dock again on 9 November for a middling repair.[47]

1791: Finally completed at an overall cost of £12,110, *Agamemnon* was undocked on 15 August 1791.[48] While the ship was later hailed as 'Nelson's favourite', from the amount of refit work undertaken it could be considered that ships built under contract in private yards were not as robust as navy-built ships. Adams, her builder, was known for late finishing contracts (*Euryalus* and *Swiftsure*), and as seen later, by 1796 *Agamemnon* was quite worn out and her weakness would prove disastrous.

1793: When the French king, Louis XVI, was executed on 21 January, war with revolutionary France seemed inevitable. *Agamemnon* was therefore docked at Chatham to be fitted out for sea service. The ship's new commander, Captain Horatio Nelson, commissioned the ship on 31 January.[49] Next day France declared war on Britain. *Agamemnon* was completed in March at a cost of £1,505 for hull, masts and yards and £3,377 for rigging and stores.[50] Nelson sailed from Chatham on 24 April for the Nore. Nelson, elated with his ship, wrote: 'We appear to sail very fast; we went, coming out, nearly as fast, without any sail, as the *Robust* did under her top sails'.[51] Under Nelson's command *Agamemnon* sailed for the Mediterranean and joined Admiral Hood's fleet blockading the French ships in Toulon, Hood flying his flag in the *Victory* (100). After capturing 19 ships of the Toulon fleet, Hood then prepared to take possession of the city in support of the royalists. Although the British fleet was aided by allied Spanish ships, he needed further assistance. Hood sent Nelson in *Agamemnon* to Naples to seek reinforcements from King Ferdinand IV. The ship anchored there on 12 September. Months at sea had taken its toll on the crew of the *Agamemnon*, as Nelson wrote:

SPECIFICATIONS: *AGAMEMNON*

Class Name	Ardent	Length on the Deck	160 ft 3½ ins	Ordnance – Upper Gun Deck	26 x 18 pounders
Rate	3rd	Length of Keel for Tonnage	131 ft 8 ins	Ordnance – Quarter Deck	10 x 9 pounders
Design Date	1761	Extreme Breadth	44 ft 4 ins	Ordnance – Forecastle	2 x 9 pounders
Designer	Slade	Depth in Hold	18 ft	Iron Ballast	70 tons
Builder	Henry Adams	Draught afore	12 ft 1 ins	Shingle Ballast	277 tons
Yard	Buckler's Hard	Draught abaft	17 ft 3 ins	Draught Forward when victualled	20 ft 11 ins
Ordered	5 February 1777	Tons Burthen	1376. 47/94.	Draught aft when victualled	2 ft 7 ins
Keel Laid	May 1777	Complement	500	Foremost Gun Port from waterline	4 ft 10 ins
Launched	10 April 1781	Ordnance – Lower Gun Deck	26 x 24 pounders	Midship Gun Port from waterline	4 ft 4 ins

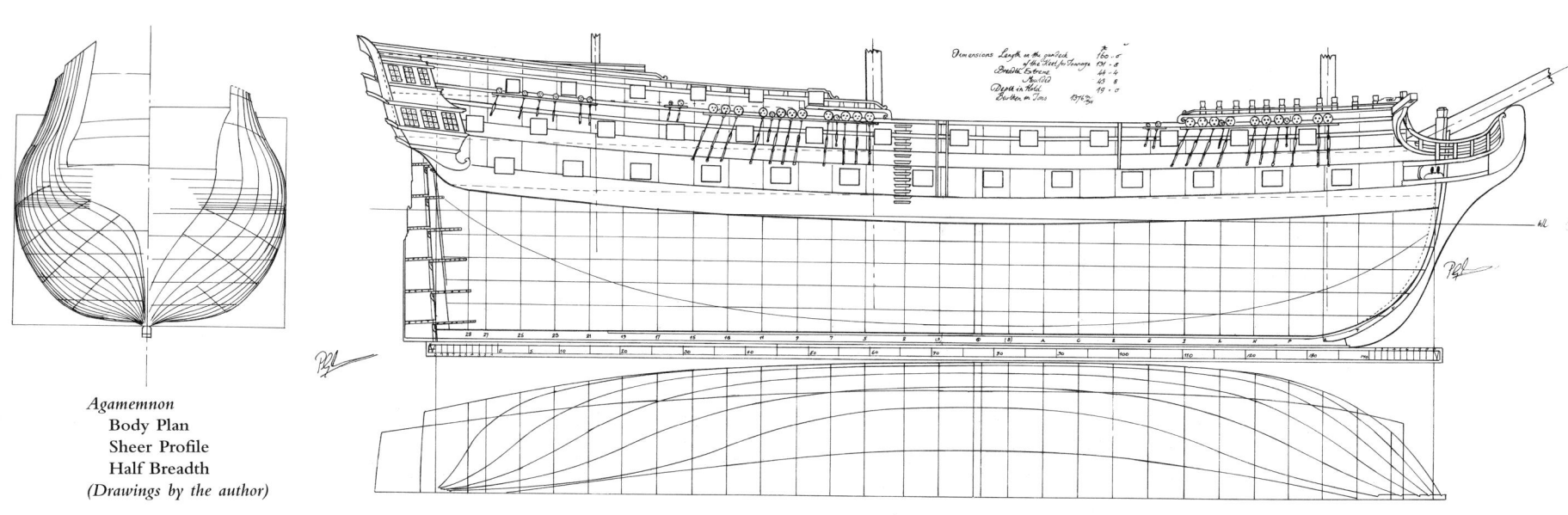

Agamemnon
Body Plan
Sheer Profile
Half Breadth
(Drawings by the author)

My poor fellows have not had a morsel of fresh meat or vegetables for nineteen weeks, and in that time I have only had my foot twice on shore, at Cadiz. We are absolutely sick with fatigue.[52]

King Ferdinand agreed to provide 4,000 troops and Nelson celebrated his success by holding a dinner for the king and his entourage, including the British Envoy Sir William Hamilton and his wife Emma, aboard *Agamemnon*, catering facilities provided from the Embassy kitchens ashore. When *Agamemnon* rejoined Hood at Toulon on 5 October the city was under siege by French forces. New orders sent *Agamemnon* to join Commodore Robert Linzee's squadron at Cagliari, Sardinia. Operating 20 leagues north of Cagliari on 22 October, Nelson sighted five suspect vessels. The frigates proved to be *Melepomène* (40), *Minerve* (38), *Fortune* (36) *Mignonne* (28) and *Hasard*. *Agamemnon* hauled up astern of *Melepomène* and engaged in a running battle which, after some three hours becalmed and crippled, ended with all hopes of pursuit lost, *Agamemnon* suffering one killed and six wounded.[53]

Returning to Cagliari for a long overdue refit, Nelson wrote: 'I would not say *Agamemnon* was unable to go in search of the Enemy, we worked all night fixing our masts and yards and stopping shot holes, mending sails and splicing our rigging'.[54] *Agamemnon* then sailed with Linzee's squadron to Tunis to open negotiations with the Bey for support against the French but proving unsuccessful *Agamemnon* rejoined Hood on 30 November. When Toulon fell to the revolutionary forces commanded by an outstanding artilleryman named Napoleon Bonaparte in December, *Agamemnon* retreated with Hood's squadron to Hyères Bay.[55]

1794: Deciding to support the Corsican partisan General Pasquale de Paoli to fight against the French forces on the island, Hood sent *Agamemnon* with a small flotilla to harrow French supply ships and attack their shore batteries. Nelson attacked a French store at San Fiorenza on 21 January and 'landed sixty soldiers and seaman. In spite opposition at landing the sailors threw all the flour into the sea, burned the mill the only one they have, and returned on board without the loss of a man'. Seven days later when Hood joined Nelson's squadron, the ships were hit by a fierce storm: 'The *Agamemnon* did well but lost every sail in her...The *Victory* was very near lost'.[56]

Throughout February *Agamemnon* was engaged in encounters off the Corsican coast, burning four vessels at Centuri on the 6th; attacking Maginaggio and destroying eight ships on the 8th; and took the tower of Miomo near Bastia on the 19th. Rejoining Hood's fleet at San Fiorenzo after three months at sea, *Agamemnon* was in a terrible condition and because her decks urgently needed re-caulking, Nelson told Hood that 'not a man has slept dry for many months'. Nelson also complained that he had no 'wine, beef, pork, flour and almost no water: Not a rope, canvas, twine or nail in the Ship. The Ship is so light, she cannot hold her side to the wind'.[57] Hood then decided to reduce the French stronghold of Bastia so *Agamemnon* sailed with part of Hood's squadron from San Fiorenzo on 2 April, arriving off Bastia two days later. Once anchored troops commanded by Lieutenant Colonel Vilettes and seamen from *Agamemnon* under Nelson, were landed just north of the town. In all the force comprised 1,248 officers and men. Nelson's 'Agamemnons' landed eight 24 pounder guns from the ship and eight 13 mortars supplied from King Ferdinand IV of Naples.[58] Saturday 5 April *Agamemnon*'s log reads: 'Landed the troops equipage & 2 days provisions. Left on shore several sail for tents of the officers and seamen. People employed making sandbags for the batteries. Empd getting two 24-pounders, sent them on shore with sundry other stores'. Because of the rough and steep terrain, the heat and the weight of the guns, such work was extremely arduous: one 24 pounder gun with its carriage weighed 3.5 tons (3.55 tonnes). On Wednesday 9 April 150 barrels of powder (weight 6.7 tons or 6.8 tonnes) were landed, together with 'a quantity of grape & canister shot'. Within three days the batteries were set up overlooking the town. Hood then sent a letter of truce to the French governor, General Lacombe Saint-Michel, who refused to read the communication. Consequently Hood signalled Nelson by running up a red flag to the truck of *Victory*'s main mast which Nelson acknowledged by hoisting his own colours above his battery. His 'Agamemnons' gave three cheers and opened fire: 'At ? past 9 our Batteries opened upon the Enemy's Redoubts, the Mortars upon the Town'.[59] The siege of Bastia lasted 40 days, the French finally surrendering on the 21 May. Although Hood's forces were opposed by 4,500 men, casualty rates on the British side were low: 14 killed and 40 wounded or missing. Of the dead five were out of *Agamemnon*, as for the wounded Nelson himself received a 'sharp cut in the back'. Enemy losses amounted to over 200 dead and 540 wounded.[60] With most of her guns re-embarked *Agamemnon* sailed to Gibraltar for urgent repairs before returning to Corsica with *Dolphin* (44) and *Lutine* (36) and 15 transports.[61]

Anchoring south of the republican held town of Calvi on 18 June, Nelson and General Stuart reconnoitred the land to establish where to land guns and stores and agreed to use the small cove of Porto Argo three miles from Calvi to effect their attack. Early next day the ships anchored off Port Galere, boats were lowered and troops and seamen were disembarked taking with them various stores, spars, sails, 91 hammocks, a four pounder field gun and 2,400 sand bags. Provisions landed comprised six casks of pork, five casks of beef, 25 bags of bread and three pipes of wine. Bad weather however forced *Agamemnon* to cut her cable, leaving her best bower anchor and stand out to sea until weather eased, after which one 24 and two 18 pounders, two howitzers and two mortars were landed. More guns were removed from the ship and manhandled up the craggy rock faces to their

THE 64 GUN SHIP *AGAMEMNON*

positions. Hood arrived with more ships on 27 June and landed more guns, some from his own ship *Victory*, and some removed from the recently acquired French prize *Commerce de Marseille*. With a total of 35 guns sent on shore, *Agamemnon*'s carpenter set about constructing gun platforms. With the first battery complete the siege commenced on 4 July. Six days later the French directed their fire upon the one of the batteries and destroyed a 32 pounder from *Victory* and two 24 pounders from the *Agamemnon*.[62] During this barrage a shot shattered the defensive earthworks of the battery and Nelson was struck in the face and chest with grit and sand. This led to the loss of sight in Nelson's right eye.[63] The siege, lasting 51 days, ended when the French governor surrendered on 10 August. Military casualties on the British side were 23 dead and 53 wounded, naval losses being naval killed, six of whom were from *Agamemnon*, and five wounded. On Tuesday 12 August *Agamemnon*'s crew returned to the ship and put to sea.[64]

Arriving at Genoa on 20 September, Nelson successfully negotiated docking facilities for British ships after which *Agamemnon* returned to Hood's fleet off Toulon. When Vice-Admiral William Hotham assumed command of the Mediterranean fleet in November and hoisted his flag in the *Britannia* (100), he withdrew his ships to San Fiorenzo and sent the *Agamemnon* to Leghorn to refit.

1795: Meagrely refitted, *Agamemnon* sailed in mid-January but poor weather made it difficult for the ships to keep station watching Toulon.[65] Taking advantage of the withdrawal of the British blockading fleet, Rear Admiral Martin sailed from Toulon on 3 March with 15 line of battle ships, six frigates, and two brigs. Receiving news of their escape six days later, Hotham, now flying his flag in *Victory* (100), ordered his ships, including *Agamemnon*, to weigh and make sail, his squadron comprising 33 vessels as follows:[66]

Guns	100	98	90	80	74	64	32	28	24	20	18	14	12	Cutter
No.	2	3	1	1	14	2	1	1	1	2	1	1	1	1

Note: Two of the 74s and one of the frigates were Neapolitan.

Shortly afterwards British and French fleets engaged on 13 March. The French *Ça Ira* (80), having carried away her own fore and main topmasts when running foul with the *Victoire* (80), fell back from her consorts and being crippled was immediately engaged by Thomas Freemantle's frigate *Inconstant* (36). At 9.a.m. *Vestale* (36) came to *Ça Ira*'s support and their joint gunfire drove *Inconstant* away. At around 10.45 a.m. Nelson placed *Agamemnon* off the quarter of *Ça Ira*, and assisted by *Captain* (74), maintained a constant fire into the French ship. This situation continued until 2.45 p.m. when fast approaching French ships forced Nelson to withdraw and regroup with Hotham's squadron. In the engagement *Agamemnon* suffered only 13 wounded. When *Censeur* (74) took *Ça Ira* in tow that night they became isolated from the French fleet. Unable to fight because of high casualties, both ships were captured next day by *Captain* (74) and *Bedford* (74).[67]

Hotham's entire fleet then returned to San Fiorenzo to make repairs. *Agamemnon* put to sea again on 4 July with the frigates *Meleager* (32),

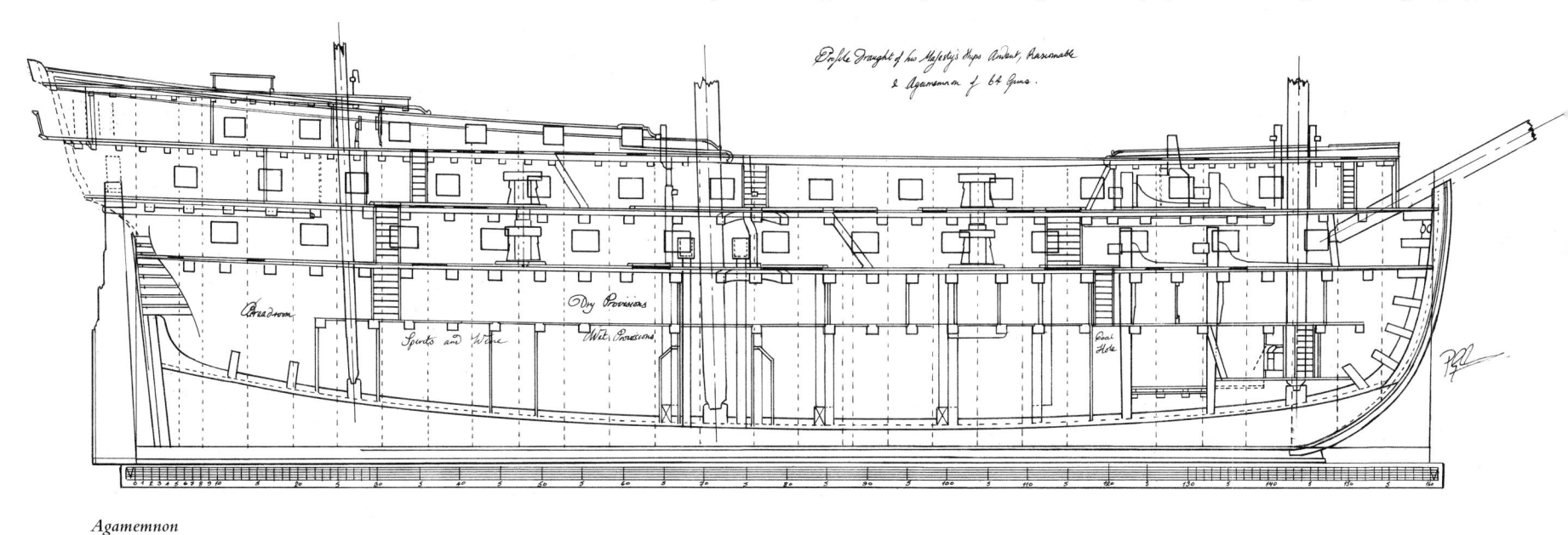

Agamemnon
Inboard profile
Lower Gun Deck Plan
Orlop Deck Plan with Hold underneath
(Drawings by the author)

Moselle (24), *Ariadne* (20) and the brig *Mutine* (12). Three days they later sighted the Admiral Martin's Toulon fleet of 22 sail of the line and accompanying frigates 5 leagues NW of Cape de Helle. Nelson's small force was soon chased off. Returning to San Fiorenzo at 7.20 a.m. next day he alerted Hotham by signalling with *Agamemnon*'s guns but adverse winds prevented Hotham's ships weighing until 9 p.m. *Agamemnon* rejoined the fleet and sighting Martin's squadron south of Hyéres on 13 July, Hotham gave the signal 'general chase' and ordered his ships to clear for battle. Although partial action commenced around 12.30 p.m. it was 2 p.m. when *Agamemnon*, together with *Blenheim* (90), *Captain* (74) *and Defence* (74), got into battle. When the wind fell off, disadvantaging the French at 2.45. p.m., Hotham amazingly signalled his ships to break off the action. Failing to resume action later, Hotham was much criticised for this response. Sustaining no casualties *Agamemnon* returned to station blockading Toulon on 8 August.[68]

Needing to support the Austrian and Sardinian armies fighting the French in Genoese territory, Hotham again despatched Nelson with *Agamemnon* (64), *Inconstant* (36), *Meleager* (32), *Southampton* (32), *Tartar* (28), *Ariadne* (20) and 14 gun brig/sloop *Speedy* to patrol off Genoa. Nelson's squadron cut out two French brigs, two 5 gun galleys and five store-ships and sank two other vessels. At the end of 1795 Hotham was relieved by Admiral Sir John Jervis.[69]

1796: On 23 April Jervis sent *Agamemnon*, *Diadem* (64), *Meleager* (32) and the sloop *Petrel* (16) to blockade Genoa and harass French shipping off that coast. Two days later Nelson captured four enemy store-ships carrying supplies for the French army anchored in Loano Bay. Cruising off Oneglia in May Nelson's squadron fell in with six French ships and chased them into harbour but in doing so came under fire from the shore batteries. These were soon silenced by the gunnery of the *Agamemnon* and supporting fire from *Meleager* (16*)*, *Petrel* (16) and *Speedy* (16). Nelson sent boats inshore to cut out the French ketch and gunboat. To avoid capture, the accompanying French transports laden with guns and stores, needed for the planned siege of Mantua, ran themselves on shore. Although this operation was relatively minor, it had far-reaching effects as the French siege of Mantua failed because of Nelson's actions.[70] Promoted to Commodore on the 11 March, Nelson now raised his broad pendant in *Agamemnon*. When he left his 'favourite' ship and transferred into *Captain* (74) on 10 June he was succeeded by Captain John Samuel Smith.[71] Much fatigued with continual sea service, *Agamemnon* was sent home to refit, arriving at Chatham on 10 September. Nine days later Smith paid off the ship, *Agamemnon* went into dock on 3 October for a 'Middling Repair' and her old copper was removed and replaced with new.[72] While in dock *Agamemnon* was recommissioned under Captain Robert Devereux Fancourt on 23 November. However, according to the entry in the Progress Book, the ship came out the dock on the 31 October. This date appears to have been erroneously recorded, for Fancourt's log on Wednesday 30 November reads: 'D.o W.r [Ditto weather] Artificers employ'd AM took the ship out of Dock and Transported her to the moorings, found the Ship make a great deal of Water'.[73] Because of serious problems, she was, according to the Progress Book, docked again on the 29 November to 'stop a leak & Refit[te]d' and have her 'copper repaired'. *Agamemnon*'s log actually states: 'Thursday 1st December 1796 Bearings In Dock Light Breezes and Cloudy PM emp.d pumping the Ship out AM took the Ship into Dock Artificers employ'd variously'.[74] The overall cost for her refit amounted to £10,623. Accepting the difference between ship time and actual time, the Progress Book date corresponds better with the log date. With remedial work completed two weeks later the ship was, according to the Progress Book, undocked on 14 December 1796, again a date which conflicts with the log book. Artificers were employed working on the ship in the dock until 15 December.[75] Next day, Friday 16 December, *Agamemnon* was back at her moorings where she remained for the next eight weeks taking on stores and finishing repairs.

1797: On Thursday 9 February *Agamemnon* left Chatham for the Nore and throughout March and April was with the North Sea squadron between the Texel and Yarmouth Roads watching over the Dutch fleet. Following the mutiny of the Channel fleet at Spithead 17 April, the *Agamemnon*, along with 25 other vessels of the fleet anchored at the Nore, mutinied on 4 June. When the signal was made on 29 May for the fleet to sail few ships complied and those that did sailed back into Yarmouth Roads. *Agamemnon*'s seamen cut the cable but did not refuse to make sail. There was no sign of mutiny within *Agamemnon* until after dinner when the crew did not answer when the Boatswain called the hands. One petty officer went aft to report that that the men had withdrawn to the fore part of the lower deck. Lieutenant Brenton, one of *Agamemnon*'s officers, stated:

> I was at the time officer of the watch and fourth Lieutenant, I acquainted the captain, who desired me to accompany him down to speak to them. We went forward on the lower deck, and found the men had made a barricade of hammocks from one side of the ship to another, just before the fore hatchway, and had left an embrasure each side, through which they had pointed two 24-pounders; these being loaded, and threatened to fire in case of resistance on the part of the officers. The captain spoke to them, but, being treated with much contempt, returned to the quarter deck. A few minutes after a number of the people came up; some seized the wheel, while others rounded in the weather braces and wore the ship round, passing under the stern of the *Venerable*.[76]

When Admiral Duncan signalled his ships to come to windward on a larboard tack, the seamen hoisted the signal of inability - a red/white flag over blue/yellow. While the mutineers steered for Yarmouth Roads, Captain Fancourt and his officers went to dinner and Lieutenant Brenton remained standing the watch. He approached Axle, the Master-at-Arms who said that the ship had been given away even though 'the best part of the men and all the marines', were not in support. Brenton told Captain Fancourt there was a chance of retaking the ship from the mutineers. Brenton then reports:

> His answer I shall never forget, 'Mr Brenton, if we call out the marines some of the men will be shot, and I could not bear to see them lying in convulsions on the deck; no, no, a little patience, and we shall all hail unanimity again'. I quitted the cabin, and walked the deck until my watch was out, too much irritated to say a word more.[77]

As the mutiny at the Nore become more critical greater pressure was brought upon the ships stationed in Yarmouth Roads. *Agamemnon*'s log for Monday 5 June records that delegates supporting the Nore mutineers arrived in a cutter from Sheerness at 2.30 p.m. to incite further disharmony and 'came on board and took Command of the ship demanding the Keys of the Magazine the first Lieut.t refused them, the Capt.n not being on board'. *Agamemnon* then weighed and put to sea with 'a red flag at the Fore Top Gall.t mast head', with ships '*Ardent*, *Leopard*, *Isis*, and *Ranger* Sloop in Company'. *Agamemnon* moored at the Great Nore on Wednesday 7 June where, two days later, 'the Delegates in the Name of the Ships C.o demanded the Arms out of the Wardroom, which they got & took away & also all the Arm Chests of the Poop & stow'd all below' and at '8 mann'd the Yards & hoisted the Red Flag'.[78] Hoping to bring pressure upon the Admiralty the seditious fleet now prevented merchant trading vessels entering or leaving the Thames. Trying to break from the mutiny on Saturday 10 June, *Leopard* and *Repulse* slipped their moorings to run into Sheerness but when *Repulse* ran aground she came under 'a perpetual fire from the *Monmouth* & *Director*'. Eventually floating free she ran into harbour. Likewise when *Ardent* got under way at 11.30 she was fired upon 'from the *Sandwich*, & 2 other ships' and like *Leopard* earlier, suffered some casualties. *Agamemnon*'s log of 10 June then states that Captain Knight went on board *Sandwich* where he 'met all the Delegates, in the presence of a Mr. Parker leading Officer of Rebellion'. That afternoon 'the greatest part of the Merchant Ships, got under way, our boat return'd with one of the Delegates with

Orders to hoist a Blue Flag at the Mizon Peek as an Answer to the Proposals, as did several others'. The mutiny was collapsing and at 12.20 Tuesday 13 June the boatswain's mate of *Iris* went on board *Agamemnon* with a 'Paper which exprest [sic] no Pardon for any one concern'd in this Mutiny'. Half an hour later *Montague* made a signal for all seditious representatives to repair on board for a meeting. When the delegates returned to *Agamemnon* they 'came into the Wardroom, saying all Officers must go on shore, for as we find we are not to be pardoned, we must do the best we can for ourselves'. With little hope of retaining hold of the situation any longer, reluctant crews ended the dispute by overthrowing hard line insurgents. After a struggle *Agamemnon*'s loyal seamen and marines ejected their 13 representatives after which, 'our People came aft & said they was willing to resign the Command, if Captⁿ. Fancourt would pass his Honour to petition the Admiralty for a Pardon, at which time resign'd the Command & ? before 11 weigh'd & made sail up the River' with *Nassau* (64), *Standard* (64), *Isis* (50) and *Vestal* (28). This action was undertaken in fear of being fired upon by the remaining mutineers. Next day *Agamemnon* anchored at Gravesend Reach with 'the *Nassau*, *Standard*, *Iris* & *Vestal* in C^o'. Once moored Captain Fancourt disembarked into the cutter and went ashore to Gravesend, returning at 11.30 'with a Promise of Pardon for His Ships Comp:^y'.[79] Vice-Admiral Buckner then sent marines into *Sandwich* to arrest Richard Parker, 30 of his fellow protagonists and following a court martial in the *Sandwich* at Sheerness, Parker was hanged from the topgallant yardarm of the *Sandwich* on 29 June. *Agamemnon*, with the other ships, was recalled from Gravesend to witness the event. Other leading mutineers were executed, imprisoned, or flogged round the fleet.[80] *Agamemnon* remained operating from Yarmouth and the Nore throughout the remainder of 1797 and 1798.

1799: On 19 February *Agamemnon* arrived at Sheerness dockyard for minor maintenance and rigging work, £22 was spent on her hull and £181 on rigging and stores. Sailing to Chatham on 8 March she went into dock on 23 March to have her copper repaired. She was refitted at a cost of £2,603 for her hull and masts and £2,136 on rigging and stores. Undocked on 20 April 1799, the ship sailed on 18 May.[81]

1800: In the first part of the year *Agamemnon* was deployed in the Channel. Entering Plymouth dockyard on 30 March, she was docked on 8 April to have her copper repaired. Coming out of the dock on 6 May, after she had 'made good repairs', the ship sailed on 20 June to return to her North Sea station. No refit costs are recorded for this or succeeding work in the Progress Book.[82]

1801: Following the recent embargo imposed by the Armed Neutrality of the North which prevented Britain importing raw materials essential to the navy, the British government decided to send a fleet to break the alliance between Baltic States and attack the Danes at Copenhagen. This fleet, placed under the overall command of Admiral Sir Hyde Parker with Vice-Admiral Lord Nelson second in command, comprised 38 vessels as follows:[84]

Rate	Guns	Ships' names (guns borne where applicable)
2nd	98	London, St George
3rd	74	Bellona, **Defence, Defiance**, Edgar, Elephant, Ganges, Monarch, Ramillies, Russell, Saturn, Warrior
3rd	64	**Agamemnon**, Ardent, **Polyphemus**, Raisonnable, Veteran
4th	54 - 40	Glatton - 54. Isis -50. Désirée - 40
5th	38 - 30	Amazon - 38. Blanche - 36. Alcème - 32. Arrow - 30. Dart - 30
6th	26 - 18	Jamaica - 26. Cruiser - 18. Harpy - 18
Bombs	various	Discovery - 16. Hecla - 10. Sulphur - 10. Explosion - 8. Terror - 8. Volcano - 8. Zebra - 16
Fireships	14	Otter, Zephyr

Author's Note. Ships' names denoted in bold type later fought at Trafalgar.

Anchored off Copenhagen on 2 April, Nelson's flotilla weighed anchor at 9.30 a.m. and proceeded down the Outer Channel to navigate around the southern tip of the Middle Ground before returning north towards the city. Leading the line was *Edgar* (74), which commenced firing into the *Prövesteen*. Making considerable sail *Agamemnon* followed in her wake but unable to weather the point, had to bring up and was grounded. This left *Edgar* unsupported for a period until *Polyphemus* (64) breached *Agamemnon*'s position. Following *Agamemnon*'s fate, *Bellona* (74) and *Russell* (74) also grounded on the Middle Ground at around 1 p.m. and all three ships were flying distress signals. Already their situation was affecting Nelson's general situation and it was probably the combination of these factors that prompted Parker to call off the action. Consequently signal No. 39, 'Discontinue Action', was hoisted from the Commander in Chief; Nelson however successfully pressed on the attack. During the night of the 2nd and 3rd *Agamemnon*, together with the *Bellona* and *Russell*, were eventually rescued from their plight. Hampered by squally weather and snow the ship rejoined the fleet four days later. *Agamemnon* remained off Copenhagen until the 19 April and was deployed in the Baltic until finally sailing for England on 11 July.[84]

1802: Arriving at Sheerness on 12 April *Agamemnon* sailed up river to Chatham where Fancourt paid off the ship. Considering her condition it is very likely that she would have either been hulked or broken up but war resumed in May 1803.

1804: Brought out of ordinary, *Agamemnon* went into dock to be 'Fitted' on 12 April. After her copper was replaced the ship undocked 21 July. Ten days later the ship was recommissioned under Captain John Harvey.[85] After spending a further month rigging and storing *Agamemnon* sailed from Chatham on 30 September to join Cornwallis's Channel fleet.[86]

1805: In the summer Cornwallis deployed *Agamemnon* in a separate squadron under Admiral Sir Robert Calder watching over Ferrol, Calder flying his flag in the *Prince of Wales* (98). Receiving orders from Lord Barham, First Lord of the Admiralty, on the 8 July, Calder stood his fleet some 35 leagues west of Finisterre in wait for Villeneuve's fleet returning from the West Indies. At around 11 a.m. on 22 July Calder sighted Villeneuve's combined fleet of 29 ships steering in three columns ESE towards Ferrol.

Although outnumbered, Calder prepared to engage and at 12 noon signalled his squadron to form two columns and clear for battle and at 1 p.m. brought his ships into line ahead on a starboard tack. Unfortunately the weather was contrary with light winds and hazy, making it difficult to close with the French. After successive manœuvres the British fleet began to converge on their adversaries and by 6 p.m. a general engagement ensued during which *Agamemnon* lost her mizzen topmast and fore topsail yard. By 8.30 p.m. Calder's ships had become scattered as the fog closed in again. With two Spanish prizes *San Rafael* (80) and *Firme* (74) taken the enemy suffered 476 killed or wounded as opposed to 198 British. Next morning the two fleets lay 17 miles apart with Calder's advance squadron of *Barfleur*, *Hero*, *Triumph* and *Agamemnon* laying five miles to windward of the enemy van. Even though Calder had attained a small victory with a numerically inferior squadron he was recalled home to face a court martial. Although acquitted, he was severely reprimanded because he had failed to take the initiative to bring about a decisive action, thereby giving the enemy the opportunity to re-mobilise and meet the British fleet off Cape Trafalgar.[87]

Now 24 years old, *Agamemnon* returned to refit at Portsmouth on 6 September. Docked seven days later for re-coppering she came out the dock on the 17 September and at 9 o'clock that same day Captain Sir Edward Berry Kt 'came on board and took command of the above Ship Must^d. By Divisions [and] sent a Man to the Hospital'.[88] Berry's First Lieutenant Hugh Cook also joined that day. After repairs, embarking guns and stores and provisioning for six months, including 1,200 pounds of fresh beef, the ship moved out to Spithead on Saturday 28 September. At 1.30 p.m. on Thursday 3 October *Agamemnon* 'Weighed and Made Sail, [and] run through the Needles', to join Nelson's squadron blockading Villeneuve's combined Franco-Spanish fleet in Cadiz. Next morning Berry punished seaman James Mounslow for deserting.[89] After meeting heavy weather off Cape Finisterre on Thursday 12 October *Agamemnon* fell in with Admiral Allemand's French squadron out of Rochefort, her log reporting: 'at day light made the Private signal to a Squad[n] which was not answered found the Strange Ships to be an Enemy Consisting of 6 Sail of the Line 2 Frigates & 1 Brig 4 Small Vessels in tow', then at 8 weather 'Carried away the Starb[d] Fore Tops[l] Steer[g] Sail Boom Cut away the Lower & Tops[l] Steering sails got another Boom on the Yard'. When Allemand detached ships to intercept the *Agamemnon* Berry recorded 'at 8.30 a Three decker & a Ship of 80 Guns coming up with us Started 30 Tons of Water and threw the Casks overboard, fired Several Guns and made the Sig[l]. for an Enemy in sight The Enemy still gaining upon us Cutaway the Yawl from the Larb[d] Quarter at 11 the Enemy left off the Chace'. Berry then watched Allemand's ships bear down on a convoy. Evading the Frenchmen, the *Agamemnon* arrived 50 miles west of Cadiz on 13 October and was immediately deployed as part of the inshore squadron.

TRAFALGAR

After *Agamemnon*'s crew had 'Washed Decks & Cloaths [the canvas cloths covering the hammocks in the nettings] on Saturday 19 October, Berry 'hoisted the Boats out to board a Brig in the NW', which proved to be American. Continuing next day the log states: 'at 8 Boats return[d] with part of the Brigs Men', after which *Agamemnon* 'took the Brig in Tow'. By this time Nelson had been informed that the 'Enemy has their topsail yards hoisted' and were coming out of port. Berry states next morning 'at 7 Observed a strange fleet East at 8 the Euryalus made the Sig[l] for an Enemy Counted 30 Sail of them Cast off the tow', and made good his escape.[90]

Agamemnon's log Monday 21 October starts:

PM Fresh Breezes & Squally at 3 Came on a heavy Squall Carried away the M[n] Topm[t] lost the Royal & Top G[t]. Y[d] Overboard Empl[d] getting up another Topmast AM Light airs & clear got the M[n] G[t]. Yard up & Set the sail at Daylight Enemy ESE Ans[d]. Gen[l]. Sig[l]. Prepare for Battle Ans[d]. Sig[l]. N[o]. 50 & 63 at Noon Bearing down on the Enemy's fleet.

Agamemnon lay seventh in line of Nelson's division, ahead of her lay *Britannia* (100), astern *Ajax* (74). *Agamemnon*'s log then states:

At Meridian the Action Commenced at 1.10 Opened our Fire on the Enemy at 1.20 Observed a Spanish Ship which had been Engaged by the *Roy[l]. Sovereign* to Strike her Colours at 1.40 Observed the Ship we was engaging to loose [sic] her masts at 2 Observed a Spanish 4 Decker which was engaged by the *Neptune Conqueror* and *Agamemnon* loose [sic] her Main & Miz[n] Mast at 2.30 She lost her Foremast at 2.35 Observed the Royal Sovereign loose [sic] her Main & Miz[n] Mast at 2.40 hailed a Ship which we had engaged and She struck desired her to hoist English Colours - We was prevented from taking Possession of the 4 Decker by 4 Ships of the Line which kept up a heavy fire upon us...

When *Agamemnon* got into action she opened both her broadsides, her larboard battery pouring into the French *Héros* (74), her starboard guns firing into the great Spanish four decker *Santísima Trinidad* (136). Berry then closed to support *Neptune* (98) and *Conqueror* (74) pounding *Santísima Trinidad* into submission. Having intensely mauled their huge adversary and brought down all her masts, the pride of the Spanish fleet, suffering some 216 dead and 116 wounded, hauled down her colours. When Admiral Dumanoir's previously isolated van division had finally turned and bore down on the windward side of the British line Hardy, now captain of the fleet, signalled his ships to oppose Dumanoir's unscathed vessels. Coming onto a larboard tack, *Agamemnon*, together with *Britannia* (100), *Neptune* (98), *Ajax* (74), *Conqueror* (74), *Leviathan* (74), and *Africa* (64), turned north to engage. Reacting to this manœuvre, three ships in Dumanoir's squadron, *Rayo* (100), *San Francisco de Asis* (74) and *Héros* (74), took this opportunity to leave the battle and make for Cadiz. Shortly after these British ships engaged the French *Intrépide* (74) as they sailed north to cut off the fleeing Spanish ships. *Agamemnon*'s log then states:

... at 5.30 1 of the Prizes blew up Ans[d]. Gen[l]. Sig[l]. N[o]. 99 Killed & Wounded Killed Rob[t]. Paine & Tho[s]. Moore (Seamen) Wounded Edw[d]. Badger, Ham[h] Donaldson, Rich[d]. Heatherly, And[w]. Campbell, Ja[s]. Longley, Alen Schanks, Cha[s] Bland & Angus Campbell - 1 Shot Hole in the Upper Counter 1 in the Larb[d] Q[tr] 3[F] 1[l] under Water which kept the Pumps constantly going 3 in the Larb[d] Side 5 in the Star[d] Side 5 in the Fore Yard, 1 in the Larb[d] Cheek of the Main Mast Shot away in the Action a White Ensign & Seceral Numeral Flags repeating Sig[ls] At 6 took H. M. Ship *Colossus* in Tow being much Cut up in Action Carpenter's repairing Shot Holes on Ships Hull Sailmakers Repairing d[o] in the Sails People Empl[d] at the Pumps 4 feet of Water in the Hold Counted 16 of the Enemys fleet that had Struck & the rest making their Retreat, AM. D[o] W[r] Fleet & Prizes in Comp[y] *Colossus* in Tow.

On Wednesday and Thursday *Agamemnon*'s First Lieutenant 'Served a Gill of Spirits p[r] Man p[r] Captains orders'. The log also records that the fore yard was fished and that the ship was making three feet of water in the hold an hour and on Friday 25 October the rope towing *Colossus* parted but was recovered. Hampered by great storms it took six days for *Agamemnon* to sail the 55 mile voyage towing *Colossus* towards Gibraltar. Arriving there Monday 28 October, *Agamemnon* 'Came to with the Best Bower in Gibraltar Bay in 20 fms Cast off the *Colossus* Moored East & West a cable each way'.[91] The wounded were sent on shore to the hospital and having made repairs the ship returned to Collingwood's squadron blockading Cadiz.

In December Collingwood sent *Agamemnon* with seven other ships to the West Indies in pursuit of Vice-Admiral Leissègues' fleet carrying 1,000 troops and to reinforce the garrison on Santo Domingo. In command of this detached squadron was Vice-Admiral Sir John Duckworth flying his flag in *Superb* (74).

1806: *Agamemnon*, with the other ships, reached Carlisle Bay, Barbados, on 2 January and spent the next twelve days refitting. Duckworth's ships sailed on 14 January and arrived at Basse Terre Roads, St Kitts five days later. Receiving news that Vice-Admiral Leissègues' fleet had been sighted off Santo Domingo disembarking troops, Duckworth immediately put to sea, reaching the east end of Santo Domingo on the 5 February. Joined by other ships, Duckworth's squadron now contained eleven ships as follows:[92]

Guns.	80	74	64	40	36	14
No.	1	6	1	1	1	1

Realising he had been discovered, Leissègues' squadron of eight ships put to sea on 6 February and sailed westwards to Punta Palenque. Seeing Duckworth's ships bearing down he formed his squadron into line of battle in two columns of four. Duckworth divided his eight line of battle ships into two columns and steered to cross the French line, *Superb* (74) leading the weather line, *Canopus* (80) to leeward, the attack beginning around 8 a.m. While the lead ships were running before the wind at 8 knots, *Agamemnon* dropped astern and failed to get into action until around 11 a.m. When *Agamemnon* reached the affray, she assisted Duckworth's *Superb* in engaging Leissègues' flagship *Impérial* (120), their combined broadsides hammering the flagship and bringing down her main and mizzen masts. Out of control, *Impérial* ran on shore at 11.40 a.m., her foremast collapsing, her hull stove in by the rocks. *Superb* only just avoided a similar fate. The French *Diomède* (84) also ran onshore, all her masts going by the board as she slammed into the rocks but she continued to fire guns until her com-

Britannia, 100 guns, with the 74s *Bedford* and *Egmont*, and the cutter *Resolution*, in the Gulf of Genoa, March 1795. *(Courtesy of Derek Gardner, RSMA)*

Royal Sovereign, flagship of Vice-Admiral Hon. William Cornwallis, furling sails at Spithead, May 1795. *(Courtesy of Derek Gardner, RSMA)*

'Trafalgar Dawn'; "... at 6 observed the Enemy bearing E b S distant 10 or 12 Miles bow up to the Eastd. out all reefs Topsails..." (Master's log, HMS *Victory*, 21 October 1805).
(Oil on canvas, by Geoff Hunt, RSMA)

'The Power and the Glory.' Nelson's *Victory* and the British fleet, 2.30 p.m. approx., 21 October 1805 (Nautical Day). *(Taken from an original oil painting by Robin Brooks. © Published by Black Dog studios as signed limited edition prints; www.blackdog-studios.com)*

'*Victory* breaks the enemy line.' The defining moment at Trafalgar, where Nelson's plan is finally realised. *(Oil on panel, by Geoff Hunt, RSMA)*

Neptune, 98 guns, in Plymouth Sound. This ship was to take on both *Bucentaure* and *Santísima Trinidad* at Trafalgar. The captured Villeneuve came aboard 3 days later. *(Courtesy of Derek Gardner, RSMA)*

'*Téméraire*'s first day under sail, June 1799.'
(Oil on panel, by Geoff Hunt, RSMA)

The remaining head from the original figurehead of the *Bellerophon* that fought at Trafalgar. *(Courtesy of the Royal Naval Museum)*

Opposite: Bellerophon opens fire at Trafalgar. *(Courtesy of Derek Gardner, RSMA)*

Bellerophon at Plymouth, August 1793. *(Courtesy of Derek Gardner, RSMA)*

'The Defining Moment, Trafalgar 1805.' *(Taken from an original oil painting by Robin Brooks. © Published by Black Dog studios as signed limited edition prints; www.blackdog-studios.com)*

The upper gun-deck, looking forward, of HMS Victory. *(Author's own photograph)*

The replica iron 'Brodie' firehearth in the galley of HMS *Victory*. These stoves varied in size and capacity for each class of warship. (*Author's own photograph*)

The hold, with iron and shingle ballast, of HMS *Victory* but common to all sailing men-of-war. (*Author's own photograph*)

The 74 gun ship *Thunderer*. On the day of the battle *Thunderer* lay 13th in line of Collingwood's leeward division and being near the rear did not get into action until relatively late. (Courtesy of Derek Gardner, RSMA)

'Eyewitness at Trafalgar: HM schooner *Pickle*.' (Oil on canvas, by Geoff Hunt, RSMA)

'I have urgent dispatches.' *Pickle* on the 1,000-mile voyage home, conveying the news of the victory at Trafalgar and Nelson's death. During the great gales which followed the battle, *Pickle* sighted another ship, HMS *Nautilus*. Pickle commenced signalling her dramatic news by flying the 1805 code signal flags 2214: "I have urgent dispatches". (© Gordon Frickers 2005. This painting was the result of close co-operation between the author and artist, and is available as a limited edition print at www.frickers.co.uk)

Quarter view of the model of the armed schooner *Pickle*. (Courtesy of the Royal Naval Museum)

Starboard broadside view of the *Pickle* model, defining her lines and rig. *(Courtesy of the Royal Naval Museum)*

Bucentaure, Villeneuve's 80 gun flagship, seen here leaving Toulon. *(Oil on panel, by Geoff Hunt, RSMA)*

Above: The port side of the model of the *Santa Ana* (112). Captured at Trafalgar, she was recaptured two days later and served the Spanish navy until broken up in 1816. (Courtesy of the Museo Naval de Madrid and Lunwerg Editores)

Right: The stern of the model of the *Santa Ana* (112) seen from the starboard quarter. Note the first and second batteries, with shutters on the portholes and the hull painted in black and yellow or red ochre strips, which became regulation for all Spanish navy ships in 1810. (Courtesy of the Museo Naval de Madrid and Lunwerg Editores)

Overleaf: Lengthwise view of the model of the 74 gun 3rd rate *San Ildefonso*. Note the way the starboard anchor is lashed to the side, the latrines and the *chinchorro* net on the bowsprit. This ship was captured by the Royal Navy at Trafalgar and taken into British service as HMS *San Ildefonso*. (Courtesy of the Museo Naval de Madrid and Lunwerg Editores)

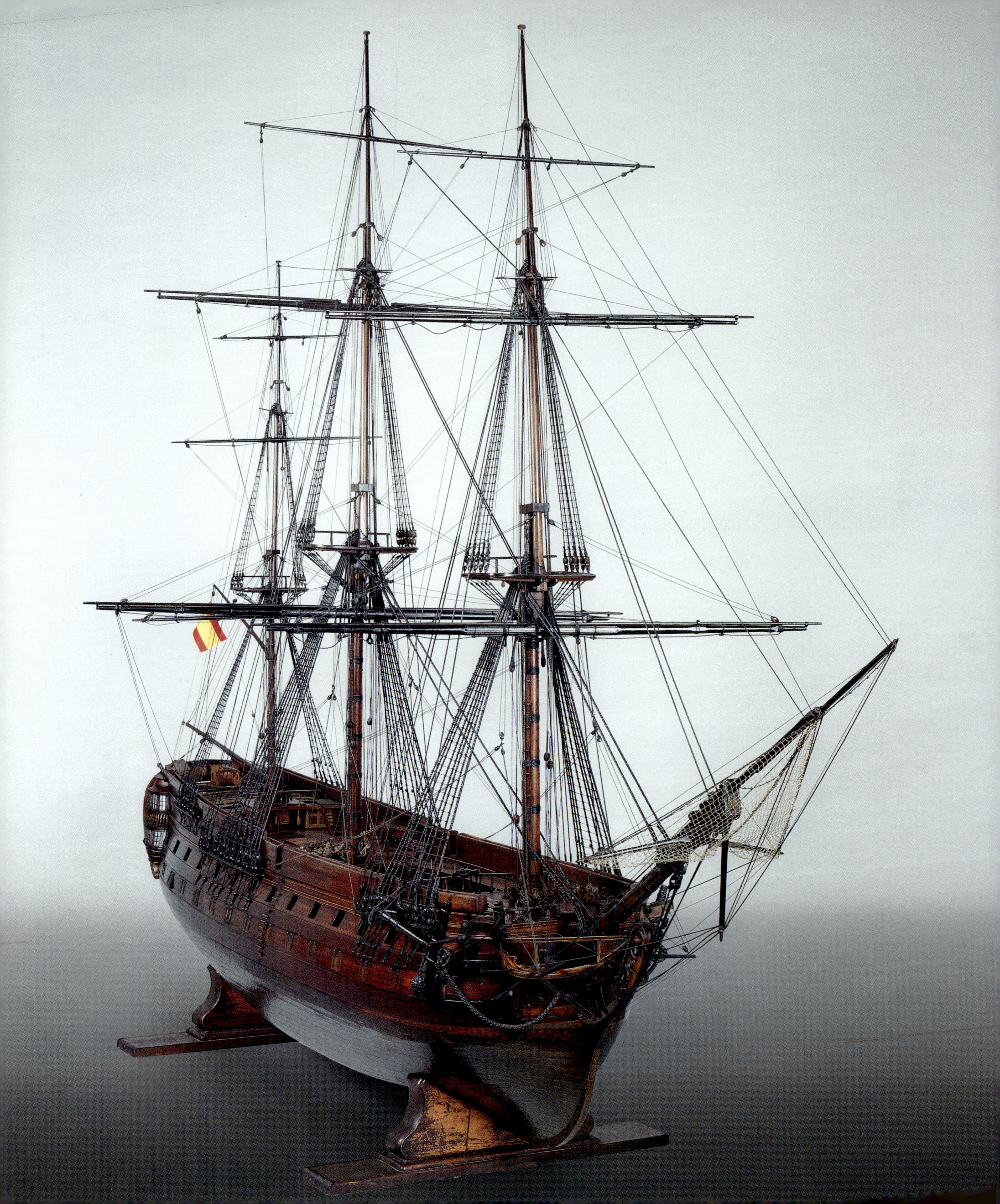

mander raised his hat in token of surrender. Acknowledging his gesture Berry gave the order to cease firing into the stricken ship. Three French ships were captured, the two grounded ships were later burnt and the three frigates escaped. British casualties were 74 killed and 264 wounded; *Agamemnon* lost one seaman, James Cavanough, and had three officers, two marines and sixteen seamen wounded. French casualties were 1,510 killed or wounded. Much damaged, *Agamemnon* went into English Harbour, Antigua, to repair.[93]

On Tuesday 18 March *Agamemnon* captured 'La Dame Ernouf French Privateer Schooner mounting 19 guns and 81 men from Guadeloupe'. On 24 March she captured a vessel which 'Struck after our firing 39 shott at her she proved to be *La Lutine National* Brig of 16 guns from Lorient bound to Martinico'.[94] At the end of June Joseph Spear briefly superseded command of the ship until succeeded by Captain Jonas Rose on 9 July.[95]

In early October *Agamemnon* left the Leeward Islands and escorted a convoy to England. Entering Chatham dockyard on 3 December to refit, the ship was docked 26 December to have her old copper removed and replaced.[96]

1807: Undocked 24 January *Agamemnon* the ship joined the North Sea fleet at the Nore on 8 March. By June fears that the Danish fleet would fall into French hands prompted the British government to present an ultimatum to Denmark on 19 July stating that if they did not hand over their fleet to Britain, it would be taken by force. To enforce this order Admiral James Gambier assembled a large fleet to sail for Copenhagen. Flying his flag in the *Prince of Wales* (98) Gambier sailed from Yarmouth Roads on 26 July with *Agamemnon* in company. By the time Gambier reached Copenhagen his fleet had expanded to 27 line of battle ships, 40 frigates, sloops gunboats and bomb vessels accompanied by 377 transports conveying 27,000 troops. Shortly after her arrival *Agamemnon* grounded by the stern but after moving guns forward and setting out two anchors astern, managed to haul herself off on the next rising tide. *Agamemnon* had suffered the same misfortune at Copenhagen six years earlier. Gambier then deployed his ships accordingly to prevent Danish ships leaving, *Agamemnon* being sent south to Kjörge Bay. Here she landed four 18 and three 24 pounder guns, and 200 rounds of shot, for shore batteries being set up overlooking the city. The siege commenced at 7.30 p.m. on 2 September, the shore batteries opening fire, which, according to *Agamemnon*'s log, started 'a great fire in Copenhagen'. The bombardment continued over the next few days causing a destructive conflagration. On 5 September *Agamemnon*'s log states: 'AM at 6 Copenhagen on fire whilst our Batteries Bombarding the Town…Copenhagen High Steeple burned down…PM the fire in Copenhagen apparently increasing'.[97] When General Peyman, the governor of the city, asked to discuss terms, firing provisionally ceased. The articles of surrender were finally declared and signed on 7 September.[98]

In November *Agamemnon* returned to Spithead and after re-provisioning and watering sailed on 6 December in company with *Foudroyant* (80) *Plantagenet* (74) and schooner *Elizabeth* (12) to join the squadron blockading Lisbon. While cruising on this station *Agamemnon* captured three Portuguese vessels, one named *Europa*.[99]

1808: On 16 February Captain Rose received new orders to sail with Rear-Admiral Sir Sidney Smith's flagship *Foudroyant*, and the 12 gun brigs *Confounder* and *Pitt* for Brazil. Reaching Río de Janeiro on 14 May, the squadron anchored in the Bay of Guanabara off Ponta de Santa Cruz in sight of the Sugar Loaf. Already in the harbour were *Mutine* (16) and the schooner *Mistletoe* (8).[100] Shortly after these ships were joined by another incoming squadron comprising *London* (90), *Marlborough* (74), *Bedford* (74), Monarch (74) and *Surveillante* frigate (38).

At Río de Janeiro it was discovered that *Agamemnon* had considerable defects: planking seams had opened, and many of the bolts fastening her hull together were worn or broken. *Agamemnon* and *Monarch* were ordered to sail for Buenos Aires, escorting the merchant vessel *Maria* on a diplomatic mission to expose a political plot against the exiled Portuguese King Dom João. Reaching the entrance of the Río de la Plata on the 11 October, *Maria* parted company and sailed to Montevideo while *Agamemnon* and *Monarch* temporarily anchored in Maldonado Bay. Avoiding Garrita Island, *Monarch* ran aground but, after lightening ship, came off the shoal unscathed. Returning to Maldonado Bay in late November, lightning struck *Agamemnon*'s mizzen topgallant mast bringing it down with the shrouds and other rigging during the storm. Disaster struck again on 11 December when *Agamemnon*'s cutter was upset with the loss of five men when watering ship. The two ships left Maldonado Bay on 28 December.

1809: Reaching Río de Janeiro on 16 January, climate and conditions had drastically affected the health of *Agamemnon*'s crew, so many were landed and sent to hospital, eleven of whom were declared unfit for further service.[101] When George Robbins, *Agamemnon*'s carpenter, surveyed the ship he discovered that the 28 year old, battle-worn veteran had many defects. Captain Rose wrote to Admiral Sir William Sidney Smith:

Defects of his Majesty's ship *Agamemnon* Jonas Rose Captain. Rio de Janeiro. March 28th, 1809.

1st. Some of the Standard Knees and hooks move considerably which requires an additional fastening.
2nd. The riders in general work much, some of them (from the labouring of the Ship) worked themselves ? of an inch in the Ceiling.
3rd. The Ship shews her weakness in general, and particularly in the Wings when blowing fresh.
4th. Several of the old Bolts are apparently broke and the beams work much in the Clamps, and the Scarfs of some of them work much, which adds to the general weakness of the Ship.
5th. Each Deck swags much and worn very thin; the Nail Heads (when labouring in the Sea) leak much, occasioned from the decay between wood and wood.
6th. The Pawl Rim of the Capstan is broke and wants replacing.
7th. The Water Cocks and Pipes want replacing.
8th. The second Pintle from the Head of the stern Post works much up Hill upon the Brace and makes the Rudder work heavy
9th. Taylors and Nobles hand Pumps are much shook which occasions them to blow and deliver but little water.
10th. The Copper Pumps are worn very thin at the lower parts and want repairs.
11th. The decks of the fore and After Cock Pits are worn very thin and want replacing.
12th. The facing piece of the Bitts is much worn.
13th. The after Hoods on the Stern frame of the Tuck are much decayed, and one Chain Plate in the fore Channels want replacing.
14th. Several of the Lower deck Ports are very much decayed and leak considerably when blowing fresh at Sea.
15th. Carried away and wants replacing the Cross Jack Yard.

Signed.
Jonas Rose, Captain
Geo. Robbins, Carpenter [102]

With few repair facilities in Río de Janeiro, little could be done to rectify the condition of her hull, moreover, her anchor cables had been much gnawed by rats. Both issues were to be raised as evidence regarding the fate of the ship.

On the 18 May Rear-Admiral Michael De Courcy arrived in *Diana* frigate (38) to relieve Sir William, bringing with him news that the French squadron at Lorient had evaded the British blockade and with Spain now allied to Britain, were intending to attack the Spanish colonies in the Río de la Plata. Hoisting his flag in *Foudroyant* De Courcey put to sea on 26 May

PROGRESS BOOK - AGAMEMNON 3rd RATE OF 64 GUNS: Source: ADM 180/7 folio 155 & ADM 180/10 folio 166

At what Port	Arrived	Docked	Coppered	When Launched or Undocked	Sailed	Built or Nature of Repair	Hull, Masts & Yards	Rigging & Stores	Total
Buckler's Hard Henry Adams	Began	May 1777		10 Apr 1781		Built	24,415. 7. 0		
							45. 2. 6 Extra Works		
							24,460. 9. 6		
Portsmouth	15 April 1781	23 April 1781	Coppered May 1781	7 May 1781	9 July 1781	Fitted	4,119. 12. 1	9,724. 13. 9	38,303. 15. 4
Chatham	3 June 1783	29 Oct 1783	Copper taken of Nov 1783 Re Copper'd Jun 1784	4 June 1784		Small Repair			
Do.		1 Nov 1787		10 Nov 1787		Partly Fitted	10,593. 0 9	2,000. 0 0	12,593. 0. 9
Do.	Taken in Hand Oct 1790 &	Completed Nov 1790				Fitted for Sea	504. 9. 7		504. 9. 7
Do.		9 Nov 1790	Copper taken of Dec 1790 Re Copper'd Aug 1791	15 Aug 1791		Between Small & Middling Repair			
Do.	Taken in Hand Jan 1793 &	Completed March 1793			23 Mar 1793	Fitted	11,764	346	12,110
Do	10 Sep 1796	3 Oct 1796	Copper taken of and Re Copper'd Oct 1796	31 Oct 1796		Refitted	1,505	3,377	4,882
Do.		29 Nov 1796	Copper repaired	14 Dec 1796	9 Feb 1797	To stop a Leak & Refit	5,207	4,815	10,623
Sheerness	19 Feb 1799				8 Mar 1799		22	181	203
Chatham	8 March 1799	23 Mar 1799	Copper repaired	20 April 1799	18 May 1799	Refitted	603	2,136	4,739
Plymouth	30 Nov 1800	6 April 1800	do.	6 May 1800	20 June 1800	made good defects			
Sheeerness	12 April 1802				12 April 1802				
Chatham	13 April 1802								
Chatham	13 April 1802	12 Apr 1802	Copper taken off April & Recopp'd July 1804	21 July 1804	20 Sep 1804	Fitted	10,083	7,612	17,695
Portsmouth	6 Sep 1805	13 Sep 1805	Copper taken off and Recopp'd Sep 1805	17 Sep 1805	24 Sep 1805	Refit	41,048	10,242	51,290
Chatham	3 Dec1806	26 Dec 1806	Copper taken off and Recopp'd	24 Jan 1807	8 Mar 1807	Refitted	39,347	7,948	39,407

Lost in 1809

BREAKDOWN OF ACTUAL EXPENDITURE (IN £) BETWEEN DATES 1804 AND LOSS

	Charge of the								Grand Total
	Hull			Masts & Yards			Rigging & Stores		
Materials	Workmen	Total	Materials	Workmen	Total	Materials	Workmen	Total	
5,935	2,725	8,660	1,214	209	1,423	7,575	37	7,612	17,695
27,422	19,259	37,701	3,041	306	3,347	10,039	203	10,242	51,290
25,238	6,201	31,448	-	11	11	7,899	49	7,948	30,407

with his squadron comprising *Bedford* (74), *Agamemnon*, *Brilliant* (28), *Mutine* (16), *Elizabeth* (12), and *Mistletoe* (8). At noon the wind died and in the wallowing swell *Agamemnon* collided with *Mutine*, damaging her own bowsprit in the accident.[103]

During the voyage the *Agamemnon* endured a furious storm and appalling weather which battered her already weakened hull; slackened shrouds and stays had to be tightened, pumps were manned continuously and, more alarmingly, the ship had to be frapped with cables to hold the hull together. De Courcy's squadron reached the entrance of Maldonado Bay on the 15 June but with daylight fading and knowing the hazards, anchoring within was deferred until the next morning.[104]

FATE

Next morning, 16 June, Captain Rose ordered Master Thomas Webb to take the cutter and mark the shoal where *Monarch* had grounded previously; in the meantime *Agamemnon* weighed and proceeded into Maldonado Bay for her third time. Following *Bedford*, *Agamemnon* worked her way between Gorreti Island and the shore; Rose was unfortunately relying on a Spanish chart. With most sails furled *Agamemnon* was carrying little way, and encountering shoaling water, quickly let go her bower anchor to check the ship. Momentarily the anchor held but lost its grasp, the ship swung to starboard and grounded. Signalling distress, Rose immediately ordered the boats to be lowered, the launch and pinnace to carry out the stream and kedge anchors respectively, however attempts to haul her off using their anchor cables soon failed. By this time *Agamemnon* was making water and pumps were manned to stem the ingress of water. The schooner *Mistletoe* came to assist by carrying out the small bower but this also failed. Captain Fabian of *Mutine* soon discovered that *Agamemnon* had run onto a bank 3? fathoms beneath the surface and that having come down on her main anchor the fluke had broken through her hull. Despite continual pumping and removing stores to lighten ship, *Agamemnon* now listed heavily starboard. Rose took bearings to ascertain his true position which later confirmed that she had grounded on an unmarked shoal. Water continued to flood the hull and by sunset had risen to the level of the lower gun deck. Rose recorded in the log:

Point of Gaula SWbyW½W, Guard Point SSE½E, Belone Point W½N; PM Fresh Breezes & cloudy all the Pumps working Empl'd unriving the running rigging & unShipping the Topmasts loading the boats with various Stores. At 3 left off Pumping water gaining fast & the Ship settling down at 5 got the Fore & main yard over for Shores Struck Topmasts at 8 Moderate & Hazy water above the Lower deck Ports on the Starb'd Side & the Orlop Deck within, at Midnight Modte & hazy Weath. to the level had risen to about 9 feet in the hold.[105]

Next morning, 17 June, masters and carpenters from the other ships came aboard to assess what measures could be taken to save the ship. Realising that she was beyond redemption, the rest of her stores and the entire crew were taken off by boats sent from the assisting vessels. Three condition reports were submitted directly to De Courcy from the captains, masters and carpenters of the attending ships respectively (see appendices).

By evening, after all stores had been removed, *Agamemnon*'s upper decks were awash. That night Captain Rose completed his log with the following entry: 'at 6 I slept with the rest of the officers'. Next day after further salvage of anchors, etc. Rose and the remaining people

The 64 gun ship POLYPHEMUS

As the first ship to bear the name *Polyphemus* in the Royal Navy, her name derives from two sources within classical Greek mythology, one a Cyclopic son of primary sea god Poseidon, the second Polyphemus being one of the 49 Argonauts who sailed with the Greek hero Jason in the ship *Argo* searching for the Golden Fleece.[107]

Ordered 1 December 1773, *Polyphemus* was a 3rd rate 64 gun ship built to the lines of the *Intrepid/Magnanime* class designed by John Williams in 1765. Laid down at Sheerness in January 1776 and built under the Master Shipwright George White, *Polyphemus* was launched 7 April 1782. That she took six years to build is probably due to other priorities during the American War of Independence. Building costs amounted to £37,218 5s 1d, of which £29,238 2s 11d was expended on her hull, masts and yards and £7,980 2s 2d for rigging and stores.[108]

Timber for her construction would have come from the nearby forests in Kent, timber being floated down the River Medway to Maidstone where the river became navigable for transporting timber by barge to the Medway dockyards. Carrying ordnance comprising twenty-six 24 pounders on the lower gun deck, twenty-six 18 pounders on the upper gun deck, ten 9 pounders on the quarter deck, and two 9 pounders on the forecastle, *Polyphemus* could fire a single broadside weight of 600 pounds.

CAPTAINS OF POLYPHEMUS (MSS 248/4 and 248/6)

Name	Time of Entry	Time of Discharge	On What Occasion
Hon William C Finch	2 May 1782	10 November 1782	Superseded
Thomas Potherby	11 November 1782	25 December 1782	Superseded Acting
John Ford	26 December 1782	27 June 1783	Paid Off at Chatham
George Lumsdaine	13 April 1794	4 August 1800	Superseded
John Lawford	5 August 1800	5 May 1802	Paid Off at Chatham
John Lawford	1 January 1804	15 June 1806	To the *Audacious*
Robert Redmill	16 June 1806	16 September 1806	Superseded
Joseph Masefield	17 September 1806	3 October 1806	Superseded
John Broughton	4 October 1806	22 October 1806	Superseded
Peter Heywood	23 October 1806	17 May 1808	Superseded
William Price Cumby	18 May 1808	25 March 1811	To the *Hyperion*
Thomas Greaves	26 March 1811	16 October 1811	Superseded
Nicholas Patishall	17 October 1811	24 November 1811	Superseded
William Manners	25 November 1811	13 December 1811	To the *Thalia*
E C Askew	14th & 29th December 1811		Naval Hospital
J G Vashon	30 December 1811		To the *Thalia*
John Boss	5th & 26th January 1812		Superseded
Peter Douglas	27 January 1812	10 November 1812	Paid Off at Chatham

SERVICE HISTORY

1782: Completed too late for the war of American War of Independence, *Polyphemus* was first commissioned under Captain the Hon. William Finch on 2 May. Finch was superseded 11 November by Captain Thomas Potherby who, only commanding in an acting capacity, was succeeded by Captain John Ford on 26 December.[109]

1783: Returning to Chatham 23 June, *Polyphemus* was paid off four days later. At the end of July she was moved downriver to Sheerness, remaining there until 30 December when she was taken back to Chatham and laid up at moorings.

1784: Docked on 7 June, *Polyphemus* was given a small repair costing in total £6,371 10s 4d.

1795. Placed under the command of Captain George Lumsdaine, *Polyphemus* was deployed on the Ireland station operating out of Queenstown. On October 22 she fell in with and captured the Dutch warship *Overijssel* (64), later added into naval service.[110]

1796: Between the 15 and 17 December a French fleet commanded by Vice-Admiral de Galles sailed from Brest to land forces in Ireland, but from its very inception this expedition had been beset with disaster. Many French vessels – warship or transport – were successfully captured by the patrolling British ships. *Polyphemus* was no exception, on 31 December she fell in with *Justine*, a French transports and in the chase caused her to run ashore and founder.[111]

1797: Still operating from Queenstown, on 5 January *Polyphemus* captured the French frigate *Tortue* (40) which had also formed part of de Galles' fleet abandoned fleet.[112]

1800: Having returned to home waters, *Polyphemus* sailed from Yarmouth on 9 August with a convoy for Denmark escorted by a squadron commanded by Vice-Admiral Dickson flying his flag in *Monarch* (74). Encountering little wind, the faster vessels were forced to take the slower in tow so it took six

SPECIFICATIONS: POLYPHEMUS

Rate	3rd	Length on the range of the gun deck	159 ft 6 ins	Ordnance - middle gun deck	26 x 18 pounders
Guns	64	Length of keel for tonnage	131 ft	Ordnance - quarter deck	10 x 9 pounders
Class	Intrepid/Magnanime 1765	Extreme breadth	44 ft 4 ins	Ordnance - forecastle	2 x 9 pounders
Designer	John Williams	Depth in hold	19 ft	Single broadside weight	600 pounds
Builder	George White	Tons burthen	1369 50/94	Fate	1813 Hulked at Chatham as a powder magazine
Dockyard	Sheerness	Draught afore	17 ft 9 ins		1826 Fitted as accommodation for Lieutenants of the Ordinary
Date ordered	1 December 1773	Draught abaft	20 ft 10 ins		
Date keel laid	January 1776	Complement	500		1827 Broken up
Date launched	7 April 1782	Ordnance - lower gun deck	26 x 24 pounders		

Source: Lyon, *Sailing Navy List*, p. 74.

days to reach the Skaw. On 16 August the entire squadron advanced to the entrance of the Sound where they were confronted by four Danish 74-gun ships anchored in line between Cronberg Castle and the Swedish shore. Gales forced the British ships to shelter in Elsinore Roads, when Dickson transferred into *Romney* ((50) and sailed to Sophienburg to speak with Lord Whitworth. Because of rising hostilities between Britain and Denmark, he was already negotiating with Danish ministers. Once matters were resolved the squadron, including *Polyphemus*, returned to Yarmouth in September.

1801: In March Captain John Lawford took command of the ship and on 12 March *Polyphemus* sailed from Yarmouth with Admiral Sir Hyde Parker's fleet to attack and bombard Copenhagen. Entering the Sound on 30 March, the British fleet began their assault on the city on 2 April, Vice-Admiral Nelson leading the main attack. Nelson's ships, including *Polyphemus*, weighed at 9 a.m. and proceeded round the southern end of the Middleground. When *Agamemnon* ran aground *Polyphemus* was ordered to take her place in line. Action commenced at 10 a.m., during which *Polyphemus* played a significant rôle engaging the block-ship *Provesteen*. During the battle *Polyphemus* suffered 31 casualties; those killed included Mr James Bell, Midshipman, four seamen and one marine. Wounded were Mr Edward Burr, Boatswain, twenty seamen and four marines. As part of Admiral Graves' division of the North Sea fleet, *Polyphemus* returned to Yarmouth from the Baltic on 13 July.[113]

Shortly after the ship was deployed with Admiral Dickson's squadron blockading the Dutch fleet in the Texel. Dickson, flying his flag in the *Veteran* (64) also had with him *Ruby* (64), brig-sloops *Espiègle* (14) and *Speedwell* (14), gun vessels *Teazer* (14), *Bruiser* (12), *Cracker* (12), *Hasty* (12) and *Pincher* (12), bomb vessels *Explosion* (12), *Sulphur* (8) and *Vesuvius* (8) and two fireships *Otter* (14) and *Alecto* (12).

1802: On 26 April *Polyphemus* returned to Sheerness and sailed that same day for Chatham. After the brief journey up the River Medway, she arrived off the dockyard next day. As the war had finished the next few weeks were spent de-storing ship and discharging powder to Upnor Castle. The ship was then re-rigged and her masts taken out. With this completed Captain Lawford paid off the ship on 5 May. No longer required for service, *Polyphemus* was laid up in ordinary for the next year.

1804: With war restarting Captain Lawford was recalled to place *Polyphemus* back in commission.[114] On 28 March the ship was taken into dock to have her old copper removed and replaced. Other refitting work was also undertaken so it was not until 6 July that *Polyphemus* was re-launched. Fitted and stored for sea service, the ship sailed from Chatham on 2 September. Unfortunately the cost of this work was not entered in the Progress Book.[115]

1805: Command of *Polyphemus* was now under Captain Robert Redmill, who was ordered in July to join the British squadron deployed off Cadiz.

TRAFALGAR

On the morning of the battle *Polyphemus* was stationed ninth from the head of Collingwood's leeward division, getting into the battle at about 2.30 p.m. *Belleisle* as we have seen, was already under considerable fire from the French *Neptune* (84), so Redmill ordered his First Lieutenant George Mowbray to place *Polyphemus* off the starboard bow of the Frenchman to draw off some of the fire directed at *Belleisle*. It was now about 3.15 p.m. her engagement with the much larger *Neptune* was brief, for having seen the British Union flag waved from her cathead, *Polyphemus* ceased firing and moved on to engage the French *Achille* (74). The part played by *Polyphemus* during the battle was modest, the ship only suffering two killed and four wounded.[116] As predicted, a great storm followed the battle, battering the beleaguered ships. When winds abated on 23 October, at 11 a.m. *Polyphemus* was hailed by *Victory* to take her in tow. The towing cable, run out through *Victory*'s larboard hawse, was passed through *Polyphemus*' wardroom windows and run forward to the head of the main capstan. Why the cable was not passed through the *Polyphemus*'s stern ports and secured around either the mizzen mast, the lower part of the main capstan or the riding bitts on the lower gun deck remains a mystery, but Redmill must have had good reason to choose the alternative. Slowly the two ships proceeded towards Gibraltar, however when the violent winds returned on Friday 25 October, the tow line parted. As dawn broke the next day Hardy in *Victory* saw the *Royal Sovereign* (100) flying a distress signal, for her consort *Africa* had now lost all her masts. Ignoring his own predicament Hardy signalled *Polyphemus* to take *Royal Sovereign* in tow, the two ships eventually anchoring in Rosia Bay, Gibraltar, late on the 28 October.[117] For the rest of the year *Polyphemus* remained stationed off Gibraltar undertaking escort duties to incoming and homebound convoys.[118]

1806: On 15 June command of *Polyphemus* was superseded by Captain Robert Redmill, Lawford, her previous commander transferring into *Audacious* (74). *Polyphemus* then joined Earl St Vincent's squadron deployed off Ushant. When news was received that two French corvettes *Cæsar* and *Teazer* with a convoy were lying off the entrance to the Garonne, plans were set in motion to capture them. *Teazer* was in fact a captured British brig. On 14 July boats from *Polyphemus* and other ships in the squadron were sent under tow by the 5th rate *Iris* to Captain Sir Samuel Hood in *Indefatigable* (64), lying off Rochefort, to conduct the attack. The expedition set out on 15 July but when weather conditions deteriorated with strong winds, the boats only managed to capture the 18-gun brig *Cæsar* leaving the other man-of-war and convoy to escape up river. In the attack many of the boats were severely damaged by shot fired from the shore batteries and the two corvettes, some of which were swamped and were cut adrift. Casualties from *Polyphemus* comprised William Anderson, Quarter Master's Mate, and William Flemming, coxswain. After this Captain Joseph Masefield briefly in command from 17 September but he only remained in the ship until 3 October. His successor, Captain John Broughton, also had a short command as he was superseded by Captain Peter Heywood. As a midshipman earlier in his career, Heywood had been tried for his part in the mutiny on board His Majesty's Armed Transport *Bounty* commanded by Lieutenant William Bligh in 1789. Pardoned of the crime, Heywood continued his career, proving a first class sea officer.

1807: Under Heywood the ship served as the flagship of Rear-Admiral Murray on the South American station.

1808: On 18 May Heywood was superseded by Captain William Price Cumby and in July *Polyphemus* sailed for Jamaica escorting a large fleet of merchantmen to undertake her new rôle as flagship of Vice-Admiral Rowley. Since the admiral resided mainly on shore, keeping his flag hoisted on the receiving ship *Shark* (14), *Polyphemus* was released for standard patrol work against the French. Cruising off Santo Domingo on the morning of 14 November, Cumby sighted an armed schooner trying to enter the harbour. The boats, placed under the command of Lieutenant Joseph Daly, were immediately lowered to give chase. One hour later, amid a barrage of grape shot and musket fire, Daly and his men boarded and captured the schooner which proved to be the French vessel *Colibri* commanded by a *lieutenant de vaisseau* with 63 men. In the attack one marine, Samuel Compton, was killed.[119]

1809: Appointed to Rear-Admiral the Hon. Sir Alexander Cochrane's squadron in March, *Polyphemus*, in company with the flagship *Neptune* (98), *Captain* (74), *Pompée* (74) and *York* (74), sailed for the Saintes to blockade the French ships commanded by Commodore Amable-Gilles Truode lying there.[120] Although an action between the *Pompée* and *D'Haupuolt* ensued, the *Polyphemus* was not engaged. In June Cumby was appointed to command a squadron which, included *Polyphemus*, *Aurora* (28), armed schooner

PROGRESS BOOK – POLYPHEMUS 3rd RATE OF 64 GUNS: Source: ADM 180/7 Entry 142 & ADM 180/10 Entry 194

At what Port	Arrived	Docked	Coppered	Launched or Undocked	Sailed	Built or Nature of Repair	Cost of Hull, Materials £ s d	Cost of Rigging & Stores Materials £ s d	Grand Total
Sheerness	Began	January 1776		27 April 1782		Built			
Sheerness		29 April 1782	Coppered May 1782	13 May 1782	24 July 1782	Fitted	29,238. 2s. 11d.	7,980. 2s. 2d.	37,218. 5s. 1d
Chatham	23 June 1783			20 July 1783	To Sheerness				
Sheerness	30 July 1783			30 Dec 1783	To Chatham		161. 3s. 10d.	5. 0s. 6d.	166. 4s. 4d.
Chatham	30 Dec 1783	7 June 1784	Copper taken off June; Re-coppered Sep 1784	15 Sep 1784		Small Repair	4,198. 16s. 1d.	2,172. 14s. 3d	6,371. 10s. 4d
Chatham		19 Dec 1793	Copper taken off Jan & Re-coppered Jan 1794	3 Feb 1794	9 June 1794	Large Repair & Fitted	4,779	3,992	8,771
Plymouth	7 May 1796	19 May 1796	Copper Repaired	7 June 1796	7 July 1796	Refitted	1,759	3,846	5,605
Plymouth	17 June 1797	6 July 1797		8 July 1797	13 Aug 1797	Made Good Defects	926	2,061	2,987
Chatham	30 Oct 1799	29 Oct 1799	Copper taken off Nov 1799, Re-coppered Feb 1800	25 Feb 1800	29 March 1800	Made Good Defects	7,575	5,178	12,753
Sheerness	26 April 1802				26 April 1802				
Chatham	27 April 1802	8 Mar 1804	Copper taken off March, Re-coppered July 1804	6 July 1804	3 Sep 1804	Fitted			
Portsmouth	23 Jan 1808	4 Feb 1808	Copper taken off & Re-coppered Feb 1808	216 Feb 1808	17 March 1808	Refitted			
Chatham		21 Oct 1812	Taken in Hand 5 March 1813 & Completed 25 Sep 1813			Fitted for a Powder Magazine			
			Taken in Hand Feb 1826 & Completed April 1826			Fitted for the Lieut. of the Ordinary			
		9 Aug 1827	*Completed taking to Pieces 15th Sepr. 1827*						

Fleur-de-Mer (8), brig-sloops *Moselle* (18), *Thrush* (18), *Tweed* (18), *Griffon* (16), *Lark* (16), *Sparrow* (16) and the cutter *Pike* (10). Having embarked troops under Major General Carmichael, *Polyphemus* with her squadron sailed from Port Royal on 7 June to assist Spanish forces besieging the French in the town of Santo Domingo. To assist the land forces *Polyphemus* anchored at Caleta in 1 July and disembarked eight of her lower deck guns into *Sparrow*, which landed guns at Palenqui to form a battery west of the town. Needing to reinforce troops making their assault from the east, Captain Burt of *Sparrow* carried his sloop into Andre Bay and recovered two of *Polyphemus*' guns and transported them to the east battery. Transferring these guns by sea was far easier than taking them overland across 30 miles of impassable country. Defeated by the concerted efforts of British and Spanish forces, the French garrison surrendered on 6 July.

1811: In March Captain Thomas Graves took command of *Polyphemus*, Cumby transferring into *Hyperion* (32).

1812: Now under the command of Captain Cornelius Quinton, *Polyphemus* continued working out of Jamaica escorting convoys entering or leaving the island.[121] In November command of *Polyphemus* was given over to Captain Douglas who, recalled home, sailed for England. Arriving at Chatham, Douglas paid off *Polyphemus* as ordered.

FATE

In 1813 *Polyphemus* was hulked as a powder magazine at Chatham, then 1826 she was fitted out to provide accommodation for the Lieutenants of the Ordinary, officers who managed the ships laid up in reserve and the groups of assistant manpower formally referred to as the 'men of the ordinary'. Her rôle as an accommodation ship was short lived as she went to the breakers on 15 September 1827.[122]

NOTES TO PART 1: CHAPTER 4

1. Lyon, p. 189.
2. Lyon, p. 73.
3. Barnard, *Building Britain's Wooden Walls: The Barnard Dynasty c1687–1851*, pp. 51, 55.
4. TNA: PRO, ADM 180/7 Entry 137.
5. TNA: PRO, ADM 180/7 Entry 137; RNM MS 248/4.
6. *Ibid & Ibid*.
7. Clowes, 3, pp. 562–654.
8. TNA: PRO, ADM 180/7 Entry 137; RNM, MS 248/4.
9. TNA PRO, ADM 180/7 Entry 137.
10. TNA: PRO, ADM 180/7 Entry 137; RNM, MS 248/4.
11. Clowes, 5, p. 293.
12. TNA: PRO, ADM 180/7 Entry 137; RNM, MS 248/4.
13. TNA: PRO, ADM 180/7 Entry 137.
14. TNA: PRO, ADM 180/10.
15. James, 4, pp. 183, 366.
16. TNA: PRO, ADM 180/7 Entry 137.
17. RNM, MS 248/6.
18. TNA: PRO, ADM 51/1518 part 9.
19. Clowes, 5, p. 128; TNA: PRO ADM 51/1518 part 9
20. TNA: PRO, ADM 51/1518 part 9.
21. *Ibid*.
22. James, 4, p. 65.
23. TNA: PRO, ADM 51/1518 part 9.
24. *Ibid*.
25. Clowes, 5, pp. 131, 148–149, 158, 160.
26. TNA: PRO, ADM 51/1518 part 9.
27. RNM, MS 248/6.
28. *Ibid*.
29. James, 5, pp. 12–13; Clowes, 5, p. 247.
30. James, 5, pp. 16–17; Clowes, 5, p. 250.
31. James, 5, pp. 76–76; Clowes, 5, p. 420.
32. RNM, MS 248/6.
33. *Ibid*.
34. James, 6, pp. 92–93; TNA: PRO, ADM 180/10 Entry 168; RNM, MS 248/6.
35. TNA: PRO, ADM 180/10 Entry 168.
36. Goodwin, *Nelson's Ships*, p. 118.
37. TNA: PRO, ADM 180/7 folio 155; Goodwin, *Nelson's Ships*, p. 118; Lyon, *The Sailing Navy List*, p. 74; Holland, *Ships of British Oak*, and *Buckler's Hard: A Rural Shipbuilding Centre*, Emsworth, Hampshire 1985.
38. RNM, MS 248/4.
39. TNA: PRO, Adm 52/211 part 3, Master's Log; Deane, *Nelson's Favourite*, Goodwin, *Nelson's Ships*, p. 118.
40. Clowes, 4, pp. 519–520.
41. Clowes, 3, pp. 519–535.
42. TNA: PRO, ADM 52/211 part 3, master log held at Buckler's Hard Maritime Museum, Hampshire; Goodwin, *Nelson's Ships*, p. 119.
43. RNM, MS 248/4.
44. TNA: PRO, ADM 180/7 folio 155.
45. *Ibid*.
46. *Ibid*.
47. *Ibid*.
48. *Ibid*.
49. RNM, MS 248/4.
50. TNA: PRO, ADM 180/7 folio 155.
51. Nicholas, *The Dispatches and Letters of Vice Admiral Lord Viscount Nelson*, 1, p. 304.
52. Nicholas, *Op Cit*, pp. 204–207, 325; Goodwin, *Nelson's Ships*, p. 120; Deane, *Nelson's Favourite*, p. 83.
53. Goodwin, *Nelson's Ships*, pp. 120–121; Deane, *Op Cit*,

pp. 93–94.	75 TNA: PRO, ADM 51/1194; ADM 180/7 folio 155.	Cit, p. 128.
54 Nicholas, Op Cit.	76 Brenton, The Naval History of Great Britain, 1, 1783–1806, pp. 282–284.	99 Goodwin, Op Cit, p. 128; Deane, Op Cit, p. 219.
55 Clowes, 4, p. 203.		100 According to Lyon, The Sailing Navy List, and Colledge, Ships of the Royal Navy, 1, Mistletoe was not launched until 1809.
56 Nicholas, Op Cit, p. 349; Goodwin, Nelson's Ships, p. 121.	77 Ibid.	
57 Nicholas Op Cit, pp. 370–374; Goodwin, Op Cit, p. 121.	78 TNA: PRO, ADM 51/1194.	
58 Clowes, Op Cit, pp. 243–245; Tracy, Naval Chronicle, 1, pp. 32–33; Goodwin, Nelson's Ships, p. 121.	79 Ibid.	101 TNA: PRO, ADM 51/1855.Goodwin Op Cit p128.
	80 Goodwin, Op Cit, pp. 123–125; Deane, Op Cit, pp. 138–139.	102 TNA: PRO, ADM 1/5339.
59 TNA: PRO, ADM 51/1104.		103 TNA: PRO, ADM 51/1934.
60 Goodwin, Op Cit, p. 121.	81 TNA: PRO, ADM 180/7 folio 155.	104 TNA: PRO, ADM 51/1934.
61 The Lutine, which had been captured at Toulon, foundered off Vlieland on the Dutch coast 9 October 1799. Her recovered bell now hangs in Lloyd's, London.	82 Ibid.	105 TNA: PRO, ADM 51/1934.
	83 Goodwin, Op Cit, p. 125; Pope, The Great Gamble, passim.	106 TNA: PRO, ADM 51/1934.
		107 MacPherson, The Four Ages of Man: The Classical Myths, pp. 127–132; Graves, Greek Myths, p. 225.
62 Deane, Op Cit, p. 109; Goodwin, Op Cit, p. 121.	84 TNA: PRO, ADM 51/1364; Goodwin, Op Cit, p. 125; Clowes, 4, pp. 430–439.	
63 R Southey, The Life of Horatio Lord Nelson, p. 60; Clowes, Op Cit, p. 245.		108 TNA: PRO, ADM 180/7 Entry 142.
	85 RNM, MS 248/6.	109 RNM, MS 248/4.
64 TNA: PRO, ADM 51/1104. Some guns removed from the Agamemnon still remain on the site of the siege today.	86 TNA: PRO, ADM 180/7.	110 Clowes, 4, p. 558.
	87 Clowes, 5, pp. 117–118	111 Clowes, 4, pp. 304, 556.
	88 TNA: PRO, ADM 51/1576 part 7; RNM, MS 248/6.	112 Clowes, 4, pp. 304–p556.
65 Deane, Op Cit, p. 113.	89 TNA: PRO, ADM 51/1576 part 7.	113 James, 3, pp. 67–75; Clowes, 4, pp. 430–439.
66 Clowes, 4, p. 269; Goodwin, Op Cit, p. 122.	90 Ibid.	114 RNM, MS 248/6.
67 Ibid.	91 Ibid.	115 TNA: PRO, ADM 180/10 Entry 194.
68 Clowes, 4, p. 274; Goodwin, Op Cit, p. 122.	92 Clowes, 5, pp. 186–188; Goodwin, Op Cit, p. 127.	116 Clowes, 5, pp. 131–160.
69 Clowes, 4, p. 277; Goodwin, Op Cit, p. 122.	93 Goodwin, Op Cit, p. 127; Brenton, 2, pp. 105–108.	117 Pope, England Expects, pp. 340–341.
70 Clowes, 4, p. 284; Goodwin, Op Cit, p. 123.	94 TNA: PRO, ADM 51/1576.	118 Clowes, 5, p. 186.
71 RNM, MS 248/4.	95 RNM, MS 248/8.	119 James, 5, p. 87.
72 TNA: PRO, ADM 180/7 folio 155.	96 TNA: PRO, ADM 180/7 folio 155.	120 James, 5, pp. 161–164.
73 TNA: PRO, ADM 51/1194.	97 TNA: PRO, ADM 51/1855.	121 James, 6, p. 80.
74 Ibid.	98 James, 4, pp. 283–286; Clowes, 5, p. 210; Goodwin, Op	122 Colledge, 1, p. 428; Lyon, p. 74.

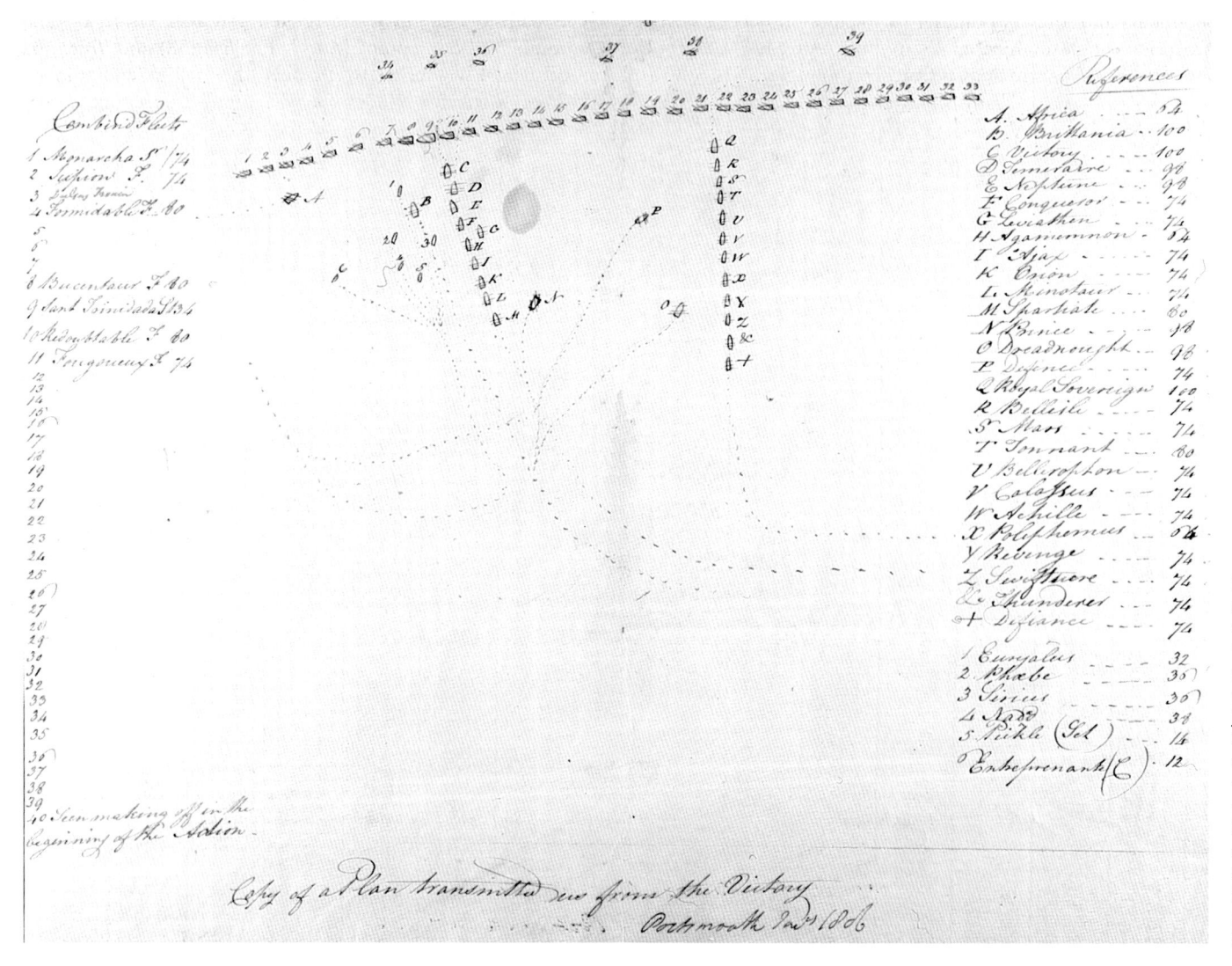

Battleplan sketch, watercolour, by John Livesay. Original caption states: 'Copy of a Plan transmitted — [unreadable] from the Victory Portsmouth Jany 1806'. This battleplan, listing the names of the ships and their stations, was drawn from first-hand verbal accounts Livesay heard from Nelson's officers in the Victory after her return to Portsmouth in December 1805. (Courtesy of the Royal Naval Museum)

PART 1: CHAPTER 5
THE BRITISH FIFTH RATE SHIPS

The 38 gun ship NAIAD

The Trafalgar *Naiad* was the second ship to bear the name in the Royal Navy, the previous *Naiad* being a 6th rate 26 gun frigate captured from the French on 1 June 1783 by *Sceptre* (64). Because the American War of Independence had concluded this *Naiad* was never commissioned and was sold 17 August 1784. In Greek mythology, a *naiad* (pl. *naiades*) was a nymph that lived in a river or freshwater spring.

The Trafalgar *Naiad*, a 5th rate of 38 guns, was the only ship built to the lines of the *Naiad* class designed by William Rule in 1795. Despite this, she was one of a group of eight 18 pounder heavy frigates ordered in the early years of the French Revolutionary Wars. Ordered 30 April 1795, *Naiad*'s keel was laid down at Limehouse September 1795, the ship was built by contractors Hill & Co. and launched 27 February 1797. Overall building costs including fitting out amounted to £24,989 of which £15,404 covered the cost of her hull.[1] Initially armed with twenty-eight 18 pounders on her main deck, eight 9 pounders and six 32 pounder carronades on the quarter deck, and two 9 pounders and four 32 pounder carronades on her forecastle, *Naiad*'s single broadside weight comprised 457 pounds. After her 'large repair' in 1815 *Naiad*'s armament was increased from 36 to 46 guns.[2]

CAPTAINS OF *NAIAD* (MSS 248/4 and 248/6)

Name	Time of Entry	Time of Discharge	On What Occasion
William Pierrepont	22 March 1797	10 November 1799	Superseded
Hon. John Murray	12 December 1799	2 April 1800	Superseded
William Henry Ricketts	11 November 1800	29 May 1801	Superseded
Philip Wilkinson	30 May 1801	2 December 1801	Paid Off at Plymouth
James Wilkins	8 September 1802	31 December 1803	New Book
James Wilkins	1 January 1804	18 October 1804	Superseded
Thomas Dundas	19 October 1804	7 October 1809	Superseded
George Cacks	28 February 1809	7 October 1809	Superseded Acting
Philip Carteret	9 July 1811	8 April 1812	Paid Off at Portsmouth
Hon. R C Spencer	12 April 1823	9 October 1826	Paid Off at Portsmouth

SERVICE HISTORY

1797: *Naiad* was first commissioned 22 March while fitting out at Deptford under Captain William Pierrepont.[3] Undocked six days later after being coppered, the ship sailed for Sheerness on 6 May where she after having various defects made good sailed on deployment 18 October.

1798: On 23 April *Naiad* with *Jason* (36) captured the French gunboat *Arrogante* (6) off Brest.[4] Returning to Plymouth 8 June *Naiad* went into dock five days later for two days to make good several defects. Completed at a cost of £1,271 the ship sailed back on patrol off the French Atlantic coast. Sighting the French *Décade* (36) commanded by Captain Villeneuve on 22 August, *Naiad* gave chase through the night. Joined by *Magnanime* next day, the two British ships brought the French frigate to action, compelling her to strike.[5] In December she went back into Plymouth to be docked to repair defects.[6]

1799: Undocked at the end of the previous year, *Naiad* remained moored in the Hamoaze but on 11 February broke from her moorings during a gale and ran aground upon the West Mud stern first. Suffering little damage she was refloated on the next high tide. Sailing from Plymouth six days later *Naiad* joined part of the Channel squadron operating off the Loire and on 5 March fell in with and captured the French privateer *Heureux Hazard* (20). In the autumn *Naiad*, in company with *Ethalion* (38) and *Triton* (32), was deployed off Ferrol where, on 16 October, they fell in with and gave chase to two Spanish frigates. While *Ethalion*, under Pierrepont's orders, pursued the foremost vessel, *Naiad* attacked the other frigate which, after a brisk engagement, surrendered. The ship proved to be *Santa Brigada* of 36 guns and 300 men commanded by Don Antonio Pillon. Command of the prize was given over to Lieutenant J Marshall, *Naiad*'s First Lieutenant. Meanwhile *Ethalion* captured *Thetis* (36) commanded by Don Juan de Mendoza. Both Spanish frigates, bound for Spain, had sailed from Vera Cruz on 21 August, the *Santa Brigada* having on board 1,400,000 dollars, the *Thetis* 1,411,526 dollars.[7] *Naiad* returned to Plymouth 9 November to make good her defects. Sailing again 3 December Pierrepont suddenly fell ill, so on the 12th command of the *Naiad* was temporarily given over to Captain the Hon. John Murray.[8]

1800: When the prize money was paid to the ship's crews on 14 January for the capture of *Santa Brigada* and *Thetis*, Pierrepont and the other two frigate captains each received £40,730 while each marine and seaman was awarded £182 (equal to 8 years 8 months' pay). This figure excluded the value of the two ships, their masts, rigging, guns, and stores. According to primary sources Captain Murray was superseded on 2 April so Pierrepont must have returned to the ship. Most of this year *Naiad* operated out of Plymouth until

SPECIFICATIONS: *NAIAD*

Rate	5th	Length on the range of the gun deck	147 ft	Ordnance - main deck	28 x 18 pounders
Guns	38	Length of keel for tonnage	122 ft 8¾ ins	Ordnance - quarter deck	8 x 9 pounders
Class	Naiad 1795	Extreme breadth	98 ft 5 ins		6 x 32 pounder carronades
Designer	William Rule	Depth in hold	13 ft 9 ins	Ordnance - forecastle	2 x 9 pounders
Builder	Hill & Co.	Tons burthen	1013 90/94		4 x 32 pounder carronades
Dockyard	Limehouse	Draught afore	19 ft 4 ins	Single broadside weight	457 pounds
Date ordered	30 April 1795	Draught abaft	21 ft 2 ins	Fate	1847 Hulked at Callao, Peru as a coal ship
Date keel laid	September 1795	Complement	264		1866 Sold
Date launched	27 February 1797				

Source: Lyon, *Sailing Navy List*, p. 12.

| Part 1: **The British Fleet** | The Ships of Trafalgar |

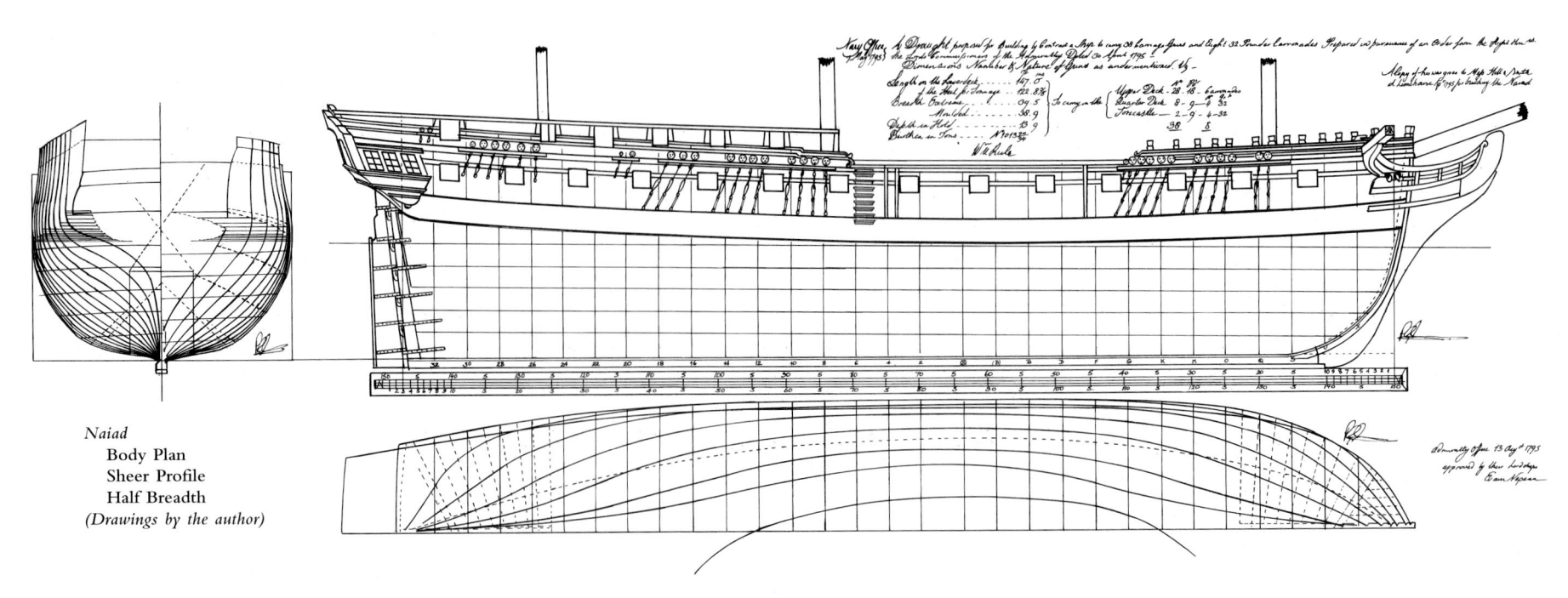

Naiad
Body Plan
Sheer Profile
Half Breadth
(Drawings by the author)

10 November. Next day command of the ship was succeeded by Captain William Henry Ricketts and on 18 November *Naiad* went into dock to have her copper repaired. Undocked 4 December, the ship sailed eight days later.[9]

1801: Operating 500 miles west of Cape Finisterre at the beginning of May, *Naiad* recaptured the Post Office packet *Phœnix*, Captain Thompson, which, after sailing from Falmouth for New York on 15 April, had been taken by a French 40-gun privateer six days later. Luckily Thompson had managed to throw any dispatches and mail overboard before being boarded. After being escorted towards home by *Naiad*, *Phœnix* reached Plymouth on 11 May. Returning to her station off the north-west coast of Spain, on 16 May boats from *Naiad* and *Phæton* (38) commanded by Lieutenant Marshall, *Naiad*'s First Lieutenant, went 10 miles up the River Pontevedra and captured the Spanish corvette *Alcudia* and destroyed the armed vessel *Rapos* lying under the protection of a battery of five 24-pounders. *Alcudia*'s sails had, under her commander Don Jean Antonio Barbuto's orders, been taken ashore therefore the boats had to tow her down river. When winds picked up, the corvette being unable to sail, was set on fire. In the attack two British seamen were wounded. Returning to Plymouth 25 May command of the ship was superseded five days later by Captain Philip Wilkinson. After taking on stores, live bullocks and vegetables *Naiad* sailed on 6 June to replenish the Channel fleet.

Cruising off Rochefort at the end of October, *Naiad* was nearly wrecked near the Isle de Rhé during a violent gale. Having run onshore, the ship lay marooned for two days under the guns of a French battery which made no attempt to fire upon her. More mystifying was that on the second day boats arrived carrying cables and anchors sent out by the French commander of the fortifications who informed Wilkinson that preliminary peace negotiations had been signed between England and France. With French assistance *Naiad* was hauled off the shoals undamaged, returning to Plymouth on 3 November. On 2 December Wilkinson paid off the ship and six days later *Naiad* was docked to have her copper removed.[10]

1802: Re-coppered, *Naiad* was undocked on 21 January, towed into the Hamoaze and laid up in ordinary for eight months. On 9 September the port admiral received orders to put *Naiad* into service to replace *Fisgard* (44) which was being paid off. Consequently Captain James Wilkins, *Fisgard*'s current commander, transferred into *Naiad* and placed her in commission. As often happened when re-manning ships, the entire crew of the *Fisgard* was turned over into *Naiad*.[11] *Naiad* was then fitted out, taking an unusually long time, for it was not until 12 November that *Naiad* proceeded to Cawsand Bay to await further orders.[12] Six days later Wallis received orders to supply men to go into *Belleisle* (74) which was currently fitting out for foreign service, but these men were not actually needed. For the present *Naiad* remained at anchor.

1803: When war with France re-opened on 16 May *Naiad* was immediately sent on station off Brest where, shortly after, boats from both *Naiad* and *Hazard* (16) cut out a brig lying near the Penmarck Rocks while under fire from French batteries. The boats also cut out and sunk an armed chasse marée from the same location. The captured brig was sent into Plymouth on 28 May. Over the next week *Naiad* added more prizes to her list. On 29 May she fell in with a French corvette in the Bay of Biscay. During the ensuing chase the French commander resorted to heaving over guns and cutting away the bower anchors to avoid capture. Eventually brought to, the vessel proved to be *Impatiente* of 10 guns and 80 men commanded by Lieutenant Hypolite Arnous out of Senegal bound for Rochefort.[13] Two days later *Naiad* captured *Chasseur*, a French merchantman bound for Lorient commanded by Lieutenant Lamer. Besides being laden with a rich cargo of coffee, sugar, and cotton, and newly coppered, the value of the prize was high. Between 2 and 4 June *Naiad*, in company with *Doris* (36), captured a Dutch sloop laden with drugs and medicines, a French corvette from Gorée carrying gum and ivory, and two French brigs one of which was the *Napoleon* bound for Nantes from Guadaloupe with sugar and coffee. The latter named vessel was sent into Plymouth on 2 July. On 4 July boats from *Naiad* commanded by her First Lieutenant Mr William Dean, accompanied by Lieutenant Irwin, Royal Marines, and midshipmen Glenny, Gordon and Stewart went inshore to cut out a French schooner anchored in inshore near Nantes. Despite negotiating rocks, shoals and strong tides in the dark, the schooner was carried off without loss. This was partly because the French lieutenant in command, M. Martres Preville, and his crew bar one man and two boys fled on shore. The vessel proved to be the *Providence* of 200 tons armed with just two guns but laden with 18, 24, and 36 pounder guns from the foundry at Nantes destined for Brest and a quantity of quality timber.[14]

Returning to Plymouth on 7 September, *Naiad* went into the Barnpool to refit her rigging then moved into the Sound. While awaiting sailing orders her crew received six months' wages on 5 October. Next morning *Naiad* sailed down Channel to join Sir Edward Pellew's squadron cruising off Ferrol and Corunna. For the next three months *Naiad* experienced very bad weather with severe gales but despite the squadron being blown off sta-

1804: Still cruising off Ferrol, *Naiad* sailed from the squadron on 8 January with dispatches for Admiral Cornwallis stationed off Ushant. Two days later Cornwallis sent *Naiad* into Plymouth with further dispatches for London, the ship arriving there on 14 January. After further cruising she arrived at Plymouth 15 May and went into dock eleven days later. Re-launched 7 June after incurring costs of £3,440, *Naiad* joined Admiral Cornwallis' squadron deployed off Brest. On 19 October Captain Henry Dundas took command of ship and cruising inshore near Douarnenez on the morning of Tuesday 27 November he sighted two gunboats attacking boats from *Aigle* (36). Giving chase, the two vessels were easily overhauled and when captured, proved to be gunboats 361 and 369 mounting brass 4 and 12 pounders apiece. On board were a lieutenant of the 63rd infantry, 36 privates and six seamen. Dundas ordered the brig-sloop *Dispatch* (18) to take the two vessels into Plymouth.

1805: Returning to Plymouth on 7 January 1805 from a cruise off the coast of Spain, *Naiad* nearly ran ashore as she entered harbour, but managing to wear in time she reached her moorings safely. Accompanying *Naiad* was a captured Spanish ship carrying 200,000 dollars and a valuable cargo of dry goods. Sailing next day to cruise to the westward, *Naiad* returned on 17 February, this time with a neutral merchantman suspected of carrying Spanish property. Entering the Hamoaze 2 April *Naiad* went into dock three days later for five days to have her copper repaired, a minor refit and a replenishment of stores. The cost of £4,170 comprised hull £910; masts and yards £203; rigging and stores £2,719.[15]

Sailing 16 April *Naiad* returned to her previous station until ordered south to join Admiral Collingwood off Cadiz in September where she was deployed with Blackwood's inshore squadron watching over the Combined Fleet.

TRAFALGAR

Between 14 and 17 October *Naiad*'s log records that the ship was cruising between latitude 36'27" and 36'29" West with *Pickle*. On Friday 18th it records: 'Mod breezes & cloudy made & short.d. Sail occas.y. *Phœbe* in C.o. reconnoitred Enemy's Fleet which consisted of twenty nine Sail of the Line AM D.o. W.r. made & short.d. Sail occas.y. emp.d. stowing the Booms at Noon calm & Clear'. Next day, Saturday 19 October, Captain Dundas wrote: 'AM D.o. W.r. At 7 observed the Enemy's Ships under weigh Answ.d & repeated several several [word duplicated in log] Signals from the *Euryalus* to the *Phœbe* at Noon Calm 11 of the Enemy's Ships outside the Light House'. Maintaining her vigilance *Naiad*'s log Sunday 20 October states; 'Light Airs & Cloudy made & repeated several signals from the *Euryalus* AM D.o. W.r. At 8 saw 12 of the enemy's Ships under sail and 22 sail of our Ships on our W.r. Quarter ans.d. various signals from the *Euryalus* at noon D.o. W.r. With Rain'.[16]

Taking up her station to the windward of the main body of Nelson's fleet as ordered, *Naiad*'s log 21 October records: 'Fresh Breezes with rain at 5 both fleets in sight repeated several Blue Lights and Sky Rockets from the *Phœbe* & *Sirius* AM D.o. W.r. saw the Enemy's fleet form line of battle, our fleet a head steering towards the enemy'. As a frigate with limited ordnance, *Naiad*, like her consorts, stood off from the close fight, consequently Captain Dundas was able to give good account of the battle as it unfolded, his log Tuesday 22 October recording:

> Winds variable NW to SW later; at 1-10 observed the *R Sovereign* commencing the action as did several other Ships of the lee line at 12-50 the Spanish Adm.l. Commenced firing and the Action became very general at 1 a Spanish 3 decker hauled down her Colours to the *R Sovereign* at 1-35 a Spanish two deck'd Ship haul[ed] down her Colours 1-50 a French two decker and a french Admiral both struck to the *Victory* and *Téméraire* at 2-10 observed several of the enemy's Ships dismasted & one of ours with her fore & Mizen Mast[s] gone at 2-20 saw the *Neptune* dismast a Spanish Commander in Chief and likewise several of D.o. strike their Colours at 2-40 the Action became general from Van to Rear at 2-45 the Main & Mizen Masts of the *R Sovereign* went by the Board 3-35 bore up to take the *Belleisle* in tow she being totally dismasted at 4- obs.d. one of the french Ships on fire at 5 the firing ceased from all the Ships at 5-10 the Ship that was on fire blew up at 6 the French Ships four in N.o. retreating to windward and fourteen to leeward rec.d. on board 95 Spanish Prisoners & sent a Petty Officer and ~~fourteen~~ [word struck through] 31 Men to take charge of the *Achille*'s Prize.

With *Belleisle* in tow, *Naiad* then prepared for the storm's expected onslaught, setting her storm staysails and 'lost signal flag N.o. 3 and the substitute in making Sig.ls. to the *Belleisle*'. While many British ships spent several days plying off Cadiz it appears that by the 24th *Naiad* with her charge appear to have sailed further south towards Cape Spartel and proceeded eastward, Gibraltar bearing ENE just 3 miles. Although safety was in sight at 5 p.m. that afternoon, the stream cable towing *Belleisle* parted. Now out of control in the heavy swell, *Belleisle* 'fell on board us in endeavouring to take her in tow', with the new cable. The log then states; 'AM set the Storm Staysails & took in the fore & Mizen topsails 3-30 wore and made the Night Signal to the *Belleisle* at 4 strong Gales & Squally 5-40 saw the *Belleisle* very near the shore to the eastward of Cape Trafalgar made sail & stood towards her at 7-30 got her in tow at 11 made our N.o. and N.o. 191 with 4 guns'. Entering Gibraltar at 1 p.m. amid strong breezes and rain on Sunday 25 October, *Naiad* 'cast of the *Belleisle* at 1.30 came too with the Best Bower in 30 fathom water Moored with the S. Bower found laying her the *Hydra Niger Juno* & *Martin* sailed a Gun Brig and arrived HM Sloop *Weazle*'. While many of the Trafalgar ships had yet to arrive, *Naiad* put to sea again. Cruising off Gibraltar Bay on Thursday 29 October Dundas recorded: 'at 2-30 the Spaniards fired five Shot at us from their Lines', on shore. The next day he entered in the log: 'Punished Samuel Roberts M [marine] with 2 Dozen Lashes for Drunkenness and Neglect of Duty'.[17]

1806: Returning home, *Naiad* moored off Sheerness on 24 June and went into dock 1 July for 16 days to make good defects and have her copper replaced and put to sea again 1 August, the cost of her refit being £3,789.[18]

1808: Between 6 June and 8 August *Naiad* was refitted at a cost of £9,055.[19]

1809: *Naiad* was now deployed with Rear-Admiral Robert Stopford's squadron, Stopford flying his flag in *Cæsar*. Anchored north-west of the Chassiron lighthouse on the evening of 23 February with *Defiance* (74), *Donegal* (74), *Amethyst* (38), and *Emerald* (36), several signal rockets were seen to the north-west. Stopford's squadron immediately got under way and stood towards the lights where, next morning, they discovered eight French sail-of-the-line and two frigates standing into the Pertuis d'Antioche. *Naiad* was detached immediately to warn Admiral Lord Gambier that a French squadron had arrived from Brest. Before *Naiad* had made three miles to the north-west she sighted three French frigates standing in for Sables d'Olonne. *Naiad* signalled instantly to Admiral Stopford who, leaving *Amethyst* and *Emerald* to watch the main French squadron, went in chase of the frigates, further supported by *Amelia* (38) and brig-sloop *Dotterel* (18). Closing inshore and anchoring under the protection of shore batteries, the French vessels were soon driven ashore by the fire of the British ships. One frigate was abandoned by her crew on 2 March, the other two, now laying on their beam ends at low water, would soon be destroyed by the elements. During this period George Cacks commanded *Naiad* in an acting capacity. Stopford's squadron, including *Naiad*, returned to blockade the main French force at the Isle d'Aix until 7 March when Admiral Gambier arrived to take command.

1810: Now under the command of Captain Henry Hill, *Naiad* suffered a stain on her career; on 26 and 27 March a court martial was held on board *Salvador del Mundo* (112) anchored in the Hamoaze. On trial were seven petty officers and seamen from *Naiad* charged with inciting mutiny by urging the ship's company to sign a bill requesting not to sail under Captain Hill because of his autocratic treatment of the crew. Found guilty, John Campbell, Henry Page and Thomas Passmore, each captains of the forecastle, were sentenced to death by hanging. The remainder were to be flogged round the fleet: Robert Cuddeford, carpenter's crew, 150 lashes; Thomas Norman, seaman, 100 lashes; William Moulton captain of the foretop and Joseph Nash, 50 lashes. In June the three men sentenced to death were pardoned, their reprieve, with a suitable caution, being read by Captain Wolley; most of those to be flogged were also pardoned. Captain Hill was superseded out of *Naiad*, considered too senior to command a frigate, and was never employed again.

1811: On 9 July command of the ship was succeeded by Captain Philip Carteret, her appointed First Lieutenant being Mr John Greenlaw. *Naiad* was now deployed with the Channel squadron stationed in the Downs. While lying at anchor off Boulogne on 20 September, at around midday Captain Carteret was able to see Napoleon Bonaparte inspecting the French invasion flotilla moored inshore under the protection of shore batteries. Watching through his glass Carteret then watched Napoleon embark in his barge and sail some three miles along the coast about three miles to inspect the vessels assembled at Wimereux and Ambleteuse. Not surprisingly a display was soon executed to impress Napoleon, seven prams put to sea and stood towards *Naiad* and getting within gun-shot, fired at the British ship. Shortly after ten brigs and a sloop came up and joining their consorts periodically discharged their broadsides at *Naiad* for the next two hours. Although *Naiad* suffered little damage, Carteret felt humiliated by this demonstration played out for the French Emperor, therefore when the tide turned slack *Naiad* weighed and stood off to get to windward and await her vengeance. Next morning the French vessels resumed their attack, however, finding that *Naiad* now had the company of the brig-sloops *Castilian* (18), *Redpole* (10) and *Rinaldo* (10), and the gun-brig *Viper* (10), the French tacked and stood inshore. The British ships bore up together and followed and once ranged within pistol shot fired their broadsides upon the flotilla and the batteries. Running aboard the pram Mr Grant, one of *Naiad*'s lieutenants, lashed her alongside. Meeting considerable resistance from her crew of some 112 seamen and soldiers, *Naiad*'s boarders eventually carried the vessel, inflicting some 35 casualties. The pram proved to be the *Ville de Lyon* armed with twelve long 24 pounders. The French captain M. Jean Barbaud was one of the wounded. *Naiad*'s casualties were two killed and 14 wounded, among whom were Lieutenant of Marines William Morgan and Midshipman James Dover. On 6 August *Naiad* captured another vessel, the French privateer *Milan*, a lugger of 16 guns and 50 men and shortly after *Requin* of Boulogne mounting only two guns but with others stowed within the hold.[20]

1812: *Naiad* returned to Portsmouth on 19 March and in early April suffered an unfortunate accident. Her gig carrying Captain Carteret was upset off Cowes; while Carteret was recovered from the sea unconscious, three seamen were drowned. Ordered to pay off *Naiad* on 8 April, Captain Carteret shifted into *Pomone* (38) formerly *Astrée* captured from the French in 1810.[21] As for *Naiad*, she was taken into Portsmouth dockyard and 'Fitted to raise the Wreck of the Qn. Charlotte Mercht. Ship'.[22] Though details of her conversion have yet to be found, in all probability each lower mast was fitted with sheer-legs, more capstans would have been fitted and her external sides fitted with additional timbers. This work was completed in November at a cost of £2,428. Having fulfilled her singular duty *Naiad* was then laid up in ordinary.

1814–1821: Taken into dock 13 July *Naiad* was given a large repair and

PROGRESS BOOK – *NAIAD* 5th RATE OF 38 GUNS:

At what Port	Arrived	Docked	Coppered
River Thames; Hill & Co.	Began	Sept 1795	
Deptford	27 Feb 1797	14 March 1797	Coppered March 1797
Sheerness	17 Sep 1797		
Plymouth	8 June 1798	13 June 1798	
Plymouth	4 Dec 1798	19 Dec 1798	
Plymouth	9 Nov 1799		
Plymouth	10 Nov 1800		
Plymouth	3 Nov 1801		
Plymouth	15 May 1804	26 May 1804	
Plymouth	2 April 1805	5 April 1805	Copper Repaired
Sheerness	24 June 1806	1 July 1806	Copper taken off and Re-coppered July 1806
Plymouth	6 June 1808	15 June 1808	Copper Repaired
Plymouth	26 Feb 1810	6 March 1810	Copper Repaired
Portsmouth	19 Mar 1812	Fitted to raise the wreck of the Queen Charlotte Merchant Ship Nov 1813	
Portsmouth	13 July 1814		Copper taken off July Re-coppered April 1815
Portsmouth			Copper taken off to Light Draft of Water Nov 1815
Portsmouth	12 Oct 1821		Copper taken off and re-coppered
Portsmouth	15 April 1823		Raised copper [to full water line]
Portsmouth	29 Sep 1826	3 April 1828	Copper taken off and re-coppered
Portsmouth			
Portsmouth		30 July 1846	Copper taken off; Felted Sheathed & Re-coppered

Sold 1866

'Housed over' to protect her from the elements while in ordinary, the overall cost of the refit being £28,062. Undocked 25 April 1825, in November the ship had her copper removed to the light waterline. Docked between 12 October and 24 December 1822 *Naiad* was recoppered.[23]

1823: Required for sea service, *Naiad* was recommissioned 12 April under Captain Robert Spencer. Three days later she went into dock at Portsmouth to be fitted for sea and have her copper 'raised' to the full waterline. Undocked 21 April, the entire costs of this refit including masts, yards, rigging and stores amounted to £15.058.[24] Spencer unfortunately found it difficult to raise a full crew due to a prejudiced attitude, somewhat unfounded, towards his First Lieutenant Michael Quinn. Consequently when *Naiad* was ready for sea it was only by Spencer's political influence that she sailed with 80 per cent complement. After cruising with the Channel fleet for a few months, in September *Naiad* sailed from Spithead for Lisbon.

1824: In January *Naiad* sailed with *Camelion* (10) for the Mediterranean to resolve a political situation concerning the Dey of Algiers who, after forcing entry into the residence of the British consul, had taken away two of his servants. On arrival Spencer found two Spanish ships interred in the harbour, their crews, like the consul's two servants, being condemned into slavery. Seeking a diplomatic audience with the Dey, Spencer reminded him that the treaty signed after Lord Exmouth's attack on Algiers in 1816 forbade the enslavement of Christians and demanded their release. When this was refused, Spencer immediately embarked the British consul and his family into *Naiad* and with *Camelion* in company, sailed on 31 January. Once outside the harbour *Naiad* gave chase to the Algerian corvette *Tripoli* (18) which had captured the Spanish vessels and fired a warning shot across her

Source: ADM 180/9 Entry 576 & ADM 180/11 Entry 321

Launched or Undocked	Sailed	Built or Nature of Repair	Cost of Hull, Masts & Yards Materials £	Workmen £	Cost of Masts & Yards Materials £	Workmen £	Cost of Rigging & Stores Materials £	Workmen £	Grand Total £
27 Feb 1797		Built	15,407						15,407
28 March 1797	6 May 1797	Fitted			3,357		6,228		9,585
18 Oct 1797		Made Good Defects 533			738		1,271		
		Made Good Defects							
		Made Good Defects							
		Made Good Defects							
		Made Good Defects							
		Fitted							
7 June 1804	20 June 1804	Defects	404	269	39	9	2,669	5-	3,440
10 April 1805	16 April 1805	Defects	707	203	198	5	3,030	27	4,170
16 July 1806	1 Aug 1806	Defects	995	479	95	23	2,143	54	3,789
20 July 1808	8 Aug 1808	Defects	3,530	2,030	1,325	26	2,084	60	9,055
7 March 1810	28 March 1810	Defects	407	300	24	2	1,666	29	2,428
			22	178	-	1	-	13	241
25 April 1815		Large Repair & Housed over	19,219	5,746	1,639	5	2,219	34	28,806
24 Dec 1821		Defects Made Good	Included in the expense of the Ordinary 3rd Article - See Master Shipwts. Letter 30 Dec 1826						
21 April 1823	7 Aug 1823	Fitted for Sea	3,391	1,553	1,775	79	8,238	22	15,058
25 June 1828		Small Repair	8.090	3.244	594	6	841	14	12,789
		Expenses to 31 Mar 1844	188	264	452	312	203	15	673
25 Sep 1846	9 Jan 1847	Fitted for a Coal Depot for Callao	3,091	1,741	883	10	5,131	259	11,115
		Expenses to 31 March 1862	42	18	-	-	1		61

bow to bring her to. Refusing to heave to, Spencer ordered his gunners to fire, *Naiad*'s timely broadsides speedily reducing *Tripoli* to a wreck before *Camelion*'s seamen boarded her, bringing off the Algerine commander and freeing seventeen Spanish captives. *Naiad* then sailed for Malta to report the incident to the Commander-in-Chief, Sir Harry Neale. On their return to Algiers two days later and finding the Dey still refusing to adhere to the treaty, the British ship set up a complete blockade of the Barbary coast.[25]

During the night of 23 May boats from *Naiad* commanded by Lieutenant Michael Quinn went in under the guns of the fortress at Bona to destroy an Algerine 16-gun brig of war. This vessel, moored head and stern with a chain cable to shore, was covered by at least 40 pieces of cannon manned by 400 Turkish soldiers as well as the crew. The brig was riding high in the water so boarding her from the boats proved troublesome. However, once carried off the British seamen set her ablaze. Burnt to the water line, the brig finally blew up and sank. In spite of the tremendous fire of cannon and small arms only a few men were hurt and none killed. The officers employed in the boats were Lieutenants Michael Quinn, Thomas Dilke and George Evans, together with Midshipmen George Davies, Searls Oldham, Frederick Grey, Charles Hotham, Thomas Lavington, David Mosseberry, John Robb, Charles Ryder, Charles Schieber, John Sealy and Edmund Seppings. Commanding the marines was Lieutenant William Knapman. While enforcing the blockade *Naiad* captured *Muni* bound for Algiers from Livorno and assisted in cutting out a grain ship from under the guns of Bona. When the Commander-in Chief assembled his squadron in the Bay of Algiers and took up positions to bombard the town, the Dey decided to bow to the inevitable. The squadron was dispersed while Captain Spencer concluded the treaty.

1824-1826: When Captain Spencer was appointed senior officer in the Ionian Islands *Naiad* spent most of this period employed in the Aegean, when Spencer took part in the negotiations between Greeks and Turks in Morea. Ordered home on 2 August 1826, *Naiad* reached Portsmouth 29 September, Spencer finally paying off the ship on 9 October.[26]

FATE

Besides having a 'Small Repair' between April and June 1828, *Naiad* remained laid up in ordinary at Portsmouth until 1846 when, on 30 July, she was docked to be 'Fitted for a Coal Depot for Callao' at a cost of £11,115. Launched 25 September that same year she sailed under the charge of William Browne, Master, for Valparaiso. In early 1847 *Naiad* sailed for Callao, Peru, where she was to remain hulked as a coal ship under successive masters. William Browne was superseded by Samuel Strong in December 1851 and was himself succeeded by William Dillon in December 1856. *Naiad* was finally sold in 1866.[27]

The 36 gun ship EURYALUS

As the first vessel to bear the name *Euryalus* in the Royal Navy, the ship also takes its name from classical Greek mythology. Euryalus, son of Mecisteus, one of the Epigoni, served as one of the 49 Argonauts that sailed in the ship *Argo* with Jason.[28] *Euryalus* was one of twenty-six 5th rate 36 gun ships built on the lines of the *Apollo/Euryalus* class frigates designed by William Rule in 1798. Ordered in 1800, the Navy Board granted the contract to the private contractor Henry Adams of Buckler's Hard. With the keel laid in October 1801, the ship was launched 6 June 1803. Built on the River Beaulieu, all the timber needed for the construction of a frigate of this size, in all about 1,590 loads amounting to 79,500 cubic feet, was extracted from some 38 acres of the New Forest in Hampshire and the Forest of Dean. Her building costs for hull, masts and yards totalled £15,568 16s. When initially armed with twenty-six 18 pounders on her main deck, six 9 pounders and six 32 pounder carronades on her quarter deck and two 9 pounders and two 32 pounder carronades on the forecastle *Euryalus* delivered a single broadside weight of 398 pounds. When her ordnance inventory was modified to carry two 9 pounders and ten 32 pounder carronades on the quarter deck and two 9 pounders and four 32 pounder carronades on the forecastle, her broadside weight was increased by 19.6 per cent to 476 pounds.

CAPTAINS OF EURYALUS (MSS 248/4 and 248/6)

Name	Time of Entry	Time of Discharge	On What Occasion
Hon. Henry Blackwood	17 June 1803	31 December 1803	New Book
Hon. Henry Blackwood	1 January 1804	11 February 1806	Superseded
Temple Hardy	30 April 1804	4 August 1806	Superseded
Hon. G H L Dundas	12 February 1806	4 March 1811	To the *Achille*

SERVICE CAREER

1803: First commissioned on 17 June under Captain the Hon. Henry Blackwood, *Euryalus* was first deployed with Admiral Gardner's squadron operating off the Irish coast.

1804: Redeployed to the Channel squadron commanded by Lord Keith, in late summer *Euryalus* was detached with Rear-Admiral Louis' squadron operating off Dungeness watching over Boulogne where the French invasion fleet was assembling. In October Blackwood received orders to make an attack upon several catamarans lying off Boulogne which proved to be specially built explosion vessels designed by Robert Fulton. Fulton, an American sympathetic to the French cause, was also responsible for the design of an early submersible.

1805: Operating off Gibraltar in late March, *Euryalus* fell in with the English privateer *Eliza* of Liverpool commanded by Captain Keene. Although Keene was able to produce a protection from the Admiralty, Blackwood pressed four men from her crew of 41 men and boys into his own ship. Blackwood's conduct was to later prove detrimental for on 4 April *Eliza*, together with the *Greyhound*, another privateer from Guernsey, captured the Spanish *Dos Amigos* off the Azores which proved to have a cargo worth £150,000. Unfortunately, as *Eliza* was now four men down on her official complement, the vessel's share of the prize money was reduced by £3,000. Consequently her owners, Messrs Hobson and partners, took their case to the King's Bench in July 1807 and sued Blackwood for £2,888 10s 6d. While the judge proved sympathetic to Blackwood's action in the interests of the service, the presiding jury opted to support the plaintiffs, awarding them full compensation. Deployed with Calder's squadron off the Iberian coast, *Euryalus* was soon to make her name. Sighting Villeneuve's combined fleet off Cape St Vincent, *Euryalus* shadowed the Franco-Spanish ships as they proceeded into Cadiz. Once they were in port Blackwood sailed north to warn Calder who in turn sailed south to join Vice-Admiral Collingwood's squadron to support the blockade of Cadiz. Collingwood, needing to inform the Admiralty and Nelson, immediately sent *Euryalus* home with dispatches. Reaching the west end of the Isle of Wight within ten days, Blackwood anchored the *Euryalus* in Alum Bay and once the ship's boat was lowered went ashore at Lymington where he hired a post-chaise to London via Merton. The hire charge Blackwood claimed amounted to £15 9s. Arriving at Merton at 5 a.m. Monday 2 September Blackwood was immediately greeted by Nelson eager for news. After this brief encounter Blackwood continued the journey to London. Blackwood later returned to his ship and on at 8 a.m. Sunday 15 September *Euryalus* weighed and came to sail from her anchorage off St Helen's, joining *Victory* with Lord Nelson on board. Progress down Channel was hampered by strong winds so *Euryalus* still lay off Portland two days later. Reaching the Lizard Thursday 19 September, *Euryalus* and *Victory* were joined by *Ajax* (74) and *Thunderer* (74) out from Plymouth.[29]

On 26 September Nelson sent Blackwood ahead to inform Collingwood that no signal guns were to be fired on his arrival. Rejoining Collingwood's fleet, *Euryalus* was immediately deployed with the inshore squadron of frigates *Hydra* (38), *Naiad* (38) and *Phœbe* (36) and the schooner *Weazle*, watching Cadiz. On 4 October *Euryalus* and *Hydra* were attacked by Spanish gunboats out from Cadiz which were quickly repelled, Blackwood being given overall command. For three weeks *Euryalus* and her squadron, which now also included *Sirius*, (36), retained their vigil diligently, waiting for signs that the combined fleet were preparing to sail. Concerned that signalling between the inshore squadron and the fleet plying some 12 leagues (50 miles) south-west of Cadiz should be possible in all forms of weather,

SPECIFICATIONS: EURYALUS

Rate	5th	Length on the range of the gun deck	145 ft 2 ins	Ordnance - quarter deck	6 x 9 pounders
Guns	36	Length of keel for tonnage	129 ft 9¾ ins		6 x 32 pounder carronades
Class	*Apollo/Euryalus* 1798	Extreme breadth	38 ft 2? ins	Ordnance - forecastle	2 x 9 pounders
Designer	William Rule	Depth in hold	13 ft 3 ins		2 x 32 pounder carronades
Builder	Henry Adams	Tons burthen	943 53/94	Single broadside weight	398 pounds
Dockyard	Buckler's Hard	Draught afore		Fate	1813 Hulked at Chatham as a convict ship
Date ordered	? 1800	Draught abaft			1847 Sent to Gibraltar as a convict ship
Date keel laid	October 1801	Complement	264		1859 Renamed *Africa*
Date launched	6 June 1803	Ordnance - main deck	26 x 18 pounders		1860 Sold

Note: Armament was later modified as: quarter deck - 8 x 9 pounders and 4 x 32 pounder carronades or 2 x 9 pounders and 10 x 32 pounder carronades, the forecastle being either 2 x 9 pounders and 4 x 32 pounder carronades or 2 x 12 pounders and 4 x 32 pounder carronades.

Source: Lyon, *Sailing Navy List*, p. 124.

THE 36 GUN SHIP *EURYALUS*

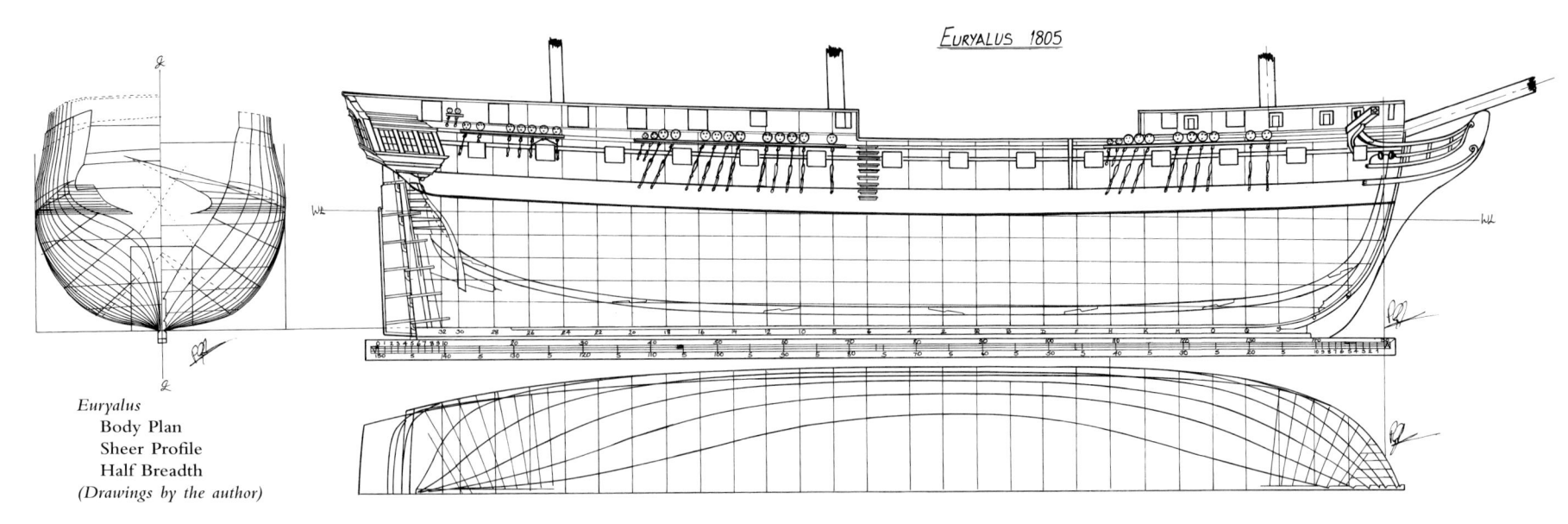

Euryalus
Body Plan
Sheer Profile
Half Breadth
(Drawings by the author)

Nelson ordered that the frigates were 'to fire a gun every three minutes and burn a rocket from the mast-head every hours', and that 'one of the Ships to be placed to windward, or rather to the eastward of the other two, to extend the distance of seeing, and I have desired Captain Blackwood to throw a Frigate to the Westward of Cadiz, for the purpose of an easy and early communication'.[30] Finally, at 9.30 a.m. Saturday 19 October, *Euryalus* indelibly marked her name in the annals of naval history when Blackwood conveyed to *Mars* (74) signal number 370, 'The enemy are coming out of port'.[31] On receipt of this message Nelson ordered the British fleet to give general chase and prepare for battle. Next morning amid heavy rain and thickening fog *Euryalus* and her accompanying frigates were pursued by ships from Admiral Magon's squadron which had put to sea.[32]

TRAFALGAR

The log book entry for *Euryalus* that day states:

> AM at 8 observed the British fleet forming the line the head most ships from the Enemy under 8 or 9 miles, the Enemys force consist of thirty three Sail of the Line, five frigates and two Brigs. Light winds & haze with a great swell from the Westw[d] English Fleet all Sail Set Standing towards the Enemy them on a Starboard tack at 8-5 answ[d] Lord Nelson's sig[l] for Captain Blackwood and went immediately on Board *Victory*.

Responding to Nelson's signal, *Euryalus* closed alongside *Victory* for Blackwood to repair on board the flagship. Most accounts state that Blackwood entered into *Victory* at 6 a.m., a statement that contradicts *Euryalus*' journal. Whilst on board Blackwood suggested that Nelson should transfer into *Euryalus* where he would be better placed to take command of the fleet but Nelson would have nothing of this. Later that morning Blackwood, together with Captain Hardy, penned his signature as witness to Nelson's codicil to his will. *Euryalus*' log entry continues:

> ... took our Station on *Victory*s Larboard Quarter and repeated the Admirals Sig[l]. at 10 observed the Enemy waring [sic] and comming [sic] to the Wind on the Larboard Tack at 11-40 repeated Lord Nelsons Telegraph Message I intend to push or go through the end of the Enemys line to prevent him getting into Cadiz Saw the Lead bearing EBN 5 or 6 leagues At 11-56 repeated Lord Nelsons Telegraph Message, England expects that every Man will do his Duty, at noon light Winds and a Great swell from the Westw[d]. Observed the *Royal Sovereign* (Admiral Collingwood) leading the Lee line bearing Down on the Enemys Rear line being then nearly within Gun Shot of them Lord Nelson leading the Weather Line bore Down upon the Enemys Center [sic]'.[33]

Shortly afterwards, generally recorded as 11.50 a.m., Blackwood quitted the deck of *Victory* to return into *Euryalus*. Taking his leave, he took Nelson's hand and said 'I trust, my lord, that on my return to the *Victory*, which will be as soon as possible, I shall find your Lordship in possession of twenty prizes'. Nelson responded saying, 'God bless you, Blackwood, I shall never speak to you again'.[34] *Euryalus*' log then states, 'Captain Blackwood returned from the *Victory* Cape Trafalgar SEBE about 5 Leagues Lat. [? large ink stain] by 12 W'.[35]

Standing off from the main battle fleet, *Euryalus* took station to relay sig-

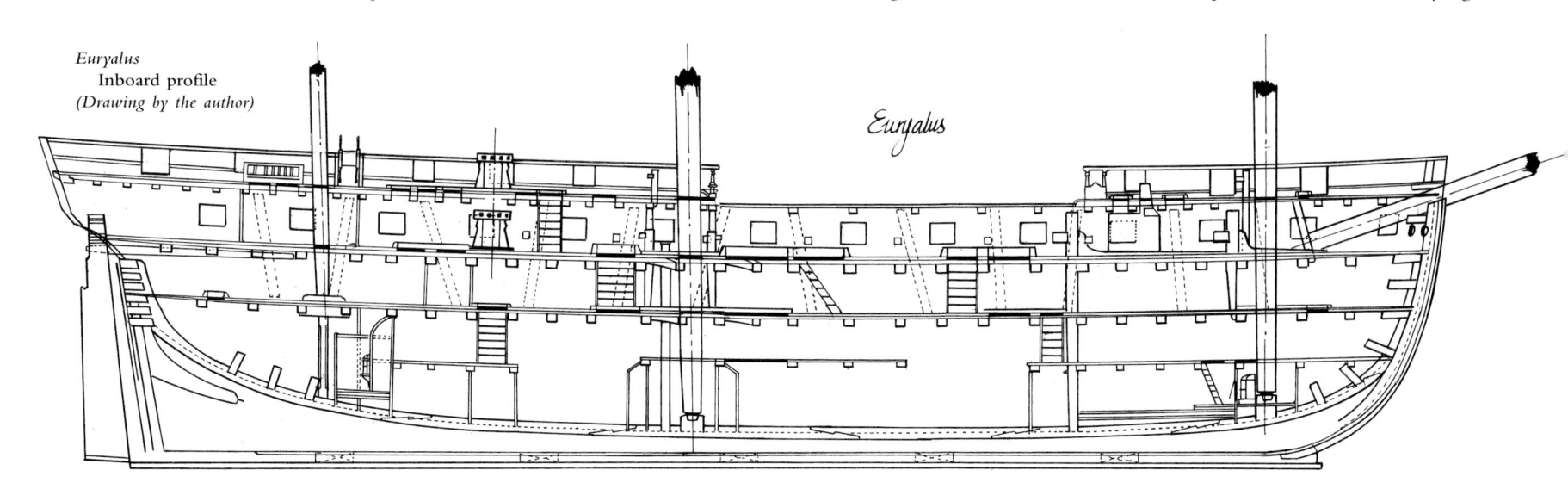

Euryalus
Inboard profile
(Drawing by the author)

would escort Napoleon to exile on the isle of Elba. *Euryalus*, however, remained at Marseilles to await further orders to sail for Gibraltar. In June *Euryalus* sailed from Gibraltar for Bermuda with a squadron commanded by Captain Andrew King escorting a convoy of transports carrying troops from Genoa.

Although the war with France had finished, the war with the American Congress continued, hence on 2 August *Euryalus* sailed from Bermuda with Vice-Admiral Cochrane's squadron for Chesapeake Bay, arriving to join Rear-Admiral Cockburns' ships waiting at the mouth of the River Potomac. Sailing on 17 August, *Euryalus*, in company with a squadron commanded by Captain James Gordon comprising *Seahorse* (38), bomb vessels *Ætna*, *Devastation* and *Meteor*, and rocket ship *Erebus*, sailed up the River Potomac. Having no pilots, progress was delayed as the ships had to negotiate the difficult part of the river known as Kettle-Bottoms with contrary winds. Moreover, while passing the flats of Maryland on the 25th the ships were beset by squalls. As *Euryalus* clewed up her sails to avoid the oncoming gusts of wind she sprung her bowsprit and the head of foremast and lost her three topmasts. Despite the damage, within twelve hours *Euryalus* was again under weigh, the squadron finally reaching Fort Washington on 27 August after running aground no less than 20 times. Anchoring, the three bomb vessels immediately began bombarding the fort and two batteries; within two hours marines and seamen landed from the squadron to complete the destruction.

Next day the town of Alexandria capitulated, the terms of surrender given by Captain Gordon witnessed by Midshipman John Fraser of *Euryalus*. All shipping lying there was seized and, under the responsibility of Lieutenant Herbert of *Euryalus*, the prizes were made ready for their journey downriver. On 31 August the brig-sloop *Fairy* (18) arrived bearing orders from Cochrane to retreat with news that the Americans had fortified the river banks downstream to oppose the British return. Captain Gordon ordered his squadron to sail but faced with contrary winds his ships, including *Euryalus*, had to warp themselves down river. Reaching the point where batteries had been set up, a boat from *Euryalus* mounted with a howitzer assisted by the guns of *Fairy* and *Meteor*, briefly repulsed the American attack, but undeterred they increased their battery to eleven guns and set up a furnace for heating shot. With wind improving on the 5 September *Euryalus* and *Seahorse* came to anchor within musket shot of the battery and firing their broadsides, silenced the enemy fire whereby the prizes passed down river unimpeded. In the action *Euryalus* suffered three men killed and ten wounded, the dead being William Fair and Edward Dobson, both Able Seamen, and Ordinary Seaman John Hogan. The wounded included Captain Napier, Quartermaster Patrick Powis, Able Seamen John Allen, James Burgoyne, John Jones, James Kelly, Lawrence Murray and William Scott and marines John Aldred and John Bourman.[47]

Shortly after *Euryalus* sailed with Cochrane's squadron to attack Baltimore and arriving off the entrance of the Patapsco on 13 September, the frigates and bomb ships commenced up the shallow river and landed troops. To support their attack and get closer to Fort Henry, *Euryalus*, together with *Severn* (50), *Havannah* (36), and *Hebrus* (36), each lightened ship to reduce their draught. Drawing less water, the bomb vessels closed and began bombarding Fort Henry and Fort Star, the frigates giving supportive fire. Meeting considerable resistance on land, the British troops retired next day, re-embarked into the ships and retreated downstream to rejoin Cochrane's main force. Shortly after this campaign *Euryalus* returned home to Spithead.[48]

1815: In May Napier embarked 400 seamen from *Prince* (98) into *Euryalus* and sailed for the Scheldt. Shortly afterwards, on 12 June, Captain Thomas Huskinson took command of the ship. Huskinson brought *Euryalus* home into Woolwich on 20 August and paid off the ship the following day.[49] Docked on 4 December for a 'small to middling repair', work progressed slowly and although her copper was completely removed that month it was another nine months before it was replaced.[50]

1816: Completing her refit at an unrecorded cost, *Euryalus* was undocked on 4 October and sailed for Chatham on 27 November. Reaching there two days later the ship was left at moorings for eighteen months.[51]

1818: Required for service in the West Indies, *Euryalus* was taken in hand during May and 'Fitted for Sea'.[52] Nearing completion, the ship was put back into commission by her previous commander, Captain Huskinson, on 27 July.[53] Sailing on 18 October, the ship would remain deployed on this station until recalled three years later.

1820: While in the West Indies Huskinson fell ill and was invalided out of the ship on 31 December.

1821: With Huskinson removed, it appears that command was temporarily undertaken by the ship's First Lieutenant until formally relieved by Captain J F Chapman on 18 April. Three days later Chapman was superseded by Captain William Bigland.[54] Recalled to England *Euryalus* arrived at Portsmouth 13 August where she was paid off on 28 August. Docked that same day *Euryalus* was taken in hand, refitted and launched again on 18 September.[55] On 22 October *Euryalus* was recommissioned under Captain A H Clifford.[56]

1822: Leaving Portsmouth 22 January *Euryalus* sailed for the Mediterranean where she remained on deployment until 1825.

1825: Recalled home, *Euryalus* arrived at Deptford on 30 April where Captain Clifford paid her off on 9 May.

FATE

On 27 July *Euryalus* was taken down the River Thames and taken into Chatham where, going into dock on 30 August, she was 'Fitted for Convicts'. She also had her 'Copper rep[d.] [repaired] & fixed Protectors'. What is meant by 'protectors' is uncertain, but it could relate to copper sheathing, possibly some form of sacrificial anodes were being employed to protect iron fittings from the effects of electrolysis. Alternatively protectors may have been baulks of timber fitted to protect the copper from vessels coming alongside. However, the fact that 'protectors' are intrinsically related to remarks about the copper suggests that the former interpretation appears more probable. Completed at an overall expense of £7,936, of which £2,221 covered labour costs, *Euryalus* was launched again on 10 November.[57] She was laid up in the River Medway fulfilling her new rôle as a gaol for criminals for the next 20 years. Moved from her moorings 21 November 1845, the ship was taken down to Sheerness to await her future. Docked at Sheerness 31 July 1846, *Euryalus* was 'Fitted for a Convict Ship for Gibraltar', during which time her copper was removed after which she was then felted, sheathed in timber and then coppered. The overall cost of this refit amounted to £11,104 of which, £6,781 was spent on her hull including labour, £768 for masts and yards and £3,855 for rigging and stores.[58] Coming out of the dock 20 October, she sailed for Gibraltar on 12 February 1847 where she fulfilled this rôle for the next 13 years. Renamed *Africa* in 1859, she was 'Sold at Gibraltar to Mr A C Recano 16 August 1860 for £337 6s 8d', her stores being sold off separately beforehand.[59]

The 36 gun ship PHŒBE

The 5th rate 36 gun frigate *Phœbe* that accompanied the fleet at Trafalgar was the first ship to carry this name in the Royal Navy. One of five vessels built to the lines of the *Phœbe* class introduced in 1794, her design in fact a lengthened variation of Hunt's *Perseverance* class of 1780. The other ships of the *Phœbe* class were *Caroline*, *Doris*, *Dryad* and *Fortune*.[60] In Greek mythology the name *Phœbe* (or *Phœb'us*) relates to Apollo and Artemis personified respectively as goddesses of the sun and moon.

Ordered 24 May 1794, *Phœbe's* keel was laid down at Dudman's yard in Deptford June 1794 and built under contract. Launched 24 September 1795, the cost for her hull was only £15,791 with a further £1,069 spent on her copper sheathing. The ship was then moved into Deptford dockyard for fitting out, complete with masts, yards, rigging and stores adding another £9,118 to her overall cost.[61] Her ordnance comprised twenty-six 18 pounders on the main deck, eight 9 pounders on the quarter deck, and two 9 pounders on the forecastle, giving her a single broadside weight of fire of 279 pounds. In May 1811 *Phœbe's* ordnance was increased to 44 guns, the additional guns comprising six 9 pounders, one 12 pounder carronade and one 18 pounder carronade which increased her maximum broadside weight to 351 pounds.[62]

CAPTAINS OF PHŒBE (MSS 248/4 and 248/6)

Name	Time of Entry	Time of Discharge	On What Occasion
Robert Barlow	15 November 1795	25 June 1801	Superseded
Thomas Barker	26 June 1801	27 May 1802	Superseded
James K Shepard	28 May 1802	12 September 1802	Superseded
Hon. Thomas B Capel	13 September 1802	31 December 1803	New Book
Hon. Thomas B Capel	1 January 1804	6 January 1806	Superseded
James Oswald	7 January 1806	7 November 1808	Superseded
Hasard Stackpoole	8 November 1808	25 July 1809	Dismissed by Sentence of a Court Martial
James Hillyer	29 July 1809	28 August 1815	Paid Off at Plymouth

SERVICE HISTORY

1795: *Phœbe* was first put into commission under Captain Robert Barlow at Deptford 15 November and sailed to join the Channel fleet on 23 December.[63]

1796: She was deployed with Captain Sir Edward Pellew's inshore squadron off Brest. When the French fleet under De Richery was seen approaching the port on 11 December, Pellew despatched *Phœbe* to Vice-Admiral Sir John Colpoys' squadron on their arrival while a second frigate, *Amazon* (36) carried the same news to England. Having returned on station *Phœbe* was again sent to Colpoys on 15 December, this time with word that the French were getting out to sea.[64] On 3 November she went into Plymouth to make good various defects, sailing again on the 19th.[65]

1797: Operating in the Western approaches, Cape Clear bearing NNW 20 leagues, *Phœbe* fell in with a French corvette and gave chase. After a pursuit lasting eight hours, *Phœbe* brought the corvette to into close action and forced her to surrender. The vessel proved to be *Atalante* of 16 guns and 112 men commanded by Lieutenant Dordeli. On inspection by the prize agents *Atalante* had a keel length of 80 feet and well coppered. On 20 December *Phœbe* was in action again, this time with the French *Néréide* (36) commanded by Captain Canon. The engagement commenced at 9 a.m. and during the ensuing chase *Néréide* began to fire astern on *Phœbe*, damaging her rigging and masts. After changing tack several times, the two ships converged towards each other and at a range of some 300 yards, the two ships fought a running battle for some 45 minutes until *Néréide* briefly ran aboard the *Phœbe*. Getting free, *Phœbe* resumed firing deadly broadsides which, at 10.45 a.m. obliged the very battered French ship to surrender. In the action *Phœbe* lost three men killed and ten wounded, *Néréide* having 20 dead and 55 wounded. Once repaired *Néréide* was entered into the Royal Navy under her own name, serving with *Phœbe* in 1810.[66]

1798: Having gone into Plymouth the previous October, *Phœbe* went into dock 1 February for one day to have her copper repaired and sailed on 5 March. This repair obviously proved unsatisfactory for the ship was again docked at Plymouth between 8 October and 8 November the same year to have her copper replaced. Work on her hull on this occasion amounted to £4,056 compared to £94 previously.[67]

1799: Further work to eradicate defects was carried out on the ship at Plymouth between 17 November and 29 December, costing £796.[68]

1800: Still operating in the Western Approaches, on 21 February *Phœbe* captured the French privateer *Bellegarde* of St Malo of 14 guns and 114 men. This vessel had, in the last 16 days, captured the *Chance* merchantman of London and the brig *Friends* of Dartmouth. Later, on 5 March *Phœbe* fell in with the French privateer *Heureux* (22) which, mistaking *Phœbe* for an Indiaman, fired upon her only to realise the error within musket shot range. Hurriedly wearing across *Phœbe's* bow and hauling to windward, *Heureux* fired at *Phœbe's* masts and rigging while attempting to make good her escape. Outgunned, *Heureux* soon succumbed to *Phœbe's* broadsides and struck her colours. In the action *Phœbe* lost three men killed and three wounded whereas *Heureux* suffered 18 killed and 25 wounded.[69] Following this action *Phœbe* returned to Plymouth 27 March to make good her defects

SPECIFICATIONS: PHŒBE

Rate	5th	*Date launched*	24 September 1795	*Ordnance - main deck*	26 x 18 pounders
Guns	36	*Length on the range of the gun deck*	142 ft 6 ins	*Ordnance - quarter deck*	8 x 9 pounders
Class	Phœbe 1794	*Length of keel for tonnage*	118 ft 10½ ins	*Ordnance - forecastle*	2 x 9 pounders
Designer	Lengthened variation of Hunt's *Perseverance* class of 1780	*Extreme breadth*	38 ft	*Single broadside weight*	279 pounds
		Depth in hold	13 ft 5 ins	*Fate*	1826 Hulked at Plymouth as a receiving ship then a slop ship
Builder	Dudman	*Tons burthen*	913 13/94		1841 Sold
Dockyard	Deptford	*Draught afore*	17 ft 9 ins		
Date ordered	24 May 1794	*Draught abaft*	19 ft 0 ins		
Date keel laid	June 1794	*Complement*	264		

Author's Note: In May 1811 the ordnance on *Phœbe* was increased to 44 guns. The additional guns comprised six 9 pounders, one 12 pounder and one 18 pounder carronades which increased her maximum broadside weight to 351 pounds. James, 5 p. 21, pp. 284–285.

Source: Lyon, *Sailing Navy List*, p. 123.

Part 1: The British Fleet

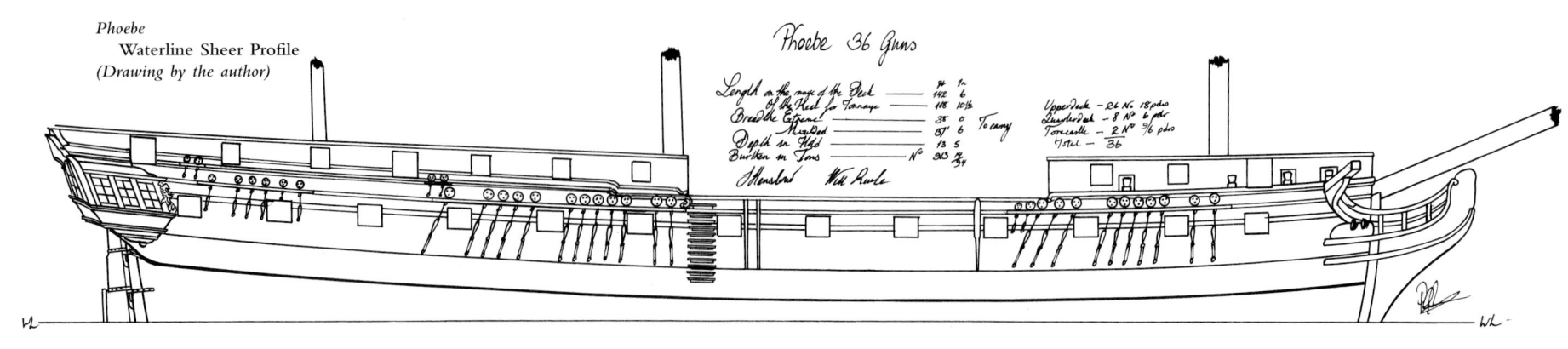

Phoebe
Waterline Sheer Profile
(Drawing by the author)

and put to sea again on 4 May.[70] Cruising some 650 miles WSW of Cape Clear on 11 May, *Phœbe* fell in with and captured another French privateer, the 16 gun *Grand Ferrailleur*, 16 days out of Bordeaux. Unlike the previous prize, this vessel had made no captures. In September *Phœbe* went into Plymouth for minor work.

1801: Deployed off the Iberian coast some six miles east of Gibraltar, at about 4 p.m. Thursday 19 February *Phœbe* sighted a French frigate off Ceuta, Morocco, steering eastward. After shadowing the vessel for two and a half hours, Captain Barlow brought the ship to close action within pistol-shot. A fierce engagement ensued, *Phœbe* ranged up on her adversary's quarter and maintained a steady raking fire inflicting high casualties and dismounting guns. After two hours *Phœbe*'s continuous broadsides reduced her opponent to a wreck. On capture the frigate proved to be *Africaine* of 44 guns comprising twenty-six 18 pounders and eighteen 9 pounders, flying the broad pendant of Commandant la Division Saunier. Commanded by Captain Magendie, who was later to fight at Trafalgar, the frigate had a crew of 315 officers and men and 400 troops under General Desfourneaux bound for Egypt. French casualties amounted to 200 killed and 143 wounded; among the former was the Commandant Saunier, the Chef de Brigade and two army captains, the latter group comprised Captain Magendie and General Desfourneaux.

The reason for such horrific slaughter was that the French troops, despite not being able to perform an active rôle in a naval ship, refused honourably to go below during the battle. Crowded upon the decks, they suffered much from shot and grape. Besides the carnage, *Africaine* was also on fire in several places, had over five feet of water in the hold and many guns were dismounted. Remarkably *Phœbe* had few casualties; seaman Samuel Hayes was killed, Mr Holland, First Lieutenant, Mr Griffiths, the ship's Master, and ten seamen were wounded. As to the ship, masts, sails and rigging were severely damaged so after making temporary repairs *Phœbe* made for Port Mahon with her prize. After considerable repairs *Africaine* was entered into the Royal Navy under her own name and remained in service until broken up in 1816.[71] In 1849 surviving members of *Phœbe*'s crew received naval medals. Returning to Plymouth 22 May, *Phœbe* went into dock on 3 June for one day to have her copper repaired at a cost of £1,103, with a further £1,554 spent on rigging and stores.[72] Sailing from the Hamoaze on 15 June, *Phœbe*'s command was taken by Captain Thomas Barker eleven days later.[73]

1802: Although war with France had ended, *Phœbe* remained operational with the Channel squadron and on 28 May Captain James Shepard assumed command of the ship. Entering Sheerness 3 June the ship was docked to repair her copper before returning to duty on 3 September. Ten days later Captain the Hon. Thomas B Capel took command of the ship.[74]

1803: When war with France resumed on 16 May, *Phœbe*, still under Capel's command, was sent to the Mediterranean to join Nelson's squadron blockading Toulon.[75]

1804: Cruising off Hyères with Nelson's squadron on 13 June, a signal was made to Nelson that two sail had been seen east of Porquerolles. *Phœbe* and *Amazon* (36), were sent in chase. By noon the next day the two frigates arrived off the Grand Passe and signalled that the vessels, which proved to be French frigates, had moored under Porquerolloes Fort. As *Phœbe* and her consort moved closer inshore, at 5.30 p.m. guns from the fort opened their fire upon them. Within 15 minutes both *Phœbe* and *Amazon* had cleared for action and anchored with springs, but seeing that the whole of the French fleet in the outer harbour of Toulon had were now standing out for sea, they weighed immediately and put to sea.[76]

1805: When Villeneuve left Toulon with his fleet on 19 March he evaded the British until sighted by *Phœbe* and *Active* two days later thirty miles south of Cape Cicié. After tracking Villeneuve's ships overnight, *Phœbe* made sail for the Gulf of Palma to inform Nelson. When Nelson sailed in pursuit of Villeneuve's fleet on 3 April, *Phœbe* with four frigates and two

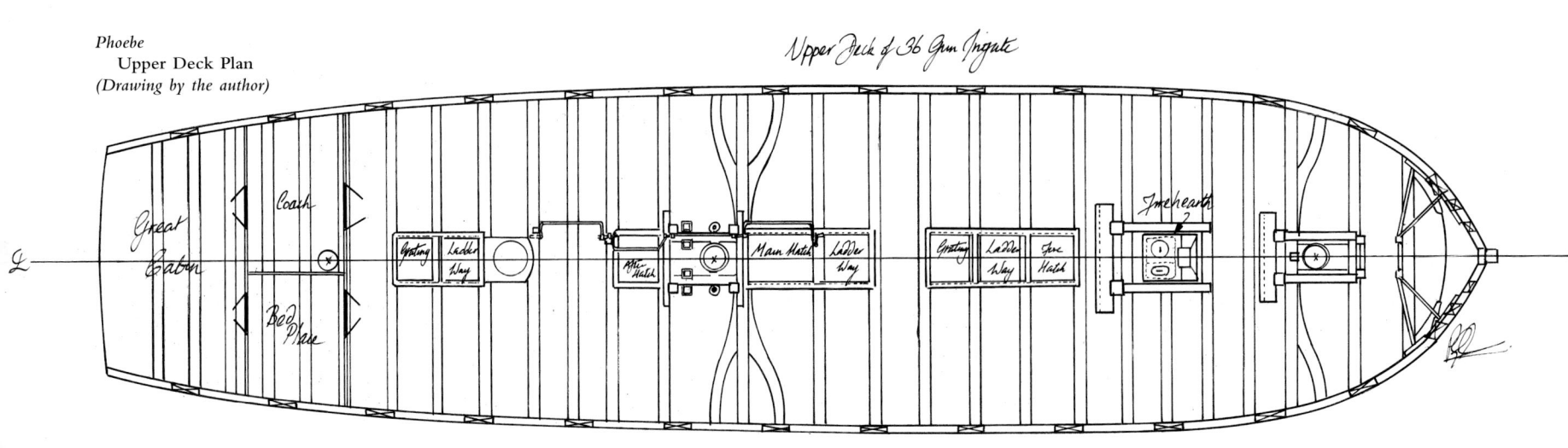

Phoebe
Upper Deck Plan
(Drawing by the author)

146

bomb vessels remained to protect Malta, Sicily, Sardinia and the route to Egypt, Captain Capel assuming overall command. Remaining on this station until late summer, *Phœbe* joined the squadron blockading Cadiz.[77]

TRAFALGAR

Like the other frigates deployed with Nelson's fleet, *Phœbe* played a more active rôle before and after the battle. During the days preceding the great fleet action *Phœbe* was deployed with the inshore squadron watching for movement of the combined fleet within Cadiz. Lieutenant Young's log on board *Phœbe* dated Monday 21 October records:

> PM Squally with rain Obs[d.] a Line of Battle Ship to windward with her Main Topmast gone at 5 saw the Enemy to Windward Consisting of 34 sail of the Line frigates & 2 Brigs at 6 Tack'd ship burnt several blue Lights & Rocketts AM D[o.] W[r.] spoke H M Ship *Mars* at 2 hove too at 2.30 filled at 4 wore ship at 5 saw the Enemy's fleet to Leeward at 6 wore Ship & made all sail Repeated several signals from the *Victory* at Noon the fleet nearly within gunshot of the Enemy's Fleet …[78]

Phœbe then took her station to windward of Nelson's line her log of 22 October revealing as follows:

> PM Light airs & Fine Weather at 5 minutes past 12 Obs[d.] the enemy senter [sic] commence Firing at the Van of our Fleets at 15 minutes past 12 came to the Wind on a larb[d.] Tack at 17 minutes past 12 the *Victory* began firing at 30 minutes past 12 the Action became general at 1-10 No 269 was made to the *Ajax* at 1.05 2 French Ships of the Line struck their Colours at 1.55 saw a French ship of the Line with her Main & Mizen Mast shot away at 2.18 Obs[d.] a Spanish Line of Battle Ship with English Colours over Spanish at 2.19 Obs[d.] the *Royal Sovereign* with her Main & Mizen Masts gone at 2.30 the Spanish Four Decker lost her mast at 3 saw another French Ship dismasted & on Fire at 5-4 Obs[d.] 11 of the Enemy's Ships of the line had bore up at 5-6 a Spanish Ship of the line struck to the *Minotaur* at Sun set saw 17 of the enemy's ship's of the line in possession of the English.

Next morning the log states: 'AM Fresh Breezes & squally at Day light saw front of the Fleets much scattered with the Prizes in Tow Employed all Night getting the Prize in Tow past 3 Hawsers & one hundred fathoms of Rope Prize in Tow Strong breezes & squally'.[79]

After the conflict weather rapidly deteriorated and by the night of 22 October it was blowing a heavy gale which proved extremely hazardous to the battle-torn ships of both fleets. The much damaged Spanish *San Juan Nepomuceno* (74), struggling in the rising seas, would have foundered had it not been for the exertions of *Phœbe* and *Donegal* (74) taking her in tow.[80]

While *Phœbe* had sustained no damage, next day Capel sent his carpenter into the prize for 'stopping shot holes', and on the Thursday 24 October recorded: 'Crossed Top gall[t.] Yards saw the remains of the Enemy Fleet standing towards us HMS *Thunderer* Cast off her Tow the Enemy's Fleets standing towards her Obs[d.] One of their Ships take the hulk in Tow…'.

After heaving to off San Sebastian, on the 25th Capel 'sent a boat on board the Prize for wounded Prisoners'. Suffering the effects of gales and squally weather, *Phœbe* was running under close reefed topsails with winds so strong that 'two of the main shrouds were carried away', but were soon deftly secured 'to the mast with the runners and tackles', moreover the 'small bower cable also parted'. Two days later *Phœbe* came to anchor off St Lucars.[81] *Phœbe* eventually returned to Portsmouth 19 December.

1806: On 7 January command of *Phœbe* was superseded by Captain James Oswald. Two days later the ship was taken into dock to be refitted and have her copper replaced. Undocked on the 6 February her materials costs amounted to £3,446 for her hull, £842 on masts and yards, and £3,317 for rigging and stores. Labour costs were £1,186, £69, and £3,377 respectively, bringing the grand total to £8,920.[82] *Phœbe* sailed 4 April to join the Channel fleet. Following reports in July that a French squadron comprising the *Revanche* (40), *Guerrière* (40), *Sirène* (36) and *Néarque* (16), commanded by Commodore Leduc, were attacking Swedish whaling ships. *Phœbe*, with *Blanche* (38) and *Thames* (32) were despatched to the Arctic. Although the *Blanche* captured *Guerriére* on 19 July, *Phœbe* and *Thames* went in search of *Revanche* and *Syrène* but failed to find them.[82] Returning to Plymouth *Phœbe* was docked on 1 August for four days to have her copper dressed, repaired and re-nailed, sailing again on the 19th.[84]

1808: Now deployed with the Channel fleet, *Phœbe*'s command was succeeded on 8 November by Captain Hasard Stackpoole.[85] In October the ship went into dock at Portsmouth to have her copper dressed and re-nailed for a second time which infers that the same work undertaken the previous year was not adequate.[86]

1809: When Captain Stackpoole was 'Dismissed by Sentence of a Court Martial' on 25 July command of the ship was succeeded four days later by Captain James Hillyar.[87] Why Stackpoole was dismissed is unclear at the time of writing.

1810: In January *Phœbe* was docked at Plymouth to have her copper repaired after which she remained within the port until docked again on 21 March to be completely re-coppered and undertake a 'small to Middling Repair' in preparation for foreign service. Fitted out at a total cost of £18,427, *Phœbe* sailed on 14 July for the Cape of Good Hope and deployment in the Indian Ocean.[88] In November Hillyar received orders to join

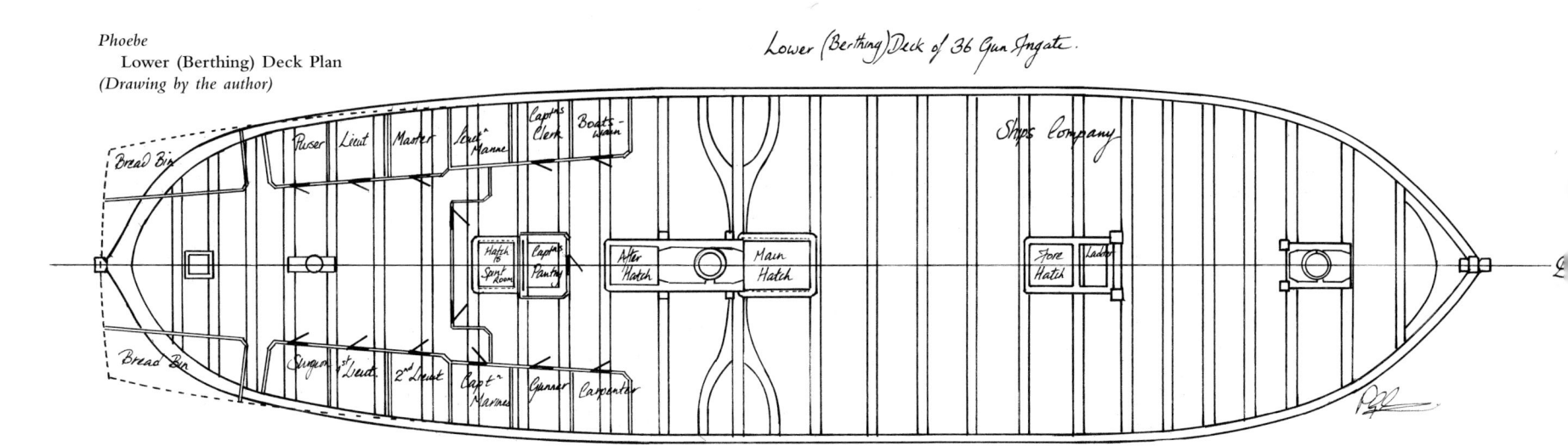

Phoebe
Lower (Berthing) Deck Plan
(Drawing by the author)

Vice Admiral Albemarle Bertie's squadron being assembled to undertake an expedition to attack Isle de France in Mauritius. Bertie, flying his flag in *Cornwallis* (44), was supported by *Illustrious* (74), the 38 gun frigates *Africaine, Boadicea, Clorinde, Menelaus, Néréide* and *Nisus;* the 36 gun frigates *Cornelia* and *Doris;* 32 gun frigates *Ceylon* and *Psyché;* sloops *Hecate* and *Hesper;* gun-brigs *Actæon, Emma* and *Staunch.* Also there were many transports carrying 10,000 troops, mainly grenadiers of the 12th, 33rd, 56th, and 59th Regiments commanded by Major-General Abercromby. This fleet, numbering about 70 vessels in all, including *Phœbe*, anchored in Grande Baie four leagues NE of Port Louis on 29 November. Although reefs along the coast provided poor anchorage the extensive survey undertaken by the navy resolved any problems. The troops were successfully landed and by 2 December Isle de France capitulated. Losses on the British side amounted to 28 killed, 94 wounded and 45 missing.[89]

1811: In May Hillyar decided to increase *Phœbe*'s armament from 36 to 44 guns by adding six 9 pounders and one 18 and one 12 pounder carronade as broadside guns. He also fitted four swivel guns aloft: one in her fore top, two in the main top, and one in the mizzen top.[90] Three years later this was to prove beneficial. Meanwhile, when Commodore François Roquebert sailed from Brest in *Renommeé* (40) on 2 February news had not yet reached France that Isle de France, his destination, had fallen. In convoy were the frigates *Clorinde* (40) and *Néréide* (40), all three vessels carrying munitions and 200 troops for Isle de France. Arriving off Isle de la Passe on 7 May, Roquebert became suspicious when the French flag flying over the fort was not accompanied by private signals and sent in three boats to investigate. Next morning five vessels appeared off the coast which, giving the secret signals, allayed Roquebert's suspicions. Unknown to Roquebert three of the five sail were British men-of-war, *Phœbe, Galatea* (36) and the brig-sloop *Racehorse* (18) which, following intelligence, had been deployed to cruise off Isle de France by Rear-Admiral Stopford to await the arrival of French ships. When only one boat returned, the others having been captured, did Roquebert learn of Isle de France's plight and hence ordered his ship to tack and stand to the east. *Phœbe* and her consorts followed in pursuit. Next day at 8 a.m. the French ships bore up and stood on towards the three British ships which counteracted by wearing to westward. The chase continued and on the 9 May when *Phœbe* was joined by *Astraea* (36) the three British frigates steered for Port Louis, anchoring there on the 12th and put to sea again two days later. The French squadron, in the meantime, stood on for Isle Bourbon and then on towards Madagascar. Finally at 3.50 p.m. on 20 May the two adversaries closed and within ten minutes the long awaited engagement ensued. *Phœbe*, following *Astraea*, opened fire as the three British frigates bore down in succession. Unfortunately the French had the wind and *Phœbe* like *Galatea* abreast of her, found her starboard quarter exposed to the guns of *Renommeé* and *Clorinde*. Backing her sails to support her consort, *Phœbe* continued to defend her starboard quarter and at 6.30 p.m. when the wind picked up, Hillyar manœuvred *Phœbe* into a position to rake *Néréide*'s stern. After 25 minutes *Phœbe*'s guns had silenced *Néréide* but with *Renommeé* and *Clorinde* bearing down to assist *Néréide*, *Phœbe* was obliged to haul off. Later that evening *Astraea* fought a hot engagement with *Renommeé* during which Commodore Roquebert was killed. After *Renommeé* struck her colours around 10 p.m., *Phœbe* and *Astraea* went in chase of *Clorinde*; however *Phœbe* lost her fore topmast around 2 a.m. on the 21st, compelling both ships to retire. In the action *Phœbe* lost seven killed and 24 wounded, among whom was Midshipman John Wilkie. For his efforts George Scott, *Phœbe*'s First Lieutenant, was promoted to commander.[92] In August *Phœbe* was deployed in the East Indies with Admiral Stopford's fleet, involved with operations against the Dutch in Java.[92] In September Stopford despatched *Phœbe, Nisus* and *Présidente* to receive the surrender of Cheribon.[93]

1812: Recalled home, *Phœbe* went into Plymouth 30 September and into dock on 8 October for two days to have her copper repaired and make

PROGRESS BOOK – *PHŒBE* 5th RATE OF 36 GUNS:

At what Port	Arrived	Docked	Coppered
River Thames; Dudman.	Began	June 1794	
Thames		30 Sep 1795	Coppered
Deptford	27 Oct 1795		
Plymouth	3 Nov 1796		
Plymouth	29 Dec 1797	1 Feb 1798	Copper Repaired
Plymouth	5 Oct 1798	8 Oct 1798	Copper taken off and Re-coppered Nov 1798
Plymouth	17 Nov 1799	Taken in Hand Nov and completed Dec 1799	
Plymouth	27 Mar 1800		
Plymouth	1 Sep 1800	13 Sep 1800	Defects Made Good 414 1,754 2,168
Plymouth	22 May 1801	3 June 1801	Copper Repaired
Sheerness	3 June 1802	17 June 1802	Copper Repaired
Portsmouth	19 Dec 1805	9 Jan 1806	Copper taken off and Re-coppered Jan 1806
Plymouth	25 July 1807	1 Aug 1807	Copper Dressed, Repaired and Re-nailed
Portsmouth	26 Oct 1808	2 Nov 1808	Copper Dressed, Repaired and Re-nailed
Plymouth	6 Jan 1810	12 Jan 1810	Copper Repaired
Plymouth		21 Mar 1810	Copper taken off and Re-coppered June 1810
Plymouth	23 Jan 1812	13 Feb 1812	Copper Repaired
Plymouth	30 Sep 1812	8 Oct 1812	Copper Repaired
Plymouth	25 Nov 1814	16 Dec 1814	Copper taken off and Re-coppered
Plymouth	14 Feb 1815		
Plymouth	15 Aug 1815	Copper taken off to Light Draft of Water Oct 1815	
Plymouth		Hove on the Graving Slip copper & turned off 2 May	
Plymouth		Taken in hand Jan 1823 Completed Oct 1826	
Plymouth		Defects from 1 April 1833 to 27 May 1841	
		Sold 27 May 1841 to Mr Joseph Custall £1750	

good any defects. Sailing again 3 November, *Phœbe* proceeded westward for her new deployment involved with the American War.

1814: Now operating on the Pacific side of South America, *Phœbe* searched for the USS *Essex*. In company with the ship-sloop *Cherub* (18) she arrived off Valparaiso on 8 February to find *Essex*, with her prizes *Essex-Junior* and *Hector*. Like the situation with the German pocket battleship *Graf Spee* during World War II 128 years later, Hillyar could not make any moves towards the American ships while they were lying in a neutral port. Next day Captain Porter of *Essex*, meaning to antagonise the British ships, hoisted a white flag bearing the motto 'Free Trade and Sailor's Rights'. Hillyar replied by hoisting a St George's flag with an equally pretentious motto, 'God and Country, British Sailors' Best Rights: Traitors Offend Both'. To this the crew of *Essex* manned their rigging and gave three cheers, *Phœbe*'s men replying the same. On the 12th Captain Porter hoisted another flag, this one reading, 'God, Our Country, and Liberty, Tyrants Offend Them'. When *Essex-Junior* was towed out of the harbour at 7 a.m. three days later *Phœbe* and *Cherub* weighed and put to sea after her. Unable to escape the American ship returned to the safety of the port and passed *Phœbe* within pistol shot before anchoring, this act further antagonizing the British ships. While *Phœbe* and *Cherub* continued to cruise off the harbour, *Essex* attempted to get to sea on the 23rd but returned. Two days later Porter had his prize *Hector* towed out of the port and set on fire, an act that also has parallel with the *Graf Spee* episode. At 6.45 p.m. on 27th *Essex* and *Essex-Junior* put to sea and stood towards *Phœbe*. Taking this as an offer to fight, Hillyar cleared for battle, backed his main topsail, hoisted his colours and waited. At 7.30 p.m. *Phœbe* weared to bring her starboard batteries to bear, at which point the two Americans hauled to onto a starboard tack, fired a single gun and

Source: ADM 180/9 Entry 565 & ADM 180/11 Entry 397

Launched or Undocked	Sailed	Built or Nature of Repair	Cost of Hull, Materials £	Workmen £	Cost of Masts & Yards Materials £	Workmen £	Cost of Rigging & Stores Materials £	Workmen £	Grand Total £
29 Sep 1795		Built	14,722 hull only						14,722
Oct 1795		Transported to Deptford	1,069 for coppering						
23 Dec 1795		Fitted	3,016			6,102		9,118	
19 Nov 1796		Defects Made Good	317			1,227		1,554	
2 Feb 1798	5 Mar 1798	Defects Made Good	94				1,343		1,443
8 Nov 1798	18 Dec 1798	Defects Made Good							
	29 Dec 1799	Defects Made Good	4,506				4,589		9,095
4 May 1800		Defects Made Good	166			630		796	
4 June 1801	15 June 1801	Fitted	1,103				1,554		2,657
2 July 1802	3 Sep 1802	Defects Made Good	1,143				1,549		2,691
6 Feb 1806	4 April 1806	Refitted	3,446	1,186	842	69	3.317	60	8,920
4 Aug 1807	19 Aug 1807	Defects	402	243	50	4	5,042	49	5,790
7 Nov 1808	1 Dec 1808	Refitted	433	347	712	18	1,354	31	2,895
18 Jan 1810		Defects							
13 June 1810	14 July 1810	Between a Small & Middling Repair & Fitted for Sea	10,327	4,061	558	67	3,322	92	18,427
18 Feb 1812	1 April 1812	Defects							
9 Oct 1812	3 Nov 1812	Defects	1,275	829	1,494	67	4,963	148	8,776
27 Dec 1814	29 Jan 1815	Defects							
21 Feb 1815		Defects	1,887	392	918	22	369	31	2,807
2 May 1817 repaired									
		Fitted for a Slop Ship	968	835					1,803
			22	213					235

returned to port again, frustrating Hillyar more than ever. After another abortive attempt by *Essex-Junior*, Porter finally quit the harbour in *Essex* on 3 March hoping to draw *Phœbe* and *Cherub* off, allowing *Essex-Junior* to escape. At 1 a.m. on the 28th Porter hoisted a blue light and fired rockets, enticing *Phœbe* and *Cherub* further away while he and his consort returned yet again to port. Porter's luck however began to fail for when the wind freshened that afternoon *Essex* parted her larboard cable and drifted, dragging her starboard anchor, seaward. Making sail *Essex* got under way and just as he rounded the westward point a heavy squall brought down the ship's main topmast, forcing Porter to anchor at 3.40 half a mile off shore east of Point Caleta. He then hoisted motto flags at the fore and mizzen head and American colours at the mizzen peek and shrouds. The British ships, not to be outdone, amply displayed motto flags, ensigns and union flags from their own spars before standing in to the American. Passing *Essex* at 4.10 *Phœbe* opened her fire into the American's stern, *Cherub* coming up doing likewise. Running three long 12 pounders out through her stern *Essex* gallantly defended herself. Running close inshore *Phœbe* and *Cherub* wore ship onto a starboard tack at 4.30. p.m. For *Phœbe* this manœuvre was hampered because a round shot coming to rest on her main course clew garnets prevented the sail from being reset, moreover her fore, main and mizzen stays were shot through, rendering her rig tender and her jib-boom splintered. Finally getting round ten minutes later Hillyar stood towards *Essex* and signalling that he intended to anchor informed Captain Tucker that he should keep *Cherub* under way. At 5.35 p.m. *Phœbe* closed with the American and firing her bow chase guns forced Porter to hoist his jib, cut his cable and get under weigh with his fore coarse and topsail. Running onshore all endeavours were made to remove any bullion into boats while English captives made their escape. Shortly after Porter reported that 'flames were bursting up each hatchway', and leaped from the ship. Porter's ruse about the flames created confusion and at 6.20 *Essex* struck her colours, *Phœbe*'s men taking possession. In all 31 American lost their lives and a further 16 were rescued from the sea, the remainder getting ashore safely. Beside damage to mast and rigging, *Phœbe* had received seven 32 pound round shot between wind and water and one 12 pound shot some three feet below. Of her 278 men and 22 boys only William Ingram, *Phœbe*'s, First Lieutenant, and three seamen were killed and four seamen and marines wounded. This was the last notable action in which *Phœbe* was involved, the ship being recalled at the end of the American War and decommissioned.[94]

1815-1826: After refitting at Plymouth for seven days *Phœbe* put to sea again on 21 February on her last patrol cruise, returning into Plymouth 15 August. Not required for further service, Hillyar paid her off on 28 August 1815.[95]

FATE

Now laid up in ordinary her copper was removed down to her light waterline in October 1815, then in 1817 *Phœbe* was put into a graving dock to repair her copper after which she returned to her moorings in the Hamoaze amid other redundant hulks. Taken in hand by the dockyard workforce in January 1823, *Phœbe* was 'Fitted for a Slop Ship', work being completed in October 1826. Initially employed as a receiving ship, *Phœbe* spent the best part of next 15 years serving as a slop (clothing) ship until 1841 when *Phœbe* was sold for £1750.[96]

The 36 gun ship SIRIUS

Named after the Dog Star, a brilliant white star in the constellation of Canis Major, *Sirius* was the second ship in the Royal Navy to bear the name. The previous vessel, originally named *Berwick*, was a storeship named of 22 guns purchased into the navy in November 1781. Converted into a 6th rate and renamed *Sirius* October 1786, she was wrecked on Norfolk Island on 15 March 1790.[97]

The Trafalgar *Sirius*, a 5th rate of 36 guns, was a one-off vessel built to the lines of the French *San Fiorenzo* captured in 1794. Ordered 30 April 1795, her keel was laid at Deptford in September 1795, her construction overseen by Dudman who had only just launched the *Phœbe*. Launched on 12 April 1797, *Sirius* mounted twenty-six 18 pounders on the main deck, six 9 pounders on the quarter deck, and two 9 pounders on her forecastle, *Sirius* delivered a single broadside weight of 270 pounds.[98]

SERVICE HISTORY

1797: Fitted for sea service, *Sirius* was first commissioned under Captain Richard King in June and deployed with the North Sea fleet under the orders of Admiral Lord Duncan.

1798: Operating off the Texel on 24 October, *Sirius* fell in with and gave chase to two Dutch ships and coming up upon one of them with musket shot range, fired a shot to windward to bring her to. While this vessel hauled down her colours her consort kept her course making more sail as she continued. Leaving her prize *Sirius* went on and after a running fight lasting half an hour the Dutchman, having lost eight men and 14 wounded, surrendered. Respectively the prizes proved to be the Dutch *Waakzaamheid* (24) and the French *Furie* (36) carrying some 290 French troops and 4,000 muskets, pistols and small arms. From her crew of 261 *Sirius* suffered one man wounded in the affray. Both prizes were entered into the Royal Navy, *Furie* as *Wilhemena*, *Waakzaamheid* under her own name. Later detached with the Channel fleet, *Sirius* captured *Favorie* (6) carrying camphor, cotton and indigo from Cayenne for Bordeaux and the Spanish brig from Corunna carrying iron and other commodities to Montevideo.

1801: Operating off the Portuguese coast on 28 January *Sirius* intercepted the French frigate *Dedaigneuse* (36) which, for the past two days, had been pursued by the 36 gun frigate *Oiseau* (formerly the French *Cleopatre* captured 19 January 1793). The action between *Sirius* and *Dedaigneuse* ensued for 45 minutes before the French ship surrendered. On capture *Dedaigneuse* was found to be carrying dispatches to Rochefort from Cayenne. Putting his First Lieutenant in command of the prize Captain King sent her into Plymouth where she was repaired and entered into the navy. Joining company with *Amethyst* the same day, *Sirius* assisted in the capture of *Charlotta* (16), a Spanish letter of marque out of Ferrol, about 20 miles off Cape Belem. Not all was glorious for *Sirius*, for on 2 September a court martial was convened aboard *Cambridge* (80) in the Hamoaze to try Lieutenant Lewis of the *Sirius* for leaving the quarter deck during the night watch when the ship was look-out frigate of the inshore squadron cruising off Brest. Found guilty, Lewis was dismissed the service. Three courts-martial were held in the *Cambridge* one week later, the first for *Sirius*'s master, the second for her gunner, each charged with drunkenness and neglect of duty, the master being dismissed from the ship, the gunner acquitted. Third on trial was Mr Rains, *Sirius*'s First Lieutenant who was charged with drunkenness and leaving his post during action, but the evidence being obscure, Rains was honorably discharged.

1802: When the war with France terminated most ships were decommissioned, *Sirius* however served a short time actively employed as the senior ship of a small squadron operating in the Channel against smugglers until she herself was paid off in August.

1803: Peace was short and *Sirius* was taken from her moorings in the Hamoaze and taken into the Barnpool on 31 July to be rigged and put into commission under the command of Captain William Prowse. Manned and victualled for four months she sailed from Plymouth on 15 August to cruise with the squadron lying off Brest.

1804: Returning to Plymouth on 28 February she disembarked Captain Wilkinson and survivors of *Hussar* (38) who had escaped in their cutter when their ship was wrecked early that month near the Saints in the Bay of Biscay and got on board one of the cruisers. For the remainder of the year *Sirius* cruised in the Channel.

1805: Returning to Plymouth, *Sirius* was docked 8 May for five days to have her 'Copper taken off and Coppered'.[99] Re-launched on 13 May *Sirius* sailed for duty on 3 June and joined the division of the Channel squadron cruising off Ushant and Penmarck and later took part in Vice-Admiral Sir Robert Calder's action against Villeneuve's combined fleet on 22 July. Because of the appalling mists that hampered this engagement, Calder ordered *Sirius*, with *Egyptienne* (40) to shadow the French ships and report their movements. After the battle *Sirius* took tow of the Spanish prize *Firme* (74).[100] In September *Sirius*, together with other cruisers *Naiad*, *Phœbe*, *Juno* and *Niger*, joined Collingwood off Cadiz operating as part of Blackwood's inshore squadron. At 4.30 Monday 14 October Captain Prowse records on his log that he went on board *Euryalus* to receive orders from Blackwood. Although the combined fleet was assembling in Cadiz, day to day routines in *Sirius* continued, Prowse stating on Thursday 17 October, '1.05 examined an imperial Brig from Vigo bound to Leghorn Squadron in C⁰⋯ made & shorten'd sail occasionally & Joined C⁰ HMS *Defiance*'. Next day; '*Naiad* & *Phœbe* ENE made & short.d sail occasionally Sound in 20 f^{ms} People work-

SPECIFICATIONS: *SIRIUS*

Rate	5th	Date launched	12 April 1797	Complement	274
Guns	36	Length on the range of the gun deck	148 ft 10 ins	Ordnance - main deck	26 x 18 pounders
Class	Sirius 1795	Length of keel for tonnage	124 ft 0¾ ins	Ordnance - quarter deck	6 x 9 pounders
Designer	Lines of French *San Fiorenzo* 1794	Extreme breadth	39 ft 7 ins	Ordnance - forecastle	2 x 9 pounders
Builder	Dudman	Depth in hold	13 ft 3 ins	Single broadside weight	270 pounds
Dockyard	Deptford	Tons burthen	1033 66/94	Fate	1810 Destroyed to avoid capture when grounded at Grand Port, Mauritius
Date ordered	30 April 1795	Draught afore	17 ft 10 ins		
Date keel laid	September 1795	Draught abaft	19 ft 0 ins		

Source: Lyon, *Sailing Navy List*, pp. 123-124.

Sirius
  Sheer Profile
  (Drawing by the author)

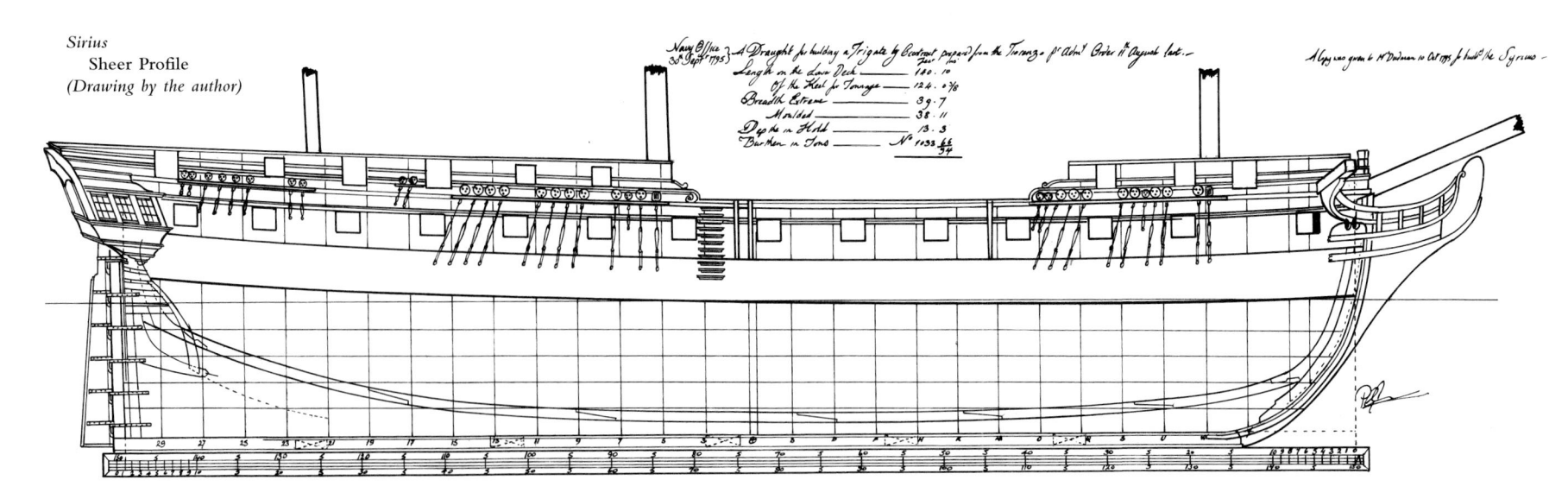

ing up junk'. The log also states that two seamen were punished with twelve lashes for drunkenness and neglect of duty. Carrying out surveillance Saturday 19 October the log states:

> 3.45 p.m. Obs^d the enemy continually making Signals on Shore 4.05 Obs^d part of the enemy's fleet under weigh and the rest with topsail & TG^t Yards hoisted up made the Sig^l N° 307 & ans^d 108 at 7 y^e *Phœbe* made all sail and fired Minute guns at 8 Light House NEbE 7 miles at 9 *Weazle* & *Pickle* parted C^o at wore Ship Captn went on B^d y^e *Euryalus* 10.30 Shorten'd sail & hove to At Noon 4 Sail of the Enemy's Line Anchored in the mouth of ye Harbour seven other under weigh one of which wore a Rear Adm^{ls} Flag.[101]

TRAFALGAR

As the combined fleet got ready to leave Cadiz, Prowse continued his log Sunday 20 October:

> Light airs from the WNW observed a french Rear Adm^l & sail of French Line of battle ships & 1 Spanish with 2 frigates outside of the Light House at 2 filled & made sail 2.30 tack'd ship ans^d Sig^l 108 from y^e *Euryalus* send for a Captain Tack^d Ship at 4 Obs^d 3 more ships of the Line come out of the harbour 4.20 Short^d sail hove to Captn went on b^d y^e *Euryalus* in C^o *Defence* & *Agamemnon* W?N *Naiad* & *Phœbe* WbS Enemy's Fleet ENE 4 Miles at 8 Obs^d ye Enemy's Ships to be on ye Larb^d Tack to the Northw^d of the Light House spoke y^e *Euryalus* 9.40 saw a Rocket sound^d occasion^{ly} from 28 to 34 f^{ms}. AM Light Airs & Hazy cadiz Light House NE 6 or 7 miles *Euryalus* NWbN made and Short^d sail occasion^{ly} reconnoitring the Enemy's fleet at 4 Mod. & Cloudy tack^d Ship *Euryalus* & *Naiad* in C^o wore ship & spoke y^e *Euryalus* at 6 9 sail of the Enemys ships standing out from the Light House made all sail in Chace of an American Ship NNW boarded Do. from Belfast bound to Gibraltar.

As Prowse's log shows it was at this point that *Sirius* and her consorts *Euryalus*, *Naiad* and *Phœbe* were driven off by the enemy observation squadron; moreover the American vessel being neutral was to suffer further harassment.[102] The log continues:

> ... wore Ship & made all sail being chaced [sic] by a Squadron of the Enemy 7.50 one of the Enemy's Squadron fired a broadside at us at 8 Fresh breezes & Squally 9.15 Obs^d the french Line of battle Ship that fired at us board the American Ship 9.40 made ye Sig^l N° 1 with 2 Guns & N° 11 East at 10 the Enemy's fleet tack^d Short^d sail & Wore Ship at 11 the Enemy's fleet EbN on the Larb^d Tack 11.30 fired 4 Minute guns 11.45 . D^o at Noon Strong breezes & Squally with Rain Centre of the Enemy's fleet NNE fire 4 Guns.[103]

Although *Sirius* was to play no key role in the ensuing battle Prowse's log provides a detailed insight into the events unfolding between the two fleets as they shadowed each other through the night beforehand, so much so that one can sense the tension rising as the hours pass. *Sirius*'s log Monday 21 October commences:

> Strong breezes & Squally with Rain 12.10 fired 4 Guns saw a Line of Battle Ship supposed to be the *Agamemnon* down Jib & Spanker heard the report of 4 Signal guns to windward at 1 it [the weather] cleared up saw ye Enemy's fleet NEbN 1.20 made sail 2.15 saw our Fleet from the North^d head SbE 2.25 bore up 3.15 came to the Wind on a Larboard Tack 3.30 Obs^d the Enemys fleet wear and come to the Wind on the Starb^d tack handed TG^t sails and wore ship the Enemys fleet NNE part of our Fleet in sight S^o 1 of the enemys Line of battle Ships and 2 Frigates chaced [sic] us at 5.50 they tacked bearing N?E 2? Miles [these ships formed part of Gravina's observation squadron] at 6 Fresh breezes & Hazy wore towards the Enemys fleets bearing NNE 6 or 7 miles our Fleet Sw^d continued burning blue lights and Rockets as did the *Phœbe Euryalus Naiad* and all our Look out Ships 7.15 wore and set the Courses Obs^d ye French Adm^l w up EbN 3 or 4 Miles 7.40 wore Enemys fleet from ESE to NE making Signals with Guns Rockets &c saw our Admiral SWbS 5 or 6 Miles 9.35 fired 3 guns and continued burning blue Lights & Rockets as before came to the Wind on ye Starb^d Tack heard the report of 6 guns from our Fleet at 10 set the Spanker and Mainsail still reconnoitring the Enemys fleet and making signals 11.30 wore & hove to a 4 Light Airs inclinable to calm Enemys fleet East 6 Miles and both fleets making Signals tried Soundings no bottom 4.45 wore Ships 5.10 up Mainsail and bore up to close with the enemy.

As the morning sun broke on Monday morning, Prowse continued his journals, stating:

> ... at Day Light Obs^d the Enemys fleet form the line of Battle on the Larb^d Tack consisting of 33 Sail of ye Line 5 Frigates and 2 Brigs our Fleet to wind^d of them about 5 L^{gs} 6.30 wore & hove to saw ye Land about Cape Trafalgar NE 7.45 *Vict^y* made our Sig^l for a captain at 8 our Captn went on b^d ye Adm^l wore & hove to Admiral SWbS 1 mile Centre of the enemys fleet EbE 4 Leagues forming the Line on the Larb^d Tack our fleet running down under all sail.[104]

Prowse, like the other frigate captains, went on board *Victory* for a final briefing from Nelson. From this point *Sirius* took up station to windward, running on a parallel course with the main body of the British fleet.

Tuesday 22 October:

> ... at 12 Centre of the Enemys fleet SEbE about 3½ Miles our fleet running down in two columns 12.5 a french Ship in the centre opend her fire on the *Royal sovereign* 12.20 she broke thro' the enemys Line and commenced firing from both sides offering herself ——— ——— [words illegible] to a Spanish Three

Decker at the same time the —— [illegible] began firing upon the *Victory* 12.35 she broke thro' the enemys line between the 14 & 15 Ship and commenced a heavy firing on a Ship astern of a Spanish four Decker hauling up for the said Spaniard and at 1 our Capt[n.] ret[d] from the *Victory* the Action became more general at 2 most of our Ships in hot action the abovementioned three Decker dismasted & surrendered 2.15 Obs[d] the four Deckers fore & Mizen Mast go over the Side and several other of the enemys Ship dismasted & struck 2.35 the Spanish four Decker with 5 other of the Enemys Ships taken possession of the whole of our Ships in Action and some boarding the Enemys Ships at the same time the enemys van of which had separated by Lord Nelsons breaking the Line wore wore [word repeated in log] to protect their Centre which being cut up in all directions but in so doing several of their sternmost Ships were dismasted and fell to out hand 2.40 Ans[d] Sig[l]. N[o.] 186 bore up to take a dismasted Ship in Tow 3.45 Fleets still Engaging and 1 of the Enemys Ships in our possession Obs[d] her to be on fire, sent Boats to let go the Anchors of several of the Enemys Ships that had struck 4.40 Tack[d] Ship sent boats to y[e] *Tonnant* she having lost her topmasts 5.10 Action ceased having 18 of the Enemys Line of Battle Ships in our possession including the four decker and a three decker (Spanish the remainder of y[e] Combined fleet of which at the commencement of the Action) consisted of 33 sail of y[e] Line 4 Frigates & 2 Brigs) to leeward of our Fleet bearing NE except 4 sail of the Line bearing SbW one on the Starb[d] Tack 5.15 PM Tack[d] Ship Cape Trafalgar EbS?S 5 Leagues Cape Spartel SbE 8 L[gs] 5.40 one of our Prizes after burning 2 hours blew up took y[e] *Téméraire* in Tow and made sail the *Victory Rl. Sovereign* and most of our Fleet dismasted 6.30 sent 2 Boats to take possession of the *swiftsure* French Ship 7.40 sounded in 27 f[ms.] at 8 in 14 f[ms] sent Boats to inform 3 Ships to leeward of the Shoalsness of y[e] Water at 9 a–pened our Water to 45 f[ms] spoke the *defiance* 11.20 boats ret[d] made & short[d] Sail occasionally *Téméraire* in Tow at 1 AM saw a blue Light NNW 1.15 wore Ship at 4 Moderate & Cloudy *Téméraire* in Tow at 6 Fresh breezes and Cloudy Cape Spartel SbE?E 8 Leagues —— 47 sail in C[o] disabled ships and prizes in tow by part of the fleet 9.30 struck the royal Yards & Masts ans[d]. y[e] Sig[l]. N[o.] 108 at 10 bore up at 11 in 2[d] refs of the Topsails and haul[d] off on y[e] Larb[d] Tack 11.40 up foresail and back[d] the Mizen topsail at Noon Strong breezes & Squally with rain *Victory* NE 2 Mile Fleet in C[o] *Téméraire* in Tow.[105]

Next day mention is made that of two prizes found adrift one was taken in tow as the weather deteriorated to strong gales, *Sirius*'s log also states that 'at 9.45 sent our Carpenter and part of his crew on b[d]. y[e] *Téméraire*' to assist with leak stopping caused by shot holes. Moreover on Thursday 24 October Prowse records in the log that after sending his boats to both the '*Prince* which had the Spanish four Decker in tow', and *Achille* who had a Prize in tow a little after 4 p.m. 'a squadron of y[e] Enemy EbS consisting of 5 Sail of y[e] Line 3 frigates & a Brig Obs[d] them retake a Spanish three Decker which the *Thunderer* was obliged to cast off being chaced by them'. Realising that this squadron probably comprised fresh ships from Cadiz which presented some threat to the British fleet and their prizes, as Prowse records at 5.15 p.m., they took measures to retaliate: '8 or 9 of our Line of Battle ships with the *Euryalus* formed in Line of Battle edging towards the Enemy bore up & set the Studding sails steering towards 2 Ships of the Line 1 Frigate and 2 Prizes separated from our Fleet'. Later the day *Sirius* communicated with *Orion* with her prize in tow and by noon the weather had turned to 'Strong Gales with Lightning'.[106] In December we find *Sirius* deployed with *Polyphemus* (64) escorting a convoy from Gibraltar.[107]

1806: Now deployed in the Mediterranean, on the afternoon of 17 April, Captain Prowse sighted a French squadron while *Sirius* was cruising 20 miles east of Civita Vecchia. The French ships, comprising the sloop *Bergère*, brigs *Abeille*, *Légère*, and *Janus*, one bomb vessel, five gunboats and a cutter, were standing towards Gaeta to attack the Neapolitan frigate *Minerve*. Making sail *Sirius* immediately went in pursuit and at sunset found the flotilla lying six miles off the mouth of the Tiber near dangerous shoals. Running in at 7 p.m. *Sirius* and her consorts opened fire upon the French ships within pistol shot, the ensuing engagement lasting two hours before *Bergère*, having sustained considerable damage and casualties, finally surrendered. The other craft, drawing less water, got inshore to safety beyond the shoals. *Bergère*, armed with eighteen long 12-pounders and 189 men and captained by Commander Chauney Duolvis, was entered into the navy under the same name and remained in service until broken up in October 1811. During the action *Sirius* suffered considerable damage and casualties; those killed comprised William Adair, Master's Mate, five seamen and three marines with another seaman dying of his wounds later; among the 20 wounded were James Brett, the ship's Acting Master; Mr Meyricke, Midshipman; and John Robinson, Master's Mate.[108]

1807: Throughout this year *Sirius* continued to operate in the Mediterranean until recalled to refit.

1808: Arriving at Sheerness on 11 April *Sirius* spent the next week disembarking powder, guns, and other stores. Having completed this the ship sailed for Chatham on 20 April, arriving the same day. After de-rigging and having her masts removed *Sirius* went into dock on 28 April to begin her 'Small & Middling Repair', the costs of which are not recorded. Re-coppered, the ship was undocked on 4 October and placed back in commission under Captain Samuel Pym.[109]

1809: *Sirius* was now deployed in the East Indies where French cruisers and privateers operating out of St Paul's on the island of Bourbon (Réunion) repeatedly attacked British merchant shipping in the Indian Ocean. Plans were made to attack the island, therefore 386 troops, commanded by Lieutenant-Colonel Henry Keating, were embarked from the island of Rodriguez into the frigate *Néréide* (36), sloop *Otter* (18), and the HEIC's schooner *Wasp* on 16 September. These vessels were joined by *Sirius*, *Raisonnable* (64) and *Boadicea* (38) off Mauritius. The attack was made on 21 September. Covered by gunfire from *Sirius* and her consorts, the troops plus 136 royal marines and 100 seamen were landed near Pointe du Galet at 5 a.m. After marching seven miles to St Paul's the troops soon occupied the batteries of Lambousière and La Centière overlooking the harbour and trained the guns on shipping in the harbour. After taking possession of the battery of La Neuf, the two remaining forts fell shortly afterwards and by 8.30 a.m. the entire town, including magazines, eight field guns and 117 different calibre guns were in British hands and destroyed. With the guns

PROGRESS BOOK – *SIRIUS* 5th RATE OF 36 GUNS: Source: ADM 180/11 Entry 391

At what Port	Arrived	Docked	Coppered	Launched or Undocked	Sailed	Built or Nature of Repair	Cost of Hull, Masts & Yards Materials £ s d	Cost of Rigging & Stores Materials £ s d	Grand Total
Plymouth	May 1805	8 May 1805	Copper taken off and Coppered May 1805	13 May 1805	3 June 1805	Defects			
Sheerness	11 April 1808			20 April 1808					
Chatham	10 April 1808	28 April 1808	Copper taken off May Re-coppered October 1808	4 October 1808	10 Jan 1810	Small & Middling Repair			
			Lost in 1810						

Authors Note: No expenses are listed in the original document.

silenced the three British men-o-war stood into the harbour and *Sirius*, anchoring within 80 feet of the French frigate *Caroline*, began to beat the ship into submission with her heavy broadsides. *Caroline* struck her colours after 20 minutes of this punishment. The captive vessels comprising the brig of war *Grappler*, and the two East Indiamen *Europe* and *Streatham* were retaken and brought off. Afterward *Sirius* resumed her patrols off Isle de France (Mauritius).[110]

1810: Following the previous attack on Isle de Bourbon (Réunion), preparations were now made to capture the island fully. *Sirius* was cruising off Mauritius with *Iphigenia* (38) and *Magicienne* (32), Captain Pym in overall commander of the flotilla. These ships received orders to rendezvous off the island with *Boadicea* (38), *Néréide* (36) and several transports on 6 July. Distributed between the ships and transports were 3,650 troops which, again under the overall command of Lieutenant Keating, were landed next day from different points. As ordered *Sirius* hoisted a flag of truce and anchored in St Paul's Bay where she was fired upon instantly from the shore batteries. Captain Pym noticed a French brig making preparations to sail so at 11 p.m. he sent in his barge under the command of Lieutenant George Norman to cut out the vessel. Unfortunately the brig had sailed two hours earlier but not wishing to lose the opportunity of a prize Norman's crew rowed for twelve hours after her and catching up with the brig boarded her. After a fierce skirmish they took possession. The brig proved to be the privateer *Edward* of four 12 pounders and 30 men taking dispatches to France.[111]

Having captured Bourbon it was decided to attack the Isle de la Passe lying at the entrance to Port Sud-est, Mauritius. *Sirius* was joined by *Iphigenia*, *Néréide* and the gun-brig *Staunch* (12) and boats from the three frigates, carrying 400 men, began their attack on 10 August. The assault however had to be aborted, as due to very poor weather, any attempt to deceive the French was lost so the squadron made sail and cruised to the other side of the island. On 12 August *Sirius* and *Iphigenia* returned to make a second attack, Captain Pym sending in five boats, three from *Sirius* and two from the *Iphigenia* with 70 officers and men under the command of Lieutenant Norman. Other officers were lieutenants Henry Chads and John Watling. Making for the shore Chads became separated and landed unopposed. The other four boats got past the first two gun batteries but as the sky cleared, were spotted and fired upon by the third battery, several men being wounded. On landing Lieutenants Norman and Watling and their men were beaten back as they tried to scale the fortifications, Norman being shot clear through his heart. Watling's second attempt succeeded and he was soon joined by Lieutenant Chads and his men. *Sirius*'s casualties comprised five killed and twelve wounded, with the loss of Lieutenant Norman. For their endeavours both Chads and Watling were commended, Watling being promoted First Lieutenant in *Sirius*. Captain Pym's letter to Vice-Admiral Bertie via Commodore Rowley stated:

I had the honour to transmit to you, on 31st of August Captain Pym's report of a gallant and successful attack by his boats on the Isle de la Passe, and beg to second his recommendation of these two Lieutenants: and consequently, in our humble view, Lieutenant Chads took command after the death of Lieutenant Norman.

Pym wrote:

'I do further certify, that the conduct of the said Lieutenant Watling in the attack on Isle de la Passe, under Lieutenant Norman of the *Sirius*, was truly gallant, and that after the latter was killed, by his (Lieutenants W's) side in the moment of victory, he took command.

One week later two boats from *Sirius* commanded by Lieutenant Watling and Midshipman John Andrews with eleven seamen went in at night and under the shore batteries cut out the British East Indiaman *Wyndham* of 26 guns recently taken by two French frigates. Arriving alongside the Indiaman it was discovered that no arms had been placed in the boat therefore using the boat stretchers as clubs, Watling's seamen carried out the attack with alacrity. Having secured *Wyndham* they had to bring the ship out under fire from the batteries.[112]

FATE

Having captured the Ile de Bourbon (Réunion) on 13 August, *Néréide* (36), Captain Willoughby, proceeded to attack Grand Port, Mauritius. While landing troops on the 20th the assault was jeopardised by the arrival of a French squadron comprising *Bellone* (40), *Minerve* (40), *Victor* (18) *Ceylon* (18) and two East Indiamen prizes. On 22nd Willoughby signalled to the remainder of the squadron, *Sirius*, *Magicienne* (32) and *Iphigenia* (36), for assistance. Leading the attack that afternoon *Sirius* ran aground as she entered the harbour but managed to get free, only to run onto a shoal again at 5 p.m. and stuck fast when *Magicienne*, steering clear of *Sirius*, likewise ran aground. Just a mile away *Néréide* was now totally unsupported as *Iphigenia was* prevented from joining her because of shoals. The French were therefore able to devote all their effort against *Néréide* which came under sustained heavy fire from *Bellone* and was obliged to surrender after losing 230 killed and wounded out of 281. On board *Sirius* Pym made every effort using the kedge anchor to get her free but to no avail. Next morning a tow was passed to *Iphigenia* but this too failed. The ship was now making water so Pym ordered all stores, provisions and men to transfer into *Iphigenia*. Since *Sirius* and *Magicienne* could not be moved both were set on fire on 25 August to avoid capture, *Sirius* exploding at about 11 am. *Iphigenia*, the only vessel to survive, low in powder, shot, and supplies, and burdened with men removed from *Magicienne* and *Sirius*, was forced to surrender to a squadron of three French 40 gun frigates on 28 August.[113]

❧ NOTES TO PART 1: CHAPTER 5 ❧

[1] TNA: PRO, ADM 180/9 Entry 576.
[2] Ibid.
[3] RNM, MS 248/4.
[4] Clowes, 4, p. 510.
[5] Clowes, 4, pp. 516, 556.
[6] TNA: PRO, ADM 180/9 Entry 576.
[7] Clowes, 4, pp. 525–526, 560.
[8] RNM, MS 248/4.
[9] TNA: PRO, ADM 180/9 Entry 576; RNM, MS 248/4.
[10] TNA: PRO, ADM 180/9 Entry 576; RNM, MS 248/4.
[11] RNM, MS 248/4.
[12] TNA: PRO, ADM 180/9 Entry 576.
[13] Clowes, 5, p. 316.
[14] Clowes, 5, p. 320.
[15] TNA: PRO, ADM 180/10 Entry 321.
[16] TNA: PRO, ADM 51/1518 part 5.
[17] Ibid.
[18] TNA: PRO, ADM 180/10 Entry 321.
[19] Ibid.
[20] James, 5, pp. 337–339; Clowes, 5, p. 993.
[21] RNM, MS 248/6.
[22] TNA: PRO, ADM 180/10 entry 321.
[23] TNA: PRO, ADM 180/10 entry 321.
[24] TNA: PRO, ADM 180/10 entry 321.
[25] James, 6, p. 395.
[26] RNM, MS 248/6.
[27] TNA: PRO, ADM 180/10 entry 321.
[28] Graves, *Greek Myths*, p. 224.
[29] Pope, *England Expects*, pp. 135–137.
[30] Schom, *Trafalgar*, p. 286.
[31] Schom, *Trafalgar*, p. 295.
[32] Schom, *Trafalgar*, p. 312; Clowes, 5, pp. 127–132.
[33] TNA: PRO, ADM 51
[34] Southey, *The life etc. Lord Nelson*, p. 211; Pope, *England Expects*, p. 239.
[35] TNA: PRO, ADM 51
[36] Clowes, 5, p. 161.
[37] TNA: PRO, ADM 180/11 Entry 386.
[38] Clowes, 5, p. 565.
[39] TNA: PRO, ADM 180/11 Entry 386.
[40] Clowes, 5, p. 559.
[41] TNA: PRO, ADM 180/11 Entry 386.
[42] TNA: PRO, ADM 180/11 Entry 386.
[43] Clowes, 5, p. 289.
[44] RNM, MS 248/6.
[45] Clowes, 5, p. 527; James, 6, p. 168; *Naval Chronicle*, 30, p. 77.
[46] Clowes, 5, p. 561.

47 James, 6, pp. 312–315.
48 James, 6, pp. 320–321.
49 RNM, MS 248/6.
50 TNA: PRO, ADM 180/11 Entry 386.
51 Ibid.
52 Ibid.
53 RNM, MS 248/6.
54 Ibid.
55 TNA: PRO, ADM 180/11 Entry 386.
56 RNM, MS 248/6.
57 TNA: PRO, ADM 180/11 Entry 386.
58 Ibid.
59 Ibid.
60 Lyon, Sailing Navy List, p. 123.
61 TNA: PRO, ADM 180/9 Entry 565.
62 James, 5, pp. 21, 284–285.
63 TNA: PRO, ADM 180/9 Entry 565; RNM, MS 248/4.
64 Clowes, 4, pp. 229–300.
65 TNA: PRO, ADM 180/9 Entry 565.
66 Clowes, 4, p. 508.
67 TNA: PRO, ADM 180/9 Entry 565.
68 TNA: PRO, ADM 180/9 Entry 565.
69 James, 3, p. 33–34.
70 TNA: PRO, ADM 180/9 Entry 565.
71 Colledge, 1, p. 27.
72 TNA: PRO, ADM 180/9 Entry 565.
73 RNM, MS 248/4.
74 Ibid.
75 Clowes, 5, p. 54.
76 Clowes, 5, p. 74.
77 Clowes, 5, p. 97–98.
78 TNA: PRO, ADM 51/1531 part 4.
79 Ibid.
80 Clowes, 5, p. 128–132.
81 TNA: PRO, ADM 51/1531 part 4.
82 TNA: PRO, ADM 180/11 Entry 397.
83 Gardiner, The Victory of Seapower, pp. 35–36.
84 TNA: PRO, ADM 180/11 Entry 397.
85 RNM, MS 248/6.
86 TNA: PRO, ADM 180/11 Entry 397.
87 RNM, MS 248/6.
88 TNA: PRO, ADM 180/11 Entry 397.
89 James, 5, p. 325–326; Gardiner, The Victory of Seapower, p. 96–97; Clowes, 5, p. 294.
90 James, 5, pp. 21, 284–285.
91 James, 6, pp. 15–26; Clowes, 5, p. 486; Gardiner, The Victory of Seapower, p. 98–99.
92 Gardiner, p. 108; James, 6, pp. 33–39; Clowes, 5, p. 298.
93 Clowes, 5, pp. 302, 560, 567.
94 James, 6, p. 285–289.
95 RNM, MS 248/6.
96 TNA: PRO, ADM 180/11 Entry 397.
97 Colledge, p. 74.
98 Lyon, pp. 123–124.
99 TNA: PRO, ADM 180/11 Entry 391.
100 Clowes, 5, pp. 112–116.
101 TNA: PRO, ADM 51/1595.
102 Clowes, 5, p. 132.
103 TNA: PRO, ADM 51/1595.
104 Ibid.
105 Ibid.
106 Ibid.
107 Clowes, 5, p. 186.
108 Clowes, 5, p. 379.
109 TNA: PRO, ADM 180/11 Entry 391; RNM, MS 248/6.
110 James, 5, pp. 197–198; Clowes, 5, pp. 444–445.
111 James, 5, pp. 271–272; Clowes, 5, pp. 457–458.
112 James, 5, pp. 274–276; Clowes, 5, pp. 457–458.
113 James, 5, pp. 281–296.

PART 1: CHAPTER 6
THE OTHER BRITISH SHIPS

The Armed Schooner *PICKLE*

As the second vessel to be named *Pickle* in the Royal Navy the origins of this schooner present at Trafalgar are somewhat confusing. The first *Pickle* listed was a 6 gun vessel employed as tender to Admiral Lord Seymour's flagship *Sans Pareil* (80) stationed in the West Indies. Initially named *Sting* this vessel was purchased by Seymour at Curacao after the capture of this island in October 1800. Although it is recorded that she was purchased for the sum of £2,500 in December that year details regarding her origin are omitted from the correspondence dated 21 December 1800 and 31 January 1801.[1] It is quite possible that *Sting* was built in Bermuda as a mercantile schooner but there is no hard evidence to support this, only that such fast vessels were commonly used in the West Indies and the Eastern American seaboard. When Seymour died in 1801 this vessel deployed as a tender to his flagship and brought his body from the West Indies to Portsmouth but whether this is the vessel that was later renamed *Pickle* remains obscure.[2] An alternative origin is that another vessel, originally named *Sting*, was a 'West Country' vessel built at Plymouth, Cornwall, possibly by Pope & Burns. Consequently there is reason to surmise that the schooner rig, generally American in its origin, had already become well adopted by West Country trading companies by the latter part of the eighteenth century. Purchased and renamed *Pickle*, her presence in the navy at Plymouth dates from 7 July 1802 when entries begin in *Pickle*'s Progress Book. Remaining in Plymouth until sailing on 6 August, *Pickle* is listed as being 'Made Good' a common occurrence after a purchase. Unfortunately as no costs are entered within the Progress Book we cannot ascertain the extent of the work undertaken. However as *Pickle* was not taken into dock it is inferred that she was 'made good' fit for naval service, in other words she was modified to carry guns and have a magazine installed.[3] Classified as an armed schooner or armed tender, she carried, according to Lyon, six 12 or 18 pounder carronades on her main deck giving her single broadside of either 36 or 54 pounds.[4] The model of *Pickle* researched and made by Rear-Admiral C M Blackman in 1968 and displayed in the Royal Naval Museum, Portsmouth, however, shows the ship mounting ten rather than eight carronades, this number being more appropriate as the vessel, apart from her rig, very much corresponds to armed cutters of similar proportions.

CAPTAINS OF *PICKLE* (MSS 248/4 and 248/6)

Name	Time of Entry	Time of Discharge	On What Occasion
Pellatier	1802	30 March 1803	Superseded
John Richard Lapenotière	31 March 1803	2 December 1805	Superseded
Daniel Callaway	3 December 1805	13 April 1807	Superseded
Moses Cannadey	14 April 1807		Ship Lost

SPECIFICATIONS: *PICKLE*

Rate	Schooner/Armed Tender	Date keel laid	Unknown	Draught afore	9 ft Approx
Guns	8	Date launched	Unknown	Draught abaft	11 ft Approx
Class	*Sting* (Mercantile)	Length on the range of the gun deck	73 ft	Complement	30 – 35
Designer	? West Country	Length of keel for tonnage	56 ft 3¾ ins	Ordnance - main deck	8 x 12 pounder carronades
Builder	Unknown	Extreme breadth	20 ft 7 ½ ins	Single broadside weight	48 pounds
Dockyard	Devon/Cornwall?	Depth in hold	9 ft 6 ins	Fate	1802 Renamed *Pickle*
Date ordered	Purchased 1800	Tons burthen	127.		27 July 1808 Wrecked off Cadiz

Source: Lyon, *Sailing Navy List*, p. 255.

SERVICE HISTORY

1802: When *Sting* was bought into the navy in 1802 she was renamed *Pickle* and placed in commission as a dispatch vessel at Plymouth under the command of Lieutenant Pellatier. With his crew Pellatier sailed from Plymouth on 6 August, possibly for sea trials and to hone his crew into shape as the vessel was of unfamiliar rig to the Royal Navy, and returned to Plymouth on 24 September. After taking in stores and provisions *Pickle* sailed again on 12 October for Malta as ordered with dispatches and left the island in late December for home.

1803: After a six week voyage *Pickle* returned into Plymouth on 16 February, the last leg of her journey from Gibraltar taking only 14 days. Taking this distance into account and excluding tacking, *Pickle*'s speed averaged 6 knots. According to the progress book *Pickle* reached Plymouth on 7 February.[5] First going on shore to report to Admiral Dacres, Pellatier hired a post-chaise and four and set off to the Admiralty at Whitehall with his dispatches. *Pickle* in the meantime, was quarantined in Coney Cove, Stonehouse Pool, Plymouth.

1803: Undergoing a refit at Plymouth under management of the Master Shipwright Joseph Tucker the following works were undertaken to *Pickle* between the dates 15 March and 27 April, the entire costs for labour amounting to £139 5s 9d. During this refit the ship was taken into dock on 22 March for one day only to have her copper taken off and replaced. The details of *Pickle*'s entire refit are as follows:

> **Hold:** - trimd & bolted a piece of apron, bored for & drove 14 bolts in the keelson & crutches, cut & set up 6 well stantions, trimd & fastend 5 pallating beams, flat 50 feet, bulkheads to well & coalhole 118 feet, & shifted jambs round the foremast. - **Platform:** - fitted & bolted 2 Iron breasthooks; trimd & fastend one beam, shifted platform 46 feet, bulkhead to storeroom 181 feet & unhung & rehung 2 doors made one scuttle lid, repaired 2 hatches & fitted & fastend lead copper & tin in the galley; **Upperdeck:** - got in place bored off & bolted 14 iron hanging knees, trimd & bolted 6 carronade chocks & one lodging knee; shifted the hawse pieces; drove out & redrove 22 ring bolts; split down a knee, unbolted trimd over & rebolted a crosspiece to the bolts, & 3 ranges - took off refitted & fastened birthing 104 feet, trimd & let down 14 port sills, made milds for & fitted 7 and refitted 34 hammock stantions, trimd & fitted short timbers, hammock boards 127 feet & a wood lock for the rother; cleard & took off plansheer & trimd & bolted 6 arch pieces over the ports, built a case to the rother, repaired the roundhouse; refitted hammock boards 24 feet & fitted & fastend lead on the flat 32 feet - made 6 half ports; one cap scuttle & one ladder; repaired 13 scuttle lids & 2 ladders - **Withoutboard:** Grounded & lifted the schooner in the mast pond; took off the copper & dubd the bottom, split out 7 blocks, shifted staples & copperd the false keel, bolted & leaded the gripe, punched up & plugd 3112 nails & bored for & drove 3112 nails & squared & copperd the bottom, unhung took ashore & shifted the main piece of the rother & unbolted took off refitted & rebolted the pintles; trimd & bolted the hawse bolster & cheek to the head & trimd & fastend the counter & quarter rails, shifted wale 14 feet birthing 148 feet & made & hung 2 rowport lids - got up & let in 3 deadeyes; drove out & redrove 17 chain plate bolts & 2 ring bolts & fitted & fastend 4 iron plates to channels - made stages for the above works; cut out & put in 19 pieces and performed works incident to rigging.[6]

Recommissioned under Lieutenant John Lapenotière after the outbreak of war, *Pickle* was deployed with the Channel fleet and sailed Plymouth on 15 October. John Richards Lapenotière, a Devon man born at Ilfracombe in 1770, was 33 years old when he took this command. Lapenotière had earlier served in the transport *Assistance* which accompanied Captain Bligh on his second voyage to attain breadfruit in 1793. Cruising in the Channel on 22 October *Pickle* captured the American vessel *Resolution*, brought her into Plymouth and sailed again on 28 December.

1804: *Pickle* remained cruising on station until hit by heavy gales on 19 January when she lost her main topmast and fore yard, forcing her to return into Plymouth 31 January to refit. Refitted with new masts and yards *Pickle* sailed again on 22 February carrying dispatches for Admiral the Hon. Sir William Cornwallis, Commander-in Chief of the Channel fleet stationed off Ushant. While off Brest *Pickle* went to the aid of *Magnificent* (74) which had been wrecked on an uncharted rock near Pierres Noires on 25 March. Standing by the stricken ship Lapenotière ordered his boat over the side to rescue the people just before *Magnificent* capsized and sank. Also assisting were boats from the cutter *Fox*. Shortly afterwards the survivors were transferred out of *Pickle* and *Fox* into the far roomier *Colossus* (74) which took them home to Plymouth, *Pickle* returning later.

While operating off Brest one crew member of the ship incited insurrection.[7] Lapenotière quelled the potential sedition and confined the ringleader. When *Pickle* returned to Plymouth a court martial was held on 26 July aboard the flagship lying in the Hamoaze to try the man for mutiny. Found guilty the man was sentenced to be flogged around the fleet, consequently the flagship made the appropriate signal for all ships to sent boats manned and armed to attend the punishment. The same day a seaman from *Doris* (36) was likewise flogged around the fleet for maiming a shipmate with intent to kill him. Then *Pickle* put to sea and cruising off Finisterre in October fell in with and captured two French coastal craft carrying supplies for Brest and brought them into Plymouth.

1805: Still deployed off Ferrol in the new year, on Thursday 3 January *Pickle* sailed for Plymouth with important dispatches from Rear-Admiral Alexander Cochrane, arriving there on Saturday in only 49 hours. Not accounting for tacking her average speed for this passage was 14.25 knots (about 16 miles per hour). *Neptune* (98) which arrived the same day had, although delayed by earlier gales, taken 10 days' passage, her average speed being just 3 knots. The remainder of the year was relatively uneventful, *Pickle* returning to Plymouth in August to refit. It was while undergoing these small repairs that Lapenotière received the following order on 5th September:

> You are hereby directed and required to put to sea in the gun vessel you command the moment she shall be ready, and wind and weather permit, and use your best endeavours to join Vice-Admiral Nelson agreeably to the accompanying rendezvous; and having so done, put yourself under his command and follow his orders for your further proceedings.[8]

Leaving Plymouth on 25 September *Pickle* made a fast passage, joining Nelson's squadron off Cadiz Tuesday 1 October. Four days later, after *Entreprenante* joined the fleet, she was immediately deployed with Blackwood's inshore squadron observing Villeneuve's combined fleet.[9] Besides Lapenotière *Pickle*'s crew comprised 17 Englishmen, nine Irish, two Americans, one of whom was George Almy, the ship's second master and pilot, one Norwegian, one Scot, one Welshman and one Channel Islander. Charles Hawkins was sub-lieutenant, Mr L G Britton the surgeon and John Kingdom midshipman.[10] With *Pickle* were the frigates *Euryalus*, *Naiad*, *Phœbe* and *Sirius* and the new-built brig-sloop *Weazle* (18).[11] The master's log of the *Pickle* for Sunday 20 October records the following events:

> PM Mod^t Breezes & Cloudy at 1 Cape Trafalgar E½S 4 or 5 leagues…at ½ p[ast] 5 saw the fleet to the NW supposed it was the Enemy made sail at 6 discoverd it was admiral Nelson's fleet tack^d & made all posible [sic] sail towards them at 8 Cape Spartell SSE 7 or 8 leagues fresh Breezes & Squally at 9 found the Commander in Chief out Boat the Commander [Lt. Lapenotière] went on Board with his Orders at 10 the Boat Returnd in Boat & made sail in Company with the *Phœbe*.[12]

Pickle's other master's log commencing 20 October states:

PM Strong Breezes & Squally tack[d] & wore occasionally at 2 answerd a Signal to Reconoitre in the NW at 3 discovered the Enemy fleet consisting of thirty three sail of the line fore [sic] frigates & two Brigs Bereing [sic] NbE & standing to the SW out Reefs and made sail towards them at 4 Tack[d] from the Enemy Repeated Signal from *Sirius* to the fleet Tack[d] occasionally keeping sight of the Enemy, AM Mod[t] Breezes & Cloudy at 4 wore towards the Enemy up Fore & Fore Topsail Yards & made sail at 8 the Enemy Bore E——[illegible] 4 or 5 Leagues the Commander in Chief WSW 2 or 3 leagues at 9 the fleet made sail towards the Enemy which had formed their line And appeared Ready for battle at 10 the Commander in chief made the signal to prepare for action with a number of other signals which was answerd by the fleet. At Noon the Commander in chief was with for A Bout [about] 2 leagues of the Enemy which kept their former station.[13]

TRAFALGAR

On this crucial day *Pickle* was attached to Nelson's weather division at the onset of the ensuing events and followed to leeward of the main column of ships. Although she was too small to play no greater rôle than that of a bystander witnessing this very decisive battle, it was by her involvement in the aftermath of battle that the ship's name *Pickle* became indelibly stamped in the annals of naval history. Her log, beginning at Noon recalls:

PM Light airs & Clear at ½ p12 the *Royal Sovring* [sic] Comenced her fire on the Enemy An Broke thru the Enemy line The Enemy —— [illegible] a warm fire on the afore mentioned Ship untill she was Coverd By the *Victory* & other Ships at ½ p 2 we discovered fore [sic] of the Enemys Ships dismasted the Wind Being light our Ships were not Not all yet in action at 4 discoverd foure [sic] of the Enemy Ships making their Escape at ½ p 4 the Enemy Ceast [sic] their fire Except 4 Ships which was trying to effect their Escape to windward and was attacted [sic] By two of our Ships their rigging Being Shatterd The Enemy got off Nineteen struck and one blew up in the action.[14]

At this point the French *Achille* (74) took fire at about 4 p.m. and *Pickle* performed her first act. With explosion of the stricken French ship imminent, *Pickle*, with the cutter *Entreprenante* and boats from *Prince* (90) and *Swiftsure* (74) went to *Achille*'s assistance. While *Pickle*'s log simply records: 'out Boats & saved 150 men', for those undertaking the act of rescue the scene was horrific. The entire ship was engulfed from head to stern in flames, their reflections playing on the surrounding waters together with the noise of burning, cracking and collapsing timber as her people, some like flaming torches, jumped into the water. Although the awesome spectacle was the direct result of the firepower meted out by their own British colleagues, the people in the water, friend or foe, were seamen in distress so each man lay on his oar with dogged determination to speed towards the wreck. As the boats made their approach towards the people screaming from the water some British seamen lost their lives in the attempt as preloaded guns within the French ship, heated by the fires, discharged themselves scattering round shot in all directions. Among the flotsam *Pickle*'s boat found a virtually naked woman clinging to wreckage. Once brought on board the schooner she was immediately given a pair of seaman's trousers, a shirt and a neckerchief to cover her womanhood and her burns around her neck and shoulders treated. *Pickle* took 120 survivors on board, outnumbering her own crew, and it was feared that the French prisoners could overtake the ship. Consequently all were transferred into the *Revenge* (74) at the earliest opportunity. The other log completing the story that day states:

Nineteen of them Struck & one took Fire & Blew up out Boats to save the men at 6 the Boats Returnd in Cutter And made sail saved one hundred and twenty or thirty men at 8 mod[t] Breezes & Hazy Empl[d] Assisting the disabled Ships at 12 ditto weather the Commander [Lt. Lapenotière] went on Board the *Victory* at 2 the Boat Returnd in Boat Employed as before At 4 fresh Breezes & Cloudy at 8 the Breeze freshend down fore and fore topsail yards at 10 Reef[d] the main sail and middle jib the jolly Boat Empd Carrying Prisoners on board of different Ship all prizes in tow.[15]

Besides giving an eyewitness account of events, *Pickle*'s master's log books provide insight into her rig. Although *Pickle* carried only a fore topsail, a square sail that described as a fore yard was in fact a spread yard that served the same function as a crossjack fitted on a mizzen mast of a ship rigged vessel. In both cases the yard simply acted as a spreader for the foot of the topsail. Also mentioned in the logs are a square-sail which, bent to a light yard, was hoisted up behind and just above the fore yard and set 'flying' below the topsail. This follows the earlier sail plan of armed cutters; consequently *Pickle*'s topsail was gored deeply across its foot to allow the square sail yard to be set at its full height, its halyard running through a block stropped to the head of the fore mast.[16] Much reference in the logs is also made to the ship having a middle jib, a middle jibboom and a gaff topsail. While the first two items are relatively self-explanatory, the gaff topsail appears to be an innovation that predates what later became commonly used in merchant trading vessels of the nineteenth century. Triangular in shape, the gaff topsail set with its luff to the topmast and its foot spread long the upper side of the gaff.

As weather deteriorated into the great storm on Wednesday 23 October *Pickle*'s log recalls: 'PM Strong Breezes & Squally wore Ship occasionally Boat Employed Carrying Prisoners on Board different Ships'. This was necessary as the number of prisoners on board *Pickle* far outnumbered her ship's crew. Living space had also become problematic. Labouring in the heavy swell *Pickle*'s seamen handled the mainsail and standing jib. By this point, according to this account the fleet had to scatter and 'several Prizes Broke their tow Ropes'. When the weather moderated Lapenotière set the fore topsail, storm jib main trysail and reset the standing jib and main sail. At 10 a.m. the boats were swayed out again, the task of transferring prisoners continued and signals were made to resume towing the prizes. At 11 a.m. the signal was made that: 'the Enemy were coming out', from Cadiz to recapture the prize ships, so 'at ½ p 11 the Sig[l]. was made to prepare for Battle at anchor'. The threat, however, disappeared.[17]

On Thursday 24 October there were 'fresh Breezes & Cloudy with a heavy Swell from the West[d].', during which Lieutenant Lapenotière 'Sent two Boats Loads of Prisoners on Board the *Victory*'. Later Lapenotière went on board *Euryalus* to speak to Collingwood, returning at 5.30. By noon the storm had become more violent and squally winds continued to batter Collingwood's ships in the angry seas between Cape Trafalgar and Gibraltar. Lapenotière also went on board *Prince*. Shortly after signals were made to 'take the Prisoners out of the Prizes And Cut their anchors from their Bows to let them go'. Collingwood had resorted to scuttling the battered prize fleet.

Next day *Pickle*

Tack[d] made & Shortend sail occasionally at 2 Sent other Boat on Board the *Prince* at ½ p 2 the Boat Returnd made sail several Ships at anchor at 5 ans[d] the Sig[l] to come within hale of the Commander in Chief at ½ p 5 Sent the Boat on Board [the *Euryalus*] at 6 the Boat Returnd Bore up for the *Prince* at 7 in Boat at 8 Saw one of the Prizes Blow up...

Later that day as the gale freshened Lapenotière had the rig reduced to steady the ship. This involved sending down the fore topmast, taking in the middle jibboom and resetting the main sail, standing jib and main trysail.

On Saturday 26 October Collingwood ordered Blackwood to hail *Pickle* alongside in order to transfer his dispatches for England. *Pickle*'s pendant number followed by flag numbers 8 and 4 (8, a complete white flag set above 4, quartered red and white) were immediately hoisted from the *Euryalus*'s yardarm signalling *Pickle* to 'pass within hail'. *Pickle*'s log records 'ans[d] 'the Sig[l]. to Come in Hale of the Commander in Chief Bore up & made sail'. Under the direction of George Almy, an American from Newport, Rhode Island serving as *Pickle*'s second master, *Pickle* was deftly manœuvred across the violently tossing sea and hove to upon the lee side

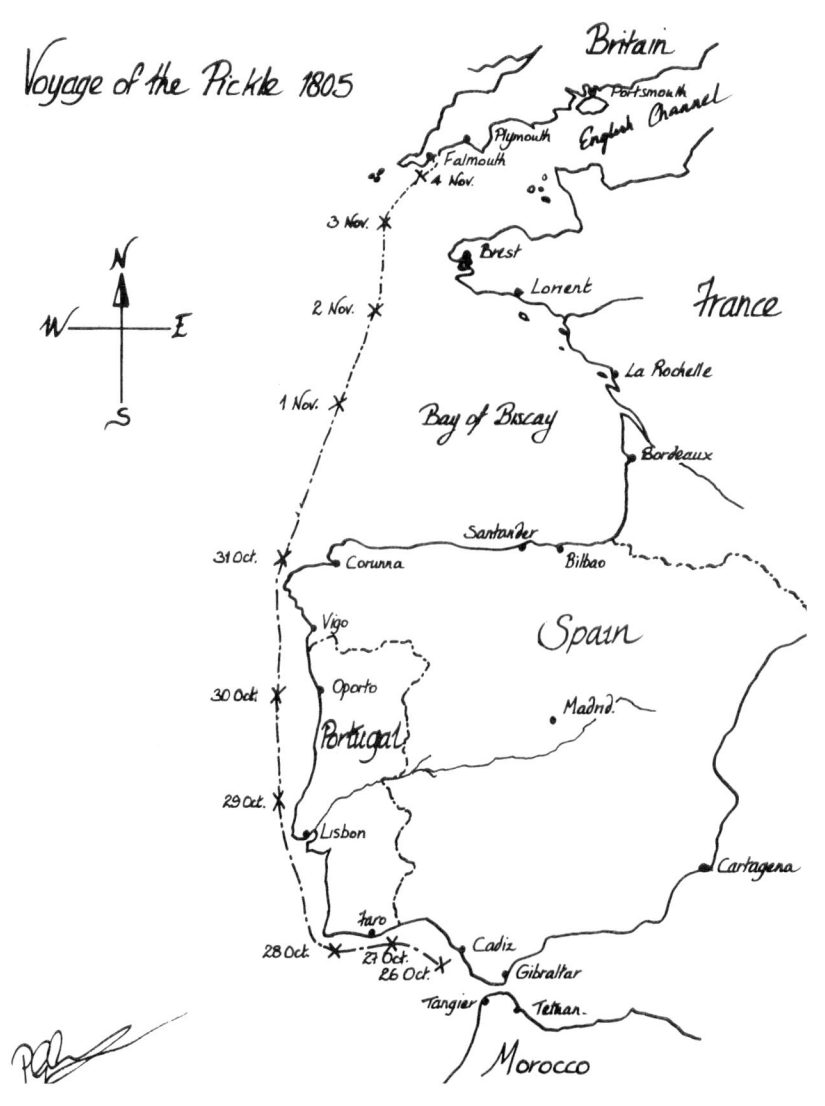

The voyage of the Pickle, *26 October–4 November 1805 (Author's drawing)*

of *Euryalus* where, 'at 9 out Boat the Com^d (Lapenotière) Went on Board of the Commander in Chief'. Despite the raging waters *Pickle*'s boat was lowered and Lapenotière went on board the frigate. Receiving strict orders from Collingwood, the admiral stated that Lapenotière was to make all possible haste to deliver the dispatches personally to William Marsden, Secretary to the Board of the Admiralty. *Pickle*'s log then records: 'at 10 Discharged all the Prisoners Us to the *Revenge* at Noon the Boat Returnd In Boat & made sail for England'. *Pickle* crammed as much sail as possible under the conditions, pitching in the heavy swell, and hauled away. Having set a course WNW past Cape St Vincent, set off on her momentous passage to England, conveying the victorious news of Trafalgar and the death of Lord Nelson. The log commencing noon Sunday 27 October: 'at ½ p 12 parted Comp^y with the Commander in Chief'. As soon as weather permitted Lapenotière ordered ' up main top mast & set the Gaff top Sail at 5 in Gaff Top…at 2 AM a shift of wind' forced *Pickle* to sail towards the bay above Cape St Vincent on an opposite course to that intended but soon veered bringing the ship back some 5 leagues off Cape St Mary. While sounding they 'lost the deepsea lead & Ninety fathom of line'.

The log on Monday 28 October records little until 11 o'clock when they saw 'a strange sail in the NNW standing towards us'. Seeing a sloop bearing down upon them Lapenotière took no chances and having first made more sail gave the private signal. Returning the number 451, the sloop proved to be *Nautilus* (18) commanded by Captain Sykes. The log entry Tuesday 29 October records 'At ½ p 3 hove to & Spoke H.M.S. *Natlis* [*Nautilus*] the Captain of the *Natlis* [sic] Came on board…' After receiving the news of Trafalgar, Sykes returned to *Nautilus* and proceeded to Lisbon to inform the British ambassador. Shortly after the two ships parted company but remained in sight for the next two days as *Pickle* resumed her course. On 30 October *Pickle* was NW of Lisbon and meeting heavy weather again was obliged to send down her topgallant yard and reef as necessary.

By Thursday *Pickle* had rounded Finisterre. No sooner had she entered the Bay of Biscay than she suffered the ravages of the heavy seas. With constant changes in weather *Pickle*'s crew were kept busy making alterations to her sails. A leak opened up in the fore part of the hull and finding the foremost limber holes blocked prevented water to drain from her fore peak to the pumps, the men had to bale the ship to prevent her becoming heavy at the bow. Recording this the log 31 October states:

> … at ½ p 8 Reeft the middle Jib & Main [sail] and down Fore yard at 12 fresh Gales & Squally with a heavy head Swell At 4 AM down fore topsail yard & got in the flying Jib & Ring Tail Booms And Reeft the Fore sail… at 9 in Middle jib Boom carried away the Spritsail yard People Emp^d Bailing the Water out of the fore Peak limbers being Stopt…

Friday 1 November fared no better, for *Pickle*'s tiny crew there was no respite; wretched in their wet clothing and bruised through knocks and falls as they laboured continuously on deck, they had no dry bedding or hot meals to give them a small comfort. Despite this the crew continued baling the ship, 'one pump continually Going at 5 the Gale increased'. With a heavy swell reaching from the ENE and the sea state increasing with wind pressure, mercilessly buffeted, *Pickle* pitched and rolled endlessly, every wave threatening to roll out the masts or turn her over onto her beam ends. Concerned that he needed to ease the ship's motion Lapenotière called all hands on deck and 'hove four guns with their carriages over Board'. The four 12 pounder carronades complete with their slides jettisoned, the ship eased. At 10 a.m. further sail had to be reduced, the crew hazarding another climb aloft to battle with flogging canvas as they tied reefs or passed gaskets while others slipping on the wet canted decks hauled on buntlines, clews, sheets and halyards as required. As the testing day passed the wind marginally eased, allowing more sail to be set. At 5 a.m. Lapenotière sent up the 'fore topmast and fore yard & Set the square sail'. The log then states, 'at 6 up fore topsail yard and made sail…at 10 out middle Jiboom & set the Jib and top mast lower Studding sails'.

By Saturday 2 November *Pickle* had passed Ushant and entering the Channel, made more sail. By dead reckoning the Lizard lay some 150 miles away. Sailing under an easy wind there was opportunity to square off the ship; the 'people clearing the after hold at 6 fresh breezes with Rain'. As the wind fell off with the rain, mists began to shroud the ship with the result that by Sunday 3 November the entry in the log records: 'PM light airs & fogg People Emp^d at the Sweeps to Keep the vessels Head the Right way'. With three men stationed at each oar the *Pickle* was propelled at a speed of no more than 1½ knots. After labouring at the sweeps for some hours, 'at 4 a Breeze from the East, wore & made sail', the sweeps were shipped inboard as the sails began to fill and 'at 5 the Breeze freshend in fore Topsail & down fore yard'. At 7.30 Monday morning two sail were seen and at 9 o'clock *Pickle* made 'the Private Sig^l & our No. & 387 & 311 & 216 all answ^d then ans^d their Sig to come within Hale made the Sig^l 351 which was ans^d out Boat our Com^d went on Board HMS *Superbe* [sic]'.[18]

The 74 gun *Superb* was making her way to Cadiz to join Nelson's squadron completely unaware that the great battle had already been fought. As soon as *Pickle* had hoisted number 351: 'I have some intelligence to communicate', the two vessels hove to. *Pickle*'s boat was lowered, Lapenotière went over to the *Superb* to speak with Captain Richard Gardiner Keats. Keats was utterly shocked at the news because as a friend of Nelson he had only been in Merton some seven weeks previously, listening to the admiral's plan of attacking the combined fleet. Keats and his crew had also missed

PROGRESS BOOK – *PICKLE* ARMED SCHOONER OF 8 GUNS: Source: ADM 180/8

At what Port	Arrived	Docked	Coppered	Launched or Undocked	Sailed	Built or Nature of Repair	Cost of Hull, Masts & Yards Materials £ s d	Cost of Rigging & Stores Materials £ s d	Grand Total
Plymouth	7 July 1802				6 Aug 1802	Made Good [Defects]			
Plymouth	24 Sep 1802				12 Oct 1802	-			
Plymouth	7 Feb 1803	22 Mar 1803	Copper taken off & Coppered Mar 1803	22 March 1803	9 May 1803				
Plymouth	19 July 1803			22 July 1803					
Plymouth	9 Sep 1803			20 Sep 1803					
Plymouth	30 Nov 1803			28 Dec 1803					

playing an active rôle in the battle. When the two ships parted company *Pickle* was less than 70 miles from the Lizard. Shortly afterwards *Pickle*, according to the parish records at Madron Church, Penzance, fell in with Cornish fishermen from Penzance working off Mousehole and gave them the news of Trafalgar. While *Pickle* maintained her course for Falmouth the fishermen hauled in their nets and made for Penzance. Getting on shore they immediately went to the Assembly Rooms (now part of the Union Hotel) to inform the Mayor who was holding a civic reception. Standing in the gallery overlooking the hall the Mayor hushed the proceedings and disclosed the first news of Trafalgar and the death of Nelson to the English public. Following this the Mayor led a procession to Madron Parish Church where the Vicar, the Rev. William Borlase MA, held a memorial service for the victory and death of Nelson, the church bells being rung to indicate the news.[19] The log entry for Monday 4 November commencing at noon records:

'PM Fresh Breezes & Cloudy all Sail Set to advantage at 4 mod^t & cloudy At 6 Sounded in 65 fathoms several sail in sight at 12 Sounded in 52 fathoms AM ditto weather at 2 the Lizard Light Bore EbN 3 leagues'.[20]

As the evening closed, the light high on the cliff of Lizard Point shone distant some eight miles, and rounding the Lizard *Pickle* had just 23 miles to go. When dawn broke Monday morning proper, the treacherous Manacles lay well to larboard and Lapenotière could see Falmouth Bay dead ahead crowned by Pendennis Castle to the left of the harbour and the smaller fort of St Mawes on the right hand bank. The log then states: 'at 4 ditto Light NNEbE at 6 Set all Sail at 8 the Lizard WNW1/2N dist^t 4 Leagues at 9.45 shortend Sail', and after her ten day passage from Cape Trafalgar *Pickle* finally hove to. The log then recalls 'out Boat our Commander went on Shore at falmouth with his dispatches for London At Noon mod^t & cloudy Pendennis castle NNW 2 or 3 Miles Tack^d ocassionally'.[21]

Despite the appalling weather *Pickle* had covered approximately 1,500 miles at an average speed of 6.5 knots. Once Lapenotière landed from *Pickle*'s boat he went on shore and ordered a post chaise and four to set out for London, a distance of 266 miles.[22] The route taken by the coach, the stops to change horses and take meals, can be reconstructed from Lapenotière's expense claim submitted to the Admiralty.

Account of Expenses of Lieut. Lapenotière for Express with Dispatches from Adm^l Lord Nelson to the Admiralty from Falmouth - Viz -

Falmouth to Truro	-	£1:	2s:	6d
To the Blue Anchor	-		2:	17: -
To Bodman [sic]	-		1:	19: -
To Launceston	-		3:	6: 6
To Oakhampton	-		3:	4: -
To Crockernwell	-		1:	16: 6
To Exeter	-		1:	17: 6
To Honiton	-		2:	14: -
To Axminster	-		1:	11: 7
To Bridport	-		1:	16: 6
To Dorchester	-		2:	14: 6
To Blandford	-		2:	10: 6
To Woodyates	-		2:	5: -
To Salisbury	-		1:	17: 6
To Andover	-		2:	15: -
To Overton	-		1:	13: -
To Basingstoke	-		1:	14: -
To Hertford [sic] bridge	-		1:	15: 6
To Bagshot	-		1:	12: -
To Staines	-		1:	17: 6
To Hounslow	-		1:	14: 6
To the Admiralty	-		2:	5: -
	-		46:	19: 1

[Signed] JR Lapenotière

From the above the estimated rate equated to approximately 3 shillings and 6 pence (32 pence) per mile, private hire coach travel being quite expensive.

After a journey of some 37 hours, hampered in parts by fog, at 1 a.m. Wednesday 6 November the coach turned down the empty streets of Whitehall, and passing through the gate of the Admiralty Building, the horses came to a clattering halt on the wet cobbled courtyard, whinnying and exhaling their steaming breath into the cold damp air. Lapenotière, stiff from the journey, alighted from the coach, mounted the steps and hammered on the door. Moments later a light was seen flickering in the hall, and the door was opened by the porter. The porter immediately took Lapenotière to William Marsden, Secretary to the Board of the Admiralty, who was still awake working late on important papers. Marsden later recalled that it was 'about one o'clock a.m. of the 6th November, when I was in the act of withdrawing from the Board Room to my private apartments, after having opened the common letters received in the course of the evening', when he was disturbed by the porter. Without preamble Lapenotière handed Marsden the dispatches, saying, 'Sir, we have gained a great victory; but we have lost Lord Nelson'. Marsden broke the seal and read the despatch:

Euryalus. Off Cape Trafalgar, Oct 22, 1805

The ever-to-be lamented death of Vice-Admiral Lord Nelson, who, in the late conflict with the enemy, fell in the hour of Victory, leaves me the duty of informing my Lords Commissioners of the admiralty, that on the 19th instant it was communicated to the Commander-in-Chief, from the ship watching the motions of the enemy in Cadiz, that the Combined Fleet had put to sea…On Monday the 21st instant, at daylight, when Cape Trafalgar bore E by S about seven leagues, the enemy was discovered six or seven miles to the eastward, the wind about west, and very light.

The Commander-in-Chief immediately made the signal for the Fleet to bear up in two columns, as they are formed in order of sailing; a mode of attack his Lordship had previously directed, to avoid the inconvenience and delay in forming the line of battle in the usual manner… The Commander-in-Chief, the *Victory*, led the weather column, and the *Royal Sovereign*, which bore my flag, the lee. The action began at Twelve o'clock by the leading ships breaking through the enemy line. The enemy ships were fought with a gallantry highly honourable to their officers; but the attack on them was irresistible, and it pleased the Almighty Disposer of all events to His Majesty's arms a complete and glorious victory.

His lordship received a musket ball in his left breast, about the middle of the action... I have also to lament the loss of those excellent officers, Captains Duff, of the *Mars*, and Cooke of the *Bellerophon*.

The Secretary then left to wake Lord Barham. On entering his room he drew aside the curtains and, stated Marsden later, 'with candle in hand, I awoke the old peer from a sound slumber; and to the credit of his nerves be it mentioned that he showed no symptoms of alarm or surprise, but calmly asked: "What news, Mr M?"'. Copies of Collingwood's despatch were immediately made, one sent direct to Prime Minister Pitt at 3 a.m., another by Admiralty messenger at 6.30 a.m. to the King at Windsor. Later that day Collingwood's second despatch, previously sent overland but later transferred into *Nautilus*, was delivered to the Admiralty by Captain Sykes. That afternoon the news of Trafalgar was published in the *Gazette Extraordinary*, and given full coverage in the *Times* Thursday 7 November.[23] In fact these were not the first publications of the news for on 24 October a letter from Collingwood to Lieutenant-General Fox, Governor of the fortress, was published first in the *Gibraltar Gazette*.

For his efforts in bringing home Collingwood's dispatches Lapenotière was promoted to the rank of commander on 6 November and received the sum of £500. He also received a silver sifter from the King's breakfast table and was later presented with a sword valued at 100 guineas donated from the Committee of the Patriotic Fund.[24]

As for the *Pickle*, she soon got under way for Plymouth, the log commencing at noon Tuesday 5 November continues:

PM Mod^t & loudy Tack^d occasionally standing off & on waiting for the Boat at 2 the Boat Return^d in Boat & made sail to the East^d Several sail in sight at 6 saw land NE 6 or 7 miles at 7 the wind hauld to the East^d tack^d made & shortend sail occasionally at ? p 7 down fore yard At 8 the Eddystone light SEbE 6 or 7 miles fresh Breezes & Cloudy at 12 the Ram head [Ramehead] NNE 3 miles Tack^d as before AM ditto weather Emp^d Working in to the Sound at ? p 7 more mod^t up fore yard & made sail Working in to Plymouth Sound at ? p 8 out Boat & Sent the Letters on Shore at 9 anchored in Stonehouse pool with the Best Bower anchor in 17 fathoms water & Run a hawser on to the shore people employd unbending sails at Noon mod^t & cloudy.[25]

For the first time in weeks *Pickle*'s crew could have uninterrupted sleep and for the next few weeks the ship remained in Stonehouse pool.

1806: Succeeding Lapenotière's promotion, command of *Pickle* was superseded by Lieutenant Moses Cannadey and she was redeployed in the Channel operating out of Plymouth.

1807: While cruising five leagues off the Lizard on 3 January *Pickle* fell in with and engaged a French privateer which was being chased by the brig-sloop *Scorpion* (18). On boarding the vessel she proved to be the cutter *Favourite* of 14 guns and 70 men out of Cherbourg commanded by M. Eduoard. J. Boutruche. The vessel was only two months old. In the affray *Pickle* suffered three wounded, Acting Master George Almy, Lieutenant Charles Hawkins and a seaman whilst boarding. The French prisoners were removed into *Scorpion* and landed at Falmouth.

FATE

Still commanded by Lieutenant Moses Cannadey in 1808, *Pickle* was deployed carrying dispatches from England to Admiral Collingwood's squadron laying off Cadiz. Approaching Cape Santa Maria near Cadiz on 26 July, at 6 p.m. Cannadey altered course but by midnight water could be seen breaking on shore. Despite putting the helm hard over to larboard to avoid driving *Pickle* aground she struck hard on the Chipona Shoal. All hands were called and the boat was lowered over the side to carry a kedge anchor out to warp the ship off but their actions were in vain for the vessel began to fill causing her to heel over to larboard. With little to do the entire crew abandoned the ship and took to boats and landed safely on the Spanish coast. Next morning Cannadey, accompanied by the carpenter and others, returned to the wreck to find her hull was well stove in and filled with water. At the ensuing courts martial Cannadey was reprimanded for making an unaccountable error in dead reckoning the distance travelled.[26] Luckily the dispatches for Collingwood covering instructions for his return into the Mediterranean to blockade Toulon were not lost, for the 'admiral found out a Maltese diver, who after three days' exertion found them'.[27]

The Armed Cutter ENTREPRENANTE

Entreprenante is the only vessel to bear this name in the Royal Navy. Although listed as being captured from the French in 1798, no immediate records indicate where or by whom she was taken. In design she probably differed little from the standard English cutters of the period. According to Lyon she was armed with ten 12 pounder carronades and therefore could deliver a single broadside of 60 pounds.

CAPTAINS OF *ENTREPRENANTE* (MSS 248/4 and 248/6)

Name	Time of Entry	Time of Discharge	On What Occasion
William Swiney	1801	30 November 1803	Superseded
James Brown	1 December 1803	11 April 1804	Superseded
Robert B Young	12 April 1804	3 December 1807	Superseded
Peter Williams	4 December 1807	1812	Paid Off

SPECIFICATIONS: *ENTREPRENANTE*

Rate	Armed Cutter	*Date keel laid*	Unknown	*Draught afore*	9 ft 0 ins approx
Guns	10	*Date launched*	Unknown	*Draught abaft*	11 ft 0 ins approx
Class	French *Entreprenante*	*Length on the range of the gun deck*	67 ft	*Complement*	40
Designer	Unknown	*Length of keel for tonnage*	51 ft 6 ins	*Ordnance - main deck*	10 x 12 pounder carronades
Builder	Unknown	*Extreme breadth*	21 ft 6 ins	*Single broadside weight*	60 pounds
Dockyard	Unknown	*Depth in hold*	Unknown	*Fate*	1812 Broken up.
Date ordered	Captured from French 1798	*Tons burthen*	123.		

Source: Lyon, *Sailing Navy List*, p. 255.[28]

SERVICE HISTORY

1801: First commanded by Lieutenant William Swiney, *Entreprenante* was deployed with Lord Keith's fleet which sailed for Egypt and landed troops in Abu-Kir Bay to attack the French occupational forces. During this expedition troops were landed at 9 a.m. 2 March under the direction of Captain the Hon. Alexander Cochrane. The landings were covered by a flotilla of smaller vessels comprising *Entreprenante*, together with *Minorca* (18), *Peterell* (16), *Cameleon* (16), *Malta* (10), *Cruelle* (8), *Tartarus* (8), *Dangéreuse* (6), *Janissary* (6), *Negresse* (6), and *Fury* (4), plus armed launches. At this event Clowes lists *Entreprenante* as carrying 14 guns, however most armed cutters carried twelve or fewer guns.[29] *Malta*, according to Colledge, had in fact been renamed *Gozo* in 1801.[30]

1802: Recalled to England, *Entreprenante* went into Portsmouth on 28 November.[31]

1803: On 4 October *Entreprenante* went into dock at Portsmouth to have her copper replaced. Undocked on 29 October the vessel was then fitted out and recommissioned on 1 December under her new commander Lieutenant James Brown.[32] For the remainder Brown set his crew to setting up the rigging and taking in stores.

1804: *Entreprenante* finally sailed out of Portsmouth on 7 January and moored at Spithead to await orders. During this period Lieutenant Brown had obviously found some defects, so he took the ship back into Portsmouth on 29 January to undertake minor refitting. Having completed this work and taken on fresh provisions *Entreprenante* sailed again on 2 February.[33] On 12 April command of the *Entreprenante* was superseded by Lieutenant Robert Benjamin Young who remained in the ship throughout the Trafalgar campaign. On 7 November the ship had to go back into Portsmouth to have her copper repaired, and sailed 13 days later. Unlike standard naval vessels it appears that because of her size *Entreprenante* did not always require to be dry-docked for simple underwater repairs but merely taken up on a slipway.[34]

1805: On Thursday 8 August *Entreprenante* moored at Spithead awaiting orders and four days later while laying at anchor at Yarmouth Roads, Young wrote in his log: 'rec^d 21 supernumeraries from the *Royal William* weighed at 5 pm and sailed cruising between Portland and Needles' the vessel returning to Spithead and anchoring off St Helens on Saturday 7 September.[35] Receiving new orders to join Nelson's fleet off Cadiz, *Entreprenante* sailed Wednesday 11 September and with a fall in wind came to a single anchor in Shanklin Bay three days later. Afterwards shifting to moor at the Motherbank, *Entreprenante* finally proceeded down the Channel on Thursday 19 September. Reaching her destination on Wednesday 2 October, Young recorded that Cadiz light lay 10 miles off.[36] Pope states that the ship arrived Friday 4 October.[37] On arrival, *Entreprenante* was immediately deployed with *Pickle* and frigates of Blackwood's inshore squadron watching over Cadiz.

TRAFALGAR

In *Entreprenante*'s log of Monday 21 October, Lt Young records:

> Squally with rain reeft the mainsail, shifted Jibs and close reeft the Bowsprit Tk^d per signal with the fleet AM Moderate and cloudy at Daylight observed the Enemy consisting of 35 Sail to the Eastw^d observed the fleet wear and stood towards them under all sail at noon Light breezes and cloudy the Body of the Enemy's fleet ESE 3 miles.

Tuesday 22nd:

> Light breezes and cloudy at 1 PM observed the van of our fleet bring the Enemy's fleet to Action observed a very heavy fire on both sides at 5 saw one of the Enemy's ships on fire made sail to her sent our boat to save her people which were floating on different spars belonging to the ship at 5.30 the ship blew up saved from Different wrecks 168 Men observed 16 sail of the Enemy strike their Colours several of which were dismasted AM Mod.e & breezy Cape Spartel SSE 8 Leagues noon signals...

Wednesday 23rd:

> Strong Gales and squally at 2 answered signal made by HM Ship *Euralus* [sic] to pass within hail Tk.d occasionally receieved from H M Ship *Polyphemus* one cask of water took the small boat from the stern spoke several ships with the Enemy's Hulks in tow down topsail yard and struck the Topmast double reeft the main sail at midnight heavy squalls hove to with the Cutter's head to the NW AM more moderate at Daylight the body of the fleet ESE 7 or 8 Miles out all reefs up Topmast and topsail Yard at 8 spoke HM Brig *Scout* hoisted signal of Distress Received from the *Scout* 5 casks of water and a jolly Boat...

On Thursday 24th the ship 'observed several of the Enemy's Hulks at an anchor AM Hard Gales and squally lost the Jolly Boat from the stern at 7 split the after back of the main sail carried away the topmast'.

On Friday 25th the ship was hailed by *Euryalus* and 'discharged 5 of the Prisoners into HMS *Ajax* AM Hard Gales with a heavy swell set the Try Sail and Storm Jib at noon Stormy shifted several heavy scars — made signal of Distress for want of water'.

Saturday 26th:

> Stormy with heavy sea several seas broke in upon the Cutters Decks thought it necessary for the preservation of the Cutter to hove 5 Guns overboard besides shot and the old mainsail split the fore sail and storm Jib at AM more moderate at 8 made signal of Distress with Guns to several ships at noon Vb.le with heavy swell anchored off St. Lucars with the best bower on 16 fathoms wore away the whole cable...

Sunday 27th:

> Strong Gales and squally Employed splicing cables and returning Prisoners into HM Ships *Orion* at midnight wore away two cables p.r —— to assist one of the Enemy Hulks in Distress AM Squally with a heavy swell at 8 slipt our cables and made sail at noon spoke one of the Spanish Hulks the English Officers of which informed us that they were in Distress they had 1 1/7 feet of water in her old [sic] and had no Pumps nor rudder and had given her up to the Enemy Observed one of the Hulks run on shore off St Lucars at noon... [Laying off Faro on 30th the ship hove to and] 'came on board a pilot and took charge of the Cutter at 6 anchored off the Bar in 12 fathoms AM Moderate and hazy at 6 weighed and made sail for faro harbour Struck several toomes crossing the Bar, at 8 anchored with the stream.

Being such a small vessel *Entreprenante* did not play a major part in the action off Cape Trafalgar but cruised near the fleet, acting in support where required. Her most significant part came towards the end of the action at about 5.45 p.m. when she, with *Pickle* and boats from *Prince* (90) and *Swiftsure* (74), rescued people abandoning the French *Achille* (74) which had caught fire. Despite the danger *Entreprenante* and the forenamed ships saved 200 people from the raging inferno *Achille* had become before she blew up.[38] In the aftermath of battle, according to a report by Lieutenant Paul Nicholas of *Belleisle* (74), 'a boat with a lieutenant from the cutter *Entreprenante* shortly came on board, on his return from the *Victory*, to announce the death of Nelson. The melancholy tidings spread through the ships in an instant and the paralysing effect was wonderful'.[39] When the weather abated a few days later *Entreprenante* was sent to Faro with copies of Collingwood's dispatches and later returned to England.

1806: Going into Plymouth 10 January *Entreprenante* went into dock three days later to have her copper replaced. Re-launched on 6 February the vessel sailed again 11 March for her new deployment in home waters watching the French in the Channel. That the vessel was docked again at Plymouth 28 November to have her copper repaired and re-nailed implies that the previous work undertaken was insufficient.[40]

PROGRESS BOOK - *ENTREPRENANTE* ARMED CUTTER OF 10 GUNS Source: ADM 180/4 & ADM 180/13 Entry 692

At what Port	Arrived	Docked	Coppered	Launched or Undocked	Sailed	Built or nature of Repair
Portsmouth	28 Nov 1802	4 Oct 1803	Copper taken off Re-coppered Oct 1803	29 Oct 1803	7 Jan 1804	Fitted
Portsmouth	29 January 1804			2 February 1804		
Portsmouth	7 Nov 1804		Copper Repaired		20 Nov 1804	Refitted
Plymouth	10 January 1806	13 Jan 1806	Copper taken off Jan Re-coppered Feb 1806	6 February 1806	11 March 1806	Defects
Plymouth						Defects
Plymouth	22 Nov 1806 2	8 Nov 1806	Copper Repaired & Re-nailed	4 December 1806	2 January 1807	Defects
Plymouth	12 April 1807				3 May 1807	Defects
Plymouth	20 July 1807				8 August 1807	
Plymouth	29 Sep 1807				9 October 1807	Defects
Plymouth	25 Nov 1807	4 Dec 1807	Copper taken off and re-coppered Dec 1807	9 December 1807	25 December 1807	Defects
Plymouth	20 March 1808			30 March 1808		
Plymouth	13 May 1808				28 May 1808	
Plymouth	9 July 1808				15 July 1808	
Plymouth	29 August 1808			13 September 1808		
Plymouth	7 October 1808			15 October 1808		Defects
Plymouth	24 Nov 1808		Copper Repaired		20 December 1808	Defects
Plymouth	17 January 1809			9 February 1809		Defects
Plymouth	7 July 1809				16 July 1809	
Plymouth	24 Feb 1810	1 March 1810	Copper Repaired	6 March 1810	22 March 1810	Defects
Plymouth	30 March 1812	13 May 1812				
	Taken to Pieces June 1812					

1807: *Entreprenante* continued working in the Channel, entering Plymouth on four occasions in April, July, September and November to make good her defects. On 4 December Lieutenant Peter Williams assumed command of the vessel the same day. Under her new commander *Entreprenante* sailed on Christmas Day back on deployment. Williams remained in command until she paid off in 1812.[41]

1808-1809: *Entreprenante* continued operating in the Channel, going into Plymouth every few months to re-provision and make good any defects. On no occasion did she go into dock even though repairs were made to her copper in November 1808.[42]

1810: Preparing for her new deployment in the Mediterranean, *Entreprenante* was recalled into Plymouth on 24 February and docked on 1 March to make good her defective copper. Undocked on 6 March the ship took in stores, carried out maintenance on her rigging and sailed out of the Hamoaze on 22 March.[43] *Entreprenante*'s crew, excluding Lieutenant Williams, seems to have comprised 33 men and boys. Lying becalmed off Malaga on 12 December, at 8 a.m. Williams sighted four lateen rigged vessels lying under the fort at Faro. One hour later all four craft put to sea towards *Entreprenante* and at 10.30 a.m. hoisted French colours. These vessels proved to be privateers, one of which was armed with four guns and two long 18 pounders and 75 men, the second carrying five guns and 45 men, the smaller craft both having just 2 guns and 25 men each. *Entreprenante* was both out-gunned and out numbered. By now Williams had cleared his cutter for action and at 11 a.m. opened fire at the Frenchmen as they drew up one off the starboard quarter, one off the starboard bow, the other two directly astern. A vigorous action ensued at pistol shot range, grape shot being used as well as round, muskets also being brought into play. Within the hour *Entreprenante* suffered much damage aloft, shot carrying away her topmast, gaff peak halliards, fore jeer tackle and falls, various blocks and the jib halliard. With one carriage gun and one swivel put out of action one of the privateers saw the opportunity to board *Entreprenante* but they were beaten back by the foremost guns and musketry fire. A second attempt to board also failed, however on this occasion one of *Entreprenante*'s men was killed and four were wounded. Williams then ordered the sweeps to be manned to manœuvre the ship to bring her larboard guns to bear and firing two broadsides obliged the attackers to stand off. By this time *Entreprenante*'s ammunition was low, having expended all her canister and musket shot, however the gunners took care and directed two well-aimed broadsides into their opponents, bringing down masts and rigging. A third attempt was made to board but this was also repulsed. By 2.30 p.m. a further two of *Entreprenante*'s guns were dismounted but despite this loss the remaining two guns fired a shattering double shotted broadside into the dismasted privateer. This volley forced the enemy to retire. While towing their vessels clear by boat *Entreprenante* continued to fire into them until out of range at 3 p.m. Williams and his crew had gallantly defended the cutter against overwhelming odds for besides being outgunned 2 to 1, the *Entreprenante* was out-manned 5 to 1. *Entreprenante* suffered 33 per cent casualties; one killed and ten wounded whereas French casualties numbered nearly 50 per cent. Getting into Gibraltar afterwards Williams and *Entreprenante*'s crew were publicly acclaimed by the commander on that station, Commodore Charles Penrose. Surprisingly, however, Williams was not promoted, which would normally have been the case under similar circumstances.[44]

1811: On 25 April *Entreprenante* went into Malaga Bay under a flag of truce to deliver a letter to the Governor, General Sabastini. Having received a reply for Governor Campbell at Gibraltar *Entreprenante* made sail and while working out of the bay Williams sighted a privateer with a prize in company making for port. Williams cleared *Entreprenante* for action and closed with the vessel. The ensuing action lasted some 15 minutes, both vessels running towards the shore. Fortunately *Entreprenante* tacked in time but her opponent ran aground. Coming up alongside Williams boarded and carried the privateer which proved to the Spanish brig *Saint Joseph* out of Cadiz bound for Tarragona. Two miles away on the mole at Malaga hundreds of spectators witnessing the entire action now watched as *Entreprenante* took the *Saint Joseph* in tow ashore. During the affray *Entreprenante* suffered not a single casualty.

1812: Completing her deployment in the Mediterranean, *Entreprenante* was recalled home, arriving at Plymouth on 30 March. Shortly after Lieutenant Williams paid off the ship.[45]

FATE

As with most small vessels such as armed cutters, *Entreprenante* had a short hull life and was consequently surveyed. Docked on 13 May *Entreprenante* was 'Taken to Pieces June 1812'.[46]

Notes to Part 1: Chapter 6

1. TNA: PRO, ADM 1/250 and ADM 1/251.
2. Cross, 'Unpickling the Pickle', *The Trafalgar Chronicle* (Yearbook of the 1805 Club), p. 204.
3. TNA: PRO, ADM. 180/8.
4. Lyon, *Sailing Navy List*, p. 255.
5. TNA: PRO, ADM 180/8.
6. RNM, portfolio 1 (3); Account of Work by Shipwrights on the Hulls of Ships, Plymouth 1803, Joseph Tucker – Master Shipwright.
7. Schom, *Trafalgar*, p. 166.
8. Pope, *England Expects*, p. 128.
9. Pope, *England Expects*, pp. 161–177.
10. TNA: PRO, ADM 36/1650; Pope, *England Expects*, p. 20.
11. Schom, *Trafalgar*, pp. 288, 311.
12. TNA: PRO, ADM 52/3669/16.
13. TNA: PRO, ADM 52/3669 part 20.
14. *Ibid*.
15. *Ibid*.
16. Goodwin, *The Naval Cutter Alert 1777*, *passim*.
17. TNA: PRO, ADM 52/3669/20.
18. *Ibid*.
19. Madron Parish Records research papers by Canon Michael Hocking, Vicar of Madron Parish Church.
20. TNA: PRO, ADM 52/3669 part 20.
21. *Ibid*.
22. Pope, *England Expects*, pp. 15–27.
23. Pope, *England Expects*, pp. 33–37.
24. Clowes, 5, p. 168.
25. TNA: PRO, ADM 52/3669 part 20.
26. Clowes, 5, p. 552; Hepper, p. 124; James, 5, p. 392.
27. Tracy, *Naval Chronicle*, 4, p. 167.
28. James, 5, p. 242. James list *Entreprenante* as carrying eight 4-pounder carriage guns instead of 12-pounder carronades. If armed with 4 pounders her broadside weight was only 16 pounds.
29. Clowes, 4, pp. 454–455.
30. Colledge, 1, p. 343.
31. TNA: PRO, ADM 180/4.
32. TNA: PRO, ADM 180/4; RNM, MS 248/4.
33. TNA: PRO, ADM 180/4.
34. TNA: PRO, ADM 180/13 Entry 692.
35. TNA: PRO, ADM 51/1443 part 3.
36. *Ibid*.
37. Pope, *England Expects*, pp. 164, 216.
38. Clowes, 5, p. 157; Pope, *England Expects*, p. 317.
39. Pope, *England Expects*, p. 337.
40. TNA: PRO, ADM 180/13 Entry 692.
41. RNM, MS 248/6; TNA: PRO, ADM 180/13 Entry 692.
42. TNA: PRO, ADM 180/13 Entry 692.
43. *Ibid*.
44. James, 5, pp. 242–243; Clowes, 5, p. 476.
45. RNM, MS 248/6.
46. TNA: PRO, ADM 180/13 Entry 692.

The Ships of Trafalgar

PART 2
THE FRENCH FLEET

The French fleet present at the battle of Trafalgar comprised 25 ships in total, consisting of 18 line of battle ships, five 5th rate frigates, and two brigs. Like the British fleet, not all were French built; two of the 74 gun ships, *Berwick* and *Swiftsure*, were prizes captured from the British and one 74 gun ship, *Intrépide*, had been given by Spain. The main body of the French Trafalgar fleet comprised ships of Vice-Admiral Villeneuve's squadron which, having evaded Nelson earlier, had sailed from Toulon on a diversionary course for West Indies to draw off the English Channel fleet. The other ships came from squadrons based at Brest and Rochefort that had rendezvoused at Cadiz. The number of French present would have been greater but the 74 gun ship *Atlas* and frigates *Guerièrre*, *Revanche* and *Syrène* had been docked at Vigo for repairs after their encounter with Admiral Calder on 22 July 1805, and the corvettes *Observateur* and *Téméraire* had been redeployed.[1] The French part of Villeneuve's combined fleet that finally fought at Trafalgar comprised the following ships, flag officers and commanders:

Ship's Name	Rate or Type	Guns	Flag Officer and/or Commander
Bucentaure	3rd	80	Vice-Admiral Pierre Villeneuve & Captain J J Magendie
Formidable	3rd	80	Rear-Admiral P M R E Dumanoir Le Pelley & Captain J M Lettelier
Indomptable	3rd	80	Captain J J Hubert
Neptune	3rd	80	Commodore E T Maistral
Achille	3rd	74	Captain G Deniéport
Aigle	3rd	74	Captain P P Gourrège
Algésiras	3rd	74	Captain Le Tourneur
Argonaute	3rd	74	Captain J Epron
Berwick	3rd	74	Captain J G Filhol-Camas
Duguay Trouin	3rd	74	Captain Claude Touffet
Fougueux	3rd	74	Captain L A Baudoin
Héros	3rd	74	Captain J B J R Poulain
Intrépide	3rd	74	Captain L A C Infernet
Mont Blanc	3rd	74	Captain J G N La Villegris
Pluton	3rd	74	Commodore J M Cosmao-Kerjulien
Redoutable	3rd	74	Captain J J E Lucas
Scipion	3rd	74	Captain Charles Bellanger
Swiftsure	3rd	74	Captain C E l'Hôpitalier-Villemadrin
Cornélie	5th	40	Captain de Martinenq
Hermione	5th	40	Captain Mahé
Hortense	5th	40	Captain La Marre La Melilerie
Rhin	5th	40	Captain Chesneau
Thémis	5th	40	Captain Jugan
Furet	Brig	18	Lieutenant Dumay
Argus	Brig	16	Lieutenant Tailliard

Of the eighteen 80 and 74 gun line of battle ships, 15 (83 per cent) were designed by one man, Jacques Noel Sane, who was as innovative a ship designer as his English counterpart Thomas Slade. That most of the ships were designed by Sane meant that French warships were, compared with the British ships at Trafalgar, more standardised in their construction. This uniformity was advantageous because refitting and repair would, in theory, be far easier as specifications would be standardised. The remaining three 74 gun ships comprised a Spanish vessel, previously named *Intrepido*, designed by the renowned Spanish designer Romero y Landa and given to France in 1800, and the two captured British ships *Berwick* and *Swiftsure*, both *Elizabeth* class vessels designed by Thomas Slade. Irrespective of their origins the French ships at Trafalgar had all been well designed, although the principles of their construction differed from that of the British and Spanish vessels and contributed to comparatively high French casualties in close action.[2]

Ship's Name	Rate or type	Guns	Designer	Dockyard Built	Date Launched	Age in 1805
Bucentaure	3rd	80	Jacques Noel Sane	Toulon	1803	2
Formidable	3rd	80	Jacques Noel Sane	Toulon	1795	10
Indomptable	3rd	80	Jacques Noel Sane	Brest	1788	17
Neptune	3rd	80	Jacques Noel Sane	Toulon	1803	2
Achille	3rd	74	Jacques Noel Sane	Rochefort	1802	3
Aigle	3rd	74	Jacques Noel Sane	Rochefort	1802	3
Algésiras	3rd	74	Jacques Noel Sane	Lorient	1804	1
Argonaute	3rd	74	Jacques Noel Sane	Lorient	1798	7
Berwick	3rd	74	Thomas Slade	Portsmouth	1775	30
Duguay Trouin	3rd	74	Jacques Noel Sane	Toulon	1797	8
Fougueux	3rd	74	Jacques Noel Sane	Lorient	1785	20
Héros	3rd	74	Jacques Noel Sane	Rochefort	1795	10
Intrépide	3rd	74	Romero y Landa	Ferrol - Spain	1800	5
Mont Blanc	3rd	74	Jacques Noel Sane	Rochefort	1789	16
Pluton	3rd	74	Jacques Noel Sane	Toulon	1805	9 months
Redoutable	3rd	74	Jacques Noel Sane	Brest	1790	15
Scipion	3rd	74	Jacques Noel Sane	Lorient	1798	7
Swiftsure	3rd	74	Thomas Slade	Deptford	1787	18
Cornélie	5th	40	Jacques Noel Sane	Brest	1794	11
Hermione	5th	40	André Geofrey	Lorient	1803	2
Hortense	5th	40	Jacques Noel Sane	Toulon	1803	2
Rhin	5th	40	Jacques Noel Sane	Toulon	1802	3
Thémis	5th	40	René A Haran	Bayonne	1796	9
Furet	Brig	18	Unknown	Unknown	1801	4
Argus	Brig	16	Unknown	Unknown	1799	6

Most of the French ships were built within their principal arsenals: seven at Toulon, five at Lorient, four at Rochefort and three at Brest; the rest, excluding the British and Spanish ships, at Bayonne and smaller unrecorded yards. Timber for their construction, mainly oak, would have been procured from nearby forests. The French Trafalgar fleet comprised 80 and 74 gun line of battle ships only. Ships carrying 90 guns or more which had been more evident in the early stages of conflict had been considered too costly to construct at this stage of the war; while vessels of less than 74 guns had been virtually eliminated from the French fleet after the American War of Independence, because 50 and 64 gun ships had insufficient firepower and were not as cost effective as the more versatile 74s.[3] Unlike the British ships, 18 of the French Trafalgar fleet, 72 per cent, comprised vessels of 10 or fewer years old. This percentage relates to the fact that France had sustained considerable ship losses from the start of the Revolutionary War in 1793. Large fleet actions, especially battles such as the Glorious First of June in 1794 and the Nile in 1798 had taken their toll. Following these setbacks France had to undertake a comprehensive building programme. Around 52 per cent of French ships at Trafalgar were built after 1798, with only three vessels, excluding the two British, before 1794. One ship, *Achille*, blew up at the battle of Trafalgar; of the eight captured vessels, five foundered in the storm afterwards, *Algésiras* was recaptured and went into Cadiz and *Intrépide* blew up. The only prize to survive was *Swiftsure* which was returned to England where she served as a prison ship until broken up in 1816. The 16 French ships that evaded capture at Trafalgar had varying fates: Strachan's squadron captured four on 4 November 1805 and two were captured in

1806. Of the remaining vessels that reached Cadiz, one was laid up as a hulk and the others remaining in harbour were surrendered to the Spanish in June 1808 after Spain declared war on France.

Ship's Name	Initial Fate	Final Fate
Bucentaure	Captured at Trafalgar 21 October 1805	Foundered in storm October 1805
Formidable	Escaped at Trafalgar & Captured 4 November 1805	Broken up 1816
Indomptable	Escaped at Trafalgar	Surrendered to Spain 16 July 1808
Neptune	Escaped at Trafalgar	Surrendered to Spain 14 June 1808
Achille	Surrendered & Blew up at Trafalgar	
Aigle	Captured 21 October 1805	Foundered in storm 25 October 1805
Algésiras	Captured at Trafalgar and Recaptured afterwards	Surrendered to Spain 14 June 1808
Argonaute	Escaped at Trafalgar	Surrendered to Spain 14 June 1808
Berwick	Captured at Trafalgar	Foundered in storm 2 October 1805
Duguay Trouin	Escaped at Trafalgar & Captured 4 November 1805	Scuttled 1949
Fougueux	Captured at Trafalgar	Foundered in storm 22 October 1805
Héros	Escaped at Trafalgar	Surrendered to Spain 14 June 1808
Intrépide	Captured at Trafalgar	Blew up off Trafalgar 23 October 1805
Mont Blanc	Escaped at Trafalgar & Captured 4 November 1805	Sold and broken up 1819
Pluton	Escaped at Trafalgar	Hulked at Cadiz
Redoutable	Captured at Trafalgar	Foundered in storm 23 October 1805
Scipion	Escaped at Trafalgar & Captured 4 November 1805	Broken up 1819
Swiftsure	Captured at Trafalgar	Prison Ship then Broken up 1816
Cornélie	Escaped at Trafalgar	Surrendered to Spain 14 June 1808
Hermione	Escaped at Trafalgar	Surrendered to Spain 14 June 1808
Hortense	Escaped at Trafalgar	Surrendered to Spain 14 June 1808
Rhin	Escaped at Trafalgar & Captured 28 June 1806	Sold & Broken up 1884
Thémis	Escaped at Trafalgar	Unknown
Furet	Escaped at Trafalgar & Captured 12 February 1806	Unknown
Argus	Escaped at Trafalgar	Unknown

Ordnance carried in the entire French fleet of 25 ships including frigates amounted to 1,718 guns comprising 1600 carriage guns, 42 howitzers and 76 carronades. This quantity of ordnance weighed 3,534.3 tons (3,590.3 tonnes) in total. Regarding the actual armament statistics carried by the 18 line of battle ships, this amounted to 1,452 guns comprising 1,406 carriage guns, 42 howitzers and 2 carronades weighing 3,148.9 tons (3,198.2 tonnes)

THE FRENCH FLEET OF 25 SHIPS

Gun Type & Calibre	No. Of Guns	Average weight per Gun in cwt (cwt = 112 lbs)	Total weight in cwt (C = A x B)	Total weight in Tons (D = C divided by 20)	Total Weight in Tonnes (E = D x 1.016)
(Weight of shot)	A	B	C	D	E
36 pounder carriage gun	464	60	27,840.0	1,392.0	1,414.3
32 pounder carriage gun	56	55	3,080.0	154.0	155.5
24 pounder carriage gun	124	50	6,200.0	310.0	315.0
18 pounder carriage gun	554	42	23,268.0	1,163.0	1,182.0
9 pounder carriage gun	34	23	5 799.0	40.0	40.6
8 pounder carriage gun	368	22	8,096.0	404.8	411.3
32 pounder howitzer	42	17.25	725.0	36.3	36.8
18 pounder carronade	76	9.00	684.0	34.2	34.8
TOTAL	1,718	-	-	3,534.3	3,590.3

THE 18 FRENCH LINE OF BATTLE SHIPS

Gun Type & Calibre	No. Of Guns	Average weight per Gun in cwt (cwt = 112 lbs)	Total weight in cwt (C = A x B)	Total weight in Tons (D = C divided by 20)	Total Weight in Tonnes (E = D x 1.016)
(Weight of shot)	A	B	C	D	E
36 pounder carriage gun	464	60	27,840.0	1,392.0	1,414.3
32 pounder carriage gun	56	55	3,080.0	154.0	155.5
24 pounder carriage gun	124	50	6,200.0	310.0	315.0
18 pounder carriage gun	414	42	17,388.0	869.4	883.3
9 pounder carriage gun	34	23.5	799.0	40.0	40.6
8 pounder carriage gun	314	22	6,908.0	345.4	350.9
32 pounder howitzer	42	17.25	725.0	36.3	36.8
18 pounder carronade	4	9.00	36.0	1.8	1.8
TOTAL	1,452	-	-	3,148.9	3,198.2

Notes

[1] A Schom, *Trafalgar: Countdown to Victory* (London, 1990), p. 391.
[2] D Pope, *England Expects* (London, 1959), p.357.
[3] Hubert Granier, *Histoire de Marines Français* (Nantes, 1998), p.33.

PART 2: CHAPTER 1
THE FRENCH THIRD RATE 80 GUN SHIPS

The 80 gun ship BUCENTAURE

The 80 gun *Bucentaure* was the first ship in the French navy to bear this name, taken from the elaborate Italian barge *Bucentaur* used by the Doges of Venice before it was captured and destroyed when France took possession of that city and its arsenal in 1797. Designed by Jacques Noel Sane, her lines are virtually identical to contemporary 80 gun ships *Indomptable*, *Formidable*, and *Neptune*, which also fought at Trafalgar. She was also similar to *Tonnant* which, captured at the battle of the Nile in 1798, fought on the British side at Trafalgar. The two-decked 80 gun ships employed in the French navy proved far superior in design to the cumbersome and crank three-decked 80 gun ships previously used in the Royal Navy. When built *Bucentaure* would have required 3,500 to 3,700 loads of timber for her construction which relates to between 175,000 and 185,000 cubic feet of wood before conversion. This amount of timber would have been taken from 80 acres of woodland from the surrounding region of Provence and further afield. When first launched *Bucentaure* probably carried thirty 36 pounders on her lower gun deck, thirty-two 24 pounders on her upper gun deck, twenty 8 pounders on her quarter deck and forecastle and either four or six 32 pounder brass howitzers on her poop. This gave her a single broadside weight of 1,052 or 1,112 pounds. Before Trafalgar her quarter deck and forecastle armament was altered to carry a number of carronades.

THE 80 GUN SHIP *BUCENTAURE*

Bucentaure 80 Guns

Bucentaure
Body Plan
Sheer Profile
Half Breadth Plan
(Drawings by the author)

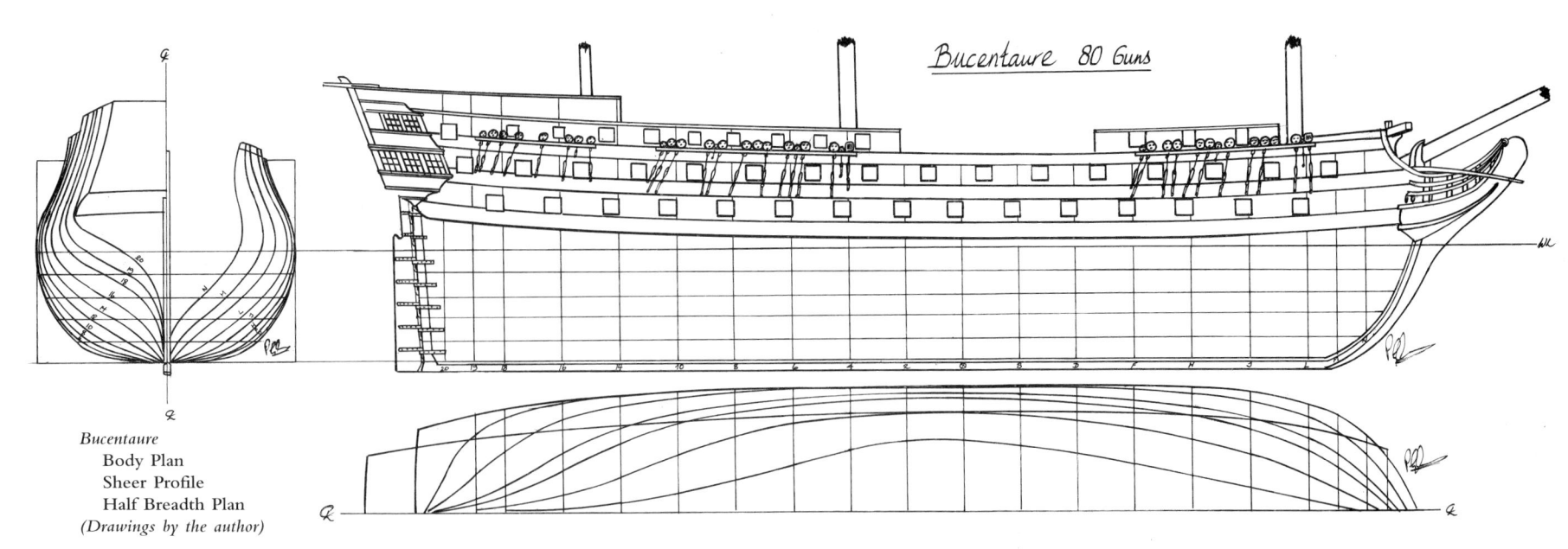

SERVICE CAREER

1803: When war with France resumed in May *Bucentaure* was one of five ships on the stocks building at Toulon, the others being a sister ship *Neptune* (80), and the 74 gun ships *Borée*, *Phæton* and *Pluton*. In command of the French Toulon fleet at the time was Vice-Admiral René Madeleine de Latouche-Tréville. Even though war had just recommenced, the British Mediterranean fleet commanded by Rear-Admiral Sir Richard Hussey Bickerton was already stationed off Toulon blockading the port.[1]

1804: Launched by May, *Bucentaure* was immediately put in commission as flagship to Latouche-Tréville under the command of Captain Jean-Jacques Magendie. Magendie remained in her for the next eighteen months. Over the next few weeks she was fitted out and completed with her masts, yards, rigging and stores. On 18 August Latouche-Tréville suddenly died and command of the Toulon fleet passed to Vice-Admiral Pierre Charles Jean Baptiste Silvestre de Villeneuve. Villeneuve was one of the few officers who had fought and escaped from Nelson at the Battle of the Nile in 1798. Villeneuve, however, did not raise his flag in *Bucentaure* until 16 November.[2]

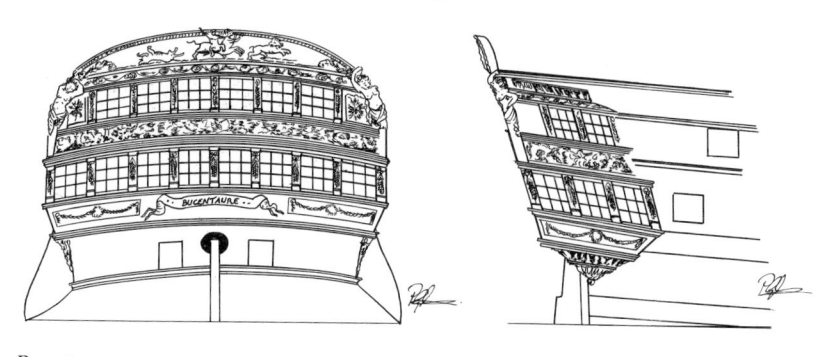

Bucentaure
Stern View   Quarter Gallery View
(Drawings by the author)

He would have embarked earlier when the Toulon fleet was expected to sail on 21 October after receiving some 6,500 troops under General Lauriston, but sailing was postponed because of the dogged alertness of Nelson's blockading ships.

1805: Taking advantage of a NNW wind and the forced withdrawal of the main body of Nelson's watching ships, *Bucentaure* finally sailed with the Toulon fleet on 17 January. Villeneuve's squadron comprised 20 vessels as follows:

Rate or Type	Guns	Ships' Names	No.
2nd	80	*Bucentaure*, *Formidable*, *Indomptable* and *Neptune*	4
3rd	74	**Annibal**, **Atlas**, *Berwick*, *Mont Blanc*, *Intrépide*, *Scipion*, and *Swiftsure*	7
5th	40	*Cornélie*, *Hortense*, *Rhin*, *Thémis*, and **Uranie**	5
5th	38	*Incorruptible*	1
5th	36	*Sirène*	1
Brig	18	*Furet*	1
Brig	16	*Naïade*	1
Total ships			20
Total gunpower			1146

NOTE: Those denoted in bold type were NOT present at Trafalgar.

Unfortunately for Villeneuve, his fleet was sighted at 6.30 p.m. by frigates *Active* (38) and *Seahorse* (38) which had remained on station. Moreover, as the French sailed westward into the Gulf of Lyons, the weather deteriorated, dispersing their ships and compelling Villeneuve to return to Toulon on 20 January.[3]

Under new orders *Bucentaure* with her consorts finally sailed from Toulon on 29 March. Evading Nelson, Villeneuve sailed for Cartagena as instructed, arriving there on 6 April. Here he was to be joined by six Spanish ships commanded by Admiral Salcedo. However Salcedo refused to leave the harbour. Wasting no more time, Villeneuve sailed through the Straits of Gibraltar two days later and after taking on provisions at Cadiz, sailed for

SPECIFICATIONS: *BUCENTAURE*

Rate	3rd	Length on the range of the gun deck	195 ft 2 ins	Ordnance - lower gun deck	30 x 36 pounders
Guns	80	Length of keel for tonnage		Ordnance - upper gun deck	30 (or 32) x 24 pounders
Class	Sane-Border 1787	Extreme breadth	51 ft 4 ins	Ordnance - quarter deck	12 x 8 pounders
Designer	Jacques Noel Sane	Depth in hold	23 ft 2 ins	Ordnance - forecastle	6 x 8 pounders
Builder	Dockyard	Tons burthen	2231 tons	Ordnance - poop deck	4 (or 6) x 36 pounder howitzers
Dockyard	Toulon	Draught afore		Single broadside weight	1052 (or 1112) pounds
Date ordered		Draught abaft		Fate	Foundered in storm after battle of Trafalgar
Date keel laid	1801/02	Complement	690		
Date launched	1803				

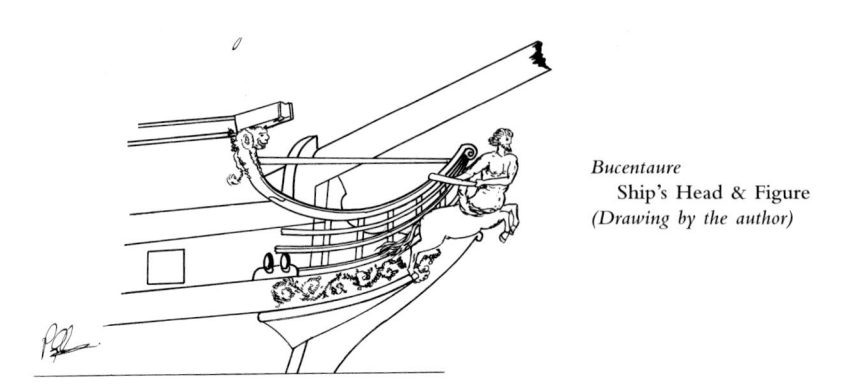

Bucentaure
Ship's Head & Figure
(Drawing by the author)

the West Indies as ordered. *Bucentaure* with 17 sail of the line, seven frigates and several smaller vessels anchored off Fort Royal (Port du France), Martinique on 3 May. In company was the English sloop *Cyane* (18) and a storeship captured en route. While waiting for Admiral Ganteaume, *Bucentaure*'s crew made good rigging repairs. On 29 May Villeneuve detached vessels to attack Diamond Rock. After Villeneuve received new orders from Napoleon on 1 June, *Bucentaure* put to sea with the rest of the fleet on 4 June, reaching Guadeloupe two days later where they met Ganteaume with *Achille* and *Algésiras*. Troops were then embarked for the next stage of the campaign, which was to attack British colonies, particularly Antigua with its dockyard. Instead Villeneuve captured a British convoy of 15 sail of merchantmen that had sailed from Antigua on 7 June carrying cargo valued at £200,000. These ships were taken into Guadeloupe by the frigate *Sirène* (40). When Villeneuve received news that Nelson had arrived in the West Indies he aborted his plans, disembarked the troops at Guadeloupe and sailed for Europe.[4]

Around noon on 22 July *Bucentaure* and Villeneuve's fleet fell in with Rear-Admiral Sir Robert Calder's squadron off Finisterre. Due to poor visibility and little wind the initial engagement did not begin until after 3 p.m. and for the next five hours fighting was sporadic, with ships firing at opponents when they materialised out of the fog. When action discontinued around 8.30 p.m. only two Spanish ships, *Firme* and *San Rafael*, had been taken. Next day Villeneuve took the initiative and, despite his objective of keeping his fleet intact to support the next stage of Napoleon's invasion plan, he decided to bear down upon Calder's damaged ships. Realising that poor wind conditions would not allow him to close with them until after nightfall Villeneuve resumed his original design to join the Brest fleet. Although Calder had won a small victory against the numerically superior Franco-Spanish fleet, he had failed to take the initiative to bring about a decisive action. Villeneuve could now re-mobilise. Calder was recalled home to face a court-martial. Although acquitted, he was severely reprimanded.[5]

Bucentaure had played little part in the action. Relatively unscathed she made sail and entered Vigo Bay on 27 July, moving round into Ferrol on 2 August. After making necessary repairs *Bucentaure* and her consorts weighed on the evening of the 9 August. Failing to rendezvous with Rear-Admiral Allemand's Rochefort squadron as intended, Villeneuve contravened his orders and sailed south for Cadiz. While passing Cape St Vincent on 18 August *Bucentaure* and her consorts captured and burnt three merchantmen. As he approached Cadiz at 10 a.m. on 20 August, Villeneuve detached a number of ships to chase off Collingwood's blockading ships, *Dreadnought* (98), *Achille* (74), and *Colossus* (74). *Bucentaure* anchored in Cadiz later that evening.[6] Villeneuve's decision to go into Cadiz instead of going north towards Brest was, if Napoleon's invasion of England was to succeed, a strategic error. For Villeneuve it was political suicide.

The failure of the French naval squadrons to combine forces and enter the English Channel forced Napoleon to abort his invasion plan against Britain. Moreover a Third Coalition against France had been formed between Britain, Austria, Russia and Sweden. Outflanked and threatened from the east Napoleon, decamped his invasion forces and moved them east to face the Austrian army. To support this new theatre of war against the Austro-Russian forces and dissuade Prussia from entering this Third Coalition, Villeneuve received new orders to take the combined fleet into the Mediterranean. To achieve this he had to break out through the Nelson's blockading fleet stationed off Cadiz.

TRAFALGAR

Bucentaure and the combined fleet began leaving Cadiz on 19 October. Assembled next morning they sailed towards Gibraltar in three divisions shadowed by Nelson's ships. Later that night the combined fleet regrouped into line ahead. By Monday 21 October Villeneuve realised that action could not be evaded. At 8.30 a.m. he ordered his fleet to wear together and come round on a larboard tack northward towards Cadiz, each ship clearing for action. This put his flagship *Bucentaure* in the centre, lying eleventh in line from the head of the van. Ahead lay the mighty *Santísima Trinidad* (136), astern *Neptune* (80) and on her larboard quarter, *Redoutable*. The nearest frigate, *Hortense* (40), lay some four cables distant (half a mile) off *Bucentaure*'s starboard quarter.

Just before noon as *Victory* was making her approach leading Nelson's windward division, Captain Magendie ordered the colours to be raised in *Bucentaure*. At about 12.20 p.m. *Bucentaure*, in unison with *Santísima Trinidad*, *Neptune*, and *Redoutable*, commenced firing at the British column, concentrating their 185 guns upon *Victory*. Just before 1 p.m. *Victory* crossed *Bucentaure*'s stern at a range of barely 28 feet and firing her larboard batteries, raked her with double and treble shotted guns. Upwards of 1.5 tons of solid iron round shot, together with grapeshot, slammed through the entire length of *Bucentaure*'s decks, up-turning guns, cutting through timber and scything down men. Reeling from the effects, Captain Magendie found the entire stern of *Bucentaure* reduced to match-wood, 20 guns out of action

SHIPS ENGAGED IN ACTION OFF CAPE FINISTERRE 22 JULY 1805

Guns	Fr/Sp	Combined Franco-Spanish fleet Ships' Names	Guns	British fleet Ships' Names
90	Spanish:	*Argonauta*	98	*Barfleur*, *Glory*, *Prince of Wales* and *Windsor Castle*
80	French:	*Bucentaure*, *Formidable*, *Indomptable* and *Neptune*	80	*Malta*
	Spanish:	*San Rafael* [captured]		
74	French:	*Achille*, *Aigle*, *Algésiras*, *Berwick*, *Intrépide*, *Mont Blanc*, *Pluton*, *Scipion*, *Swiftsure*, and *Firme* [captured]	74	*Ajax*, *Dragon*, *Hero*, *Repulse*, **Thunderer**, *Triumph*, and *Warrior*
	Spanish:			
–	–	–	64	*Agamemnon* and *Raisonnable*
40	French:	*Cornélie*, *Didon*, *Hortense*, *Rhin*, *Sirène* and *Thémis*	40	*Egyptienne*
–	Spanish:	*Santa Magdalena*	36	*Sirius*
18	French:	*Furet*	Lugger	*Nile*
16	French:	*Naïade*	Cutter	*Frisk*
TOTAL SHIPS	25		18	
TOTAL GUNS	1424		1194	

NOTE: Those denoted in bold type WERE present at Trafalgar.

and some 200 killed and wounded in this one devastating salvo.[7] Within 15 minutes the English *Neptune* (98) ranged up across *Bucentaure*'s stern and raked her with trebled shotted guns. This volley, containing forty-two 32 pound balls, eighty-seven 18 pound balls and thirty 12 pound balls, brought a second wave of devastation, taking every remaining 24 pounder gun off its carriage and killing half the remaining men manning *Bucentaure*'s lower deck 36 pounders. Turning to larboard, *Neptune* then poured another broadside into *Bucentaure*'s starboard side before passing on to engage *Santísima Trinidad*. This last salvo wounded Captain Magendie, who was sent below, relieved by Lieutenant Joseph Daudignon. The few men remaining on *Bucentaure*'s upper decks went below to reinforce the depleted guns' crews. There was a short reprieve: *Bucentaure* was raked in succession by *Leviathan* (74) and *Conqueror* (74), these broadsides bringing down her main and mizzen masts and, ironically, Villeneuve's signal for Dumanoir's squadron to turn back into action. *Conqueror* then came to *Bucentaure*'s starboard quarter, ready to fire again. While Lieutenant Daudignon, now also wounded, was relieved by Lieutenant Fournier, *Bucentaure*'s foremast collapsed over the side. Unable to fly any colours Midshipman Donadieu bravely clasped the French Eagle to his chest and conspicuously stood on the upper deck as *Conqueror* fired another salvo. Amid the thunderous destruction Villeneuve grievously complained to Prigny, his Chief of Staff, 'that he was spared amidst so many balls, grape and splinters'. Hit in his right leg by a splinter Prigny fell to the deck before making any reply. Despite the fact that *Bucentaure* had now been reduced to a total wreck, she was further fired upon from *Britannia*. Villeneuve recorded that the boat prepared to transfer him to another command ship had been smashed or lost. All other boats stowed on the skid beams had been shot to pieces. Villeneuve then said, 'I had the *Santísima Trinidad*, which was ahead of us, hailed to know if she could send a boat and give us a tow. I had no reply; this ship was herself engaging vigorously with a three decker [*Neptune*]'. He continued:

> In the end, surrounded by the enemy ships which had congregated on my quarters, astern and abreast to leeward; being powerless to do them any injury, the upper-works and the 24 pounder gun-deck being deserted and strewn with dead and wounded; the lower-deck guns dismounted or masked by the fallen mats and rigging; the ship isolated in the midst of the enemy, lying motionless, and it being impossible to make any movement, I was obliged to yield to my fate and put an end to a slaughter already vast, which was from henceforward useless.

To this end a white handkerchief of surrender was waved towards *Conqueror*. Before being boarded Fournier had the French Eagle smashed and cast overboard to avoid it becoming a trophy of war. Magendie, with his wounds dressed, returned on deck at this poignant moment as James Atcherley, Captain of Marines plus marine corporals, privates and seamen from *Conqueror* entered *Bucentaure* to take her surrender. Villeneuve, Captain Magendie and several of the admiral's aides went down the side into *Conqueror*'s boat with Atcherley, leaving Prigny to deal with the ship and her casualties.[7] Final casualties in *Bucentaure* amounted to 40 per cent of her complement, comprising 197 dead and 85 wounded.[8] Considering the tremendous multi-shotted raking fire she received, let alone the close broadsides from *Neptune* and *Conqueror*, this figure is far less than expected.

Taken in tow by *Conqueror*, *Bucentaure* had now been placed under the command of Lieutenant Richard Spear. Next day the rising storm began to take its toll on the British ships and their prizes and repairs were hastily made within *Bucentaure* to keep her seaworthy. On the morning of Wednesday 23 October, when Captain Cosmao-Kerjulien ventured out of Cadiz in a gallant attempt to recapture some of the prizes, *Bucentaure* was cast off her tow as *Conqueror* made provision to counter attack this threat. Taking advantage of this opportunity, French prisoners within *Bucentaure* overwhelmed the prize crew and retook the ship. Their victory was short lived, however. While endeavouring to get into Cadiz, *Bucentaure* drifted onto the Puercos rocks near the harbour entrance and went to pieces. Barely 18 months old, this great ship was no more. Despite the raging storm, most of the French seamen and the prize crew were rescued by boats from two French warships. The prize crew, Lieutenant Spear included, were detained at Cadiz and treated with dignity. They were later released back to Collingwood under a flag of truce.[10]

The 80 gun ship FORMIDABLE

Formidable was the second 80 gun ship of the French revolutionary navy to bear this name. Her predecessor, launched at Rochefort as *Lion*, later changed to *Marat* and then renamed *Formidable*, was captured in Lord Bridport's action off Isle de Groix against Villaret on 23 June 1795. Once entered in the British navy this *Formidable* was renamed *Belleisle*. The Trafalgar *Formidable* was launched at Toulon in 1795 under her original name of *Figuières*. Designed by Jacques Noel Sane, her lines are virtually identical to her 80 gun contemporaries *Bucentaure*, *Indomptable* and *Neptune*, which fought at Trafalgar, and *Tonnant* which fought on the British side.

When first launched *Figuières/Formidable* carried thirty 36 pounders on her lower gun deck, thirty two 24 pounders on her upper gun deck, twenty 8 pounders on her quarter deck and forecastle and either four or six 32 pounder brass howitzers on her poop. She could deliver a single broadside weight of 1,076 or 1,112 pounds.

SERVICE CAREER

1795: Although built under the name *Figuières*, this 80 gun ship was

SPECIFICATIONS: *FORMIDABLE*

Rate	3rd	Length on the range of the gun deck	194 ft 6 ins	Ordnance - upper gun deck	32 x 24 pounders
Guns	80	Length of keel for tonnage	159 ft 7¼ ins	Ordnance - quarter deck	12 x 8 pounders
Class	Sane-Border	Extreme breadth	51 ft 5½ ins	Ordnance - forecastle	8 x 8 pounders
Designer	Jacques Noel Sane	Depth in hold	26 ft 6 ins	Ordnance - Poop	4 or 6 x 32 pounder brass howitzers
Builder	Dockyard	Tons burthen	2249 tons	Single broadside weight	1,076 (or 1112) pounds
Dockyard	Toulon	Draught afore		Fate	Captured by Sir Richard Strachan's squadron 4 November 1805. Renamed *Brave* and entered into British navy. Hulked 1808 as a Prison Ship, Converted to a Powder Hulk in 1814. Broken up 1816.
Date ordered	1794	Draught abaft			
Date keel laid		Complement	690		
Date launched	1795	Ordnance - lower gun deck	30 x 36 pounders		

Source: Lyon, *Sailing Navy List*, p. 267.

renamed *Formidable* after the capture of her namesake by the British on 23 June 1795. After her launch it appears that *Formidable* saw no true service until 1800.

1800: During this year *Formidable* was deployed with the Brest fleet commanded by Rear-Admiral Honoré Ganteaume. In command of the ship was Captain J Allary. Shortly afterwards Rear-Admiral C A L Durand, Compte de Linois, hoisted his flag in the ship. Prior to attaining flag rank, he had served as captain on the previous *Formidable* when she was captured by Lord Bridport off Isle de Groix in 1795.

1801: On 7 January *Formidable* sailed from Brest with Ganteaume's squadron of ten ships, Ganteaume flying his flag in *Indivisible* (80). The rest of the squadron comprised *Indomptable* (80), the 74 gun ships *Desaix*, *Dix Août* (ex-*Tyrannicide*), *Constitution* and *Jean Bart*, accompanied by *Créole* (40), *Bravoure* (40) and the 12 gun lugger *Vautour*. As soon as these ships attempted to make their way through the Passage du Raz on 8 January, the blockading ships under Vice-Admiral Henry Harvey made chase, forcing Ganteaume to anchor off the mouth of the Vilaine before returning to Brest. On 23 January *Formidable* sailed again with the Brest fleet, appalling weather having driven off Harvey's ships. Although suffering some damage to topmasts and rigging, *Formidable* and her consorts evaded the British squadrons, passing through the Straits of Gibraltar to arrive at Toulon on 19 February.[11]

Receiving new orders from Napoleon, Ganteaume's squadron sailed from Toulon on 27 April for Egypt. He was also to call in and reduce Porto Ferrajo, Elba, en route. When they put into Leghorn, Ganteaume ordered *Formidable* and several other short-handed ships back to Toulon. Command of *Formidable* was superseded by Captain Laindet Lalonde. Still flying his flag in the ship, the Compte de Linois received orders to proceed to Cadiz where he would pick up six French and six Spanish line of battle ships carrying 1,560 troops. *Formidable* sailed from Toulon on 13 June with *Indomptable*, *Desaix*, and *Muiron* (40) and sailed westwards, driving off the cruising British frigates. *Formidable* and her consorts approached Gibraltar on 1 July, capturing a British brig, *Speedy* (14), commanded by Lord Cochrane. Finding that Rear-Admiral Sir James Saumarez was cruising with a British squadron of reasonable force off Cadiz, *Formidable* and her flotilla bore up for Algeciras and anchored off Gibraltar on 4 July. Saumarez, flying his flag in *Cæsar* (80), sailed with the 74 gun ships *Audacious*, *Hannibal*, *Pompée*, *Spencer* and *Venerable*. They arrived off Algeciras on 6 July and disregarding the shore batteries sited along the coast, drove into the bay to attack Linois' anchored ships. Action commenced around 8 p.m. with *Formidable* coming under close fire from *Pompée* just 45 minutes later, Meanwhile *Formidable* was being warped closer inshore. The other ships closed and by 10 a.m. firing from both sides was heavy. Seeing that *Pompée* was only able to use her foremost guns into *Formidable*, Saumarez ordered *Hannibal* to 'go and rake the French admiral'. Captain Ferris cut *Hannibal's* cable, tacked and attempted to bring his ship between *Formidable* and the shore, but in doing so ran aground. Completely stranded, *Hannibal* was severely mauled. Losing her fore and main masts and with many guns disabled, she was compelled to strike her colours. Action continued until 1.35 p.m. when Saumarez, under sustained fire from French ships and shore batteries, ordered his squadron to cease fire and withdrew, leaving *Hannibal* in French possession. British casualties amounted to 121 killed and 252 wounded. Although Linois' ships had put up a superb defence, casualties were high: 306 dead and 280 wounded. Among the dead was *Formidable's* commander Laindet Lalonde.

On Lalonde's death command of *Formidable* was succeeded by Commander Aimable Gilles Troude. On 9 July *Formidable* and her squadron were reinforced by a Spanish squadron from Cadiz commanded by Vice-Admiral Don Juan Joaquin de Moreno, which included *Argonauta* (80) which would later fight off Trafalgar. This Franco-Spanish fleet now comprised two 112, one 94, three 80, three 74, three 44 and 40 gun frigates and

PROGRESS BOOK: *BRAVE* (EX-*FORMIDABLE*)

At what Port	Arrived	Docked	Coppered
Plymouth	11 Nov 1805		Copper Repaired 1808
Plymouth		Taken in Hand 25 July and completed	

Taken to Pieces April 1816

a 14 gun brig, in all 918 guns. Getting into Gibraltar, Saumarez's squadron had also been strengthened but comprised only one 80, four 74s, one 32 gun frigate, one 14 gun polacre and an 8 gun brig, total armament a mere 430 guns. The two fleets came to action off Cabareta Point in late evening of 12 July, the action continuing through the night, by which time both Moreno and Linois had long since transferred into the Spanish frigate *Sabina* (44). At 5.15 next morning *Formidable* got into close action against *Venerable* (74) and by 5.30 a.m. her broadsides had taken down *Venerable's* mizzen topmast. Within fifteen minutes *Thames* (32) drew up and commenced raking *Formidable's* stern. The fierce duel between *Formidable* and *Venerable* continued and at 6.45 a.m. *Venerable's* main mast went by the board. When action ceased around 8 a.m. *Formidable* is reported to have lost some 25 killed and wounded which, compared to her adversary, appears a small number.[12] *Formidable* eventually returned to Toulon and refitted.

1803: When war with France reopened in May *Formidable* was one of six ships afloat in Toulon harbour serving with the French fleet commanded by Vice-Admiral Latouche-Tréville. The British Mediterranean fleet stationed off Toulon was commanded by Rear-Admiral Sir Richard Hussey Bickerton.[13]

1805: Flying the flag of Rear-Admiral Pierre Renée Marie Etienne Dumanoir Le Pelley (hereafter Dumanoir), and commanded by Captain Jean Marie Letellier, *Formidable* put to sea with Vice-Admiral Villeneuve's fleet on 17 January. Meeting violent gales in the Gulf of Lyons two days later, many of Villeneuve's ships sustained so much damage aloft they were forced to run back into port, *Formidable* being no exception. She finally sailed from Toulon with Villeneuve's combined fleet on 30 March and successfully evaded Nelson's blockading ships. With Villeneuve, *Formidable* sailed to the West Indies and on her return took part in Vice-Admiral Sir Robert Calder's action west of Cape Finisterre on 22 July. Like many ships that day, British or French, *Formidable* played little part during the battle. With Villeneuve's ships, *Formidable* put into Vigo Bay on 27 July and then into Ferrol on 2 August. After refitting and provisioning *Formidable* put to sea on 9 August. When Villeneuve failed to rendezvous with Admiral Allemand's Rochefort squadron he headed south, *Formidable* entering Cadiz 21 August.

TRAFALGAR

When *Formidable* put to sea with the combined fleet on 19 October, Rear-Admiral Dumanoir commanded the rear division. After the combined fleet turned north and reversed its sailing order on the morning of 21 October *Formidable*, lay fourth in line from the head of Villeneuve's fleet, ahead was the Spanish *Rayo* (100), astern *Duguay Trouin* (74). Once battle had opened and Nelson's division had cut through the line Dumanoir's van of ten ships became isolated and with little wind available five of Dumanoir's ships, *Neptuno*, *Scipion*, *Rayo*, *Duguay Trouin*, *Mont Blanc* and his own *Formidable* found themselves unable to tack to return and support Villeneuve's centre. Some of his ships used their boats to turn their ship's heads back through the wind, but when Dumanoir's ships eventually hauled their wind and re-entered the battle, the British ships had already gained the advantage. With *Formidable* leading the line, followed by *Duguay Trouin*, *Mont Blanc*, and *Scipion*, Dumanoir attempted to give support but came under raking fire from *Minotaur* (74) and *Spartiate* (74) which were just entering the battle.

THE 80 GUN SHIP FORMIDABLE

3rd RATE OF 80 GUNS: Source: ADM 180/10 Folio 44

Launched or Undocked	Sailed	Built or Nature of Repair	Cost of Hull, Masts & Yards Materials £	Workmen £	Cost of Masts & Yards Materials £	Workmen £	Cost of Rigging & Stores Materials £	Workmen £	Grand Total £
		Fitted for a Prison Ship	2,191	1,589			652	12	4,444
	Oct 1814	Fitted for a Powder Ship							

Apart from engaging with these two and firing long range at whatever British ships presented themselves, Dumanoir had lost the opportunity of pressing home a counter-attack which could very well have changed the entire course of the battle. By 4.30 p.m. *Formidable* and her three consorts, unscathed, sailed from the mêlée and made good their escape. Although *Formidable* did not play a considerable part in the battle three of her guns were dismounted and she had received some damage aloft. As for casualties, she suffered just 22 killed and 45 wounded.[14]

Sailing off Cape Finisterre on 2 November, *Formidable*, accompanied by *Duguay Trouin*, *Mont Blanc* and *Scipion*, was sighted by *Phœnix* (36), Captain Thomas Baker. After giving chase Baker steered south to inform Captain Sir Richard Strachan who was lying off Ferrol with his squadron comprising the following 8 ships:

Guns	Ships' Names	Total
80	Cæsar	1
74	Bellona, Courageux, Hero, Namur	4
38	Révolutionnaire	1
36	Santa Margarita	1
32	Æolus	1

Joined by *Phœnix* (36), Strachan, flying his pendant in *Cæsar*, immediately set off with his squadron in pursuit. During the chase Captain Letellier ordered twelve of *Formidable*'s quarter deck 12 pounders to be thrown overboard to lighten the ship. The loss of these, plus the three guns put out of action at Trafalgar, put this ship at a disadvantage. Next afternoon *Bellona*, being a poor sailer, parted company. By morning 4 November Strachan's ships had closed within six miles of Dumanoir's squadron. At around 11.45 a.m. *Cæsar*, *Courageux* and *Hero* formed line ahead and commenced running down upon the four Frenchmen. Dumanoir ordered his ships to take in their small sails and come to on a starboard tack NE by E. Dumanoir then formed his squadron into line ahead with *Duguay Trouin* leading the line by *Formidable*, *Mont Blanc* and *Scipion*. Action commenced at 12.15 p.m. with Strachan's ships coming up on Dumanoir's windward side and opening their fire from their larboard guns. A hot contest ensued during which Strachan signalled for close action and brought his ship *Cæsar* into action with *Formidable*. After an hour Dumanoir's ships tacked to larboard, the British ships giving chase. At around 2 p.m. battle resumed with *Hero* engaging *Scipion*. Shortly afterwards *Hero* drew alongside *Formidable*'s windward side and having fore-reached her, stood off her weather bow and commenced pouring her broadsides into Dumanoir's ship. When *Hero* was joined by *Namur* at 2.45 p.m. *Formidable* found herself hard pushed to sustain herself under fire from two ships. Although she gave a good account, when the refitted *Cæsar* joined at 3.05 p.m. Dumanoir was compelled to strike his colours within just ten minutes. While *Namur* took possession of *Formidable*, *Scipion* also struck, with *Duguay Trouin* and *Mont Blanc* striking shortly after. It had been a hard pressed fight with French casualties amounting to 750 killed and wounded compared to just 24 killed and eleven wounded within Strachan's squadron. *Formidable* was taken into Plymouth on 11 November.[15] As there was already a 98 gun ship named *Formidable* serving in the Royal Navy, *Formidable* was renamed *Brave*, after which she was simply laid up in ordinary in the Hamoaze.

1808: During this year *Brave* had her copper repaired and was then fitted 'for a Prison Ship' at a cost of £2,191 for materials and £1,589 for labour. With further charges for stores at £664, the total cost of this conversion amounted to £4,444. Serving her new rôle detaining French prisoners of war she was commanded by the following officers:

CAPTAINS OF *BRAVE* (MS 248/6)

Name	Time of Entry	Time of Discharge	On What Occasion
John Ribouleau	10 January 1808	2 February 1810	Discharged Dead
Edmund Nepean	1 March 1810	14 September 1810	Superseded
George A Aire	14 September 1810	29 December 1810	Superseded
George Hayes	21 December 1810	20 April 1811	Superseded
Henry Raye	29 April 1811	18 October 1812	Discharged Dead
William Stylis	24 October 1812		

FATE

No longer required as a prison hulk when the war ended in 1814, *Brave* was 'Taken in hand 25 July' and 'Fitted for a Powder Ship', the work being completed that October. Fulfilling this rôle for two years, *Brave* was 'Taken to Pieces' in April 1816.[16]

The 80 gun ship INDOMPTABLE

Built to the standard 80 gun lines designed by Jacques Noel Sane, *Indomptable* was launched at Brest in 1788, her name meaning indomitable, invincible. Her specification differed very little from those of the *Bucentaure*, *Formidable* and *Neptune*. She would also have carried an identical configuration of ordnance on her respective decks with the possibility of having some guns substituted with carronades by 1805. Her single broadside weight was in the range of 1,052 or 1,112 pounds.

SERVICE CAREER

1794: As part of the Brest fleet under the command of Admiral Villaret-Joyeuse, *Indomptable* put to sea on 16 May with 24 other ships of the line, several frigates and corvettes. Their object was to meet and escort an incoming convoy from America carrying much needed grain and other necessities essential to the French economy. Three days later *Indomptable* with Villaret's ships captured a Dutch Lisbon convoy. Admiral Howe's fleet was already at sea intent on joining Rear-Admiral Montague's smaller squadron which, already pursuing the French, may have been in danger. The two fleets of Villaret and Howe confronted each other first on 28 May. *Indomptable* was not directly involved. A second action commenced at 8 a.m. next day. However it was not until after 1.30 p.m. that *Indomptable* came

SPECIFICATIONS: *INDOMPTABLE*

Rate	3rd	Length on the range of the gun deck	194 ft 0 ins	Ordnance - lower gun deck	30 x 36 pounders
Guns	80	Length of keel for tonnage		Ordnance - upper gun deck	30 (or 32) x 24 pounders
Class	Sane-Border	Extreme breadth	51 ft 4½ ins	Ordnance - quarter deck	12 x 8 pounders
Designer	Jacques Noel Sane	Depth in hold	23 ft 2 ins	Ordnance - forecastle	6 x 8 pounders
Builder	Dockyard	Tons burthen	2231 tons	Ordnance - poop deck	4 (or 6) x 36 pounder howitzers
Dockyard	Brest	Draught afore		Single broadside weight	1052 (or 1112) pounds.
Date ordered		Draught abaft		Fate	Survived the battle of Trafalgar and surrendered over to Spain 16 July 1808
Date keel laid		Complement	690		
Date launched	1788				

under fire from Vice-Admiral Hood's *Royal George* (100) and Rear-Admiral Gardner's flagship *Queen* (98). During this engagement *Indomptable*, like her consort *Tyrannicide* ahead of her, suffered considerable damage. *Indomptable* was then hotly engaged by *Barfleur* (98) and *Orion* (74). Despite suffering further damage and rising casualty figures, *Indomptable* continued to fight with her colours flying for the best part of an hour until she and *Terrible* were rescued by Villaret's ships driving down to give assistance. Severely damaged, *Indomptable* was sent home escorted by *Mont Blanc*.[17]

1796: Commanded by Commodore Bedout and flying the flag of Vice-Admiral Morard de Galles, *Indomptable* sailed from Brest for Ireland on 15 December. By this point, following common French practice, de Galles had transferred into the frigate *Fraternité* (40). Ill fated from its outset, this expedition, carrying some 18,000 troops under the command of General Hoche, became dispersed within the first two days of leaving port. *Indomptable* with part of the fleet under Rear-Admiral Bouvet eventually reached Bantry Bay on 21 December. Beset with appalling weather the ships had to stand off; unable to anchor, troops were not landed. As the provision ships had also failed to reach their destination Bouvet aborted the invasion and sailed for Brest, *Indomptable* reaching there with *Fougueux*, *Redoutable*, *Mucius*, and *Patriote* on 1 January 1797, remaining in port under successive British blockading fleets.[18]

1801: Napoleon, realising that a British fleet under Lord Keith was preparing to expel the French from Egypt, directed Rear Admiral Honoré Ganteaume to assemble the Brest fleet and sail for Alexandria with reinforcements. Besides *Indomptable*, now commanded by Commodore Moncousu, Ganteaume's squadron comprised the following ten ships:

Rate or type	Guns	Ships' Names	No.
3rd	80	*Indivisible*, *Indomptable* and *Formidable*	3
3rd	74	*Constitution*, *Desaix*, *Dix Août* and *Jean Bart*	4
5th	40	*Créole* and *Bravoure*	2
Lugger	12	*Vautour*	1

Flying his flag in *Indivisible*, Ganteaume sailed on 7 January with *Indomptable* and anchored in Bertheaume Roads to await other French ships acting as decoys, to draw off the blockading British ships. With this accomplished Gauteaume weighed next day and stood through the Passage du Raz. However, to his consternation, his ships were discovered by a division of the Channel squadron under Vice-Admiral Sir Henry Harvey. *Indomptable* and her consorts stood back into the coast and anchored, creating a ruse to pretend to Harvey that the fleet had no other notions. Ganteaume's ships remained anchored off Brest for two weeks waiting for the wind to back round to the north and drive the blockading ships off station. When the wind finally rose to storm force on 23 January *Indomptable* and the squadron weighed and put to sea. Two days later when *Indomptable* was off Cape Finisterre with *Formidable*, *Constitution*, *Desaix*, *Dix Août*, *Jean Bart* and *Bravoure*, they were sighted by *Concorde* (36). This British frigate was, after being chased by one of Commodore Moncousu's 74s and in action with *Bravoure*, obliged to stand off. Moncousu then took *Indomptable* and his detachment south and after rejoining Ganteaume, steered eastwards passing through the Straits of Gibraltar on 9 February. It was at this point that *Success* frigate (32) took up pursuit. The following day *Indomptable* and her consorts captured and scuttled the cutter *Sprightly* (12). *Success* caught up with Ganteaume's ships on 12 February but becoming too close, she was fired upon by *Indomptable* and other two deckers. Unable to escape, *Success* was compelled to strike her colours at 3 p.m. From her prisoners Ganteaume was falsely told that Lord Keith was already off Egypt and that another British squadron under Sir John Borlase Warren was in pursuit. Here Ganteaume erred; instead of engaging Warren's smaller force, he sailed for Toulon.

Detached from Ganteaume's ships, *Indomptable* remained at Toulon until sailing with Rear-Admiral Linois on 13 June. In company were Linois' flagship *Formidable* (80), *Desaix* (74) and *Muiron* (40). Carrying 1,560 troops under Brigadier-General Devaux, these ships had been ordered to sail for Cadiz and join forces with the French and Spanish ships within that port. En route, *Indomptable* and her consorts drove off the British frigates cruising off Marseilles, captured a brig on 2 July and next day captured the brig-sloop *Speedy* (14) commanded by Lord Cochrane.

Indomptable and the squadron then proceeded through the Straits of Gibraltar and anchored off Algeciras, where, on 6 July, they were attacked by Rear-Admiral Sir James Saumarez's squadron of five ships: *Cæsar* (80) and 74 gun ships *Audacious*, *Hannibal*, *Pompée* and *Spencer*. During the ensuing action, which commenced just before 8 a.m., *Indomptable* ran aground while trying to warp further inshore. For two hours firing was heavy from both sides during which Captain Moncousu of *Indomptable* and Captain Lalonde of *Formidable*, were killed. The British attack was unsuccessful for, besides not getting in close enough for fear of grounding, the French ships were well covered by shore batteries. *Hannibal*, which had grounded and became partially dismasted and severely damaged from gun fire, was compelled to strike her colours. Saumarez's ships then retired to Gibraltar. Both sides suffered high casualties: French losses were 306 killed and 280 wounded; British 115 killed and 220 wounded.[19]

With Moncousu's death, command of *Indomptable* was succeeded by Captain Lucas who later commanded *Redoutable* at Trafalgar. Linois' squadron was joined by Vice-Admiral Don Juan Joaquin de Moreno's Spanish squadron from Cadiz on 10 July. This raised the strength of the fleet to two 112s, one 94, three 80s, three 74s, three 44 and 40 gun frigates and the 14 gun brig. Hurriedly refitted, Saumarez's squadron sailed from Gibraltar on 12 July and by late evening the two fleets came to action off Cabareta Point. By midnight the Spanish *Real Carlos* (112) had taken fire and blown up, *San Hermengildo* (112) exploded shortly after, with only 300 people recovered from these two vessels. Fighting continued through the night during which *St Antoine* (74) was captured. As for *Indomptable*, her rôle in this engagement does not appear to have been significant.[20]

1803: When war restarted in May *Indomptable* was one of seven ships lying at moorings in Toulon. The rest of the ships in this port that would later form part of Villeneuve's Trafalgar fleet that were on the stocks building.

1805: Now under the command of Commodore Jean Joseph, *Indomptable* sailed with Villeneuve's twenty ships on 17 January but after being sighted by Nelson's patrolling frigates and meeting poor weather in the Gulf of Lyons, she returned to harbour three days later.[21]

When *Indomptable* finally sailed from Toulon with Villeneuve's fleet on 29 March for the West Indies, her movements from this point follow exactly those of *Bucentaure*. *Indomptable* was also with Villeneuve's fleet when it fought with Rear-Admiral Sir Robert Calder's squadron off Finisterre on 22 July. Relatively unscathed, *Indomptable* eventually arrived at Cadiz on 20 August with the rest of the fleet after making good her repairs off Ferrol.[22]

TRAFALGAR

Indomptable sailed from Cadiz on 19 October. After Villeneuve's combined fleet formed line ahead sailing northward on the morning of Monday 21 October *Indomptable* lay at the centre, seventeenth from the van. Ahead on her larboard bow lay *Santa Ana* (112), on her starboard bow *San Justo* (74) and astern on her larboard quarter *Fougueux* (74). Taking her lead from *Fougueux*, *Indomptable* commenced firing her larboard broadsides just before noon at the approaching ships of Collingwood's leeward division. As Collingwood's *Royal Sovereign* (100) crossed the stern of *Santa Ana* (112) and ranged up upon *Santa Ana*'s starboard side, *Indomptable* raked the British warship and continued firing into her starboard quarter from a distance of five hundred yards and give support to the great Spanish three-decker. After *Belleisle* (74) had crossed and raked the *Santa Ana* in turn she then ported her helm and turned across the stern of *Indomptable* to rake her. *Indomptable* however was saved by the intervention of *Fougueux* which then poured a couple of broadsides into *Belleisle*. Suffering few casualties, Captain Hubert chose to carry *Indomptable* away from the battle and made for Cadiz; it was barely 1 p.m.[23]

FATE

On Tuesday 23 October *Indomptable* sailed from Cadiz with Commodore Cosmao-Kerjulien's ships in an attempt to save some of the damaged prizes. In company were *Neptune*, *Pluton*, *Rayo*, and *San Francisco de Asis*. Also with *Indomptable* were the frigates *Cornélie*, *Hermione*, *Hortense*, *Rhin*, *Thémis*, and the brigs *Argus* and *Furet*. After clearing the harbour the wind veered round to WSW and rose to storm force and although Kerjulien's intentions were highly honourable the ensuing weather conditions were far from perfect for salvaging unmanageable ships. As Kerjulien's ships approached the British ships towing their prizes they obviously posed a considerable threat. As recorded in log books, ten British ships cast off their prizes and formed line of battle to protect them. These records also imply that a second action off Trafalgar was fought. Kerjulien's force was outnumbered, and to attempt an attack with his already battle-damaged ships was foolhardy but his frigates did retake the Spanish ships *Santa Ana* (112) and *Neptuno* (80). During this sortie *Indomptable* embarked 500 survivors from *Bucentaure* before turning back for Cadiz. Next morning on 24 October *Indomptable* ran aground off Rota and, battered by the heavy seas, rapidly went to pieces with terrible loss of life. Including those taken out of *Bucentaure*, nearly 1,000 men perished.[24]

The 80 gun ship *NEPTUNE*

Like her British and Spanish namesakes, the 80 gun *Neptune* was named after the Roman god of the sea. Designed by Jacques Noel Sane, her lines are virtually identical to her contemporary 80 gun ships *Bucentaure*, *Indomptable*, and *Formidable*. She was also similar to *Tonnant* which fought on the British side at Trafalgar. Built at Toulon, *Neptune* was launched in 1803 ready for the restart of the war. The amount of timber used in construction before conversion was virtually the same as that used in *Bucentaure*. She would have carried an identical configuration of ordnance on her respective decks with the possibility of having some guns substituted with carronades by 1805. Her single broadside weight was in the range of 1,052 or 1,112 pounds.

SERVICE CAREER

1803: Although on the stocks when war restarted, *Neptune* was launched shortly afterwards and fitted out with masts, yards and standing rigging. It is very unlikely that she was put in commission immediately.[25]

1804: Towards the end of the year *Neptune* was placed in commission under the command of Commodore Esprit Tranquille Maistral and prepared ready to sail on 21 October with the rest of the Toulon fleet, now commanded by Vice-Admiral Villeneuve.[26] This fleet, carrying 6,500 troops, could not sail because of the British blockading fleet cruising off Cape Sicié.

1805: *Neptune* finally put to sea with Villeneuve's squadron of twenty ships on 17 January, only to return three days later after being sighted by the patrolling frigates of Nelson's inshore squadron and because deteriorating weather in the Gulf of Lyons dispersed the ships.[27]

Neptune eventually sailed from Toulon with Villeneuve's fleet on 29 March and followed the admiral to the West Indies, anchoring off Fort Royal, Martinique on 3 May. *Neptune*'s movements from this point follow exactly those of *Bucentaure*.[28] *Neptune* was also present when Villeneuve's fleet fought Rear-Admiral Sir Robert Calder's squadron off Finisterre on 22 July. Like *Bucentaure*, *Neptune* came out of the battle comparatively unharmed and after entering Vigo Bay four days later, moved into Ferrol on 2 August. On 9 August *Neptune* made sail with the rest of the fleet and arrived at Cadiz on 20 August.[29]

TRAFALGAR

Having received new orders from Villeneuve, Commodore Maistral prepared *Neptune* for sea and with the rest of the fleet left Cadiz on 19 October. On the morning of the battle, Monday 21 October, after the combined fleet had weared onto a northerly course, *Neptune* lay twelfth in line from the head of the van. Ahead on her larboard quarter lay Villeneuve's flagship *Bucentaure* (80), and astern on her larboard quarter *Redoutable* (74). It was some 25 minutes after battle opened that *Neptune*

SPECIFICATIONS: *NEPTUNE*

Rate	3rd	Length on the range of the gun deck	195 ft 2 ins	Ordnance - lower gun deck	30 x 36 pounders
Guns	80	Length of keel for tonnage		Ordnance - upper gun deck	30 (or 32) x 24 pounders
Class	Sane-Border 1787	Extreme breadth	51 ft 4½ ins	Ordnance - quarter deck	12 x 8 pounders
Designer	Jacques Noel Sane	Depth in hold	23 ft 2 ins	Ordnance - forecastle	6 x 8 pounders
Builder	Dockyard	Tons burthen	2231 tons	Ordnance - poop deck	4 (or 6) x 36 pounder howitzers
Dockyard	Toulon	Draught afore		Single broadside weight	1052 (or 1112) pounds
Date ordered		Draught abaft		Fate	Survived the battle of Trafalgar and surrendered over to Spain 14 July 1808.
Date keel laid	1801/02	Complement	690		
Date launched	1803				

was able to open fire on *Victory* and ships of Nelson's division as they approached. By this point *Neptune* had fallen off to leeward and astern of *Redoutable*. When *Victory* had passed and raked *Bucentaure*, *Neptune* fired her larboard batteries into Nelson's flagship, causing considerable damage to her foremast, bowsprit, spritsail yards, her foremost hull planking and beakhead bulkhead, and damaged her anchors. After discharging this salvo, Commodore Maistral ordered the jib to be run up in order to bring *Neptune* out of range should *Victory* run aboard her. It was now about 12.45 p.m. Standing off to leeward, *Neptune*'s gunners reloaded and after re-sighting their guns upon a new target, fired. Accurately time, *Neptune* poured her larboard broadsides into *Téméraire*, severing the British ship's rigging, bringing down her fore yard and main topmast, and severely damaging her fore mast and bowsprit, so much so that *Téméraire* became unmanageable. *Neptune*'s fire into *Téméraire* was equalled by broadsides from *San Justo* laying astern of *Neptune*.[30] Shortly afterwards Commodore Maistral ported his helm and turned eastward to avoid engaging *Leviathan*.[31] At about 2.30 p.m. Maistral brought *Neptune* off the starboard bow of *Belleisle* and supported the other French ships pummelling this isolated British 74 and also engaged *Polyphemus* (64). Towards the end of the battle *Neptune* gave supporting fire to protect *Principe de Asturias* as she made her escape with other rallying ships to run for Cadiz, *Neptune* doing likewise.[32] In the battle *Neptune* sustained just 54 casualties; 15 dead and 39 wounded.[33]

Having gained the safety of Cadiz relatively intact, *Neptune* put to sea again on Wednesday 23 October to support Commodore Cosmao-Kerjulien's noble attempt to recapture some of the prize ships. Sailing with *Neptune* were *Rayo* (100), *Indomptable* (80), *Pluton* (74), and *San Francisco de Asis* (74). Accompanying these line of battle ships were the French 40 gun frigates, *Hortense*, *Cornélie*, *Hermione*, *Thémis* and the brigs *Furet* (18) and *Argus* (16). Although this force was hampered by the ensuing storm and found itself confronting a defensive British line, the frigates did manage to retake the Spanish ships *Santa Ana* (112) and *Neptuno* (80). However, three of these did not make it back to Cadiz. *Indomptable* grounded off Rota and went to pieces and *San Francisco de Asis* went on shore in Cadiz Bay. To avoid running on shore *Rayo* anchored off San Lucar. While riding out the storm she rolled out her masts in the heavy seas and consequently surrendered to *Donegal* (74). Having survived all this *Rayo* finally went on shore on Saturday 26 October and became a total wreck. *Neptune* in the meantime returned safely to Cadiz.[34]

FATE

Confined by the British blockade, *Neptune* remained in Cadiz for the next two and a half years under the command of Vice-Admiral de Rosily. When Spain changed her allegiance and declared war on France on 4 July 1808 de Rosily realised that his ships were now dangerously moored within range of the Spanish shore batteries. Besides *Neptune* his squadron comprised the 74 gun ships *Algésiras*, *Argonaute*, *Héros*, *Pluton* and the 40 gun frigate *Cornélie*. Cautiously he moved his squadron out of the harbour, but on 9 June was attacked by Spanish forces from land and sea. After unsuccessfully negotiating to retain his squadron de Rosily was compelled to surrender *Neptune* and the other French ships to the Spanish on 14 June. *Neptune* was entered into the Spanish navy as *Neptuno*, replacing the Spanish ship of that name lost at Trafalgar. *Neptuno* continued serving in the Spanish Royal Navy until broken up in 1820.[35]

NOTES TO PART 2: CHAPTER 1

1. Clowes, 5, p. 52.
2. Clowes, 5, pp. 73–77.
3. Clowes, 5, p. 92.
4. Clowes, 5, pp. 101–110.
5. Clowes, 5, pp. 112–117.
6. Clowes, 5, p. 121.
7. Clowes, 5, p. 140.
8. Pope, *England Expects*, pp. 260–263.
9. Pope, *England Expects*, p. 357.
10. Fraser, *The Enemy at Trafalgar*, pp. 303–304.
11. Clowes, 4, pp. 447–450.
12. Clowes, 4, pp. 159–169.
13. Clowes, 5, p. 52.
14. Clowes, 5, pp. 149, 161.
15. TNA: PRO, ADM 180/10/44; Clowes, 5, pp. 170–174.
16. TNA: PRO, ADM 180/10/44; Lyon, *Sailing Navy List*, p. 267.
17. Clowes, 4, pp. 220–225; see also Duffy & Morriss, *The Glorious First of June*.
18. Clowes, 4, pp. 297–301.
19. Clowes, 4, pp. 460–465.
20. Clowes, 4, pp. 466–469.
21. Clowes, 5, pp. 89–92.
22. Clowes, 5, pp. 112–121.
23. Pope, *England Expects*, 275–281; Clowes, 5, pp. 15–163.
24. Pope, *England Expects*, p. 339; Clowes, 5, pp. 162–163.
25. Clowes, 5, p. 52.
26. Clowes, 5, pp. 73–77.
27. Clowes, 5, p. 92.
28. Clowes, 5, pp. 101–110.
29. Clowes, 5, pp. 112–121.
30. Clowes, 5, p. 146.
31. Pope, *England Expects*, p. 260.
32. Clowes, 5, pp. 155–156.
33. Pope, *England Expects*, p. 357.
34. Clowes, 5, 162–163.
35. Clowes, 5, pp. 246, 558; Schom, *Trafalgar*, p. 403.

PART 2: CHAPTER 2
THE FRENCH THIRD RATE 74 GUN SHIPS

The 74 gun ship ACHILLE

The French 74 gun ship *Achille* is named after Achilles, Homer's Greek hero of the Trojan War who was killed by Paris shooting an arrow into his vulnerable heel. As a ship *Achille* is perhaps most acclaimed for her spectacular destruction at the end of the battle of Trafalgar and for the rescue of Jeanette, the wife of one of her crew. Her predecessor, also 74 guns, had fought under Captain de La Villegris with Rear-Admiral Villaret's fleet against Admiral Howe at the Glorious First of June in 1794. Although this *Achille* gave good account of herself during this engagement, and nearly struck after having her masts shot away, she was eventually captured by *Ramillies* (74) and entered into the British fleet.[1]

Designed by the celebrated constructor Jacques Noel Sane, the Trafalgar *Achille* was laid down at Rochefort and eventually launched in 1802. Her sister ships at Trafalgar were *Aigle*, *Duguay Trouin*, *Héros*, *Mont Blanc*, *Redoutable* and *Scipion*. The construction of *Achille* required some 170,270 cubic feet of timber before conversion, which at 50 cubic feet per load comprised some 2,405.4 loads of which 153,243 cubic feet (90 per cent)

SPECIFICATIONS: *ACHILLE*

Rate	3rd	Length on the range of the gun deck	182 ft 6 ins	Ordnance - lower gun deck	28 x 36 pounders
Guns	74	Length of keel for tonnage (estimated)	157 ft	Ordnance - upper gun deck	30 x 18 pounders
Class	Sane-Border			Ordnance - quarter deck	12 x 8 pounders
Designer	Jacques Noel Sane	Extreme breadth	49 ft 0 ins	Ordnance - forecastle	6 x 8 pounders
Builder	Dockyard	Depth in hold	21 ft 3 ins	Ordnance - Poop	4 or 6 brass howitzers
Dockyard	Rochefort	Tons burthen	1929 tons	Single broadside weight	846 pounds
Date ordered		Draught afore	22 ft 0 ins	Fate	Took fire and blew up at the battle of Trafalgar 21 October 1805.
Date keel laid		Draught abaft	23 ft 0 ins		
Date launched	1802	Complement	550/600		

Note: Ordnance listed as for 1803/1805 Trafalgar campaign.

Source: Lyon, *Sailing Navy List*, pp. 70-71.

was oak. This quantity of timber equates to approximately seventy acres of woodland. These figures are estimated from those recorded in John Charnock's *History of Naval Architecture*.[2] Timber for *Achille*'s masts and yards, fir, pine, or spruce, would have been imported mainly from Norway and other Baltic States. Carrying twenty-eight 36 pounders on her lower gun deck, thirty 18 pounders on her upper gun deck, and eighteen 8 pounders on her quarter deck and forecastle, *Achille* could deliver a single broadside weight of 846 pounds (387.7 kg). Compared with an average English 74 gun ship, *Achille* had far greater firepower. For *Achille* to fire one broadside she would use about 282 pounds (127 kg) gunpowder.

SERVICE CAREER

1802: When *Achille* was launched at Rochefort the French Revolutionary War had already been ended with the signing of the Treaty of Amiens on 27 March.

1803: The fragile peace was short lived and when war declared against Napoleon on 16 May *Achille* was already being fitted for sea service and placed in commission under the command of Captain Gabriel Deniéport. Completed, the ship remained at Rochefort until required.

1805: In spring Deniéport received orders to join Villeneuve's forces in the West Indies. In company with *Algésiras* (74), *Achille* sailed from Rochefort on 1 May under the flag of Rear-Admiral Charles Magon de Médine, reaching Guadeloupe on 29 May. The two ships sailed again on 2 June and joined Admiral Villeneuve's squadron as directed and eventually returned across the Atlantic, only to fall in with Vice-Admiral Calder's squadron off Finisterre on 22 July.[3] It appears that *Achille* played little part in the ensuing action, after which she sailed with the rest of the fleet for Cadiz.

TRAFALGAR

Still under the command of Deniéport, *Achille* made sail with the rest of Villeneuve's ships on 19 October and by 1 p.m. had cleared Cadiz. Once all the fleet had assembled next morning *Achille* had been placed in the second division of Admiral Gravina's observation squadron which, taking a south-westerly course, led the entire combined fleet. At 6 p.m. on the 20th *Achille* signalled *Bucentaure* (80) that 18 British sail of the line had been seen bearing up on the rear of the combined fleet. At this point Villeneuve ordered the fleet to clear for battle. When Villeneuve ordered his ships to wear at 8 p.m. on the morning of the 21 October, *Achille* was fourth from the rear of the combined fleet, ahead lay *San Ildefonso* (74), astern Gravina's flagship *Principe de Asturias* (112).[4]

Achille got into close action around 1.30 p.m., Deniéport bringing his ship across the stern of the British *Belleisle* (74) and firing a heavy cannonade into her larboard quarter. Shortly after *Achille* was supported by *Aigle* (74), *San Leandro* (74) and *San Justo* (74), further threatening the surrounded British ship. Relatively unhindered, *Achille* continued engaging *Belleisle* and various British ships until about 3.30 p.m. when she received a raking broadside through her stern from the British *Swiftsure* (74). *Swiftsure* then drew up on the larboard side and commenced pouring broadsides into Deniéport's ship, her starboard side being simultaneously engaged by *Polyphemus* (64). Without support *Achille* began to succumb as concerted volleys poured into her hull. Besides having her wheel shot to pieces, losing her fore yard, main topmast and mizzenmast, *Achille*'s gallant commander Gabriel Deniéport was killed during the barrage, leaving Lieutenant Cauchard in command. At 4 p.m. *Prince* (98) ranged up alongside and fired her heavy broadside into *Achille*, bringing down her mainmast. Alarmingly, fire broke out in *Achille*'s fore top which quickly set fire to the sails and rigging. Hastily *Achille*'s crew left their guns to cut away the rigging and send the remaining mast overboard, but their actions were too late. A second broadside from *Prince* brought the flaming foremast down, destroying boats in the waist and worse still, smashing the fire engine. Uncontrollable fire began to spread through the ship, burning débris falling through the decks below. With no fire-fighting facilities, the French had little chance of saving the ship. At this point Lieutenant Cauchard gave orders for the sea-cocks to be opened and flood the ship while Lieutenants Lachasse and Clamart organised the men to jettison anything overboard that would give aid to those abandoning ship. While all ships nearby hauled off to avoid damage from the inevitable explosion when the flames reached *Achille*'s magazines, they lowered their boats to pick up survivors leaping overboard. Inside the inferno a woman named Jeanette, wife of one of *Achille*'s maintopmen, ran from her station in the passage from the fore magazine. With most ladders smashed she found herself trapped. Guns and burning debris began falling through as the planking of the main deck above burnt through. Scrambling over wreckage, overturned guns and dead, Jeanette made her way to the gun room and climbed out through a stern port. Climbing onto the rudder Jeanette found herself being dripped upon by molten lead oozing from the lining of the rudder helm port. Stripping off her clothes she plunged into the water and clung to some wreckage until rescued by one of *Pickle*'s boats. Later transferred into *Revenge* Jeanette was, by fortune, reunited with her husband. Meantime *Achille* had become a blazing inferno and at around 5.30 p.m., when the fires reached her magazines, with a tremendous explosion she blew up, adding a grand finale to the battle.[5]

It appears, according to Lieutenant Halloran of *Britannia*, that Jeanette was not the only woman saved from *Achille*: 'This poor creature,' he wrote, 'was brought on board with scarcely any covering and our senior subaltern, Lt. Jackson, gave her a cotton dressing-gown for clothing'.

The 74 gun ship AIGLE

Meaning 'Eagle', the 74 gun ship *Aigle* was launched at Rochefort in 1794. Designed by Jacques Noel Sane, her specifications would have been virtually identical to the other vessels built to his lines. Likewise as a standard 74 gun ship *Aigle* carried an armament of twenty-eight 36 pounders on her lower gun deck, thirty 18 pounders on her upper gun deck, twenty 18 pounders on her quarter deck and forecastle thus *Aigle's* single broadside firepower was 890 pounds. Her predecessor, which served during the American War of Independence, was a 40 gun frigate which, under the command of Captain (later Admiral) La Touche-Treville, fought a three hour indecisive engagement with *Hector* (50) on 4 September 1782 and eight days later captured the British brig *Racoon* (14). Pursued up the Delaware by a squadron commanded by Captain the Hon. George Elphinstone, comprising *Lion* (64), *Warwick* (50), *Vestal* (28) and *Bonetta* (14), this *Aigle* ran aground. Although La Touche-Tréville cut away her masts and bored holes to sink her before being captured, the prize *Aigle* was repaired and refloated. Entered into the Royal Navy, this 38 gun frigate ship was wrecked off Cape Farina 18 July 1798.[6]

SERVICE HISTORY

1794: After her launch it appears that *Aigle* remained at Rochefort for a number of years before sailing to join French squadrons in the West Indies. When exactly she was sent on this deployment is uncertain.

1803: After operating from Santo Domingo, *Aigle* returned home with nine other vessels. When she became separated from these ships during their passage across the Atlantic she put into Cadiz and here remained under blockade.

1805: By the end of 1804 *Aigle* had been recommissioned under Captain P P Gourrège and prepared for sea service. As planned, Villeneuve had finally left Toulon with the French Mediterranean fleet and passed through the Straits of Gibraltar on 8 April. Evading the British blockade, he anchored off Cadiz at 4 p.m. and sent in the frigate *Hortense* (40) with orders for *Aigle* and her consorts *Torche* and *Argus* to make sail. The Spanish ships *Argonauta* (80), *San Rafael* (80), *Firme* (74), *Terrible* (74), *América* (64) and *España* (64) also joined Villeneuve that evening. *San Rafael* grounded in the process and had to follow later. Next morning *Aigle* sailed with Villeneuve for the West Indies, arriving off Fort Royal, Martinique on 13 May. On her return *Aigle* fought in the action off Finisterre against Vice-Admiral Calder on 22 July. After making repairs off Ferrol she sailed with Villeneuve's combined fleet, reaching Cadiz on 9 August.[7]

TRAFALGAR

Like a number of Villeneuve's ships, *Aigle* did not clear Cadiz until the morning of Sunday 20 October. Divided into five columns, Villeneuve's fleet came about on a larboard tack at 5 p.m. and headed for the Straits of Gibraltar. At this point *Aigle* was detached with Admiral Gravina's observation squadron successfully chasing off the British frigates *Euryalus*, *Naiad*, *Phœbe* and *Sirius* under command of Captain Blackwood. Then, at 7.30 p.m., *Aigle* signalled that 18 of Nelson's fleet had been sighted standing in line ahead to the south. Captain Gourrège's communication put Villeneuve on the alert.

Next morning after Villeneuve had grouped his ships into line of battle and altered course to northward *Aigle* was standing twenty-second from the head of the combined fleet. Ahead of her lay the Spanish *Bahama* (74), astern *Montañez* (74). Getting fully into action at around 12.50 p.m., *Aigle* got herself entangled with *Bellerophon* (74). A sharp engagement followed during which Gourrège made two unsuccessful attempts to board. Hauling off at about 1.40 p.m., Gourrège then placed *Aigle* off the starboard beam of *Belleisle* (74); supported by the 74 gun ships the French *Achille* and Spanish *San Justo* and *San Leandro*, he maintained a heavy fire into the

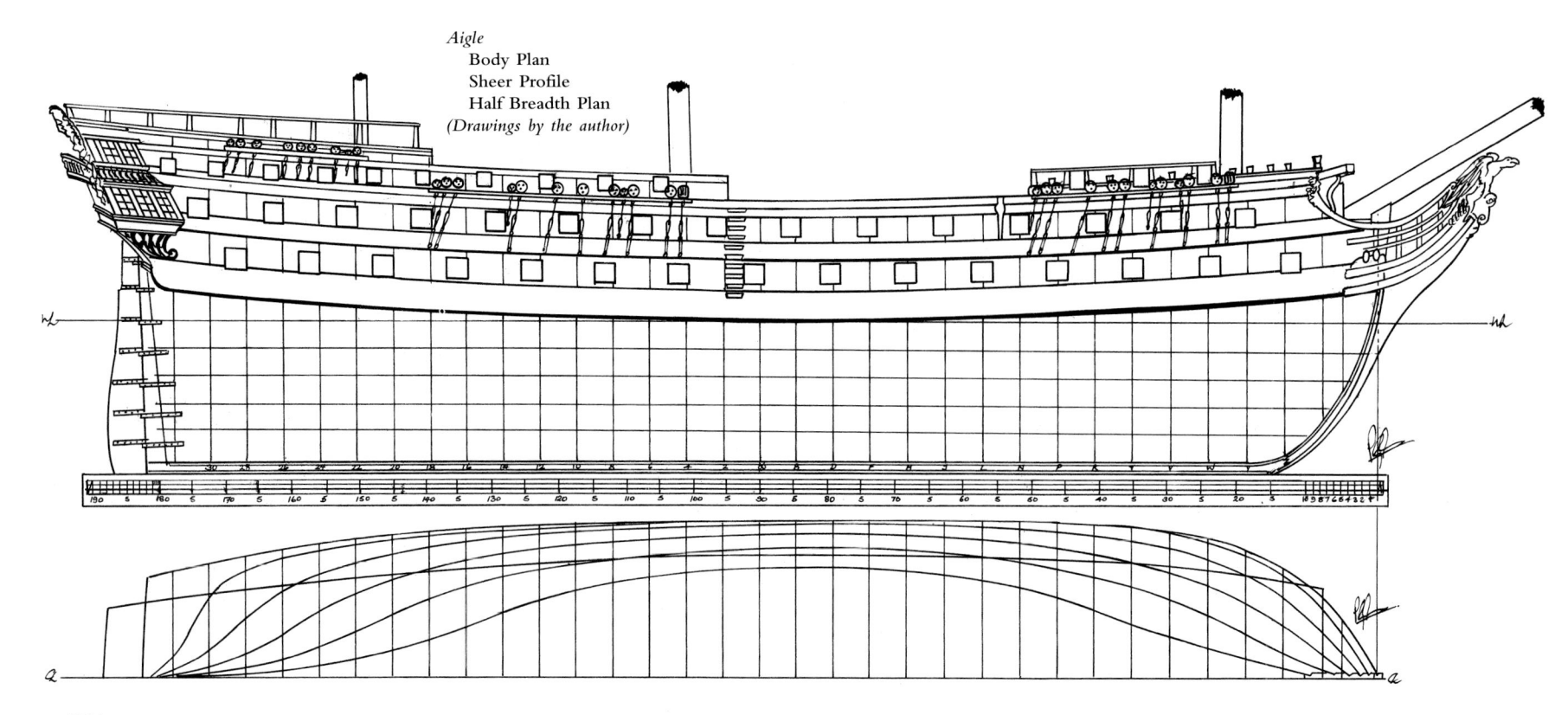

Aigle
Body Plan
Sheer Profile
Half Breadth Plan
(Drawings by the author)

SPECIFICATIONS: AIGLE

Rate	3rd	Date launched	1794	Complement	640
Guns	74	Length on the range of the gun deck	182 ft 6 ins	Ordnance - lower gun deck	28 x 36 pounders
Class		Length of keel for tonnage	148 ft 11⅝ ins	Ordnance - upper gun deck	30 x 18 pounders
Designer	Jacques Noel Sane	Extreme breadth	48 ft 11 ins	Ordnance - quarter deck	14 x 8 pounders
Builder	Dockyard	Depth in hold	21 ft 3 ins	Ordnance - forecastle	6 x 8 pounders
Dockyard	Rochefort	Tons burthen	1929 tons	Single broadside weight	890 pounds
Date ordered	-	Draught afore		Fate	Unknown
Date keel laid		Draught abaft			

already dismasted British ship. At about 3 p.m. *Aigle* came under fire from *Defiance* (74) which quickly lashed herself alongside and sent over boarders. When these were repelled *Defiance* let go her lashings and standing off just 30 feet, commenced to beat *Aigle* into submission, killing Captain Gourrège. After some 20 minutes of this cannonade *Aigle* finally capitulated to *Defiance*. Of the French ships fighting that day *Aigle* had put up a gallant defence and suffered 270 casualties in total.[8]

FATE

Taken in tow as a prize, *Aigle* did not survive the encroaching storm and on the night of Friday 25 October ran upon the rocks laying off Puerto Santa Maria and went to pieces with substantial loss of life.[9]

The 74 gun ship *ALGÉSIRAS*

Named after the port of Algeciras, the 74 gun ship *Algésiras* was launched at Lorient in 1804. Probably designed by Sane, she carried a standard armament of twenty-eight 36 pounders on her lower gun deck, thirty 18 pounders on her upper gun deck, and twenty 18 pounders on her quarter deck and forecastle. *Algésiras* could deliver a single broadside weight of 854 pounds.

SERVICE HISTORY

1805: Under the command of Captain Laurant Le Tourneur, and flying the flag of Rear-Admiral C Magon de Médine (hereafter Magon), *Algésiras* sailed from Rochefort on 1 May with *Achille* (74) for the West Indies. Napoleon's direct orders were that both ships were to reinforce Villeneuve's fleet. Making good time, *Algésiras* and her consort arrived at Guadeloupe on 29 May and made their rendezvous with Villeneuve. On 6 June *Algésiras* sailed with Villeneuve's fleet for Antigua to land troops and capture the island and, equally important, its small strategic British dockyard. Villeneuve, however, aborted this plan when he received news that a convoy, homebound for England, had just sailed from Antigua. With the rest of Villeneuve's ships *Algésiras* set off in pursuit and by 8 June 15 sail of merchantmen, carrying cargoes worth £200,000, had been captured.[10] *Algésiras* then returned with the combined fleet to Europe where, on 22 July, it fell in with and fought against Vice-Admiral Sir Robert Calder's squadron laying off Finisterre. As with many of the ships, *Algésiras* appears to have little part during this action. After a short stay laying off Ferrol refitting, *Algésiras* sailed south to Cadiz.[11]

TRAFALGAR

Still under the command of Captain Le Tourneur, and flying the flag of Rear-Admiral Magon, *Algésiras* hoisted her sails and made her way out of Cadiz with part of Villeneuve's combined fleet on the evening of Saturday 19 October. In company were just seven line of battle ships comprising the *Neptune*, *Achille*, *Argonaute*, *Duguay Trouin*, *Héros* and *Bahama* and the three frigates *Hermione*, *Rhin* and *Thémis*. Because the rest of the combined fleet had failed to leave the harbour by 10 p.m., *Algésiras* and her consorts had to cruise off Rota until daybreak.[12]

Forming part of Admiral Gravina's observation squadron, on the morning of 21 October *Algésiras* lay ninth in line from the rear. Ahead lay the Spanish *Montañez* (74), astern *Argonauta* (80), and to leeward the frigate *Thémis* (40). It was not until about 12.30 p.m. that *Algésiras* engaged Collingwood's ships and within 15 minutes found herself receiving heavy fire from the starboard batteries of *Tonnant* (80) which was also engaging *Monarca* (74). Intending to rake *Tonnant* through her stern with his starboard guns, Tourneur quickly turned *Algésiras* to larboard. Outwitted when *Tonnant* counter-manœuvred to starboard, *Algésiras* unavoidably ran aboard the British ship amidships. Locked together and unable to use her guns, *Algésiras* was severely raked with double shotted guns, bringing down her mizzen mast. *Tonnant*'s carronades, loaded with grape and musket balls, scythed through Tourneur's ship causing high casualties and stripping down her rigging. With sharpshooters stationed in *Algésiras*' main and fore tops maintaining a heavy fire upon *Tonnant*'s decks, Admiral Magon gave orders to board his adversary. Led by Lieutenant Verdreau, *Algésiras*' boarders swarmed across her bowsprit, only to be repelled by further fusillades of musket and grape shot from *Tonnant*'s carronades. *Algésiras* then swung broadside on to *Tonnant* and with their hulls grinding close together the two ships hotly exchanged broadsides for the next hour, guns being fired without being run out. During this contest *Algésiras* lost her fore mast. Fires caused by burning wads started below in her boatswain's

SPECIFICATIONS: ALGÉSIRAS

Rate	3rd	Date launched	1804	Complement	670
Guns	74	Length on the range of the gun deck	181 ft 6 ins	Ordnance - lower gun deck	28 x 36 pounders
Class	Sane-Border	Length of keel for tonnage	148 ft 11½ ins	Ordnance - upper gun deck	30 x 18 pounders
Designer	Jacques Noel Sane	Extreme breadth	48 ft 11 ins	Ordnance - quarter deck	14 x 8 pounders
Builder	Dockyard	Depth in hold	22 ft 0 ins	Ordnance - forecastle	6 x 8 pounders
Dockyard	Lorient	Tons burthen	1896. 22/94 tons	Single broadside weight	854 pounds
Date ordered	-	Draught afore		Fate	Captured at Trafalgar 21 October 1805 but retaken. Surrendered to the Spanish at Cadiz 16 June 1808.
Date keel laid	1801	Draught abaft			

store. Further fires started between the two ships but were soon doused. While busily encouraging his men amid the confusion of battle, Magon was hit by musket ball in the arm and a splinter in his thigh but, undeterred, stayed on deck. Casualties mounted: Captain Tourneur was wounded in the shoulder and taken below, closely followed by Morel, his First Lieutenant. Lieutenant Leblond-Passon, *Algésiras'* navigating officer, was shot in the chest and Admiral Magon, who had refused to go below earlier, was killed outright with a musket ball in his chest. Despite the fact that few men were left to man the 18 pounder guns, *Algésiras'* lower deck gunners continued to hammer shot into *Tonnant* with their 36 pounders, causing equally high casualties within the British ship. *Algésiras* then lost her main mast which caused considerable damage on going over the side as it ripped through the partners at each deck level. At about 2.15 p.m. *Algésiras* ceased firing, at which point 60 men from *Tonnant*, led by Lieutenant Charles Bennet, boarded and took possession. With casualties of 77 dead and 142 wounded, *Algésiras* had put up a courageous fight; Tourneur, her commander, later died of his injury.[13]

During the storm after the battle Lieutenant Bennet and his men were hard pressed to keep the battered *Algésiras* from foundering. On the morning of Wednesday 23 October, when the ship appeared to be standing into danger, Bennet was compelled, for humane reasons, to bring the French prisoners up on deck. Noble this may have been, but Bennet's action cost him the ship; being outnumbered the ship was retaken and carried into Cadiz. The French repossession of *Algésiras* probably saved, including Bennet and his prize crew, 500 lives.[14]

FATE

For the next three years *Algésiras* remained in Cadiz with the remnants of the French fleet under the command of Vice-Admiral de Rosily until Spain declared war on France on 4 June 1808. After his ships were attacked five days later de Rosily was forced to surrender *Algésiras* together with *Neptune* (80), *Argonaute* (74), *Héros*, *Pluton* (74), and the frigate *Cornélie* (40) to the Spanish on 16 June. *Algésiras*, renamed *Algeciras*, continued serving in the Spanish Royal Navy until lost in 1826.[15]

The 74 gun ship ARGONAUTE

Named after the men who sailed with Jason in the ship *Argos* in the classical Greek legend, *Argonaute* was another 74 gun ship designed by Jacques Noel Sane. With respect to timber used in her construction, cast, and the number and type of ordnance she carried, these statistics were virtually identical to those of her contemporaries.

SERVICE CAREER

1805: Placed under the command of Captain Jacques Epron, *Argonaute*, like *Fougueux*, appears to have joined Villeneuve's combined fleet at Ferrol sometime around 26 July and sailed for Cadiz with them on 9 August, arriving at that port eleven days later.[16]

TRAFALGAR

Sailing with Villeneuve's fleet from Cadiz on 19 October, *Argonaute* was deployed with Admiral Gravina's observation squadron. Her relative position after the combined fleet had weared and turned northward on the morning of the battle was sixth from the rear. Ahead and lying to leeward of *Argonaute*'s starboard bow was *Swiftsure* (74), and astern on her starboard quarter *San Ildefonso* (74).[17] It was comparatively late when Argonaute got into action, engaging *Colossus* (74) of Collingwood's division, which having passed astern of *Swiftsure* ported her helm and ran aboard *Argonaute*'s lar-

board side. Yardarm to yardarm *Argonaute* and *Colossus* ferociously delivered broadsides into each other during which Captain Morris of *Colossus* had his leg severed by a round shot. After some ten minutes when virtually every larboard gun within *Argonaute* had been silenced, she drifted away, only to be raked by her adversary as she did so. This last broadside caused much damage to *Argonaute*'s masts and severely crippled her steering. With her rudder shot to pieces and unable to manœuvre, *Argonaute* withdrew from the mêlée and made for Cadiz, completely losing her rudder en route. Much damaged, *Argonaute* never ventured to sea again. According to Captain Epron casualties within the ship comprised 55 dead and 132 wounded.[18]

FATE

Unfit for service due to damage, *Argonaute* remained in Cadiz with the other French ships *Neptune*, *Algésiras*, *Héros*, *Pluton*, and *Cornélie*, all of which were seized by Spain on 14 June 1808.[19] Entered into the Spanish navy, *Argonaute* was renamed *Argonauta* to replace the Spanish *Argonauta* (74) which had been captured at Trafalgar and sunk in the storm afterwards. Under her revised name, *Argonauta* the French prize continued to serve in the Spanish Royal Navy until she was wrecked, ironically in Cadiz Bay, in 1810.

SPECIFICATIONS: *ARGONAUTE*

Rate	3rd	Length on the range of the gun deck	183 ft 2 ins	Ordnance - lower gun deck	28 x 36 pounders
Guns	74	Length of keel for tonnage	149 ft 7½ ins	Ordnance - upper gun deck	30 x 18 pounders
Class	Sane-Border	Extreme breadth	48 ft 8¼ ins	Ordnance - quarter deck	14 x 8 pounders
Designer	Jacques Noel Sane	Depth in hold	20 ft 6 ins	Ordnance - forecastle	6 x 8 pounders
Builder	Dockyard	Tons burthen	1886 tons	Single broadside weight	854
Dockyard	Lorient	Draught afore		Fate	Survived the battle of Trafalgar and surrendered over to Spain 14 July 1808
Date ordered		Draught abaft			
Date keel laid	1794	Complement	650		
Date launched	1798				

The 74 gun ship BERWICK

Originally a British warship, the *Berwick* that fought on the side of the French at Trafalgar was the fourth ship to bear this name in the Royal Navy. The name derives from the town and strategic castle situated at the east of the English-Scottish border. The first *Berwick*, a 3rd rate ship of 70 guns launched at Chatham in 1697, was, after being rebuilt in 1700, hulked in 1715 and broken up in 1742. The second *Berwick*, likewise a 3rd rate of 70 guns, was built at Deptford in 1723. After serving at the siege of Gibraltar of 1727, the Wars of Jenkin's Ear and Austrian Succession, she was hulked in 1743 and broken up in 1783. The third *Berwick*, a 70 gun ship, was launched at Deptford in 1743. After seeing some service in the East and the West Indies during the Seven Years' War, she was broken up at Chatham in 1760.[20]

As a British ship *Berwick* was one of eight *Elizabeth* class 3rd rate 74 gun ships designed by Thomas Slade in 1766. Sister ships were *Elizabeth*, *Resolution*, *Cumberland*, *Bombay Castle*, *Powerful* and *Defiance*, the latter of which fought within Nelson's Trafalgar fleet. *Berwick*, which also fought as part of Villeneuve's combined fleet at Trafalgar, had been captured from the British off San Fiorenzo on 7 March 1795 by the French frigates *Minerve* (38), *Alceste* (36) and *Vestale* (36). Ordered on 12 October 1768, the keel of *Berwick* was laid down at Portsmouth in May 1769 and launched 18 April 1775. Most of the 160,000 cubic feet of timber (about 3,250 trees) used in her construction was taken from the New Forest and Forest of Bere in Hampshire. Her building costs, which totalled £30,774 15s 11d comprised £25,862 8s 5d for hull, masts and yards and £4,912 7s 6d stores and rigging.[21] Armed with twenty-eight 32 pounders on the lower gun deck, twenty-eight 18 pounders on the upper gun deck, fourteen 9 pounders on the quarter deck and four 9 pounders on the forecastle, *Berwick* could deliver a single broadside weight of 781 pounds.[22]

SERVICE CAREER

1777: Although launched in 1775 when England had entered a war with her rebel American colonists, *Berwick* was not put into sea service. Docked at Portsmouth between 27 June and 5 July, she was graved with a compound containing white lead to protect her hull from shipworm. She was again docked on 16 October for four days to have her bottom sheathed with deal boards, secured with many flat headed iron nails and again graved for the same purpose at a cost of £1,956 13s 0d and a further £2,292 16s 7d spent on rigging and stores.[23] When it appeared likely that France would support the Americans *Berwick* was commissioned on 27 December 1777 under Captain the Hon. Keith Stewart, a Scotsman of some social standing.

1778: Deployed with Admiral Augustus Keppel's Grand Fleet, *Berwick* sailed from Portsmouth on 9 July to cruise off Ushant, where on 27 July the fleet engaged a large French squadron commanded by Admiral Compte d'Orvilliers, during which *Berwick* played little part in this somewhat indecisive action.[24] The ship re-entered Portsmouth on 9 November.[25]

1779: On 4 January *Berwick* docked at Portsmouth for one day to be graved and after a short refit sailed on 2 March. *Berwick* was docked again at Portsmouth on 3 December. This time, following recent Admiralty legislation, all her timber sheathing boards were removed and replaced entirely with copper sheathing. Undocked on 24 December the total cost of this and her previous refit amounted to £9,763 12s 6d, of which £6,689 2s 4d was expended on stores and rigging refit. Although the ship's Progress Book gives a collective expenditure of £3,074 10s 2d for hull, masts and yards, the exact cost of her coppering cannot be determined.[26]

1780: *Berwick* sailed on 20 January and was later deployed to the West Indies, where, between 4 and 16 October, violent hurricanes inflicted severe losses to British shipping. At this time *Berwick* was at sea with Rear-Admiral Rowley's squadron NE of Santo Domingo comprising the 74 gun ships *Grafton*, *Hector*, *Ruby*, *Thunderer* and *Trident*, *Stirling Castle* (64), and *Bristol*

CAPTAINS OF BERWICK (MSS 248/4 and 248/6)

Name	Time of Entry	Time of Discharge	On What Occasion
Hon Keith Stewart	27 December 1777	8 March 1781	Made Commander-in-Chief Scotland
John Ferguson	9 March 1781	17 March 1782	Superseded
Hon Charles Phipps	18 March 1782	24 June 1783	Paid off
Benjamin Caldwell	28 August 1790	6 December 1790	Paid off at Portsmouth
Sir John Collins Kt.	25 January 1793	24 March 1794	Dead at Sea
William Shield	30 March 1794	26 April 1794	To *Sincere*
George Campbell	27 April 1794	25 May 1794	To *Terrible*
George Henry Towry	26 May 1794	27 June 1794	To *St Fiorenzo*
Andrew Sutherland	1 July 1794	10 October 1794	Superseded
William Smith	11 October 1794	28 January 1795	Superseded
Rt. Hon Gambier Middleton	17 January 1795	28 January 1795	Superseded Acting
Adam Littlejohn	29 January 1795		Killed in Action 7 March 1795
French Officers			
Jean-Gilles Filhol-Camas	March 1805	21 October 1805	Ship recaptured and foundered
Post Trafalgar			
James Macnamara	10 March 1810	21 October 1811	Superseded
Sir Robert Laurie	22 October 1811	30 November 1811	Superseded
Edward Bruce	1 December 1811	9 July 1816	Paid Off
James Nash	10 July 1816	28 October 1816	Paid Off (Recommissioned)

SPECIFICATIONS: BERWICK

Rate	3rd	Length on the range of the gun deck	168 ft 6 ins	Ordnance - lower gun deck	28 x 32 pounders
Guns	74	Length of keel for tonnage	138 ft 3⅛ ins	Ordnance - upper gun deck	28 x 18 pounders
Class	*Elizabeth* class 1766	Extreme breadth	46 ft 10 ins	Ordnance - quarter deck	14 x 9 pounders
Designer	Thomas Slade	Depth in hold	19 ft 9 ins	Ordnance - forecastle	4 x 9 pounders
Builder	Dockyard	Tons burthen	1612.88/94	Single broadside weight	781 pounds
Dockyard	Portsmouth	Draught afore		Fate	Recaptured from the French at Trafalgar 1805 and wrecked off St Lucar in the storm after the battle.
Date ordered	12 October 1768	Draught abaft			
Date keel laid	May 1769	Complement	550/600		
Date launched	18 April 1775				

Source: Lyon, *Sailing Navy List*, pp.70-71.

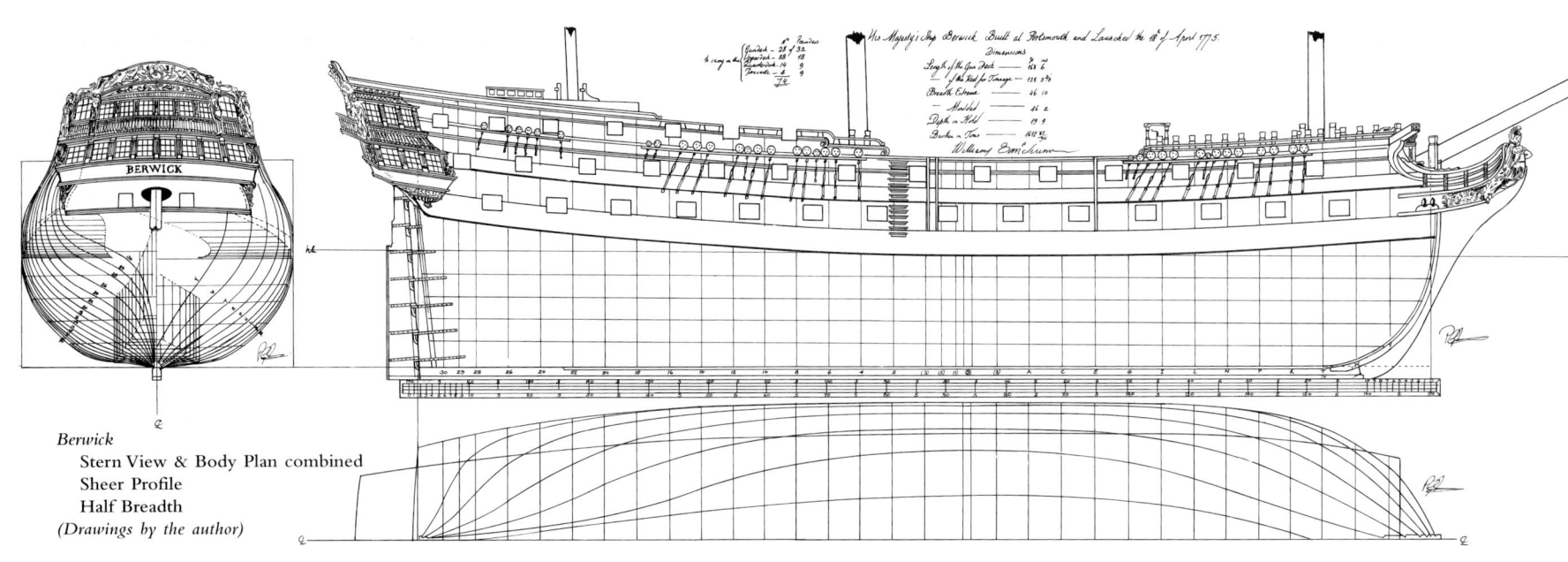

Berwick
   Stern View & Body Plan combined
   Sheer Profile
   Half Breadth
(Drawings by the author)

(50). Hit by furious winds on the night of 5 October *Thunderer* completely disappeared, *Grafton Hector, Ruby, Trident* and *Bristol* were all dismasted, and *Stirling Castle* ran on shore and went to pieces with only 50 survivors.[27] *Berwick* was so badly damaged that she was compelled to run direct for England. Returning to Plymouth Dockyard on 5 December she went into dock ten days later to have 'sevl Sheets of Copper' shifted and refit after her ordeal.[28]

1781: Undocked on 13 January, *Berwick* sailed for duty on 23 February. Her refit had cost £9,194 16s 8d, of which £3,784 10s 0d covered expenditure for hull, masts and yards. When Stewart was promoted to Commander-in-Chief, Scotland, Captain John Ferguson superseded command of the *Berwick* on 9 March.[29] Not only had Spain entered the war against Britain, by this year the Dutch had also intervened. In the spring *Berwick* was detached with Vice-Admiral Hyde Parker's squadron escorting a convoy of 700 merchantmen from Leith to the Baltic. Besides Parker's flagship *Fortitude* (74), *Berwick* was accompanied by Princess Amelia (80), *Buffalo* (60), *Bienfaisant* (64), *Preston* (50), *Dolphin* (44), six frigates and five sloops and cutters. While Parker's fleet was returning home with a convoy carrying essential materials from the Baltic they fell in with Dutch squadron of virtually equal force commanded by Rear-Admiral Johann Arnold Zoutman off Dogger Bank on 5 August. Although the ensuing battle, which commenced at 8 a.m., was hotly contested, it was indecisive. Action ceased at 11.30 a.m. after which Zoutman recovered his convoy and bore away for the Texel. English casualties amounted to 104 killed and 339 wounded, the Dutch had 142 killed and 403 wounded.[30] In all *Berwick* suffered 16 killed including two midshipmen and the pilot and 58 wounded, among whom were Lieutenants Shipley and Maxwell, Captain Campbell and Lieutenant Stewart of the Marines, and six midshipmen. Following this action *Berwick* went into Sheerness on 13 August for repairs. Although not requiring docking, work undertaken incurred costs of £866 1s 5d, for her hull, etc. and £3,194 16s 1d for rigging and stores. Completed, the ship sailed on 5 September.[31]

1782: On 18 March Captain the Hon. Charles Phipps was appointed to command the ship.[32] Needing to refit again, *Berwick* entered Portsmouth dockyard on 5 April and was docked three weeks later for two days to have her copper repaired. Finished at a cost of £6,233 11s 0d, of which £4,880 8s 4d was expended on rigging and stores, she sailed for duty on 18 May.[33]

1783: When the American War of Independence ended *Berwick* returned to Portsmouth on 16 June and was paid off 8 days later.[34] Before being laid up

in ordinary the ship went into dock on 12 August for one day to have her bottom examined. As a result some of her copper sheathing was repaired at a cost of £12 8s 6d with a further £2 14s 0d spent on stores.[35]

1786-87: On 27 April 1786 the ship was docked for a 'Between Small & Middling Repair'. Besides having her bottom completely re-sheathed with copper, she was refitted with new timbers, planking, hanging knees, and like many ships was fitted with top and breadth riders to strengthen her hull. Finally completed at a cost of £18,546 1s 8d for hull masts and yards and just £1,115 17s 7d expended on rigging and stores, *Berwick* was launched 31 May 1787 and replaced in ordinary.[36]

1790: Following the Spanish re-armament, like many naval vessels, *Berwick* was recommissioned on 28 August under Captain Benjamin Caldwell. However, as the threat dissipated Caldwell paid off the ship at Portsmouth on 6 December.[37]

1793: When war was declared between Britain and France *Berwick* was taken out of ordinary, commissioned under Captain Sir John Collins Kt on 25 January and taken into dock at on 2 March for eleven days to have her copper repaired. Fitted for sea at a total cost of £3,532, *Berwick* left Portsmouth on 2 May and eventually arrived off Toulon in mid-August, forming part of Admiral Lord Hood's Mediterranean fleet.[38]

1794: When Captain Sir John Collins unexpectedly died on 24 March, command of the ship was temporarily superseded by Captain William Shield six days later. When Shield transferred into *Sincere* on 26 April he was succeeded by Captain George Campbell. However Campbell's stay in *Berwick* was short, for on 25 May he took command of *Terrible* (74). His successor, Captain George Henry Towry, also remained in the ship for only a month and having turned over into *St Fiorenzo* on 27 June, was superseded on 1 July by Captain Andrew Sutherland.[39] In June, when *Berwick* lay off Bastia with the rest off Hood's squadron, Hood's ships put to sea in pursuit of Admiral Martin who had sailed from Toulon on 5 June. According to James,[40] *Berwick* was still commanded by William Shield at the time and not Towry as given on the official commanders' lists.[41] Once the French ships anchored under the two forts protecting Gourjean Bay, as part of his plan of attack Hood sent *Berwick* to draw off fire from the western battery. Finding the French had set up considerable defences the attack was aborted and Hood withdrew his ships. On 11 October Captain William Smith succeeded Sutherland.[42]

1795: This year proved fateful to *Berwick*. On 16 January while the ship lay in San Fiorenzo Bay refitting with the Mediterranean fleet, Captain Smith had, under the recommendation of her master, ordered that all *Berwick*'s lower masts be stripped of their shrouds for re-rigging. While this was considered routine maintenance, having all three masts insufficiently supported was a grave error. The sea was generating a heavy cross-swell which rolled all three masts over the ship's side. Besides their loss this accident would have caused considerable damage to the ship's partners, the beam and decking structure which supported masts at each deck level. Vice-Admiral Hotham, now commanding the fleet and flying his flag in *Britannia* (100), immediately convened a court-martial. Placed on trial were *Berwick*'s captain, her First Lieutenant, and her master, each of whom were charged with negligence and not taking sufficient precautions to secure the masts.[43] Consequently all three officers were dismissed from the ship, Captain Smith being temporarily relieved of command by the Rt Hon. Gambier Middleton on 17 January. Middleton, commanding only in an acting capacity, was superseded by Captain Adam Littlejohn on 29 January.[44] Admiral Hotham's incautious decision to sail for Leghorn shortly after leaving the disabled *Berwick* further sealed the fate of the ship. When news reached Rear-Admiral Martin at Toulon that Hotham had removed his fleet from Corsica, the French prepared to retake the island. Martin's fleet, comprising 15 sail of the line, six frigates and two brig-corvettes, sailed from Toulon on 3 March. Meanwhile foul winds detained *Berwick* from sailing from Corsica to join Hotham. As Martin's advance frigates approached Cape Corse on 7 January, they discovered *Berwick* leaving San Fiorenzo rigged with under masts. As a ruse the French ships were initially flying Spanish colours. The lead French frigate *Alceste* (36), Captain Lejoille, passed to leeward of *Berwick*'s bow, and once within pistol shot range, changed her colours for French and fired into *Berwick*, cutting through her rigging and shredding her sails. *Alceste*'s consorts *Minerve* (38) and *Vestale* (36) then hauled up on *Berwick*'s quarter. According to British accounts they were joined shortly by two line of battle ships. As *Berwick* retaliated by firing her broadsides, a bar-shot fired from *Alceste* carried away Captain Littlejohn's head, leaving Lieutenant Nesbit Palmer in command. So far only Littlejohn had been killed and four seamen had been wounded. Palmer gathered his officers who, agreeing that fighting against such overwhelming odds was utterly futile, compelled Palmer to strike *Berwick*'s colours. The action had lasted only 15 minutes. Once boarded by the French, *Berwick*'s officers and men were distributed between the French ships; their treatment was scandalous, however, as none were permitted to take any clothes save what they were wearing. When they eventually returned home and were tried by court-martial for the loss of the ship, all were honourably acquitted.[45]

Under French colours *Berwick* was initially carried into Gourjean Bay escorted by a frigate before going into Toulon. Here *Berwick* remained until autumn, when the French Government decided to send a squadron to Newfoundland and afterwards strengthen the Brest fleet. This force was placed under the command of Rear-Admiral Joseph de Richery, a Provençal who had been expelled from the French navy during Robespierre's reign of terror. Richery's squadron, comprising *Victoire* (80), *Barras* (74), *Jupiter* (74), *Berwick* (74), *Guerrière* (74), *Duquesne* (74) and frigates *Embuscade*, *Félicité* and *Friponne*, sailed from Toulon 14 September. Although British ships under Rear-Admiral Robert Man finally went in pursuit three weeks later, *Berwick* with de Richery's squadron had already broken out into the Atlantic. Cruising off Cape St Vincent on 7 October, de Richery's ships fell in with Captain Thomas Taylor's squadron of three line of battle ships and four frigates escorting a convoy of 63 merchantmen from Gibraltar to England. That afternoon's action, with *Berwick* participating, resulted in de Richery capturing 30 of Taylor's convoy, recapturing *Censeur* (74) and carrying them into Cadiz.[46]

1796: It appears that *Berwick*, with de Richery's squadron, remained in Cadiz under blockade by Rear-Admiral Man. On 19 August the treaty allying Spain with France was signed at Madrid. This coalition effectively doubled the naval forces acting against the British navy. Before the treaty was signed de Richery exercised its rights and called upon the Spanish ships to escort his squadron out of Cadiz. Accompanied by 20 Spanish sail of the line, 14 frigates and corvettes commanded by Admiral Don Juan de Langura, *Berwick* sailed with de Richery's squadron on 4 August. Once 300 miles into the Atlantic, de Richery's ships continued their voyage along the North American coast, arriving off the Banks of Newfoundland on 28 August.[47]

Going into St Johns in early September, de Richery found the defences set up by Vice-Admiral Sir James Wallace Kt and Captain Thomas Graves too complex, and consequently bore away. *Berwick*, with de Richery's squadron, entered the Bay of Bulls on 4 September where their crews plundered and destroyed the houses and boats of the Landing fishermen. Next day de Richery detached *Censeur*, *Duquesne* and *Friponne* to the Bay of Castles in Labrador while his remaining force, including *Berwick*, sailed for St Pierre and Miquelon where they again destroyed houses and boats. Having caused havoc, *Berwick*, along with de Richery's flagship *Victoire* (80), *Barras*, *Jupiter*, *Guerrière* and frigates *Embuscade* and *Félicité*, sailed for home, reaching Rochefort on 5 November.[48] After this date *Berwick* appears to have remained inactive until 1805.

1803: When war restarted in May Rear-Admiral Sir Richard Bickerton was already stationed in the Mediterranean with a force of just ten ships; *Berwick* was laid up afloat in Toulon along with the vessels *Formidable* (80), *Indomptable* (80), *Atlas* (74), *Intrépide* (74), *Mont Blanc* (74), and *Scipion* 74). It is unlikely that she had either crew or commander at this time.

1804: Once Napoleon had determined to invade Britain, *Berwick*, together with the other French ships in Toulon, was fully prepared for sea service and placed under the command of Captain Jean-Gilles Filhol-Camas. The appointed fleet commander, Vice-Admiral Pierre-Charles Jean-Baptiste Villeneuve arrived at Toulon 19 December and hoisted his flag in *Bucentaure* (80).

1805: Under orders from Decrès, the French Minister de la Marine,

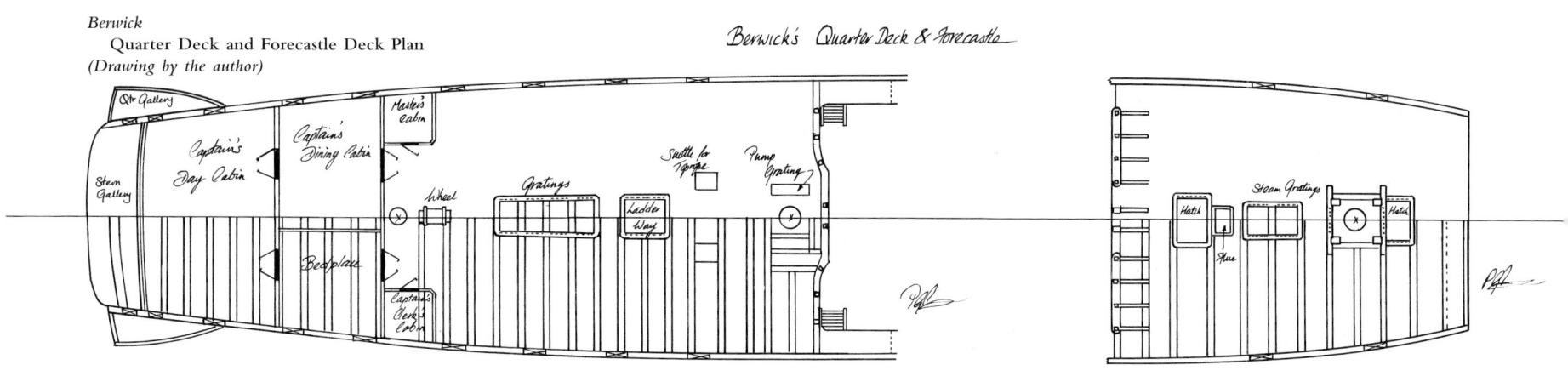

Berwick
Quarter Deck and Forecastle Deck Plan
(Drawing by the author)

Villeneuve ordered his fleet to sea and sailed from Toulon on 18 January. Including *Berwick* the French fleet comprised the following ships:

Guns	Ship's Names	No.
80	*Bucentaure*, **Formidable**, *Neptune* and *Indomptable*	4
74	*Annibal*, **Atlas**, **Berwick**, **Intrépide**, **Mont Blance**, **Scipion**, and **Swiftsure**	7
40	*Cornélie*, *Hortense*, *Rhin*, *Thémis* and *Uranie*	5
38	*Incorruptible*	1
36	*Sirène*	1
18	*Furet*	1
16	*Naïade*	1
TOTAL		20

Note: Those denoted in bold type would fight at Trafalgar

Villeneuve's entire squadron was immediately struck by strong north-westerly winds which battered his ships, forcing him to return to port. Despite the fact that Nelson's fleet had withdrawn temporarily to Corsica, Villeneuve's sally had been seen by the British frigates still patrolling off Toulon. *Berwick* with the same squadron of ships finally evaded Nelson's ships and put to sea on the evening of 29 March and sailed westwards to the West Indies as planned, anchoring off Fort de France (Fort Royal), Martinique, on 13 May.

On 29 May Villeneuve detached *Berwick* with *Pluton* (74), *Sirène* (36), *Argus* (16), the armed schooner *Fine* and eleven gunboats to attack HM Sloop *Diamond Rock*. Although given a ship's classification this was in fact a strategic gun battery mounted upon the summit of Diamond Rock positioned six miles SE of Fort de France. Manned by 107 naval personnel under the command of Commander James Maurice, its guns could readily fire upon French ships entering or leaving the port. Reaching the rock on 31 May *Berwick* got within pistol shot and at 7.50 a.m. commenced her bombardment, her consorts following suit at 8 a.m. The action continued until 4.30 p.m. on 2 June when Maurice, with little powder remaining, hoisted a flag of truce. Although the British lost two killed and one wounded, the French lost three gunboats and 65 casualties. When Maurice was tried for the loss of *Diamond Rock* at the court martial held on board the *Circe* at Carlisle Bay, Barbados, on 24 June, the sitting officers wrote:

> The Court cannot dismiss Captain James Wilkes Maurice without expressing their admiration for his conduct in the whole of the occasion; and also express the highest approbation of the support given by the officers and men under his command; a circumstance that does high honour of them; does no less credit and honour to the discipline by captain J.W. Maurice; and there do unanimously and honourably acquit the said officers and ship's company, and they are unanimously and honourably acquitted accordingly.[49]

Shortly afterwards *Berwick*, with Villeneuve's combined Franco-Spanish fleet, sailed for Europe to effect the next stage of Napoleon's invasion plan.

PROGRESS BOOK - *BERWICK* 3RD RATE OF 74 GUNS:

At what Port	Arrived	Docked	Coppered
Portsmouth	Begun	May 1769	Graved April 1775
Portsmouth		24 June 1777	Graved July 1777
Portsmouth		16 Oct 1777	Sheathed and Graved October 1777
Portsmouth	9 Nov 1778	4 Jan 1779	Graved January 1779
Portsmouth	1 Dec 1779	10 Dec 1779	Sheathing taken off Coppered Dec 1779
Plymouth	5 Dec 1780	15 Dec 1780	Shifted several Sheets of Copper
Sheerness	13 Aug 1781		
Portsmouth	5 April 1782	26 April 1782	Copper Repaired April 1782
Portsmouth	16 June 1783	12 Aug. 1783	Copper Repaired August 1783
Portsmouth		27 April 1786	Copper taken off May 1786; Re-coppered May 1787
Portsmouth		2 March 1793	Copper Repaired March 1793
Taken by French in 1795			

When approaching Cape Finisterre on 22 July Villeneuve's fleet fell in with Vice-Admiral Sir Richard Calder's squadron deployed to meet the combined fleet. The action was indecisive, with Calder capturing just two Spanish ships. *Berwick* with the combined fleet turned southward and entered Cadiz on the night of 20 August.

TRAFALGAR

The French *Berwick* put to sea with the rest of the combined fleet on 19 October and proceeded SE towards Gibraltar to enter the Mediterranean. The fleet comprised three squadrons and when ordered to form a single line ahead at 11 p.m. on the 20th the observation squadron, commanded by Admiral Federico Gravina flying his flag in *Principe de Asturias*, took the lead; *Berwick* lay second in line.

At 8 a.m. when Villeneuve ordered his fleet to wear together and bear up towards the British fleet and Cadiz on 21 October 1805, *Berwick* found herself second from the rear of the combined fleet. Astern lay *San Juan de Nepomuceno* and ahead *Principe de Asturias*. When *Defiance* attempted to cut through the line astern of *Principe de Asturias* to assist *Revenge*, *Berwick* surged ahead to close the gap, but in so doing ran aboard *Defiance* and lost her bowsprit in the process. *Defiance* did not engage, thus it was not until around 2.30 p.m. that *Berwick* was finally in action, by which time the battle had become a free-for-all. Seeing the Spanish *Argonauta* suffering considerably under heavy fire from the British *Achilles*, Filhol-Camas drove his ship between them and commenced firing his larboard broadside into *Achilles*. Besides drawing fire from the already battered Spaniard, *Berwick*'s intervention effectively drew off British fire from the French *Achille* lying

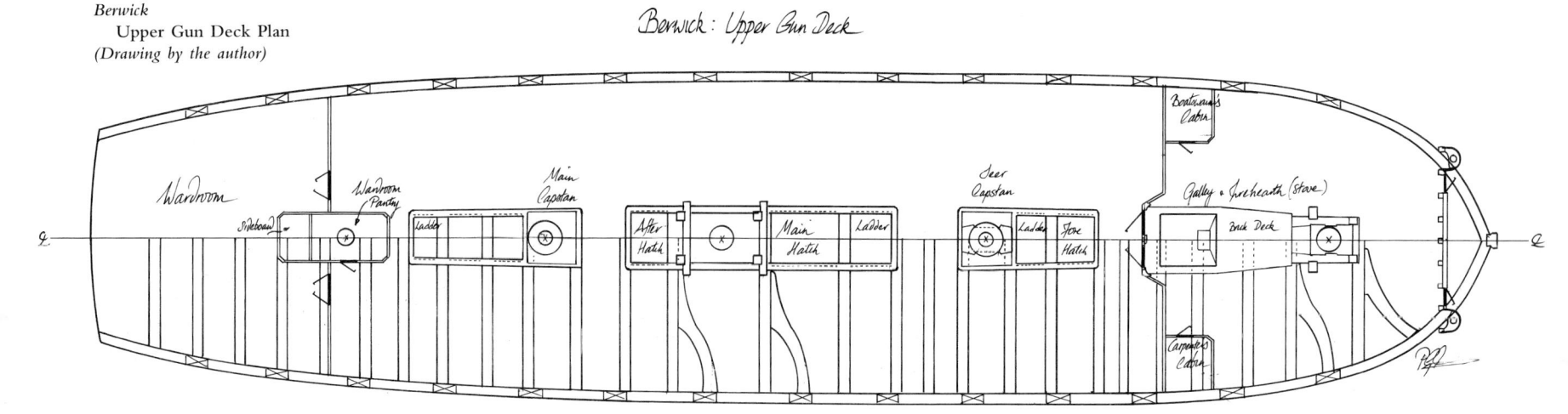

Berwick
Upper Gun Deck Plan
(Drawing by the author)

Source: ADM 180/6 Folio 42

Launched or Undocked	Sailed	Built or Nature of Repair	Cost of Hull, Masts & Yards Materials £	Workmen £	Cost of Masts & Yards Materials £	Workmen £	Cost of Rigging & Stores Materials £	Workmen £	Grand Total £
18 April 1775		Built	25,862. 8s. 5d.		-		4,912. 7s. 6d.		30,774. 15s. 11d.
5 July 1777		Tr Toirn g [?]							
20 Oct 1777	19 May 1778	Fitted	1,956. 13s.0d				2,292. 16s. 7d.		4,249. 9s. 7d.
5 Jan 1779	2 Mar 1779	Refitted	3,,074. 10s.2d				6,689. 2s. 4d		9.763. 12s. 6d.
24 Dec 1779	20 Jan 1780	Refitted	Inc. above				Inc. above		Inc. above
13 Jan 1781	23 Feb 1781	Refitted	3,784. 10s.0d				5,410. 6s. 8d		9,194. 16s. 8d.
	5 Set 1781	Refitted	657.0s.6d		209.0s.11d.		3,194.15s. 0d		4,060. 17s. 5d.
27 April 1782	18 May 1782	Refitted	1,353. 2s.8d				4,880. 8s. 4d		6,233. 11s. 0d
13 Aug 1783		Examined the bottom	12.8s.6d				2.14s. 0d		15. 2s. 6d
31 May 1787		Between Small & Middling Repair	18,546 1s.8d				1,115. 17s. 7d		19,661.19s. 3d
13 March 1793	2 May 1793	Fitted	1,198				2334		3,532

to larboard of her British namesake. *Achille* then hauled off ahead, leaving *Berwick* and the English *Achille* to fight it out alone. The duel between these two ships continued for another hour, during which *Berwick* sustained high casualties, her 'quarter-deck having thrice been cleared', among whom was Captain Filhol-Camas. With over 50 dead and 200 wounded *Berwick* was forced to strike at 3.15 p.m. A prize crew from *Achille* secured the ship and for the remainder of the day *Berwick* wallowed in the chaos of battle aftermath. In the storm afterwards, while *Berwick* lay anchored near *Donegal* (74), some of her crew, in a fit of desperation and fear, cut the cables to free the ship. *Berwick* was immediately driven onto the shoals off San Lucar, lost her masts and instantly went to pieces. Virtually all on board, including the British prize crew, perished.[50]

The 74 gun ship DUGUAY TROUIN

Named after the renowned French privateer and naval commander M. René Duguay-Trouin (1673-1736) who became the Lieutenant-Général des Armées Navales, *Duguay Trouin* that fought at the battle of Trafalgar was designed by Jacques Noel Sane. Launched at Rochefort in 1800, she should not be confused with the 74 gun *Duguay Trouin* launched in 1789. This predecessor was burnt along with nine other vessels under Admiral Hood's orders at Toulon in 1793.[51] The second *Duguay Trouin*, a frigate of 28 guns, was captured on 5 May 1794 in the East Indies by *Orpheus* (32) commanded by Captain Henry Newcome.[52]

Like her Trafalgar contemporaries *Achille*, *Aigle*, *Héros*, *Mont Blanc*, *Redoutable*, and *Scipion*, the Trafalgar *Duguay Trouin* was constructed using some 170,270 cubic feet of timber before conversion. Carrying twenty-eight 36 pounders on her lower gun deck, thirty 18 pounders on her upper gun deck, and twenty 8 pounders on her quarter deck and forecastle, *Duguay Trouin* could deliver a single broadside weight of 854 pounds (384.3 kg).

SERVICE CAREER

1802: Under the command of Captain Pierre L'Hermite, *Duguay Trouin* was deployed in the West Indies serving with the French squadron off Santo Domingo where she was involved in suppressing a rebellion.

1803: Still deployed in the West Indies under Pierre L'Hermite, *Duguay Trouin* sailed on 24 July amid heavy weather from Cape François in company with *Duquesne* (74), Commodore Pierre Maurice Julian Querangel, and the 40 gun frigate *Guerrière*. On clearing the harbour the ships set a westerly course in the hope of evading a nearby British squadron of 74 gun ships *Bellerophon*, *Elephant*, *Theseus* and *Vanguard*, and the 18 pounder frigates *Æolus* and *Tartar*. At about 9 p.m. the three French ships separated, *Duguay Trouin* taking an easterly course, whereupon *Elephant* was immediately ordered to give chase. Next morning when *Elephant* was off Cape Picolet Captain Dundas found *Duguay Trouin* just a mile distant and wore in pursuit. At 6 a.m. *Duguay Trouin* commenced firing her stern chase guns

SPECIFICATIONS: *DUGUAY TROUIN*

Rate	3rd	Length on the range of the gun deck	181 ft 6 ins	Ordnance - quarter deck	14 x 8 pounders
Guns	74	Length of keel for tonnage	148 ft 11⅜ ins		(later 2 x 12 pdrs. & 12 x 32 pdr carronades)
Class	Sane-Border	Extreme breadth	48 ft 11 ins	Ordnance - forecastle	6 x 8 pounders
Designer	Jacques Noel Sane	Depth in hold	22 ft 0 ins		(later 2 x 12 pdrs. & 2 x 32 pdr carronades)
Builder	Dockyard	Tons burthen	1896. 22/94 tons	Single broadside weight	854 pounds (later 966 pounds)
Dockyard	Rochefort	Draught afore		Fate	Captured by Sir Richard Strachan's squadron on 4 November 1805 and renamed *Implacable*, she entered the Royal Navy. Sold in 1855, later used as a training ship. Scuttled and sunk off Selsey Bill 3 December 1949.
Date ordered	-	Draught abaft			
Date keel laid	1797	Complement	670		
Date launched	1800	Ordnance - lower gun deck	28 x 36 pounders (later 32 pounders)		
		Ordnance - upper gun deck	30 x 18 pounders		

Source: Lyon, *Sailing Navy List*, p. 267.

into *Elephant* with great accuracy. Despite this, *Elephant* drew up and opened a distant fire upon *Duguay Trouin*'s starboard quarter. The chase continued until the frigate *Guerrière* arrived, compelling *Elephant* to discontinue. As a result *Duguay Trouin* returned to Europe unscathed; her consort *Duquesne*, however, was not so lucky.[53]

When *Duguay Trouin* and her accompanying frigate *Guerrière* approached the port of Ferrol on 29 August they fell in with *Boadicea* (38), Captain John Maitland. At about 2 p.m. *Boadicea* came up within quarter of mile of *Duguay Trouin* and opened fire. Although it is said that *Boadicea* brought down *Duguay Trouin*'s topsail yard and that she was holed by several round shot, return broadsides from *Duguay Trouin* were enough to compel Maitland to retire. On 2 September *Duguay Trouin* and *Guerrière* were sighted by Sir Edward Pellew's squadron and at 11.50 a.m. *Culloden* (74) brought the two French ships to action. Having the weather gauge, *Duguay Trouin* got into Corunna. When the French shore batteries opened fire, *Culloden* was obliged to stand off, allowing *Guerrière* to enter port shortly afterwards.[54] *Duguay Trouin* remained in Ferrol until 1805.

1805: Now under the command of Captain Claude Touffet, *Duguay Trouin* sailed from Ferrol with Villeneuve's combined Franco-Spanish fleet on 9 August to seek out Rear-Admiral Allemand's squadron from Rochefort. At this point Villeneuve's fleet comprised the 28 ships of the line below. Not finding Allemand, Villeneuve turned south, arriving at Cadiz on 20 August.

French

Rate	Guns	Name	No.
2nd	80	Bucentaure, Formidable, Indomptable, Neptune	4
3rd	74	Achille, Aigle, Algésiras, Argonaute, Berwick, Duguay Trouin, Intrépide, Fougueux, Héros, Mont Blanc, Pluton, Redoutable, Scipion, Swiftsure and Terrible	15

Spanish

Rate	Guns	Name	No.
1st	112	Principe de Asturias, Neptuno	2
3rd	74	Monarca, Montañez, San Augustin, San Francisco de Asis, San Fulgencia, San Ildefonso, San Juan Nepomuceno	7
TOTAL			28

TRAFALGAR

Duguay Trouin put to sea with the combined fleet on 19 October. Initially she lay in the rear division commanded by Rear-Admiral Dumanoir. When the combined fleet turned north, reversing its sailing order at 8 p.m. on 21 October, *Duguay Trouin* lay fifth in line from the head of Villeneuve's fleet. Ahead lay Dumanoir's flagship *Formidable* (80), astern *Mont Blanc*, and to leeward the frigate *Cornélie* (40). Once the battle had opened Dumanoir's van of ten ships became isolated from those ships brought into action by Nelson's division. With little wind to tack, five of his ships, *Neptuno*, *Scipion*, *Rayo*, *Formidable*, *Duguay Trouin* and *Mont Blanc* were unable to return and support Villeneuve's centre. Some used their boats to turn their ship's heads back through the wind, so Dumanoir's ships eventually hauled their wind and re-entered the battle. As they did so *Duguay Trouin*, following *Formidable*, came under raking fire from *Minotaur* (74) and *Spartiate* (74). By 4.30 p.m. *Formidable*, followed by *Duguay Trouin*, *Mont Blanc*, and *Scipion*, sailed south of the battle, leaving the Spanish *Neptuno* closely engaged with *Minotaur* and *Spartiate*. *Rayo* had turned north and was making her escape with *San Francisco de Asis* and *Héros*. Although *Duguay Trouin* played little part in the battle because she was initially isolated, and suffering just 20 killed and 24 wounded, ultimately she would not fully evade the British navy.[55]

Sailing in company with *Formidable*, *Mont Blanc*, and *Scipion*, *Duguay Trouin* was sighted by *Phœnix* (36), Captain Thomas Baker, off Cape Finisterre on 2 November. After giving chase Baker steered south to inform Captain Sir Richard Strachan who was laying off Ferrol with his squadron comprising the following eight ships:

Guns	Ships' Names	Total
80	Cæsar	1
74	Bellona, Courageux, Hero, Namur	4
38	Révolutionnaire	1
36	Santa Margarita	1
32	Æolus	1

Joined by *Phœnix* (36), Strachan, flying his pendant in *Cæsar*, set off in pursuit immediately with his squadron. The next afternoon *Bellona*, a poor sailer, parted company. By the morning of 4 November Strachan's ships had closed to within six miles of Dumanoir's squadron. At around 11.45 a.m. *Cæsar*, *Courageux* and *Hero* formed line ahead and commenced running down upon the four Frenchmen. Following Dumanoir's orders, *Duguay Trouin* took in her small sails and hauled up on a starboard tack, heading NE by E. Dumanoir then formed line ahead with *Duguay Trouin* leading, followed in order by *Formidable*, *Mont Blanc* and *Scipion*. Signalling to Gardner in *Hero* that he intended to attack the centre and rear of the French ships, Strachan's ships commenced action at 12.15 p.m., coming up on Dumanoir's windward side and opening fire from their larboard guns. A hot

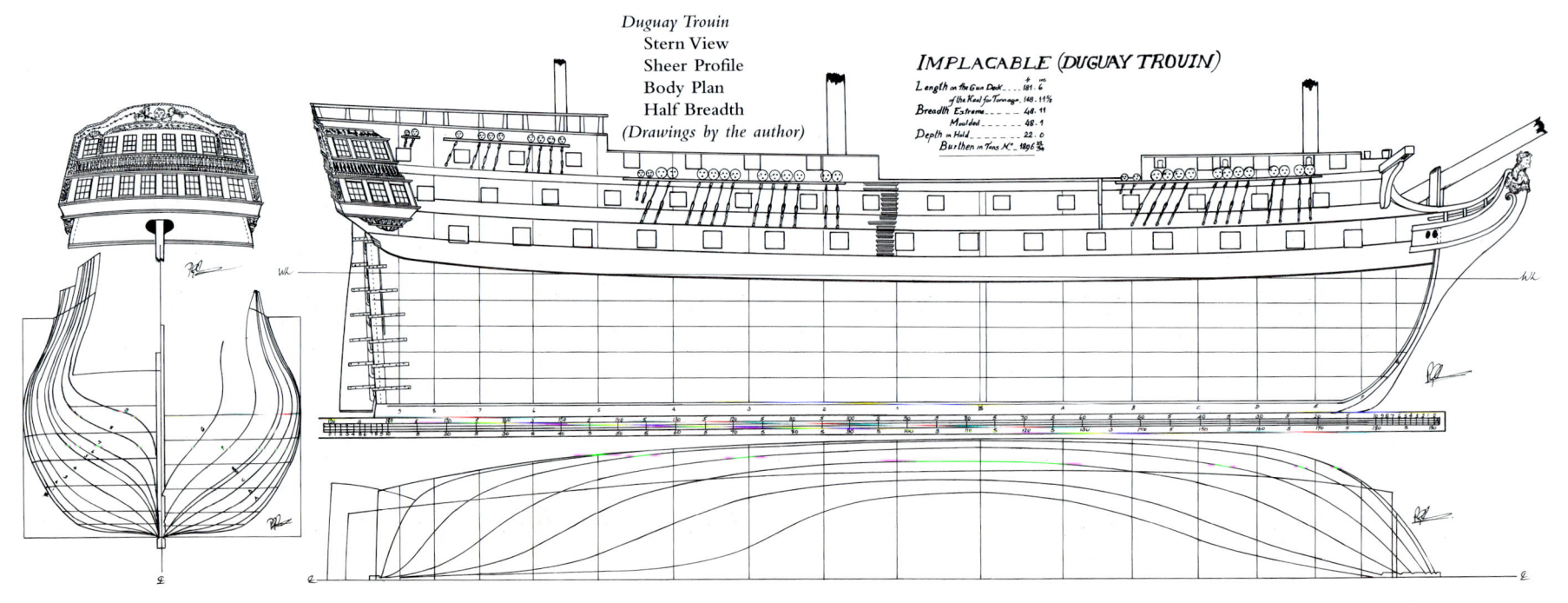

Duguay Trouin
Stern View
Sheer Profile
Body Plan
Half Breadth
(Drawings by the author)

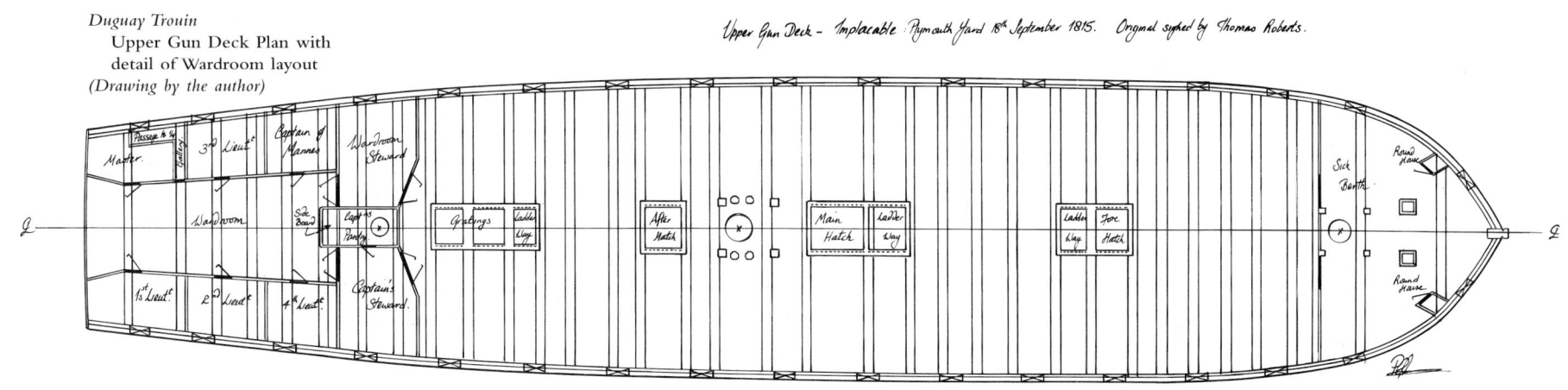

Duguay Trouin
Upper Gun Deck Plan with
detail of Wardroom layout
(Drawing by the author)

contest ensued with Strachan signalling for close action. Around 12.55 p.m. when *Duguay Trouin* luffed to cross and rake *Cæsar's* bow, Strachan's ship counter-manœuvred by doing likewise. In her attempt to tack, *Duguay Trouin* unfortunately missed stays and losing weigh did, for a short time, come under considerable fire from *Cæsar* and *Hero*. Action eased and when the French ships came onto a port tack at 1.20 p.m. the British ships made chase. With *Namur* joining at 2 p.m., battle recommenced and by 3.15 p.m. *Formidable* and *Scipion* had struck. Meanwhile *Duguay Trouin* and *Mont Blanc* make good their escape but were soon overhauled by *Cæsar* and *Hero*. After twenty minutes' close action *Duguay Trouin* and *Mont Blanc* simultaneously struck at 3.35 p.m. Total French casualties amounted to 750 killed and wounded; among the dead was Claude Touffet, *Duguay Trouin's* captain. British casualties were just 14.8 per cent of the French. All four French ships were taken into Plymouth on 10 November. Appropriately renamed *Implacable* and entered in the Royal Navy, the ship was laid up in the Hamoaze until 1807.[56]

CAPTAINS OF *IMPLACABLE* (MSS 248/6 and 248/7)

Name	Time of Entry	Time of Discharge	On What Occasion.
Thomas Byam Martin	13 January 1808	1 September 1808	Appointed Captain of the Fleet
P Pipon	2 September 1808	13 October 1808	To the *Daphne*
G C McKenzie	14 October 1808	8 March 1809	Superseded
Thomas Byam Martin	9 March 1809	6 February 1810	Superseded
George Cockburn	7 February 1810	22 April 1811	To the *Alfred*
Joseph R Watson	23 April 1811	7 November 1812	Paid Off at Plymouth
Edward Harvey	January 1839	31 January 1842	Paid Off

1807: Surveyed and deemed suitable for sea service *Implacable* was docked at Plymouth on 2 September and refitted, with her copper being removed and replaced. Undocked on 30 November, the overall costs of this refit amounted to £34,585; £19,393 for her hull, £5,602 for masts and yards, and £9,590 for stores and rigging labour costs inclusive.[57]

1808: On 13 January *Implacable* was placed under the command of Captain Thomas Byam Martin and prepared for sea service.[58] To meet Admiralty requirements she was re-armed with twenty-eight 32 pounders on her lower gun deck, thirty 18 pounders on her upper gun deck, two 12 pounders and twelve 32 pounder carronades on the quarter deck, and two 12 pounders and two 32 pounder carronades on the forecastle. This gave her a broadside weight of 966 pounds. Towards the end of May *Implacable* assembled with Admiral James Saumarez's fleet in the Baltic, Saumarez flying his flag in *Victory* (100). Other Trafalgar ships present were *Mars*, *Orion*, *Africa* and *Euryalus*. When Vice-Admiral Hanickoff's Russian fleet sailed from Kronstadt in August *Implacable* was deployed with *Centaur* (74), Rear-Admiral Sir Samuel Hood, to reinforce Rear-Admiral Nauckhoff's Swedish squadron of seven sail of the line and four frigates laying at Oro Roads. Just after *Implacable* and *Centaur* joined the Swedes on 20 August, the Russian fleet was observed off the Swedish coast. At 6 a.m. 25 August the Anglo-Swedish fleet put to sea to intercept and by 9 a.m. had sighted the Russian squadron off Hango Udd. Being faster, *Implacable* and *Centaur* closed with the enemy next morning and after two hours' close pursuit *Implacable* brought *Sewolod* (74) to action. By 7.45 a.m. *Implacable* had drawn up alongside *Sewolod's* lee side and, firing her broadside, brought down the Russian colours. The cannonade continued for some 20 minutes, when Captain Rudnov surrendered *Sewolod's* colours. Shortly after *Centaur* signalled that the remaining Russian ships were making their approach, Captain Martin was obliged to haul *Implacable* clear and make repairs. Meanwhile one of the Russian frigates took the crippled *Sewolod* in tow. With the other Russian ships coming up to give *Sewolod* assistance, they made their way into the port of Rogersvik (Tallin). Shortly afterwards *Implacable* and *Centaur* resumed the chase and forced the frigate to slip her tow, allowing *Sewolod* to run aground, but she was soon re-floated. Boats from the harbour then came out to tow *Sewolod* into port, but were beaten off by *Centaur*. Drawing alongside, Hood lashed *Sewolod's* bowsprit to *Centaur's* mizzen-mast and hand-to-hand fighting ensued. At this point *Implacable* anchored a cable length away, ready with her guns loaded and run out, obliging the Russian to strike. During this action *Centaur* and *Sewolod* ran aground. While *Centaur* was eventually freed, the Russian ship could not be re-floated. With no alternative option, Hood had all prisoners and wounded removed, then ordered *Sewolod* to be burnt. In the action *Implacable* suffered six seamen and marines killed, among whom were Quarter Gunners Robert Miller and William Chugg; Ordinary Seaman David Coming and Lewis Grouville, Marine Private Titus Netherwood and Boy Third Class George Quinton. Among the 26 wounded were Thomas Pickerwell, Master's Mate; Nicholas Drew, Captain's Clerk, and 24 seamen and marines, two of whom later died of injuries and three had limbs amputated. Afterwards Captain Martin commended his First Lieutenant Mr Augustus Baldwin and his Master Mr Moore for their part in the action. Shortly after, command of the ship was placed under Captains Peter Pipon and George McKenzie, both serving in an acting capacity. At the end of the year *Implacable* returned home to refit after which she was deployed to the Iberian peninsular.[59] After this action when Captain Martin was appointed Captain of the Fleet, command of *Implacable* was succeeded by Captain P Pipon on 2 September. Pipon remained in the ship until only 13 October when he was appointed into *Daphne*. Next day he was superseded by Captain G C McKenzie.[60] On 8 November *Implacable* returned to Plymouth to make good various defects before sailing to Spain under new orders on 8 December.[61]

1809: *Implacable* arrived at Vigo in early January where she joined *Victory*, other warships and many transports. Their purpose was to recover the remnants of General Sir John Moore's army which, having supported the Spanish, had been left fighting a rearguard action against French troops. Arriving off Corunna on 15 January, *Implacable* commenced embarking Moore's army on the night of the 16th. By 17 January only the rearguard of 2,000 men remained on shore. These men were under continuous fire from the French batteries above the beach, giving this evacuation many parallels with the recovery of the British Expeditionary Force at Dunkirk in 1940 131 years later. Making matters worse, the weather deteriorated, heavy seas prolonging the evacuation a day further. Many transports lost their anchors and ran out to sea without embarking troops, while others ran on shore and were abandoned by their crews. Some of the boats from the men-of-war were lost.

When *Implacable* returned home Captain Byam Martin resumed command on 9 March.[62] Throughout the summer the ship was re-deployed in the Baltic, harassing Russian trade operating off the Finnish archipelago. In company with *Implacable* were *Bellerophon* (74), *Melpomene* (38) and *Prometheus* (18). At 9 p.m. on 7 July boats from these ships, under the command of Lieutenant Joseph Hawkey, went into Barö Sound and made a successful attack on eight Russian gunboats, each mounting one 32 and 24-pounder gun and 46 men, and a convoy of transports laden with timber, spars, cordage, together with powder and provisions for the Russian army. Despite the British coming under a destructive fire of grape from the gunboats, six of the gunboats were taken, a seventh was sunk and twelve of the transports were captured. Of the 270 British men involved 17 were killed and 37 were wounded. Among the dead were Lieutenants Hawkey and Stirling, and Midshipman William Mountney. Shortly afterwards boats from *Implacable*, *Melpomene* and *Prometheus* discovered and captured a further three transports in a creek nearby.[63]

1810: *Implacable* returned to Plymouth on 2 January and went into dock for four days to have her copper repaired. Undocked on 7 January, the ship continued to refit, the overall cost totalling £9,268.[64] Completed, the ship sailed out to the anchorage off Cawsand on 3 February where, four days later, Byam Martin was superseded by Captain George Cockburn.[65] Shortly afterwards *Implacable* sailed for Quiberon Bay, where, under cover of darkness, her boats landed Baron de Kolli whose express mission was to arrange the escape of the Spanish King Ferdinand VII imprisoned by the French at Valençay. Hoisting the flag of Rear-Admiral Sir Richard Goodwin Keats, *Implacable* then sailed for Cadiz, arriving there on 17 July. The purpose of this expedition was raise the blockade of the island of Leon, defended by 4,000 British and Germans, 16,500 Spaniards and 1,400 Portuguese against French forces commanded by Marshal Victor. With *Implacable* were eleven British and Spanish line-of-battle ships.

This expedition was launched against the French at Moguer on 23 August. Under the direction of Captain Cockburn, Spanish troops and horses were landed from the transports. While they marched the 22 miles along the beach towards the French stronghold they were accompanied by eleven flatboats from *Implacable* commanded by Lieutenant George Westphal; Westphal had served as a midshipman in *Victory* at Trafalgar. When the troops arrived at Moguer on the morning of 24 August, Westphal's flatboats were employed to ferry them across the river. Faced by such a large force the French army of some 1,100 strong, mainly cavalry, retreated to Seville.

Off Cadiz on 2 September, Rear-Admiral Keats shifted his flag out of *Implacable* into *Milford* (74). Four days later *Implacable*, now a 'private ship', (without a flag officer) sailed from Cadiz for Havana with two Spanish three-deckers. *Implacable* then remained in the West Indies until 1811.

1811: *Implacable* returned home from her deployment in the West Indies on 18 February carrying 6,000,000 dollars on board. On 24 April command of the ship was succeeded by Captain Joseph Rowley Watson and *Implacable* was sent to the Mediterranean to join Vice-Admiral Pellew's fleet blockading Toulon.[66]

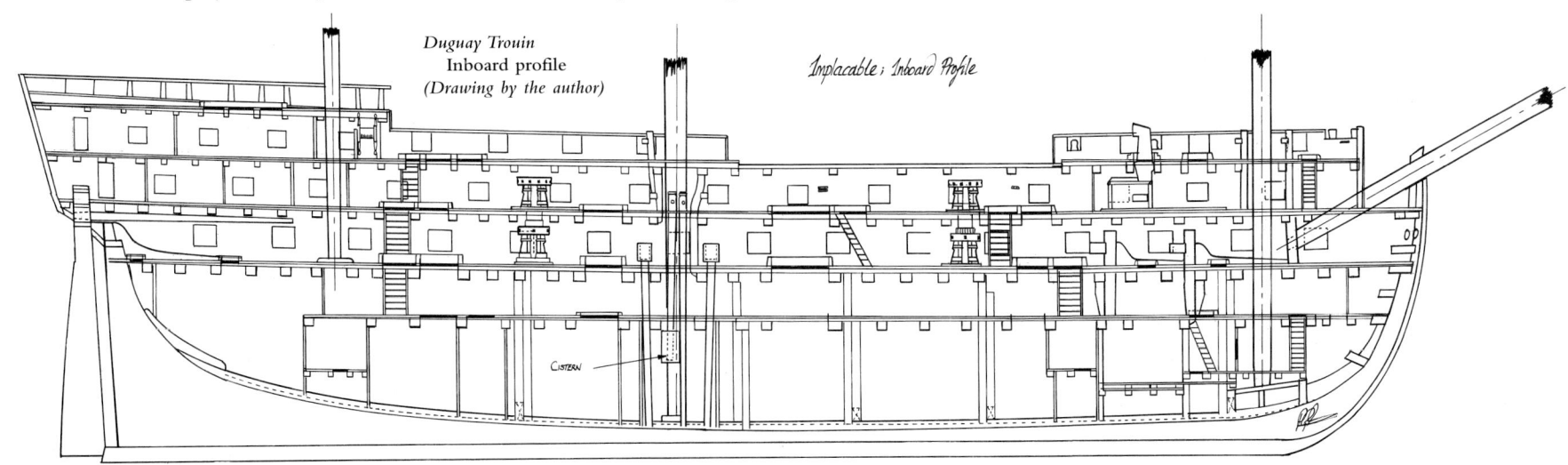

PROGRESS BOOK - *IMPLACABLE* 3rd RATE OF 74 GUNS

At what Port	Arrived	Docked	Coppered
Plymouth	10 Nov 1805	2 Sept 1807	Copper taken off Sep. Re-coppered Nov. 1807
Plymouth	11 Nov 1808		
Plymouth	2 Jan. 1810	6 Jan 1810	Copper Repaired
Plymouth	29 Sep 1812	22 Oct 1812	Copper taken off Jan 1812 [error - this should read 1813 ?] Re-coppered Jan 1815
Plymouth		23 July 1819	Copper Repaired
Plymouth		8 Feb 1826	Copper taken off and recoppered and fixed Protectors
Plymouth		8 Nov 1832	Protectors taken off
Plymouth		22 Mar 1833	Repaired Copper
Plymouth		4 Feb 1836	Raised and Dressed the Copper
Plymouth		14 Feb 1839	
Plymouth	13 May 1841		
Plymouth	17 Jan 1842	12 Feb 1842	Copper taken off and recoppered
Foreign years			
Plymouth		20 Dec 1843	Dressed Copper
Plymouth		26 Sep 1848	Repaired Copper
Plymouth		25 June 1855	Repaired and Dressed Copper
Plymouth			
Plymouth			
Plymouth		11 Jan 1860	Repaired Copper on Bottom
Plymouth			
Plymouth			

Carried to Abstract of Progress No. 9 Folio 289

Duguay Trouin
Inboard profile
(Drawing by the author)

Implacable: Inboard Profile

Source: ADM 180/10 Folio 156

Launched or Undocked	Sailed	Built or Nature of Repair	Cost of Hull, Masts & Yards Materials £	Workmen £	Cost of Masts & Yards Materials £	Workmen £	Cost of Rigging & Stores Materials £	Workmen £	Grand Total £
30 Nov 1807	21 March 1808	Fitted	13,389	6,004	5,436	166	9,482	108	34,585
	8 Dec 1808	Defects	Incl. above	Do.	Do.	Do.	Do.	Do.	Do.
7 Jan 1810	3 Feb 1810	Defects	452	462	796	23	7,474	61	9,268
25 Jan 1815		Very Large Repair	38,17712	15,8965	5,163-	59-	7,505-	57-	66,85717
Aug 1819			1,999	908	-	-	20	-	2,927
28 Dec 1816		Small Repair	14,219	5,405	-	10	876	-	20,510
7 Nov 1832			1,071	1,130	651	40	1,687	-	4,579
22 April 1833		Defects	287	420	-	9	-	-	716
16 Feb 1836		Fitted for a Demonstration Ship	1,912	1,610	-	-	192	13	3,727
16 Feb 1839	9 April 1839	Fitted for Sea	677	648	1,372	15	9,836	4	12,552
3 July 1841		Defects	4915	451	-	81	218 -	1,199	3- 1181,304
26 April 1842		Repaired Advanced Ship	1,914	515	1,510353	--	--	--	-- 3,451
23 Dec 1843		Defects	309	491	-	-	-	-	800
27 sep 1848		Defects	177	393	-	-	-	-	570
6 July 1855		Do to 31 March 1855 Training Ship Ditto	627 888	750 1,262	- 1,121	- -	1,428	- -	1,377 4,699
		Paid Off 1858 Expense to March 1839	296	161	2	-	278	-	145 [135 credit]
16 Jan 1860		Fitted for Training Ship May 1860	273	750	466	-	4,249	-	5,742
		Defects 19 Jan 1861	44	72	2 -	-	89	-	205
		Defects (Sep) 1861 Expenses included with Defects Feb 1862							
			115,017 Total		15,439 Total		44,561 Total		175,017

1812: Much in need of a refit, *Implacable* returned to Plymouth on 29 September and went into dock on 22 October for a 'Very Large Repair'. Although she was in dock Captain Watson did not officially pay off the ship until 1 November.[67]

1813: During January *Implacable* had her entire copper sheathing removed, enabling her frames and outer planking to be replaced. With no urgency to get her back to sea, this refit continued for another two years.

1815: Finally completed and recoppered, *Implacable* was re-launched on 25 January. The costs for this refit, which totalled £66,857, comprised £38,177 for her hull with £15,896 for labour; £5,163 for masts and yards with £59 for labour; and £7,505 for rigging and stores with £57 for labour. An additional £17 was also spent on her hull, of which £5 covered labour.[68] *Implacable* was laid up in ordinary for a period of some 26 years.

1839: In February *Implacable* was recommissioned under Captain Edward Harvey and sent back into the Mediterranean.

1840: While on this station *Implacable* saw action off the Syrian coast against the Egyptian fleet and was deployed with the fleet blockading Alexandria.

1842: Voted the smartest ship in the Mediterranean fleet, *Implacable* carried a golden cock at her masthead.[69] When *Implacable* was recalled home Captain Harvey paid off the ship on 31 January at Devonport (Plymouth), after which she was laid up in the Hamoaze where she remained until decisions were made to convert her into a training ship.

1855: Probably considered too obsolete for participating in the Crimean War, *Implacable* was taken into the dockyard and converted into a training ship. Completed in June, the ship was placed under the command of Captain Arthur Lowe who received her first intake of naval trainees aged 15 to 18. By this period conscription into the navy by means of the impressment had ceased with the end of the war with Napoleon in 1815. The Victorian navy, which *Implacable* now served, was made up of volunteers who needed proper naval training before going to sea. Old ships such as *Implacable* proved useful for this purpose. This concept had started with the establishment of the training ship *Illustrious* at Portsmouth in 1854.

1860: During this year *Implacable* was joined by *Lion* (74). Anchored stern to stern, the two ships formed a combined training establishment under the single name of HMS *Lion*.

1865: In January command of *Implacable* was superseded by Commander Edward Hay. By this time the ship was mainly used for training boys for the navy. Following this example *Ganges* (84) was converted in the succeeding year and set up as a training ship at Falmouth. *Ganges* was later moved to Harwich and laid up off Shotley Point where the rivers Ouse and Orwell converge. This renowned establishment, although later moved on shore, remained a training ship for boys well into the mid-1970s.[70]

1877: In October Commander (later Admiral) Carr succeeded command of *Implacable*. Besides *Implacable* and *Lion*, contemporary photographs show many other old 'wooden walls' laying in the Hamoaze.

1879: In November Carr was superseded by Commander Thomas Jackson.

1905: At the centenary of the battle of Trafalgar *Implacable*, still moored at Devonport, and *Victory* lying in Portsmouth harbour were the only surviving ships from that battle. It was planned to sell off *Implacable*.

Explosive charges are detonated within the hull of Implacable *off the Isle of Wight on 2 December 1949. (Chrysalis Picture Library)*

With White Ensign and Tricolour flying, Implacable *begins to sink beneath the waves. (Chrysalis Picture Library)*

1908: On 6 October *Implacable* was put up for sale, but not being sold, was loaned to Wheatly Cobb to use as a training ship. This move was made following the loss of Cobb's training ship *Foudroyant* (80) on Blackpool Sands on 16 June 1897 and his search for another vessel. He purchased the 46 gun frigate *Trincomalee* for £1,323. This ship, first laid up at Cowes and renamed *Foudroyant*, was moved to Falmouth and then Portsmouth to continue training duties until the late 1980s. Taken to Hartlepool and renamed *Trincomalee*, she has since been restored and is now open as a public attraction. Shortly afterwards the navy lent *Implacable* to Cobb to fulfil the boys' training ship role. *Implacable* was therefore taken to Falmouth in 1912 and moored ahead of Cobb's training frigate *Foudroyant* where she remained until the 1930s, providing a superb summer training school for boys.[71]

1920: By this year the oak hull of the *Implacable* needed urgent repairs and although the Admiralty still owned the ship they notified Cobb that he was responsible for refitting expenses. Despite this the Admiralty reversed their decision and docked the ship at Devonport and effected the necessary repairs at a cost of £6,180.

1926: Still needing considerable repairs to her hull, *Implacable* was docked at Devonport and refitted, the cost of which was borne by an appeal made by the Trustees of the ship. This however did not cover the expenditure and although some of the work was undertaken at the navy's expense, further cash was required. Supporting the Trustees, Admiral of the Fleet Lord Beatty wrote to the *Times* on 21 July stating:

> As the time for which the Trafalgar ship *Implacable* can be retained in dock at Devonport is drawing to a close, I feel I ought to let you know the result of my appeals for funds to save the old vessel, which you were good enough to publish on 20th October and 30 November last, and also how work has progressed. The amount subscribed up to date is just over £19,000, which is about £6,000 short of the £25,000 for which I originally appealed.

1935: Following completion of the restoration of the Trafalgar ship *Victory* (100) at Portsmouth in 1928, the Society for Nautical Research turned their attentions to the *Implacable* which was much used by Sea Scouts. Brought to Portsmouth in 1932, she was refitted, when dockyard shipwrights could be spared, to eradicate sagging beams and decks. This involved fitting her with Doric columns throughout, fashioned from an original surviving stanchion. New beams were fitted under her poop and new hanging and lodging knees were made from teak taken out of the composite sloop *Dragon*. Work was supervised by the ship's carpenter Mr Cole. From March 1935 some 918 men and boys made use of the ship under her newly appointed Superintendent, Commander R Michell.[72]

1936: Further restoration was undertaken on *Implacable*. Part of her stern framing and deck transoms were replaced; her taffrail and the upper finishing of each quarter gallery were rebuilt with advice from Messrs Ralfe and Winsor.[73]

1937: With little funding available the work of restoring *Implacable*'s poop and constructing a new bulkhead was left to the resources of Colonel Harold Wyllie and his onboard staff. This year saw 2,000 young people training in the ship, a rise of 40 per cent from the previous year. Not just boys; during August 270 girl Sea Rangers drawn from 35 counties throughout Britain, the colonies, including Australia and Bermuda, entered into the ship. It is noted that their boat drill, manning the capstan, knotting and slicing promoted considerable admiration from the visiting Trustees and Lady Baden-Powell who, as Chief of the Girl Guide movement, inspected the girls on 26 August.[74]

1939: *Implacable*'s accounts ending 31 December this year show that victualling costs for 1,638 boys, girls and visitors amounted to £1277 16 6d, restoration had cost £852 4s 10d, and mooring fees paid to the Admiralty totalled £50. Despite her valuable rôle the war that had started three months earlier would bring about the demise of *Implacable*.[75]

1943: During the Second World War, *Implacable* was passed back to the Royal Navy and joined by the training ship *Foudroyant*, brought up from Milford Haven, the two vessels were combined together forming the naval training establishment HMS *Foudroyant* for senior sea cadets. These boys, colloquially called the 'Bounty Boys', lived on board where they received comprehensive training in signalling and telegraphy ready to join the fleet as communication ratings.

1947: No longer further required for training purposes HMS *Foudroyant* was dissolved, the frigate *Foudroyant* being anchored in Portsmouth harbour to resume her boy training rôle, while *Implacable* was brought into the dockyard. When inspected *Implacable*'s hull structure was found to have deterio-

The Ships of Trafalgar

THE 74 GUN SHIP *DUGUAY TROUIN*

rated seriously and was beyond reasonable restoration without heavy funding from the Royal Navy. Hard pushed for financial support after the war, the Admiralty was left with little choice but to dispose of her. An attempt was made by Harold Wyllie and Frank Carr to revive the *Implacable* Committee and proposed that this Trafalgar ship be berthed in a dock at Greenwich near to the National Maritime Museum. This dock was eventually used for the tea-clipper *Cutty Sark*.

1949: Needing little short of £500,000 for restoration, the inevitable decision was made to dispose of *Implacable*. Before doing so her figurehead was removed, together with parts of her stern, and transferred into the National Maritime Museum. Likewise drawings recording her carved works were made. Finally towed out of Portsmouth flying both a British white ensign and French tricolour, *Implacable* was scuttled off Selsey Bill on 2 December 1949. Even at this point *Implacable* remained defiant, for when the charges exploded, her bottom, weighted with ballast, sank, leaving the broadsides of her upper hull a floating hazard. Eventually breaking up, timbers of *Implacable* drifted and washed up on the French shore, some pieces not far from Rochefort.

This act of destruction became an infamous episode in the annals of maritime ship preservation. Marking a tribute to her renowned designer Sane and the Rochefort Frenchmen who built her, the entire stern of *Duguay Trouin* with its carvings, balustrades and stern lights is now exhibited in the National Maritime Museum. Moreover, when the World Ship Trust was founded in 1979 to prevent pertinent historic ships being lost, it adopted the motto '*Implacable*, Never Again'.

The 74 gun ship **FOUGUEUX**

Meaning fiery and spirited, the 74 gun *Fougueux* was launched at Rochefort in 1795. Designed by Jacques Noel Sane, *Fougueux* was built using some 175-180,000 cubic feet for her construction. This figure equates to about 3,500 trees, ninety per cent of which was oak, taken from neighbouring forests. Initially carrying twenty-eight 36 pounders on her lower gun deck, thirty 18 pounders on her upper gun deck, fourteen 8 pounder on her quarter deck and four 4 pounders on her forecastle, *Fougueux* delivered a single broadside weight of 854 pounds. By the time of Trafalgar this complement of ordnance had been upgraded, her quarter deck bearing two 12 pounder carriage guns and twelve 32 pounder carronades, and her forecastle carrying two 12 pounder carriage guns and four 32 pounder carronades. This 19 per cent increase gave *Fougueux* a broadside weight of 1,054 pounds.

SERVICE CAREER

1795: The first fact in English history recorded about *Fougueux* dates from 3 January shortly after her launch and fitting out. On that day *Diamond*, Captain Sir William Sidney Smith, sighted *Fougueux* off Brest with the frigate *Virginie* (40). It appears that command of *Fougueux* was placed with Commodore E T Maistral who remained in the ship until 1801. At Trafalgar Maistral would command *Neptune* (80). In June that same year *Fougueux* joined the combined squadrons of Admirals Vence and Villaret and took part in Admiral Lord Bridport's action off Isle de Groix on 23 June during which she played little part due to her position within the fleet.[76] After this engagement *Fougueux* returned to Brest.

1796: Towards the end of this year France made plans to invade Ireland and incite rebellion. The invasion fleet, including *Fougueux*, comprised 17 ships of the line, 13 frigates, six brigs, seven transports and a powder vessel. In overall command was Admiral Morand de Galles. After embarking 18,000 troops commanded by General Hoche the fleet sailed from Brest on 15/16 December. De Galles was expecting to be joined by more ships bearing troops from Toulon under the command of Rear-Admiral Villeneuve; this squadron however did not arrive. From this point the expedition turned to failure as the fleet was dispersed off Ushant, mainly through poor and confusing signalling. *Fougueux* was in the van of the fleet which comprised de Galles' flagship *Indomptable* (80), *Mucius* (74), *Redoutable* (74), *Patriote* (74) and *Revolution* (74). Also with the van were four frigates and two brigs. While some of the fleet under Rear-Admiral Bovet managed to get into Bantry Bay, the remainder, including *Fougueux*, driven by bad weather, returned to Brest on 1 January 1797.[77]

1803: When war restarted in May *Fougueux* was based at Brest where she remained until joining Villeneuve's combined fleet in late summer 1805.

1805: As the plans for invading England gained momentum, *Fougueux* was placed under the command of Captain Louis Alexis Baudoin. While it was expected that *Fougueux* would have been detached with Admiral Ganteaume's Brest fleet and sail with those ships as ordered, this is not the case. For unknown reasons *Fougueux* joined Villeneuve's combined fleet at Ferrol around 26 July and sailed for Cadiz with them on 9 August, arriving at that port eleven days later.[78]

TRAFALGAR

When *Fougueux* sailed with the combined fleet on 19 October, her crew, like many of the French fleet, had not received any pay for 16 months. After Villeneuve altered course to northward on the morning of the battle *Fougueux* lay seventeenth in line from the head of the combined fleet. Ahead on her starboard bow was *Indomptable* (80), and abaft on her starboard quarter *Intrépide* (74). About one mile away off *Fougueux*'s starboard beam lay *Rhin*, one of the escorting French 40 gun frigates. As Collingwood's division commenced their final approach Captain Baudoin

SPECIFICATIONS: *FOUGUEUX*

Rate	3rd	Length on the range of the gun deck	183 ft 2 ins	Ordnance - lower gun deck	28 x 36 pounders
Guns	74	Length of keel for tonnage	149 ft 7ins	Ordnance - upper gun deck	30 x 18 pounders
Class	Sane-Border	Extreme breadth	48 ft 8ins	Ordnance - quarter deck	14 x 8 pounders
Designer	Jacques Noel Sane	Depth in hold	20 ft 6 ins	Ordnance - forecastle	6 x 8 pounders
Builder	Dockyard	Tons burthen	1886 tons	Single broadside weight	854
Dockyard	Rochfort	Draught afore		Fate	Captured at the battle of Trafalgar 21 October, she ran on shore and went to pieces during the storm on 22 October 1805.
Date ordered		Draught abaft			
Date keel laid		Complement	650		
Date launched	1794				

watched carefully, continuously calculating when they would come within range. Then, just before noon, Baudoin gave the order to fire. This opening broadside placed *Fougueux* forever on historical record as the first ship to fire at Trafalgar. Recalling events, Commander Bazin, *Fougueux*'s second in command, later wrote 'Captain Baudoin had the colours and the French pendant hoisted and fired the whole broadside at the foremost ship; from that minute the action commenced vigorously on both sides'.[79] *Fougueux*'s opening salvo, to which Bazin referred, was directed at Collingwood's *Royal Sovereign* (100) as she and those following in her wake pressed home their attack. Within moments the 170 guns from the *Santa Ana* (112), *Indomptable* (80), *San Leandro* (74) and *San Justo* (74), all double shotted, added their weight to *Fougueux*'s opening broadside. By this point Baudoin had the main topgallant sail set to drive *Fougueux* forward to close the gap astern of *Santa Ana* (112) towards which the *Royal Sovereign* was sailing. At 12.10 p.m. *Royal Sovereign* passed through the line, raking *Santa Ana* with her double shotted larboard batteries to considerable effect. At the same time Collingwood's flagship raked *Fougueux* with her starboard guns. Those that passed through beakhead bulkhead ranged through her upper gun deck, causing considerable casualties. To avoid collision with *Royal Sovereign* Baudoin had already backed *Fougueux*'s main topsail. When Collingwood turned his ship to larboard to run aboard *Santa Ana*'s starboard quarter Captain Baudoin saw his oportunity to retaliate and smartly ported his helm, bringing *Fougueux* round to starboard. Now well positioned to use her larboard guns, *Fougueux* delivered a raking broadside through *Royal Sovereign*'s exposed stern. Besides the guns of *Santa Ana*, *Royal Sovereign* was also fired upon by *San Leandro*, *San Justo* and *Indomptable*. When these ships realised that they were inadvertently firing into one another, each ceased firing and sought another opponent.[80] At this point *Fougueux* also came under heavy raking fire from *Belleisle* (74) and *Mars* (74) as they followed *Royal Sovereign* through the line. *Belleisle* then turned alongside *Fougueux* and starboard to starboard the two ships poured broadsides into each other, both vessels suffering damage and casualties. Simultaneously *Fougueux* prepared and fired her larboard guns at *Mars* which now lay off her larboard bow. This one broadside slammed into the the starboard quarter of *Mars*, instantly killing her commander Captain Duff.

With her lower and topsail yards carried away *Fougueux* disengaged herself from *Belleisle* and drifted north-west in an unmanageable condition. Shortly before 2 p.m. she came up within one hundred yards of the dismasted *Téméraire* (98). As *Fougueux* loomed out of the battle smoke *Téméraire*'s starboard batteries opened fire. The fusillade of round shot and grape ripped into *Fougueux*, killing Captain Baudoin and many others. Commander Bazin immediately assumed command although he had already been wounded several times. Unmanageable without her course and topsails, *Fougueux* drifted further towards *Téméraire*, the inevitable collision bringing down *Fougueux*'s wounded main and mizzen masts. Anticipating that she would be boarded Bazin ordered his crew to take up arms to defend the ship as another broadside hit them followed by a volley of musket balls fired from *Téméraire*'s carronades. Needing assistance to repel boarders Bazin sent for his senior lieutenant but he had already been killed. The next officer was also dead and the fourth in command was dying. The one remaining lieutenant who had been commanding the lower gun deck reported that nearly every seaman manning the 36 pounders was dead. *Fougueux*'s upper gun deck battery of 18 pounders fared no better; Midshipman Dudrésit, the only officer left standing reported that only 15 seamen had survived and every gun was out of action. Bazin had little choice but surrender. Recording this later Bazin wrote:

> Seeing the impossibility of repelling boarding, or of defending the ship against the number of enemies who are getting aboard, I gave orders to cease firing and dragged myself, in spite of my wounds, as far as the Captain's cabin to get and throw into the sea the box containing the signals and instructions for the ship, and reappearing on the quarter-deck, I was taken and conveyed on board the English ship; the enemy hauled down the colours and gradually the slaughter ceased.

Honourably defended, the casualty rate in *Fougueux* reached a staggering 84 per cent; of her complement of 650 some 546 had been killed or wounded.[81] That evening the frigate *Phœbe* (38) took *Fougueux* in tow.

FATE

Fougueux was the first prize ship to be lost by the British. At around midnight when the wind shifted to the south-west and began to rise *Fougueux* broke adrift from *Phœbe*. Recording the events on board *Fougueux* during the night of 21 October, Pierre Servaux, *Fougueux*'s master-at-arms, reported:

> The ships was in a terrible condition, cut down to a hulk, without masts, or rigging left. She was, too, without a boat that could swim, while the whole vessel was full of holes as a sieve, shatterd from stem to stern and two enormous gaps forced in the starboard side at the water line, through which the sea poured in a stream. The water had risen almost to the orlop deck. Everywhere one heard the cries of the wounded and dying, as well as the noise and shouts of insubordinate men who refused to man the pumps and only thought of themselves. The scenes of horror on board the ship that night were really the most awful and fearful that imagination can call up.

Next morning, Tuesday 22 October, as the wind blew harder *Phœbe*'s log states that she had been 'Employed all Night getting the Prize in Tow past 3 Hawsers & one hundred fathoms of Rope Prize in Tow AM Fresh Breezes & squally'.[82] The tow however did not hold and in the rising storm *Fougueux* was driven on shore and rapidly beaten to pieces upon the rocks. As *Fougueux* neared the rocks Servaux escaped the wreck by jumping out of a lower deck port and swam to a boat sent from *Orion* (74).[83]

The 74 gun ship HÉROS

Simply meaning 'Hero', *Héros* was another 74 gun ship designed by Jacques Noel Sane launched at Rochefort in 1795 and consequently resembled her Trafalgar contemporaries *Achille*, *Aigle*, *Duguay Trouin*, *Mont Blanc* and *Redoutable*. Carrying twenty-eight 36 pounders on her lower gun deck, thirty 18 pounders on her upper gun deck, twenty 18 pounders on her quarter deck and forecastle and possibly two 18 pounder carronades or howitzers on her poop, *Héros* could deliver a single broadside weight of 908 pounds. Her predecessor, also a 74 gun ship, served in the East Indies during the American War of Independence, where she captured the British *Hannibal* (50) in 1782.[84] Anchored in the inner roads of Toulon in 1793, this *Héros* was one of many ships destroyed during the evacuation of Toulon on 18 December.[85]

SERVICE HISTORY

1795: After her launch it appears that *Héros* remained in Toulon for the duration of the French Revolutionary War.

1805: When hostilities re-opened with the declaration of war on 16 May

SPECIFICATIONS: *HÉROS*

Rate	3rd	Length on the range of the gun deck	182 ft 1½ ins	Ordnance - lower gun deck	30 x 36 pounders
Guns	74	Length of keel for tonnage	150 ft 0⅝ ins	Ordnance - upper gun deck	30 x 18 pounders
Class	Sane-Border	Extreme breadth	48 ft 7½ ins	Ordnance - quarter deck	14 x 8 pounders
Designer	Jacques Noel Sane	Depth in hold	21 ft 10 ins	Ordnance - forecastle	6 x 8 pounders
Builder	Dockyard	Tons burthen	1887 39/94 tons	Ordnance - Poop	2 x 18 pounder carronades
Dockyard	Rochefort	Draught afore		Single broadside weight	908 pounds
Date ordered	-	Draught abaft		Fate	Given over to Spanish 14 June 1808
Date keel laid		Complement	640		
Date launched	1795				

1803 it seems that *Héros* was not in Toulon but had already transferred to the Atlantic coast of France. By the beginning of August 1805 she was inside the Spanish port of Ferrol. In command of *Héros*, was Captain J B J T Poulin. On 26 July Villeneuve anchored his battered ships off Ferrol after his action against Calder. When they had refitted and provisioned *Héros*, with *Duguay Trouin* and *Swiftsure*, joined the combined fleet which sailed south for Cadiz on 9 August. With these three ships the combined fleet, now comprising 29 sail of the line, several frigates and smaller vessels, evaded Collingwood's division and got into Cadiz.

TRAFALGAR

When *Héros* put to sea with the rest of the combined fleet on 19 October she was one of those fortunate vessels which cleared the harbour by nightfall. On the morning of 21 October *Héros* was placed ninth in line of the combined fleet with the Spanish *San Agustin* (74) ahead of her, leading Villeneuve's division. Astern of *Héros* was the great *Santísima Trinidad* (136), while on her starboard beam lay the 18 gun brig *Furet*. As Nelson's weather division slowly made their approach at about 11.50 a.m. Captain Poulin ordered *Héros*'s gunners to try a ranging shot, the first of which fell short. Giving more time for the British ships to close, *Héros* prepared a second broadside. Firing almost simultaneously, *Héros*, *Santísima Trinidad*, *Bucentaure* and *Redoutable* discharged their broadsides, 182 guns in all, into *Victory* (100), *Téméraire* (98), and *Neptune* (98) causing considerable damage. This firepower, dealing out death with no fire returned, continued for some 25 minutes, round, bar and chain shot ripping through *Victory*'s fore topsail. At around 12.30 p.m. after *Victory* had turned to starboard after making her feint, *Héros* came under concentrated fire from *Téméraire*'s larboard batteries as she passed in *Victory*'s wake. *Héros* maintained her fire in brisk retaliation. While most ships in Nelson's division concentrated themselves on *Bucentaure* and *Santísima Trinidad*, *Héros* became isolated and from 1 p.m. onwards *Héros* appears to have been firing sporadically at any ships within range. At some point during these engagements Captain Poulin was mortally wounded and dying very shortly after, left command to his First Lieutenant. When Dumanoir's division finally turned and re-entered the battle *Héros* was brought about and with *San Agustin* (74) standing abreast to leeward, bore down to meet the British counter-attack led by *Leviathan* (74) and *Conqueror* (74). At 4.30 p.m. Admiral Gravina signalled the remaining ships of the combined fleet to rally to leave the battle. Captain Poulin, finding that his rudder was damaged, tacked *Héros* to larboard and followed *Rayo* (100) and *San Francisco de Asis* (74) towards Cadiz. Besides her damaged rudder *Héros* suffered some damage aloft. Her casualties amounted to twelve killed and 24 wounded.[86]

Héros was one of nine French ships of the line that survived the battle; of this figure four, *Formidable*, *Duguay Trouin*, *Mont Blanc* and *Scipion* were captured two weeks later. *Héros* remained at Cadiz for the next two years with her consorts.

FATE

Spain declared war on France on 4 June 1808, putting those French ships still lying at Cadiz, most of which had escaped from Trafalgar, into grave danger. Realising that his ships now lay within range of the defensive gun batteries, their commander, now Vice-Admiral Francois Etienne de Rosily, immediately ordered his fleet to weigh and move out into the channel leading to Caraccus. Outside the harbour lay a British squadron of ten ships commanded by Rear-Admiral John Purvis, who offered the Spanish assistance in reducing the French. Preferring to act alone the Spanish mounted an attack on de Rosily's ships from land and sea on 9 June. Next day de Rosily negotiated terms which the Spanish patriots refused. Finally on 14 June de Rosily capitulated and under a more satisfactory agreement surrendered *Héros* together with *Neptune* (80), *Algésiras* (74), *Argonaute* (74), *Pluton* (74), and *Cornélie* (40) to the Spanish. Clowes states that there was also an unnamed corvette but does not later verify this. Once entered into the Spanish Royal Navy *Héros* was renamed *Heroe* and continued in service until lost in 1839.[87]

The 74 gun ship INTRÉPIDE

Named after her predecessor, a 74 gun ship lost during a great hurricane in the West Indies in October 1780, the 74 gun ship *Intrépide* which fought at Trafalgar was originally the Spanish *Intrepido*.[88] *Intrepido*, which means brave, was launched at Ferrol in 1790 (when Spain was re-arming, causing Britain to mobilise her forces.) It appears that this ship had a relatively uneventful career before being transferred into the French Navy in 1801. Why the Spanish gave her to the French is not clear.[89]

SERVICE CAREER

1801: *Intrepido* was transferred into the French Navy and renamed *Intrépide*.[90]

1803: When war restarted in May *Intrépide* was laid up afloat in Toulon along with seven other vessels. A further three were in dock and five were building. In command of the Toulon fleet at the time was Vice-Admiral Madeleine de Latouche-Tréville, with vessels *Formidable* (80), *Indomptable* (80), *Atlas* (74), *Mont Blanc* (74), and *Scipion* (74). It is very unlikely that she had either crew or commander at this time.

1804: At the end of this year *Intrépide* was placed under the command of Captain Lêonore Deperonne and fully fitted for sea service; command of the Toulon fleet having now been appointed to Villeneuve.

1805: On 18 January *Intrépide* put to sea with Villeneuve's fleet which, off Cape Sepet, was immediately struck by strong north-westerly winds. Much

SPECIFICATIONS: *INTRÉPIDE*

Rate	3rd	Date launched	1790	Complement	550/600
Guns	74	Length on the range of the gun deck		Ordnance - lower gun deck	28 x 36 pounders
Class		Length of keel for tonnage		Ordnance - upper gun deck	28 x 24 pounders
Designer		Extreme breadth		Ordnance - quarter deck	12 x 8 pounders
Builder	Dockyard	Depth in hold		Ordnance - forecastle	4 x 8 pounders
Dockyard	Ferrol	Tons burthen		Single broadside weight	
Date ordered		Draught afore		Fate	Blew up off Cape Trafalgar 23 October after the battle of Trafalgar.
Date keel laid		Draught abaft			

Source: Lyon, *Sailing Navy List*, pp. 70-71.

battered, *Intrépide* with her consorts was forced to return to port. On the evening of the 29 March *Intrépide* finally broke out of Toulon with Villeneuve's squadron and sailed for the West Indies as planned, arriving off Fort de France, Martinique, on 13 May.[91]

Intrépide sailed for Europe with Villeneuve's combined Franco-Spanish fleet. Meeting with Vice-Admiral Sir Richard Calder's squadron west of Cape Finisterre on 22 July. After fighting in this indecisive action *Intrépide* turned southward and entered Cadiz on the night of 20 August with the rest of the Villeneuve's combined fleet. While in harbour command of the ship was superseded by Provençal Captain Louis A C Infernet who would prove a formidable and courageous commander in the forthcoming battle.[92]

TRAFALGAR

Intrépide sailed with the combined fleet on 19 October. When Villeneuve ordred his fleet to form single line ahead at 11 p.m. on 20 October *Intrépide* lay in the centre.

On 21 October 1805 Villeneuve ordered his fleet to wear together and bear up towards the British fleet and Cadiz at 8 a.m. *Fougueux* (74) lay ahead of *Intrépide* and *Monarco* was astern (74). This position is open to doubt, however, as it appears that *Intrépide* had moved further forward at the opening of the battle joining the van division.[93] When battle opened *Intrépide* maintained her fire on the approaching ships of Nelson's windward division. When Admiral Dunmanoir finally turned and re-entered the battle in the mid-afternoon *Intrépide* also wore but collided with *Mont Blanc* whose flying jibboom cut *Intrépide*'s foresail. Infernet's main objective was to save his admiral Villeneuve. Recalling his actions, he 'crowded on canvas and set my course for the ships foul of each other and dismasted'. When he saw *Bucentaure* was among these ships he stated that he 'observed with sorrow' the condition of Villeneuve's flagship. *Intrépide*, as with the rest of Dumanoir's ships, were now confronted with a renewed threat as the *Leviathan* (74), *Conqueror* (74), *Britannia* (100) *Africa* (64) and *Neptune* (98) bore down upon them. When *Leviathan* turned and run aboard *San Agustin* and lashed her alongside to take possession, *Intrépide* drew up ahead of the British ship and raked her. Infernet brought *Intrépide* alongside *Leviathan*'s starboard side and fired his starboard battery into her. *Intrépide* was then attacked by *Africa* (64) while also receiving fire from *Britannia*, *Neptune*, *Ajax*, and *Agamemnon*. The close action between *Intrépide* and *Africa* remained brisk for 40 minutes. At this point one of Infernet's lieutenants, the Marquis Giquel des Touches who was posted on the forecastle, prepared his men to board and in doing so sent a midshipmen to inform Infernet of his intentions. Going to the quarter deck shortly after to speak with the captain personally the Marquis 'found my midshipman, laying flat on the deck terrified at the sight of *Téméraire* which ship had come abreast of us within pistol shot and was thundering into us from her lofty batteries. I treated my emissary as he deserved – I gave him a hearty kick'. The ship ranging alongside was in fact *Britannia*. Reaching Infernet, the Marquis found him brandishing a sabre which came close to his face. 'Do you want to cut my head off Captain?' the Marquis demanded. Infernet replied in the negative but that was what he intended 'for the first man who speaks of surrender'.

By this point the Marquis's plans to board were too late, *Orion* wore round *Intrépide*'s stern, ranging up on larboard bow and raked her, 'letting fly a murderous broadside'. It was now about 3 p.m. and when *Britannia* fired her deadly broadside into *Intrépide* a nearby infantry colonel tried to shelter behind Infernet. The gallant captain retorted 'Ah Colonel, do you think I am sheathed metal then?'. The broadside cleared most men from *Intrépide*'s upper decks and shattered much of the ship's rigging. At 3.45 when Infernet sent the remaining men below to help man the lower batteries, *Intrépide*'s mizzen yard, from where her colours were flying, was shot away. Infernet 'immediately ordered a flag to be flown from the mizzen shrouds to starboard and larboard'. At 4 o'clock when the wheel, tiller, tiller quadrant and ropes were shot away the secondary tiller was put into action. Fifteen minutes later *Intrépide*'s mizzen mast fell by the board, her main mast following four minutes later. Infernet continued to fight, using musketry and what few guns that had not been dismounted. Infernet recorded, 'At 5.53 p.m. the foremast fell; I was left without masts or sails; seeing myself surrounded by enemies and not being able to escape, having, moreover, no French ships in sight to come to my assistance, the enemy keeping up a terrible fire into me, having about half my crew killed… I was obliged to yield to the seven enemy ships that were engaging me'. (Infernet's time was one hour out, it was in fact 4.53 p.m.). Besides having no rigging, masts, guns, there was eight feet of water in the hold despite the pumps still being operable. One of the last two ships of the combined fleet to capitulate, *Intrépide*'s casualties amounted to 306 dead and wounded; some 45 per cent of her crew. For Infernet's valiant defence and 'noble madness' France later called him 'Intrépide Infernet'.[94]

Much damaged from battle and with the pumps working continuously, *Intrépide* suffered considerably during the storm. On Thursday 24 October Collingwood sent orders to *Britannia*, *Ajax* and *Orion* to commence removing the prisoners out of *Intrépide* and other very disabled prizes before destroying them. According to Lieutenant des Touches in *Intrépide*, while the storm was gathering, 'we had to pass through a leeward gunport more than eighty wounded who were incapable of moving into the small English boats. We succeeded with infinite trouble by means of a bed-frame and capstan bars, Afterwards we were towed by an English frigate which we followed while rolling from side to side and leaking everywhere'. Realising that the men working at the pumps had slowed down, des Touches found that a storeroom had been breached and that both English and French seamen had broached the liquor. Moreover the lieutenant had to stamp out a fire when spilled brandy came in contact with a candle flame. Then 'with kicks and punches I had the storeroom cleared, I barricaded the door, and I agreed with the English officer how to avert the danger that was threatening'. Des Touches then went to sit with his colleague Lieutenant Poullain, who was too badly wounded to transfer out of the hulk. By the time Poullain died, there were just three men remaining, des Touches, a captain of artillery and a midshipman. Describing the scene before leaving *Intrépide*, des Touches stated that their situation became worse every minute. 'In the midst of these bodies and the spilt blood, the silence was no longer disturbed only by the sound of the sea, but by a subdued murmuring that the water was making as it rose in the hold and spread through the vessel'. Later finding a lanthorn which they fixed to a rod, 'by a lucky chance, the *Orion* passed within earshot; we hailed it and a small boat came to take us off'. At 8 p.m. seamen from the *Britannia* set *Intrépide* on fire. *Orion*'s log records: 'At 8 received all the Prisoners from her. At 8.30 perceived the Fire to have taken At 9.30 the *Intrépide* blew up'.[95] The fire and subsequent explosion of *Intrépide* is recorded in most log books of the British ships present.[96]

The 74 gun ship MONT BLANC

Named after the highest mountain in the European Alps, *Mont Blanc* was launched at Rochefort under her original name *Républicain* in 1789. Like many of her Trafalgar contemporaries this 74 gun ship was designed by Jacques Noel Sane although her dimensions differ marginally. Unlike her some of her Trafalgar contemporaries, *Mont Blanc* carried two additional guns on her lower gun deck broadside and was therefore armed with thirty 36 pounders on her lower gun deck, thirty 18 pounders on her upper gun deck, and twenty 8 pounders on her quarter deck and forecastle. *Mont Blanc* could deliver a single broadside weight of 890 pounds (400.5 kg).

SERVICE CAREER

1789: At some point between her launch and 1794 *Républicain* had her name altered to *Mont Blanc*, her former name being given, perhaps more appropriately, to a new built ship of 110 guns.

1794: In May *Mont Blanc* sailed with the Brest fleet commanded by Rear-Admiral Villaret, the objective to rendezvous with much needed grain convoys arriving from America at a point 400 miles west in the Atlantic. When news of this reached Admiral Earl Richard Howe he went in pursuit and on 28 May fell in with and engaged Villaret's fleet. *Mont Blanc* played little part in this action. A second action ensued the next day, after which Villaret detached *Mont Blanc* to accompany the crippled *Indomptable* home to refit.[97] On the 1 June the fleets of Villaret and Howe met again for a final engagement later known as the Glorious First of June. And while this battle has been praised as an overwhelming victory for Howe, Villaret did not lose, for by strictly adhering to his orders he attained his two objectives; to protect the grain convoy, which did get home intact, and not to engage the British fleet unless necessary.[98] When the grain convoy, together with 16 prize ships captured off America, were brought into Bertheaume Bay on 12 June under escort by Rear-Admiral Vanstabel, *Mont Blanc* was with them.[99]

1795: Deployed to reinforce the French fleet at Toulon, *Mont Blanc* sailed from Brest on 22 February with a squadron commanded by Rear-Admiral Renaudin: 74 gun ships *Formidable*, *Jemmapes*, *Jupiter*, *Révolution* and *Tyrannicide*, together with three frigates and several smaller vessels. Successfully evading Admiral Hotham's blockading ships, *Mont Blanc* and her consorts arrived at Toulon on 4 April. Having joined forces, these additional ships gave France naval superiority in the Mediterranean.[100] It also demonstrated Hotham's general incompetence for in September *Mont Blanc*, flying the broad pendant of Commodore Honoré Ganteaume, escaped from Toulon with five frigates and a brig to intercept a convoy with no pursuit from Hotham.[101] It appears that with the withdrawal of the British fleet from the Mediterranean *Mont Blanc* rarely ventured from Toulon until the restart of war in 1803.

1803: When war with France reopened in May *Mont Blanc* was lying in Toulon harbour with six other ships while others were hurriedly being refitted or completed. Watching over Vice-Admiral Latouche-Tréville's ships at Toulon was a small British Mediterranean squadron commanded by Rear-Admiral Sir Richard Hussey Bickerton.[102]

1805: Placed under the command of Captain J G N La Villegris, *Mont Blanc* sailed with Vice-Admiral Villeneuve's fleet on 17 January, only to return into port when faced with violent gales. Finally leaving Toulon on 30 March, *Mont Blanc* sailed with Villeneuve's fleet to the West Indies. On her return she took part in Vice-Admiral Sir Robert Calder's action west of Cape Finisterre on 22 July, where she gave support to prevent the Spanish *Espana* (64) from being overwhelmed. Then she reached Cadiz.[103]

TRAFALGAR

Placed in Rear-Admiral Dumanoir's rear division of Villeneuve's combined fleet, *Mont Blanc* sailed from Cadiz on 19 October. When Villeneuve ordered the fleet to turn northward on the morning of 21 October *Mont Blanc* was sixth in line from the head of the fleet. Ahead of her lay *Duguay Trouin* (74), astern the Spanish *San Francisco de Asis* (74), and to leeward on her starboard bow the 40 gun frigate *Cornélie*. With the rest of Dumanoir's van, *Mont Blanc* became isolated and with little wind available was initially unable to tack and return to support Villeneuve's centre. By the time *Mont Blanc* re-entered the melée, there was little she could do but make good her escape in company with *Formidable* (80), *Duguay Trouin* (74) and *Scipion* (74). *Mont Blanc* had not a single casualty on board.[104]

Two weeks later on 4 November *Mont Blanc*, in company with *Formidable*, *Duguay Trouin* and *Scipion*, was brought to action by Captain Sir

SPECIFICATIONS: MONT BLANC

Rate	3rd	Length on the range of the gun deck	183 ft 2 ins	Ordnance - upper gun deck	30 x 18 pounders
Guns	74	Length of keel for tonnage	149 ft 7½ ins	Ordnance - quarter deck	14 x 8 pounders
Class	Sane-Border	Extreme breadth	48 ft 8 ins		(later 2 x 12 pdrs & 12 x 32 pdr carronades)
Designer	Jacques Noel Sane	Depth in hold	20 ft 6 ins	Ordnance - forecastle	6 x 8 pounders
Builder	Dockyard	Tons burthen	1886 tons		(later 2 x 12 pdrs & 2 x 32 pdr carronades)
Dockyard	Rochefort	Complement	650	Single broadside weight	890 pounds (later 998 pounds)
Date ordered	-	Ordnance - lower gun deck	30 x 36 pounders	Fate	Captured by Sir Richard Strachan's squadron 4 November 1805. Never fitted for sea and converted into a powder hulk 1811. Sold 1819.
Date keel laid	1789		(later 32 pounders)		
Date launched	1791				

Source: Lyon, *Sailing Navy List*, p. 268.

PROGRESS BOOK - MONT BLANC 3RD RATE OF 74 GUNS Source: ADM 180/10 Folio 158

At what Port	Arrived	Docked	Coppered	Launched or Undocked	Sailed	Built or Nature of Repair	Cost of Hull Masts & Yards Materials £ s d	Cost of Rigging & Stores Materials £ s d	Grand Total
Plymouth	10 Nov 1805								
	(Powder Hulk) Sold - 8 March 1819 to Mr Jn° Sedger for £5,510								

Richard Strachan's squadron of eight ships off Cape Finisterre. As ordered by Dumanoir, *Mont Blanc* took in her small sails and come up on a starboard tack, course NE by E. During the first part of the action which commenced at 12.15 p.m. *Mont Blanc* tacked to support *Duguay Trouin*, which having missed stays was under fire from Strachan's *Cæsar* (80) and *Hero* (74). When *Formidable* and *Scipion* struck their colours at 3.10 p.m. *Mont Blanc* and *Duguay Trouin* attempted to escape but were brought into close action by the heavy broadsides of *Hero*. Shortly after *Cæsar* joined, *Mont Blanc* struck her colours at about 3.35 p.m. Having placed boarding parties into each ship Strachan sent all four French prizes into Plymouth on 10 November.[105]

FATE

At the time of her capture *Mont Blanc* was already 16 years old. Following the results of the survey undertaken at Plymouth it was agreed that no expense would be made to fit her for sea service and consequently she was laid up in ordinary. Converted into a powder hulk in 1811, for which no expenses are recorded, *Mont Blanc* was eventually sold on 8 March 1819 to Mr John Sedger for £5,510 and inevitably broken up.[106]

The 74 gun ship **PLUTON**

Named after the planet Pluto, the 74 gun ship *Pluton* was launched at Toulon in 1805, replacing her predecessor, in service since her launch in 1778. In all probability *Pluton* was designed by Jacques Noel Sane to similar lines as the other 74 guns ships present at Trafalgar. Following French practice her armament would have been standard for a 74 gun ship carrying twenty-eight 36 pounders on her lower gun deck, thirty 18 pounders on her upper gun deck, twenty 18 pounders on her quarter deck and forecastle. *Pluton* could deliver a single weight of 854 pounds. She may well have been armed with 4 or 6 brass howitzers or carronades on her poop.

Pluton's predecessor had fought in the West Indies during the American War of Independence and had engaged *Leander* (50), Captain John Payne, on 19 January 1783.[107] Clowes states that the name of the French ship engaged in this action was not identified but also suggests it was *Couronne* whereas James names her as *Pluton*.

In 1796 *Pluton* had formed part of Vice-Admiral Morard de Galles' ill-fated expeditionary fleet that sailed from Brest on 15 December to land a force of 25,000 troops under General Hoche to support and incite rebellion in Ireland. De Galles' force comprised the following ships and transports.[108]

Rate	Guns	Ships' names	Total
2nd	80	Indomptable	1
3rd	74	Cassard, Constitution, Droits de L'Homme, Eole, **Fougueux**, Mucius, Nestor, Patriote, Pégase, **Pluton**, **Redoutable**, Révolution, Séduisant, Trajan, Tourvile, and Wattignies	16
4th	44	Inpatiente, and Scévole	2
5th	40	Bellone, Bravoure, Cocarde, Fraternité, Immortalité, Romaine, Résolue, Sirène, and Tortue,	9
5th	36	Charente, Surveillante	2
Brig	20	Atalante	1
Brig	16	Affronteur, Renard, Vautour, and Voltigeur	4
Brig	14	Mutine	1
Powder ship		Fidele	1
Transports		Allègre, Experiment, Fille Unique, Justine, Nicodème, Suffren, and Ville de Lorient	7
TOTAL			44

Note: Those denoted in bold type later fought at Trafalgar.

After this date it is not whether this *Pluton* was broken up, lost or rebuilt at Toulon.

SERVICE HISTORY

1803: When war re-opened in May the Trafalgar *Pluton*, according to Clowes, was on the stocks building at Toulon. What is unclear is whether this was an entirely new ship designed by Sane or the previous 1778 *Pluton* designed by Clairin-Deslauriers undergoing a rebuild or a 'large repair' due to her age. If this were the case then she would have been the oldest French ship in Villeneuve's combined fleet at Trafalgar.[109]

1805: When Villeneuve was re-assembling his fleet after attempting to venture out of Toulon in January, the entire ship's company of *Annibal* (74) which had been found unfit for service, was turned over into *Pluton*. Placed under the command of Commodore Julien Marie Cosmao-Kerjulien, *Pluton* sailed from Toulon with the rest of Villeneuve's fleet on the evening of 29 March. After reaching the coast off Cartagena on 6 April and passing through the Straits of Gibraltar two days later, *Pluton* stood into Cadiz with the rest of the squadron. Here they were joined by the Spanish ships *Argonauta* (80) *Firme* (74), *Terrible* (74) *América* (64), *España* (64), and French ships *Aigle* (74), the corvette *Torche* and the brig *Argus*. *Pluton* then sailed with Villeneuve's fleet for the West Indies, arriving off Fort Royal, Martinique on 13 May. On 29 May Villeneuve detached *Pluton* with *Berwick* (74), *Sirène* (36), *Argus* (16), schooner *Fine* and eleven gunboats to attack Diamond Rock lying six miles off the entrance of Fort Royal Bay. HM Sloop *Diamond Rock*, as it was formally listed, comprised a series of gun platforms built into the cliff face manned by 108 officers and men under Commander James Wilkes Maurice. The fortifications comprised two major batteries: halfway up was Hood's Battery comprising 24 pounders, and on the summit, named Fort Diamond, were 18 pounders. These strategically placed batteries had long been a thorn in the side for French shipping entering or leaving Port Royal. *Pluton* and her force arrived off Diamond Rock on 31 May and bombarded the fortifications from 8 a.m. until 4.30 p.m. On 2 June Maurice, short of shot and powder, was compelled to surrender. British losses comprised just two killed and one wounded, whereas Kerjulien lost three gunboats and 50–60 men. Besides being honourably acquitted at his later court-martial for the loss of HM Sloop *Diamond Rock*, Maurice received recognition for his noble defence.[110]

Back with Villeneuve's squadron, *Pluton* sailed across the Atlantic where, on 22 July, the entire force fell in with Vice-Admiral Calder's squadron laying off Finisterre. In the ensuing action Kerjulien gallantly carried *Pluton* out of the line of battle to give firing support to the Spanish *Firme* (74) and then *España* (74) which were both under considerable fire from Calder's ships.[111] Four days later *Pluton* anchored at Ferrol and after making repairs sailed for Cadiz on 9 August.

TRAFALGAR

Sailing with the combined fleet on 19 October, *Pluton* found herself placed twenty-first from the head of Villeneuve's fleet on the morning of 21 October. Ahead lay the Spanish *Monarca* (74), astern *Bahama* (74). Being towards the rear of the line, *Pluton* came under attack from Collingwood's leeward division as the battle opened. At about 11.58 a.m. when *Mars* (74) and *Tonnant* (80) were making their final approach to cut through Villeneuve's line, *Pluton*, using her larboard guns, opened fire on both ships. At 12.10 when *Monarca* was engaging *Mars* (74), *Pluton* crammed on more sail and passed to the leeward of *Monarca* and got across the bows of *Mars* and raked her. To avoid this *Mars* tuned to larboard and surged northward

SPECIFICATIONS: PLUTON

Rate	3rd	Length on the range of the gun deck	182 ft 6 ins	Ordnance - lower gun deck	28 x 36 pounders
Guns	74	Length of keel for tonnage	157 ft (estimated)	Ordnance - upper gun deck	30 x 18 pounders
Class	Sane-Borda	Extreme breadth	49 ft 0 ins	Ordnance - quarter deck	14 x 8 pounders
Designer	Jacques Noel Sane	Depth in hold	21 ft 3 ins	Ordnance - forecastle	6 x 8 pounders
Builder	Dockyard	Tons burthen	1929 tons	Ordnance - Poop	4 or 6 brass howitzers
Dockyard	Toulon	Draught afore	22 ft 0 ins	Single broadside weight	854 pounds
Date ordered	-	Draught abaft	23 ft 0 ins	Fate	Reached Cadiz in a sinking condition 23 October 1805.
Date keel laid	1804	Complement	550/600		
Date launched	1805				

to assist engaging *Santa Ana* (112). Briefly *Pluton* and *Mars* were now running on a parallel course firing broadsides into each other; at about 12.45 p.m. *Pluton* hauled up to starboard and using her larboard battery commenced raking her stern, clearing away the upper decks of *Mars*. Now under fire from *Pluton*, *Santa Ana* and *Fougueux* (74), *Mars* was heavily mauled; a shot decapitated Captain Duff commanding *Mars*, and also killed one of his sons. Kerjulien then put *Pluton's* helm to port and fired a final salvo through the stern of *Mars* as she paid off to avoid further damage. *Pluton* had been under considerable fire throughout from various ships; with 60 killed and 132 wounded and taking in a great amount of water, Kerjulien veered her off to the SE to join Admiral Gravina's *Principe de Asturias* (112). With *Neptune* (80) and *San Justo* (74) he made for Cadiz, *Pluton* in a sinking state.[112]

Despite *Pluton's* appalling condition, Commodore Cosmao-Kerjulien set out from Cadiz on 23 October to succour some of the damaged prizes. With her were *Indomptable*, *Neptune*, *Rayo*, and *San Francisco de Asis*, together with the frigates *Cornélie*, *Hermione*, *Hortense*, *Rhin*, *Thémis*, and the brigs *Argus* and *Furet*. As soon as *Pluton* and her consorts got out of harbour the wind veered, rising to storm force from the WSW. Although Kerjulien's intentions were noble and can certainly be deemed brave, the deteriorating weather conditions were not ideal for salvaging unmanageable ships. On seeing his approach ten British ships with prizes in tow cast off their hawsers and formed line of battle to protect them. Such actions are clearly noted in the log books of the various British ships involved. These records verify that Kerjulien's ships posed a considerable threat which could have resulted in a second action off Trafalgar. Outnumbered, and with his ships already battle damaged, Kerjulien did not attempt to attack, but his frigates did retake the Spanish ships *Santa Ana* (112) and *Neptuno* (80). Having made this sortie *Pluton* and her force, including the recaptured prizes, put back into Cadiz.[113]

FATE

Like the other French ships that had escaped capture at Trafalgar or Strachan's action two weeks later, *Pluton* was still lying at Cadiz when Spain declared war on France on 4 June 1808. When Vice-Admiral de Rosily realised that his ships were now dangerously moored within range of the gun batteries he moved his squadron out of the harbour where, on 9 June, they were attacked by Spanish forces from land and sea. After unsuccessful negotiations, de Rosily finally surrendered his vessels on 14 June. Renamed *Montañez* to replace the ship of the same name wrecked after the battle of Trafalgar in 1805, *Pluton* served in the Spanish navy until broken up in 1816.[114]

The 74 gun ship REDOUTABLE

Meaning redoubtable or uncompromising, the 74 gun ship *Redoutable* is perhaps, by virtue of her association with both *Victory* (100) and the death of Lord Nelson, the most acclaimed French ship to fight at the battle of Trafalgar. Designed by Jacques Noel Sane and launched at Brest in 1790, *Redoutable* was certainly the third oldest French ship in Villeneuve's fleet. With lines and specifications similar to other 74 guns within the French fleet, *Redoutable* carried thirty 36 pounders on her lower gun deck, thirty 18 pounders on her upper gun deck, twenty 18 pounders on her quarter deck and forecastle. This gave her a single broadside weight of 890 pounds. If *Redoutable*, like other 74 gun ships, carried four or six additional 36 pounder brass howitzers or iron carronades on her poop her single broadside weight was increased to either 962 or 988 pounds.

SERVICE HISTORY

1793: When war with revolutionary France opened in February *Redoutable* was probably blockaded within Brest by the British Channel fleet and does not appear to have undertaken any sea service until 1795.

1795: In early June *Redoutable* sailed from Brest with Rear-Admiral Villaret's fleet which joined with Rear-Admiral Vence's squadron on 15 June. Once united, this French fleet comprised the following ships:[115]

Rate or Type	Guns	Ships' Names	No
1st	120	*Peuple*	1
3rd	74	*Alexandre*, *Droits de l'Homme*, *Formidable*, *Fougueux*, *Jean Bart*, *Mucius*, *Nestor*, *Redoutable* and *Wattignies*	9
4th	50	*Brave* and *Scévola*	2
5th	40	*Fraternité*, *Proserpine*	2
	36	*Dryade*, *Fidèle*, *Cocarde*, *Régénérée*, and *Insurgente*	5
Misc.	4		
Brigs	2		
Cutters	2		
TOTAL	**27**		

With Villaret's squadron *Redoutable* fell in with Admiral Lord Bridport's fleet of 14 sail of the line, five frigates and five lesser ships off Isle de Groix on 23 June and took part in the ensuing action. One of the three French prizes taken was the 74 gun ship *Formidable*. Renamed *Belleisle*, she would later fight with distinction at Trafalgar.[116]

1796: On 15 December *Redoutable* sailed from Brest for Ireland with a large fleet comprising 44 warships and transports commanded by Vice-Admiral Morard de Galles. On board were 18,000 troops under General Hoche's command. The intention was to land these forces and incite rebellion in

193

SPECIFICATIONS: *REDOUTABLE*

Rate	3rd	Length on the range of the gun deck	182 ft 6 ins	Ordnance - lower gun deck	30 x 36 pounders
Guns	74	Length of keel for tonnage	157 ft (estimated)	Ordnance - upper gun deck	30 x 18 pounders
Class	Sane-Border	Extreme breadth	49 ft 0 ins	Ordnance - quarter deck	14 x 8 pounders
Designer	Jacques Noel Sane	Depth in hold	21 ft 6 ins	Ordnance - forecastle	6 x 8 pounders
Builder	Dockyard	Tons burthen	1929 tons	Ordnance - Poop	4 or 6 x 36 pdr howitzers or carronades
Dockyard	Brest	Draught afore	22 ft 0 ins	Single broadside weight	890 pounds (maximum 988 pounds)
Date ordered	-	Draught abaft	23 ft 0 ins	Fate	Captured at the battle of Trafalgar 21 October 1805 then sank in the storm afterwards.
Date keel laid		Complement	550/600		
Date launched	1790				

Ireland. The expedition failed, however, when the squadron became divided due to confused signalling; some ships sailing through the Passage d'Iroise, others through the Passage du Raz; few made their destination.[117] *Redoutable*, in company with the *Indomptable*, *Fougueux*, *Mucius*, and *Patriote*, returned eventually to Brest on 1 January 1797.[118]

1805: Placed under the command of Captain Jean-Jacques Lucas, *Redoutable* did not effectively join Villeneuve's combined fleet until it had entered Ferrol on 1 August. Eight days later *Redoutable* sailed south with Villeneuve's squadron and entered Cadiz on 20 August. *Redoutable* was a remarkable fighting vessel and under her commander Captain Lucas, a particularly efficient French naval officer, she was well officered and manned. When she had been placed in commission, Lucas stated to Admiral Decrès that 'nothing was omitted on board to instruct the ship's company in every form of exercise My thoughts ever turned on boarding my enemy in any action I fought, and I so counted on finding an opportunity that I made that form of attack part of our daily exercises, so as to ensure success when the hour arrived'.

So meticulous was Lucas that gun captains were issued canvas cartridge cases for holding two grenades, complete with tin tubes to hold quick-match. He also stated that:

> At all our drills on board ship I practised the men at flinging dummy hand grenades made of pasteboard, to ensure rapidity and expertness, and while at Toulon also I often landed parties to practice with iron grenades. By that means, in the end, they had so acquired the art of flinging the grenades that on the day of battle my topmen were able to fling two grenades at a time. I had a hundred muskets fitted with long bayonets sent on board also. The picked men to whom these were served out were specially trained in musketry and stationed in the shrouds.

Lucas also states that his men were trained in cutlass drill, the use of pistols, and skill of throwing grappling irons. Concluding his statement Lucas says: 'On the drums beating branle-bas de combat before Trafalgar, every man went to his post fully accoutred, and with his weapon loaded, and they placed them at hand by their guns, in racks between the ports'.[119]

While *Redoutable* was confined in Cadiz Lucas continued to train his crew, the result of which would later prove invaluable, for by its precise execution Nelson's flagship *Victory* was nearly defeated.

TRAFALGAR

Redoutable sailed with the combined fleet 19 October. At about 7 a.m. on 21 October, Captain Lucas recorded, the admiral signalled the whole fleet to form 'dans l'ordre naturel', with the flag officers stationed at the heads of their divisions, and bring their ships onto a starboard tack.[120] Once this manœuvre was executed *Redoutable* was positioned thirteenth from the head of Villeneuve's fleet. Ahead of her starboard bow was *Neptune* (84), astern *San Leandro* (74), and just off her starboard quarter, the frigate *Hortense* (40). When battle opened *Redoutable*'s gunners concentrated their fire upon *Victory* as she made her approach and when shot holes appeared in *Victory*'s fore topsail, denoting that the guns had found their mark, cheers ranged up from *Redoutable*'s lower gun deck. Seeing *Neptune* veer off to leeward causing a large gap to open behind Villeneuve's flagship, Captain Lucas quickly luffed to close the gap, both to protect the admiral and prevent *Victory* breaking through the line. In so doing *Redoutable*'s flying jib boom ran over the taffrail of *Bucentaure*. *Victory* drove through, firing a deadly broadside through *Bucentaure*'s stern and at the same time running aboard the *Redoutable* on her larboard bow. It was now about 1.10 p.m.; locked in combat the two ships drifted leeward. To prevent boarding through the lower deck, Lucas immediately ordered his men to shut the lower deck gun port lids; he then concentrated his fire into *Victory* from his main deck guns. This, supported with a hail of musketry fire from *Redoutable*'s fore, main and mizzen tops, put out most of *Victory*'s upper deck guns. Besides showering *Victory*'s deck with grenades, 200 in all, Lucas had brass cohorns mounted in his tops which, loaded with grape, inflicted high casualties within Nelson's ship. The small arms exercises undertaken in *Redoutable* at Cadiz proved proficient as a hail of fire rained onto *Victory*'s quarter deck. At about 1.25 p.m. one of the sharpshooters stationed in *Redoutable*'s mizzen top shot Lord Nelson from a distance of 15 yards. According to English records Midshipman John Pollard almost immediately took up a musket and turning to fire into *Redoutable*'s mizzen top brought down the admiral's assailant. Alternative records reveal that the sharpshooter lived to tell his story of how he shot Nelson. While the mortally wounded admiral was taken below, unrelenting fire from *Redoutable* killed most of those remaining on *Victory*'s open decks. With few men left to resist any attack Lucas's men prepared to board the higher sides of *Victory*. This proved more difficult than expected, however, and only Ensign Yeo and four men managed to get across onto *Victory*'s sheet anchor. Their bid was unexpectedly repelled, as marines came up from below *Victory*'s decks. Undeterred, Lucas ordered the main yard to be lowered to form a bridge for his men to cross. It was now about 1.40 p.m. and as his men massed themselves for a second attempt they were brought down by a murderous fusillade of grapeshot fired from the upper deck carronades of the *Téméraire* drawing up on *Redoutable*'s starboard side. 'The slaughter that ensued', Lucas said, 'is indescribable. More than two hundred of our men were killed'. The remainder was sent below to re-man the guns and engage *Téméraire*. Tenaciously Lucas continued to defend *Redoutable* against *Téméraire* to starboard and *Victory*, using whatever guns remained. Her main and mizzen masts had gone by the board and fires had broken out on her bowsprit and forecastle. *Redoutable* was further hampered when *Téméraire*'s main mast fell on her. *Redoutable* was now a shambles both within and without; her lower gun deck and orlop had been ripped to pieces when *Victory*'s gunners had depressed their guns to avoid firing through the ship into *Téméraire*. Out-gunned by two three-decked ships, Lucas finally struck his colours at 2.30 p.m. Casualties within *Redoutable* were high. Of her '643h. d'équipage' (complement) Lucas stated, '522 étaient hors de combat, dont 300 tués et 222 grièvement blessés, du nombre desquels se trouvait en totalité l'état major et dix aspirants sur 12' There were 300 dead and 222 badly wounded, among whom were all his senior and ten of his junior officers. When Lucas later reported his reasons for surrendering, his statement reveals the true state of damage inflicted upon *Redoutable*. Both main and mizzen masts had gone, the tiller, helm, rudder gear, and part of the stern post had been destroyed. Most of her guns had been dismounted during the initial collision with *Victory*, many by shot; furthermore, two guns, one 18 pounder carriage gun and one 36 pounder carronade, had burst during firing. Her poop had been entirely smashed and many of her stern counter timbers and adjacent deck beams had been shot to pieces. In short her stern was little more that a large cavity. Nearly every single gun port had been destroyed while internally her decks were riddled and fires had broken out astern. Adding to the carnage many of the wounded lying in the orlop had been killed outright when *Victory* depressed her guns. *Redoutable* was also making water and with nearly every pump shattered by shot, Lucas feared that the ship 'might go down under our feet'. Referring to the *Victory*'s casualties in his statement Lucas wrote that 'il a en beaucoup de monde hors de combat et particulièrment l'amiral Nelson, à 'l'abordage par le feu de notre mousquesterie'. (Nelson was killed by a musket shot during the attempt to board).[121]

FATE

At 7 o'clock Tuesday 22 October *Redoutable* was taken in tow by the British *Swiftsure* (74). After the ship had been secured Captain Lucas, Lieutenant Dupotet and M. Ducrest were removed into *Swiftsure*. *Redoutable*, however, was in a terrible condition and by noon was making considerable water. According to *Swiftsure*'s log entry at 3 p.m., *Redoutable*'s prize officer 'made the signal of distress' for assistance. Boats from *Swiftsure* soon arrived and took out 'as many of the Prisoners as possible'. According to Lucas, 119 men were removed. By 7 p.m. the stern of *Redoutable* was under water and there was little more that could be done; at 8.15 p.m. *Swiftsure*'s boats were recovered. *Swiftsure*'s log then states, '10.13 *Redoutable* Prize in Tow went down cut the Tow & lost two cables of 8 Inch & one of 15 to her'. When *Redoutable* sank her wounded went down with her. At 3.30 a.m. Wednesday 23 October *Swiftsure*'s log recalls, 'heard the cries of some people a short distance from us picked up part of the Remaining Crew of Prize who to save their lives had made a raft succeeded in taking them all on board served some Slops [clothes] to those who were destitute of Cloaths'. Then at 8.15 a.m. *Swiftsure* 'discovered 2 rafts full of men who saved themselves from the wreck of *Redoutable* when sinking sent Boats & brought them on board'.[122] Counting those on the rafts this brought the total recovered from the wreck to 169.[123]

The 74 gun ship **SCIPION**

Originally named *Orient* to replace the great 120 gun ship that blew up at the battle of the Nile in 1 August 1798, *Scipion* as she was later called, was launched at Lorient in late 1798. Designed by Jacques Noel Sane, she very much resembled her Trafalgar contemporaries *Achille*, *Aigle*, *Duguay Trouin*, *Héros*, *Mont Blanc*, and *Redoutable*. Carrying thirty 36 pounders on her lower gun deck, thirty 18 pounders on her upper gun deck, twenty 8 pounders on her quarter deck and forecastle and probably two 18 pounder carronades or howitzers on her poop, *Scipion* could deliver a single broadside weight of 908 pounds. This figure was increased after she was captured and re-armed in 1805. *Scipion* had three predecessors of the same name within the French revolutionary navy. The first was a 74 gun ship taken by Admiral Lord Hood at Toulon on 29 August 1793 which was accidentally burnt off Leghorn on 20 November that same year.[124] The second *Scipion*, an 80 gun ship built to replace the former, foundered in a gale on 28 January 1795.[125] The third *Scipion* was a 20 gun ship captured off Guadeloupe on 16 February 1798 by *Alfred* (74) commanded by Captain Thomas Totty.[126]

SERVICE CAREER

1798: After her launch *Orient* remained at Lorient primarily because the port was blockaded by British ships.

1801: During this year *Orient* was renamed *Scipion*.[127]

1803: It appears that while the brief peace prevailed during 1802 *Scipion* finally got to sea and joined the French Mediterranean fleet based at Toulon. Consequently she was one of six ships afloat in that port when war with France reopened in May.[128]

1805: Under the command of Captain Charles Bellanger, *Scipion* sailed from Toulon with Vice-Admiral Villeneuve's fleet on 17 January, meeting violent gales in the Gulf of Lyons two days later. Returning to port *Scipion* finally sailed from Toulon with Villeneuve's fleet on 30 March and successfully evaded Nelson's blockading ships. *Scipion* sailed to the West Indies with Villeneuve's fleet and fought a minor part in Vice-Admiral Sir Robert Calder's action west of Cape Finisterre on 22 July.

TRAFALGAR

As part of Rear-Admiral Dumanoir's rear division, *Scipion* put to sea with the combined fleet on 19 October. On the morning of 21 October *Scipion* found herself in second place in head of the combined fleet once they had reversed course at 8 a.m. Ahead lay the Spanish *Neptuno* (80), astern *Rayo* (100). Like Dumanoir's *Formidable* and the other ships now forming the van, *Scipion* found herself isolated. Like her consorts *Formidable*, *Duguay Trouin* and *Mont Blanc*, *Scipion* was late getting into the mêlée and left the action by 4.30 p.m, virtually unscathed. *Scipion* was one of two French ships that bore no casualties.[129]

On 4 November *Scipion* and Dumanoir's consorts fell in with Sir Richard Strachan's squadron off Cape Finisterre. Although the battle opened before noon, it was not until 2 p.m. that *Scipion* was brought into action by *Hero*

SPECIFICATIONS: *SCIPION*					
Rate	3rd	Length on the range of the gun deck	182 ft 1½ ins	Ordnance - lower gun deck	30 x 36 pounders (later 32 pounders)
Guns	74	Length of keel for tonnage	150 ft 0⅞ ins	Ordnance - upper gun deck	30 x 18 pounders
Class	Sane-Border	Extreme breadth	48 ft 7½ ins	Ordnance - quarter deck	14 x 8 pounders
Designer	Jacques Noel Sane	Depth in hold	21 ft 10 ins		(later 2 x 12 pdrs & 12 x 32 pdr carronades)
Builder	Dockyard	Tons burthen	1887 39/94 tons	Ordnance - forecastle	6 x 8 pounders (later 2 x 12 pdrs & 2 x 32 pdr carronades)
Dockyard	Lorient	Draught afore		Ordnance - Poop	2 x 18 pounder carronades
Date ordered	-	Draught abaft		Single broadside weight	890 (later 1016) pounds
Date keel laid		Complement	640	Fate	Captured by Sir Richard Strachan's squadron 4 November 1805 and entered into British navy under the name *Scipion*. Broken up 1819.
Date launched	1798				

Source: Lyon, *Sailing Navy List*, p. 268.

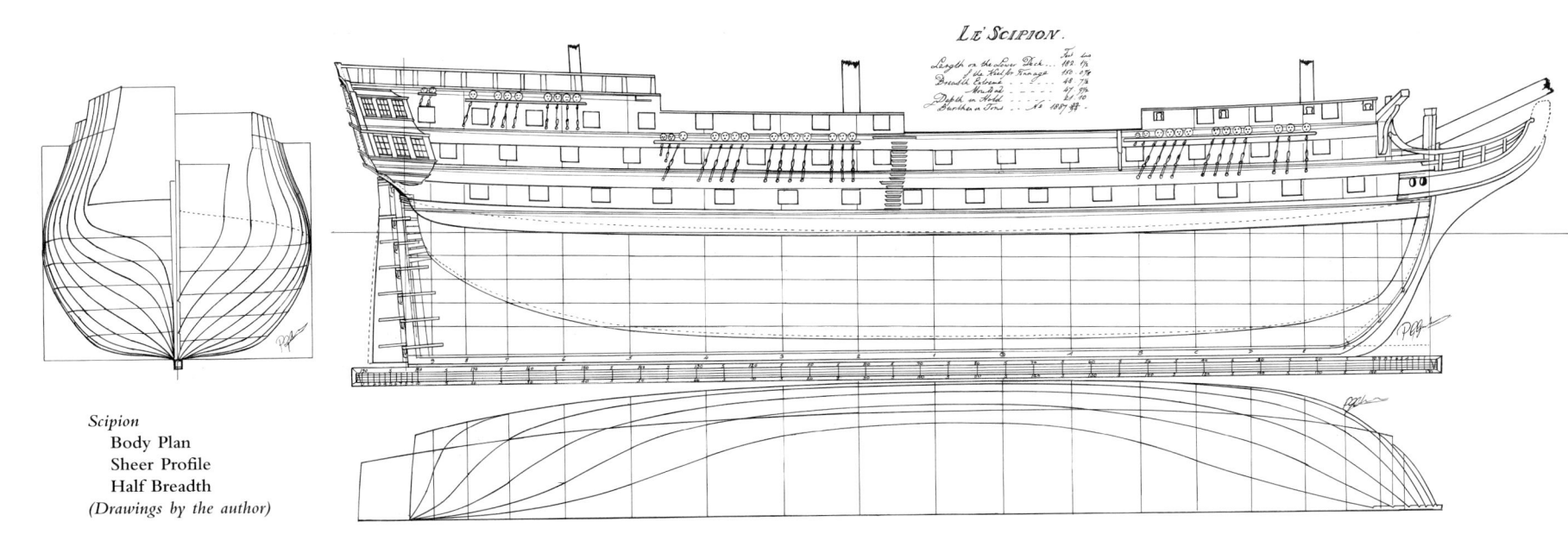

Scipion
 Body Plan
 Sheer Profile
 Half Breadth
(Drawings by the author)

(74), firing her starboard broadsides into Bellanger's ship. *Scipion*'s main topmast fell off to leeward and she came under fire from *Courageux* (74). Under constant fire and suffering considerable casualties, *Scipion* struck her colours at 3.10 p.m. Once Strachan's forces had taken possession, *Scipion*, with *Duguay Trouin*, *Formidable* and *Mont Blanc* were taken to Portsmouth on 10 November.[130] After survey *Scipion* entered the Royal Navy under her own name *Scipion* and laid up for an opportune time to be refitted.

1808: On 9 June *Scipion* was docked at Portsmouth for a 'large repair and fitted', when her old copper sheathing was removed.

1809: With her hull defects made good and her bottom recoppered in July, *Scipion* was re-launched on 26 July and over the next few months received her masts and rigging, the costs of which are not recorded. From this point *Scipion* would serve under the following commanders.

BRITISH CAPTAINS OF *SCIPION* (MSS 248/6 and 248/7)

Name	Time of Entry	Time of Discharge	On What Occasion.
C P B Bateman	25 September 1809	30 September 1809	Superseded
James Johnstone	1 October 1809	30 April 1812	Superseded
Henry Heathcote	1 May 1812	15 October 1814	Per Order ship
		7 November 1814	Paid Off at Portsmouth

1809: On 25 September *Scipion* was placed in commission under Captain Charles Bateman, who was succeeded on 1 October by Captain James Johnstone. Fully stored and provisioned *Scipion* sailed from Portsmouth for her new deployment in the East Indies on 5 November.

1811: Still stationed in the East Indies under the command of Captain James Johnstone, *Scipion* was now carrying the flag of Rear-Admiral the Hon. Robert Stopford. In April Stopford assembled a large force at Madras prepared for the reduction of the Dutch colony of Batavia, Java. With *Scipion* as flagship the entire squadron sailed in two divisions by 24 April, comprising the following naval ships, East India Company vessels and transports:

Rate	Guns	Ship's Names	No.
3rd	74	*Illustrious*, *Minden*, and *Scipion*	3
3rd	64	*Lion*	1
4th	44	*Akbar*	1
5th	38	*Hussar*, *Phaeton*, *Présidente*, and *Nisus*	4
5th	36	*Bucephalus*, *Caroline*, *Doris*, *Leda*, *Moleste*, and *Phœbe*	6
5th	32	*Cornelia*, *Psyche*, and *Sir Francis Drake*	3
Sloops	18	*Baracouta*, *Dasher*, *Hesper*, *Harper*, *Hecate*, *Procris*, and *Samarang*	7
HEIC cruisers		*Ariel*, *Aurora*, *Malabar*, *Mornington*, *Nautilus*, *Psyche*, *Thetis* and *Vestal*	8
TOTAL			33

Reaching Penang on 21 May, the two divisions of Stopford's fleet sailed for Malacca three days later, where after embarking further units of troops commanded by Lieutenant-General Sir Samuel Auchmuty, this expedition now comprised some 11,960 officers and men. *Scipion* left Malacca on 11 June, sailing by way of Singapore, and Port Samba, Borneo to rendezvous with her consorts off the Island of Boompjes on the coast of Java. Once re-assembled, Stopford's fleet sailed from Boompjes on 2 August and anchored off Chillingching just twelve mile east of Batavia two days later and commenced disembarking 800 troops. Although Batavia surrendered on 8 August, the Dutch force entrenched in camp at Meester Cornelis nine miles away under the command of Governor-General Janssens put up considerable resistance until finally defeated on 27 August.[131]

1812: Returning to England, *Scipion* was paid off at Portsmouth on 30 April and recommissioned on 1 May under the command of Captain Henry Heathcote.[132] Once ready for sea the ship sailed for the Mediterranean where she would be deployed with Vice-Admiral Sir Edward Pellew's squadron blockading Toulon.

1813: In November, when the main body of Pellew's ships had been driven off station by bad weather, *Scipion*, with her inshore squadron comprising *Armada* (74), *Mulgrave* (74) and *Pembroke* (74), remained on station working off Cape Sicié. Taking advantage of Pellew's absence, the Toulon fleet, comprising fourteen sail of the line, six frigates and a schooner under the command of Vice-Admiral Comte Emeriau, came out of port on 5 November for manœuvres. Once out of harbour the wind shifted, forcing Emeriau to head back into Toulon, at which point *Scipion* with her frigates attempted to cut off the French van to leeward, led by Admiral Cosmao-Kerjulien flying his flag in *Wagram* (130). Despite the fact that there were five French sail of the line and four heavy frigates, Heathcote carried *Scipion* into attack. At 12.34 *Scipion* was joined by *Pompée* (74) which had come up from Pellew's division, the two ships continuing a running battle until Pellew, flying his flag in *Caledonia* (120), together with *San Josef* (112) and *Boyne* (98), entered the affray. Overwhelmed, the French ships made good their escape into Toulon, never to venture out again.[133]

1814: *Scipion* returned to Portsmouth on 11 October. On 15 October Heathcote relinquished command to his First Lieutenant, who remained with the ship until paying her off on 7 November.[134]

FATE

Scipion remained laid up at Portsmouth where, in February 1817 her copper was removed to her 'light draught of water' line. Docked on 15

PROGRESS BOOK - *SCIPION* 3RD RATE OF 74 GUNS: Source: ADM 180/10 Folio 157							
At what Port	Arrived	Docked	Coppered	Launched or Undocked	Sailed	Built or Nature of Repair	Cost of Hull, Masts & Yards Materials £ s d	Cost of Rigging & Stores Materials £ s d	Grand Total
Portsmouth	10 Nov 1805	9 June 1808	Copper taken off June 1808. Re-coppered July 1809	26 July 1809	5 Nov. 1809	Large Repair and Fitted	No costs recorded	-
Portsmouth	11 Oct 1814		Copper taken off to Light Draught of Water February 1817					
Portsmouth		15 Sept 1818	Copper taken off *Taken to Pieces January 1819*			Middling Repair		

September 1818, she commenced a 'Middling Repair', during which her entire copper sheathing was taken off. The decision to refit her for service was, however, rescinded and she was finally taken to pieces in January 1819.[135]

The 74 gun ship SWIFTSURE

Originally a British warship, the *Swiftsure* that fought on the side of the French at Trafalgar was the fourth ship to bear this name in the Royal Navy. The first *Swiftsure*, a 3rd rate ship of 70 guns launched at Chatham in 1697, was, after being rebuilt in 1700, hulked in 1715 and broken up in 1742. The next *Swiftsure*, also a 3rd rate of 70 guns, was built at Deptford in 1723, hulked in 1743 after serving at the siege of Gibraltar 1727, through the wars of Jenkin's Ear and Austrian Succession and broken up in 1783. The third *Swiftsure*, a 64 gun ship, was launched at Deptford in 1743. After seeing some service in the East and the West Indies during the Seven Years' War, she was broken up at Chatham in 1760.[136]

As a British ship the *Swiftsure* was one of eight *Elizabeth* class 3rd rate 74 guns ships designed by Thomas Slade in 1766. The sister ships comprised the *Elizabeth, Resolution, Cumberland, Berwick, Bombay Castle, Powerful,* and *Defiance*, the latter of which fought within Nelson's Trafalgar fleet. The *Berwick*, which fought as part of Villeneuve's combined fleet at Trafalgar, had been captured from the British off San Fiorenzo on 7 March 1795 by the French frigates *Minerve* (38), *Alceste* (36) and *Vestale* (36). Ordered on 19 June 1782, the keel of the *Swiftsure* was laid down at Deptford in May 1784 and constructed by John Wells. It was launched three years later on 4 April 1787. In all about 3,250 loads of timber taken from forests in Kent, Sussex and Essex were used in her construction. This equates to approximately 160,000 cubic feet of timber (about 3,250 trees) before conversion into individual components. Armed with twenty-eight 32 pounders on the lower gun deck, twenty-eight 18 pounders on the upper gun deck, fourteen 9 pounders on the quarter deck and four 9 pounders on the forecastle, *Berwick* could deliver a single broadside weight of 781 pounds.[137]

SERVICE CAREER

1790: *Swiftsure* was first put in commission on 24 June under the command of Captain Sir James Wallace, who remained in the ship until he paid her off

CAPTAINS OF *SWIFTSURE* (MSS 248/4, 248/6 and 248/7)			
Name	Time of Entry	Time of Discharge	On What Occasion.
Sir James Wallace	24 June 1790	13 September 1791	Paid Off
Charles Boyles	1 July 1792	6 December 1795	To the *Raisonnable*
Robert Parker	7 December 1795	19 October 1796	Superseded
Arthur Phillips	20 October 1796	27 September 1797	To the *Blenheim*
John Irwin	28 September 1797	25 October 1797	To the *Lively*
Benjamin Hallowell	26 October 1797	18 January 1801	Paid Off day of Court Martial Ship captured
French Officers			
Jean-Gilles Filhol-Camas	March 1805	21 October 1805	Ship recaptured off Cape Trafalgar 21 October 1805
English Officers			
George Digby	4 April 1806	24 June 1806	Paid Off at Chatham

on 13 September 1791, after which the ship laid up in ordinary until war with France opened in 1793.[138]

1793: Fitted for sea *Swiftsure* was recommissioned under Captain Charles Boyles on 1 July and sent to the West Indies on the Jamaica station under the overall command of Rear-Admiral William Parker.[139]

1795: Still operating out of Jamaica, command of *Swiftsure* was superseded by Captain Robert Parker on 7 December. Her previous commander, Captain Boyles, had transferred into *Raisonnable* (64).[140]

1796: Still deployed in the West Indies, *Swiftsure* sailed from Jamaica with Admiral Parker's fleet in March to attack the French forces occupying the island of Santo Domingo. On 21 March *Swiftsure*, with *Leviathan* (74) and *Africa* (64), bombarded the town of Port au Prince. Meeting greater oppo-

SPECIFICATIONS: *SWIFTSURE*	
Rate	3rd
Guns	74
Class	*Elizabeth* class 1766
Designer	Thomas Slade
Builder	Wells
Dockyard	Deptford
Date ordered	19 June 1782
Date keel laid	May 1784
Date launched	4 April 1787
Length on the range of the gun deck	168 ft 6 ins
Length of keel for tonnage	138 ft 3⅜ ins
Extreme breadth	46 ft 10 ins
Depth in hold	19 ft 9 ins
Tons burthen	1612.88/94
Draught afore	
Draught abaft	
Complement	550/600
Ordnance - lower gun deck	28 x 32 pounders
Ordnance - upper gun deck	28 x 18 pounders
Ordnance - quarter deck	14 x 9 pounders
Ordnance - forecastle	4 x 9 pounders
Single broadside weight	781 pounds
Fate	Recaptured from the French at Trafalgar 1805 and renamed *Irresistible*. Used as a prison ship. Broken up at Chatham 1816

Source: Lyon, *Sailing Navy List*, pp. 70-71.

Swiftsure
Sheer Profile
(Drawing by the author)

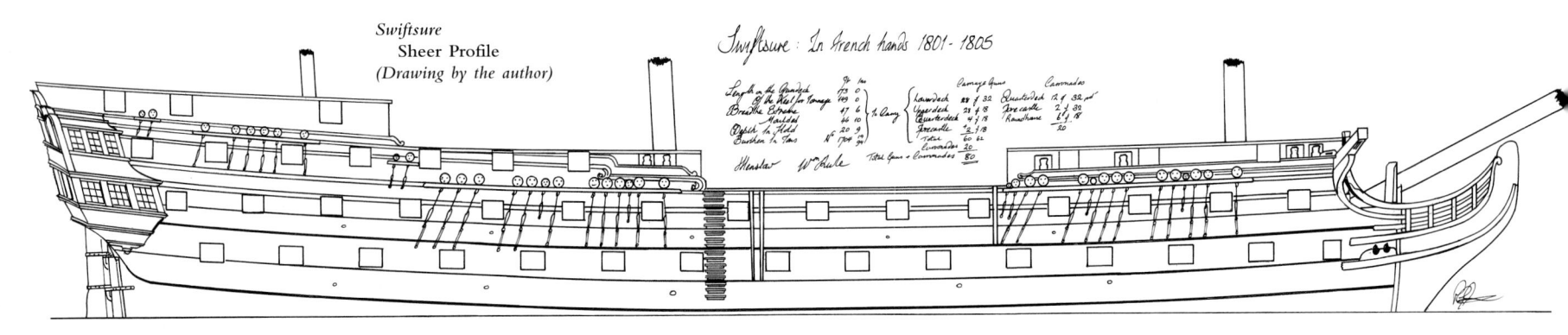

sition than anticipated, and with several ships much damaged aloft, Admiral Parker was obliged to recover the troops which had been landed and withdraw.[141] On 19 October command of the *Swiftsure* was superseded by Captain Arthur Philips.[142]

1798: Now under the command of Captain Benjamin Hallowell, the *Swiftsure* was sent into the Mediterranean to join Nelson's small squadron pursuing the French fleet from Toulon, commanded by Vice-Admiral de Brueys. Reaching Alexandria on 1 August, Nelson detached *Swiftsure* and *Alexander* (74) to reconnoitre the port, to find the harbour empty of French warships. Just before 1 p.m. *Zealous* (74) brought news that de Brueys' ships were anchored further east in Abu-Kir Bay. Recalled at 2.15 p.m., *Swiftsure* and *Alexander* made sail to rejoin the British fleet. When Nelson entered the bay in the late afternoon to attack, *Swiftsure* and *Alexander* were still to the west. Carrying a press of sail, they arrived at about 8 p.m. On entering battle *Swiftsure* immediately fell in with a dismasted ship drifting without lights. Cautiously hailing the stricken vessel before opening his fire, Hallowell fortunately identified her as *Bellerophon* which, being much damaged, was leaving the action. Amid the chaos and smoke of gunfire Captain Hallowell was briefly confused and after anchoring by the stern found that he had brought *Swiftsure* up between Admiral de Brueys' flagship *Orient* (120) and Rear-Admiral Blanquet du Chayla's flagship *Franklin* (80). Nearby lay *Tonnant* (80), which by the end of the day would be captured, entered into the British navy, and later fight at Trafalgar. *Swiftsure* began firing into *Orient*'s bow and *Franklin*'s quarter. Seeing that *Orient* was already damaged from her encounter with *Bellerophon* and had taken fire, Hallowell concentrated *Swiftsure*'s broadsides into her; *Alexander* was pouring more shot into the same area. By this time de Brueys had been severely wounded, then killed outright, and Casa Bianca, *Orient*'s flag captain, lay dangerously wounded. Unable to extinguish the fires, many of the French crew began to jump overboard and swim to nearby ships, ten men and the ship's First Lieutenant being rescued by *Swiftsure*'s crew. As the conflagration began to envelop the French flagship's entire hull, it was inevitable there would be an almighty explosion when the flames reached her magazines. Consequently the British ships nearby began to move away. Instructing John Waters, *Swiftsure*'s First Lieutenant, Hallowell ordered his crew to remove any powder from *Swiftsure*'s upper decks. At 10 p.m. *Orient* exploded, showering burning débris and people among the ships, much of which landed upon *Franklin* and *Alexander*, causing initial fires. As *Swiftsure* was closer to the conflagration she received less wreckage and suffered no immediate casualties. For some ten minutes the battle paused, the silence being broken when *Franklin* reopened her fire into *Swiftsure*. When the battle finally ceased around 8 a.m. next morning *Swiftsure* had suffered considerable damage aloft and having received a shot below the waterline, her pumps had to be continually manned throughout the battle, the water in the hold never falling below four feet. *Swiftsure*'s casualties comprised seven killed and twenty-two wounded. In all nine French ships were captured, of which *Tonnant* (80) and *Spartiate* (74) were each to serve in Nelson's fleet at Trafalgar. The main body of the British line of battle ships departed over the next two weeks, leaving *Swiftsure* together with the 74s *Goliath* and *Zealous* and frigates *Emerald* (36), *Alcmène* (32), *Seahorse* (28), and *Bonne*

Citoyenne (20) remaining in Alexandria under the command of Captain Samuel Hood.[143] On 8 August Captain Hallowell took *Swiftsure* close inshore and took possession of the island of Abu-Kir. Having cast all the existing iron guns into the sea, he carried off two brass mortars and two brass 12-pounders. Two days later *Swiftsure* was cruising towards Damietta when she fell in with and captured the corvette *Fortune* of 16 guns and 70 men. When taken, her French surgeon learnt that he had lost his brother in *Orient*. Later, on 21 October, *Swiftsure* with three gunboats attacked the castle of Abu-Kir and nearby French camp based on Lake Madieh, using shell and incendiaries taken from the French *Spartiate*.[144]

1799: Sailing from Alexandria on 14 February, *Swiftsure*, in company with *Culloden* (74), *Zealous* (74), *Seahorse* (38), and the bomb vessels *Bulldog* and *Perseus*, rejoined Nelson at Palermo on 18 March. Detached by Nelson to blockade Naples, *Swiftsure* sailed again on 31 March with a small squadron commanded by Captain Troubridge. Arriving off the Italian port on 2 April, Troubridge's ships landed marines and took possession of Capri, Ischia, Ponzo and Procida, then rejoined Nelson at Palermo on 17 April.[145] Six days later Hallowell presented Lord Nelson with a coffin made from the mainmast of *Orient*, wishing that it would be fitting if he would later be buried in this trophy of war. As second in command to Captain Troubridge, Hallowell with men from the *Swiftsure* went on shore at Naples and set up trenches before the castle of St Elmo to besiege Neapolitan rebels within the fort. Assisted by Russians under General Suvorof, batteries were erected and began firing on the fort. After a short barrage the rebels surrendered. With marines and seamen out of their respective ships Hallowell and Troubridge travelled 15 miles north to Capua, erected more batteries and in four days forced the rebels to capitulate. After these events *Swiftsure* put to sea and cruised off Maritimo and sailed for Civita Vecchia on 7 August, where Captain Hallowell was expected to negotiate surrender terms with the French. Before these terms could be ratified *Swiftsure* was orded to sail for Gibraltar. Joining the 74s *Bellerophon*, *Leviathan*, *Powerful* and *Vanguard*, she proceeded to Lisbon, arriving there on 30 November. Cruising off the Portuguese coast on 6 December, *Swiftsure* captured two merchant vessels.

1800: While cruising off the Spanish coast near Cadiz in February, *Swiftsure* was so badly damaged in a gale that she had to go into Gibraltar for repairs. Returning to her station patrolling off Cadiz on 5 April, *Swiftsure*, with *Leviathan* (74), flagship of Rear-Admiral Sir John Duckworth and the frigate *Emerald* (36), sighted twelve head of sail and gave chase. This convoy, which had sailed from Cadiz three days before, was bound for Lima. Next day *Emerald* caught up and captured part of a convoy carrying 140 tons of mercury, together with the 34 gun frigates *Carmen* and *Florentina* and a Spanish vessel of 10 guns and 70 men. However, the frigate *Sabina* and four remaining merchantmen escaped. Being too far to leeward, *Swiftsure* had no part in this action but on 12 April she did capture a Spanish schooner bound for Vera Cruz from Malaga.[146] Continuing her deployment blockading, *Swiftsure* later carried the flag of Rear Admiral Sir Richard Bickerton.

1801: At the end of the previous year Admiral Lord Keith had assembled a squadron at Gibraltar to make an assault on the French in Egypt. Flying his

THE 74 GUN SHIP *SWIFTSURE*

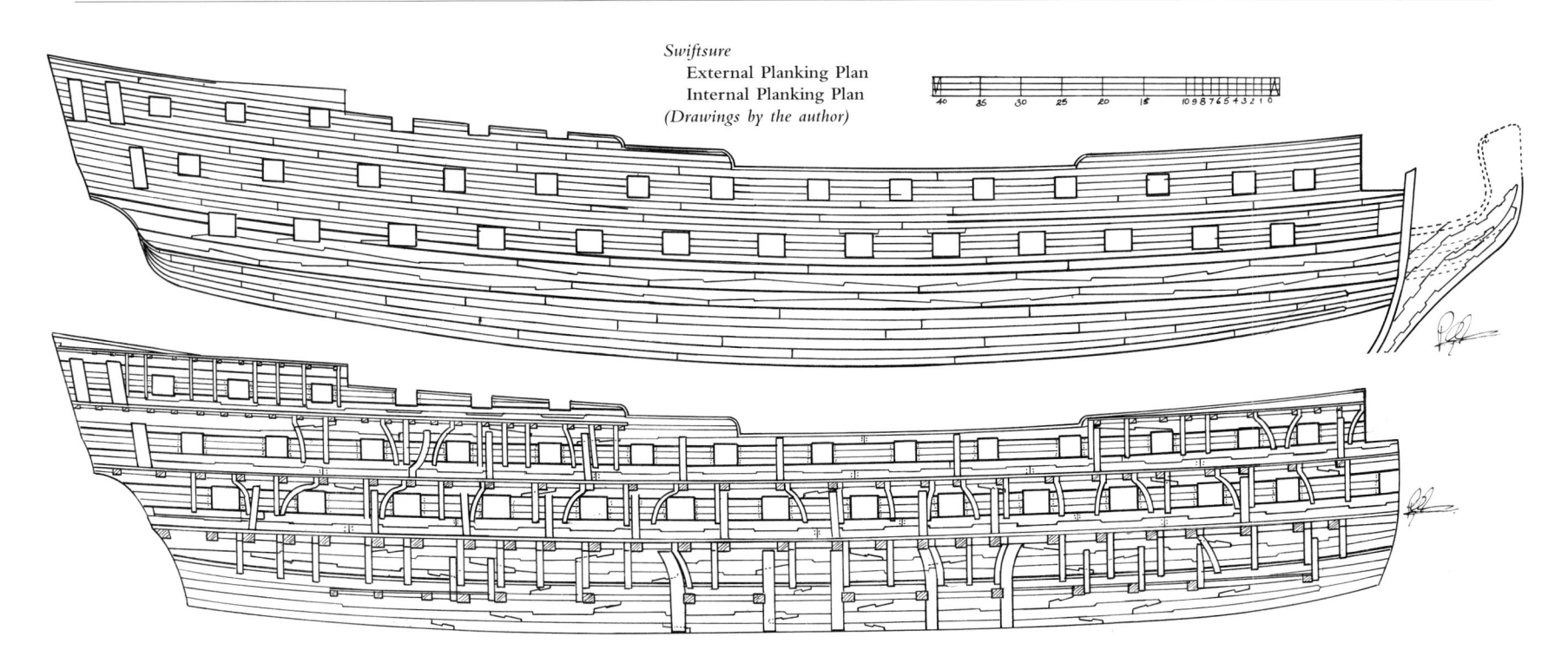

Swiftsure
External Planking Plan
Internal Planking Plan
(Drawings by the author)

flag in *Foudroyant* (80), the main body of his fleet comprised the 74 gun ships *Kent*, flagship of Rear-Admiral Sir Richard Bickerton, *Ajax*, *Minotaur*, *Northumberland*, *Tigre* and *Swiftsure*. The remainder of the fleet consisted of a further 16 sail of the line, 37 frigates and sloops, and 80 transports carrying 18,000 troops commanded by General Sir Ralph Abercromby. Anchoring off Marmorice on 31 January, the British fleet was joined by Turkish forces eager to drive the French from Egypt. Reaching Egypt at the beginning of March, landings were made at Abu-Kir Bay on 8 March, when Midshipman John Finchley and one seaman from *Swiftsure* were wounded. The initial attack was hampered by poor weather, high winds and strong tides. Meeting greater resistance than anticipated, casualties were high with a considerable number being lost as their boats neared the shore. Many of *Swiftsure*'s officers and seamen served on shore under the command of Captain Sir William Sidney Smith. Getting within four miles of Alexandria on 21 March, Abercromby's army was confronted with a French force of some 11–12,000 men which put up a defiant defence. Although the French were eventually repulsed, the British suffered very high casualties. Smith's naval brigade lost four killed and 20 wounded, among the latter being Lieutenant Davis and four seamen from *Swiftsure*; and 59 men were sick on board *Swiftsure*. Throughout the following days *Swiftsure*, like the other ships, played only a supportive rôle to the troops on shore.[147]

Cruising off Cape Derna on the Barbary Coast on 24 June with a convoy to reinforce Rear-Admiral Sir John Borlase Warren's squadron at Malta, *Swiftsure* unwittingly fell in with Admiral Ganteaume's squadron. By 2 p.m. the leading French ships *Créole*, *Dix Août* and *Indivisible* had out-sailed *Swiftsure* and came within gun shot. Taking the best gamble, Hallowell decided to bear down and attack the nearest of the three ships before making good his escape from this greater force. However, just after 3 p.m. the French ships tacked and, cramming on sail, stood towards *Swiftsure*. Opening their fire into Hallowell's ship at 3.30 p.m., *Swiftsure* was out-manœuvred by the superior sailing abilities of the Frenchmen. This was mainly because *Swiftsure* leaked badly and was much in need of having her bottom cleaned of marine growth. Hallowell engaged all three vessels as best he could but, to add to his predicament, at 4.37 p.m. the three French ships were joined by *Jean Bart* and *Constitution*. Much damaged about her spars and rigging and fighting against such odds, Hallowell had little choice but to surrender. Casualties within *Swiftsure* comprised only two dead, two mortally wounded and six injured, one being Lieutenant Davis; French casualties comprised 33 killed and wounded. Having taken possession, the French eventually carried *Swiftsure* into Toulon on 22 July. Her crew were interned and some officers, Hallowell included, were exchanged. News of her capture first reached England through the French newspaper *Moniteur*, dated 23 July. On his release Hallowell was tried on 18 August before a court martial held on board *Généreux* at Malta for her loss. Although Hallowell had left the convoy he was escorting, he was honourably acquitted.[148]

1803: When war resumed in May *Swiftsure* was one of two ships in dock undergoing a refit at Toulon.[149] At the time the Toulon squadron was commanded by Vice-Admiral René Madeleine de Latouche-Tréville. Here she remained until able to break out in 1805.

1805: Under the command of Captain C E l'Hôpitalier-Villemadrin, *Swiftsure* finally sailed from Toulon with Villeneuve's fleet on 30 March, to join Admiral Gravina's squadron at Cadiz before sailing for the West Indies.[150] Like her counterpart *Berwick*, *Swiftsure* would follow the same course of actions with Villeneuve's fleet, both in the West Indies and in the indecisive engagement between the combined fleet and Vice-Admiral Sir Richard Calder's squadron off Ferrol on 27 July. *Swiftsure* finally reached the safety of Cadiz on 21 August where she remained until sailing with Villeneuve's combined fleet for the Mediterranean on 19 October. As part of Gravina's observation squadron she was involved in chasing off Blackwood's frigates on the evening of the 20th July.

TRAFALGAR

Once Villeneuve had given the order for all ships to wear together on the morning of the battle, *Swiftsure* was stationed 26th in line ahead of the combined fleet. Ahead of her lay the Spanish *Argonauta* (80) and astern *San Ildefonso* (74) and on her larboard quarter *Argonaute* (74). Also nearby standing to leeward was the French frigate *Thémis* (40). It was about 1 p.m. when *Swiftsure* got into close action. She stood off the starboard quarter of *Bellerophon* (74) and added her fire into this already hard pressed British ship. Fifteen minutes later *Swiftsure* came under fire from *Colossus* (74). To counter-attack Villemadrin, attempted to drive *Swiftsure* across the stern of *Colossus* and rake her but failed to do so when the British ship unexpectedly wore. Having outwitted Villemadrin with this manœuvre, *Colossus* commenced firing her starboard batteries into his ship with deadly effect, completely carrying away *Swiftsure*'s mizzen mast and main topmast. Almost simultaneously *Orion* (74) ranged up, luffed and poured three rapid broad-

199

PROGRESS BOOK – IRRESISTIBLE (EX-SWIFTSURE) 3rd RATE OF 74 GUNS Source: ADM 180/10 Folio 98

At what Port	Arrived	Docked	Coppered	Launched or Undocked	Sailed	Built or Nature of Repair	Cost of Hull, Masts & Yards Materials £ s d	Cost of Rigging & Stores Materials £ s d	Grand Total
River Thames [John & William Wells]	Began May 1784			4 April 1787	4 April 1787	Built	31,241. 3s.5d		31,241. 3s.5d. Hull Only
Deptford	4 April 1787	-	-	-	22 May 1787	To Woolwich	3,548	7,095	10,643
Woolwich	22 May 1787	2 June 1787	Coppered June 1787	15 June 1787	21 Aug 1787	To Plymouth	1,577	58	1,635
Plymouth	28 Aug 1787	-	Copper Repaired July 1790	-	24 Aug 1791	Fitted for CS [Channel Service]	3,356	3,100	6,456
Plymouth	16 Nov 1790	Taken in Hand Feb[y] & Complet'd		Mar. 1791	4 Mar 1791	Refitted	3,373	8,040	11,413
Plymouth	5 Sep 1791	10 June 1793	Copper taken off June 1793; Re-coppered June 1793	23 June 1793	14 Oct 1793	Fitted	4,917	4,,753	9,670
Plymouth	18 July 1794	28 July 1794	-	30 July 1794	14 Aug 1794	Made Good Defects	717	2,119	2,836
Portsmouth	3 Sep 1796	18 Sep 1796	Copper taken off Sep 1796; Re-coppered Oct 1796	5 Oct 1796	12 Nov 1796	Refitted	4,961	4,304	9,265
			Taken by the French 24 June 1801. Retaken in 1805						
Chatham	11 June 1806	17 July 1806	Copper taken off Aug. Re-coppered with old copper August 1806	15 Aug. 1806		Repaired	1,723	1,015	2,738
			Taken to Pieces January 1816						

sides into *Swiftsure*'s stern, which, according to Villemadrin, 'brought down my main mast, carried away part of the taffrail, the wheel, and dismounted most of the guns on the main deck and killed many of the people'. Pummelled from both sides, *Swiftsure* reeled from the effects of these broadsides, her fore mast went over the side and casualties rose. Besides supporting *Colossus*, the arrival of *Orion* had prevented *Swiftsure* opening fire into *Victory* (100). With his ship unable to withstand any more punishment and, as Villemadrin stated, 'five feet of water in the hold – I gave orders to cease fire and hauled down my colours'. Completely dismasted, *Swiftsure* was taken possession by *Colossus*. In the action *Swiftsure* lost 68 killed and 123 wounded.[151]

Of the 17 actual ships captured (*Achille* having blown up), *Swiftsure* was one of only four prizes that survived the great storm and reached Gibraltar under tow. After refitting sufficiently to make her seaworthy, *Swiftsure* sailed for England escorted by *Britannia* (100). Also accompanying *Britannia* home were the prizes *Bahama* (74), *San Ildefonso* (74) and *San Juan Nepomuceno* (74).[152]

FATE

When *Swiftsure* eventually arrived at Chatham with *Bahama* on 11 June 1806, she was renamed *Irresistible*, there already being a *Swiftsure* in service. *Irresistible* was docked at Chatham on 11 July that same year for repairs, her copper taken off and replaced. Re-launched on 15 August, the cost of this refit amounted to £2,738, of which £1,723 covered hull materials and £1,0215 labour. *Irresistible* was then laid up as a prison ship until finally taken to pieces in January 1816.[153]

NOTES TO PART 2: CHAPTER 2

1. Clowes, 4, pp. 226–335.
2. Charnock, *History of Naval Architecture*, pp. 148–149.
3. James, 3, pp. 337–338.
4. Schom, *Trafalgar*, pp. 312–313.
5. Pope, *England Expects*, pp. 316–318.
6. Clowes, 4, pp. 86–89, 115, 549.
7. Clowes, 5, pp. 112, 121.
8. Clowes, 5, pp. 120–156.
9. Clowes, 5, p. 163.
10. Clowes, 5, p. 107.
11. Clowes, 5, p. 112.
12. Pope, *England Expects*, p. 184.
13. Clowes, 5, p. 152; Pope, *England Expects*, pp. 284–288.
14. Clowes, 5, p. 162.
15. Clowes, 5, pp. 246, 558.
16. Clowes, 5, p. 120.
17. Clowes, 5, p. 136.
18. Schom, *Trafalgar*, pp. 346–356.
19. Clowes, 5, p. 558.
20. Lyon, pp. 71–72.
21. TNA: PRO, ADM 180/6 folio 42.
22. Lyon, 71–72.
23. TNA: PRO, ADM 180/6 folio 42.
24. Clowes, 3, p. 415.
25. TNA: PRO, ADM 180/6 folio 42.
26. Ibid.
27. Clowes, 4, pp. 57–58.
28. TNA: PRO, ADM 180/6 folio 42.
29. RNM, MS 248/4.
30. Clowes, 3, pp. 505–508.
31. TNA: PRO, ADM 180/6 folio 42.
32. RNM, MS 248/4.
33. TNA: PRO, ADM 180/6 folio 42.
34. RNM, MS 248/4.
35. TNA: PRO, ADM 180/6 folio 42.
36. Ibid.
37. RNM, MS 248/4.
38. James, 1, p. 65.
39. TNA: PRO, ADM 248/4.
40. James, 1, p. 192.
41. TNA: PRO, ADM 248/4.
42. RNM, MS 248/4.
43. James, 1, p. 254; Clowes, 4, p. 267.
44. RNM, MS 248/4.
45. James, 1, pp. 254–255; Clowes, 4, p. 268.
46. Clowes, 4, pp. 277–278.
47. Clowes, 4, p. 286.
48. Clowes, 4, pp. 290–291.
49. Tracy, *Naval Chronicle*, 3, pp. 147–149; James, 3, 337.
50. NMM, MS LBK/38.
51. Clowes, 4, pp. 203–204.
52. Clowes, 4, p. 553.
53. James, 3, pp. 191–192.
54. James, 3, p. 193.
55. Clowes, 5, pp. 149, 161.
56. TNA: PRO, ADM 180/10/156; Clowes, 5, pp. 170–174.
57. TNA: PRO, ADM 180/10/156.
58. RNM, MS 249/6.
59. James, 5, pp. 12–16.
60. RNM, MS 248/6.
61. TNA: PRO, ADM 180/10/156.
62. RNM, MS 248/6.
63. James, 5, pp. 180–181; Gardiner and Woodman, *Victory of Seapower*, pp. 126–127.
64. TNA: PRO, ADM 180/10/156.
65. RNM, MS 248/6.
66. RNM, MS 248/6; James, 5, p. 329.
67. TNA: PRO, ADM 180/10/156; RNM, MS 248/6.
68. TNA: PRO, ADM 180/10/156.
69. Trustees of the *Implacable: Appeal for the Implacable Fund*, 1926.
70. The author started his naval career at HMS *Ganges*, 17 October 1966.
71. The 80 gun *Foudroyant* served as Nelson's flagship in the Mediterranean, 1799–1800. P Goodwin, *Nelson's Ships*, pp. 170–195. Aged 13 the author spent time in *Foudroyant* doing sea training.
72. Annual Report for the Society for Nautical Research, 1938.
73. Ibid.
74. Ibid.
75. Ibid.
76. Clowes, 4, pp. 254 255, 262.
77. Clowes, 4, pp. 289–301.
78. Clowes, 5, p. 121.
79. Pope, *England Expects*, p. 233.
80. Clowes, 5, pp. 146–148.
81. Pope, *England Expects*, pp. 269–284.
82. TNA: PRO, ADM 51/1531.
83. Fraser, *The Enemy at Trafalgar*, pp. 297–299.

84 Clowes, 4, p. 77.
85 Clowes, 4, pp. 203, 210, 552.
86 Pope, *England Expects*, pp. 321–322, 327–329; Clowes, 5, p. 120.
87 Clowes, 5, pp. 246, 558.
88 Clowes, 4, p. 114.
89 Harbron, *Trafalgar and the Spanish Navy*, 172.
90 *Ibid*.
91 Clowes, 5, p. 89.
92 Clowes, 5, pp. 112, 120.
93 Clowes, 5, p. 131.
94 Pope, *England Expects*, pp. 327–329; Fraser, *The Enemy at Trafalgar*, pp. 189–192; Clowes, 5, pp. 148–149. The magnificent defence of *Intrépide* by Louis Infernet certainly equals that of the British ship *Belleisle* by Captain Hargood and perhaps more so as *Intrépide* had to contend with at least one three decker, *Britannia*, with *Neptune* nearby.
95 Des Touches, pp. 421–423.
96 TNA: PRO, ADM 51, *passim*; Fraser, *The Enemy at Trafalgar*, p. 310.
97 Clowes, 4, p. 225.
98 Duffy & Morriss, *The Glorious First of June*.
99 Clowes, 4, p. 239.
100 Clowes, 4, p. 255.
101 Clowes, 4, p. 278.
102 Clowes, 5, p. 52
103 Clowes, 5, pp. 89, 112, 115.
104 Clowes, 5, pp. 131, 149, 161.
105 TNA: PRO, ADM 180/10/158; Clowes, 5, pp. 170–174.
106 TNA: PRO, ADM 180/10/158; Lyon, p. 268.
107 James, 2, p. 268; Clowes, 4, p. 92.
108 Clowes, 4, pp. 297–301.
109 Clowes, 5, p. 52.
110 Clowes, 5, pp. 106–107.
111 Clowes, 5, pp. 112–115.
112 Pope, *England Expects*, pp. 282–285; Clowes, 5, pp. 151–152.
113 Clowes, 5, pp. 162–163.
114 Clowes, 5, pp. 246, 558; Schom, *Trafalgar*, p. 403.
115 Clowes, 4, p. 255.
116 Clowes, 4, pp. 255–262.
117 Clowes, 4, p. 298.
118 Clowes, 4, p. 301.
119 Fraser *The Enemy at Trafalgar*, pp. 146–147.
120 Fraser, *The Enemy at Trafalgar*, p. 112.
121 Fraser, *The Enemy at Trafalgar*, pp. 153–157.
122 TNA, PRO, ADM 51/1533 part 1.
123 Fraser, *The Enemy at Trafalgar*, pp. 156–157.
124 Lyon, p. 263; Clowes, 4, pp. 548, 552
125 Clowes, 4, pp. 254, 553.
126 Clowes, 4, p. 555.
127 Lyon, p. 268.
128 Clowes, 5, p. 52.
129 Clowes, 5, pp. 149, 161.
130 TNA:ADM 180/10/157; Clowes, 5, pp. 170–174.
131 Clowes, 5, pp. 297–300.
132 RNM, MS 248/7.
133 Clowes, 5, pp. 304–305.
134 RNM, MS 248/7
135 TNA: PRO, ADM 180/10/157.
136 Lyon, pp. 71–72.
137 *Ibid*.
138 RNM, MS 248/4.
139 *Ibid*.
140 *Ibid*.
141 Clowes, 4, p. 293.
142 RNM, MS 248/4.
143 Clowes, 356–373.
144 Clowes, 4, p. 377.
145 Clowes, 4, pp. 390–391.
146 James, 3, p. 37.
147 James, 3, pp. 26, 98–110.
148 James, 3, pp. 94–95; Clowes, 4, p. 453.
149 Clowes, 5, p. 52.
150 Clowes, 5, p. 89.
151 Pope, *England Expects*, p. 302; Clowes, 5, pp. 152–154; James, 4, pp. 55, 360.
152 Fraser, *The Enemy at Trafalgar*, p. 312.
153 TNA: PRO, ADM 180/10/98; Lyon, p. 71.

PART 2: CHAPTER 3
THE FIVE FRENCH FRIGATES OF 40 GUNS

CORNÉLIE

Designed by Jacques Noel Sane, *Cornélie* was built at Brest and launched in 1794.

SERVICE HISTORY

1799: Her history, sparse as it is from English sources, first records her on 9 April 1799 when she is sighted with two other frigates by the British cruisers *Amelia* (38) and *San Fiorenzo* (36), lying off Belle Isle. As the two British frigates closed a sudden squall carried away *Amelia*'s main topmast and fore and mizzen topgallant masts, rendering her easy prey for the French ships. *Cornélie* and her consorts *Vengeance* (40), *Sémillante* (36) and a gunboat, immediately stood out and attacked the two British ships. A running battle ensued during which the two British ships suffered considerable damage to rigging and spars. After three hours *Cornélie* and her accomplices retired.[1]

1805: *Cornélie* sailed with Villeneuve's fleet from Toulon on 17 January under the command of Captain de Martinenq. While many of the French ships were forced by bad weather to return to port, *Cornélie* operated off Corsica. Here, on 21 January, she actively chased off *Seahorse* (38), one of Nelson's frigates, as she was standing into Pulla Bay. Afterwards she took shelter off Genoa from the deteriorating weather and finally got back into Toulon on 24 January.[2] *Cornélie* remained at Toulon until sailing for the West Indies with the main body of Villeneuve's fleet at the end of March and was consequently present at Calder's action off Cape Finisterre on 22 July. *Cornélie* eventually entered Cadiz on 20 August where she carried out necessary maintenance to rigging and re-provisioned.

TRAFALGAR

Sailing with the rest of the combined fleet on 19 October, *Cornélie* took up station with Rear-Admiral Dumanoir's van on the morning of the battle, standing to leeward of *Duguay Trouin* (74) and *Mont Blanc* (74). As frigates were too lightly armed to stand in the line of fire, *Cornélie* remained a respectable distance to leeward for the entirety of the battle and returned to Cadiz afterwards.

On 23 October *Cornélie* put to sea with Cosmao-Kerjulien's squadron to attempt the recapturing of prizes. During this sortie she assisted the other frigates in recapturing the Spanish ships *Santa Ana* (112) and *Neptuno* (80) and escorting them back into Cadiz.[3]

FATE

Cornélie remained in Cadiz with the rest of the surviving Trafalgar ships, now all placed under the command of Vice-Admiral de Rosily, and was surrendered to Spain on 14 June 1808 after Spain declared war on France on 4 June.[4] What happened to *Cornélie* after she was entered into the Spanish navy remains unclear.

HERMIONE

Designed by André Geofry, *Hermione* was built and launched at Lorient in 1803.

SERVICE HISTORY

1805: At some point between 1803 and early March 1805 *Hermione* sailed for Toulon. While Villeneuve was preparing his fleet to undertake the first part of Napoleon's invasion plan he removed the entire crew out of the *Uranie* and transferred them into *Hermione*, the better of the two vessels.[5] Placed under the command of Captain Mahé, *Hermione* sailed with Villeneuve's fleet from Toulon on 29 March for the West Indies and arrived at Martinique on 14 May. Two days beforehand *Hermione* and *Hortense* had captured the 18 gun sloop *Cyane*. When Villeneuve received news that Nelson and his fleet were in the West Indies he abandoned his initial plans and sailed back to Europe. First he had to disembark the troops embarked at Martinique and Guadeloupe. These were put on board *Hermione* and the other frigates and landed. Following orders, Mahé and the other frigate captains were to rejoin Villeneuve's combined fleet off the Azores. En route, *Hermione* and her consorts captured a convoy and their escort *Syrène* on 26 June. These prizes were burnt next day when it was conceived that a British squadron of reasonable force was near at hand. *Hermione* and the frigate squadron rejoined Villeneuve off Corvo on 30 June. Although with the fleet, *Hermione* did not get involved in Calder's action off Cape Finisterre on 22 July but did eventually enter Cadiz on 20 August.[6]

TRAFALGAR

When she sailed from Cadiz on 19 October *Hermione* was deployed with Admiral Gravina's observation squadron. After the combined fleet had wore and turned northward at 8 a.m. of the morning of the battle, *Hermione*'s position appears well to windward of the rearmost ship in the fleet, *San Juan Nepumuceno* (74). Why *Hermione* took up station to windward instead of to leeward, as the other frigates and brigs had, is not at all clear. Returning to Cadiz after the action, *Hermione* sailed again on 23 October with Commodore Kerjulien's squadron to recapture some of the prizes. During this sally she helped retake the Spanish ships *Santa Ana* (112) and *Neptuno* (80).[7]

1806: *Hermione* remained in Cadiz until 1806. Finding that strong easterly winds had driven off the British blockading fleet, Commodore La Marre La Meillerie, senior frigate captain, decided to break out of port with the frigates and make for the West Indies. *Hermione*, in company with *Hortense*, *Rhin*, *Thémis* and the 18 gun brig *Furet*, sailed on 26 February. Besides carrying troops each frigate was provisioned for six months. Unfortunately the five vessels were sighted that evening at 9.15 by the British frigate *Hydra* (38) and brig-sloop *Moselle* (18), with the result that the *Furet* was captured.[8]

Later that year, *Hermione*, with the same three frigates sailed from the West Indies for France. As they arrived off Rochefort on 27 July they were sighted by *Mars* (74). In the following chase *Rhin* was captured while *Hermione*, *Hortense* and *Thémis* made good their escape to Bordeaux.[9]

FATE

What happened to *Hermione* after 1806 is uncertain.

HORTENSE

Like *Cornélie*, the frigate *Hortense* was designed by Sane, built at Toulon and launched in 1803.

SERVICE HISTORY

1805: Under the command of Captain (later Commodore) La Marre La Meillerie, *Hortense* sailed with Villeneuve's first sally out of Toulon on 17 January 1805. While much of the fleet was forced by poor weather to return to harbour three days later, *Hortense* did not return to Toulon for a further two months.[10] During this period she operated off the Algerian coast in company with *Incorruptible* (38). On 3 February the two ships fell in with and shadowed a convoy from Malta escorted by *Arrow* (28) and the bomb ship *Acheron* (8). At 4.45 a.m. next day *Hortense* closed with *Arrow* on an opposite tack and hailed her, then overhauled the *Acheron* and did the same, only this time she fired her broadside into the bomb ship, causing much damage to her hull and carrying away the main and topgallant yards. *Arrow* and *Acheron* returned their fire and after bearing up raked *Hortense*. *Incorruptible*, too far off to give support, finally ranged up at 5.30 a.m., by which time *Acheron* had made some running repairs to rigging. By 7.30 a.m. *Hortense* and *Incorruptible* were again on an opposing tack, bearing down upon the two British ships, *Incorruptible* in the lead. While *Incorruptible* maintained her fire into *Acheron*, *Hortense* concentrated her attention on *Arrow*. The two French ships then wore and, passing a second time, reversed their opponents: *Hortense* engaging *Acheron*, *Incorruptible* the *Arrow*. The British ships were no match for the heavy French frigates and at 8.30 a.m. *Arrow* struck her colours to *Incorruptible*. *Acheron*, unable to out-sail *Hortense*, capitulated at 8.45 a.m. The two British ships were so damaged in the action that neither was worth taking as a prize. Once prisoners had been transferred to the two French frigates *Acheron* was burnt and *Arrow* simply sank due to severe hull damage. Although both escorts had put up a considerable defence, only armed with short range carronades their defeat was inevitable against the long guns of *Hortense* and *Incorruptible*. After this the French frigates captured three of the convoy.[11]

Hortense next sailed from Toulon on 29 March with Villeneuve's fleet. After passing through the Straits of Gibraltar on 8 April, Villeneuve ordered Captain L C A La Marre to sail on ahead of the fleet to inform the authorities at Cadiz of his impending arrival. *Hortense* then sailed with the rest of the fleet for the West Indies and in company with *Hermione* captured the 18 gun sloop *Cyane* on 12 May, two days before arriving at Martinique. While in the West Indies *Hortense*'s movements follow those of *Hermione* as stated above. During her voyage home *Hortense* and the other frigates captured *Syrène* and her convoy. *Hortense* rejoined the main body of Villeneuve's fleet off Corvo on 30 June. Like her consorts *Hortense* did not take part in Calder's action off Cape Finisterre on 22 July but did go into Cadiz on 20 August.[12]

TRAFALGAR

At the opening of the battle *Hortense* was stationed near the centre of the fleet standing to leeward of *Redoutable* and *San Leandro*. Once battle com-

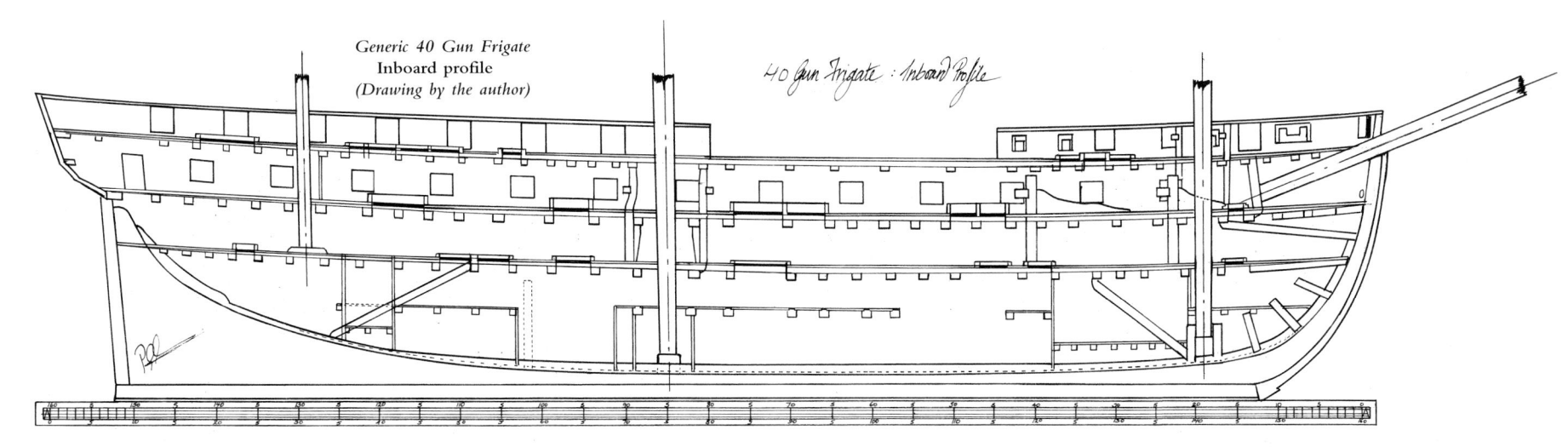

Generic 40 Gun Frigate
Inboard profile
(Drawing by the author)

menced and the centre was broken by Nelson it is obvious that Captain La Marre would have taken his ship further to leeward as the *Victory* and *Redoutable* locked in combat drifted in that direction. With Captain La Marre being the senior of the French frigate captains it is plausible that should Villeneuve have been able to leave his striken flagship *Bucentaure*, he would have transferred his flag into *Hortense* to continue directing the battle. After returning to Cadiz *Hortense* sailed again two days later with Commodore Kerjulien to retake some of the prizes and like her consorts helped recapture *Santa Ana* (112) and *Neptuno* (80).[13]

1806: *Hortense* remained in Cadiz until February 1806, when Commodore La Marre La Meillerie decided to break out of port with the frigates and make for the West Indies. Besides carrying troops all the frigates had embarked six months' provisions. Taking advantage of the strong easterly winds which had driven off the British blockading fleet, *Hortense* with *Hermione*, *Rhin*, *Thémis* and the 18 gun brig *Furet* sailed on 26 February. All five vessels were sighted that evening with the result that *Furet* was later captured.[14] When *Hortense* and the three frigates were returning to Rochefort on 27 July 1806 they fell in with *Mars* (74). *Rhin* was captured as *Hortense*, *Hermione* and *Thémis* escaped into Bordeaux.[15]

1808: In April *Hortense* formed part of the Rochefort squadron under Commodore Gilbert Faure which anchored between the southern end of Isle d'Aix as part of the defences against Admiral Lord Gambier's concerted attack in the Basque Roads. When fireships were sent in on the night of 11 April under Captain Lord Cochrane *Hortense* and the other frigates made sail, got to windward and fired several broadsides into the oncoming vessels before taking suitable shelter beyond the larger ships. Confusion ensued throughout the French fleet, causing many ships to cut their cables; in the panic many vessels collided with each other in the darkness and all but two ships ran aground. *Hortense* was no exception; by next morning she was hard aground on the Fontenelles. She finally got afloat on 14 April and moved up the River Charente to avoid further danger.[16]

FATE
The fate of *Hortense* after 1808 is unknown.

RHIN

Like *Cornélie* and *Hortense*, *Rhin* was designed by Sane, built at Toulon and launched in 1802.

SERVICE HISTORY
1805: Under the command of Captain M J A Chesneau, *Rhin* sailed from Toulon on 17 January in Villeneuve's first attempt to break out into the Atlantic, but meeting appalling weather conditions in the Gulf of Lyon, was forced to re-enter harbour three days later. After re-provisioning and making good repairs to rigging, *Rhin* sailed from Toulon on 29 March with Villeneuve's fleet for the West Indies and arrived at Martinique 14 May. While in the West Indies she assisted the other frigates with the transfer of troops embarked at Martinique and Guadeloupe. After this her movements were identical with those of the other frigates within the combined fleet until finally reaching Cadiz on 20 August.

TRAFALGAR
After Villeneuve had altered course to northward on the morning of the battle *Rhin* found herself stationed at a considerable distance to leeward of the centre of the combined fleet. Far to her larboard lay *Fougueux*, *Intrépide* and *Indomptable*, all 74 gun ships. Apart from relaying signals *Rhin* played little part in the ensuing battle and returned to the safety of Cadiz that evening as the storm moved in from the West. Like the other frigates forming part of the battle fleet, *Rhin* put to sea again on 23 October supporting Commodore Kerjulien's bid to recapture some of the prizes. While undertaking this sortie *Rhin* helped to recapture the Spanish ships *Santa Ana* (112) and *Neptuno* (80).[17]

1806: Taking advantage of the strong easterly winds that had driven off Collingwood's blockading ships, *Rhin* sailed from Cadiz on 23 February with Captain La Marre La Meillerie's squadron of three other frigates and the gun brig *Furet* (18). The frigates in company are discussed above. It was La Marre's intention to make for the West Indies but after being sighted later that evening by British patrols, *Furet* was captured next day.[18]

Having successfully accomplished their mission, *Rhin* and her consorts *Hermione*, *Hortense* and *Thémis* sailed for France. When the squadron arrived off Rochefort on 27 July they were sighted by *Mars* (74) which had been detached inshore from Captain Richard Goodwin Keats' squadron blockad-

CAPTAINS OF *RHIN* (RNM, MS 248/6)			
Name	Date of entry	Date left	Occasion
Hon. J W Aylmer	25 June 1809	25 November 1809	To the *Narcissus*
Charles Malcolm	20 July 1810	26 August 1815	Paid Off at Sheerness

ing the port. In command of *Mars* was Captain Robert Oliver. Recording the events leading to the capture of *Rhin*, Captain Oliver wrote in his log on Sunday 27 July 1806:[19]

> At 6 Robert Cutt [the spelling of this surname is unclear] Seaman fell overboard short^d Sail & picked him up & took every approved means of restoring animation but without desired effect. ? past 7 Tk^d Short^d Sail *Superb* NNE 8 or 9 miles. Wore & performed divine Service. Fresh Breezes *Superb* 10 or 11 Miles'.
>
> PM Fresh Breezes at 1.50 Tk^d at4 Do W^r *Superb* NNE 8 or 9 miles at 4.35 bore up East at 5 hauled to the wind on the Starb^d Tack & hove too Answered the signal of Recall at 6 discovered 4 strange sail SSW made the signal N$^{os.}$ 394, 372, 922, 360, 758 with ESE Comp^s Sig^l ans^d Signals 3, 13, 26, & 23 – ans^d by Telegraph impossible say^n --- Commodore NNE 5 or 6 Miles. At 7.48 *Superb* made Sig^l N° 26 with *Mars* Pend^{ts} at 8 headmost Ship of the chase bore SWbW 7 or 8 Miles & the *Africa* NE about 5 Miles & *Superb* NNE 8 or 9 Miles Shewed a light in the Poop Lanthorn – the chase making all sail from us – *Superb* made N° 13 Genl cleared Ship for Action at 9 lost sight of the Chase observed a Ship astern (supposed the *Africa*) burn several blue lights & set off rockets. D^o W^r still in chace – *Africa* out of sight'.

Continuing his log next day Monday 28 July Oliver recorded:

> Fresh Breezes & cloudy with lightning & Rain In chase all night, Saw one of the chase bearing SbW at 5 split the fore topgall^t Sail & shifted it & obs^d the other 3 Ships - at 7 the headmost 3 tacked & formed in order of Battle with the sternmost one – Committed the Body of Robt Cutt to the Deep with the customary funeral Rites. Strong Breezes & squally with hard rain Sprung the Foretop-mast in 2nd reefs of topsails & fitted and additional Backstay to the foretopmast – still in chase. Fresh Gales with heavy squalls of wind & rain split the Jib shifted it – set & took in the maintopgal^t Sail occasionally. Still in chase all hands at Quarters.

At noon the log continues:

> Fresh gales with frequent squalls set the Jib & Spanker occas^{ly} ½ past observed the 3 headmost ships of the Chase part C^o with the rearmost one & steer more easterly continued on the chase of the latter. Shewed our Colours – the Chase hoisted French D^o At 6 during a heavy squall of wind & rain came up with her & fired a shot between her masts which was returned by firing two guns & striking her colours – Hoisted the Boats out & boarded her she proved to be the *Rhin* French Frigate of 44 Guns & 318 Men from Porto Rica the[y] informed us the 3 Frigates in C^o with her were the *Hortense*, *Hermione* &

PROGRESS BOOK – *RHIN* 5TH RATE OF 40-44 GUNS:

At what Port	Arrived	Docked	Coppered
Plymouth	8 Aug 1806	17 Mar 1809	Copper taken off Mar. Re-coppered May 1809
Plymouth	15 Sep 1811		Coppered
Plymouth	9 Jan 1812		Copper Repaired
Plymouth	9 Oct 1812	23 Oct 1812	Copper Repaired
Plymouth	10 Feb 1813		
Plymouth	5 Oct 1814	10 Oct 1814	Copper taken off and recoppered
Plymouth	28 Apr 1815	8 May 1815	Copper repaired and dressed down
Sheerness	17 Aug 1815	3 May 1817	Copper taken off May 1817; Re-coppered Aug. 1820
Sheerness		12 Feb 1827	Copper repaired, re-nailed, dressed down – and fitted with Iron Protectors
Other expenses appended to the original document in pencil			
Chatham	18 Dec 1833	26 May 1838	Copper taken off and recoppered
Medway -Sheerness			

Sold to Mr Castle 26 May 1884

Themis French Frigates Sent 2 Lieut^s & a party of men on b^d the Prize - & brought on b^d her Captn several officers & 120 men – in Boats & made sail. Fresh Breezes & squally Prize in C^o.

Although *Hortense*, *Hermione* and *Thémis* tacked and formed line of battle to meet *Mars*, they then crammed on more sail and made good their escape to Bordeaux, leaving *Rhin* unsupported. As shown by Oliver's entry in the log of the *Mars*, both James and Clowes falsely state that *Rhin* capitulated without firing a shot.[20] The two guns fired by *Rhin* were purely a gesture 'pour l'honneur du pavillon'. Once the prisoners had been transferred, the prize crew got *Rhin* under weigh and took her into Plymouth, arriving there on 8 August. She was laid up in the ordinary in the Hamoaze and officially entered into the Royal Navy under the name *Rhin*.[21]

1809: On 17 March *Rhin* was docked at Plymouth and fitted out for sea service. While in dock her copper was removed and renewed in May. Undocked on 31 May, the ship remained in harbour until sailing on 31 August. Finding various defects, this refit had changed into a 'Middling Repair' at a total cost of £24,302, of which £5,609 covered labour costs. Total individual expenditure comprised £14,894 on her hull, £1,900 on masts and yards, and £7,508 on rigging stores.[22]

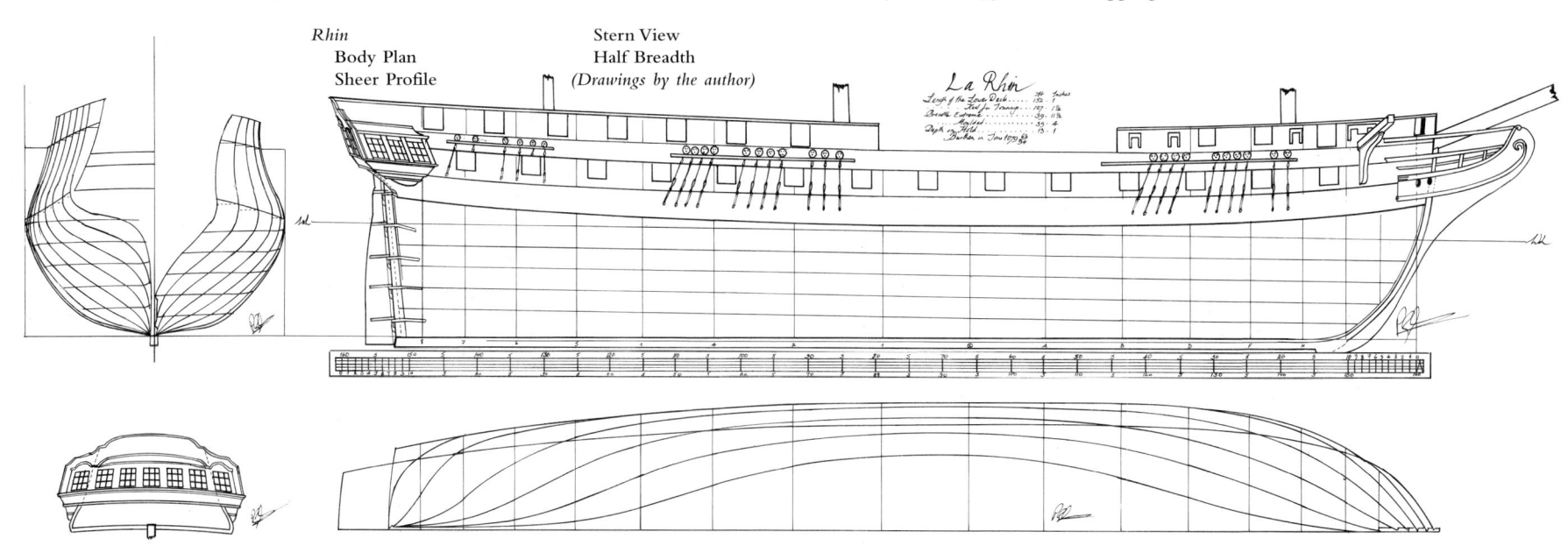

Rhin
Body Plan
Sheer Profile
Stern View
Half Breadth
(Drawings by the author)

Source: ADM 180/1 Folio 361

Launched or Undocked	Sailed	Built or Nature of Repair	Cost of Hull, Masts & Yards Materials £	Workmen £	Cost of Masts & Yards Materials £	Workmen £	Cost of Rigging & Stores Materials £	Workmen £	Grand Total £
31 May 1809	31 Aug 1809	Fitted (Middling Repair)	9,355	5,539	1,839	61	7,499	9	24,302.
	22 Oct 1811	Defects	585	190	420	19	2,697	34	3,945
	22 Jan 1812	Defects	844	465	652	50	5,337	87	7,435
24 Oct 1812	23 Nov 1812	Defects	Incl. above		Incl. above		Inc. above		Incl. above
	28 Feb 1813	Defects	160	62	714	17	3,352	49	4,354
14 Oct 1814	5 Nov 1814	Defects	1,795	811	562	30	3,497	2	6,747
9 May 1815	12 May 1815	Defects	228	123	291	11	3,811	66	4,530
9 Aug 1817		Large Repair	22,039	6,930	3	41	108	83	29,204
			522	481	-	9	9	1	1,022
24 Feb 1827	18 Dec 1833	Defects	325	227	4	14	-	-	570 (corrected)
			587	34	25	46	9	12	713
21 Sep 1838	17 Oct 1838	Fitted for the Quarantine Department	950	1,228	-	-	61		2,239
		Expenses 1859/60	-61	2					2
		Total Expenses	53,482		4,808		26,773		85,063

1812: Now commanded by Captain Charles Malcolm, *Rhin* was deployed with Captain Sir Home Popham's squadron operating off the north coast of Spain. In late June the ship lay off the town of Lequeito and the small island of San Nicholas in company with the frigates *Surveillante* and *Medusa*. Besides detachments of seamen and marines, each ship landed one carronade apiece to support the Spanish patriots against the French. Throughout the first two weeks of July Popham's squadron, including *Rhin*, moved westward along the coast to land parties as required and destroy batteries and works that had been utilised by the French. After this *Rhin* supported Popham's combined attack on Santander carried out on 30 July and 1 August.[23] Returning to Plymouth on 9 October, *Rhin* was docked on 23 October for one day to have her copper repaired, costing £844 for materials and £465 for labour.[24]

1813-1815: Between these years *Rhin* continued operating out of Plymouth, docking as required to have her copper repaired or replaced, the costs and dates of which are shown in the Progress Book.[25] Leaving Plymouth on 12 May 1815, she went into Sheerness on 17 August and paid off.[26]

1817: Taken in hand at Sheerness, *Rhin* was docked on 3 May to begin a 'Large Repair', her copper being removed first to allow her planking to be stripped off and her futtocks and toptimbers to be replaced where required. Now at peace, there was no urgency to complete the ship.[27]

1820: Re-coppered in early August, *Rhin* finally came out of dock on 9 August. The cost for this 'Large Repair' amounted to £29,204, with additional expenses of £1,022 (total £30,226). Individual expenditure including labour comprised £29,972 for her hull, £53 for masts and yards and £101 for rigging and stores. That so little money was spent on masts, yards, rigging and stores implies that she was not rigged afterwards, and the money spent on spars probably related to booms or derricks.[28]

FATE

Taken into dock on 26 May 1838, *Rhin* was 'Fitted for the Quarantine Department' at an overall expense of £2,239 of which £2,178 covered modifications to her accommodation facilities. She was also recoppered. *Rhin* was undocked on 17 October 1838. While the Progress Book infers that she immediately undertook the role of a quarantine hulk, other sources (Lyon and Colledge) suggest 1841. The grand total expended on *Rhin* between 1859 and 1861 was just £2. Gross expenditure from the date *Rhin* was first brought into Plymouth in 1806 amounted to £85,063 covering £53,482 expended on her hull, £4,808 for spars, and £26,773 for rigging and stores. After 45 years *Rhin* was sold on 26 May 1884 to shipbuilder Castle at Charlton.[29]

THÉMIS

Thémis was built and launched at Bayonne in 1796. Unlike most other 40 gun frigates which followed lines designed by Jacques Sane, *Thémis* was designed by R A Haran. Regarding her ordnance, the number, type and weight of each gun carried complied with the standard for French 40 frigates.

SERVICE HISTORY

1805: Little is recorded about the career of *Thémis* before her rôle in the Trafalgar campaign, which began when Villeneuve first sallied out of Toulon with his fleet on 17 January in an attempt to evade Nelson's blockading ships. When *Thémis* sailed as part of this squadron she was under the command of Captain Jugan who would remain in the ship for the duration. Like most of the fleet *Thémis* was compelled to return to port within three days. As the deployment of *Thémis* before the battle of Trafalgar follows exactly that of her counterparts *Cornélie*, *Hermione*, *Hortense* and *Rhin*, there is no need to repeat her movements.

TRAFALGAR

On the morning of the battle *Thémis* was stationed to leeward of Admiral Gravina's observation squadron at the rear of the fleet. On her larboard bow lay the Spanish *Argonauta* (80), on her larboard quarter, *Swiftsure* (74). Once battle commenced Captain Jugan stood *Thémis* further to leeward where he was better placed to repeat any signals and also to avoid heavy fire from the well armed ships of the line. After returning to Cadiz after the battle *Thémis* sailed again two days later with Commodore Kerjulien's squadron and assisted the other frigates to recapture *Santa Ana* (112) and *Neptuno* (80).[30]

1806: *Thémis* remained in Cadiz until sailing on 26 February with Commodore La Marre La Meillerie's squadron of frigates and the 18 gun brig *Furet* for the West Indies. *Thémis* was present next day when *Furet* was later captured[31] and when *Mars* (74) captured the frigate *Rhin* off Rochefort (see above). Not staying to defend her, *Thémis* escaped into Bordeaux with her consorts *Hortense* and *Hermione* and she remained there under blockade.[32]

1808: *Thémis*, with *Pénélope* (40), finally escaped from Bordeaux on 21 January and cruised in the Atlantic before re-entering the Mediterranean. Having passed through the Straits of Gibraltar without hindrance on 17 March, *Thémis* and *Pénélope* went into Ajaccio on 23 March before anchoring off Toulon 5 days later. During this voyage *Thémis* and her consort had taken or destroyed British shipping worth £250,000.[33]

FATE

Whatever happened to *Thémis* after 1808 is unknown.

NOTES TO PART 2: CHAPTER 3

1. Clowes, 4, p. 522.
2. Clowes, 5, pp. 90–92.
3. Clowes, 5, pp. 282–263.
4. Clowes, 5, pp. 246, 558.
5. Clowes, 5, p. 94.
6. Clowes, 5, p. 108.
7. Clowes, 5, pp. 282–263.
8. James, 4, pp. 213–214; Clowes, 5, pp. 197–198.
9. James, 4, pp. 253–254; Clowes, 5, p. 387.
10. Clowes, 5, pp. 89–92.
11. Clowes, 5, pp. 353–355.
12. Clowes, 5, p. 108.
13. Clowes, 5, pp. 282–263.
14. James, 4, pp. 213–214; Clowes, 5, pp. 197–198.
15. James, 4, pp. 253–254; Clowes, 5, p. 387. After this *Hortense* got back into Rochefort.
16. James, 5, pp. 110–111; Clowes, 5, pp. 255–267.
17. Clowes, 5, pp. 282–263.
18. James, 4, pp. 213–214; Clowes, 5, pp. 197–198.
19. TNA: PRO, ADM 51/4472.
20. James, 4, pp. 253–254; Clowes, 5, p. 387.
21. TNA: PRO, ADM 180/11 folio 361.
22. *Ibid*.
23. James, 6, pp. 62–63; Clowes, 5, pp. 508–509.
24. TNA: PRO, ADM 180/11 folio 361.
25. See Progress Book.
26. TNA: PRO, ADM 180/11 folio 361.
27. *Ibid*.
28. *Ibid*.
29. Colledge, 1, p. 463.
30. Clowes, 5, pp. 282–263.
31. James, 4, pp. 213–214; Clowes, 5, pp. 197–198.
32. James, 4, pp. 253–254; Clowes, 5, p. 387.
33. Clowes, 5, p. 244.

PART 2: CHAPTER 4
THE TWO FRENCH BRIGS

Beside the five 40 gun frigates accompanying Villeneuve's 18 line of battle ships, there were two brigs, *Furet* (18) and *Argus* (16), both of which were far too lightly armed to stand in the line of battle. Their primary purpose was to act as scouts and relay signals, being too small even to tow damaged ships out of action. Without extensive research little has been discovered about these two vessels.

FURET

Simply named after a ferret, *Furet* was a traditional brig, a two masted vessel carrying square sails on her fore and main masts. Armed with eighteen long 8 pounder guns on her open upper deck *Furet* could deliver a single broadside weight of just 72 pounds. It is surprising that *Furet* was not armed with 12 pounder carronades on slides, for by this date this weapon had become more popular in the smaller classes; being proportionately lighter than a long gun, they could fire a heavier projectile. Having such guns would have increased *Furet's* broadside weight by 50 per cent. *Furet* carried a complement of 130 men.

SERVICE HISTORY

Launched in 1801, the story of *Furet* starts in Toulon in late 1804. Under the command of Lieutenant de Vaisseau Pierre Antoine Toussaint Dumay, she was ordered to join Villeneuve's fleet preparing to support Napoleon's invasion plan. From this time *Furet's* story follows Villeneuve's other ships which attempted to get out of Toulon 17 January 1805 and finally sailed for the West Indies on 29 March. She was also present at Calder's action 22 July and arrived at Cadiz on 20 August.

TRAFALGAR

On the morning of the battle *Furet* was stationed well to leeward with *San Agustin* (74) and *Héros* (74) on her larboard side and remained a respectable distance to leeward for the entirety of the battle. She then returned to Cadiz where she remained until 1806.

1806: Stored with five months' provisions, *Furet* sailed from Cadiz on 26 February with Commodore La Marre La Meillerie's squadron of frigates comprising *Hermione*, *Hortense*, *Rhin*, and *Thémis*. That evening the five vessels were sighted at 9.15 p.m. by the frigate *Hydra* (38) and brig-sloop *Moselle* (18). Bearing up onto a parallel course, for the next two days the two British ships shadowed the French squadron. Recording events, the log of *Hydra* dated 26 February states that the wind was SE by E and the ship was sailing NW by W making between 8 and 9 knots but sometimes slowing to four. A signal recorded was No. 2161 to *Moselle*. The log then states: 'At 1 [a.m.] Strong Breezes At 4 wore ship *Moselle* in Company At 8 D°. W[r]. at 9.15 Cadiz light House &c 4 miles observed 4 Frigates and a Brig coming out of Cadiz, made all sail, *Moselle* in Company. Beat to quarters and continued to fire signal Guns and rockets'.[1] Once it had been established that Commodore La Marre La Meillerie's vessels were continuing to proceed westwards at 11 p.m. Captain George Mundy, commanding *Hydra*, sent *Moselle* away to inform the main body of Collingwood's blockading fleet standing over the horizon. Maintaining the chase on his own Mundy then wrote 'at 12 d°. W^r. lost sight of the *Moselle*'. Next day, 27 February, *Hydra*'s log records the wind direction as W by W, ship's course NNE doing 8 knots. At 7 *Hydra* 'Exchanged No.s with HM Ship *Thunderer*'. Captain Mundy then wrote: 'Fresh gales and squally made and short^d Sail occasy to keep sight of the strangers, and came Sin--d [word illegible] to fire Signal Gins & rockets also fired several shot at the sternmost vessel of the Chases, at 2.10 lost sight of the frigates and made all sail in chase of the Brig'. *Furet* had virtually been abandoned by her consorts and was soon overhauled by *Hydra*. Captain Mundy then wrote: 'at 4.10 she fired her Broadside and surrendered, 4.20 took possession of *Furet* French Man of war Brig mounting 18 guns, employed in taking the prisoners out'.[2] From *Hydra*'s log it appears that Lieutenant Dumay fired his guns 'pour l'honneur du pavillon' [for the honour of the flag] before hauling down his colours. While Mundy's log statement complies with that given by the historian James, it conflicts with the narrative given by Clowes who wrongly implies that *Hydra* fired the broadside, causing *Furet* to strike.[3] In the meantime *Hermione*, *Hortense*, *Rhin* and *Thémis* made good their escape to Bordeaux.

FATE

Although *Furet* was captured as *Hydra*'s prize, the records do not indicate what happened to her. If she was entered into the Royal Navy then her name was certainly changed but this is not evident within the Progress Books. Alternatively she may have been sold outright as a prize.

ARGUS

Argus, like *Furet*, was a traditional brig. She was armed with sixteen long 8 pounder guns on her open upper deck which gave her a single broadside weight of just 64 pounds. Like *Furet* it seems quite surprising that *Argus* had not been re-armed with 12 pounder carronades on slides; this would have increased her broadside weight by 25 per cent. Launched in 1799, her complement would have been about 110 men.

SERVICE HISTORY

1805: Under the command of Lieutenant de Vaisseau Talliard, *Argus* does not appear to have joined Villeneuve's combined fleet until it had arrived off Cadiz on 8 April. Also joining Villeneuve at this rendezvous were the French seventy-four *Aigle* and the corvette *Torche*, together with the Spanish ships *Argonauta* (80), *Firme* (74), *Terrible* (74), *América* (64), *España* (64) and the frigate *Santa Magdalena*. In command of the Spanish squadron was Admiral Don Federico Gravina. *Argus* then sailed with Villeneuve's combined fleet for the West Indies, arriving at Martinique on 14 May. On 29 May *Argus* was detached with a squadron under Commodore Cosmao-Kerjulien to attack Diamond Rock. Besides *Argus* this flotilla comprised *Berwick* (74), *Pluton* (74), *Sirène* (36), *Fine*, armed schooner and eleven gunboats. The attack on the Diamond Rock, which began on 31 May, was over by 2 June, after which *Argus* returned to join the fleet off Guadeloupe.[4] From this point it appears that the story of *Argus* follows the same line as Villeneuve's other ships although she does not appear to have been present at Calder's action on 22 July and because of this it is not clear when she actually got into Cadiz. Apart from noting that *Argus* was stationed to leeward of *Algésiras* (74) at the beginning of the battle there is else to say about her part at Trafalgar other than she returned intact to Cadiz afterwards.

1807: It appears that sometime after Trafalgar *Argus* sailed from Cadiz, for, on 27 January she is sighted in company with *Favourite* (18) off the Guiana coast by the British frigate *Jason* (32), commanded by Captain Thomas Cochrane. Her consort *Favourite* was a British man-of-war captured off the Canaries a year previously. Cochrane immediately brought *Favourite* to action and compelled her to strike but while he was transferring prisoners into *Jason*, *Argus* managed to escape. Little more is known about *Argus*.[5]

NOTES TO PART 2: CHAPTER 4

[1] TNA: PRO, ADM 51/1560/6.
[2] *Ibid*.
[3] James, 4, pp. 213–214; Clowes, 5, pp. 197–198.
[4] Clowes, 5, pp. 106–107.
[5] Clowes, 5, p. 397.

PART 3
THE SPANISH FLEET

The Spanish fleet under the command of Admiral Federico Carlos Gravina present at the battle of Trafalgar comprised 15 line of battle ships carrying between 136 and 64 guns. In the Spanish navy a ship of the line was a *navio*. The number of Spanish ships present at the battle of Trafalgar could have been greater but the 74 gun ships *Firma* and *San Rafael* had been captured by Admiral Calder's squadron on 22 July, while *España* (74) and *America* (74) which had been damaged during that action had gone into dock at Vigo for repair. The 64 gun *San Fulgencio*, frigate *Flora* (34) and corvettes *Mercurio* and *Indagora* which had sailed with Villeneuve's combined fleet from Ferrol in August 1805 had all been redeployed; therefore there were no frigates or other smaller Spanish vessels at Trafalgar. Unlike the British and French fleets which contained some prize vessels, all of Gravina's ships were Spanish built. The Spanish part of Villeneuve's combined fleet comprised the following ships, flag officers and commanders.

Ship's Name	Rate or Type	Guns	Flag Officer and/or Commander
Santísima Trinidad	1st	136	Admiral B Hidalgo de Cisneros Captain Francisco Javier Uriarte
Principe de Asturias	1st	112	Admiral Don Federico Gravina Rear-Admiral Don A Escaño
Santa Ana	1st	112	Vice-Admiral Don Ignacious M de Alava Captain Don Juan Gardoqui
Rayo	1st	100	Captain Don Enrique McDonel
Neptuno	3rd	80	Captain Don H Cayetano Valdès
Argonauta	3rd	74	Captain Don A Parejo
Bahama	3rd	74	Commodore Don D A Gallano
Monarca	3rd	74	Captain T Argumosa
Montañez	3rd	74	Captain Don J Alcedo
San Agustin	3rd	74	Captain Don F X Cagigal
San Francisco de Asis	3rd	74	Captain Don Luis de Florès
San Ildefonso	3rd	74	Commodore Don Jose de Varga
San Juan Nepomuceno	3rd	74	Commodore Don Cosmé Churruca
San Justo	3rd	74	Captain Don M Gaston
San Leandro	3rd	64	Captain Don Jose Quevado

Of the 15 Spanish ships, eight were designed by the prominent Spanish designer Romero y Landa and three by Jorge Juan. That the newer ships

THE SPANISH FLEET AT TRAFALGAR

Ship's Name	Rate or type	Guns	Designer	Dockyard Built	Date Launched	Age in 1805
Nuestra Señora de Santísima Trinidad	1st	136	Mateo Mullàn	Havana	1769	36
Principe de Asturias	1st	112	Romero y Landa	Ferrol	1784	21
Santa Ana	1st	112	Romero y Landa	Ferrol	1784	21
Rayo (San Padro)	1st	100	Pedro de Torres	Havana	1749	56
Neptuno	3rd	80	Romero y Landa	Ferrol	1795	10
Argonauta	3rd	80/84	Romero y Landa	Ferrol	1798	7
Bahama	3rd	74	Francisco Guatier	Cartagena	1784	21
Monarca	3rd	74	Romero y Landa	Ferrol	1794	11
Montañez	3rd	74/80	Romero y Landa	Ferrol	1794	11
San Agustin	3rd	74/80	Jorge Juan	Guarnizo	1768	37
San Francisco de Asis	3rd	74	Jorge Juan	Guarnizo	1767	38
San Ildefonso	3rd	74	Romero y Landa	Cartagena	1785	20
San Juan Nepomuceno	3rd	74	Jorge Juan	Guarnizo	1766	39
San Justo	3rd	74	Francisco Guatier	Cartagena	1779	26
San Leandro	3rd	64	Romero y Landa	Ferrol	1794	11

THE 15 SPANISH LINE OF BATTLE SHIPS

Gun Type & Calibre	No. Of Guns	Average weight per Gun in cwt (cwt = 112 lbs)	Total weight in cwt (C = A x B)	Total weight in Tons (D = C divided by 20)	Total Weight in Tonnes (E = D x 1.016)
(Weight of shot)	A	B	C	D	E
36 pounder carriage gun	124	60	7,440.0	372.0	378.0
32 pounder carriage gun	10	54	540.0	27.0	27.4
24 pounder carriage gun	532	50	26,600.0	1,330.0	1,351.3
18 pounder carriage gun	274	42	11,508.0	575.4	584.6
12 pounder carriage gun	64	31	1,984.0	99.2	100.8
8 pounder carriage gun	242	22	5,324.0	266.2	270.5
4 pounder carriage gun	6	12	72.0	3.6	3.7
24 pounder howitzer	6	12	72.0	3.6	3.7
4 pounder howitzer	8	4	32.0	1.6	1.6
48 pounder carronade	24	24	576.0	28.8	29.3
32 pounder carronade	2	17.25	34.5	1.7	1.8
24 pounder carronade	6	12.25	73.5	3.7	3.8
18 pounder carronade	216	9	1,944.0	97.2	98.8
4 pounder stone mortar	5	5	20.0	1.0	1.1
TOTAL	1,519	-	-	2811.0	2856.4

were built to Landa's designs meant that the Spanish ships, like the French, were far more standardised in their construction than the British and this uniformity was an advantage when refitting and repairing. Built in the *artilleros reales* (royal dockyards), seven were built in Ferrol, three in Guarnizo (Santander), three in Cartagena; the remaining two, *Santísima Trinidad* (136) and *Rayo* (100) were built in Havana. These two 'foreign built' ships were also the oldest Spanish ships present. *Rayo* was in fact the oldest ship at Trafalgar; launched in 1749, she had been in service for 56 years. Like the British fleet many of the other Spanish *navios* had served many years, the youngest vessel being *Argonauta* (74), launched in 1798.

Of the nine ships captured during the battle of Trafalgar only two vessels

SPANISH FLEET: INDIVIDUAL SHIP FATES

Ship's Name	Initial Fate	Final Fate
Nuestra Señora de Santísima Trinidad	Captured 21 October 1805	Foundered 23 Oct 1805
Principe de Asturias	Broken up 1814	
Santa Ana	Captured 21 October	Recaptured 23 October 1805 & Broken up 1816
Rayo (San Padro)	Foundered 23 Oct 1805	
Argonauta	Captured and Scuttled	
Montañez	Broken up 1810	
Neptuno	Captured 21 October	Recaptured & Foundered 23 Oct. 1805
San Agustin	Captured 21 October 1805	later Burnt
Bahama	Captured, served as a Prison Ship	Broken up 1814
Monarca	Foundered in storm October 1805	
San Francisco de Asis	Captured 21 October	Recaptured & Foundered 23 Oct. 1805
San Ildefonso	Captured 21 Oct. 1805	Served as Victualling Ship Broken up 1816
San Juan Nepomuceno	Captured 21 Oct. 1805 and remained at Gibraltar	Broken up 1814
San Justo	Disposed of 1828	
San Leandro	Broken up 1813	

were taken to England as prizes, *Bahama* and *San Ildefonso*. A third prize, *San Juan Nepomuceno*, remained hulked at Gibraltar due to her damaged condition. Of the other six vessels three were recaptured and taken into Cadiz, the remainder being destroyed in the storm after Trafalgar. The six Spanish ships that escaped from Trafalgar continued in active service until disposed of eventually.

The ordnance carried in the entire Spanish fleet of 15 ships amounted to 1,519 guns comprising 1,252 carriage guns, 14 howitzers and 248 carronades. This quantity of ordnance weighed 2,811 tons (8,856.4 tonnes) in total.

PART 3: CHAPTER 1
THE SPANISH FIRST RATE SHIPS

The 136 gun ship SANTÍSIMA TRINIDAD

Nuestra Señora de la Santísima Trinidad, meaning 'Our Lady of the Most Holy Trinity', was the seventh ship to bear this name in the Spanish Royal Navy. The first *Santísima Trinidad* served with the great Armada sent by Philip II to invade England in 1588. The Trafalgar *Santísima Trinidad* was initially built as a three decked 120 gun ship designed by Matthew Mullen, although it has been suggested that her design could be attributed to Pedro de Acosta. Irish by birth, Mullen had migrated to Spain from England with his son Ignatius in 1750 to take up a position in La Carraca dockyard at Cadiz. Mullen had been hired along with many others to improve Spanish ship design. When Mullen married a Spanish noblewoman in 1754 they modified their names to Mateo and Ignacio Mullàn. Ignacio soon equalled his father as a ship designer and constructor. On 11 November 1766 Mullàn received orders to supervise ship construction in the Royal Arsenal of Havana and before his departure in April the following year he submitted his plans for building a large 112 gun ship. Once *San Luis* (80) had been launched at Havana on 30 September 1767 work on Mullàn's ship began but he was never to see his concept materialise. Dying of the 'black vomit'[1] on 25 November 1767, the design and construction of this great and yet unnamed ship was transferred to Ignacio. Mullàn's ship was named *Nuestra Señora de la Santísima Trinidad* (hereafter *Santísima Trinidad*) by royal proclamation on 12 March 1768. Built at a cost of 140,000 pesetas (40,000 pesos), the *Santísima Trinidad* was launched at 11.30 a.m. on 3 March 1769.[2]

Measuring almost 213.66 Burgos feet on the waterline and about 57.75 Burgos feet in breadth, some 360,000 cubic feet of timber was consumed in her construction. At 50 cubic feet per load, or tree, this volume of timber equates to 7,200 trees taken from about 120 acres of land. Like all Spanish ships built in Havana, the *Santísima Trinidad* was built with Cuban mahogany and cedar. Timber for her masts and spars was imported from the Baltic as the more local supply of pine from the forests of Mexico had already been depleted.

SERVICE CAREER

1769: *Santísima Trinidad* was launched as a 120 gun ship at the Artillero Real (royal dockyard), Havana at 11.30 a.m. on 3 March and fitted for sea service. She received a royal order on 30 March to sail for El Ferrol. Command of the ship was appointed to Captain Joaquín de Marguna Echezarreta who took up his post on 1 December. Initially armed with just thirty-two 24 pounders and fourteen 12 pounders the ship was given a crew of 960 men.[3]

1770: Ready for sea, *Santísima Trinidad* sailed from Havana for Ferrol on 19 February in company with the *San Francisco de Paula*, and anchored off Vigo on 12 April. After repairing some damage to her fore and mizzen yards she sailed again on 9 May and entered Ferrol six days later. Between 21 July and 9 August *Santísima Trinidad* underwent sea trials in company with the *Guerrero* and *Santo Domingo*. While on trials she was armed with thirty 24 pounders on her lower gun deck, thirty-two 24 pounders on her middle gun deck, thirty-two 12 pounders on her upper gun deck, two 8 pounders and sixteen 6 pounders on her quarter deck and four three pounder stone mortars on her forecastle. This gave her a single broadside weight of 998 pounds. It was during these trials that serious concerns were raised about her stability, for although she was carrying some 39,500 quintals (1,816 tonnes) of ballast, the ship listed so badly that she could not use her lower deck gun battery in calm water. After this the ship was then laid up in ordinary.[4]

SPECIFICATIONS: *SANTÍSIMA TRINIDAD*

Rate	1st	Length on the range of the gun deck	100 cubits (57.47 m)	Complement	960 (1110)
Guns	120 (136)	Length of keel for tonnage	85 cubits 6 ins (49 m)	Ordnance - lower gun deck	30 x 36 pounders (34 x 36 pounders)
Class	Santísima Trinidad	Extreme breadth	27 cubits (15.52 m)	Ordnance - middle gun deck	32 x 24 pounders (34 x 24 pounders)
Designer	Mateo Mullàn	Depth in hold	13 cubits 12 ins (7.76 m)	Ordnance - upper gun deck	32 x 12 pounders (34 x 18 pounders)
Builder	Artillero Real (Royal Dockyard)	Tons burthen	4920 tons (7.443.7 cubic metres)	Ordnance - quarter deck	22 x 8 pounders (18 x 8 pounders)
		Draught afore	12 cubits 6 ins (7.2 m)	Ordnance - waist	6 x 4 pounders
Dockyard	Havana	Draught abaft	13 cubits (7.47 m)	Ordnance - forecastle	(10 x 24 pounder carronades)
Date ordered	23 October 1767	Floor of the hold	13 cubits 12 ins (7.76 m)	Single broadside weight	1204 lbs (1530 lbs)
Date keel laid	October 1767	Dead works with floor of the hold	12 inches	Fate	Captured at the battle of Trafalgar and sank in the storm afterwards 23 October 1805
Date launched	3 March 1769	Span between each port from stem to stern	1 cubit 17 ins (0.98 m)		

Notes: The dimensions and ordnance details cover her initial build.
The 22 x 8 pounders listed also served the forecastle albeit to what proportion is unclear.
Her Trafalgar complement of men and armament are given in enclosed brackets.
Dimensions given as a proportion of a cubit.

Source: *Modelos de Arsenal del Museo Naval*, pp. 306-307.

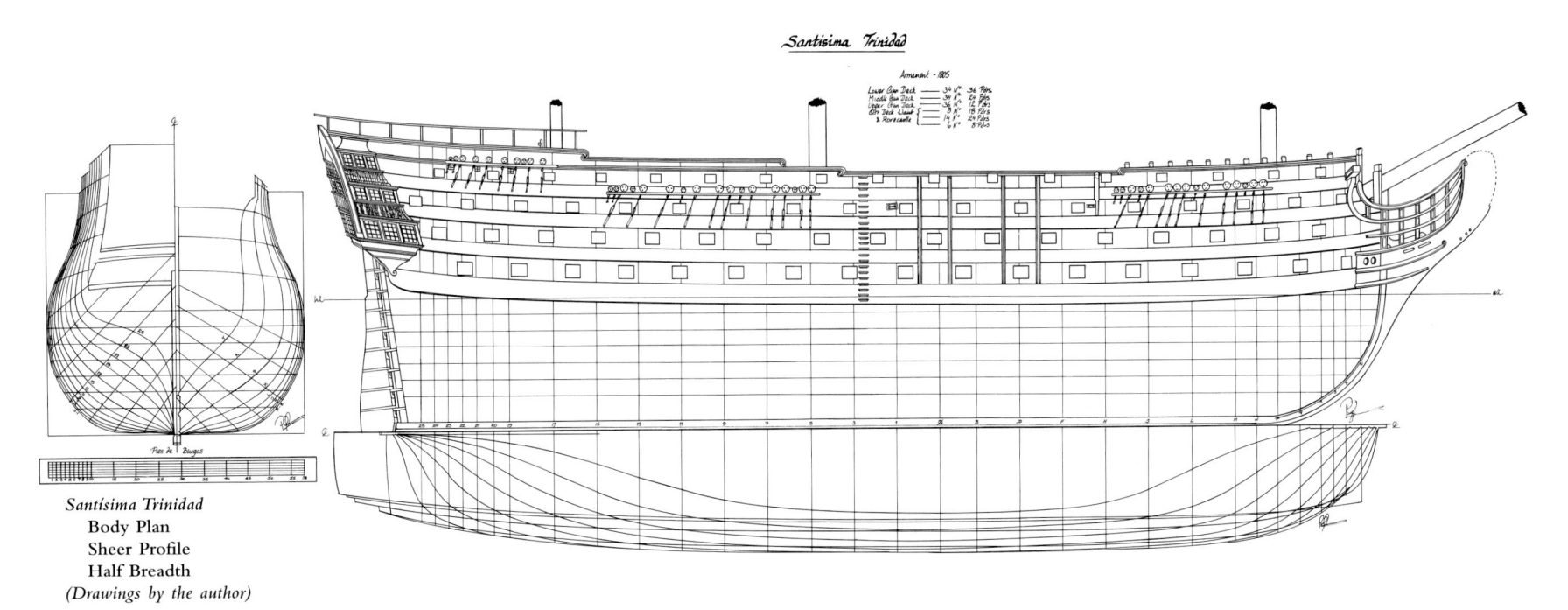

Santísima Trinidad
Body Plan
Sheer Profile
Half Breadth
(Drawings by the author)

1771: On 14 March *Santísima Trinidad* was taken into dock at El Ferrol to attempt to eliminate her stability problems. Besides fitting a deep false keel, the works undertaken to lower her centre of gravity and her metacentric height to improve her righting moment comprised lowering her deck housing and lowering the height of her decks. Besides this her stern post, rudder and various other items were modified including altering the steeve (angle) of her bowsprit.

1778: Placed in commission under the command of Captain Fernadoz Daoíz, *Santísima Trinidad* went to sea where on 7 August Daoíz reported that she still continued to have stability problems.[5]

1779: On 22 June Spain declared war on Britain and entered the American War of Independence. Still under the command of Captain Daoíz, *Santísima Trinidad* sailed from Cadiz as the flagship of Lieutenant-General Don Luis de Córdoba, deployed as part of the French invasion fleet commanded by Admiral Comte d'Orvilliers. As flagship of the observation squadron she had in company sixteen line of battle ships and two frigates. When the invasion plan was dissolved *Santísima Trinidad* then served as part of the Spanish fleet blockading Gibraltar.[6]

1780: Still flying the flag of Córdoba, *Santísima Trinidad* was involved in a number of sorties between 9 and 18 July. On 31 July she took up station off Cape St Vincent. While on this deployment she participated in the capture of a British convoy transporting troops and supplies to both Bombay and Jamaica on 9 August.[7]

1781: Córdoba took *Santísima Trinidad* to sea again on 23 July and joined forces with the French fleet of 20 sail under Admiral the Comte de Guichen. Now comprising over 50 warships, the intention of this combined fleet was to recapture Minorca. Over the next few months *Santísima Trinidad* was involved in the capture of a British convoy off Sisargas and supported the blockade of Gibraltar from Algeciras. Returning to Cadiz on 23 September, *Santísima Trinidad* went into dock on 5 October to have her hull careened and her bottom coppered in compliance with recent legislation authorised by the Spanish navy.[8]

1782: After *Santísima Trinidad* was undocked on 23 April she rejoined the combined Franco-Spanish fleet and took part in the battle against Admiral Lord Howe's fleet off Cape Spartel on 20 October. During this action the ship suffered one man killed and four wounded.[9]

1783: After peace had been signed on 23 April *Santísima Trinidad* returned to Cadiz where she was withdrawn from service although she remained

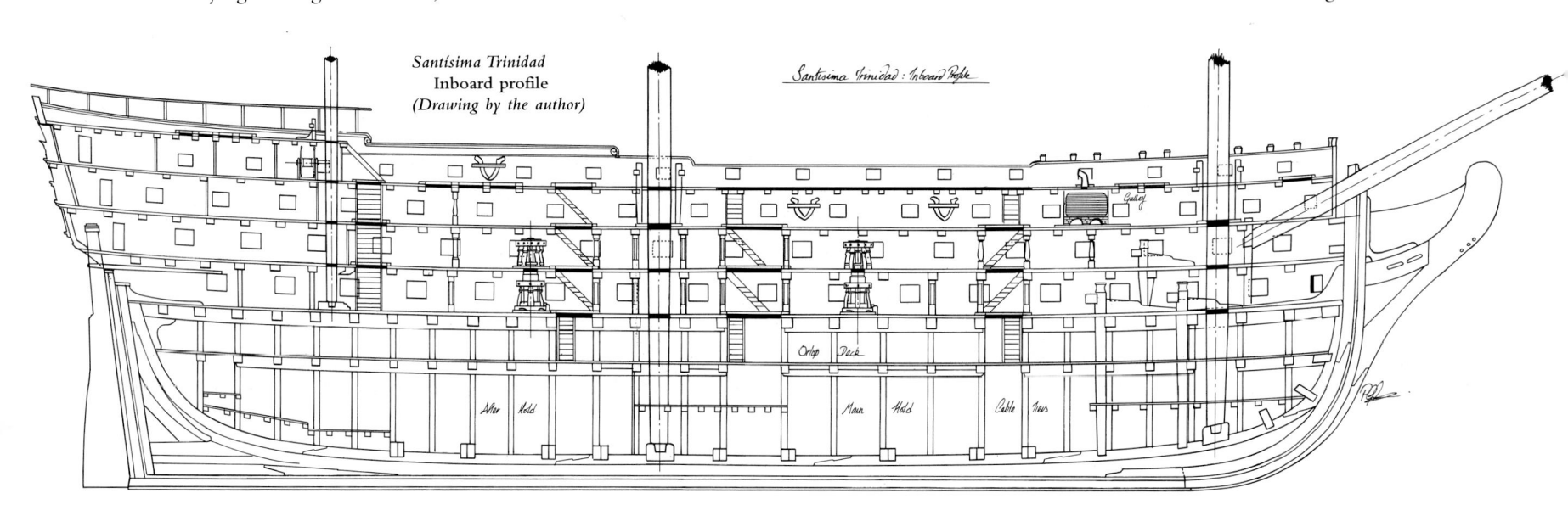

Santísima Trinidad
Inboard profile
(Drawing by the author)

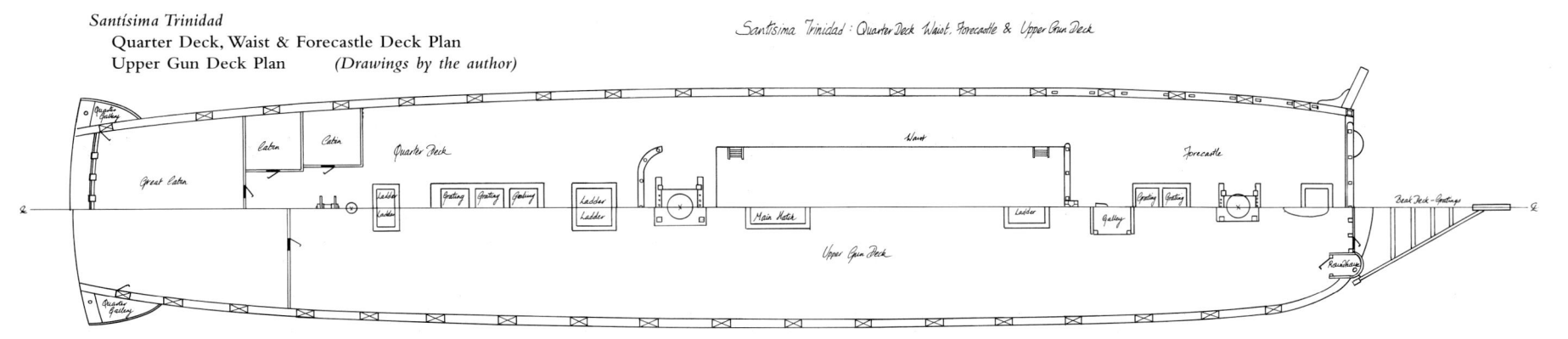

Santísima Trinidad
Quarter Deck, Waist & Forecastle Deck Plan
Upper Gun Deck Plan   *(Drawings by the author)*

under the command of Brigadier Pedro Autrán.[10]

1796: Under Brigadier Rafael Orozco's command and flying the flag of Admiral Juan de Lángara, *Santísima Trinidad* sailed from Cadiz with a squadron for the Mediterranean, cruising off Corsica and Italy. Going into Toulon in November, she sailed again in October, escorting Rear-Admiral Villeneuve's ships bound for Brest. Having cleared the convoy, *Santísima Trinidad* went into Cartagena on 20 December. Command of the Spanish squadron was now superseded by Lieutenant-General (Admiral) Don José de Córdoba y Ramos who hoisted his flag in the *Santísima Trinidad*, although Orozco still held command of the ship.[11]

1797: Receiving orders to sail for Cadiz, Córdoba put to sea on 1 February with his fleet, comprising 27 ships of the line, twelve frigates, a brigantine and some smaller vessels. After re-provisioning at Cadiz Córdoba's fleet was to sail for Brest where it would join forces with the Dutch and French squadrons already assembled to invade England. Besides *Santísima Trinidad* the other ships that had sailed from Cartagena with Córdoba on 1 February which would later fight at Trafalgar were *Principe de Asturias* (112), *Neptuno* (80), *Bahama* (74), and *San Ildefonso* (74). The Spanish fleet fell in with Admiral Sir John Jervis's squadron of 25 ships off Cape St Vincent on 14 February. In the ensuing battle *Santísima Trinidad* was simultaneously engaged under concentrated fire from the 74 gun ships *Blenheim, Excellent, Irresistible* and *Orion*. Despite her greater size and firepower *Santísima Trinidad* would have struck her colours had it not been for the intervention of Rear-Admiral Cisneros who arrived in time to give support and draw off British fire. Under fire for nearly five hours, *Santísima Trinidad* sustained heavy damage, she was totally dismasted and her larboard side had been virtually destroyed. Moreover she had been hulled by 60 round shot below the waterline causing her to take in three feet of water per hour. Her casualties amounted to 69 dead and 407 wounded. While Córdoba transferred his flag into the frigate *Diana*, *Santísima Trinidad* under jury masts was partially escorted by the frigate *Mercedes* towards Cadiz. After losing contact with *Mercedes* the ship was sighted by another British squadron en route. To avoid action, Captain Orozco hoisted British colours above the Spanish so the patrolling ships would think she had British prisoners on board. The subterfuge worked and the ship was able to get into Zafi, Morocco, where she remained until making sail again on 28 February. That night *Santísima Trinidad* was attacked by the frigate *Terpsichore* which was driven off by her four 24 and 36 pounder stern chase guns. She received more damage and suffered one man killed and five wounded. *Santísima Trinidad* finally reached Cadiz on 3 March.[12] Once in port Admiral José de Mazarredo, captain-general of Cadiz, questioned *Santísima Trinidad*'s ability in battle against smaller ships. Having also found her unseaworthy, Mazarredo proposed that *Santísima Trinidad* be beached at Cadiz as a defensive gun platform. Mazarredo's recommendations were however overruled and the great ship was refitted and laid up until 1804.[13]

1799: Because she had been extensively damaged during the battle of St. Vincent, *Santísima Trinidad* had to go into dock in February for extensive repairs and was thoroughly careened. While in dock she was she was modified by extending her planking between the quarter deck and forecastle to mount more guns and consequently became the world's only four-decked fighting ship, although this alteration further compromised her sailing quality and handiness. Already a colossal three-decked ship of 120 guns with a broadside weight of 1,204 pounds when built, she now had 16 additional gun ports. When rearmed on 12 February this allowed her to mount six 4 pounder carriage guns in her waist and ten 24 pounder carronades on her forecastle. This increased her a total broadside weight of fire by 132 pounds to 1,530 pounds. In all her firepower was 25 per cent greater than Nelson's *Victory*.

Santísima Trinidad's dimensions at this time were recorded as follows:

Length on the range of the gun deck	220 ft 6 ins (63.36 m)
Length of keel for tonnage	188 ft (54.02 m)
Extreme breadth	58 ft 0 ins (16.67 m)
Depth in hold	28 ft 9 ins (8.26 m)
Floor of the hold	29 ft 10 ins (8.57 m)
Displacement	2,475 tons (3,758 cubic metres)
Ballast	20,000 quintals
Draught afore	27 ft 0 ins (7.76 m)
Draught abaft	29 ft 7 ins (8.5 m)
Complement (including servants)	1096
Ordnance - lower gun deck	32 x 36 pounders
Ordnance - third gun deck	34 x 24 pounders
Ordnance - second gun deck	36 x 12 pounders
Ordnance - quarter deck	18 x 8 pounders
Ordnance - waist	4 x 4 pounder howitzers
Ordnance - forecastle	10 x 24 pounder howitzers
Single broadside weight	1300 pounds

Source: *Modelos de Arsenal del Museo Naval*, pp. 307-308
Note: Clowes lists *Santísima Trinidad* as being armed with 130 guns which implies that the ship did not have the six 4 pounder carriage guns mounted in her waist until after 1797; therefore her broadside weight would have been marginally less than 1,530 pounds at this time.[14]

1804: When Spain allied herself to France and entered the war against Britain, Napoleon virtually doubled the size of his operational navy to support his plan to invade England. Fitted for sea *Santísima Trinidad* was placed in commission under the command of Don Francisco Javier de Uriarte y Borja.

1805: Lying in Cadiz harbour ready to sail with Villeneuve's combined fleet, *Santísima Trinidad* clearly stood out from her consorts. Besides having four gun decks, her sides were painted, according to Lieutenant William Lovell serving on British *Neptune* (98) at Trafalgar, 'with four distinct lines of red, with a white ribbon between them'. After hoisting the flag of Rear-Admiral Báltasar Hidalgo de Cisneros, *Santísima Trinidad* sailed from Cadiz with the combined fleet on 19 October, Captain Uriarte in command.

Only *Santa Ana* (112) with her completely black hull could equal her majestic appearance.[15]

TRAFALGAR

After Villeneuve manœuvred his fleet at about 8 a.m. *Santísima Trinidad*, lying in the centre of the fleet, found herself tenth in line ahead; before her was the 74 gun *Héros*, astern Vice-Admiral Villeneuve's flagship *Bucentaure* (80). When battle opened around noon *Santísima Trinidad*'s gunners directed their fire upon Nelson's *Victory* (100) as he approached. Uriarte then luffed, letting *Santísima Trinidad* fall off the wind in order to fall back and close the space between her and *Bucentaure*, thereby protecting Villeneuve, all the while concentrating the fire from her 68 larboard guns into *Victory*. As *Victory* and successive ships passed within range and fired into *Santísima Trinidad*, Uriarte's ship began to suffer from the onslaught. At about 1.45 p.m. the British *Neptune* (98) drew up and commenced firing her larboard battery into *Santísima Trinidad*'s starboard side, causing considerable damage and casualties. These devastating broadsides were soon joined by those of *Leviathan* (74) and *Conqueror* (74), leaving her completely dismasted and covered in the debris of her fallen spars, rigging and rent sails. During the interim *Santísima Trinidad* was boarded by Lieutenant John Smith from *Africa* (64) who, finding that she had not yet struck her colours, discreetly removed himself from the ship before being noticed. Despite the fact that few men were alive on her upper decks and poop and the ship was in an appalling condition, *Santísima Trinidad* continued to fight and it was not until about 5.30 p.m. that Uriarte eventually struck her colours. *Prince* (98) took possession but the British seamen found it difficult to get her under tow. Matters were further complicated by the fact that *Santísima Trinidad* had five feet of water in her hold, adding considerable dead weight. Casualties within *Santísima Trinidad* were high: 216 dead and 116 wounded. When Cisneros gave his report to Gravina on 31 October he placed the dead at 300, his figures based on the number of dead cast overboard after the battle and successive days. Five officers had been killed. Besides Cisneros and Uriate, officers wounded included the second officer Ignacios de Olaeta; the third officer José Sartorio and a further 13 officers. A final report, submitted by Antonio de Escaños to the Principe de la Paz, stated 205 dead and 103 wounded.[16]

Taken in tow by *Prince* every effort was made to keep *Santísima Trinidad* afloat, the pumps being manned continuously. However, the storm finally claimed the great Spanish ship. By midday on the 24 October Vice-Admiral Collingwood gave orders for *Santísima Trinidad* and other prize ships be scuttled. John Edwards, Third Lieutenant in *Prince* feared, as their tow rope had parted twice, that they would not weather the coast. It was 'impossible to describe the horrors the morning presented, nothing but distress signals flying in every direction guns firing, and so many large ships driving on shore'. Every endeavour was made to remove her prisoners while her wounded were lowered with ropes from the stern and quarter galleries into the waiting boats sent from *Neptune*, *Prince* and *Ajax*. Regarding the wounded Edwards stated that:

> We had to tie the poor mangled wretches round their waists, or where we could, and lower them into a tumbling boat, some without arms, others no legs, and lacerated all over in the most dreadful manner. About ten o'clock we had got all out, to about thirty-three or four, which we believe it was impossible to remove without instant death. The water was now at the pilot deck, the weather dark and boisterous, and taking in tons at every roll, when we quitted her, and supposed this superb ship could not remain afloat longer thatnten minutes.

A seaman from *Revenge* stated that Spanish seamen who could not be removed 'displayed their bags of dollars and doubloons' as a reward for their deliverance, 'but it was not within our power to rescue them'. One lieutenant in the last boat from *Ajax* stated that 'Everything alive was taken out down to the ship's cat', which, according to his narrative, had 'ran out on the muzzle of one of the lower deck guns and by a plaintive mew seemed to beg for assistance; the boat returned and took her in'. Midshipman Badcock from *Neptune* recorded:

> I was sent on board the *Santísima Trinidada* a few days after the action to assist in getting out the wounded men previous to destroying her. She was a magnificent ship, and ought to be in Portsmouth Harbour. Her top-sides it is true were perfectly riddled by our firing, and she has, if I recollect right, 550 killed and wounded, but from the lower part of the sills of the lower-deck ports to the water's edge, few Shots of consequence had hurt her between wind and water, and those were all plugged up. She was built of cedar, and would have lasted for ages, a glorious trophy of the battle, but 'sink, burn and destroy' was the order of the day, and after a great deal of trouble, scuttling her in many places, hauling up her lower-deck ports - that when she rolled a heavy sea might fill her decks - she did at last unwillingly go to the bottom.

Describing her last moments Captain Brenton recalled: 'Night came on - the swell ran high - three lower-deck ports on each side were open, and in a few minutes the tremendous ruins of the largest ship in the world were buried in the deep. The waves passed over her, she gave a lurch, and went down', 26 miles south of Cadiz.[17]

The 112 gun ship **PRINCIPE DE ASTURIAS**

Based on the lines of the *Santa Ana* of 1784, the 1st rate 112 gun *Principe de Asturias* was designed by José Joaquín Romero y Fernàndez de Landa, hereafter referred to as Romero Landa. Her name was the Spanish equivalent of the Prince of Wales. Built at Havana with some 335,000 cubic feet of Cuban mahogany and cedar equating to approximately 6,700 trees taken from 112 acres of woodland, *Principe de Asturias* was launched in 1794. Once fitted out the ship was armed with thirty 32 pounders on her lower gun deck, thirty-two 24 pounders on her middle gun deck, thirty 12 pounders on her upper gun deck and eighteen 8 pounders and two 24 pounder carronades on her quarter deck and forecastle. *Principe de Asturias* delivered a single broadside weight of 1,200 pounds. Before Trafalgar her quarter deck was re-armed with fourteen 48 pounder carronades and her forecastle with six 24 pounder carronades, increasing her broadside to 1,512 pounds. It is also probable that like her counterparts she had four 4 pounder howitzers mounted on her poop at Trafalgar. The sister ships of *Principe de Asturias*, also built to the lines of *Santa Ana*, were *Mexicano* (1786), *Salvador del Mundo* (1787), *Real Carlos* (1787), *San Hermenegildo* (1789) and *Reina Luisa* (1791).[18]

SERVICE HISTORY

1794: Once fitted out, armed and manned, *Principe de Asturias* sailed for Spain where she was eventually deployed with Spain's Mediterranean squadron based at Cartagena until Spain allied herself to revolutionary France.

1797: Deployed with the fleet of Lieutenant-General (Admiral) Don José de Córdoba y Ramos who hoisted his flag in *Santísima Trinidad*, *Principe de Asturias* put to sea from Cartagena on 1 February with 27 ships of the line,

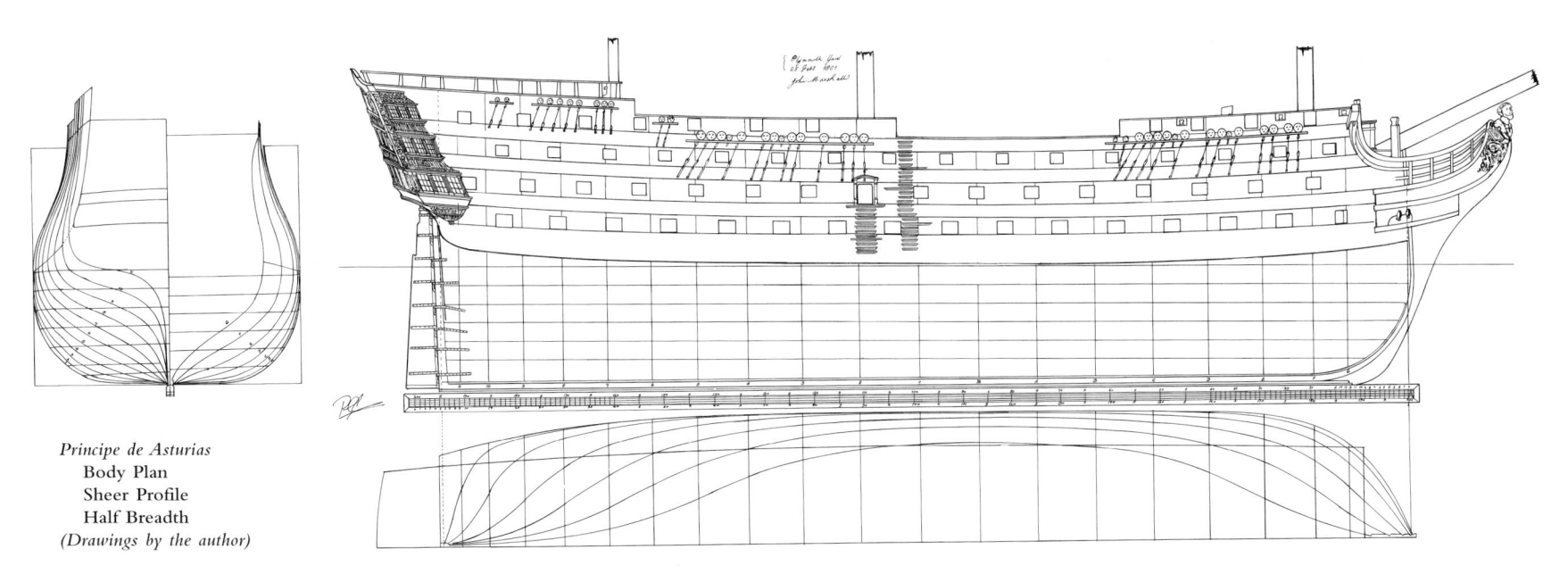

THE 112 GUN SHIP *PRINCIPE DE ASTURIAS*

Principe de Asturias
Body Plan
Sheer Profile
Half Breadth
(Drawings by the author)

twelve frigates, a brigantine and some smaller vessels. After re-provisioning at Cadiz *Principe de Asturias* was to sail for Brest with Córdoba's fleet to join forces with the Dutch and French squadrons already assembled to invade England. Besides *Principe de Asturias* and *Santísima Trinidad* the other ships that had sailed from Cartagena with Córdoba on 1 February later to fight at Trafalgar were *Neptuno* (80), *Bahama* (74), and *San Ildefonso* (74). The Spanish fleet fell in with Admiral Sir John Jervis's squadron of 25 ships off Cape St Vincent on 14 February. Like a number of ships within the Spanish fleet *Principe de Asturias* did not get into close action and managed to get into Cadiz afterwards without suffering too much damage or casualties.[19]

After this *Principe de Asturias* remained in harbour.

1805: Placed under the command of Commodore Rafael de Hore and hurriedly refitted for sea service, *Principe de Asturias* joined Villeneuve's fleet and sailed from Ferrol on 9 August with many of the other Spanish ships for Cadiz. On arrival on 20 August *Principe de Asturias* was appointed flagship for Admiral Don Federico Gravina who was to command Villeneuve's observation squadron; the ship was also directed to carry the flag of Rear-Admiral Don Antonio Escaño. Commodore Hore survived the forthcoming battle of Cape Trafalgar but died three years later in 1808. Command of

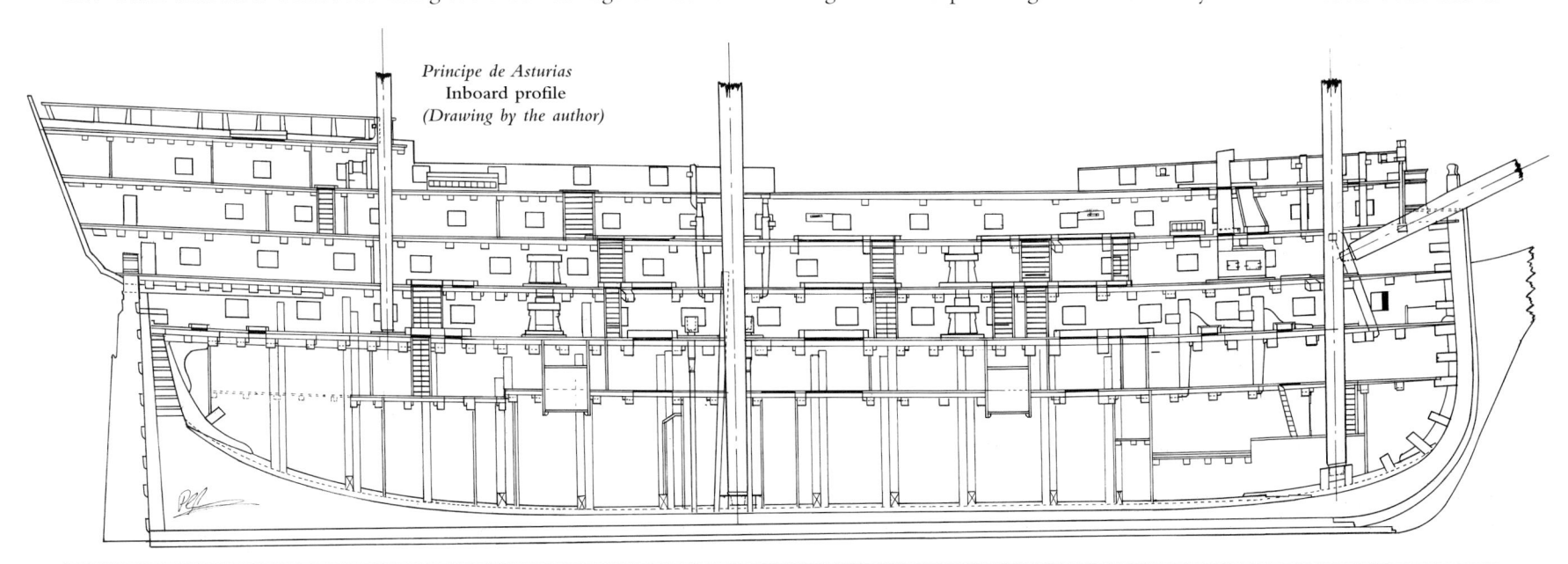

Principe de Asturias
Inboard profile
(Drawing by the author)

SPECIFICATIONS: *PRINCIPE DE ASTURIAS*

Rate	1st	*Length on the range of the gun deck*	210 Burgos feet (60.34 m)	*Ordnance - lower gun deck*	30 x 36 pounders (30 x 36 pounders)
Guns	112	*Length of keel for tonnage*	185 ft 10 ins (53.40 m)	*Ordnance - middle gun deck*	32 x 24 pounders (32 x 24 pounders)
Class	Santa Ana	*Extreme breadth*	58 ft 0 ins (16.67 m)	*Ordnance - upper gun deck*	30 x 12 pounders (32 x 12 pounders)
Designer	Romero Landa	*Depth in hold*	27 ft 6 ins (7.90 m)	*Ordnance - quarter deck and forecastle*	18 x 8 pounders & 2 x 24 pounder carronades (14 x 48 pounder carronades & 6 x 24 pounder carronades)
Builder	Artillero Real (Royal Dockyard)	*Tons displacement*	2,308 tons (3.4504.70 cubic metres)		
Dockyard	Havana				
Date ordered		*Draught afore*	26 ft 1 ins (7.5 m)		
Date keel laid		*Draught abaft*	28 ft 1 ins (8.07 m)	*Ordnance - poop*	(4 x 4 pounder howitzers)
Date launched	1794	*Floor of the hold*	29 ft 0 ins (8.33 m)	*Single broadside weight*	1200 (1520) pounds
		Complement	1113	*Fate*	Broken up in 1814.

Source: *Modelos de Arsenal del Museo Naval*, p. 314.

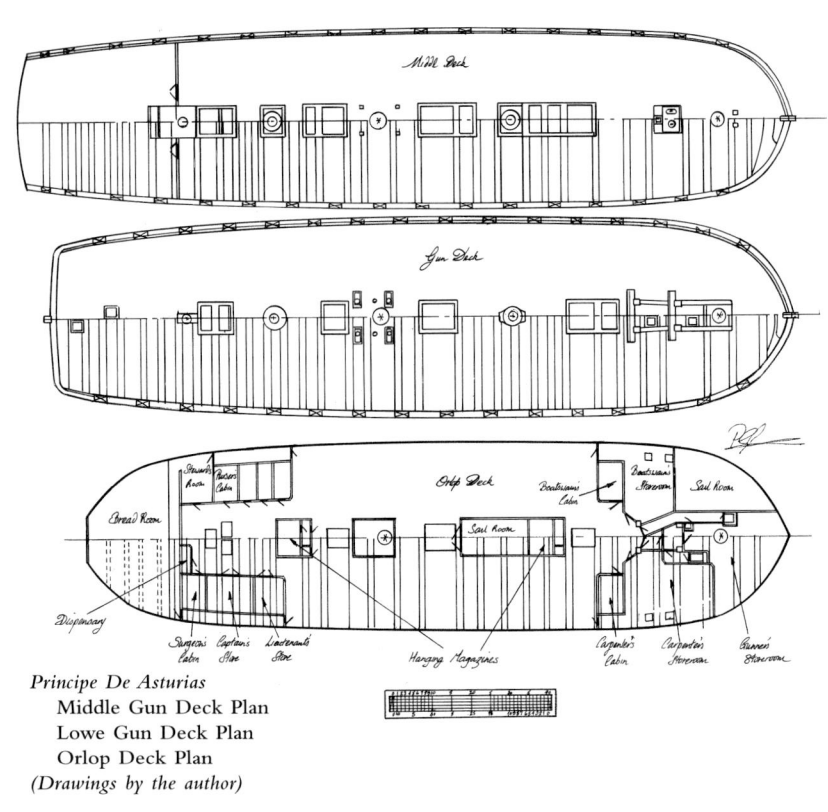

Part 3: The Spanish Fleet

Principe De Asturias
Middle Gun Deck Plan
Lowe Gun Deck Plan
Orlop Deck Plan
(Drawings by the author)

Principe de Asturias was to have been given to Commodore Cosme Churruca but Churruca chose instead to go into *San Juan Nepomuceno*.[20]

TRAFALGAR

It was not until 18 October that Villeneuve went on board *Principe de Asturias* to inform Gravina that he had received new orders to sail at once. Over the next 24 hours the combined fleet made preparations to sail. As principal ship of Gravina's observation squadron *Principe de Asturias* commenced getting under weigh on 19 October but was delayed as the tide was too strong. Once the ship finally got to sea she took her station with her division. Next day when winds became stronger she split her reefed topsails. When the combined fleet had formed a single line and wore in succession onto a northerly course just after 8 a.m. on 21 October, *Principe de Asturias*, instead of being in the foremost squadron, found herself stationed third from the rear of the line. Ahead of her lay the French *Achille* (74), astern the French *Berwick* (74). With her topsails and topgallants set, *Principe de Asturias* proceeded north with the wind from the west shivering her sails. When she got into action finally at about 1 p.m. her broadsides prevented *Defiance* breaking through the line. Turning to starboard she fired a tremendous broadside into the starboard quarter of *Revenge* (74) which, according to the British ship's chaplain, killed 28 men, wounded 51 others and severely shot away her masts and yards. At about 3 p.m. *Principe de Asturias* was raked from ahead by *Thunderer* (74) as she passed through the line. After further action with *Prince* (98), *Principe de Asturias* had suffered some 15 per cent casualties comprising 54 killed and 109 wounded. Alternative sources suggest 52 dead and 116 wounded.[21] In all, despite her casualties and damage Gravina's flagship had proved her mettle as an adversary throughout the affray but with the battle turning into a rout Gravina hoisted a signal to rally the other ships and steered his flagship away from the mêlée. *Principe de Asturias* was joined by *San Justo*, *San Leandro*, *Pluton* and *Neptune* who supported their admiral making for Cadiz. In the rising storm that followed *Principe de Asturias* lost her weakened main and mizzen masts but despite this handicap reached harbour safely.[22]

At 9 a.m. on the morning of Tuesday 22 October Admiral Escaño convened a council of war to determine whether the sounder ships should put to sea to recapture the prizes. This initiative was very much promoted by Commodore Cosmao-Kerjulien. This plan was executed but *Principe de Asturias* did not put to sea, having only one mast standing.[23]

FATE

After the battle *Principe de Asturias* rarely put to sea and after just 20 years' service this proud ship was broken up in 1814.

The 112 gun ship SANTA ANA

Designed by the renowned Spanish naval architect Romero Landa, the 1st rate 112 gun *Santa Ana* was initially ordered 9 November 1782 although she was neither named, nor given royal proclamation until May 1783. Once plans had been approved in June that same year construction began under the master shipwright Miguel de la Puente at the Royal Arsenal at Ferrol. Smaller than *Santísima Trinidad* but larger than *Royal Sovereign*, the amount of timber required to build the *Santa Ana* before conversion would have been about 335,00 cubic feet of timber which at 50 cubic feet per tree equates to approximately 6,700 trees. This number of trees would have been taken from some 112 acres of woodland. Although Romero Landa was only appointed as Surveyor of the Navy in the British sense, the equivalent to Sir Thomas Slade and Sir John Henslow, in March 1782, he was also responsible for the many improvements related to timber procurement and forestry management. Initially armed with thirty 32

SPECIFICATIONS: *SANTA ANA*

Rate	1st	Length on the range of the gun deck	210 Burgos feet (60.34 m)	Ordnance - lower gun deck	30 x 36 pounders (30 x 36 pounders)
Guns	112 (126)	Length of keel for tonnage	185 ft 10 ins (53.40 m)	Ordnance - middle gun deck	32 x 24 pounders (32 x 24 pounders)
Class	Santa Ana	Extreme breadth	58 ft 0 ins (16.67 m)	Ordnance - upper gun deck	30 x 12 pounders (32 x 12 pounders)
Designer	Romero Landa	Depth in hold	27 ft 6 ins (7.90 m)	Ordnance - quarter deck and forecastle	18 x 8 pounders (10 x 8; 10 x 8; 2 x 32 and 6 x 24 pounders)
Builder	Artillero Real (Royal Dockyard)	Tons displacement	2,308 tons	Ordnance - poop	4 x 4 pounder howitzers
		Draught afore	26 ft 1 ins (7.5 m)	Single broadside weight	1176 lbs (1508 lbs)
Dockyard	Ferrol	Draught abaft	28 ft 1 ins (8.07 m)	Fate	Captured at Trafalgar 21 October 1805 and recaptured 23 October 1805. Broken up in 1816.
Date ordered	9 November 1782	Floor of the hold	29 ft 0 ins (8.33 m)		
Date keel laid	June 1783	Complement	948 (1053)		
Date launched	29 September 1784				

Notes: The dimensions and ordnance details cover her initial build.
Her Trafalgar complement of men and armament are given in parentheses.
The distribution of her various quarter and forecastle deck guns is unclear.

Source: *Modelos de Arsenal del Museo Naval*, p. 314.

THE 112 GUN SHIP SANTA ANA

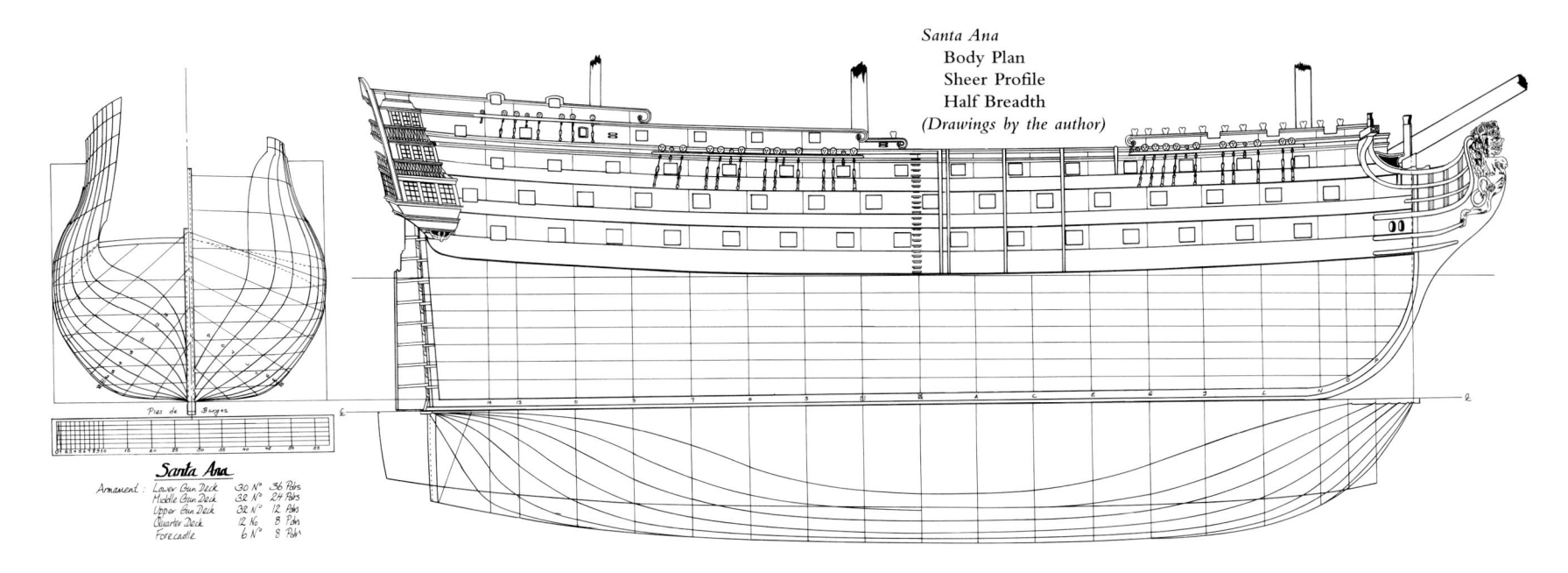

pounders on her lower gun deck, thirty-two 24 pounders on her middle gun deck, thirty 12 pounders on her upper gun deck and eighteen 8 pounders on her quarter deck and forecastle, the *Santa Ana* could deliver a single broadside weight of 1,176 pounds. After her ordnance was upgraded *Santa Ana*'s broadside weight at Trafalgar was 22 per cent greater.[24] The previous *Santa Ana*, a minor vessel carrying just eleven guns, had been captured and burnt by the Royal Navy on 14 September 1782 at the Siege of Gibraltar. Also captured and burnt that day were the Spanish ships *Pastor Paula Prima* (31) *Talla Piedra* (31) *Rosario* (29), *San Cristóbal* (28), *Principe Carlos* (15), *Paula Segunda* (13), *San Juan* (13), and *Delores* (10).[25] *San Miguel* (72), which had been driven ashore and taken by the garrison, was later added to the Royal Navy and sold in December 1791.[26]

SERVICE CAREER

1784: Constructed at Ferrol, *Santa Ana* was launched during the afternoon of 29 September 1784. Nelson, who was to indirectly oppose *Santa Ana* at Trafalgar, was celebrating his 26th birthday when this great ship took to the water. *Santa Ana* was first commissioned under Brigadier (Captain) Santiago Muñoz de Velasco on 30 November that same year. Once fitted out, the ship sailed from Ferrol on 15 December for Cadiz. On board was Brigadier Félix de Tejada, the Royal Spanish Navy's Inspector General.[27]

1785: On 28 February *Santa Ana* put to sea from Cadiz for her sea trials which proved her a stable ship. Unlike *Santísima Trinidad*, she could still use her lower battery in a fresh wind with a heavy sea. Following the British format of recording sailing qualities the following observations were recorded.[2]

In a strong gale of wind under 3rd reefed topsails and the fore topmast staysail; the ship bearing 6? points off the wind
Close hauled under all courses, topsails and topgallants with the wind abaft
Running under all courses, topsails and topgallants bearing 12 points off the wind
Rolls slow and easy and never makes leeway over 9 degrees.
Makes 8 knots on a smooth sea and only makes 2 and 3 degrees of leeway
Makes 10 knots

The report also indicated that in a storm and heavy sea she could lay too under lower sails unfurled and that she responded well to her helm. It was also noted that when she heeled she only went over to the top of her lower wale. So impressed were the naval authorities with the ship's sailing performance and that on 12 December 1786 a royal command was issued authorising that all three decked ships were to be built on the lines of *Santa Ana*.[29]

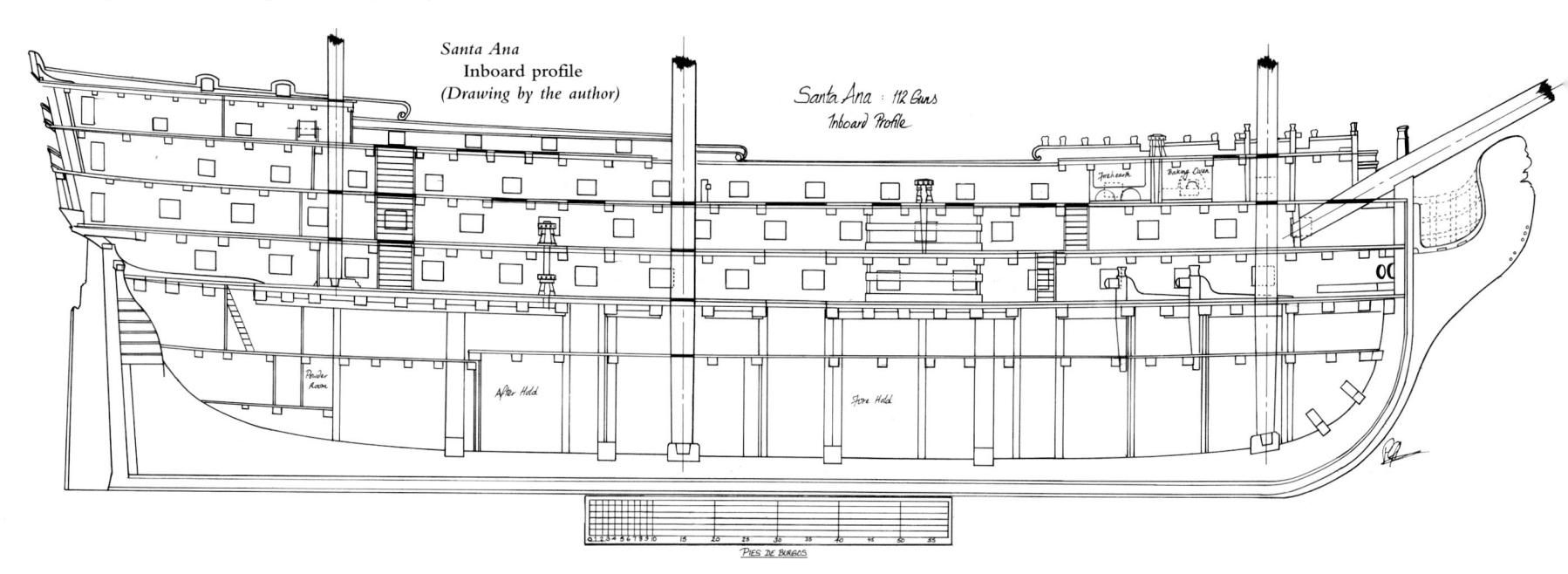

1787-1789: Command of the ship was superseded by Brigadier Juliàn Sànchez Bort who was himself succeeded two years later by Brigadier Francisco Javier Winhuysen of Dutch descent. *Santa Ana* remained in Cadiz all this time.[30]

1791: In June *Santa Ana* was taken into dock to refit, during which she was careened, sheathed in copper and had her 'bridges' repaired. It is uncertain what is meant by bridges. It may simply relate to the two gangboards fitted fore and aft along the ship's side between the quarter deck and forecastle. However, this does not explain why *Santísima Trinidad* was fitted with four bridges, unless two of them ran fore and aft amidships. Alternatively, if these bridges resembled a narrow platform spanning the ship athwartships above her decks, then this feature certainly predates the concept used in later nineteenth century ships. During this refit surveys revealed that some of her timbers were rotten; these were subsequently replaced.[31]

1792: Taken out of commission, *Santa Ana* remained laid up until 1796.

1796: Although *Santa Ana* was recommissioned on 18 February under the command of Brigadier Andrés de Valderrama, the ship was completely overhauled in July to prepare her for sea service. By the end of this year Spain found herself dragged into the war between Britain and France.[32]

1797: In January *Santa Ana* was appointed to the fleet being assembled under Gravina. On 9 March Valderrama was dismissed from the ship and superseded three days later by Brigadier Don Balthasar Hidalgo de Cisneros. Later holding the rank of rear-admiral, Cisneros would fly his flag in the *Santísima Trinidad* at Trafalgar. Since the defeat of Córdoba off Cape St Vincent on 14 February, the port of Cadiz had remained under constant blockade by the British fleet commanded by Earl St Vincent Admiral Sir John Jervis. During the nights of 3 and 5 July men and boats from *Santa Ana* made successive attacks on Jervis's inshore squadron in order to prevent them bombarding Cadiz. In command of the inshore squadron was Rear-Admiral Nelson.[33]

1798: *Santa Ana* finally put to sea on 6 February with Rear-Admiral Mazarredo's fleet comprising 22 line of battle ships, five frigates and two brigantines to drive off the British blockading ships. Having driven them south to Cape St Vincent, *Santa Ana* and the squadron returned to Cadiz on 13 February. This was far too soon, for four days later Jervis's ships reappeared on station, forcing *Santa Ana* to remain in harbour.[34]

1799: When the blockade eased somewhat *Santa Ana* prepared for sea. Flying the flag of Lieutenant-General Pérez de Grandallana, she sailed for the Mediterranean on 12 May with a fleet comprising 43 ships. Intending to recapture Minorca, this foray failed, as the ships were hit by storms in the Gulf of Vera and had to put into Cartagena for repairs. While here, the French fleet under Bruix entered port and an agreement was made between Mazarredo and Bruix that the Spanish fleet should follow the French to Brest to support the invasion of Britain. The Spanish fleet, including *Santa Ana*, sailed from Cartagena on 29 June and after anchoring off Cadiz between 11 and 12 July to take on provisions, sailed for Brest. However, as *Santa Ana* was leaving harbour she unfortunately went aground on the beach off Rota. Refloated with great difficulty because of her size and because she had taken in water she went back into Cadiz for repairs escorted by *Mexicano* (112) Using this opportunity of docking the ship, *Santa Ana* was careened and re-coppered. In the meantime Cisneros, her commander, left the ship.[35]

1800: On 10 January command of the *Santa Ana* was succeeded by Brigadier Pedro Ristory who remained in the ship until superseded by Diego González Guiral in June 1801.

1801: With Spain virtually out of the war and the restoration of peace imminent Guiral took on the responsibility of having the *Santa Ana* overhauled. Taken into dock at Carraca, *Santa Ana* commenced a prolonged refit or 'large repair' which lasted four years.[36]

1805: Ready for sea after her extensive refit, Brigadier (Captain) José de Gardoqui assumed command of *Santa Ana* on 16 February. At the same time *Santa Ana* was appointed as flagship for Lieutenant-General (Vice-Admiral) Ignacio Mariá de Álava, commander of the Escuadra del Océano, although he did not hoist his flag until 6 May. While part of the Spanish fleet joined forces with Vice-Admiral Villeneuve and had sailed for the West Indies the *Santa Ana* remained at Cadiz. After Álava temporarily transferred into *Santísima Trinidad* (136) on 4 August he re-hoisted his flag in *Santa Ana* 1 September. By this point Villeneuve's combined Franco-Spanish fleet was in Cadiz. Within weeks, after receiving new orders to sail into the Mediterranean for Italy, *Santa Ana* and her consorts would be fighting off Cape Trafalgar.[37]

TRAFALGAR

Flying the flag of Vice-Admiral Álava and under the command of Captain José de Gardoqui, *Santa Ana* prepared for sea. Second in command was Francisco de Riquelme. While most of Villeneuve's combined fleet had already got out of harbour by the evening of Saturday 19 October, it was not until dawn Sunday 20 October that *Santa Ana* cleared Cadiz with other delayed ships. Once the entire fleet was at sea it formed into five divisions. *Santa Ana*, placed between *Fougueux* and *Indomptable* in line ahead, took her station to the left of Villeneuve's central division. As Álava's flagship the *Santa Ana* was to lead the van of the combined fleet.

After the combined fleet changed course at 8 a.m. Monday 21 October, *Santa Ana* lay in the centre of the fleet, her position sixteenth from the head of the line. Ahead on her starboard bow lay the Spanish *San Justo* (74), abaft on her starboard quarter *Indomptable* (74) and directly astern, *Fougueux* (74). Unlike the broadsides of most ships which were painted in a livery of black and yellow horizontal bands of various combinations, *Santa Ana* was unique in that her sides were painted entirely in black.[38]

As battle commenced just before noon *Santa Ana* opened her broadsides into Collingwood's flagship *Royal Sovereign* (100) as she made her approach on a bearing SE by S. To close the gap between herself and *Fougueux* astern, *Santa Ana* backed her mizzen topsail to slow down. At 12.10 p.m. *Royal Sovereign* passed under *Santa Ana*'s stern and raked her. Double and trebled shotted, every ball of this broadside found its mark as it tore through the entire length of the *Santa Ana*'s crowded decks, overturning 14 guns, smashing carriages into match-wood, scything down her crew and sending deadly splinters in every direction. This one salvo killed and wounded some 400 men. After the battle Vice-Admiral Álava revealed that 350 men were killed instantly, although this figure does not comply with the official casualty list. *Royal Sovereign* then turned to larboard and ran down *Santa Ana*'s starboard side. Stunned from the first bloody fusillade, *Santa Ana*'s crew were stood aghast as a second broadside from *Royal Sovereign* slammed in through her starboard bow, dealing out more destruction and adding more numbers to the carnage. Ten minutes later she was raked a third time, through her starboard quarter as *Belleisle* (74) crossed her stern. Recoiling, the Spanish gunners stood back to their guns and recommenced firing broadsides into Collingwood's flagship. The ferocious duel between *Santa Ana* and *Royal Sovereign* lasted until 2.15 p.m. by which time the starboard side of the *Santa Ana* was, to quote Collingwood, 'almost entirely beaten in' and her stern had been shot to pieces, and her decks, clamps and stringers ripped open. The two ships drifted apart and when *Santa Ana* broached to in the rising swell the sudden motion shook her weakened masts which collapsed over the side. It was now 2.30 p.m. and unable to sustain any further resistance Captain Gardoqui finally struck his colours. *Santa Ana* had fought hard; *Royal Sovereign* was in virtually the same condition, so much so that Collingwood had to hail Captain Blackwood to take possession of *Santa Ana* and send her admiral into *Royal Sovereign*. Vice-Admiral Álava had been seriously wounded and could not be removed out of the ship, so Blackwood took Captain Gardoqui in his stead. *Santa Ana*'s casualties, according to the official list, comprised 5 officers and 90 men killed and 10 officers and 127 men wounded which equate to eight per cent and 11.5 per cent respectively of her complement of 1,188. Alternative figures submitted by Antonio de Escaño state 97 dead and 141 wounded.[39]

Throughout that evening and on Tuesday 22 October the British prize crew, assisted by the Spanish seamen, endeavoured to secure the *Santa Ana* for the oncoming storm and tend to the many wounded. When Commodore Cosmao-Kerjulien sailed out of Cadiz with his ships and frigates on the afternoon of Wednesday 23 October to rescue some of the prizes the Spanish seamen overwhelmed the sentinels and recaptured the *Santa Ana* from her prize crew. *Santa Ana* was then taken in tow by one of the French frigates towards Cadiz and after enduring the storm she eventually anchored off Puntales on 7 November. Five days later *Santa Ana* was taken into Carraca for extensive repairs.[40]

1806: *Santa Ana* went into dock on 20 February to begin what was essentially a complete 'rebuild', the work being overseen by her commander, Captain Gardoqui, who would remain with the ship until 21 November 1807. With her hull repaired and her bottom re-sheathed in copper *Santa Ana* came out of the dock 9 December that same year. Although without a crew the *Santa Ana* remained in Cadiz as part of the Armada del Océano commanded now by Admiral Álava, Gravina having died on 9 March.

1808: When Spain allied herself to Britain and declared war on France on 4 July she deprived France of her fleet. Moreover, those French ships still in the Spanish ports of Cadiz and Ferrol were commandeered and entered into the Spanish Royal Navy. Between 6 October and 27 December *Santa Ana* was commanded by Miguel Orozco.

1809: Fitted out again in January for sea service, on 13 February Captain Gardoqui was re-appointed commander of *Santa Ana*. Gardoqui would remain in the ship until superseded on 1 March 1810. Probably at this time *Santa Ana* was repainted in the new authorised livery of black/yellow or black/red horizontal bands.

1810: When Cadiz came under siege from Napoleon's troops, steps were taken to safeguard the Spanish fleet from falling into French hands. Consequently on 6 September *Santa Ana* and *Principe de Asturias* (112) sailed for Havana escorted by British ships including *Implacable* (74), formerly the French *Duguay Trouin*.

FATE

When *Santa Ana* finally reached Havana in November 1810 she was short of provisions and many of her crew sick. After decommissioning she was laid up as a depôt ship in the dockyard and over the next few years deteriorated. Although refitted in July 1815 the ship became very much neglected and over the next two years she sank into her mud berth. In 1820 all ships that had virtually foundered within Havana harbour were sold. Although *Santa Ana* was sold her hull was, according to a report by Salazar, still protruding out of the mud in October 1834.

The 80/100 gun ship **RAYO**

Initially built as the 80 gun ship *San Padro* at the royal dockyard at Havana, *Rayo* was launched in 1749. It is not known when her name was changed but it was not long after her launch. Giving 56 years' service before she foundered after the battle thus made *Rayo* the oldest ship serving in the Spanish fleet at Trafalgar. Designed by Pedro de Torres and built under the supervision of Master Shipwright Juan de Acosta, *Rayo* was constructed with Cuban mahogany and tropical cedar, timbers which obviously influenced her longevity. Their drawback was that their splinters easily set up infection in wounds sustained in action. The amount of timber consumed in her construction before conversion is estimated at about 4,300 loads which equates to 215,000 cubic feet of wood before conversion. Another ship built at Havana of similar timber to *Rayo*'s lines with an equally long life was *Fénix* (alias *San Alezandro*). Once launched it was 20 years before *Rayo* needed a major refit. The cost of building *Rayo* amounted to 143,000 pesos which was just 43.5 per cent of the cost of building a 112 gun ship. Building costs were low as much of the labour was supplied by levées of cheap slaves. When first built as an 80 gun ship *Rayo* carried thirty 36 pounders on her lower gun deck, thirty 28 pounders on her upper gun deck, and twenty 8 pounders on her quarter deck and forecastle. This gave her a broadside weight of fire of 890 pounds. In 1803 the ship was enlarged to carry 100 guns, increasing her broadside weight by twelve per cent.[41]

SERVICE CAREER

The longevity of the *Rayo*'s career as a serving warship and the fact that she had few refits suggests that she did not have a very active career before the Trafalgar campaign. From this it can only be assumed that she undertook a limited sea service rôle and probably spent much of her early years stationed at Havana and laid up in a dockyard unmanned. She certainly does not appear to have played an active part when Spain entered the war of American Independence.

1803: During this year *Rayo* went into dock at Cartagena for what was vir-

SPECIFICATIONS: *RAYO*

Rate	1st	Length overall	198 ft 0 ins (56.98 m)	Ordnance - lower gun deck	30 x 36 pounders (30 x 36 pounders)
Guns	80/100	Length of keel for tonnage	165 ft 0 ins	Ordnance - upper gun deck	30 x 18 pounders (32 x 18 pounders)
Class	San Padro/Rayo	Extreme breadth	57 ft (14.89 m)	Ordnance - quarter deck	
Designer	Pedro de Torres	Depth in hold	28 ft 3 ins	and forecastle	20 x 8 pounders (32 x 8 pounders)
Builder	Artillero Real (Royal Dockyard)	Tons displacement	1889 tons	Ordnance - poop	(6 x 18 pounder carronades)
Dockyard	Havana	Draught afore	27 ft 0 ins	Single broadside weight	890 (1010) pounds
Date ordered		Draught abaft	27 ft 0 ins	Fate	Ran aground on Gordos beach near Rota and foundered after the battle of Trafalgar
Date keel laid		Complement	670 (830)		
Date launched	1749				

Notes: Dimensions are given in English feet.
The ordnance and complement listed above in brackets reflects *Rayo*'s statistics at Trafalgar.

Source: Harbron, *Trafalgar and the Spanish Navy*, p. 38.

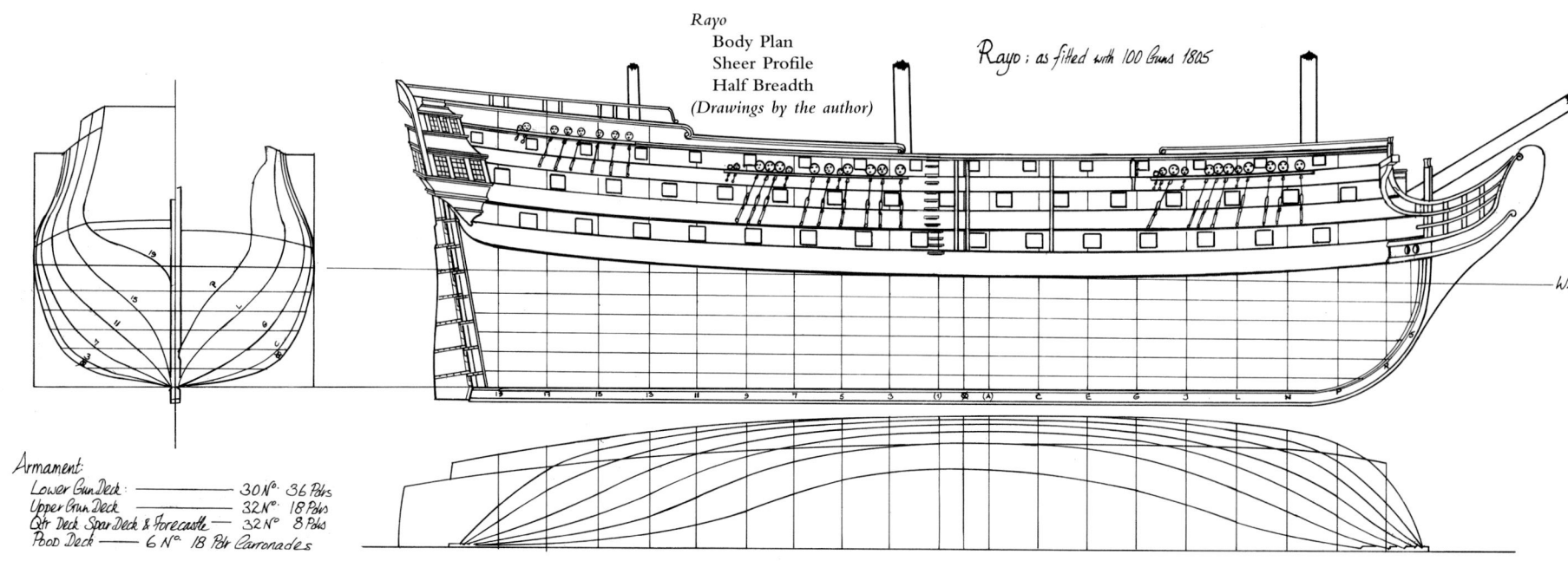

Rayo
Body Plan
Sheer Profile
Half Breadth
(Drawings by the author)

Rayo: as fitted with 100 Guns 1805

Armament:
Lower Gun Deck: — 30 N°. 36 Pdrs
Upper Gun Deck — 32 N°. 18 Pdrs
Qtr Deck Spar Deck & Forecastle — 32 N°. 8 Pdrs
Poop Deck — 6 N°. 18 Pdr Carronades

tually a rebuild, the work undertaken by the head constructor Bouyon. Her reconstruction was quite unique for she was enlarged to carry 100 guns, an increase of 20 per cent. Quite remarkably this was accomplished without having to build a third full gun deck. It was achieved by closing the waist between the quarter deck and forecastle with what was effectively a spar deck. A similar modification had been carried out on the *Santísima Trinidad*; consequently the concept of closing in the waist, a feature that did not appear in English ships until circa 1832, appears to be wholly a Spanish innovation. Now a two decked 1st rate ship of 100 guns, *Rayo* was armed with thirty 36 pounders on her lower gun deck, thirty-two 18 pounders on her upper gun deck, sixteen 8 pounders on her quarter deck, ten 8 pounders on her spar deck (waist), six 8 pounders on the forecastle and six 18 pounder carronades on her poop deck. This increase gave *Rayo* a single broadside weight of 1,010 pounds. Her complement was increased from 670 to 830 men. It was not until Sir Robert Seppings became Surveyor of the Royal Navy in 1813 that the idea of building two decked ships carrying well beyond 80 guns was conceived in the British navy. Before the end of his period of office in 1832 Seppings introduced the 92 gun two decker *Rodney* class of 1833. Seppings' successor, Sir William Symonds, introduced the two decked 90 gun *Albion* class in 1842. Such ships saw service in the Crimean War (1854-1856).

1805: Gravina asked the Spanish prime minister for Captain Enrique MacDonnell to command *Rayo*: 'his skills, his accredited valour encourage me to request that Your Excellency may restore him to his rank and seniority given the circumstances of the day, to the Navy List'. In his reply written at the court of Aranjuez dated 26 February 1805 Godoy wrote, 'I approve and I have commanded that Don Enrique MacDonnell may be returned to active service in the fleet in his rank and seniority in order to take over the *Rayo*'.[42] *Rayo* did not sail with Villeneuve's fleet to the West Indies and so she did not get involved in Calder's action on 22 July.

TRAFALGAR

Appointed to Rear-Admiral Dumanoir's squadron, *Rayo* was one of the last ships of Villeneuve's combined fleet to sail from Cadiz and did not get out of harbour until 10 a.m. Sunday 20 October. Her delay was caused by the wind veering around to the south-east. Once *Rayo* had finally weighed and set her topsails the brig *Furet* (16), acting like a sheep dog, signalled to Villeneuve that she was under way. Originally sailing towards the rear of the line, when the fleet turned northward on the morning of 21 October, *Rayo* took up station third from the head of the line. Ahead of her was *Scipion* (74) and abaft Dumanoir's flagship *Formidable* (80). Being one of the foremost ships, *Rayo* did not get into action until late. Like the rest of Dumanoir's division, because of light winds she was unable to turn and get back into action once Nelson's windward division had broken the line. Her support, together with *Formidable*, the Spanish *Neptuno* (80), the 74 gun ships *Duguay Trouin*, *Mont Blanc*, and *Scipion*, may well have changed the balance of the battle had they succeeded in re-entering the mêlée earlier. As Dumanoir's squadron approached to meet the British line led by *Leviathan* (74) they split into three groups: *Formidable*, *Duguay Trouin Scipion* and *Mont Blanc* forming one; *Intrépide Héros* and *Neptuno* the second; *San Agustin*, *San Fransisco de Asis* and *Rayo* the third. While the first and second divisions steered towards the British ships the third group with *Rayo* rearmost used this opportunity to quit the battle and turned eastward, *Héros* following suit. As they veered away *Rayo* and her consorts were fired upon from the starboard batteries of *Britannia* (100), *Ajax* (74) and *Conqueror* (74), the range however was not effective. Hardly surprisingly *Rayo* suffered just 18 casualties in action: four killed and 14 wounded.[43]

FATE

After the battle *Rayo* was forced to anchor off San Lucar to ride out the storm and, buffeted by heavy seas, rolled out her masts. Now in a precarious situation *Rayo* officially surrendered to *Donegal* (74) newly out from Gibraltar. Although safe for a few days, disaster struck on Saturday 26 October. After dragging her anchors, *Rayo* was driven on shore. Following Collingwood's orders regarding prizes, once *Rayo*'s prisoners had been removed she was set on fire and went to pieces.[44]

∽ NOTES TO PART 3: CHAPTER 1 ∽

1. A fatal symptom of yellow fever, a virus carried by mosquitoes.
2. *Modelos de Arsenal del Museo Naval* (Madrid, 2004), pp. 306-307.
3. *Modelos de Arsenal del Museo Naval*, p. 307.
4. *Ibid*.
5. *Ibid*.
6. *Ibid*.
7. *Modelos de Arsenal del Museo Naval*, p. 308.
8. *Ibid*.
9. *Ibid*.
10. *Ibid*.
11. *Ibid*.
12. *Modelos de Arsenal del Museo Naval*, pp. 308-309; Clowes, 4, pp. 312-317.
13. Harbron, *Trafalgar and the Spanish Navy*, p. 100.
14. Clowes, 4, p. 309.
15. Clowes, 5, p. 26.

[16] *Modelos de Arsenal del Museo Naval*, pp. 309-310; Clowes, 4, pp. 138-149.
[17] Fraser, *The Enemy at Trafalgar*, pp. 314-317.
[18] Harbron, *Trafalgar and the Spanish Navy*, p. 44.
[19] Clowes, 4, pp. 309-310.
[20] Harbron, *Trafalgar and the Spanish Navy*, pp. 141,144.
[21] Harbron, *Trafalgar and the Spanish Navy*, p. 119.
[22] Clowes, 5, pp. 155-156; Clayton & Craig, *Trafalgar*, pp. 144-245.
[23] Clayton & Craig, *Trafalgar*, pp. 298-308.
[24] *Modelos de Arsenal del Museo Naval*, p. 314.
[25] Clowes, 4, p. 115.
[26] Colledge, p. 484.
[27] Ibid.
[28] Ibid.
[29] Ibid.
[30] Ibid.
[31] Ibid.
[32] *Modelos de Arsenal del Museo Naval*, p. 315.
[33] Ibid.
[34] Ibid.
[35] Ibid; Clowes, 4, p. 387.
[36] *Modelos de Arsenal del Museo Naval*, p. 316.
[37] Ibid.
[38] Clowes, 5, p. 26.
[39] Clowes, 5, pp. 137-138; Pope, *England Expects*, pp. 269-279, 319.
[40] Pope, *England Expects*, p. 317.
[41] Harbron, *Trafalgar and the Spanish Navy*, passim.
[42] Harbron, *Trafalgar and the Spanish Navy*, p. 124.
[43] Pope, *England Expects*, pp. 322-327.
[44] Pope, 339; Clowes, 5, p. 163.

PART 3: CHAPTER 2
THE SPANISH THIRD RATE SHIPS

The 80 gun ship ARGONAUTA

Designed by Romero Landa, the 80 gun *Argonauta* (not to be confused with the French 74 gun ship *Argonaute*) was built and launched at the royal dockyard at Ferrol in 1798. In all some 4,200 loads of timber or an equivalent number of trees were used for her construction. In volume this relates to 210,000 cubic feet of wood before conversion. *Argonauta* was armed with thirty 24 pounders on her lower gun deck, thirty-two 18 pounders on her upper gun deck, fourteen 8 pounders on her quarter deck, four 8 pounders on her forecastle, and four 18 pounder carronades on her poop giving her a single broadside weight of 756 pounds.

SERVICE CAREER

1800: *Argonauta* first saw active service when she was deployed with Admiral Mazzaredo's fleet being assembled at Ferrol that summer. At the time she was under the command of Captain Don Juan Herrera. Besides *Argonauta*, this squadron was comprised of *San Hermenegildo* (112), *Real Carlos* (112), *San Fernando* (96), *San Antonio* (74) and *San Agustin* (74). The position of these ships became perilous, for in June they were attacked by a squadron commanded by Rear-Admiral Sir John Borlase Warren, flying his flag in *Renown* (74). Besides transports carrying troops under Lieutenant-General Sir James Pulteney, Borlase's squadron comprised the following ships:

Rate	Guns	Name	No.
2nd	98	*London*	1
3rd	78	*Impétueux*	1
3rd	74	*Captain, Courageux* and *Renown*	2
4th	44	*Amelia* and *Indefatigable*	2
5th	38	*Amethyst*	1
5th	32	*Stag*	1
5th	28	*Brilliant*	1
6th	18	*Cynthia*	1
Total			10

Although troops, seamen and field guns were landed on 25 June and these forces took control of the heights around Ferrol by next morning, Pulteney failed to press home a concerted attack and take the town and consequently *Argonauta* and her consorts were safe.[1]

1801: Still commanded by Captain Herrera, *Argonauta* was deployed with a small squadron commanded by Vice-Admiral Don Juan Joaquin de Moreno. Moreno's ships, comprising five Spanish, including *Argonauta*, and one French sail of the line, three frigates and a lugger, moved out of harbour and anchored off Cadiz on 8 July. Next day Moreno's squadron made sail and joined, as planned, Rear-Admiral Linois' French squadron lying off Algeciras. This Franco-Spanish force now comprised the following ships:

Rate	Guns	Name	No.
1st	112	*Real Carlos* and *San Hermenegildo*	2
2nd	94	*San Fernando*	1
3rd	80	*Argonauta, Formidable* and *Indomptable*	3
3rd	74	*San Agustin, Desaix* and *St Antoine*	3
4th	44	*Sabine*	1
5th	40	*Liberté* and *Muiron*	2
6th	14	*Valour*	1
Total			13

When the Franco-Spanish ships made sail on 12 July they met with Rear-Admiral Sir James Saumarez's squadron of nine ships off Cabareta Point that evening. By 8 p.m. a chase had ensued which continued through the night with ships firing at each other as the opportunity arose. At 11.20 p.m. the *Real Carlos*, *San Hermenegildo* and the French *St Antoine* were brought to action and within half an hour the French ship struck. *Real Carlos*, which had already caught fire, collided with *San Hermenegildo*, and although the two broke away from each other they both blew up just after midnight. Of the 2,000 men manning these two great ships there were only 300 survivors. The *Argonauta* in the meantime managed to keep her distance from the pursuing British ships and got into Cadiz.[2]

1805: Now under the command of Captain Don Rafael Hore, *Argonauta* was appointed flagship for Admiral Don Federico Gravina. Also flying the flag of Rear Admiral Don Antonio Escaño, *Argonauta* lay in Cadiz with Admiral Gravina's squadron waiting to join Villeneuve's French fleet from Toulon. When Villeneuve's ships stood into Cadiz Bay at 4 p.m. on 8 April *Argonauta* and her consorts made sail. United with the French, they set sail for the West Indies. Villeneuve's combined fleet now comprised the following ships:

SPECIFICATIONS: *ARGONAUTA*

Rate	3rd	Length on the range of the gun deck	186 ft 0 ins Burgos (51.83 m)	Ordnance - lower gun deck	30 x 24 pounders
Guns	80			Ordnance - upper gun deck	32 x 18 pounders
Class	-	Length of keel for tonnage	-	Ordnance - quarter deck	14 x 8 pounders
Designer	Romero Landa	Extreme breadth		Ordnance - forecastle	4 x 8 pounders
Builder	Artillero Real (Royal Dockyard)	Depth in hold		Ordnance - Poop	4 x 18 pounder carronades
Dockyard	Ferrol	Tons burthen		Single broadside weight	756 pounds
Date ordered	-	Draught afore		Fate	Captured at Trafalgar 21 October 1805 and sunk during the following storm
Date keel laid		Draught abaft			
Date launched	1798	Complement	683		

Sources: *Modelos de Arsenal del Museo Naval*; Pope, *England Expects*, p. 357.

French/Spanish	Rate	Guns	Name	No.
French	3rd	80	*Bucentaure, Formidable, Neptune* and *Indomptable*	4
Spanish	3rd	80	*Argonauta*	1
French	3rd	74	*Aigle, Annibal, Atlas, Berwick, Intrépide, Mont Blanc* and *Swiftsure*	7
Spanish	3rd	74	*Firme, Terrible* and *San Rafael*	3
Spanish	3rd	64	*America* and *España*	2
French	5th	40	*Cornélie, Hortense, Rhin, Thémis* and *Uranie*	5
French	5th	8	*Incorruptible*	1
French	5th	36	*Sirène*	1
Spanish	5th	36	*Santa Magdalena*	1
French	6th	18	*Furet* and *Naïade*	2
French	Corvette	16	*Torche*	1
French	Brig	16	*Argus*	1
TOTAL				28

Note: *San Rafael* joined the fleet later as she had run aground when getting out of Cadiz.

With the other ships *Argonauta* reached Martinique on 13 May, *San Rafael* joining them three days later. Her movements from this point follow those described in previous chapters. After sailing back to Europe, she was present at Calder's action off Finisterre on 22 July. While it appears that *Argonauta* did not get into close action at this battle, it is recorded that when the opportunity arose for her to engage the frigate *Sirius* (38), she passed by without firing a single shot, thereby upholding a protocol that ships of the line did not fire into non-line of battle ships. This respect was also shown by the Spanish ships *América* and *Terrible*. *Argonauta* finally went into Cadiz on 20 August after making repairs off Ferrol after the battle.[3]

TRAFALGAR

Once in Cadiz Admirals Gravina and Escaño lowered their flags and left the ship. Shortly after command of the *Argonauta* was passed over to Captain A Parejo. After sailing with Villeneuve's combined fleet on 19 October as part of Gravina's observation squadron on the morning of 21 October, *Argonauta* was stationed eighth from the rear of the line. Ahead lay *Algésiras*, astern on her starboard quarter *Swiftsure*. At about 1.30 p.m. *Argonauta* engaged the British *Achille* which had drawn up upon her larboard side. The two ships fought at very close quarters for an hour during which she sustained considerable casualties including Captain Parejo. Regarding the condition of the ship Parejo later wrote:

> ... all the guns on the quarter deck and poop dismounted, a great number of guns in the batteries out of action, as much as on account of the pieces [being damaged] as from want of crews... the whole rigging was destroyed, so that there were no shrouds left to the masts save one on the main mast and that they were threatening to fall every minute, being shot through.

He then recorded that 'it was very evident that the ship could make but slight and feeble resistance'. Before being taken below to have his wounds dressed Captain Parejo ordered his men to cease firing and shut the lower deck port lids which indicated that she had surrendered. *Argonauta* attempted to make sail but with her masts about to fall she simply drifted off to leeward unable to escape. Her hull had also received a fierce beating. Shortly afterwards the one remaining boat from *Belleisle* bearing William Hudson, ship's master and John Owen, Lieutenant of Marines, came alongside to take possession of the Spanish ship. *Argonauta* had sustained 44 per cent casualties comprising 100 killed and 203 wounded.[4]

FATE

In the storm that followed the battle *Argonauta*'s dismasted hull proved too weak to withstand the constant battering of the sea and no matter what measures were taken by her prize crew to keep the ship afloat, hopes of getting her to Gibraltar became doubtful. Following Collingwood's orders given on 24 October to scuttle all ships beyond redemption the Spanish prisoners and wounded were removed. Once the prize had crew undertaken the necessary actions to scuttle her *Argonauta* was abandoned and left to founder.

The 80 gun ship MONTAÑEZ

Designed by Romero Landa and built at Ferrol, the 80 gun ship *Montañez* was launched in 1794. First of her class, *Montañez*'s lines were in fact an upgraded version of Landa's *San Ildefonso* class of 1785. In many respects *Montañez* was considered the best designed Spanish naval ship of the late eighteenth century. Other ships built on similar lines of the *Montañez* class include *Argonauta, Monarca* and *Neptuno*, although the latter was actually designed to carry 80 guns. Overall building work of the *Montañez* class 74 and 80 gun ships was overseen by Julién de Retamosa who, in 1793, was placed in charge of Spanish arsenals and shipyards. Armed with twenty-eight 24 pounders on the lower gun deck, thirty 18 pounders on the upper gun deck, fourteen 8 pounders on the quarter deck and four 8 pounders on the forecastle, the *Montañez* could deliver a single broadside weight of 678 pounds. Later supplemented with four 18 pounder carronades on her poop, her broadside weight was increased by five per cent to 714 pounds.[5]

SERVICE CAREER

1805: Like many of her contemporaries *Montañez* was not employed in any major fleet deployment until 1805. At the time she was laid up at Ferrol along with the Spanish ships *Principe de Asturias* (112), *Argonauta* (80),

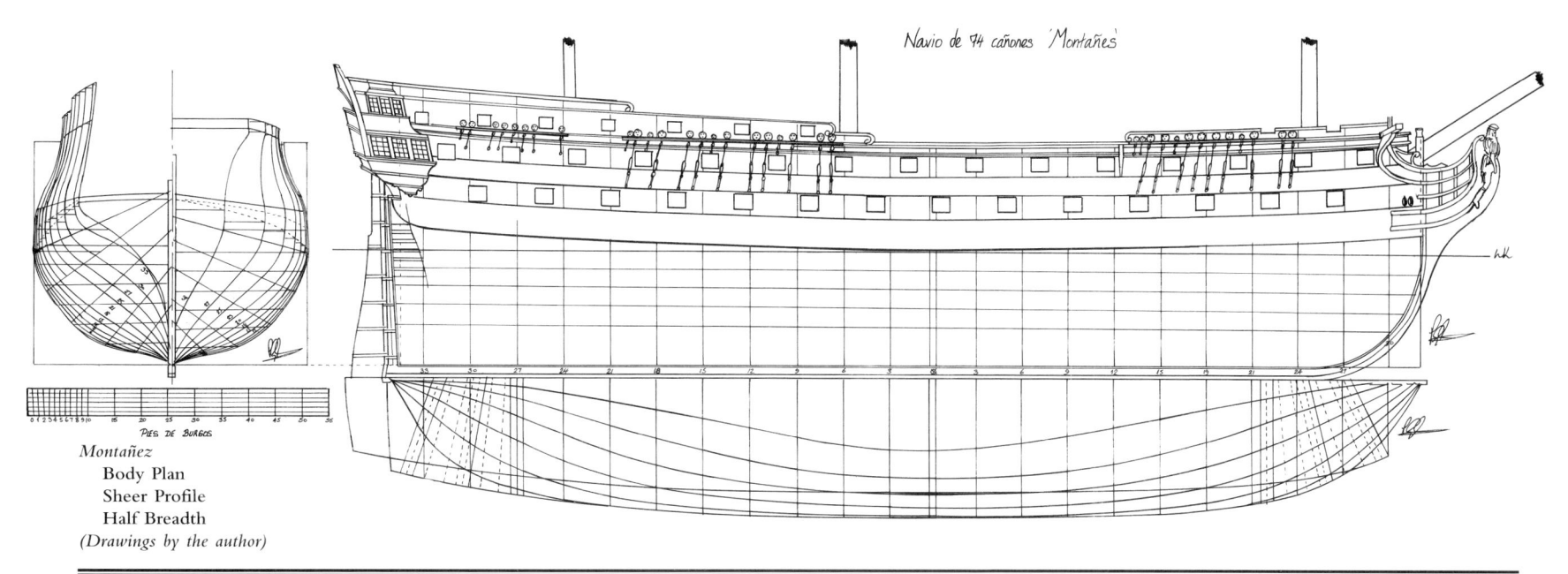

THE 80 GUN SHIP MONTAÑEZ

Montañez
Body Plan
Sheer Profile
Half Breadth
(Drawings by the author)

SPECIFICATIONS: *MONTAÑEZ*

Rate	3rd	Length on the range of the gun deck	90 Burgos feet (54.60 m) [175 ft 3 ins Eng.]	Draught abaft	23 ft 3 ins (6.48 m)
Guns	74 (80)			Complement	715
Class	Montañez (based on San Ildefonso class)	Length of keel for tonnage	181 ft 0 ins (5043 m)	Ordnance - lower gun deck	28 x 24 pounders (28 x 24 pounders)
		Extreme breadth	51 ft 0 ins (14.21 m) [48 ft 5½ ins Eng.]	Ordnance - upper gun deck	30 x 18 pounders (30 x 24 pounders)
Designer	Romero Landa				
Builder	Artillero Real (Royal Dockyard)	Depth in hold	25 ft 6 ins (7.11 m) [20 ft 10 ins Eng.]	Ordnance - quarter deck	14 x 8 pounders
				Ordnance - forecastle	4 x 8 pounders
Dockyard	Ferrol	Tons burthen	1753 tons Eng. Tons displacement 1,815.5 tons (2,756.83 cubic metres)	Ordnance - poop	(4 x 18 pounder carronades)
Date ordered					
Date keel laid		Ballast	12,000 to 13,000 quintals (552 to 598 tons)	Single broadside weight	678 (714) pounds
Date launched	1794			Fate	Broken up in 1810
		Draught afore	26 ft 7 ins (7.39 m)		

Neptuno, (80), *Monarca* (74), *San Agustin* (74), *San Fransisco de Asis*, (74), *San Ildefonso* (74), *San Juan Nepomuceno* (74), *Terrible* (74), and *San Fulgencio* (64). Although *Montañez* did not sail with the Spanish contingent of Villeneuve's fleet to the West Indies and back, she did join Villeneuve's fleet when it arrived off Ferrol in July and sailing on 9 August, steered south for Cadiz.

TRAFALGAR

Under the command of Captain Francisco Alcedo y Bustamente, *Montañez* sailed with the combined fleet from Cadiz on 19 October. Taking up her station within the fleet at the beginning of the battle on 21 October, *Montañez* was positioned twenty-third from the head of the line. Ahead on her starboard bow lay the French ship *Aigle* (74) and astern on her starboard quarter *Algésiras* (74); further astern lay Admiral Gravina's observation squadron. During the ensuing action *Montañez* got into close action with the British *Achille* during which *Montañez* lost her fore mast. This engagement lasted only some ten minutes before *Montañez* veered off to avoid further damage and bloodshed. At this point she had sustained 49 casualties: 20 dead, including her commander Captain Bustamente, and 29 wounded. Making sail as best as she could, *Montañez* then steered for Cadiz.[6]

FATE

After completing essential repairs *Montañez* appears to have remained in Cadiz for the duration of the war and was broken up in 1810.

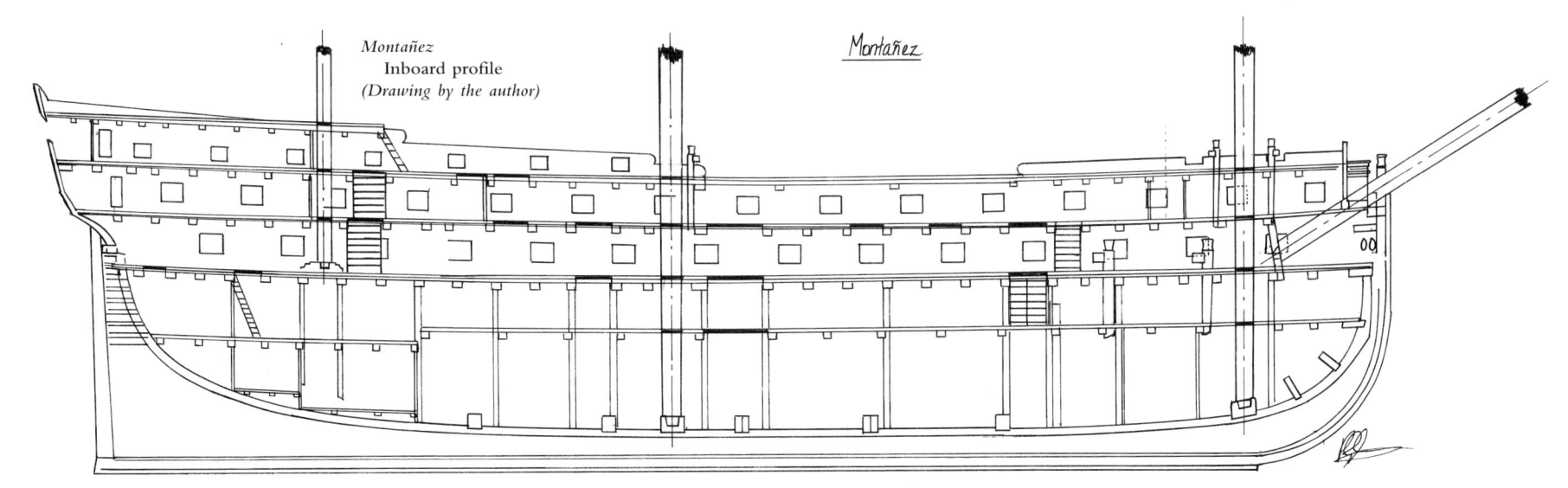

Montañez
Inboard profile
(Drawing by the author)

221

The 80 gun ship NEPTUNO

Based on the lines of the *Montañez* class designed by Romero Landa, the 80 gun ship *Neptuno* was built at Ferrol and launched in 1794. Like *Montañez*, *Neptuno* and her other sister ships, *Argonauta* and *Monarca* were in fact upgraded versions of Landa's *San Ildefonso* class of 1785 and were considered well designed ships. Overall building work of the *Montañez* class 74 and 80 gun ships was overseen by Julién de Retamosa. Armed with twenty-eight 24 pounders on the lower gun deck, thirty 18 pounders on the upper gun deck, fourteen 8 pounders on the quarter deck and four 8 pounders on the forecastle, *Neptuno* could deliver a single broadside weight of 678 pounds. Later supplemented with four 18 pounder carronades on her poop, her broadside weight was increased by five per cent to 714 pounds.[7]

SERVICE CAREER

1796. Before this date *Neptuno* appears to have been fitting out and undertaking sea trials before transferring to Admiral Don José de Córdoba's Mediterranean fleet assembled at Cartagena. Shortly afterwards Spain joined France and entered the war against Britain and commenced preparing to support the French invasion plan.

1797: On 1 February *Neptuno* sailed from Cartagena with Córdoba's fleet of 27 sail of the line, twelve frigates, one brig, and several smaller craft. After passing though the Straits of Gibraltar on 5 February, *Neptuno* was sent into Algeciras with *Bahama* (74), *Terrible* (74), *Nuestra Señora del Guadeloupe* (34) and various gunboats. After rejoining Córdoba's fleet *Neptuno* went into Cadiz to take on provisions before proceeding north to join the Franco-Dutch fleet assembled at Brest ready to invade Britain. Unable to get into Cadiz due to prevailing easterly winds, *Neptuno* with the rest of Córdoba's Spanish fleet, fell in with and were brought to action by Admiral Sir John Jervis's squadron off Cape St Vincent on 14 February. As with many ships, *Neptuno* did not get into close action during the ensuing battle and eventually reached Cadiz afterwards.[8]

1805: Stationed at Ferrol and placed under the command of Captain Don H Cayoteno Valdès, *Neptuno* sailed on 9 August from Cadiz in Villeneuve's combined fleet, with the Spanish ships that would fight off Cape Trafalgar in two months' time.

TRAFALGAR

Originally at the rear of Admiral Dumanoir's squadron, after the combined fleet altered course northward on the morning of the 21 October *Neptuno* was at the head of the line. Like the other leading ships in Dumanoir's squadron *Neptuno* soon found this a disadvantage, for once the battle opened she was unable to turn around and consequently became isolated from supporting the main body of the fleet. Still trying to get his fleet into an orderly line, at about 10.15 a.m. Villeneuve signalled *Neptuno* to hug the wind while other ships continued to get on station. In the opening stages *Neptuno* was fired upon by *Africa* (64) as she came in from the north to join Nelson's division, but being at distant range these broadsides had little effect. When Dumanoir's squadron finally turned south to enter the fray *Neptuno* was one of only five vessels that bore up to give consolidated support to *Bucentaure* (80), the other four being *Formidable* (80), *Duguay Trouin* (74), *Mont Blanc* (74) and *Scipion* (74). The remaining ships veered off to the east, joining Admiral Gravina. It appears that to help Admiral Villeneuve, Valdès was prepared to launch his boats in the attempt to recapture *Bucentaure*. However this noble plan was rejected when Valdès found all *Neptuno*'s boats shot to pieces. Just after 4 p.m. *Neptuno* found herself cut off by the two rearmost ships of Nelson's division and came into close action with *Minotaur* (74) and *Spartiate* (74). For the next hour *Neptuno* gallantly exchanged broadsides with these two 74 gun ships, during which her rigging was very much damaged, her mizzen mast was shot away and Captain Valdès was wounded in the head and neck. Having lost consciousness temporarily Valdès was taken below for a short period to recover, the third time Valdès had been wounded in the action. For the best part of an hour *Neptuno* was under continuous fire and lost her fore topmast, the fore top, fore yard and fore shrouds. Next to go were her main top mast and the main stay. With all her masts and rigging shot away *Neptuno* struck her colours at 5.10 p.m. Reporting later, Valdès wrote: 'Finally a few minutes before sunset, having thirty-seven dead and forty-seven wounded, totally dismasted and overwhelmed by the superior number of the enemy who

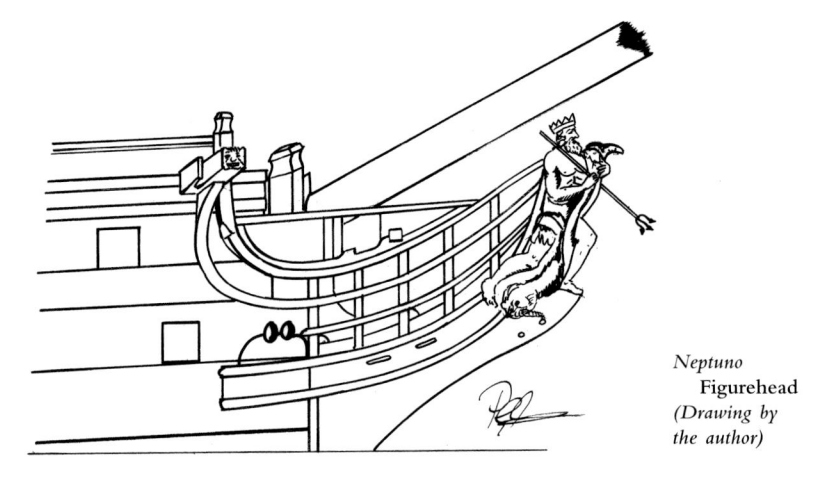

Neptuno Figurehead (Drawing by the author)

SPECIFICATIONS: NEPTUNO

Rate	3rd	Length on the range of the gun deck	190 Burgos feet (54.60 m) [175 ft 3 ins Eng.]	Draught abaft	23 ft 3 ins (6.48 m)
Guns	74 (80)			Complement	715
Class	Montañez (based on San Ildefonso class)	Length of keel for tonnage	181 ft 0 ins (5043 m)	Ordnance - lower gun deck	28 x 24 pounders (28 x 24 pounders)
		Extreme breadth	51 ft 0 ins (14.21 m) [48 ft 5½ ins Eng.]	Ordnance - upper gun deck	30 x 18 pounders (30 x 24 pounders)
Designer	Romero Landa			Ordnance - quarter deck	14 x 8 pounders
Builder	Artillero Real (Royal Dockyard)	Depth in hold	25 ft 6 ins (7.11 m) [20 ft 10 ins Eng.]	Ordnance - forecastle	4 x 8 pounders
				Ordnance - poop	(4 x 18 pounder carronades)
Dockyard	Ferrol	Tons burthen	1753 tons Eng. Tons displacement 1,815.5 tons (2,756.83 cubic metres)	Single broadside weight	678 (714) pounds
Date ordered				Fate	Captured at the battle of Trafalgar 21 October 1805. Recaptured 23 October but went on shore and foundered.
Date keel laid		Ballast	12,000 to 13,000 quintals (552 to 598 tons)		
Date launched	1795	Draught afore	26 ft 7 ins (7.39 m)		

Sources: *Modelos de Arsenal del Museo Naval*; Pope, *England Expects*, p. 357.

surrounded my ship – which was the only one in those waters – we decided to strike to such superior forces'.9 Alternative reports suggest that *Neptuno* had 38 killed and 35 wounded. As her casualties were relatively low it would appear that her submission, as Valdès states, was greatly influenced by declining morale because of isolation rather than damage and injuries. That casualties were relatively light would prove advantageous in due course.10 The British boarding party sent to take possession of *Neptuno* comprised 48 men from *Minotaur* led by Marine Second Lieutenant Thomas Reeves. As Valdès was below in the cockpit receiving medical attention the ship was surrendered formally by Antonio Miranda, *Neptuno*'s First Lieutenant, who went immediately into *Minotaur* and submitted his sword to Captain Charles Mansfield.

FATE

At 3.30 a.m. Tuesday 22 October *Minotaur* took *Neptuno* in tow. When daylight broke the prize crew commenced clearing the ship of wreckage and heaving masts and yards overboard. All the while the wind was increasing, causing the tow hawser to break, with *Neptuno* at risk of running onto a lee shore. Later that day the remaining part of *Neptuno*'s mainmast toppled and fell across the poop deck, smashing the captain's cabins below. In this accident Diego de Soto, the Spanish paymaster, was crushed to death and a member of the prize crew was also killed. Besides rendering the ship completely mastless, the quarterdeck beams had to be shored up to prevent the deck collapsing. Throughout the day all means to save the ship from foundering were made, jury sails were rigged to the mast stumps, and anchors were prepared for letting go. On Wednesday 23 October Commodore Churruca assembled his squadron and sailed out from Cadiz intent on rescuing some of the prize ships from the British fleet. To Churruca's advantage the British ships cast off their prizes as they prepared for a counter attack. As Churruca's escorting frigates *Cornélie*, *Hortense*, *Rhin* and *Thémis* harassed the British ships, *Hermione* (40) took *Neptuno* in tow and the Spanish seamen on board retook their ship. The prize crew, now prisoners themselves, worked at the pumps while *Neptuno* came to anchor in Cadiz Bay. That night as the storm started to rise again *Neptuno* dragged her anchors and drifted inshore. According to William Thorpe, one of the British prize crew who survived, lines were passed quickly from ship to shore through the efforts of the prize crew, to aid evacuation from the ship. These lines were rigged to the cathead, bowsprit and remains of the fore mast. Thorpe also states that the Spanish seamen hurriedly constructed rafts, which conveyed more men to safety. One raft plied to and fro removing groups of twenty men at a time, but it eventually capsized, sending men to their deaths. No further attempts were made that day to rescue the remaining people on board. Over the succeeding days most of the survivors, including Captain Valdès who was still recovering from his wound, were removed by fishing boats and another raft. Abandoned, stranded on a lee shore and crushed mercilessly by heavy seas *Neptuno* quickly went to pieces.11 In 1808 after Spain had declared war against France the French *Neptune* was seized at Cadiz on 14 June and entered into the Spanish navy under the name *Neptuno*, replacing the ship lost at Trafalgar. This *Neptuno* continued serving in the Spanish Royal Navy until broken up in 1820.12

The 74 gun ship *BAHAMA*

Designed by Francisco Gautier, the 74 gun *Bahama*, also named the *San Cristóbal*, was built and launched at the Royal Dockyard, Havana, in 1780. The lines and specifications of the *Bahama* and *San Leandro* follow those of the *San Ildefonso* class. She was built of native Cuban mahogany and Mexican cedar, in the same quantities as that required for any other Spanish 74 gun ship. Initially armed with twenty-eight 24 pounders on her lower gun deck, thirty 18 pounders on her upper gun deck, fourteen 8 pounders on her quarter deck and four 8 pounders on her forecastle, the *Bahama* could deliver a single broadside weight of 678 pounds. This was later increased by five per cent to 714 pounds when *Bahama* was fitted with four 18 pounder carronades on her poop. Under her alternative name, *Bahama*'s predecessor *San Cristóbal* was a 28 gun frigate that had been burnt in action on 14 September during the siege of Gibraltar in 1782.13

SERVICE CAREER

1796: Before this date *Bahama* does not appear to have been involved with any major campaign and probably spent much of her time escorting the vital convoys plying continually between South America and Spain. In the latter part of this year *Bahama* was prepared for sea ready to sail with Admiral Don José de Córdoba's fleet being assembled at Cartagena.

1797: On 1 February *Bahama* sailed from Cartagena in company with Córdoba's fleet of 27 sail of the line, twelve frigates, one brig and several smaller craft. When *Bahama* passed though the Straits of Gibraltar four days later she was sent into Algeciras with *Neptuno* (80), *Terrible* (74), *Nuestro Señora del Guadeloupe* (34) and various gunboats. After rejoining the fleet, Córdoba next intended to go into Cadiz and take on provisions before proceeding north to join forces with the French and Dutch fleets assembling at Brest to invade Britain. As stated earlier, however, easterly winds prevented the Spanish from entering Cadiz, and they fell in with the British squadron commanded by Admiral Sir John Jervis off Cape St Vincent on 14 February. Like many ships, *Bahama* did not get into close action during this battle and eventually reached Cadiz.14

SPECIFICATIONS: *BAHAMA*

Rate	3rd	Length on the range of the gun deck	92 Burgos feet 2 ins (53.55 m)	Ordnance - lower gun deck	28 x 24 pounders
Guns	74	Length of keel for tonnage	167 ft 3 ins (48.06 m) estimated	Ordnance - upper gun deck	30 x 18 pounders
Class	San Ildefonso	Extreme breadth	51 ft 0 ins (14.48 m)	Ordnance - quarter deck	14 x 8 pounders
Designer	Francisco Gautier	Depth in hold	24 ft 6 ins (6.83 m)	Ordnance - forecastle	4 x 8 pounders
Builder	Royal Dockyard	Tons burthen	1676 tons	Ordnance - Poop	(4 x 18 pounder carronades)
Dockyard	Havana	Draught afore		Single broadside weight	678 (714) pounds
Date ordered	–	Draught abaft		Fate	Captured at Trafalgar 21 October 1805. Entered into Royal Navy as *Bahama*. Taken to pieces 1814.
Date keel laid		Complement	690		
Date launched	1780				

Notes: Dimensions are given in English feet.
The ordnance listed above in brackets reflects *Bahama*'s statistics at Trafalgar.

Source: Lyon, *Sailing Navy List*, p. 267.

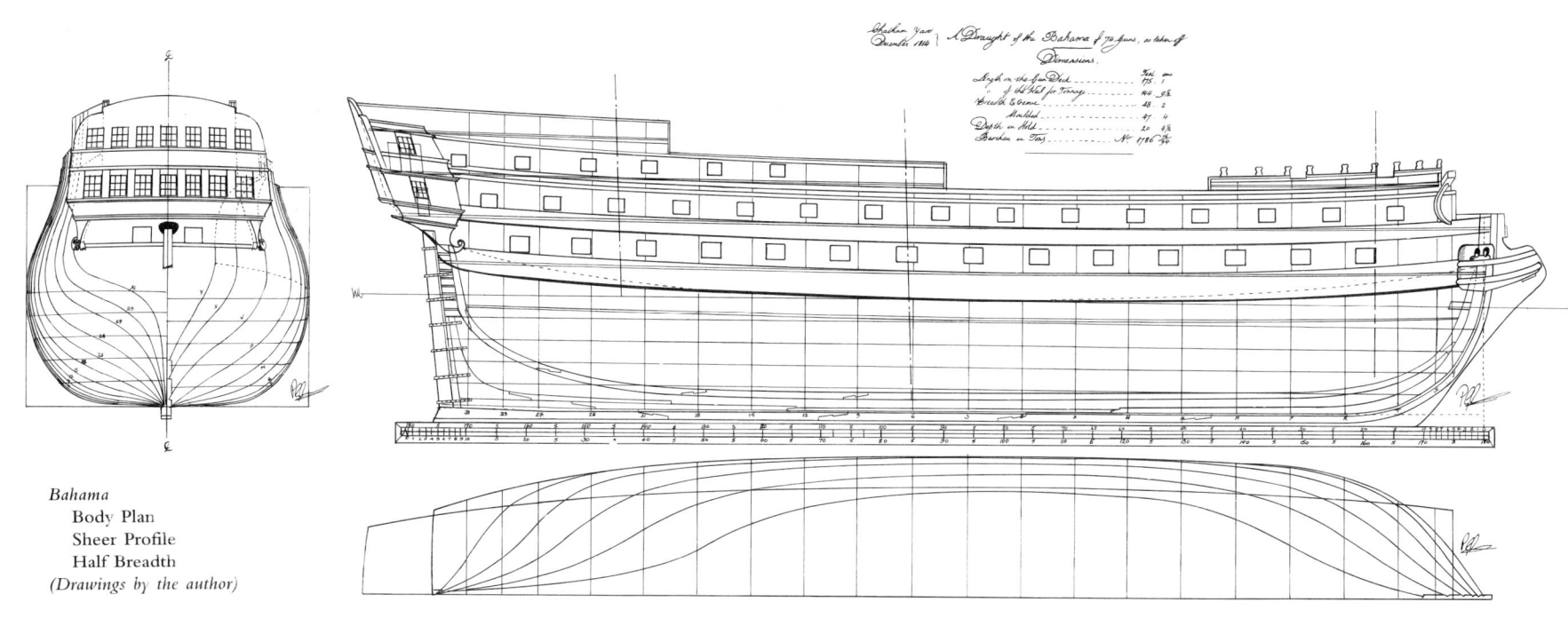

Bahama
  Body Plan
  Sheer Profile
  Half Breadth
(Drawings by the author)

1804: When Spain declared war on Britain on 3 December *Bahama* was prepared for active service and placed under the command of Captain Dionisio Alcalá Galiano. Earlier in his career Galiano was renowned as an explorer and navigator, charting the west coasts of North and South America. Although not always historically accredited, his reputation and legacy are comparable with those of Captain James Cook.[15]

1805: Unlike some of the Spanish fleet *Bahama* did not sail with Villeneuve's combined fleet to the West Indies and consequently did not take part in the action against Calder off Finisterre on 22 July.

TRAFALGAR

By the time *Bahama* had been appointed to join Villeneuve's Franco-Spanish fleet, Captain Galiano had been promoted to the rank of commodore. With the rest of the fleet *Bahama* began to leave Cadiz on the evening of 19 October, but once out of harbour she was compelled to anchor and await the next tide and got under way the next morning. At noon Monday 21 October the *Bahama* was stationed twenty-second from the head of the line; ahead on her larboard bow lay *Pluton* (74), and astern on her starboard quarter *Aigle* (74). Placed near the centre of the fleet, *Bahama* would meet the full weight of Collingwood's attack and opened her fire as the British ships came within range.

Just before 1 p.m. *Bellerophon* bore up and fired through *Bahama*'s stern as she broke through the line, before meeting the unified broadsides of *Monarca* (74), *Aigle* (74) and *Swiftsure*. *Bahama* then added her weight and fired into *Bellerophon* and with the concerted broadsides of the other three ships soon brought down the *Bellerophon*'s main and mizzen topmasts and killed her captain. *Bahama* then came under heavy fire from *Colossus*. Fighting between the two ships continued for 30 minutes during which time *Bahama*'s gunners could only maintain a steady fire against a rapid barrage from her opponent. Although briefly shielded as *Swiftsure* passed between them, *Bahama* soon felt the shock as broadsides from *Colossus* resumed. At this point Commodore Galiano gathered his officers together and reminded them that the flag was nailed to the mast. He then turned to Captain Butron commanding the troops, saying 'I charge you to defend it,

CAPTAINS OF *BAHAMA*: (MS 248/6)

Name	Time of Entry	Time of Discharge	On What Occasion
James Stewart	31 March 1806	28 June 1806	Paid Off at Chatham
J Milne	4 May 1807	24 October 1812	Superseded
H Wilson	24 October 1812	17 October 1814	Paid Off

adding, 'No Galiano ever surrenders, and no Butron should either'. By this point much of *Bahama*'s rigging had been slashed to pieces and her hull holed below the waterline. Still, broadsides poured into the Spanish ship, causing dreadful splinters, one tearing into Galiano's foot, another gashing his head. Refusing to go below for treatment, Galiano continued manning the quarter deck and giving orders to his gunners. When *Colossus* fired again a round shot carried away the telecope in Galiano's hand. As Galiano's coxswain picked up the telescope a round shot severed him in two, covering the commodore in blood. A second round shot then carried away Galiano's head. While his body was being covered by a flag *Bahama*'s surviving officers held a quick council of war and, unable to maintain a sustained defence any longer, struck the colours from *Bahama*'s main mast. Shortly afterwards the mizzen mast went crashing over the side.

Bahama had fought bravely, suffering 20 per cent casualties: of her crew of 690, 75 were killed and 66 wounded. Alternative sources suggest 100 killed and 150 wounded. Despite the fact that *Bahama*'s officers had nailed a British Union flag as a sign of capitulation, *Colossus* was unable to send over a prize crew, consequently *Bahama* simply drifted out of battle flying English colours over Spanish before being taken in tow to Gibraltar.[16]

1806: Over the following weeks *Bahama* was fitted out at Gibraltar to prepare her for sea. Placed under the command of Captain James Stuart on 31 March, she eventually sailed for England. After arriving at Chatham on 12 June, Stuart paid off the ship on 28 June. Over the next few months *Bahama* was fitted out as a prison hulk at an expense of £4,444, of which £652 covered costs for rigging and stores with a further £12 for labour.[17] Completed, she was laid up in the Medway.

PROGRESS BOOK – *BAHAMA* 3rd RATE OF 74 GUNS: Source: ADM 180/10 Folio 160

At what Port	Arrived	Docked	Built or Nature of Repair	Cost of Rigging & Stores Materials £	Workmen £	Grand Total £
Chatham	12 June 1806	15 Oct 1814	Fitted	652	12	4,444
			Taken to Pieces December 1814			

FATE

In her new rôle housing French prisoners of war, Bahama was commanded by Lieutenant A Milne who took up his appointment on 4 May 1807. Because of their lower status, lieutenants commanded prison hulks. According to the ex-French prisoner of war Baron de Bonnefoux, Milne was a 'savage martinet' who left the body of a drowned prisoner exposed on the mud to rot, although there is no evidence to substantiate this anecdote. Bonnefaux also states that Milne held 'disgraceful carouses' on board. During one such he accidentally set Bahama on fire and ordered the prisoners to be shot rather than saving them.[18] After five years in the post Milne was superseded by Lieutenant H Wilson on 24 October 1812. While under Wilson's command the Bahama housed 300 American prisoners of war. 'I never saw', wrote Dr Benjamin Waterhouse in his *Journal of a Young Man of Massachusetts*, published in 1816, 'a set of more ragged, dirty men in my life'. He continued: 'Several persons now prisoners here, and I rank myself among that number, had an idea of British humanity prior to out captivity; but we have been compelled to change our opinion of the people from whom we descended'. Wilson was, Waterhouse implies, compared with the heinous Milne, a passionate quick-tempered man with some sense of justice. Waterhouse also disclosed that Lieutenant Wilson's first mate was always drunk and that during the winter of 1813-14 there had been a serious epidemic of smallpox in the ship.[19] Prison hulks suffered high fatalities. In 1812 one inmate of Bahama was stabbed to death after attempting to steal another's tobacco.[20] When the wars against Napoleon and the American Congress drew to an end Bahama was no longer required. Consequently she was taken into dock at Chatham on 15 October 1814 where, two days later, Wilson finally paid off the ship. The last entry regarding the Bahama states 'Taken to Pieces December 1814'.[21]

The 74 gun ship MONARCA

Designed by Romero Landa, Monarca was the second ship of the Montañez class 74 gun ships built at Ferrol and launched in 1794. The Montañez class was in fact an improved version of Landa's San Ildefonso class of 1785. Monarca's construction was overseen by Julién de Retamosa, in charge of Spanish arsenals and shipyards. Armed with twenty-eight 24 pounders on the lower gun deck, thirty 18 pounders on the upper gun deck, fourteen 8 pounders on the quarter deck and four 8 pounders on the forecastle, Monarca could deliver a single broadside weight of 678 pounds. Like Montañez, Monarca was supplemented with four 18 pounder carronades on her poop increasing her broadside weight by 5 per cent to 714 pounds.[22] Monarca's predecessor of the same name, also of 74 guns and launched at Ferrol in 1756, was captured by Admiral Rodney at the Moonlight Battle 16 January 1780 and sold in 1791.[23]

SERVICE CAREER

1805: It was not until Villeneuve's fleet anchored off Ferrol to make repairs after its encounter with Calder on 22 July that Monarca became involved in the Trafalgar story. At this point Monarca was laid up in Ferrol along with Principe de Asturias (112), the 80 gun ships Argonauta and Neptuno, the 74 gun ships Montañez, San Augustin, San Fransisco de Asis, San Ildefonso, San Juan Nepomuceno and Terrible, and the 64 gun San Fulgencio. Under the command of Captain Don T Argumosa, Monarca joined Villeneuve's combined fleet when these ships sailed from Ferrol for Cadiz on 9 August.

TRAFALGAR

Still commanded by Captain Argumosa, Monarca sailed from Cadiz on 19 October. Stationed twentieth from the head of the line on the morning of the battle, she would meet the full attack of ships in Collingwood's division. Ahead and astern of her lay the French ships Algésiras (74) and Pluton (74) respectively, each bearing further to leeward. As the battle opened Monarca fired into the approaching British ships, carrying away the ensign of Belleisle (74). When Belleisle returned her fire a round shot cut Prudencio Ruiz Alegria in two as he was taking charge of Monarca's Spanish ensign. At about 12.15 p.m. Monarca turned to starboard to fire her larboard broadside into Mars (74) which was bearing down upon Pluton, which by this point had overtaken Monarca to close the gap in the line. Shortly afterwards Tonnant (80) crossed through the line and fired her double shotted larboard broadsides through Monarca's stern, bringing down her fore course and crossjack yards. After severely raking the Spanish ship, Tonnant ran close alongside Monarca's starboard side and pummelled her for three quarters of an hour, during which time fires broke out briefly below deck and several officers, including Lieutenant Ramón Amaya, were killed. Very much beaten and unable to fire her guns, Monarca drifted downwind and according to Spartiate's log, at '1-7 a Spanish two Decker struck to the Tonnant'.[24] Monarca's colours were soon re-hoisted, however, at which point she then crossed Tonnant's bow and raked her before going on to engage Bellerophon (74), which was also engaged on her opposite side by the French Aigle (74). Despite the British ship being surrounded, her broadsides continued to pour into Monarca, compelling Captain Argumosa to finally strike her colours. Casualties within Monarca comprised 101 dead and 154 wounded. As for damage, much of her rigging had been severely cut, leaving her masts in a very unsafe condition.

FATE

Lieutenant Edward Thomas, Midshipman Henry Walker and eight men from Bellerophon took possession. Walker later recalled that as they were

SPECIFICATIONS: MONARCA

Rate	3rd	Length on the range of the gun deck	190 Burgos feet (54.60 m) [175 ft 3 ins Eng.]	Draught abaft	23 ft 3 in. (6.48 m)
Guns	74 (80)			Complement	715
Class	Montañez (based on San Ildefonso class)	Length of keel for tonnage	181 ft 0 ins (5043 m)	Ordnance - lower gun deck	28 x 24 pounders (28 x 24 pounders)
		Extreme breadth	51 ft 0 ins (14.21 m) [48 ft 5½ ins Eng.]	Ordnance - upper gun deck	30 x 18 pounders (30 x 24 pounders)
Designer	Romero Landa			Ordnance - quarter deck	14 x 8 pounders
Builder	Artillero Real (Royal Dockyard)	Depth in hold	25 ft 6 ins (7.11 m) [20 ft 10 ins Eng.]	Ordnance - forecastle	4 x 8 pounders
Dockyard	Ferrol	Tons burthen	1753 tons Eng. Tons displacement 1,815.5 tons (2,756.83 cubic metres)	Ordnance - poop	(4 x 18 pounder carronades)
Date ordered				Single broadside weight	678 (714) pounds
Date keel laid		Ballast	12,000 to 13,000 quintals (552 to 598 tons)	Fate	Foundered in the storm October 1805 after the battle of Trafalgar.
Date launched	1794	Draught afore	26 ft 7 in. (7.39 m)		

securing *Monarca* the ship was fired upon by Dumanoir's ships as they passed in retreat. After the battle great efforts were made by the prize crew to get *Monarca* in some condition to endure the forthcoming storm, while Spanish seamen manned the pumps continuously. Throughout Wednesday 23 October, according to Midshipman Walker, *Monarca* began to drift while riding at her anchor and was in serious distress. Walker also noted that she was making three feet of water in her hold per hour and that the additional prize crew put on board had broken into the spirit room and become intoxicated. During the night of Thursday 24 October, when the storm was at its worse, *Monarca* rolled out her masts. The next morning she ran onshore at Arenas Gordos, just north of San Lucar, and went to pieces, taking 170 people to their deaths.[25]

The 74 gun ship SAN AGUSTIN

Designed by Jorge Juan and built to the lines of the *San Juan Nepomuceno* class 74 gun ships, *San Agustin* was launched at Guarnizo, Santander in 1769. In many respects her sister ships were *San Francisco de Asis* and *San Justo*. Like all her class *San Agustin* was armed with twenty-eight 24 pounders on the lower gun deck, thirty 18 pounders on the upper gun deck, fourteen 8 pounders on the quarter deck and four 8 pounders on the forecastle giving her a single broadside weight of 678 pounds. In 1800 her ordnance was supplemented with four 18 pounder carronades on her poop, increasing her broadside weight by five per cent to 714 pounds.[26]

SERVICE CAREER

1800: Before this date *San Agustin* played little part in any major operation other than escorting the Spanish mercantile fleets plying between Cuba, the West Indies, and South America or alternative voyages in the Mediterranean. Her first campaign deployment came in June 1800 when she was appointed to form part of Admiral Mazzaredo's fleet being prepared at Ferrol. Flying his flag in *San Hermenegildo* (112), Mazzaredo's squadron also comprised *Real Carlos* (112), *San Fernando* (96), *Argonauta* (80) and *San Antonio* (74). Although Ferrol came under attack by ships from Rear-Admiral Sir John Borlase Warren's squadron and troops under Lieutenant-General Sir James Pulteney in late August, the British attempt to take the town and destroy Mazzaredo's ships failed.[27]

1801: Placed under the command of Captain Don R Topete, *San Agustin* took part in the action off Algeciras against Rear-Admiral Sir James Saumarez's squadron on 12 July. The combined Franco-Spanish fleet present at this battle jointly commanded by Vice Admiral Moreno and Rear-Admiral Linois is as follows:

Franco-Spanish

Rate or type	Guns	Ships' Names	No.
1st	112	*Real Carlos* and *San Hermenegildo*	2
2nd	94	*San Fernando*	1
3rd	80	*Argonauta*, *Formidable*, and *Indomptable*	3
3rd	74	*San Antonio*, *San Agustin*, and *Desaix*	3
4th	44	*Sabina*	1
5th	40	*Liberté* and *Nurion*	2
Lugger	14	*Vautour*	1
TOTAL			13

British

3rd	80	*Cæsar* (Flagship)	1
3rd	74	*Audacious*, *Spencer*, *Superb*, and *Venerable*	4
5th	32	*Thames*	1
Polacre	14	*Calpe*	1
	–	*Carlotta* (Portuguese)	1
Brig	8	*Louisa*	1
TOTAL			8

Although *San Agustin* did not get fully involved in this action, *Real Carlos* and *San Hermenegildo* both blew up after taking fire. *San Antonio* was captured and entered into the British navy, but never went to sea again.[28]

1805: Like many of the Spanish ships that fought at Trafalgar, *San Agustin*, under the command of Captain Don Felipe Jado Cagigal, joined Villeneuve's fleet at Ferrol and sailed for Cadiz on 9 August. She also sailed from Cadiz with the combined fleet for the Mediterranean on 19 October. On the day of the battle *San Agustin*, stationed eighth in line from the head of the fleet, was leading Villeneuve's squadron. Ahead of her lay *San Francisco de Asis* (74), astern *Héros* (74). To leeward on her starboard quarter lay the French brig *Furet* (18). When battle opened *San Agustin* fired her broadsides towards *Victory* (100) as she approached, but once Nelson's division had made its attack and cut through the line of the fleet, *San Agustin* found herself detached from the main body of the fleet. Following the rest of Dumanoir's squadron *San Agustin* continued northward, unable to give support to the battle astern of her. When she finally acknowledged Villeneuve's signal to wear she bore down bravely upon *Leviathan* (74), leading the British column, and prepared to rake her. Following in *San Agustin*'s wake were *San Francisco de Asis* (74) and *Rayo* (100). Despite the fact that Cagigal had *San Agustin*'s guns crew ready to fire, he found himself quickly outmanœuvred as *Leviathan* ported her helm and came up around the *San Agustin*. Using her larboard batteries she poured a treble shotted broadside into *San Agustin*'s starboard quarter which carried away her mizzen mast and her colours. Within minutes *Leviathan* ran aboard *San Agustin*, pummelled her with another heavy broadside and boarded her without further opposition, compelling Cagigal to strike his colours. The boarding party of seamen and marines was led by Lieutenant John Baldwin. Although only in close action for a short while *San Agustin* sustained many casualties from *Leviathan*'s ferocious broadsides; in all, 184 dead and 201 wounded.

SPECIFICATIONS: *SAN AGUSTIN*

Rate	3rd	Date launched	1769	Complement	683
Guns	74	Length on the range of the gun deck	196 ft 0 ins Burgos (54.61 m)	Ordnance - lower gun deck	28 x 24 pounders
Class	San Juan Nepomuceno	Length of keel for tonnage	–	Ordnance - upper gun deck	30 x 18 pounders
Designer	Jorge Juan	Extreme breadth	51 ft 4 ins Burgos (14.30 m)	Ordnance - quarter deck	14 x 8 pounders
Builder	Artillero Real (Royal Dockyard)	Depth in hold	25 ft 5 ins Burgos (7.12 m)	Ordnance - forecastle	4 x 8 pounders
Dockyard	Guarnizo, Santander	Tons burthen	1600 tons (1740 tons - English measurement)	Ordnance - Poop	(4 x 18 pounder carronades)
Date ordered	–	Draught afore		Single broadside weight	678 (or 714) pounds
Date keel laid		Draught abaft		Fate	Captured at the battle of Trafalgar 21 October 1805 and burnt afterwards.

Explaining his capitulation, Captain Cagigal later reported: 'It was inevitable to surrender to superior numbers and having been boarded twice I had not sufficient men to repel a third boarding, the few who remained being on the gun-decks continued firing into the other ships which were closing round me at pistol shot range'.[29]

While *San Agustin* surrendered, *San Francisco de Asis* and *Rayo* continued to steer away south east to avoid further action. *San Agustin* was taken in tow by *Leviathan*.

FATE

At some point during the following two days the tow appears to have parted and was not reconnected by *Leviathan* until 10 a.m. on Wednesday 23 October, and even then only for a short while. When ships of Rear-Admiral Cosmao-Kerjulien sailed from Cadiz to threaten the British ships and their prizes, *Leviathan* cast off the tow at 4 p.m. as she prepared for action. At this point *San Agustin* was taken in tow by *Bellerophon*. When Collingwood gave orders to sink, burn and destroy the prizes, boats from *Dreadnought* took 149 Spanish seamen from *San Agustin* before the full fury of the storm threatened the safety of the ship; a further 116 were removed by boats from the British *Swiftsure*. When the weather abated somewhat on Saturday 26 October the remainder of *San Agustin*'s crew were taken off. According to one of *San Agustin*'s lieutenants the ship was quite tight and only making eight inches of water in the hold per hour. Despite this the ship, now rudderless, was in too poor a condition to salve and following orders *San Agustin* was set alight on 28 October and continued to burn until she foundered.[30]

The 74 gun ship SAN FRANCISCO DE ASIS

Named after Saint Francis of Assisi, *San Francisco de Asis* was launched at Guarnizo, Santander, in 1767. Designed by Jorge Juan, her lines and specifications were virtually identical to those of the *San Juan Nepomuceno* class 74 gun ships which he had introduced the previous year. Although *San Francisco de Asis* was 38 years old when she fought at Trafalgar this was not uncommon among the Spanish ships. Spain, it must be remembered, was not at war with Britain for as many years as France; therefore, compared with the French, fewer of her ships were captured or destroyed. Even from the time Spain entered the American War of Independence her ships mainly fought a defensive campaign in home waters, for example the siege of Gibraltar. As with most of her class, *San Francisco de Asis* was armed with twenty-eight 24 pounders on the lower gun deck, thirty 18 pounders on the upper gun deck, fourteen 8 pounders on the quarter deck and four 8 pounders on the forecastle. This gave *San Francisco de Asis* a single broadside weight of 678 pounds. Like many of the Spanish ships her original ordnance was supplemented with four 18 pounder carronades on her poop, increasing her broadside weight by 5 per cent to 714 pounds.[31]

SERVICE CAREER

1805: Placed under the command of Captain Don Luis de Florès at Ferrol, *San Francisco de Asis* did not join Villeneuve's fleet until it anchored off Ferrol making repairs after its encounter with Calder on 22 July. With nine other Spanish ships *San Francisco de Asis* sailed from Ferrol with Villeneuve's combined fleet on 9 August and entered Cadiz eleven days later.

TRAFALGAR

Remaining under the command of Captain Florès, *San Francisco de Asis* sailed for the Mediterranean with the combined fleet on 19 October. Forming part of Rear-Admiral Dumanoir Le Pelley's van squadron, *San Francisco de Asis* was stationed seventh in line from the head of the fleet. Ahead on her larboard bow lay *Mont Blanc* (74), astern on her starboard quarter *San Agustin*. Once action had begun and the British weather division had joined the affray, *San Francisco de Asis* appears to have been engaged first briefly with *Britannia* (100). Placed in the foremost part of the fleet, *San Francisco de Asis*, with the rest of Dumanoir's ships, continued sailing northward, experiencing some difficulty in turning about to re-enter the battle and give support to the centre. When *San Agustin* and *San Francisco de Asis* finally wore, with *Rayo* (100) following in their wake, the three ships found themselves bearing down upon *Leviathan* (74) and six other British ships. To avoid an overwhelmingly close confrontation *San Agustin*, *San Francisco de Asis* and *Rayo* each turned to larboard and sailed eastward out of the battle. At 5 p.m. Dumanoir gave the signal to rally the ships of his division. Consequently *San Francisco de Asis*, *Argonauta*, *Montañez*, *Rayo*, *Héros*, and Dumanoir's *Indomptable* made for Cadiz. Although *San Francisco de Asis* come through the battle virtually unscathed, suffering just five killed and twelve wounded, she would later pay a far higher price.

FATE

Despite the storm *San Francisco de Asis* sailed out of Cadiz on 23 October with Conmmodore Cosmao-Kerjulien's squadron, intent on succouring some of the damaged prizes in British hands. Once out of harbour the wind veered, rising to storm force from the WSW. In the face of the deteriorating weather, *San Francisco de Asis* and her consorts pressed on and managed to retake *Santa Ana* (112) and *Neptune* (80). That night, however, *San Francisco de Asis* was forced to anchor. Continuously battered by heavy seas, she dragged her anchors, ran ashore in Cadiz Bay, and went to pieces.[32]

SPECIFICATIONS: *SAN FRANCISCO DE ASIS*

Rate	3rd	Date launched	1767	Complement	683
Guns	74	Length on the range of the gun deck	196 ft 0 ins Burgos (54.61 m)	Ordnance - lower gun deck	28 x 24 pounders
Class	San Juan Nepomuceno	Length of keel for tonnage	-	Ordnance - upper gun deck	30 x 18 pounders
Designer	Jorge Juan	Extreme breadth	51 ft 4 ins Burgos (14.30 m)	Ordnance - quarter deck	14 x 8 pounders
Builder	Artillero Real (Royal Dockyard)	Depth in hold	25 ft 5 ins Burgos (7.12 m)	Ordnance - forecastle	4 x 8 pounders
		Tons burthen	1600 tons (1740 tons - English measurement)	Ordnance - Poop	(4 x 18 pounder carronades)
Dockyard	Guarnizo, Santander			Single broadside weight	678 (or 714) pounds
Date ordered	-	Draught afore		Fate	Recaptured after the battle of Trafalgar and ran onshore and went to pieces 23 October 1805.
Date keel laid		Draught abaft			

wounded in the left arm and chest by flying splinters and taken below to the surgeon, command of *San Ildefonso* was in the hands of the second in command, Frigate Captain (First Lieutenant) Amselmo Gomendio. At around 3 p.m. *Defence* (74) drew up alongside *San Ildefonso* and commenced firing into her starboard side with great intensity, bringing down her masts, smashing into her hull and dismounting guns. At 3.45 p.m. Gomendio sent Lieutenant Benito Garisoaín to Captain Vagras concerning the condition of the ship and her casualties; Vagras refused to surrender. Close action between *San Ildefonso* and *Defence* continued and within half an hour *San Ildefonso*'s hull had been breached in many places at the waterline, especially near her sternpost. Although all four pumps were manned, she was making considerable water. *San Ildefonso*'s situation was now critical; much damaged and unable to defend her any longer, Gomendio once again sent word to Vagras. This time Vagras agreed and at 4.30 p.m. *San Ildefonso* struck her colours. Casualties within *San Ildefonso* comprised 34 dead, among whom were lieutenants Agustín Monzón and José de Rozo; of her 148 wounded, six were officers, including Captain Vagras. Alternative figures suggest 36 dead and 129 wounded.[50] Once seaman and marines had taken possession, Gomendio went into *Defence* but after half an hour was released by Captain George Hope to return and prevent *San Ildefonso* from sinking. After the battle *San Ildefonso* was one of the few ships to anchor. The others, besides *Defence*, were the prize ships *Bahama* (74) and the French *Swiftsure* (74). Taken under tow *San Ildefonso* was taken into Gibraltar where necessary repairs were effected to make her seaworthy for her voyage to England.[51]

FATE

San Ildefonso was taken to Portsmouth and entered into the Royal Navy under her original name *San Ildefonso*. Until a decision was made concerning her future she was simply laid up. On 3 April 1806 she was placed under the command of John Quilliam who had served as First Lieutenant in *Victory* at Trafalgar. Williams remained in the *San Ildefonso* until she paid off at Portsmouth on 19 June 1806. On 22 July 1808 *San Ildefonso* was briefly recommissioned under Captain Edward Harvey until reduced and used as a victualling storeship at Portsmouth later that year.[52] According to Lyon, she was moored at Spithead as a victualling ship. As no Progress Book exists it is assumed that no work was carried out during her eleven years laid up as a hulk. Being of no further use and well beyond her years at the end of the war, *San Ildefonso* was finally broken up in July 1816.[53]

ENGLISH CAPTAINS OF *SAN ILDEFONSO* (MS 248/6)

Name	Time of Entry	Time of Discharge	On What Occasion
John Quilliam	3 April 1806	19 June 1806	Paid Off at Portsmouth
Edward Harvey	22 July 1808		

The 74 gun ship SAN JUAN NEPOMUCENO

Designed by Jorge Juan, *San Juan Nepomuceno* was launched at the Artillero Real, Guarnizo, Santander, in 1766. Consequently she was one of the older Spanish 74 gun ships serving at Trafalgar. Built to marginally larger dimensions than her English counterparts, 3,500 to 4,000 loads of timber were used for her construction which in volume relates to between 175,00 and 200,000 cubic feet of wood before conversion. Armed with twenty-eight 24 pounders on her lower gun deck, thirty 18 pounders on her upper gun deck, fourteen 8 pounders on her quarter deck and four 8 pounders on her forecastle, this gave *San Juan Nepomuceno* a single broadside weight of 678 pounds. Later fitted with four 18 pounder carronades on her poop deck, her broadside weight was increased by just five per cent to 714 pounds.

SERVICE CAREER

1785: Little is recorded in English sources about *San Juan Nepomuceno*'s career before this date. However, it is known that the she was in sea trials during August of this year, where her sailing capabilities were tested against the new built ship *San Ildefonso*. Also present during these trials were the frigates *San Brigada* and *San Casilda*. The results of this experiment proved that the *San Ildefonso* designed by Romero Landa proved far superior: *San Juan Nepomuceno* was slower and could not sail to windward as well as the *San Ildefonso*. During these trials *San Juan Nepomuceno* visited Algiers.[54]

1797: Attached to the Mediterranean fleet, *San Juan Nepomuceno* was based at Cartagena where on 1 February she sailed with the fleet of Lieutenant-General (Admiral) José de Córdoba y Ramos for Brest. After passing through the Straits of Gibraltar on 5 February *San Juan Nepomuceno* intended to put into Cadiz with the other 26 ships of the line for provisions. However prevailing easterly winds prevented this. As a result Córdoba was forced to stay at sea west of Cadiz and consequently fell in with the British blockading fleet commanded by Admiral Sir John Jervis on 14 February. Like quite a number of ships *San Juan Nepomuceno* does not appear to have been heavily engaged during the ensuing battle and reached Cadiz afterwards. Three ships were captured, *San Josef*, *San Nicolas* and *San Ysidro*.[55] *San Juan Nepomuceno* then remained for the most part laid up in port until deployed with Vice-Admiral Villeneuve's combined fleet in 1805.

1804: Once Spain entered the war on the side of France there was much activity in her dockyards preparing ships for sea and re-arming shore batteries. *San Juan Nepomuceno*, placed back into commission at Ferrol, com-

SPECIFICATIONS: *SAN JUAN NEPOMUCENO*

Rate	3rd	Date launched	1766	Ordnance - lower gun deck	28 x 24 pounders
Guns	74	Length overall	196 ft 0 ins Burgos (54.61 m)	Ordnance - upper gun deck	30 x 18 pounders
Class	San Juan Nepomuceno	Length of keel for tonnage	-	Ordnance - quarter deck	14 x 8 pounders
Designer	Jorge Juan	Extreme breadth	51 ft 4 ins Burgos (14.30 m)	Ordnance - forecastle	4 x 8 pounders
Builder	Artillero Real (Royal Dockyard)	Depth in hold	25 ft 5 ins Burgos (7.12 m)	Ordnance - Poop	(4 x 18 pounder carronades)
		Tons burthen	1600 tons (1/40 tons - English measurement)	Single broadside weight	678 (or 714) pounds
Dockyard	Guarnizo, Santander	Draught afore		Fate	Captured at Trafalgar 21 October 1805. Entered into Royal Navy and renamed *Berwick*, then *San Juan*. Harbour service. Broken up 1814.
Date ordered	-	Draught abaft			
Date keel laid		Complement	683		

Source: *Modelos de Arsenal del Museo Naval*; Colledge, p. 482; Lyon, *Sailing Navy List*, p. 268.

THE 74 GUN SHIP *SAN JUAN NEPOMUCENO*

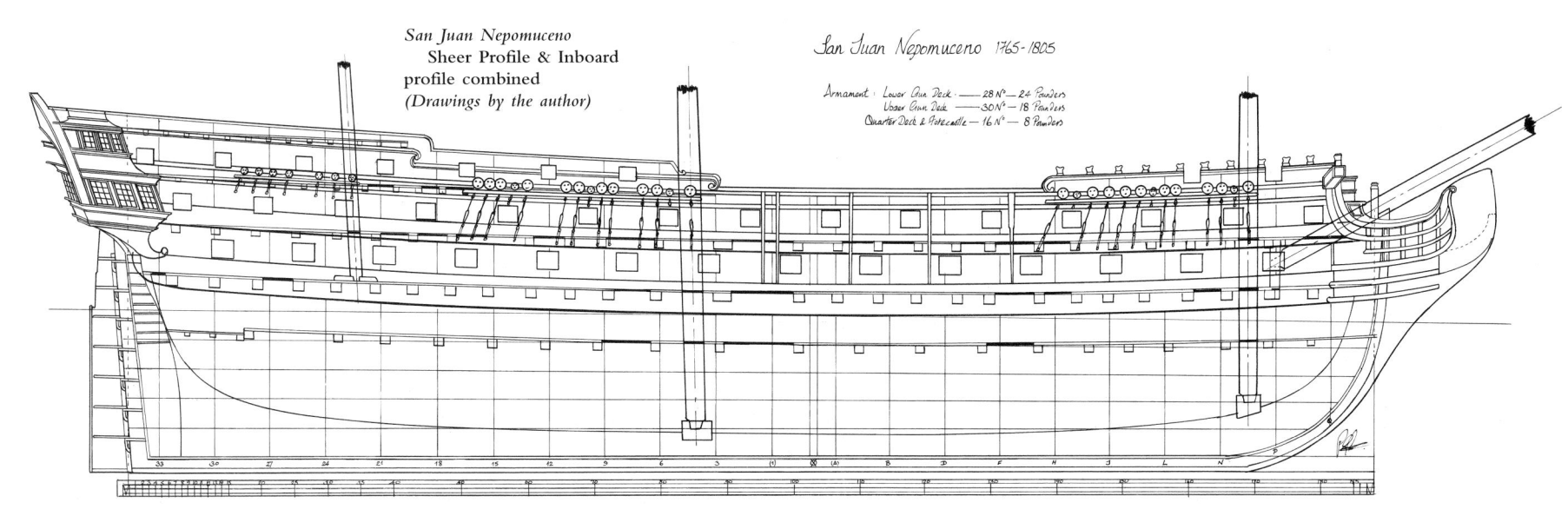

San Juan Nepomuceno
Sheer Profile & Inboard profile combined
(Drawings by the author)

menced fitting out under Commodore Don Cosmé Damián Churruca. According to Admiral Cochrane, who looked into Ferrol on 13 November, *San Juan Nepomuceno* and *Principe de Asturias* (112) were both fitting out and having their lower masts stepped.[56]

1805: *San Juan Nepomuceno* remained in harbour until Villeneuve's combined fleet anchored off Ferrol after their action against Calder on 22 July. While in harbour, troops from the Regimento de Soria, Regimento de Africa and the Regimento de Corona were embarked into Spanish ships to supplement limited crews, *San Juan Nepomuceno* being no exception.[57] As part of Admiral Gravina's squadron *San Juan Nepomuceno* sailed from Ferrol on 9 August with Villeneuve's fleet. The total Spanish ships joining Villeneuve were as follows:

Rate	Guns	Name	No.
1st	112	*Principe de Asturias*	1
3rd	80	*Argonauta* and *Neptuno*	2
3rd	74	*Terrible*, *Monarca*, *Montañez*, *San Agustin*, *San Francisco de Asis*, *San Ildefonso* and *San Juan Nepomuceno*	8
3rd	64	**San Fulgencio**	1
Total			11

Note: Those denoted in bold type were NOT present at Trafalgar

Instead of going north to support the invasion of Britain, the entire fleet sailed south to Cadiz, arriving there on 20 August. Once in port Commodore Churruca continued to recruit more men into his ship; manning the fleet with prime seamen had proved particularly difficult. A few days before the fleet sailed Churruca married a young bride who, within the week, would become a widow.

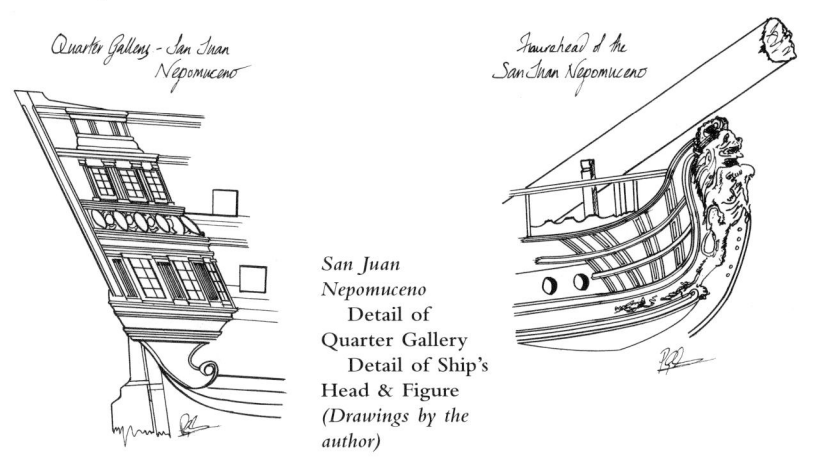

San Juan Nepomuceno Detail of Quarter Gallery Detail of Ship's Head & Figure *(Drawings by the author)*

TRAFALGAR

Deployed with Gravina's observation squadron, *San Juan Nepomuceno* sailed from Cadiz in the early morning of Sunday 20 October. Once the combined fleet had left harbour and commenced sailing towards the Straits of Gibraltar, *San Juan Nepomuceno* was effectively the leading ship. This however was to change. After the fleet altered course northward at 8 a.m. on the morning of the battle, *San Juan Nepomuceno* was stationed last in line of battle. The next ship ahead of her was *Berwick* (74). Being the rearmost ship, it was 12.45 p.m. before the *San Juan Nepomuceno* actually engaged with any British ships. Using her starboard batteries, she first exchanged broadsides at a distance with *Defiance* (74). She also exchanged fire with *Belleisle* and carried away her main topmast. At about 1.30 p.m. *San Juan Nepomuceno* came under distant fire from *Tonnant*. Fifteen minutes later *San Juan Nepomuceno* engaged *Bellerophon*. Shrouded by battle smoke, Churruca's ship fired a raking broadside into *Bellerophon*'s stern with good effect. Preparing to fire a second and equally effective salvo into *Bellerophon*, *San Juan Nepomuceno* suddenly found herself fired upon by *Dreadnought* (98), ranged up upon her starboard side. Totally outgunned, *San Juan Nepomuceno* fought against the great three-decker. Churruca kept his nerve throughout. The ceaseless barrage continued for ten minutes, during which Churruca went below to give further directions to the gunners. As he returned to the quarter deck he was hit in the right leg with a round shot 'with such violence as almost to take it off, tearing it across the thigh in the most frightful manner'. Attempting to raise himself on one arm, 'his face was as white as death', and yet he boldly said 'It is nothing - go on firing'. While his officers encouraged him to go below he dismissed them; then, finding that his second officer Moyna had been killed, he ordered the officer on the upper gun deck to assume command. He too had been wounded but once on deck Churruca agreed to go down to the surgeon but before doing so ordered that the flag be nailed to the mast and that the ship must not surrender while he still lived. Once down in the cockpit Churruca began to fade fast but despite his condition insisted that the men should be thanked for their courage. He then spoke with the chaplain and resigned himself to prayer before he died. Describing his conduct later a Spanish report stated that he 'directed the battle with gloomy calmness. Knowing that only care and skill could supply the place of strength, he economised our fire, trusting entirely to careful aim, and the consequence that each ball did terrible havoc on the foe. He saw to everything, settled everything, and the shot flew round him and over his head without his ever once even changing colour'.

The horrendous battering sustained from *Deadnought* combined with the high casualties and the loss of their commander quickly broke the morale of *San Juan Nepomuceno*'s crew and within ten minutes she struck her colours. Suffering 37 per cent casualties, there were 103 dead and 151 wounded. As for the ship, many of her guns were out of action, her hull was

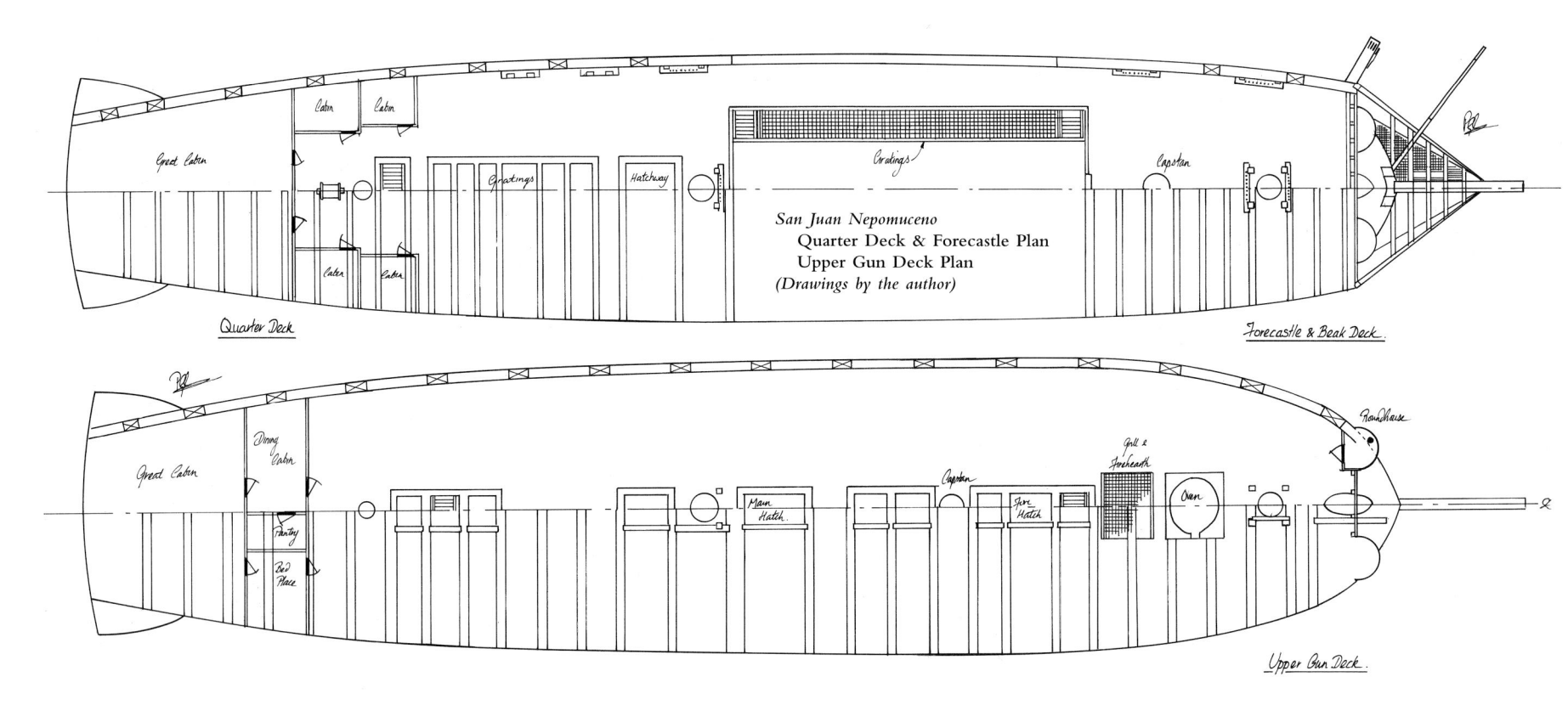

San Juan Nepomuceno
Quarter Deck & Forecastle Plan
Upper Gun Deck Plan
(Drawings by the author)

riddled with shot, her rudder was shot to pieces and only her main mast remained standing. Unable to steer or make sail she attempted to withdraw. Shortly after the *Defiance* took possession of *San Juan Nepomuceno* and took her under tow. That evening *San Juan Nepomuceno* was one of the few vessels that anchored to ride out the storm. She was one of only four prize ships that actually arrived at Gibraltar, the others being lost or recaptured.[58]

FATE

Brought to England, *San Juan Nepomuceno* went into Chatham on 12 June 1806. Renamed HMS *San Juan* and then *Berwick*, she was laid up in ordinary in the River Medway for eight years, during which she appears to have had nine commanders. Because she was re-rated a sloop her officers were commanders by rank, not captains. Whatever work and associated expenses were made to cover refit work during this period is not entered into the ship's Progress Book. On 15 October *San Juan* was taken into dock at Chatham and 'Taken to Pieces December 1814'.[59] This is at variance from Lyon's statement that she was not brought back to Britain but retained at Gibraltar until sold in 1818; Colledge simply states that she was in service until 1816.[60]

ENGLISH CAPTAINS OF *SAN JUAN NEPOMUCENO*:
(MS 248/6)

Name	Time of Entry	Time of Discharge	On What Occasion
Thomas Spence	1 September 1805		
John Gourly	13 November 1808	25 November 1808	To *Atlas*
Thomas Spence	26 November 1808	6 March 1809	Acting Lieutenant of the Ship
John Gourly	7 March 1809	1 July 1810	Superseded
Thomas Vivian	2 July 1810	12 September 1810	Superseded
C V Penrose	13 September 1810	11 January 1813	Superseded
James Tillard	12 January 1813	4 November 1813	Superseded Invalided
F E Thomas	8 February 1814	27 May 1814	Superseded
G H Guion	28 May 1814	28 July 1814	To *Elizabeth*
Charles McKenzie	27 September 1814	6 November 1816	Paid Off

EXTRACT OF PROGRESS BOOK – *SAN JUAN NEPOMUCENO* 3rd RATE OF 74 GUNS: Source ADM 180/10

At what Port	Arrived	Docked	Coppered	Launched or Undocked
Chatham	12 June 1806	15 Oct 1814		

Taken to Pieces December 1814

The 74 gun ship *SAN JUSTO*

Based on *San Ildefonso*'s lines and designed by Francisco Gautier, *San Justo* was launched at Cartagena in 1779. In many respects *Bahama*, similarly designed, was a sister ship to *San Justo*. Armed with twenty-eight 24 pounders on the lower gun deck, thirty 18 pounders on the upper gun deck, fourteen 8 pounders on the quarter deck and four 8 pounders on the forecastle, the *San Justo* delivered a single broadside weight of 678 pounds. This was increased by five per cent to 714 pounds when four 18 pounder carronades were added to her poop.[61]

SERVICE CAREER

1805: Before this year *San Justo* does not appear to have been involved in any major campaign; neither was she present at the siege of Gibraltar nor the battle of Cape St Vincent, as one would have expected. In the summer of 1805 *San Justo* was in dock refitting at Ferrol under the command of Don Francisco Javíer Garstón, her newly appointed captain.[62] Garstón, like MacDonnell commanding *Rayo*, had been recalled from retirement to serve in the Spanish Royal Navy. Besides being hastily refitted and commissioned,

THE 74 GUN SHIP SAN JUSTO

SPECIFICATIONS: SAN JUSTO

Rate	3rd	Length on the range of the gun deck	192 Burgos feet 2 ins (53.55 m)	Ordnance - lower gun deck	28 x 24 pounders
Guns	74	Length of keel for tonnage	167 ft 3 ins (48.06 m) estimated	Ordnance - upper gun deck	30 x 18 pounders
Class	San Ildefonso	Extreme breadth	51 ft 0 ins (14.48 m)	Ordnance - quarter deck	14 x 8 pounders
Designer	Francisco Gautier	Depth in hold	24 ft 6 ins (6.83 m)	Ordnance - forecastle	4 x 8 pounders
Builder	Royal Dockyard	Tons burthen	1676 tons	Ordnance - Poop	(4 x 18 pounder carronades)
Dockyard	Cartagena	Draught afore		Single broadside weight	678 (714) pounds
Date ordered	-	Draught abaft		Fate	Reached Cadiz after the battle of Trafalgar 21 October 1805. Disposed 1828.
Date keel laid		Complement	694		
Date launched	1779				

Garstón's crew were mainly raw recruits with little seamanship experience, a factor that would affect her ability in the battle.[63] Once completed *San Justo* joined Villeneuve's fleet with the other appointed Spanish ships of the line and sailed from Ferrol for Cadiz on 9 August.

TRAFALGAR

San Justo sailed from Cadiz on 19 October and on the morning of the battle found herself stationed at the centre of the fleet in fifteenth position from the head of the line. Ahead and to windward on her larboard bow lay *San Leandro* (74) and astern to windward on her larboard quarter *Santa Ana* (112) and the French *Indomptable* (80).

When firing began just before noon, *San Justo* was so badly placed to leeward of *Santa Ana* that she could hardly bring her guns to bear on *Royal Sovereign* (100) and other approaching British ships. When *Téméraire* (98) made her turn to come to *Victory*'s aid and was engaged by *Santa Ana*, *San Justo* with *San Leandro* poured their broadsides jointly into the British 98. The inexperience of *San Justo*'s crew began to tell as they failed to manoeuvre the ship into close action with British ships as they came into range. *San Justo* continued to bear off to leeward and as she, with *San Leandro*, fell back and passed *Belleisle*, both ships fired their broadsides into her. At this point *Belleisle* was surrounded and taking fire from every quarter. After this *San Justo* gave support to *Principe de Asturias* (112) as she also removed herself from the battle.[64] Blame for *San Justo* not getting into close action was conveniently placed upon the crew. Reporting afterwards, Captain Garstón publicly stated that his crew had had inadequate training, the reason why she remained well to leeward instead of going to windward to give support. *San Justo* came through the battle virtually unscathed, suffering just seven wounded.[65]

San Justo did not go directly into Cadiz but, on the morning of 23 October, tried to help the stricken *Algésiras*. Later that day she sailed with Cosmao-Kerjulien's squadron of ships comprising *Pluton*, *Neptune*, *Héros*, *Rayo*, *San Francisco de Asis* and several French frigates and brigs to recapture some of the prizes captured by the British fleet. During this sortie *San Justo* lost her main and mizzen masts. Considering that *San Justo*'s crew had already proved their inexperience as seamen it is remarkable that her officers considered making this attempt in such appalling weather.

FATE

San Justo was repaired at Cadiz and continued to operate in the Spanish navy until disposed of in 1828 after giving 49 years' service.

The 64 gun ship SAN LEANDRO

Although some sources suggest that *San Leandro* was a two decked ship of 74 guns, she was in fact built as a 64 gun ship, the only one of her class within the Spanish fleet present at the battle of Trafalgar. Designed by Romero Landa, she was built at the Royal Dockyard in Ferrol and launched in 1787. Although *San Leandro* was a smaller class of ship, her lines were based on those of the 74 gun *San Ildefonso*, also designed by Landa. Being larger than the British equivalent, it is estimated that some 2,870 loads of timber were used in her construction. At 50 cubic feet of timber per load, this equates to 143,500 cubic feet of wood before conversion. The Spanish 64 gun ships were generally armed with twenty-six 24 pounders on the lower gun deck, twenty-six 18 pounders on the upper gun deck, ten 8 pounders on the quarter deck and four 8 pounders on the forecastle. *San Leandro* could thus deliver a single broadside weight of 602 pounds. Whether she carried additional carronades at the time of Trafalgar is uncertain. It is quite probable the *San Leandro* was enlarged to carry 74 guns before Trafalgar. In this case two additional ports would have been cut in the lower and upper gun decks and her quarter deck and forecastle. After this modification her new complement of ordnance would have comprised twenty-eight 24 pounders on her lower gun deck, twenty-eight 18 pounders on the upper gun deck, twelve 8 pounders on the quarter deck and six 8 pounders on the forecastle. This increase of nine per cent gave her a revised broadside weight of 660 pounds.

SERVICE CAREER

1804: Before this date the career of *San Leandro* does not appear to have had any great significance. As a relatively small ship it is highly probable that she spent much of the previous 17 years undertaking escort duties, rather than forming part of a battle fleet such as those that fought off Cape St

SPECIFICATIONS: SAN LEANDRO

Rate	3rd	Date launched	1787	Complement	606
Guns	64	Length on the range of the gun deck	192 Burgos feet 2 ins (53.55 m)	Ordnance - lower gun deck	26 x 24 pounders
Class	San Leandro	Length of keel for tonnage	167 ft 3 ins (48.06 m) estimated	Ordnance - upper gun deck	26 x 18 pounders
Designer	Romero Landa	Extreme breadth	51 ft 0 ins (14.48 m)	Ordnance - quarter deck	10 x 8 pounders
Builder	Royal Dockyard	Depth in hold	24 ft 6 ins (6.83 m)	Ordnance - forecastle	4 x 8 pounders
Dockyard	Ferrol	Tons burthen	1676 tons	Single broadside weight	602 pounds
Date ordered	-	Draught afore		Fate	Taken to pieces 1813.
Date keel laid		Draught abaft			

Note: Dimensions are given in English feet. The ordnance listed above in brackets reflects *San Leandro*'s statistics at Trafalgar.

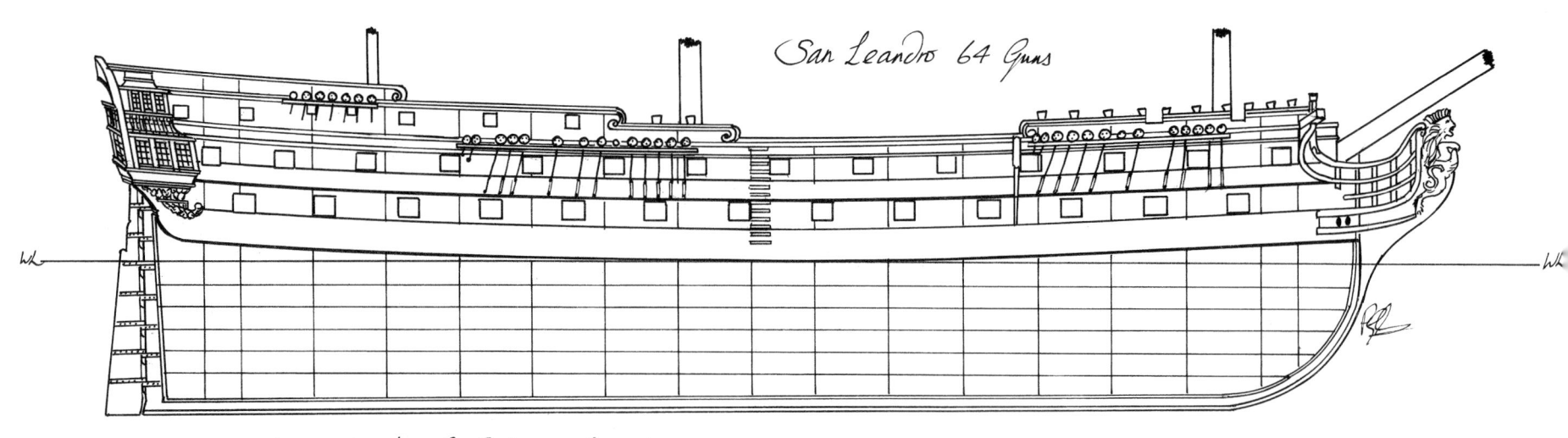

San Leandro
Sheer Profile
(Drawing by the author)

Armament - Lower Gun Deck - 26 N° 24 pdrs
Upper Gun Deck - 26 N° 12 pdrs
Quarter Deck - 10 N° 8 pdrs
Forecastle - 4 N° 8 pdrs

Vincent in 1797. For the most part Spain had remained neutral, but this was to change. When Spain entered the war against Britain on 3 December, *San Leandro* was taken out of reserve and recommissioned under the command of Captain Don José Quevedo. She was then prepared quickly for active service.

1805: *San Leandro* did not sail with Villeneuve's combined fleet to the West Indies and consequently did not take part in the action against Calder off Finisterre on 22 July. She did, however, find herself committed to Villeneuve's combined fleet as it made preparations to sail on a new campaign to the Mediterranean.

TRAFALGAR

Still under the command of Captain Quevedo, *San Leandro* sailed from Cadiz with the rest of the fleet on 19 October. Just before battle commenced at noon on 21 October *San Leandro* was stationed fourteenth in line from the head of the combined fleet. Ahead of her lay *Redoutable* (74), astern the *San Justo* (74), while distant on her starboard beam, the French frigate *Hortense* (40). Besides opening fire upon Collingwood's ships as they made their approach, *San Leandro* did not get into close action until *Royal Sovereign* (100) ran alongside *Santa Ana* (112). At this point Quevedo ordered the braces to be manned, and wearing ship, brought *San Leandro* round to starboard and fired a raking broadside into *Royal Sovereign*. *San Justo* did likewise and with *San Leandro* fired their starboard batteries into *Royal Sovereign*. Although *San Leandro* does not appear to have played any significant part in the battle after this point by getting into close action with any particular opponent, she did suffer damage to her masts, rigging and hull. With most of her adversaries having a far greater firepower, *San Leandro* with just 64 guns of lower calibre was at a disadvantage so it is quite understandable that Captain Quevedo remained somewhat prudent when choosing his opponents. At the end of the day *San Leandro* rallied with Dumanoir's ships and made for Cadiz. Casualties within *San Leandro* were low, with just eight killed and 22 wounded.[66]

FATE

The *San Leandro* reached the safety of Cadiz before the storm really set in. Closely blockaded by Collingwood's squadron *San Leandro* remained in Cadiz until Spain declared war on France in 1808. Although she may have been employed for minor duties or just simply laid up in ordinary, *San Leandro* remained in service until broken up in 1812.

NOTES TO PART 3: CHAPTER 2

1. Clowes, 4, pp. 424-425.
2. Clowes, 4, pp. 466-469
3. Clowes 5, pp. 99-115.
4. Clowes, 5, pp. 151; Pope, *England Expects*, pp. 303-305.
5. *Modelos de Arsenal del Museo Naval*; Harbron, *Trafalgar and the Spanish Navy*, pp. 42-46.
6. Pope, *England Expects*, 290-201.
7. *Modelos de Arsenal del Museo Naval*; Harbron, *Trafalgar and the Spanish Navy*, 42-46.
8. Clowes, 4, pp. 307-309.
9. Pope, *England Expects*, p. 234.
10. Clowes, 5, pp. 149-150.
11. Clayton & Craig, *Trafalgar: the Men, the Battle, the Storm*, pp. 299-307.
12. Clowes, 5, pp. 246, 558; Schom, *Trafalgar*, pp. 190, 403.
13. Clowes, 4, p. 115.
14. Clowes, 4, pp. 307-309.
15. Harbron, *Trafalgar and the Spanish Navy*, p. 84.
16. Pope, *England Expects*, pp. 300-301, 341.
17. TNA: PRO, ADM 180/111 folio 160.
18. Garneray, *The Floating Prison*, p. 224 and *Mes Pontons*; Branch-Johnson, *The English Prison Hulks*, p. 55.
19. Branch-Johnson, *The English Prison Hulks*, pp. 77-79.
20. Branch-Johnson, *The English Prison Hulks*, p. 84.
21. RNM, MS 248/6; TNA: PRO ADM 180/111 folio 160.
22. *Modelos de Arsenal del Museo Naval*; Harbron, *Trafalgar and the Spanish Navy*, pp. 42-46.
23. Lyon, p. 215.
24. TNA: PRO, ADM 51/1543 part 1.
25. Clayton & Craig, *Trafalgar: the Men, the Battle, the Storm*, pp. 224-334.
26. *Modelos de Arsenal del Museo Naval*; Harbron, *Trafalgar and the Spanish Navy*, pp. 42-46.
27. Clowes, 4, pp. 424-425.
28. Clowes, 4, pp. 466-467.
29. Pope, *England Expects*, pp. 225-227.
30. Clayton & Craig, *Trafalgar*, pp. 299-337.
31. *Modelos de Arsenal del Museo Naval*; Harbron *Trafalgar and the Spanish Navy*, 42-46.
32. Pope, *England Expects*, p. 339.
33. *Modelos de Arsenal del Museo Naval*, pp. 317-318.
34. *Ibid*.
35. *Ibid*.
36. *Ibid*.
37. *Ibid*.
38. *Ibid*.
39. *Ibid*.
40. *Ibid*.
41. *Ibid*.
42. *Ibid*.
43. Clowes, 4, pp. 306-313.
44. *Modelos de Arsenal del Museo Naval*, p. 319.
45. *Ibid*.
46. *Ibid*.
47. *Ibid*.
48. *Ibid*.
49. *Ibid*.
50. Pope, *England Expects*, p. 357.
51. Pope, *England Expects*, p. 316; *Modelos de Arsenal del Museo Naval*, p. 320.
52. RNM, MS 248/6 & 7.
53. Lyon, p. 268; Colledge, 1, p. 483.
54. *Modelos de Arsenal del Museo Naval*, pp. 317-318.
55. Clowes, 4, pp. 306-313.
56. Schom, *Trafalgar*, p. 179.
57. Pope, *England Expects*, p. 148.
58. Clowes, 5, p. 156; Schom, *Trafalgar*, pp. 339-355; Pope, *England Expects*, pp. 314-316.
59. TNA: PRO, ADM 180/10.
60. Lyon, p. 268; Colledge, p. 482.
61. *Modelos de Arsenal del Museo Naval*; Harbron, *Trafalgar and the Spanish Navy*, pp. 42-46.
62. Clowes, 5, p. 131, wrongly gives the name as M Garstón.
63. Clayton & Craig, *Trafalgar*, pp. 87, 143.
64. Clayton & Craig, *Trafalgar*, pp. 142-221.
65. Harbron, *Trafalgar and the Spanish Fleet*, pp. 119, 122, 123, 134.
66. Pope, pp. 273-275; Clowes, 5, pp. 137-139.

CONCLUSION

To reiterate the introduction, an objective of this book is to evaluate the matériel, industrial technology and manufacturing capacity required to place the British, French and Spanish ships off Cape Trafalgar. How much effort was implemented by each nation? To this end the conclusion examines several key elements: dockyards and manpower, ship designers and builders, ships' draughts, timber quantities and procurement, block manufacture, copper sheathing, rigging cordage, sail manufacture, ordnance and firepower. There is also a brief evaluation of what prize money could have been realised had captured ships neither foundered in the great storm nor been recaptured after the action.

DOCKYARDS AND THEIR MANPOWER

Besides seamen, the fighting capability of any fleet was dependent upon the support given by its dockyards, whose would require innumerable volumes to cover the subject fully and accurately. The naval dockyards were the mightiest industrial complexes in existence, designed to build, repair and fit out naval ships for war. In Britain there had been a marked expansion utilising technological advances made in the last two decades of the eighteenth century. Many recent changes had been driven by Brigadier-General Sir Samuel Bentham who, appointed Inspector-General of Naval Works in 1796, had modified the dockyards to meet the demands of the present war. Bentham was sustained by key engineers and inventors Henry Maudslay, Marc Brunel, Matthew Boulton and James Watt, and installed Admiralty chemist James Sadler, architect and engineer Samuel Bunce and mechanist Simon Goodrich. Besides expanding facilities with new and deeper docks, Bentham introduced innovations utilising steam plant: sophisticated pumping systems for emptying and filling docks, mechanical saw mills, block-making machinery, metal mills, and dredgers. Each of these attributes guaranteed the speedier construction and repair of naval ships at the crucial time of war. The block-making machinery, designed by Marc Brunel, was perhaps the most innovative introduction; by combining and refining existing machine processes Brunel created the world's first mass production unit which not only reduced manpower but also increased annual productivity tenfold. Installed in 1803 producing 12,000 blocks up to 10 inches long annually, by 1808 the Block Mills were producing some 150,00 blocks of all sizes per annum. Such an infrastructure gave Britain the edge over her adversaries and it was very much these aspects that aided the defeat of the Franco-Spanish fleet off Trafalgar.[1] Four of the dockyards had ropewalks.[2] That at Chatham still operates today although in the private ownership of Master Ropemakers Ltd. As a commercially viable concern supplying rope for private customers, this company also manufactures rope for refitting Nelson's *Victory* and serves as a working museum as part of the Chatham Historic Dockyard experience.

French and Spanish dockyards both had adequate stone-built docks and basins, but no innovative steam machinery and associated plant. Fully reliant on conventional facilities, repairing and refitting ships remained a slower process. This point explains why these two navies, the French particularly, were reluctant to risk damaging their ships in bad weather or action and why, irrespective of British blockades, their ships remained in harbour for long periods. The French, we know, had adopted machinery for piercing copper plating with nail holes but this process was, compared with British mechanisation, relatively minor.

The other factor preventing modernisation related to dockyard manning. Since the start of the war with France in 1793 the workforce employed within the British dockyards expanded yearly as the demands of war increased until it was reached 10,000 in 1805. The increase in skilled men at Portsmouth dockyard alone rose from 1,331 in 1793 to 2,668 by 1813. Of this number there were no fewer than 1,428 shipwrights and 322 apprentices.[3] Joseph Tucker, master shipwright at Plymouth in 1803, provided a detailed description covering the actual scope of work undertaken within a six month period at the restart of the war to prepare ships, twelve of which would fight at Trafalgar. The work in each ship was tremendous: besides detailing how much planking was fitted, how many ladders, gratings and doors were refitted, and iron work fitted, this document provides a host of fitting out information that is rarely found in other primary sources or plans. Tucker itemised additional items fitted for war time, such as constructing ready-use shot lockers around the masts, fitting fireproof iron staircases to maintain communication between decks, copper voice pipes to communicate to alternative steering positions, and cisterns for flooding magazines, to name but a few.

Besides skilled wood and metal workers, there were teams of lesser skilled labour that coppered the ships. Once a ship was docked gangs set up staging around areas of the hull. Although access was reasonable from the steps and altars of the dock, scaffolding was needed around the bow and stern. They stripped off the old copper, removed reluctant nail heads and scraped away residual brown paper. After making good any hull planking needing repair and filling up nail holes with wooden spyles or plugs these teams paid[4] the hull with brown paper coated with tar before fitting up and nailing the new copper sheathing in place. Ship's Progress Books show us is that ships' bottoms were partially or fully coppered remarkably quickly, the work being counted in days rather than weeks, allowing a quick return of vessels to sea. This could only have been achieved by large and well organised work gangs who would then move on to the next ship in a similar manner to its twentieth century equivalent of 'Jenny's Side Party' in Hong Kong. What is not clear is whether this work force was supplemented by the ships company of the ship in dock which would seem highly plausible as well as practical; we know that ship's crew were involved with breaming (burning off barnacles and weed) and paying the hulls.

French and Spanish dockyards built ships far more quickly than British. Most ships, even the great *Santísima Trinidad*, appear to have been constructed within two years. How? The skilled workforce within French and Spanish dockyards appears to have been supplemented by large contingents of convicts who moved materials, leaving the skilled artisans to concentrate on their work, whereas British dockyards used only convicts for groundbreaking and building. The workforce in the Spanish dockyard at Havana also included a high percentage of slaves. While African slaves had been sold or loaned to Jamaica and Antigua dockyards by West Indies merchants since the 1730s and trained as shipwrights and caulkers, the British West Indian dockyards did not build ships.[5] In England all shipbuilding was undertaken by a smaller force of paid skilled men.

The second factor relates to geography. All British yards were subject to prolonged periods of inclement weather and shorter days in winter. While similar conditions affected Brest, Rochefort, Guarnizo (Santander), Ferrol and to a lesser extent Cadiz, the Mediterranean dockyards of Toulon and Cartagena were far warmer, likewise Havana. A third point may relate to shipbuilding practices. In Britain shipwrights would leave the oak hull 'in frame' to season for at least a year before planking. This practice was formally introduced in the 1770s as a precautionary measure against dry rot. Whether the French and Spanish stood their hulls in frame for a period is uncertain. *Santísima Trinidad* and *Rayo*, built of cedar and mahogany in Havana, would not have needed seasoning.

Demand also affected building time. France needed to rebuild her fleet to replace ship losses of the 1790s whereas the policy in England was to reduce shipbuilding in peacetime. *Victory*, laid down in 1759 during a war, was intended to be built in 30 months, but with the war drawing to a close the workforce was reduced to save money so was not completed until 1765.

The worst example was *Dreadnought* which, laid down in 1788, was on the stocks for 13 years. Spain appears to have built ships fast whether at peace or war. A final factor may relate to the standardisation of French warship design where components were semi-mass-produced with ships being constructed assembly-line fashion.

SHIP DESIGNERS AND BUILDERS

By the end of the eighteenth century the art of designing and building wooden naval ships in Britain, France and Spain had reached its zenith. Ironically it was France, defeated at Trafalgar, that had taken initial steps to design ships using scientific evaluation. This concept was driven during the reign of Louis XIV by the innovative authority of Jean-Baptiste Colbert, the French Minister of the Marine. From 1671 he initiated a scientific approach to ship design using mathematicians and applied technological skills to redevelop the French fleet.[6] In 1673 Colbert introduced a 'reglement' that standardised dimensions for each class of ship and in 1683 had individual ship models made for training shipwrights and designers.[7]

This gave rise to similar systems being introduced in Spain and Britain. The English master shipwright and Navy Commissioner Sir Anthony Deane had written his theoretical *Doctrine of Naval Architecture* in 1670 and William Petty of the Navy Board and Royal Society had experimented with ship design. The first specification Royal Navy establishment, authorised by the Navy Board, was introduced in 1706. It was amended in 1719, 1733, 1741 and 1745 but fixed specifications tended to restrict innovative development. France had already found this a handicap. As a result Henri Louis Duhamel du Monceau, Inspector General of the French Navy, set up a training school for students to study theoretical ship design in 1741.[8] Duhamel followed up this initiative and published his comprehensive treatise *Architecture Navale* in Paris 1752. A similar work based on Duhamel entitled *Treatise on Shipbuilding and Navigation* was published by Mungo Murray in England two years later. The shortcomings of the establishment system in England was soon proved during the War of the Austrian Succession (1740-1748) when the Royal Navy confronted better designed French and Spanish ships. Master Shipwright Sir Thomas Slade, appointed Surveyor of the Navy in 1755, persuaded the Admiralty to amend establishments and designed ships based on the lines of captured French ships. The best British, French or Spanish designers, men like Sir Thomas Slade, Sir John Henslow, Romero y Landa and Jacques Noel Sane, all built on theory and experience. Each country drew on further experience of conflict, the Seven Years' War (1756-1763), the American War of Independence (1775-1783) and war with revolutionary France which started in 1793. A decade after Trafalgar a new breed of ships, constructed of new materials and techniques spurred by innovations in wrought iron production by Henry Cort,[9] emerged under Sir Robert Seppings, Surveyor of the Navy 1813-1832 and his successor Sir William Symonds. Although these vessels were never put to the same test of unremitting warfare, they were extremely robust and, with a very rigid hull form, adapted to take steam machinery.

SHIP DRAUGHTS

Close examination of ship draughts shows considerable variation in ship design between the three fleets. The lines of British ships differ very little, irrespective of individual designer, one 74 gun ship looks very much like another. British ships generally had a greater sheer (the rise of the wales afore and abaft) than their foreign equivalents to counteract hogging, the tendency for the keel to fall at its extremities. Plans of *Prince* (98), *Ajax* and *Revenge* are of particular interest because of their modifications. *Prince* was lengthened by 17 feet. How was the hull divided before a middle section was inserted? The plausible solution is that the ship was run into an inclined dock at high tide. Once the water was pumped out the entire midship section could be stripped of all planking, wales and other longitudinal timbers including a section of the keelson, leaving just the keel to be cut through. Using high water the stern-most section would then be partially floated and hauled down the incline some distance. A new section of keel and hog would then be fitted upon which new frames, made to the same moulding as the original adjacent frames, would then be erected. Work was then completed by rebuilding with a new length of keelson, followed by beams, knees, internal and external planking. Further research into lengthening ships is needed. The sheer draught of *Ajax* (74) shows that she was lengthened by ten feet and later fitted with the round stern introduced by Sir Robert Seppings, Surveyor of the Navy 1813-1832. An example of this type of stern can be seen on the frigate *Unicorn* preserved at Dundee and in the plans of *Revenge* (74). Frame drawings of British frigates indicate that they were fitted with sweep ports equidistant between the midship gun ports. Sweep ports permitted the ship to be rowed like a galley when there was no wind and were generally fitted during wartime and boarded up in peacetime.[10] A later draught of *Euryalus* shows her fitted as a convict ship with poop deck, non-seagoing fittings, squared off bulwarks and iron grills closing off her gun ports. Most notably the plan shows the hand-cranked ventilation through-deck system fitted to provide air to each cell. Reference to a similar type of ventilating system is mentioned in *Mes Pontons* written by French prisoner-of-war Louis Garneray.[11]

Of the French vessels, *Tonnant* (80) is typical. Her lines are straighter, far less sheer, and she has built up solid bulwarks at her poop, quarterdeck and forecastle. French two-decked ships had a thicker band of planking forming what was virtually a third wale above the upper gun deck ports, which gave better structural support to the frames at the head of the top-timber line. It also appears that each wale was faired in with planking above and below. The fact that the edges of the wales are smooth and fair is evident because French ships were not fitted with two vertical fenders at the dead flat. These fenders, common in British ships, were fitted to assist in parbuckling casks up the ship's side when storing ship. The rabbet line running along the top edge of the keel to receive the garboard strake (lowest plank) differs from British ships inasmuch that it extends right aft to the stern post. This French practice ensured that all the dead and rising wood was fully planked in. French ships also had a longer knee of the head, giving more graceful lines to their head rails and figure. Their rudders were simpler, with an angled straight back without hances (stepping). Similar rudders were later introduced briefly in English vessels before the cranked rudder head was adopted. French sterns varied. Some had a similar profile to British ships, while others, like *Spartiate*, had the classic horseshoe shape. *Spartiate* also had an open gallery at the level of the upper gun deck but unlike the English practice before the introduction of the closed stern, it did not protrude beyond the line of the stern timbers. *Scipion*, *Tonnant* and *Duguay Trouin* differed in that they had closed sterns, although this may reflect English modifications after capture. The stern of *Duguay Trouin/Implacable* may be seen at the National Maritime Museum, Greenwich.

Internally, French ship plans show a shorter mizzen mast stepped on the lower gun deck and not the keelson. The shorter mast may have been introduced because of mast timber procurement difficulties and less need for a long one. Dominant features are deeper hatch coamings which prevented sea water passing to other decks, keeping ships drier. Short mizzen masts and high hatch coamings were introduced in British ships a few years after Trafalgar. Unusual features in *Implacable*'s plans are her main and jeer capstans. The trundlehead of each capstan appears to be furnished with just six sockets for capstan bars instead of twelve. The latter figure, with 14 sockets in the drumhead of the capstan on the deck above, would operate the capstan with a maximum of 260 men. This is shown in other ship draughts. Why this trundlehead is fitted with just six sockets is uncertain but a recent discovery in *Victory* indicates that a reduction of capstan bars, and consequently manning, may have become common after Trafalgar. This development is still being investigated.

Although French heavy frigates were well armed, fast and manoeuvrable, *Rhin*'s plans show that her hold capacity was limited. This fact is supported by the draught of the 38 gun *Unité*.[12] Limited hold space would reduce operational time at sea without replenishment. Besides having little space afore and abaft at hold level, the height of *Rhin*'s berthing deck is also low, making living spaces cramped. Like the larger ships, French frigates also had a heavy band of planking at the top-timber line, solid built bulwarks and simpler rudder forms.

The Spanish ships fall into two categories, old and new. The older vessels had similar lines to British ships with a relatively high rise in their sheer, a shorter knee of the head and an open stern with galleries. Later vessels reflect French influence, with a very reduced sheer and solid built bulwarks with squared hancings at the poop, quarterdeck and forecastle. Most notable in the Spanish ships is the angle of the cathead. Where in British and French ships the cathead was set at an angle of 45-60 degrees off the centre line, in newer Spanish ships the cathead was set virtually at 90 degrees. Whether this proved more efficient when 'catting' the anchor is debatable, but it made timber procurement easier because the piece needed shaping in two planes rather than three. If the protruding arm of the cathead remained in the same plane as the heel it could be soundly bolted to the catbeam, whereas if the cathead arm was angled in a third plane then the fastenings were subjected to additional torque or twist.

A notable Spanish feature in *Bahama*'s draught is the design of the after part of the keel. The piece of timber forming the aftermost section of the keel does not remain parallel in depth as the other sections but rises by a height of 15-20 per cent towards its after extremity. The advantages of this are twofold: greater depth makes it easier to cut deeper mortises to receive the heel tenons of the stern and inner posts, producing greater jointing and support; second, the angled rise in height gives a quicker rise to the deadwood. The after end of the keel was also not squared off as in British practice, but angled downward and backward to its tread, common practice in French ships. Also like the French ships the rabbet line for the garboard strake is carried along the entire length of the keel. The sterns of the Spanish ships varied according to the age of the vessel, older ships having open sterns and galleries, the newer vessels having the closed horseshoe shape stern. Internally Spanish plans show a stepped orlop deck at the after end. Generally 20-25 feet long, this appears to be a feature carried over from a much earlier Elizabethan ship design when ships were fitted with a 'nether orlop'.[13] This practice was originally introduced to give sufficient height and more decks aft to provide additional cabin space. Drawings of *Santísima Trinidad* and *Rayo* clearly show alterations to increase their complement of armament between quarterdeck and forecastle by modifying the gangways running fore and aft at the waist. Re-planked with thicker boards to carry the weight of the guns, these gangways were broadened by fitting additional longitudinal carlings between the skid beams and filling the space with gratings to provide a 'bridge' between the quarter deck and forecastle referred to in *Santísima Trinidad* in Part 3, Chapter 1. While close examination of the draughts provides much unrecorded evidence about ship design and fitting out, written notes on each plan reveal data of equal importance. This subject alone demands much more investigation.

TIMBER SOURCES AND QUANTITATIVE CONSUMPTION

The amount of timber used for the ships of Trafalgar is astounding but the navies were not the sole cause of deforestation in Britain, France and Spain. While the Royal Navy did consume vast quantities of timber for shipbuilding, much was also expended in iron-smelting, glass-blowing, canal-building, mercantile and fishing fleets, farming and civil construction. Smaller trades such as cooperage also contributed to forest depletion. The same situation prevailed in France and Spain although the latter country was already building ships in Havana where deforestation had yet to take effect. Building a standard 3rd rate ship of 74 guns such as *Orion* required 3,500 loads of which 90 per cent was oak. As each load equalled 50 cubic feet, 1 tree, or approximately 1 ton (1006 kg) of timber, then the amount of timber to build a ship of this size before being converted into individual ship components totalled 175,000 cubic feet (4,952.5 cubic metres) of wood. As one acre of land yielded a maximum of 60 suitable trees of 80-120 years old then the acreage required for a 74 gun ship averaged 65 to 75 acres (30 to 35 hectares). Obviously the number of loads varied according to the size of vessel built, the amount increasing exponentially for the larger ships, although this figure did not alter much for the smaller vessels. This is understandable as the larger ships, the 100 gun *Britannia* for example, required more bulk in proportion to her size. These same constraints and timber quantities also governed the construction of the French and Spanish ships, although French ships were built marginally lighter in their upperworks as shown in the sailing report for *Implacable/Duguay Trouin*.[14] Estimates of timber expended in the construction of each ship type in Trafalgar ships as a whole are given in the appendices.

Given the following conversion factors, the overall figures of volume of timber expended in building the total ships at Trafalgar, as shown in the table below, was extracted from an aggregate area of 6.61 square miles. This relates to an area roughly the size of the City of Westminster, London, the island of Portsea (Portsmouth, England) or the island of Bequia, the largest of the Grenadines in the St Vincent group in the West Indies.

Conversion factors:
1 load = 50 ft^3 and/or 1 tree   1 ft^3 = 0.028 m^3
1 acre = 0.4047 hectares   640 acres = 1 square mile^2

TOTAL ESTIMATE OF TIMBER EXPENDED ON BUILDING THE 73 BRITISH, FRENCH & SPANISH SHIPS AT TRAFALGAR

Fleet	Total No. of Ships	Total No. of Loads (Tons)	Total No. of Trees	Total Cubic Feet	Total Cubic Metres	Total Acres of Woodland	Total Hectares of Woodland	Square Miles of Woodland
British	33	115,725	115,725	5,786,250	162,015	1,902.06	769.76	2.97
French	25	74,570	74,570	3,728,500	104,398	1,244.81	503.77	1.95
Spanish	15	65,090	65,090	3,250,000	91,000	1,084.32	438.82	1.69
TOTAL	73	255,385	255,385	12,764,750	357,413	4,231,19	1,712.35	6.61

These figures do not cover timber used for masts, yards, spars, ships' boats, gun carriages, pulley blocks for rigging and guns and deadeyes. See tables below.

French ships were built lighter above the waterline ('She is well timbered and kneed below but is weak in her topsides'),[15] with thinner framing and planking, raising several points. While hull thickness was reduced to produce greater speed and manoeuvrability, ability to withstand heavy gunfire and extreme weather was severely compromised. British gunners delivered broadsides at a greater rate, but shot penetration of thinner bulwarks inflicted greater damage and injury within French ships. This is clearly evident in French casualty statistics at Trafalgar - in total some 6,350 were dead and wounded although about 25 per cent died in the storm afterwards.[16]

Weather was equally important. Masts needed good support for their shrouds. If the bolts fastening the shroud preventer plates to the hull were driven through thinner material the shrouds were less effective, so when these ships hit heavy weather and seas the chance of rolling out masts increased. With these design weaknesses it is understandable that French ships avoided putting to sea when weather conditions were severe. This can be seen when Villeneuve ventured first from Toulon in early 1805; hit by poor weather, his battered ships were soon forced back into harbour.

MAST TIMBER

Timber for masts and yards was generally pine, spruce and fir imported from the Baltic. With 69 ship-rigged vessels present at Trafalgar, the cumulative length of timber is again notable. As masts and spars were generally manufactured proportional to the length and breadth of the vessel they fitted, and were proportional to each other, to assess each of the ships individually would be time-consuming. If however we use the average mast and yard specifications for ship types, the 100 gun *Victory*, a typical 74 gun, and a rough calculation for the brigs, the following estimates are derived in the following table.

Ship Type	Overall length of masts per ship	Overall length of yards per ship	Total length of masts and yards timber per ship	No. of ships	Accumulative length of mast and yard timber	Accumulative length of mast and yard timber	
		feet	feet		feet	metres	miles
	A	B	C = A + B	D	E = C x D	E x 0.3048	E ÷ 5280
1st Rate	760	815	1575	7	11,025	3,360.4	2.10
2nd Rate	757	810	1567	4	6,268	1,910.5	1.20
3rd Rate	520	665	1185	49	58,065	17,698.2	11.00
5th Rate	395	505	900	9	8,100	2,469.9	1.50
Brigs, etc.	240	320	560	4	2,240	682.7	0.42
TOTAL	-	-	-	73	85,698	26,121.7	16.22

For simplicity this table only covers basic rig; spars such as royal yards, studding sail booms and yards have been omitted. Also unaccounted for is the fact that composite made lower masts were manufactured from seven to nine trees and that larger yards were made in two pieces scarphed together. As shown, the estimated length of timber used extends to about 85,500 feet (26,000 m). If spar lengths for royal yards, studding sail booms and yards, were accounted for, this figure would exceed 106,000 feet (32,500m) - about the distance across the English Channel at its narrowest point, ironically between Dover and Boulogne. For all fleets, masts and yards required maintenance or replacement due to damage, therefore the supply of this timber from the Baltic was essential, hence the need for Napoleon to control Russia and the Baltic states to deprive Britain of this material as well as tar, turpentine and hemp.

BLOCKS

The final timber-related item to be assessed is rigging pulley blocks. Apart from two French brigs and the British schooner and cutter, the remaining 69 vessels were ship-rigged vessels with three masts. Whether they were a 1st rate or a frigate each employed a similar number of blocks for their rigging. Using tables given in Steel's *Element of Mastmaking, Sailmaking and Rigging*, dated 1794, the average number of blocks employed in a ship-rigged vessel generally totalled 768. An approximate figure of 250 blocks can be given for the brigs, the schooner and the cutter. Added to this would be blocks for the anchor gear, ship's boats and miscellaneous uses, averaging 60 each. Each carriage gun required six blocks, four for their side tackles and two for their train tackle. Carronades generally had eight blocks, four for their side tackles and four for their two train tackles. Estimating the number of carriage guns and carronades carried within each fleet, the overall number of blocks employed follows. A breakdown for each individual fleet is given in the following table.

	British	French	Spanish	Total
Ship-rigged vessels	22,272	17,664	11,520	51,456
Total non-ship-rigged vessels	1,000	500	0	1,500
Total no. of carriage guns	13,116	9,540	7,512	30,168
Total no. of carronades, howitzers,&c	1,472	944	267	2,683
Misc. blocks: anchor gear, boats, etc.	1,980	1,500	900	4,380
Total no. of blocks in each fleet	39,840	30,148	20,199	90,187
OVERALL TOTAL				90,187

As the average size of pulley block was 12 inches, whether single or double purchased, the average volume of timber required for one block was about 1 cubic foot. The volume of timber required for the 90,187 blocks stated would then be 90,187 cubic feet of elm or ash. This equals 1,804 loads or tons of timber, enough to build a 40 gun frigate. It took about eight hours for a skilled blockmaker to manufacture one good sized block, therefore the manufacturing output to produce this quantity of blocks amounted to 721,496 hours (82 years 131 days). Taking the 39,840 blocks of the British fleet alone, to produce this quantity manually would equate to 318,720 hours (36.4 years). Although Britain could, by mid-1803, mechanically mass-produce about 12,000 blocks a year in the new Portsmouth Block Mills, it would still have taken three years four months to manufacture this quantity using this method. The above does not account for the quantity of *lignum vitae* imported for manufacturing block shivers/sheaves (pulley wheels).

COPPER

This essential material was used for bolts, sheathing and nails. Because the number of copper and 'mixed metal' bolts used for fastening hull timbers cannot be ascertained, copper sheathing and its fastenings alone are analysed. Since the 1780s all three navies had sheathed the underwater bodies of their ships with copper plating to protect against the marine boring worm *teredo navalis*. This was essential, for while this species lived predominantly in tropical waters, as mercantile trade increased during the eighteenth century, returning ships brought *teredo navalis* into European waters where they could live and occasionally breed.

Copper ore could be imported from Sweden but much of Britain's supply was mined in Cornwall and Anglesey. Production of copper bolts and sheathing was centred in South Wales which had a plentiful supply of coal for smelting although there were also smaller companies in Lancashire. Ironically copper plating was also exported to France, thus most of the Trafalgar ships were coppered with British sheathing. The main source of Spanish copper ore came from the Rio Tinto (Red River) mines located 50 miles up river from the port of Huelva, itself some 90 miles north of Cape Trafalgar. These mines, which had been worked by the Phoenicians, Carthaginians and Romans, were one of the richest sources of copper in Europe. Its principal customer was the great cannon foundry at Seville. *Victory* was sheathed with 3,923 plates, each four feet by 14 inches; the number of plates fitted on *Santísima Trinidad* would have exceeded this figure. Although many ships were smaller than *Victory* the volume of their underwater hulls would not have varied by more than 25 per cent, therefore most were sheathed with 2,500-3,000 plates, the brigs and schooners requiring perhaps 1,000. As shown in the table below, the Trafalgar ships were sheathed with 216,900 copper sheets. Each sheet had an area of 4.64 square feet; thereby covering a total area of 1,006,416 square feet (190.6 square miles). On average 144 nails were used to fasten each copper plate around the edges and in three lines across the surface. On estimate over 31 million nails would have been used. Although the copper could be drawn through rollers beforehand, until Portsmouth Metal Mills mass-produced them the final process relied on someone handcrafting each nail individually. The amount of metal used in brass coaks and sheaves has also not been analysed.

Ship types	guns	No. of ships	Average no. copper sheets	Total no. copper sheets	Average no. nails per sheet	Total no. nails expended
		A	B	A x B = C	D	C x D
1st Rates	136 - 100	7	4000	28,000	144	4,302,000
2nd Rates	98	4	3850	15,400	144	2,217,600
3rd Rates	80 - 64	49	3000	147,000	144	21,168,000
Frigates	40 - 36	9	2500	22,500	144	3,240,000
Brigs, etc.	18 - 10	4	1000	4000	144	576,000
TOTAL		73	2,870	216,900	-	31,233,600

For all three navies the gauge of copper plating was generally 28-32 ounces (0.79 and 0.91 kg) per square foot, the heavier plates being fitted where water turbulence was greater.[17] As the average plate weighed 8.7 pounds (3.9 kg), the cumulative weight of copper sheathing the 73 Trafalgar ships totalled 842 tons (856 tonnes). As each single nail weighed 0.16 ounces (100 nails being 16 pounds), the total weight of nails is estimated at 139 tons (141.2 tonnes). The overall statistics are given in the following table. Individual fleet information is given in the appendices.

OVERALL COPPER STATISTICS FOR TRAFALGAR SHIPS

Ship types	No of ships	Average no. copper sheets per ship	Total no. copper sheets	Total weight of copper tons	Total no. nails expended	Total weight of nails tons	Overall weight of copper & nails tons
BRITISH	33	2,870.0	99,400	385.06	14,313,600	63.90	448.96
FRENCH	25	2,166.6	68,500	266.05	9,864,000	44.04	310.09
SPANISH	15	3,500.0	49,000	190.31	7,056,000	30.70	221.03
TOTAL	73	2,836.6	216,900	841,42	31,233,600	138.64	980.08

Another commodity, often overlooked, is the tarred brown paper applied to a ship's hull before sheathing with copper. Vast quantities must have been employed but the actual amount used on the Trafalgar ships is at present unknown. A sheet of the copper removed from *Victory* (fitted well after Trafalgar) indicates that the brown paper was large enough to cover at least one copper plate. What has yet to be researched is the size and thickness of brown paper used and whether the sizes of these sheets reflect standard measurements today. Currently the largest sheet of brown paper, a quad imperial, measures 58 by 45 inches (147.3 x 114.5 cm).[18] Copper sheeting was also employed to line the magazines, although the quantity was minimal. The number of sheets employed to cover the bulkheads, deck and deckhead of one hanging magazine in *Victory* during recent restoration required 90 sheets with 20 for the entrance and light room. Copper tubing, as described in Joseph Tucker's work lists, was used for voice communication pipes.[19] Other non-ferrous metals comprised lead sheeting for magazine passageways, cisterns and powder bins, the upper finishing of quarter galleries and canopies of roundhouses. Large quantities of lead piping were also used for scuppers. Tucker shows that tinplate was used extensively in many locations including lining breadrooms.[20] It is difficult to ascertain the quantity of lead or tin used.

RIGGING CORDAGE

Rigging cordage, made from hemp, was supplied mainly from Russia although it was also imported from elsewhere. The demand for this material was so great that the East India Company was using Indian hemp for sail canvas as well as rope. Not only was rope manufactured in the dockyards, but ropewalks could be found extensively throughout each country as rope was used in all industries. The quantity of rope needed for rigging sailing ships was vast, especially as it had to be replaced frequently through wear. One only has to read the logbooks of British naval vessels at this period to realise how often rigging failed.[21] Nelson's *Victory* (100) for example, a standard three masted rigged vessel, required 26.2 miles (23,056 fathoms) of rigging; a 3rd rate ship about 22 miles (19,360 fathoms) of rigging, and the frigate classes about 17 miles (14,960 fathoms). Using these criteria estimates are given in the two tables of standing and running rigging (above, right) for the ship rigged and the four non-ship rigged vessels.

Added to this was the quantity of cordage used for each gun, breeching ropes, side and train tackles, where lengths varied according to gun size. A 32 pounder carriage gun required a breeching rope 34 feet (10.4 m) long and 54 feet (16.5 m) of rope for each side tackle and train tackle, in all 196 feet (59.75 m). As the 73 ships at Trafalgar ships carried a total of 5,607 carriage guns and carronades, each requiring an average of 158 feet (47.25 m) of cordage, the overall estimate of rope required for guns is 885,906 feet (147,651 fathoms or 268,480 m). Added to the rigging total this gives:

Total Estimates	fathoms	miles	kilometres
Standing & running rigging ship-rigged vessels	1,331,420	1,512.75	2,420.40
Standing & running rigging - brigs, cutters, &c	16,400	30.00	48.00
All gun cordage	147,651	167.80	268.48
TOTAL	1,495,471	1,710.55	2,736.88

Rope was used for other applications such as anchor cables, towing hawsers, anchor buoys, gun port lid ropes, port tackle falls and port runner falls

TOTAL ESTIMATE OF STANDING & RUNNING RIGGING FOR ALL SHIP-RIGGED VESSELS

Ship type	Ships No.	Estimated length of rigging per ship fathoms	miles	Total estimate of rigging fathoms	miles
1st Rate	7	23,100	26.25	161,700	183.75
2nd Rate	4	21,560	24.50	86,240	98.00
3rd Rate	49	19,360	22.00	948,640	1,078.00
Frigates	9	14,960	17.00	134,640	153.00
Brigs	2	8,360	9.50	16,720	19.00
Others	2	4,840	5.5	,9680	11.00
TOTAL	69	-	-	1,331,420	1,512.75

ESTIMATE OF STANDING & RUNNING RIGGING FOR BRIGS, SCHOONERS & CUTTERS

Ship type	Ships No.	Estimated length of rigging per ship fathoms	miles	Total estimate of rigging fathoms	miles
Brigs	2	8,360	9.50	16,720	19.00
Others	2	4,840	5.5	9,680	11.00
TOTAL	4	-	-	16,400	30.00

(about 9.5 fathoms per port), gun muzzle lashings (each generally 4 fathoms in length), gun lashings (7 fathoms each) and miscellaneous tackle for storing ship. As this quantity varied from ship to ship no sensible estimate can be made.

SAILS

Sail canvas was generally made from flax woven into bolts of cloth 39 yards long and 2 feet in width, the width limited by the size of loom. The main centres for canvas manufacture were Dundee and Arbroath in Scotland, with smaller supplies from Northern Ireland and Dorset. The main contractor in Dundee at the time was William Baxter who subcontracted out the work to a multitude of Dundee weavers working at looms set up in their own homes termed 'manufactories'. The names of individual contractors are on trade stamps printed on *Victory*'s original fore topsail now displayed at Portsmouth. Finished bolts of canvas were sold to the navy under contract and supplied to the dockyards where the canvas was made into sails by sailmakers in sail lofts.[22]

The quantities of canvas manufactured to supply the fleets, as shown in the tables below, were enormous. One suit of sails for a ship-rigged vessel comprised 37 individual sails and it was not unusual for a vessel to carry 15 spare sails. Demand during wartime necessitated sailmaking to be contracted out to private companies, for example Ratsey and Lapthorn near Portsmouth.

To evaluate the quantity of canvas used for the ship's sails at Trafalgar, statistics for the following tables have been taken from Rees's *Naval Architecture 1819-20*.[23] Taking one set of figures calculated from Rees, the total length of canvas used for a 100 gun ship was 12,130 yards. If each seam required three rows of stitching at three yards an hour, the cumulative number of hours is 12,130. Assuming a working day of eight hours, one man would produce 24 yards, a standard team of 20 sailmakers 480 yards per day, with each seam requiring three rows of stitching, so the total time to make a set of sails was 75 days. This statistic is supported by the fact that during the 1780s twenty Chatham sailmakers took 83 days to make one suit of 37 sails for *Victory*. Estimating the time taken to make sails for every British ship present at Trafalgar where 345,232 yards of canvas was used, this quantity seamed with three rows of stitching (3 x 345,232 yards) totals 1,035,696 hours (129,462 working days). See Appendices for detailed estimates per fleet.

The final figures surrounding the quantities of canvas, the estimated sail area, and time taken to manufacture the sail for all 73 Trafalgar ships are given below. In brief the total length of canvas is 423.25 miles (677 km), covering an estimated area of 282.16 square miles (451.33 km^2) requiring a manufacturing output of 1,324,784 hours (290,598 working days). This lat-

CONCLUSION

ter figure applies to making the sails only and does not cover the time taken to weave the cloth. No account has been taken of the quantity of rope used for the bolt ropes for each sail.

ESTIMATED QUANTITY OF CANVAS EMPLOYED, SAIL AREA AND TIME TO MANUFACTURE ALL SAILS FOR THE 73 BRITISH, FRENCH AND SPANISH SHIPS

Fleet	Ships in fleet	Total quantity of canvas required	Total no. of bolts of canvas required	Total estimated sail area	Estimated time to manufacture all sails	
	No.	Yards C (A x B)	No. C ÷ 39 yards	Square Yards D (C x 2/3)	Man Hours E (C x 3)	Man Days F (E ÷ 8)
BRITISH	33	345,232	8,852.0	230,154.6	1,035,696	129,462
FRENCH	25	253,915	6,521.9	169,570.5	761,745	95,218
SPANISH	15	175,781	4,507.2	117,187.2	527,343	65,918
TOTAL	73	774,928	17,881.1	516,912.3	1,324,784	290,598

ORDNANCE

The total armament in the British fleet present at Trafalgar, including the four frigates, the *Pickle* schooner and the cutter *Entreprenante* was 2,370 guns consisting of 2,186 standard carriage guns and 184 carronades of various calibre. Taking the average weight for each type and calibre of ordnance, the standard weight of a gun measured in hundredweights (1 cwt. = 112 lbs), the total weight of guns carried in the British fleet is estimated at 4,945.2 tons (5,025 tonnes) (See table). Applying the same data, ordnance statistics for the 27 British line of battle ships in action are given in the appendices.

THE BRITISH FLEET OF 33 SHIPS

Gun type & calibre	No. of guns	Average weight per gun in cwt (cwt = 112 lbs) (A x B = C)	Total weight in cwt	Total weight in tons (C ÷ 20)	Total weight in tonnes (D x 1.016)
(Weight of shot)	A	B	C	D	E
32 pounder carriage gun	624	55	43,320.0	1,716.0	1743.5
24 pounder carriage gun	374	50	18,700.0	935.0	950.0
18 pounder carriage gun	756	42	31,752.0	1,587.6	1,613.0
12 pounder carriage gun	162	32	5,184.0	259.2	263.4
9 pounder carriage gun	238	23.5	5,593.0	279.7	284.1
6 pounder carriage gun	32	19	608.0	30.4	30.9
68 pounder carronade	2	32.5	65.0	3.3	3.3
32 pounder carronade	128	17.25	2,208.0	110.4	112.8
24 pounder carronade	6	12.25	73.5	3.7	3.8
18 pounder carronade	30	9.00	270.0	13.5	13.7
12 pounder carronade	18	7.13	128.3	6.4	6.5
TOTAL	2,370	-	-	4,945.2	5,025.0

NOTE: New evidence reveals that two 74 gun ships (*Conqueror* & *Spartiate*) had substituted carriage guns for carronades therefore the number of 18 and 24 pounder carriage guns and carronades could now vary.

Ordnance carried in the French fleet of 25 ships including the frigates and brigs was 1,718 guns comprising 1,600 carriage guns, 42 howitzers and 76 carronades. Applying the same average gun weights used in the table above, the estimated weight of ordnance carried in the French fleet is 3,534.3 tons (3,590.3 tonnes). (See table). Applying the same data the ordnance statistics related to the 18 French line of battle ships in action are given in the appendices.

The 15 vessels of the Spanish fleet collectively carried 1,519 guns comprising 1,252 carriage guns, 246 carronades, 14 howitzers and 4 stone mortars. The types and calibre of Spanish ordnance was far more varied than in the other two fleets. Applying the same average gun weights as used in the tables above the estimated weight of ordnance carried in the Spanish fleet is 2,811 tons (2,856.4 tonnes):

THE FRENCH FLEET OF 25 SHIPS

Gun type & calibre	No. of guns	Average weight per gun in cwt (cwt = 112 lbs) (A x B = C)	Total weight in cwt	Total weight in tons (C ÷ 20)	Total weight in tonnes (D x 1.016)
(Weight of shot)	A	B	C	D	E
36 pounder carriage gun	464	60	27,840.0	1,392.0	1,414.3
32 pounder carriage gun	56	55	3,080.0	154.0	155.5
24 pounder carriage gun	124	50	6,200.0	310.0	315.0
18 pounder carriage gun	554	42	23,268.0	1,163.0	1,182.0
9 pounder carriage gun	34	23.5	799.0	40.0	40.6
8 pounder carriage gun	368	22	8,096.0	404.8	411.3
32 pounder howitzer	42	17.25	725.0	36.3	36.8
18 pounder carronade	76	9.00	684.0	34.2	34.8
TOTAL	1,718	-	-	3,534.3	3,590.3

THE 15 SPANISH LINE OF BATTLE SHIPS

Gun type & calibre	No. of guns	Average weight per gun in cwt (cwt = 112 lbs) (A x B = C)	Total weight in cwt	Total weight in tons (C ÷ 20)	Total weight in tonnes (D x 1.016)
(Weight of shot)	A	B	C	D	E
36 pounder carriage gun	124	60	7,440.0	372.0	378.0
32 pounder carriage gun	10	54	540.0	27.0	27.4
24 pounder carriage gun	532	50	26,600.0	1,330.0	1,351.3
18 pounder carriage gun	274	42	11,508.0	575.4	584.6
12 pounder carriage gun	64	31	1,984.0	99.2	100.8
8 pounder carriage gun	242	22	5,324.0	266.2	270.5
4 pounder carriage gun	6	12	72.0	3.6	3.7
24 pounder howitzer	6	12	72.0	3.6	3.7
4 pounder howitzer	8	4	32.0	1.6	1.6
48 pounder carronade	24	24	576.0	28.8	29.3
32 pounder carronade	2	17.25	34.5	1.7	1.8
24 pounder carronade	6	12.25	73.5	3.7	3.8
18 pounder carronade	216	9	1,944.0	97.2	98.8
4 pounder stone mortar	5	5	20.0	1.0	1.1
TOTAL	1,519	-	-	2,811.0	2,856.4

The following tables provide comparable ordnance statistics between the three fleets. The first table states that estimated weight of ordnance carried in all 73 ships comprised a total of 11,290.5 tons (11,471.7 tonnes) of iron. The second table, which covers the 60 ships of the line that actually fought the battle only, gives a total estimated weight of ordnance as 10,569 tons (10,738.5 tonnes) of iron. By comparison with the army the quantity, weight, and firepower of ordnance employed in naval fleet actions like Trafalgar was immense. At the battle of Waterloo 16 June 1815 Wellington and his allies had 163 guns comprising sixty 9 pounders, seventy 6

TOTAL WEIGHT OF ORDNANCE OF THE BRITISH, FRENCH & SPANISH FLEETS (73 SHIPS)

Fleet	Total guns	Total weight in tons	Total weight in tonnes	Total weight in cwt	Total weight in lbs
British	2,370	4,945.2	5,025.0	98,904	11,077,248
French	1,718	3,534.3	3,590.3	70,686	7,916,832
Spanish	1,519	2,811.0	2,856.4	56,220	6,296,640
TOTAL	5,607	11,290.5	11,471.7	225,810	24,290,720

TOTAL WEIGHT OF ORDNANCE OF THE 60 BRITISH, FRENCH & SPANISH LINE OF BATTLE SHIPS

Fleet	Total guns	Total weight in tons	Total weight in tonnes	Total weight in cwt	Total weight in lbs
British	2,166	4,610.0	4,683.9	92,200	10,326,400
French	1,452	3,148.9	3,198.2	62,978	7,053,536
Spanish	1,519	2,811.0	2,856.4	56,220	6,296,640
TOTAL	5,137	10,569.9	10,738.5	211,398	23,676,576

pounders, and thirty-one 24 pounder howitzers. This gave Wellington and his forces a total firepower of 1,704 pounds. Nelson's *Victory* could fire a single broadside of weight of 1,148 pounds which alone amounts to 67 per cent of the total firepower at Wellington's disposal. Even if we combined Wellington's 163 with the 246 guns of Napoleon's French forces the overall figure is only 409 guns. This figure represents just 7.3 per cent of the 5,607 guns carried in the 73 ships at Trafalgar and only 7.9 per cent of the 5,137 guns carried in the 60 line of battle ships.[24] Many of the British guns were cast by Walker & Co of Rotheram. Between 1793 and 1815 it is estimated that this company produced 13,000 tons of guns for the army and navy. Other gun manufacturers were the Carron Ironworks near Falkirk and Alexander Brodie, who had originally made iron stoves for naval ships, at his iron works on the River Severn.

FIREPOWER

Although not specifically quantitative in the material form, firepower in conjunction with the ordnance was the most essential capability requirement of each fleet. The standard gunpowder charge to fire a standard carriage gun was one-third the weight of the shot fired, and that for a carronade was one-twelfth of the shot. If all 33 British ships fired their 2,370 guns with one single round only, as shown in the table, the total weight of iron discharged would be 51,944 lbs (23,375 kg) expending a total of 16,032 lbs. (7,175 kg) of gunpowder (160 full barrels). The individual total for carriage guns is 48,812 lbs (21,066 kg) of iron using 15, 604 lbs (6, 981 kgs) of gunpowder; and for carronades 5,132 lbs. (2,309 kgs.) of iron using 428 lbs (194 kgs)

FIREPOWER OF THE BRITISH FLEET OF 33 SHIPS

Gun type and calibre	Total no. of guns	Total broadside weight of iron expended if all guns fired one round			Total quantity of gunpowder expended if all guns fired one round		
		lbs.	tons	kgs	lbs	tons	kgs
32 pounder carriage gun	624	19,968	8.91	8,986	6,656	2.97	2,954
24 pounder carriage gun	374	8,976	4.01	4,039	2,992	1.34	1,346
18 pounder carriage gun	756	13,608	6.08	6,124	4,536	2.03	2,041
12 pounder carriage gun	162	1,944	0.87	875	648	0.29	292
9 pounder carriage gun	238	2,124	0.96	956	708	0.32	319
6 pounder carriage gun	32	192	0.09	86	64	0.03	29
Intermediate total A	*2,186*	*46,812*	*20.92*	*21,066*	*15,604*	*6.98*	*6,981*
68 pounder carronnade	2	136	0.06	61	12	0.005	6
32 pounder carronnade	128	4,096	1.83	1,843	341	0.15	154
24 pounder carronnade	6	144	0.06	65	12	0.005	6
18 pounder carronnade	30	540	0.24	243	45	0.02	20
12 pounder carronnade	18	216	0.10	97.2	18	0.008	8
Intermediate total B	*184*	*5,132*	*2.29*	*2,309*	*428*	*0.19*	*194*
TOTAL (A + B)	2,370	51,944	23.21	23,375	16,032	7.17	8,175

Further analysis of the ordnance data indicates that while it is commonly believed (probably through the survival of *Victory*), that the standard ordnance in the British fleet comprised the heavier 32 and 24 pounder carriage guns, the most common gun carried in the British ships was in fact the long 18 pounder. This was primarily because this gun type formed the upper gun deck armament of the 74 gun ships. By calculation the number of 18 pounder guns exceeds the 32 pounder by 21 per cent and the 24 pounder by 49 per cent. Looking at the main battle-fleet comprising 27 ships of the line, the statistics relating to broadside firepower and gunpowder are given in the appendices. This gives an overall total of 2,166 guns firing 48,010 lbs (21,604 kg) of iron using 15,079 lbs (6,787 kg) of powder (150 barrels). For the 2,038 carriage guns alone the figures are 44,310 lbs (19,939 kg) of shot to 14,770 lbs (6,647 kg) of powder; and the 128 carronades 3,700 lbs of iron using 309 lbs of powder.

Although frigates carrying 18 pounder guns are excluded from the table given in the appendices, the 18 pounder gun still dominated the British battle-fleet. While the number of 12 pounder carriage guns remains the same at 162, if we were to deduct the 44 fitted on *Victory*, then the number of 12 pounders carried within the fleet remained marginal at 118, most being disposed on the other 1st rate ships *Royal Sovereign* and *Britannia*.

The firepower of the French fleet differed from the British because their heavier carriage guns and carronades fired a shot of 36 pounds rather than 32 pounds. This is rational because 36, having an incremental factor of 6 or 12, was a logical progression following the 12, 18 and 24 pounders. French ships also carried 36 pounder howitzers as an alternative to carronades. The howitzer, suited to land or sea service, was the most common piece of ordnance available and, having standard trunnions, could be mounted on a sea service carriage. Carronades needed a completely different form of carriage. French ships also carried 8 rather than 9 pounders for their uppermost armament.

If all 25 French ships, including their five frigates and two brigs, fired their 1,718 guns with one single round only, as shown in the table, the total weight of iron discharged would be 37,502 lbs (16.908 kg) expending a total of 11,804 lbs. (5,313 kg) of gunpowder (118 full barrels). The individual total for the 1,600 carriage guns is 34,694 lbs (15,612 kg) of iron using 11,564 lbs (5,204 kg.) of gunpowder; and for the carronades and howitzers 2,808 lbs (1,296 kg.) of iron using 240 lbs (109 kgs) of gunpowder. Gunpowder was made from saltpetre, sulphur and charcoal (produced specifically from crack alder and willow).

FIREPOWER OF THE FRENCH FLEET OF 25 SHIPS

Gun type and calibre	Total no. of guns	Total broadside weight of iron expended if all guns fired one round			Total quantity of gunpowder expended if all guns fired one round		
		lbs.	tons	kgs	lbs	tons	kgs
36 pounder carriage gun	464	16,704	7.46	7,517	5,568	2.49	2,505
32 pounder carriage gun	56	1,792	0.80	806	597	0.27	269
24 pounder carriage gun	124	2,976	1.33	1,339	992	0.44	446
18 pounder carriage gun	554	9,972	4.45	4,487	3,324	1.48	1,496
9 pounder carriage gun	34	306	0.14	138	102	0.05	46
8 pounder carriage gun	368	2,944	1.31	1,325	981	0.44	442
Intermediate total A	*1,600*	*34,694*	*15.49*	*15,612*	*11,564*	*5.17*	*5,204*
36 pounder howitzer	42	1,512	0.68	680	126	0.06	58
18 pounder carronnade	76	1,368	0.61	616	114	0.05	51
Intermediate total B	*118*	*2,808*	*1.29*	*1,296*	*240*	*0.11*	*109*
TOTAL (A + B)	1,718	37,502	16.78	16,908	11,804	5.28	5,313

NOTES: For the purpose of comparison with the British ordnance this table contains the standard one-third charge of gunpowder for carriage guns and one-twelfth charges for howitzers and carronades. Likewise for comparison, the weights are calculated in Imperial tons.

Like the British, the dominant French gun was the 18 pounder mounted mainly on the upper deck batteries of the 74 gun ships. Second to the 18 pounder was the 36 pounder which, like the British equivalent 32 pounder, was used on the lower batteries. It appears that no 12 pounder guns were employed in the French fleet as they preferred 8 pounders. The lighter 8 pounder was more suitable for mounting on upper decks because the upper-works of French ships were much lighter built. The 32 and 9 pounder guns listed above were not standard pieces of French ordnance but simply reflected the number of guns of this calibre mounted within the two British prize ships *Berwick* and *Swiftsure*. Howitzers, more commonly used on land, were still being carried within the French fleet as an alternative to the carronade and although readily in supply, were probably used to supplement deficiencies in carronades.

Looking at the main French battle-fleet comprising 18 ships of the line, the statistics relating to broadside firepower and gunpowder are given in the appendices. The total weight of iron fired by the 1,452 guns, carronades and howitzers is estimated at 33,158 lbs (14,920 kg) of iron using 10,580 lbs (4,814 kg) of powder (106 barrels). For the 1,406 carriage guns alone the figures are 31,742 lbs (14,283 kg) of shot to 10,580 lbs (4,761 kg) of powder and the 46 howitzers; and carronades 1,416 lbs of iron using 118 lbs of powder.

CONCLUSION

Spanish firepower differed from the British in that they had 30 pounder carriage guns, 48 pounder carronades, 4 pounder howitzers and 4 pounder stone mortars. Like the French, the Spanish favoured the larger 36 pounder and lighter 8 pounder carriage guns.

If all 15 Spanish line of battle ships fired their 1,519 guns with one single round only, as shown in the table below, the total weight of iron discharged would be 30,636 lbs (13,816 kg) expending a total of 8,851 lbs (3,984 kg) of gunpowder (88.5 full barrels). The individual total for the 1,252 carriage guns is 25,192 lbs (11,366 kg) of iron using 8,397 lbs (3,779 kgs) of gunpowder; and for the 267 howitzers and carronades 5,444 lbs (2,450 kgs) of iron using 454 lbs (205 kgs) of gunpowder.

The comparison of firepower between the three fleets is disclosed in the following two tables. The first compares the 73 ships; the second table, the 60 line of battle ships only. Finally, the third table compares the difference between the 60 line of battle ships of the two opposing fleets formally in action. Although the 27 British line of battle individually outgunned the 18 French ships by 33 per cent and the 15 Spanish ships by 30 per cent, collectively Villeneuve's combined Franco-Spanish fleet outgunned the British by 805 guns. This gave Villeneuve a numerical advantage of 37 per cent guns with a firepower advantage of 33 per cent.

COMPARISON OF FIREPOWER BETWEEN THE 73 SHIPS OF THE BRITISH, FRENCH & SPANISH FLEETS

Gun type and calibre	Total no. of guns	Total broadside weight of iron expended if all guns fired one round (lbs.)	(tons)	(kgs)	Total quantity of gunpowder expended if all guns fired one round (lbs)	(tons)	(kgs)
BRITISH	2,370	51,944	23.21	23,375	16,032	7.17	8,175
FRENCH	1,718	37,502	16.78	16,908	11,804	5.28	5,312
SPANISH	1,519	30,636	13.65	13,816	8,851	3.94	3,984
TOTAL	5,607	120,082	53.64	54,099	36,687	16.39	16,471

COMPARISON OF FIREPOWER BETWEEN THE 60 BRITISH, FRENCH & SPANISH LINE OF BATTLE SHIPS

Gun type and calibre	Total no. of guns	Total broadside weight of iron expended if all guns fired one round (lbs.)	(tons)	(kgs)	Total quantity of gunpowder expended if all guns fired one round (lbs)	(tons)	(kgs)
BRITISH	2,166	48,010	21.43	21,604	15,079	6.75	6,787
FRENCH	1,452	33,158	14.81	14,920	10,698	4.78	4,814
SPANISH	1,519	30,636	13.65	13,816	8,851	3.94	3,984
TOTAL	5,137	111,804	49.89	50,340	34,628	15.47	15,585

DIFFERENCE OF FIREPOWER BETWEEN THE 60 BRITISH AND FRANCO-SPANISH LINE OF BATTLE SHIPS

Gun type and calibre	Total no. of guns	Total broadside weight of iron expended if all guns fired one round (lbs.)	(tons)	(kgs)	Total quantity of gunpowder expended if all guns fired one round (lbs)	(tons)	(kgs)
FRANCO-SPANISH	2,971	63,794	28.46	28,736	19,549	8.72	8,798
BRITISH	2,166	48,010	21.43	21,604	15,079	6.75	6,787
DIFFERENCE	805	15,784	7.03	7,132	4,470	1.97	2,011

PRIZE MONEY

The 17 ships captured initially at Trafalgar represented 51.5 per cent of the Franco-Spanish line of battle fleet. The eighteenth ship, the 74 gun *Achille*, cannot be counted as she blew up. Eight were French and nine Spanish, representing 44 and 60 per cent respectively of each fleet. However, battle damage and the great storm soon wrenched material victory from the British fleet and the expected prize money sank before the victors' eyes. Of the eight French ships five foundered and one was burnt. Of the remaining two only the English-built 74 gun *Swiftsure* remained in British hands. The

FIREPOWER OF THE 15 SPANISH LINE OF BATTLE SHIPS

Gun type and calibre	Total no. of guns	Total broadside weight of iron expended if all guns fired one round (lbs.)	(tons)	(kgs)	Total quantity of gunpowder expended if all guns fired one round (lbs)	(tons)	(kgs)
36 pounder carriage gun	124	4,464	1.99	2,009	1,488	0.66	670
30 pounder carriage gun	10	300	0.13	135	100	0.04	45
24 pounder carriage gun	532	12,768	5.70	5,775	4,256	1.90	1,915
18 pounder carriage gun	274	4,932	2.20	2,219	1,644	0.73	740
12 pounder carriage gun	64	768	0.34	346	256	0.11	115
8 pounder carriage gun	242	1,936	0.86	871	645	0.29	290
4 pounder carriage gun	6	24	0.01	11	8	0.003	4
Intermediate total A	1,252	25,192	11.23	11,366	8,397	3.733	3,779
24 pounder howitzer	6	144	0.06	65	12	0.005	5.4
4 pounder howitzer	8	32	0.01	14	3	0.001	1.4
48 pounder carronnade	24	1,152	0.51	518	96	0.043	43.2
32 pounder carronnade	2	64	0.03	29	5	0.002	2.3
24 pounder carronnade	6	144	0.06	65	12	0.005	5.4
18 pounder carronnade	216	3,888	1.74	1,750	324	0.145	146.0
4 pounder stone mortar	5	20	0.01	9	2	0.001	1.0
Intermediate total B	267	5,444	2.42	2,450	454	0.202	204.7
TOTAL (A + B)	1,519	30,636	13.65	13,816	8,851	3.935	3,983.7

NOTES: For the purpose of comparison with the British ordnance this table contains the standard one-third charge of gunpowder for carriage guns and one-twelfth charges for howitzers and carronades. For comparison, the weights are calculated in Imperial tons.

other vessel, *Algésiras*, was recaptured by her crew and taken into Cadiz. The British fleet fared little better with the Spanish prizes. *Santa Ana* was recaptured, five foundered, leaving just three in possession, the 74 gun ships *Bahama*, *San Ildefonso* and *San Juan Nepomuceno*. Consequently the total number of ships captured was reduced to four, which represented just nine per cent of the 33 strong battlefleet. In terms of prize money this was a disaster, as the loss of two 1st rates and eleven 3rd rates was a severe financial blow to the British. The maximum valuation for these 13 ships was expected to be about £625,000 (£65,000 for a 1st rate and £45,00 for a 3rd rate) the minimum, due to battle damage, being about £420,000. With only four 3rd rate 74 gun ships remaining after the storm, at best the prize money was only about £180,000 (28 per cent) Taking the prize money value of the entire Franco-Spanish battle-fleet of 33 ships to be estimated at £1,560,000 (4 1st rates and 29 3rd rates), the final sum of £180,000 is just 11.5 per cent of the total projected value.

To conclude, Nelson's victory at the battle of Trafalgar did not save Britain from invasion because that threat had already passed. More important, and much ignored, it did mean that Napoleon could not utilise any troops that Villeneuve was carrying to support the proposed Italian campaign against the Austrians, the arrival of which may have changed history. The cost in men, time, labour, equipment, matériel, industrial support, ship building and repair, of bringing together the fleets of Britain, France and Spain to fight the battle off Cape Trafalgar on Monday 21 October 1805 was an enormous financial burden for all the governments and people. For Britain the financial burden placed upon William Pitt, his government and the nation was perhaps greatest. Besides the Trafalgar fleet there was the cost of maintaining Cornwallis's fleet blockading the French ports. However the victory at Trafalgar eventually brought its rewards. The battle was won not only by expertise in seamanship, ship organisation, tactics and gunnery, but also by the capability of the dockyards and other industrial organisations. When finally peace in 1815 opened an era of *Pax Britannia* Britain expanded her global empire, bringing greater commercial wealth and political rewards, while consolidating her position as the world's leading industrial and technological nation, a position which had borne the fruits of victory in October 1805.

Notes to the Conclusion

1. Coad, Jonathan, 'The Introduction of Steam Power into the Royal Dockyards; the genesis of the Block Mills', a paper given to Portsmouth Dockyard in the Age of Nelson, Naval Dockyard Society Conference, 2005; Coad, J, *The Portsmouth Block Mills* (English Heritage, 2005). See also Gilbert, K R, *The Portsmouth Blockmaking Machinery* (HMSO, 1965), passim.
2. Chatham, Portsmouth, Devonport and Woolwich.
3. Morriss, R, *The Royal Dockyards during the Revolutionary and Napoleonic Wars* (Leicester University Press, 1983), 106; Wilkin, F S, 'Portsmouth – The Royal Dockyard – Contribution to the Success of the Royal Navy in the Napoleonic War 1793 - 1815', Portsmouth Dockyard in the Age of Nelson, Naval Dockyard Society Conference 2005.
4. Coated with a protective substance.
5. Nicholson, D, *et al*, 'Nelson's Dockyard Antigua', *Dockyards*, vol. 8, issue 1 (Naval Dockyards Society, August 2003), pp. 10-12.
6. De la Ronciere, Charles, *Historie de la Marine Française*, vol. 5 (Paris, 1899-1932), pp. 373-379. See Goodwin, P, 'The Influence of Industrial Technology and Material Procurement on the Design, Construction and Development of HMS *Victory*' (MPhil Dissertation, University of St Andrews, 1998), p. 34.
7. Pardies, I G, *Statique, ou la Sciences des Forces Mouvantes* (Paris, 1673).
8. Boudriot, J, *The Seventy Four Gun Ship*, vol. 1 (Rotherfield, 1986), p. 12.
9. Goodwin, P, 'The influence of iron in ship construction 1660-1830', *Proceedings of the 3rd international conference in the technical aspects of the preservation of historic vessels* (San Francisco 1997); reprinted *The Mariner's Mirror*, vol. 84, 1 (1998).
10. Gardiner, D, *The Heavy Frigates* (London, 1994), passim; Gardiner, D, *The 18 Pounder Frigates* (???), passim.
11. Translated by R Rose and republished as *The Floating Prison* (Conway Maritime Press, London, 2003).
12. Goodwin, P, *Nelson's Ships* (London, 2002), p. 219.
13. Goodwin, P, 'The development of the orlop deck in HMS *Victory*', *The Mariner's Mirror*, vol. 83, 4 (1997).
14. TNA: PRO, ADM 95/47/25.
15. TNA: PRO, ADM 95/47/25.
16. Pope, D, *England Expects*, p. 357.
17. Goodwin, P, 'The Influence of Industrial Technology and Material Procurement on the Design, Construction and Development of HMS *Victory*' (MPhil Dissertation, University of St Andrews, 1998), p. 44.
18. Chapman, Colin R, *How Heavy, How Much and How Long* (Dursley, 1995), p. 29.
19. RNM MS Portfolio I (3), passim
20. RNM MS Portfolio I (3).
21. Goodwin, P, *Nelson's Ships*, passim.
22. Goodwin, P, '*Victory's* foretopsail', *The Mariners Mirror*, vol. 83, 4 (1997).
23. Rees, Abraham, *Naval Architecture 1819-20* (2nd Edn., Newton Abbott, 1970).
24. Chandler, D, *The Campaigns of Napoleon* (London, 1993), p. 1121.

APPENDICES

Appendix 1: GUNNERY TABLE

Cutt	Length	Weight of Piece	Weight of Carriage	Bore Diameter	Powder Charge	Range -Point Blank	Range - maximum at 6 degrees	No. of gun's Crew
	(Ft. Ins.)	(Cwt. Qtrs lbs.)	(Cwt. Qtrs lbs.)	(ins.)	(lbs.)	(yds)	(yds)	(Full Min.)
42 Short	9 6	65 0 0	13 0 0	6.9	14	400	2,740	16 8
32 Long	10 0	58 0 0	11 2 11	6.35	10.66	400	2,640	14 7
32 Short	9 6	55 0 0	10 2 0	6.35	10.66	400	2,640	14 7
24 Long	10 0	52 0 0	9 3 17	5.74	8	400	1,980	12 6
24 Short	9 0	47 2 0	9 2 0	5.74	8	400	1,980	12 6
18 Long	9 6	42 0 0	8 1 16	5.24	6	340-360	1,920 –2,300	10 5
18 Short	9 0	40 0 0	8 0 0	5.24	6	340-360	1,920 –2,300	10 5
12 Long	9 0	32 0 0	6 1 17	4.64	4	375	1,320	10 5
12 Short	7 6	29 1 0	5 3 12	4.64	4	375	1,320	10 5
9 Long	7 6	24 2 0	4 3 18	4.20	3	330	1,730-1,800	8 4
9 Short	7 0	23 0 0	4 2 11	4.20	3	330	1,730-1,800	8 4
6 Long	8 0	22 0 0	4 1 17	3.69	2	320	1,500-1,600	4 2
6 Short	6 0	16 2 0	3 1 6	3.69	2	320	1,500-1,600	4 2

Note: Specifications for the French and Spanish 36 and 8 pounder guns would vary little from that given for the 32 and 9 pounders stated above. For further details of armament, see *Nelson's Ships* (Conway Maritime Press, 2002).

Appendix 2: ACCOUNT OF THE WORKS PERFORMED BY THE SHIPWRIGHTS ON THE HULLS OF HIS MAJESTY'S SHIPS, AT THE PORT OF PLYMOUTH FROM THE 11TH OF MARCH (BEING THE COMMENCEMENT OF THE EQUIPMENT) TO THE 30TH OF SEPTEMBER 1803 PORTFOLIO 1 (3)

HM Ship *Prince* – Page 8

Prince 98 Guns: - Hold & Magazine cut and set up 13 stantions, turned and fastened plank to bulkhead: 535 feet, cants to the sides 81 feet, ceiling 311 feet, flat 714 feet and lining to bulkheads 2001 feet; trimd & let down pallating & platform beams; refitted & fastened flat 179 feet, refitted the timber boards made mold for & bolted an iron knee against the transom. Took down fitted and refitted battens and rack drawers & fitted and fixed the lanthorns, fitted & hung the sashes, copperd the bulkheads, repaird & fitted wing pannels, lead the flat of light & filling rooms and made a scuttle & 2 ladders in the fore magazine & lightroom: - batten'd the fronts of the bulkheads.

Orlop & Platforms. Took down storeroom bulkheads, binns lockers &c 551 feet, cut and set up 60 stantions, trimd and fastened bulkheads & built binns lockers &c 3594 feet, lined the flat 1330 feet trimd & fastend cieling 178 feet large cants 220 feet a cistern to the foremast; flat 78 feet, 14 wing ledges. hammock racks 60 feet & dunnage battens 192 Feet, made a drawer & desk & fitted shelves &c in the steward room, fitted and guarded 2 lanthorns took down & refitted racks, battens &c 250 feet refitted & fasten'd 30 wing ledges; easd & refitted 22 doors, made 4 cisterns for paint, one ladder, 2 scuttles 3 doors & 3 hatches repaired 9 gratings 5 doors & one ladder fitted 2 hatch bars. leaded the passages & cased over water pipes.

Gun Deck. Trim'd & fasten'd waterways 66 feet, flat 820 feet, manger boards 30 feet hammock racks 217 feet, linings on lodging knees 136 feet, 13 chocks behinds riders cabin cants 51 feet & filling between the Transoms 80 feet: returnd & fastend old waterways 239 feet, flat 357 feet: shifted flat 101 feet and shut in the air openings to the sides: trimd & fitted bucklars bars cants & rollers & 32 washboards to the ports; trimmed & bolted shot cants 154 feet relayd chocks bored off & bolted 2 Iron standards & 2 wood standards; fitted 2 Tillers with Ironwork. complete repayd & refittd shotgarlands 113 feet refitted & fastend shot cants 41 feet & manger boards 90 feet; let in & fastend 16 Iron plates to hatchways: refitted 2 crosspieces to mooring bitts, 4 hawse plugs & 2 scuttles, took down & replaced 14 pillars, let out & turnd 14 scuppers, built gun room cupboards; turned a portsill, made fitted with Ironwork 2 port rollers & shifted 31 port rope pipes; drove out & redrove 13 bolts in the sides & bored for & drove 15 knee bolts; repaired the armourers bench, 3 ladders, 6 gratings & one cap scuttle.

Middle Deck. Trimed & fastend stuff in the air openings; trimd & fitted 32 port bars & one Sampsons post shifted flat 19 feet & 39 port rope pipes: Trimd & fasten'd cabin cants 55 feet 64 port slices & hammock rack 124 feet – leaded, trimd & copper'd the galley, built cooks lockers & made & hung tables with cranks complete, fitted 2 Iron staircases & 2 deadlights: refitted 2 rother chocks & 3 sampsons posts: drove out & redrove 26 bolts in & reduc'd the heads of 26 topriders: made the armourers bench, 5 gratings & one half port. repaired 17 gratings & eased in 31 half ports, - took down guarding stations & berthing round the fireplace.

Upper Deck. Took down the Ordinary galley, trimd & fastened cabin cants 114 feet & made the steam funnel, trimd & bolted 4 ranges: shifted bulkheads in the roundhouses, refitted 7 pillars, trimd & fitted 2 sampsons posts drove out & redrove 20 rider bolts, cased in lead pipes & bored for & drove 20 belaying pins repaired 6 gratings & one ladder.

Forecastle, Waiste, QuarterDeck & Roundhouse. Unbolted & took off plan–sheers 275 feet & 4 sweep pieces over ports, took up 13 short timbers, split out 4 cat blocks & took out 4 port sills – trimd out scarphs for & trimd let down, & bolted 78 timbers to receive the birthing, trimd & let down between the timbers 141 fillings, trimd let in & bolted 8 portsills & trimd & fastend birthing plank 2060 feet – cut off 65 timberheads & made tenons to receive the plansheer, trimd & bolted. 10 carronade chocks, plansheer 121 feet, 4 blocks 4 ranges shroud racks 96 feet, combing 30 feet, 84 headledges – trimd & fastened 3 inch cants on the gangways 228 feet, rubbing pieces to skid beams 75 feet, shortstuff 42 feet spirketting 12 feet, & 6 drifts, trimd & fitted roughtree rail 259 feet hammock board 278 feet & 2 rollers with Ironwork – made molds for & fitted 58 Iron stantions, fitted & fixed stern lanthorns &c, refitted & fastend 2 boom chocks; & cabin cants 47 feet – refitted & bolted 2 ranges, fitted & got in plane hammocks boards 150 feet, refitted an Iron stair case, trimd & set up 8 pillars, lined gratings 219 feet, bored for let thro & cased 6 lead pipes bored for & drove 88 ring & eyebolts & 80 belaying pins. – made 16 half ports, 3 gratings, one ladder & 2 lopers for tiller rope – took off housing from the gear, galley &c & unbolted awning stantions.

Withoutboard. Unbolted & took off harbour hawse bolsters. Refayed & bolted the hawse bolsters, trimd & fastend filling & louvre boards to the cheeks & refayed & fastend filling & louver boards to the cheeks & refayed's & fastened the washboards: - took off & refitted the Channel rails, got in place & fitted 64 deadeyes to the channels, 28 plates preventer with washers & forelocks & refitted & bolted 4 goose necks: - shifted middle wale 102 feet & topside plank 98 feet – trimd & bolted 2 anchor bolsters; refittd & bolted the bumpkins & chock of the bowsprit; got in place the accommodation stantions, carlings & gratings – made 2 trunks to the roundhouses & 2 cisterns in the head; made & hung 3 port lides with scuttles – made molds for & bolted 4 Iron knees under the gunroom ports & 4 under the stools – repaired 11 port lids & 27 scuttle lids – renailed & card in all the port & scuttle lid trimd & fastend 94 port & scuttle riggles; 8 balusters, eking under the wale 272 feet, shook to the sides, lining of the anchor 21 feet & 3 steps, fitted & secured 4 boats Davits, got in place & bolted 4 cranks for sheets; refitted & fastend 14 steps, took off 15 & fitted & nailed 380 sheets of copper – drove out 146 & bored for & drove 16 bolts.- made stages to perform the above works; cut out & put in 229 pieces in different parts of the ship; squared with the caulkers & performed works incident to rigging.

HM Ship *Mars* - Page 13

Mars 74 Guns. Hold. Trimd & fastend thick stuff in air openings 136 feet bulkhead plank 134 feet; cut & set up 6 stantions fittd & fastend bulkhead for dry provisions & shut in air openings in the bulkheads 622 feet, fitted & fastend lining to bulkheads; breadrooms &c 1592 feet lead in magazine & c 351 feet 33 sheets of copper 2105 tin plates fitted magazine & powder room lanthorns card the drawers & doors, fitted & bolted 6 wing panels capt over air openings 116 feet & fitted & fastend battens to the bulkheads 71 feet.

Orlop & Platforms; - trimd & fastend thick stuff in air opening 107 feet, fitted & fastend flat 214 feet; fitted shelves built binns & shut in openings to storerooms 594 feet, lined bulkheads & flat 202 feet; fitted & leaded the cistern to the foremast & cut & set up 4 stanchions; fitted in place 4 storeroom lanthorns & nailed 77 tin plates – make molds for & fastend 4 Iron bars over the wing ledges; made one desk & one door; eas'd 7 doors & one scuttle & repaird on grating – capt over an air opening 73 feet & took off the ordinary battens &c.

Gun Deck took up flat 614 feet, trimd & fastend fillings between the transoms 56 feet, shortstuff 121 feet & flat 718 feet; got in place & fastend flat 876 feet; retrimd got in place & fastend waterways 328 feet, trimd & bolted 6 showels & relayd & bolted 6 iron standards; bored for & let out 56 port rope pipes & 16 scuppers; easd in 30 port & 28 scuttle lids, trimd & fastend 28 washboards to ports; a cross chock to the bowsprit partners & cabin cants 36 feet, refitted bars; bucklers & messenger rollers with Iron work; trimd & bolted chocks for & refitted & got in place the manger boards; trimd & fastened cants & made 2 caps with bars to the pumpdale scuppers; unshipt refitted & reshipt the tiller & cross piece to the mooring bitts, refitted 2 shot lockers & trimd & hung 2 shores to mooring bits; trimd & fitted arm battens 240 feet & trimd & fitted with Iron-work 2 port cants; refastend shot cants 105 feet & took down deadeye racks guarding & lanthorns &c.

Upper Deck Took down the ordinary galley & birthing to the foreheath & shifted 192 feet of lead, trimd & fastend shortstuff 86 feet. Cabin cants 116 feet & 3 urns to the masts – bored & let out 8 scuppers & cased in lead pipes; fayd & bolted 4 iron standards & 4 Iron knees to the bitts, made molds for & fitted an iron staircase; trimed & fitted 2 shot lockers, refitted & bolted 8 ranges & 4 blocks, set up 6 pillars; bolted the fireheath made cooks table & ladder & built lockers, bored for & drove 4 ring & eyebolts & repaird 3 half ports. Forecastle waiste quarter-deck & roundhouse; fitted in place 95 Iron stantions; trimd & fitted hammock board 446 feet roughtree rail 250 feet, refitted hammock boards 38 feet & roughtree rails 84 feet ript off & shifted breadthing pieces from carronade chocks & hacked off 40 bolts, trimd & fastend 32 legs & relayd & bolted 22 carronades chocks trimd & fastened flat 51 feet shortstuff 118 feet, one bolster for the main stay, 2 urns for the masts shotlockers 25 feet cabin cants 80 feet & 2 boom chocks; trimd & bolted 16 blocks, 2 additional bittpins, 2 anchor chocks & 2 kivels one range & shroud racks 47 feet, refitted & bolted on range 6 blocks, cut two additional ports to the quarter deck; shifted the fore brace bitts & crosspiece & bored for & drove an Iron horse, shifted combing 12 feet & 2 headledges; got in place & bolted the accommodation carlings &c drove 2 tybolts fitted & fastend 27 Iron cranks to beams; bored for let down & easd in a voice pipe, trimd & fitted 2 sampsons posts & 2 rollers with ironwork; refitted 2 galley cisterns – made 5 gratings, 4 half ports & 2 cup scuttles. repaird 2 half ports, bored for & drove 54 & drove out & redrove 12 upbolts, unbolted awning stantion & took off housings from the gear &c.

Withoutboard: - Got up & fitted 70 deadeyes with preventer plates to the Channels, bolted 4 goosenecks, refitted & fastend the channel rails; rebolted & took down harbour bolstens & fayd & bolted hawse & anchor bolsters & chesstress; trimd & let down & fastend solid washboards & gammoning bolsters & trimd & bolted billboards; trimd chocks for & got in place & bolted the bumpkins; cut down 6 ledges in the head, built 2 seats; made 2 Trunks to the roundhouses & made leaded one cistern – trimd & fastend arras pieces under the wale 152 feet, lining of the anchor 36 feet, 28 ports & 28 scuttle riggles, 32 steps to the sides & 2 cleats for davits; made & fastend 14 shoots & refayd & fastend 25 steps; made molds for & bolted 2 Iron knees under gunroom, ports & fitted 2 Iron plates to pumpdale & scuppers; trimd & fitted with Ironwork 2 rollers for mainsheets & fitted & bolted 4 iron cranks for sheets & tacks trimd & bolted 2 fixt; blocks, fitted & fixed stools & got in place & secured with stays & c the stern lanthorns – fitted boat davits & drove logel [sic] bolts in the channels; repaird the steeping cistern & dead lights – drove out 30 & bored for & drove 12 eyebolts - made stages for performing the above works, cut down & put in 62 pieces, made & drove 299 plugs and performed works incident to rigging.

HM Ship *Temeraire* - Page 8

Temeraire 98 Guns – Hold and Magazine Took off lining bulkheads 1738 feet, cleard & took down bulkhead plank 584 feet, board 168 feet, 30 stantions & took up flat 635 feet – trimd and fastend cieling 502 ft trimd & bolted 2 half & 2 whole beams, trimd & fastend pallating beam & took up & fastend 6 – trimd & let down 12 Carlings & 12 ledges, trimed & fastend flat in the magazine & hanging storeroom 935 feet – refayd & fastend bulkhead plank 696 feet, pallating 95 feet and large cants 76 feet cut & set up 6 pillars, 35 stantions & 3 sampsons posts – trimd & fastend bulkhead plank 569 feet, board 463 feet lining 8530 feet featheredge lining in breadroom &c 2946 feet & 4 inch cants 166 feet, trimd & fitted timber boards 94 feet & examined and refitted 254 feet, let in & fastend the lanthorn & trimd & fastend stool bracket &c in the after powderroom – refitted & hung 8 door & one scuttle – fore magazine, Trimd rabbetted & set up the jambs, took up and refitted 36 scuttles, 36 boxes, refayd & fastend 31 carlings made & fitted 11 scuttles, 2 cisterns, one ladder & 2 blinds: took down & refitted bottoms battings [sic] racks drawers & wing pannels [sic] leaded jambs and filling room; coppered the bulkhead &c fitted in place complete the lanthorns & made molds for & fitted & hung the sashes-

Orlop and Platform: Cleard & took down lining from bulkheads &c 626 feet, storeroom bulkheads 6685 feet & 70 stantions; split down & trimd out scarphs for 4 end beams, trimd & bolted 4 end pieces of beams, unbolted chocks & rebolted 2 lodging knees, drove out & redrove 30 bolts in knees &c, trimd & let down 10 carlings & 33 ledges; shifted flat 197 feet refayd & fastend flat 380 feet trimd & fastend cieling (thickstuff) 161 feet; trimd & set up 35 stantions & refitted & set up 14, trimd & let in 9 sills birthed up & canted storeroom bulkheads 3298 feet trimd & fastend lining & cants 2839 feet, took down & refitted & fastened framing drawers, &c in the carpenters & Gunners storerooms – cut holes thro' the bulkhead & let in guarded lanthorns made molds for & let in & bolted 6 Iron plates to hatchways & fitted 9 hatch bars; trimd & fastend. thick cants 34 feet & leaded the magazine & lightroom passages. made the stewards desk, 4 scuttles one grating & one roller, got in place & fitted the cheese rack repaird & hung 4 scuttles repaird 10 gratings one ladder & 2 doors. Unhung refitted and hung 10 doors & shifted 24 locks.

Gun Deck; made molds for & fitted 42 Iron plates to the ends of the beams, & bolted 6 end pieces of beams – unbolted trimd & bolted one breadth rider, one lodging knee & one hanging knee – trimd & fastend firrings [illegible word] 124 feet, deck flat 856 feet, waterways 207 feet, plank in air openings 207 feet – refayd & fastend waterways 136 feet deck flat 399 feet & 2 face pieces to the bitts: unbolted chocks & rebolted a standard against the Bitts & mouthd 6 ends of Beams, made molds for & bolted 22 Iron hanging knees trimd & bolted 8 large cleats under beam ends – cut holes & let out & trimd 18 scuppers – trimd & bolted the manger stantions &c trimd & fitted manger boards, bucklers bars rollers &c &c – trimd & fastend shot cants 174 feet, trimd & fitted with Ironwork complete 5 port cants & 2 rollers and refitted with Ironwork 25 port cants & 2 rollers – made molds for & fitted gooseneck bolted Iron Straps & fitted 2 Tillers – made molds for & fitted 6 hatch bars, let in & fastened 2 Ironplates to hatchways: built gunroom cupboards; trimd let down & bolted combing 10 feet trimd & let up 5 carlings & 2 angle chocks & 20 ledges – made one cap scuttle: repaired 3 ladders & 14 gratings, fitted & fastend hammock rack 299 feet & shifted 9 port rope pipes – bored for & drove 56 bolts in ends of waterways & 5 eyebolts drove & redrove 2 butt & 3 rider bolts & took down guarding stantions deadeye racks etc.

Middle deck – Cleard & took up flat 366 feet, binding strakes 61 feet & waterways 22 feet – unbolted trimd & bolted deckhook with long ekings & the bowsprit partners – reduced the heels of 15 topriders & hackt off & reclenchd 15 bolts – trimd & let down 4 carlings & 9 ledges; trimd & fastend flat 406 feet, waterways 22 feet – made molds for and bolted 11 Iron hanging knees, made molds for & fitted an Iron staircase – unbolted chocks & bolted one hanging knee – leaded & copperd the galley, bolted the fireheath & built cook's cupboards & lockers – trimd & fastend shot cants 156 feet, cabin cants 96 feet, unbolted trimd & bolted one range, trimd & fitted 4 rollers, 26 port cants with Iron work – refitted a shot locker 4 sampsons posts 2 rother chocks & refitted with Ironwork 24 port cants – shifted the lead to the helm port, 21 port rope pipes & one scupper – let on hoops & refitted the Tiller; fitted & fastened hammock racks 839 feet forced home with an engine the hanging knees & reclenched the bolts: bored for & drove 35 additional bolts in riders & knees & drove out & redrove 8 ring bolts – made one ladder 3 cooks tables & 2 half ports; repair'd 19 gratings 6 ladders, 26 half ports & 8 deadlights.

Upper deck Took down the ordinary galley, cleard & took up flat 34 feet, trimd & let down 15 ledges & one head ledge – split down an end beam & trimd out a scarph, turnd & bolted one end beam – shifted flat 587 feet & clamps 21 feet, trimd & fastend plank in air openings 111 feet – unbolted, shifted & bolted 3 lodging & 3 hanging knee – made molds for & bolted 10 Iron stantions 216 Iron knees under the beams & bored holes for & drove 25 additional bolts in knees & clamps – unbolted & rebolted 2 Iron pillars; forced home with an engine hanging knees & reclenched the bolts; shifted one cheek block & 14 scuppers, trimd & fastend shot cants 170 feet hammock board 723 feet, 4 bolsters to bitts & 8 bulls eyes; refitted 2 Iron stantions 4 sampsons posts & 2 rollers, made 4 half ports, 2 gratings & the steam trunk; repaird 13 half ports 18 gratings & 5 ladders-took up refayed & fastend cabin cants 61 feet.

Forecastle, Waiste, Quarterdeck and Roundhouse, Cleard & took off birthing plank 694 feet flat 98 feet plansheer 198 feet roughtreerail 137 feet 8 drifts & 8 sweep pieces over ports, trimd out scarphs for & trimd let down & bolted 86 timbers for raising the berthing, cut off 84 timberheads to recieve plansheer & trimd & bolted 8 short timber heads: trimd & fastend birthing planking 1118 feet, spirketting 137 feet, plank in the openings 38 feet & 2 cheek blocks; trimd & bolted plansheer 217 feet, shifted flat 258 feet & fiferail 25 feet; refayd & fastened spirketting 52 feet unbolted 11 hanging knees & 5 lodging knees; trimd & bolted 15 & refayd & bolted 2 hanging knees – made molds for & bolted 27 Iron hanging knees – made molds for & fitted 46 Iron stantions: trimd & fitted hammock boards 812 feet, – unbolted 2 roughtreerails 62 feet refitted 35 Iron stantions and roughtreerail 278 feet-unbolted shifted & bolted the brace bitts, drove out 95 ring & eyebolts, bored for & drove 108 ring & eyebolts, 13 bolts in portsills & 48 belaying pins – refayd & bolted 2 belaying racks & 2 anchor chocks: trimd & fastened 22 bolsters to beams &c 8 bulls eyes & lopers ? for tiller rope – bored holes let out trimd & easd over 26 lead pipes & leaded the Taffrel – made 20 half ports, 3 gratings & 2 ladders – repaird one ladder & 3 gratings – trimd & bolted 2 ranges & shroud racks 52 feet – unbolted awning stantions, & took down guarding stantions housings &c.

Withoutboard Docked & shored the ship, shifted 397 sheets of copper trimd & fastend ekings under the wale 77 feet, dubbed the bottom 1500 feet & undocked the ship– shifted Topside plank 148 feet cleard & fastend channel rails got in place & fitted channel rail 60 feet & 2 billboards – unbolted the harbour bolsters, refayd & bolted hawse bolsters with fillings, refayd & fastend solid washboards. under the cheeks & trimd & fastend washboards to upper cheeks, made molds for & bolted 2 Ironplates above & below the upper cheeks & fitted & bolted 4 cranks for sheets &c. refayd & bolted the chesstrees & anchor bolsters trimd & fastend 6 stantions for lining of the anchor & made molds for & fitted and 3 Iron plates refitted & bolted the bumpkins & 2 cranks for mainbrase – took down & rebuilt the roundhouses – shifted the beakhead bulkhead & part of the flat, fitted & bolted the Bowsprit chock, trimd & let down 12 ledges & 2 carlings, took up & refastend 3 Iron plates trimd & built up seats & Trunks made and steeping cistern with chocks & secured with iron clamp: trimd & fastend 74 port riggles; 15 scuttle riggles 12 steps & 5 bolsters for stays. trimd & bolted 2 bolsters for main Tack & 2 large cleats – unhung and rehung 6 port scuttles, trimd out the sides of 12 & cut stops to 8 ports; made and fastend the shoots to the sides and 2 cisterns to quarter galleries; refayd & fastend the 2 upper finishings & 3 rails to the same; Trimd & fitted 3 stools for stern lanthorns & shifted leads on stools 510 feet – refitted & fastend 12 steps; drove out 28 eyebolts & 64 plugs from portrope holes – made stages to perform the before mentioned works – cut out & put in 389 pieces in different parts of the ship; squared with the caulkers & performed works incident to rigging.

HM Ship *Tonnant* - Page 12

Tonnant 80 Guns – Hold Trimd & fastend fillings in air openings 424 feet bulkhead plank 596 feet trimd & fastend 70 feet & flat 304 feet cut & set up 10 stantions & bored for and drove 7 eyebolts.
Magazine & powder Room Trimd & fastend oak lining 1904 feet bulkhead board 470 feet, filled & fas-

tend lead 4012 feet & 72 tin plates, copperd bulkheads 563 feet fitted the lanthorns, cisterns cants & birthing, easd drawers, refitted the battins [sic] & made a scuttle & lid in the powderroom.

Orlop and Platforms Took down storeroom bulkheads 311 feet, made a desk & fitted the steward room, birthd up storeroom bulkheads 339 feet, lined the flat 895 feet, capt over the openings in the wings 286 feet lead the magazine & lightroom passages, refitted the cistern to the foremast, cut & set up 4 stations, fitted 4 storeroom lanthorns, made 4 doors & one roller, easd 4 hatches & 7 scuttles, dubd the flat 210 feet & took down guarding stanters &c.

Gundeck Trimd & fastend the flat 210 feet, fillings to air openings 144 feet, shot cants 48 feet, cabin cants 36 feet shotlockers 28 feet, cut holes let out & trimd 22 scuppers; bored for & let out 64 lead pipes for port ropes, trimd & fitted fillings between the deck & transon refayd & bolted shot racks 131 feet, refitted manger boards &c. trimd & fitted 32 wash boards to ports fitted a tiller with Iron work, cut & set up 2 pillars, dubd off flat 452 feet drove 10 eyebolts & took down deadeye stantions & racks guarding stantions &c. (crossed out in original) made armourers [sic] bench.

Upper deck Took down the ordinary galley & bulkheads round the fireheath, took up lead 137 feet, got in place fitted bored off & bolted 22 Iron standards; cut holes let out & trimd 10 scuppers – trimd & fastend galley cants 28 feet, fitted & fastend lead 280 feet & 204 tin plates, lined the beams, bolted the firehearth, fitted cranks & made cooks tables & cupboards & ladders – trimd & fastend fillings in air openings 124 feet, cabin cants 173 feet, shotlockers 24 feet hammock rack 35 feet, trimd & bolted 4 ranges; 2 carlings for top tackle eye bolts, fitted chocks & bolted shot racks 128 feet trimd & fitted with Iron worn 4 rollers, trimd & set up 2 cleats & 4 sampsons posts, fitted canted & cut holes in 32 half ports, fitted battens & cleats for arms 144 feet; made one half port, repair 4 gratings, fitted casing around the tiller ropes, fayd & bolted 6 ranges & bored for & drove 36 eyebolts.

Forecastle, waiste, Quarter Deck & roundhouse Trimd & bolted 6 carronade chocks, fitted in place drove eyebolts for & stapled 92 Iron stantions, hammock board 876 feet & roughtree rail 200 feet – fitted & bolted 10 Iron stantions, let out 14 scuppers, cut thro' the sides & let out 40 lead pipes, fayd & bolted anchor chock & 6 cheek blocks, trimd & bolted shroud racks 92 feet, 22 blocks 8 ranges , 2 headledges & combings 33 feet trimd & fastend shotlockers 35 feet & fillings in air openings 140 feet, refitted 4 Iron stantions, cut down 2 carronade ports, made molds for & fastend Iron cranks between beams, made 9 gratings, 4 scuttles & 6 half ports; unshipt & reshipt the steering wheel & shifted one of the stantions – bored for & drove 85 ring & eyebolts & 113 belaying pins, drove out & redrove 8 ring & eyebolts – unbolted awning stantions, ript off housing from the gear, took down the crane, roughtreerails, stantions louvering over openings &c &c.

Withoutboard Took off & refastend the channel rails, got in place & fitted 80 deadeyes & 50 preventer plates, bored off & bolted 4 goosenecks & drove 4 swivel bolts, unbolted & took down the harbour bolsters, fitted bored off & bolted the hawser bolsters, trimd & fastend the fillings & fayd & fastend the washboards, fayd & bolted the anchor bolsters with ekings trimd & fastend lining of the anchor 56 feet, 2 billboards & fitted & fastend 2 Iron plates; got in place & fitted the accommodation stations, carlings, gratings &c got in place chocked & bolted the bumpkins with clasps made & fitted 2 trunks to the roundhouses & 6 cisterns – fitted & fasten'd 304 copper sheets on the bottom, made molds for & bolted 2 Iron knees under gunroom ports, made molds for & bolted 4 outriggers for tacks & sheets; fayd, bolted & morticed, the chesstrees with bolsters, made & bolted 14 shoots, trimd & fastend 6 & fitted & fasten'd 38 steps – 32 port & 32 scuttle riggles, easd the port lids, took off & refastend the upper finishings & fitted in place the stern lanthorns with stools & stays – bored for & drove 51 eyebolts & drove out 32 – made stages for performing the above works, cut out & put in 26 pieces in different parts of the ship & performed works incident to rigging.

Works performed in making good defects page 29/30/31

HM Ship *Neptune*
Neptune 98 guns – hold Shifted the greater part of the bulkheads to well shotlockers fish & spirit rooms & hanging storerooms dubbed the cieling & riders for inspection, unbolted trimed & bolted four third futtock riders, shifted 2 shifts of clamp & 7 shifts of cieling, lined fish & spiritrooms bulkheads; refitted the limberboards & built bulkheads for dry provisions.

Magazine and Lightroom Shifted the beams carlings flat jambs bulkheads &c.
Orlop unbolted shifted & bolted 3 halfbeams & 2 lodging knees, shifted part of the flat & the carlings to the forehatch, made & repaird hatches & gratings, took down & rebuilt storerooms & leaded the passageways.

Gundeck Shifted 37 shifts of the flat & 8 scuppers bored for and drove 36 additional bolts in knees & drove out & redrove the stopper & train bolts, made molds for & bolted 12 Iron knees under beams, trimed & bolted shot racks, refayd the manger boards &c refitted tillers, made the armourers bench repaired bowsprit partners & trimed & fitted washboards to the ports & messenger rollers.

Middle Deck trimd & fastened shot cants shifted 7 scuppers & made & repaird half ports, ladders gratings & port cants.
Upperdeck Fayd & bolted 22 Iron hanging knees, trimed & bolted the shot cants shifted 4 scuppers & made & repaired half ports ladders & gratings.
Quarterdeck, Waiste, & Forecastle Shifted 2 shifts of the flat trimed and bolted 8 hanging knees to skid beams & fayd & bolted 18 Iron knees under the beams.

Withoutboard Shifted 4 shifts of topside & 2 of sheetstrake. Docked & sustained the ship took off the copper sheathing shifted lead under the gripe, coppered the bottom & undocked the ship – unbolted, shifted & bolted one & refayd & bolted one hawser bolster shifted the filling between the cheeks and eased in the ports.

HM Ship *Thunderer*
Thunderer 74 guns – Gundeck Took down & refastend manger boards & shifted 2 scuppers.
Upperdeck repaired the flat.
Withoutboard unbolted & rebolted chain plates & repaired copper sheathing.

HMS *Minotaur*
Minotaur 74 Guns – **Withoutboard** Trimd & fastend bumpkins & lining of the anchor.

HM Ship *Naiad*
Naiad 38 Guns – Lowerdeck trim'd & fitted a tiller & repaired gratings.
Magazine raised the flat & made 36 scuttles.
Upper Deck shifted 2 shifts of the flat took down & rebuilt 2 roundhouses & let out 3 scuppers.
Withoutboard repair the copper sheathing shifted 7 steps & repaired air scuttle.

Appendix 3: AN ACCOUNT OF THE EXPENSE OF BOATSWAINS STORES ON BOARD HIS MAJESTY'S SHIP *BRITANNIA* CHAS BULLEN ESQ. COMMANDER

Page 1
An Account of the Expense of Boatswains Stores on Board His

Day of the Month	For what Use expended, with the Occasion of Extraordinary Accidents and Conversions Year 1805 Month October	Species	Number or Quantity In Words
21st	To Fore Topmast Sya the old shot away in Action What was left was used for spunyarn Tackle Fall for Do. Shot away in action to Do.	Bouy Rope 8 _ In. Rope 3 In. Rope 1 In.	One in No. Twenty four fms. Ten fms.
	Cut away Towing a sterne being sunk by the Enemy	Cutter 25 feet	One In No.
	Lost with the Cutter	Oars Cutter Sails Cutter Rope 3 In. Fore Topsail Main Topsail Mizen Staysail Steering Sails Fore Dead Eyes 18 In. Block 14 Ins. Rope 3 In.	Six in No. On in No. Seventy fms. One in No. One in No. One in No. One in No. One in No. One in No. Thirty fms.
	Shot away in Time of Action		
	Main Deadeyes and Fore Clew Garnet		
	To Reeving Fore Tiopmast Stay sail Halyd the old shot away		
	Do. Fore Top sail Braces Old Shot away Do.	Rope 3 In.	122 fms.
	Do. Main Top Sail Braces Old Do.	Rope 3 In.	106 fms.
	Do. Davit Tackle Falls for a Cutter on the Quarter Do.	Rope 3 In.	Seventy two fms.
	Do. Main Braces Old Shot away Do.	Rope 4 In.	120 fms.
	Do. To Jibb Outhauler Old do.	Rope 2 In.	Thirty fms.
	Do. To Spanker Brails having no 2 In. & 6	Rope 1 In.	Thirty fms.
	Do. To Mizen Royal Braces Ols Do. In Action	Rope 1 _ In.	Fifty Four fms.
	Do. To Main Royal Braces Do.	Rope 1 _ In.	Eighty fms.
	Do. To Lanyard for Bowsprit Shrouds Old Do.	Rope 2 In.	Twelve fms.
	To Fitting New Jibb Pendants	Rope 3 _ In.	Twelve fms.
	To Reeving Davit Toping [sic] Lifts Old Do.	Rope 3 In.	Twenty fms.
22nd	To Do. For Main Mizen & Mizen Peak Halyds	Rope 1 _ In.	302 fms.
	To Mizen Top Gallt Truck Old Do.	Truck	One In No.
	To Signal Blocks Old Do.	Block Brass Shiver	Four In No.
	Cut up to Woold the Bowsprit being Shot	Rope Jibb Halyard &	Main Top Gallt
	Lifts		
	Do. To Woold the gaff being new fished	Ropeold MizTopGallt	lifts & Royal

Used Woolding Bowsprit Gaff & ----- of the Ship

		Halyd Woolding Nails	Two Hundred
	Lost Woolding Bowsprit & Splicing Do.	Crows	Two in No.
	To Do.	Handspikes	Ten in No.
	To Do.	Marlin Spikes	Eight in No.
	To Do.	Junk Axes	Two in No.
	To Do.	Hatchets	Four in No.
	Found Missing after the Action	Haversacks	160 in No.

Page 2.
Majesty's Ship the *Britannia* Chas Bullen Esq. Commander

Day of the Month	For what Use expended, with the Occasion of Extraordinary Accidents and Conversions Year 1805 Month October	Species	Number or Quantity In Words
23rd	Shot away in time of Action & reptd as defects	Blocks 12 In.	Five in No.
	Do.	Blocks 7 In.	Four in No.
	Do.	Blocks 6 In.	Six in No.
	Do.	Futtock Hooks	Four in No.
	Do.	Tackle Hooks	Eight in No.
	Do.	Thimbles	Thirty in No.
	Do.	Cringles	Fifty in No.
	Do.	Half Hour Glasses	Three in No.
24th	To Mizen Flag Staf [sic] Stay Ols Shot away in Action	Rope 1 In.	Twenty fms.
	To Mizen top sail Braces Old Do.	Rope 2 In.	Sixty One fms.
	To Mizen Top Gallt Bowline Old Do.	Rope 1 In.	Forty Eight fms.
	To Main Top Gallt Steering Sail Tack Old Do.	Rope 1 In.	Twenty seven fms.
24th	Lost out of the Boats in Getting [sic] Prisoners abd Four in No.		Bowles Wood
	To Repairing F. M. & Mizn Top Gallt Sails & Jibb	Twine Canvas No. 7	Twenty Five Yds. Two Lbs.
	Do. To Cott [sic] Clews & Lanyds for men Wounded	Rope In.	Forty fms.
25th	To fiting [sic] New fore Top sail Bowlines & Bridles	Rope 3 In.	Fourteen fms.
	To Earings	Rope 1 In.	Forty fms.
	To Repairing Flags &c this Month	Buntin [sic]	Fifty Yds.
	To Heading Flags & Line	Lines White Twine	Five in No. One Lb.

245

Part 1: The British Fleet — The Ships of Trafalgar

		Shot away in Action	Ensign White 3/4	One in No.
		Do	Jacks 16 Breadth	One in No.
		Do	Linen Flag	One in No.
		Do	Flags of sorts	Fifteen in No.
		Do.	Pendants of sorts	Six in No.
26th		To Repairing Fore Top Gt Steering sails being shot through in Diff places	Canvas No. 7	Ten Yds.
			Twine	One Lb
		Covering sides Repairs To Cott [sic] Clews &c	Kersey	Nine Yds
			Linen Cabbin [sic]	Four in No.
27th		To Repairing M. Mast Steering sails shot in action Gaff Top sail &c	Canvas No. 7	Fifty Two Yds.
			Twine	Three Lb.
27th		Broke & Lost &c by Sail Maker	Palms sailmakers	Six in No.
		Broke & Lost this Month	Locks Hanging	Four in No..
		Do.	Lanthorns	Two in No.
29th		To Strops for Diff. Blocks shot away	Rope 3 In.	Twenty Twp fms.

Page 3
Majesty's Ship the *Britannia* Chas Bullen Esq. Commander

Day of the Month	For what Use expended, with the Occasion of Extraordinary Accidents and Conversions Year 1805 Month October	Species	Number or Quantity In Words
	To Do.	Rope 3 In.	Nineteen fms.
	To Do.	Rope 2 In.	One fms
	To Do.	Rope 1 In.	Twenty One fms.
	To Do.	Rope – In.	209 fms
31st	Used Keeping Ship Clean this Month	Buckets Iron Bound	Six in No.
	Do.	Brushes large	Two in No.
	Do.	Shovels Iron	Two in No.
	Cut away being on Fire & Cut up for Swabs	Hammocks	112 in No.
	Broke & Lost in Action	Leather Buckets	Twenty in No.

C. Bullen Captain.
J Frances Master
Thos...... Boatswain

Appendix 4: AN ACCOUNT OF THE EXPENSE OF CARPENTERS STORES ON BOARD HIS MAJESTY'S SHIP *AFRICA* 64 GUNS HENRY DIGBY ESQ. COMMANDER

Page 1
An Account of the Expense of *Carpenters* Store on Board His

Day of the Month	For what Use expended, with the Occasion of Extraordinary Accidents and Conversions Year 1805 Month October	Species	Number or Quantity In Words
21st	Shot away in Action & Throwed Over Board	Mn Topsail Yard	One in No.
	Lost in Action, from the Hatchways	Tarporlins [sic]	Three in No.
	Wounded on the Booms	F & M Topmasts	One each
		Jib Booms	Two No.
	Shot to Pieces with the Barge and thrown [sic] overboard	Barge Mast	Three No
		Yards	Three No.
		Bowspritt [sic]	One in No.
		Hooks	One in No.
	Shot away in Action	Port Hinges	Two in No.
	Chain Plate	Formed in Chains	Two No.
		Tea [sic] Plates	Two No
	To Repairing Damages After the action	Oak – 4 Inch	Twenty Eight ft.
		Plank Elm – 4 Inch	Twelve ft.
		Board Elm	Eighty ft.
22nd	To Making over & Stopping Shot Holes	Oak Board	Forty ft.
		Deales [sic] Ordinary	Ten in No.
		Oak – 3 Inch	Fourteen ft.

Page 2.
Majesty's ship Africa 64 Guns. Henry Digby Esq. Commander

Day of the Month	For what Use expended, with the Occasion of Extraordinary Accidents and Conversions Year 1805 Month October	Species	Number or Quantity In Words
22nd	Used for Making over & Stopping Shot Holes	Coper [sic] Sheets	Three in No.
	Used for Making over ....Ditto	Sheet Lead	Four Hundred Lbs.
22nd	Used for Tallow Mugs	Tallow	132 Lbs.
	Used for ....Ditto	Oakum Black	Two Hunderd Lbs.
	Lost in Making the Lead over the Shot Holes	Hammer Clench	Two in No.
	To Making a Fish for the Bowsprit	Anchor Stock	Half
23rd	Used for Fishing the Mizen Mast	Spars Barling	Two in No.
		Boom	Two in No.
	To Fishing the Main Mast	Capstan Bars Fur [sic]	Three in No.
	Lost with the Fore Mast	Fore Mast	One in No.
	Ditto	FT Mast with Sheves	One in No.
	Ditto	F Yd with Boom Irons	One in No.
	Ditto	FTYard with Boom Irons	One in No.
	Ditto	Stunsail Booms	Foure [sic] in No.
	Ditto	Stunsail Yards	Foure [sic] in No.
24th	Lost with the Maine [sic] Mast	Maine Mast	One in No.
	Ditto	MT Mast with Sheves	One in No.
	Ditto	M Yd with Boom Irons	One in No.
	Ditto	MTYard with Boom Irons	One in No.
	Ditto	Topand T'Gallant Stunsail Booms	Four in No.
	Ditto	Stunsail Yards	Foure [sic] in No.
	Lost with the Mizen [sic] Mast	Mizen Mast	One in No.
	Ditto	Mizen Top Mast	One in No.
	Ditto	Cross Jack Yd	One in No.
	Ditto	Mizen Top Sl Yd	One in No.
	Ditto	Trysail Gaff	One in No.
		Fids for Top Mast	Three in No.
	Carried away & lost by the Foremast Goin [sic]	Flying Jibb Boom	One in No.
		Jibb Boom	One in No.
	Lost in the Gales by the Mizzen Mast goin [sic] over side	Spreets	Two in No.

Page 3
An Account of the Expense of *Carpenters* Store on Board His

Day of the Month	For what Use expended, with the Occasion of Extraordinary Accidents and Conversions Year 1805 Month October	Species	Number or Quantity In Words
24th	Lost by the Mast Goin [sic]	Top Chest	Three No.
	Broke & Lost by the Mast Going over the Side	Iron Honshores ?	Twenty Seven
25th	Used for a Jury Fore mast	Mast Norway 14 Hands	One No.
26th	Used for a jury Maine [sic] Mast	Miz Mast	One No.
	Used for Steps for Jury Mast	Anchor Stock	Half
27th	Used for a Jury Mizen Mast	Mn TopGall. Mast	One No.
	Cut into Bolts for securing the Jury Mast	Iron New	One Hundred Weight
	To Fitting Cross Trees and Tressle [sic] Trees for Jury Mast	Tressle Trees	Three No.
28th	The Former Lost with the Wreck	Cross Trees	Five No.
		Cross Tree Bitts	Ten No.
	Used for Repairing the Pinnace the Former Stove in Action	Winscott [sic]	Forty ft.
		Copper Sheeting	Four Lbs.
		Coper [sic] Boat Nails	Twelve Lb.
		Roves & Clinches	Eight Lb.
		Spik [e] of weight ?	Forty Lb.
		Sharp – 40 ?	Nineteen Lb.
		Do. – 30	Eighteen Lb
		Do. – 24	Forty Lb.
	Used in Lew [sic] of Woolding Nailes [sic] having none on Board & Port	Do. – 20	Forty Five Lb.
		Do. – 10	Twenty Lb.
		Do. – 6	Ten Lb.
		Do. – 4	Eight Lb.
		Do. – 3	Seven Lb.
		Do. – 2	Six Lb.
30th	Used the Above this Month		

Page 4
Majesty's ship Africa 64 Guns. Henry Digby Esq. Commander

Day of the Month	For what Use expended, with the Occasion of Extraordinary Accidents and Conversions Year 1805 Month October	Species	Number or Quantity In Words
30th		Boats 1 Oz 6	Four Lb.
		Brads	One Lb.
		Deck Boats	Six Lb.
		Lead Nails	Eighteen No.
		Scuper [sic] Do.	Twenty Five
		Tacks	One Lb
30th	Used for the Arm Chest the former Broke in Action	Hasps & Stapels [sic]	Nine in No
	Split & Broke in Securing the Steps of the Jury Mast	Wedges	Thirty No.

H Digby Capt.n
Lt. G Barnard Master
Thos. Coates Carpenter

Received from Mr. Coates Carpenter
of HM Ship Africa the undermentioned Carpenter's Stores
for the use of HM Ship Donegal – Viz
P.r Order of Capt.n Digby
Board Elm – Fifty One feet
Boat Nails – Ten Pounds

Tho.s Hughes Carpenter's Mate

Donegal Gibraltar Bay
5th Nov. 1805   Approved H Digby

246

Appendix 5: AN ACCOUNT OF THE EXPENSE OF CARPENTERS STORES ON BOARD HIS MAJESTY'S SHIP THE *VICTORY* T M HARDY ESQ. COMMANDER

Page 1
Majesty's Ship the *Victory* Thos. M Hardy Esq. Commander

Day of the Month	For what Use expended, with the Occasion of Extraordinary Accidents and Conversions	Species	Number or Quantity In Words
	Year 1805		
	Month October		
15th	To Hoses to Port Ropes and on the upper Edge of the Middle Deck Ports to keep the Deck Dry	Canvas New	Twenty Seven Yds.
19th	To repairing the Poop Lanthorns & Lead Pipe	Plate White Single	
Eight lbs.		Solder	Four No.
21st	Broke to Pieces and thrown over Board in Clearing Ship for Action	Hen Coops	Eight No.
		Turkey Coops	One No.
21st	Carried away in the Action with the French and Spanish combined fleet off Cape Trafalgar – Shot to Pieces and lost overboard	Mizen Mast	One No.
		Mizen Top Mast	One No.
		Mizen Top Gallt Mast	One No.
		Boom Driver	One No.
		Gaff Do.	One No.
		Cross Jack Yard	One No.
		Mizen Topsail Yard	One No.
		Mizen Top Gallt Yard	One No.
		Mizen Royal Yard	One No.
		Fore Yard	One No.
		Spritsail Yard	One No.
		Do. Topsail Yard	One No.
		Flyg Gib [sic] Boom	One No.
		Studg Sail Booms	Six No.
		Do. Yards	Six No.
	Shot to Pieces asnd lost with the Boats and on the Booms	Boats Masts	Seven No.
		Boats Sprits	Nine No.
		Spars small	Fifteen No.
22nd	Converted into a Jury Mizen Mast	Jibb [sic] Boom.	One No.
	To Fishing the Main Mast being Wounded by Shot	Plank Oak 4 In.	Forty Eight feet
		Plank Oak 3 In.	Fort feet
25th	Carried away in a Squall being Wounded by Shot and lost overboard	Main Yard	One No.
26th	To Strengthening the Fore and Main Topsail Yards for Lower Yards	Spars Cant	Four No.
	Do.	Spars Barling	Four No.
27th	Converted into a Jury Fore Top Mast being damaged by Shot	Top Mast Fore	One No.
	Do. for a Fore Top Gallt Mast	Top Mast Stump	One No.
	Do. for a Fore Top Sail Yard	Jibb [sic] Boom	One No.
	Do. for a Main Top Sail Yard	Mast Norway 15 _ Hands	One No.
	Do. for a Main Top Gallt Mast being Shot	Top Mast Stump	One No.
29th	To the Main Chains the old Shot away	Chain Plate with Chains for shifting	
One No.			
	Cut up for a Step for the Mizen Mast and fitting Jury Geer [sic]	Plank Oak 3 In.	Ten feet
		Elm 4 In.	Fifteen feet
From 22nd to 31st	Shot away, thrown overboard with the Bulk Heads in Clearing Ship and Missing after the Action	Marine Arm Chest	Two No.
		Do. For Tops & Boats	Three No.
		Port Sashes	Fifteen
		Half Ports	? [not listed]
		Sampsons Post	Four No.
		Armourers Benches	Two No.
		Airing Stoves	One No.
		Back & Two Iron of the Ca--- Fore ?	One
		Anvil	One

Page 2.

An Account of the Expense of Carpenters Stores on Board His

Day of the Month	For what Use expended, with the Occasion of Extraordinary Accidents and Conversions	Species	Number or Quantity In Words
	Year 1805		
	Month October		
Between the 22nd and 31st	Shot away, thrown overboard with the Bulk Heads in Clearing Ship & Missing after the Action	Brimmer Stock	One No.
	Do.	Grinding Stone	One No.
	Do.	Bell Cabin	One No.
	Do.	Cavas Births	Fourteen No.
	Do.	Poop Lanthorns with Reflectors	Five No.
	Do.	Braces	Eight No.
	Do.	Nutts [sic] & Screws	Three sets
	Do.	Stools	Three No.
	Do.	Outriggers for Boats	Five
	Do.	Tables Deal small	Twelve
	Do.	Wainscott Hounds Ear	Six
	Do.	Wainscott Stools	Three
	Do.	Wainscott Pantry	One
	Do.	Nettin [sic] Stations	Six
	Do.	Brass Locks 8 In.	Fourteen
	Do.	Door Stays with Eyes	Seven
	Do.	Round Plate Bolts	Ten
	Do.	Quadrant	One Pr.
	Do.	Hinges Lath 10 In.	Two
	Do.	Do. Side Small	Two
	Do.	Table Fastenings	Three
	Do.	Pins & Chains	Twelve
	Do.	Venetian Blinds	Nine
	Do.	Bell Cranks	Four
	Do.	Valves & Plugs	Four Sets
	Do.	Glass Ground Fixed	208 Panes
	Do.	Fore Top Mast Cross Trees	One Set
	Do.	Fore Top Mast Tressletrees	One Set
	Do.	Bars Capstan	Nine No.
	To Repairing Hanging Ports, Putting in Pieces Covering Shot Holes fixing up screens for the Wounded and Officers Births and Repairing Different Damages	Plank Oak 4 In.	Eighteen Feet
		Do. Do. 3 In.	Thirty Feet
		Do. Do. 2 _ In.	Forty Feet
	Do.	Do. Do. 2 In.	Sixty Feet
	Do.	Do. Do. 1 _ In.	Seventy Feet
	Do.	Board Elm	150 Feet
	Do.	Do. Oak	110 Feet
	Do.	Wainscott	100 Feet
	Do.	Deals Ordinary	Thirty in No.
	Do.	Canvas Old	140 Yds.
	Do.	Floor Cloth	One No.
	Do.	Hinges Port	Four No.
	Do.	Port Hooks	Four No.
	Do.	Oaham [sic] Black	Fifty Six Lbs.
	Do.	Tallow	148 Lbs.
	Do.	Lead Sheet	296 Lb.
	Do.	Wedges	Fifty No.
	Do.	Port Staples	Twenty Seven
	Do.	Rope Old	350 fms

Page 3
Majesty's Ship the *Victory* T M Hardy Esq. Commander

Day of the Month	For what Use expended, with the Occasion of Extraordinary Accidents and Conversions	Species	Number or Quantity In Words
	Year 1805		
	Month October		
	Repairing Damages Continued.	Ballast Baskets	Nine No.
	Do.	Staples Large	Eighteen
	Do.	Staples Small	Twelve
	Do.	Hinges Butt	Four Prs.
	Do.	H[inges] L[arge]	Two Prs
31st	Do.	Fearnought	Forty Yds.
	Do.	Hasps & Staples	Eight No.
	Do.	Twine	Four & Half Lbs.
	Do.	Needles Sail	Twelve No.
	To Securing the aforesaid Work, Cleets [sic] &c for the Wounded and Repairing and the Different Damages Sustained in the Action &c this Month	Nails Spike & Weight	136 Lbs.
		Nails – 40 Penny	Thirty Lbs
		Do. – 30 Penny	Forty Five Lbs
		Do. – 24 Penny	Thirty Four Lbs.
		Do. – 20 Penny	Twenty Lbs.
		Do. – 10 Penny	Seventy Lbs.
		Do. – 6 Penny	Fifty Lbs.
		Do. – 4 Penny	Twenty Five Lbs.
		Do. – 3 Penny	. Eighteen Lbs
		Do. – 2 Penny	Twenty Lbs
		Boat [nails] 10 & 6	Thirty Lbs.
		Brads	Five Lbs.
		Deck Dble	Twelve Lbs.
		Deck Single	Ten Lbs.
		Lead	Eighty Lbs.
		Pump	Seven
		Scupper	Forty nine
		Woulding [sic]	Sixty Five
		Tacks	Four Lbs.
	To repairing and making knees and Sundry Iron works for the Boats, Repairing Boom Irons, Netting Stations and Port Fastenings this Month	Iron New	160 Lbs
		Coals	Six Bushels

TM Hardy — Captain
Thos Atkinson — Master
W Bunce — Carpenter

Trafalgar Ships Monthly Accounts – Boatswain and Carpenter
Source RNM MS. 1064/83 Record number 2376
NOTE – Account Commencing 21 October 1805

247

Appendix 6: SELECTED SAILING QUALITIES

For further details of sailing qualities, see *Nelson's Ships* (Conway Maritime Press, 2002).

Source: TNA: PRO; Adm 95/47/25

7th Day of July 1812

{ A REPORT of the Sailing and other Qualities of His Majesty's Ship
{ *Implacable* as found in strict Observation thereof, between the
{ *Twenty Third* of *April 1812* and this Date

		Ft.	Ins.
Her light draught of Water was stated to be	{ Forward	Dont know	
	{ Abaft		
The draught of Water which was estimated by the Builder to be her best trim	{ Forward	Dont know	
	{ Abaft		
The draught of Water found on trial to be her best sailing trim	{ Forward	21	10
	{ Abaft	23	6

What should be the difference between her draught of Water forward and abaft, to give her the best possible trim, when from circumstances she happens to be

- Considerably deeper than her best sailing draught as above stated .... 20 inches by the Stern
- Considerably lighter than ditto .... 17 inches D°.

		Tons.
Quantity of Ballast necessary to bring her to her best trim	{ Iron	236 ?
	{ Shingle	None

Quantity of Water she stows 300
Quantity of Water whereof is contained in Iron Tanks .... None

				Ft.	Ins.
When Stored for	{ Channel Service	{ Draught of Water	{ Forward		
	Foreign Service		Abaft		
			Forward		
			Midships	Dont Know	
		{ Height of Ports	Abaft		
			Forward	21	10
		Draught of Water	Abaft	23	6
			Forward	7	3
			Midship	6	1
		Height of Ports	Abaft	6	8

			No.	Pounders.
	On the Lower Deck {	Guns	30	32
		Carronades	–	–
	On the Mdd^l Deck {	Guns	–	–
		Carronades	–	–
How armed {	On the Gun Deck {	Guns	30	18
		Carronades	–	–
	On the Quart^r Deck {	Guns	2	12
		Carronades	12	32
	On the Forecastle {	Guns	2	12
		Carronades	2	32
	On the Roundhouse {	Guns	–	–
		Carronades	1	24

How does she stow her provisions	Very well
Does she ride easy at her anchors	Very easy
How does she stand under her sails	Not very well but which I think may be remedied by altering her stowage
How does she carry her lee ports	Very fare [sic]
Does she roll easy or uneasy in a trough of sea	Rolls deep but very easy
Does she pitch easy	Very easy
Is she, generally speaking, an easy or uneasy ship	An easy Ship
How does she in general carry her helm	When in Trim astern a Weather but when too much by the stern, a Lee
How does she steer	Very well when in trim
How does she Wear & Stay	Very quick
Is she weatherly or leewardly compared with other ships	Weatherly
How does she behave laying too	Very well

		Knots.	Fathoms.
	Under whole or single topsails or topgallant sails	9?	
Close hauled - {			
She has run per hour by	Under double reefed topsails	7	
the log with as much win {	Under courses	–	
as she safely can bear	Large under all sail that could with priority be set	12	
	Before the wind under similar circumstances	11	

What is her best point of sailing	On a wind
Comparative rate of sailing with other Ships	Has in many instances been a good advantage
Is she generally speaking a well built and strong ship or does she shew {sic} any unusual symptoms of weakness	She is well timbered and kneed below but is weak in her topsides

Remarks; stating the grounds of such of the present avowes to differ from those in last report, and any other observations tending to form accurate judgement on the qualities of the ship.

Source: TNA: PRO; Adm 95/39/93

The OBSERVATIONS of the Quality of His Majesty's Ship *Britannia*

	Ft.	Ins.	
Her best Sailing Draft of Water when Victualled and Stored for Channel Service being given this 22nd Day of December 1797	{ Afore 23 { Abaft 23	10? 10?	} or as much lighter (at the same Difference) as she is able to bear Sail }
Her Lowest Gundeck Port will be above the surface of the Water		5	2 or more

    In a Topgallant Gale . . . .   *By the wind Leeward 4 knots with a large wind 7 to 8 knots*

    In a Topsail Gale   *By the wind Leeward 4 knots with a large wind 8 to 9 knots*

Query the 1st . . . How she Steers, and how she Wears and Stays . . . .   *-*

    Under her... { Reeft

Topsails . . . .   *Steers very east Wears very slow Stays pretty well but requires her mainsail and after sails 3 to 4 knots easy in a sea easy a weather helm*

Courses . . . .   *2? to 3 knots leewardly easy in a sea*

And Query, Whether she will Stay under her Courses . . . .   *No*

2nd. In each Circumstance above mentioned (in Sailing with Other Ships) in what Proportion she gathers to Windward, and in what proportion she forereaches, and in general her Proportions in leeway . . . .   *In general leewardly – leeway in a topgallant Gale ? a point to 1 point Gale 1? points to 2 points under courses 3 to 4 points*

3rd. How she proves in Sailing thro' all the variations of the Wind from its being two feet abaft the Beam, to its Veering forward upon the Bowline in every Strength of Gale, especially if a stiff Gale and a Head sea, and how many Knots she runs in each Circumstance and how she carries her Helm . . . .   *Sails pretty well with a large wind and stiff gale runs 8 to 9 knots carries a weather helm upon a bowline in a head sea leewardly and sails slow*

4th. The most knots she runs before the Wind; and how she Rolls in a trough of Sea   *10 knots rolls easy*

5th. How she behaves in Lying Too, or a Try, under a Mainsail, also under a Mizon balanc'd . . . .   *Very well*

6th. What a Roader she is, and how she Careens . . . .   *Pretty good*

		Ft.	Ins.
7th.	If upon Trial the best sailing Draft of water given as above should not prove to be so what is her best sailing Draft of Water	{ Afore { Abaft	24 3 25 5
		Ft.	Ins.
8th.	What is her best Draft of water when victualled for six Months, and Stored for Foreign Service	{ Afore { Abaft	24 5 23 0
		Ft.	Ins.
9th.	What height is her lowest Gundeck-Port above the Surface of the Water {Midships . . . . { Abaft	{ Afore	4 9

10th. Trim of the Ship . . . .   *All the masts raking a little aft*

11th. How she stand under sails   *She stand very well under her Sails*

12th. The Quantities of Iron and Shingle Ballast on Board . . . .   *80 Tons of Iron Ballast stowed in the three midship rooms on each side and 211 Tons of shingle Ballast*

13th. How she stows her Provisions and water and What Quantity of the latter she carries with four and

  to six Months provisions; also the at Quantity of Shingle or Iron Ballast which may be put out when she is victualled for Six Months . . . .   *She will not stow six months provisions in the After Hold Will stow 243 Tons of Water 4 Months provisions*

  230 Tons of Water and 6 Months provisions – no occasion to put out shingle or Iron ballast

14th. The Weight of the Provisions taken on Board, in Consequence of being stored for the above time . . . .   *The gross weight of provisions for six months for 500 men is 565600 pounds and the weight for four months for the same is 3370665 pounds*

Source: TNA: PRO; Adm 95/44/19

The OBSERVATIONS of the Quality of His Majesty's Ship *Revenge*

	Ft.	Ins.	
Her best Sailing Draft of Water when Victualled and Stored for Channel Service being given this 10th Day of Septr 1804	{ Afore { Abaft	22 0 24 2	} or as much lighter (at the same Difference) as she is able to bear Sail }

Her Lowest Gundeck Port will be above the surface of the Water . . . .   5 4 or more

    In a Topgallant Gale . . . .   *Will out carry most Ships Runs 8 knots 4 fathoms*

    In a Topsail Gale . . . .   *Behaves remarkably well Runs 8 knots*

Query the 1st . . .How she Steers, and how she Wears and Stays . . . .   *Steers and Wears, and Stays remarkably well*

    Under her . . . { Reeft Topsails . . . .   *Behaves well Runs 7 knots*

Courses   *Behaves well Runs 5 knots*

And Query, Whether she will Stay under her Courses. . . . . *Never Tried*

2nd. In each Circumstance above mentioned (in Sailing with Other Ships) in what Proportion she gathers to Windward, and in what proportion she forereaches, and in general her Proportions in leeway . . . .   *Sails well with other ships. Is Weatherly, and fore reaches on most ships Makes very little Leeway when the Weather will permit of carrying Sail*

3rd. How she proves in Sailing thro' all the variations of the Wind from its being two feet abaft the Beam, to its Veering forward upon the Bowline in every Strength of Gale, especially if a stiff Gale and a Head sea, and how many Knots she runs in each Circumstance and how she carries her Helm . . . .   *Sails well in all points Best point of sailing Winds abaft the Beam with a Strong Breeze*
  Rate of Sailing {Under all sail close hauld - 8 knots 4 fathoms
      Under double reeft topsails - 8 knots
      Large under all sail - 11 knots 4 fathoms
  Carries her helm two spokes to half a turn a Weather under a pres of sail nearly Midships

4th. The most knots she runs before the Wind; and how she Rolls in a trough of Sea . . . .   *11 knots and Rolls remarkably easy*

5th. How she behaves in Lying Too, or a Try, under a Mainsail, also under a Mizon balanc'd . . . .   *Behaves remarkably well with her Main Topsail and storm Staysails never tried other Sails*

6th. What a Roader she is, and how she Careens . . . .   *Very good Roader and easy Careened to a certain bearing*

			Ft.	Ins
7th.	If upon Trial the best sailing Draft of water given as above should not prove to be so . . . . . . { Afore what is her best sailing Draft of Water . . . . { Abaft		21 24	7 0
			Ft.	Ins
8th.	What is her best Draft of water when victualled for six Months, and Stored for . . . . { Afore Foreign Service . . . . { Abaft		22 24	5 8
			Ft.	Ins
9th.	What height is her lowest Gundeck-Port above the Surface of the Water		4	9

10th. Trim of the Ship . . . .   *2 Feet 5 Inches by the Stern*

11th. How she stand under sails   *No remarkably stiff but well —— [word illegible] with most ships*

12th. The Quantities of Iron and Shingle Ballast on Board . . . .   *152 Tons of Iron, no shingle*

13th. How she stows her Provisions and water and What Quantity of the latter she carries with four to six Months provisions; also the at Quantity of Shingle or Iron Ballast which may be put out when she is victualled for Six Months . . . .   *Stows provisions and water remarkably well, Will stow 303 Tons of Water with Six Months Provisions 351 Tons with Four Months Forty Eight tons of Ballast may be taken out complete with 6 Months*

14th. The Weight of the Provisions taken on Board, in Consequence of being stored for the above time . .   *Six Months Provisions 144 Tons and Four Months 96 Tons*

Source: TNA: PRO; Adm 95/39/36

The OBSERVATIONS of the Quality of His Majesty's Ship *Bellerophon*

	Ft. Ins.
Her best Sailing Draft of Water when Victualled and Stored for Channel Service { Afore	20 9 } or as much lighter (at the same Difference) as she is able to bear Sail
being given this 25th Day of *April* 1800 { Abaft	23 3 }
Her Lowest Gundeck Port will be above the surface of the Water	5 1? or more
In a Topgallant Gale	8 knots
In a Topsail Gale	7 knots
Query the 1st ...How she Steers, and how she Wears and Stays	Very well
Under her ... { Reeft Topsails	6? knots, close reeft topsail 5 knots
Courses	3? knots
And Query, Whether she will Stay under her Courses	She will not Stay
2nd. In each Circumstance above mentioned (in Sailing with Other Ships) in what Proportion she gathers to Windward, and in what proportion she forereaches, and in general her Proportions in leeway	She gathers to windward & fore reaches equal to the generality of Line of Battle Ships and her proportion of leeway in the above circumstances from half a point to three points.
3rd. How she proves in Sailing thro' all the variations of the Wind from its being two feet abaft the Beam, to its Veering forward upon the Bowline in every Strength of Gale, especially if a stiff Gale and a Head sea, and how many Knots she runs in each Circumstance and how she carries her Helm	With the wind Two Points abaft the Beam and a stiff gale she will run 11 knots With the wind on the Beam 10 knots. One Point before the Beam 9 knots and close to the wind with a head sea 5 knots
4th. The most knots she runs before the Wind; and how she Rolls in a trough of Sea	12 knots she rolls deep but very easy
5th. How she behaves in Lying Too, or a Try, under a Mainsail, also under a Mizon balanc'd	Very well & very weatherly
6th. What a Roader she is, and how she Careens	A very good Roader and careens very well
	Ft. Ins
7th. If upon Trial the best sailing Draft of water given as above should not prove to be so { Afore	20 9
what is her best sailing Draft of Water { Abaft	22 3
	Ft. Ins
8th. What is her best Draft of water when victualled for six Months, and Stored for { Afore	21 2
Foreign Service { Abaft	23 0
	Ft. Ins
9th. What height is her lowest Gundeck-Port above the Surface of the Water { Afore	4 9
{Midships	
{ Abaft	
10th. Trim of the Ship	All the masts raking a little aft
11th. How she stand under sails	She stand very well under her Sails
12th. The Quantities of Iron and Shingle Ballast on Board	80 Tons of Iron Ballast stowed in the three midship rooms on each side and 211 Tons of shingle Ballast
13th. How she stows her Provisions and water and What Quantity of the latter she carries with four and to six Months provisions; also the at Quantity of Shingle or Iron Ballast which may be put out when she is victualled for Six Months	She will not stow six months provisions in the After Hold Will stow 243 Tons of Water 4 Months provisions 230 Tons of Water and 6 Months provisions – no occasion to put out shingle or Iron ballast
14th. The Weight of the Provisions taken on Board, in Consequence of being stored for the above time	The gross weight of provisions for six months for 500 men is 565600 pounds and the weight for four months for the same is 3370665 pounds

Source: TNA: PRO; Adm 95/39/108

The OBSERVATIONS of the Quality of His Majesty's Ship *Spartiate*

	Ft. Ins.
Her best Sailing Draft of Water when Victualled and Stored for Channel Service { Afore	20 9 } or as much lighter (at the same Difference) as she is able to bear Sail
being given this 30th Day of *August* 1799 { Abaft	23 3 } - Never tried
Her Lowest Gundeck Port will be above the surface of the Water	or more - Uncertain
In a Topgallant Gale	The ship having come
In a Topsail Gale	To England
Query the 1st ...How she Steers, and how she Wears and Stays	Under Jury
Under her ... { Reeft Topsails	Mast -
Courses	No opinion
And Query, Whether she will Stay under her Courses	can be
2nd. In each Circumstance above mentioned (in Sailing with Other Ships) in what Proportion she gathers to Windward, and in what proportion she forereaches, and in general her Proportions in leeway	Formed of
3rd. How she proves in Sailing thro' all the variations of the Wind from its being two feet abaft the Beam, to its Veering forward upon the Bowline in every Strength of Gale, especially if a stiff Gale and a Head sea, and how many Knots she runs in each Circumstance and how she carries her Helm	her quality in any of
4th. The most knots she runs before the Wind; and how she Rolls in a trough of Sea	These apsects
5th. How she behaves in Lying Too, or a Try, under a Mainsail, also under a Mizon balanc'd	
6th. What a Roader she is, and how she Careens	Never tried
	Ft. Ins
7th. If upon Trial the best sailing Draft of water given as above should not prove to be so { Afore	Uncertain
what is her best sailing Draft of Water { Abaft	
	Ft. Ins
8th. What is her best Draft of water when victualled for six Months, and Stored for { Afore	Never tried 0
Foreign Service { Abaft	
	Ft. Ins
9th. What height is her lowest Gundeck-Port above the Surface of the Water	Uncertain
10th. Trim of the Ship	Uncertain
11th. How she stand under sails	
12th. The Quantities of Iron and Shingle Ballast on Board	
13th. How she stows her Provisions and water and What Quantity of the latter she carries with four to six Months provisions; also the at Quantity of Shingle or Iron Ballast which may be put out when she is victualled for Six Months	Never tried
14th. The Weight of the Provisions taken on Board, in Consequence of being stored for the above time	Uncertain

Charles H Passent Captain ??????

Source: TNA: PRO; Adm 95/44/141

The OBSERVATIONS of the Quality of His Majesty's Ship *Euryalus* – between 12 June & 28 August 1815

			Ft.	Ins.	
Her best Sailing Draft of Water when Victualled and Stored for Channel Service being given this 28th Day of *August* 1815		{ Afore { Abaft	18 19	0 } 7? }	or as much lighter (at the same Difference) as she is able to bear Sail

Her Lowest Gundeck Port will be above the surface of the Water		7 2 or more
	In a Topgallant Gale	Over single reef Topsails wind 2 Points abaft the Beam Smooth Water – Has gone Twelve knots
	In a Topsail gallant Gale	Over double reeft topsails moderate swell - Nine knots
Query the 1st	How she Steers, and how she Wears and Stays	While in Trim quick and not doubtful without a heavy head sea
	Under her double{ Reeft Topsails	8 knots 4 fathoms
	Treble reeft Topsails & fore sail large .... Courses	9 knot and 4 fathoms. Never under them (only) during my command
	And Query, Whether she will Stay under her Courses	Never had the opportunity of ascertaining
2nd.	In each Circumstance above mentioned (in Sailing with Other Ships) in what Proportion she gathers to Windward, and in what proportion she forereaches, and in general her Proportions in leeway	From the state of the Copper &c under her Bottom & having been onshore several Times ion the American Coast could not form any opinion what she ought to do in Complete Order except her being Weatherly with most of His majestiy's Ship in Company
3rd.	How she proves in Sailing thro' all the variations of the Wind from its being two feet abaft the Beam, to its Veering forward upon the Bowline in every Strength of Gale, especially if a stiff Gale and a Head sea, and how many Knots she runs in each Circumstance and how she carries her Helm	Never had the opportunity of ascertaining
4th.	The most knots she runs before the Wind; and how she Rolls in a trough of Sea	The most ...... ling the above period 10 Knots
5th.	How she behaves in Lying Too, or a Try, under a Mainsail, also under a Mizon balanc'd	Never
6th.	What a Roader she is, and how she Careens	Never had a Gale during my Command
		Ft. Ins
7th.	If upon Trial the best sailing Draft of water given as above should not prove to be so { Afore what is her best sailing Draft of Water { Abaft	17 8 19 6
		Ft. Ins
8th.	What is her best Draft of water when victualled for six Months, and Stored for { Afore Foreign Service { Abaft	Never completed [sic] for that time
		Ft. Ins
9th.	What height is her lowest Gundeck-Port above the Surface of the Water	Never considered for the above period cannot say
10th.	Trim of the Ship	One foot 10 Inches by the Stern
11th.	How she stand under sails	Well
12th.	The Quantities of Iron and Shingle Ballast on Board	Iron 164 Tons Stone Tons
13th.	How she stows her Provisions and water and What Quantity of the latter she carries with four to six Months provisions; also the at Quantity of Shingle or Iron Ballast which may be put out when she is victualled for Six Months	Water 91 Tons never being Completed [sic] for Six Months – cannot say
14th.	The Weight of the Provisions taken on Board, in Consequence of being stored for the above time	Never completed [sic] by Three Months

Hotchkiss Captain   J Buncle Master

Source: TNA: PRO; Adm 95/39/159 & 160

The OBSERVATIONS of the Quality of His Majesty's Ship *Neptune*

			Ft.	Ins.	
Her best Sailing Draft of Water when Victualled and Stored for Channel Service being given this 29th Day of *April* 1802		{ Afore { Abaft	23 25	9 } 0 }	or as much lighter (at the same Difference) as she is able to bear Sail

Her Lowest Gundeck Port will be above the surface of the Water		4 3 or more
	In a Topgallant Gale	From 6 to 7 knots
	In a Topsail Gale	From 5 to 6 knots
Query the 1st	How she Steers, and how she Wears and Stays	Steers remarkably well, wears quick and never refuses Stays if going 3 knots
	Under her ... { Reeft Topsails	With 2 reefs in, from 4 to 5 knots
		With 3 reefs - from 3 to 4? knots
		Close reef'd about 3 to 3? knots
	Courses	From 2? to 3 knots
	And Query, Whether she will Stay under her Courses	Never have tried her
2nd.	In each Circumstance above mentioned (in Sailing with Other Ships) in what Proportion she gathers to Windward, and in what proportion she forereaches, and in general her Proportions in leeway	Has been generally considered in the Fleet as a fast sailing and weatherly Ship for her class, Leeway from ? a point to 3 or 3? points according to the degree of Wind and Head sea
3rd.	How she proves in Sailing thro' all the variations of the Wind from its being two feet abaft the Beam, to its Veering forward upon the Bowline in every Strength of Gale, especially if a stiff Gale and a Head sea, and how many Knots she runs in each Circumstance and how she carries her Helm	Has been considered as a remarkable fast sailer off the Wind, particularly with the Wind abaft the Beam, and all variations of its strength - goes 1 to 10 knots with a fair Wind and is very easy in pitching in a head sea - in general carries a weather helm
4th.	The most knots she runs before the Wind; and how she Rolls in a trough of Sea	About 10 knots - rolls moderately and very easy, never straining or carrying away her Spars or Rigging
5th.	How she behaves in Lying Too, or a Try, under a Mainsail, also under a Mizon balanc'd	never tried under any if the circumstances mentioned; under storm sails she lies to very well and easy, not coming up or falling off more than 2 to 2? points
6th.	What a Roader she is, and how she Careens	Very good Roader - having never parted a cable or started and Anchor in 6 Months at Torbay - has never been careened
		Ft. Ins
7th.	If upon Trial the best sailing Draft of water given as above should not prove to be so { Afore what is her best sailing Draft of Water { Abaft	As above afore and abaft
		Ft. Ins
8th.	What is her best Draft of water when victualled for six Months, and Stored for { Afore Foreign Service { Abaft	Never tried
9th.	What height is her lowest Gundeck-Port above the Surface of the Water	Ditto
10th.	Trim of the Ship	15 Inches by the Stern
11th.	How she stand under sails	Not particularly stiff but nearly as other Ship of her Class
12th.	The Quantities of Iron and Shingle Ballast on Board	Iron 430 Tons, Shingle 60
13th.	How she stows her Provisions and water and What Quantity of the latter she carries with four to six Months provisions; also the at Quantity of Shingle or Iron Ballast which may be put out when she is victualled for Six Months	Stows Provisions for 5 Months very wel, and 325 Tons of beer & Water cannot answr. The later part of the Query having never tried

14th.	The Weight of the Provisions taken on Board, in Consequence of being stored for the above time	Weight of provisions for { 4 } Months { 131 }
		                                                { 5 } { 164 }
		                                                { 6 } { 196 }

James McMaster Captain

Geo Paton Master

Source: TNA: PRO; Adm 95/46/159

3rd of June 1812

{ A REPORT of the Sailing and other Qualities of His Majesty's Ship
{ *Entreprenante* as found in strict Observation thereof, between the
{ *First* of *January 1812* and this Date

			Ft.	Ins.
Her light draught of Water was stated to be .... { Forward			*French Built*	
		{ Abaft		
The draught of Water which was estimated by the Builder to be her best trim .... { Forward			*French Built*	
		{ Abaft		
The draught of Water found on trial to be her best sailing trim .... { Forward			8	0
		{ Abaft	12	0

What should be the difference between her draught of Water forward and abaft, to give her the best possible trim, when from circumstances she happens to be { Considerably deeper than her best sailing draught as above stated .... *Aft 4 feet*

Considerably lighter than ditto ....

		Tons.
Quantity of Ballast necessary to bring her to her best trim .... { Iron		20
Shingle {		20
Quantity of Water she stows		*7 Tons*
Quantity of Water whereof is contained in Iron Tanks		*None*

			Ft.	Ins.
When Stored for { Channel Service	{ Draught of Water .... { Forward		7	11
		Abaft	11	11
		Forward	3	10
		Midships	3	2
	{ Height of Ports .... Abaft		3	4
		Forward	8	0
	Draught of Water .... Abaft		12	0
Foreign Service		Forward	3	9?
		Midship	3	1?
	Height of Ports .... Abaft		3	3?

How does she stow her provisions	*Ten weeks complete very well*
Does she ride easy at her anchors	*Very easy*
How does she stand under her sails	*Middling stiff*
How does she carry her lee ports	*Fair for a small ship*
Does she roll easy or uneasy in a trough of sea	-
Does she pitch easy	*Easy*
Is she, generally speaking, an easy or uneasy ship	*Pretty easy*
How does she in general carry her helm	*Easy*
How does she steer	*Weatherly*
How does she Wear & Stay	*Stays very well in Smooth water, Wears but Middling*
Is she weatherly or leewardly compared with other ships	*Weatherly*
How does she behave laying too	*Very well*

		Knots.	Fathoms.
Close hauled - {	Under whole or single topsails or topgallant sails	8	4
She has run per hour by the log with as much win {	Under double reefed topsails	6	4s
as she safely can bear	Under courses	4	4
	Large under all sail that could with priority be set ..... {	9	4
	Before the wind under similar circumstances	10	

What is her best point of sailing	*Before the Wind*
Comparative rate of sailing with other Ships	*When turning to Windward & Weatherly*
Is she generally speaking a well built and strong ship or does she shew {sic} any unusual symptoms of weakness	*Upper works weak*

Remarks; stating the grounds of such of the present avowes to differ from those in last report, and any other observations tending to form accurate judgement on the qualities of the ship.

Appendix 7: ROPE SIZES FOR GUNS, CARRONADES AND PORT ROPES, ETC.

Sizes for Carriage Gun Breeching, Side & Train Tackle Ropes

Gun		Breeching Rope (Left Hand laid)		Side & Train Tackle Ropes (Right Hand laid)	
Pounder	Length of Piece	Size in Inches Circumference	Length in Feet	Size in Inches Circumference	Length in Feet
32 Pdr	10 ft - 9 ft 6 ins	8	34	3	54
24 Pdr	9 ft 6 ins - 9 ft	7	32	3	54
24 Pdr	8 ft - 6 ft	7	22	2?	42
18 Pdr	9 ft - 8 ft	6?	28	2?	48
12 Pdr	9 ft 6 ins - 8 ft 6 ins	6	27	2?	42
12 Pdr	8 ft - 7 ft 6 ins	6	25	2?	40
9 Pdr	8 ft 6 ins - 7 ft	5	24	2	30
6 Pdr	7 ft - 6 ft	4	23	2	30

Source: TNA. WO 44/649. Ordnance Board Letters dated 11th April 1811 and 29th May 1811

Sizes for Carronade Breeching, Side & Train Tackle Ropes

Pounder	Breeching Rope (Left Hand laid)		Side & Train Tackle Ropes (Right Hand laid)	
	Size in Inches Circumference	Length in Feet	Size in Inches Circumference	Length in Feet
32	7	20	2	30
32	7	20	2	24
24	7	20	2	24
18	6	16	1?	20
12	5	15	1?	20

Sizes for Gun Port Ropes and Gun Lashing Ropes

Item	Deck Location	Size in Inches Circumference	Length in Feet
Port Rope Lanyards	Lower or Middle Decks	3	21
Port Tackle Falls	Lower Decks	2	28
Port Tackle Falls	Middle Decks	2	25
Port Runner Falls	Lower or Middle Decks	2?	10
Muzzle Lashings	Lower Decks	2?	30
Muzzle Lashings	Middle Decks	2	25
Lashing for Securing Guns	Lower Decks	3	42
Lashing for Securing Guns	Middle Decks	2?	42

Appendix 8: COMPARISON TABLE OF ENGLISH & FRENCH ROUND SHOT DIAMETERS

Weight of Shot (lbs)	*English Dia. (ins)*	*Notes*	*French Dia. (ins)*	*Notes*
1	1.92	Grape Shot for 6, 9 & 12 pdrs	2.01	Used as Grape Shot
2	2.42	Grape Shot for 18 & 24 pdrs	2.53	Used as Grape Shot
3	2.77	Grape Shot for 32 pdrs	2.90	Used as Grape Shot
4	3.05		3.19	
6	3.49		3.66	
8	3.84	Used as Case Shot only for all 24 & 32 pdr guns and all carronades	4.02	Standard French gun size
9	4.00		4.18	
12	4.40		4.60	
18	5.04		5.27	
24	5.54		5.80	
32	6.10		6.39	
36	6.35	Not a standard English gun size	6.64	
42	6.68		6.99	
68	6.85		NOT USED	

Source: Robert Wilkinson-Latham, *British Artillery on Land and Sea 1790–1820* (Newton Abbot, 1973), p. 26 and p. 29.

Appendix 9: GENERAL PROPORTION OF ROUND SHOT FOR ALL RATES OF SHIP

Number of Solid Shot carried for Channel Service

Type	*32 lb*		*24 lb*		*18 lb*		*12 lb*		*9 lb*		*6 lb*	
	No.	*Imp. Tons*	*No.*	*Imp. Tons*	*No.*	*Imp. Tons*	*No.*	*Imp. Tons*	*No.*	*Imp. Tons*	*No.*	*Imp. Tons*
1st Rate	2760	39.40	2380	25.50	2450	19.68	560	3.00	–	–	–	–
2nd Rate	2800	40.00	2170	23.25	2170	17.44	2240	12.00	–		–	
3rd Rate	2760	39.40	2380	25.50	2450	19,68	560	3.00	560	2.25		
4th Rate	–	0	420	4.50	1510	12.13	1680	9.00	140	0.56	140	0.11
5th Rate	840	0.45	2170	23.25	2170	17.44	560	3.00	560	2.25	140	0.11
6th Rate	960	13.71	960	10.28	480	3.86	60	0.32	60	0.24	120	0.05

Number of Solid Shot carried for Foreign Service

Type	*32 lb*		*24 lb*		*18 lb*		*12 lb*		*9 lb*		*6 lb*	
	No.	*Imp. Tons*	*No.*	*Imp. Tons*	*No.*	*Imp. Tons*	*No.*	*Imp. Tons*	*No.*	*Imp. Tons*	*No.*	*Imp. Tons*
1st Rate	4080	58.28	3400	36.43	3500	28.13	800	4.29	–		–	
2nd Rate	4120	58.85	3100	33.21	3100	24.91	3200	17.14	–		–	
3rd Rate	4080	58.20	3400	36.43	3500	28.13	800	4.29	800	3.21	–	
4th Rate	600	8.57	2260	24.21	2400	19.29	230	1.23	230	0.92	–	
5th Rate	1200	17.14	3100	33.21	3100	24.91	800	4.29	800	3.21	180	0.48
6th Rate	1440	20.57	1440	15.43	720	5.79	90	0.48	90	0.36	180	0.48

Source: Lieut. T S Beauchant, RMA, *The Naval Gunner* (London, 1828), pp 106-121.

Appendix 10: MAST AND YARD SPECIFICATIONS FOR 40 GUN FRIGATE *RHIN*

Item	*Mast Length yards*	*Yard Diameter inches*	*Length inches*	*yards*	*Diameter inches*	*inches*
Main Mast	30	24	26 ¾	27	26	19 ⅞
Main Topmast	18	14	16 ⅞	20	9	12. ⅝
Main Topgallant Mast	9	7	9 ⅜	12	13	7 ⅜
Fore Mast	28	3	8	24	7	16 ¾
Fore Topmast	16	7	16 ½	18	2	11 ¼
Main Topgallant Mast	8	3	8	11	0	6 ½

Item	*Mast Length yards*	*Yard Diameter inches*	*Length inches*	*yards*	*Diameter inches*	*inches*	
Mizzen Mast	21	18	19	14	16	18. ½	*Gaff*
Mizzen Topmast	13	28	11. ½	13	26	8. ¼	
Mizzen Topgallant Mast	6	32	6. ⅞	9	24	5. ½	
Bowsprit	19	0	28. ½	18	2	11. ¼	
Jib Boom	13	12	12	11	0	6. ½	
Crossjack Yard	-	-	-	20	9	12. ⅝	

Source: Ship's Draught NMM.

BIBLIOGRAPHY

Primary Sources

HMS *Victory* Archive

VLDA 2000, Letter & Document Archive

VPA 2000, Photographic Archive

The National Archives: Public Record Office, Kew

ADM 51 Series: Captains' Log Books

ADM 52 Series: Masters' Log Books

ADM 95 Series: Observations on the Quality of Sailing of His Majesty's Ships

ADM 180 Series: Progress Books

WO 44/649 Breeching rope sizes for guns and carronades, Ordnance Board 11 April 1811

WO 44/649 Dimensions and length of rope for gun tackle falls and port rope gear in HM Ships of War, Office of Ordnance, 29 May 1811

ADM 160/154, Inventory of HMS *Agamemnon*'s Ordnance

National Maritime Museum, Greenwich

MSS POR/F/2, Portsmouth Dockyard Papers

Navy Board to Admiralty vol. 24

Admiralty Sailing Navy Collection (Ship Draughts)

Admiralty Library, Portsmouth

Le Calve Franck, Roche Jean-Michel, *Liste des Batiments de la Flotte de Guerre Française de 1700 à Nos Jours* Société Française d'Histoire Maritime, October 2001).

Royal Naval Museum Admiralty Library Manuscript Collection, Portsmouth

MSS 248, Volume 4, Ships and Captains

MSS 248, Volume 5, Ships and Captains

MSS 248, Volume 6, Ships and Captains

MSS 259, Portfolio I (3), Account of Work by Shipwrights on the Hulls of Ships – Plymouth 1803 (Joseph Tucker, Master Shipwright)

MSS 1064/83 2376, Record of the Carpenter's and Boatswain's Stores and Expenses for *Africa*, *Britannia*, and *Victory* (July-December 1805)

MSS 1986/573 (11), Rivers' Papers, Journal of Midshipman William Rivers in *Victory*

MSS 1998/41, Rivers' Papers, Journals of Master Gunner William Rivers in *Victory* 1793-1811

Primary Published

Barnes G, and Owen J (eds), *The Sandwich Papers 1771-1782*, vol 3 (Navy Records Society, no 75, 1936).

Beatty W, *The Death of Lord Nelson: The Authentic Narrative* (2nd Edn, London, 1985).

Freemantle A (ed.), *The Wynne Diaries*, vol 3, 1798-1820 (Oxford, 1940).

Graham G S & Humphreys R A (eds), *The Navy and South America 1807-1823* (NRS no 104, 1962).

Jackson T S (ed.), *Logs of the Great Sea Fights: 1794-1805*, vol 1 (NRS, no 16, 1899)

——*Logs of the Great Sea Fights: 1794-1805*, vol 2 (NRS, no 18, 1900)

Lavery B (ed.), *Shipboard Life and Organisation 1731-1815* (NRS no 138, 1998).

Patents for Inventions. Abridgements of the Specifications Relating to ShipBuilding Repairing, Sheathing and Launching Etc (London, 1862).

Thursfield H G (ed.), *Five Naval Journals 1798 –1817* (NRS no 91, 1951).

Tracy N (ed.), *The Naval Chronicle, The Contemporary Record of the Royal Navy at War 1793-1815*, 5 vols (London, 1998 to 1999).

Personal Narrative of Events 1799-1815 (2nd Edn, 1879)

Des Touches (1905)

Secondary Sources: Books

Addis C P, *The men who fought with Nelson in HMS* Victory *at Trafalgar* (Nelson Society, 1988).

Adkins R, *Trafalgar: A Biography of a Battle* (London, 2004).

Albion R G, *Forests and Seapower: The Timber Problem of the Royal Navy 1652-1862* (Cambridge, 1926).

Banbury P, *Shipbuilders of the Thames and Medway* (Newton Abbot, 1971).

Barnard J E, *Building Britain's Wooden Walls* (London, 1997).

Beauchant T S, *The Naval Gunner* (Devonport, 1828).

Branch-Johnston, W, *The English Prison Hulks* (London, 1957).

Brenton E P, *The Naval History of Great Britain: 1783-1836*, vols 1 & 2 (London, 1837).

Bryant A, *The Years of Endurance 1793-1802* (London, 1942).

——*The Years of Victory 1802-1812* (London, 1944).

Boudriot J, *The Seventy Four Gun Ship*, vol. 1 (Rotherfield, 1986).

Buglar A R, *HMS Victory: Building Restoration & Repair* (HMSO, 1966).

Callender G, *The Story of HMS* Victory (London, 1914).

——*The Naval Side of British History* (London, 1924).

——*The Campaigns of Napoleon* (London, 1993).

Chandler D, *Dictionary of the Napoleonic Wars* (Ware, 1999).

BIBLIOGRAPHY

Chapman C, *How Heavy, How Much and How Long: Weights and other Measures used by our Ancestors* (Dursley, 1995).
Charnock J, *History of Naval Architecture*, 3 vols (London, 1800-1802).
Clayton T & Craig P, *Trafalgar: The Men, The Battle, The Storm* (London, 2004).
Clowes, W Laird, *The Royal Navy: A History from the Earliest Times to 1900*, vols 1-7 (London, 1996/1997).
Clarke J, *The Men of HMS* Victory *at Trafalgar* (Dallington, 1999).
Coad J, 'The Introduction of Steam Power into the Royal Dockyards; the genesis of the Block Mills', in Coad, J, *The Portsmouth Block Mills* (English Heritage, Swindon, 2005).
Coats C, Riley R, (eds), *Transactions of Portsmouth Dockyard in the Age of Nelson Conference* (Naval Dockyards Society, Portsmouth, 2005)
Colledge J J, *Ships of the Royal Navy*, vol 1 (Newton Abbot, 1969).
Cordingly D, *Billy Ruffian: The Bellerophon and the Downfall of Napoleon (the biography of a ship of the line 1782-1836)* (London, 2003).
Deane A, *Nelson's Favourite: HMS* Agamemnon *at War 1781-1809* (London, 1996).
Egerton J *Turner; The Fighting Temeraire* (London, 1995)
Fincham J, *An Introductory Outline of the Practice of Shipbuilding* (London, 1821).
——*A History of Naval Architecture* (London, 1851).
Fraser E, *The Enemy at Trafalgar* (London, 1906).
Gardiner R, *The First Frigates* (London, 1992).
——*The Line of Battle: The Sailing Warship 1650-1840* (London, 1992).
——*The Navies of the American Revolution 1775-1783* (London, 1992).
——*The Heavy Frigates* (London, 1994).
——*The Heavy Frigate, Eighteen-pounder Frigates: Volume 1, 1778-1800* (London, 1995)
——*Fleet, Battle and Blockade: The French Revolutionary War 1793-1797* (London, 1996).
——*Nelson Against Napoleon: From the Nile to Copenhagen 1798-1801* (London, 1996).
——*The Campaign of Trafalgar 1803-1805* (London, 1997).
——*Victory and Seapower* (London, 1998).
——*Frigates of the Napoleonic Wars* (London, 2000).
Garneray L, *The Floating Prison* (Translated from Garneray's *Mes Pontons*, 1851, by Rose R, London, 2003).
Gilbert K R, *The Portsmouth Blockmaking Machinery* (HMSO/Science Museum, 1965).
Glover R, *Britain at Bay: Defence against Bonaparte 1803-1814* (London, 1973).
González-Aller H, José I, *España En La Mar. Una Historia Milenia* (Lisbon, 1998).
González-Aller H, José I, *La Campaña de Trafalgar* (Madrid, 2004).
Goodwin P, *The Construction and Fitting of the Sailing Man of War: 1650-1850* (London, 1987).
——*The Naval Cutter* Alert *1777* (London, 1991).
——*Nelson's Victory: 101 Questions and Answers on HMS Victory* (London, 2004). Previously published as *Countdown to Victory: 101 Questions and Answers on HMS Victory* (Portsmouth, 2000).
——*Nelson's Ships: A History of the Vessels In Which He Served 1771-1805* (London, 2002).
——*Man o' War: The Illustrated Story of Life in Nelson's Navy* (Carlton/National Maritime Museum, London, 2003).
Goss J, *Portsmouth-built Warships 1497-1967* (Fareham, 1984).
Granier H, *Histoire de Marines Français* (Nantes, 1998).
Grocott T, *Shipwrecks of the Revolutionary and Napoleonic Eras* (London, 1997).
Harbron J D, *Trafalgar and the Spanish Navy* (London, 1988, Revised 2004)
Harding R, *The Evolution of the Sailing Navy: 1509-1815* (Basingstoke, 1995).
Harland J, *Seamanship in the Age of the Fighting Sail* (London, 1984).
Harris J R, *The Copper King* (Liverpool, 1964).
——*Industrial Espionage and Technology Transfer: Britain and France in the Eighteenth Century* (Aldershot, 1998).
Haythornthwaite P, *Who was Who in the Napoleonic Wars* (London, 1998)
Hepper D J, *British Warship Losses in the Age of Sail 1650-1859* (Rotherfield, 1994).
Hierro et al, *Modelos de Arsenal del Museo Naval: Evolución de la construcción naval española, siglos XVII-XVIII* (Lunwerg, 2004).
Hill J R, *The Oxford Illustrated History of the Royal Navy* (Oxford, 1995).
——*The Prizes of War: The Naval Prize System in the Napoleonic Wars 1793-1815* (Stroud, 1998).
Holland A J, *Ships of British Oak* (Newton Abbot, 1971).
—— *Buckler's Hard* (Emsworth, 1993).
Howarth D, *Trafalgar: The Nelson Touch* (London, 1969).
——*Sovereign of the Seas: The Story of British Sea Power* (London, 1974).
Howarth S (ed), *Battle of Cape St. Vincent: The Bicentennial Naval Conference Portsmouth 15 February 1997* (1805 Club/Shelton, 1998)
Humbart J-M & Ponsonnet B, *Napoleon et la Mer: Un Rêve d'Empire* (Musée National de la Marine, n.d.)
Hume D, Smollett T, *The History of England*, vol 3 (London, 1857).
King D, *Every Man Will Do His Duty* (London, 1997).
James W M, *The Naval History of Great Britain* vols 1-6 (London, 2002).
——*The British Navy in Adversity* (London, 1926).
Laird Clowes W, *The Royal Navy* vols 4, 5, 6 (London, 1997)
Lambert A, *Battleships in Transition: The Creation of the Steam Battlefleet 1815- 1862* (London, 1984).
——*The Last Sailing Battlefleet* (London, 1991).
Laughton L G Carr, *Old Ship Figureheads and Sterns* (2nd Edn, London, 1991).
Lavery B, *The Arming and Fitting of English Ships of War: 1600-1815* (London, 1987).
——*Nelson's Navy: The Ships, Men and Organisation 1793-1815* (London, 1989).
——*Building the Wooden Walls* (London, 1991).
——*Nelson and the Nile: The Naval War against Bonaparte 1798* (London, 1998).
——*Nelson's Fleet at Trafalgar* (National Maritime Museum, 2004).
Legg S, Hart-Davis R, *Trafalgar: An Eyewitness Account of a Great Battle* (London, 1966).
Lewis M, *The Navy of Britain* (London, 1948).
Lyon D, *The Sailing Navy List* (London, 1993).
MacDougall P, *The Chatham Dockyard Story* (Whitstable, 1987).
McGrigor M, *Defiant, and Dismasted at Trafalgar* (Barnsley, 2004).
Maine R, *Trafalgar: Napoleon's Naval Waterloo* (London, 1957).
Mahan A T, *The Influence of Seapower upon History: 1660-1783* (Cambridge, 1890).
Maxwell J, *The Spirit of Marine Law* (London, 1800).
McGowan A P, *HMS* Victory: *Her Construction, Career and Restoration* (London, 1999).
Morriss R, *The Royal Dockyards during the Revolutionary and Napoleonic Wars* (Leicester, 1983).
Müller J, *A Treatise on Artillery* (London, 1780).
Oman C, *Nelson* (London, 1947).
Padfield P, *Nelson's War* (London, 1976).
Pardies I G, *Statique, ou la Sciences des Forces Mouvantes* (Paris, 1673).
Peake J, *The Rudiments of Naval Architecture* (London, 1884).
Pope D, *England Expects* (London, 1959).
——*The Great Gamble* (London, rp. 2001).
Raistrick A, *Dynasty of Iron Founders* (Ironbridge Gorge Museum Trust, 1989).
Rees A, *Naval Architecture* (1st Edn 1819-1920, rp. Newton Abbot, 1970)
Robinson William, Warner O introduction, *Jack Nastyface, Nautical Economy or Forecastle Recollections of Events during the Last War* (1836, rp Annapolis, 2002) (deserter from HMS Revenge)
Rodger N A M, *The Wooden World: An Anatomy of the Georgian Navy* (London, 1986).
Rodger N A M, *The Command of the Ocean; A Naval History of Britain 1649-1815* (London, 2004).
De la Ronciere Charles, *Historie de la Marine Française*, vol 5 (Paris, 1899-1932).
Rowlands J, *Copper Mountain* (Anglesey, 1981).
Schom A, *Trafalgar: Countdown to Battle, 1803-1805* (London, 1990).
Southey R, *The Life of Horatio Lord Nelson* (London, 1906).
Steel D, *The Elements of Mastmaking, Sailmaking and Rigging* (London, 1794).
——*The Elements and Practice of Naval Architecture* (London, 1932).
Vattel M, *The Law of Nations* (London, 1793).
Watson J S, *The Reign of George III* (Oxford, 1960).
White C, *The Nelson Companion* (Sutton, 1995).
——*1797 Nelson's Year of Destiny* (Sutton, 1998).
Wilkinson-Latham R, *British Artillery on Land and Sea: 1790-1820* (Newton Abbot, 1973).
Woodman R, *The Victory of Seapower: Winning the War against Napoleon 1806-1 1814* (London, 1997).

Secondary Sources: Articles
Cross A, 'Unpickling the Pickle' *The Trafalgar Chronicle* (Yearbook of the 1805 Club), p. 204.
Goodwin P, 'The development of the orlop deck in HMS *Victory*' *The Mariner's Mirror*, vol. 83, 4 (1997).
——'*Victory*'s foretopsail', *The Mariners Mirror*, vol. 83, 1 (1997).
——'The influence of iron in ship construction 1660-1830', *Proceedings of the 3rd international conference in the technical aspects of the preservation of historic vessels* (San Francisco, 1997); reprinted *The Mariner's Mirror*, vol. 84, 1 (1998).
—— 'Where Nelson Died: An Historical Riddle resolved by Archaeology', *The Mariner's Mirror*, (1998).
Jones A, 'Sir Thomas Slade', *The Mariner's Mirror*, 63 (1977).
Nicholson, D, et al, 'Nelson's Dockyard Antigua', *Dockyards*, vol. 8, issue 1(Naval Dockyards Society, Aug 2003), pp. 10-12.
Paul L, 'British Ships Painting at Aboukir', *The Mariner's Mirror*, 4 (1914), pp. 266-274.
'The Trafalgar General Order Book of HMS *Mars*', *The Mariner's Mirror*, 22 (1936), p. 99.
Wilkin F S, 'Portsmouth - The Royal Dockyard - Contribution to the Success of the Royal Navy in the Napoleonic War 1793-1815', in Coats C, Riley R, eds, *Transactions of Portsmouth Dockyard in the Age of Nelson Conference* (Naval Dockyards Society, Portsmouth, 2005).

Catalogue
Rafael de la Sierra D, *El Navio 'San Juan Nepomuceno' Y La Ciudad De Santander a Finales Del Siglio XVIII* (Catalogo de la Exposicion, Concejal de Cultura del Excmo Ayuntamiento de Santander).

Unpublished Sources
Harris J R, 'The Copper Industry of North Wales and Lancashire 1760-1815' (PhD thesis, Manchester University, 1952).
Goodwin P, 'The Influence of Industrial Technology and Material Procurement on the Design, Construction and Development of HMS *Victory*' (MPhil Thesis, University of St Andrews, 1998).
Goodwin P, 'The Influence of the Carronade on Ship Design' (2000)
Goodwin P, 'The Battle of Trafalgar: A short account in two parts: The Prelude and The Battle' (1995).
Hocking Canon M, Vicar of Madron Parish Church, Madron Parish Records Research Papers

INDEX

Entries in **bold** denote ship chapters; those in *italic* denote illustrations

Abeille (Fr) 152
Aboukir, HMS 86, 94
Abu-Kir Bay 59, 96, 100, 160, 198-9
Acasta, HMS 41, 65
Acheron, HMS 202
Achille, HMS 35, **55-8**, 59, 63, 93, 166, 181, 10; at Trafalgar 57-8, 68, 73, 152, 221
Achille (Fr) 9, 81, 114, 163, 166, **172-3**, 175, 182, 164, 166, 173; at Trafalgar 15, 48, 57, 63-4, 82, 104, 107, 110-11, 132, 156, 160, 173, 175, 180-1, 200, 214, 229, 242
Actaeon, HMS 148
Active, HMS 18, 61-3, 110, 114-15, 146, 165
Adrienne (Fr) 78
Aeolus, HMS 65, 121, 169, 181; at Trafalgar 182
Ætna, HMS 65, 105, 144; at Trafalgar 20, 35
Affronteur (Fr) 192
Africa, HMS 14, 19, 87, 93, **118-22**, 183, 197; at Trafalgar 29, 40, 44, 52, 89, 93, 101, 107, 120-1, 128, 190, 212, 222, 11
Africaine, *Fr*/HMS 121, 146, 148
Agamemnon, HMS 6-7, 9, 14, 19, 25, 73, 82, 84, 93, 97, 114, **122-31**, 132, 166; at Trafalgar 14, 20, 60, 68-9, 73, 101, 128, 151,
Agincourt, HMS 39, 59
Aigle, HMS 105
Aigle (Fr) 114, 172, *174*, **174-5**, *175*, 182, 192, 207, 221, 164, 166; at Trafalgar 15, 63-4, 69, 73, 84-5, 104, 173, 224-5
Aimable, HMS
at Trafalgar 68
Ajax, HMS 7, 58-62, 78, 91, 96, 108, 114-15, 140, 142-3, 199; at Trafalgar 53, 60-1, 101, 111, 128, 147, 190, 212, 218
Ajax (Fr) 118
Akbar, HMS 196
Alava, Admiral Ignacio de 19, 142, 216-17, 228, 208
Alceste, HMS 108
Alceste (Fr) 179
Alcide, HMS 24
Alcmène (Fr/HMS) 127, 198
Alcudia (Sp) 136
Alecto, HMS 132
Alert, HMS 23
Alexander, HMS 12, 100, 198
Alexandre (Fr) 100, 193
Alexandria 95-6, 100, 106, 170, 198-9
Algeciras, battle of 168, 170, 226
Algésiras (Fr) 114, 163, 166, 172-3, **175-6**, 182, 189, 207, 221, 164, 166, 175; at Trafalgar 52, 108, 225, 233, 242
Algiers 138-9, 139, 202, 228, 230
Allemand, Admiral 74, 128, 166, 168, 182
Amaranthe, HMS 65
Amazon, HMS 63, 85, 127, 145-6
Amelia, HMS 85, 105, 137, 201, 219
Amélie (Fr) 78
America, HMS 87, 89-90
America (Fr) 114
América (Sp) 174, 192, 207
Amethyst, HMS 137, 219
Amiable, HMS 19, 48
Amiens, Peace of 7, 18, 42, 150, 173, 229
Amphion, HMS 19, 27, 62-3, 108
Amphitrite, HMS 19
Andromeda, HMS 23, 88
Annibal (Fr) 118, 180, 192, 165
Anson, Admiral Lord 11
Antigua 123, 129, 166, 176
Apollo, HMS 20
Apollon (Fr) 118
Aquilon, HMS 99
Aquilon (Fr) 95, 105
Aradne, HMS 126
Ardent, HMS 18, 126-7
Arethusa, HMS 12
Argo, HMS 30, 87
Argonauta (Sp) 114, 166, 168, 174, 176, 180, 192, 208, **219-20**, 220; at Trafalgar 57, 61, 64, 175, 180, 199, 227, 229
Argonaute (Fr) 73, 118, 172, 176, **176**, 182, 189; at Trafalgar 74, 175, 199
Argus, HMS 99
Argus (Fr) 171, 174, 180, 192, **207**, 164; at Trafalgar 193
Ariel, HMS 196
Armada, HMS 196
Armide (Fr) 93
Arrogant, HMS 24
Arrogante (Fr) 135
Arrow, HMS 74, 127, 202
Artésian (Fr) 118
Assistance, HMS 155
Astraea, HMS 18, 99, 148
Atalante, HMS 58, 93
Atalante (Fr) 145, 192
Atlante (Sp) 229
Atlas, HMS 48, 59, 83
Atlas (Fr) 114, 179-80, 189, 165
Audacious, HMS 44, 58, 64, 79-80, 87, 95-6, 100, 132, 168, 170
Aurora, HMS 87, 96, 132-3, 196
Austria 8-9, 96, 126, 166

Babet, HMS 99
Bahama (Sp) 101, 200, 211, 213, **223-5**, 229, 237; at Trafalgar 69, 73, 82, 101, 175, 192, 224, 230, 242
Baleine (Fr) 143
Balladière (Fr) 70
Baracouta, HMS 196
Barbados 8, 27, 40, 64-5, 65, 68, 88, 107, 110, 128, 180
Barfleur, HMS 16, 24-5, 99, 114, 123, 127, 170, 166
Barham, Lord 8, 159
Barö Sound 184
Barras (Fr) 179
Barrington, Admiral 24
Baudin, R/A 89
Bayntun, Captain Henry William 10, 76, 86, 88
Beagle, HMS 105
Beaulieu, HMS 18
Bedford, HMS 18, 78, 129-30
Bellegarde (Fr) 145
Belleisle, HMS (ex-*Formidable*) 14, 18, **62-5**, *63-4*, 88, 96, 110, 160, 193; at Trafalgar 19, 35, 52, 57, 63-4, 68-9, 74, 92, 110-11, 132, 137, 171-3, 188, 225, 233
Bellerophon, HMS 6-7, 17-18, 20, 30, **66-72**, 79-80, 87, 91, 95-6, 99-100, 113, 181, 198, 226, 10; at Trafalgar 53, 68-9, 73, 199, 224, 231, 11
Bellona, HMS 24, 56, 64-5, 84, 86, 105, 127, 169, 182
Bellone (Fr) 153, 192
Belvidera, HMS 121-2
Bergère (Fr) 152
Berkeley, R/A the Hon George 59, 91
Bermuda 54, 70, 144
Bertie, V/A Albemarle 148, 153
Berwick (HMS/Fr) 23, 81, 114, 143, 164, 166, **177-81**, 182, 207; at Trafalgar 57, 180-1, 214, 231
Bickerton, R/A Sir Richard 18-19, 63, 96, 165, 168, 179, 191, 198-9
Bienfaisant, HMS 178
Bittern, HMS 36-7
Blackwood, Captain the Hon Henry 9, 19, 61, 78, 88, 92, 114, 150, 216-17, 10, 59; court-martial of 61
Blanche, HMS 26, 127, 147
Blenheim, HMS 25-6, 48, 100, 126, 211
Boadicea, HMS 106, 148, 152-3, 182
Bombay, HMS 86, 94
Bombay Castle, HMS 24
Bonne Citoyenne (Fr/HMS) 100, 198
Borée (Fr) 165
Boston, HMS 25
Bounty, HMS 132, 155
Bourbon Island *see* Réunion
Bourdelois, HMS 84
Bouvet, R/A 95, 170
Bowyer, R/A 47
Boyne, HMS 196
Brave (Fr) 13, 193
Bravoure (Fr) 170, 192
Brazil 100, 129
Brest, and blockade of 6-8, 12-13, 17, 23, 27, 35, 42, 47-8, 52-4, 56, 67, 70, 79-81, 84, 90, 95, 104-5, 131, 135, 137, 145, 148, 155, 166, 168-70, 187, 191, 193-4, 211, 216, 235
Bretagne (Fr) 23
Bridport, Admiral Lord 47-8, 59, 62, 91, 95, 99, 113, 91
Brilliant, HMS 130, 219
Brilliant (Fr) 118
Bristol, HMS 118, 177-8
British Army 30, 40-1, 59, 65, 87-8, 96-7, 113, 119, 121, 124, 129, 133, 142, 144, 148, 152-3, 160, 183-4, 196, 198-9, 240-1
Britannia, HMS 7, **12-16**, 19, 24-5, 36, 48, 100; at Trafalgar 11, 14-15, 61, 97, 101
Brueys, Admiral François-Paul de 50, 67, 80, 95, 100, 106, 198
Bruiser, HMS 82, 132
Bruix, Admiral Eustache 39, 48, 84, 216
Brunswick, HMS 17, 67, 91, 121
Bucentaure (Fr) 7, 76, 114, 163-7, 171, 180, 182, 164, 166, 220; at Trafalgar 14, 28, 40, 76, 93, 101, 107, 166-7, 171, 173, 189-90, 194, 203, 212, 222
Bucephalus, HMS 71, 196
Buckler's Hard 7, 11, 36
Buckner, V/A 127
Buffalo, HMS 178
Bulldog, HMS 198
Bulwark, HMS 74
Burford, HMS 118
Byam Martin, Captain Thomas 70, 183-4

Ça Ira (Fr/HMS) 13, 25, 125
Cabareta Point 170, 219
Cadiz, and blockade of 7-10, 14-15, 19, 26, 35, 39, 42, 48, 52, 57-58, 63, 67-68, 73, 76, 81-82, 84-85, 88, 95-97, 100, 103-4, 111, 114, 120, 128, 140, 142, 147, 150, 155, 160, 163-7, 171-4, 176, 179, 184, 187, 189, 191-3, 198-9, 201-3, 207, 210-11, 215-6, 219, 223, 229-30, 234, 242
Caesar, HMS 18, 56, 64, 74, 80, 85-6, 99, 105, 137, 168-70, 192
at Trafalgar 182-3
Calcutta, HMS 87
Calder, Admiral Sir Robert 8, 26, 51, 59-60, 63, 80, 84, 114, 127, 140, 150, 166, 171, 173-5, 190, 195, 199, 202, 208, 227; court martial 19, 60, 114, 127; *see also* Cape Finisterre, actions off
Caledonia, HMS 105, 196
Calypso, HMS 18
Calypso (Fr) 85-6
Cambridge, HMS 76, 150
Cameleon, HMS 138, 160
Campbell, R/A 100
Camperdown, battle of 45
Canopus, HMS 61-3, 76, 88-9, 108, 110, 114, 128
Cape Finisterre, actions off; 1795: 99-100, 113, 193; 1805: 8, 59-60, 84, 114, 127, 150, 166, 171, 173-5, 180, 190-3, 195-6, 201-2, 224, 227, 231
Cape St Vincent 140, 179; battle of 13, 26, 100, 211, 213, 223, 233-4
Captain, HMS (ex-*Royal Sovereign*) 21, 25-6, 65, 126, 132, 219
Captivity, HMS (ex-*Bellerophon*) 72
Carmen (Sp) 88, 198
Carnatic, HMS 24, 86, 94
Caroline, HMS 145, 196
Caroline (Fr) 153
Cartagena 7-8, 96, 100, 142, 165, 192, 208, 211-12, 217-18, 223, 228-9
Cassard (Fr) 192
Castilian, HMS 138
Censeur (Fr/HMS) 13, 179
Centaur, HMS 57-8, 77, 87, 93, 104, 121, 183
Ceres, HMS 87, 119
César (Fr) 77-8, 132
Ceylon, HMS 71, 148
Ceylon (Fr) 153
Channel Fleet 10, 12, 16-18, 23-4, 34-5, 42, 47-8, 52-3, 56, 59, 62, 68, 74, 77-9, 81, 83-5, 87, 90-1, 93, 95-6, 104, 127, 135-6, 138, 140, 142, 145, 147, 150, 193
Charente (Fr) 192
Charlemagne (Fr) 111-12
Charlotta (Sp) 150
Charon, HMS 99
Chasseur (Fr) 136
Chatham 7, 11-12, 16, 22-3, 26-7, 29, 54, 56, 58-9, 66, 75, 78-9, 81-3, 85, 90, 97, 101, 111, 113, 115, 119, 121, 123, 126-7, 129, 131-3, 142, 152, 200, 235, 239, 11
Chatham, HMS 29
Cherbourg 58, 105
Cherub, HMS 65, 148-9
Christian, R/A Sir Hugh Cloberry 113
Circe, HMS 65
Cisneros, Admiral 211-12, 216, 208
Cleopatra, HMS 111
Cléopâtre (Fr) 118
Cleveland, HMS 105
Clorinde (Fr) 148
Cocarde (Fr) 192-3
Cochrane, V/A the Hon Sir Alexander 40, 54, 59, 65, 96, 107, 132, 144, 155, 160, 168, 207, 230, 59
Codrington, Admiral Edward 54, 101, 10, 100
at Trafalgar 101
Colibri (Fr) 132
Collingwood, V/A Cuthbert 10, 15-16, 19, 26, 28, 35, 39-40, 42, 44-47, 52-3, 57, 68, 72, 89, 92, 96, 101, 103-4, 107, 114, 119, 128, 137, 140, 159-60, 166, 225; at Trafalgar 14, 48, 57, 60, 63, 68, 73, 81, 84-5, 92, 108, 110, 114, 120, 132, 141-2, 167, 171, 175, 187-8, 192, 206, 212, 216, 218, 224, 227, 234
Colossus, HMS 19, 24, 26, 35, 57, **72-5**, 86, 94, 99-100, 108, 128, 155, 166, 176; at Trafalgar 19, 53, 68-9, 73-4, *74*, 92, 101, 108, 199-200, 224, 11
Colpoys, V/A Sir John 95, 145
Comet, HMS 25
Commerce de Marseille (Fr) 125
Comus, HMS 82
Concepción (Sp) 96, 229
Concorde, HMS 170
Conflict, HMS 105
Confounder, HMS 129
Conquérant (Fr) 95, 106
Conqueror, HMS 18, 40, 63, **75-8**, 88, 104, 110, 142-3; at Trafalgar 14, 40, 76-7, 88, 120, 128, 167, 189-90, 212, 218, 11
Conquestador, HMS 74
Conquestador (Sp) 229
Constitution, USS 11, 121-2
Constitution (Fr) 168, 170, 192
Constitution (GB) 87
Copenhagen 121; first battle of (1801) 42, 81, 84, 95, 106, 127, 132; second battle of (1807) 70, 82, 93, 97, 101, 129
coppering 6-7, 15-16, 18-21, 23-4, 27, 29-30, 32, 34, 37-9, 42, 44-5, 47-8, 53-4, 58-9, 69-70, 81-2, 84, 89-91, 93-4, 96, 100, 112, 114, 119-23, 126-7, 136, 142, 144-50, 160, 178, 185, 197, 204, 210, 228, 235, 238-9
Córdoba, Admiral Don José 13, 26, 100, 210-11, 222-3, 229-30
Cormorant, HMS 87, 119
Cornelia, HMS 148, 196
Cornélie (Fr) 114, 163, 171-2, 176, 180, 189, **201**; at Trafalgar 182, 191, 193, 201, 223
Cornwallis, Admiral Sir William 8, 17-18, 27, 35, 67, 90-1, 96, 127, 137, 155, 242; court-martial of 18
Cornwallis, HMS 148
Coromandel, HMS 87-8
Corsica 24-5, 50, 62-3, 76, 80, 88, 95, 110-11, 124-5, 143, 178, 180, 206
Corunna 30, 51, 85, 107, 136-7, 183-4
Cotton, R/A Sir Charles 17, 39, 48, 78, 90-1, 91
Courageous, HMS 169
Courageux (Fr/HMS) 196, 219; at Trafalgar 182
Coventry (Fr) 118
Cracker, HMS 132
Créole (Fr) 168, 170
Cressy, HMS 82
Cruelle, HMS 160
Cruiser, HMS 127, 142
Cuba 7, 184, 217, 228-9, 235, 237
Cuddalore, battle of 79, 118-19
Culloden, HMS 24-6, 51, 67, 100, 182, 198
Cumberland, HMS 23-5, 74, 83, 118
Curaçao, HMS 90
Curieux, HMS 8
Cybèle (Fr) 85-6
Cynthia, HMS 219
Cyrus, HMS 71

Dacres, Admiral 155
Dame Ernouf (Fr) 129
Dangereuse, HMS 160
Danzig 7, 142
Daphne, HMS 71
Dart, HMS 127
Dasher, HMS 196
De Courcey, R/A Michael 30, 129-30
Décade, HMS 63-4
Décade (Fr) 135
Decrès, V/A Denis 8, 50, 179
Dedaigneuse (Fr) 150
Defence, HMS 10, 25, 67, 73, **78-83**, 95, 100, 113, 118, 126-7, 10
captains' list 79
casualties 79, 82
construction and design 78-9, *79*, 79
damage, refits and repairs 79-82, 80-1
discipline 80-1
guns 10, 78
loss of 82
mutiny 80
at Trafalgar 11, 19, 81-3, 92, 151, 230, 11
Defiance, HMS 7, 23, 36, 60, **83-6**, 93, 110, 114, 137, 150; at Trafalgar 44, 64, 84-5, 88, 180, 229, 231-2
Denmark 65, 80-1, 84, 93, 97, 101, 121, 127, 131-2
Deptford 7, 11, 38, 135, 11
Desaix (Fr) 168, 170, 219
Désirée, HMS 68, 127
Devastation, HMS 144
D'Hautpoult (Fr) 41, 132
Diamond, HMS 126
Diamond Rock, HMS 180, 192, 207
Diana, HMS 74, 129
Diana (Sp) 211
Dickson, Admiral 131-2
Dictator, HMS 82, 121
Didon (Fr) 114, 166
Diomède (Fr) 128-9
Director, HMS 24, 126
Discovery, HMS 127
Dispatch, HMS 137
Dix Août (ex-*Tyrannicide*) (Fr) 168, 170
Dixon, V/A 58
dockyards 6-7, 11, 208, 235-6, 242; *see also individual dockyards*
Dogger Bank, battle of 178
Dolly, HMS 99
Dolphin, HMS 25, 87, 178
Dolphin (USA) 75
Donegal, HMS 10, 37, 62-3, 85-6, 88, 105, 110, 137, 147, 172, 218; at Trafalgar 44
Doris, HMS 52, 136, 145, 155, 148, 196
discipline 155
d'Orvilliers, Admiral Comte 23, 177, 210
Dos Amigos (Sp) 140
Dotterel, HMS 105, 137
Dragon, HMS 114, 166
Drake, HMS 88
Drake, R/A Sir Francis 24, 31
Dreadnought, HMS 7, 19, **34-8**, 49, 57, 82, 85, 96, 166, 236; at Trafalgar 97, 101, 231
Droits de l'Homme (Fr) 100, 192-3
Dromedary, HMS 88
Dryad, HMS 145
Dryade (Fr) 193
Duckworth, V/A Sir John 61, 68, 84, 87-8, 99-100, 114-15, 128, 198, 86, 100
Duguay Trouin (Fr) 7, 51, 68, 169, 172, **181-7**, *184*, 189, 192, 196, 164;at Trafalgar 96, 168, 175, 182-3, 189, 191, 195, 218, 222; *see also Implacable*, HMS
Duke, HMS 12
Duke of Wellington, HMS 32
Dumanoir le Pelley, V/A Pierre 15, 53, 62, 96, 128, 168-70, 182, 189-91, 195-6, 218, 222, 226-7
Duncan, Admiral Lord 45, 126, 150
Duncan, HMS 20
Duquesne, HMS 68
Duquesne (Fr) 50, 179, 181-2

Eagle, HMS 118
East Indies 7, 79, 148, 152, 196
Echo, HMS 68
Eclair, HMS 65, 88-90
Edgar, HMS 12, 24, 56, 121, 127
Edinburgh, HMS 143
Edward (Fr) 153
Egypt 59, 106, 147, 168, 170, 198-9; *see also* Abu-Kir, Alexandria, Nile
Egyptienne, HMS 114, 150, 166
Ejlau (Fr) 74
Elba 144, 168
Elbe (Fr) 105
Elephant, HMS 68, 80, 127, 181-2
Eliza (GB) 140
Elizabeth, HMS 78, 83, 129-30
Embuscade (Fr) 179
Emerald, HMS 88, 100, 105, 137, 198
Emeriau, V/A Maurice 78, 106, 196
Emma, HMS 148
Encounter, HMS 105
Endymion, HMS 61, 114-15
Entreprenante, HMS **159-61**; at Trafalgar 156
Eole (Fr) 67, 192
Epervier (Fr) 70-1
Erebus, HMS 144
España (Sp) 114, 174, 191-2, 207
Espiègle, HMS 132
Espoir, HMS 108
Essex, USS 148-9
Essex-Junior, USS 148-9
Essington, R/A William 97
Ethalion, HMS 30, 65, 135
Europa (Portugal) 129
Europe (GB) 153
Eurotus, HMS 71
Euryalus, HMS 7, 27, 78, 104, 114, 121, **140-4**, 150-1, 155, 174, 183, 236; at Trafalgar 19-20, 28, 40, 44, 57, 60, 84, 97, 107, 128, 137, 141-2, 151, 160
Eurydice, HMS 53, 65
Excellent, HMS 25-6, 80, 211
Exeter, HMS 118
Explosion, HMS 127, 132
Express, HMS 65

Fairy, HMS 144
Falmouth, HMS 71
Favorie (Fr) 150
Favourite (HMS/Fr) 207
Félicité (Fr) 179
Fendant (Fr) 118
Ferrol 8, 51, 58, 96, 106, 127, 135, 155, 166, 169, 171, 174, 182, 187, 189, 192, 199, 209-10, 213, 215, 219-20, 228-9, 232
Fervent, HMS 105
Fidèle (Fr) 192-3
Firme (Sp/Fr) 8, 60, 84, 114, 127, 150, 166, 174, 180, 192, 207-8, 229, 166
Fisgard, HMS 30, 80, 136
Flamand (Fr) 118
Fleur-de-Mer, HMS 133
Flora, HMS 121
Flora (Sp) 208
Florentina (Sp) 88, 198
Forester, HMS 65
Formidable, HMS 23, 30, 48, 64, 123
Formidable (Fr) 100, 114, **167-9**, 170, 179-80, 182, 189, 191, 193, 196, 219, 220, 164-6; captured and renamed HMS *Belleisle* 62, 100; at Trafalgar 96, 168-9, 182, 189, 191, 195, 218, 222
Fortitude, HMS 178
Fortune, HMS 145
Fortune (Fr) 124, 143, 198
Foudroyant, HMS 78, 87, 96, 129-30, 199
Fougueux (Fr) 100, 163, 170, 182, **187-8**, 192-4, 203, 164; at Trafalgar 19, 28, 43, 45, 52, 63, 92, 171, 187-8, 190, 192, 216
Fox, HMS 23, 25, 155
Foxhound, HMS 105
France 10, 70, 87, 93; armies 30, 50, 59, 68, 146, 170, 187, 192, 202-3; crews 9
Franklin (Fr) 67, 80, 95, 100, 198
Fraternité (Fr) 170, 192-3
Fredeickscoarn (Den) 82
Freija, HMS 58
Friponne (Fr) 179
Frisk, HMS 114, 166
Frolic, HMS 65
Fulton, Robert 140
Furet (Fr) 114, 163-66, 171-2, 180, 202-3, **206-7**, 218; at Trafalgar 193, 206-7, 218
Furie (Fr) 150
Fury, HMS 160

Galatea, HMS 148
Galgo (Sp) 228
Gambier, Admiral James, Lord 79, 82, 93, 97, 104-5, 129, 137, 203, 79
Ganges, HMS 30, 79, 82, 127, 185
Ganteaume, Admiral Honoré 8, 78, 166, 168, 170, 187, 191, 199, 229
Gardner, V/A Sir Alan 18, 70, 140, 170
Garlies, Captain Lord Viscount 68, 59, 66
Geary, Admiral Sir Francis 23, 31
Généreux, HMS 199
Genoa 13, 25, 50, 96, 112, 126, 144, 201, 228
Gibraltar 8-10, 19, 24, 26, 40, 49, 53, 58, 63-4, 68-9, 74, 80, 82, 85, 89, 93, 96, 100, 104, 107-8, 110, 121, 124, 132, 140, 142, 144, 146, 155, 161-2, 165-6, 168, 170, 192, 198, 200, 210, 229
Gibraltar, HMS 25, 62, 105, 118; at Trafalgar 101, 111
Gladiator, HMS 42, 56
Glatton, HMS 127
Gleyheid Bloodhound, HMS 29
Gloire (Fr) 93
Glorious First of June, battle of the 16-17, 66-7, 79-80, 87, 99, 112-13, 163, 191
Glory, HMS 83, 114, 166
Goliath, HMS 13, 26, 67, 93, 100, 114, 121, 198, 13
Gore, Captain Sir John 74, 104-5, 103
Gorée, HMS 65
Gorgon, HMS 121
Gower, Captain Sir Erasmus 17, 39, 39
Grafton, HMS 177-8
Grampus, HMS 18
Grand Ferailleur (Fr) 146
Grasse, R/A François Joseph, Comte de 12, 123
Graves, Admiral Thomas 16, 84
Gravina, Admiral Don Federico de 8, 175-6, 180, 189, 193, 199, 212-14, 216, 218-19, 221, 229, 208; at Trafalgar 84, 173, 222
Grenada 87, 107, 113
Greyhound (Ger) 140
Griffon, HMS 133
Growler, HMS 105
Grunstadt (Den) 114
Guadeloupe 173, 175, 203, 207
Guerrero (Sp) 209
Guerrière, HMS 121
Guerrière (Fr) 51, 68, 100, 106, 147, 179, 181-2
Guichen, Admiral Comte de 12, 122-3, 210
Guillemard (Fr) 74
Guiscardo Sannite (Naples) 25
guns and gunnery 6-7, 11, 43, 164, 194, 208-9, 238, 240-2

Hallowell, R/A Sir Benjamin 24, 54, 96
Hamilton, Sir William 124
Hanickoff, V/A 183
Hannibal, HMS 168, 170
Hannibal (Fr) 118
Hardi (Fr) 118
Hardy, Admiral Sir Charles 23, 31
Hardy, Captain Thomas Masterman 14, 27-9, 32, 61, 105, 122, 141, 10, 32; at Trafalgar 15, 76, 128
Harmonie (Fr) 113
Harper, HMS 196
Harpy, HMS 127
Harvey, Captain John 20, 89, 17, 86
Harvey, R/A Eliab 42-4, 53, 10, 42
Harvey, V/A Henry 167, 170
Harwich 7, 142, 11
Hasard (Fr) 124
Hasty, HMS 132
Haughty, HMS 65
Havannah, HMS 144
Hawke, Admiral 22
Hazard, HMS 41, 106, 136
Hebrus, HMS 144
Hecate, HMS 148
Hecla, HMS 127
Hector, HMS 177
Hector, USS 148
Henslow, Sir John 7, 10-11, 34, 38, 10
Hercule (Fr) 91
Hermione (Fr) 93, 163-4, 171-2, **202**, 203, 206; at Trafalgar 175, 193, 202, 204, 207
Hero, HMS 59, 105, 114, 118, 127, 169, 192, 195-6; at Trafalgar 182
Heron (GB) 53
Héros (Fr) 118, 163, 172, 176, 182, **188-9**, 206; at Trafalgar 28, 61, 128, 175, 182, 189, 218, 226-7, 233
Hesper, HMS 148, 196
Heureux (Fr) 51, 68, 145
Heureux Hazard (Fr) 135
Hibernia, HMS 20, 78
Hood, Admiral Samuel, Lord 13, 24, 50, 58, 87, 93, 104, 123-4, 132, 170, 178, 183, 198, 228, 31
Hood, Admiral Sir Alexander *see* Bridport, Admiral Lord
Hope, Admiral Sir George 30, 81-2, 10, 79, 86
Hornet, HMS 88
Hortense (Fr) 93, 114, 163-66, 171-2, 174, 180, 202, **202-3**, 203, *203*, 206; at Trafalgar 166, 193-4, 204, 206-7, 223, 234
Hotham, Admiral Sir Henry 70-1, 85, 83
Hotham, Admiral William 13, 24-5, 50, 79, 125-6, 179, 191
Howe, Admiral Lord 16-17, 24, 66-7, 79, 87, 95, 99, 112-13, 169, 191, 31
Hughes, Admiral Sir Edward 79, 118
Hunt, Edward 16, 10
Hunter, HMS 68
Hussar, HMS 150, 196
Hydra, HMS 140, 202, 206-7; at Trafalgar 137
Hyères 13, 25, 79-80, 124, 126, 143
Hyperion, HMS 133

Illustre (Fr) 118
Illustrious, HMS 35, 50, 52, 96, 105, 148, 196
Immortalité (Fr) 192
Impatiente (Fr) 136, 192
Impérial (Fr) 128
Impérieuse, HMS 90, 105
Impétueux, HMS 219
Impétueux (Fr) 59, 65
Implacable, HMS (ex-*Duguay Trouin*) 6, 30, 70, 121, **183-7**, *186*
Implacable (Fr) 236-7
Impregnable, HMS 24, 26
Inconstant, HMS 126
Incorruptible (Fr) 78, 180, 202, 165
Indagora (Sp) 208
Indefatigable, HMS 77, 104-5, 219
Indefatigable (Fr) 93
India 118, 147-8
Indian, HMS 111
Indienne (Fr) 105
Indivisible (Fr) 168, 170
Indomptable (Fr) 99, 114, 163, 168, **169-71**, 172, 179-80, 182, 187, 189, 192, 194, 219, 233, 164-166, 170, 220; at Trafalgar 19, 63, 104, 171, 187-8, 193, 216, 227
Inflexible, HMS 97, 118
Insolent, HMS 105
Insurgente (Fr) 193
Intrepid, HMS 65
Intrépide (Fr) 89, 95, 101, 105, 108, 114, 143, 163, 179-80, 182, **189-90**, 164-166; at Trafalgar 61, 76-7, 89, 97, 101, 108, 120, 128, 187, 190, 218
Intrepido (Sp) 189
Invincible, HMS 99
Iphigenia, HMS 87, 119, 153
Ireland 8, 57, 100, 114, 131, 140, 170, 192-4
Iris, HMS 77, 104, 126-7, 132
Irresistible, HMS 26, 99-100, 211
Isis, HMS 118, 127
Italienne (Fr) 85-6

Jacobin (Fr) 17
Jamaica 68, 87, 100, 113, 123, 132-3, 197
Jamaica, HMS 127
Janissary, HMS 160
Janus (Fr) 152
Jean Bart (Fr) 100, 105, 168, 170, 193
Jemmapes (Fr) 113, 191
Jervis, Admiral Sir John, Earl St Vincent 7, 13, 25-6, 47-8, 56, 59, 67, 80, 84, 87, 95, 100, 126, 132, 211, 213, 216, 230, 31
Juno, HMS 108, 118, 150; at Trafalgar 137
Jupiter (Fr) 179, 191
Justine (Fr) 131

Keats, R/A Sir Richard Goodwin 70, 184, 203-4
Keith, Admiral Lord 18, 39, 48, 59, 71, 80, 96, 106, 140, 160, 170, 198-9
Kempenfelt, R/A Richard 12, 23, 122-3, 31
Kent, HMS 18, 62, 96, 199
Keppel, Admiral the Hon Augustus 23, 177, 32
King George, HMS 105
Kingfisher, HMS 17

Kingsmill, Admiral 67
Kronstadt 183

Lady Elgin (GB) 53
Lagos Bay 22, 26
Lancaster, HMS 39, 48
Langara, Admiral Don Juan de 179, 228
Lark, HMS 87, 119, 133
Latona, HMS 67
Latouche-Tréville, V/A René Madeleine de 165, 168, 189, 191, 199
Leander, HMS 80, 95, 100
Leda, HMS 196
Leeward Islands 129
Légère (Fr) 152
Leghorn 13, 25, 96, 168, 179, 228
Leissègues, V/A 128
Leopard, HMS 126
Leviathan, HMS 7, 18, 63, 67, **86-90**, 94, 108, 110, 119, 197-8; at Trafalgar 53, 76, 88-9, 100, 111, 120, 128, 167, 189-90, 212, 218, 226
Leyden, HMS 97
Liberté (Fr) 219
Liberty (GB) 25
Liffey, HMS 71
Linzee, V/A Robert 124, 31
Lion, HMS 185, 196
Lion (Fr) 89
Lisbon 45, 54, 78, 80, 88, 138, 142, 157; blockade of 82, 129
Loire, HMS 97
London, HMS 78, 99-100, 127, 129, 219
Lord Nelson (GB) 51
Lorient 7, 74, 95, 105, 129, 195
Louis, R/A Sir Thomas 10, 114, 140
Lucifer, HMS 61, 114-15
Lutine (Fr) 129
Lynx (Fr) 93

Madagascar 148
Magicienne, HMS 153
Magnanime, HMS 118, 135
Magnificent, HMS 18, 24, 155
Magon de Médine, R/A Charles de 8, 141, 173, 175
Magpie (Fr) 105
Majestic, HMS 51, 66-7, 80, 87, 95, 99-100
Majorca 20
Malabar, HMS 196
Malabar (GB) 138
Malta 50, 58, 61-2, 96, 106, 114, 147, 155
Malta, HMS 76, 106, 114, 160, 166
Man, R/A Robert 24, 80, 179
Marengo (Fr) 74
Maria Antonia (Sp) 38
Marlborough, HMS 17-18, 78, 80, 87, 95, 113, 129; mutiny 48, 95
Mars, HMS 7, 17-18, 35, 52, 58-9, 67, 73, **90-4**, 92, 96, 104, 121, 141, 183, 188, 192, 204-5, 206; at Trafalgar 19-20, 40, 61, 63, 68, 76, 92-3, 101, 147, 188, 192-3, 204
Mars (Den) 97
Marseilles 143-4
Martial, HMS 105
Martin, Admiral George 72, 89, 96, 108, 178, 72
Martin, HMS 37, 137
Martin, HMS 37, 125, 125-6, 140
Martinique 8, 40-1, 123, 166, 171, 192, 202-3, 207
Mauritius 148, 152-3
Mazarredo, Admiral José de 211, 216, 229
Mazarredo, Admiral José de 39, 219, 228
McBride, R/A 94
Medea, HMS 118
Mediator, HMS 67
Mediterranean Fleet 7-8, 10, 13, 18, 27, 39, 48, 58, 62-3, 67, 72, 74, 78, 80, 87-9, 95-6, 96, 152, 178
Méduse (Fr) 70
Medway, HMS
guns 12
Megaera, HMS 99
Melampus, HMS 64-5
Meleager, HMS 125-6, 126
Melpomene, HMS 36, 70
Melpomène (Fr) 124

Menelaus, HMS 148
Mercedes (Sp) 8, 211
Mercurio (Sp) 208
Messiessy, R/A 65
Meteor, HMS 114-15, 144
Mignonne (Fr) 68, 124
Milan (Fr) 138
Milford, HMS 23, 58, 184
Minden, HMS 196
Minerva HMS 25-6
Minerve, HMS 67
Minerve (Fr) 124, 153
Minerve (Naples) 182
Minorca 48, 87, 96, 131
Minorca, HMS 160
Minotaur, HMS 30, 35, 52, 67, 70, 80, 86, 93, 168, 182, 223; at Trafalgar 96-7, 107, 182, 187, 195, 203, 218
Mistletoe, HMS 129-30
Moleste, HMS 182
Monarca (Sp) 182, 208, **225-6**; at Trafalgar 52, 58, 63, 68, 73, 92, 190, 192, 224-5
Monarch, HMS 58, 77-8, 84, 93, 104, 127, 129-31
Monarco, HMS 118
Monmouth, HMS 39, 62, 118, 126
Monsieur, HMS 105
Mont Blanc (Fr) 114, 164-6, 169-70, 172, 179-80, 182, 189, **191-2**, 196; at Trafalgar 96, 168, 182-3, 189-90, 195, 218, 222, 227
Montague (Fr) 150
Montagne (Fr) 150
Montagu, HMS 64, 127
Montague, R/A 169
Montañez, HMS 87, 199
Montañez (Fr) 99
Montañez (Sp) 182, 208, **220-1**, 221; at Trafalgar 57, 175, 221, 224
Montañez (Sp) (ex-*Pluton*) 193
Moore, General Sir John 30, 183
Morand de Galles, Admiral Justin-Bonaventure 131, 170, 187, 192-3
Moreno, V/A Don Juan Joaquin de 20, 168, 170, 219
Mornington, HMS 196
Mortar, HMS 61
Moselle, HMS 126, 133, 202, 206
Mucius (Fr) 79, 100, 170, 187, 192-4
Muiron (Fr) 168, 219
Mulgrave, HMS 196
Murray, R/A 132
Mutine, HMS 80, 100, 126, 129-30
Mutine (Fr) 192
Myrmidon, HMS 70-1

Naiad, HMS 7, 9, 85, **135-9**, 140, 150, 155; at Trafalgar 64, 137, 151
Naïade (Fr) 114, 180, s 165-6
Namur, HMS 26, 169; at Trafalgar 182-3
Naples 8, 95-6, 123-4, 152, 198, 228
Napoleon I, Emperor of the French 6, 9, 24, 30, 50-1, 138, 165-6, 170, 229; abdication 143-4; invasion plans for Britain 7-9, 84, 93, 97, 166, 179-80, 202, 206, 216, 222-3, 229, 242; move from Elba 20; on St Helena 78; surrender of 70-1
Nassau, HMS 127
Nautilus, HMS 114, 157, 196
Nautilus, USS 121
Néarque (Fr) 147
Negresse (Fr) 160
Nelson, V/A Horatio Lord 6-10, 14, 18, 25-7, 35, 50-1, 60, 62-3, 67, 73, 76, 80-1, 84, 87-8, 95, 100, 103, 106, 114, 123-4, 127, 132, 140-1, 146, 155, 157, 166, 170-1, 180, 198, 216, 229; death and funeral of 19, 28, 53, 95, 140, **145-9**, 155, 196; at Trafalgar 19, 81, 137, 147, 151, 188, 195; pursuit of Villeneuve 8, 10, 18-19, 63, 88, 107, 110, 146, 166, 202, 204-5
Neptune, HMS 7, 36-7, *Pitt*, HMS 129
Pitt (GB) 25
Plampin, R/A Robert 78
Plantagenet, HMS 76, 78, 97, 106, 129
Plover, HMS 65
Pluton (Fr) 114, 163, 165, 171-2, 176, 180, 189, 192, **192-3**, 207, 164, 166; at Trafalgar 52, 92-3, 193-3, 214, 224-5, 233
Plymouth 7-8, 10-11, 14-17, 19-21, 34, 38, 41-2, 44-5, 48-9, 51, 53-4, 56-60, 63-4, 67, 70-4, 78-80, 82, 84-5, 89, 91-3, 95-6, 98, 100, 102, 106-8, 114, 118-19, 121, 127, 135-7, 142, 145, 147-50, 155, 159-61, 178, 185, 192, 204, 235
Poictiers, HMS 74
Pole, HMS 56
Polyphemus, HMS 7, 19, 29, 41, 59, 67, 77, 104, 108, 110, 127, 135-6; at Trafalgar 44, 64, 111, 132, 152, 172-3
Pomone, HMS 138
Pomone (Swed) 114
Pompée, HMS 18, 29-30, 41, 61, 65, 74, 84, 114-15, 132, 168, 170, 196
Porcupine, HMS 23
Portsmouth 7, 11-13, 18, 20, 23-4, 27, 29-32, 34, 37-40, 47-8, 50, 54, 58-9, 65, 67-8, 70, 78, 81-2, 84-5, 93-4, 100-2, 105, 108, 110-12, 121-2, 127, 138-9, 142, 144, 154, 160, 177-8, 196, 235, 239
Portugal 18, 24, 26, 58, 78, 129, 142, 150; see also Lisbon
Powerful, HMS 83, 198
Présidente, HMS 148, 196
Preston, HMS 178
Primrose, HMS 30
Prince, HMS 7, 19, 32, 39, **46-50**, 204, 108, 236; at Trafalgar 20, 48-9, 53, 156, 160, 170, 173, 212, 214
Prince George, HMS 23, 26, 48, 56, 79, 99-100
Prince of Wales, HMS 8, 19, 59-60, 63, 77, 84, 89, 93, 97, 99, 104, 114, 127, 129, 166
Princess Amelia, HMS 178
Princess Royal, HMS 24-5, 56, 114
Principe de Asturias (Sp) 26, 182, 208, 211, **212-14**, 217, 220, 229; at Trafalgar 36, 84, 104, 114, 172-3, 180, 193, 214, 233
Print (US) 75
Procris, HMS 196
Prometheus, HMS 70-1
Proselyte, HMS 88
Proserpina (Sp) 87
Proserpine, HMS 23
Proserpine (Fr) 193
Providence (Fr) 136
Prussia 7
Psyche, HMS 168, 198
Prudente, HMS 12
Prövesteen (Den) 127, 132
Purvis, R/A John 189

Queen, HMS 12, 16, 36, 97, 99-100, 108, 170
Queen Charlotte, HMS 16, 62, 84, 87, 96, 99-100
Queen Charlotte (GB) 138

Racehorse, HMS 148
Raisonnable, HMS 114, 127, 152-3, 197, 166
Rambler, HMS 106
Ramillies, HMS 12, 59, 91, 127
Ranger, HMS 126
Rattlesnake, HMS 23
Rayo (Sp) 6, 171-2, 189, 208, **217-18**, 218, 232, 217, 235; at Trafalgar 15, 61, 128, 168, 182, 193, 195, 218, 227, 233
Real Carlos (Sp) 170, 219
Recruit, HMS 129
Redoubtable (Fr) 100, 111, 163-4, 170, 176, 182, 187, 192, **193-5**; at Trafalgar 28, 43, 111, 147, 170, 187, 192, 194-5, 202, 234
Redpole, HMS 138
Régénérée (Fr) 193
Regulus (Fr) 105
Renard, HMS 68
Renard (Fr) 192
Renaudin, R/A 191
Renommée (Fr/HMS) 19, 48, 148
Renown, HMS 12, 59, 62, 74, 80, 85, 219
Républicain (Fr) 79
Repulse, HMS 84, 114, 126, 166
Requin (Fr) 138
Résolue (Fr) 192
Resolution, HMS 83-4, 100, 105
Resolution, USS 155
Réunion Island 152-3
Revanche (Fr) 147
Revenge, HMS 7, 10, 19, 30, 58, 79, 93, **102-5**, 156-7; 236; at Trafalgar 11, 103-4, 114, 173, 180, 212, 214, 229
Révolution (Fr) 187, 191-2
Révolutionnaire, HMS 99, 169, 182
Révolutionnaire (Fr) 66, 93
Reynolds, Admiral 82
Rhin (Fr) 93, 114, 163-6, 171, 180, 202-3, **203-5**
Richery, R/A Joseph de 80, 145, 179
Rinaldo, HMS 138
Rio de Janeiro 58, 129
Rivoli, HMS 112
Robust, HMS 59, 91, 99, 113, 123
Robuste (Fr) 85
Rochefort 7-8, 51-2, 64, 58-9, 93, 100, 114, 128, 136, 172, 175, 179, 182, 202-3, 235, 11
Rodney, Admiral George 123
Rosily, R/A François de 8-9, 172, 189, 193, 201
Rotheram, Captain Edward 7, 19-20, 35, 69-70, 10, 17, 34, 66
Rotherhithe 11
Rowley, V/A 132, 177
Royal Charlotte, HMS 23
Royal George, HMS 12, 23, 45, 59, 61, 91, 95, 99, 114, 170
Royal Oak, HMS 65
Royal Sovereign, HMS 9, 10, 14, **16-21**, 18, 56, 67, 74, 85, 91, 108, 110, 132; at Trafalgar 15-16, 19-20, 27-8, 35-6, 40, 53, 57, 60-1, 63, 68, 73, 81, 84, 92, 96-7, 101, 103, 107, 111, 120, 128, 137, 141-2, 152, 156, 188, 216, 233-4
Royal William, HMS 31
Ruby, HMS 82, 132, 178
Russell, HMS 18, 79, 84, 97, 99-100, 114, 170
Russia 1, 70, 78, 80-1, 93, 114, 121, 166, 183-4, 198
Séduisant (Fr) 192
Sémillante (Fr) 201
Seniavin, V/A 78
Sérieuse (Fr) 100
Sévère (Fr) 118
Severn, HMS 144
Sewold (Russia) 183
Seymour, Admiral Lord 154
Salvador del Mundo (Sp) 229
Salvador del Mundo (Sp/HMS) 26, 74, 100
Samarang, HMS 196
San Agustin (Sp) 36, 88, 182, 219, **226-7**; at Trafalgar 61, 69, 88-9, 189-90, 218, 226
San Antonio (Sp) 170, 219, 229
San Brigada (Sp) 228, 230
San Casilda (Sp) 230
San Domingo (Sp) 229
San Fernando (Sp) 229
San Fiorenzo 25-6, 80, 124-6, 179
San Francisco de Asis (Sp) 171-2, 187, 189, 221, **227**; at Trafalgar 15, 61, 128, 182, 193, 195, 218, 227, 233
San Fulgencio (Sp) 182, 208, 221, 228-9
San Hermengilda (Sp)
San Ildefonso (Sp) 176, 182, 200, 211, 213, 221, **205-6**; at Trafalgar 175, 182, 200, 211, 219
Snake, HMS 68
Sophie, HMS 54
Sotheby, R/A Thomas 26, 38, 32
Southampton, HMS 126
Spain 6-7, 9-10, 19-20, 27-9, 47, 85, 87-8, 96, 100, 123, 129, 133, 189, **208-34**, 209, 235-40, 242; allied with Britain 24, 164, 172, 193, 201, 223, 234; allied with France 8, 51, 130, 178-9, 199, 216-17, 222, 224, 229; Peninsular War 30, 44, 53-4
Sparrow, HMS 133
Spartiate, HMS 17, 19, 63, 173, 188, 194, 202, 214, 233-4
Spartiate (Fr) 95, 198, 236
Speedwell, HMS 67
Speedy, HMS 126, 168, 170
Spencer, HMS 63, 88, 168, 170
Sphinx (Fr) 118
Spithead 17-18, 23-4, 26-7, 29-31, 30, 47-8, 66-8, 78, 88, 90, 95, 100, 102, 122, 128-9, 138, 142, 144, 160, 166, 182, 192-3, 196-7; mutiny 67, 142, 175, 83, 91, 95, 126
St Fiorenzo, HMS 178
St George, HMS 13, 25, 81-2, 127, 13
St Helena 71, 78
St Kitts 128
St Lucia 41, 113, 123
St Michel (Fr) 118
St Thomas 65
St Thomas (Den) 97
St Vincent, Admiral Earl see Jervis, Admiral Sir John
Stag, HMS 219
Standard, HMS 61, 99, 113-15, 127
Star, HMS 65
Stately, HMS 111
Staunch, HMS 148, 153
Stirling Castle, HMS 23, 177-8
Stopford, R/A the Hon Robert 17, 85, 137, 148, 196
Stork, HMS 65
Strachan, Admiral Sir Richard 64-5, 74, 108, 163, 182, 191-2, 195
Streatham (GB) 153
Stuart, General the Hon Charles 87
Success, HMS 170
Suffren, Admiral 79, 118
Sulphur, HMS 127, 132
Sultan, HMS 18, 63, 110, 118, 144, 155, 198
Suoverof, General 198
Superb, HMS 8, 62-3, 71, 74, 88, 110, 118, 121, 128, 157
Surprise, HMS 129
Surveillance, HMS 129
Surveillante (Fr) 192, 205
Suvoroff, General 198
Swallow, HMS 143
Sweden 31, 30, 80-1, 93, 121, 166, 183, 238
Swiftsure, HMS 7, 18-19, 24, 63, 67, 80, 83, 87-8, 96, 100, 108, **109-12**, 119; at Trafalgar 11, 35, 61, 64, 82, 84, 110-11, 173, 195
Swiftsure (HMS/Fr) 73, 108, 114, 163-6, 169-70, 180, 182, 189, **197-200**; at Trafalgar 101, 152, 199-200, 224, 229-30, 242
Sydney, Lord
Sylph (Fr) 93

Tartar, HMS 12, 121, 126, 181
Tartarus, HMS 160
Teazer, HMS 132
Téméraire, HMS 7, 20, 28, 30, 54, 85, **41-6**, 43, 44, 57, 61, 68, 172; at Trafalgar 40, 42-4, 53, 76, 85, 97, 101, 107-8, 152, 172, 188, 190, 194, 233
Terpsichore, HMS 100, 211
Terrible, HMS 64, 178
Terrible (Fr) 17, 87, 114, 170, 182
Terrible (Sp) 174, 192, 207, 223, 228-9
Terror, HMS 127
Texel river 85, 132, 150
Thalia, HMS 99
Thames, HMS 147, 168
Thémis (Fr) 114, 163-6, 171-2, 180, 202-3, 225 228-30; at Trafalgar 81-2, 104, 173, 199, 229-30, 242
Thérèse (Fr) 80
Theseus, HMS 26, 58, 67-8, 80, 95, 100, 105, 181
Thetis, HMS 196
Thetis (Sp) 135
Thétis (Fr) 93
Thompson, V/A Charles 13
Thornbrough, V/A Edward 20, 74, 81
Thrush, HMS 133
Thunder, HMS 105, 108, 121
Thunderer, HMS 16, 23, 60-1, 67, 87, 99, 108, 166; at Trafalgar 53, 101, 114, 147, 152, 214, 229
Tigre, HMS 63, 88, 96, 110, 199
Tigre (Fr) 100
timber 6-7, 235, 237-8
Tisiphone, HMS 12, 123
Tobago 8
Tonnant (Fr/HMS) 30, 35, **50-4**, 52, 68, 71, 74, 95-6, 106, 108, 176, 198; at Trafalgar 52-3, 63, 68, 92-3, 101, 107, 122, 175, 188, 194, 212
Tonnerre (Fr) 105
Torbay 24, 57, 68-71, 79, 114
Torche (Fr) 174, 192, 207
Fortune (Fr) 131, 192
Toulon 7-8, 13, 50, 62, 76, 87, 95, 106, 124, 142-3, 165, 168, 170-1, 178-80, 188-90, 192, 195-6, 201-3, 205, 229; blockade of 7-8, 13, 18, 24-5, 27, 58, 62, 67, 78-80, 84, 87, 127, 187, 189, 201-2, 205, 211, 213, 229, 231, 234; Atlantic crossing 18, 59-60, 63, 84, 87-8, 97, 110, 114, 140, 150, 166, 168, 171, 4-5, 180, 190-2, 194-5, 199, 202-3, 219, 221; at Trafalgar 27-9, 40, 76, 93, 166-7, 173-4, 182, 190-2, 199, 214, 222, 224, 229
Tourville (Fr) 79, 105, 192
Trafalgar, battle of 6-10, 14-19, 19-20, 27-9, 35-7, 39-40, 42-4, 48-9, 52-3, 57-8, 60-1, 63-4, 68-9, 73-4, 76-7, 80, 84-5, 88-9, 92-3, 96-7, 101, 103-4, 107-8, 110-12, 114-15, 120-1, 128, 134, 137-8, 141-2, 147, 151-2, 156-60, 160, 163, 168-9, 171-2, 171-6, 174-5, 175-6, 176, 180-3, 187-96, 198-203, 205-6, 208-9, 211-22, 216-18, 220-1, 222-3, 229-34, 235, 237, 240-1, 242
Tremendous, HMS 74, 78, 88, 110, 118, 121, 128, 157
Tribune, HMS 121
Trident, HMS 177-8
Trincomalee, HMS (ex-*Foudroyant*) 7
Triomphant (Fr) 13
Tripoli (Algiers) 138-9
Triton, HMS 135
Triumph, HMS 17-18, 64, 67, 91, 105, 114, 127, 166
Turkey 114-15
Tweed, HMS 133
Tyrannicide (Fr) 170, 191
see also Dix Août

Ulysses, HMS 65, 87
Undaunted, HMS 89, 143
Unicorn, HMS 7, 80, 105, 236
Union, HMS 12
Unité, HMS 89
Unité (Fr) 236
Uranie (Fr) 180, 202, 165
USA 70, 75, 87, 121, 144, 151, 155, 169; bombardment of Washington 54, 144; War of American Independence 12-13, 16, 23, 58, 79, 119, 123, 135, 177-8, 210, 227, 236; War of 1812 54, 70, 121, 144, 148-9
Ushant 27, 35, 38, 56, 70, 91, 104, 122, 122, 137: actions off 1778 23; 1781 12, 17-18; 1795 17-18, 67, 90-1; 1809 85-6

Valiant, HMS 12, 16-17, 23-4, 97, 99, 105, 113
Valour (Fr) 219
Vanguard, HMS 68, 80, 95, 100, 106, 121, 181, 210
Vautour (Fr) 168, 170, 192
Vence (Fr) Jean Gasper 17, 67, 187, 193
Venerable, HMS 45, 59, 91, 168
Vengeance, HMS 100
Vengeance (Fr) 201
Vengeur, HMS 30
Vengeur (Fr) 21-32, 45, 47, 50, 59, 88, 100, 105, 181
Vengeur du Peuple (Fr) 99, 113
Vengeur (Fr) 118
Venice 58, 89, 108
Vestal, HMS 127, 196
Vestale (Fr) 179
Vesuvius, HMS 132
Veteran, HMS 127, 132
Vétéran (Fr) 74
Victoire (Fr) 50, 179
Victor (Fr) 153
Victory, HMS 6-9, 11-13, 18, 21-32, 32, 46, 47, 50, 59, 62-3, 70, 82, 88, 93, 100, 103, 108, 110, 114, 121, 123-4, 125, 140, 172, 183, 185-6, 189, 229; at Trafalgar 15, 19-20, 27-9, 29, 35-6, 40, 42-3, 48, 53, 58, 60, 69, 76, 84, 88-9, 92, 101, 103-4, 107-8, 111, 122, 132, 141, 147, 151-2, 156, 160, 166, 172, 189, 194, 212
Vigo, HMS 82
Vigo Bay 8, 30, 183
Villaret-Joyeuse, V/A Louis de 16-17, 40, 47, 62, 66-7, 79, 87, 90-1, 99, 112-13, 113, 169, 187, 191, 193
Ville de Lyon (Fr) 138
Ville de Paris (Fr/HMS) 23, 26, 35, 48, 128
Villeneuve, Admiral Pierre 6, 8-10, 27, 46, 50, 60, 72, 95, 103, 114, 128, 135, 146, 155, 163-6, 170, 173-4, 179, 182, 187, 189, 192, 201-2, 205, 229; English coast 7-8, 13, 18, 24-5, 27, 58, 62, 67, 78-80, 84, 87, 128, 165-9, 176, 182, 189-90, 199, 201-2, 205, 211, 213, 229, 231, 234; Atlantic crossing 18, 59-60, 63, 84, 87-8, 97, 110, 114, 140, 150, 166, 168, 171, 4-5, 180, 190-2, 194-5, 199, 202-3, 219, 221; at Trafalgar 27-9, 40, 76, 93, 166-7, 173-4, 182, 190-2, 199, 214, 222, 224, 229
Viper, HMS 138
Virginie (Fr) 91, 187
voice pipes 28, 235, 239
Volcano, HMS 127
Voltigeur (Fr) 192

Waakzaamheid (Holland) 150
Wagram (Fr) 196
Walcheren expedition 58, 65, 142
Wallace, V/A Sir James 179
Warren, Admiral Sir John Borlase 42, 54, 80, 111, 113, 199, 219
Warrior, HMS 114, 127, 166
Warspite, HMS 78, 142
Wasp, HMS 152
Waterloo, battle of 20, 70, 240-1
Wattignies (Fr) 100, 192-3
Weazle, HMS 19, 63, 68, 108, 137, 140, 155
Wellington, Duke of 54, 97
West Indies 7-8, 12, 18, 23, 42, 44-5, 65, 68, 87-8, 90, 112-13, 123, 144, 177, 180, 184, 190, 192, 198, 202-3
see also individual islands
Whiting, HMS 105
Whitshed, R/A 42, 80, 84
Willaumez, Admiral Jean Baptiste 64-5, 85, 104
Williams, Admiral Sir Thomas 39-40, 54, 39
Windsor Castle, HMS 58, 61, 93, 114, 166
Wolverine, HMS 65
Woolwich 11-12, 16, 46, 83, 90, 94, 108, 118, 144
Worcester, HMS 118
Wyndham, HMS 153

Yarmouth 97, 121, 126-7, 129, 131-2
York, HMS 41, 65, 132
Yorke, Admiral Sir Joseph 30, 31
Zealous, HMS 25, 67, 95, 100, 198
Zebra, HMS 127
Zélé (Fr) 100
Zephyr, HMS 127